Library and Book Trade Almanac™

formerly **The Bowker Annual**

2015 | 60th Edition

Library and
Book Trade
Almanac™

WITHDRAWAL

formerly **The Bowker Annual**

2015 | 60th Edition

Editor Dave Bogart
Consultant Alan Inouye

⊞ Information Today, Inc.

Published by Information Today, Inc.
Copyright © 2015 Information Today, Inc.
All rights reserved

International Standard Book Number 978-1-57387-505-9
International Standard Serial Number 2150-5446
Library of Congress Catalog Card Number 55-12434

Page 703 constitutes a continuation of the Copyright page.

Information Today, Inc.
143 Old Marlton Pike
Medford, NJ 08055-8750
Phone: 800-300-9868 (customer service)
        800-409-4929 (editorial queries)
Fax: 609-654-4309
E-mail (orders): custserv@infotoday.com
Web Site: http://www.infotoday.com

Printed and bound in the United States of America

ISBN 13: 978-1-57387-505-9
27900>

9 781573 875059

Contents

Part 2
Legislation, Funding, and Grants

Legislation

Funding Programs and Grant-Making Agencies

Part 3
Library/Information Science Education, Placement, and Salaries

Part 4
Research and Statistics

Library Research and Statistics

Book Trade Research and Statistics

Part 5
Reference Information

Bibliographies

Ready Reference

Distinguished Books

Part 6
Directory of Organizations

Preface

The importance of access to information in today's world cannot be overemphasized. With that in mind, at its 2014 annual conference the International Federation of Library Associations and Institutions (IFLA) advanced the Lyon Declaration on Access to Information and Development, which calls on the United Nations to formally acknowledge and promote the necessity to make information—and the skills to use it effectively—readily available everywhere.

Libraries and publishers are at the forefront of that effort, and this 60th edition of the *Library and Book Trade Almanac* looks at the many ways in which the information industry is dealing with new demands and technological advances.

Our Special Reports in this edition address several related topics of current importance.

- In the multi-part "Re-Thinking the Roles of U.S. Libraries," Larra Clark, Roger E. Levien, Amy K. Garmer, and Miguel Figueroa examine how libraries are evolving in an increasingly digital atmosphere.
- In "Preservation Pending: The Future of E-Book Access in the Digital Age," Melissa Goertzen, Robert Wolven, and Jeffrey D. Carroll discuss the opportunities and obstacles involved in preserving e-books.
- In "School Libraries Meet the Challenges of Change," Christopher Harris and Barbara K. Stripling analyze the demanding situation facing K–12 school libraries, and at how opportunities can be found in the varied challenges.
- In "New Publishing and the Library: E-Books, Self-Publishing, and Beyond," James LaRue looks in depth at the questions that advancing technology poses for libraries of all types.

Part 1 continues with reports on the activities of federal libraries, federal agencies, and national and international library, publishing, and bookselling organizations.

Legislation affecting the information industry is featured in Part 2, as are the programs of two major grant-making agencies.

Part 3 contains professional information for librarians, such as advice on finding employment opportunities, salary and placement studies, job-seeking tips, and a list of the year's top library award and scholarship winners.

Part 4 offers an abundance of statistical material: book and periodical prices, reports on noteworthy research, extensive tables of library acquisition expenditures, and other useful library and book trade data.

Reference information fills Part 5, ranging from lists of major literary prize winners to lists of notable books and other resources for all ages.

Part 6 is our directory of library and publishing organizations at the state, national, and international levels, and also includes a calendar of upcoming information industry events.

The *Library and Book Trade Almanac* represents the effort of many people, and we are grateful to all those who supplied reports, assembled statistics, and responded to our many requests for information. Very particular thanks are due to Consultant Editor Alan S. Inouye for his invaluable help with planning and assembling our Special Reports section; to Contributing Editor Catherine Barr; and to Christine Weisel McNaull for her skill and diligence in turning all of this information into a book.

We believe you will turn to this milestone 60th edition frequently, and welcome your comments on how we might make it even more useful.

Dave Bogart
Editor

Part 1
Reports from the Field

Special Reports

Re-Thinking the Roles of U.S. Libraries

Larra Clark, Roger E. Levien, Amy K. Garmer, and Miguel Figueroa

Introduction

Larra Clark

America's libraries historically have been on the forefront of bringing new technology devices and information formats to their users. From microfiche to online catalogs to the "hidden Web," libraries have made more information more readily accessible, while also providing public access to new technology and helping people gain skills and proficiency in using new devices and platforms.

More recently, libraries also have worked to develop new business models and systems to ensure equitable access to information in all formats and to advance the ease of use, stability, and affordability of digital content. As the ways in which people access and use information broaden, libraries continue to strive to ensure equitable access to the world's cultural and educational riches. In the midst of the digital revolution, librarians see a vital role for their work.

Of course, not everyone has shared this view. Others (particularly in the media) have long predicted a dismal future for libraries—mostly forecasting their demise in the wake of cheaper paperback books (now everyone can afford them!), the advent of the Internet (now everything's online for free!), and the decline of the printed book as e-books and other media are downloaded and streamed (now everything's online and available with one click!).

Unfortunately, recent public library data do show declines in physical visits to public libraries, as well as decreased revenue per capita and full-time equivalent (FTE) staffing declines since 2008 and 2009.[1] While individual libraries often report increased online use, no national data have been collected to date regarding virtual library "visits." The level of upheaval in United Kingdom public libraries also sounds a caution that librarians cannot afford to be complacent about their places in the world.[2] (It is worth noting that U.S. academic libraries saw a 9 percent uptick in gate counts from 2008 to 2010, attributed at least in part to

Larra Clark is deputy director of the American Library Association's Office for Information Technology Policy. Roger E. Levien is the founder of Strategy & Innovation Consulting, a consultancy established to support senior executives. Amy K. Garmer is director of the Aspen Institute Dialogue on Public Libraries. Miguel Figueroa is director of the ALA Center for the Future of Libraries.

increased student enrollment, but staffing declined over the same period.[3] School librarian staffing declined more than the number of other K–12 educators from 2005 to 2011.[4])

Directly and indirectly, these trends have contributed to a growing drumbeat about "the future of libraries" within the library community and among its allies and supporters. These conversations in the last year or so have involved a greater consideration of the conceptual place and role of libraries, as well as new models that may extend beyond an individual library to the community of libraries. This debate is less about *what* specific services libraries offer (although this is clearly still important), but about *how* they are developed and delivered. What will guide libraries' relationships to their communities, to each other, and to national and global trends?

These are the concerns of the three essays that follow, in which writers from disparate backgrounds discuss how we might re-envision or even re-create libraries at a time when the speed of change is constantly accelerating—for our institutions, staff, and communities.

First, Roger E. Levien takes a long view that connects Andrew Carnegie and Melvil Dewey to a proposed new national infrastructure of connected libraries. Roger draws on a career devoted to assisting public and private decision makers in understanding and choosing among strategic alternatives, especially those driven by technological development. His essay provides a preview to his forthcoming book *The Once and Future Library,* and outlines five transformational shifts and systems needed to move libraries forward in meeting community needs.

Amy K. Garmer shares a view from the recent Aspen Institute Dialogue on Public Libraries that outlines a renewed vision. The dialogue is a multi-stakeholder forum to explore and champion new thinking on U.S. public libraries, with the goal of fostering concrete actions to support and transform public libraries for a more diverse, mobile, and connected society. The dialogue working group includes leaders from libraries, executives from businesses, government officials, community development visionaries, and education experts. Garmer proposes a vision based on three vital public library assets and shares strategies for success derived from the dialogue process.

Finally, Miguel Figueroa provides a peek inside the American Library Association's (ALA's) new Center for the Future of Libraries and work under way to create a "one-stop" platform for librarians and their collaborators to track trends and crowd-source innovation. The center opened its virtual doors in mid-2014 and has initiated a "trend library" and communications to engage libraries of all types in accelerating the dissemination of new ideas and bridges to experts outside the library community.

This article's three sections span conceptual frameworks to concrete resources, but several themes emerge, led by the conclusion that libraries must turn further outward. They must align their programs and services in support of community goals through deeper engagement with other community institutions, leaders, and residents. A library strategic plan should also be a community empowerment plan or a student achievement plan. Library metrics become a means to the end of advancing community priorities.

This, of course, demands flexibility, another broad theme. Library assets— whether physical place, human resources, or brokered collections—must be (re) engineered for movement and change. Part of this flexibility involves re-examining library education and further developing systems for lifelong learning within the profession.

If there is a clarion call, it is this: Tear down these walls! The authors paint a world of deeper interrelationships—among libraries and across local, national, and global contexts. The library is unbound, a place without borders, available to all.

It can be difficult to prepare for the future while meeting today's pressing demands on our time and attention. For a moment, though, I invite you to take the time to consider the broad themes laid out by Roger, Amy, and Miguel.

Great Good Fortune: Organization, Philanthropy, and the Re-Creation of the Public Library

Roger E. Levien

The community public library has been a well-known institution throughout America for just over a century. At the end of the 19th and beginning of the 20th century, libraries spread across the nation as if sown by a knowing and driven hand. Their dissemination resulted from a confluence of need, arising from the post-Civil War demand for a better-educated workforce, and great good fortune, in the form of Melvil Dewey's organizational genius and Andrew Carnegie's philanthropic ambition. In 1890 there were about 400 free, tax-supported community libraries in America, half in New England.[5] Today there are about 9,000 public library administrations (with more than 16,400 buildings) in virtually every county and most communities across the land.

Born to the Book

America's public libraries were born to a world in which virtually the only way for knowledge to be recorded and widely distributed was as text and still images printed on paper. The pinnacle medium, which all authors—whether literary or scholarly—sought to occupy, was the printed book. It alone was a vessel capable of conveying mind-sized segments of what civilization had created and learned in a portable and affordable form.

The new public libraries (thank you, Mr. Carnegie!) therefore took it to be their principal task to acquire for their communities a careful selection of available books, to organize and store them in a way that they might readily be found (thank you, Mr. Dewey!), to encourage their free borrowing and return, and to keep them in good condition for as long as needed.

Almost a century ago America's public libraries accomplished something of transcendent economic, social, and cultural importance to their patrons, their communities, and the nation: They made a tailored selection of civilization's cultural and intellectual riches freely available to anyone within range of their facilities in communities across the United States. By doing so, they strengthened and diversified the nation's economic and social development.

Collection Centered

Throughout the 20th century the model of the book-centered library continued to spread, even as books were supplemented, first by periodicals, then by audio and video recordings.

An ecosystem of supporting institutions developed in concert with libraries. States and some counties established agencies to oversee and support libraries. Suppliers of furniture and equipment and media distributors developed library specializations. Professional organizations, such as the American Library Association (ALA), were established. Schools of library science offered master's degrees to aspiring librarians under the imprimatur of ALA accreditation. Individuals attracted by a life with books and comfortable with the role of steward flowed into the field. This eco-web wrapped the library in a tight cocoon of shared concern for the stewardship of physical collections, primarily books.

The Digital Computer Enters

Even the advent of the digital computer in the second half of the 20th century did little to alter the *raison d'être* of the library. Entering as a tool to improve the efficiency of library operations, the computer then replaced the time-consuming maintenance and use of card catalogs with digital catalogs. The strongest influence of the computer on the library was as an offering, complementary to, but independent of, the collections. Personal computers, most with Internet access, became ubiquitous and heavily used as the 20th century neared its end. Nevertheless, addressing "digital divide" concerns did not displace traditional services as the principal justification for library support.

Into this smoothly evolving world, technology unleashed a torrent of progressively more disruptive innovations. In the 1980s and 1990s the Internet swept across the world, channeling instantaneous global flows of digital information. The World Wide Web rapidly became the infrastructure for an explosion of Internet information services.

Simultaneously, cellular telephony was introduced to the United States, Europe, and Japan. Through linkage with the Internet, the cellular network became a means of accessing the Web, but only on special phones whose physical keyboards limited their display size. Until the end of the 20th century, desktop computers with large displays or hefty laptop computers were the principal means of accessing the full power of Web services. Momentous as they were, these developments posed, at best, a modest threat to the library, warranting a comparable response.

Disruptive Innovation: The iPhone and iPad

In January 2007, however, the power of the technology torrent culminated in the iPhone (and competing devices). Although marketed as phones, these are really high-quality displays powered by a supercomputer. Suddenly a pocketable device gave access to almost all the information and entertainment riches of the Web. To strengthen the challenge to the paper book, the iPhone's larger sibling, the iPad, was launched in 2010 as a superior display for digital books and rich multimedia. E-book readers such as the Kindle also provided easy access.

Thus the printed paper book was confronted by a competitor capable of disrupting its more than five-century reign as the principal means to access segments of the world's knowledge, anywhere and at any time. By doing so, this new device simultaneously threatened disruption of the book-centric public library. Suddenly a smart-phone-wielding prospective library patron can access, at exactly the place and time of need, any media he or she wants without having to set foot in a library. The threat is exacerbated by the intense competition from the vast smorgasbord of new media for the library patron's attention.[6]

This threat, though potentially fatal, will build up gradually over the coming decades as technology progresses, the media landscape widens, the proportion of digital natives in the population grows, and the media ecosystem is reshaped. But at some time, perhaps in 15 or so years, the changes will achieve critical mass, becoming powerful enough to destroy well-established institutions in a way comparable to the havoc wreaked on book, music, and video stores; and will threaten newspapers, radio stations, and cable networks. In a world so transformed, will communities continue to support physical libraries with their associated costs, or will they turn to virtual libraries?

Responding to Disruption

Despite their noncommercial status, libraries can learn from the experience of iconic businesses that have confronted technological disruption, both those that survived and those that succumbed. Consider, for example, the contrasting experiences of Kodak and Xerox, both in the imaging industry, one putting images on film and the other on paper.[7] Film was the raison d'être and the cash cow of Kodak from its founding in 1890. Xerox earned its living, initially in 1960, by selling analog copiers, their supplies, and service. Both were threatened from the mid-1980s by the imminent arrival of digital technology—in the form of their own inventions: Kodak's digital camera and Xerox's digital office.

Kodak's film-centric management could not break the strong pull of film's profit stream to transition fully to the digital world. In contrast, through a series of long-term corporate strategy exercises, Xerox anticipated the threat and transitioned over two decades from *The Copier Company,* whose principal income derived from document copiers, to *The Document Company,* serving the broader customer need for document services. Kodak declared bankruptcy in 2012, unable to achieve profitability in the by-then-dominant digital world. Xerox's revenue in 2014 was greater than $20 billion, the majority from document services, and it continues to grow profitably. Benefits like those Xerox achieved by thinking strategically about sustainable customer values and acting steadily—over decades—to make changes to deliver them are available to libraries as they face a comparable disruption.

The Opportunity

The threat of fatal disruption of the collection-centric library is developing. Virtual libraries are already serving communities and the nation. The penetration of smart phones and tablets is rapidly expanding. The key to the long-term survival of physical libraries lies in establishing sustainable value that is not rooted in the collections patrons take from the library, but in the valuable connections they make at the library. Through those connections the library must serve real communities' needs.

The needs are manifold. They are severe, growing, and consequential. America's communities confront challenges both from continuous technological, economic, political, social, demographic, and environmental change; and from unpredictable storms, floods, riots, or attacks. Although the challenges are broadly the same nationally, they take varying forms and have differing consequences in different communities. National responses alone cannot resolve them. Each community needs the means to address its challenges by drawing on the best resources, whether local, national, or international.

Fortunately, a great opportunity to meet these needs lies in plain sight. The fruits of a massive, century-long nationwide buildup of facilities, capabilities, and experience, the nation's 16,400 public library locations provide the raw material for serving the needs of communities in the 21st century. As they are reshaped, libraries will be the essential engines of community adaptation, helping each locale successfully confront its challenges. By advancing the well-being of their communities, these libraries will immeasurably strengthen the nation, as the 20th century libraries did.

The 21st Century Library

But how will tomorrow's library differ from its predecessor? Three recently completed studies have addressed this question. The first, sponsored by the Aspen Institute, *Rising to the Challenge: Re-Envisioning Public Libraries,*[8] focuses on community libraries in the United States. The second, sponsored by the Royal Society of Canada, *The Future Now: Canada's Libraries, Archives, and Public Memory,*[9] is concerned with all types of libraries and archives in that nation. The third, sponsored by the U.K. Department for Culture, Media, and Sport, *Independent Library Report for England,*[10] addresses the needs of England's public libraries. Those studies' conclusions are embedded (as I interpret them) with my own[11] as five changes required to transform U.S. libraries.

1 Inward to Outward

The primary focus of the 21st century library will be outward, to the needs of its community. Librarians will actively engage with community groups, organizations, and residents to identify needs and develop responsive library activities.

2 Collections to Connections

The 21st century library's value will be the strong connections it establishes within and between media resources and people. The library will be a place where people congregate, meet, learn, collaborate, enjoy, and create together, both for personal and community benefit, facilitated by librarians. Local physical collections will constitute a small portion of all available resources; the largest portion will reside on the Web. Local librarians will curate the most relevant and reliable media.

3 Stability to Agility

The 21st century library will continually evolve in response to incremental learning and discontinuous innovation, as well as to continually changing challenges and opportunities. Rigid buildings, fixed furnishings, inflexible operations, and unchanging skills will be replaced by structures, facilities, operations, and personnel flexible enough to respond smoothly to changing needs.

4 Responsive to Proactive

Libraries of the 21st century will lead in identifying critical concerns and informing and facilitating community efforts to address the issues facing the community and its residents. They will develop programs to connect the community with otherwise inaccessible aspects of the external world, whether they be instructive, inspirational, or simply entertaining. Media, digital and physical, will be used to communicate the library's roles, goals, and activities.

5 Passive to Competitive

The physical library of the 21st century will successfully compete with the cacophony of other media for its patrons' attention. Even in a world of social media, one of the most reliable attractions for people is other people, especially when easy and serendipitous connections can be made. Libraries will attract attendees with activities that serve valuable community and personal needs.

The 21st Century Library Network

Transforming libraries will require significant changes in their operations, management, and staffs. Although many of the larger and wealthier libraries have already begun such changes, the great majority of the country's 9,000 systems have neither the flexible funds nor abundant staff capacity to transform themselves at the necessary pace. Moreover, library change cannot be achieved without complementary changes in the eco-web of supporting institutions. Such thoroughgoing changes will be difficult to achieve in the current world of self-contained library systems. Rather, the first step in bringing them about must be to create an institution through which libraries, while remaining autonomous, can operate together at scale to achieve common goals—a Network of Community Libraries, call it CONNECT/LS.

CONNECT/LS will establish the information infrastructure through which libraries can communicate the challenges they face, collaborate to innovate, share experience and the results of experiments, and inspire innovation. Within the larger network, many smaller "communities of interest" will be established to share experiences among libraries whose communities face similar challenges or have common needs. For example, libraries "serving communities with tourism-based economies," "serving small towns," or "delivering virtual reality experiences."

Three associated systems with specialized responsibilities will support libraries in ways beyond the capabilities of lone or small groups of libraries.

- PRODUCE/LS: Libraries need access to high-quality, library-specific media products providing information and experiences that compete effectively with the panoply of non-library alternatives available to library patrons. Producing a full-range of those media will require not-for-profit professional organizations that create or acquire from other sources and distribute media responsive to the specific needs of public libraries, as the Public Broadcasting Service (PBS) and National Public Radio (NPR) do for public television and radio. Each library will select and acquire materials useful for its community from PRODUCE/LS, as public radio and TV stations do for their communities.

- INNOVATE/LS: In light of each library's need for continuing adaptive change, the ability of 9,000 library systems to experiment is a considerable opportunity, but only if the results are thoroughly analyzed and widely disseminated. To complement library-based experimentation, therefore, an organization is needed whose sole focus is on the development, documentation, and dissemination of information about innovations and best practices. Each library will then select for adoption those documented changes that suit its situation.

- EDUCATE/LS: The 21st century librarian will need the mix of skills and talents suitable for a community-focused, connection-oriented, agile, proactive, and competitive institution. The organizations that train them must work closely with community libraries to learn from their experiences and convey new knowledge and opportunities. Library schools will have to change to satisfy changing professional requirements. Complementary fields of study will be a significant part of librarians' updated education and training.

- FINANCE/LS: Finally, to create these systems and establish a 21st century library system will require a substantial infusion of funding, amounting to tens of billions of dollars over the next 10 to 20 years. Although many localities will obtain government or private funds to help, a great many others will have no such opportunity. The organized aid of private philanthropy will be essential.

Consequently, creating a 21st century library system requires not only organizational innovation exceeding Melvil Dewey's, but also coordinated philanthropy even more ambitious than Andrew Carnegie's. Now, a century after their inventiveness and generosity boosted America's public libraries, libraries and their communities need once again the boon of great good fortune.

Rising to the Challenge: Re-Envisioning Public Libraries

Amy K. Garmer

Expanding access to education, learning opportunities, and social connections for all is one of the great challenges facing libraries in the digital age. It is a challenge made more urgent by the rapid transition to a new economy in which knowledge and creativity are the drivers of productivity and economic growth. But the digital revolution also opens up considerable opportunity for communities and institutions willing to champion new thinking and nurture new relationships.

The speed of technical change creates an environment in which knowledge is no longer stable over many years, and in which skills quickly become obsolete. According to John Seely Brown, co-director of the Deloitte Center for the Edge, the half-life of a skill is about five years. From this one can conclude that most learning in the future will not take place in schools.

At the same time that the half-life of a skill is shrinking, information is becoming more abundant and the means of production more accessible, which opens new channels for knowledge-sharing. A state of information abundance places a premium on the ability to navigate, create, and innovate. In this environment, success will belong to the "entrepreneurial learner," the person capable of finding resources anywhere and using them to read the world and teach themselves.

The sweeping changes under way pose new and sustained challenges for communities as well as individuals. Over the next three decades the U.S. population is expected to grow to more than 400 million. By the year 2050, 1 in 5 Americans will be an immigrant, and 30 percent of the population is projected to be Hispanic. The United States is aging too: by 2050 nearly 1 in 4 Americans will be over the age of 65.[12] Concurrent with these demographic changes are fundamental shifts in the economy that change how Americans will learn and earn a living.

The public library is uniquely positioned to provide access to and develop the skills, context, and trusted platforms needed for adapting in this new society. The eagerness of libraries to embrace changes in society, while retaining the democratic foundations that have made them welcoming places for everyone, makes them ideal partners in the digital age. Libraries have the stature and capacity to make the promise of the knowledge society available to all. The library is a core civil society institution, democracy's "maker space."

Renewed Vision for Public Libraries

The emerging value proposition of the public library is built around its three key assets—people, place, and platform. "The grand theme is that ubiquitous education and learning rises with ubiquitous computing," notes Lee Rainie, director of the Pew Research Center Internet Project. "Persistent education and learning are the reality as people march through their days with their smartphones and, soon, the Internet of Things embedded everywhere. The library as people, place, and platform is the new knowledge institution that can serve all those needs."

The Library as People

The library as people reflects the shift away from building collections to building human capital, relationships, and knowledge networks in the community. People are at the center of the library's mission to inspire and cultivate learning, advance knowledge, and nurture and strengthen communities. Measuring outcomes is more important than measuring outputs. An intelligent community, not large circulation numbers, is the primary library goal.

In this people-driven environment, skilled librarians help people navigate new technology, manage vast amounts of data and meet their information needs, delivering a high-touch, participatory experience. Library staff of the future will refine and broaden their skills to meet new needs and define the library's continuing value to the community. In particular, librarians will need to develop new competencies including:

Specialization: Communities need librarians with specialized knowledge and skills for navigating the community and curating for their communities. There is simply too much information, and knowledge changes too quickly, to make it practical for every librarian to serve as a guide to the universe of knowledge and information now available. Continuously extending the definition of the librarian (as guide, coach, mentor, and so on) is neither sustainable nor in the long-term interest of the library, according to Andrew Sliwinski, cofounder and chief maker at DIY.org. "Specialization is needed with a focus on maximizing the ability for the human capital within the library, which is one of its largest resources, to engage with patrons," he argues. "It is through this engagement that the values and the assets within each library can be most fully realized and leveraged by society."

Domain Expertise: Domain expertise is one of the new scarcities in a world otherwise overflowing with information. As noted, it is simply not practical for a library to hire new librarians to fill every need for expert knowledge and to engage with more people using the library. Libraries must use their infrastructure and assets to draw on experts in their own communities and from outside the community, and allow their domain expertise to be shared outwardly to other communities as well. Robust networks of people and technology will be vital for such wide-scale sharing.

Relationship-Building with Content Creators: Building strong relationships with content providers is an important aspect of the people-focused library. This includes not only publishers but also journalists, filmmakers, artists, and information workers. Libraries need to be deeply engaged within the ecosystem that produces the content that gets into libraries.

The Library as Place

Today's library is both a physical and virtual place, but it continues to be the physical presence of the library that anchors it most firmly in the community. In an increasingly digital world, physical library places are community assets.

The physical library will become less about citizens checking out books and more about citizens engaging in the business of making their personal and civic identities. As more information moves to digital formats, public libraries will hold less material locally in their physical collections. Library users will be able to access information digitally wherever it resides through library networks. While traditional computer workstations remain important and in demand, personal or library-provided mobile devices that provide easy connections to library wifi and high-speed broadband networks are becoming a dominant form of connection. The reduction in physical materials, greater customer mobility and the desire for more collaboration and creation are changing the nature of the public library's physical space.

The physical library must undergo a transition that embraces the openness and flexibility needed to thrive in a world of constant change. Central to this flexibility is creating spaces that can adapt to the changing operational models of libraries. Trends in library design include greater transparency among spaces, larger spaces for children and teens, meeting and activity rooms of different sizes to accommodate public events and performances or co-working and collaboration, and technology-centric spaces.

The library's virtual presence must be as engaging as its physical space and fully serve the library's mission, built around equitable access, learning, and civic development. This requires thinking beyond the transaction that characterizes many online library experiences today.

The Library as Platform

The transformations of the digital age enable individuals and communities to create their own learning and knowledge. To that end, libraries become platforms—bases on which individuals and communities create services, data, and tools that benefit the community. This allows for innovation that the platform creators cannot anticipate. Users may "customize" the platform and adapt its resources to their individual needs, whatever those needs may be. The library as a platform for community learning and creativity is the innovative proposition of the public library in the digital age.

A great library platform is a "third place"—an interactive entity that can facilitate many people operating individually or in groups. To accomplish this, libraries embody the disposition of the entrepreneurial learner: seizing opportunities wherever they may exist, engaging others in the process. The library exploits its assets—content, human capital, and expertise—to foster community dialogue that makes way for new expertise and creates new social knowledge. The library can then curate and archive the solutions created for future use.

The library as platform sees itself as "library as a service." Within the building itself, it starts with the biggest, fattest, most secure broadband "pipe" that is possible, abundant wifi, devices for borrowing, and a default embrace of new interface and display gadgets. Outside the physical library, it delivers high-quality experiences on-demand to users wherever they may be, through whatever device they may use, and for whatever purpose. Content may come from within the library's own collections, from a national content platform or anywhere in the cloud. In contrast to commercial platforms that blur the line between user and commercial interests, the library as platform is trusted to be objective and operate in the interests of its users.

Unification—getting libraries to work together, to integrate their intellectual and capital resources—is a critical platform issue. A networked society envisions public libraries connecting with other curated knowledge resources via a scalable digital network, with access to open platforms that enable discovery, creation, and sharing. It is important to think not only of how to foster connections at the local level but also how to scale up in ways that eliminate barriers traditionally imposed by geography and address long-term issues of sustainability.

Strategies for Success

The Aspen Institute Dialogue on Public Libraries has identified four strategic opportunities for action to guide the continuing transformation of public libraries and communities in the future. These are:

1 Aligning library services in support of community goals.

   Public libraries that align their people, place, and platform assets and create services that prioritize and support local community goals will find the greatest opportunities for success in the years ahead. Managers of local governments report that it is often difficult to prioritize libraries over other community services such as museums or parks and recreation departments that also serve a distinctly public mission. Libraries must be even more intentional in the ways that they deploy resources in the community, and more deeply embedded in addressing critical challenges facing the community. This will require a level of flexibility and adaptability to change as community needs evolve. It also will require collaboration among libraries, policy makers, and community partners to redefine the role of libraries as institutions that inspire learning, drive development, grow social capital, and create opportunities.

2 Providing access to content in all formats.

   As the public library shifts from a repository for materials to a platform for learning and participation, its ability to provide access to vast amounts of content in all formats is vital. Libraries face two immediate major challenges in providing access to content in all forms:

   • Being able to procure and share e-books and other digital content on a comparable (that is, equitable and affordable) basis to physical versions
   • Having affordable, high-capacity broadband that supports creation and delivery of digital content

   Dealing with both challenges has been a high priority for public libraries throughout the country. The challenges have been particularly acute for small libraries, those in rural communities, and those in some urban areas where limited budgets make access to e-books and upgrades to high-speed broadband difficult despite high community need for and interest in both. Ensuring access to e-books, other e-content, and more-than-adequate high-speed broadband is a big concern going forward because it impacts the public library's ability to fulfill one of its core missions—to procure and share the leading ideas of the day and enable everyone to participate in the world's conversations.

3 Ensuring the long-term sustainability of public libraries.

Perhaps the greatest challenge facing public libraries today is to transform their service model to meet the demands of the knowledge society while securing a sustainable funding base for the future. With limited and some-times volatile funding, however, such transformations will be uneven and incomplete. In addition, the highly local nature of public library funding and governance structures may interfere with both rapid and broad-scale progress—the kind of scale needed to compete and thrive in a world of global networks. Challenges that shape the discussion about long-term public library sustainability given their vital role in the digital era include:

- Identifying reliable sources of revenue for daily operations, as well as long-term planning and investment
- Exploring alternative governance structures and business models that maximize efficient and sustainable library operations and customer service
- Becoming more skilled at measuring outcomes rather than counting activities
- Balancing the local and national library value proposition to consider economies of scale in a networked world without compromising local control

4 Cultivating leadership.

Leadership is needed across the community—from elected officials, gov-ernment leadership staff, business and civic leaders, and librarians them-selves—to build communities and public libraries that thrive and succeed together. Vision is a critical component of leadership, and every communi-ty needs a vision and strategic plan for how to work with the public library to directly align the library and its work with the community's educational, economic, and other key goals. It must have input from all stakeholder groups in the community. Key steps in building community leadership to support the public library include improving communications with com-munity leaders, developing community champions, strengthening inter-sections with diverse communities and communities of color, reaching out to and engaging with young-professional organizations, and demonstrat-ing the collective impact of partners working together.

Facing the Challenges

Overcoming these challenges will require deeper collaboration among library leaders, policy makers at all levels of government, and community partners. It will require a new shared understanding of what makes the library uniquely valuable, beginning with its people, place, and platform assets. It also rests on the public library's uniquely *public* value proposition grounded in the principles of equity, access, opportunity, openness, and participation. These are also values at the heart of American democracy. While the vision speaks to the role of the public library and its relationship to the public, it is essentially a vision for the quality of the democratic communities that we want to nourish and sustain in the 21st century.

Trending Now—A Center for the Future of Libraries

Miguel Figueroa

The American Library Association (ALA), supported by a grant from the Institute of Museum and Library Services, formally launched the Center for the Future of Libraries in 2014. It has three primary goals: identifying emerging trends relevant to libraries and the communities they serve; promoting futuring and innovation techniques to help librarians and library professionals shape their future; and building connections with experts and innovative thinkers to help libraries address emerging issues.

The library profession, especially of late, is exploring trends and their intersections with the profession. In 2013 the International Federation of Library Associations and Institutions (IFLA) issued its Trend Report and Insights Document.[13] The first library edition of the New Media Consortium's popular Horizon Report[14] was published in 2014. ALA's Office for Information Technology Policy released in 2014 a draft meta-analysis of emerging trends[15] to serve as an input for setting a national policy agenda for libraries. And the perennial popularity of the Library and Information Technology Association's (LITA's) Top Technology Trends[16] shows no signs of waning.

Why trends? In this period of significant change and disruption, many industries, libraries included, are increasingly concerned about how best to prepare for tomorrow's needs. But, as most of us know, it's impossible to accurately predict the future. What we can identify are trends, which can be key to understanding what the future might bring.

Identifying and organizing trends helps us think about the changes happening in the world and the potential effects they will have on our futures.[17]

Awareness and understanding of trends can open new opportunities to innovate and experiment with and within these "currents" shaping society, as well as better enable us to envision the role we can play in the future. In a world of rapid change where people are more and more aware of the latest technology, news, and innovation, intentionally monitoring trends inside and outside our profession is essential to staying in step with our users.

Trends in a Trend Library

The center's focus on emerging trends follows a successful model from the Center for the Future of Museums (CFM) in engaging the museum community in conversation around a diverse range of societal, technological, political, and economic trends. The Center for the Future of Libraries actively promotes trends through ALA's social media channels, including Facebook, Twitter, and Google+, using the hashtag #libraryofthefuture. The response has been overwhelmingly positive, with followers responding to posts on topics ranging from the future of banking to robots and megacities.

Building connections between external, non-library trends and library practice has proven both popular and beneficial. Many libraries and librarians already do an exceptional job spotting trends and integrating them into their programs and services. But even the most vigilant and dedicated can be overwhelmed by the pace of change, the amount of information, and the multitude of sources and sectors from which we piece together our understandings of trends.

Designed to provide a service to the profession and help ease some of the challenges of identifying trends, the Center for the Future of Libraries began developing a "trend library."[18] Bringing together and organizing the information shared via social media and found in articles and reports from across industries, the trend library presents succinct information on trends, including how they are developing, why they matter for libraries, and links to the resources that can further explain their significance. As a collection, the trend library features coverage across categories that include society, technology, education, the environment, politics, the economy, and demographics.

Adapting a phrase popularized by *Library Journal*'s John N. Berry III ("every issue is a library issue"), the trend library helps readers see how every trend can and will be a library trend. It launched with eight entries—increases in aging, collective impact, connected learning, expanding data, the Internet of things, the maker movement, rethinking privacy, and the sharing economy. New entries, including anonymity, drones, fast casual, flipped learning, resilience, robots, unplugged, and urbanization have helped flesh out the resource. Entries are updated as new information is identified, keeping content current and useful. New entries are developed from scanning available sources and through feedback from leadership in the association and profession.

One of the most interesting things to observe within the collection is the way in which trends interrelate with and connect to each other. The Internet of things and the rapid expansion of data have clear connections, each feeding the other to sustain and expand their usefulness. The "things" will become smarter thanks in no small part to the amount of data that they can collect, generate, and share. The resulting challenges—concern for privacy, security, and technological overload—will likely grow in concert.

Drones, anonymity, unplugged movements, and changing perceptions of privacy intersect in unique and complicated ways, demonstrating how our drive for technological advancement may sometimes be at odds with our personal desires and preferences. Connected learning, the maker movement, and the sharing economy grow out of the renewed importance of individual experience and personal connection. While distinct from each other, the trends capitalize on a renewed appreciation for experience, personal connection, and independence.

And then there are the trends that seem niche or uncomplicated, but that upon closer inspection reveal the potential for significant change. An aging population seems like a simple trend that should be acknowledged in terms of service development. Diving deeper, however, reveals the potential impacts on the workplace, government, technology, and the economy and leaves planners with new challenges and considerations.

Similarly the "fast casual" concept, an important trend within the restaurant and hospitality industries, has had a profound impact on customers' expectations for service, technology, space design, and personal engagement. We can expect that as more people experience the fast casual concept, they will carry with them these new expectations whether in a restaurant, government agency, or even a library.

The trend library is not a top ten, most important, or coolest list. It's simply a curated collection meant to help librarians explore and come to their own conclusions and priorities based on their own interests, strengths, and the needs and aspirations of their community. The library is a starting place from which we can build our knowledge.

Trends to Innovation

How do we leverage knowledge and understanding of trends into experimentation and innovation? Many libraries and librarians have already demonstrated an ability to respond to trends by adapting library services, exemplified by the integration of maker spaces into libraries, the introduction of robotics and coding, and the forging of new partnerships.

The trend library will be expanded to include space for sharing these best practices and accelerating dissemination across the profession. As much as the trend library can be a place for sharing trends from outside the profession, it also can document and promote libraries' and librarians' spirit of innovation.

With support from a 2015 ASAE Foundation Innovation Grant, the center also will encourage experimentation through a new online space for crowdsourcing innovative approaches to programs and services. The platform will allow librarians and supporters to submit innovative solutions to issues within the field and leverage the wisdom of the crowd to select the most viable options. The crowdsourcing space can help incubate and improve programs or services, responsibly develop solutions that conform to shared values and standards of the profession, and provide broad-based support for innovators to launch and refine their ideas within their professional community.

More experiments and initiatives to help highlight library innovation will follow, and many of them will likely grow out of an increasing knowledge of the trends that will affect the future of library services.

Trends to Experts

Through the process of identifying trends, the center also is forging new relationships. By searching broadly across industries, the center can identify and build bridges to the people and organizations leading change in society, technology, education, the environment, and government.

In 2014 then-ALA President Barbara Stripling hosted a summit on the future of libraries, "Libraries From Now On: Imagining the Future." The event, which brought together leaders from the library community as well as supporters and partners from educational organizations, federal agencies, and foundations, provided a helpful start toward developing a community of experts to point the way to the future. Participants expressed a clear optimism about the future of libraries even as they emphasized an urgent need for libraries to look outward and adapt to current and emerging trends shaping society.

Using the summit as a launching pad, the center has begun growing a network of expert partners in business, social innovation, associations, foundations, and future-focused organizations. Overwhelmingly these organizations express optimism for the future of libraries and welcome the center's work in recognizing the trends and directions that shape our shared world.

Looking Forward

Through its first year, the Center for the Future of Libraries has worked to develop a centralized place within the profession to monitor and share new and emerging trends relevant to libraries; to bring together and promote innovations already happening within the profession; to help spur and accelerate innovations; and to lead the profession's outreach to experts and innovators interested in collaborating on the future of libraries.

In this time of rapid change, providing a dedicated space for librarians and library supporters to better understand the trends shaping libraries and the innovative responses libraries are providing is critically important. The world is changing, but libraries are changing with it. The Center for the Future of Libraries can provide a place to show the new directions libraries might take and connect with the innovations and partners that will take us there.

Conclusion

Larra Clark

So, where to now? As we gather up the threads that Roger, Amy, and Miguel have spun out for us, we see complements and tensions. One might imagine that the INNOVATE/LS that Roger calls for could be realized, at least in part, through the Center for the Future of Libraries and the systems that Miguel is putting in place. A challenge persists in connecting the local innovations taking places in libraries and communities and connecting, analyzing, and disseminating them in a way that can ease the learning curve across the profession.

Both Roger and Amy point to a concern that may be growing in a time of further constrained public dollars and political shifts at the state and national level that call for smaller government. How will we financially sustain libraries in a way that remains true to their mission of universal service—rather than devolving to a situation in which wealthy communities maintain and grow their libraries while more cash-strapped towns and cities strip down or eliminate this community asset? Libraries are a great equalizer, but they are largely dependent on the same public dollars that support schools, police, fire protection, roads, and other basic public infrastructure. Roger asks us to consider a public radio or television model for content production and distribution; are there lessons there, as well, for fund raising and supporting supersystems that feed into local libraries while allowing them to refocus constrained local budgets?

There is an increased focus on connections over collections, but access to content itself remains essential to the vision of the library as a platform. How is a collection different from a platform? Perhaps this is embedded in Roger's shift from the passive to the competitive and the responsive to proactive, from static to dynamic. In a networked world, information is no longer contained and bound, but linked and embedded. This requires developing new relationships among "stuff" to bring this interconnected vibrancy to physical and virtual library spaces. For instance, a library might present a live (or archived) webcast from the Metropolitan Opera with a local educator or aficionado to discuss and describe a wide range of digital and physical materials the library offers to continue exploration. The platform can then also encourage and capture new content or mashups that result from that exploration.

Also embedded in each essay is a demand for new skills and competencies among librarians to deliver diverse and relevant services that connect with diverse users. Master's programs like the one at the University of Maryland–College Park are undertaking their own "re-envisioning" and "hacking" of library education.[19] The Maryland program, which celebrates its 50th anniversary in 2015, is aggressively considering what's to come for the next 50 years. But library staff are subject to the same "half-life" of skills Amy describes, and even re-engineered master's programs will need to be supplemented to support continuous "entrepreneurial learning." Furthermore, there is a growing interest in shifting the human resources of the library to create greater permeability with our communities. In libraries like San Francisco Public Library and Pima County (Arizona) Public Library, social workers and nurses are working inside the library to connect library users to resources beyond information. On campuses "embedded librarians" are taking library services to the users where they are, rather than waiting for library visitors to arrive at the study carrels. How could the meanings of "library" and "librarian" change as a result?

Close to my heart in the ALA Office for Information Technology Policy is the imperative to re-engineer our national policy approaches in the same way that librarians are shifting their practice and services. This is the driving concept behind the Policy Revolution! Initiative.[20] The three-year effort has three major elements: to develop a national public policy agenda, to initiate and deepen national stakeholder interactions based on policy priorities, and to build library advocacy capacity for the long-term.

We believe the investment in libraries has lagged the opportunities that libraries present. And in the digital age, these opportunities expand considerably. Thus, the nation will be well served by increased investments in libraries, and especially in areas of notable opportunity that advance the agendas of national decision makers. Increasing understanding of how libraries are doing this work and illustrating what is possible with increased capacity establishes the basis for added support from and collaboration with national government agencies, nonprofit organizations, foundations, trade associations, and commercial entities.

Finally, the objective and venerable researchers at the Pew Research Center offer encouragement for libraries in taking bold steps. Lee Rainie, director of Internet Science and Technology Research, notes five reasons our foundation is solid: Libraries are appreciated (91 percent of Americans say libraries are important to their communities); libraries stack up well as a priority compared with others.[21]

Libraries enjoy great good will, and our campuses and communities face significant challenges that libraries' people, places, and platforms can help address. Our relevance, however, will increasingly be determined by how well we leverage and integrate these assets with community priorities. Further, librarians and library advocates must also communicate how libraries are contributing to successfully addressing these priorities to secure the resources and relationships needed to continue building capacity. About 1 in 5 Americans say they don't know very much about what public libraries offer, and 10 percent know nothing at all.[22] This must change—particularly among local, state, and national decision makers and influencers—if libraries and librarians are to have the vibrant future our communities, campuses, employers, researchers, teachers, and students need and deserve.

Notes

1. Swan, D. W., Grimes, J., Owens, T., Miller, K., Arroyo, J., Craig, T., Dorinski, S., Freeman, M., Isaac, N., O'Shea, P., Padgett, R., & Schilling, P. (2014). Public Libraries in the United States Survey: Fiscal Year 2012 (IMLS-2015–PLS-01). Institute of Museum and Library Services. Washington, D.C.

2. Flood, Alison. "Library Usage Falls Significantly as Services Shrink," *The Guardian,* December 10, 2014. http://www.theguardian.com/books/2014/dec/10/library-usage-falls-dramatically-services-visits-down-40m.

3. *2012 State of America's Libraries* report. http://www.ala.org/news/mediapresscenter/americaslibraries/soal2012/academic-libraries.

4. *2014 State of America's Libraries* report. http://www.ala.org/news/state-americas-libraries-report-2014/school-libraries.

5. Fletcher, William I. "The Public Library Movement," *Cosmopolitan Magazine*, November 1894. Fletcher, a former president of ALA, interpreted statistics from U.S. Bureau of Education, *Statistics of Public Libraries of the United States and Canada,* Government Printing Office, Washington, 1893.

6. Levien, Roger E. "Through the Google Glass, Dimly," *American Libraries* digital e-supplement, June 2014. Also available at: http://www.americanlibrariesmagazine.org/article/through-google-glass-dimly.

7. Levien was vice president for strategy at Xerox during this period. The experiences of Kodak and Xerox are described and contrasted in his forthcoming publication, *A Matter of Life and Death—Kodak and Xerox Confront Disruption.*

8. Amy K. Garmer, director, Aspen Institute Dialogue on Public Libraries. *Rising to the Challenge: Re-Envisioning Public Libraries,* The Aspen Institute. Washington, D.C. October 2014. ISBN: 0-89843-611-7.

9. Demers, Patricia (chair), Guylaine Beaudry, Pamela Bjornson, Michael Carroll, Carol Couture, Charlotte Gray, Judith Hare, Ernie Ingles, Eric Katelaar, Gerald McMaster, and Ken Roberts (2014). Expert Panel Report on *The Future Now: Canada's Libraries, Archives, and Public Memory.* Royal Society of Canada, Ottawa, ON. ISBN: 978-1-928140-01-6.

10. William Sieghart and Panel, *Independent Library Report for England.* December 18, 2014. https://www.gov.uk/government/publications/independent-library-report-for-england.

11. I have drawn upon recommendations that will be presented more fully in my forthcoming book, *The Once and Future Library,* 2015.

12. U.S. Census Bureau, "U.S. Census Bureau Projections Show a Slower Growing, Older, More Diverse Nation a Half Century from Now," news release, December 12, 2012. https://www.census.gov/newsroom/releases/archives/population/cb12-243.html.

13. http://trends.ifla.org.

14. http://redarchive.nmc.org/publications/2014-horizon-report-library.

15. http://www.districtdispatch.org/2014/08/understanding-turbulent-world-develop-library-policy-agenda.

16. http://www.ala.org/lita/ttt.

17. *Futuring: The Exploration of the Future.* Edward Cornish. World Future Society, 2005.

18. http://www.ala.org/transforminglibraries/future/trends.

19. http://mls.umd.edu/2014/09/re-envisioning-mls.

20. http://www.ala.org/offices/PR-documents.

21. http://libraries.pewinternet.org.

22. http://libraries.pewinternet.org/2013/12/11/libraries-in-communities.

Preservation Pending: The Future of E-Book Access in the Digital Age

Melissa Goertzen
Robert Wolven
Jeffrey D. Carroll

For a very long time human knowledge has been recorded on print media and passed down, or preserved, for future generations. Since the latter half of the 20th century, however, this human knowledge has been increasingly recorded in digital media. Whether we will be as successful as our predecessors at preserving human knowledge will depend on the steps we take now to identify and address the risks and threats when knowledge is stored in digital form.

This report focuses specifically on e-books as a subset of all digital media. In some respects we are lucky in that the conversation surrounding the risks and threats to journal literature as it passed from print to digital has been going on for more than two decades, and some promising models and ideas have emerged. On the other hand e-books present problems that differ from those on the journal side and that will need to be addressed from scratch, as it were, with no prior models on which to build. Nor will this report provide ready answers. Rather, by bringing the conversation here we are throwing down the gauntlet and challenging all members of the information ecosystem to think seriously about the issues and to take the steps necessary to work toward a solution that is of mutual benefit to us all.

The Evolving Challenges of Preservation and Conservation

The term *preservation* in libraries refers to the overall system of efforts aimed at maximizing the longevity of our cultural heritage and of the outputs of scholarly inquiry. Research is a cumulative activity; scholars of today build on the findings and hypotheses of scholars who have gone before. As scholarly interests and societal values change, works that may have seemed to have limited, ephemeral interest when first published may take on new importance. Libraries have been the primary means of ensuring the survival of the scholarly and cultural record. For printed materials, they have accomplished this through conservation—the treating of single items in an effort to mitigate the effects of deterioration—by storing materials in controlled environments, and by converting the content to new formats when necessary. Each of these actions is but one element of a preservation strategy. Preservation practices evolve in the delicate balance between art and science. With each new generation, volumes of intellectual and cultural output undergo rigorous

Melissa Goertzen is the e-book program development librarian at Columbia University Libraries. Her research focuses on the documentation of the e-book landscape and the development of strategic plans relating to e-book collection development programs. Robert Wolven is associate university librarian for bibliographic services and collection development at Columbia University Libraries. He is a former co-chair of the American Library Association's Digital Content and Libraries Working Group (DCWG) and a current member of the DCWG subgroup on digital preservation. Jeffrey D. Carroll is director of collection development at Columbia University Libraries. His work most recently has focused on the opportunities and challenges of cooperative collection development and vendor negotiations across multiple research institutions.

evaluations to determine which artifacts merit preservation efforts. Conservation efforts are made to preserve the item itself as well as its content. Then efforts are made to place items into a historic context that forms the basis for a common cultural heritage. However, as society becomes increasingly reliant on digital technologies to produce and disseminate information, the development of strategies to preserve this information has lagged behind. This is due in large part to the rate of technological changes taking place in the sharing of information, and the complexity involved in constructing an environment that accounts for the quick pace at which this rapidly evolving technology becomes obsolete. The preservation of digital content becomes a daunting task facing information professionals.

Today much discussion surrounds the development of e-book preservation practices. In many cases, proposed strategies to tackle this complex challenge are still theoretical and abstract. However, last year librarians at Columbia University Libraries (CUL) received an acquisition request for a unique born-digital item that rooted our preservation challenges in an entirely practical context.

In 1963 Josef Albers published *Interaction of Color,* which is hailed as the canonical work regarding the study of and relationships between colors. Albers developed the text to serve as a hands-on kit that provides an interactive environment to conduct silkscreen color studies. However, there are limits to interactivity as the book was originally published in print format. Now, 50 years after its original publication, the text has been released in a digital format that brings Albers's original vision to life. Yale University Press released the *Interaction of Color* app, which includes more than 125 color plates, 60 interactive studies, and commentary from Albers. This is a landmark publication and won the George Wittenborn Memorial Book Award for excellence in art publishing from the Art Libraries Society of North America in the past year (YaleNews, 2014).

Librarians at CUL faced a number of central challenges. Because its value to the scholarly community is tied to its interactive learning environment, we searched for a means to purchase a preservation copy that guarantees long-term access to both content and functionality. We discovered that because the app can be licensed only through iTunes (currently, there is not a business model that supports a flat-out purchase of the app), there is no way to capture and archive content. Even if there were such a method, there are no benchmarks that estimate the costs of long-term app maintenance and storage.

While there is debate regarding whether this item should be considered an e-book, it still raises valid questions about e-book preservation practices and strategies. Until recently e-versions of texts have been viewed as supplementary to print copies (Armstrong and Lonsdale, 2009). Because they were acquired to "back up" print copies, preservation of the e-version was not considered urgent or even necessary. Today we stand at a tipping point and discover an increasing number of e-books that have no print equivalent. Like the *Interaction of Color* app, many of these items have significant cultural and intellectual value that may affect the way knowledge is disseminated within the research community and general public in the coming years.

In today's information society, securing the funds and server space to preserve text-only files can be a challenge. However, this process seems straightforward compared with what e-books are becoming: interactive pieces of media that are hybrids of databases, websites, and games (Robertson, 2014). In order to develop effective preservation strategies and frameworks, the library community first must understand on an intellectual, technical, legal, and financial level what preservation means for items in the digital world (Robertson, 2014). For instance, does digital preservation apply to content, functionality, or both? Is it possible to secure legal rights to preserve content that is licensed? How do we guarantee perpetual access to content that is tied to hardware, software, and file formats that will become obsolete within the next decade?

While the answers to the above questions will shape future preservation policies, a larger challenge looms on the horizon—the sheer size of the digital universe. With an exponential growth in born-digital content, there is a massive body of electronic information at our fingertips; portions of it merit preservation while others do not. In this environment, how do librarians decide what items should be captured, stored, and managed over time? The answer will affect how our intellectual and cultural heritage is shaped for future generations of scholars, students, and readers.

The Landscape: E-Books vs. E-Journals

By 2005 the information profession faced a significant digital preservation challenge with the growth of e-journal publication and many libraries beginning to collect some journals solely in digital form. At that time, the academic community recognized a pressing need to take action to preserve scholarly electronic journals to guarantee perpetual access to information. The need for a stable and reliable preservation strategy was outlined in a report titled "Urgent Action Needed to Preserve Scholarly Electronic Journals," which was authored by library leaders representing research institutions in the United States and received the support of the Association of Research Libraries (ARL) (Kirchhoff, 2011). The document defined the initial strategy as a "way of managing risk, first, against the permanent loss of electronic journals and second, against having journal access disrupted for a protracted period following a publisher failure" (ARL, 2005). In the following years, a task force under the guidance of OCLC's Research Libraries Group (RLG) and the National Archives and Records Administration (NARA) developed standardized tools and metrics. The most notable was the Trusted Repository Audit Checklist (TRAC) based upon the Open Archival Information Systems (OAIS) Reference Model. Today, digital repositories that have passed TRAC certification have the highest level of protection and security of e-journal content. Examples of these repositories include CLOCKSS (Controlled Lots of Copies Keep Stuff Safe), Portico, and HathiTrust (Center for Research Libraries, n.d.).

Given the fact that standardized metrics now exist for e-journal preservation (and, to date, have proven successful), one may ask why TRAC has not been more widely applied to e-book preservation. After all, the two formats share similarities in their general makeup—they are both electronic resources that consist of two parts: files and metadata. However, when the surface is scratched, e-book preservation presents unique challenges that have not been encountered in the past. These include, but are not limited to, the following six issues (Kirchhoff and Morrissey, 2014; Kelley, 2014; Kirchhoff, 2011):

1 E-book versions—journal articles, once published, tend to be stable; by contrast, e-books (particularly trade books) may continue to be revised and enhanced

2 Digital rights management (DRM)—relates to the common practice of embedding technologies in e-book files or devices that restrict access to content based on licensing terms

3 Metadata—relates to managing the hierarchy of metadata at many levels of the publication (such as chapters, volumes, and series)

4 Legal issues—refers to the rights to use, share, and preserve e-books

5 Format issues—refers to the coupling of e-book content with hardware, software, or distribution platforms

6 Business models—refers to the sustainability of e-book licensing models and a fractured business landscape driven by proprietary platforms.

With this complex e-book landscape, libraries must develop preservation practices and strategies that promote perpetual accessibility, usability, authenticity, and discoverability of information. Together, these four qualities ensure "fitness of use," a primary principle that guides and informs ongoing preservation decisions, actions, and financial investments (Smith, 2004).

Global Trends

This report primarily focuses on preservation trends and challenges faced by stakeholders in the United States. However, as markets become increasingly global in nature, it is important to understand e-book landscapes outside North America as they will impact preservation strategies in the future—particularly in terms of legal rights and collection development priorities.

In the English-speaking world, the United States has the strongest e-book market; e-book sales account for approximately a third of book revenues, particularly in the segments of adult fiction and genre fiction (Rüdiger Wischenbart, 2014). Across Western Europe, the adoption of e-books by consumers varies. In Germany, which has one of the world's largest book markets, e-book purchasing trends are beginning to follow English-language markets but are approximately three years behind (Rüdiger Wischenbart, 2014). Across France, Spain, and Italy, e-book "momentum seems to be fairly limited" (Rüdiger Wischenbart, 2014, p. 20). Most surprising are trends observed in Sweden, where a "domestic e-book market has hardly taken shape, due to a mix of high prices for e-books and the role taken up by libraries who are lending significantly more e-books to readers than retail has sold so far" (Rüdiger Wischenbart, 2014, p. 20).

In other parts of the globe, a number of large markets are emerging. Below are four markets that may impact the future of online educational resources.

- China: The world's most populous country is also the world's second-largest e-book market, with 52 percent growth in 2012 (Kelbanoff, 2013). It is also estimated that there are 500 million Internet users and 1.22 billion mobile phone users in China (Kelbanoff, 2013). Based on the market potential, competition among e-book providers is growing. In 2013 Amazon launched a dedicated Chinese platform, Apple's iPhones were cleared to run on China's mobile networks, and the domestic online platform, Dangdang, offered its catalog for free (Rüdiger Wischenbart, 2014). Currently, the fastest-developing market for English-language books is focused on libraries, schools, and other institutions (Kelbanoff, 2013).

- Russia: During 2013 Russian e-book sales surpassed those in the United Kingdom and Brazil, making Russia the world's third largest e-book market (Gerden, 2014). The country has a "thriving reading culture in which writers and intellectuals occupy a prominent role in the public sphere and in which books stand at the center of the country's cultural ambitions" (Rüdiger Wischenbart, 2014, p. 58). Since 2011 the market has increased by nearly 200 percent and is expected to continue growing (Gerden, 2014). Although the sale of dedicated e-readers has declined, sales from personal computers and laptops continue to drive the market forward. Since 2012 Apple has opened an iTunes store in Russia, Google a Google Play store, and Kobo has announced plans to offer services (Rüdiger Wischenbart, 2014).

- Brazil: The Brazilian book market has shown strong growth for years with no signs of slowing down. For instance, consumers in 2013 spent 8.8 billion Brazilian reals (more than $4 billion) on books, a growth of 7 percent from the previous year (Utsumi, 2014). E-books are not widely used today, but companies including Amazon, Apple, Google, and Kobo (all of whom set up e-book stores in the country within the past two years) believe there is large potential for development. In 2013 a number of Brazilian publishers attributed 4 percent of their market shares to e-books (Utsumi, 2014). Another factor that is expected to influence the market is the fact that customers do not pay value-added taxes or sales taxes on books in Brazil (Rüdiger Wischenbart, 2014). "The Brazilian senate is discussing a bill that would officially make both e-books and dedicated e-readers tax-free. If the bill passes, the prices of E-Ink Kindles, Kobo devices, and Nooks would have to come down steadily" (Rüdiger Wischenbart, 2014, p. 65).

- India: Currently, close to 24 percent of texts published in India are English-language titles. To date "all the major publishers in India, such as Penguin Books India, Hachette India, and Westland, have digitized their English-language backlists" (Vyas, 2014, para. 2). There is also great progress taking place in terms of regional e-books. With 25 regional languages spoken in India, there is an opportunity for writers "outside of the country to make further inroads into the Indian market through getting their works translated" (Vyas, 2014, para. 4). This is especially true for self-published titles, as the legal process of forming partnerships with translation companies is less complex. On the technological side, dedicated e-readers have not made a significant market impact due to consumers' questions about their overall value, but companies such as Flipkart have successfully introduced e-reading apps that can be used on tablets and phones, allowing consumers to "read e-books on devices they are most familiar with" (Vyas, 2014, para. 9).

These global trends are likely to prove of increasing importance to U.S. libraries as well. Many public libraries acquire books from other countries to serve foreign-speaking populations. Research libraries acquire a range of publications from all world regions to serve both current and future scholarship. Just as e-book markets are developing in different ways and at different rates, though, the legal regimes, licensing terms, and business models that affect the ability of libraries to preserve this content present wide differences, and thus complicate the challenge.

Current Preservation Trends

A *Library Journal* e-book survey discovered a 93 percent increase in e-book collections among academic libraries since 2012. The survey also found that libraries anticipate e-book spending to compose 20 percent of their budgets within five years (Blummer and Kenton, 2012), a figure that could range anywhere from a half million dollars for a medium-sized academic library to more than 2 million dollars for a large one. Despite the increase in e-book acquisition, it is not clear if or how e-book content will remain accessible in years to come.

Historically, the first sale doctrine has provided a crucial underpinning for preservation work: when libraries purchase a print book, they are free to rent it out, resell it, or keep it forever (Smith, 2004). In this environment, libraries own their copy of the physical book, own the storage unit (often a bookshelf), and maintain the book for future use. Digital objects have disrupted this model. The idea of purchasing a "copy" of an e-book or "lending" it to someone else is no longer relevant. In the digital world, the first sale doctrine is no longer applicable in a legal context. In 2010 an appeals court ruling in the case *Vernor* v. *Autodesk* established that individuals cannot "buy" a piece of software, only acquire a permanent and non-transferable license to it (Smith, 2004). For libraries, this means that the legal ownership of individual titles, the storage unit (often a piece of hardware or software), and the ability to maintain files for future use are tied to the content provider (often a publisher or software developer).

Libraries license e-books, and usually these licenses do not include the legal right to capture or preserve content. In the past, the inability to preserve e-book content has not been a concern as long as a print version is available in the collection. However, as born-digital content becomes increasingly common, the information profession faces a renewed urgency to preserve content that does not have a print equivalent. This is particularly problematic when DRM restrictions prevent libraries from downloading or printing copies of e-books for archival purposes. In the current market, publishers are often not prepared to sell digital e-book files to libraries due to fears of piracy, decreased revenue, or an absence of business models that support such transactions.

On the flip side, even if publishers were prepared to sell e-book files, the majority of libraries do not have adequate infrastructure to house them. Although there are some notable exceptions, at this time most do not have an institutional repository capable of storing digital files for generations to come (Yale University Library, 2013). Also, many do not have the financial resources, server space, or ability to perform continuous file maintenance and migration activities that are components of digital preservation programs.

Given the current landscape, trade-offs between ease of access and long-term preservation are necessary. In many cases, data dependencies on hardware, software, or publishers' and distributors' servers create barriers. Information in the digital world is immaterial and must be created each time it is used (Smith, 2004), creating obstacles to access and long-term preservation (Smith, 2004; Kirchhoff, 2011). This means that even if a library owns an e-book, it is often impossible to migrate those bytes from one platform to another. In order to facilitate both information accessibility and preservation, "the intellectual content of the book must be unpacked from its reliance on a particular hardware and software and then that content must be securely stowed away and maintained by one or more preservation agencies" (Kirchhoff, 2011, p. 34). Due to the complex relationship between access and preservation, there is currently no e-book solution that "simultaneously meets both the 'current use' and 'future use' requirements" (Yale University Library, 2013, p. 7). In some cases, it may make economic sense for libraries to purchase an electronic format without thinking about long-term access. Technical manuals, for instance, are in strong demand when current, but quickly become obsolete. On the other hand, academic libraries will often purchase titles (such as new foreign literature) not because of current user demand, but to preserve the content in anticipation of future interest (Yale University Library, 2013).

In the research community, both ease of access and preservation are vital to the continued development of disciplines, as many "subjects of inquiry and methodologies rely heavily on retrospective [and] current resources" (Smith, 2004, para. 1). For the many stakeholders involved in preservation, access to information removes knowledge barriers and promotes the widespread sharing and vetting of ideas.

Preservation Stakeholders

Today e-book collections reside in the cloud, meaning that content is stored on server networks that run applications and provide online access to digital resources (GCF Global, 2015). Access to content is gained by purchasing a license, such as a subscription. In the current e-book landscape, there is no guarantee that content will be available long-term—or even next week for that matter. Events such as mergers between service providers, evolving licensing models, and the obsolescence of hardware and software can result in the discontinuation of access to countless e-book titles. The instability of e-book collections and packages is a significant barrier as preservation relies on perpetual access to content (and some suggest perpetual functionality as well).

The challenges relating to e-book preservation involve a range of stakeholders with very diverse interests, needs, and limitations. They include libraries (both public and academic), publishers, distributors, third-party storage services, and authors. The development of stable and sustainable e-book preservation programs will involve a deep understanding of the perspectives, responsibilities, and roles that each stakeholder brings to the table.

In the library profession, preservation challenges are felt in different ways by public and academic libraries. On the public side, many librarians are tasked with developing collections that meet the present information needs of diverse user communities. Much of this work involves licensing fiction and nonfiction titles, often through services such as OverDrive and 3M, released by mass-market publishers that have commercial interests. Facilitating long-term preservation has not traditionally been a necessary role for public libraries. In many cases, they do not have the legal rights, funds, or data infrastructures required to preserve this content (Ciabattari, 2013; Kelley, 2012). Some public libraries have begun to challenge this model by negotiating deals with small and nontraditional publishers that allow for e-book files to be mounted on local library servers. While their primary impetus is to gain more control over the content rather than preservation per se, in the current e-book landscape these libraries may be in the best position to preserve e-books as well.

When discussing the relationship between libraries and for-profit publishers, it is important to keep in mind that "the time horizons of the preservation community and of the commercial sectors are radically different" (Smith, 2004). In the private sector, data retention is often limited to anywhere between five and ten years (Smith, 2004). The time horizon of the preservation community "must include many generations of inquiring humans, not just the next two generations of hardware or software upgrades" (Smith, 2004, para. 35). Some have cited this fundamental difference as the reason why for-profit companies have not played a strong role in the development of preservation systems, even though they provide leadership in such areas as information technologies and digital asset management (Smith, 2004). The fundamental difference in data retention schedules is an area where creativity and experimentation will be required to develop preservation programs that promote buy-in from all sides and provide value to all stakeholders involved.

In academia, the ability to guarantee perpetual access to scholarly content is a pressing issue. In the research community, both ease of access and preservation are vital to the continued development of disciplines because inquiry and discovery rely on the utilization of current and retrospective resources (Smith, 2004). In academia, one way that librarians promote preservation is by "brokering deals with publishers and third-party storage services like Portico, which hold scholarly literature in a kind of escrow" (Robertson, 2014, para. 6). Librarians provide funding to such ventures through access fees and are guaranteed access to content when "trigger" events occur—most notably when titles go out of circulation or publishers cease operations (Robertson, 2014).

Due to the complexities and costs of digital preservation repositories, it is unlikely that individual institutions will serve as preservation centers (Smith, 2004). In the current networked environment, "one does not need access to a physical object to have access to information, [and] the relationship between ownership (and physical custody) of information and access to it will be transformed" (Smith, 2004, para. 36). It is likely that a small number of actors, such as Portico (Portico, 2015), will serve the academic community to preserve the scholarly record. In the future, third-party storage services will be an essential part of the "public good information economy that research and teaching have traditionally relied upon for core services such as preservation and collection building" (Smith, 2004, para. 36).

While preservation discussions among libraries, publishers, and third-party storage services will continue for some time, a growing volume of titles are springing up outside traditional publishing frameworks—they fall into the category of self-published e-books. Last year alone, editors at *Washington Post Book World* received 150 self-published books *each day* (Charles, 2014). Established authors such as Stephen King, along with those embarking on a writing career, are beginning to turn to services offered through Amazon and Kickstarter to fund or promote their work. This is not a trend that will disappear in the near future. In some cases, corporate publishers are beginning to step into the self-publishing arena as well. In 2012 Simon & Schuster partnered with the self-publishing company Author Solutions, Inc., to form Archway Publishing, a service that helps authors to reach audiences, achieve publishing goals, and make the leap to traditional publishing (Author Solutions, 2012; Ciabattari, 2013). The preservation challenge surrounding this type of content (besides determining which titles merit preservation efforts) lies in the fact that e-books are currently exempt from mandatory legal deposit. Further, self-published e-books do not require an International Standard Book Number (ISBN), and there is not a simple way to contact or negotiate with independent authors regarding preservation issues (Kelley, 2014). This is a particularly harrowing issue when self-published works have scholarly merit. There exists a large opportunity for preservationists and computer scientists to work with scholars to develop and document standards for resources that are self-published for research and teaching purposes (Smith, 2004).

Market Segments

If e-books are to be preserved for long-term access, the impetus for action is most likely to come from those institutions that purchase—or license—them. An understanding of market sectors, and in particular of the ways in which different categories of e-books are acquired by libraries, is thus crucial to understanding the issues, barriers, and potential solutions for e-book preservation.

Broadly speaking, the library market for e-books mirrors that for print, with two major sectors: trade books aimed at the general reading public are primarily marketed to public libraries; scholarly works are aimed at the college and university population and acquired by academic libraries. While there is some overlap, and occasional "crossover" titles such as Thomas Piketty's *Capital in the Twenty-First Century,* most publishers tend to focus on one segment or the other. This division has, thus far, resulted in significant differences in business models and in the terms under which e-books are sold—differences that have profound implications for long-term preservation and access.

While the academic e-book market is still evolving, certain core characteristics seem likely to persist. E-books are sold both as individual titles and in large groups or packages, both directly by publishers and through intermediary distributors, or aggregators, who group titles from many publishers in a common platform. Libraries will license access to some collections on a subscription basis, paying for access year by year, and losing access if payment stops. Many titles, however, are licensed for "perpetual access" with a higher one-time payment. Perpetual access licenses very often include provisions for archiving, either by defining terms under which the library may acquire and use the digital files, or by depositing those files with an agency such as CLOCKSS (www.clockss.org), LOCKSS (www.lockss.org), or Portico. All three of these agencies were founded to preserve e-journals, but CLOCKSS and Portico have since expanded to embrace e-books, with CLOCKSS holding nearly 25,000 e-books and Portico almost half a million. These arrangements reflect research libraries' common interest in long-term preservation of the scholarly record.

By contrast, most trade e-books have been available to public libraries for only the past few years, and the markets and business terms are still diverse and changing rapidly. Again, though, certain common features appear to be emerging. Most trade publishers do not sell e-books directly to libraries, but work through a small number of distributors such as OverDrive, 3M, and Baker and Taylor. While some publishers make titles available for purchase (or, more accurately, perpetual access), it is far more common for e-books to be licensed for a limited term of one or two years, or for a limited number of circulations. Even for those titles available for "purchase," long-term access depends on the distributors, with no provision for external archiving. These models reflect the practical concerns of public libraries, which primarily collect to meet current reading interests, with a high turnover in collections.

In addition to these two broad patterns, there are of course many variations and experiments. Some public libraries, notably the Douglas County (Colorado) Public Library (douglascountylibraries.org), working primarily with smaller and nontraditional publishers, have developed models for purchasing and mounting the e-book files themselves, thus securing at least the potential to preserve these books. Some academic libraries have become publishers of scholarly e-books, either on their own or in partnership with university presses. These and similar experiments offer potential alternative models for preservation that may in time prove more broadly influential.

For a large and growing number of e-books, however, library markets are virtually nonexistent. New types of publication and new methods of publishing are emerging that have not, as yet, found their way into the standard channels by which libraries acquire content. Four main categories can serve as illustrations:

1 Nonprofit publishers: Academic libraries have an interest in many works that are not produced by commercial publishers but by non-governmental organizations, government agencies, and research institutes. Many of these works are now published online, and while freely available on the Web, they are not sold to libraries. Although not often thought of as e-books, they have formed an important part of research library collections.

2 Open access publishing: Although the scholarly open access movement has thus far focused largely on journal articles, it is starting to become a force in e-book publishing as well. These works are, by design, freely available, but for that very reason don't fit existing library methods of acquisition and preservation.

3 Nontraditional publishers: The relative ease of distribution over the Web and sale through online retailers has brought a proliferation of small publishers and non-publishers (such as advertising agencies, art galleries) offering a mere handful of digital titles, often available only for individual purchase and download to personal e-readers.

4 Self-publishing: The ease of self-publishing on the Web has led to an explosion of hundreds of thousands of titles. Most of these works are again

only available for individual purchase and download to e-readers, or as part of e-book subscription services.

For many of these publications the role libraries should play in providing access and the importance of long-term preservation remain uncertain. What does seem clear is that the need for action to secure future access will not wait for that clarity to develop.

Issues and Barriers that Require Solutions

Lack of clarity is pervasive when it comes to e-book preservation. Who should bear the responsibility? How can the costs be supported? What are the technical requirements? What legal rights are involved? Those with the strongest interest in outcomes are not at present in a position to take direct action. Yet a clearer understanding of the issues and barriers may suggest potential solutions.

Responsibility and Cost

Primary responsibility for preserving print books has long rested with research libraries, university libraries, the largest public libraries (such as New York Public Library), and (in the United States) the Library of Congress. Publishers are supportive of preservation in principle, but are perforce driven by financial considerations, and likely to preserve their output only so long as potential sales exceed the cost. Public libraries are primarily responsible for serving the current needs and interests of their communities, and are not funded to sustain access to works once demand for them has faded.

Given the opportunity, scholarly publishers and academic libraries have invested in e-book preservation, primarily through participation in CLOCKSS and Portico. Costs are shared by contributing publishers and member libraries. Although the economics are not transparent, it seems probable that at least some of the publishers' costs are passed on to libraries and other e-book purchasers in the form of higher prices. While the long-term costs and success of this model remain to be seen, it offers a reasonable prospect that most mainstream scholarly monographs will be preserved.

The situation with regard to trade books is far murkier. Many popular books of the past—bestsellers, dime novels, picture books, mysteries, science fiction, and other genre fiction—are now preserved in academic library collections. With few exceptions, however, these libraries didn't acquire such works as they were published, but long after, through donations from private collectors and secondary markets such as used book dealers. This deferred acquisition—and subsequent preservation—is made possible by the first sale doctrine, under which owners of print books have the right to dispose of them as they choose—lending, donating, or selling their copies to others. Many more popular books—from cookbooks to carpentry, self-help to devotional literature—are acquired by the Library of Congress through legal deposit (which requires that copies of each new print publication be deposited with the U.S. Copyright Office).

Currently, however, as noted above, the first sale doctrine does not apply to e-books. Instead, the rights of owners, even those who have purchased "perpetual access," are limited by licenses, and, as noted earlier, few licenses for trade books include any provisions for archiving. Unless this situation changes, research libraries will no longer be able to rely on deferred acquisition to collect and preserve these works. While copyright deposit is mandated for electronic works with no print equivalent, this requirement has thus far been applied only to e-journals, and the potential of the program to provide preservation and long-term access is imperfectly understood. If trade e-books are to be preserved, a new understanding of roles, responsibilities, and financing will need to develop, in all likelihood an understanding that actively engages publishers and public libraries, as well as research libraries.

E-books are subject to both legal and technical constraints that limit what libraries can do to ensure their preservation.

Rights and Obligations

While e-books are subject to the provisions of copyright law, as has been noted most e-book purchases are also governed by licenses that specify what actions the purchaser may take. In many cases, however, the license a library signs when purchasing an e-book is only part of the picture. Several parties are involved in the chain of creating, producing, and distributing an e-book, and each may retain certain rights. Here, as elsewhere, the situation is somewhat different for scholarly and trade publications.

Authors of scholarly monographs are generally interested in broad dissemination of their work. The contracts they sign with publishers—often university presses—may assign copyright to the publisher or leave it with the author, and may allow the author certain rights of limited distribution (such as deposit in an institutional repository), but rarely place limits on the publisher's right to distribute the work. Library purchases are often made directly from the publisher, providing a relatively straightforward process for negotiating some form of preservation rights. By contrast, both authors and publishers of trade books depend on sales for their livelihood and survival. They are thus deeply concerned about unauthorized and uncontrolled distribution. The markets, pricing, and royalty structures for c-books are volatile, and all parties involved are cautious about giving away too many rights and suspicious of potential threats.

In both spheres, scholarly and trade, rights issues are further complicated because many library e-book purchases are made not directly from the publisher but through such distributors as OverDrive, 3M, ebrary, and many more. The library's rights to the content are controlled by its license with the distributor, while the distributor's rights are in turn limited by its contracts with many publishers, whose own rights are determined by agreements with hundreds or thousands of authors. In such an environment it is no wonder that the final link, between library and distributor, is generally quite limiting and cautious.

Complicated as this may seem, e-book licenses for major publishers, both trade and academic, at least offer opportunities for negotiation with high-volume impact. For the output of small independent publishers, self-published authors, and works on the open Web, the situation is much worse. Many small publishers' and authors' works are for sale only through major online retailers—Amazon, Apple, and Barnes and Noble. As we've seen, they are marketed to individual consumers, whose rights are governed by those retailers' standard contracts, leaving little-to-no room for library negotiation of preservation, or indeed any other, terms. Any attempts to negotiate directly with authors and publishers will necessarily be scattered and diffuse.

We might then turn with a sigh of relief to a class of e-books that are freely available for download from the Web. While many of these are not what we typically think of as e-books—research reports from scientific institutes, policy briefs from think tanks and other non-governmental organizations—they are of considerable interest to academic libraries. Even here, though, rights issues are not absent. Most of these works are subject to copyright and, unless they are made available under some form of Creative Commons license, the ability to download a copy for personal use does not automatically convey the right to make further copies for preservation and access.

Technical Requirements

Securing the right to preserve an e-book does not necessarily include the ability to do so. Publishing formats for e-books are diverse, and attempts to standardize on a single format such as EPUB3 have so far met with limited success. Many are produced in multiple formats for use on different e-readers; preserving a single format therefore may or may not suffice for future use. Far more than with journal articles, e-books are aesthetic objects, where style and appearance are considered important aspects of the reading experience; preservation of the words and images is necessary but not always sufficient. Moreover, the e-books that are most at risk—those without print equivalents—are often the most challenging to preserve, incorporating multiple media and experimental features. DRM software is often part of the standard distribution package, requiring a separate format for preservation purposes.

Finally, some e-books, such as *Interaction of Color*, are beginning to be produced as apps, with the application software an integral part of the work. From a technical standpoint, these objects might better be viewed as a software preservation challenge, rather than as e-books per se. Conceptually and intellectually, however, they seem more related to books than other types of software.

A relatively small number of libraries are likely to have the wherewithal, in technical expertise, storage capacity, and back-up storage to preserve and render back e-books from diverse sources on a large scale. As with e-journal preservation, concentration of effort and collaboration around agencies such as Portico and CLOCKSS is likely to be the norm.

Recommendations for Action

For years to come, attempts to preserve e-books are likely to prove messy, uncoordinated, inconclusive, and incomplete, yet that is still better than waiting for things to become simpler and clearer. Failed attempts and partial successes can help narrow the range of possible solutions. Small-scale experiments may address specific technical, legal, or financial challenges, and then build toward more systematic solutions. Engaging multiple stakeholders in different ways can help foster a sense of collective ownership of the issues. The recommendations that follow are offered not as resolutions, but as explorations.

Focus on Outcomes

Ultimately, preservation is about ensuring the survival of e-books so that they may continue to be available for future use. However, different types of content may suggest different types of use, by different groups, at different times. For any group of e-books, libraries will need to consider:

- Who is likely to want access in future? For what purposes? When?
- Is preservation of the content (text and images) sufficient? How important are other features?
- Are there classes for which a semi-dark archive, with limited or embargoed access, is sufficient?

Focusing on one standard, ideal model of preservation for all types of e-books is likely to impede incremental progress that may ultimately get us closer to the ideal.

Build Consensus on Priorities

Numerically and financially, a high percentage of the e-books purchased by libraries are still also produced in print and preserved in that form. At the other extreme, many works produced only as e-books are not purchased by libraries at all. With limited resources to devote to e-book preservation, should libraries focus on value (protecting investment, broad interest) or risk (ephemeral interest, entrepreneurial publishing)? Should they seek quick results (low-hanging fruit) or concentrate on difficult questions with potential for broad impact? Different stakeholders may well answer these questions differently. Finding like-minded partners may help organize action on multiple fronts.

Clarify Roles

There is broad consensus within the library community, and at least in principle among publishers, that preservation is important, but little discussion of who can and should take responsibility for different aspects—negotiating rights; storing content; maintaining format integrity; migrating access; supporting costs. Here again, different stakeholders are likely to have different perspectives, and roles may vary for different types of e-books. Two types of action are needed:

- Sectors within the library community organized by type (public, academic), size (large, small), and function (preservation, collection development) need to organize discussions and build consensus around willingness to act and effective locus of activity.
- Libraries, individually and through organizational channels, need to propose a variety of potential models to publishers and providers of e-books to test their willingness and ability to support specific preservation actions.

Experiment

A major barrier to e-book preservation is that it has been difficult to see how anyone can take action without massive changes in the way e-books are licensed, distributed, and stored. While systemic change is still difficult, small scale experimentation is possible.

- As noted earlier, CLOCKSS, LOCKSS, and Portico are already preserving tens of thousands of e-books. Individually and collectively, libraries can take a more active role in encouraging new publishers to participate in these programs.
- New open-access ventures such as Knowledge Unlatched have secured agreement from HathiTrust, Portico, and others to preserve and provide access to their e-book publications, a model that might be extended to additional content (HathiTrust, 2014).
- Some of the e-books most at risk are the output of innovative, start-up ventures (some of which have already suspended activity). These firms might be amenable to a "rescue" operation in which one or more libraries would secure the right to preserve (and possibly provide access to) their e-book content.
- Research libraries might explore a model used for some print archives, in which a particular publisher's e-book output would be deposited with the library for preservation, with access embargoed for an interval and/or restricted to researchers on the archive's premises.
- Many self-published books may ultimately be of more interest as a corpus than for reading as individual titles. Libraries might seek agreement from providers of self-publishing platforms to secure and preserve the content for non-consumptive use.

These examples are cited merely to suggest a range of possibilities. Ultimately, none may prove viable or extensible, but—as with e-books themselves—innovation will require a willingness to fail sometimes.

Reward Success

If innovation requires a willingness to fail, it is also true that limited successes, however imperfect, must be encouraged. Publishers and libraries that demonstrate a willingness to take risks in order to preserve e-books ought to be recognized, providing encouragement to others to follow and build on their efforts. Rewards may take many forms—favorable notice in library forums and media; formal awards and citations; and, most tangibly, increased business for those most committed to preservation. This is not to suggest that all initiatives should be received uncritically, but that acknowledgment of good-faith effort should accompany critical analysis, and that the best form of criticism is to point the way to something better.

Conclusion

At a time when the library profession is in transition because of the proliferation of technology in society, one may ask why time and resources should be invested in a complex challenge that addresses the future state of library collections. Are we borrowing trouble when we should be focused on today? In reality, the policies that guide e-book acquisition decisions can be coupled with preservation strategies. The digital universe is slowly erasing the distinction between collecting content "just in case" (that is, in case an item proves later to be valuable) and "just in time" (that is, for use today). As technologies evolve, digital items need to be optimized for preservation at the time of their creation, the time of their deposit into repositories, and managed over time (Smith, 2004) to guarantee long-term access in an environment where hardware and software obsolescence is guaranteed.

The good news is that we are in the early days of e-book collection development. There is time to develop strategies and frameworks that support the preservation of e-book content and functionality. At the same time, the knowledge that digital collections are not permanent signals that we must take action and begin experimentation. In the future, there will be "no uniqueness, no scarcity, [and] no category of 'rare'" (Smith, 2004, para. 45) when dealing with digital information. These resources are part of our national cultural heritage, and the responsibility for ensuring their survival must be shared. Publishers, foundations, and the federal government must all play a part. But action will begin only if librarians take a more active role in the stewardship of collections and build effective relationships with external stakeholders to collectively evaluate information and determine what items best represent the cultural heritage of the early 21st century. The answers will not be simple, but—as evidenced through advances in e-journal preservation—they are not impossible.

As librarians at Columbia University Libraries grappled with the preservation questions surrounding the *Interaction of Color* app, we had an opportunity to discuss preservation challenges with Yale University Press. We learned that publishers are also grappling with these issues, and there are opportunities to work together, experiment, and discuss frameworks relating to the preservation of enhanced e-books. For instance, one strategy may be to begin with the preservation of underlying images and text. While this excludes functionality, it provides a starting point that may better acquaint information professionals and publishers with the challenges at hand. As we learn from each other, we move toward sustainable, long-term preservation solutions one byte at a time.

References

ARL. (2005, October). "Urgent Action Needed to Preserve Scholarly Electronic Journals." Retrieved from http://www.arl.org/storage/documents/publications/ejournal-preservation-15oct05.pdf.

Armstrong, C., and R. Lonsdale. (2009, November). *E-Book Collection Management in UK University Libraries: Focus Group Report. Information Automation Limited, Final Report.* Retrieved from http://observatory.jiscebooks.org/reports/e-book-collection-management-in-uk-university-libraries-focus-groups-report.

Author Solutions. (2012, November 27). "Simon & Schuster and Author Solutions Launch Archway Publishing." Retrieved from http://www.authorsolutions.com/News-Events/News-Releases/2012/Simon-and-Schuster-and-Authors-Solutions-Launch-Archway-Publishing.

Blummer, B., and J. Kenton. (2012). "Best Practices for Integrating E-Books in Academic Libraries: A Literature Review from 2005 to Present." *Collection Management,* 37(2), 65–97.

Center for Research Libraries. "TRAC and TDR Checklists." Retrieved from http://www.crl.edu/archiving-preservation/digital-archives/metrics-assessing-and-certifying-0.

Charles, R. (2014, October 1). "No, I Don't Want to Read Your Self-Published Book." The *Washington Post.* Retrieved from http://www.washingtonpost.com/blogs/style-blog/wp/2014/10/01/no-i-dont-want-to-read-your-self-published-book.

Ciabattari, J. (2013, September 3). "Now There Are 5." *Library Journal.* Retrieved from http://lj.libraryjournal.com/2013/09/publishing/now-there-are-5/#_.

GCF Global. (2015). *What Is the Cloud?* Retrieved from http://www.gcflearnfree.org/what-is-the-cloud.

Gerden, E. (2014, January 9). "Russian E-Book Market Matures, Shows More Potential for Growth." *Publishing Perspectives.* Retrieved from http://publishing perspectives.com/2014/01/russia-is-now-the-worlds-third-largest-ebook-market.

HathiTrust. (2014, April). HathiTrust rights and access working group charge [Web log message]. Retrieved from http://www.hathitrust.org/rights_and_access_charge.

Kelbanoff, A. (2013, December 16). "The Tantalizing English Language eBook Opportunity in China." *Digital Book World.* Retrieved from http://www.digitalbookworld.com/2013/the-tantalizing-english-language-ebook-opportunity-in-china.

Kelley, M. (2012, October 18). "Random House Says Libraries Own Their E-books." *Library Journal.* Retrieved from http://lj.libraryjournal.com/2012/10/opinion/random-house-says-libraries-own-their-ebooks-lj-insider.

Kelley, M. (2014, October 3). "How Libraries Preserve E-Books." *Publishers Weekly.* Retrieved from http://www.publishersweekly.com/pw/by-topic/industry-news/libraries/article/64271-check-it-out-with-michael-kelley-how-libraries-preserve-e-books.html.

Kirchhoff, A. (2011). "E-Books: The Preservation Challenge." *Against the Grain* 23(4). Retrieved from http://docs.lib.purdue.edu/atg/vol23/iss4/10.

Kirchhoff, A., and S. Morrissey. (2014, June 1). *Technology Watch Report 14-01: Preserving E-Books.* Retrieved from http://www.dpconline.org/advice/technology-watch-reports.

Portico. Our Organization. Retrieved March 17, 2015 from http://www.portico.org/digital-preservation/about-us/our-organization.

Robertson, A. (2014, May 9). "The Fight to Save Endangered E-Books." *The Verge.* Retrieved from http://www.theverge.com/2014/5/9/5688146/the-fight-to-save-endangered-ebooks.

Rüdiger Wischenbart Content and Consulting. (Spring 2014). *Global eBook: A Report on Market Trends and Developments.* Retrieved from www.wischenbart.com/upload/1234000000358_04042014_final.pdf.

Smith, A. (2004). "Preservation." In S. Schreibman, R. Siemens, and J. Unsworth (eds.), *A Companion to Digital Humanities.* Oxford: Blackwell.

Utsumi, I. (2014, March 10). *The Brazilian Book Market.* The Brazil Business. Retrieved from http://thebrazilbusiness.com/article/the-brazilian-book-market.

Vyas, H. (2014, September 11). "India's Ebook Industry Shows Great Potential." *Digital Book World.* Retrieved from http://www.digitalbookworld.com/2014/indias-ebook-industry-shows-great-potential.

Yale University Library. (2013, March 3). *The eBook Strategic Plan Task Force: Report of Findings and Recommendations.* Retrieved from http://www.library.yale.edu/departments/collection-development/Yale-ebook-task-force-rpt.pdf.

YaleNews. (2014, May 14). 'Interaction of Color' App Wins George Wittenborn Memorial Book Award [Web log message]. Retrieved from http://news.yale.edu/interaction-color-app-wins-george-wittenborn-memorial-book-award.

School Libraries Meet the Challenges of Change

Christopher Harris

Barbara K. Stripling

Perhaps no character from children's literature better exemplifies the attitude of school librarians today in facing the challenges of technology and a changing environment than Corduroy. No matter what happens to that lovable little bear, Corduroy responds with a positive attitude: "Could this be a mountain? . . . I think I've always wanted to climb a mountain" (Freeman, 1968). School librarians, by their very nature, turn challenges into opportunities, creating a yin-yang culture of school librarianship.

School libraries have been integral to K–12 education for many decades; however, changes in society, economics, the national educational scene, and the nature of resources and technology have combined to redefine and, in some cases, marginalize the role of school libraries in the educational process. Although data from the National Center for Education Statistics for 2011–2012 show that 79,000 of the 85,500 traditional public schools and nearly half of charter schools (2,200 out of 4,500) had a library media center (NCES, 2013), the misapplication of the term "library media center" reveals a deeper problem. Only two-thirds of the traditional public school library media centers were staffed by a full-time, state-certified library media specialist, and only one-third of the charter schools were so staffed. In fact, 20 percent of the traditional public school media centers and 56 percent of charter school media centers had no professional staff at all (NCES, 2013). A "library media center" without a librarian is simply a room with books, not a library.

Even more troubling are the declines that have occurred since 2011–2012. The number of certified school librarians staffing the libraries of the 600 Chicago public schools declined from 454 in 2012–2013 to 313 the next year and then saw a deep dip to 254 in September 2014 (Vevea, 2014). About half of Los Angeles Unified's 600 schools are without a librarian or even an aide to keep the doors open (Watanabe, 2014).

One must understand the impact of school libraries on teaching and learning to realize the devastating effect of shuttered libraries on children. In an article about the closing of Philadelphia's school libraries, Stephen Segal issues a battle cry: "The library is the single most important operation in any school. It's more important than each and every classroom. The library is where students engage their own minds. The library is the place that embodies the concept of intellectual activity being something for a person to *choose*" (Segal, 2013).

Certainly, numerous research studies point to the positive impact on student achievement of school libraries staffed by a certified school librarian. Studies in

Christopher Harris is the director of the School Library System for the Genesee Valley (New York) Educational Partnership and serves as a fellow for Youth and Technology Policy Issues with the Office for Information Technology Policy of the American Library Association. In addition, he is the author of the Teaching Through Games series of professional books from Rosen Publishing. Barbara K. Stripling has had a lifelong career in school libraries, both as a high school librarian and as director of library services for the Fayetteville, Arkansas, and New York City schools. She is currently an assistant professor and senior associate dean at the School of Information Studies, Syracuse University, and immediate past president of the American Library Association.

more than 20 states confirm that school librarians and school libraries affect academic achievement, lifelong learning, 21st century skills, and reading (Lance and Hofschire, 2011; 2012; Kachel, 2013).

Many studies confirm the strong difference in reading achievement that the presence of a qualified school librarian makes. A national reading expert, Stephen Krashen, emphasizes the impact of school libraries and librarians on reading, especially for children in poverty: "Research consistently shows that when children have access to good libraries with plenty of good books and with adequate staffing, they read more, and thus do better on reading tests. For children of poverty, libraries are typically the only possible source of reading material" (Krashen, 2004).

Student achievement, of course, has a much deeper meaning than performance on tests. School libraries are especially effective in that deeper context of learning, when students are going beyond gathering information to developing personal understanding. In the school library, students learn how to inquire and pursue both academic and personal learning, because the school librarian teaches essential 21st century critical thinking, inquiry, technology, and literacy skills. School librarians are often cited for their expertise in integrating these independent and lifelong learning skills throughout the curriculum in collaboration with classroom teachers at all levels and in all subject areas.

The increasing proliferation of information and the continuing rapid development of technology have made the role of the school librarian in teaching and learning even more critical. Students need to learn sophisticated digital inquiry, digital citizenship, presentation, and communication skills in order to thrive in the digital world. Students must learn the skills and attitudes of evaluating information and authority, interpreting and making sense of an abundance of disorganized bits of knowledge, detecting bias and persuasive techniques in media, interpreting digital primary sources presented out of context, and developing an empathetic stance toward information received from cultures and societies across the world.

Indeed, changes in technology and society have led to a redefinition of the school library and school librarian role. This article examines some of the challenges faced by school librarians as they adapt to changes in the demographics of their students, the educational focus of the schools dictated by national standards and testing, the concept of lifelong reading and new literacies demanded by new technologies, and the complexities of resources and technology offered through the digital environment. More importantly, it explores the ways in which librarians are transforming those challenges into opportunities. Although each librarian faces unique combinations of all the factors affecting students and schools, the article concludes with the fundamental principles that guide all school library practice—how to maintain library principles in a technological world, how the role of school librarians must change, and what challenges school libraries may face in the future.

The Challenge of Changing Demographics

Predictions are that by 2044 the United States will become a "majority minority" nation (Frey, 2014). That change in demographics has already hit the schools. The U.S. Department of Education predicted that enrollment in public schools in fall 2014 would flip to majority minority with minority students composing 50.3

percent and white students 49.7 percent, although final statistics will not be available for a few years (Krogstad and Fry, 2014). The racial/ethnic picture of many schools is quite complex; the number of Hispanic students has doubled and the percentage of Asian students has increased by 46 percent since 1997, along with an increased recognition of mixed-race students (Krogstad and Fry, 2014). In the 100 largest school districts in the United States, about 63 percent of the students are black or Hispanic (based on National Center for Education Statistics [NCES] data from the 2007–2008 school year) (Samuels, 2011, p. 5).

Immigration is also changing the demographic composition of U.S. schools. In the next ten years, the percentages of the U.S. population who are first- or second-generation immigrants are expected to climb back to the levels of the 1930s. That upward trend is expected to continue for decades (Taylor, 2014, p. 8).

Educational policy makers have looked at the relationship between demographic composition of school populations and student achievement for a number of years; however, the decision makers are increasingly recognizing what school librarians have long known: that socioeconomic factors have a larger impact on students' educational success than race, ethnicity, or even non-native English speaking (Benner and Wang, 2014). One study found that students who were socioeconomically marginalized at school (that is, fewer than 15 percent of the students were their socioeconomic peers) had lower grade point averages, lower academic attainment, and poorer school attachment (which led to lower academic performance) than students who were racially/ethnically marginalized or students who fit the majority demographic (Benner and Wang, 2014).

The Opportunity of Changing Demographics

School librarians are dedicated to empowering all students to be independent and thoughtful learners. Librarians have begun using data to identify the needs of their students, including socioeconomic status, ethnic and racial composition of the school, reading levels, languages, special education needs, and test scores. They have been able to respond to the increasing diversity in their schools by providing resources in languages other than English, by assuring equitable access to computers and other technologies through the library, by purchasing databases at different reading levels, by differentiating their teaching to accommodate different languages and abilities, and by teaching students to create information using digital tools and graphics. Librarians have also recognized that parents play a big role in the developing literacy of their young children and that they can offer many opportunities (parent workshops, parent access to computers) and resources (books in other languages, parenting materials) that invite parents into the educational process, no matter what language is spoken at home or how many books are in the home.

Library support for diverse students goes beyond academics. Recognizing that many students may feel disconnected and marginalized from their school community because they struggle academically or they speak English as a second language, librarians have focused on several areas of social and emotional support. In fact, in many schools the library is the only space that provides a caring climate of shared learning, collaboration, and conversation. In terms of development of the whole child, school librarians are capitalizing on the diversity of the students, enabling each student to feel welcome, offering opportunities for discovery of personal interests and answers to personal problems, and facilitating conversations among students of different backgrounds. The common ground of the library enables individual students to feel safe, to develop self-confidence, and to connect to a caring adult beyond their own family.

The Challenge of Changing Educational Focus

The "restructuring of public education" conversation has been around since at least the 1980s. Most educators can offer a litany of theories, innovations, and best practices that have been tried, ignored, and then tried again. The bottom line continues to be that, taken as a whole, U.S. students are not achieving at a level that signifies solid preparation for college and career. Although the racial/ethnic and gender achievement gaps seem to be narrowing, as measured by the 2012 National Assessment of Educational Progress (NAEP), only the 13-year-olds made gains from 2008 to 2012 (NCES, 2013). In the snapshot view of the Organisation for Economic Co-operation and Development (OECD) Programme for International Student Assessment (PISA) results for 2012 (involving 510,000 students and 65 countries, or 80 percent of the world economy), students from the United States performed below the OECD average (OECD, 2014).

To counter this lag in achievement, new national standards in literacy and math were developed, called the Common Core State Standards. Added to the standards themselves was a heightened national focus on accountability through testing, despite the many educational voices that wanted to separate the high expectations of the standards from emphasis on testing and accountability.

In many states the Common Core rollout also coincided with new teacher accountability standards demanded by the federal government as a part of federal funding. In many states, teacher effectiveness is determined in large part by how well students perform on standardized tests. The testing and accountability requirements have become so much a part of public understanding about the Common Core that communities are unable to separate the standards from the testing. As a result, there has been a backlash against the Common Core as seen in the national opt-out movement that blames the new standards for testing (for example, see http://saynotocommoncore.com).

Implementation of the Common Core and its testing component has been somewhat spotty and variant. Some states, among them New York, have rolled out a comprehensive series of resources, guiding documents, sample units, training, and professional development tools, although actual implementation decisions on teaching to the standards are left to local districts. Criticisms of the Common Core have proliferated in a number of states, with objections that have included the following:

- Testing is so integral that teachers must "teach to the test"
- The Common Core challenge was handed to teachers without adequate preparation or professional development
- The expectations for students are too high and not developmentally appropriate

- This is so comprehensive that elementary schools no longer have time to teach social studies and science
- Teachers at all grade levels do not have time to incorporate in-depth units or engaging projects

The Opportunity of Changing Educational Focus

Many school librarians have celebrated the new opportunities made possible by the Common Core. An analysis of the skills embedded in the Common Core shows very strong alignment with the American Association of School Librarians (AASL) national standards, as outlined in *Standards for the 21st Century Learner* (AASL, 2007), and with information fluency continuums that have been developed in a number of states and districts. New York, for example, has adopted the *Empire State Information Fluency Continuum,* with a comprehensive delineation of the literacy, critical thinking, information, and technology skills to be taught at every grade level (K–12) as a part of the library curriculum and an explicit alignment of those skills to the Common Core.

Librarians are prepared to teach those skills; many classroom teachers, especially in social studies and science, have focused on teaching content and have never been expected to teach those skills. School librarians have stepped into the breach and collaborated with classroom teachers to design instruction that integrates the teaching of Common Core/information fluency skills with content—at all grade levels and in all subject areas. Increasingly, educators and administrators are discovering what librarians have always known, that the librarian provides a connective tissue of independent learning skills for an entire school. As students enter higher education or a career, their success in managing information, in making solid decisions based on evidence, and in communicating through various media is often based on the skills they learned from their school librarian.

Other opportunities have also arisen from changing emphases in education. Inquiry and independent student research are integral to the Common Core (and should be an essential component of any child's education). Classroom teachers, who may never have had training in an inquiry model or the skills of inquiry, flourish when given the chance to partner with their school librarian on inquiry projects. Students are both excited and engaged by projects that enable them to ask their own questions and probe deeply to discover answers and draw their own conclusions.

Constructivist learning, in which the learner constructs his own understanding, has long been the mantra of many librarians in their quest to provoke critical thinking and independent learning. Many educators are rethinking their pedagogy to design more constructivist learning experiences. Wise librarians seize the opportunity to foster this minds-on and active learning by collaborating with teachers and bringing students into the active library environment, creating makerspaces and production labs, teaching production and presentation skills, and enabling teachers and students to create (as well as consume) information.

Although an oft-repeated criticism of the Common Core is that it eliminates creativity, in fact the standards call for much higher levels of creative thinking and resource use. Instead of textbooks, Common Core classrooms should be filled with high-quality, literary nonfiction texts—a staple of the modern school library. Noted nonfiction author Marc Aronson, school library system director at the Erie 2 Board of Cooperative Educational Services (BOCES) Sue Bartle, and others have developed exemplar lists to help librarians enrich their collections with creative nonfiction titles (see http://nonfictionandthecommoncore.blogspot.com).

The Challenge of Fostering Lifelong Reading

It has always been a delightful challenge for school librarians to motivate and engage students in independent reading by helping them find just the right book at the right time. That's part of the art of librarianship. The art of guiding student reading is particularly rewarding for school librarians because students are developing and changing interests and reading ability so rapidly during their school years. Librarians know that students are motivated by choice, being able to "see" themselves in the story, learning exportable knowledge that they can inject into conversations with their peers, books that are trendy and popular with their friends, and books that they can read with fluency. Every librarian learns to ask the questions that elicit the reading interests and abilities of young people without violating their privacy or self-confidence. Every librarian recognizes that we are all formed by our own reading journeys and that librarians play a pivotal role in helping students map their journeys. In fact, reading guidance is a crucial role for school librarians, because other educators have neither the resources nor the training to help students navigate their own reading identities.

School librarians have also always been intimately involved in teaching literacy—not the basic developmental reading skills of decoding sounds, letters, and words, but the skills of comprehension, interpretation, and responses to texts. Many of those traditional literacy skills typically taught by librarians (like finding the main idea and determining point of view) are embedded within the Common Core.

The demands of literacy have changed dramatically since the advent of the Internet and the explosion of information and technology. Many educators and researchers are using the term "new literacies" to describe the literacy skills required for the 21st century. Researchers Leu, Kinzer, Coiro, and Cammack have developed a definition for new literacies as a framework for understanding the new demands (Leu et al., 2004):

> The new literacies of the Internet and other ICTs [information and communications technologies] include the skills, strategies, and dispositions necessary to successfully use and adapt to the rapidly changing information and communication technologies and contexts that continuously emerge in our world and influence all areas of our personal and professional lives. These new literacies allow us to use the Internet and other ICTs to identify important questions, locate information, critically evaluate the usefulness of that information, synthesize information to answer those questions, and then communicate the answers to others.

Most interesting for school librarians about the above definition is the congruency of new literacies with the inquiry process and some of the related information skills that librarians teach. The literacy skills that students need to thrive in our technology-rich and information-abundant world are the skills that librarians consider part of their curriculum. Libraries have moved way beyond traditional "library skills" (like simply finding a book on the shelf). Instead, librarians are challenging themselves and their students to develop the thinking skills needed to navigate and make sense of information presented in multiple formats and genres that are constantly changing.

The exciting challenge for school librarians, then, is to teach the multiple literacies required to learn and communicate in a world of constantly changing technologies, diverse cultural contexts, and globalization. New literacies involve problem solving, civic engagement, media literacy, making sense of linked information, locating and evaluating information presented through multiple formats and changing technologies, participating in virtual interactions, using a variety of tools to produce and communicate information through multiple media forms, and interpreting the impact of social and cultural context on information.

The Opportunity of Fostering Lifelong Reading

The need for students to develop new literacies enables school librarians to balance the dual facets of the library curriculum. On the one hand, students need to learn fundamental and critical literacy skills that underlie any communication (no matter what technology is used). On the other hand, the curriculum must be dynamic and flexible enough to enable students to adapt to and use rapidly changing information and technology.

Leu and his coauthors say that new literacies place greater importance on the role of the teacher, but that role must change (Leu et al., 2004). Students are engaged in using new technologies on their own. As a result, they are coming to school with many skills that teachers and librarians may not have. The teachers and librarians must shift their emphasis from teaching simple access and communication skills to designing complex learning experiences, teaching critical literacy skills that students may not learn on their own, and co-learning new literacy skills with students. For example, librarians increasingly are confronting students with authentic media messages that are created to persuade or influence the viewer or reader. Librarians are helping students to evaluate these messages that bombard them every day, to become critical consumers, and to resist biased and inaccurate information. Students are learning the power of color, placement on a Web page, icons and graphics, targeted messages, and multiple other techniques that may obfuscate the underlying meaning. The opportunity presented by new literacies, then, is for librarians to create a constructivist learning environment that both supports and provokes students to develop ever more sophisticated literacy skills.

The Challenge of Changing Resources

The development of digital, media, and other new literacies is especially critical in the face of the shifting nature of library collections. In school libraries, as in most other types, content is increasingly being accessed digitally. This shift is opening new possibilities for information use, but also brings a new set of challenges. Digital content is licensed, not purchased, and so may include contract terms that are not fully compatible with the usage scenarios unique to school libraries. Digital content from the largest trade publishers is offered under terms created for public library usage; school libraries tend to need more simultaneous readers to accommodate teacher-directed use cases for novels. Content from publishers that focus on the K–12 market is often much more accessible. Most nonfiction offerings from K–12-focused publishers are licensed for unlimited, simultaneous use in a school building. The challenge then becomes one of educating teachers and administrators about the high-quality content that is more easily accessed versus the less accessible content from the major publishers.

School libraries are working to provide increased access to digital content through e-books, databases, and curated Web content. To leverage the full potential of digital content, however, libraries must also have adequate levels of both hardware and connectivity. In poor districts these can both be lacking; broadband access is an especially difficult issue in rural areas where the infrastructure may simply not be available to provide the necessary levels of connectivity. Federal Communications Commission (FCC) Chairman Tom Wheeler noted in a November 2014 update titled "Closing the Digital Divide in Rural America" that "Forty-one percent of America's rural schools couldn't get a high-speed connection if they tried" (Wheeler, 2014). Steps taken by FCC to modernize the E-rate program, which provides financial support for broadband access, should help schools and libraries increase connectivity. Even so, Wheeler's concerns about a rural broadband gap remain valid; 41 percent of rural schools lack adequate connectivity, compared with only 31 percent of urban schools (Wheeler, 2014).

Another major challenge school libraries face in shifting to digital content is the availability of resources at a reasonable price. Going digital with reference collections and periodicals is trivial from a technical and content acquisition perspective when hardware and connectivity issues are solved. A 2012 review of statewide subscription database programs found that 38 states provided some level of statewide access to online resources, with all of them having at least a basic periodical index offering (Krueger, 2012). This statewide access may be the only digital subscription content available in some school libraries. These statewide purchases are often made possible through Library Services and Technology Act (LSTA) funding administered by the federal Institute of Museum and Library Services (IMLS). There is no direct federal funding for school library materials, and most states do not provide specific support for library materials, so the pass-through nature of LSTA funding that provides statewide access to databases is especially critical for underfunded schools.

Licensing other resources primarily focused on research needs is also relatively easy thanks to strong relationships between school libraries and the many K–12-focused publishers (Harris, Hasenyager, and Russell, 2014). When it comes to fiction, though, school libraries face a unique set of challenges beyond those shared with public libraries. In many cases, fiction e-book titles are being sought for use as instructional resources in a teacher-directed activity as opposed to student-selected reading. When students are selecting books to read, they remain more likely to prefer a print book (54 percent) to an e-book (18 percent), according to reading research from Nielsen as reported in *Publishers Weekly* (Gilmore and Burnett, 2014). Licensing fiction for teacher-directed uses can be difficult, as it often requires simultaneous access to multiple copies of an e-book for group reading assignments. The current license offerings from major publishers have been developed around public library use scenarios and do not provide any method for schools to easily secure access to a large number of simultaneous-use copies.

The Opportunity of Changing Resources

Although full utilization of digital resources requires both hardware and broadband access, school libraries without these two critical prerequisites are still preparing students to be digital users of information. Broadband rollout in rural communities has accelerated in recent years thanks to the National Broadband Plan, with further access proposed through ConnectED, a plan from the Obama White House that seeks to connect 99 percent of students to high-speed broadband by 2018 (http://www.whitehouse.gov/issues/education/k-12/connected). This is the ideal time for school libraries that do not yet have full broadband access to upgrade their capacity.

This proactive approach to new resources and technologies can be seen in a renewed focus on the same instructional methods called for by the Common Core: constructivism, project-based learning, and social engagement around knowledge. These foundational elements of the AASL Standards for the 21st Century Learner can be utilized for digital preparation even absent the technology. For example, students can be asked to write blog posts and share them for peer-commenting on paper if 1:1 devices or computer labs are not available. Being part of the development of a wiki is as much a mindset as a technology skill.

School libraries are also using digital access to provide highly relevant resources to teachers to support Common Core instruction. The Teaching with Primary Sources program from the Library of Congress supports teachers and school librarians with resources and professional development on primary sources from the extensive collections housed at the Library of Congress. With increasing digitization of local holdings at small libraries and historical societies around the country, the new challenge is discovery and management of an overwhelming flood of potential resources. One example of statewide primary resource discovery collaboration is the New York Heritage project (http://www.newyorkheritage.org). Even within tools like this, a key role of the school librarian is curation of applicable resources that directly align with classroom instruction.

This role of curation expert is part of the dramatic change in modern school libraries—and has been for many years. "To find the right materials for the right child at the right time is not a new goal for librarians," readers of the *Library Trends* article "The Changing Nature of School Library Collections" in 1969 were reminded, "but the means of achieving it have changed and expanded and, for the first time, give more realistic promise of fulfillment" (Crawford, 1969, p. 1). With the new opportunities of 1:1 computing, broadband access, and digital content delivery, librarians certainly have a much more realistic promise of matching students with the resources they need. In some cases, this new model is being referred to as a learning commons with both physical and virtual components to meet all types of needs (Loertscher and Koechlin, 2014). The virtual learning commons model highlights librarian-created learning guides to help students and teachers navigate the many available resources to find the best information on a specific topic. Far from being a static warehouse of knowledge, the new learning commons model calls for a dynamic presence online that can adapt to meet daily teaching and learning needs through tele-presence librarianship, personalized resource lists, and custom screen capture how-to guides.

The learning commons model of school librarianship also places a strong focus on content creation. School libraries are being redesigned to include makerspaces, music or video studios, and other areas for students to create. This isn't just about students being engaged with technology and having fun in the library; there are real instructional outcomes related to these project spaces. "The act of making these products demonstrates authentic evidence of critical understanding of complex concepts while simultaneously teaching the students how to use media production tools they can apply on their own later" (Wolf, Jones, and Gilbert, 2014, p. 7).

Internationally, school libraries are also being reimagined and rebranded as learning commons (Canada) or modern library learning environments (New Zealand) highlighting the new aspects of teaching and learning incorporated in the spaces. These new spaces focus not only on resources but also on other opportunities for student engagement. This may include makerspaces, media production tools, games and game design, and other high-interest creative elements.

Maintaining Principles in a Technological World

One unfortunate result of technological changes in the wider world has been an increased level of tension between intellectual property rights holders and consumers of content. In the digital world, creating perfect replicas of content is much easier and rights holders have vigorously attacked real (and perceived) violations. This tension can be seen in school libraries through the rise in plagiarism. Though more of an ethical violation than an actual breach of copyright, the two are very closely related to an underlying change in how students understand and interpret intellectual property. In a Pew study from 2011 more than half of colleges surveyed reported that plagiarism cases had increased in the previous decade; 89 percent of the respondents blamed this increase on computers and the Internet (Parker, Lenhart, and Moore, 2011). The challenge for school libraries today is to teach ethical use of information while also pushing back against rights holders to maintain allowed uses of information.

Teaching about intellectual property and the ethical use of information is a key element of school library instruction. The challenge, though, is in finding a positive message that resonates with students who have been desensitized by over-the-top antipiracy campaigns. The Electronic Frontier Foundation offers a potential curriculum at http://www.teachingcopyright.org that respects students' rights to fair use of content while also encouraging respect of the work of others. Beyond the issue of student copying/pasting, librarians also often have to serve as copyright advisers for faculty. These are complicated legal issues, yet school librarians must help colleagues navigate the waters of fair use, educational use, and other use scenarios.

Overly zealous responses to perceived issues relating to students or teachers and technology seems to be the norm. Just as music downloading was met with a barrage of lawsuits, teen sexting incidents in schools are often escalated to the level of federal child pornography crimes. Meanwhile, proactive education about online safety and privacy are hampered by a lack of access to social sites to be used in instruction about positive online behavior (Batch, 2014, p. 25).

An overzealous implementation of the Children's Internet Protection Act (CIPA) in many school districts has led to severe restrictions on information access. In Rhode Island, the filtering denies access to content that "ranges from political websites under the category 'Terrorist/Militant/Extremist,' such as those of Hezbollah and the Black Panther Party; to social websites under the 'Social Opinion' category, such as those of the American Civil Liberties Union (ACLU), People for the Ethical Treatment of Animals (PETA), the National Organization for Marriage, and Planned Parenthood; as well as other content deemed 'controversial, inappropriate, or time-wasting' by the school administration" (Batch, 2014, p. 21). Policies and practices for having specific websites made accessible vary from district to district, but in most cases the decision making and implementation of unlocking websites are not under the librarian's control.

The intrusion of technology also has serious implications for student privacy. Filtering software intended to block access to Web content is increasingly militarized, with schools being sold on a filter's ability to defend against students as if they were enemy combatants. One filter advertises a "Live Threat Dashboard [that] provides immediate insight into threats, suspicious events, and liability risks that can result in AUP [acceptable use policy] or regulatory violations, data loss, or costly litigation" (iBoss, 2015). Filters often either block or decrypt secure traffic, rendering student searches visible to detection. This, combined with default block lists that often include even sites educating about sex, can have a chilling effect on a student's ability to seek answers to potentially difficult questions. In the print-based history, access might have been similarly restricted by a school's decision not to purchase content, but this is a challenge that is reasserting itself when there is no longer a basis for its existence. School librarians must maintain constant pressure to ensure the most open access possible to all information.

Changing Role of School Librarians

School librarians, like the little bear Corduroy, will encounter many mountains in their professional lives. The library profession as a whole is undergoing massive changes brought on by the shift to digital content, the proliferation of personal computing devices, and declining budgets. In school libraries, these changes are often magnified by the fact that most school librarians are the sole library/information professional in the building. In an increasing number of unfortunate situations, there might be a single accredited, certified librarian in a district overseeing clerks. The school librarian must handle library tasks including collection development, cataloging, processing, interlibrary loan, technical services, and website development that in public or academic libraries are often addressed by entire departments.

In addition to all of the library tasks, school librarians are also teachers; they fill instructional roles that have grown in importance over the past five years. School librarians design and deliver professional development for their colleagues. They are expected to be familiar with and able to assist in instructional design tasks across the entire breadth of the curriculum. After lessons are developed, the school librarian is also expected to be a master teacher capable of showing finesse with multiple pedagogical strategies. The role of the school librarian has so greatly expanded that it is now more closely aligned with the principal in a building than with other teachers; the most successful librarians are functioning in a quasi-administrative role as instructional leaders within their buildings (Wolf, Jones, and Gilbert, 2014, p. 14).

Needs and Challenges of the Future

Although it is impossible to predict the future of school library programs, especially in the context of constantly changing resources and technology, the way librarians have handled the challenges and opportunities of the past demonstrates that school librarians both acknowledge and embrace change.

Certainly, resources will continue to evolve, as will the balance between print and digital. Digital resources will be increasingly integrated throughout the curriculum, especially with the escalating focus on digitization and access to digital primary sources through museums, archives, civic organizations, science centers, and libraries of all kinds. The Digital Public Library of America is one signal that portends the importance of digital access in the future. As students increasingly turn to the Web as their first-search strategy, librarians will be called upon to enable teachers and students to find the most credible and authoritative sources by exercising a critical curation role and teaching sophisticated digital literacy and inquiry skills.

School libraries will support a different type of learning in the future. Instruction by the librarian in new literacies will empower students to explore ideas in multiple formats and to make sense of them. Students will have increasing opportunities to use technology tools for creating their own products, moving beyond remixing to original creation. School libraries will emphasize active learning through makerspaces, learning commons, virtual learning commons, and production centers.

The virtual environment will posit both challenges and exciting opportunities for school libraries. The need to offer around-the-clock access to resources through mobile technology will become an increasing pressure, as will the need for librarians to provide continuing virtual guidance. Online learning will offer experiences for students that will both deepen and extend the access to education for many students, especially at high school age. Librarians will have to think creatively to support the learning of distance students through resources, teaching, and guidance.

Finally, libraries will need to confront new ways to integrate technology. Increasingly, schools will figure out how to open access to social media for educational purposes; learning, therefore, will be both active and interactive. Many libraries will turn to bring-your-own-device (BYOD) procedures, blended with circulation of e-readers and other technologies in order to provide access to electronic textbooks, e-books for independent reading, databases, and other resources. Some schools will implement a 1:1 approach, so that every student in the school has a computer for continuous access to learning through technology.

Seizing the Moment

It would be easy for school librarians to allow the challenges of change to block their vision of the wonderful opportunities for students that new developments can bring. But that's not the way school librarians are reacting. Despite the difficult circumstances caused by limited resources, technology, space, and support, school librarians are seizing the moment. They are building on the strengths of their demographically diverse students. They are not only acknowledging the changes in educational focus, but they are integrating the teaching of critical information and inquiry skills throughout the curriculum of the school.

The focus on lifelong reading and the teaching of new literacies has become an even more essential part of the librarian's job. That job has been enhanced with the addition of e-resources and by the co-learning of new literacy skills with technologically savvy students. The constantly changing formats and characteristics of digital resources provide a dynamic landscape for serving the needs of teachers and students. As librarians adapt to changes in the information environment, they must invite others to be part of the change process. Everyone involved in the educational enterprise, from teachers and administrators to publishers and media producers, must contribute to the changing dynamics of the school library profession.

As much as librarians adapt to change, they remain true to the abiding principles of their profession: equity, intellectual freedom, and social responsibility. The focus of school librarians, and of all those who have a part in the development of youth, will always be on empowering all students to be productive citizens.

Sources

AASL (American Association of School Librarians). (2007). *Standards for the 21st Century Learner*. ALA. Accessed February 23, 2015, at http://www.ala. org/aasl/standards.

Batch, K. (2014). *Fencing Out Knowledge*. ALA. Accessed January 20, 2015, at http://connect.ala.org/files/cipa_report.pdf.

Benner, A. D., and Y. Wang. (2014). "Demographic Marginalization, Social Integration, and Adolescents' Educational Success." *Journal of Youth and Adolescence* 43, 1611–1627.

Crawford, L. (1969). "The Changing Nature of School Library Collections." *Library Trends*. Accessed January 20, 2015, at https://www.ideals.illinois.edu/ bitstream/handle/2142/6460/librarytrendsv17i4g_opt.pdf.

Freeman, D. (1968). *Corduroy*. Penguin.

Frey, W. H. (2014, December 12). "New Projections Point to a Majority Minority Nation in 2044." *The Avenue*. Accessed February 23, 2015, at http://www. brookings.edu/blogs/the-avenue/posts/2014/12/12-majority-minority-nation-2044-frey.

Gilmore, N., and M. Burnett. (2014, December 16). "Crunching Numbers at the Nielsen Children's Book Summit." *Publishers Weekly*. Accessed January 20, 2015, at http://www.publishersweekly.com/pw/by-topic/childrens/childrens-industry-news/article/65068-kids-are-thriving-reading-and-hungry-for-more-crunching-numbers-at-the-nielsen-children-s-book-summit.html.

Harris, C., R. Hasenyager, and C. Russell. (2014, June). "School Library Ebook Business Models." *American Libraries.* Accessed January 20, 2015, at http://www.americanlibrariesmagazine.org/article/school-library-ebook-business-models.

iBoss. Accessed January 20, 2015, at http://www.iboss.com/tec/threat_event_console.html.

Kachel, D. (2013). *School Library Research Summarized: A Graduate Class Project,* revised ed. Mansfield University. Accessed February 18, 2015, at http://sl-it.mansfield.edu/upload/MU-LibAdvoBklt2013.pdf.

Krashen, S. (2004). *The Power of Reading: Insights from the Research,* 2nd ed. Libraries Unlimited.

Krogstad, J. M., and R. Fry. (2014, August 18). "Dept. of Ed. Projects Public Schools Will Be 'Majority-Minority' This Fall." Pew Research Center. Accessed January 16, 2015, at http://www.pewresearch.org/fact-tank/2014/08/18/u-s-public-schools-expected-to-be-majority-minority-starting-this-fall.

Krueger, K. (2012, April 17). "The Status of Statewide Subscription Databases." *School Library Research.* Accessed February 18, 2015, at http://www.ala.org/aasl/sites/ala.org.aasl/files/content/aaslpubsandjournals/slr/vol15/SLR_StatusofStatewide_V15.pdf.

Lance, K. C., and L. Hofschire. (2011, September). "Something to Shout About: New Research Shows That More Librarians Means Higher Reading Scores." *School Library Journal* 57(9).

Lance, K. C., and L. Hofschire. (2012, October). "School Librarian Staffing Linked with Gains in Student Achievement, 2005 to 2011." *Teacher Librarian* 40(1), 15–19, 4.

Lenhart, A., and M. Madden. (2005). *Teen Content Creators and Consumers.* Pew Research Center. Accessed January 20, 2015, at http://www.pewinternet.org/2005/11/02/57-of-teen-internet-users-create-remix-or-share-content-online.

Leu, D. J., Jr., et al. (2004). "Toward a Theory of New Literacies Emerging from the Internet and Other Information and Communication Technologies." Preprint of chapter in Unrau, N. J., and R. B. Ruddell (eds.). (2004). *Theoretical Models and Processes of Reading,* 5th ed. International Reading Association. Accessed January 16, 2015, at http://www.readingonline.org/newliteracies/leu.

Loertscher, D., and C. Koechlin. (2014, March) at *Knowledge Quest.* Accessed January 20, 2015, at http://www.ala.org/aasl/sites/ala.org.aasl/files/content/aaslpubsandjournals/knowledgequest/docs/KQ_MarApr14_Climbingto Excellence.pdf.

NCES (National Center for Education Statistics). (2013, August). *Characteristics of Public Elementary and Secondary School Library Media Centers in the United States: Results from the 2011–12 Schools and Staffing Survey* (NCES 2013-315). Institute of Education Sciences, U.S. Department of Education. Accessed February 18, 2015, at http://nces.ed.gov/pubs2013/2013315.pdf.

NCES (National Center for Education Statistics). (2013, June). *The Nation's Report Card: Trends in Academic Progress 2012* (NCES 2013-456). Institute of Education Sciences, U.S. Department of Education. Accessed January 16, 2015, at http://nces.ed.gov/nationsreportcard/subject/publications/main2012/pdf/2013456.pdf.

OECD. (2014). *PISA 2012 Results in Focus: What 15-Year-Olds Know and What They Can Do with What They Know.* OECD. Accessed January 16, 2015, at http://www.oecd.org/pisa/keyfindings/pisa-2012-results-overview.pdf.

Parker, K., A. Lenhart, and K. Moore. (2011). *The Digital Revolution and Higher Education.* Pew Research Center. Accessed February 21, 2015, at http://www.pewinternet.org/2011/08/28/the-digital-revolution-and-higher-education.

Samuels, C. A. (2011, March 30). "District Demographics: Characteristics of the 100 Largest Public Elementary and Secondary School Districts in the United States: 2008–09." *Education Week* 30(26), 5.

Segal, S. (2013, September 13). "Closing School Libraries? This Means War." PhiladelphiaWeekly.com. Accessed February 18, 2015, at http://www.philadelphiaweekly.com/news-and-opinion/editors-note/Closing-school-libraries-This-means-war-223651501.html.

Taylor, P. (2014, April 10). *The NEXT America.* Pew Research Center. Accessed January 16, 2015, at http://www.pewresearch.org/next-america/#Immigration-Is-Driving-Our-Demographic-Makeover.

Vevea, B. (2014, September 1). "Librarians Are a Luxury Chicago Public Schools Can't Afford." *NPR Ed.* Accessed February 18, 2015, at http://www.npr.org/blogs/ed/2014/09/01/344905087/librarians-are-a-luxury-chicago-public-schools-cant-afford.

Watanabe, T. (2014, February 23). "Many L.A. Unified School Libraries, Lacking Staff, Are Forced to Shut." *Los Angeles Times.* Accessed February 18, 2015, at http://www.latimes.com/local/la-me-lausd-libraries-20140224-story.html#page=1.

Wheeler, T. (2014). "Official FCC Blog." Accessed February 18, 2015, at http://www.fcc.gov/blog/closing-digital-divide-rural-america.

Wolf, M. A., R. Jones, and D. Gilbert. (2014). *Leading In and Beyond the Library.* Alliance for Excellent Education. Accessed January 20, 2015, at http://all4ed.org/wp-content/uploads/2014/01/BeyondTheLibrary.pdf.

New Publishing and the Library: E-Books, Self-Publishing, and Beyond

James LaRue

For publicly funded libraries of all kinds, 2014 was about being tossed in an uncertain sea by alternately converging and clashing currents. Should libraries invest more in print or more in e-books? What percent of purchases should go to the mainstream publishers (the Big Five in public libraries, the Big Deal for academic) and what percent to the huge, bewildering surge of independent and self-published material? How much attention should go to the rise of "library as publisher," in which the institution moved from distributor of content to partner in production? Had supply chains and pricing settled down? Finally, how on earth were libraries to pay for all of this?

Librarians are no strangers to change. We have been largely unfazed by the format shifts of the consumer market: 16 mm film to VHS to DVD to streaming; book to cassette to CD to mp3 player. Technology has long been a familiar house guest: We made room for public PCs, Internet stations, and wireless hotspots; we're not even shaken by spikes in indie and small-scale publishing (see Tkach and Hank's "Before Blogs, There Were Zines."[1])

But there is a shared sense among librarians that this time is different. There are *fundamental* changes in our environment. This article will focus on some of the publishing patterns that emerged in the library world in 2014.

E-Book Sales in the United States

First, let's look at the larger numbers. In 2013 traditional print book production dropped slightly to a projected 304,912 titles; nontraditional publishing produced slightly over a million.[2] Self-published books alone, both print and electronic, rose 16.5 percent to 458,564.[3]

Jim Milliot reported in *Publishers Weekly* that small publishers registered 46,654 ISBNs in 2013, placing that group fourth among companies that registered ISBNs. The Big Three in 2013 were Amazon's CreateSpace, which registered 186,926 ISBNs, followed by Smashwords, which registered 85,500, and Lulu, which registered 74,787. The various Author Solutions divisions had 44,574 ISBNs. The CreateSpace figure reflects only print ISBNs, while Smashwords includes only registered e-books.[4]

In 2014 *unit sales* [my emphasis] of print books reported to Nielsen Bookscan rose 2.4 percent. Milliot concluded that ". . . the 2014 figures are further evidence that print books are selling better than they have since sales of e-books exploded in 2010 and Borders closed its doors in 2011."[5] Clearly, the print market is still alive, even if there are some new players at the table. Publishing itself has seen the largest expansion in human history.

James LaRue is CEO of the consulting firm LaRue and Associates. He was the director of the Douglas County (Colorado) Libraries from March 1990 through January 2014, and is a member of the American Library Association's Digital Content Working Group.

Availability, Infrastructure, and Pricing

One big story of the year was the very public fight between Amazon and Big Five publisher Hachette Book Group. Amazon apparently withheld preorders, and possibly delayed shipping, to put pressure on Hachette during price negotiations. The dispute was resolved in November,[6] but publishing continued its migration to Amazon as a platform. According to the July 2014 Author Earnings Report[7] (which tracks book sales through Amazon), "self-published authors then accounted for 31 percent of total daily e-book sales regardless of genre. This makes indie authors, as a cohort, the largest publisher of e-books on Amazon.com in terms of market share."

However, Amazon doesn't sell e-books to libraries directly; in fact, its licensing agreement expressly forbids library lending of e-books.[8] (Libraries may purchase and lend print books from Amazon; further, many libraries lend Kindles with content pre-loaded.) So for public libraries, the only way to gain access to Amazon-specific e-book titles, and many other self-published materials, has been through e-book distributor OverDrive. On May 20, 2014, OverDrive announced a deal with e-book publisher and distributor Smashwords to make some 80,000 self-published authors and independent presses available to customers.[9] For many libraries, this was the first time they had been able to purchase books that may be bestsellers, and may not be available in print. Indeed, the rising demand for e-books may be encouraging libraries to purchase from nontraditional sources generally.

There continues to be, however, a significant price discrepancy between some Big Five titles and self-published e-books. Random House sells some e-book titles to libraries for $84 a copy; the deal with OverDrive sets a minimum price of $1.99, and in practice has an average of around $4.00 per title. Many authors, it seems, want their books in libraries, and are willing to offer significant discounts to that end. In both cases, the "license" allows only one user at a time, paralleling the use of print. But this example illustrates several key issues affecting libraries and e-books:

- Publishers (or authors) have to agree to sell their books to libraries. The good news: thanks in part to the persistent efforts of the American Library Association (ALA) (see this report from ALA's Alan Inouye[10]), all of the Big Five (Penguin Random House, HarperCollins, Hachette, and in 2014 both Macmillan and Simon & Schuster) now sell their full catalogs of e-books to public libraries, although their business terms vary. (See ALA's "Big Five Publishers and Library Lending."[11]) All limit use of digital files to one user at a time.
- Few libraries have the technological expertise or financial wherewithal to build their own e-book management platforms. Absent those systems (their own servers for storage of e-books and software to integrate the discovery of the content with the traditional library catalog), libraries require the services of a distributor to deliver e-books to their patrons. The primary public library e-book distributors continue to be OverDrive, 3M, Baker and Taylor, and EBSCO, although newer challengers (Total Boox, BiblioLabs, and Odilo) have stepped up their presence in the marketplace, each with its own

wrinkles; Total Boox, for instance, offers simultaneous use, and charges the library only for what is actually read. Unglue.it[12] continues its creative campaign to liberate books not just from digital rights management (DRM), but from restrictive copyright, and now offers a free platform for libraries.[13] Several state libraries (among them Kansas, Colorado, Massachusetts, Connecticut, and Arizona[14]) have stepped into the gap, and each is building a shared infrastructure for managing digital content. Moreover, some integrated library systems (such as SirsiDynix's eResource Central) now offer tools to acquire and manage such content, regardless of the source.

• Pricing varies widely for such content, but, generally speaking, libraries still spend some five times more per title than would the average consumer.[15] However, this price differential is driven by the Big Five's "suggested" retail price and distributor margin. There are many hundreds of publishers in the United States, and some of them have agreed to sell directly to libraries at prices that offer more traditional library discounts (40 percent to 45 percent of consumer retail).[16] Given the more "library friendly" orientation of new publishers eager to get into the library market, this may herald a reorientation of library purchasing patterns. At present, however, anecdotal evidence suggests that few libraries have made this shift.

There seems to be no consistent percentage of funding going to e-book purchasing. Through discussions with those in the public library field, I hear that something like 10 percent to 15 percent of the collection budget is going to e-books. In academic and research libraries, it isn't uncommon to see a combination of journal and e-book subscriptions exceed 80 percent of the budget. Libraries tend to lump their "electronic resources" budgets together—not only e-books, but journals, databases, language and homework help services, and more. That makes tracking of individual trends difficult. School librarians, with average materials acquisition budgets of $6,970 a year, were spending $1,100 on e-books (or about 16 percent of their budgets) in 2012–2013. But these numbers are based only on those who report buying e-books: 57 percent of them don't.[17]

Public Funding

Bosch and Henderson also address the issue of public funding. While noting that the "overall economic news appears positive . . . public funding and spending in [academic and research] libraries have not yet recovered to 2008 level adjusted for inflation or population growth."[18]

Having less money is a problem when the marketplace features both exorbitant pricing by a handful of big publishers and distributors and an explosion of cheaper but sometimes less-vetted content from more nontraditional publishing platforms (midlist, independent, and self-publishers).

Self-Publishing

Some of the statistics about self-publishing were touched on above. But the trend is so significant—now outpacing the production of traditional titles—that it is worth a closer look.

Betty Kelly Sargent wrote in *Publishers Weekly*[19] about 2014's third quarterly Author Earning Report, based on the top-selling 7,000 digital genre titles on Amazon's category bestseller lists. Among its findings:

- The Big Five traditional publishers now account for only 16 percent of the e-books on Amazon's bestseller lists.
- Digital rights management (DRM) "harms e-book sales at any price point."
- Self-published books now represent 31 percent of e-book sales on Amazon's Kindle Store.
- Indie authors are earning nearly 40 percent of the e-book dollars going to authors.
- Self-published authors are "dominating traditionally published authors" in sci-fi/fantasy, mystery/thriller, and romance genres, but—and here is the surprise—they are also taking "significant market share" in all genres.

In the same article, Sargent listed some findings from Mark Coker, CEO of self-published e-book distributor Smashwords, who reported:

$2.99 and $3.99 are currently the pricing sweet spots for most e-book bestsellers. In general, authors who price their books modestly earn more than those whose prices are higher, but 99 cents is "no longer the path to riches."

Readers prefer longer e-books. In fact, bestselling books tend to be over 100,000 words.

Series books outsell standalone books, but series books under 50,000 words are at a sales disadvantage.

Free still works as a marketing tool, especially when an author offers the first book in a series for free, but it is much less effective than before, primarily because so many authors are taking advantage of it.

Pre-orders give authors a sales advantage. "I think pre-orders today are where free was five years ago," says Coker. "The first authors to effectively utilize pre-orders will gain the most advantage just as the first authors to enter new distribution channels gain the most advantage."

Nonfiction earns more at higher prices . . . "Nonfiction buyers are less price sensitive," says Coker. "It appears as if most nonfiction authors are underpricing their works, and they should experiment with higher prices," he says.

Lawrence Grobel, author of several celebrity biographies, commented on the changing publishing environment from the writer's perspective.[20] Through traditional publishers, authors typically make 8 percent to 15 percent royalties on a book. Through CreateSpace, Amazon offers 70 percent. Smashwords offers 85 percent. Moreover, self-published authors can retain greater control over the content and even the design of their work. There is a lot of gatekeeping in traditional publishing: authors have to clear the hurdles of agent and "slush pile" (competing manuscripts vying for attention). Self-published work gets to market faster, better reflects the author's intent, and (if successful) makes the author more money.

But self-published authors don't get advances, either, making it harder to get the book finished. They have to pay for their own editing. They may find that all of the work to market their book falls entirely on them (although many traditional publishers also require authors to assist in the marketing).[21] Taking on all of these tasks can be daunting, expensive, and, of course, takes authors away from writing. Grober concludes, "I agree that there are more options for writers today, but . . .

how many of these options allow a writer to actually earn a living from his writing[?]" That issue should matter to libraries.

Reviews

A significant problem for author and librarian alike is that it's also harder for self-published authors to get their works reviewed. Absent reviews, books often don't make it into library collections. Again, there are more than 458,000 self-published titles annually. Librarians cannot possibly keep up with the flow of new materials. The good news: there are beginning to be more sources for reviews of self-published content. Among them are aNobii (anobii.com), BlueInk Review (blueinkreview.com), Foreword (forewordreviews.com), Goodreads (goodreads.com), IndieReader (indiereader.com), Reader2 (reader2.com), *Kirkus Review*'s Indie Book Reviews (https://www.kirkusreviews.com/book-reviews/indie), and *Publishers Weekly*'s BookLife (http://booklife.com).[22]

Another option is *Library Journal*'s new Self-e platform.[23] And some libraries have begun to experiment with self-published e-book "approval plans"—simply placing a standing order for all starred reviews from a given source.

Despite lingering suspicions about the quality of some self-published works among librarians, successful self-published author Hugh Howey put it this way: "the indie movement in literature is not a blip and not a gold rush."[24] It has found a place at the library table.

Library as Publisher

Stephen Arnold writes, "Libraries often have unique content that is not available elsewhere."[25] That content tends to be local, either concerning the history of an area, or work produced by or about the immediate community. It might be the work of scholars, professionals, or amateurs. But because such content is part of an institutional mission, or the larger professional mission of the preservation of knowledge, many libraries find themselves moving from being collectors of content to being producers and publishers.

Often libraries undertake this work (especially in the digital world) because no one else has or will—collecting residents' photographs of a local flood, for instance. Digital archives tend to be multimedia, incorporating not just digitized texts but photos, voice recordings, and more.

Academic Libraries

In the academic world, there's another reason to get into publishing. Vardi laments the rise of commercial, "predatory publishing, whose main goal is to generate profits rather than promote scholarship."[26] He notes that "An informal directory of predatory publishers and journals has over 50 entries."[27] The problem of predatory publishing is not just moral: it threatens the academy itself, raising prices so sharply that libraries must curtail what they can collect, thereby impeding scholarly activity, which builds on the works of others. For many libraries, electronically publishing their own peer-reviewed content is literally the only way they can afford it.

Amid ongoing charges of predatory pricing of journal and "Big Deal" monopolies (in which university libraries must buy pre-bundled packages to get a subset of more popular titles), many academic and research libraries have begun to explore open access (OA) publishing, in which universities retain the right to publish the work of their own scholars on local repositories, or host their own e-journals. According to Bosch and Henderson,[28] "Although there are many different approaches to OA, 'green' (authors deposit a copy of their work in an OA repository for free) and 'gold' (authors pay processing charges to have an article published immediately and freely available to all) are the two most common designs. There has always been tension between the two models and this year was no exception, as green advocates found much to criticize."

Rizor and Holley argue that "gold OA has fared better and has more potential for economic stability than green OA. As commercial publishers have found ways to live with and even profit from open access, the movement has not yet achieved its goal of reducing costs for libraries. The future remains uncertain for OA as the means to meeting its goals need more critical evaluation and revision."[29]

Nonetheless, Bosch and Henderson note that in 2014 "Congress passed an OA mandate. Under the bill, federal agencies under the jurisdiction of the Labor, Health, and Human Services, Education and Related Agencies (LHHS) Committee that have research and development expenditures in excess of $100 million per year must develop a policy that provides for free online public access to final peer-reviewed manuscripts or published versions of funded research not later than 12 months after the official date of publication. Though the scope is limited and some argue that the embargo period is too long, this does represent progress in support of public access to the results of research funded by the U.S. government."

In 2014 academic and research libraries seem to be far ahead of the public in the library-as-publisher movement. Examples cited in Arnold's "Libraries as Publishers" article[30] include:

- Open access journal publisher PLOS (plos.org) is more than a decade old and publishes seven journals. Another, even older, service is ArXiv.org, technically an e-print archive.
- The Library Publishing Directory, compiled by the Library Publishing Coalition (librarypublishing.org), provides a snapshot of the publishing activities of 115 academic and research libraries, including information about the number and types of publications they produce, the services they offer authors, how they are staffed and funded, and the future plans of institutions that are engaged in this growing field.[31]
- The University of Louisville, for example, has an extensive collection of images (louisville.edu/library/archives).

Arnold also mentions the vast resources of the Library of Congress's American Memory Project, a collection of digitized American historical materials.[32]

Bepress's Digital Commons published a report on library-based journal data and benchmarks,[33] which "shows that the dramatic growth in library-based e-journals since 2007 has truly become a sustainable model for library publishing.

By the end of 2013, total downloads on the Digital Commons platform exceeded 14 million and continue to grow."[34] Bepress is only one platform used, however. Many libraries use OJS and some use DSpace for journal publishing. Also of note is the Library Publishing Toolkit,[35] "a united effort between Milne Library at SUNY Geneseo and the Monroe County (New York) Library System to identify trends in library publishing, seek out best practices to implement and support such programs, and share the best tools and resources."

HathiTrust, which offers more than 13 million digitized titles through partnerships with 100 libraries, announced that on January 6, 2015, the remaining plaintiffs in *Authors Guild* v. *HathiTrust* resolved their dispute with HathiTrust institutions,[36] thereby preserving public access to its collections.

Bridging the academic and public libraries, uniting a host of digital archival materials across the nation, is the Digital Public Library of America (DPLA), which celebrated its first anniversary in April 2014. It has numerous projects under way, involving digital hub infrastructure, digital rights, educational uses of DPLA-linked content, and partnerships with public libraries.[37] Going forward, its plans include completing its hub network, building out the technology platform, pursuing an outreach plan, and achieving sustainability through revenue diversification.[38]

The Public Library

The first and best known public library as publisher remains the Internet Archive. Among its more interesting new collections is classic game software, with 2,500 new titles added in January 2015.[39] While not really in the business of content creation, the Internet Archive is now often the only remaining or extant "publisher" of many kinds of multimedia content.

A few other libraries launched a variety of publishing projects. In 2013 Smashwords CEO Mark Coker put out the call for library as portal.[40] His hometown library in Los Gatos, California, followed up with several things, including a public education program, then a dedicated portal for self-published authors. More recently,[41] the library "created two self-publishing mobile labs; each includes a MacBook Air, ten iPads, and a charging cube. Building on an existing partnership with Smashwords and expanding outreach efforts to the local high school, town librarian Henry Bankhead worked with Los Gatos High School teacher Tonya McQuade and 120 freshman students to publish a poetry anthology e-book, *Windows to the Teenage Soul*. . . . Bankhead said such projects allow libraries to help writers "promote the logical progression from a culture of reading to a culture of authorship with the library as a springboard."

Other notable projects include:

- Provincetown (Massachusetts) Public Library "curates content and enables authors to distribute their work digitally through Provincetown Public Press . . . [and] undertake[s] publishing efforts as a way to demonstrate the viability of self-publishing to their customers and communities."[42]
- Since 2012 and its popular National Novel Writing Month programs, the Topeka and Shawnee County (Kansas) Public Library has published four

"Community Novel Project titles." They have been "serialized weekly on the library's website, published as free e-books through Smashwords, and released as audiobooks." The titles are also available print-on-demand through Amazon for $5.99, and sold in the library's Booktique.[43]

• Sacramento (California) Public Library used Print on Demand and its Espresso Book Machine to produce "The Slender Poe," a collection of the works of Edgar Allan Poe. The e-book (and a host of marketing material) was designed in house. The book was then was lent, sold, and packaged with book club kits. The program's innovative promotion (involving the use of advertising in bus shelters and the creation of a custom beer, Edgar Allan Porter, by a local brewer) won several awards.[44] This effort underscores a real need for libraries: how to let patrons know about local content, particularly content that cannot be physically displayed (see "Library as Bookseller" below).

Vendors

While print-on-demand can be contracted out to various vendors (Amazon, Lulu, Scribd) as a service, electronic publishing moves the library catalog farther upstream. While e-book aggregators can perform in standalone silos (OverDrive, 3M, Total Boox, and so forth), greater integration is now possible in some cases. In the above-mentioned statewide e-book platforms, BiblioLabs (the successor to BookSurge, which was acquired and rebranded as CreateSpace by Amazon) enables libraries to take local content directly to integrated storage, discovery, and delivery platforms. BiblioLabs has also teamed with *Library Journal* to form Self-e, a platform that encourages local writers to contribute their content to the local library in exchange for exposure.[45] Also as mentioned earlier, SirsiDynix's eResource Central, and Odilo, allow for the stitching together of content from external vendors (such as OverDrive, 3M, EBSCO, Baker & Taylor, and others), leased hosting through SirsiDynix, and internal servers. In this more integrated approach, and aided by clean metadata and robust application program interfaces (APIs), the library catalog itself becomes the discovery tool not only for broader cultural content, but for what has been locally produced.

Music

There were a couple of interesting experiments with locally produced music and libraries in 2014. A library first was Ann Arbor (Michigan) Library District's agreement with indie music label Ghostly Records.[46] In brief, the library paid a flat fee to offer the entire catalog of Ghostly and subsidiary label Spectral Sound for streaming and downloading to local library patrons. Musicians tend to make more money from performing than from the sale of music; the local exposure made sense for local artists.

A second experiment was Denver Public Library's (DPL's) Volume service.[47] DPL solicited and paid Colorado musicians directly for the non-exclusive right to offer 37 DRM-free albums. The program hopes to grow to as many as 100 new albums a year. The music is available to any DPL cardholder for two years as a downloadable file; after that, it will be archived by the library, and may be rebroadcast, although it will no longer be freely downloadable.

In some respects, both of these initiatives are more about distribution than publishing. They parallel the efforts of indie publishers reaching out to libraries to market their own explosion of digital works. Uniting them all, however, is the attempt to capture the public libraries' extraordinary foot traffic, as producers seek to solve the marketing problem in an era of fewer record and book stores. Librarians are making common cause with new content partners.

Library as Bookseller

Many public libraries have long had temporary or permanent book sales. Some run in-house boutiques or gift stores. Other libraries have offered a purchase option for library holdings, right in the catalog, through a variety of local vendors, as a patron convenience and community business partnership (with or without commissions on sales referrals). But when Simon & Schuster finally agreed to sell e-books to libraries (the last of the Big Five to do so), it mandated a condition: all libraries that purchased digital content from them also had to offer it for sale to consumers. Typically, this was accomplished through one of the big distributors (OverDrive, 3M, Baker & Taylor), although not always easily.[48] The so-called "buy-it-now button" proved controversial. For some, the issue was philosophical—a reluctance to move from public servant to corporate shill. Others pointed to the experience of such libraries as Boston Public, which had offered the service for years, and reported that although its patrons didn't complain, they didn't buy much, either. Ultimately, Simon & Schuster backed down.[49]

Again, the issue is marketing. Right now, the library isn't seen by most library patrons as a place to buy new content. UK-based Bilbary, a product developed by Tim Coates, launched in 2012[50] and offered a full catalog of Big Five material, available for purchase from library websites. By 2014 it was gone. Changing consumer behavior isn't easy.

3-D Printing and Makerspaces

On January 6, 2015, ALA's Office of Information Technology Policy made available a report called "Progress in the Making: 3D Printing Policy Considerations Through the Library Lens," by Charlie Wapner.[51] Wapner reported that "A small, but rapidly growing number of public libraries—currently about 250 locations—in every part of the United States are adopting 3D printers and making them available for patron use." The uses are more like custom manufacturing than "publishing." For instance, a Boy Scout troop in Fort Wayne, Indiana, printed wheels for its robot team. "In Kansas, a high school junior created a functioning prosthetic hand for a nine-year-old family friend using the 3D printer at the Johnson County Public Library."[52] But 3-D printing in libraries also supports educational aims: printing mathematical models and multicolor globes for university and high school students, or designing and producing jewelry as part of elementary school geology lessons.

Wapner noted that 3-D printing raises many issues: intellectual property, intellectual freedom, individual liberty, and, arguably, public safety. Three-D printers can produce all or part of firearms. Should such uses be forbidden? Licensed? At this point, little has been done in a regulatory sense. In 2013 Philadelphia became the first U.S. city to ban the 3-D printing of firearms. Also in 2013 U.S. Attorney General Eric Holder mentioned 3-D printed guns in a public statement recommending the extension of the Undetectable Firearms Act, which bans guns with low metal content. However, in December 2013 a ten-year extension of the act made no explicit mention of 3-D printed firearms.[53]

The capabilities of 3-D printers are extensive. Depending upon the "ink" of a printer, one might be able to print pharmaceuticals or narcotics. It is clear that 3-D printing is a revolutionary technology, and new technology is often disruptive. Library policies will probably have some catching up to do.

The "maker movement" continues in libraries, in ways too numerous to cover adequately here. While libraries have always provided space for at least some kinds of "making" (many authors got their start at libraries, and many continue to write there), the maker movement embraces creation more broadly. Typically, this seems to mean a combination of computer labs (often incorporating 3-D printing, but not always), other digital technologies (recording of music and voice, production of video, digitization of art), public spaces (for maker stations or makerspaces that use other technologies, such as quilting or other crafts), public programming, and various exhibits to show off the results. The focus has shifted, for some, to ensuring the accessibility of these spaces[54]—a sign that makerspaces are being more completely integrated into library operations.

Conclusions

What can we conclude from this brief survey of the still-expanding ripples of the digital publishing revolution in the pond of American librarianship?

Some predictions are safe:

- People will still want print books for some time. It's unlikely that the sales mix of print to digital has stabilized. The shift to digital publishing is inexorable. But one will never extinguish the other.

- Self-publishing will continue to grow. There are three reasons. First, people want to write and publish, and the means for doing so are now far more available. Second, successful authors who have found their audiences can make more money by striking out on their own. Third, in the academic world, "self-publishing" (or peer-reviewed institutional publishing) is essential to the survival of scholarship.

- Independent publishing—alternatives to the Big Five—will also continue to grow. Again, technology gives smaller publishers not only the ability to produce works more quickly, but to distribute them globally.

- Both self- and indie publishers will continue to seek ways to work with libraries. Particularly after the contraction of bookstores in the United States, libraries are rightly seen as the place where readers can be found.

- The Big Five in the public world, and the Big Deal in the academic world, will continue to try to hold onto their near-monopolies and profit margins as long as possible, as will the e-book distributors.
- New vendors will try to get into the act, incorporating more nontraditional publishing and formats (especially music and video), and better integrating them into the library catalog. Their potential market niches will likely center around discounts and vetted content from new sources.
- If history is any guide (and sometimes it isn't), the conflict between old vendors and new will lead to a new class of winners.
- The "maker movement" will continue, as libraries continue to explore the shift from content distribution to content co-creation and publication.

In other areas, the digital publishing ecosystem needs attention. I would offer the following observations and recommendations:

- The key issues are ownership, price, and integration.
- Big Five licensing arrangements—particularly the expiration after a specific number of circulations or months—require a significant, new, and recurring method of managing library collections. The license-based business models of the Big Five don't work for libraries. Libraries need a mix of permanent purchase and pay for use, or whole-catalog subscriptions. That's the only way out of the limit of "one copy, one user"—a restriction that makes no technological sense. Tying our collections to specific vendor relationships (without ownership of the content) is contrary to the public good. We should be able to preserve what we purchase with public dollars.
- Big Five/Big Deal pricing is too high. Libraries have less money than before. The enforced scarcity of predatory e-book pricing injures patron and publisher alike; patrons don't suddenly buy what they can no longer borrow, but they often do buy what they borrowed and liked. If libraries have fewer copies, fewer people read the e-book, and fewer people talk about it, decreasing the probability that a title catches fire. High pricing encourages libraries to look for better deals with those new vendors. Moreover, libraries *should* be looking for better deals, and taking them.
- Library distributors need to restore discounts. We know that publishers sell to them at discounts. Publishers should not then be able to dictate the final retail price. Libraries are still volume purchasers, and one of the best bets for authors to find readers.
- E-content distributors and integrated library system vendors need to work on their application program interfaces (APIs). Libraries and patrons despair of yet another silo. They are looking for consistent, comprehensive, simple, single discovery tools that are available on any device.
- Libraries need to build their own e-content platforms. The technological investment is daunting for individual libraries. But at the regional, statewide, or even national level (as has been done in other countries), libraries can recoup that investment quickly by cutting out the middleman of distributors, and negotiating directly with publishers. The growth of statewide platforms is an encouraging sign.

A few more thoughts:

Libraries need to more deliberately sample the work of indie publishers and self-published authors. More and more high-quality work is rising here; better to set aside some of the money formerly used for Big Five licenses (whose content we already have in print) to build the business relationships of the future.

If publishers want our help to sell books more directly, then they need to invest in library marketing. Rather than punishing libraries for their purchases, publishers should spend real marketing dollars to help libraries highlight and promote new works. We know that in-library displays generate interest in content; publishers could help libraries solve that problem for e-books. Libraries, because of their presence in virtually every community across the country, have the potential to shore up or fill the gap of bookstores. But if we are to succeed at that, we'll need real commitment from the private sector to change buying habits. "Library as bookseller" is a culture change for libraries and consumers both. It can't be mandated. It would require a long-term, national marketing campaign, and it would have to be a partnership, meaning that both sides get something. Private profit needs to be balanced with public gain.

Authors need to step into the game. As we saw in the Amazon/Hachette conflict, authors can have real power. Many authors don't seem to know under what terms their books are sold to libraries; when they find out, they're shocked. Libraries and authors are allies—perhaps better allies than traditional publishers have been, and perhaps better than Amazon is becoming. Libraries need to build new partnerships with authors, linking them, for example, to library publishing platforms in which we help them promote their books. This is perfectly in stride with the maker movement; libraries are the homes of creators. Let the renaissance—a fountain of new literature, music, and art—start here.

In sum, libraries continue to grapple with the transformative technologies of digital publishing, a disruption that calls into question long-standing supply chains and business practices. At the same time, there is a shift in the professional and public perception of the purpose of the library, a new energy that celebrates the creativity of the human spirit. Despite some post-recessionary budget challenges, 2014 was an exciting year for the library world, and 2015 looks equally promising.

Notes

1. Tkach, David, and Carolyn Hank. 2014. "Before Blogs, There Were Zines: Berman, Danky, and the Political Case for Zine Collecting in North American Academic Libraries." *Serials Review* 40:1, 12–20. Academic Search Premier, EBSCOhost, accessed January 7, 2015.

2. Bowker. "Traditional Print Book Production Dipped Slightly in 2013." http://www.bowker.com/en-US/aboutus/press_room/2014/pr_08052014.shtml, accessed January 10, 2015.

3. Milliot, Jim. "Self-Published Books Topped 450,000 in 2013," October 8, 2014. http://www.publishersweekly.com/pw/by-topic/industry-news/manufacturing/article/64305-output-of-self-published-isbns-rises-again.html, accessed January 10, 2015.

4. Ibid.

5. Milliot, Jim. "For Books, Print Is Back," January 2, 2015. http://www.publishersweekly.com/pw/by-topic/industry-news/bookselling/article/65172-print-is-back.html?utm_source=Publishers+Weekly&utm_campaign=cc91c20e3a-UA-15906914-1&utm_

medium=email&utm_term=0_0bb2959cbb-cc91c20e3a-304524509, accessed January 10, 2015.

6. Streitfield, David. "Amazon and Hachette Resolve Dispute," November 13, 2014, *New York Times,* http://www.nytimes.com/2014/11/14/technology/amazon-hachette-ebook-dispute.html, accessed January 10, 2015.

7. Author Earnings. http://authorearnings.com/report/july-2014-author-earnings-report/, accessed January 10, 2015.

8. "Kindle Store Terms of Use, Limitations," http://www.amazon.com/gp/help/customer/display.html?nodeId=201014950, accessed January 10, 2015.

9. Enis, Matt. 2014. "Publishing: Smashwords, OverDrive Pair." *Library Journal* 139:11. Academic Search Premier, EBSCOhost, accessed January 7, 2015.

10. Inouye, Alan. "Librarians Do New York," December 9, 2014. http://www.digitalbookworld.com/2014/librarians-do-new-york, accessed January 10, 2015.

11. "Big Five Publishers and Library Lending," http://www.ala.org/transforminglibraries/sites/ala.org.transforminglibraries/files/content/Big%20Five%20Ebook%20Terms%20091314.pdf, accessed January 10, 2015.

12. http://www.unglue.it.

13. "Unglue.it for Libraries," https://unglue.it/libraries, accessed January 12, 2015.

14. "Connecticut to Build a Statewide eBook Delivery Platform," June 5, 2014, http://www.americanlibrariesmagazine.org/blog/connecticut-build-statewide-ebook-delivery-platform, accessed January 10, 2015.

15. DCL e-book report, http://www.americanlibrariesmagazine.org/blog/dcl-ebook-report-september-2014, accessed January 10, 2015.

16. E-book publisher contact list, http://evoke.cvlsites.org/files/2013/05/DCL-eBook-Publisher-Contact-List.pdf, accessed January 10, 2015.

17. Barack, Lauren. 2014. "Spending Smarter, Stretching Further." *School Library Journal* 60:4. Academic Search Premier, EBSCOhost, accessed January 12, 2015.

18. Bosch, Stephen, and Kittie Henderson. "Steps Down the Evolutionary Road," *Library Journal* 139:7 (April 15, 2014).

19. Sargent, Betty Kelly. "Surprising Self-Publishing Stats." *Publishers Weekly* 261:34 (August 25, 2014). Business Source Premier, EBSCOhost, accessed January 7, 2015.

20. Grobel, Lawrence. 2015. "Adventures in the Kindle Trade." *Saturday Evening Post* 287: 1: MasterFILE Premier, EBSCOhost, accessed January 7, 2015.

21. Wiener, Jessica. "The Benefits of Self-Publishing vs. Traditional Publishing," http://www.amarketingexpert.com/the-benefits-of-self-publishing-vs-traditional-publishing/#sthash.uHomVeWx.dpuf, accessed January 10, 2015.

22. Herther, Nancy K. "Today's Self-Publishing Gold Rush Complicates Distribution Channels." *Online Searcher* 37:5 (September–October 2013) p. 22. Available from: MasterFILE Premier, Ipswich, Mass., accessed January 6, 2015.

23. "SELF-e: Connecting Self-Published Authors, Libraries, and Readers," http://reviews.libraryjournal.com/self-e/, accessed January 10, 2015.

24. Sargent, Betty Kelly. "Surprising Self-Publishing Stats."

25. Arnold, Stephen E. "Libraries as Publishers." *Online Searcher* 38:6, Nov./Dec. 2014, 51–55.

26. Vardi, Moshe Y. Predatory Scholarly Publishing. *Communications of the ACM* [serial online]. July 2012; 55(7):5. Available from: Business Source Premier, accessed January 6, 2015.

27. See http://scholarlyoa.com.

28. Bosch, Stephen, and Kittie Henderson. "Steps Down the Evolutionary Road," *Library Journal* 139:7, April 15, 2014.

29. Rizor, Sara L., and Robert P. Holley. "Open Access Goals Revisited: How Green and Gold Open Access Are Meeting (or Not) Their Original Goals." *Journal of Scholarly Publishing* [serial online]. July 2014; 45:4, 321–335. Available from: Academic Search Premier, accessed January 6, 2015.

30. Arnold, 2014.

31. Ibid.

32. The Library of Congress American Memory Project: About Us, http://memory.loc.gov/ammem/about/about.html, accessed January 11, 2015.

33. Busher, Casey, Irene Kamotsky, and Ann Taylor. "Library-led Publishing Data and Benchmarks: Journal Data Collected from the Digital Commons Platform" (2014). *Publishing Journals Using Digital Commons,* Paper 3. http://digitalcommons.bepress.com/journals/3, accessed January 11, 2015.

34. Huwe, Terence K. "Building Digital Libraries." *Computers in Libraries.* 34:8, October 2014, pp. 31–33.

35. Library Publishing Toolkit, http://www.publishingtoolkit.org/about-us/about-the-project, accessed January 6, 2015.

36. Statement on the Resolution of *Authors Guild* v. *HathiTrust,* http://www.hathitrust.org/resolution_authors_guild_hathitrust, accessed January 11, 2015.

37. Digital Public Library of America: Projects, http://dp.la/info/about/projects, accessed January 11, 2015.

38. Digital Public Library of America Strategic Plan: 2015–2017, http://dp.la/info/wp-content/uploads/2015/01/DPLA-StrategicPlan_2015–2017 Jan 7 pdf, accessed January 11, 2015.

39. Internet Archive News, https://archive.org/post/1029210/all-those-ms-dos-games-youve-dreamt-of-replaying-are-now-available-to-download, accessed January 11, 2015.

40. Coker, Mark. "Libraries to Become Community Publishing Portals," *Huffington Post,* published March 28, 2013, accessed January 8, 2015.

41. Staley, Lissa. "Leading Self-Publishing Efforts in Communities." *American Libraries* 46:1/2 (January 2015): 18. MasterFILE Premier, EBSCOhost, accessed January 7, 2015.

42. Ibid.

43. Ibid.

44. Schwartz, Meredith. 2014. "DIY One Book at Sacramento PL." *Library Journal* March 9, 2014. Academic Search Premier, EBSCOhost, accessed January 7, 2015.

45. See http://biblioboard.com/SELF-e.

46. Raymer, Miles. "Libraries Are Branching Out into Digital." *Fortune* March 26, 2014. http://fortune.com/2014/03/26/libraries-are-branching-out-into-digital, accessed January 6, 2015.

47. LaRue, James. "Turn Up the Volume," August 19, 2014, http://www.americanlibrariesmagazine.org/blog/turn-volume, accessed January 6, 2015.

48. Maier, Robert C. "Libraries and Buy It Now: A Difficult Decision?" *American Libraries* website. November 5, 2014. http://www.americanlibrariesmagazine.org/blog/libraries-and-buy-it-now-difficult-decision, accessed January 11, 2015.

49. Simon & Schuster Strips "Buy It Now" from Library E-Book Program, http://www.digitalbookworld.com/2014/simon-schuster-strips-buy-it-now-requirement-from-library-ebook-program, accessed January 11, 2015.

50. Price, Gary. "eBooks: Bilbary Goes Live for U.S. Users, More than 340,000 Titles Currently Available for Purchase," posted March 20, 2012. http://www.infodocket.com/2012/03/20/

ebooks-bilbary-goes-live-for-u-s-users-more-than-340000-titles-currently-available-for-purchase, accessed January 14, 2015.

51. Wapner, Charlie. "Progress in the Making: 3D Printing Policy Considerations Through the Library Lens," http://www.ala.org/offices/sites/ala.org.offices/files/content/3D%20 Library%20Policy-ALA%20OITP%20Perspectives-2015Jan06.pdf, accessed January 12, 2015.

52. Ibid.

53. Ibid.

54. Brady, Tara, Camille Salas, Ayah Nuriddin, Walter Rodgers, and Mega Subramaniam. 2014. "MakeAbility: Creating Accessible Makerspace Events in a Public Library." *Public Library Quarterly* 33:4, 330–347. Library, Information Science & Technology Abstracts with Full Text, EBSCOhost, accessed January 12, 2015.

Federal Agency and Federal Library Reports

Library of Congress

10 First Street S.E., Washington, D.C. 20540
202-707-5000
World Wide Web http://www.loc.gov

James H. Billington
Librarian of Congress

Founded in 1800, the Library of Congress is the nation's oldest federal cultural institution and the largest library in the world, with more than 160 million items in various languages, disciplines, and formats. As the world's largest repository of knowledge and creativity, the library's mission is to support the U.S. Congress in fulfilling its constitutional duties and to further the progress of knowledge and creativity for the benefit of the American people.

The library's collections are housed in its three buildings on Capitol Hill and in climate-controlled facilities for books at Fort Meade, Maryland. Its audiovisual materials are held at the Packard Campus for Audio-Visual Conservation in Culpeper, Virginia. The library also provides global access to its resources through its popular website, http://www.loc.gov.

Legislative Support to Congress

Serving Congress is the library's highest priority, particularly in the area of legislative support. The library provides such support through the Congressional Research Service (CRS), the Law Library of Congress, and the U.S. Copyright Office.

During the past year CRS marked its centennial with a series of events and activities planned by its divisions and offices. These included staff events; a CRS-themed issue of the *Library of Congress Magazine* (May/June 2014); a display at the library during July; the publication of a book, *The Congressional Research Service at 100: Informing the Legislative Debate 1914*; and a committee print, *The Evolving Congress*.

During the year CRS supported Congress with policy analyses as it considered key domestic issues such as the minimum wage, federally funded earnings supplements, employment and training benefits reauthorized by the Workforce In-

Report compiled by Audrey Fischer, Public Affairs Specialist, Library of Congress

novation and Opportunity Act, and concerns about unaccompanied alien children. CRS experts answered congressional questions regarding treatment and domestic preparedness following the outbreak of Ebola in West Africa, as well as its economic and political effects. In the area of foreign affairs, CRS supported congressional review of developments in Iraq and Syria and the emergence of the organization calling itself the Islamic State. These posed major challenges to U.S. global interests, as did situations in Iran and Libya and armed conflict in Gaza between Israel and the Palestinians. Congress also called on CRS to analyze and interpret the potential impact of rapidly evolving situations in Russia and China and the need for strengthened U.S. alliances in Asia.

CRS responded to more than 593,000 congressional reference requests. In addition, online research products were accessed on the CRS website by congressional clients on more than 656,000 occasions. The library circulated approximately 20,600 volumes from its collections to members of Congress.

The Law Library—the world's largest law library, comprising more than 5 million items, including 2.91 million volumes—provided Congress with comprehensive international, comparative, and foreign law research based on the most current information available. During the year law library staff prepared 464 legal research reports, special studies, and memoranda in response to congressional inquiries. Foreign law specialists provided reports relating to many pressing U.S. legislative issues, including firearms control, mental health provisions, judicial tort systems, laws on the sale of human organs, government authority to conduct electronic surveillance, humanitarian exemptions from import duties, and European Union merger regulations. Many of these reports are accessible by the public on the law library's website.

The U.S. Copyright Office provided policy advice and technical assistance to Congress on important copyright laws and related issues. Throughout the year the Copyright Office continued to assist the comprehensive review of the nation's copyright laws initiated in 2013 by Rep. Bob Goodlatte (R-Va.), chair of the House Judiciary Committee. In 2014 the committee held 12 copyright review hearings on a wide range of issues, from piracy to fair use. Copyright Office legal experts testified at two of the hearings. The chief of the library's Packard Campus for Audio-Visual Conservation also testified at one of these hearings.

In 2014 the Copyright Office conducted three major policy studies in support of congressional work. These studies addressed: whether Congress should enact a federal resale royalty right for visual artists; whether and how to update the provisions of the Copyright Act that govern music licensing, including the activities of songwriters, music publishers, record labels, and digital delivery services; and the implementation by the United States of certain treaty provisions regarding the right of copyright owners to make their works available online. For these studies, scheduled for publication in early 2015, the Copyright Office invited stakeholder comments and held public roundtables.

On September 18, 2014, the House Judiciary Committee convened an oversight hearing of the Copyright Office. Register of Copyrights Maria Pallante was the sole witness, appearing before the committee's Subcommittee on Courts, Intellectual Property, and the Internet. Among other issues, members of Congress questioned the register about budgetary, technology, and staffing needs; modernization challenges; and the stature of the Copyright Office within the federal government.

Legislative Transparency

To support transparency in government, the Library of Congress, in collaboration with the U.S. Congress and the Government Printing Office, is working to make the nation's legislative information accessible online. On September 26, 2014, Congress.gov officially transitioned from a beta site to its permanent role as the official site for free federal legislative information from the U.S. Congress and related agencies. The site replaces the nearly 20-year-old THOMAS.gov system for public use and the Legislative Information System used by Congress. The site provides bill status, summary, and text from the 103rd through the current Congresses; member profiles; the *Congressional Record*; committee reports; direct links from bills to cost estimates from the Congressional Budget Office; legislative process videos; committee profile pages; and historic documents and metadata reaching back to the 93rd Congress.

The library continued to manage the House Streaming Video Project to stream House Committee hearings to the public and maintained an online archive of these videos. The library also participated in the Bulk Download Task Force created by House leadership to continue discussing how to better create and share legislative information with congressional offices and the public.

The Library of Congress, at the request of the House of Representatives, used the Challenge.gov platform to advance the exchange of legislative information worldwide. Administered by the U.S. General Services Administration in partnership with ChallengePost, Challenge.gov empowers the U.S. government and the public to propose solutions to the nation's challenges. During fiscal year (FY) 2013, the library issued two data challenges. The first invited competitors to apply the Akoma Ntoso schema to U.S. federal legislative information so it can be analyzed alongside legislative documents created in other countries. Akoma Ntoso is a framework used in many other countries to annotate and format electronic versions of parliamentary, legislative, and judicial documents. The second data challenge invited competitors to map the Akoma Ntoso schema to established U.S. and United Kingdom legislative markup languages. Winners of the two challenges, which each offered a $5,000 prize, were announced in February 2014.

Security

The library's Office of Security and Emergency Preparedness focused during the year on strengthening collections security, personnel security, and protective services. The office conducted Site Assistance Visits (SAVs) and implemented needed access control to protect the library's highest-level collections and financial assets. The office promoted awareness and provided training to key staff members responsible for planning and execution to enhance service unit understanding of how mission-essential functions will be performed during an emergency.

The Information Technology Services Office (ITS) ensures that the library's mission-critical systems are reliable and secure and that the technology infrastructure that supports these systems is uncompromised. ITS also ensures continuity of operations in the event of a pandemic or other emergency, including enhancing the Alternate Computing Facility and remote access.

Throughout the year ITS ensured that the library's information technology infrastructure and the services it provides continued to adapt to new technology and respond to other changes and requirements. The library's current IT infrastructure includes five data centers in four building locations. These facilities support more than 650 physical servers, 540 virtual servers, 250 enterprise systems and applications, 8 petabytes of disk storage, and 15 petabytes of backup and archive data on tape. The IT infrastructure includes a wide-area network, a metropolitan-area network and local-area networks that consist of 350 network devices. ITS supports more than 8,600 voice connections, 14,700 network connections, and 5,300 workstations. During the year the ITS Help Desk resolved more than 23,000 trouble reports from end users.

Strategic Planning

During the year the library made significant progress in updating and implementing its strategic plan for FY 2011–2016 and the related planning and budgeting framework. The plan describes goals and strategies for serving Congress and the people and demonstrates the organization's commitment to the Government Performance and Results Act. The framework integrates planning and budgeting processes, adds rigor to the library's planning and budgeting activities, and enhances the organization's ability to measure progress toward achieving the plan's outcomes and goals. In 2014 the Librarian of Congress continued development of a Futures Program to chart a course for the institution and to lay the foundation for a new Strategic Plan.

Budget

Following a 16-day government-wide shutdown, the library operated under two continuing resolutions from October 17, 2013, until January 17, 2014. The president signed the Omnibus Appropriations Act, 2014 (P.L. 113-76) on January 27, 2014, providing an appropriation for the library of $618.8 million, including authority to spend up to $39.8 million in offsetting receipts. This represented an increase of $20.3 million or 3.4 percent over FY 2013 funding, following budget cuts in the previous three fiscal years. At the end of FY 2014, the legislative funding bill had not yet been passed. FY 2015 began with a continuing resolution, signed by the president on September 19, 2014, which provided funding from October 1 through December 11, 2014.

Development

The library's development efforts in 2014 raised a total of $9.52 million, representing 880 gifts from 614 donors. Those gifts—including $4.93 million in cash gifts, $2.59 million in new pledges, $474,500 in in-kind gifts, and $1.52 million received through planned gifts—were made to 75 library initiatives.

Gifts from the James Madison Council, the library's private sector advisory group, totaled more than $1.75 million. The library forged partnerships with 226 first-time donors, who gave a total of $3,903,888. Private gifts supported a variety of new and continuing initiatives throughout the library, including exhibitions, acquisitions, scholarly programs, and the 2014 Library of Congress National Book Festival.

Madison Council member and co-chair of the National Book Festival Board David M. Rubenstein, Wells Fargo, the Institute of Museum and Library Services, and additional donors gave nearly $1.9 million to support the 2014 festival. Led by a key gift from the Federalist Society for Law and Public Policy Studies, the library received more than $362,000 to support the exhibition "Magna Carta: Muse and Mentor," which opened at the library in November 2014.

Educational Outreach

Administered by the Educational Outreach Team in the Office of Strategic Initiatives, the library's outreach to teachers focuses on the use of primary sources in the classroom. Over the past two decades, digital technology has allowed the Library of Congress to make many of its collections accessible in K–12 classrooms around the world. Access to these resources assists educators in meeting curriculum goals and creating lifelong learners. The Teachers Page, the library's Web-based resource for teachers, includes lesson plans that meet curriculum standards. The site recorded more than 10 million page views during the year.

The Educational Outreach Team worked with Web Services to develop the Interactive Student Discovery Series for Apple iPads, which can be downloaded free of charge on iBooks. Based on content, including primary-source documents, from the library's Teachers Page, the first six discovery sets cover the U.S. Constitution, Symbols of the United States, Immigration, the Dust Bowl, the Harlem Renaissance, and Understanding the Cosmos.

The library offered an array of professional development opportunities for teachers. These include five summer teacher institutes held at the library in July and August 2014. Participants in the summer program totaled 136 educators from 33 states, representing 104 congressional districts. For the first time, the program included a seminar for science educators and a civil rights institute in conjunction with the library's exhibition on the Civil Rights Act of 1964.

Through its Teaching with Primary Sources Program (TPS), the library is providing educators with methods and materials that build student literacy skills, content knowledge, and critical-thinking abilities. During the year, through workshops, conferences and webinars, the TPS program involved more than 23,000 teachers in 374 congressional districts. Many of these received instruction through the TPS Consortium, composed of the library's 28 partner institutions across the country.

The library sought to connect with educators around the nation. The Educational Outreach Team attracted more than 5,000 new followers to @TeachingLC, the library's Twitter feed for K–12 educators, offering primary sources, inspiration, and ideas. The team also published 106 posts on its "Teaching with the Library of Congress" blog, to showcase the library's collections and strategies for using them in the classroom, and to encourage readers to share their teaching strategies.

Literacy Promotion

The Library of Congress promotes reading and literacy through the Center for the Book, the National Book Festival, the appointment of a National Ambassador for Young People's Literature, and through its popular literacy-promotion website, http://www.Read.gov.

With its network of affiliates in all 50 states and more than 80 organizational partners, the Center for the Book leads the library's reading-promotion efforts and administers the Young Readers Center and the Poetry and Literature Center. [For more information on the center and its activities, see the following article, "Center for the Book"—*Ed.*]

Collections

During 2014 the size of the library's collections grew to more than 160 million items, an increase of more than 2.8 million over the previous year. This figure included more than 37 million cataloged books and other print materials, 69 million manuscripts, 16.9 million microforms, 14.9 million visual materials (photographs, posters, prints, and drawings), 7.1 million pieces of sheet music, 5.5 million maps, 3.5 million audio materials, 1.7 million moving images, and more than 3.3 million items in miscellaneous formats.

The library's policy to process only one copy of U.S. monographs, rather than two, was implemented in 2014. This policy change will result in fewer copies of books on the library's shelves and will alleviate a future budget obligation of an estimated $100 million to $250 million over the next 100 years for the storing and preserving of these additional service copies. Arrangements were made with two major nonprofit organizations to distribute withdrawn service copies to African and Asian libraries. A Digital Collections Coordinating Committee was established during the year to address the issues of digital-collections management. The committee was tasked with surveying and collecting information about library-wide digital collecting. At year's end, the committee had begun to finalize a report based on its survey that identifies and categorizes the library's incoming and existing digital content.

Important New Acquisitions

The library receives millions of items each year from copyright deposits, federal agencies, and purchases, exchanges, and gifts.

The U.S. Copyright Office forwarded more than 700,000 copies of works with a net value of $32 million to the library's collections in FY 2014; more than 407,000 of these copies were received from publishers under the mandatory-deposit provisions of the law. This includes hundreds of electronic serial publications, which were acquired through the special eDeposit program and are being managed pursuant to Copyright Office regulations and agreements with copyright owners.

Contributions from the James Madison Council helped the library acquire a number of iconic items, including a collection of Calvin Coolidge materials and

George M. Cohan's original rough sketch for the World War I-era song "Over There."

The library also acquired many significant items and collections by gift or purchase, including the following:

- The Asian Division purchased a reproduction of an encyclopedia compiled during the Ming dynasty in the early 15th century—the world's largest known general encyclopedia at its time.
- The Manuscript Division received donations of the papers of former Federal Reserve Chairman Alan Greenspan and former Secretary of State Madeleine Albright.
- The Motion Picture, Broadcasting, and Recorded Sound Division received the donation of the HistoryMakers Digital Archive, consisting of 2,600 videotaped interviews with African Americans, totaling 9,000 hours of content.
- The Motion Picture, Broadcasting, and Recorded Sound Division acquired the personal collection of actor, screenwriter, and producer Jerry Lewis under a gift-purchase agreement.
- The Music Division acquired the personal papers of jazz drummer Max Roach, including letters, business papers, musical scores and manuscripts, photographs, recordings, and videos.
- The Prints and Photographs division received, through a gift/purchase agreement with photographer Camilo Vergara, more than 4,000 photographs documenting U.S. urban ghettos from the 1980s to the present.

Cataloging

The library provided cataloging records to the nation's 122,000 public, school, academic, and research libraries and other institutions that rely on its bibliographic data. In FY 2014 the library cataloged in its Voyager system 359,072 new works on 275,112 separate bibliographic records. Production of full- and standard-level original cataloging totaled 186,657 bibliographic records. The library and other member institutions of the international Program for Cooperative Cataloging created 281,111 name and series authority records, and 3,350 subject authorities. The library served as secretariat for the program and created 77,652 of the name and series authority records and 1,786 of the subject authorities. Dewey Decimal Classification numbers were assigned to 86,630 titles as a service to other libraries throughout the world that use that system to organize their collections.

Bibliographic Framework Initiative

Since 2011 the Library of Congress has been leading a bibliographic framework initiative (BIBFRAME) to plan for the evolution from the present framework to the future, not only for the Library of Congress but also for the institutions that depend on bibliographic data shared by the library and its partners. In FY 2014 the library continued to support the BIBFRAME initiative, sought to increase publicity for the initiative and provided metadata creators with a greater understanding of the initiative. In June 2014 the library expressed its desire to work with the Program for Cooperative Cataloging (PCC) to assure that the development and fine-tuning of BIBFRAME is informed by input, feedback, and support from the cooperative cataloging community. On June 24 the library distributed a survey to PCC members and numerous electronic discussion lists. A total of 860 individuals responded to the survey. Many respondents noted that they were unaware that they could participate in BIBFRAME developments and testing. In August PCC developed a new Web page, "BIBFRAME and the PCC."

Standards

March 2013 marked nationwide implementation of RDA: Resource Description and Access, a cataloging standard designed to better meet the demands of the digital age. RDA replaced the Anglo-American Cataloguing Rules, second edition (AACR2), a standard used by libraries throughout the English-speaking world since 1981. The new standard offers better tools to describe digital and nonprint resources, such as digital maps, streaming videos, sound recordings in various formats, and e-books. Following the release of RDA, the library continued to participate in refining the new standard and making it more accessible to librarians. The library was represented on the Joint Steering Committee for Development of RDA (JSC), which met in Washington, D.C., in November 2013. JSC discussed 48 proposals and discussion papers. Five papers were submitted by the library. The primary development work on RDA accomplished during FY 2014 included a major release of the online RDA Toolkit (April 2014) and two updates, issued in November 2013 and February 2014. With the Program for Cooperative Cataloging, the Acquisitions and Bibliographic Access Directorate began planning to recode the remaining portion of the library's Name Authority File (NACO) into alignment with RDA and to populate existing name records with additional enhancements whenever possible.

Reference Services

During the year more than 982,000 items were circulated for use by patrons working at the library. Staff responded to more than 467,000 reference requests. Of these, more than 165,000 were received online, including queries that were handled through the Ask a Librarian service.

Patrons continued to register in person for the library-issued user card. Those patrons submit hundreds of requests for materials using the Integrated Library System's (ILS) automated Call Slip function in the Library of Congress Online Catalog. The library circulates approximately 200,000 items per year to patrons using ILS. The system contains 9 million authority records that provide references from variant forms of names and from narrower to broader subject headings within the Library of Congress subject headings.

The library added 155 new encoded archival description finding aids online, bringing the total to 2,138 Web-accessible finding aids covering more than 58.3 million archival items in the library's Manuscript, Music, American Folklife Center, Prints and Photographs, and Motion Picture, Broadcasting, and Recorded Sound divisions, and other Library of Congress research centers.

Online Resources

The library continued to add high-quality digital resources to its website. During the year, 7.1 million new digital files were added, bringing the total to 52.3 million, including files from the National Digital Newspaper Program. The library's website, http://www.loc.gov, gives users access to the institution's vast resources, such as its online catalogs; selected collections in various formats; copyright, legal, and legislative information; its exhibitions; and videos and podcasts of library events. Consistently recognized as one of the top federal sites, the website recorded more than 78.1 million visits and 489.3 million page views during the year.

The library continued work on "Project ONE," its enterprise-wide effort to manage its existing website content and provide a base upon which to develop new capabilities. With oversight from its Web Governance Board, the library-wide Web strategy governs three Web content areas: Congress, the Copyright Office, and the National Library. FY 2014 marked year three of a multiyear strategic project to deliver legislative content under the library's new unified Web architecture, which includes the legislative information service Congress.gov, mentioned above.

Social Media

The library continued to participate in media-sharing and social networking sites such as Flickr, YouTube, Facebook, iTunes U, and Twitter. The library's YouTube channel continued to grow with the addition of nearly 500 new videos. Since its debut in 2009, the YouTube channel has garnered almost 7.8 million video views by users around the world. Content on the library's iTunes U channel has been viewed or heard via downloads and streams more than 3.5 million times since its launch in June 2009. New content added in fiscal 2014 included tutorials on Congress.gov and the NLS BARD application, copyright roundtables on orphan works and mass digitization, scholarly symposia, poetry readings, concerts, and presentations from the 2013 and 2014 National Book Festivals.

Thousands of enthusiasts continued not only to access but also help identify library photos from the early 1900s through the photo-sharing project on Flickr. During the year the library added nearly 2,500 images to its Flickr account, bringing the total to more than 22,000. The photos have received 164 million views since 2008.

In addition to its main Facebook site, which has more than 200,000 "friends," the library offers Facebook pages for the Law Library, the American Folklife Center, Performing Arts, and the National Digital Information Infrastructure and Preservation Program. The library's Twitter presence includes feeds for the World Digital Library, the digital preservation program, the Congressional Research Service, teacher resources, and the Register of Copyright's Twitter feed. The library's main Twitter account gained 80,000 followers during the year, bring the total to 630,000.

In June 2014 the library launched its presence on Pinterest, a social-media platform for those seeking creative content and inspiration. At year's end the library's account had 14 boards featuring seasonal content from its collections, exhibitions, publications, and events, including the National Book Festival.

The library's main blog—which was among the first federal blogs at the time of its launch in April 2007—has since been joined by blogs generated by the Copyright Office; the Law Library; the National Digital Information Infrastructure and Preservation Program; the Music, Prints and Photographs, and Science, Technology, and Business divisions; the Poetry and Literature Center; the Educational Outreach Office; and the American Folklife Center. In FY 2014 new blogs were introduced by the National Library Service for the Blind and Physically Handicapped for its special-format music materials; the Packard Campus for Audio-Visual Conservation, featuring early sound and film treasures; and for the John W. Kluge Center, to highlight the center's scholarly research.

Global Access

The Library of Congress acquires global resources through cooperative agreements and exchanges with other nations, and through its overseas offices and the World Digital Library initiative. The overseas offices collect and catalog materials from 86 countries, in some 150 languages and 25 scripts, from Africa, Asia, Latin America, and the Middle East. These items are accessible in the library's area studies reading rooms. Selected items have been digitized, many through cooperative digitizing projects, and are accessible on the library's website.

Overseas Offices

The library's six overseas offices (in Cairo, Islamabad, Jakarta, Nairobi, New Delhi, and Rio de Janeiro) acquired, cataloged, and preserved materials from parts of the world where the book and information industries are not well developed. Those offices acquired 234,341 items for the Library of Congress and, on a cost-recovery basis, provided 347,187 items to other U.S. libraries through their Cooperative Acquisitions Programs. In FY 2014 the library continued the West Africa Acquisitions Pilot Project, a collaboration that began in 2011 with the Council of American Overseas Research Centers to select, purchase, and provide bibliographic services for materials from West African countries. In FY 2014 the project acquired 4,926 collection items published in 11 countries, more than double the number of items acquired the previous year. These acquisitions strengthen the library's holdings in the areas of literature, social sciences, and current events in West Africa.

World Digital Library

The World Digital Library (WDL) is a website, accessible from anywhere in the world, which presents in digital form, free of charge, documents of historical significance about numerous countries and cultures. Proposed by the Librarian of Congress, the site was launched in 2009. Since then participation has grown to 181 partners in 81 countries.

A highlight of the year was the development of a revamped and updated user interface for the WDL website. The beta version was released to partners for testing and comments on September 15, 2014. Among its many improvements, the new interface was designed to better accommodate access on mobile devices. In

FY 2014 the WDL website recorded more than 3.7 million visits and 24 million page views.

With the addition of a set of 16th century gospel books from Ethiopia in March, the site reached the milestone of 10,000 items online. At year's end the WDL website contained 10,689 items, comprising more than 492,498 images, in 116 languages.

Other noteworthy content added to the site from partner institutions included the *Cervera Bible,* Spain, 1299–1300, National Library of Portugal; *Cosmography,* England, circa 1190, Walters Art Museum; "Fragment from Major Alfred Dreyfus's Memoirs" (sound recording), 1912, National Library of France; the parchment manuscript *Collection of Texts on Mathematical Astronomy and the Natural Sciences,* Germany, 818 A.D., Bavarian State Library; *Ramayana,* Burma, 1870, British Library; *Qur'an,* Malaysia or Thailand, circa 1850–1899, British Library; and the photograph album *Views of Great Tibet* circa 1900–1901, University of Wisconsin–Milwaukee Libraries.

A key objective of the WDL project is to build digital library capabilities in the developing world. To that end, WDL continued to operate digital-conversion centers at the National Library and Archives of Egypt in Cairo, the Iraqi National Library and Archives in Baghdad, and the National Library of Uganda in Kampala. Established with private funding, these centers contribute to the capacity-building mission of WDL and are digitizing rare and at-risk material that otherwise would be inaccessible to U.S. and international audiences.

Preservation

Preserving its unparalleled collections—from cuneiform tablets to born-digital items—is among the library's major activities. During the year more than 7 million items from the library's collections were bound, repaired, mass-deacidified, and microfilmed or otherwise reformatted. The Preservation Directorate surveyed the preservation needs of nearly 1.2 million items from the library's general and special collections, including books, photographs, maps, audiovisual materials, and other formats. Of these, nearly 66,000 items were housed in protective containers, of which 58,000 were paper-based. Nearly 1.1 million units (volumes/sheets) were deacidified and more than 5.6 million pages were microfilmed, including 2.3 million items microfilmed by the library's office in New Delhi.

The congressionally mandated National Digital Information Infrastructure and Preservation Project, administered by the library's Office of Strategic Initiatives, continued to collect and preserve at-risk digital content of cultural and historical importance.

Books

During the year the library transferred 274,470 trackable items to its climate-controlled offsite storage facility at Fort Meade, Maryland, and to its storage facility at Landover, Maryland, bringing the total to more than 5.6 million items housed off site. In most cases, items can be retrieved and sent to Capitol Hill within 24 hours. To address overcrowding in the book stacks of the Thomas Jefferson and

John Adams Buildings on Capitol Hill, plans were made to explore additional leased storage space.

The library continued to sustain the book digitization program created in 2008 with a grant of $2 million from the Alfred P. Sloan Foundation to address at-risk "brittle books" in the library's public-domain general collection. The program's scanning facilities are shared by the library with other federal libraries through a FEDLINK master contract. The scanned materials are accessible for reading online or for downloading on the Internet Archive's website. At the end of FY 2014 a total of 143,000 volumes comprising 30 million images had been scanned since the project's inception.

Through the Internet Archive, the Biodiversity Heritage Library (BHL)—a subject-oriented digital repository for books relating to biodiversity scanned by American and other libraries and museums—identified 60,000 digitized items from the Library of Congress collections as candidates for BHL inclusion. During the year the library began the process of categorizing and tagging those items by format and subject. The library continued as a member of the HathiTrust, a digital repository for books scanned by American libraries, having contributed more than 89,000 digitized volumes from its collection to the project. All the works contributed to BHL and to HathiTrust are pre-1923 American imprints, or foreign imprints published before 1893, and thus in the public domain and freely available on the Internet.

Newspapers

The Library of Congress, in partnership with the National Endowment for the Humanities, sponsors the National Digital Newspaper Program, a project to digitize and provide free public access to American newspapers that are in the public domain. During 2014 more than 1.4 million newspaper pages were scanned, bringing the total to 8.1 million pages since the project's inception. Since March 2007 the library has been making this material accessible on the Chronicling America website, a free, national, searchable database of 800 historic American newspapers published between 1836 and 1922.

Audiovisual Collections

The Packard Campus for Audio-Visual Conservation in Culpeper, Virginia, houses the library's sound, film, and video collections—the world's largest and most comprehensive. In FY 2014 the Packard Campus Film Laboratory processed 1,401 reels of nitrate film. Of these, 832 reels were digitized and 569 were preserved on analog film. Each reel of original nitrate film was inspected, cleaned, and hand-repaired prior to transfer to safety-preservation copies. A total of 8,746 recorded sound items and 24,888 video collection items were digitally preserved. The library continued its collaboration with physicists at the Lawrence Berkeley National Laboratory to further develop imaging technology, known as IRENE (Image, Reconstruct, Erase Noise, Etc.), that provides noninvasive preservation and access to endangered recorded-sound collections.

Films

It is estimated that half the films produced before 1950, and 80 percent to 90 percent of those made before 1920, are gone forever. The Library of Congress is working with many organizations to prevent further losses. Under the terms of the National Film Preservation Act of 1988, the Librarian of Congress, with advice from the National Film Preservation Board, began selecting 25 films annually to be preserved for the National Film Registry. The films are chosen on the basis of whether they are "culturally, historically, or aesthetically significant."

On December 17, 2014, the library announced the following additions to the National Film Registry, which brought the total of films on the list to 650.

The Big Lebowski (1998)

Down Argentine Way (1940)

The Dragon Painter (1919)

Felicia (1965)

Ferris Bueller's Day Off (1986)

The Gang's All Here (1943)

House of Wax (1953)

Into the Arms of Strangers: Stories of the Kindertransport (2000)

Little Big Man (1970)

Luxo Jr. (1986)

Moon Breath Beat (1980)

Please Don't Bury Me Alive! (1976)

The Power and the Glory (1933)

Rio Bravo (1959)

Rosemary's Baby (1968)

Ruggles of Red Gap (1935)

Saving Private Ryan (1998)

Shoes (1916)

State Fair (1933)

Unmasked (1917)

V-E + 1 (1945)

The Way of Peace (1947)

Willy Wonka and the Chocolate Factory (1971)

The legislation also directs the library to support archival research projects that would investigate the survival rates of American movies produced in all major categories during the 19th and 20th centuries. During the year the library released a report, *The Survival of American Silent Feature Films: 1912–1929,* commissioned by the library's National Film Preservation Board. The study was written by historian-archivist David Pierce and published by the Council on Library and Information Resources. The report concluded that of the estimated 11,000 silent feature films produced and distributed domestically from 1912 through 1929, about 1,575 exist in their original format. Five percent of those that survived in their original 35 mm format are incomplete. Eleven percent of the films that are complete only exist as foreign versions or in lower-quality formats. Pierce prepared an inventory database of information on archival, commercial, and private holdings—who has custody of the films, how complete they are, the films' formats, and where the best surviving copies can be found.

Sound Recordings

The National Recording Preservation Act of 2000 mandates the preservation of the nation's historic sound recordings, many of which are at risk of deterioration. It directs the Librarian of Congress to name sound recordings of aesthetic, historical, or cultural value to the National Recording Registry; to establish an advisory National Recording Preservation Board; and to create and implement a national plan to assure the long-term preservation and accessibility of the nation's audio heritage.

On April 14, 2014, the Librarian of Congress announced the addition of 25 sound recordings to the 2014 National Recording Registry, bringing the total to 400. These were:

"The Laughing Song," George Washington Johnson (c. 1896)

"They Didn't Believe Me," Harry Macdonough and Alice Green (1915)

"Brother, Can You Spare a Dime?" Bing Crosby; Rudy Vallee (1932)

"Recordings of Kwakwaka'wakw Chief Dan Cranmer," Franz Boas and George Herzog (1938)

"Were You There," Roland Hayes (1940)

"The Goldbergs: Sammy Goes Into the Army" (radio broadcast, July 9, 1942)

"Caldonia," Louis Jordan (1945)

"Dust My Broom," Elmore James (1951)

"A Night at Birdland" (Vols. 1 and 2), Art Blakey (1954)

"When I Stop Dreaming," Louvin Brothers (1955)

"Cathy's Clown," Everly Brothers (1960)

"Texas Sharecropper and Songster," Mance Lipscomb (1960)

"The First Family," Vaughn Meader (1962)

Lawrence Ritter's Interviews with Baseball Pioneers of the Late 19th and Early 20th Century (1962–1966)

"Presidential Recordings of Lyndon B. Johnson (November 22, 1963–January 10, 1969)"

"Carnegie Hall Concert with Buck Owens and His Buckaroos" (1966)

"Fortunate Son," Creedence Clearwater Revival (1969)

"Theme from Shaft," Isaac Hayes (1971)

"Only Visiting This Planet," Larry Norman (1972)

"Celia & Johnny," Celia Cruz and Johnny Pacheco (1974)

"Copland Conducts Copland: Appalachian Spring," Aaron Copland (1974)

"Heart Like a Wheel," Linda Ronstadt (1974)

"Sweeney Todd," original cast recording (1979)

"The Joshua Tree," U2 (1987)
"Hallelujah," Jeff Buckley (1994)

Oral History

The Library of Congress has been collecting and preserving the nation's oral history since the 1930s when the Works Progress Administration's (WPA's) Federal Writers' Project documented the experiences of former slaves and of Americans living through the Great Depression. The American Folklife Center in the Library of Congress became the repository for these oral histories and others, such as the man-on-the-street interviews after the attack on Pearl Harbor, on December 7, 1941, and similar interviews following the terrorist attacks of September 11, 2001.

In 2000 the library launched the Veterans History Project, an oral history program that preserves the memories of those in the U.S. armed services and others who were part of America's wartime experience in the 20th and early 21st centuries. In 2014 the project collected more than 5,000 personal recollections, bringing the total to more than 94,000 since the project's inception. Many of these stories are accessible on the project's website.

Under the Civil Rights History Project Act of 2009 (P.L. 111-19), Congress directed the library and the Smithsonian Institution's National Museum of African American History and Culture to conduct a survey of existing oral history collections with relevance to the civil rights movement, and to record new interviews with people who participated in the movement. The library's American Folklife Center cataloged the new interviews and added them to the project website.

Inspired by the library's WPA collections, in 2003 documentary producer Dave Isay launched StoryCorps, an oral history project in which Americans record one another's stories. The more than 47,600 audio interviews that comprise the StoryCorps project reside in the Library of Congress. In addition to weekly broadcasts on National Public Radio's "Morning Edition," selected interviews are available as downloadable podcasts from NPR and as animated shorts on the StoryCorps website.

Digital Preservation and Management

The National Digital Information Infrastructure and Preservation Program (NDIIPP) was mandated by Congress in 2000 to develop a nationwide strategy to collect and preserve high-risk digital materials.

NDIIPP works with a network of national and international collaboratives, including the National Digital Stewardship Alliance (NDSA), a membership organization. In September 2014 NDSA released the "2015 National Agenda for Digital Stewardship," a set of recommendations that provides insight into emerging technological trends, gaps in capacity, and key opportunities for results in digital stewardship research and development.

NDIIPP also disseminated information about digital stewardship to a wide audience through social media channels, newsletters, podcasts, videos, and its popular blog "The Signal." The Digital Preservation Outreach and Education Program continued to foster education and training about digital preservation on a national scale through a network of dedicated trainers.

Web Archiving

In 2014 the library's Web Archiving Team continued to provide project management and technical support for a growing number of Web archive collections for Library Services and the Law Library, and continued to develop tools and strengthen the infrastructure for the long-term storage and preservation of Web archive content. During the year the Web Archiving Team managed 29 Web archive collections comprising more than 9.2 billion files or 582 terabytes of data.

U.S. Copyright Office

The U.S. Copyright Office administers certain major provisions of U.S. copyright law and provides expert and impartial advice about copyright law and policy to Congress, federal agencies, the courts, and the public. Congress enacted the first copyright law in May 1790; in 1870 it centralized the national copyright function in the Library of Congress. The library's collections have been created largely through the copyright deposit system.

During 2014 the Copyright Office registered more than 476,000 copyright claims, of which 89 percent were filed online, and recorded thousands of copyright transfer documents. Additionally, the office processed hundreds of notices terminating transfers of copyrights made in the 1970s, most of which pertained to musical works.

The Copyright Office completed digitizing its 36 million catalog cards, including historical copyright records created between 1870 and 1977. The office is now exploring how best to make the newly digitized card images searchable online.

In May 2014 the Copyright Office implemented an updated fee schedule, following a two-year study and opportunities for public comment. In August 2014 the office released a public draft on its website of the third edition of the *Compendium of U.S. Copyright Office Practices*. The new edition is the first revision in decades of the publication, which serves as the office's administrative manual regarding its core statutory duties under the Copyright Act.

The Copyright Office continued work to bring its document recordation function online. A major goal of the project is to provide for online filing and processing of documents submitted for public recordation, such as assignments and transfers, licenses, terminations of grants, and other records reflecting copyright ownership.

Copyright Royalty Judges

The Copyright Royalty Judges administer the provisions of Chapter 8 of Title 17 of the Copyright Act, which is related to setting royalty rates and terms as well as determining the distribution of royalties for certain copyright statutory licenses. In FY 2014 licensees remitted approximately $318 million in royalties. The judges approved distributions of nearly $2.5 million from six different royalty funds. The judges finalized eight proceedings by stipulation or adjudication, published an agreed partial distribution for comment, and commenced two rate-determination proceedings. The judges also published final rates and terms for three statutory licenses and cost-of-living adjustments for two established rates.

National Library Service for the Blind and Physically Handicapped

The National Library Service for the Blind and Physically Handicapped (NLS) was established in 1931 when President Herbert Hoover signed the Pratt-Smoot Act into law. In FY 2014 NLS circulated more than 23 million copies of braille and recorded books and magazines to some 890,000 reader accounts through a network of more than 100 cooperating libraries.

NLS contracted for the production of 3,224 audiobooks, 480 braille titles, and the conversion of more than 6,000 legacy titles from analog to digital format. Under its agreement with Hachette Book Group, NLS continued to provide copies of the publisher's audiobooks for use in the program at no cost to the library.

Through its digital talking-book program, NLS distributed digital players and audiobooks on flash-memory cartridges in specially designed mailing containers to libraries nationwide. NLS continued to evaluate options for on-demand duplication of digital talking books on flash-memory cartridges. This lays the groundwork for the introduction of a distribution model that would make it easier for NLS patrons to receive any NLS digital title on flash-memory cartridges.

On July 4, 2014, the library released a report titled *The Future of Braille* at the National Federation of the Blind national convention in Orlando. The report details the proceedings of a Braille Summit held by NLS in partnership with the Perkins School for the Blind in Watertown, Massachusetts, in June 2013. Participants recognized that collaboration is the way forward for strengthening braille literacy. They recommended that NLS support efforts to update braille technology and specifications. The report is available at http://www.loc.gov/nls/other/futureofbraille.html.

John W. Kluge Center

The John W. Kluge Center was established in 2000 with a gift of $60 million from the late John W. Kluge, Metromedia president and founding chairman of the James Madison Council, the library's private sector advisory group. Located within the library's Office of Scholarly Programs, the center's goal is to bring leading world thinkers to the Library of Congress to use the institution's vast resources and interact with policymakers in Washington.

During the year the Kluge Center brought to Washington 110 scholars and interns in the humanities and social sciences. Senior scholars, pre- and post-doctoral fellows, and interns researched topics of historical and contemporary significance in the fields of humanities, social sciences, foreign policy, and law.

Highlights of the year included a congressional hearing on astrobiology research, with Steven Dick, Baruch S. Blumberg NASA/Library of Congress Chair in Astrobiology, testifying before the House Committee on Science, Space, and Technology; the launch of a C-SPAN American History television interview series with Kluge scholars; and the announcement of the first-ever Kluge Center Fellowship in Digital Studies.

Publications

Each year the library publishes books, calendars, and other printed products featuring its vast content. All told, more than 200 library publications are in print and can be purchased in bookstores nationwide and from the Library Shop.

Among titles published in 2014 were volumes featuring items drawn from the library's map, photographic, and folklife collections. Among them were *Michigan-I-O: Alan Lomax and the 1938 Library of Congress Folksong Expedition* by Todd Harvey (in association with Dust to Digital and the iBookstore), which celebrates the 1938 folklife survey of the Great Lakes region by folklorist Alan Lomax; and the *Christopher Columbus Book of Privileges: The Claiming of a New World* by John W. Hessler, Chet Van Duzer, and Daniel De Simone (in association with Levenger Press), which contains the first authorized facsimile of the library's copy—one of four in existence—of the royal charters, writs, grants, and papal letters that comprise Columbus's "Book of Privileges." In addition, the library (in association with Skira/Rizzoli) published *The Forgotten Fifties: America's Decade from the Archives of Look Magazine* by James Conaway, which brings the 1950s to life through more than 200 photographs drawn from the more than 4 million images in the library's *Look* Magazine Collection, covering the period 1937–1971. Late in the year the library (in association with Thomson Reuters) published *Magna Carta: Muse & Mentor,* the companion book to the library's exhibition of the same title that opened November 6.

Exhibitions

From pre-Columbian artifacts to rare 15th century Bibles, from Thomas Jefferson's personal library to the art and architecture of the Library of Congress building named for him, continuing exhibitions offer numerous attractions. The library's exhibitions can be viewed online at http://www.loc.gov/exhibits.

In 2014 the library celebrated the centennial of the American Society of Composers, Authors and Publishers (ASCAP) with an exhibition ("One Hundred Years and Beyond") of 45 objects, including sheet music, photographs, pamphlets, and posters. Also included was the first ASCAP license, issued to Rector's Restaurant in New York City (Broadway at 44th Street) in 1914.

The African and Middle Eastern Division explored the literary tradition of the Persian language over the last millennium from illuminated manuscripts to contemporary publications in "A Thousand Years of the Persian Book."

The Music Division marked the 75th anniversary of the American Ballet Theatre and the recent donation of the company's archive to the Library of Congress with a display of items highlighting the dance company's vibrant history ("American Ballet Theatre: Touring the Globe for 75 Years").

To celebrate the 50th anniversary of the Civil Rights Act of 1964, the library mounted an exhibition to highlight the legal and legislative struggles and victories that led to the passage of this landmark legislation that outlawed discrimination based on race, color, religion, sex, or national origin ("The Civil Rights Act of 1964: A Long Struggle for Freedom").

At year's end the library opened "Magna Carta: Muse & Mentor" to commemorate the 800th anniversary of the creation of Magna Carta, the charter of liberties that England's King John granted to his barons in 1215 in order to halt their rebellion and restore their allegiance to his throne. The centerpiece of the display is the Lincoln Cathedral Magna Carta, one of only four existing manuscript copies of Magna Carta that date to 1215.

Special Events

During 2014 the library presented hundreds of public events such as poetry and literary programs, concerts, film screenings, lectures, and symposia, many of which were broadcast live or archived on the library's website at http://www.loc.gov/webcasts. For a list of upcoming events, visit http://www.loc.gov/loc/events. For concert information, go to http://www.loc.gov/concerts.

Literary Events

The 14th annual Library of Congress National Book Festival, held August 30, 2014, drew a capacity crowd of book-lovers to the free, public event in a new, indoor venue, the Walter E. Washington Convention Center in Washington, D.C. The theme of the festival, which celebrates the joy of reading and the importance of lifelong learning and literacy, was "Stay Up With a Good Book," a nod to the fact that the 12-hour event continued into the evening hours for the first time.

The Center for the Book sponsored more than 25 public programs during the year. Many of these were part of the popular Books and Beyond literary series, which highlights new books by authors who drew on the library's vast resources to produce their works. Among the notable speakers were Nicholas A. Basbanes discussing his book on the history of paper and Maureen Corrigan offering her perspective on *The Great Gatsby.*

The Poetry and Literature Center offered numerous poetry readings and literary events during the year. Natasha Trethewey concluded her tenure as the library's 19th Poet Laureate Consultant in Poetry with an evening lecture in the library's Coolidge Auditorium on May 14. On September 25 Charles Wright gave his inaugural reading as the 20th Poet Laureate Consultant in Poetry for the 2014–2015 season. The center also sponsored programs celebrating the birthdays of such writers as Philip Roth, Vladimir Nabokov, and Countee Cullen.

Concerts

Since 1925 the library's Coolidge Auditorium has provided a venue for world-class performers and world premieres of commissioned works. Sponsored by the Music Division with support from private donors, the 2013–2014 season of concerts featured world-class chamber music, jazz, bluegrass, country, American music theater, pop, rock, and electronica. The concerts were complemented by guest speakers, curators, panels, film screenings, and displays of rarely seen manuscripts, letters, and memorabilia from the library's holdings. All concerts were presented free of charge.

The library's 88th concert season celebrated American history and culture through performances by musicians including Rosanne Cash, who came to the library for a three-day residency that included a live debut of her new album "The River and the Thread." The concert season also commemorated the 200th birthdays of Giuseppe Verdi and Richard Wagner, the bicentennial of "The Star-Spangled Banner," the 75th anniversary of the founding of the Blue Note Records label, and the 50th anniversary of the March on Washington. The noontime folklife concert series known as "Homegrown: The Music of America," presented by the American Folklife Center in cooperation with the Kennedy Center Millennium Stage, the series ran from June through September.

Symposia and Lectures

Various library divisions sponsored programs and lectures on a wide range of topics during FY 2014, providing an opportunity to share ideas, celebrate diversity, and showcase the library's collections. The following are examples of these programs:

The African and Middle Eastern Division sponsored approximately 30 programs, including a symposium on the Persian book in conjunction with the Persian book exhibition. The African Section and the Poetry and Literature Center jointly sponsored a lecture series featuring African poets and writers.

The American Folklife Center presented more than 20 public programs during the year, including those that were part of its Benjamin Botkin lecture series.

The Copyright Office offered a number of programs as part of its "Copyright Matters" lecture series. It again offered a program on World Intellectual Property Day, on April 18, this time featuring movies and the copyright law, with remarks from Francis Gurry, director general of the World Intellectual Property Organization (WIPO).

The Daniel A. Murray African American Culture Association sponsored a lecture by civil rights activist Dick Gregory.

The European Division hosted the "Second Conference on Latvian Diaspora Archives, Libraries, and Material Culture." Held on September 11, the event was sponsored jointly with the American Latvian Association and the Embassy of Latvia.

The Geography and Map Division hosted the annual Jay I. Kislak Lecture on the archaeology and history of the Early Americas, which was delivered by noted archaeologist Richard Hansen on April 2. On May 15 the division joined the Philip Lee Phillips Society in sponsoring a major conference on the history of 20th century cartography.

The Hispanic Division sponsored more than 20 events including a two-day symposium on "The Spanish Language of the United States," organized with the North American Academy of the Spanish Language, and jointly sponsored by the Embassies of Mexico and Spain.

The John W. Kluge Center sponsored more than 25 public programs on such topics as foreign policy, religion, American history and government, world history, astrobiology, the Earth and the environment, and arts and culture. Notable events included the Ninth Annual International Seminar on Decolonization and the second annual NASA/Library of Congress Astrobiology Symposium focused on the potential impacts on society and humanity of finding microbial or complex life beyond Earth.

The Law Library marked Law Day (May 1) with a lecture by Jeffrey Rosen of the National Constitution Center on the influence of the courts and Congress on civil and voting rights. The Law Library marked Constitution Day on September 16 with a lecture by law professor Akhil Amar on the ways in which the United States has both drawn upon and broken with English constitutional precursors such as Magna Carta and the English Bill of Rights of 1689. In conjunction with the library's Magna Carta exhibition, the Law Library launched a Magna Carta lecture series, cosponsored by the American Bar Association Standing Committee on the Law Library of Congress.

Film Screenings

The library's Packard Campus Theater continued its popular film screenings that showcase the film, television, radio, and recorded sound collections. The theater is one of only five venues in the United States equipped to show original classic film prints on nitrate film stock as they would have been screened in theaters before 1950. The theater also features a custom-made organ that provides live musical accompaniment for silent movies. During 2014 the theater offered 140 public screenings of more than 200 titles held by the library, and more than 11,000 people attended these screenings.

Honors and Awards

Gershwin Prize for Popular Song

The Library of Congress celebrated pianist, composer, and singer Billy Joel's 50-year career and his selection as the 2014 recipient of the Library of Congress Gershwin Prize for Popular Song with a series of events, culminating in a concert at DAR Constitution Hall on November 19. Joel is the sixth top-selling artist of all time and the third top-selling solo artist of all time, according to the Recording Industry Association of America. His multiple Grammy wins include Song of the Year ("Just the Way You Are," 1978), Record of the Year ("Just the Way You Are," 1978), Album of the Year ("52nd Street," 1979), and back-to-back wins for Best Rock Vocal Performance, Male for two of his 13 multi-platinum albums, "52nd Street" and "Glass Houses." The Gershwin Prize honors a living musical artist's lifetime achievement in promoting the genre of song as a vehicle of cultural understanding, entertaining and informing audiences, and inspiring new generations. Previous recipients are Paul Simon, Stevie Wonder, Sir Paul McCartney, songwriting duo Burt Bacharach and the late Hal David, and Carole King.

Library of Congress Prize for American Fiction

Acclaimed fiction writer E. L. Doctorow received the Library of Congress Prize for American Fiction during the National Book Festival on August 30. The prize honors an American writer whose body of work is distinguished not only for its mastery of the art but for its originality of thought and imagination.

For other Library of Congress awards, see "Literary Awards" in Part 5 of this volume.

Additional Sources of Information

Library of Congress website	http://www.loc.gov
Main telephone	202-707-5000
Reading room hours and locations	http://www.loc.gov/rr
	202-707-6400
General reference	http://www.loc.gov/rr/askalib
	202-707-3399
	TTY 202-707-4210
Visitor information	http://www.loc.gov/visit
	202-707-8000
	TTY 202-707-6200
Exhibitions	http://www.loc.gov/exhibits
	202-707-4604
Copyright information	http://www.copyright.gov
	202-707-3000
Copyright hotline (to order forms)	202-707-9100
Library catalogs	http://catalog.loc.gov
Cataloging information	http://www.loc.gov/aba
Services for the Blind and Physically Handicapped	http://www.loc.gov/nls
	202-707-5100
	TDD 202-707-0744
Teachers Page	http://www.loc.gov/teachers
Legislative information	http://www.Congress.gov
Library of Congress Shop (credit card orders)	http://www.loc.gov/shop
	888-682-3557
Literacy promotion	http://www.read.gov

Center for the Book

World Wide Web http://www.read.gov, http://www.loc.gov/cfbook

John Y. Cole
Director

Congress established the Center for the Book in the Library of Congress by statute (Public Law 95-129) in 1977. The center's purpose—to use the resources and prestige of the Library of Congress to stimulate public interest in books and reading—has since expanded substantially. Today it also includes promoting both literacy and libraries and encouraging the historical study of books, reading, libraries, and print culture, both nationally and internationally.

To help carry out these ambitious goals, the center has developed two national partnership programs. Its network of affiliated state centers, comprising all 50 states plus the District of Columbia and the Virgin Islands, began in 1984 with the launch of the Florida Center for the Book, hosted by the Broward County Library.

The creation of its national network of nonprofit reading promotion partners, which today includes more than 80 organizations and several U.S. government agencies, was stimulated in 1989 by the center's "Year of the Young Reader" national reading promotion campaign. First Lady Barbara Bush served as the campaign's honorary chair. Internationally, the center has inspired the creation of similar organizations in several countries, including South Africa and Russia.

The Center for the Book is an early example of a successful governmental public-private partnership. The Library of Congress supports its six staff positions; all of its projects, programs, conferences, and other activities are supported by contributions from individuals, corporations, or foundations, or transfers of project funds from other government agencies.

Highlights of 2014

During 2014 the Center for the Book

- Successfully led the Library of Congress Literacy Awards, a five-year awards program, through its second year
- Played a major role in the organization and development of the 2014 Library of Congress National Book Festival in August
- In cooperation with the Office of the Librarian of Congress, assumed the overall direction of the National Book Festival
- Through its Books and Beyond noontime author series, and the programs of its Poetry and Literature Center and Young Readers Center, sponsored more than 75 public events at the Library of Congress or in the Washington, D.C., area
- In collaboration with the Poetry and Literature Center and the Office of the Librarian of Congress, managed the Library of Congress Prize for American Fiction program

Library of Congress Literacy Awards

The Center for the Book continued its administration of the Library of Congress Literacy Awards. The five-year program, initiated in 2013, is funded by philanthropist David M. Rubenstein, a major donor to the Library of Congress. On January 31 a call for applications was issued for the three prizes: the David M. Rubenstein Prize ($150,000), to an organization making outstanding and measurable contributions in increasing literacy levels over a sustained period of time; the American Prize ($50,000), to a U.S. organization making a significant and measurable contribution to increasing literacy levels or national awareness of the importance of literacy; and the International Prize ($50,000), to an organization outside the United States or a national entity that has made a significant and measurable contribution to increasing literacy levels.

Three prize committees drawn from a national advisory board of literacy experts narrowed the number of applications from 89 to a small number of candidates for each prize. The winners, chosen by Librarian of Congress James H. Billington, were introduced at the National Book Festival on August 30. They also were featured, along with 14 Best Practices honorees, at the awards ceremony at the Library of Congress on October 8.

The winner of the Rubenstein Prize was Room to Read, a San Francisco-based organization focused on literacy among children in Africa and Southeast Asia; the American Prize went to Start Making a Reader Today (SMART), a program of the Oregon Children's Foundation that annually serves approximately 9,000 children in Oregon; and the International Prize went to the Mother Child Education Foundation (AÇEV), the largest literacy organization in Turkey.

The three winning projects, plus those of the 14 Best Practices honorees, are described in a 26-page booklet, *Library of Congress Literacy Awards 2014: Best Practices,* available as a pdf at http://read.gov/documents/best-practices2014-for-web.pdf.

Poetry and Literature Center

The Poetry and Literature Center of the Library of Congress, which became part of the Center for the Book in February 2013, sponsored or cosponsored 38 events in 2014. It collaborated with 10 different Library of Congress divisions or centers and more than 20 organizations outside the library. While most of the events took place either at the library or in the Washington, D.C., area, programs also were held in Georgia, Oklahoma, Texas, Pennsylvania, and New York City.

The center expanded its International Literature series to include an annual program with the literary magazine *MANOA,* and developed three new series. Its Conversations with African Poets and Writers series continued on the library's website, at http://www.loc.gov/poetry.

Natasha Trethewey, the 19th Poet Laureate Consultant to the Librarian of Congress, concluded her second term in the post in May 2014. During the year she continued her signature second-term project, "Where Poetry Lives," with PBS NewsHour and the Poetry Foundation.

In June the Librarian of Congress appointed Charles Wright as the 20th Poet Laureate. Wright began his term with a reading on September 25 in the library's Coolidge Auditorium. All evening poetry readings at the library were recorded digitally for the library's Literary Archives and posted as webcasts on the Poetry and Literature Center website.

National Book Festival

The Center for the Book played a major role in the presentation of the library's annual National Book Festival, as it has done since the festival was created in 2001. For the first time, the 2014 festival was held indoors, on August 30 at the Walter E. Washington Convention Center in downtown Washington. Standing-room-only crowds filled the new venue. The program featured the first evening hours in the festival's history and the debut of three new festival pavilions: Culinary Arts, Science, and Picture Books. More than 100 authors, illustrators, and poets participated. Other highlights included expanded coverage of graphic novels, a poetry slam, and an evening film program with authors discussing the films based on their books.

In addition to E. L. Doctorow, winner of the 2014 Library of Congress Prize for American Fiction, featured writers and illustrators at the festival included Paul Auster, Bryan Collier, Billy Collins, Kate DiCamillo, Jack Gantos, Doris Kearns Goodwin, Cynthia Kadohata, Alice McDermott, Meg Medina, Anchee Min, Sandra Day O'Connor, Cokie Roberts, Richard Rodriguez, Lisa See, Raina Telemeier, Jacqueline Woodson, and Gene Luen Yang.

Young Readers Center

Opened in 2009, the Young Readers Center serves children and youth 16 and younger who are accompanied by an adult. In 2014 it continued to draw an increasing number of families to the Library of Congress, hosting approximately 38,000 visitors.

In June the center sponsored its first program aimed primarily at adults, a symposium on "The Reluctant Reader." The audience of more than 200 included educators, parents, caregivers, and professionals in the field of early childhood learning. Panelists included a pediatrician representing Reach Out and Read (which won the center's 2013 Rubenstein Prize); a school psychologist, and two popular graphic novelists, Jarrett J. Krosoczka and Stephan Pastis, who signed their most recent books after the program.

Other major 2014 activities included weekly storytime events for toddlers, a popular program that attracted a full house each Friday; special events coordinated with holidays, including Presidents Day in February (400 visitors) and the Cherry Blossom Festival in April (500 visitors); hosting, with author Meg Medina, its first bilingual program, which celebrated El Día de los Niños/El Día de los Libros (Day of the Child/Day of the Book); and a May 12 film program celebrating Children's Book Week that featured author Lois Lowry and film producer Nikki Silver.

They discussed the forthcoming film version of Lowry's *The Giver,* her classic and award-winning dystopian novel.

National Ambassador for Young People's Literature

Award-winning author Kate DiCamillo was inaugurated as the fourth National Ambassador for Young People's Literature in a ceremony at the Library of Congress on January 10, 2014. Her theme during her two-year ambassadorship, which includes presentations at special events around the country, is "Stories Connect Us." Her appearances during 2014 included the launching of Children's Book Week in New York City and the 2014 National Book Festival.

Former national ambassadors are Jon Scieszka (2008–2009), Katherine Paterson (2010–2011), and Walter Dean Myers (2012–2014). The Librarian of Congress names the national ambassador based on recommendations from a selection committee representing many segments of the book community. The selection criteria include the candidate's contribution to young people's literature and ability to relate to children. The position was created by the Center for the Book, the Children's Book Council, and Every Child a Reader, the council's nonprofit foundation. Financial support is provided by several publishers of books for children and teens.

Displays and Other Continuing Programs

In 2014 the center initiated a series of small 30-day public displays centering on aspects of the history of the Library of Congress. Developed in cooperation with the library's Manuscript Division, the home of the Library of Congress Archives, the first two displays focused on the interior decoration of the Jefferson Building, which opened in 1897. A display on the building's sculpture was presented in April, and murals and decorative pointing were the topics in August.

Annual idea exchanges at the Library of Congress during 2014 were hosted for the Center for the Book's two national organizational networks. The reading and literacy partners met March 4, the state Center for the Book affiliates on May 1 and 2.

The Letters About Literature reading and writing program for grades 4–12, established by the center in 1992, received more than 50,000 entries in 2014. State Center for the Book affiliates play a major role in the program, each designating three winners who then are eligible for one of the three national prizes.

For more than a dozen years, the center and the Hispanic Division have joined with the Consortium of Latin American Studies Program at the University of Wisconsin–Milwaukee to present the Americas Award. Works by writers for children and young adults are recognized for "authentically and engagingly portraying Latin America, the Caribbean, or Latinos in the United States."

For the fifth consecutive year, the center hosted the awards ceremony for the National Collegiate Book Collecting Contest. The three winners were announced at the Library of Congress on October 17. Cosponsors of the contest and ceremony are the Antiquarian Booksellers Association of America, the Fellowship of American Bibliographic Societies, and the Library of Congress Rare Book and Special Collections Division.

Federal Library and Information Network (FEDLINK)

Kathryn Mendenhall

Interim Executive Director

Summary

During fiscal year (FY) 2014 the Federal Library and Information Network (FED-LINK) continued its mission to achieve better utilization of federal library and information resources; provide the most cost-effective and efficient administrative mechanism for providing necessary services and materials to federal libraries and information centers; and serve as a forum for discussion of federal library and information policies, programs, and procedures, to help inform Congress, federal agencies, and others concerned with libraries and information centers.

FEDLINK's Advisory Board focused its bimonthly meetings on a variety of broad federal information issues including strategic sourcing and the Library of the United States project; FEDLINK's research agenda; federal science, technology, engineering, and medicine (STEM) collections; access to federally funded scientific research; the National Digital Stewardship Alliance (NDSA); and support of American Indian libraries. The board created two new working groups: the American Indian Libraries Working Group and the Research and Metrics Working Group.

The governing body structure of FEDLINK includes a number of committees, working groups, and ad hoc committees that all completed an ambitious agenda in FY 2014. Notably, the Education Working Group completed the third edition of the *Handbook of Federal Librarianship* for release in FY 2015, and the Preservation Working Group presented to the National Digital Stewardship Alliance on digital preservation standards and practices. The FEDGrey Working Group hosted Stefania Biagioni and Carlo Carlesi from ISTI-CNR (Institute of Information Science and Technologies of the National Research Council of Italy) via the online "unified learning system" iCohere, for the presentation "Guide to Good Practice in Grey Literature."

The FEDLINK Awards Committee announced the following awards:

- 2013 Federal Library/Information Center of the Year (large library/information center category, staff of 11 or more employees): Information Services Office (ISO), National Institute of Standards and Technology (NIST), Gaithersburg, Maryland
- 2013 Federal Library/Information Center of the Year (small library/information center category, staff of ten or fewer employees): Joint Base Librar-e and Resource Commons (JB LRC), 87th Force Support Squadron, Joint Base McGuire-Dix-Lakehurst, New Jersey
- 2013 Federal Library Technician of the Year: Brandan Carroll, Veterans Health Administration / Veterans Integrated Service Network 1 (VISN1), Bedford, Massachusetts

The Human Resources Working Group released its Federal Librarian Professional Development Roadmap. This guide assists library professionals with their career development; it is organized according to the Federal Librarian Competencies developed by the working group in 2011.

During FY 2014 FEDLINK continued its publication program as a digital communication provider and used the FEDLIB listserv to communicate critical advocacy and program information to more than 2,000 electronic subscribers. New resources for FY 2014 included expanding the *Handbook of Federal Librarianship*, the FEDLINK Strategic Sourcing page, and a number of research documents.

FEDLINK continued to enhance its fiscal operations while providing its members with $83.3 million in transfer-pay services, $7.5 million in direct-pay services, and an estimated $68.4 million in "direct express" services, saving federal agencies more than $30.1 million in vendor volume discounts and approximately $42.4 million more in cost avoidance.

FEDLINK staff participated in national conferences including the Annual Conference of the American Library Association (ALA), Computers in Libraries, the National Contracts Management Association World Congress, and the Government Contracts Management Symposium. Staff also represented FEDLINK at such regional events as the House of Representatives Subscription Fair and the Federal Communications Commission Information Fair. Staff members also assisted the ALA Federal and Armed Forces Librarians Round Table (FAFLRT) in tracking activities affecting federal libraries and by hosting programs at the Annual Conference on working in a federal library and on best practices for library internships. They participated in additional conferences, workshops, and meetings, including the national Digital Preservation Conference. FEDLINK representatives also attended regular meetings of the Office of Management and Budget's (OMB's) Strategic Sourcing Leadership Council and worked with OMB to improve usability of its OMB Max tool for procurement-related data gathering and analysis.

FEDLINK gave federal agencies cost-effective access to automated information retrieval services for online research, cataloging, and resource sharing. FEDLINK members procured print serials, electronic journals, books and other publications, document delivery, online language-learning systems, digitization, preservation, and other library support services via Library of Congress/FEDLINK contracts with approximately 150 companies. The program obtained further discounts through consortia and enterprise-wide licenses for journals, aggregated information retrieval services, and electronic books.

Highlights of the Year

American Indian Libraries

The mission of the FEDLINK American Indian Libraries Working Group is to support the consortial work of agencies responding to Presidential Executive Order 13592 of December 2011 to "increase the capacity of educational agencies and institutions, including our Nation's public schools and Tribal Colleges and

Universities, to deliver high-quality education and related social services to all American Indian and Alaskan Native students."

FEDLINK's standing working group will work tangentially with the Library of Congress/Library Services Ad Hoc Committee to form an American Indian Library Initiative that spans efforts by both the Library of Congress and FEDLINK's member agencies and organizations. FEDLINK's working group will develop strategic goals to support its member agencies in their effort to build an information culture among all levels from local to local and from local to national; create a clearinghouse of resources among participants; identify federal efforts to support American Indian libraries in their preservation, digitization, cataloging, and reference services efforts; integrate event and training opportunities on core information competencies; and promote existing federal resources in legal and STEM (science, technology, engineering, and mathematics) knowledge collections of value to American Indian libraries.

Research and Metrics

The FEDLINK Research and Metrics Working Group was organized primarily to serve as an advisory group in support of FEDLINK's research agenda. Research coordination across the federal enterprise is essential to making sound investments with the resources available. To that end FEDLINK, in collaboration with its members and other national organizations, investigates current trends and issues facing the information community. With relevant metrics, data sets, analysis, training, and education, FEDLINK ensures that federal libraries and information centers have the expertise and other resources necessary to make critical decisions about their services and programs. The working group has six areas as priorities for research: demonstrating value, collections management, information marketplace, information technology, management tools, and cross-cutting areas. In addition to advising on the biennial Federal Library Census, the working group also supports FEDLINK's research agenda in the following areas: identifying trends among members, vendors, and information science thought leaders; identifying priorities for research and inviting collaboration; creating a research agenda based on identified trends and priorities; conducting research consistent with these priorities and agenda; and providing the federal community and larger library and information science community with useful research and information.

Expositions

FEDLINK held two expositions in FY 2014, "Accessing Information in a Changing Federal Environment" and "Developing an Information Culture in Federal Agencies: Training for Today's Knowledge Navigator."

Strategic Sourcing Initiative

FEDLINK's Strategic Sourcing Initiative continued throughout the fiscal year with research reports on federal spending on information and efforts with OMB and the General Services Administration (GSA) to develop further strategic sourcing of information resources for federal agencies.

Working Groups

Education

During FY 2014 the FEDLINK Education Working Group, in concert with other FEDLINK working groups, sponsored seminars, workshops, and brokered conferences for more than 1,200 members of the federal library and information center community. The working group also sponsored sessions at FEDLINK Expositions on e-books and on the Library of the United States program. The working group also sponsored a series of orientations to libraries and information centers to provide the opportunity for federal librarians to become acquainted with a variety of institutions and collections in the Washington, D.C., area. These included the National Library of Education, the U.S. Supreme Court, the Department of Justice Library, the Martin Luther King Library, and the Holocaust Museum Library.

FedGrey

The FedGrey Working Group focused its efforts on contributions to the FEDLINK expositions. At the Spring (2014) Expo, the group focused on "Guide to Good Practice in Grey Literature: A Community Driven Open Resource Project." At the Fall Expo, the group sponsored "GreyMatters! Expand Your World View: Conversation About the International Conference Series on Grey Literature."

Human Resources

The Human Resources Working Group (HRWG) released its Federal Librarian Professional Development Roadmap. The guide is designed to help library professionals with career development and is organized according to the Federal Librarian Competencies developed by the working group in 2011. Librarians can find resources, training, and information to assist in developing a given competency. HRWG also hosted a workshop on Succession Planning at the Spring Expo. The presenters outlined how the information culture can be a strategic asset when a library considers all of the processes it can put in place to ensure development of its future leaders. Succession planning is one method of examining the current workforce to better address the changing workforce environment and put staff development and other programs in place.

Preservation

The Library of Congress Preservation Directorate, the FEDLINK Preservation Working Group, and the Federal Library Safety Net (a voluntary federal library network for disaster response) regularly collaborate to present disaster planning and response educational opportunities. The FEDLINK Preservation Working Group sponsored two programs in conjunction with the Spring Expo, including an update on digital preservation standards and practices at the Library of Congress.

Library Technicians

The Library Technicians Working Group presented a number of programs to the technicians community including a five-day institute and a brown bag session on customer service. Training featured discussion on continuing education, cross training, technology developments, and individual development planning. The institute featured a variety of speakers on the subjects of federal contracting, acquisitions, preservation, disaster preparedness, budgeting, and career development.

Publications and Education

FEDLINK continued its publication program as a digital communication provider and used the FEDLIB listserv to communicate critical advocacy and program information to more than 2,000 electronic subscribers.

It continued to develop targeted resources to support the FEDLINK program, including strategic sourcing communications, and development of supporting materials for both exposition programs and working group events. It produced the minutes of the FEDLINK Advisory Board meetings, as well as all FEDLINK program promotional and support materials.

Staff members continued to convert all publications, announcements, alerts, member materials, meeting minutes, and working group resources into accessible pdf formats and created new graphics for exhibits. New resources for FY 2014, in addition to the expanded *Handbook of Federal Librarianship,* included the Strategic Sourcing page and a number of research documents. Staff worked on quality assurance efforts with Library Services and the Office of Strategic Initiatives. FEDLINK staff also supported photographic coverage of all FEDLINK programs and off-site tours.

FEDLINK supported distance-learning offerings by using Web conferencing software for a number of its free events and routinely incorporated electronic versions of PowerPoint and other presentation materials to enhance access to the resources available at educational programs.

In conjunction with the Education Working Group and other working groups, FEDLINK offered 21 seminars, workshops, brokered conferences, and lunchtime discussions to more than 1,200 members of the federal library and information center community. Staff also hosted a variety of vendor sessions with more than 100 attendees.

Network Operations

FEDLINK continued in FY 2014 to provide federal agencies with cost-effective access to an array of automated information resources for online research and support for federal library functions. FEDLINK members procured a variety of publications in various formats, including print and electronic journals, print and electronic books, sound recordings, audiovisual materials, items via document delivery and interlibrary loan, and access to databases of full text, indexes, abstracts, and a variety of other data. Via Library of Congress/FEDLINK contracts with more than 150 information vendors, federal libraries obtained support for such functions as acquisitions, cataloging and related technical processing services, staffing support, information management, resource sharing, copyright royalty payment, information industry market research and library services benchmarking, integrated library systems, digitization, digital archiving, and preservation and conservation services.

FEDLINK issued many Requests for Proposals (RFPs) and Requests for Quotes (RFQs). An RFP "open season" established new agreements for preservation and conservation services with six companies, bringing the total to 27 vendors, and expanding the range of services available. Two other "open season" RFPs added a serials subscription agent and several information retrieval vendors. FEDLINK awarded a contract for interlibrary loan fee management and renewed option years for staffing support and bibliographic resources. In total, FEDLINK issued 40 RFQs for agencies' requirements for these services.

Approximately 140 contracts and agreements were renewed, including a contract to support CENDI, an interagency working group of senior scientific and technical information (STI) managers from 14 U.S. federal agencies representing 97 percent of the federal research and development budget, and an Interagency Agreement with Department of Energy to support Science.gov.

FEDLINK representatives also worked with OMB to improve usability of its OMB Max tool for procurement-related data gathering and analysis and developed a FEDLINK section for StrategicSourcing.gov.

Fiscal Operations

FEDLINK continued to enhance its fiscal operations during FY 2014, and throughout the fiscal year worked on both its performance standards and the criteria for its Balanced Scorecard Dashboard. By the end of the year, staff members established all criteria and began developing measurement tools for each item. FEDLINK will review and implement new tools for auditing vendor "direct express" transactions.

FEDLINK Fees

The final budget for FY 2015 held membership fees steady for transfer-pay customers to 6 percent on amounts exceeding $100,000; 6.75 percent below $100,000, and 4 percent on amounts equal to or exceeding $1,000,000. Direct-pay fees remained at FY 2009 levels, as did "direct express" fees of 0.75 percent for all participating commercial online information services vendors.

Accounts Receivable and Member Services

FEDLINK processed registrations from federal libraries, information centers, and other federal offices for a total of 349 signed Interagency Agreements (IAAs) and more than 800 IAA amendments for agencies that added, adjusted, or ended service funding. It executed service requests by generating 2,803 delivery orders that the Library of Congress/Office of Contracts and Grants Management issued to vendors.

Accounts Payable Services

Staff members efficiently processed vendor invoices and earned $7,658 in discounts in excess of interest payment penalties levied for the late payment of invoices to FEDLINK vendors. FEDLINK continued to maintain open accounts for three prior years to pay publications service invoices for members using books and serials services. It completed the closing of FY 2009. Statements are issued to members for the current year and prior years.

'Direct Express' Services

The "direct express" program now includes 92 vendors offering database retrieval services. The program is set up to provide customers procurement and payment options similar to those of GSA in which the vendors pay a quarterly service fee to FEDLINK based on customer billings for usage.

National Agricultural Library

U.S. Department of Agriculture, Abraham Lincoln Bldg.,
10301 Baltimore Ave., Beltsville, MD 20705-2351
E-mail agref@nal.usda.gov
World Wide Web http://www.nal.usda.gov

Jennifer Gilbert
Special Assistant to the Director

The U.S. Department of Agriculture's National Agricultural Library (NAL) is one of the world's largest and most accessible agricultural research libraries, offering service directly to the public via its website, http://www.nal.usda.gov.

The library was instituted in 1862 at the same time as the U.S. Department of Agriculture (USDA). It became a national library in 1962 when Congress established it as the primary agricultural information resource of the United States (7 USCS § 3125a). Congress assigned to the library the responsibilities to

- Acquire, preserve, and manage information resources relating to agriculture and allied sciences
- Organize agricultural information products and services and provide them within the United States and internationally
- Plan, coordinate, and evaluate information and library needs relating to agricultural research and education
- Cooperate with and coordinate efforts toward development of a comprehensive agricultural library and information network
- Coordinate the development of specialized subject information services among the agricultural and library information communities

NAL is located in Beltsville, Maryland, near Washington, D.C., on the grounds of USDA's Henry A. Wallace Beltsville Agricultural Research Center. Its 15-story Abraham Lincoln Building is named in honor of the president who created the Department of Agriculture and signed several of the major U.S. laws affecting agriculture.

The library employs about 100 librarians, information specialists, computer specialists, administrators, and clerical personnel, supplemented by about 50 volunteers, contract staff, and cooperators from NAL partnering organizations.

NAL's reputation as one of the world's foremost agricultural libraries is supported and burnished by its expert staff, ongoing leadership in delivering information services, expanding collaborations with other U.S. and international agricultural research and information organizations, and its extensive collection of agricultural information, searchable through AGRICOLA (AGRIcultural On-Line Access), the library's bibliographic database.

In 2012 NAL reorganized to better align its functions with its overall strategic plan, which includes simplified access to all NAL content, expansion of digital content, and the integration of scientific data sets and discovery tools.

The Collection

The NAL collection dates to the congressionally approved 1839 purchase of books for the Agricultural Division of the Patent Office, predating the 1862 establishment of USDA itself. Today NAL provides access to billions of pages of agricultural information—an immense collection of scientific books, journals, audiovisuals, reports, theses, artifacts, and images—and to a widening array of digital media, as well as databases and other information resources germane to the broad reach of agriculture-related sciences.

The library's collection contains nearly 8.1 million items, dating from the 16th century to the present, including the most complete repository of USDA publications and the world's most extensive set of materials on the history of U.S. agriculture.

Building the Collection

NAL has primary responsibility for collecting and retaining publications of USDA and its agencies, and it is the only U.S. national library with a legislated mandate to collect in the following disciplines: plant and animal health, welfare, and production; agricultural economics, products, and education; aquaculture; forestry; rural sociology and rural life; family and consumer science; and food science, safety, and nutrition. In addition to collecting as comprehensively as possible in these core subject areas, NAL collects extensively in many related subjects, such as biology, bioinformatics, biochemistry, chemistry, entomology, environmental science, genetics, invasive species, meteorology, natural resources, physics, soil science, sustainability, water quality, and zoology.

Rare and Special Collections

The NAL Rare and Special Collections program emphasizes access to and preservation of rare and unique materials documenting the history of agriculture and related sciences. Items in the library's special collections include rare books, manuscripts, nursery and seed trade catalogs, posters, objects, photographs, and other rare materials documenting agricultural subjects. Materials date from the 1500s to the present and include many international sources. Detailed information about these special collections is available on the NAL website at http://special collections.nal.usda.gov.

Special collections of note include the following:

- The U.S. Department of Agriculture History Collection (http://special collections.nal.usda.gov/usdahistory), assembled over 80 years by USDA historians, includes letters, memoranda, reports, and papers of USDA officials, as well as photographs, oral histories, and clippings covering the activities of the department from its founding through the early 1990s.
- The U.S. Department of Agriculture Pomological Watercolor Collection (http://usdawatercolors.nal.usda.gov) includes more than 7,000 detailed, botanically accurate watercolor illustrations of fruit and nut varieties de-

veloped by growers or introduced by USDA plant explorers. Created between 1886 and the 1940s, the watercolors served as official documentation of the work of the Office of the Pomologist and were used to create chromolithographs in publications distributed widely by the department. Although created for scientific accuracy, the works are artistic treasures in their own right. The full collection has been digitized and is now available online.

- The Henry G. Gilbert Nursery and Seed Trade Catalog Collection (http://specialcollections.nal.usda.gov/guide-collections/henry-g-gilbert-nursery-and-seed-trade-catalog-collection), begun in 1904 by USDA economic botanist Percy L. Ricker, has grown to comprise more than 200,000 U.S. and foreign catalogs. The earliest items date from the late 1700s, but the collection is strongest from the 1890s to the present. Researchers commonly use the collection to document the introduction of plants to the United States, study economic trends, and illustrate early developments in American landscape design.

- The Rare Book Collection (http://specialcollections.nal.usda.gov/guide-collections/rare-book-collection) highlights agriculture's printed historical record. It covers a wide variety of subjects but is particularly strong in botany, natural history, zoology, and entomology. International in scope, the collection documents early agricultural practices in Britain and Europe, as well as the Americas. Of particular note are the more than 300 books by or about Carl Linnaeus, the "father of taxonomy," including a rare first edition of his 1735 work *Systema Naturae*.

- Manuscript collections (http://specialcollections.nal.usda.gov/guide-collections/index-manuscript-collections), now numbering more than 400, document the story of American agriculture and its influence on the world.

NAL continues to digitize these and other unique materials to share them broadly via its website and has published detailed indexes to the content of many manuscript collections to improve discovery. AGRICOLA, NAL's catalog, includes bibliographic entries for special collection items, manuscripts, and rare books. The library provides in-house research and reference services for its special collections and offers fee-based duplication services.

Preservation/Digitization

NAL is committed to the preservation of its print and non-print collections. It continues to monitor and improve the environmental quality of its stacks to extend the longevity of all materials in the collection. The library has instituted a long-term strategy to ensure the growing body of agricultural information is systematically identified, preserved, and archived.

NAL's digital conversion program has resulted in a growing digital collection of USDA publications and many non-USDA historical materials not restricted by copyright. NAL is in the midst of a large-scale project to digitize agricultural literature and provide online access to the general public. Important and distinctive items were selected from the NAL collection, with an initial focus on USDA-issued publications and nursery and seed trade catalogs. In 2014 NAL digitized and created citation information for 38,698 items. Publications are accessible at https://archive.org/details/usdanationalagriculturallibrary.

NAL Digital Collections

NAL has undertaken several projects to digitize, store, and provide online access to more than 1.5 million pages of historic print documents and images, primarily from USDA. In an effort to unify all digital content, the library launched an interface for the NAL Digital Collections (http://naldc.nal.usda.gov) accompanied by policies for collecting, storing, and making publicly available federally funded research outcomes published by USDA scientists and researchers. Long-range plans include collecting, maintaining, and providing access to a broad range of agricultural information in a wide variety of digital formats. The result will be a perpetual, reliable, publicly accessible collection of digital documents, data sets, images, and other items relating to agriculture. As of the end of 2014 NAL's digital repository of full-text content comprised nine collections, including nearly 50,000 peer-reviewed journal articles authored by USDA researchers, and more than 30,000 historical documents and reports. The public downloaded nearly 3 million full-text items during the year.

AGRICOLA

AGRICOLA comprises an online catalog and citation database of NAL collections and delivers worldwide access to agricultural information through its searchable Web interface (http://agricola.nal.usda.gov). Alternatively, users can access AGRICOLA on a fee basis through several commercial vendors, or they can subscribe to the complete AGRICOLA file, also on a fee basis, from the National Technical Information Service within the U.S. Department of Commerce.

The AGRICOLA database covers materials in all formats, including printed works from the 16th century onward. The records describe publications and resources encompassing all aspects of agriculture and allied disciplines. AGRICOLA, updated daily, includes the following two components:

- NAL Public Access Catalog, containing more than 1 million citations to books, audiovisual materials, serial titles, and other materials in the NAL collection. (The catalog also contains some bibliographic records for items cataloged by other libraries but not held in the NAL collection.)
- NAL Article Citation Database, consisting of more than 3 million citations to serial articles, book chapters, reports, and reprints. NAL has chosen and is implementing automated indexing/text analytics software to produce its Article Citation Database. This application combines semantic analysis, machine learning, and human rules to automatically assign subject terms to journal articles.

LCA Digital Commons

NAL launched the LCA Digital Commons, a life cycle inventory database, to address the lack of information resources regarding the life cycle of agricultural products. The LCA Digital Commons provides, through a fully searchable Web interface (http://www.lcacommons.gov), peer-reviewed crop production data sets for commodity crops measuring the material and energy flows to and from the environment. In 2014 more than 13,000 downloadable data sets were added to the database.

Information Management and Information Technology

Over the past quarter century, NAL has applied increasingly sophisticated information technology to support the ever more complex and demanding information needs of researchers, practitioners, policymakers, and the general public. Technological developments spearheaded by the library date back to the 1940s and 1950s, when NAL Director Ralph Shaw invented "electronic machines" such as the photo charger, rapid selector, and photo clerk. Over the years NAL has made numerous technological improvements, from automating collections information to delivering full-text and image collections digitally on the Internet.

NAL has fully implemented the Voyager integrated library management system from Ex Libris, Ltd. The system supports ordering, receiving, and invoice processing for purchases; creating and maintaining indexing and cataloging records for AGRICOLA; circulating print holdings; and providing a Web-based online catalog for public searching and browsing of the collection. In addition, the system is fully integrated with an automated interlibrary loan and document delivery system by Relais International that streamlines services and provides desktop delivery of needed materials.

English-Spanish Agricultural Thesaurus and Glossary

NAL is known for its expertise in developing and using a thesaurus, or controlled vocabulary, a critical component of effective digital information systems. The NAL Agricultural Thesaurus (NALT) (http://agclass.nal.usda.gov/agt.shtml) is a hierarchical vocabulary of agricultural and biological terms, organized according to 17 subject categories. It comprises primarily biological nomenclature, with additional terminology supporting the physical and social sciences.

In January 2015 NAL released the 14th edition of NALT, which has grown to approximately 110,000 terms. Taxonomic terms from every biological kingdom were expanded in this edition, along with common names of species. Plant species were added following taxonomic verification by the Germplasm Resources Information Network (GRIN). Terminology for genetic soil types was modified according to *USDA Keys to Soil Taxonomy, Twelfth Edition,* 2014. Fish taxonomy was expanded following taxonomic verification from Fishbase. Other subject areas expanded include terms in chromatography, receptors, bacteria, fungi, breeds of animals, endangered species, insects, chemicals, enzymes, economics, food, wood, and forestry.

NALT continues to be available as Linked Open Data. NAL can now connect its vocabulary to other linked data vocabularies, which, in turn, will connect NALT to the larger semantic Web. Such interconnections will help programmers create meaningful relationships that will make it easier to locate related content.

Associated with NALT, the NAL Glossary provides definitions of agricultural terms. The 2015 edition contains 4,488 definitions, ranging across agriculture and its many ancillary subjects, an increase of 667 definitions from last year. Most definitions are composed by NALT staff. (Suggestions for new terms or definitions can be sent by e-mail to agref@ars.usda.gov.)

NAL publishes Spanish-language versions of the thesaurus and glossary, which carry the names *Tesauro Agrícola* and *Glosario,* respectively. Both are updated concurrently with the annual release of the English-language version. The 2015 edition of the Spanish-language version of NALT contains more than 87,500 terms and 4,465 definitions.

The thesaurus and glossary are primarily used for indexing and for improving the retrieval of agricultural information, but they can also be used by students (from fifth grade up), teachers, writers, translators, and others who are seeking precise definitions of words from the agricultural sciences. Users can download all four publications—English and Spanish thesaurus and glossary—in both machine-readable (MARC 21, RDF-SKOS, and XML) and human-readable (doc, pdf) formats at http://agclass.nal.usda.gov/download.shtml.

Library Services

NAL serves the agricultural information needs of customers through a combination of Web-based and traditional library services, including reference, document delivery, and information center services. The NAL website offers access to a wide variety of full-text resources, as well as online access to reference and document delivery services. In 2014 the library provided nearly 8,000 reference transactions, fulfilled more than 1.2 million full-text article requests, and satisfied more than 5,000 requests for interlibrary loans.

The main reading room in the library's Beltsville facility features a walk-up service desk, access to an array of digital information resources (including full-text scientific journals), current periodicals, and an on-site request service for materials from NAL's collection. Services are available 8:30 to 4:30 Monday through Friday, except federal holidays.

NAL's reference services are accessible online using the Ask a Question form on the NAL Web pages; by use of e-mail addressed to agref@ars.usda.gov; by telephone at 301-504-5755; or by mail to Research Services, National Agricultural Library ARS/USDA, 10301 Baltimore Avenue, Beltsville, MD 20705. Requesters receive assistance from Research Services staff in all areas and aspects of agriculture, but staff particularly answer questions, provide research guidance, and make presentations on topics not addressed by the seven subject-focused information centers of the library.

NAL's seven information centers are reliable sources of comprehensive, science-based information on key aspects of U.S. agriculture, providing timely, accurate, and in-depth coverage of their specialized subject areas. Their expert staff offer extensive Web-based information resources and advanced reference services. Each NAL information center has its own website and is a partner in AgNIC.

- The Alternative Farming Systems Information Center (AFSIC) (http://afsic.nal.usda.gov) specializes in identifying and accessing information relating to farming methods that maintain the health and productivity of the entire farming enterprise, including the world's natural resources. This focus includes sustainable and alternative agricultural systems, crops, and livestock.
- The Animal Welfare Information Center (AWIC) (http://awic.nal.usda.gov) provides scientific information and referrals to help ensure the proper care and treatment of animals used in biomedical research, testing, teaching, and exhibitions, and by animal dealers. Among its varied outreach activities, the center conducts workshops for researchers on meeting the information requirements of the Animal Welfare Act.
- The Food and Nutrition Information Center (FNIC) (http://fnic.nal.usda.gov) provides credible, accurate, and practical resources for nutrition and health professionals, educators, government personnel, and consumers. FNIC maintains a staff of registered dietitians who can answer questions on food and human nutrition.
- The Food Safety Research Information Office (FSRIO) (http://fsrio.nal.usda.gov) delivers information on publicly funded—and, to the extent possible, privately funded—food safety research initiatives. Its Research Projects Database, with more than 8,500 projects cited, provides ready access to the largest searchable collection of food safety research being conducted within U.S. and international governmental agencies.
- The National Invasive Species Information Center (NISIC) (http://www.invasivespeciesinfo.gov) delivers accessible, accurate, referenced, up-to-date, and comprehensive information on invasive species drawn from federal, state, local, and international sources.
- The Rural Information Center (RIC) (http://ric.nal.usda.gov) assists local officials, organizations, businesses, and rural residents working to maintain the vitality of rural areas. It collects and disseminates information on such diverse topics as community economic development, small business development, health care, finance, housing, environment, quality of life, community leadership, and education.
- The Water Quality Information Center (WQIC) (http://wqic.nal.usda.gov) collects, organizes, and communicates scientific findings, educational methodologies, and public policy issues relating to water quality and agriculture.

In addition to these information centers, NAL manages the popular Nutrition.gov website (http://www.nutrition.gov) in collaboration with other USDA agencies and the Department of Health and Human Services. This site provides vetted, science-based nutrition information for the general consumer and highlights the latest in nutrition news and tools from across federal government agencies. The site is an important tool for disseminating the work of multiple federal agencies in a national obesity prevention effort. A team of registered dietitians at NAL's Food and Nutrition Information Center maintains Nutrition.gov and answers questions on food and nutrition issues.

Web-Based Products and Services

The NAL websites, which encompass nearly all the content and services described here, collectively receive millions of pageviews per month from people seeking agricultural information.

DigiTop

DigiTop, USDA's Digital Desktop Library, delivers the full text of thousands of journals and hundreds of newspapers worldwide, provides 17 agriculturally significant citation databases, supplies a range of digital reference resources, and offers focused, personalized services. Navigator is a component of DigiTop that allows cross-searching of multiple bibliographic databases. This system includes AGRICOLA; AGRIS; BIOSIS; CAB Abstracts; Fish, Fisheries, and Aquatic Biodiversity Worldwide; Food Science and Technology Abstracts; GEOBASE; GeoRef; MEDLINE; Wildlife and Ecology Studies Worldwide; Scopus; and Zoological Record. The Navigator service allows researchers to access nearly 79 million records at once and is updated weekly. DigiTop is available to the entire USDA workforce worldwide—more than 100,000 people—around the clock. NAL staff provide help desk and reference services, continuous user education, and training for DigiTop users.

Document Delivery Services

NAL's document delivery operation responds to thousands of requests each year from USDA employees and from libraries and organizations around the world. NAL uses the Relais Enterprise document request and delivery system to support document delivery. With Relais fully integrated with the Voyager library system, with DigiTop, and with other Open-URL and ISO ILL compliant systems, NAL customers can request materials or check on the status of their requests via the Web, and the needed materials can easily be delivered electronically. Document requests can also be submitted via OCLC (NAL's symbol is AGL) and DOCLINE (NAL's libid is MDUNAL). Visit http://www.nal.usda.gov/services/request.shtml for details.

Networks of Cooperation

The NAL collection and information resources are supplemented by networks of cooperation with other institutions, including arrangements with agricultural libraries at U.S. land-grant universities, other U.S. national libraries, agricultural libraries in other countries, and libraries of the United Nations and other international organizations.

AgNIC

The library serves as secretariat for the Agriculture Network Information Center (AgNIC) Alliance, a voluntary, collaborative partnership that hosts a distributed network of discipline-specific agricultural information websites at http://www. agnic.org. AgNIC provides access to high-quality agricultural information selected by its 53 partner members, which include land-grant universities, NAL, and other institutions globally. Together they offer more than 80 information and subject specialists, more than 60 topics covered comprehensively, and links to more than 5 million full-text and bibliographic items.

AGLINET

Through the Agricultural Libraries Network (AGLINET), NAL serves as the U.S. node of an international agricultural information system that brings together agricultural libraries with strong regional or country coverage and other specialized collections. NAL functions as a gateway to U.S. agricultural libraries and resources, fulfilling requests for information via reciprocal agreements with several other libraries, information centers, and consortia. As an AGLINET member, NAL agrees to provide low-cost interlibrary loan and photocopy service to other AGLINET libraries. Most materials requested through AGLINET are delivered digitally, although reproductions via fiche or photocopy are used when appropriate. AGLINET is administered by the Food and Agriculture Organization of the United Nations.

National Library of Medicine

8600 Rockville Pike, Bethesda, MD 20894
301-496-6308, 888-346-3656, fax 301-496-4450
E-mail publicinfo@nlm.nih.gov
World Wide Web http://www.nlm.nih.gov

Kathleen Cravedi

Director, Office of Communications and Public Liaison

Melanie Modlin

Deputy Director, Office of Communications and Public Liaison

The National Library of Medicine (NLM) is one of the 27 Institutes and Centers of the National Institutes of Health (NIH). Founded in 1836 as the Library of the Surgeon General of the Army, NLM has evolved into the world's largest biomedical library.

In today's increasingly digital world, NLM carries out its mission of enabling biomedical research, supporting health care and public health, and promoting healthy behavior by

- Building and providing electronic information resources used billions of times each year by millions of scientists, health professionals, and members of the public
- Creating and maintaining information systems that provide free public access to results of biomedical research supported by NIH and by other government and private funders
- Supporting and conducting research, development, and training in biomedical informatics, computational biology, data science, and health information technology
- Coordinating a 6,300-member National Network of Libraries of Medicine that promotes and provides access to health information in communities across the United States

Through its information systems, a cutting-edge informatics research portfolio, and extensive partnerships, NLM plays an essential role in catalyzing and supporting the translation of basic science into new treatments, new products, improved practice, useful decision support for health professionals and patients, and effective disaster and emergency preparedness and response.

The range of information that NLM organizes and disseminates is enormous, including genetic, genomic, biochemical, and toxicological data; images; published and unpublished research results; decision support resources; scientific and health data standards; informatics tools for system developers; and health information for the public. Scientists, health professionals, and the public can search or download information directly from an NLM website, find it via an Internet search engine, or use an app that provides value-added access to NLM data. Thousands of commercial and nonprofit system developers regularly use the applications programming interfaces (APIs) that NLM provides to fuel private sector innovation.

Delivering High-Quality Information Services

Central to NLM services is the world's largest, continually expanding collection of biomedical literature in all media and a broad array of authoritative digital databases encompassing information for scientists, health professionals, the public, and the librarians and information specialists who serve them. NLM develops and uses sophisticated information systems to support the complex operations necessary to acquire, describe, index, archive, and provide rapid access to physical and digital materials. Special attention is given to developing systems to build and refine electronic databases and services and to responding to changes in user needs and behaviors.

In 2014 NLM greatly expanded the quantity and range of high-quality information readily available to scientists, health professionals, and the general public. Advances included:

- The indexing of more than 765,000 new journal articles for PubMed/MEDLINE, NLM's most heavily used database, which contains more than 24 million references to articles in the biomedical and life sciences journals and delivers information to about 2 million users a day
- Growth in the PubMed Central (PMC) digital archive, which now provides public access to the full-text versions of more than 3.3 million research articles, including those produced by NIH-funded researchers
- Expansion of ClinicalTrials.gov, which now includes more than 181,000 registered studies and summary results for more than 15,700 trials, including many not available elsewhere
- A doubling of the number of tests in the Genetic Testing Registry, where users can find detailed information on more than 33,000 genetic tests
- More than 20 percent growth in the database of Genotypes and Phenotypes (dbGaP), which connects individual-level genomic data with individual-level clinical information and now contains nearly 600 studies involving more than 840,000 people
- Improved dissemination methods and new tools to aid the use of the U.S. clinical terminology standards required for interoperability of electronic health records

NLM also continued to expand access to its rare and unique historical collections by digitizing rare books, manuscripts, pictures, and historical films. In 2014 a total of 2,460 printed historic books, 4,319 historic images, and 895 manuscripts were digitized and added to NLM's Digital Collections, a free online archive of biomedical books and videos. These collections are heavily used by scholars, the media, and the general public.

As the percentage of users accessing NLM databases with mobile phones and tablets continues to rise, NLM is redesigning many of its Web interfaces so that the information display adjusts automatically to the size of the device. In 2014 the library released new "responsive design" versions of AIDS*info*, the Department of Health and Human Services (HHS) authoritative source of HIV/AIDS treatment and prevention information, and of DailyMed, which includes Food and

Drug Administration (FDA)-approved structured label information for medications marketed in the United States. NLM continued to be a leading player in social media among HHS agencies with active Facebook, Twitter, Flickr, Pinterest, and YouTube accounts (including the very popular @medlineplus Twitter feed and a Spanish-language counterpart), several online newsletters, and its National Network of Libraries of Medicine, which covers the United States and hosts 8 Facebook pages, 10 Twitter feeds, and 12 blogs. NLM is consistently ranked among the most liked, most followed, and most mentioned organizations among small government agencies with social media accounts.

Promoting Public Access to Information

NLM has extensive outreach programs to enhance awareness of its diverse information services among biomedical researchers, health professionals, librarians, patients, and the public. To improve access to high-quality health information, NLM works with the National Network of Libraries of Medicine and has formal partnerships such as Partners in Information Access for the Public Health Workforce and the Environmental Health Information Outreach Partnership with Historically Black Colleges and Universities, tribal colleges, and other minority serving institutions.

The member institutions of the National Network of Libraries of Medicine are valued partners in ensuring that health information, including NLM's many services, is available to scientists, health professionals, and the public. The network is coordinated by eight regional medical libraries and is composed of academic health sciences libraries, hospital libraries, public libraries, and community-based organizations.

In 2014 dozens of community-based projects were funded nationwide to enhance awareness of and access to health information, including in disaster and emergency situations, and to address health literacy issues. As part of its outreach efforts, NLM continually solicits feedback from users on how existing resources can be improved.

NLM also fosters more informal community partnerships and uses exhibitions, the media, and new technologies in its efforts to reach underserved populations and to promote interest among young people in careers in science, medicine, and technology. The library continues to expand its successful traveling exhibitions program as another means to enhance access to its services and promote interest in careers in science and medicine. Examples of these exhibitions include "Every Necessary Care and Attention: George Washington and Medicine" and "Surviving and Thriving: AIDS, Politics, and Culture."

With assistance from other NIH components and outside partners, NLM continues to increase the distribution of *NIH MedlinePlus* magazine, and its Spanish-language counterpart, *NIH Salud*. The magazine, which is also available online in Spanish and English, is distributed to doctors' offices, health science libraries, Congress, the media, federally supported community health centers, select hospital emergency and waiting rooms, and other locations where the public receives health services.

Information Systems, Standards, Research Tools

NLM's advanced information services have long benefitted from its intramural research and development (R&D) programs. The library has two organizations that conduct advanced R&D on different aspects of biomedical informatics: the Lister Hill National Center for Biomedical Communications (LHC) and the National Center for Biotechnology Information (NCBI). Both apply their research results to the development of new information services and tools for scientists, informatics researchers, and software developers.

LHC, established in 1968, conducts and supports research in such areas as the development and dissemination of health information technology standards; the capture, processing, dissemination, and use of high-quality imaging data; medical language processing; high-speed access to biomedical information; and advanced technology for emergency and disaster management.

NCBI, created in 1988, conducts R&D on the representation, integration, and retrieval of molecular biology data and biomedical literature, in addition to providing an integrated, genomic information resource consisting of more than 40 databases for biomedical researchers at NIH and around the world. NCBI's development of large-scale data integration techniques with advanced information systems is key to its expanding ability to support the accelerated pace of research made possible by new technologies such as next-generation DNA sequencing, microarrays, and small molecule screening. GenBank at NCBI, in collaboration with partners in Britain and Japan, is the world's largest annotated collection of publicly available DNA sequences. GenBank contains 175 million sequences from more than 310,000 different species. NCBI's Web services for access to these data provide the information and analytic tools for researchers to accelerate the rate of genomic discovery and facilitate the translation of basic science advances into new diagnostics and treatments.

NLM was also a pioneer in developing and sharing novel medical language resources and innovative algorithms and tools, including the UMLS (Unified Medical Language System), MetaMap, Medical Text Indexer (MTI), and SemRep, to advance research in natural language understanding and biomedical text mining. This research has been applied to indexing, information retrieval, question answering, and literature-based discovery to assist NLM's high-volume data creation and service operations, to help other NIH components to identify and summarize new knowledge useful in updating clinical guidelines, and to add standard terminology and codes to clinical and clinical research data to enhance their research value. NLM has many joint research activities with other NIH components and other federal agencies, including collaborations with FDA to use natural language processing and NLM terminology resources to extract adverse event data from publications indexed for PubMed/MEDLINE and drug-drug interactions from product labels submitted by manufacturers.

NLM has also made advances that will facilitate health information exchange and meaningful use of electronic health records (EHRs). NLM researchers have developed advanced and heavily used APIs for medication data, nomenclature, and high-quality pill images, including information submitted to FDA; produced novel algorithms for validating vocabulary components of electronic clinical quality measure specifications in cooperation with the Centers for Medicare and

Medicaid Services; and analyzed frequency data from multiple private healthcare organizations and the Veterans Health Administration to produce manageable subsets of large standard clinical vocabularies. They have also developed effective techniques for mapping clinical vocabularies to administrative code sets and have established partnerships to test the use and impact of personal health records.

NLM's Personal Health Record (PHR) project has developed open source software components that can be used by PHR and EHR developers to provide capabilities that help individuals to manage health and health care for themselves and their families. The strong use of vocabulary standards in the NLM PHR software components enables many computer-generated features such as personalized reminders, automatic calculation of health measures, and direct links to such information sources as MedlinePlus. The use of standards in these components will also enable the direct importing of the consumer's own data from clinical sources.

Administration

The director of the Library, Donald A. B. Lindberg, M.D., is guided in matters of policy by a board of regents consisting of 10 appointed and 11 ex officio members.

Table 1 / Selected NLM Statistics*

Library Operations	Volume
Collection (book and non-book)	26,648,261
Items cataloged	18,755
Serial titles received	17,439
Articles indexed for MEDLINE	765,850
Circulation requests processed	259,285
For interlibrary loan	188,912
For on-site users	70,373
MEDLINE/PubMed Searches	2,650,894,898
Budget Authority	$328,000,000
Staff	830

*For fiscal year ending September 30, 2014

National Technical Information Service

U.S. Department of Commerce, Alexandria, VA 22312
800-553-NTIS (6847) or 703-605-6000
World Wide Web http://www.ntis.gov

The National Technical Information Service (NTIS) is the nation's largest and most comprehensive source of government-funded scientific, technical, engineering, and business information produced or sponsored by U.S. and international government sources. NTIS is a federal agency within the U.S. Department of Commerce.

Since 1945 the NTIS mission has been to operate a central U.S. government access point for scientific and technical information useful to American industry and government. NTIS maintains a permanent archive of this declassified information for researchers, businesses, and the public to access quickly and easily. Release of the information is intended to promote U.S. economic growth and development and to increase U.S. competitiveness in the world market.

The NTIS collection of more than 2.5 million titles contains products available in various formats. Such information includes reports describing research conducted or sponsored by federal agencies and their contractors; statistical and business information; multimedia training programs; databases developed by federal agencies; and technical reports prepared by research organizations worldwide. NTIS maintains a permanent repository of its information products.

More than 200 U.S. government agencies contribute to the NTIS collection, including the National Aeronautics and Space Administration; the Environmental Protection Agency; the departments of Agriculture, Commerce, Defense, Energy, Health and Human Services, Homeland Security, Interior, Labor, Treasury, Veterans Affairs, Housing and Urban Development, Education, and Transportation; and numerous other agencies. International contributors include Canada, Japan, Britain, and several European countries.

NTIS on the Web

NTIS offers Web-based access to information on government scientific and technical research products. Visitors to http://www.ntis.gov can search the entire collection dating back to 1964 free of charge. NTIS provides many of the technical reports for purchase on CD, paper copies, or downloaded pdf files. RSS feeds of recently catalogued materials are available in major subject categories.

NTIS Database

The NTIS Database offers unparalleled bibliographic coverage of U.S. government and worldwide government-sponsored research information products acquired by NTIS since 1964. Its contents represent hundreds of billions of research dollars and cover a range of important topics including agriculture, biotechnology, business, communication, energy, engineering, the environment, health and safety, medicine, research and development, science, space, technology, and transportation.

The NTIS Database can be leased directly from NTIS and can also be accessed through several commercial services. To lease the NTIS Database directly from NTIS, contact the NTIS Office of Product Management at 703-605-6515.

NTIS National Technical Reports Library

The National Technical Reports Library (NTRL) enhances accessibility to the NTIS technical reports collection. Subscription rates are based on institutional FTE levels. NTRL operates on a system interface that allows users to do queries on the large NTIS bibliographic database. The intent is to broadly expand and improve access to more than 2.5 million bibliographic records (pre-1960 to the present) and more than 700,000 full-text documents in pdf format that are directly linked to that bibliographic database.

NTIS offers several valuable research-oriented database products. To find out more about accessing the databases, visit http://www.ntis.gov/products/ntrl.

AGRICOLA

As one of the most comprehensive sources of U.S. agricultural and life sciences information, the AGRICOLA (Agricultural Online Access) Database contains bibliographic records for documents acquired by the U.S. Department of Agriculture's National Agricultural Library. It is available at http://www.ntis.gov/products/databases/agricola.

AGRIS

The International Information System for the Agricultural Science and Technology (AGRIS) Database is a cooperative system for collecting and disseminating information on the world's agricultural literature. More than 100 national and multinational centers take part in the system. References to citations for U.S. publications given coverage in the AGRICOLA Database are not included in AGRIS. To access AGRIS, go to http://www.ntis.gov/products/databases/agris.

Energy Science and Technology

The Energy Science and Technology Database (EDB) is a multidisciplinary file containing worldwide references to basic and applied scientific and technical research literature. The information is collected for use by government managers, researchers at the national laboratories, and other research efforts sponsored by the U.S. Department of Energy, and the results of this research are transferred to the public. The database is available at http://www.ntis.gov/products/databases/energy-science-technology.

FEDRIP

The Federal Research in Progress Database (FEDRIP) provides access to information about ongoing federally funded projects in such fields as the physical sciences, engineering, and life sciences. To access FEDRIP, go to http://www.ntis.gov/products/databases/federal-research-in-progress.

Online Subscriptions

NTIS offers quick, convenient online access, on a subscription basis, to the following resources:

U.S. Export Administration Regulations

U.S. Export Administration Regulations (EAR) provides the latest rules controlling the export of U.S. dual-use commodities, technology, and software. Step by step, EAR explains when an export license is necessary and when it is not, how to obtain an export license, policy changes as they are issued, new restrictions on exports to certain countries and of certain types of items, and where to obtain further help.

This information is available through NTIS in loose-leaf form, on CD-ROM, and online. An e-mail update notification service is also available.

World News Connection

World News Connection (WNC) was an NTIS online news service accessible via the World Wide Web. It made available English-language translations of time-sensitive news and information culled from non-U.S. media in more than 100 countries. WNC was provided by the Open Source Center (OSC), operated by the Central Intelligence Agency (CIA), and its content was updated throughout every government business day. It was made available by NTIS through the Dialog Corporation. The service ceased operation at the end of 2013.

Special Subscription Services

NTIS eAlerts

More than 1,000 new titles are added to the NTIS collection every week. NTIS prepares a list of search criteria that is run against all new studies and research and development reports in 16 subject areas. An NTIS cAlert provides a twice-monthly information briefing service, by e-mail, covering a wide range of technology topics. For more information, call the NTIS Subscriptions Department at 703-605-6060.

NTIS Selected Research Service

NTIS Selected Research Service (SRS) is a tailored information service that delivers complete electronic copies of government publications based on customers' needs, automatically, within a few weeks of announcement by NTIS. SRS includes the full bibliographic information in XML and HTML formats. Users choose between Standard SRS (selecting one or more of the 320 existing subject areas) or Custom SRS, which creates a new subject area to meet their particular needs. Custom SRS requires a one-time fee to cover the cost of strategy development and computer programming to set up a profile. Except for this fee, the cost of Custom SRS is the same as the Standard SRS. Through this ongoing subscription service, customers download copies of new reports pertaining to their field(s) of interest as NTIS obtains the reports. To place an order, call 800-363-2068 or 703-605-6060.

This service is also available in CD-ROM format as Science and Technology on CD, which delivers the documents digitized and stored in pdf format.

Federal Science Repository Service

Collections of scientific and technical documents, images, videos, and other content represent the mission and work of an agency or other institution. To help preserve these collections, NTIS formed a joint venture with Information International Associates, Inc. of Oak Ridge, Tennessee, to develop for federal agencies a searchable, digital Federal Science Repository Service (FSRS). FSRS provides a supporting infrastructure, long-term storage, security, interface design, and content management and operational expertise. An agency can utilize this entire service or select components, resulting in the design of an agency-specific repository that serves as a distinct gateway to its content. For more information, visit http://www.ntis.gov/products/fsrs.

NTIS Customer Service

NTIS's automated systems make shopping online at NTIS safe and secure. Electronic document storage is fully integrated with NTIS's order-taking process, allowing it to provide rapid reproduction for the most recent additions to the NTIS document collection. Most orders for shipment are filled and delivered anywhere in the United States in five to seven business days. Rush service is available for an additional fee.

Key NTIS Contacts for Ordering

Order by Phone

Sales Desk 800-553-6847 or 703-605-6000
8:30 A.M.–5:00 P.M. Eastern time, Monday–Friday

Subscriptions 800-363-2068 or 703-605-6060
8:30 A.M.–5:00 P.M. Eastern time, Monday–Friday
TDD (hearing impaired only) 703-487-4639
8:30 A.M.–5:00 P.M. Eastern time, Monday–Friday

Order by Fax

24 hours a day, seven days a week 703-605-6900

To verify receipt of fax, call 703-605-6090, 7:00 A.M.–5:00 P.M. Eastern time Monday–Friday

Order by Mail

National Technical Information Service
5301 Shawnee Rd.
Alexandria, VA 22312

RUSH Service (available for an additional fee)   800-553-6847 or 703-605-6000
Note: If requesting RUSH Service, please do not mail your order

Order Online

Direct and secure online ordering   http://www.ntis.gov

Note: In early 2015 legislation was introduced in the U.S. House of Representatives that would effectively do away with the National Technical Information Service. The "Let Me Google That for You Act" (H.R. 443) echoed a measure introduced in both houses of Congress in 2014 that died in committee. In both sessions, the measure's supporters have said NTIS should be abolished because much of the government information it provides is available free of charge from other sources. At the time this report was prepared, there had been no further action on the 2015 bill—*Ed.*

United States Government Publishing Office

732 North Capitol St. N.W., Washington, DC 20401
World Wide Web http://www.gpo.gov

Gary Somerset
Media and Public Relations Manager
202-512-1957, e-mail gsomerset@gpo.gov

The U.S. Government Printing Office (GPO) was created when President James Buchanan signed Joint Resolution 25 on June 23, 1860. GPO opened its doors for business nine months later on March 4, 1861, the same day Abraham Lincoln took the oath of office to become the 16th president of the United States. On that day GPO began operation in buildings purchased by Congress, at the same address it occupies today.

A historic moment occurred for GPO in December 2014 when President Barack Obama signed into law a bill changing the agency's name to the U.S. Government *Publishing* Office. The new name reflects the increasingly prominent role that GPO plays in providing access to government information in digital formats through GPO's Federal Digital System (FDsys), apps, e-books, and related technologies. The information needs of Congress, federal agencies, and the public have evolved beyond only print, and GPO has transformed itself to meet its customers' needs.

Under Title 44 of the United States Code, GPO is responsible for the production and distribution of information products for all three branches of the federal government. These include the official publications of Congress, federal agencies, and the courts. Today GPO provides products in print and a variety of digital forms, all of which are born digital. In addition GPO produces passports for the Department of State and secure credentials for many government agencies.

As the federal government's official, digital, secure resource for gathering, producing, cataloging, providing access to, and preserving published information in all forms, GPO has disseminated millions of publications to the public.

GPO's Superintendent of Documents and its Library Services and Content Management (LSCM) organizations administer and manage the four programs required by Title 44:

- The Federal Depository Library Program (FDLP)
- Cataloging and indexing (C&I)
- Distributing government publications to the International Exchange Service
- The By-Law Program, under which certain government publications are distributed to members of Congress and to other government agencies as mandated by law

FDLP dates back to 1813 when Congress first authorized legislation to ensure the provision of certain congressional documents to selected universities, historical societies, and state libraries. At that time, the secretary of state was responsible for distributing publications. In 1857 the secretary of the interior assumed oversight of printing and the designation of depositories. In the Printing Act of 1895 the governance of the depository program was transferred to the Office of the Superintendent of Documents at GPO. Duties remained largely unchanged until 1993, when Public Law 103-40, the Government Printing Office Electronic Information Access Enhancement Act, amended GPO's duties to not only provide public access to printed publications but to Internet-accessible publications as well. Two centuries after the start of FDLP, the program continues to serve a vital need of the public through the partnership with federal depository libraries located in nearly every congressional district.

GPO is obviously a much different agency in the digital age than it was years ago. While its name has changed, its mission—"Keeping America Informed" is as important and relevant as ever. FDLP and GPO's information dissemination programs are examples of the agency's longstanding commitment to permanent public access to U.S. government information.

Collaboration

Digital Partnerships with Federal Depository Libraries

Since 1997 GPO has developed strategic partnerships with federal depository libraries and other federal agencies to increase access to electronic federal information. All branches of federal government are transitioning away from print, and federal materials are coming to GPO for publishing. This is due to budgetary pressures, open government initiatives, and increasing access to electronic solutions.

One avenue to address this has been to develop strategic partnerships to ensure permanent public access to electronic content, assist depositories in providing access to electronic material, and help libraries better manage their depository collections. Partnerships also allow GPO to take advantage of the expertise and services of federal depository librarians and federal agencies.

Partnership Updates

GPO currently maintains partnerships with sixteen depository libraries, eight federal agencies, and two institutions. During fiscal year (FY) 2014 LSCM signed three new partnership agreements:

- University of North Texas (UNT)—This partnership ensures permanent public access to the university's large current and future digital collections of U.S. government content that are within scope of FDLP. These collections now contain approximately 50,000 federal government information products on a wide range of interesting topics. Notable examples are World War II newsmaps; documents on early aircraft, engines, and more from the National Advisory Committee for Aeronautics; and annual reports from the U.S. Department of Agriculture's experiment stations from 1901 to 1954. Under the agreement, GPO guarantees public access to these materials in perpetuity.
- University of Colorado, Boulder—This is a cooperative cataloging partnership. The university is creating bibliographic records for historic publications from the U.S. Geological Survey Bulletins series and the Bureau of

Mines Reports of Investigations series. GPO will enhance the records by verifying the Superintendent of Documents Classification System (SuDoc) number and performing needed authority work to the subject headings and corporate names. The records will then be available through GPO's Catalog of U.S. Government Publications (CGP) and OCLC.

- Boston Public Library (BPL)—In commemoration of the 50th anniversary of the release of the Warren Commission report on the assassination of President John F. Kennedy, GPO made the complete report and the 26 volumes of hearings testimony available on FDsys through a partnership with BPL. The hearing transcripts were digitized by BPL. This partnership ensures permanent public access to Warren Commission resources.

During FY 2014 LSCM renewed one partnership:

- University of Illinois at Chicago—This partnership ensures permanent public access to the content in DOSFAN, a digital library of electronically archived information produced by the U.S. Department of State from 1990 to 1997 that includes the archived websites of the U.S. Arms Control and Disarmament Agency and the U.S. Information Agency.

Work continued on several cooperative cataloging partnerships:

- University of Florida—LSCM's partnership with the University of Florida combines cooperative cataloging and permanent public access to digitized content. As material is digitized, the university will share bibliographic records with GPO. Records will be added to CGP, and records for the digitized versions will be created with persistent URLs (PURLs). During FY 2014 work was completed on more than 1,600 bibliographic records for titles from the National Recovery Administration.
- University of Iowa—LSCM completed work to convert the University of Iowa's Dublin Core records for their digitized poster collection to 1,454 MARC records. Each poster was also assigned a PURL, and these records are available through CGP.
- University of Montana—LSCM began working with the university's Mansfield Library in 2011 to add bibliographic records to CGP for historic U.S. Forest Service publications. Mansfield Library staff members create bibliographic records for Forest Service publications and submit them to LSCM. Cataloging and classification staff at LSCM verify the SuDoc class and item number and add subject and corporate name headings to the records. As a result of this partnership, more than 1,900 Forest Service records have been added to CGP.
- University of North Texas—LSCM's partnership with the university combines cooperative cataloging and permanent public access to digitized content. During FY 2014 LSCM staff created or updated bibliographic records for titles in the following university digital collections: Federal Register, Congressional Record, World War I, Government Documents General, World War II Newsmaps, and U.S. Experiment Station Reports.

GPO and DPLA

GPO also developed a new partnership with the Digital Public Library of America (DPLA), a repository of digitized content from U.S. libraries, archives, and museums, all available to the public free of charge. In September 2014 GPO and DPLA partnered to increase public access to government information made available through CGP. More than 150,000 records from CGP are available to the public via the DPLA website (http://dp.la). Examples of records include the federal budget; federal laws, such as the Patient Protection and Affordable Care Act; federal regulations; transcripts of congressional hearings; and reports and other documents. GPO continuously adds records to CGP, which will also be available through DPLA, increasing public discoverability of and access to federal government information. GPO adds approximately 1,000 new records to DPLA each month.

During the year LSCM staff participated in and collaborated with a number of outside groups in support of FDLP and the Cataloging and Indexing Program, including CENDI and the CENDI Policy Working Group (CENDI is an interagency working group of senior scientific and technical information managers representing 14 U.S. federal agencies): the CENDI Digitization Specifications Working Group, Ex Libris Users of North America, the Federal Agencies Digitization Guidelines Initiative (FADGI) Preservation Working Group, the FADGI Audio-Visual Working Group, the FADGI Still Image Digitization Working Group, the FADGI Still Image File Format Working Group, the Federal Library and Information Network (FEDLINK), the American Indian Libraries Initiative, the Federal Web Archiving Coordination Group (National Archives and Records Administration, Library of Congress, and GPO), the International Internet Preservation Consortium, the National Digital Strategy Advisory Board, OCLC, the Program for Cooperative Cataloging (Library of Congress), the Science.gov Alliance, the Society of American Archivists, and the Society for Imaging Science and Technology.

Key GPO Tools

Federal Digital System (FDsys)

GPO's Federal Digital System (FDsys) (http://www.fdsys.gov) provides free online access to official publications from the three branches of the federal government. The content in FDsys is available in multiple formats including pdf, XML, audio, and photographs. FDsys provides access to digitized historical content and serial publications that are updated daily.

GPO adds content to FDsys regularly and continuously implements enhancements to system functionality. FDsys offers the public access to approximately 50 collections of government information, and more than 10 million documents are indexed by the FDsys search engine. As of September 2014 FDsys provided access to more than 856,000 searchable online titles and received an average of 34 million retrievals a month.

Catalog of U.S. Government Publications (CGP)

Under the requirements of sections 1710 and 1711 of Title 44, GPO is charged with cataloging a comprehensive index of public documents issued or published by the federal government that are not confidential in character. The goals of the Cataloging and Indexing Program are to:

- Develop a comprehensive and authoritative national bibliography of U.S. government publications
- Increase the visibility and use of government information products
- Create a premier destination for information searchers

This undertaking serves libraries and the public nationwide and enables people to locate desired government publications in all formats. The main public interface for the access of cataloging records is CGP.

The identification and creation of online bibliographic catalog records for new U.S. federal government publications, in all published formats, is accomplished through daily operations. A separate retrospective effort is necessary to build online bibliographic records for historical and fugitive (uncataloged but relevant) materials. This effort is known as the National Bibliographic Records Inventory Initiative (NBRII).

NBRII endeavors to provide an online bibliographic record or serial holding record for historical records not currently captured in CGP. These records include:

- Fugitive materials, with a focus on publications issued prior to 1976
- Older publications where bibliographic records exist only in a non-electronically available resource, such as a catalog card or other paper bibliographic record.
- Materials that were previously cataloged with such minimal information that they require critical record enhancement to reach a full-level bibliographic record

Enhancement/Progression/Innovation

Notable additions to FDsys during FY 2014 included the following:

Warren Commission Report and Hearings

GPO made available the official, digital version of the Warren Commission hearings on FDsys in FY 2014. Georgetown University's Lauinger Library provided a copy of the report to GPO for digitizing, and the Boston Public Library digitized the 26 hearing volumes. The commission was created by President Lyndon Johnson and chaired by Chief Justice Earl Warren and presented its findings on September 24, 1964. The commission also released 26 volumes of hearing transcripts, produced by GPO, composed of testimony from 550 witnesses and other evidence.

U.S. Courts Opinions Collection

GPO enhanced the U.S. Courts Opinions Collection by providing public access to the opinions of the U.S. Court of International Trade, along with the opinions of 31 additional courts (appellate courts, bankruptcy courts, and district courts).

The number of courts available on FDsys was expanded from the initial 29 courts in FY 2012 to 95 by the end of FY 2014. The collection saw almost 51 million content retrievals on FDsys for FY 2014.

U.S. House of Representatives Bill Summaries

In February 2014 GPO partnered with the Library of Congress to make House of Representatives bill summaries available in XML format for bulk data download from FDsys. Bill summaries are prepared by the Library of Congress's Congressional Research Service and describe the most significant provisions of a piece of legislation. They also detail the effects the legislative text may have on current law and federal programs. The bill summaries are part of the FDsys bulk data repository starting with the 113th Congress. Making House bill summaries available in XML permits data to be reused and repurposed for mobile Web applications, data mashups, and other analytical tools by third party providers, which contributes to openness and transparency in government. This project commenced at the direction of the House Appropriations Committee and is in support of the task force on bulk data established by the House.

CIA Audiobook

GPO made an audiobook available for the first time on FDsys in FY 2014. Published by the Central Intelligence Agency (CIA), the audiobook, "Getting to Know the President: Intelligence Briefings of Presidential Candidates, 1952–2004," is a historical account of the information-sharing process between the intelligence community and presidential candidates and presidents-elect during campaigns and administration transitions. The audiobook is available in an MP3 format on FDsys.

Historic Bound Congressional Record

GPO has been collaborating with the Library of Congress to digitize volumes of the Bound Congressional Record dating from 1873 to 1998 and to provide access through FDsys. The entire Digitized Bound Congressional Record (DBCR) project, covering the period 1873 to 1998, contains approximately 2,085 parts and a total of 2.6 million pages. The digitized content must be reviewed and descriptive content metadata must be identified and recorded prior to providing access on FDsys. As of the end of FY 2014 nearly all volumes of the Bound Congressional Record had been digitized.

Cataloging and CGP Accomplishments

GPO Among Top Ten Original Catalogers

GPO was again named one of the world's top ten original catalogers in OCLC's annual report for FY 2013 (released in FY 2014). During FY 2013 GPO added 13,793 new records for U.S. government information products to WorldCat, a database of bibliographic information built by libraries around the world and OCLC.

GPO was a founding member of the OCLC network in 1976, and has reached several important milestones as an active contributor to WorldCat. In 1992 a GPO cataloger contributed the 100,000th record to the OCLC Bibliographic Database, and in 1999 another GPO cataloger contributed the 43,000,000th record.

National Bibliographic Records Inventory

Projects associated with the National Bibliographic Records Inventory in FY 2014 included the following:

* Historic Shelflist Transcription—LSCM continued transcribing all non-OCLC cards in its historic shelflist. Contract staff transcribe the shelflist cards, check in serial issues, and add Library of Congress subject headings and corporate name authority to records. By the end of FY 2014 there were 157,623 shelflist records available through CGP.
* Monthly Catalog Transcription—Beginning in January 2013 LSCM initiated an effort to transcribe entries from volumes of the *Monthly Catalog of U.S. Government Publications*. In FY 2014 transcription of entries from the 1895 and 1898 volumes was completed. More than 9,600 Monthly Catalog records are available through CGP.
* Serials Management Plan—In FY 2014 more than 54,770 serial issues were checked into CGP, and 559 publication patterns were created for serial titles. In addition, 785 previously uncataloged serial titles were identified, and new bibliographic records for those titles were created and added to CGP.
* LSCM Internal Manual Records Conversion—Beginning in June 2013 GPO staff have been adding information for historic and current serial issues of government publications from internal GPO sources of CGP. In FY 2014 information for 41,500 historic serial issues of U.S. government publications from internal GPO sources were added to CGP.

E-Books Added to FDLP

In February 2014 GPO introduced more than 100 titles in new e-book formats to FDLP. The new formats, MOBI and EPUB, are available to the public free of charge using CGP. All e-book titles available through CGP are federal publications of public interest or educational value within the scope of Title 44, sections 1902–1903. The titles made available through this program were previously self-distributed on federal websites and available to the public at no cost; they join the growing number of online resources that have been a vital part of FDLP for more than 20 years.

By the end of FY 2014 more than 150 e-book titles were available through CGP through this program. More information is available at FDLP.gov's e-books page.

Resource Description and Access

After the successful implementation of Resource Description and Access (RDA) in early 2013 Library Technical Services librarians engaged in training and outreach to the FDLP community in 2014 to assist in RDA application. GPO librarians presented three webinars in GPO's Library Technical Services Webinar and Webcast Series, all of which cover the interpretation of RDA for government documents—Congressional Publications: An Overview; Name Authority Records in RDA; and Archiving and Cataloging Federal Agency Websites.

Cataloging Record Distribution Program

The Cataloging Record Distribution Program (CRDP) continued in FY 2014 through a contract with MARCIVE, Inc. Through this program, 82 libraries receive free bibliographic records that correspond to their item number selection profile. The annual survey of participants validated the success of the program, with nearly all of the libraries indicating that the CRDP meets expectations and increases access to government information or has made it easier for the libraries to provide it.

FDLP Academy

FDLP Academy was launched by LSCM in FY 2014 as a new resource for educational tools on government information. This educational program was created to support the FDLP community and to advance federal government information literacy. The mission of FDLP Academy is to create and deliver enhanced educational opportunities to the FDLP community by fostering collaboration, by facilitating knowledge sharing, and through the application of new methods and use of multiple media.

FDLP Academy enhances federal government information knowledge through events and conferences coordinated by GPO and webinars and webcasts on a wide variety of government information topics. Many sessions are presented by GPO staff, while others are presented by staff from other federal agencies and from members of the FDLP community, as recruited and hosted by GPO.

Through this program, 51 live webinars were presented to 3,803 attendees, eight recorded webcasts had more than 900 views, and four live classroom sessions attracted 41 attendees during the fiscal year. Collaborators with GPO through this program have included representatives of the U.S. Department of Energy, the U.S. Census Bureau, the National Institutes of Health, the U.S. Department of Health and Human Services, the National Oceanic and Atmospheric Administration, and many more.

FDLP Academy resources include

- An FDLP Events Calendar with information on upcoming events and related registration information
- A Webinars and Webcasts Archive with links to recordings and handouts of all past webinars and webcasts, categorized by learning track (FDsys, GPO, Agency, or FDLP Community)
- An Events and Conferences page with information about GPO's annual FDLP events
- An Events and Conferences Archive with links to recordings and handouts of all past FDLP events and conferences that have been broadcast virtually
- A collection of FDsys training videos

- A form to request specialized training or to volunteer to share expertise through a webinar hosted by GPO

Web Archiving Initiative

GPO continues to be an Archive-It partner for website-level harvesting and has made a number of advances in collection development. LSCM staff members have completed archiving the websites of the Y3 SuDoc classification scheme, which encompasses the committees, commissions, and independent agencies, and have begun to develop a concept for special collections of online content. The first effort began as a request from the Superintendent of Documents to archive federal Web resources that would be beneficial to the Native American community. LSCM envisions similar special collections in the future.

Since the beginning of this program, LSCM staff have focused on increasing the number and types of agencies being archived. LSCM also wants to focus on maintenance of existing collections by completing regular crawls. A workflow has been developed for improving the frequency of crawls on existing collections, and implementation began in FY 2014.

LSCM continues to welcome nominations for Web archiving. The FDLP community can nominate websites through a number of avenues, including Document Discovery, askGPO, or through a direct e-mail to LSCM's Web Archiving team.

The current size of GPO's collection in Archive-It is 3.5 terabytes with more than 24 million documents crawled. There are 57 agencies represented on GPO's Archive-It site and 65 records in CGP.

To avoid duplication of effort, GPO has worked with other federal agencies that are Web archiving in order to foster better communication and cooperation relating to long-term preservation and access initiatives.

In fall 2014 GPO joined with the Library of Congress and the National Archives and Records Administration in forming a Federal Web Archiving Working Group. The group meets monthly to discuss Web archiving strategies and coordinated efforts. Members plan to expand outreach and communication efforts in 2015.

There is an extensive project page on FDLP.gov that provides more information and FAQs on the Web archiving program.

Recognizing Depository Libraries

On April 30, 2014, during the Depository Library Council Meeting and Federal Depository Library Conference, GPO recognized four libraries for their achievements and initiatives in 2013 and 2014. These "libraries of the year" were selected for their leadership, educational outreach, and commitment to providing free public access to federal government information.

These were the honorees:

The University of Iowa Libraries, the state's regional depository library, was honored for its successful blending of partnerships and projects within the institution, the local community, GPO, and the nation. The libraries were found to be exemplary in their cataloging and preservation initiatives. One project included the identification, cataloging, and digitization of nearly 1,500 large-format posters issued by the federal government.

The Ottenheimer Library at the University of Arkansas, Little Rock, was honored for its leadership in scholarship activities that promote government information and depository libraries nationwide. The library is a leader in coordinating federal documents activities at the state level. It was instrumental in acquiring support and financing for the online U.S. Congressional Serial Set while continuing to preserve and maintain the tangible volumes on campus under a cooperative agreement with other institutions in the area.

The State Library of Arizona was honored for its active participation in the electronic distribution of online cataloging records project, creation of the state master plan for depository libraries, and collaboration in the development of a biennial multi-state virtual depository library conference.

Brooklyn College Library was honored for its leadership and mentoring activities for library staff in the greater New York City area. The library provides access and staff with expertise for a wide range of tangible and electronic resources for the public, providing a basis for transitioning from a traditional to a modern library.

Depository Library Spotlight

GPO Depository Library Spotlight highlights a federal depository library and describes the unique services it offers. This feature appears on the GPO website, gpo. gov, and in the *FDLP Connection* newsletter.

The following depositories were highlighted in FY 2014: Hesburgh Libraries, University of Notre Dame; San Diego Public Library; Las Vegas Library of the Las Vegas-Clark County Library District; and Arizona State University Libraries.

LSCM Metrics

Notable LSCM Metrics for FY 2014:

- New titles acquired (online and tangible): 13,384
- Number of serial issues checked in: 64,779
- Searches of CGP: 25,605,364
- Total titles cataloged: 13,697
- Total PURLs created: 11,345
- Total titles distributed: 6,193
- Total copies distributed: 1,363,635
- Number of federal depository libraries: 1,174
- Total titles available through GPO: 1,286,466

Public Access Assessment

Regular communication and consultation between individual depository libraries and GPO staff strengthen and benefit FDLP. A Public Access Assessment (PAA) is a review by a GPO librarian of an individual federal depository library's operation and services; it is one of the significant ways in which GPO communicates and shares information with individual libraries in FDLP. PAAs are intended to support each library through sharing of best practices, recognition of notable achievements, and recommendations so the library can continue enhancing its operation and services. The assessment involves a review of library documentation and a conference call with depository library personnel.

GPO also performs PAAs, pursuant to 44 U.S.C. §19, to ensure that resources distributed to federal depository libraries are readily accessible to all library users, including the general public, and that libraries are complying with requirements and regulations outlined in "Legal Requirements and Program Regulations of the Federal Depository Library Program." If necessary, GPO advises libraries on how to reach greater compliance and requests related follow-up action. Information about PAAs is available to depository library personnel in featured newsletter articles, a webcast, and an FDLP.gov guidance article. In FY 2014 GPO completed 107 PAAs in Colorado, Indiana, Louisiana, Montana, Nevada, New York, Oklahoma, Pennsylvania, Tennessee, and Wisconsin.

National Archives and Records Administration

700 Pennsylvania Ave. N.W., Washington, DC 20408
202-357-5000
World Wide Web http://www.archives.gov

The National Archives and Records Administration (NARA), an independent federal agency, is the nation's record keeper. NARA safeguards and preserves the important records of all three branches of the federal government so that the people can discover, use, and learn from this documentary heritage. NARA ensures continuing access to records that document the rights of American citizens, the actions of government officials, and the history of the nation.

NARA carries out its mission through a national network of archives and records centers stretching from Boston to San Francisco and Atlanta to Seattle, in addition to 13 presidential libraries that document administrations back to that of Herbert Hoover—a total of 46 facilities nationwide.

The agency includes the National Historical Publications and Records Commission (NHPRC), the grant-making arm of NARA; the Office of the Federal Register, which publishes the official records of the actions of the government; the Information Security Oversight Office (ISOO), which oversees the government's classification programs; the National Declassification Center (NDC), which is streamlining the declassification process; and the Office of Government Information Services (OGIS), which reviews agencies' Freedom of Information Act (FOIA) administration and practices.

NARA also assists federal agencies, the courts, and Congress in documenting their activities by providing records storage, offering reference service, administering records management programs, scheduling records, and retiring non-current records to federal records centers. NARA also provides training, advice, and guidance on many issues relating to records management.

NARA's constituents and stakeholders include educators and their students at all levels, a history-minded public, family historians, the media, the archival community, and a broad spectrum of professional associations and researchers in such fields as history, political science, law, library and information services, and genealogy.

The size and breadth of NARA's holdings are staggering. NARA's electronic records holdings amount to approximately 574 terabytes of data, which includes the 2010 census. This consists of records that were "born digital" and managed in a digital form throughout their life cycle.

In addition, NARA maintains traditional holdings that will be converted to digital form for preservation purposes and to ensure access to them far into the future. This, along with the ever-growing quantity of "born digital" records, creates a big data challenge for NARA and the federal government.

NARA's current traditional holdings include more than 11 billion pages, 18 million maps, 50 million photographs, 600,000 artifacts, and 360,000 motion picture films. In addition, 18 Federal Records Centers (FRCs), located around the country, provide storage for about 75 billion pages of non-current records for 400 federal agencies.

NARA is currently operating under a Strategic Plan for fiscal years 2014 to 2018, which sets its long-term objectives. It has four strategic goals: Make Access

Happen, Connect with Customers, Maximize NARA's Value to the Nation, and Build Our Future Through Our People. Specific initiatives are under way at NARA to reach each goal.

Records and Access

Information Security Oversight Office

The Information Security Oversight Office (ISOO) is responsible to the president for policy and oversight of the government-wide security classification system, the National Industrial Security Program, and the emerging federal policy on "controlled unclassified" information. ISOO receives policy and program guidance from the assistant to the president for national security affairs and National Security Council staff in the Executive Office of the President.

ISOO oversees the security classification programs (classification, safeguarding, and declassification) in both government and industry. It is also responsible for exercising NARA's authorities and responsibilities as the executive agent for controlled unclassified information. ISOO contributes materially to the effective implementation of the government-wide security classification program and has a direct impact on the performance of thousands of government employees and contract personnel who work with classified national security information. For more information on ISOO, visit http://www.archives.gov/isoo.

National Declassification Center

In December 2009 President Barack Obama directed an overhaul of how documents created by the federal government are classified and declassified. This initiative aims at promoting transparency and accountability of government. The president also directed the creation of the National Declassification Center (NDC), located within NARA.

NDC is leading the streamlining of the declassification process throughout the federal government. In particular, it is accelerating the processing of historically valuable classified records in which more than one federal agency has an interest. NDC met the president's initial December 31, 2013, goal for the center by successfully addressing referrals and quality assurance problems within the backlog of 352 million pages of accessioned federal records at NARA that were previously subject to automatic declassification. NDC maintained that momentum by meeting its 2014 quality assurance goals as well.

NDC also oversees the development of common declassification processes among agencies, and it is prioritizing declassification based on public interest and the likelihood of declassification. For more information about NDC, go to http://www.archives.gov/declassification.

Office of Government Information Services

Congress refers to the Office of Government Information Services (OGIS) as "the Federal FOIA (Freedom of Information Act) ombudsman." OGIS serves as a bridge between requesters and agencies, particularly in situations where clear, direct communication has been lacking.

OGIS was created within NARA when the Open Government Act of 2007 amended FOIA. Its key responsibilities include reviewing compliance by federal agencies and proposing any changes in FOIA to Congress; mediating disputes between persons making FOIA requests and agencies; and serving as ombudsman for the agencies and the public regarding the administration of FOIA and to improve communications between agencies and requesters.

OGIS also provides dispute resolution training for the FOIA staff of federal agencies, and it works closely with key FOIA stakeholders, including the requester community and open-government advocates. For more information about OGIS, visit http://ogis.archives.gov.

In cooperation with the Environmental Protection Agency and the Department of Commerce, OGIS developed and established a Web portal, FOIAonline, at https://foiaonline.regulations.gov. The public can submit FOIA requests, track their progress, communicate with the participating agency, file appeals, and find records that have been released to the public under FOIA.

Electronic Records Archives

The Electronic Records Archives (ERA) system captures electronic records and information, regardless of format, saves them permanently, and provides access to them. ERA development was completed at the end of fiscal year (FY) 2011, and ERA moved to an operations and maintenance phase at the beginning of FY 2012.

The focus then shifted to increasing the use of ERA by federal departments and agencies in anticipation of ERA becoming mandatory by the end of 2012 for federal agency use in scheduling and transferring permanent electronic records to NARA. The adoption of ERA by federal agencies has led to the transfer of increasing volumes of electronic records to NARA for preservation and eventual access through its public access portal, the Online Public Access System (OPA).

From 2013 through 2014 NARA made several improvements to better meet the needs of all stakeholders that rely on the ERA system to schedule, transfer, preserve, and provide access to the permanently valuable digital heritage of the federal government.

In early 2015 ERA held 602 terabytes of information in electronic form. For 2015 NARA will continue to evolve the ERA system to improve its capabilities and performance to meet the growing challenges in preserving and providing access to electronic records. For more information about ERA, see http://www.archives.gov/era.

Applied Research Division

NARA's Applied Research Division serves as the agency's center for advanced and applied research capabilities in the fields of computer science, engineering, and archival science. The division's staff conducts research on new technologies, both to be aware of new types of electronic record formats that will need to be preserved and to evaluate new technologies that might be incorporated into electronic records management and preservation systems at NARA to increase their effectiveness. The staff also helps NARA managers and employees acquire the knowledge and skills they need to function effectively in e-government through presentations on new technologies. For more information, visit http://www.archives.gov/applied-research.

National Archives Catalog

Today anyone with a computer connected to the Internet can search descriptions of more than 86 percent of NARA's nationwide holdings and view digital copies of some of its most popular documents through NARA's updated National Archives Catalog. By the end of 2016 NARA will have 95 percent of its vast holdings described in the catalog. Currently the catalog contains more than 8 million descriptions of archival holdings. Included are more than 2,186,000 digital copies of high-interest documents, representing many of the holdings highlighted on NARA's numerous social media platforms and in the Public Vaults, NARA's permanent interactive exhibition. The catalog is available on the Internet at http://www.archives.gov/research/catalog.

NARA's Website

The online entrance to the National Archives is its award-winning website, http://www.archives.gov, which provides the most widely available means of electronic access to information about and services available from NARA. Links to various sections provide help to the particular needs of researchers, including veterans and their families, educators and students, and the general public—as well as records managers, journalists, historians, information security specialists, members of Congress, and federal employees.

The NARA website provides

- Directions on how to contact NARA and do research at its facilities around the country
- Direct access to certain archived electronic records at http://www.archives.gov/aad
- Digital copies of selected archived documents
- An Internet Web form, at http://www.archives.gov/contact/inquire-form.html, for customer questions, reference requests, comments, and complaints
- Electronic versions of *Federal Register* publications
- Online exhibits
- Selected articles about U.S. history from *Prologue* (http://www.archives.gov/publications/prologue), the agency's quarterly magazine
- Classroom resources for students and teachers
- Online tools such as eVetRecs (http://www.archives.gov/veterans/military-service-records), which allows veterans and their next-of-kin to complete and print, for mail-in submission, requests for their military service records

Copies of military pension records from the American Revolution through World War I, census pages, land files, court records, and microfilm publications can be ordered online at http://www.archives.gov/shop. Researchers can also submit reference questions about various research topics online. In FY 2014 NARA had 63 million visits to its websites.

Digitization Projects

Within its Office of Innovation, NARA is working to digitize its traditional (paper) holdings to preserve them and provide greater access to them. The Office of Innovation will accelerate NARA's innovation activities and culture, support innovation in public access delivery, and demonstrate leadership in the archival and information access field.

While NARA's online catalog gives users the ability to identify the archival holdings it has attached to descriptions and made available through the catalog, the amount of material digitized and fully made available online is limited.

Most of NARA's holdings currently are available only from the archival facility in which they are stored. Through a series of digitization projects, NARA is working to vastly increase online public access to more of its holdings. In 2008 the agency created a strategy to deal with digitization efforts, which includes working with partners in the private sector. In 2015 NARA will be adding millions of images to the catalog. These images were created by its private industry digitization partners. More information about the digitization partnerships is available at http://www.archives.gov/digitization/index.html.

Social Media

The National Archives uses multiple social media platforms to increase access to the records in its holdings, which is at the heart of its mission. The main goals of social media at NARA are to increase awareness about archival holdings and programs and to enrich the agency's relationship with the public through conversations about its services and holdings. In addition to expanding access, use of social media creates a more collaborative work environment and increases communication and knowledge sharing both within NARA and externally with other federal agencies.

The National Archives has more than a dozen blogs, including one by the Archivist of the United States. NARA also offers historical videos from its holdings and videos of recent public events on the agency's YouTube channel. The agency shares photographs and documents from its collections through Flickr Commons.

The National Archives also uses Facebook, Twitter, Instagram, Tumblr, GitHub, HistoryPin, Pinterest, Foursquare, Google+, and Storify. Followers can also use Really Simple Syndication (RSS) feeds of the "Document for Today" feature, NARA news, and press releases. Several mobile apps and e-books have been developed and are available free of charge in the iTunes store and Android Market for Today's Document, DocsTeach, and recent exhibits.

Social media also allow NARA's researchers, friends, and the public to become "citizen archivists" at the National Archives by tagging, sharing, and transcribing documents. For more information, go to http://www.archives.gov/citizen-archivist.

Additional information about NARA's social media projects is available at http://www.archives.gov/social-media.

National Archives Museum

The National Archives Museum, a set of interconnected resources made possible by a public-private partnership between NARA and the National Archives Foundation, provides a variety of ways to explore the power and importance of the nation's records.

The Rotunda for the Charters of Freedom at the National Archives Building in Washington, D.C., is the centerpiece of the National Archives Museum. On display are the Declaration of Independence, the Constitution, and the Bill of Rights—known collectively as the Charters of Freedom. The Public Vaults is a 9,000-square-foot permanent exhibition that conveys the feeling of going beyond the walls of the Rotunda and into the stacks and vaults of the working archives. Dozens of individual exhibits, many of them interactive, reveal the breadth and variety of NARA's holdings.

Complementing the Public Vaults, the Lawrence F. O'Brien Gallery hosts a changing array of topical exhibits based on National Archives records. The 290-seat William G. McGowan Theater is a showplace for NARA's extensive audio-visual holdings and serves as a forum for lectures and discussions. It also is home to the Charles Guggenheim Center for the Documentary Film at the National Archives.

An expanded museum shop opened in 2012, and a new exhibition gallery and visitor orientation plaza opened in 2013. The David M. Rubenstein Gallery houses a new permanent interactive exhibit, "Records of Rights," which documents the struggles and debates over civil rights and liberties throughout American history. The Rubenstein Gallery is also the new home for a 1297 copy of the Magna Carta, owned by Rubenstein.

Inside the Boeing Learning Center, the ReSource Room is an access point for teachers and parents to explore documents found in the exhibits and to use NARA records as teaching tools. The center's Constitution-in-Action Learning Lab is designed to provide an intense field trip adventure for middle and high school students that links to curriculum in the classroom.

DocsTeach (http://www.docsteach.org) is an education website designed to provide instruction to teachers in the best practices of teaching with primary sources. Using documents in NARA's holdings as teachable resources, DocsTeach strongly supports civic literacy. This tool gives all teachers access to primary sources, instruction in best practices, and opportunities to interact with their counterparts across the nation.

When developing the DocsTeach site, the agency established an online community that served as a virtual meeting place for NARA's education team and colleagues from schools, institutions, and organizations nationwide to collaborate and share innovative ideas and best practices for this online resource.

The National Archives Museum has expanded to the National Archives in New York City, which is located in the Alexander Hamilton U.S. Custom House at the southern tip of Manhattan. There NARA has not only a new research area but also a learning center for education and public programs and a welcome center with exhibit space. The new Learning Center incorporates many of the resources and activities found in the Washington, D.C., building.

At its Kansas City, Missouri, field office at 400 West Pershing Road, NARA also has a welcome center, changing exhibitions, workshops, and other public programs.

A set of Web pages now makes the National Archives Museum available anywhere. An illustrated history of the Charters of Freedom can be found there, as well as information on educational programs, special events, and current exhibits at the National Archives.

Those traveling to Washington can bypass the public line during peak tourist season by making online reservations at http://www.recreation.gov. For more information, see "The National Archives Museum" at http://www.archives.gov/nae. An online version of the "Records of Rights" exhibition is available at http://recordsofrights.org.

NARA facilities hosted about 4.2 million physical visitors in FY 2014, of which about 3.5 million were visiting to see exhibits, 600,000 were for public programs, and 104,000 were headed to research rooms. More than a million visited the National Archives Museum in Washington, and exhibits in the 13 presidential library museums were visited by about 2.5 million.

Research Services

Few records repositories serve as many customers as NARA. In FY 2014 there were nearly 104,000 researcher visits to NARA facilities nationwide, including archives, presidential libraries, and federal records centers. More than a million people requested information in writing.

National Archives Research Centers

At the Robert M. Warner Research Center in the National Archives Building in Washington, D.C., and the Steny Hoyer Research Center at the National Archives at College Park, Maryland, researchers can consult with staff experts on federal records held in each building and submit requests to examine original documents.

The Warner Research Center holds approximately 275,000 rolls of microfilmed records, documenting military service prior to World War I, immigration into the United States, the federal census, the U.S. Congress, federal courts in the District of Columbia, the Bureau of Indian Affairs, and the Freedmen's Bureau. The center also contains an extensive, ever-expanding system of reference reports, helping researchers conduct research in federal documents.

Executive branch records housed in the National Archives Building include those of the Bureau of Indian Affairs and of civilian agencies responsible for maritime affairs. Military records in this building include records of the Army before World War I and the Navy and Marine Corps before World War II. In addition, the National Archives Building holds many records relating to the federal government's interaction with individuals; these are often consulted for genealogical research.

The Hoyer Research Center in College Park holds textual records of civilian agencies from 1789, investigative records and military holdings that include records from the Army and Army Air Forces dating from World War I and Navy, Marine Corps, intelligence, defense-related, and seized enemy records dating from World War II. In addition to textual records, special media records include motion pictures, still photographs and posters, sound recordings, maps, architectural drawings, aerial photographs, and electronic records. A research room for accessioned microfilm holds records of the Department of State's Berlin Document Center and other World War II-era captured documents.

Regional Archives

NARA has 12 regional archives where the public can do research. They are located in or near Boston, New York, Philadelphia, Atlanta, Chicago, St. Louis, Kansas City, Fort Worth, Denver, Riverside (California), San Francisco, and Seattle. Archived records of regional significance, as well as, in some locations, immigration records, are available for use by the public in these regional archives.

Presidential Libraries

NARA operates the libraries and museums of the 13 most recent U.S. presidents, beginning with Herbert Hoover, whose library is in West Branch, Iowa. The others are Franklin D. Roosevelt, Hyde Park, New York; Harry S. Truman, Independence, Missouri; Dwight D. Eisenhower, Abilene, Kansas; John F. Kennedy, Boston; Lyndon Baines Johnson, Austin; Richard Nixon, Yorba Linda, California; Gerald R. Ford, Ann Arbor (library) and Grand Rapids (museum), Michigan; Jimmy Carter, Atlanta; Ronald Reagan, Simi Valley, California; George Bush, College Station, Texas; William J. Clinton, Little Rock; and George W. Bush, Dallas.

In FY 2014 about 2.5 million people visited exhibits in the presidential library museums; the libraries had more than 10,000 researcher visits. At http://www.archives.gov/presidential-libraries, visitors can learn about the presidential library system as a whole and link to individual library websites to learn about the lives of the presidents and the times in which they served.

Federal Records Centers

NARA also serves federal agencies, the courts, and Congress by providing records storage, reference service, training, advice, and guidance on many issues relating to records management.

A network of 18 Federal Records Centers (FRCs) stores 30 million cubic feet (about 75 billion pages) of non-current records for 400 agencies. In FY 2014 these records centers replied to more than 7 million requests for information and records, including more than 1 million requests for information regarding military and civilian service records provided by the National Personnel Records Center in St. Louis.

In addition, NARA has records centers in or near Atlanta; Boston; Chicago; Dayton; Denver; Fort Worth; Kansas City; Kingsridge (near Dayton), Ohio; Lee's Summit, Missouri; Lenexa, Kansas; Philadelphia; Pittsfield, Massachusetts; Riverside, California; San Francisco; Seattle; and Suitland, Maryland.

Genealogy Research

Genealogy research brings hundreds of thousands of people to NARA facilities every year. In its holdings NARA has census records dating back to 1790, records dealing with immigration, land and pension records, and passenger lists from ships arriving from all over the world.

NARA is often considered the first stop in searching for one's ancestry, at its facilities in the Washington, D.C., area or one of its 12 regional archives around the country. At these locations, NARA staff offers genealogy workshops to show the public how to look through documents dating back to the Revolutionary period. A "Genealogy Tool Kit" has been published to assist individuals in tracing their family histories.

NARA also offers an annual Genealogy Fair, which is now a "virtual" event at which NARA staff provides tips and techniques for researching genealogy records at the National Archives. Lectures are designed for experienced genealogy professionals and novices alike.

NARA also maintains close relationships with genealogical associations as well as organizations such as Ancestry.com, which can be accessed without charge at any NARA location.

The National Archives has the census schedules on microfilm available from 1790 to 1940. (Most of the 1890 Census was destroyed in a Department of Commerce fire, although partial records are available for some states.)

Archives Library Information Center

The Archives Library Information Center (ALIC) provides access to information on American history and government, archival administration, information management, and government documents. ALIC is located in the National Archives at College Park. Customers also can visit ALIC on the Internet at http://www.archives.gov/research/alic, where they will find "Reference at Your Desk" Internet links, staff-compiled bibliographies and publications, and an online library catalog. ALIC can be reached by telephone at 301-837-3415.

Government Documents

Government publications are generally available to researchers at many of the 1,250 congressionally designated federal depository libraries throughout the nation. A record set of these publications also is part of NARA's archival holdings. Publications of the U.S. Government (Record Group 287) is a collection of selected publications of government agencies, arranged by the SuDoc classification system devised by the Office of the Superintendent of Documents, U.S. Government Publishing Office (GPO).

The core of the collection is a library established in 1895 by GPO's Public Documents Division. By 1972, when NARA acquired the library, it included official publications dating from the early years of the federal government and selected publications produced for and by federal government agencies. Since 1972 the 25,000-cubic-foot collection has been augmented periodically with accessions of government publications selected by the Office of the Superintendent of Documents as a byproduct of its cataloging activity. As with the federal depository library collections, the holdings in NARA's Record Group 287 comprise only a portion of all U.S. government publications.

NARA Publications

Historically NARA has published guides and indexes to various portions of its archival holdings. Many of these are still in print, though the most up-to-date information about NARA holdings now is available almost exclusively through online searches at http://www.archives.gov. The agency also publishes informational leaflets and brochures and NARA's flagship publication, *Prologue,* a scholarly magazine published quarterly.

Some publications appear on NARA's website, at http://www.archives.gov/publications/online.html, and many are available from NARA's Customer Service Center in College Park, by calling 800-234-8861 or 866-272-6272 (in the Washington, D.C., area, 301-837-2000) or faxing 301-837-0483. The NARA website's publications homepage, http://www.archives.gov/publications, provides more detailed information about available publications and ordering.

General-interest books about NARA and its holdings that will appeal to anyone with an interest in U.S. history, exhibition catalogs, and facsimiles of certain documents are published by the National Archives Foundation. They are for sale at the foundation's myArchives Store in NARA's downtown Washington building and via the NARA website's eStore page at http://www.myarchivesstore.org.

Federal Register

The *Federal Register* is the daily gazette of the U.S. government, containing presidential documents, proposed and final federal regulations, and public notices of federal agencies. It is published by the Office of the Federal Register and printed and distributed by GPO. The two agencies collaborate in the same way to produce the annual revisions of the *Code of Federal Regulations* (*CFR*). Free access to the full text of the electronic version of the *Federal Register* and *CFR,* and to an unofficial, daily-updated electronic *CFR* (the *e-CFR*), is available via http://www.fdsys.gov. Federal Register documents scheduled for future publication are available for public inspection at the Office of the Federal Register (800 North Capitol St. N.W., Washington, DC 20002) or online at the electronic Public Inspection Desk (http://www.federalregister.gov/public-inspection). Federalregister.gov provides access to proposed rules and rules published in the *Federal Register* and open for public comment (the website https://www.federalregister.gov and the multiagency website http://www.regulations.gov also provide means to comment on these documents).

The full catalog of other Federal Register publications is posted at http://www.ofr.gov and includes the *Compilation of Presidential Documents, Public Papers of the President,* slip laws, *U.S. Statutes at Large,* and the *United States Government Manual.* Printed or microfiche editions of Federal Register publications also are maintained at federal depository libraries (http://www.gpo.gov/libraries).

The Public Law Electronic Notification Service (PENS) is a free subscription e-mail service available for notification of recently enacted public laws. Varied subscriptions to the daily *Federal Register* are available from http://www.federalregister.gov. Additional information about Federal Register programs appears on Facebook (http://www.facebook.com/federalregister) and Twitter (@ FedRegister).

The Office of the Federal Register also publishes information about its ministerial responsibilities associated with the operation of the Electoral College and ratification of constitutional amendments and provides access to related records. Publication information concerning laws, regulations, and presidential documents and services is available from the Office of the Federal Register (telephone 202-741-6070). Information on Federal Register finding aids, the Electoral College, and constitutional amendments is available through http://www.archives.gov/federal-register.

Publications can be ordered by contacting GPO at http://bookstore.gpo.gov, or by toll-free telephone at 866-512-1800. To submit orders by fax or by mail, see http://bookstore.gpo.gov/help/index.jsp.

Grants

The National Historical Publications and Records Commission (NHPRC) operates the grantmaking affiliate of NARA's national grants program. The Archivist of the United States chairs the commission and makes grants on its recommendation. NHPRC's 14 other members represent the president (two appointees), the Supreme Court, the Senate and House of Representatives, the departments of State and Defense, the Librarian of Congress, the American Association for State and Local History, the American Historical Association, the Association for Documentary Editing, the National Association of Government Archives and Records Administrators, the Organization of American Historians, and the Society of American Archivists.

The commission carries out a statutory mission to ensure understanding of the nation's past by promoting nationwide the preservation and use of essential historical documents. The commission supports the creation and publication of documentary editions and research in the management and preservation of authentic electronic records, and it works in partnership with a national network of state archives and state historical records advisory boards to develop a national archival infrastructure. NHPRC grants help state and local governments—as well as archives, universities, historical societies, professional organizations, and other nonprofit organizations—to establish or strengthen archival programs, improve training and techniques, preserve and process records collections, and provide access to them through finding aids, digitization of collections, and documentary editions of the papers of significant historical figures and movements in American history. For more information about the commission, visit http://www.archives.gov/nhprc. For more information about the projects it supports, go to http://www.facebook.com/nhprc.

Customer Service

Few records repositories serve as many customers as NARA. In FY 2014 there were about 104,000 researcher visits to NARA facilities nationwide, including archives, presidential libraries, and federal records centers. At the same time, more than a million customers submitted written requests for information.

NARA also maintains an Internet form (http://www.archives.gov/contact/ inquire-form.html) to facilitate continuous feedback from customers about what is most important to them and what NARA might do better to meet their needs.

Administration

The head of NARA is David S. Ferriero, who was appointed Archivist of the United States in 2009 by President Obama. As of January 31, 2015, the agency employed 3,002 people, of whom about 2,645 were full-time permanent staff members working at NARA locations around the country.

National Center for Education Statistics

U.S. Department of Education, Institute of Education Sciences
1990 K St. N.W., Washington, DC 20006

Bao Le
Academic Libraries, Integrated Postsecondary Education Data System

Chelsea Owens
School Library Media Centers, Schools and Staffing Survey

In an effort to collect and disseminate more-complete statistical information about libraries, the National Center for Education Statistics (NCES) initiated a formal library statistics program in 1989 that included surveys on academic libraries, school library media centers, public libraries, and state libraries.* At the end of December 2006, the Public Libraries Survey and the State Library Agencies Survey were officially transferred to the Institute of Museum and Library Services (IMLS). The Academic Libraries Survey and the School Library Media Centers Survey continued to be administered and funded by NCES. However, the School Library Media Centers Survey was incorporated into the School and Staffing Survey (SASS), and the Academic Libraries Survey was incorporated into the Integrated Postsecondary Education Data System (IPEDS). [For detailed information on the surveys now being handled by IMLS, see "Institute of Museum and Library Services Library Programs" in Part 2 and "Highlights of IMLS and NCES Surveys" in Part 4—*Ed.*]

The surveys conducted by NCES are designed to provide comprehensive nationwide data on the status of libraries. Federal, state, and local officials, professional associations, and local practitioners use these surveys for planning, evaluating, and making policy. The data are also available to researchers and educators.

Past information about elementary and secondary public school library media centers is available on the School and Staffing Survey website, http://nces. ed.gov/surveys/sass. The Library Statistics Program's website, http://nces.ed.gov/ surveys/libraries, provides links to data search tools, data files, survey definitions, and survey designs for the Academic Libraries Survey from 1996 to 2012. The IPEDS Academic Libraries Information Center, http://nces.ed.gov/ipeds/resource/ alscenter.asp, contains current survey definitions and designs, and the IPEDS Data Center at http://nces.ed.gov/ipeds/datacenter contains data files for the Academic Libraries component beginning in 2014. The two library surveys conducted by NCES are described below.

Academic Libraries

The IPEDS Academic Libraries (AL) component provides descriptive statistics from academic libraries in the 50 states, the District of Columbia, and, if appli-

---

*The authorization for the National Center for Education Statistics (NCES) to collect library statistics is included in the Education Sciences Reform Act of 2002 (PL 107-279), under Title I, Part C.

cable, the outlying areas of the United States (Guam, the Commonwealth of the Northern Mariana Islands, Puerto Rico, and the U.S. Virgin Islands).

NCES surveyed academic libraries on a three-year cycle between 1966 and 1988. From 1988 to 1998 AL was a component of IPEDS collected on a two-year cycle. From 2000 to 2012 the Academic Libraries Survey (ALS) separated from IPEDS but remained on a two-year cycle as part of the Library Statistics Program. IPEDS and AL data were still linked by the identification codes of the postsecondary education institutions. In aggregate, these data provide an overview of the status of academic libraries nationally and by state. Beginning with the 2014–2015 collection cycle, AL was reintegrated back into IPEDS.

AL collects data on libraries in the entire universe of degree-granting postsecondary institutions using a Web-based data collection system. The survey component collects counts of library books, e-books, media, and databases, both in the physical and electronic formats. Academic libraries are also asked to report salaries, wages, and fringe benefits, if paid from the library budget; materials and services expenditures; operations and maintenance expenditures; and total expenditures. Libraries with reported total expenditures over zero but equal to or less than $100,000 were required to report collections data, while those with expenditures greater than $100,000 were required to report collections and detailed expenditures data.

A First Look report, "Academic Libraries: 2012" (NCES 2014-038), was released on the NCES website in February 2014, as were the final data file and documentation for the 2012 ALS (NCES 2014-039). NCES has developed a Web-based peer analysis tool for AL called "Compare Academic Libraries." This tool currently uses AL 2012 data. Future library data collected will be available via the IPEDS Data Center tool. Academic library statistics information can be obtained from Bao Le, Integrated Postsecondary Education Data System (e-mail bao.le@ed.gov).

School Library Media Centers

National surveys of school library media centers in elementary and secondary schools in the United States were conducted in 1958, 1962, 1974, 1978, and 1986, 1993–1994, 1999–2000, 2003–2004, and 2007–2008. Data collection for the 2011–2012 School Library Media Centers Survey has been completed.

NCES, with the assistance of the U.S. Bureau of the Census, conducted the School Library Media Center Survey as part of the Schools and Staffing Survey (SASS). SASS is the nation's largest sample survey of teachers, schools, and principals in K–12 public and private schools. Data from the school library media center questionnaire provide a national picture of public school library staffing, collections, expenditures, technology, and services. Results from the 2011–2012 survey can be found in *Characteristics of Public Elementary and Secondary School Library Media Centers in the United States: Results from the 2011–2012 Schools and Staffing Survey* (NCES 2013-315).

NCES also published a historical report about school libraries titled *Fifty Years of Supporting Children's Learning: A History of Public School Libraries and Federal Legislation from 1953–2000* (NCES 2005-311). Drawn from more than 50 sources, this report presents descriptive data about public school libraries since 1953. Along with key characteristics of school libraries, the report also presents national and regional standards, and federal legislation affecting school library media centers. Data from sample surveys are presented at the national, regional, and school levels, and by state.

SASS is currently undergoing a redesign and will become the National Teacher and Principal Survey (NTPS). NTPS will be focused on teachers, principals, and the schools in which they work. The redesigned study will collect counts of the number of school library media centers. Additional information on school library media center statistics can be obtained from Chelsea Owens, Schools and Staffing Survey (e-mail chelsea.owens@ed.gov).

NCES has added some library-oriented questions relevant to the library usage and skills of the parent and the teacher instruments in the new Early Childhood Longitudinal Study (ECLS). For additional information, visit http://nces.ed.gov/ecls. Library items also appear in National Household Education Survey (NHES) instruments. For more information about that survey, visit http://nces.ed.gov/nhes.

NCES included a questionnaire about high school library media centers in the Education Longitudinal Study of 2002 (ELS: 2002). This survey collected data from tenth graders about their schools, their school library media centers, their communities, and their home life. The report, *School Library Media Centers: Selected Results from the Education Longitudinal Study of 2002 (ELS: 2002)* (NCES 2005-302), is available on the NCES website. For more information about this survey, visit http://nces.ed.gov/surveys/els2002.

How to Obtain Printed and Electronic Products

Reports are currently published in the First Look format. First Look reports consist of a short collection of tables presenting state and national totals, a survey description, and data highlights. NCES also publishes separate, more in-depth studies analyzing these data.

Internet Access

Many NCES publications (including out-of-print publications) and edited raw data files from the library surveys are available for viewing or downloading at no charge through the Electronic Catalog on the NCES website at http://nces.ed.gov/pubsearch.

Ordering Printed Products

Many NCES publications are also available in printed format. To order one free copy of recent NCES reports, contact the Education Publications Center (ED Pubs) at http://www.edpubs.org, by e-mail at edpubs@edpubs.ed.gov, by toll-free telephone at 877-4-ED-PUBS (1-877-433-7827) or TTY/TDD 877-576-7734, by fax at 703-605-6794, or by mail at ED Pubs, P.O. Box 22207, Alexandria, VA 22304.

Many publications are available through the Education Resources Information Center (ERIC) system. For more information on services and products, visit http://www.eric.ed.gov. [Also see the article "Education Resources Information Center" on Pages 157–160—*Ed.*]

Out-of-print publications and data files may be available through the NCES Electronic Catalog on the NCES website at http://nces.ed.gov/pubsearch or through one of the 1,250 federal depository libraries throughout the United States (see http://catalog.gpo.gov/fdlpdir/FDLPdir.jsp). Use the NCES publication number included in the citations for publications and data files to quickly locate items in the NCES Electronic Catalog. Use the GPO number to locate items in a federal depository library.

Defense Technical Information Center

Fort Belvoir, VA 22060
World Wide Web http://www.dtic.mil

Michele Finley
Public Affairs Officer

The Defense Technical Information Center (DTIC) is responsible for developing, coordinating, and enabling a strong scientific and technical information (STINFO) program for the Assistant Secretary of Defense for Research and Engineering, and for the Department of Defense (DoD) scientific and technical (S&T) enterprise. In this role, DTIC sets policy for scientific and technical information exchanges for the research and engineering community. DTIC's aim is to maximize the availability, use, and collaboration of technical information resulting from DoD-funded technical activities while ensuring restrictions to safeguard national security, export control, and intellectual property rights.

Since its inception in 1945 DTIC has served as a vital link in the transfer of defense-related information. The center offers access to approximately 4 million research records to engineers, researchers, scientists, and information professionals in laboratories, universities, and the acquisition field. DTIC's mission is to provide essential, technical, research, development, test, and evaluation information rapidly, accurately, and reliably to support DoD customers' needs. As a DoD field activity, DTIC is under the office of the Under Secretary of Defense for Acquisition, Technology, and Logistics and reports to the Assistant Secretary of Defense for Research and Engineering (ASD[R&E]).

In 2013 DTIC marked nine years as a DoD field activity and saw the renewal of its field activity charter. Signed by Deputy Secretary of Defense Ashton B. Carter, the charter, in force until 2018, reaffirmed DTIC's position as DoD's central scientific, research, and engineering information support activity for ASD(R&E). In 2013 DTIC also saw the approval of DoD Instruction 3200.12, "DoD Scientific and Technical Information Program (STIP)." Now an instruction, this issuance establishes policy and responsibilities and proposes procedures for DTIC to carry out STIP. The instruction outlines the vital role played by DTIC in collecting, indexing, cataloging, and providing storage for scientific and technical information obtained from DoD components and their contractors, non-DoD organizations, and foreign sources.

The instruction reiterates that DoD should sustain a coordinated program to manage scientific and technical information, which will maximize resources while eliminating duplication of effort by the reuse of DoD research, development, test, and evaluation investments and assets. DoDI 3200.12 can be found on the DoD Issuances website, http://www.dtic.mil/whs/directives/corres/pdf/320012p.pdf.

In 2014 DoD Manual 3200.14, Volume 2, "Principles and Operational Parameters of the DoD Scientific and Technical Information Program (STIP): Information Analysis Centers (IACs)," was updated. DoD establishes IACs to acquire, digest, analyze, evaluate, synthesize, store, publish, and distribute scientific and technical information and engineering data in a clearly defined specialized field or subject area of significant DoD interest or concern. Additionally IACs provide advisory and other user services to their authorized user community. The updated document describes the DoD IAC program and implements its policy, principles, and concepts for procedural functions. This volume is available at http://www. dtic.mil/whs/directives/corres/pdf/320014vol2.pdf.

Early in 2015 the Defense Acquisition Regulation Supplement clause on Electronic Submission of Technical Reports was updated to require electronic submissions instead of paper copies of approved final scientific or technical reports of research funded by DoD. This reaffirms the requirement for all final scientific and technical reports on DoD-funded research to be submitted to DTIC.

Reaching Customers

DTIC offers its suite of services to a diverse population of the defense community. Because of the nature of the information it handles, some of DTIC's products are accessible only to the federal government and its contractors. While DTIC also has a public website and search, there are advantages to accessing the secured sites. These value-added services include having research assistance from trained information professionals and having access to "limited" (not publicly available) information. More information about who is eligible to access DTIC's suite of products can be found at http://www.dtic.mil/dtic/registration/Eligibility.html.

Who uses DTIC information? Some of its more than 25,000 users are:

- Acquisition community
- Active duty military personnel
- Congressional staff
- DoD and federal contractors
- Engineers
- Faculty and students at military schools
- Historians
- Information professionals/librarians
- Intelligence community
- Logistics management specialists
- Researchers
- Scientists
- Security managers
- Software engineers and developers

Resources

DTIC's holdings include technical reports on completed research; research summaries of planned, ongoing, and completed work; independent research and development summaries; defense technology transfer agreements; DoD planning documents; budget data; DoD directives and instructions; international agreements; conference proceedings; security classification guides; command histories; and special research collections that date back to World War II. DoD-funded researchers are required to search DTIC's collections to ensure that they do not undertake unnecessary or redundant research. The general public can access "unclassified, unlimited" information, including many full-text downloadable documents, through the public DTIC website at http://www.dtic.mil. The information on the site is free of charge, and no registration is required.

Information Sources

DTIC information is derived from many sources, including DoD organizations (civilian and military) and DoD contractors; the Information Analysis Centers, U.S. government organizations, and their contractors; nonprofit organizations working on DoD scientific, research, and engineering activities; academia; and foreign governments. DTIC accepts information in print, nonprint (CDs and DVDs), and electronically over the Web. DTIC gets information from the defense community, for the defense community, on defense topics and more. Having a full range of science and technology and research and development information within the DTIC collection ensures that technological innovations are linked to defense development and acquisition efforts. New research projects can begin with the highest level of information available. This avoids duplication of effort, maximizing the use of DoD project dollars and saving taxpayer dollars.

Creating Tools for DoD

DTIC continues to play a key role in DoD by producing collaboration tools (often not available to the public) to help the defense research and engineering community work in a secure environment. In order to utilize many of these websites, individuals must be eligible to access DTIC's products.

The culture of DoD has encouraged communities to keep their projects closely held. But, in a more networked world, the defense workforce needs the tools that will help them create, share, and reuse knowledge developed both within DoD and by its external partners (industry and academia, for example). DTIC has made strides in creating and hosting sites aimed at enhancing the ability of DoD to connect internally and externally. In addition, DTIC is working to map relationships to enable users to access the life cycle of research projects from planning to final results. DTIC employs technology to verify and validate information submitted and improve user confidence in DoD research documentation.

The Research and Engineering (R&E) Gateway provides the means to connect the acquisition enterprise (DoD Labs); Federally Funded Research and Development Centers (FFRDCs); Program Executive Offices; and Acquisition, Technology, and Logistics (AT&L) commands and Combatant commands (CCMDs). In an access-controlled environment, all of DTIC's unclassified assets, tools, and community interaction capabilities foster innovation, competition, and identification of solutions. DoD conducts research at its more than 60 labs, in the FFRDCs, in DTIC's IACs, through contracts and grants, and across 17 distinct priority area communities of interest. This work is available through the R&E Gateway. In addition, the gateway offers access to official defense scientific and technical information, collaborative tools, and subject matter experts. The gateway helps the defense S&T community build on past work, collaborate on current projects, and avoid duplication of effort. With better connections within DoD, the development and delivery of technologies to the armed forces can be accelerated.

The R&E Gateway is the entry point to DTIC's suite of tools. Some of the tools within the gateway are:

- DTIC Collection Search—This tool aids in the quick discovery of public and access-controlled DoD research projects and documents, as well as people (subject matter experts), places (organizations), and content (past and current research) from DoDTechSpace. DTIC continually works to enable additional features within its search capabilities and from commercial partners to improve information discovery and relevance.

- DoDTechipedia—Designed by DTIC in 2008, DoDTechipedia was one of the first DoD scientific and technical wikis. A secure online system, it facilitates transparency and communication among DoD scientists, engineers, program managers, and the armed forces. It helps members of the DoD S&T community collaborate and identify solutions for technology challenges. Among its numerous features are interest area pages for DoD personnel and DoD contractors to work together on challenges and solutions.

- DoDTechSpace—A social business tool, DoDTechSpace is a place for DTIC's customers to collaborate, share, find, and post information. It connects the defense research and engineering community, DoD laboratories, and other DoD agencies, while providing current and next-generation researchers with advanced Web 2.0 tools. Offering real-time discussions on capability needs and solutions, events, and people, this collaborative environment can support community activities, social networking, lessons learned, and discussions.

- DoD Budget Tools—DTIC publishes searchable congressional budget data shortly after release and offers both public and access-controlled sites to review and analyze DoD research and engineering funding data. The center posts reports from the House and Senate committees that oversee the DoD budget information, all of which can be found on the public site http:// www.dtic.mil/congressional_budget. DTIC posts this reformatted budget data within days of release on the Congress.gov legislative information website operated by the Library of Congress. The figures are thoroughly checked prior to posting, ensuring accuracy and reliability.

- Defense Innovation Marketplace—The Defense Innovation Marketplace was launched in late 2011 and continues to be used as an online resource (both public and access-controlled) for the purpose of "connecting industry with government customers." Creation of this site was a direct result of a "better buying power" initiative within DoD, which called for the department to deliver better value by improving the way it was doing business. In short, industry submits information about DoD-related ideas and projects, which helps DoD to see what industry is developing. The site helps the department plan acquisitions and identify gaps that are being encountered in research.

These tools are available through DTIC's public website at www.dtic.mil/dtic.

DoD Information Analysis Centers (IACs)

DoD IACs, established under DoD Instruction 3200.14, serve as a vital resource in providing timely, relevant information directly to users when and where it is needed. IACs serve as a bridge between the armed forces and the acquisition/research community, providing essential technical analysis and data support to a diverse customer base, to include the Combatant Commands (CCMDs), the Office of the Secretary of Defense, Defense Agencies, and the military services. IACs actively partner and collaborate with DoD R&E focus groups and communities of interest in specialized fields or specific technologies. The IACs create and maintain comprehensive knowledge analysis centers that include historical, technical, scientific, and other data and information collected worldwide. They are staffed with scientists, engineers, and information specialists to provide research and analysis to customers with diverse, complex, and challenging requirements.

IAC operations directly support the fighting forces and play an ongoing and critical role in solving key CCMD operational issues such as cybersecurity, unmanned aerial vehicle visual/audible signature reduction, and improvements to the ballistic resistance of body armor. More information on the IACs is available at http://iac.dtic.mil.

Expanding Free Training Opportunities

Webinars have been mainstays of the opportunities offered to DTIC registered users to learn about DTIC's products and services. Three webinars, on DoDTechSpace, DoDTechipedia, and DTIC Search, are offered monthly.

"DTIC Boot Camp: S&T Resources for the DoD Community" offers hands-on training (at DTIC headquarters), including sessions about the center's numerous resources as well as instruction about submitting documents. DTIC users can request additional training sessions at DTIC headquarters or at their own locations.

DoD Scientific and Technical Information (STINFO) training can be held at DTIC or requested off-site. DTIC provides instruction on the management and conduct of an organizational STINFO program.

Public Access to Federally Funded Research

DTIC has a leading role in DoD's efforts to implement public access to published journal articles and digital data from research funded by taxpayers. In this role, DTIC is actively working with partners across the armed services, components, other federal agencies, and publishers.

DTIC is a registered service mark of the Defense Technical Information Center.

Education Resources

National Library of Education

Knowledge Utilization Division
National Center for Education Evaluation and Regional Assistance
Institute of Education Sciences, U.S. Department of Education
400 Maryland Ave. S.W., Washington, DC 20202
World Wide Web http://ies.ed.gov/ncee/projects/nle

Pamela Tripp-Melby
Director
202-453-6536, e-mail pamela.tripp-melby@ed.gov

The U.S. Department of Education's National Library of Education (NLE), created in 1994, is the primary resource center for education information in the federal government, serving the research needs of the Department of Education, the education community, and the public. NLE resides in the National Center for Education Evaluation and Regional Assistance, Institute of Education Sciences.

NLE was created by Public Law 103-227, the Educational Research, Development, Dissemination, and Improvement Act of 1994, and reauthorized under Public Law 107-279, the Education Sciences Reform Act of 2002. The act outlines four primary functions of NLE:

- Collect and archive information, including products and publications developed through, or supported by, the Institute of Education Sciences; and other relevant and useful education-related research, statistics, and evaluation materials and other information, projects, and publications that are consistent with scientifically valid research or the priorities and mission of the institute, and developed by the department, other federal agencies, or entities
- Provide a central location within the federal government for information about education
- Provide comprehensive reference services on matters relating to education to employees of the Department of Education and its contractors and grantees, other federal employees, and the public
- Promote greater cooperation and resource sharing among providers and repositories of education information in the United States

NLE works closely with the Education Resources Information Center (ERIC). ERIC collects and archives information and provides a central location within the federal government for information about education. Because ERIC serves as the major public program, it is covered separately. [See "Education Resources Information Center" below.—*Ed.*]

The primary responsibility of NLE is to provide information services to agency staff and contractors, the general public, other government agencies, and other libraries. Located in the agency's headquarters building in Washington, D.C., the library houses current and historical collections and archives of information on education issues, research, statistics, and policy; there is a special emphasis on agency publications and contractor reports, as well as current and historical federal education legislation.

NLE has a staff of 12 as of 2015, four full-time federal staff and eight contract librarians. Staffing and organizational structure are kept flexible to support changing needs and to allow for fast, competent response to customer requests, institutional initiatives, and advances in technology. NLE's primary customer base includes about 5,000 department staff nationwide; department contractors performing research; education organizations and media; and academic, special, and government libraries. All services are supported by NLE's budget, which in fiscal year 2015 is approximately $2 million.

Collections

The focus of NLE's collection is on education issues, with an emphasis on research and policy, with some materials on related topics including law, public policy, economics, urban affairs, sociology, history, philosophy, psychology, and cognitive development. In addition to current materials, the collection has books dating from the early 19th century, including approximately 800 books on education research in the United States and more than 25,000 historical textbooks. Some of these books were donated to the library by Henry Barnard, the first U.S. Commissioner of Education.

NLE maintains collections of historical documents associated with its parent agency, the U.S. Department of Education, having a complete collection of ERIC microfiche; research reports reviewed by the What Works Clearinghouse and special panels; and publications of or relating to the department's predecessor agencies, including the National Institute of Education and the U.S. Office of Education in the Department of Health, Education, and Welfare. These collections include reports, studies, manuals, statistical publications, speeches, and policy papers. NLE also serves as a selective federal depository library under the U.S. Government Publishing Office program.

Services

NLE provides reference and other information services, including legislative reference and statistical information services, to department staff, to the education community at large, and to the general public, as well as offering document delivery services to department staff and interlibrary loan services to other libraries and government agencies.

Contact Information

The U.S. Department of Education Research Library can be contacted by e-mail at askalibrarian@ed.gov. The library's reference desk is available by telephone from 9 A.M. to 5 P.M. weekdays, except federal holidays, at 800-424-1616 (toll free) or 202-205-5015, and by fax at 202-401-0547. For the hearing-impaired, the toll-free number for the Federal Relay Service is 800-877-8339.

Located in the department's headquarters building at 400 Maryland Ave. S.W., the library is open to researchers by appointment from 9 A.M. to 5 P.M. weekdays, except federal holidays.

Education Resources Information Center

Knowledge Utilization Division
National Center for Education Evaluation and Regional Assistance
Institute of Education Sciences, U.S. Department of Education
555 New Jersey Ave. N.W., Washington, DC 20208
World Wide Web http://eric.ed.gov

Erin Pollard
Program Officer, ERIC
202-219-3400, e-mail erin.pollard@ed.gov

The Education Resources Information Center (ERIC) is the world's largest and most frequently used digital library of education resources. It is composed of more than 1.5 million bibliographic records and more than 340,000 full-text materials indexed from 1966 to the present. Each ERIC bibliographic record contains an abstract of a journal article or non-journal document (for example, a technical report or conference paper), along with such indexed information as author, title, and publication date.

Background

ERIC has served the information needs of schools, institutions of higher education, educators, parents, administrators, policymakers, researchers, and public and private entities for decades, through a variety of library services and formats—first in paper copy, then in microfiche, and today exclusively in electronic format. ERIC provides service directly to the public via its website, http://eric.ed.gov.

With more than 50 years of service to the public, ERIC is one of the oldest programs in the U.S. Department of Education. As the world's largest education resource, it is distinguished by two hallmarks: free dissemination of bibliographic records and the collection of gray literature such as research conference papers and government contractor reports.

The authorizing legislation for ERIC is part of the Education Sciences Reform Act of 2002, Public Law 107-279. This legislation envisioned ERIC subject areas or topics (previously covered by the ERIC Clearinghouses) as part of the totality of enhanced information dissemination to be conducted by the Institute of Education Sciences. In addition, information dissemination includes material on closing the achievement gap and on educational practices that improve academic achievement and promote learning.

ERIC Mission

ERIC's mission is to provide a comprehensive, easy-to-use, searchable, Internet-based bibliographic and full-text database of education research and information for educators, researchers, and the general public. Terms defining the ERIC mission are as follows:

- *Comprehensive:* The ERIC digital library consists of journal articles and non-journal materials, including materials not published by commercial publishers that are directly related to education and education research.
- *Easy-to-use and searchable:* ERIC users will be able to find the education information they need quickly and efficiently.
- *Electronic:* ERIC is an entirely electronic system comprising the ERIC website and the digital library. It links to libraries, publishers, and commercial sources of journal articles, and is made available to commercial database vendors through authorization agreements.
- *Bibliographic and full-text:* Bibliographic records convey the information that users need in a simple and straightforward manner, and, whenever possible, full-text journal articles and non-journal materials are included free of charge in the digital library. Other full-text articles and materials, whenever possible, will be immediately available for purchase through an online link to the publisher's website.

Selection Standards

The selection policy provides that all materials added to the ERIC database are rigorous and relevant sources of research directly related to the field of education. The majority of the journals indexed in ERIC are peer-reviewed, and peer-reviewed status is indicated for all journals indexed since 2004 when this data began to be documented by the ERIC system. The collection scope includes early childhood education through higher education, vocational education, and special education; it includes teacher education, education administration, assessment and evaluation, counseling, information technology, and the academic areas of reading, mathematics, science, environmental education, languages, and social studies.

To be considered for selection, all submissions must be in digital format and accompanied by author permission for dissemination. For individual document submissions, authors (copyright holders) can upload materials through a link on the ERIC website. Journal publishers, associations, and other entities with multiple documents also submit electronic content following guidance and instructions consistent with provider agreements from ERIC.

ERIC Collection

In addition to being the largest education library, ERIC is one of the few collections to index non-journal materials as well as journal literature. The largest share of the collection consists of citations to journal articles (more than 825,000 records), and a smaller portion consists of non-journal materials (more than 725,000 records). The non-journal materials are frequently called gray literature, materials that are not easy to find and are not produced by commercial publishers. In ERIC, the gray literature consists of research syntheses, dissertations, conference proceedings, and such selected papers as keynote speeches, technical reports, policy papers, literature reviews, bibliographies, congressional hearings and reports, reports on federal and state standards, testing and regulations, U.S. Department of Education reports (such as those produced by the department's What Works Clearinghouse and the National Center for Education Statistics), and working papers for established research and policy organizations.

The ERIC selection policy was recently revised and can be found at http://eric.ed.gov/?selection. The list of journals approved for indexing can be found at http://eric.ed.gov/?journals, and the list of non-journals approved for indexing can be found at http://eric.ed.gov/?nonjournals.

To facilitate electronic access to more archived materials, ERIC launched a microfiche digitization project in 2006; this project was concluded in 2009. The project scope was to digitize and archive microfiche full-text documents containing an estimated 43 million pages and to provide copyright due diligence by seeking permission from the copyright holders to make the electronic version available to users.

Approximately 340,000 full-text documents, indexed 1966–1992, were converted from microfiche to digital image files, and more than 65 percent of these documents were added to the ERIC digital library.

In 2010 ERIC established a partnership with ProQuest to begin indexing education-related doctoral dissertations from 700 academic institutions worldwide. More than 17,900 recent records from the ProQuest Dissertations and Thesis Database have been added to the ERIC collection.

ERIC Website

In August 2013 ERIC released a new website to provide an improved level of service to the community at a reduced cost to taxpayers. The new home page has a light visual design that emphasizes ERIC's most crucial features—Search and Thesaurus. The search feature is fast, robust, and fully comparable to widely used commercial search products. Additionally, the ERIC Thesaurus is integrated with ERIC Search, increasing its ease of use. Easy-to-find limiters allow searchers to retrieve only records with full text in ERIC and/or only peer-reviewed materials. The goal of the website is to make its use easier and more productive for novice users and skilled searchers alike. New functionality is being added on an ongoing basis, and there are plans for new support tools designed especially for practitioners and new ERIC users.

Automated systems for acquisition and processing help to reduce the total time required to produce a database record, and most records are processed in fewer than 30 days. New content is added to the ERIC database every day, and ERIC publishes approximately 4,000 new records to the ERIC digital library each month. New updates to the database will be available to download at eric.ed.gov/download.

The website also provides links to find ERIC on Facebook and Twitter. This feature provides frequent news updates, links, and downloadable materials, with the goal of broadening ERIC outreach.

ERIC Access

Use of ERIC continues to grow. In addition to the government-sponsored website at http://www.eric.ed.gov, ERIC is carried by search engines including Google and Google Scholar, MSN, and Yahoo!, as well as by commercial database providers including EBSCO, OCLC, OVID, ProQuest, SilverPlatter, and Dialog. ERIC is also available through statewide networks in Ohio, Texas, Kentucky, and North Carolina.

The ERIC digital library can be reached toll-free by telephone in the United States, Canada, and Puerto Rico at 800-LET-ERIC (800-538-3742), Monday through Friday, 9 A.M. to 7 P.M. eastern time. Questions can also be transmitted via the message box on the "Contact Us" page on the ERIC website.

National Association and Organization Reports

American Library Association

50 E. Huron St., Chicago, IL 60611
800-545-2433
World Wide Web http://www.ala.org

Courtney L. Young
President

The American Library Association (ALA)—the oldest, largest, and most influential library association in the world—was founded in 1876 in Philadelphia and later chartered in the Commonwealth of Massachusetts. ALA has approximately 55,300 members, including librarians, library trustees, and other interested people from every state and many nations. The association serves public, state, school, and academic libraries, as well as special libraries for people working in government, commerce and industry, the arts, and the armed services or in hospitals, prisons, and other institutions.

ALA's mission is "to provide leadership for the development, promotion, and improvement of library and information services and the profession of librarianship in order to enhance learning and ensure access to information for all."

ALA is governed by an elected council, which is its policy making body, and an executive board, which acts for the council in the administration of established policies and programs. In this context, the executive board is the body that manages the affairs of the association, delegating management of its day-to-day operation to the executive director. ALA also has 37 standing committees, designated as committees of the association or of the council. ALA operations are directed by the executive director and implemented by staff through a structure of programmatic offices and support units.

ALA is home to 11 membership divisions, each focused on a type of library or library function. They are the American Association of School Librarians (AASL), the Association for Library Collections and Technical Services (ALCTS), the Association for Library Service to Children (ALSC), the Association of College and Research Libraries (ACRL), the Association of Specialized and Cooperative Library Agencies (ASCLA), the Library and Information Technology Association (LITA), the Library Leadership and Management Association (LLAMA), the Public Library Association (PLA), the Reference and User Services Association (RUSA), United for Libraries, and the Young Adult Library Services Association (YALSA).

ALA also hosts 20 round tables for members who share interests that lie outside the scope of any of the divisions. A network of affiliates, chapters, and other organizations enables ALA to reach a broad audience.

Key action areas include diversity, equitable access to information and library services, education and lifelong learning, intellectual freedom, advocacy for libraries and the profession, literacy, transforming libraries, and organizational excellence.

ALA offices address the broad interests and issues of concern to ALA members; they track issues and provide information, services, and products for members and the general public. Current ALA offices are the Chapter Relations Office (CRO), the Development Office, the Governance Office, the International Relations Office (IRO), the Office for Accreditation, the Office of Government Relations (OGR), the Office for Human Resource Development and Recruitment (HRDR), the Office for Information Technology Policy (OITP), the Office for Intellectual Freedom (OIF), the Office for Library Advocacy (OLA), the Office for Diversity, Literacy, and Outreach Services (ODLOS), the Office for Research and Statistics (ORS), the Public Information Office (PIO), the Public Programs Office (PPO), and the Washington Office.

ALA's headquarters is in Chicago. OGR and OITP are located at ALA's Washington Office, and United for Libraries is located in Philadelphia. ALA also has an editorial office for *Choice,* a review journal for academic libraries, in Middletown, Connecticut.

ALA is a 501(c)(3) charitable and educational organization.

Leadership and Strategic Planning

Courtney L. Young, head librarian at Penn State Greater Allegheny, was inaugurated as ALA president at the 2014 Annual Conference in Las Vegas.

Young's presidency has focused on advocacy and outreach and the value of membership as demonstrated through diversity, career development, and engagement. Young encouraged all librarians to become advocates and to commit to spending an hour every week on library advocacy. She also focused on diversity as an essential value for the profession, and partnered with ALA chapters to provide training for a national cohort of 25 librarians from a cross-section of libraries to become certified career development facilitators.

Sari Feldman, executive director of the Cuyahoga County Public Library, Parma, Ohio, became ALA president-elect in the 2014 election and will be inaugurated as ALA president at the 2015 Annual Conference in San Francisco.

Four new executive board members were elected by the council in a vote at the 2014 ALA Midwinter Meeting. Peter D. Hepburn, Gina A. Persichini, and Gail A. Schlachter are each serving three-year terms that will conclude in June 2017. Mike L. Marlin was also elected to a five-month term (January 28 through July 1, 2014) on the executive board to complete the unexpired term of Sylvia K. Norton.

In a planning retreat at the 2014 Midwinter Meeting, the executive board identified three areas of strategic direction to guide the association into the future: advocacy, information policy, and professional and leadership development. Throughout 2014 in-person and virtual forums provided the broadest possible opportunity for member groups to contribute to the vision, assumptions, goals, strategies, and objectives in each of the three strategic directions. Draft plans will be available for comment, and the plan will go to council for approval at the 2015 Annual Conference.

Highlights of the Year

Washington, D.C., Advocacy

ALA continued to work closely and aggressively in tandem with partners in several coalitions to reform the multiple statutes that provide the government with various forms of surveillance and investigatory authority. In June 2014 ALA joined more than 30 other organizations concerned with civil liberties and privacy in writing to key members of the Senate to support the modification of the USA Freedom Act so that it ends the "bulk collection" of telephone business records and builds transparency and additional oversight into court-approved surveillance activities.

In April 2014 ALA leaders participated in "Libraries and Broadband: Urgency and Impact," a public hearing hosted by the Institute of Museum and Library Services (IMLS) that explored the need for high-speed broadband in American libraries.

ALA's Washington Office launched "Libraries Matter," a series of videos showcasing the ways in which libraries use federal funding to support early literacy, high-speed Internet access, small business owners, and immigrants. Library champions were urged to send the videos to policymakers before or after their scheduled advocacy meetings as part of National Library Legislative Day in early May, when hundreds of library supporters met with their members of Congress to advocate for library funding. On May 6 ALA hosted "Responding to the Second Digital Divide," a National Press Club briefing that explored the ways in which governments, schools, and communities can better support libraries in bridging the growing skills-based digital divide.

In July President Barack Obama signed the Workforce Innovation and Opportunity Act, a law that will open access to federal funding support to public libraries for effective job training and job search programs.

In December the Federal Communications Commission (FCC) approved a landmark E-rate modernization order to address the broadband capacity gap facing many public libraries and schools. The FCC vote confirmed that it will add an additional $1.5 billion to the yearly program for libraries and schools. OITP staff served as the lead library advocates on behalf of libraries.

In February 2015 FCC voted to assert the strongest possible open Internet protections—banning paid prioritization and the blocking of lawful content and services. ALA, a longtime network neutrality advocate, applauded this step forward in ensuring a fair and open Internet.

Declaration for the Right to Libraries

The Declaration for the Right to Libraries was the cornerstone document of 2013–2014 ALA President Barbara Stripling's presidential initiative, Libraries Change Lives. The declaration serves as a strong public statement about the value of libraries for individuals, communities, and the nation. During Stripling's presidency and continuing into Young's presidency, more than 100,000 people signed the declaration, either virtually or during in-person signing events.

Creating the Future

With funding from IMLS, ALA established a Center for the Future of Libraries in April 2014. The center will provide library planners and community leaders with information resources and tools that will help them better understand the trends reshaping their libraries and communities and help them incorporate foresight into their planning processes.

Eighty librarians and representatives of organizations that work with libraries met at the Library of Congress on May 2 and 3, 2014, for the ALA Summit on the Future of Libraries. Inspired by five nationally recognized speakers and their own table discussions, participants engaged in wide-ranging conversations about the trends in society that libraries will have to address and how librarians might prepare, respond, and, in fact, lead libraries and their communities into that future.

Focus on School Libraries and Librarians

In March 2014, as the spring budget season arrived, ALA began to see a rise in the requests for assistance from school libraries facing budget cuts and loss of positions. In response to multiple school library crises, OLA led an ALA crisis team and assisted Stripling and AASL President Gail Dickinson in sending letters to decision-makers. OLA also published "School Libraries Make the Difference," on I Love Libraries, ALA's library website for the public. Written specifically with parents in mind, it focuses on the importance of high-quality school libraries and certified school librarians for student success at all education levels. Created in consultation with AASL, this resource complements AASL's "School Libraries Transform Learning," a digital supplement produced by *American Libraries* magazine.

AASL released two new video public service announcements (PSAs) featuring Jeff Kinney, bestselling author of the Diary of a Wimpy Kid series. Kinney was the national spokesperson for the 2014 observance of School Library Month, and in the PSAs he encouraged viewers to "celebrate how school libraries change lives." Also during School Library Month, Stripling wrote two op-eds that passionately made the case for the value of libraries. The op-eds appeared in the April/May edition of *Our Children,* a publication of the National PTA, and in the *Huffington Post.*

Fifty research scholars from across the nation gathered in Chicago to participate in AASL's IMLS-funded research summit. Focused on setting an agenda for future school library research, the summit, "Causality: School Libraries and Student Success (CLASS)," took place April 11–12, 2014. The researchers worked to create a national focus and agenda on causal research that can provide empirical evidence that school libraries make positive contributions to student achievement. A white paper from the summit was published in May 2014.

AASL challenged leaders in all fields to bring about an evolution in student learning with its adoption of a new mission statement and strategic plan. During the 2014 ALA Annual Conference, the AASL Board of Directors voted unanimously to approve the mission statement: "The American Association of School Librarians empowers leaders to transform teaching and learning."

Internet Over-Filtering in Schools and Libraries

Schools and libraries nationwide are routinely filtering Internet content far more than the Children's Internet Protection Act (CIPA) requires, according to *Fencing Out Knowledge: Impacts of the Children's Internet Protection Act 10 Years Later,* a report released by OITP and OIF. The report was based on a year-long study that included a two-day symposium during the summer of 2013 and other research.

Task Force on Equity, Diversity, and Inclusion

The ALA Task Force on Equity, Diversity, and Inclusion was created in spring 2014 with a charge to develop a plan and strategic actions to build more equity, diversity, and inclusion among ALA members, the field of librarianship, and communities. At the 2015 Midwinter Meeting, participants came together for lively small-group discussions on these issues.

Trends in Digital Content

In May 2014 ALA's *American Libraries* magazine released "Digital Discoveries," a new digital supplement in which library visionaries and experts discussed trends in digital content technology and the current state of library e-book lending. Developed by ALA's Digital Content Working Group (DCWG), the digital supplement examined the ways in which public and school libraries are defining their roles in the evolving digital publishing environment. The digital supplement also detailed ALA's progress in advocating for equitable access to e-books.

In December an ALA leadership delegation met with executives of New York-based publishers to discuss library e-book issues. The delegation was led by ALA President Young and the co-chairs of DCWG, Carolyn Anthony and Erika Linke. Sari Feldman, Barbara Stripling, ALA Executive Director Keith Michael Fiels, and OIPT Director Alan S. Inouye also participated in the delegation. Also in December, *Publishers Weekly* lauded former DCWG co-chairs Sari Feldman and Robert Wolven in the publication's annual "Publishing People of 2014" for their role in advocating for fair library e-book lending practices.

In January 2015 OITP released "Progress in the Making: 3D Printing Policy Considerations Through the Library Lens," a report that encourages libraries to take a proactive role in developing institutional policies that address the social, technological, and political complexities that will result from the rise of 3D printing. The report also examines various intellectual freedom issues raised by 3D printing, with OIF offering guidance to library professionals seeking to craft acceptable use policies in accord with library values.

Leadership Development

The Emerging Leaders program enables newer librarians to participate in problem-solving work groups, network with peers, gain insight into ALA structure, and have an opportunity to serve the overall profession in a leadership capacity.

There were 56 participants in 2014; nearly 700 people have participated in the program since it began as an initiative of ALA Past President Leslie Burger in 2007.

In August 36 mid-career librarians were selected from a highly competitive pool to participate in the 2014 Leadership Institute, ALA's four-day immersive leadership development program for future library leaders. The institute is designed to help participants develop and practice leadership skills in areas critical to the future of the libraries and allow them to form a vibrant learning community and network. With content based on real world cases and nuanced situations, participants explored topics relating to the challenges and possibilities of leadership in a future that may be marked by turbulence and ambiguity.

Diversity in Library Programs and Material Collections for Children

In April 2014 ALSC released a white paper titled *The Importance of Diversity in Library Programs and Material Collections for Children,* written for ALSC by Jamie Campbell Naidoo. The paper explores the critical role libraries play in helping children make cross-cultural connections and develop skills necessary to function successfully in a culturally pluralistic society.

PLA Strategic Plan

At the 2014 ALA Annual Conference, the PLA Board of Directors approved an updated three-year strategic plan building on PLA's successes to date, regarding two strategic goal areas in particular—Advocacy and Awareness, and Leadership and Transformation. The aim of the planning process is to guide and create clarity on how PLA should invest its resources to meet the future needs of its members and other stakeholders.

Teen Services

In January 2014 YALSA released "The Future of Library Services for and with Teens: A Call to Action," a report recommending ways in which libraries can evolve in order to better meet the needs of 21st century teens.

With funding from the Dollar General Literacy Foundation, YALSA released a free Teen Book Finder app for Apple and Android platforms. The app features thousands of titles of recommended reading and offers a "find it" feature so that users can identify libraries holding the title in their collections.

Skype Consulting Service

United for Libraries instituted a Skype consulting service in 2014. Libraries needing support for their boards or friends groups can arrange for a one-hour interactive session via Skype with appropriate experts.

Banned Books Week

Libraries, schools, and bookstores across the country celebrated the freedom to read during Banned Books Week 2014 by hosting special events and exhibits. ALA partnered with Sage Publications to host a free webinar to discuss efforts to "un-ban" books. Sage and OIF also hosted a Banned Books Virtual Read-Out Booth at the ALA Annual Conference. Videos from that event were posted on the Banned Books Week YouTube channel.

Choose Privacy Week

Choose Privacy Week 2014 featured a webinar and guest bloggers discussing privacy topics ranging from surveillance to the art of developing library privacy policies. The webinar introduced the revised ALA privacy toolkit and provided an introduction to key online privacy concepts to help librarians act as better stewards of patron privacy as well as their own.

Freedom to Read

In spring 2014 ALA and the Freedom to Read Foundation (FTRF) joined a broad coalition of bookstores and other organizations in filing a friend-of-the-court brief in *Susan B. Anthony List* v. *Driehaus*. An adverse decision in this case could have negatively affected the right to challenge laws that infringe on the First Amendment prior to their enforcement. On June 16, 2014, the Supreme Court issued its opinion, holding in a unanimous 9–0 ruling that "a credible threat of enforcement" is sufficient to establish standing in cases with First Amendment implications. The case represents an important victory for ALA, FTRF, and other organizations that protect the right of free expression, freedom of the press, and the right to receive information by filing pre-enforcement challenges to statutes that appear to violate the First Amendment.

November marked the 45th anniversary of FTRF, and to commemorate this milestone there was an online celebration featuring FTRF President Julius C. Jefferson, Jr. and others discussing the history and future of the foundation. The event launched a year-long series of online and in-person events to help build the foundation's profile and resources.

Preservation Week

Hundreds of libraries offered special events during Preservation Week 2014. More than 1,500 individuals and libraries participated in ALCTS-produced webinars on low-cost personal archiving and preserving scrapbooks. Among partners for Preservation Week 2014 were the Library of Congress, Society of American Archivists, American Institute for Conservation, and Heritage Preservation.

Notable Anniversaries

The Coretta Scott King Book Awards marked 45 years of excellence in children's literature with a program at the 2014 Annual Conference. Publisher and author Andrea Davis Pinkney spoke with previous award and honor authors and illustrators at "Let Our Rejoicing Rise: 45 Years of the Coretta Scott King Book Awards."

The Library Bill of Rights, the library profession's major policy document on intellectual freedom, celebrated its 75th anniversary in 2014.

ACRL marked its 75th anniversary during 2014, and its review publication *Choice* magazine celebrated its 50th.

Programs and Partners

Campaign for America's Libraries

The Campaign for America's Libraries focused in 2014 on promoting the value to the public of libraries and librarians. The theme of 2014 National Library Week was "Lives change @ your library." Judy Blume served as honorary chair. Blume is the author of 28 books published in 32 languages and is a longtime advocate of intellectual freedom. She has worked closely with the National Coalition Against Censorship as well as OIF to protect the freedom to read.

Legendary comic book creator Stan Lee served as honorary chair of Library Card Sign-up Month in September. "Having a library card, it's like having a key to all the information in the world," Lee said. "When you have a library card you can read anything about anything, and I have found that whatever you read . . . it increases your fund of knowledge. So a library card is the 'Open Sesame' to all the knowledge in the world."

Ten librarians from public, school, and academic libraries were selected as recipients of the Carnegie Corporation/*New York Times* I Love My Librarian Award. The 2014 recipients were selected for the role they play in transforming lives through education. As part of the nominating process, more than 1,000 library patrons submitted detailed stories about how a librarian had a positive impact on their communities and lives. Each recipient received a $5,000 award at the December 2 ceremony and reception in New York City, hosted by the *New York Times*.

National Bookmobile Day

The fifth annual celebration of National Bookmobile Day was held on April 16, 2014. The observance is a collaborative effort between ALA, the Association of Bookmobile and Outreach Services, and the Association for Rural and Small Libraries. Downloadable publicity materials were made available free of charge from the online resource center (http://www.ala.org/bookmobiles) to provide libraries and bookmobile agencies with the tools to host their own National Bookmobile Day celebrations. The "Why We Love Our Bookmobile" virtual celebration gave libraries the opportunity to submit videos highlighting their services and Bookmobile Day celebrations.

American Dream Starts @ your library

In Spring 2014 the Dollar General Literacy Foundation renewed its commitment to "The American Dream Starts @ your library," a literacy initiative for adult English-language learners and their families, by providing a fourth round of funding to ALA to build on the project's success. A total of 22 libraries in 15 states were selected to receive one-time grants up to $15,000 to add or expand literacy services. This funding will help libraries build print and digital ESL collections, increase computer access, train tutors, hold writing classes, facilitate GED and citizenship training, and heighten public awareness of library services. The selected fourth-round American Dream libraries join a cohort of 144 previously funded programs.

Relief for School Libraries Affected by Disaster

The Dollar General Literacy Foundation renewed its commitment to AASL and school libraries by dedicating an additional $258,000 in grants to AASL's "Beyond Words: The Dollar General School Library Relief Fund." This donation brings the foundation's support of rebuilding school libraries affected by disaster to a total of $1.8 million. The Beyond Words grant program supports public school libraries nationwide that have suffered material losses because of a major natural disaster or acts of terrorism.

Everyone Reads @ your library

ALSC and YALSA received grant support from the Dollar General Literacy Foundation for the "Everyone Reads @ your library" initiative. ALSC used grant funds to continue to support the Día de los Niños/Día de los Libros program. YALSA offered $1,000 grants to libraries for summer reading resources and summer intern initiatives.

Money Smart Week @ your library

A total of 700 libraries in 48 states participated during April 2014 in the fourth year of "Money Smart Week @ your library," an ALA/Federal Reserve Bank of Chicago partnership to provide financial education programming for all ages. Thanks to emphasis on financial education by ACRL President Trevor A. Dawes, more than 50 academic libraries collaborated with other departments within their institutions to help students improve their financial literacy.

Public Programming

Grants from PPO enable libraries of all types, sizes, and budgets to boost their offerings and infuse their communities with new ideas. In 2014 PPO brought seven programs and exhibitions to more than 1,000 libraries. Four of the programs were "Muslim Journeys," a National Endowment for the Humanities-supported initiative that highlights the people, places, histories, beliefs, practices, and cultures of Muslims; "Discover Earth: A Century of Change," an interactive multimedia exhibition funded by the National Science Foundation that shows how the global environment changes and is changed by local environments; "StoryCorps @ your library," a two-year program funded by IMLS that provides equipment, training, and resources for public libraries to take part in the StoryCorps oral history project; and "Dust, Drought, and Dreams Gone Dry," a traveling exhibition exploring the causes and consequences of the Dust Bowl through oral histories, essays, letters, and photographs, funded in part by the National Endowment for the Humanities.

Guadalajara International Book Fair Program

One hundred and twenty ALA members from 25 states and the District of Columbia took advantage of the 15th year of the ALA Free Pass Program to travel to Mexico for the 2014 Guadalajara Book Fair to review and purchase Spanish-language materials. The group included many first-timers to the book fair, including five library students from Dominican University interested in pursuing careers in libraries with Spanish-speaking populations.

Adult Literacy Through Libraries

ODLOS worked closely with partners at ProLiteracy to advance the Adult Literacy Through Libraries Action Agenda, released in early 2014, as a product of work funded by IMLS and led by ODLOS, ProLiteracy, and the Onondaga County (New York) Public Library. The action agenda is a series of recommendations, organized into priority areas with specific outcomes and concrete action steps, to assist libraries in providing literacy and basic skills services to adult learners.

Conferences and Workshops

2014 Annual Conference

The 2014 ALA Annual Conference in Las Vegas brought 18,626 attendees and exhibitors together in the shared endeavor of "Transforming Our Libraries, Ourselves." The schedule included more than 2,700 programs, sessions, and events.

At the President's Program, 2014 President Barbara Stripling interviewed two-time Newbery Medal winner and Margaret A. Edwards Award winner Lois Lowry, along with actor Jeff Bridges, star of the movie based on Lowry's *The Giver.* The closing general session featured B. J. Novak, actor and author of *The Book With No Pictures,* talking about the power of words.

The newly formed IMLS-supported ALA Center for the Future of Libraries launched its work as an association-wide incubator for experimentation. Stripling hosted a related panel to stimulate thinking about the future and the place libraries will have in it.

Topics high on the conference agenda included e-book lending and usability, digital content, community engagement, the impact and potential of the newest technologies, digital literacy, the state of the school library, innovative outreach, privacy and surveillance, and best practices on a wide range of library-related concerns. Some content was organized around the three strategic directions on which ALA plans to focus in the coming years: advocacy, information policy, and professional and leadership development. Policy sessions hosted by the ALA Washington Office explored net neutrality, copyright trends, e-book access, e-government services, and surveillance.

Libraries Transforming Communities, a two-year ALA initiative that seeks to strengthen libraries' roles as core community leaders and change agents by developing and distributing tools and support for library professionals, offered four related "Turning Outward to Lead Change in Your Community" training sessions.

Sharjah International Book Fair/ALA Library Conference

ALA's largest-ever international professional development event was held in November 2014 in Sharjah, United Arab Emirates, where more than 600 librarians from 20 countries gathered at the Sharjah International Book Fair (SIBF) for the first two-day SIBF/ALA Library Conference. ALA President Courtney Young's opening keynote address on the transformation of libraries was followed by 15 concurrent sessions presented by an international roster of experts.

2015 Midwinter Meeting

A total of 10,637 attendees crowded more than 1,800 meetings, events, and social gatherings that offered lively conversations, updates, productive problem-solving, and networking during the 2015 ALA Midwinter Meeting in Chicago.

"News You Can Use" offered 38 sessions presenting the latest in library-related policy, research, statistics, legislation, technology, and trend-monitoring. Sessions included the Washington Office update featuring Sen. Richard Durbin (D-Ill.) and others addressing the importance of advocating for libraries to safeguard government funding.

Ferguson, Missouri, Library Director Scott Bonner spoke, after a standing ovation, to a packed room about the often-difficult judgment calls made during the violent protests that had wracked his city a few months earlier.

Grants and Contributions

Libraries Transforming Communities

The Bill and Melinda Gates Foundation awarded ALA a grant of $1.5 million to fund a two-year project, Libraries Transforming Communities. The project will develop and distribute new tools, resources, and support for librarians to engage with their communities in new ways; strengthen librarians as community leaders and change agents; and strengthen ALA's capacity as a lead library-support entity. During the grant period, ALA will work with the Harwood Institute for Public Innovation to provide training opportunities and learning resources. A Public Innovators cohort representing ten libraries nationwide was selected for an intensive 18-month training and coaching experience.

Policy Revolution! Initiative for Libraries

OITP began work on a national public policy agenda and action plan for U.S. libraries with support from a grant from the Gates Foundation. Nearly $1 million in funding over three years will enable ALA to increase library visibility and build capacity for sustained action on the national level. The three-year initiative includes three major components: establishing policy priorities, engaging decision makers and influencers to advance policy goals, and upgrading ALA policy advocacy practice and capabilities for long-term sustainability.

Impact of Public Programming

PPO received an IMLS National Forum research planning grant for "Assessing the National Impact of Library Public Programs." The project supported the development of a comprehensive research agenda and five-year implementation plan to understand and document the characteristics, audiences, outcomes, and value of public programming in libraries at a national level. A comprehensive research agenda was developed and released as a white paper.

Assessment in Action

ACRL selected 100 teams from higher education institutions to participate in the second year of "Assessment in Action: Academic Libraries and Student Success" (AiA), made possible by a grant from IMLS. AiA employs a blended learning environment and a peer-to-peer community of practice over the course of the 14-month program, which runs from April 2014 to June 2015. Undertaken by ACRL in partnership with the Association for Institutional Research and the Association of Public and Land-grant Universities, the program is a cornerstone of ACRL's Value of Academic Libraries initiative.

Knowledge Alliance Recruitment Initiative

The Knowledge Alliance recruitment initiative, developed with support from IMLS, deployed 35 racially and ethnically diverse early-career librarians to participate in career and graduate education fairs targeting students from under-represented groups. The librarians offer support and guidance to engage potential library professionals at every step of their journey, from initial interest to selecting a graduate program and to pursuing professional opportunities.

Public Library Training

PLA received a 2014 Laura Bush 21st Century Librarian Program Grant for the project "Navigating Change, Building Community: Outward-Focused Public Library Leadership Training." The three-year grant will allow PLA to further refine and implement the PLA Leadership Academy (originally presented in 2012) and measure its impact on participants and their libraries. In addition, PLA will convene a meeting of leadership training providers to share evaluation results and best practices and further raise awareness and understanding of the PLA leadership model.

Performance Measures for Libraries

PLA was awarded a grant of $2.9 million from the Gates Foundation for the development of performance outcome measures. This grant will enable PLA to accelerate development of its performance measurement project and build an active community of informed users. Surveys will be created for libraries to collect patron outcomes. Related training and support tools will guide libraries in using outcome data for advocacy, planning, and decision making. By collecting outcomes, participating libraries will be able to demonstrate the difference they make in the lives of patrons and the vital role they play in communities.

Digital Inclusion Study

Results from the 2014 Digital Inclusion Study found that nearly 100 percent of U.S. public libraries offer workforce development training programs, online job resources, and technology skills training. Overall, libraries report technology improvements—including nearly ubiquitous public wifi, growing mobile resources, and a leap in e-book access—but the study also documented digital differences among states and an urban/rural divide. The study is funded by IMLS and is conducted by ORS and the Information Policy and Access Center at the University of

Maryland–College Park. Grant partners include OITP and the International City/ County Management Association.

Financial Literacy Education

RUSA, with the support of an IMLS grant, prepared "Financial Literacy Education in Libraries: Guidelines and Best Practices for Service." These guidelines and best practices will facilitate the provision of financial literacy education in libraries nationwide. A webinar to launch the guidelines was held in September and is archived and available on the ALA website.

Publishing

ALA Editions / ALA Neal-Schuman

The ALA Editions publishing strategy focuses on professional development titles and the Neal-Schuman publishing strategy on library education. Together the two imprints published 68 titles in fiscal year (FY) 2014. Lead titles on the professional development side included Robert Maxwell's *Handbook for RDA* and *Customer-Based Collection Development,* edited by Karl Bridges. Lead titles on the library education side included the third edition of Peggy Johnson's *Fundamentals of Collection Development and Management* and *Rare Books and Special Collections* by Sidney Berger.

ALA TechSource

ALA TechSource, which continues to be the source for two enduring periodicals, *Library Technology Reports* and *Smart Libraries Newsletter,* also develops and presents online content for professional development through webinars and e-courses. It produces both original and re-purposed content (from ALA Editions and Neal-Schuman authors) for its growing list of programs. It produces the "AL Live" series for *American Libraries* magazine. AL Live streams live interviews and panel discussions that are underwritten by industry sponsors and are free of charge to attendees. These live events can be viewed in real time and allow viewers to interact with hosts and expert panelists via active live chat. Popular sessions have included such topics as "RDA for Music," "Dynamic One-Shot Library Instruction," and "Re-thinking Readers Advisory."

RDA: Resource Description and Access

RDA subscriptions increased from 2,668 in FY 2013 to 2,879 in FY 2014, an 8 percent rise. The pricing model was modified to allow lower price points for smaller institutions. Germany has adopted RDA as its national cataloging standard. French and German translations are in the RDA Toolkit. Mandarin, Spanish, and Swedish translations are being made.

Training in RDA and related issues is offered by a number of sources, including regular, well-attended, and free "RDA Toolkit Essentials" webinars that introduce users to the site and offer updates. These webinars are archived on the RDA Toolkit site (http://www.rdatoolkit.org). Workshops offered by ALA TechSource continue to sell out. ALCTS runs well-attended programs, and outreach to LIS instructors and students continues to help them integrate RDA into their teaching/ learning.

ALA Graphics: Celebrities, Characters, Collaboration

Celebrities, beloved book characters, tie-ins with movies adapted from books, and event-related themes all continue to inspire ALA Graphics products and customers.

Collaborating with units across ALA to create new posters, bookmarks, and other products for library-related celebrations is a hallmark of Graphics' success every year. Projects in 2014 included National Library Week (April) and Library Card Sign-up Month (September) with PIO; Banned Books Week (September) and Choose Privacy Week (May) with OIF; Teen Read Week (October) and Teen Tech Week (March) with YALSA; School Library Month (April) with AASL; Día (April) with ALSC; and National Friends of Libraries Week (October) with United for Libraries.

Four catalogs mailed and distributed in FY 2014 introduced a host of new products. The posters feature popular book characters, READ celebrities, TV series, and book-to-movie-inspired images, many with accompanying bookmarks.

Booklist Publications

Booklist Publications includes *Booklist* magazine, *Booklist Online, Book Links* magazine, and (new in FY 2014) the Booklist Reader, a website hosting a compendium of electronic newsletters and blogs and news on the publishing industry of interest to librarians.

Subscriptions to the magazine now include access to *Booklist Online*. The number of popular electronic newsletters and blogs continues to grow. In conjunction with RUSA, *Booklist* cosponsors the Andrew Carnegie Medal for Excellence in Fiction and Nonfiction. Programming at the ALA Annual Conference also continues to be robust. Along with the long-standing Books for Youth Forum and Reference Books program, the conference now includes the Booklist Author Forum in conjunction with the Exhibitor's Round Table.

The current multi-platform suite of 12 products (double the number produced in 2006) includes the 22 print issues of *Booklist* and four of *Book Links*; *Booklist Online*; seven revenue-generating e-newsletters (some with exclusive sponsorships, some selling advertising on an issue-by-issue basis); *Booklist* webinars (sponsor-supported online programs, free to registrants); and Booklist Delivers (an e-blast service delivering sponsors' HTML promotions).

Booklist webinars have continued to be a success, with more than 60,000 registrants (averaging 400 for each program) for the 40 programs moderated by *Booklist* editors and guests. Registrants who are unable to attend can access archived recordings. In post-webinar surveys, 91.2 percent of attendees said the programs were useful.

American Libraries

American Libraries magazine offered more content in more channels during FY 2014 and increased its social media presence. It has extended its evolution from a monthly print magazine to serving news and other information daily through a suite of products that includes print and digital options.

AmericanLibrariesMagazine.org, now part of the ALA website, is developing a fresh look to continue to attract and keep reader and advertiser interest. On the financial front, *American Libraries* exceeded its annual revenue budget by more than $100,000 and reduced its subscription allocation by $148,000. Social media engagement and outreach has exceeded 24,000 Twitter followers and 5,000 Facebook fans. On Pinterest, *American Libraries* added two boards, and now has 24 boards with more than 3,000 pins.

The publishing calendar includes six print issues, one digital issue, and six digital supplements, which included coverage of school libraries, the state of American Libraries, e-content, and e-learning. *American Libraries* also offers AL Live, an interactive, streaming, sponsored webinar produced in conjunction with ALA TechSource.

After some nine years in its current format, the digital newsletter AL Direct was slowing down in terms of online analytics and advertiser support. Research supported the decision to shorten the number of entries, increase its frequency, convert it to a responsive design that would allow it to reformat for mobile devices, and create an app to allow access on mobile devices. Both open rates and ad click rates went back up to levels not seen since the advent of the publication.

Freedom of Information Awards

During the 16th Annual Freedom of Information Day in Washington, D.C., ALA awarded the James Madison Award to President Obama's Review Group on Intelligence and Communications Technologies, the body of intelligence and legal experts tasked with assessing the United States' surveillance practices. The award honors, celebrates, and recognizes groups and individuals who have championed public access to government information.

ALA awarded the grassroots advocacy Eileen Cooke Award to the Open Government Project of the American Civil Liberties Union of New Jersey.

American Booksellers Association

333 Westchester Ave., White Plains, NY 10604
914-406-7500
World Wide Web http://www.bookweb.org

Founded in 1900, the American Booksellers Association (ABA) is a national not-for-profit trade organization that works to help independently owned bookstores grow and succeed.

ABA's core members are key participants in their communities' local economy and culture. To assist them, ABA creates relevant programs; provides education, information, business products, and services; and engages in public policy and industry advocacy. It is governed by a volunteer board of ten booksellers, and actively supports and defends free speech.

At the end of 2014 ABA members reported another year of growth in overall business, capped by strong holiday sales. The national resurgence in independent stores continued, with numerous new stores opening and a new generation coming into the business as both owner/managers and frontline booksellers.

During the year ABA welcomed 59 independent bookstores that opened in 25 states, the District of Columbia, and the U.S. Virgin Islands. This was the largest number of new stores joining ABA in a single year since the start of the recession in 2008. The new stores include nine branches or satellites of existing businesses and five stores selling primarily used books. A total of 29 established ABA member businesses were bought by new owners.

ABA members reported healthy sales in 2014 and an equally encouraging start to 2015. Small Business Saturday, November 29, launched a successful national holiday bookselling season, boosted by "buy local" campaigns and widespread promotional media coverage.

ABA reported that unit sales of books maintained the growth seen over the past few years, based on the figures provided by the approximately 500 stores reporting to the weekly Indie Bestsellers List. In addition, based on reports from the ABA board and Booksellers Advisory Council, average total bookstore sales for December were up more than 9 percent over 2013, and annual sales more than 6 percent.

In a January 2015 letter to the association membership, ABA President Steve Bercu wrote, "This great [holiday] season kicked off with 'Indies First on Small Business Saturday' and just kept going. After our many years of hard work, customers are realizing the importance of shopping at locally owned stores. Of course, the widespread media coverage touting local bookstores and other local businesses as the places to be didn't hurt."

Indies First on Small Business Saturday was a strong day for independent bookstores for the second year in a row. The event was marked by solid sales, increased customer traffic in stores, and a festive national partnership between authors and booksellers.

In more than 420 bookstores nationwide, 1,200-plus authors volunteered as booksellers for a day, handselling their favorite titles, gift wrapping purchases, and demonstrating their commitment to the indie bookstore channel as a key to discovering new writers.

Throughout the day, store events were shared on social media, and, overall, the #indiesfirst hashtag produced more than 56 million impressions.

Unit sales of books in independent bookstores for the week rose 4.6 percent over 2013, an increase that outpaced other independent businesses. And while average consumer spending in dollars was down overall from the previous year, American Express reported that Small Business Saturday spending with independent businesses and restaurants increased by 2.1 percent over 2013.

The sales gains among independent booksellers were in clear contrast to national retail numbers; total retail spending fell 11 percent for Thanksgiving weekend, according to the National Retail Federation.

Survey Highlights Growth

According to the results of the 2015 Independent Business Survey, ABA member bookstores and other independent businesses experienced strong sales growth during 2014. The eighth annual survey, conducted by the Institute for Local Self-Reliance in partnership with Advocates for Independent Business, gathered data from more than 3,000 locally owned businesses.

Respondents reported brisk sales during the year, with revenue growing 8.1 percent on average, up from a growth rate of 5.3 percent in 2013. Independent retailers, which made up about half the sample, saw revenue increase by 5.1 percent in 2014, versus 2.3 percent in 2013. Holiday sales at local stores also grew by an average of 4.8 percent, beating the performance of many national chains and coming in well ahead of the 0.9 percent decline in December retail sales reported by the U.S. Department of Commerce.

The survey results suggest that the strength of the independent sector is owed partly to an improving economy and partly to the spread of the "buy local" movement. Businesses located in cities with active Local First campaigns reported sales growth of 9.3 percent, compared with 4.9 percent for businesses located elsewhere. Survey respondents cited a wide range of direct benefits from "buy local" campaigns, with half saying the initiatives had generated new customers and 45 percent saying the projects had resulted in more support from municipal officials.

Association and Governance

The results of balloting by the bookstore members of ABA to elect three directors to serve three-year terms on the ABA Board (2014–2017) were announced in May 2014.

Elected to her first three-year term as an ABA director was Jamie Fiocco of Flyleaf Books in Chapel Hill, North Carolina. Elected to their second three-year terms on the board were John Evans of DIESEL, A Bookstore, with locations in Brentwood, Larkspur, Malibu, and Oakland, California, and Matthew Norcross of McLean & Eakin Booksellers in Petoskey, Michigan.

In keeping with a 2011 amendment to ABA's bylaws, which established two-year terms for board officers, Steve Bercu of BookPeople in Austin and Betsy Burton of The King's English Bookshop in Salt Lake City began their second years as ABA president and vice president/secretary, respectively.

Continuing on the ten-member board are Sarah Bagby of Watermark Books and Café in Wichita; Valerie Koehler of Blue Willow Bookshop in Houston; Annie Philbrick of Bank Square Books in Mystic, Connecticut; Robert Sindelar of Third Place Books in Lake Forest Park, Washington; and Jonathon Welch of Talking Leaves . . . Books in Buffalo. Leaving the board at the end of his second three-year term was Ken White of Books Inc. in San Francisco.

Book Awards

The winners of the 2014 Indies Choice Book Awards and the E. B. White Read-Aloud Awards, as voted by independent booksellers nationwide, were announced in April.

Life After Life by Kate Atkinson, published by Reagan Arthur, was judged adult fiction book of the year; the adult nonfiction book of the year was *The Boys in the Boat: Nine Americans and Their Epic Quest for Gold at the 1936 Berlin Olympics* by Daniel James Brown (Viking). Adult debut book of the year went to the novel *A Constellation of Vital Phenomena* by Anthony Marra (Hogarth), and young adult book of the year was *Eleanor and Park* by Rainbow Rowell (St. Martin's Griffin).

The winners of the E. B. White Read-Aloud Awards were: (picture book) *The Day the Crayons Quit* by Drew Daywalt, illustrated by Oliver Jeffers (Philomel); and (middle readers) *Flora and Ulysses* by Kate DiCamillo, illustrated by K. G. Campbell (Candlewick).

The Indie Champion Award went to James Patterson. The award is presented to an author or illustrator who has most impressed booksellers with a sense of the importance of independent bookstores to their communities at large and has shown the strongest personal commitment to foster and support the mission and passion of independent booksellers.

Indie booksellers choose three classic picture books each year for induction into the Picture Book Hall of Fame. The 2014 inductees were *Brown Bear, Brown Bear, What Do You See?* by Bill Martin, Jr., and Eric Carle (Holt); *Goodnight Moon* by Margaret Wise Brown, illustrated by Clement Hurd (HarperCollins); and *Stellaluna* by Janell Cannon (Houghton Mifflin Harcourt).

In September, for the fifth consecutive publishing season, two panels of booksellers chose ten debut adult titles and ten children's titles for the Indies Introduce Debut Authors and New Voices promotion. Featured winter/spring titles include fiction and nonfiction, middle grade and YA publishing between January and June 2015.

Member Education

The tenth anniversary celebration of ABA's Winter Institute, held in Asheville, North Carolina, February 8–11, 2015, drew more than 500 ABA member booksellers, 100-plus authors, and close to 20 guests from Canada, Australia, New Zealand, Sweden, and France.

The institute featured three days of featured speakers, education sessions, publisher/bookseller focus groups, and breakout sessions, and received the support of lead sponsor Ingram Content Group and a record-breaking 63 publisher sponsors.

Immediately before the institute, 25 booksellers, representing 17 established or prospective businesses, participated in an "introduction to bookselling" workshop presented by ABA and facilitated by Mark and Donna Paz Kaufman of the bookstore training group Paz & Associates. This year's class was the largest since 2009.

Topics addressed included trends in the book industry; claiming a competitive advantage in the current retail environment; the importance of choosing the right location and judging a community's ability to support an independent bookstore; and understanding the financial dynamics of retail bookselling—how much it would cost to open, what can be expected as a return on investment, and how much a new bookstore can earn.

ABA's programming regarding children's bookselling also continued to grow. The ABC Children's Group of ABA welcomed 130 booksellers from 32 states to San Antonio in April 2014 for its children's institute. Lead sponsor was Baker & Taylor.

ABA again published its annual financial survey of participating independent bookstores, the ABACUS report. Stores participating in the ABACUS project received a customized report analyzing their financial results, including comparisons with other businesses based on multiple criteria (such as sales level, store size, and community type) in addition to year-to-year trending information.

ABACUS helps participants benchmark key economic indicators and create a plan for growth and profitability. ABACUS data are used in aggregate by ABA to create education offerings for member stores.

Throughout the year ABA's e-commerce platform for member bookstores, IndieCommerce, continued the migration of several hundred stores' websites to the Drupal 7 platform. ABA staff worked with bookstores in a number of ways, including dedicated e-mail updates, twice-weekly conference calls, a series of webinars, and in-person meetings at the industry trade show BookExpo America.

Advocacy

ABA's advocacy efforts on behalf of member bookstores continued during the year. It joined the Marketplace Fairness Coalition, which includes a diverse array of trade associations and businesses of all sizes, to more effectively work with the federal government on behalf of ABA members. In addition, the Advocates for Independent Business, a coalition of independent trade associations and businesses co-founded by ABA in late 2013, worked on behalf of a federal e-fairness solution to sales tax inequities. Its initiatives included a social media campaign, #efairnessnow.

ABA created testimonial videos featuring member bookstore owners that highlighted the negative impact of current sales tax policy. And, in advance of a U.S. House of Representatives Judiciary Committee hearing on sales tax fairness, ABA coordinated local meetings between bookstore members and their members of Congress.

In addition, ABA CEO Oren Teicher and Barnes & Noble CEO Michael P. Huseby jointly wrote to Judiciary Committee Chairman Bob Goodlatte (R-Va.) in support of sales tax fairness. ABA also continued to support state efforts on behalf of e-fairness.

ABA provided its members with key information about the Affordable Care Act, such as how to claim healthcare tax credits and how to purchase insurance through exchanges.

The association also sent out updates on a class action settlement over rapidly rising Visa and MasterCard swipe fees.

In September the American Booksellers Foundation for Free Expression (ABFFE) joined five Arizona bookstores in challenging a new law making it a felony to sell books containing nude photos without the permission of the people depicted. The purported goal of the law was to suppress the posting of so-called "revenge porn" on the Internet. However, the law applies to the distribution of nude images in any medium, creating a serious threat to booksellers who sell books with such historical images as the young girl running from a napalm attack during the Vietnam War.

ABFFE continued to seek the restoration of protections for customer privacy that were eliminated by the USAPatriot Act, endorsing the latest congressional vehicle for reforms to such legislation, the USA Freedom Act.

ABFFE joined the protest over the South Carolina state legislature's effort to punish two state colleges that had assigned students books that included homosexual characters. Through its sponsorship of the Kids' Right to Read Project, ABFFE opposed efforts to ban dozens of books in schools around the country. ABFFE also sponsors Banned Books Week, the annual celebration of the freedom to read.

At the end of the year, ABFFE merged with ABA to reduce the administrative burden on its small staff and make it possible to devote more time and resources to program activities. Under its new name, American Booksellers for Free Expression (ABFE), it continues to be the bookseller's voice in the fight against censorship.

Association of Research Libraries

21 Dupont Circle N.W., Washington, DC 20036
202-296-2296, e-mail arlhq@arl.org
World Wide Web http://www.arl.org

Kaylyn Groves
Senior Writer and Editor

The Association of Research Libraries (ARL) is a nonprofit organization of 125 research libraries in the United States and Canada. ARL's mission is to influence the changing environment of scholarly communication and the public policies that affect research libraries and the diverse communities they serve. ARL pursues this mission by advancing the goals of its member research libraries, providing leadership in public and information policy to the scholarly and higher education communities, fostering the exchange of ideas and expertise, facilitating the emergence of new roles for research libraries, and shaping a future environment that leverages its interests with those of allied organizations.

ARL and its member libraries addressed a number of strategic issues in 2014. Perhaps the most important of the many milestones achieved was the completion of the first half of a Strategic Thinking and Design (ST&D) process, which developed a framework and a system of action to guide the association in the near term. During 2015 ARL is implementing the system of action—fostering efforts in collective collections, the scholarly dissemination engine, the "Libraries that Learn" series, the ARL Academy, and the Innovation Lab.

Key issue-oriented accomplishments for ARL in 2014 were in the areas of access to research, accessibility, copyright and intellectual property, diversity and leadership, federal funding, library management and assessment, net neutrality, scholarly communication, surveillance reform, and workforce transformation. Organization-oriented accomplishments included fund raising and two Membership Meetings, in addition to the ST&D work.

The following are highlights of the association's achievements in 2014. For links to additional information about these accomplishments, visit http://www.arl.org/about/arl-key-accomplishments-in-2014.

Strategic Thinking and Design

ARL spent much of 2014 actively engaging in the ST&D process that it embarked upon in mid-2013. Fueled by the desire of the ARL membership to rise to the challenges facing higher education, and enabled by grants from the Institute of Museum and Library Services (IMLS) and the Andrew W. Mellon Foundation, the association tackled this unprecedented project in order to reimagine the future of the research library and reshape its organization to help bring that future into being.

Inspired by the work of John Seely Brown, a researcher who specializes in organizational studies, and working with design consultant Ann Pendleton-Jullian, ARL's ST&D Work Group engaged more than 360 people—drawn from throughout the library community, both within ARL and beyond, and from the academic, funding, and association communities—in a technique called "worldbuilding" to develop a "system of action" for ARL to achieve its desired future. In fall 2013 and winter-spring 2014, ARL convened ten regional design meetings (singular workshops of large groups of people who offered ideas, experiences, insights, and concepts relating to the future of research libraries) and five design studios (sessions with sustained participation over time by a smaller group of people who identified, synthesized, and designed convergences coming out of the regional meetings).

In February 2014 the ARL board held a retreat during which it built upon the work of the early regional design meetings and design studios to draft a vision and system of action for ARL. That vision and system of action was tested in later design meetings in spring 2014 and was the focus for member review at the spring 2014 Membership Meeting.

Over the summer ARL developed a strategic framework, based on the vision and system of action, to guide the association for the next two to three years. ARL shared the working framework with the membership prior to the fall 2014 Membership Meeting and will publish the final framework in 2015. The framework outlines a system of action that currently consists of five initiatives for ARL to focus on for the near future, recognizing that over time new initiatives will be identified.

In early 2015 an ST&D transition team is working with the ARL committees and senior staff to develop recommendations for implementing the new framework. The team will report their preliminary recommendations to the ARL board in February 2015 and will report to the membership soon thereafter.

Issue-Oriented Accomplishments

Access to Research

In 2014 ARL—in collaboration with the Association of American Universities (AAU) and the Association of Public and Land-grant Universities (APLU)—made considerable progress in developing the SHARE ("SHared Access Research Ecosystem") initiative, higher education's venture to promote good stewardship and accessibility of research. In February SHARE released its Notification Service Project Plan; in March IMLS and the Sloan Foundation awarded SHARE $1 million to develop the notification service; in June SHARE selected the Center for Open Science as its development partner for the notification service; in September SHARE launched a logo and brand; in October SHARE began to test its notification service prototype, Tyler Walters was appointed SHARE's founding director, and SHARE held a community meeting at which more than 60 SHARE working group members, notification service prototype participants, technical partners, and other interested parties discussed challenges and opportunities as SHARE moves to its next phase of development.

Throughout the year, ARL supported legislation to advance open and public access to federally funded research. In addition, ARL worked with U.S. federal agencies as the agencies developed public access plans in response to the Office of Science and Technology Policy memorandum on increasing access to federally funded research.

In November ARL sponsored three individuals to participate in OpenCon, the student and early-career researcher conference on open access, open data, and open educational resources.

Accessibility

On Global Accessibility Awareness Day, May 15, ARL launched a Web accessibility toolkit to promote the principles of accessibility, universal design, and digital inclusion and to help research libraries achieve digital accessibility. The lead author was Molly Schwartz, a National Digital Stewardship Residency fellow who was in residence at ARL for six months in 2013–2014.

In October ARL appointed Katya Pereyaslavska as a visiting program officer for accessibility and universal design. Pereyaslavska is scholars portal accessibility librarian at the Ontario Council of University Libraries and the University of Toronto Libraries. She will work with the ARL Accessibility and Universal Design Working Group to develop an outreach program, directed at the international scholarly publishing community, to raise awareness of the obligations and responsibilities of publishers with respect to providing accessible content to libraries serving students and researchers with print disabilities.

In October and November ARL and the American Library Association (ALA) filed comments with the Federal Communications Commission (FCC) opposing a request by the Coalition of E-Reader Manufacturers to waive compliance with disability law in manufacturing e-readers such as the Kindle. The law requires that equipment used for advanced communication services (ACS) be accessible to, and usable by, individuals with disabilities.

Copyright and Intellectual Property

In April ARL, as part of the Library Copyright Alliance (LCA), endorsed the testimony of James G. Neal, vice president for Information Services and university librarian, Columbia University, before the House Judiciary Subcommittee during the ongoing copyright review. Neal spoke to issues concerning preservation and the reuse of copyrighted works. In June LCA endorsed the testimony of Greg Cram, associate director of copyright and information policy at the New York Public Library, at a Judiciary Subcommittee hearing focused on the first sale doctrine. In addition to endorsing these two statements, in 2014 LCA submitted written statements for seven other Judiciary Subcommittee copyright review hearings.

ARL participated in two cases regarding fair use, accessibility, higher education, and libraries. In June LCA applauded the decision by the U.S. Court of Appeals for the Second Circuit in *Authors Guild* v. *HathiTrust,* finding in favor of fair use. In July LCA released "What Does the *HathiTrust* Decision Mean for Libraries?" by copyright attorney Jonathan Band. In November ARL released a video of Band discussing the *HathiTrust* case in depth and presenting the implications of the ruling. In another important case for higher education and libraries, LCA filed a friend-of-the-court brief in a Georgia State University case concerning the use of excerpts of academic books for electronic course reserves. In its ruling, the U.S. Court of Appeals for the Eleventh Circuit reversed the decision and remanded it to the district court. In doing so, the appeals court upheld the importance of the flexible application of fair use.

In October ARL published an infographic that shows how libraries are champions for academic freedom and balanced copyright. The infographic explains the threat of unbalanced copyright to academic freedoms, including the freedom to research, to teach and learn, and to publish. The infographic is freely available to embed on blogs and websites and to print and hand out at events.

Also in October ARL released three videos that show the value of the "Code of Best Practices in Fair Use for Academic and Research Libraries," an easy-to-use statement of reasonable approaches to fair use of copyrighted material, developed by and for librarians who support academic inquiry and higher education. With support from the Andrew W. Mellon Foundation, the videos capture how the code has assisted many communities by providing guidance about the scope of best practice when fair use comes into play.

Diversity and Leadership

In January, at the ALA Midwinter Meeting, ARL hosted the tenth annual leadership symposium for MLIS students participating in ARL diversity recruitment programs. The symposium focuses on topics relating to the major strategic areas of ARL, as well as transitioning into, and building career networks in, research libraries and archives. Thirty-eight students participated in the three-day event.

In June, at the ALA Annual Conference, the ARL Leadership and Career Development Program (LCDP) 2013–2014 cohort celebrated its closing ceremonies. The LCDP is an 18-month program to prepare mid-career librarians from traditionally under-represented racial and ethnic minority groups to take on increasingly demanding leadership roles in ARL libraries.

In summer 2014 seven ARL partner institutions hosted internships for the 2014 ARL Career Enhancement Program fellows. Thirteen MLIS students from under-represented racial and ethnic minority groups participated in a six- to twelve-week practical field experience as a major component of this diversity recruitment fellowship. The program is funded by IMLS and ARL member libraries.

In July ARL and the Music Library Association (MLA) selected four MLIS students to participate in the 2014–2016 ARL/MLA Diversity and Inclusion Initiative. This initiative—funded by IMLS, ARL, and MLA—seeks to address the growing need for professional staff in music and performing arts libraries to better reflect the changing demographics of students and faculty in those fields.

Also in July ARL and the conference planning committee awarded five individuals Library Assessment Conference travel awards for 2014 to fund attendance at the conference in Seattle in August. These grants are offered to students and early-career professionals from under-represented racial and ethnic groups who have demonstrated a strong interest in assessment.

In August ARL chose 13 MLIS students to participate in the 2014–2016 Initiative to Recruit a Diverse Workforce (IRDW) as ARL Diversity Scholars. Underwritten by ARL member libraries, the initiative offers financial benefits and leadership development to participants.

Also in August a selection committee chose five recipients for the 2014 ARL/Digital Library Federation (DLF) Forum fellowships for under-represented groups. Each fellow received financial support to attend the forum in Atlanta October 27–29. The fellows wrote blog posts reflecting on their experiences at the forum.

In September ARL and SAA selected five MLIS students specializing in archival studies to participate in the 2014–2016 ARL/Society of American Archivists (SAA) Mosaic Program. Funded by IMLS, the program strives to promote diversification of the archives and special collections professional workforce.

In October the ARL Leadership Fellows Program celebrated its tenth anniversary at the ARL Membership Meeting. The program, known as the Research Library Leadership Fellows Program from 2004 through 2012, is designed and sponsored by ARL member libraries to develop future senior-level leaders in large research libraries and archives. In the program's first decade, 115 fellows have participated, and 18 have gone on to become ARL library directors.

Also in October ARL appointed Carlette Washington-Hoagland as a visiting program officer for diversity and leadership. Washington-Hoagland is coordinator of staff development and diversity programming at the University of Iowa Libraries. She will take the lead in managing the assessment of the ARL Leadership and Career Development Program, will organize a review of ARL mentor programs to inform component enhancements, will contribute to the planning of the annual ARL Leadership Symposium, and will support other research projects and programs as needed.

In December ARL and six partner institutions recruited a 2015 cohort of Career Enhancement Program fellows. The new class was announced in January and the selected fellows participated in the 11th ARL Annual Leadership Symposium in Chicago at the end of the month. The Career Enhancement Program is funded by IMLS and the partner institutions.

Federal Funding

Throughout 2014 ARL participated in a campaign to "Close the Innovation Deficit," urging Congress to allocate more funding to research and higher education. More than 130 other higher education, scientific, and business organizations are supporting this campaign.

Library Management and Assessment

In March and November ARL offered a new seminar and webcasts on "Leading a Strategic Assessment Program in a Research Library" geared toward new assessment professionals. The program was to be offered again in May 2015.

In July the association published the *ARL Annual Salary Survey 2013–2014*, which analyzes salary data for all professional staff working in the 125 ARL member libraries during that year. A poster using data from the salary survey, "Minority Representation in U.S. ARL University Libraries as of 2012–2013: Taking a Closer Look at the Evidence," was presented at the Library Assessment Conference in August.

ARL completed a cohort development in applying the balanced scorecard approach to libraries. Based on this experience, University of York (England) Library's Stephen Town and ARL's Martha Kyrillidou wrote a paper on "Developing a Values Scorecard" that can be used alongside the balanced scorecard to draw a more value-oriented picture of library strengths and impact. Town and Kyrillidou's paper was recognized as the Outstanding Paper of 2014 by the journal *Performance Measurement and Metrics*.

In August ARL and the University of Washington cosponsored the fifth biennial Library Assessment Conference (LAC), hosted in Seattle by the university.

With 600 participants in 2014, LAC is the largest conference of its kind. ARL supported five individuals from under-represented racial and ethnic groups in attending the event. The next LAC is scheduled to take place in Arlington, Virginia, October 31–November 2, 2016. The proceedings of the 2012 Library Assessment Conference in Charlottesville, Virginia, are available at http://libraryassessment.org/archive/2012.shtml.

In August and September ARL published SPEC Kit 340, *Open Source Software*; SPEC Kit 341, *Digital Collections Assessment and Outreach*; and SPEC Kit 342, *Next-Gen Learning Spaces*.

In October ARL published *ARL Statistics 2012–2013, ARL Academic Health Sciences Library Statistics 2012–2013,* and *ARL Academic Law Library Statistics 2012–2013*. These are the latest in a series of annual publications that describe the collections, staffing, expenditures, and service activities of ARL's 125 member libraries.

In fall 2014 ARL, Montana State University, OCLC Research, and the University of New Mexico were awarded an IMLS grant for the project "Measuring Up: Assessing Use of Digital Repositories and the Resulting Impact." The grant will fund research over the next three years in this area, complementing and building on the knowledge base developed by ARL's current suite of library assessment services: LibQUAL+, ClimateQUAL, MINES for Libraries, and the new LibValue Toolkit.

Net Neutrality

In July 2014 ARL collaborated with ten other library and higher education organizations to develop net neutrality principles that they recommended form the basis of an upcoming FCC decision to protect the openness of the Internet. The groups believe network neutrality protections are essential to protecting freedom of speech, educational achievement, and economic growth.

Later in July ARL, EDUCAUSE, and ALA filed comments with FCC on net neutrality. These comments largely expanded on the points made in the principles, going into greater detail and making specific suggestions to strengthen the proposals made in FCC's Notice of Proposed Rulemaking (NPRM).

In September 12 library and higher education organizations, including ARL, filed reply comments with FCC on net neutrality in response to the NPRM to protect and promote the open Internet.

Scholarly Communication

In July ARL began hosting an American Council of Learned Societies (ACLS) Public Fellow, Rikk Mulligan, to work with ARL member institutions on implementing the recommendations of the ARL/AAU Task Force on Scholarly Communication. Mulligan will work to promote the use of the enhanced capabilities of digital technology to move the academy toward new, sustainable, affordable, innovative forms of scholarship. He was appointed as an ARL program officer for scholarly publishing for a two-year term.

In October ARL hosted the Fall Forum 2014, "Wanted Dead or Alive—The Scholarly Monograph," in Washington, D.C. Organized by ARL's Steering Committee for Advancing Scholarly Communication and ARL staff, the forum engaged the ongoing debate about the viability of the monograph, challenged the research library community's thinking about the monograph's future, and considered the changing nature of scholarship.

Also in October ARL published SPEC Kit 343, *Library Support for Faculty/ Researcher Publishing*. In December ARL published SPEC Kit 345, *Shared Print Programs*.

Surveillance Reform

Throughout the year ARL urged Congress to reform the National Security Agency surveillance program. In July the association joined two coalitions in letters to congressional leadership supporting a compromise version of the USA Freedom Act introduced by Sen. Patrick Leahy (D-Vt.). In November ARL expressed disappointment that the Senate failed to advance Leahy's version of the act. ARL remains hopeful that meaningful reform can still be achieved as the fight over bulk collection of records continues.

In June 2014 ARL applauded the House of Representatives for achieving majority support for the E-mail Privacy Act. This legislation would update an outmoded law from 1986 known as the Electronic Communications Privacy Act (ECPA) and ensure that important Fourth Amendment privacy protections extend to online communications. In September ARL joined a coalition in running an advertisement in the privately owned Capitol Hill newspaper *Roll Call* urging congressional leaders to bring ECPA reform to a vote. The coalition also sent letters to House and Senate leaders, urging passage of the ECPA legislation.

Workforce Transformation

In January and June 2014 ARL hosted an ARL Liaison Supervisor meeting at the ALA Midwinter Meeting and the ALA Annual Conference, building on ARL's 2013 New Roles for New Times report *Transforming Liaison Roles in Research Libraries*. More than 50 people attended each meeting, and there was consensus on the need for liaison retraining, toolkits, and community.

From March through November ARL and SAA offered a weeklong package of Digital Archives Specialist courses at five ARL institutions: Syracuse University, the University of Alberta, Emory University, the University of Minnesota, and the U.S. National Archives.

In June ARL's Transforming Research Libraries Steering Committee launched a monthly Web column, "Workforce Transformation Stories." The committee hopes this column will enable library leaders to point to evidence of trends and general truths, and to support organizational change. Collectively the community will build a shared understanding of what it means to work in a research library and what skills and competencies are required.

In November ARL published SPEC Kit 344, *Talent Management*.

Organization-Oriented Accomplishments

Fund Raising

In addition to the $1 million grant from IMLS and the Sloan Foundation to develop and launch SHARE, mentioned above, IMLS awarded a $500,000 three-year

National Leadership Grant to four partner organizations—ARL, Montana State University, OCLC Research, and the University of New Mexico—for "Measuring Up: Assessing Use of Digital Repositories and the Resulting Impact." This project will investigate the challenges libraries face in producing accurate reports of the use of their digital repositories and will recommend best practices to improve data collection and information sharing.

Membership Meetings

Then-ARL President Carol Pitts Diedrichs convened the 164th ARL Membership Meeting in Columbus, Ohio, May 6–8. Almost all of the program sessions at this meeting focused on the ARL ST&D process, upon which the association embarked in the fall of 2013 to define its role in higher education and to maximize ARL's ability to be agile and responsive to changing priorities and member needs. The meeting also included a panel discussion of SHARE.

Diedrichs convened the 165th ARL Membership Meeting in Washington, D.C., October 7–8. This meeting began with program sessions on four ARL endeavors: ST&D, the SHARE initiative, possible rebranding of ARL, and the tenth anniversary of the ARL Leadership Fellows Program.

During the October 8 Business Meeting, the ARL membership ratified the ARL board's election of Larry Alford as ARL vice president/president-elect. Three new board members were elected by the membership to serve three-year terms: Susan Gibbons of Yale, Bonnie MacEwan of Auburn University, and John Wilkin of the University of Illinois at Urbana-Champaign. Additionally, Ann Thornton of New York Public Library was elected to serve a one-year term that was open due to a retirement. At the end of the meeting, Diedrichs transferred the president's gavel to Deborah Jakubs of Duke University, who is serving a one-year term as her successor.

The fall Membership Meeting concluded with program sessions on archiving born-digital government information, fostering innovation, enhancing library fund raising, providing accessible digital content, and operating data-management programs.

SPARC—The Scholarly Publishing and Academic Resources Coalition

Heather Joseph

Executive Director

21 Dupont Circle, Suite 800, Washington, DC 20036
202-296-2296, e-mail sparc@arl.org
World Wide Web http://www.sparc.arl.org

Background and Mission

SPARC—the Scholarly Publishing and Academic Resources Coalition is a global organization that promotes the expanded sharing of scholarship in the networked digital environment. It is committed to faster and wider sharing of outputs of the research process to increase the impact of research, fuel the advancement of knowledge, and increase the return on research investments.

Established in 1997, SPARC was launched by the Association of Research Libraries (ARL) to act on libraries' concern that the promise of the Internet to improve scholarly communication was being inhibited by pricing and access barriers in the journals marketplace. SPARC has since been an innovative leader in the rapidly expanding international movement to make scholarly communication more responsive to the needs of researchers, students, the academic enterprise, funders, and the public.

SPARC is a catalyst for action. Its pragmatic agenda focuses on collaborating with other stakeholders to stimulate the emergence of new scholarly communication norms, practices, and policies that leverage the networked digital environment to support research, expand the dissemination of research findings, and reduce financial pressures on libraries.

The growth of SPARC's influence parallels that of the open access movement, which is expanding in scale and becoming more global. Open access is now a factor in the valuation of companies and a considerable force gaining power. SPARC is supported by a global membership of more than 800 academic and research libraries.

Strategy

SPARC's strategy focuses on reducing barriers to the access, sharing, and use of scholarship. Its highest priority is advancing the understanding and implementation of policies and practices that ensure open access to scholarly research outputs, including journal literature, digital data, and educational resources.

SPARC's work centers on three key program areas:

- Educating stakeholders about the problems facing scholarly communication and the opportunities for them to play a role in achieving positive change

- Advocating policy changes that advance scholarly communication and explicitly recognize that dissemination of scholarship is an essential, inseparable component of the research process
- Incubating demonstrations of new publishing and sustainability models that benefit scholarship and academe

Priorities

SPARC activities will advance acceptance and long-term sustainability of a global open system for scholarly communication, with a primary focus on advancing open access models for publishing and archiving the outputs of scholarly research. SPARC will partner with key stakeholders, with a particular emphasis on "next generation" groups, to promote changes in both the infrastructure and culture needed to make open access the norm in scholarly communication.

The following were among SPARC's key priorities in 2014:

Advocacy/Policy Strategy—To raise the public policy profile of open access to results research including journal articles, data, and educational resources by

- Leading efforts to advocate for policies that provide for open access to journal articles, data, and educational resources on the institutional, state, national, and international levels
- Supporting research on the social/economic benefits of open access to research outputs
- Working with media outlets to promote public awareness of open access
- Working with public and private research funders to create and implement open access policies
- Participating in and promoting productive collective efforts to build scalable capacity to support effective implementations of open access policies

Member Outreach/Campus Education—To expand SPARC's programs to support members' campus education and advocacy activities by

- Providing members-only services and resources to promote the position and mission of libraries
- Establishing an open educational resources (OER) library liaison network in partnership with the Right to Research Coalition
- Supporting an open access/OER education "roadshow" for member campuses
- Building out SPARC's resources for promoting/supporting the adoption of campus-based, faculty-driven open access policies and funds
- Sponsoring Open Access Week and its related activities
- Producing and promoting targeted educational materials

Continuing Priorities

Globalization—SPARC continues to promote the updated SPARC brand as a reflection of broad global presence, deploying SPARC-branded activities in new regions and establishing partnerships with key library and advocacy groups.

Student campaign—SPARC supports student involvement and promotes campus inclusion in the open access and OER movements. Through the Right to Research Coalition, it is working to strengthen joint advocacy efforts with member organizations and expanding involvement of international students and early-career researchers. In 2014 SPARC cosponsored an international conference on open access, open education, and open data, and supported the participation of 110 students from 40 countries in the event.

Open access infrastructure support—SPARC continued its leadership role in promoting digital repositories and open access journals. It is actively partnering with open access publishers and key digital repository organizations to promote education programs and awareness.

Publisher Partnership and Incubation Program—SPARC collaborates with university presses, scholarly societies, and others to explore transition strategies to move from subscription-based to open access models. It works to develop education materials and highlights successful alternative publishing models.

Advocacy/Policy Strategy—SPARC continued to raise the public policy profile of open access through its initiative to advance public access to the results of federally funded research, including articles, data, and educational resources.

Program Activities and Outcomes in 2014

Advocacy and Policy

- SPARC launched an OER program focusing on education and advocacy to support the creation and adoption of OER on campuses and by policymakers.
- It supported the expansion of the National Institutes of Health (NIH) Public Access Policy to the Departments of Labor, Health and Human Services, and Education through the fiscal year 2014 Omnibus Appropriations Act, and led a successful effort to strip a broad, anti-open access provision from the Frontiers in Innovation, Research, Science, and Technology (FIRST) Act (H.R. 4186).
- SPARC supported new U.S. legislation on OER, promoting the introduction of the Affordable College Textbook Act (ACTA), and organized advocacy events to promote the bill that included a well-attended Capitol Hill briefing.
- It created an advocacy coalition in California that led to passage of the California Public Access to Research Act, which provides public access to articles resulting from state-funded public health research.

- To more efficiently leverage its efforts to conduct international advocacy, SPARC cofounded and helped launch the Open Policy Network, a collaboration of global organizations including Electronic Information for Libraries (EIFL), UNESCO, and Creative Commons that will focus on collective advocacy for open access, OER, and open data policies.
- SPARC provided incubation support for the student-led "Open Access Button" project, a browser-based app that lets users register when they find an article behind a paywall, maps those instances, and is intended to ultimately provide access to an open version of the article where possible.
- The coalition released an updated version of its widely used *HowOpenIsIt?* resource, which outlines the core components of reuse rights associated with open access. SPARC is currently collaborating with the Open Access Scholarly Publishers Association (OASPA) and the Public Library of Science (PLOS) on a corollary project, which will provide a numerical ranking system to quickly determine how open a journal publishing policy actually is.
- SPARC continued to lead the work of the U.S.-based Open Access Working Group (OAWG), an alliance of leading organizations that support open access, and served as the organizational focal point for the Alliance for Taxpayer Access (ATA). SPARC also strengthened its ties with the open science and OER communities.
- Internationally, SPARC worked to ensure that emerging global open access policies are aligned with the library community's values. SPARC Europe played a central role in supporting effective open access policy language adopted by the European Commission, and contributed to consultations on open access and open data policies in the United Kingdom, Canada, and across Europe.

Communication and Media

During 2014 SPARC highlighted the work of open access champions. It honored Stanford University's John Willinsky and the international organization EIFL with its Innovator Award. Details and full profiles of both honorees can be found on the SPARC website.

In response to media requests for information on public access issues, SPARC provided materials to reporters and expert sources for interviews with the *Washington Post, Times Higher Education, Science,* the *Guardian, Inside Higher Ed,* and the *Economist.* SPARC staff have also authored articles for various publications. For examples of SPARC in the press, see http://www.sparc.arl.org/news/in-the-news.

Campus Education

SPARC supported campus-based policy action in conjunction with a panel of experts to promote resources that support data-driven, community-engaging, and successful open access policy development. SPARC provides Web and administrative support for the Coalition of Open Access Policy Institutions (COAPI), a group of 44 U.S. and Canadian institutions that have implemented or are in the process of implementing campus-based open access policies.

Global Open Access Week 2014 featured thousands of participants in more than 100 countries. This year's event was jointly sponsored by SPARC and the World Bank, and had a town-hall-style dialogue on the role of students and early career researchers in the open access movement.

SPARC and the Right to Research Coalition developed and hosted OpenCon, an event attended by 150 students and early-career researchers from 39 countries to catalyze projects led by the next generation of scholars to advance the open access, OER, and open data movements.

SPARC also supported its member institutions by providing resources including guides, talking points, templates, and expert counsel on the formulation and adoption of campus open access funds, and campus open access policies. SPARC also serves as a platform for the work of COAPI.

Right to Research Coalition staff toured five campuses in the University of California system to raise awareness of the system's open access policy and open education resources.

SPARC-ACRL Forums

A major component of SPARC's community outreach occurs at meetings of the American Library Association (ALA) when SPARC works with ALA's Association of College and Research Libraries (ACRL) and its scholarly communication committee to bring current issues to the attention of the community.

In January 2014 the SPARC-ACRL midwinter forum was "Connecting Articles and Data to Expand Open Access to Research," which was repeated in Philadelphia and Washington, D.C. In June, a second forum, "Evaluating the Quality of Open Access Content," took place in Las Vegas.

SPARC continued to provide a full suite of educational tools and opportunities, ranging from "directors only" calls connecting SPARC members to thought leaders in scholarly communication to regular webcasts on such topics as open licenses.

Governance

SPARC is guided by a steering committee. The 2014 committee members were Jun Adachi (Japanese National Institute of Informatics, for SPARC Japan), Lorraine Haricombe (University of Kansas), Lee Van Orsdel (Grand Valley State University), Richard Clement (Utah State University), Kevin Smith (Duke University), Deborah Jakubs (Duke University), Mary Case (University of Illinois at Chicago), Barbara I. Dewey (Pennsylvania State University), Mary Marlino (National Center for Atmospheric Research), Alma Swan (for SPARC Europe), Loubna Ghaouti (Université Laval), Vivian Lewis (McMaster University), and John Ulmschneider (Virginia Commonwealth University).

Council on Library and Information Resources

1707 L St. N.W., Suite 650, Washington, DC 20036
202-939-4754
World Wide Web http://www.clir.org
Twitter @CLIRNews @CLIRDLF @CLIRHC

Kathlin Smith
Director of Communications

The Council on Library and Information Resources (CLIR) is an independent, nonprofit organization that forges strategies to enhance research, teaching, and learning environments in collaboration with libraries, cultural institutions, and communities of higher learning. Its staff of 13 is led by its president, Charles Henry.

CLIR is supported by fees from sponsoring institutions, grants from public and private foundations, contracts with federal agencies, and donations from individuals. CLIR's board of directors establishes policy, oversees the investment of funds, sets goals, and approves strategies for their achievement. A full listing of CLIR board members is available at http://www.clir.org/about/governance.

Stephen G. Nichols, Bethany Nowviskie, and Elliott Shore continued their affiliations with CLIR as distinguished presidential fellows through 2014. Nichols is James M. Beall Professor Emeritus of French and Humanities and Research Professor at Johns Hopkins University. Nowviskie is director of the Scholars' Lab and department of Digital Research and Scholarship at the University of Virginia Library; and Shore is executive director of the Association of Research Libraries. In 2014 two new distinguished presidential fellows were appointed: Michael Edson, director of Web and new media strategy at the Smithsonian Institution; and John Unsworth, vice provost, university librarian, and chief information officer at Brandeis University.

Activities

CLIR seeks to identify models of collaboration that could redefine the research library and produce more cost-effective services and programs to improve support of research and teaching. This goal is reflected across the organization's activities.

Digital Library Federation Program

CLIR's Digital Library Federation (DLF) program is a resource and catalyst for collaboration among digital library developers, project managers, and all who are invested in digital library issues. DLF promotes work on digital library standards and best practice; research and data management; aggregation and preservation services for digital collections; and digital library services that expand access to digital resources for research, teaching, and learning. DLF staff and activities are integral to CLIR programs—from the CLIR/DLF Postdoctoral Fellowships in Data Curation to the Committee for Coherence at Scale for Higher Education.

The annual DLF Forum is an important venue for the exchange of information that will lead to a better understanding of the elements and complexity of digital library evolution, as well as for collaboration on practical work. The 2014 DLF Forum, held October 27–29 in Atlanta, drew a record attendance of more than 400 participants. Many of the sessions, including the keynote presentations, were livestreamed and are available at http://www.diglib.org/forums/2014forum/livestream-schedule.

In August 2014 DLF Director Rachel Frick left CLIR to join the staff of the Digital Public Library of America. CLIR expects to name a successor in late winter 2015.

E-Research Peer Network

Building on the success of earlier e-science institutes, and responding to participants' desire for an ongoing support network for e-science practice, DLF launched the E-Research Peer Network Mentoring Group in May 2014. The group is focused on developing a network of practitioners through the process of sharing information on implementing research data management services and on fostering participant-directed learning and shared skill development. A select group of consultants work with participants to assess each institution's service layers and identify next steps about planning and implementing research data management services. DLF will continue the program in 2015 as the E-Research Network.

Study on Continuing Education for Managing Cultural Heritage Data

In September 2013 the Institute of Museum and Library Services (IMLS) awarded CLIR a grant to examine federally mandated plans for open access and their implications for continuing education needs for libraries, museums, and other cultural heritage institutions. Under this grant, CLIR is conducting research in three areas. Part 1 involves a highly structured content analysis of select federal agency plans for supporting open access to data and publications, identifying the commonalities and differences among the plans with emphasis on access to data. Part 2 takes the results of the content analysis and traces its implications for IMLS program areas and the cultural heritage institutions they serve. Part 3 identifies gaps in current continuing education opportunities and approaches for cultural heritage professionals, assessing the readiness of the current professional workforce and identifying how best to address the needs and close the gaps in the immediate and longer term. Final results will be released in summer 2015.

Committee on Coherence at Scale

CLIR established the Committee on Coherence at Scale for Higher Education in October 2012, in partnership with Vanderbilt University. The committee's charge is to examine emerging national-scale digital projects and their potential to help transform higher education in terms of scholarly productivity, teaching, cost-efficiency, and sustainability. The committee currently comprises 22 members, representing university and college presidents and provosts, heads of national education associations and other organizations, and library and information science deans. The committee meets twice a year. A brief video about the committee's aims is available at http://vimeo.com/103828743.

In April 2014 the Andrew W. Mellon Foundation awarded two grants relating to the committee's work. The first, a strategic planning grant, went to Vanderbilt

University. The second, awarded to the University of Pittsburgh's iSchool, supports a new doctoral fellowship program for information sciences students worldwide. The grant will support ten "iFellows," to be named in 2015 and 2016, who will supplement the work of the committee with independent dissertation research.

In September CLIR appointed Hannah Standing Rasmussen research fellow for the committee. Rasmussen, formerly a CLIR Postdoctoral Fellow in knowledge and library services at Harvard Business School, will focus her research on business models for operating analog repositories more coherently and efficiently at a larger scale.

Additional information about the committee is available on its website, http://coherence.clir.org, and in an update written by CLIR President Charles Henry, at http://www.clir.org/pubs/issues/issues101/issues101#COC.

Postdoctoral Fellowship Program

CLIR's Postdoctoral Fellowship Program offers recent Ph.D. graduates an opportunity to work on projects that forge and strengthen connections among library collections, educational technologies, and current research. The program was initiated a decade ago as the Postdoctoral Fellowships in Academic Libraries. In 2012 it expanded to offer data curation fellowships in the social sciences and sciences, with funding from the Alfred P. Sloan Foundation; and in medieval studies, with funding from the Andrew W. Mellon Foundation. In 2013, with Mellon funding, CLIR added a fellowship track in data curation for early modern studies. Both Mellon-funded fellowships were awarded for only one application cycle.

In 2014 CLIR appointed 27 fellows, its largest cohort to date. Also in 2014 CLIR introduced postdoctoral fellowships in data curation for visual studies. Visual Studies Fellows will be appointed by early summer 2015, and will join newly appointed Postdoctoral Fellows in Academic Libraries and Data Curation Fellows in Social Sciences and Sciences at the annual summer seminar at Bryn Mawr College. The event is designed to introduce new fellows to the possibilities of the fellowship through ten days of seminar-style conversations, guest speakers, and discussions of readings about current issues in librarianship, research, and the academy.

Cataloging Hidden Special Collections and Archives

In December 2014 CLIR announced the final group of Cataloging Hidden Special Collections and Archives program awardees. The program, established in 2008 with funds from the Andrew W. Mellon Foundation, supported projects to expose unknown or underused materials in cultural heritage institutions to communities of scholars and others who need them for their work.

Also in December CLIR announced a new program, focused on digitization, to succeed the Cataloging Hidden Collections program. The new program, also supported by the Andrew W. Mellon Foundation, supports a national competition for digitizing collections of rare and unique content in cultural memory institutions. The program evolved after extensive conversations with the foundation and with experts in the community, and after a review of relevant literature and publicly available data about projects recently funded through national-level programs.

Several values informed the design of the new initiative: transforming scholarship, exposing large quantities of rare and unique materials, encouraging deep inter-institutional collaboration, promoting sustainable practices, and maximizing open access to digital collections and metadata.

CLIR issued a call for proposals for the new Digitizing Hidden Special Collections Awards in January.

Mellon Dissertation Fellowships

Seventeen graduate students were selected in 2014 to receive Mellon Dissertation Fellowships. The fellowship program, initiated in 2002, is intended to help graduate students in the humanities and related social science fields pursue doctoral research using original sources and gain skill and creativity in using primary source materials in libraries, archives, museums, and related repositories. To date, the program has supported 179 graduate students who have carried out their dissertation research in public and private libraries and archives worldwide.

Leading Change Institute

CLIR and EDUCAUSE hosted the second Leading Change Institute (LCI) June 1–6, 2014. Thirty-nine participants joined deans Elliott Shore, executive director, Association of Research Libraries; and Joanne Kossuth, vice president for operations and CIO, Olin College of Engineering. Following the institute, participants were invited to join deans Shore and Kossuth for regular hour-long discussions, allowing them to continue exchanges beyond the institute and to provide ongoing support and advice for one another.

LCI shares the same goal that inspired the Frye Institute, to which it is the successor: to prepare and develop the next generation of leaders in libraries, information services, and higher education by engaging those who seek to further develop their skills for the benefit of higher education.

Chief Information Officers Group

CLIR's Chief Information Officers Group is composed of 29 directors of organizations that have merged their library and technology units on liberal arts college and university campuses.

The group, which meets semi-annually, devoted its December 2013 meeting to a discussion of the future of library and information technology services (LITS), and how their organizations could position themselves for that future. The discussion formed the basis for a white paper, written by CIOs Richard Holmgren of Allegheny College and Gene Spencer of Ursinus College, that CLIR published in September 2014. The white paper, *The Changing Landscape of Library and Information Services: What Presidents, Provosts, and Finance Officers Need to Know,* explores emerging opportunities for colleges and universities, the potential role of LITS organizations in realizing that potential, and the core competencies that LITS organizations will need to support positive institutional change in the decade ahead. The report was also the topic of a CLIR Sponsors' Webinar in October.

Rovelstad Scholarship in International Librarianship

Janetta Pegues, a library science student at the University of Wisconsin–Madison, was awarded the 2014 Rovelstad Scholarship. Pegues became interested in international librarianship while volunteering at a school in Gonaives, Haiti.

Instituted in 2002, the Rovelstad Scholarship encourages library students who have an interest in international library work by enabling them to attend the World Library and Information Congress, the annual meeting of the International Federation of Library Associations and Institutions (IFLA). The 2014 meeting was held in Lyon, France.

More information on CLIR's activities is available at www.clir.org.

Publications and Communications

CLIR's weekly blog series "Re: Thinking" continued throughout 2014. The series features perspectives from a variety of contributors on topics relating to the emerging digital environment, research, and higher education.

CLIR Issues, the bimonthly newsletter, continued publication with issues 97–102.

Reports

Participatory Design in Academic Libraries, New Reports and Findings. Nancy Fried Foster, editor. February 2014. Available at http://www.clir.org/pubs/reports/pub161. This report looks at how staff at eight academic institutions gained new insight about the ways in which students and faculty use their libraries, and how the staff are using these findings to improve library technologies, space, and services. The report is based on a series of presentations at the second CLIR Seminar on Participatory Design of Academic Libraries, held at the University of Rochester's River Campus June 5–7, 2013.

The Changing Landscape of Library and Information Services: What Presidents, Provosts, and Finance Officers Need to Know. Richard Holmgren and Gene Spencer. September 2014. Available at http://www.clir.org/pubs/reports/pub162. In late 2013 CLIR sponsored a workshop that explored the ways in which library and information technology services (LITS) organizations and academic institutions will need to evolve. Workshop participants—members of CLIR's Chief Information Officers (CIOs) group, responsible for integrated library and information technology services organizations—identified changes they would be likely to face in the next decade and what strategies they should adopt to prepare themselves for this future. CIOs Richard Holmgren of Allegheny College and Gene Spencer of Ursinus College draw on the workshop discussions to summarize the key challenges and opportunities facing LITS organizations.

CLIR Annual Report 2013–2014. December 2014. Available at http://www.clir.org/pubs/annual.

Association for Library and Information Science Education

2150 N. 107th St., Suite 205, Seattle, WA 98133
206-209-5267, fax 206-367-8777, e-mail office@alise.org
World Wide Web http://www.alise.org

Clara M. Chu
President 2014–2015

The Association for Library and Information Science Education (ALISE) is an independent, nonprofit professional association, founded in 1915 as the Association of American Library Schools (AALS). It changed to its current name in 1983 to reflect more accurately the mission, goals, and membership of the association. Its mission is to promote innovation and excellence in research, teaching, and service for educators and scholars in library and information science and cognate disciplines internationally through leadership, collaboration, advocacy, and knowledge creation.

The association celebrated its centennial at the 2015 ALISE Conference, held January 27–30 in Chicago.

Membership

Membership in ALISE is open to individuals and institutions. Personal members can include anyone interested in the objectives of the association, with categories including full-time (faculty member, administrator, librarian, researcher, or other interested individual); new professional (doctoral students as they transition to faculty-member status, maximum of three years); part-time/retired (part-time or adjunct faculty, or retired professionals); and student (doctoral or other students, maximum of six years). Institutional members include schools with programs accredited by the American Library Association (ALA) and other U.S. and Canadian schools that offer a graduate degree in library and information science or a cognate field. International affiliate institutional membership is open to any school outside the United States or Canada that offers an educational program in library and information science at the professional level as defined or accepted by the country in which the school is located. Associate institutional membership status is accorded to libraries and organizations other than schools of library and information science.

Structure and Governance

Operational groups within ALISE are the board of directors; committees; the council of deans, directors, and program chairs; school representatives; and special interest groups (SIGs). The association was managed from 2006 to July 2014 by the Medical Library Association, with Kathleen Combs as executive director. After a national search, SBI Management, Inc., in Seattle was selected to manage ALISE, starting in August 2014, with Andrew Estep as executive director. The board of directors is composed of seven elected officers serving three-year terms. Officers for 2014–2015 were Clara M. Chu (University of North Carolina at Greensboro), president; Samantha K. Hastings (University of South Carolina), vice president/ president-elect; Eileen Abels (Simmons College), past president; Steven Mac-Call (University of Alabama), secretary/treasurer; Laurie Bonnici (University of Alabama), director for membership services; Carol Tilley (University of Illinois at Urbana-Champaign), director for external relations; and Don Latham (Florida State University), director for special interest groups. At the end of the January 2015 ALISE Annual Conference, Abels and Latham concluded their terms on the board and two newly elected officers joined the board. The new officers are Louise Spiteri (Dalhousie University), vice-president/president-elect, and Denice Adkins (University of Missouri), director for external relations.

The board establishes policy, sets goals and strategic directions, and provides oversight for the management of the association. Face-to-face meetings are held in January in conjunction with the Annual Conference and in spring and fall to focus on policy, planning, and other matters. For the remainder of the year, business is conducted through teleconferences and e-mail.

Committees play a vital role in carrying out the work of the association. Since fall 2008 an open call for volunteers to serve on committees has been used to ensure broader participation in committee service, with members for the coming year appointed by the vice president/president-elect for most committees. Principal areas of activity include awards, budget and finance, conference program planning, governance, nominations, publications, research competitions, and tellers (see http://www.alise.org/mc/page.do?sitePageId=86452 for a full list). Each committee is given an ongoing term of reference to guide its work as well as the specific charges for the year. Task forces can be charged to carry out tasks outside the scope of the existing standing committees. For example, the board established the ALISE Committee on Accreditation Reform in Education (CARE), chaired by Tula Giannini (Pratt Institute), to address concerns regarding the quality and process of accreditation of LIS professional education. It is working with the ALA Subcommittee on Accreditation to enhance the quality of LIS education and the accreditation process.

The ALISE Council of Deans, Directors, and Program Chairs consists of the chief executive officers of each ALISE institutional member school. The group convenes at the Annual Conference and discusses issues via e-mail in the interim. Giannini and Seamus Ross (University of Toronto) are co-chairs for 2014–2015.

Within each institutional member school, a school representative is named to serve as a direct link between the membership and the ALISE board. These individuals communicate to the faculty of their school about ALISE and the association's events and initiatives and provide input on membership issues to the ALISE board.

Special interest groups enable members with shared interests to communicate and collaborate, with a particular emphasis on programs at the Annual Conference. New SIGs are established as new areas of interest emerge among ALISE members. Ongoing SIGs, grouped by thematic clusters, are:

- *Roles and Responsibilities:* Assistant/Associate Deans and Directors, Doctoral Students, New Faculty, Part-time and Adjunct Faculty, Student Services

- *Teaching and Learning:* Curriculum, Distance Education, Innovative Pedagogies
- *Topics and Courses:* Archival/Preservation Education; Development and Fund Raising; Gender Issues; Historical Perspectives; Information Ethics; Information Policy; International Library Education; Multicultural, Ethnic, and Humanistic Concerns; Research; School Library Media; Technical Services Education, Youth Services

Communication

ALISE communication channels are mainly electronic. The organization's presence on social media including Facebook, LinkedIn, and Twitter has grown.

ALISE conducted hot-topic polls in 2013 to obtain member feedback to inform the development of its 2014–2017 strategic plan, and in June 2014 it conducted one to gauge member input on the association's name. The results indicated an interest (55.4 percent or 82/148) to change the E in ALISE from "Education" to "Educators." The newly appointed ALISE Brand Task Force, chaired by Lynne Howarth (University of Toronto), will be addressing the question. The task force will examine the association's branding, including its name, and will submit its findings and recommendations to the ALISE board at the 2015 fall meeting.

Publications

The ALISE publications program has four components:

- The *Journal of Education for Library and Information Science* (*JELIS*) is a peer-reviewed quarterly journal edited by Peta Wellstead (Open Polytechnic of New Zealand/Kuratini Tuwhera). The journal is a scholarly forum for discussion and presentation of research and issues within the field of library and information science education. Wellstead transitioned *JELIS* to an online journal, with its first electronic issue published in January 2015.
- The *ALISE Directory of LIS Programs and Faculty in the United States and Canada* is published annually in electronic format and is available to ALISE members. Listings of faculty for each school include their teaching and research areas, using codes from the LIS Research Areas Classification Scheme that ALISE maintains. The classification is currently under revision.
- The *ALISE Library and Information Science Education Statistical Report* publishes data collected annually from its institutional members on their curriculum, faculty, students, income and expenditures, and continuing professional education. A new, fully online system to collect data was launched in 2014. In the coming year an interactive reporting system will be developed that will offer individualized searching and production of on-demand reports, as well as a single collection of data for ALISE and ALA-accreditation purposes. ALISE members can gain free access to existing reports on the members-only area of the association's website.

- The ALISE website is the public face of the association and provides information about association activities and opportunities of interest to members. It also gives login access to MemberClicks, where members can access members-only benefits (such as reports, a member directory, and so forth), renew their membership, register for conferences and webinars, and access other services. Under the guidance of ALISE's new association management company, the website was redesigned and relaunched in December 2014.

Centennial Celebration

ALISE commemorated its 100th anniversary at the January 2015 Annual Conference with activities featuring LIS education and association history. Activities to commemorate the centennial were started two years earlier under the direction of Elizabeth Aversa (University of Alabama), who chaired the Centennial Campaign Committee to raise funds for the ALISE endowment, and Michèle V. Cloonan (Simmons College), who chaired the Centennial Celebration Committee. The centennial campaign funds will support three member-driven initiatives: building leadership for the future, recognizing and rewarding excellence, and developing a 21st century ALISE infrastructure.

The committee has coordinated three activities:

- LIS education timeline—Hosted by the Web platform Viewshare, the timeline provides an overview of significant moments in LIS education, including general information about LIS education as well as specific information about colleagues and ALISE member institutions. It can be accessed at http://viewshare.org/views/SLISinitiatives/alise-timeline-december.
- Centennial Conversations—To create a digital archive, the centennial committee and ALISE members have interviewed colleagues about their roles in LIS education.
- A special issue of *JELIS*—The first online issue of the journal and the first issue published during the centennial year was dedicated to the "Centenary of ALISE: Looking Back, Moving Forward." It included selected *JELIS* content from the publication's early years (1961–1985) with commentary from current members.

Annual Conference

The ALISE Annual Conference is held immediately before the ALA Midwinter Meeting. The 2015 conference drew more than 400 attendees to Chicago January 26–30 to explore the theme "Mirrors and Windows: Reflections on Social Justice and Re-imagining LIS Education." The focus was on bringing social justice from the periphery to the center of LIS education and research, and examining how information advances equitable, inclusive, and just communities. Program co-chairs Kendra S. Albright (University of South Carolina) and Bharat Mehra (University of Tennessee, Knoxville), with 2014–2015 ALISE President Chu, planned traditional conference offerings (presentations, poster sessions, and networking and placement opportunities), and for the centennial introduced some conference firsts, including an opening session featuring "A Conversation with Association Leadership About the Future of LIS Education," and "Community conn@CT," a space for ALISE members to connect with social justice organizations and each other to create solutions to advance the organizations' missions. ALISE members also had the opportunity to submit proposals to receive micro-grants to support community information projects. The ALISE President's Program centered on LIS education and social issues from an international perspective, and an "unconference," the unCommons, provided a gathering place to share, debate, brainstorm, and network, as well as wellness/yoga sessions.

A WISE Pedagogy pre-conference workshop was held on community engagement in online education, as was an ALISE Academy on social justice in the LIS classroom. The keynote address was presented by Saskia Sassen, Robert S. Lynd Professor of Sociology at Columbia University, who spoke on "The Larger Ecologies of Meaning Within Which We Use Technology and Experience Globalization."

The centennial was celebrated as part of the annual awards reception.

Professional Development

Starting in spring 2014 the association launched the ALISE Xchange Forums, a webinar series offered free to members to facilitate virtual engagement with research and other membership interests between conferences. The webinars have been successful, and ALISE plans to continue them. A committee was established in January 2015 to review the offering of professional development opportunities.

ALISE is also contributing to the future direction of professional development nationally. It is a founding member of the Coalition to Advance Learning in Archives, Libraries and Museums (http://coalitiontoadvancelearning.org), which is supported by grants from the Institute of Museum and Library Services and the Bill and Melinda Gates Foundation, with administration provided by OCLC. The goal of the group is to work in deliberate coordination across organizational boundaries to devise and strengthen sustainable continuing education and professional development programs that will transform the library, archives, and museum workforce in ways that lead to measureable impact on the nation's communities.

Grants and Awards

ALISE supports research and recognizes accomplishments through its grants and awards programs, respectively. Research competitions include the ALISE Research Grant Competition, the ALISE/Bohdan S. Wynar Research Paper Competition, the ALISE/Dialog Methodology Paper Competition, the ALISE/Eugene Garfield Doctoral Dissertation Competition, the ALISE/Linworth Youth Services Paper Award, and the OCLC/ALISE Library and Information Science Research Grant Competition. Support for conference participation is provided by the University of Washington Information School Youth Services Graduate Student Travel Award, the Doctoral Student to ALISE Award, and the new ALISE Diversity Travel Award, which funds travel to the ALISE Annual Conference; this award was created in collaboration with the ALA Office for Diversity's Spectrum Scholarship Program, which created a parallel award, the ALA/ALISE Spectrum Travel Award to ALISE, partially funded by ALISE.

Awards recognizing outstanding accomplishments include the ALISE/Norman Horrocks Leadership Award (for early-career leadership), the ALISE/Pratt-Severn Faculty Innovation Award, the ALISE Service Award, the ALISE Award for Professional Contribution, and the new ALISE/Connie Van Fleet Award for Research Excellence in Public Library Services to Adults, made possible by Libraries Unlimited (ABC-CLIO) and an anonymous donor. The ALISE Award for Teaching Excellence (1993–2014) has been replaced by the new LJ/ALISE Excellence in Teaching Award, sponsored by ProQuest, in collaboration with *Library Journal*. [For a list of award winners, see http://www.alise.org/awards-grants and "Library Scholarship and Award Recipients, 2014" in Part 3 of this volume—*Ed.*]

Collaboration with Other Organizations

ALISE seeks to collaborate with other organizations on activities of mutual interest. In January 2015, for the third time, a subset of presentations at the ALISE Annual Conference were showcased at the ALA Midwinter Meeting, including a presentation by the Spectrum Doctoral Fellows who are developing an LIS social justice toolkit. Another important collaboration with ALA involves revising accreditation of professional LIS education. ALISE members serve as representatives to national organizations including the Library of Congress's FEDLINK Network, the 2016 IFLA World Conference National Committee, the ALA Committee on Education, the ALA Library Services and Technology Act Committee, the Association of College and Research Libraries Committee on Education, and the Coalition to Advance Learning in Archives, Libraries, and Museums mentioned above.

ALISE is continuing to build its international connections. It cosponsored the IFLA Section on Education and Training 40th anniversary summit, and ALISE's international reach has been strengthened by members serving on IFLA standing committees concerned with education and research and through its support of initiatives to address access to information.

Conclusion

ALISE is guided by a new strategic plan, "Setting in Motion a New Century of Leadership—Strategic Directions, 2014–2017." It is clear that ALISE is thriving as a century-old association and has a solid foundation based on traditions, but more importantly on the strength of its membership. There is much to look forward to as ALISE embarks on its second century, including professional development offerings, the review of ALISE's branding, and active member engagement using a variety of communication channels.

International Reports

International Federation of Library Associations and Institutions

P.O. Box 95312, 2509 CH The Hague, Netherlands
Tel. 31-70-314-0884, fax 31-70-383-4827, e-mail ifla@ifla.org
World Wide Web http://www.ifla.org

Beacher Wiggins
Director for Acquisitions and Bibliographic Access, Library of Congress
American Library Association Representative to the Standing Committee on
Government Libraries, 2011–2015

The International Federation of Library Associations and Institutions (IFLA) is the preeminent international organization representing librarians, other information professionals, and library users. Despite budgetary pressures, throughout 2014 IFLA promoted its four core values: freedom of access to information and expression, as stated in Article 19 of the Universal Declaration of Human Rights; the belief that such access must be universal and equitable to support human well-being; delivery of high-quality library and information services in support of that access; and the commitment to enabling all members of IFLA to participate without regard to citizenship, disability, ethnic origin, gender, geographical location, political philosophy, race, or religion.

Throughout 2014 IFLA promoted an understanding of libraries as cultural heritage resources that are the patrimony of every nation.

World Library and Information Congress

The World Library and Information Congress (WLIC)/80th IFLA General Conference and Council attracted 3,222 registered attendees from 132 countries to Lyon, France, August 16–22, 2014. Of these, 2,590 registered for the entire conference while 632 registered for a single day. The attendance represented a gratifying increase over the 2,704 registered full and one-day participants at the 2013 WLIC in Singapore and the 2,486 who registered for the 2012 WLIC in Helsinki, Finland. Bruno Racine, president of the Bibliothèque Nationale de France, chaired the national committee for the Lyon conference, the first IFLA WLIC to take place in France since 1989. The conference theme, "Libraries, Citizens, Societies: Confluence for Knowledge," was particularly appropriate for Lyon, a UNESCO World Heritage site founded at the confluence of the Rhône and Saône rivers. Philosopher Bernard Stiegler delivered the conference keynote address, on "The Future of

Reading." On the final day of the conference, the national committee offered tours of libraries in metropolitan Lyon and day-long excursions to libraries in other French and Swiss cities.

Twenty-two satellite meetings, organized by IFLA sections, afforded more-detailed discussions on specific topics such as art libraries and electronic publishing; reading habits of 15- to 20-year-olds around the world; ethical questions in librarianship; and linked data in libraries. The satellite meetings were held throughout France and Switzerland, with some taking place in Italy, Germany, England, and Ireland. A satellite meeting at the Deutsche Nationalbibliothek in Frankfurt was devoted to "RDA: Resource Description and Access—Status and Perspectives 2014," as the German library community prepared to implement RDA as its cataloging standard in 2015.

The next World Library and Information Congress will take place in Cape Town, South Africa, in August 2015. WLIC will return to the United States in August 2016, meeting in Columbus, Ohio. Under the current WLIC conference planning guidelines, the conference cities are selected three years in advance, and at each WLIC the IFLA Governing Board announces the specific location of the conference that will take place two years later. The 2016 conference in Columbus will be followed by conferences in Europe (2017), Latin America or the Caribbean region (2018), and again in Europe (2019). The IFLA Governing Board is committed to continuously improving both the conference experience for participants and the financial security of the organization. Although the exhibitor fees and registration are higher than for most conferences in the library community, WLIC does not make money for IFLA, and the custom of convening all registered participants in opening and closing ceremonies limits the number of cities that can host the conference to those with conference halls seating at least 3,000 people. Furthermore, member organizations have commented that it is difficult to send representatives to both the general conference and the numerous specialized satellite meetings that occur at a distance from the general conference site. The current seven-year planning cycle and conference model were adopted after a consultation in early 2010 that Pleiade Management and Consultancy of Amsterdam conducted for IFLA. In the resulting model, each IFLA conference is organized around tracks or themes. At the past three conferences (2011–2013), the five tracks were: Open Access and Digital Resources; Policy, Strategy, and Advocacy; Users Driving Access and Services; Tools and Techniques; and Ideas, Innovation, and Anticipating the New. Through its governing board, IFLA retains overall ownership of each conference, and the governing board, IFLA headquarters, and the conference national committee (the local organizing committee) are responsible for each conference overall. Program content is guided by the IFLA Professional Committee. Actual conference planning and services are contracted to a "congress secretariat" or event management company. The Helsinki, Singapore, and Lyon conferences were managed by the K.I.T. Group of Berlin. A more extensive review of conference governance, the host city selection process, the planning cycle, and financial management is planned for 2015/2016, after the site of the 2018 conference is announced and all of IFLA's regions have hosted at least one recent conference.

Five Key Initiatives

In 2010 the IFLA Governing Board adopted a new Strategic Plan for the years 2010–2015. The plan, grounded in the four core values, sets forth four strategic directions: empowering libraries to enable their user communities to have equitable access to information; building the strategic capacity of IFLA and that of its members; transforming the profile and standing of the library profession; and representing the interests of IFLA's members and their users throughout the world. The five key initiatives for 2010–2015 are the digital content program, international leadership development for librarianship, outreach for advocacy and advancement of the profession, cultural heritage disaster reconstruction, and the multilingualism program. The governing board determines priority activities every two years under the strategic plan.

Digital Content Program

In its digital content program, IFLA advocates vigorously for open access to digital content and for the right of libraries to benefit from fair use and exemptions from copyright restrictions. The federation's position is that the current framework of copyright exceptions is not adequate for the digital era. Through participation in the World Intellectual Property Organization's (WIPO's) Standing Committee on Copyright and Related Rights (SCCR), IFLA has worked toward a binding international instrument on copyright limitations and exceptions that will enable the world's libraries to continue their historic mission of providing universal access to knowledge and information. With the International Council on Archives (ICA), Electronic Information for Libraries (EIFL), and Corporación Innovarte, IFLA's Committee on Copyright and Other Legal Matters drafted the Treaty Proposal on Copyright Limitations and Exceptions for Libraries and Archives (TLIB). It would protect libraries in the areas of preservation, right of reproduction and supply of copies, legal deposit, library lending, parallel importation, cross-border uses, orphan works, retracted and withdrawn works, liability of libraries and archives, technological measures of protection, contracts, and the right to translate works. In 2013 IFLA and its partners worked intensively to gain the support of WIPO member states for the proposed TLIB. At the close of the year, on December 19 and 20, the SCCR discussed the TLIB or similar instruments in depth for the first time. While members from Latin America, the Caribbean, and Africa voiced strong support, the European Union (EU), Central Eastern European, and Baltic states opposed making it a priority for 2014. Throughout 2014 IFLA continued to press for a binding international framework for copyright limitations and exceptions for libraries and archives. In April the SCCR met without reaching a conclusion on the proposed copyright exceptions. In May IFLA and about 90 other signatories sent an open letter to the EU asking that it support constructive dialogue on copyright exceptions for libraries and archives at WIPO. However, at the next SCCR meeting in Geneva, June 30–July 4, the member states again adjourned without reaching a conclusion, and the talks essentially collapsed for the second time in a year. The WIPO General Assembly held in Geneva, September 22–30, similarly failed to reach a conclusion regarding copyright exceptions or even how the SCCR should continue. In press releases, IFLA made clear that it believed the developed countries—including the United Kingdom, the other EU nations, Australia, and the United States—were to blame. A press release from IFLA on October 1, 2014, talked about the developed countries' "blocking tactics to prevent progress" and said that group of member states "does not appear to recognise the global nature of the Internet" (retrieved from http://www.ifla.org/node/9075?og=5852, February 27, 2015). IFLA raised the issue again at the December 2014 meeting of the SCCR and planned to press further at the SCCR meeting in May 2015.

IFLA continues to be an active participant in follow-up to the World Summit of the Information Society (WSIS), which held two summits, in Geneva (2003) and Tunis (2005). The federation sends representatives to the Internet Governance Forum, a series of annual follow-up meetings to WSIS; in 2014 the forum took place in Istanbul. IFLA is responsible for reporting to UNESCO on two of the eleven WSIS action lines, Action Line C3: Access to Information and Action Line C8: Cultural Diversity and Identity, Linguistic Diversity, and Local Content. The follow-up activities have become part of the "WSIS+10" review that commenced in 2013, ten years after the Geneva summit. In January 2013 the IFLA Governing Board issued a revised Position on Internet Governance that states clearly the issues IFLA believes should be addressed in any post-WSIS framework, especially the right of equitable public access to the Internet, and advocates a multi-stakeholder model of Internet governance. The WSIS+10 Review was scheduled to be presented to the United Nations General Assembly in 2015, and IFLA's membership and officers devoted much energy in 2014 to ensuring that the post-2015 agenda for WSIS recognizes the essential role of libraries in providing access to information and cultural heritage in a digital age.

At the Lyon WLIC in August 2014 IFLA promulgated the Lyon Declaration on Access to Information and Development and publicly invited other stakeholders in the information society to co-sign. The declaration states that access to information has a central role in sustainable development for all of the world's people, and it calls on member states of the United Nations to acknowledge the necessity of access to information and the skills to use information effectively, and to ensure that this necessity is recognized in the United Nations' post-2015 development agenda. The declaration has attracted more than 500 co-signers. Most are libraries, library associations, or institutions of higher education, but the co-signers also include the Wellcome Foundation, Wikipedia Foundation, and Engineers for Social Responsibility.

International Leadership and Advocacy Program

Planning for the key Building Strong Library Associations initiative essentially began at the 2012 WLIC in Helsinki and is being carried out through IFLA's existing Action for Development Through Libraries (ALP) program. The initiative provides training materials and mentoring to help library associations build capacity. The ALP International Leaders program sponsored in-person sessions for emerging library leaders at the WLIC in 2012, 2103, and 2014.

Cultural Heritage Disaster Reconstruction Program

IFLA was a founding member in 1996 of the International Committee of the Blue Shield (ICBS) to protect cultural property in the event of natural and human disasters. Its current partners in ICBS are ICA, the International Council on Monuments and Sites, the International Council of Museums, and the Co-ordinating Council of Audiovisual Archives Associations. In 2014 the IFLA North American regional center for preservation and conservation, hosted at the Library of Congress, continued to develop a network of colleague institutions to provide a safety net for library collections during emergencies.

In April 2012 the IFLA Governing Board endorsed Principles of Engagement for cultural heritage recovery, spurred by IFLA's support of cultural reconstruction in Haiti after the massive earthquake of January 2010. The principles guide IFLA and its members in deciding when and how to provide assistance in natural disasters that threaten libraries and cultural heritage objects. In 2014 IFLA and UNESCO continued efforts to establish an online registry of at-risk areas where cultural heritage may be jeopardized by war or natural disaster.

Multilingualism Program

Recognizing that the Internet is now a prevalent means of communication and resource sharing, IFLA continues efforts to make its website at http://www.ifla.org multilingual. To assist libraries in China, francophone Africa, the Arab world, and Russia, IFLA maintains four language centers, at the National Library of China in Beijing; the Central Library of Cheikh Anta Diop University in Dakar, Senegal; the Bibliotheca Alexandrina in Alexandria, Egypt; and the Russian State Library in Moscow.

Grants and Awards

The federation continues to work with corporate partners and national libraries to maintain programs and opportunities that would otherwise not be possible, especially for librarians and libraries in developing countries. The Jay Jordan IFLA/OCLC Early Career Development Fellowships provide four weeks of intensive experience, based in OCLC headquarters in Ohio, for library and information science professionals from countries with developing economies who are in the early stages of their careers. The fellows for 2014 were from Bhutan, El Salvador, Nigeria, the Philippines, and Sri Lanka. (The American Theological Library Association has ended its cosponsor role, and OCLC and IFLA welcome inquiries from potential cosponsors.) Since its inception in 2001 the program has supported 75 librarians from more than 35 developing countries.

The Frederic Thorpe Awards, established in 2003, are administered by the IFLA Libraries Serving Persons with Print Disabilities Section and the Ulverscroft Foundation of Leicester, England, which Thorpe founded to support visually impaired people. The Ulverscroft Foundation renewed the program as the

Ulverscroft/IFLA Best Practice Awards (Frederic Thorpe Awards) in 2006, 2007, 2008, 2010, and 2011, with no award in 2009 or 2012. In 2013 the Ulverscroft Foundation again began funding the award. The most recent award, announced in 2013, went to Dragana Milunovic, Library Advisor Section for Blind and Visually Impaired, National Library of Serbia, to visit the studios of the Royal National Institute of Blind People (RNIB) National Library for the Blind in the United Kingdom to study preparation of digital materials as part of a digital library for the blind project.

The Bill and Melinda Gates Foundation Access to Learning Award in 2014 was presented at the Lyon conference to Sri Lanka's e-Library Nenasala Program, a government initiative to increase digital literacy and access to technology among the nation's poorest residents living in remote rural areas. The Access to Learning Award from 2000 through 2014 was an annual award of up to US$1 million to libraries, library agencies, or comparable organizations outside the United States that have been innovative in providing free public access to information. To IFLA's regret, the Gates Foundation announced in 2014 that it would conclude its Global Libraries program within the next three to five years, and that the award to the Nenasala Program would be the final Access to Learning Award.

Numerous awards and grants encourage travel to the annual IFLA conferences. The IFLA International Marketing Award includes a stipend and travel to the conference for representatives of the winning libraries. Emerald Group Publishing has sponsored the award since 2008. In 2014 the first-place winner was the Jirí Mahen Library in Brno, Czech Republic, for its innovative partnership program "Library in the Tram—Tram to the Library." The 2013 first-place winner was the University of Tartu Library, Finland, for its "Talking Textbooks" project to assist blind or visually impaired students.

The Council on Library and Information Resources (CLIR) sponsors the Rovelstad Scholarship in International Librarianship that brings one international library science student to the WLIC each year. Janetta Pegues, a library science student at the University of Wisconsin–Madison, was awarded the 2014 scholarship.

The Dr. Shawky Salem Conference Grant and the Naseej (Arabian Advanced Systems Co.) Conference Grant support conference attendance from Arab countries. While many national library professional associations subsidize travel to the IFLA conference, the Comité français IFLA supports travelers from any francophone country. In 2014 a total of 40 French citizens and 25 citizens of other francophone countries received support from the committee to attend the Lyon conference. The Aspire Award supports travel to conferences of IFLA and of CILIP, the Chartered Institute of Library and Information Professionals, in memory of Bob McKee (1950–2010), who was chief executive of CILIP.

The De Gruyter Saur/IFLA Research Paper Award consists of €1,000 and travel support to attend the IFLA conference. The IFLA Academic and Research Libraries Section cosponsors this annual essay contest, awarding conference registration and travel support for three contestants from Africa, Latin America, and the Asia/Pacific region. The Section on Education and Training sponsors a Student Paper Award, funded by the library services vendor ekz (ekz.bibliotheksservice GmbH), for library science students.

With IFLA, the commercial publisher Brill sponsors the Open Access Award for initiatives in the area of open access monograph publishing. The first award, in 2013, recognized Open Book Publishers, Cambridge (United Kingdom), a not-for-profit independent publisher of open access, peer-reviewed monographs in the humanities and social sciences. In 2014 the award was presented to Knowledge Unlatched, a U.K. project to ensure that scholarly publications are open accessible once the costs of publication have been met. The award includes funding to attend the WLIC and a cash award of €1,000.

The IFLA Honorary Fellowships, the IFLA Medal, and the IFLA Scroll of Appreciation recognize service to IFLA by individuals. The IFLA Scroll of Appreciation was presented to the National Committee for the Lyon WLIC in 2014. The IFLA Medal was presented to the Bibliothèque nationale de France (BnF) in recognition of its having hosted the Strategic Program for Preservation and Conservation from 1992 through 2013. The medal was also presented to Pascal Sanz of BnF; J. Peter Lor, the first National Librarian of South Africa and a former IFLA secretary general; and Jesus Lau, library science educator and former president of the Mexican Library Association. Alex Byrne, State Librarian of New South Wales and a former president of IFLA (2005–2007), was named an IFLA Honorary Fellow.

Membership and Finances

IFLA has more than 1,500 members in 150 countries. Initially established at a conference in Edinburgh, Scotland, in 1927, it has been registered in the Netherlands since 1971 and has headquarters facilities at the Koninklijke Bibliotheek (Royal Library) in The Hague. Although IFLA did not hold a General Conference outside Europe and North America until 1980, there has since been steadily increasing participation from Asia, Africa, South America, and Australia. The federation now maintains regional offices for Africa (in Pretoria, South Africa), Asia and Oceania (in Singapore), and Latin America and the Caribbean (in Mexico City since 2011; formerly in Rio de Janeiro, Brazil). The organization has seven official working languages: Arabic, Chinese, English, French, German, Russian, and Spanish. Its four language centers contribute to more effective communication with their respective language communities by providing translations of IFLA publications and becoming involved in local or regional professional events.

IFLA offers a range of membership categories: international library associations, national library associations, other associations (generally regional or special library associations), institutions, institutional sub-units, one-person libraries, school libraries, association affiliates, personal affiliates, student affiliates, new graduate members, and nonsalaried personal members. Association and institution members have voting rights in the IFLA General Council and IFLA elections and may nominate candidates for IFLA offices. Institutional sub-units, one-person libraries, and school libraries have limited voting rights for section elections; affiliates and personal members do not have voting rights but may submit nominations for any IFLA office, and individuals may run for office themselves. Except for affiliates, membership fees are keyed to the UNESCO Scale of Assessment and the United Nations List of Least Developed Countries, to encourage participation regardless of economic circumstances. The IFLA Core Activity Fund is supported by national libraries worldwide.

UNESCO has given IFLA formal associate relations status, the highest level of relationship accorded to nongovernmental organizations by UNESCO. In addition, IFLA has observer status with the United Nations, WIPO, the International Organization for Standardization (ISO), and the World Trade Organization, and associate status with the International Council of Scientific Unions. The federation continues joint activities with the World Summit on the Information Society despite mounting friction over the issue of copyright exceptions for libraries.

The federation has extended consultative status to many organizations in the information field, including the Arab League Educational, Cultural, and Scientific Organization; the Conference of Directors of National Libraries; the European Dyslexia Association; ICA; the ISSN International Centre; the International Board on Books for Young People; ISO; the International Publishers Association; the World Blind Union; and the World Federation of the Deaf.

More than a dozen corporations in the information industry have formed working relationships with IFLA as corporate partners, providing financial and in-kind support and in turn gaining the opportunity to convey information about their products and services to IFLA members and others who follow IFLA's publications and activities. Several levels of corporate partnership are available. Most prominently, in 2014 OCLC became IFLA's first and sole "platinum partner," providing support at an extraordinary level. Most corporate partners choose to support IFLA at one of three levels: gold (annual support equaling €3,500), silver (annual support equaling €2,000), or bronze (annual support equaling €1,000). Gold corporate partners in 2014 were Emerald Group Publishing and Sage Publications. De Gruyter Saur became a silver partner, and bronze partners were Brill, Elsevier, Gale Cengage Learning, Innovative Interfaces, ProQuest, and Sabinet. The federation also welcomed Annual Reviews, Axiell, Harrassowitz, and NBD Biblion as associate partners. A review of the current corporate partnership program began in 2012 and continued through 2014.

The IFLA Foundation (Stichting IFLA) was established in 2007. The foundation accepts private donations and bequests and also is funded by other IFLA income. It gives funding priority to proposals and projects that promise to have a long-term impact in developing and strengthening IFLA, are clearly related to at least one of IFLA's strategic priorities, and are not likely to be funded by other bodies. The foundation's board of trustees consists of IFLA's president, president-elect, treasurer, secretary general, and an appointed expert in foundation law and management.

Personnel, Structure, and Governance

The Secretary General of IFLA is Jennefer Nicholson, former executive director of the Australian Library and Information Association. At IFLA headquarters, Fiona Bradley manages development programs, Joanne Yeomans is professional support officer, and Julia Brungs is the policy and projects officer. Stuart Hamilton was named deputy secretary general in 2014 and continues as director for policy and advocacy. The editor of the quarterly *IFLA Journal* is J. Stephen Parker. IFLA's communications staff includes communications officers Susan Schaepman, who is also responsible for the voucher program, and Louis Takács, who is Web content editor. The manager for conference and business relations is Josche Ouwerkerk. Christine Zuidwijk is IFLA's financial officer.

New officers and board members took office at the close of the 2013 Singapore conference and will serve through the conclusion of the 2015 conference in Cape Town. Sinikka Sipilä, secretary general of the Finnish Library Association, is president of IFLA, succeeding Ingrid Parent, university librarian, University of British Columbia, Vancouver. Sipilä's presidential theme is "Strong Libraries, Strong Societies." Donna Scheeder of the Congressional Research Service, Library of Congress, is the president-elect and will succeed Sipilä as president in 2015. The treasurer is Frédéric Blin, head of preservation and heritage collections, Bibliothèque nationale et Universitaire de Strasbourg, France.

Under the revised 2008 IFLA Statutes, the 19 members of the governing board (plus the secretary general, ex officio) are responsible for the federation's general policies, management, and finance. Additionally, the board represents the federation in legal and other formal proceedings. The board is composed of the president, president-elect, secretary general (ex officio), ten directly elected members, the chair of the professional committee, the chairs of each IFLA division, and the chair of the standing committee of the Management of Library Associations Section, currently Gerald Leitner, secretary general of the Austrian Library Association. Current members, in addition to Sipilä, Scheeder, Nicholson, and Leitner, are Kent Skov Andreasen (Denmark), Blin, Ingrid Bon (Netherlands), Genevieve Clavel-Merrin (Switzerland), Loida Garcia-Febo (United States), Ngian Lek Choh (Singapore), Barbara Lison (Germany), Inga Lundén (Sweden), Ellen Ndeshi Namhila (Namibia), and Glòria Pérez-Salmerón (Spain), plus the chairs of the IFLA Professional Committee and divisions, named below.

The governing board delegates responsibility for overseeing the direction of IFLA between board meetings, within the policies established by the board, to the IFLA Executive Committee, which includes the president, president-elect, treasurer, chair of the professional committee, two members of the governing board (elected every two years by members of the board from among its elected members), and IFLA's secretary general, ex officio. The current elected governing board members of the executive committee are Lison and Lundén.

The IFLA Professional Committee monitors the planning and programming of professional activities carried out by IFLA's two types of bodies: professional groups—five divisions, 43 sections, and special interest groups—and strategic programs (formerly called core programs or core activities). The professional committee is composed of one elected officer from each division, plus a chair elected by the outgoing committee; the president, the president-elect, and the professional support officer, who serves as secretary; the chairs of the CLM and FAIFE committees, and two elected members of the governing board, currently Skov Andreasen and Clavel-Merrin. Lynne M. Rudasill, associate professor of library administration, University of Illinois at Urbana-Champaign, chairs the professional committee.

The five divisions of IFLA and their representatives on the professional committee are (1.) Library Types (Andrew McDonald, United Kingdom); (2.) Library Collections (Russell S. Lynch, United States); (3.) Library Services (Maria-Carme Torres i Calvo, Norway); (4.) Support of the Profession (Clara Chu, United States); and (5.) Regions (Dan Dorner, New Zealand). The chair of the Copyright and

Other Legal Matters Committee is Victoria Owen, head librarian, University of Toronto, Scarborough (Canada). The chair of the Freedom of Access to Information and Freedom of Expression Committee is Martyn Wade, National Librarian of Scotland. The 43 sections focus on topical interests, such as statistics and evaluation, library theory and research, and management and marketing, or on particular types of libraries or parts of the world.

The six strategic programs, which replace the former five core activities, are Action for Development through Libraries (ALP, originally Advancement of Librarianship); Preservation and Conservation (PAC); the IFLA UNIMARC Strategic Program, which maintains and develops the Universal MARC Format, UNIMARC; Committee on Standards; Free Access to Information and Freedom of Expression (FAIFE); and Copyright and Other Legal Matters (CLM). The UNIMARC Strategic Program has a separate office headed by Maria-Inês Cordeiro at the National Library of Portugal in Lisbon. Two other longstanding IFLA projects are the IFLA World Wide Web site and the IFLA Voucher Scheme, which replaced the IFLA Office for International Lending. The voucher scheme enables libraries to pay for international interlibrary loan requests using vouchers purchased from IFLA rather than actual currency or credit accounts. By eliminating bank charges and invoices for each transaction, the voucher scheme reduces the administrative costs of international library loans and allows libraries to plan budgets with less regard to short-term fluctuations in the value of different national currencies. The voucher scheme has also encouraged participating libraries to voluntarily standardize their charges for loans.

To ensure an arena within IFLA for discussion of new social, professional, or cultural issues, the professional committee approves the formation of special interest groups for a limited time period. There currently are discussion groups for Access to Information Network/Africa (ATINA); Agricultural Libraries; E-Metrics; Environmental Sustainability and Libraries; Indigenous Matters; LGBTQ (Lesbian, Gay, Bisexual, Transgender, Queer/Questioning) Users; Library and Information Science Education in Developing Countries; Library History; National Information and Library Policy; National Organizations and International Relations; New Professionals; Religious Libraries in Dialogue; RFID; Semantic Web; and Women, Information, and Libraries.

Library and Archives Canada: 2014 in Review—LAC Unbound

Guy Berthiaume

Librarian and Archivist of Canada

A book without a cover, a map without a binding, a text without protection—to a conservator, that's what "unbound" means. Safeguarding unbound documents means taking steps to ensure their long-term preservation. But the word itself comes from the verb "to unbind," which means to set free. This is the paradox facing all librarians, archivists, conservators, and other stewards of historical records in the 21st century. Bound or not—how to preserve these records while "freeing" them so they can be accessed now and in the future. Resolving the paradox requires a bold new mix of technology, innovation, and human ingenuity. In 2014 Library and Archives Canada (LAC) put this new mix to work, and like Prometheus, found itself well on the way to becoming unbound.

In June 2014 Guy Berthiaume became the new Librarian and Archivist of Canada after five years at the helm of Bibliothèque et Archives Nationales du Québec. He brought from his experience a sensitivity to the public face of library and archival work, a love of books and culture, an academic background in history and the classics, and a tenacious belief that libraries and archives are here to stay.

There were many questions to be answered. How would LAC retain its place on the national and international stage? What should the focus of Canada's national library and archives be? Where should limited resources be put to work? What were the best ways of adapting to the digital world? How to define quality of service for the future?

To frame some of these questions, and to help this modern-day Prometheus find his way, Berthiaume proposed four basic commitments for the organization. This article has been organized around these four commitments.

A Matter of Service

LAC is an institution that is dedicated to serving all its clients, including government, universities, researchers, students, librarians, archivists, genealogists, donors, and the general public.

At one time, LAC's clients were a rather specialized group, but the era of Google and Amazon has changed all that. An expanded cross-section of clients from specialists to generalists now want direct and immediate access to LAC's collections. One of the first ways to offer service to all of these clients is by digitizing the content.

Between 2013 and 2016 LAC expects to nearly quadruple its digital content, for a total of more than 75 million images. With so much content to choose from, the process of deciding what to digitize continues to be a difficult one. Decisions are based on a number of factors—the popularity of the material, how easy it would be to digitize, questions of preservation, and whether or not accompanying metadata is already available.

Report prepared by Sandra Nicholls, Senior Writer, Library and Archives Canada

However, one popular resource surfaced quickly above all the others. Each month LAC receives more than 800 consultation and reproduction requests for the service files of Canadian Expeditionary Force (CEF) personnel from World War I. The files have been housed in 12,216 containers—boxes that if placed end to end would stretch 3.25 kilometers (more than two miles). These century-old records represent unique portraits in time, providing details from more than 640,000 files—files that tell the stories of the soldiers, nurses, chaplains, and others who served in the Great War. Once the digitization project is complete, some 32 million images will be available for online research, offering unprecedented access to the files.

Released through technology from their captivity in storage boxes, the files include everything from training records to photographs, from personal letters to paychecks, and tell the stories of thousands of individual men and women. And while the stories are powerful, the paper they are written on is extremely fragile. The plan to scan and digitize them constitutes one of the biggest and most ambitious historical preservation projects ever undertaken at LAC.

A Matter of Access

LAC in 2014 was guided by a vision of access: that all Canadians can discover, engage with, and share its content when, where, and how they want it. Projects like the digitization of the CEF files mean that clients have direct access to LAC's content, and can use it and even repurpose it to create new knowledge. This mirrors a vision of access, but also of service. And in the 21st century, the main service delivery vehicle is digital. Digital partnerships are particularly successful—for example, the microfilm digitization partnership between LAC and Canadiana.org, a coalition dedicated to providing broad access to the nation's documentary heritage. Together, Canadiana.org and LAC have digitized 34.5 million images from more than 20,000 microfilm reels, covering a wide range of material that includes immigration and land records, documents relating to Canada's aboriginal history, documents from government departments, military history, and papers from a variety of prominent Canadians. And there is more to come.

In another example, in 2014 LAC and the Treasury Board of Canada Secretariat launched the first phase of the virtual library service for the government of Canada, which will offer open data sets and put thousands of government publications within easy online reach. These include government publications as well as documents, reports, white papers, and presentations. All of this information will be accessible and searchable through a single Web portal.

While much of LAC's service is being delivered through digital means, its vision of service is not limited to digitizing content. With access to holdings remaining a strong focus for the organization, quality of service also means making sure that search applications are user-friendly, offering better tools to search for and access content. LAC is concentrating on a diversified approach, providing searchers with both general reference and specialized services to facilitate content searches. In 2014 LAC continued to offer more traditional library services; for example, lending services pulled more than 91,000 requested items to circulate to clients. And within reference services, LAC continued to offer genealogy services, providing one-on-one consultation and help in locating family and family records.

Ongoing access to LAC's full range of holdings is still offered through on-site services and reading rooms in its main building at 395 Wellington Street in Ottawa. And through institutional lending, clients can access unique materials that are only available in LAC's collection.

The Leading Edge

This brings us to LAC's second commitment.

LAC is an institution at the leading edge of archival and library science and new technologies.

Above and beyond the tremendous work in digitization that took place in 2014, LAC staff also made great strides in improving and enhancing a number of technological processes vital to preservation. The first is the migration of audio-visual records, which has already made it possible to save 91,392 hours of at-risk content to sustainable media. In July 2014 the Treasury Board of Canada Secretariat cited this initiative as an ideal example of modernizing an operational process.

The second example involves digitizing LAC's microfilms. LAC staff have reduced the time it takes to transfer digital images to hard drives; while 270,000 images had been digitized by April 2013, by March of 2014 that number had climbed to 1.6 million.

LAC staff have risen to the challenges of preservation that affect all memory institutions. But more challenges lie ahead. LAC serves as the continuing memory of the government of Canada. And starting in 2017 the format of choice for the transfer of federal government records will be digital.

At present it is difficult to assess the full impact of this change. A current priority is to develop tools to accommodate this massive influx of records. LAC is implementing a new digital strategy, so that it can offer departments solid guarantees regarding the management of their digital archives.

This strategy will lead to the establishment of a Trusted Digital Repository that meets the most stringent international standards. It's not just a matter of archiving; it's a matter of democracy. Part of LAC's mandate is to help the government of Canada meet its obligation to be accountable to Canadians.

Indeed, LAC is a key player in Canada's Action Plan on Open Government 2.0, made public on November 6, 2014. Among its goals, this plan aims to broaden access to government data, and to ensure government transparency and accountability.

A Matter of Engagement

LAC's third commitment is:

LAC is an institution proactively engaged with national and international networks in an open and inclusive way.

Collaboration is a general trend in the growth and development of all memory institutions, and LAC is no exception. It makes sense. Every second, 29,000 gigabytes of information are published worldwide, the equivalent of 6,000 high-definition films. It's estimated that the volume of digital information will double every year between now and 2020. To keep up with it requires new partnerships.

There will also be a demand for client services that LAC will be able to provide only by working in concert with these new partners.

LAC is continuing to strengthen its position, both nationally and internationally. It participates in many international forums and organizations, such as the International Federation of Library Associations and Institutions (IFLA), the International Council on Archives (ICA), and the International Organization for Standardization (ISO), all of which support international collaboration. LAC has also renewed its participation in the Association Internationale des Archives Francophones (AIAF) and the Réseau Francophone Numérique (RFN).

LAC is taking an active role in mobilizing and supporting the Canadian library and archival communities. It created the Stakeholders Forum, which brings together 12 of LAC's partners, including the major library and archival associations in Canada.

Partnership is also behind the retrofit of one of LAC's most popular services: the AMICUS database. AMICUS houses LAC's published catalog as well as the national Union Catalog, which contains more than 25 million bibliographic descriptions, location, and holdings information for more than 1,000 Canadian libraries. AMICUS receives more than 1 million queries a month. But AMICUS was built on pre-Internet technology, meaning that the kind of search tools LAC clients now expect are simply not available. The costs of trying to maintain it are also rising.

In 2014 LAC began work to replace AMICUS and to bring the catalog up to 21st century standards. The requirements and features of the new catalog reflect extensive consultations with the Canadian library community.

With provincial and territorial archivists, LAC is also working on a national collaborative approach to acquisitions, which will ensure that it broadens its collections in a transparent and meaningful way.

In 2014 LAC continued to add to its collection, including a fascinating sketchbook by renowned artist Emily Carr that captures the funeral procession for Queen Victoria in 1901. It also acquired 17 new collections from notable Canadians during the 2013–2014 fiscal year, including those of retired Canadian politician Marc Lalonde, photographer Malak Karsh, and novelist and essayist Nancy Huston.

LAC's Public Face

LAC's fourth commitment is:

LAC is an institution with greater public visibility, highlighting the value of its collections and its services.

LAC is, above all, a cultural institution, but this reality has taken a back seat in the last few years. We are now setting in motion a full range of public programming aimed at a variety of audiences and developing collaborative arrangements with such partners as universities, museums, and galleries. The first season of programming is 2015.

LAC's stately building at 395 Wellington Street in Ottawa was once a vibrant presence in the heart of the capital city, a stone's throw from the Supreme Court of Canada, the Parliament buildings, and the Canadian War Museum. By introducing public programming, LAC's presence in the capital will be re-established, while its collaboration with other memory institutions will increase LAC's visibility.

In 2014 museums and other cultural institutions turned to LAC not simply to borrow works and records, but to collaborate on exhibitions. The National Gallery of Canada provided a showcase for LAC's collection of war photographs, allowing Canadians to step back in time by recreating a room from an exhibition of official Canadian war photographs from the First World War that was first seen in 1916 at the Grafton Galleries in London. This was made possible because LAC is the official repository of the negatives created by Canada's official war photographers, preserved in their original glass plate format.

LAC also lent some of its collection to the Hockey Hall of Fame in Toronto for an exhibition titled "Hockey Marching As to War: The First World War and a Century of Military Ties to the Game." The exhibition, which opened in November 2014, illustrates the impact of the war on hockey players, and how it transformed organized hockey leagues in Canada. LAC's content includes 50 reproductions of photographs, maps, and posters, as well as copies of the Canadian Expeditionary Force service files and Attestation Papers of more than 30 Hall of Fame inductees.

Thanks to a partnership between LAC and the newly opened Canadian Museum of Human Rights in Winnipeg, a number of rarely seen documents from some key moments in Canada's history went on display in 2014. These include the Royal Proclamation of 1763, an important first step in recognizing aboriginal land rights, the 1960 Canadian Bill of Rights, and the 1982 Proclamation of the Constitution Act, which formally enacted Canada's newly patriated constitution and which enshrines the guarantees contained in the Canadian Charter of Rights and Freedoms.

The 1982 Proclamation was signed outdoors on Parliament Hill, and still bears the marks of the raindrops that fell on that historic day. To protect the document from excessive light, and to preserve the ink of the signatures, LAC worked with the Canadian Conservation Institute to create unique climate-controlled glass cases with low-heat LED lighting.

LAC has been working closely with the Canadian Museum of History in Gatineau, Quebec, across the river from Ottawa, and has already lent 55 items for the museum's exhibition "1867—Rebellion and Confederation," which opened in November 2014. LAC also working with the museum to research and identify items for long-term loan to the new Canadian History Hall, the museum's signature permanent gallery set to open July 1, 2017. The hall will occupy roughly 4,000 square metres, about half of the museum's entire exhibition space, and will tell the story of Canada from the dawn of human habitation to now. LAC has already provided collection expertise and physical access to more than 400 items.

LAC's presence is also being felt through its continuing social media presence. LAC continues to guide its users to self-serve channels, such as its Flickr account, which has attracted 6 million visitors to date, and its well-received podcasts, eight of which rank among the top ten federal government productions. LAC's website continues to be one of the most popular of all federal government departments and agencies, with an average of 1.5 million visits a month. In 2014 LAC launched its 15th podcast, "Out of the Ordinary: Rare Books," highlighting a collection that has grown from relatively modest beginnings into one of the finest collections of rare printed material in Canada. In late 2014 the 16th podcast, "William Hind: Illustrating Canada from Sea to Sea," was also launched.

In early February 2014 LAC signed an agreement with Canada's public film producer and distributor, the National Film Board of Canada (NFB), to enable Canadians to have greater access to the nation's cultural heritage, no matter where they live. The first joint project between LAC and NFB is already online: a comprehensive playlist of films, an educator's guide, and fact sheets for each of Canada's 22 prime ministers.

In 2014 LAC also had its first "viral" hit on YouTube. A rare newsreel film of the 1919 World Series was "rediscovered" as part of a unique cache of rare films originally buried in permafrost in the Yukon. This footage (British Canadian Pathé News, 81A; 1919 World Series excerpt) and 500 other films were dug up accidentally by a construction crew in 1978 and sent to Canada's National Archives. When a U.S. filmmaker researching Dawson City came across the film in 2014 he alerted LAC's conservators, who immediately posted the rare footage relating to the infamous "Black Sox scandal" in which eight Chicago White Sox players were accused of taking bribes to deliberately lose. More than 360,000 people tuned in on YouTube.

A Matter of Knowledge

LAC marked its tenth birthday on April 22, 2014, celebrating the merger of two venerable Canadian institutions. On this date in 2004, LAC was created, launching a single gateway into the records of our collective memory, establishing a new mandate, and introducing the revolutionary concept of "documentary heritage." As former Librarian and Archivist of Canada Ian Wilson put it, back in 2004, LAC became Canada's oldest and newest knowledge institution. Thanks to the commitment, passion, professionalism, integrity, and energy of its staff, LAC succeeded where many others failed. The merger of the National Archives and the National Library created an institution that could handle the 21st-century needs of its clients.

A statue greets all visitors to LAC's main building at 395 Wellington Street. It is the work of Canadian artist Lea Vivot titled "The Secret Bench of Knowledge," and shows a boy and a girl sitting on a bench, sharing an apple. What makes this sculpture special is that it is covered in written messages about the joys of reading. There are messages from writers, from children, from private citizens, even one in Braille. Taken together, these scraps of ideas exert a powerful message about the desire to learn, to grow, and to change. "Knowledge belongs to all, and what is not written is forgotten," Vivot has said of her work.

"I am struck by these words," said Berthiaume, "not only for what they say about our mandate as a public institution, but about the importance of memory in our society. And about the unending role of knowledge in the 21st century. As we move toward the future, increasingly in public and private partnerships, I am encouraged by and curious about what lies ahead. Ensuring that all of our heritage, past, present and future, continues to be unbound is a role that would make Prometheus proud."

International Board on Books for Young People (IBBY)

Nonnenweg 12, Postfach, CH-4009 Basel, Switzerland
E-mail ibby@ibby.org

Wally de Doncker
President, 2014–2016

Liz Page
Executive Director

The founding of the International Board on Books for Young People (IBBY) was the result of the visionary commitment of Jella Lepman (1891–1970). Born in Stuttgart, Germany, she became a politically active journalist. In 1936 she emigrated with her son and daughter from Nazi Germany to London and became a British citizen, working for the British Foreign Office and the BBC during World War II and, from 1941, for the American Broadcasting Station in Europe.

When the war ended, she was engaged at the American headquarters in Germany as adviser for questions relating to children and young people. Despite a lack of funds, she organized an exhibition of children's illustrations and children's books from 20 countries in Munich in 1946. Three years later, with initial funding from the Rockefeller Foundation, she established the International Youth Library in Munich and was its director until 1957.

In the postwar years, individuals actively engaged in the field of children's literature in many countries became aware of the importance of children's books as a means in promoting international understanding and peace. They realized that children everywhere should have access to books with high literary and artistic standards and thus become enthusiastic and informed readers.

With this vision in mind, Lepman organized a meeting in Munich under the title "International Understanding Through Children's Books" in November 1951. The goal of the meeting was the foundation of an international organization to promote children's books. The speeches and discussions at this conference were covered by news media worldwide. The meeting resulted in the establishment of a committee to form the International Board on Books for Young People—IBBY.

The committee met in Munich in 1952 and made a formal declaration of intent. The meeting was chaired by Swiss publisher Hans Sauerländer and the effort was international in character from the beginning; the meeting included representatives from Austria, Germany, the Netherlands, Norway, Sweden, and Switzerland.

The success of this preparatory work resulted in the establishment of IBBY, which was registered as a nonprofit organization in Switzerland when the new organization's first General Assembly and Congress were held at the Swiss Federal Institute for Technology (ETHZ) in Zurich in October 1953. The congress brought together founding members including the authors Erich Kästner, Lisa Tetzner, Astrid Lindgren, Jo Tenfjord, Fritz Brunner, and Pamela Travers; the Swiss illustrators Alois Carigiet and Hans Fischer, publishers Hans Sauerländer and Bettina Hürlimann, and specialists in reading research including Richard Bamberger.

The initial capital for the founding of IBBY was donated by the Swiss foundation Pro Juventute, and its secretary general, Otto Binder, was elected as IBBY's first president. In the early years IBBY also received support from the International Youth Library. However, the dues from the ten national sections that had joined IBBY by 1956 were not sufficient to establish a permanent office, and IBBY's activities were mainly carried out through donations and voluntary work. The organization of the administration was the task of the acting presidents who served for two-year terms during the first decade. Succeeding Otto Binder were Swedish publisher Hans Rabén (1956–1958), Italian professor of education Enzo Petrini (1958–1960), and Lepman (1960–1962).

A notable professionalization of IBBY and an extension of membership were achieved during the presidency of Bamberger (1962–1966). In addition, the publication of IBBY's quarterly journal, *Bookbird,* edited by Lepman, Bamberger, and Lucia Binder, became a permanent activity at this time. During the presidencies of Slovenian publisher Zorka Persic (1966–1970) and Finnish school principal Niilo Visapää (1970–1974), IBBY grew so large that it was no longer possible to rely entirely on voluntary work. In 1974 a permanent office, the IBBY Secretariat, was established in Basel. Leena Maissen was appointed its director and remained in that post until her retirement in 2003. Currently the post is held by Liz Page.

IBBY is a nonprofit organization that represents an international network of people who are committed to bringing books and children together. The annual dues from the national sections are IBBY's only source of regular income; projects are supported by sponsors. IBBY cooperates with many international organizations and children's book institutions around the world and exhibits at the International Children's Book Fair in Bologna and other international book fairs.

The biennial IBBY Congresses, which have taken place in 20 countries, have become increasingly important meeting points for the worldwide membership, now comprising more than 75 national sections, to share information and experiences.

Mission and Programs

IBBY's mission is

- To promote international understanding through children's books
- To give children everywhere the opportunity to have access to books with high literary and artistic standards
- To encourage the publication and distribution of quality children's books, especially in developing countries
- To provide support and training for those involved with children and children's literature
- To stimulate research and scholarly works in the field of children's literature
- To protect and uphold children's rights as outlined in the United Nations Convention on the Rights of the Child

As part of its mission, IBBY administers two major international awards: the biennial Hans Christian Andersen Award, which is presented to an author and illustrator whose body of works has made lasting contributions to children's literature; and the IBBY-Asahi Reading Promotion Award, which is given biennially to two groups or institutions whose activities are judged to be making lasting contributions to reading promotion programs for children and young people. Both awards will next be made in 2016.

The IBBY Honour List is a biennial selection of outstanding recently published books, honoring writers, illustrators, and translators from IBBY member countries. An annotated catalog is published for each Honour List selection.

The IBBY Documentation Centre of Books for Young People with Disabilities offers information, consultation, and documentation services for organizations, research workers, teachers, students, librarians, publishers, authors, illustrators, policymakers, and the media who work with young people with special needs. A selective list, Outstanding Books for Young People with Disabilities, is prepared biennially and presented in an annotated catalog. The center is based at the North York Central Library Branch of the Toronto (Canada) Public Library.

Traveling exhibitions of the IBBY Honour List and the Outstanding Books for Young People with Disabilities selections are available from IBBY. Detailed information can be found on the IBBY website (http://www.ibby.org).

IBBY established International Children's Book Day in 1967 to inspire a love of reading and to call attention to children's books. Each year the day is sponsored by an IBBY national section and is celebrated on or around Hans Christian Andersen's birthday, April 2.

The IBBY Yamada workshop and project program relies on its international network to help produce and develop book cultures for children within regions that have special needs and lack support.

IBBY established its Children in Crisis program to provide support for children whose lives have been disrupted by war, civil disorder, or natural disaster. The two main activities supported are the therapeutic use of books and storytelling in the form of bibliotherapy, and the creation or replacement of collections of selected books that are appropriate to the situation.

The Sharjah/IBBY Children in Crisis Fund was established in 2012 and supports long-term projects in the region stretching from North Africa to the Middle East and Central Asia that bring children and books together.

Congresses

IBBY's biennial World Congresses, hosted by different national sections, bring together IBBY members and other people involved in children's books and reading development from all over the world. In addition to lectures, panel discussions, seminars, and book exhibitions, the IBBY Membership Assembly takes place. The presentation of the Hans Christian Andersen Awards, the IBBY-Asahi Reading Promotion Awards, and the IBBY Honour list are highlights of the biennial congresses. The 2016 congress is scheduled for August 18–21 in Auckland, New Zealand.

IBBY national sections also organize regional conferences to improve communication, networking, and professional exchange, and to strengthen ties of friendship and cooperation between the sections in the region.

Bookbird: A Journal of International Children's Literature is a refereed quarterly journal published by IBBY and is open to any topic in the field of international children's literature. *Bookbird* also has occasional themed issues. Calls for manuscripts are posted on the IBBY website. Regular features include coverage of children's literature studies, IBBY activities, and children's literature awards around the world. *Bookbird* also pays special attention to reading promotion projects worldwide. Its editor works in cooperation with an international editorial review board, guest reviewers, and correspondents who are nominated by IBBY national sections.

IBBY cooperates with several international organizations, including the Canadian Organization for Development Through Education (CODE), the International Federation of Library Associations and Institutions (IFLA), and the International Reading Association (IRA).

IBBY's U.S. National Section

The United States Board on Books for Young People, USBBY, is the U.S. national section of IBBY. It is a nonprofit organization devoted to building bridges of international understanding through children's and young adult books. The Friends of IBBY in the United States was founded in 1976 and became a national section of IBBY in 1984. Membership in USBBY is open to individuals and organizations interested in its mission.

A volunteer board includes USBBY's president, president-elect, past president, recording secretary, treasurer, and 12 directors, four elected and eight appointed, representing the membership as well as the patron organizations that support USBBY, such as IRA, the Children's Book Council (CBC), the American Library Association (ALA), and the National Council of Teachers of English (NCTE).

USBBY offers a forum for those interested in national and international activities relating to children's literature. It publishes a semiannual newsletter for its members, creates an annual list of the most outstanding international literature published or distributed in the United States for children and young adults, maintains an active website, sponsors a biennial regional conference that features speakers of international interest, and cosponsors sessions held at annual conferences of ALA, IRA, and NCTE.

USBBY sponsors the publication of a series of annotated bibliographies of outstanding international literature for young people, the Bridges to Understanding series, published by Scarecrow Press.

It also sponsors the creation of an annual USBBY Outstanding International Books (OIB) list, published yearly in *School Library Journal* and distributed via the USBBY website, http://www.usbby.org/res/2014_USBBY_OIB_Bookmark.pdf, and at meetings and conferences throughout the year.

The OIB committee selects international books that are deemed most outstanding of those published during the calendar year. Books selected for the list represent the best of children's literature from other countries; introduce American readers to outstanding authors and illustrators from other countries; help American children see the world from other points of view; provide a perspective or address a topic otherwise missing from children's literature in the United States; exhibit a distinct cultural flavor; and are accessible to American readers. Committee members judge the books based on artistic and literary merit, originality or creativity of approach, distinctiveness of topic, uniqueness of origin, and qualities that engage and appeal to children.

USBBY also submits nominations for the Hans Christian Andersen award and prepares a biennial selection of outstanding recently published books for the IBBY Honour List and the IBBY list of Outstanding Books for Young People with Disabilities. In addition, it nominates programs for the IBBY-Asahi Reading Promotion Award.

USBBY's Bridge to Understanding Award formally acknowledges the work of adults who use books to promote international understanding among children. The award was established in memory of Arlene Pillar, an educator who served USBBY as newsletter editor from 1984 until her death in 1990. Organizations eligible for this award include schools, libraries, Scout troops, clubs, and bookstores. The winning program may be a one-time event or an ongoing series that serves children ranging in age from kindergarten through tenth grade. The award carries a prize of $1,000 and a certificate. Recent winners included "Promoting Global Awareness in Second Graders," a project in the Madeira City School District in Cincinnati that involved four second-grade teachers as well as the elementary art, music, library, gym, and computer teachers. The project was described as helping students to "make personal connections to the characters of the books, develop empathy, and relate to other children of the world through literature."

Other USBBY activities include support of IBBY's Hands Across the Sea Fund that lends assistance to underfunded IBBY sections.

USBBY has an active twinning relationship with five other IBBY national sections, allowing USBBY members to know and work closely with specific countries and to internationalize USBBY perspectives. Specific initiatives within the twinning program may include payment of IBBY dues for under-funded national sections; provision of funding to purchase books or other needed resources for classrooms and libraries; providing funding or training for writers, illustrators, editors, librarians, and publishers; facilitating fellowships for writers, illustrators, editors, librarians, and publishers, or persons who want to study children's literature; supporting cultural exchange and visits between members of USBBY and twinning national sections; developing reciprocal website postings of newsletters, information about projects, lists of children's books published in each country, and relevant websites; and including news about twinning partners in "Global Partnerships," a regular column in the USBBY newsletter, *Bridges*. Current USBBY twinning partners are Haiti, Lebanon, Palestine, South Africa, and Zambia.

The USBBY Secretariat is at the Center for Teaching Through Children's Books at National Louis University, 5202 Old Orchard Road, Suite 300, Skokie, IL 60077. It can be reached by telephone at 224-233-2030, and its e-mail is secretariat@usbby.org. USBBY's executive director is V. Ellis Vance, 5503 N. El Adobe Drive, Fresno, CA 93711-2363, e-mail executive.director@usbby.org.

Canadian Library Association

1150 Morrison Drive, Suite 400, Ottawa, ON K2H 8S9
613-232-9625, fax 613-563-9895
E-mail info@cla.ca
World Wide Web http://www.cla.ca

Valoree McKay
Executive Director

The Canadian Library Association/Association Canadienne des Bibliothèques (CLA) is the national voice for Canada's library communities, representing the interests of libraries, library workers, and all those concerned about enhancing the quality of life of Canadians through information and literacy. It is predominantly English-language, with selected activities also in French. Its mission states: "CLA is the national voice for Canada's library communities. As members, we champion library values and the value of libraries; influence public policy impacting libraries; inspire and support member learning. We collaborate to strengthen the library community."

Founded in 1946, CLA is a federally incorporated not-for-profit charitable organization. It is governed by a seven-person executive council, which is advised by appointed advisory and standing committees and task forces. Membership consists of institutional members (libraries of all types and related organizations that serve a similar purpose), personal members (all individuals interested in librarianship, library and information services, and information management), associate members (organizations that align with and support libraries, such as library boards, friends groups, school boards, and other associations), and corporate members (any company that supports the mission of CLA).

There are numerous ways in which CLA members and, in some cases, non-members of the library community can engage with CLA. Members can apply for and be appointed to CLA committees and task forces. There are CLA student chapters at all seven English-language and one bilingual library and information science postgraduate programs in Canada, and there is a student chapter at one library technician program. To facilitate sharing of information in specific areas of interest, CLA has created "networks" focusing on topics as diverse as accessible collections and services, evidence-based library and information practice, human resources, library history, government library and information management professionals, and voices for school libraries. There are currently 25 networks.

Governance

In January 2014 the role of CLA president was assumed by Marie DeYoung, university librarian at Patrick Power Library, Saint Mary's University. She succeeded Pilar Martinez, deputy chief executive officer at the Edmonton Public Library. Others serving as officers for 2014 were vice president/president-elect Sandra Singh (Vancouver Public Library), and treasurer Michael Ridley (University of Guelph). CLA's executive director is Valoree McKay.

The association underwent a bylaw revision as a requirement of the new Canada Not for Profit Corporations Act (CNCA). Bylaws compliant with the new law were approved by the membership in June 2014 to take effect in September 2014. Industry Canada approved the changes and provided the association with its official certificate of continuance under the new act.

Major Activities

CLA leads a variety of national advocacy initiatives and hosts a National Conference and trade show. Major activities have focused on these two elements, with federal advocacy taking a predominant role. In addition to its traditional activities, CLA began a process of re-evaluating its current structure and mandate in order to ensure long-term sustainability and relevance to the library and information community. The work continues in 2015.

Advocacy and Public Awareness

CLA continues to monitor both the media and political activities to ensure library values are maintained, and has issued a number of official statements on a wide variety of issues. A sample of the statement topics includes

- Funding of prison libraries
- Budget cuts to Statistics Canada and the Long Form Census (Bill C-626)
- The Protecting Canadians from Online Crime Act (Bill C-13)
- Rural broadband access
- Response to the Royal Society of Canada's November 2014 report on libraries and archives

CLA has been monitoring transition and budget cuts at Library and Archives Canada. It has met with Guy Berthiaume, the newly appointed Librarian and Archivist of Canada, a number of times and continues to build a relationship with this important partner in the library community. CLA has also actively lobbied the government to revisit departmental library closures, and to consult the library community for input from experts in the consolidation and digitization of materials. CLA remains concerned at the lack of transparency and involvement of experts in this process and remains committed to encouraging access to information for all Canadians. It has also participated in the Open Government consultations.

Copyright continues to be a priority, and planning began in 2014 for the 2015 federal election and the anticipated review of the Copyright Act.

CLA tracks intellectual freedom issues in Canada through its annual survey of challenges to library materials and policies. The survey, conducted in English and French, captures details of challenges from libraries of all types.

The association also spearheads Canadian Library Month/Le Mois Canadien des Bibliothèques, partnering with provincial, regional, and territorial library associations and governments. Under the theme "Libraries Inspire! / Les bibliothèques, une source d'inspiration!," this collection of events helped raise awareness during 2014 of all types of libraries and how they have touched lives and opened new opportunities for Canadians of all ages. The public was asked to share stories about how libraries have inspired them, and these were published on the Canadian Library Month website. In addition, small packages were sent to members of Parliament to promote Canadian Library Month. This outreach included a declaration that MPs were invited to sign. Many MPs were photographed signing the declarations, and these pictures were shared via social media, thereby broadening awareness about the month-long observance.

Professional Development

CLA's major contribution to continuing professional development is its annual National Conference. The 2014 National Conference and Trade Show was held in Victoria, B.C., May 28–31, and the 2015 conference was set for June 3–5 in Ottawa.

CLA made a decision in 2014 to no longer pursue continuing professional development activities outside its National Conference. It will be supporting the activities of The Partnership's Education Institute, a continuing education program for library information workers.

International Activities

CLA maintains strong contact with the international library community, mainly through its involvement with the International Federation of Library Associations and Institutions (IFLA). CLA 2014 President Marie DeYoung, along with a large Canadian delegation, attended the 2014 IFLA Congress in Lyon, France. CLA also maintains observer status with the World Intellectual Property Organization's (WIPO's) Standing Committee on Copyright and Related Rights. In addition, CLA is a signatory to IFLA's Lyon Declaration on Access to Information and Development and has advocated for the Canadian government to sign WIPO's Marrakesh Treaty to Facilitate Access to Published Works for Persons Who Are Blind, Visually Impaired or Otherwise Print Disabled.

Communications

As information professionals, Canadian librarians depend on timely and attractive publications and other resources from their professional association, and those outside the community look to the major national association as a significant source of information.

CLA's bimonthly publication *Feliciter,* published since 1956, explores core themes in the library community. In 2012 CLA transitioned *Feliciter* from a print publication to an online magazine. A second publication, *CLA Digest,* is a biweekly e-newsletter for members, with links to in-depth news items.

Awards and Honors

CLA recognizes individuals from the library and information community with annual awards and honors.

The association's most significant award is for Outstanding Service to Librarianship. It is presented only in years when there is a candidate deemed worthy to receive it. In 2014 CLA presented the award to Linda Cook of Edmonton Public Library.

The CLA Award for the Advancement of Intellectual Freedom was presented to Dale Askey of McMaster University for his commitment to the exercise of academic freedom and freedom of speech and his courage in defending intellectual freedom against human rights violations. Since 1988 the award has recognized outstanding contributions to intellectual freedom of individuals and groups, both in and outside the library community.

The CLA/OCLC Award for Innovative Technology was presented to the Alberta Library (TAL) for TAL Online's "Where Are You From?" (WAYF) application, interface, and administrative panel. The award is given in recognition of innovative use of technology to foster community awareness and engagement in the political process.

Denise Scott was the winner of the CLA Student Article Award for "The Language of Library Services for 'At-Risk' Youth." *Curse of the Dream Witch* by Allan Stratton, published by Scholastic Canada, won the 2014 CLA Book of the Year for Children Award; *Graffiti Knight* by Karen Bass, published by Pajama, was the winner of the 2014 CLA Young Adult Book Award, and *The Dark* (HarperCollins), illustrated by Jon Klassen and written by Lemony Snicket, was the winner of the 2014 Amelia Frances Howard-Gibbon Illustrator's Award.

[For additional CLA awards, see "Library Scholarships and Awards" in Part 3—*Ed.*]

Conclusion

CLA is constantly adapting to meet the needs of its members and the broader library community in Canada. The association achieved tangible success with the government on some key files, and efforts continued to advance such issues as copyright and services provided by government libraries, including Library and Archives Canada. Promoting public awareness of the role and importance of libraries and literacies remains a key function of the association.

Part 2
Legislation, Funding, and Grants

Legislation

Legislation and Regulations Affecting Libraries in 2014

Emily Sheketoff
Executive Director

Jazzy Wright
Press Officer

Washington Office, American Library Association

As of this writing, virtually every major news outlet in the United States has dubbed the 113th U.S. Congress of 2013–2014 yet another "Do-Nothing Congress," ironically a term coined in the 1940s to describe a legislature we would now consider hyper-productive measured by its output. According to the Pew Research Center, the 113th Congress barely avoided the dubious distinction of being the least productive ever, and did so only as the result of 51 bills being signed by the president in the waning days of its lame duck session (many of them purely ceremonial, such as bills renaming post offices).

Even with that flurry of legislative activity, the 113th Congress managed to pass just four more substantive bills (212) and nine more ceremonial bills (84) than its immediate predecessor, which retains the title of least productive Congress ever. By contrast, the high water mark in the past 15 years was set by the 106th Congress, which passed 580 pieces of legislation between the beginning of 1999 and the end of the millennium, 80 percent of them substantive.

The 113th Congress's anemic performance affected every aspect of society and the economy, including libraries, and the issues of most concern to their institutions and professionals, such as literacy, privacy, copyright, and access to government information. Most notably, budget gridlock and the resulting "sequestration" of funds took a blunt ax to federal program funding across the board on key library-backed programs, such as the Library Services and Technology Act (LSTA) and the U.S. Department of Education's Innovative Approaches to Literacy (IAL) grants program.

In the non-fiscal sphere, Congress not only failed to broadly overhaul the tangle of complex laws that facilitate domestic and foreign government surveillance, but was not able even to end the National Security Agency's (NSA's) wholesale collection of phone records and "metadata" in the United States and abroad.

The American Library Association (ALA) collaborated with partners in several coalitions to support robust versions of the USA Freedom Act that would have meaningfully improved the balance between national security and personal privacy protection. A much weaker variation of that bill passed in the House; the Senate, however, failed to bring a related ALA-backed bill to the floor for debate. With the slated expiration of key parts of the USAPatriot Act on June 1, 2015, including the "library provision" (Section 215), a battle royal over privacy, cyber-security, and surveillance law reform early in the 114th Congress seems assured.

Additionally, although a majority of all members of the House (including a large number in the Democratic majority) actually cosponsored a bill in the 113th Congress to update the Electronic Communications Privacy Act (ECPA), the bill was not taken up by the House Committee on the Judiciary and did not reach the floor. It has since been reintroduced in both chambers of the 114th Congress with, once again, more than half of all members of the House listed as cosponsors.

Legislation to improve government transparency, through changes in the Freedom of Information Act (FOIA) suffered a reverse fate. Although the FOIA Improvement Act—intended to improve public access to released records—passed the U.S. Senate in December, the House failed to take it up.

Happily, there were some positive privacy developments in the judicial branch. In March 2014 ALA and the Internet Archive joined forces to file an am-icus (friend of the court) brief in *David Leon Riley* v. *State of California* and *United States* v. *Brima Wurie,* two appellate cases consolidated by the U.S. Su-preme Court to permit it to examine the constitutionality of warrantless cell phone searches after police arrests. In the amicus brief, both organizations argued that such searches violate the Fourth Amendment. In June the Supreme Court agreed, unanimously ruling that the Fourth Amendment requires police officers to obtain a warrant before they can lawfully search an arrestee's cell phone.

Federal Library Funding

In December 2014 President Barack Obama signed a $1.1 trillion omnibus spend-ing bill and continuing resolution—the so-called CRomnibus bill—funding much of the federal government through October 2015. The continuing resolution was necessary because of the failure to pass funding bills by October. Programs sup-ported by the library community received level funding or slight adjustment. LSTA received level funding at $180,909,000. LSTA funding is the primary source of federal funding for libraries and was originally authorized at $232 million, but has never received funding at that level. Most LSTA funding supports direct grants to states, which then determine how these funds will be allocated for such programs as job-searching databases, résumé workshops, and summer reading programs.

Under the CRomnibus spending bill:

- Grants to states programs received level funding of nearly $154 million.
- National Leadership grants received level funding of $12 million.
- Laura Bush 21st Century Librarian grants received level funding of $10 million.
- Grants for Native American and Native Hawaiian library services received level funding of $3.9 million.

- IAL, a competitive grant program that requires that at least half of the funds go to low-income school libraries, was level-funded at $25 million.
- Funding for the Institute of Museum and Library Services, which administers the LSTA program, received an increase of $1 million to $227 million, but the increase is largely due to anticipated costs to move the agency's office in Washington, D.C.

On February 2, 2015, the president sent to Congress his proposed nearly $4 trillion budget request to fund the federal government for fiscal year (FY) 2016. The budget request was sent several months earlier than the previous year. Although the request is only the first step in the appropriations process, it does indicate the president's priorities for the year. Obama included in his request $8.8 million in funding for a national digital platform for library and museum services, which would provide free and electronic access to the resources of libraries, archives, and museums by promoting the use of technology. The president requested an increase of nearly $6 million for overall LSTA funding, although grants to states would drop by $348,000.

Workforce Bill Passes

In July the president signed the Workforce Innovation and Opportunity Act (WIOA), intended to open access to federal funding support to public libraries for effective job training and job search programs. In a statement, ALA President Courtney Young applauded the presidential signing of the act and thanked Sen. Jack Reed (D-R.I.) and Rep. Rush Holt (D-N.J.) for their efforts to include libraries in the legislation. ALA will keep a close watch on the Department of Labor's implementation of WIOA over the next year. In October ALA hosted a webinar, "$2.2 Billion Reasons to Pay Attention to WIOA," an interactive event that focused on ways public libraries can receive funding for employment skills training and job search assistance under the act.

Months before the passage of WIOA, Rep. Holt announced his retirement from the House of Representatives after 16 years of service. Holt, who was a leader on the passage of WIOA, introduced the Workforce Investments through Local Libraries (WILL) Act to integrate libraries into job training efforts. He has also been a consistent supporter of LSTA.

Library E-book Lending Talks Continue

Throughout 2014 ALA leaders continued to meet with executives of major publishers including Macmillan, Penguin Random House, and Hachette to discuss the current state and future of library e-book lending. At the core of these discussions was a look at the ways in which authors, publishers, and libraries could work together more closely in areas of common agreement. E-book pricing models were high on the agenda; at the time this report was prepared, each publisher offered one e-book lending model.

There was some e-book access movement in the publishing world. In June Simon & Schuster expanded its pilot library e-book lending program to serve all U.S. libraries. In November ALA and its Digital Content Working Group welcomed Simon & Schuster's announcement that it would allow libraries to opt into the "Buy It Now" merchandising program, which enables library users to directly purchase a title rather than check it out from the library.

On the state and local levels, many libraries are exploring new and innovative ways to offer e-books and other digital resources to their patrons. In June 2014 Connecticut lawmakers passed a bill giving the state library's board of trustees authority to create a statewide e-book collection accessible by library patrons. State legislators earmarked $2.2 million in the state budget to cover startup costs and initial collection development.

Other continuing key issues include digital preservation, accommodation for people with disabilities, digital rights management, and privacy.

Victory for E-rate Modernization

In December 2014 the Federal Communications Commission (FCC) approved a landmark E-rate modernization order that addresses the broadband capacity gap facing many public libraries and schools. FCC will add $1.5 billion to the yearly program in an effort to maximize options for schools and libraries seeking to purchase high-speed broadband connectivity. The passage of the E-rate order marks the culmination of more than 18 months of extensive advocacy by ALA. Among other things, ALA advocated that FCC address both the lack of affordable high-capacity broadband for the majority of libraries and the long-term funding shortage of the E-rate program.

In February ALA announced the launch of "Got E-rate?"—an initiative that encourages library leaders to apply for Internet discounts under the E-rate program. The funding increase and other program changes provide new opportunities for libraries to rethink their broadband networks and make progress toward the broadband speeds necessary for today's and tomorrow's library services.

Net Neutrality Campaign Continues

Overall, 2014 was a busy year for net neutrality advocacy. In January the U.S. Court of Appeals struck down most of the Open Internet Order, giving commercial companies the legal authority to block Internet traffic, offer preferential treatment to certain Internet services or applications, and steer users to websites based on commercial interests. Beyond challenges to equitable access to information and intellectual freedom, higher education and libraries are generators of and subscribers to critical educational and cultural content and could suffer under a two-tier or "fast-lane" approach to network neutrality. In response to the ruling, ALA actively engaged with library and education allies, including the Association of Research Libraries (ARL) and EDUCAUSE, to influence FCC and Congress on the issue.

ALA was one of the first to file when FCC opened the docket in February. ALA, ARL, and EDUCAUSE followed up with key FCC staff and shared the perspective of education, research, and learning organizations and examples of what is at stake for the library community and library patrons.

Copyright Update

The U.S. Second Circuit Court of Appeals in 2014 upheld a lower court's holding in *Authors Guild* v. *HathiTrust*. In a significant victory for libraries and the public, the Second Circuit ruled that providing a full-text searchable database and access to works for people with print disabilities are both "fair use." This decision affirms that libraries can engage in mass digitization to improve the discovery of works and provide full access to those works to students at HathiTrust digital library institutions with print disabilities. The Library Copyright Alliance (LCA), of which ALA is a member, filed an amicus brief in the case.

In October the U.S. Court of Appeals for the 11th Circuit handed down an important decision in *Cambridge University Press et al.* v. *Carl V. Patton et al.* concerning the permissible fair use of copyrighted works in electronic reserves for academic courses. Although publishers sought to bar the uncompensated excerpting of copyrighted material for "e-reserves," the court rejected all such arguments and provided new guidance for how "fair use" determinations by educators and librarians should best be made in the states within the 11th Circuit's jurisdiction. Remanding the case to the lower court for further proceedings, the appeals court ruled that fair use decisions should be based on a flexible, case-by-case analysis of the four factors of fair use rather than rigid "checklists" or "percentage-based" formulae.

The Google Books case continued into December 2014 when the U.S. Court of Appeals for the Second Circuit held a hearing for the Authors Guild's appeal of the U.S. District Court for the Southern District of New York's ruling to uphold the fair use doctrine in *Authors Guild* v. *Google et al.* LCA filed an amicus brief focusing on the issue of class certification in the case. The Google case questioned the legality of Google's searchable book database, which allows the public to search more than 20 million books. In his dismissal of the case in 2013 Judge Denny Chin referenced an amicus brief submitted by LCA and enumerated the public benefits of Google Book Search by calling the project a fair use under the copyright law.

ALA's Washington Office continues to actively meet with and lobby both the U.S. Copyright Office and Patent and Trademark Office at senior levels in support of the fastest, and least legislatively complicated, ratification of the Marrakesh Treaty to promote the worldwide flow of copyrighted material to the print-disabled. Specifically, ALA and its coalition colleagues continue to urge both agencies, consistent with the position taken by the U.S. delegation in Marrakesh, to recommend "clean" ratification of that agreement without proposing any changes to existing U.S. law, particularly Section 121 of Title 17, the "Chaffee Amendment." ALA continues to coordinate closely with major national advocacy groups for the blind and print-disabled in these efforts.

Library Legislative Day

Hundreds of library supporters met in Washington, D.C., with their members of Congress May 5–6, 2014, to advocate for libraries during ALA's 40th annual National Library Legislative Day. U.S. Sen. Angus King (I-Maine) started the event by addressing library advocates at the opening briefing. Additional speakers included then-Maine State Librarian Linda Lord; Gabriel Rottman, legislative counsel for the American Civil Liberties Union; Shawn Daugherty, assistant director of the Scholarly Publishing and Academic Resources Coalition (SPARC); and Peter Jaszi, intellectual property expert and professor of law at the American University Washington College of Law. Library supporters who could not attend the Washington meetings connected virtually with legislators via phone calls, e-mails, and social media platforms.

Workforce Training Study

According to an ALA study released in July 2014, nearly all U.S. public libraries offer workforce development training programs, online job resources, and technology skills training. The Digital Inclusion Survey provides a first national look at emerging trends. A sampling of these ranges from STEM (science, technology, engineering, mathematics) makerspaces (17 percent, or about 3,000 libraries, have them), to wireless printing (33 percent), to 3-D printers and hosting hackathons or other coding/application development events (about 2 percent each, or roughly 260 libraries). Overall, libraries report technology improvements—including nearly ubiquitous public wifi and a leap in e-book access—but ALA's survey also documents digital differences among states and an urban/rural divide. Less than half of rural libraries reported they increased bandwidth speeds in the last 24 months, compared with 64 percent of urban libraries and 56 percent of suburban libraries. Fewer than two-thirds of rural libraries report having access to information technology staff, far behind their counterparts. But fully two-thirds of all libraries agree that they would like to increase their broadband capacity, and say that cost is the leading barrier to doing so. The survey is managed by the ALA Office of Research and Statistics; the ALA Office for Information Technology Policy is a partner in the research project.

Internet Filtering Study

Schools and libraries nationwide are routinely filtering Internet content to a far greater extent than the Children's Internet Protection Act requires, according to "Fencing Out Knowledge: Impacts of the Children's Internet Protection Act 10 Years Later," a report released in June by the ALA Office for Information Technology Policy and the ALA Office for Intellectual Freedom. "Fencing Out Knowledge" is based on a year-long study that included a two-day symposium during the summer of 2013 and other research.

Funding Programs and Grant-Making Agencies

National Endowment for the Humanities

1100 Pennsylvania Ave. N.W., Washington, DC 20506
202-606-8400, 800-634-1121
TDD (hearing impaired) 202-606-8282 or 866-372-2930 (toll free)
E-mail info@neh.gov, World Wide Web http://neh.gov

The National Endowment for the Humanities (NEH) is an independent federal agency created in 1965. It is one of the largest funders of humanities programs in the United States.

Because democracy demands wisdom, NEH promotes excellence in the humanities and conveys the lessons of history to all Americans, seeking to develop educated and thoughtful citizens. It accomplishes this mission by providing grants for high-quality humanities projects in six funding areas: education, preservation and access, public programs, research, challenge grants, and digital humanities.

Grants from NEH enrich classroom learning, create and preserve knowledge, and bring ideas to life through public television, radio, new technologies, museum exhibitions, and programs in libraries and other community places. Recipients typically are cultural institutions, such as museums, archives, libraries, colleges and universities, and public television and radio stations, as well as individual scholars. The grants

- Strengthen teaching and learning in the humanities in schools and colleges
- Preserve and provide access to cultural and educational resources
- Provide opportunities for lifelong learning
- Facilitate research and original scholarship
- Strengthen the institutional base of the humanities

Over nearly half a century, NEH has reached millions of people with projects and programs that preserve and study the nation's culture and history while providing a foundation for the future.

The endowment's mission is to enrich cultural life by promoting the study of the humanities. According to the National Foundation on the Arts and the Humanities Act, "The term 'humanities' includes, but is not limited to, the study of the following: language, both modern and classical; linguistics; literature; history; jurisprudence; philosophy; archaeology; comparative religion; ethics; the history, criticism, and theory of the arts; those aspects of social sciences which have humanistic content and employ humanistic methods; and the study and application of the humanities to the human environment with particular attention to reflecting our diverse heritage, traditions, and history and to the relevance of the humanities to the current conditions of national life."

The act, adopted by Congress in 1965, provided for the establishment of the National Foundation on the Arts and the Humanities in order to promote progress and scholarship in the humanities and the arts in the United States. The act included the following findings:

- The arts and the humanities belong to all the people of the United States.
- The encouragement and support of national progress and scholarship in the humanities and the arts, while primarily matters for private and local initiative, are also appropriate matters of concern to the federal government.
- An advanced civilization must not limit its efforts to science and technology alone, but must give full value and support to the other great branches of scholarly and cultural activity in order to achieve a better understanding of the past, a better analysis of the present, and a better view of the future.
- Democracy demands wisdom and vision in its citizens. It must therefore foster and support a form of education, and access to the arts and the humanities, designed to make people of all backgrounds and locations masters of technology and not its unthinking servants.
- It is necessary and appropriate for the federal government to complement, assist, and add to programs for the advancement of the humanities and the arts by local, state, regional, and private agencies and their organizations. In doing so, the government must be sensitive to the nature of public sponsorship. Public funding of the arts and humanities is subject to the conditions that traditionally govern the use of public money. Such funding should contribute to public support and confidence in the use of taxpayer funds. Public funds provided by the federal government ultimately must serve public purposes the Congress defines.
- The arts and the humanities reflect the high place accorded by the American people to the nation's rich culture and history and to the fostering of mutual respect for the diverse beliefs and values of all persons and groups.

What NEH Grants Accomplish

Since its founding, NEH has awarded more than 69,300 competitive grants.

Interpretive Exhibitions

Interpretive exhibitions provide opportunities for lifelong learning in the humanities for millions of Americans. Since 1967 NEH has awarded approximately $300 million in grants for interpretive exhibitions, catalogs, and public programs, which are among the most highly visible activities supported by the endowment. During 2014 NEH support financed exhibitions; reading, viewing, and discussion programs; Web-based programs; and other public education programs at venues across the country.

Renewing Teaching

Over NEH's history, more than 100,000 high school and college teachers have deepened their knowledge of the humanities through intensive summer study supported by the endowment; tens of thousands of students benefit from these better-educated teachers every year.

Reading and Discussion Programs

Since 1982 NEH has supported reading and discussion programs in the nation's libraries, bringing people together to discuss works of literature and history. Scholars in the humanities provide thematic direction for the discussion programs. Using selected texts and such themes as "Work," "Family," "Diversity," and "Not for Children Only," these programs have attracted more than 2 million Americans to read and talk about what they've read.

Chronicling America

NEH's National Digital Newspaper Program is supporting projects to convert microfilm of historically important U.S. newspapers into fully searchable digital files. Developed in partnership with the Library of Congress, this long-term project ultimately will make more than 30 million pages of newspapers accessible online. For more on this project, visit http://chroniclingamerica.loc.gov.

Stimulating Private Support

About $2 billion in humanities support has been generated by NEH's Challenge Grants program, which requires most grant recipients to raise $3 in nonfederal funds for every dollar they receive.

Presidential Papers

Ten presidential papers projects, from Washington to Eisenhower, have received support from NEH. Matching grants for the ten projects have leveraged millions of dollars in nonfederal contributions.

New Scholarship

NEH grants enable scholars to do in-depth study. Jack Rakove explored the making of the Constitution in his *Original Meanings* and James McPherson chronicled the Civil War in his *Battle Cry of Freedom*. Projects supported by NEH grants have earned nearly 20 Pulitzer Prizes.

History on Screen

Since 1967 NEH has awarded approximately $300 million to support the production of films for broad public distribution, including the Emmy Award-winning series *The Civil War,* the Oscar-nominated films *Brooklyn Bridge, The Restless*

Conscience, and *Freedom on My Mind,* and film biographies of John and Abigail Adams, Eugene O'Neill, and Ernest Hemingway. More than 20 million people have watched Ken Burns's critically acclaimed *The War* (2007), which chronicles the United States in World War II. More than 8 million saw the April 2010 debut of *The Buddha,* a documentary made for PBS by filmmaker David Grubin, and it has been streamed into hundreds of classrooms nationwide.

American Voices

NEH support for scholarly editions makes the writings of prominent and influential Americans accessible. Ten presidents are included, along with such key figures as Martin Luther King, Jr., George C. Marshall, and Eleanor Roosevelt. Papers of prominent writers—among them Emily Dickinson, Walt Whitman, Mark Twain, and Robert Frost—are also available.

Library of America

Millions of books have been sold as part of the Library of America series, a collection of the riches of the nation's literature. Begun with NEH seed money, the nearly 200 published volumes include the works of such figures as Henry Adams, Edith Wharton, William James, Eudora Welty, and W. E. B. Du Bois.

The Library of America also received a $150,000 grant for the publication of *American Poetry: The Seventeenth and Eighteenth Centuries* (two volumes) and an expanded volume of selected works by Captain John Smith—a key figure in the establishment of the first permanent English settlement in North America, at Jamestown, Virginia—and other early exploration narratives.

Technical Innovation

NEH support for the digital humanities is fueling innovation and new tools for research in the humanities. Modern 3D technology allows students to visit things ranging from ancient Egypt to the 1964–1965 New York World's Fair. Spectral imaging was used to create an online critical edition of explorer David Livingstone's previously unreadable field diary of 1871.

Science and the Humanities

The scientific past is being preserved with NEH-supported editions of the letters of Charles Darwin, the works of Albert Einstein, and the 14-volume papers of Thomas Edison. Additionally, NEH and the National Science Foundation have joined forces in Documenting Endangered Languages (DEL), a multiyear effort to preserve records of key languages that are in danger of becoming extinct.

EDSITEment

EDSITEment (http://edsitement.neh.gov) assembles the best humanities resources on the Web, drawing more than 400,000 visitors each month. Incorporating these Internet resources, particularly primary documents, from more than 350 peer-reviewed websites, EDSITEment features more than 500 online lesson plans in all areas of the humanities. Teachers use EDSITEment's resources to enhance lessons and to engage students through interactive technology tools that hone critical-thinking skills.

Federal-State Partnership

The Office of Federal-State Partnership links NEH with the nationwide network of 56 humanities councils, which are located in each state, the District of Columbia, Puerto Rico, the U.S. Virgin Islands, the Northern Mariana Islands, American Samoa, and Guam. Each council funds humanities programs in its own jurisdiction.

Directory of State Humanities Councils

Alabama

Alabama Humanities Foundation
1100 Ireland Way, Suite 202
Birmingham, AL 35205-7001
205-558-3980, fax 205-558-3981
http://www.alabamahumanities.org

Alaska

Alaska Humanities Forum
161 E. First Ave., Door 15
Anchorage, AK 99501
907-272-5341, fax 907-272-3979
http://www.akhf.org

Arizona

Arizona Humanities Council
Ellis-Shackelford House
1242 N. Central Ave.
Phoenix, AZ 85004-1887
602-257-0335, fax 602-257-0392
http://www.azhumanities.org

Arkansas

Arkansas Humanities Council
407 President Clinton Ave., Suite 201
Little Rock, AR 72201
501-320-5761, fax 501-537-4550
http://www.arkhums.org

California

Cal Humanities
312 Sutter St., Suite 601
San Francisco, CA 94108
415-391-1474, fax 415-391-1312
http://www.calhum.org

Colorado

Colorado Humanities
7935 E. Prentice Ave., Suite 450
Greenwood Village, CO 80111
303-894-7951, fax 303-864-9361
http://www.coloradohumanities.org

Connecticut

Connecticut Humanities Council
37 Broad St.
Middletown, CT 06457
860-685-2260, fax 860-685-7597
http://cthumanities.org

Delaware

Delaware Humanities Forum
100 W. Tenth St., Suite 1009
Wilmington, DE 19801
302-657-0650, fax 302-657-0655
http://dehumanities.org

District of Columbia

Humanities Council of Washington, D.C.
925 U St. N.W.
Washington, DC 20001
202-387-8393, fax 202-387-8149
http://wdchumanities.org

Florida

Florida Humanities Council
599 Second St. S.
St. Petersburg, FL 33701-5005
727-873-2000, fax 727-873-2014
http://www.flahum.org

Georgia

Georgia Humanities Council
50 Hurt Plaza S.E., Suite 595
Atlanta, GA 30303-2915
404-523-6220, fax 404-523-5702
http://www.georgiahumanities.org

Hawaii

Hawai'i Council for the Humanities
First Hawaiian Bank Bldg.
3599 Waialae Ave., Room 25
Honolulu, HI 96816
808-732-5402, fax 808-732-5432
http://www.hihumanities.org

Idaho

Idaho Humanities Council
217 W. State St.
Boise, ID 83702
208-345-5346, fax 208-345-5347
http://www.idahohumanities.org

Illinois

Illinois Humanities Council
17 N. State St., No. 1400
Chicago, IL 60602-3296
312-422-5580, fax 312-422-5588
http://www.prairie.org

Indiana

Indiana Humanities
1500 N. Delaware St.
Indianapolis, IN 46202
317-638-1500, fax 317-634-9503
http://www.indianahumanities.org

Iowa

Humanities Iowa
100 Library, Room 4039
Iowa City, IA 52242-4038
319-335-4153, fax 319-335-4154
http://humanitiesiowa.org

Kansas

Kansas Humanities Council
112 S.W. Sixth Ave., Suite 210
Topeka, KS 66603

785-357-0359, fax 785-357-1723
http://www.kansashumanities.org

Kentucky

Kentucky Humanities Council
206 E. Maxwell St.
Lexington, KY 40508
859-257-5932, fax 859-257-5933
http://www.kyhumanities.org

Louisiana

Louisiana Endowment for the Humanities
938 Lafayette St., Suite 300
New Orleans, LA 70113-1782
504-523-4352, fax 504-529-2358
http://www.leh.org

Maine

Maine Humanities Council
674 Brighton Ave.
Portland, ME 04102-1012
207-773-5051, fax 207-773-2416
http://www.mainehumanities.org

Maryland

Maryland Humanities Council
108 W. Centre St.
Baltimore, MD 21201-4565
410-685-0095, fax 410-685-0795
http://www.mdhc.org

Massachusetts

Mass Humanities
66 Bridge St.
Northampton, MA 01060
413-584-8440, fax 413-584-8454
http://www.masshumanities.org

Michigan

Michigan Humanities Council
119 Pere Marquette Drive, Suite 3B
Lansing, MI 48912-1270
517-372-7770, fax 517-372-0027
http://michiganhumanities.org

Minnesota

Minnesota Humanities Center
987 E. Ivy Ave.
St. Paul, MN 55106-2046
651-774-0105, fax 651-774-0205
http://www.minnesotahumanities.org

Mississippi

Mississippi Humanities Council
3825 Ridgewood Rd., Room 311
Jackson, MS 39211
601-432-6752, fax 601-432-6750
http://www.mshumanities.org

Missouri

Missouri Humanities Council
543 Hanley Industrial Court, Suite 201
St. Louis, MO 63144-1905
314-781-9660, fax 314-781-9681
http://www.mohumanities.org

Montana

Humanities Montana
311 Brantly
Missoula, MT 59812-7848
406-243-6022, fax 406-243-4836
http://www.humanitiesmontana.org

Nebraska

Nebraska Humanities Council
215 Centennial Mall South, Suite 330
Lincoln, NE 68508
402-474-2131, fax 402-474-4852
http://www.humanitiesnebraska.org

Nevada

Nevada Humanities
1670-200 N. Virginia St.
P.O. Box 8029
Reno, NV 89507
775-784-6587, fax 775-784-6527
http://www.nevadahumanities.org

New Hampshire

New Hampshire Humanities Council
117 Pleasant St.
Concord, NH 03301-3852

603-224-4071, fax 603-224-4072
http://www.nhhc.org

New Jersey

New Jersey Council for the Humanities
28 W. State St., 6th floor
Trenton, NJ 08608
609-695-4838, fax 609-695-4929
http://www.njch.org

New Mexico

New Mexico Humanities Council
4115 Silver Ave. S.E.
Albuquerque, NM 87108
505-633-7370, fax 505-633-7377
http://www.nmhum.org

New York

New York Council for the Humanities
150 Broadway, Suite 1700
New York, NY 10038
212-233-1131, fax 212-233-4607
http://www.nyhumanities.org

North Carolina

North Carolina Humanities Council
122 N. Elm St., Suite 601
Greensboro, NC 27401
336-334-5325, fax 336-334-5052
http://www.nchumanities.org

North Dakota

North Dakota Humanities Council
418 E. Broadway, Suite 8
P.O. Box 2191
Bismarck, ND 58502
701-255-3360, fax 701-223-8724
http://www.ndhumanities.org

Ohio

Ohio Humanities Council
471 E. Broad St., Suite 1620
Columbus, OH 43215-3857
614-461-7802, fax 614-461-4651
http://www.ohiohumanities.org

Oklahoma

Oklahoma Humanities Council
Festival Plaza
428 W. California, Suite 270
Oklahoma City, OK 73102
405-235-0280, fax 405-235-0289
http://www.okhumanities.org

Oregon

Oregon Council for the Humanities
813 S.W. Alder St., Suite 702
Portland, OR 97205
503-241-0543, fax 503-241-0024
http://www.oregonhumanities.org

Pennsylvania

Pennsylvania Humanities Council
325 Chestnut St., Suite 715
Philadelphia, PA 19106-2607
215-925-1005, fax 215-925-3054
http://www.pahumanities.org

Rhode Island

Rhode Island Council for the Humanities
131 Washington St., Suite 210
Providence, RI 02903
401-273-2250, fax 401-454-4872
http://www.rihumanities.org

South Carolina

Humanities Council of South Carolina
2711 Middleburg Drive, Suite 203
P.O. Box 5287
Columbia, SC 29250
803-771-2477, fax 803-771-2487
http://www.schumanities.org

South Dakota

South Dakota Humanities Council
1215 Trail Ridge Rd., Suite A
Brookings, SD 57006
605-688-6113, fax 605-688-4531
http://sdhumanities.org

Tennessee

Humanities Tennessee
306 Gay St., Suite 306
Nashville, TN 37201

615-770-0006, fax 615-770-0007
http://www.humanitiestennessee.org

Texas

Humanities Texas
1410 Rio Grande St.
Austin, TX 78701
512-440-1991, fax 512-440-0115
http://www.humanitiestexas.org

Utah

Utah Humanities Council
202 W. 300 North
Salt Lake City, UT 84103
801-359-9670, fax 801-531-7869
http://www.utahhumanities.org

Vermont

Vermont Humanities Council
11 Loomis St.
Montpelier, VT 05602
802-262-2626, fax 802-262-2620
http://www.vermonthumanities.org

Virginia

Virginia Foundation for the Humanities and
Public Policy
145 Ednam Drive
Charlottesville, VA 22903-4629
434-924-3296, fax 434-296-4714
http://www.virginiafoundation.org

Washington

Humanities Washington
1015 Eighth Ave. North, Suite B
Seattle, WA 98109
206-682-1770, fax 206-682-4158
http://www.humanities.org

West Virginia

West Virginia Humanities Council
1310 Kanawha Blvd. East
Charleston, WV 25301
304-346-8500, fax 304-346-8504
http://www.wvhumanities.org

Wisconsin

Wisconsin Humanities Council
222 S. Bedford St., Suite F
Madison, WI 53703-3688
608-262-0706, fax 608-263-7970
http://www.wisconsinhumanities.org

Wyoming

Wyoming Humanities Council
1315 E. Lewis St.
Laramie, WY 82072-3459
307-721-9243, fax 307-742-4914
http://www.thinkwy.org

American Samoa

Amerika Samoa Humanities Council
P.O. Box 5800
Pago Pago, AS 96799
684-633-4870, fax 684-633-4873
http://ashcouncil.org

Guam

Guam Humanities Council
222 Chalan Santo Papa
Reflection Center, Suite 106

Hagatna, Guam 96910
671-472-4460, fax 671-472-4465
http://www.guamhumanitiescouncil.org

Northern Marianas Islands

Northern Marianas Humanities Council
P.O. Box 506437
Saipan, MP 96950
670-235-4785, fax 670-235-4786
http://northernmarianashumanities.org

Puerto Rico

Fundación Puertorriqueña de las Humanidades
109 San José St., 3rd floor
Box 9023920
San Juan, PR 00902-3920
787-721-2087, fax 787-721-2684
http://www.fphpr.org

Virgin Islands

Virgin Islands Humanities Council
1829 Kongens Gade
St. Thomas, VI 00802-6746
340-776-4044, fax 340-774-3972
http://www.vihumanities.org

NEH Overview

Bridging Cultures

Bridging Cultures is a special endowment-wide initiative that highlights the role of the humanities in enhancing understanding and respect for diverse cultures and subcultures within America's borders and around the globe.

The initiative encourages projects that explore the ways in which cultures have influenced society. With the aim of revitalizing intellectual and civic life through the humanities, NEH welcomes projects that expand both scholarly and public discussion of diverse countries, peoples, and cultural and intellectual traditions worldwide.

Contact: 202-606-8337, e-mail bridgingcultures@neh.gov.

Division of Education Programs

Through grants to educational institutions and professional development programs for scholars and teachers, this division is designed to support study of the humanities at all levels of education.

Grants support the development of curriculum and materials, faculty study programs among educational institutions, and conferences and networks of institutions.

Contact: 202-606-8500, e-mail education@neh.gov.

Seminars and Institutes

Grants support summer seminars and institutes in the humanities for college and school teachers. These faculty-development activities are conducted at colleges and universities in the United States and abroad. Those wishing to participate in seminars should submit their seminar applications to the seminar director.

Contact: 202-606-8471, e-mail sem-inst@neh.gov.

Landmarks of American History and Culture

Grants for Landmarks workshops provide support to school teachers and community college faculty. These professional development workshops are conducted at or near sites important to American history and culture (such as presidential residences or libraries, colonial era settlements, major battlefields, historic districts, and sites associated with major writers or artists) to address central themes and issues in American history, government, literature, art history, and related subjects in the humanities.

Contact: 202-606-8463, e-mail landmarks@neh.gov.

Division of Preservation and Access

Grants are made for projects that will create, preserve, and increase the availability of resources important for research, education, and public programming in the humanities.

Support may be sought to preserve the intellectual content and aid bibliographic control of collections; to compile bibliographies, descriptive catalogs, and guides to cultural holdings; and to create dictionaries, encyclopedias, databases, and electronic archives. Applications also may be submitted for education and training projects dealing with issues of preservation or access; for research and development leading to improved preservation and access standards, practices, and tools; and for projects to digitize historic U.S. newspapers and to document endangered languages. Grants are also made to help smaller cultural repositories preserve and care for their humanities collections. Proposals may combine preservation and access activities within a single project.

Contact: 202-606-8570, e-mail preservation@neh.gov.

Division of Public Programs

Public humanities programs promote lifelong learning in American and world history, literature, comparative religion, philosophy, and other fields of the humanities. They offer new insights into familiar subjects and invite conversation about important humanities ideas and questions.

The Division of Public Programs supports a wide range of public humanities programs that reach large and diverse public audiences through a variety of program formats, including interpretive exhibitions, radio and television broadcasts, lectures, symposia, interpretive multimedia projects, printed materials, and reading and discussion programs.

Grants support the development and production of television, radio, and digital media programs; the planning and implementation of museum exhibitions, the interpretation of historic sites, the production of related publications, multimedia

components, and educational programs; and the planning and implementation of reading and discussion programs, lectures, symposia, and interpretive exhibitions of books, manuscripts, and other library resources.
   Contact: 202-606-8269, e-mail publicpgms@neh.gov.

Division of Research Programs

Through fellowships to individual scholars and grants to support complex, frequently collaborative research, the Division of Research Programs contributes to the creation of knowledge in the humanities.

Fellowships and Stipends

Grants provide support for scholars to undertake full-time independent research and writing in the humanities. Grants are available for a maximum of one year and a minimum of two months of summer study.
   Contact: 202-606-8200, e-mail (fellowships) fellowships@neh.gov, (summer stipends) stipends@neh.gov.

Research

Grants provide up to three years of support for collaborative research in the preparation for publication of editions, translations, and other important works in the humanities, and in the conduct of large or complex interpretive studies, including archaeology projects and humanities studies of science and technology. Grants also support research opportunities offered through independent research centers and international research organizations.
   Contact: 202-606-8200, e-mail research@neh.gov.

Office of Challenge Grants

Nonprofit institutions interested in developing new sources of long-term support for educational, scholarly, preservation, and public programs in the humanities can be assisted in these efforts by an NEH Challenge Grant. Grantees are required to raise $3 in nonfederal donations for every federal dollar offered. Both federal and nonfederal funds may be used to establish or increase institutional endowments and therefore guarantee long-term support for a variety of humanities needs. Funds also can be used for limited direct capital expenditures where such needs are compelling and clearly related to improvements in the humanities.
   Contact: 202-606-8309, e-mail challenge@neh.gov.

Office of Digital Humanities

The Office of Digital Humanities encourages and supports projects that utilize or study the impact of digital technology on research, education, preservation, and public programming in the humanities. Launched as an initiative in 2006, Digital Humanities was made permanent as an office within NEH in 2008.
   NEH is interested in fostering the growth of digital humanities and lending support to a wide variety of projects, including those that deploy digital technologies and methods to enhance understanding of a topic or issue; those that study the impact of digital technology on the humanities; and those that digitize important

materials, thereby increasing the public's ability to search and access humanities information.

The office coordinates the endowment's efforts in the area of digital scholarship. Currently NEH has numerous programs throughout the agency that are actively funding digital scholarship, including Humanities Collections and Resources, Institutes for Advanced Topics in the Digital Humanities, Digital Humanities Challenge Grants, Digital Humanities Start-Up Grants, and many others. NEH is also actively working with other funding partners in the United States and abroad in order to better coordinate spending on digital infrastructure for the humanities.

Contact: 202-606-8401, e-mail odh@neh.gov.

A full list of NEH grants programs and deadlines is available on the endowment's website at http://www.neh.gov/grants.

Institute of Museum and Library Services
Office of Library Services

1800 M Street N.W., Ninth Floor, Washington, DC 20036-5802
202-653-4657, fax 202-653-4600
World Wide Web: http://www.imls.gov

Susan H. Hildreth
Director

Maura Marx
Deputy Director for Libraries

Vision and Mission

The vision of the Institute of Museum and Library Services (IMLS) is a democratic society where communities and individuals thrive with broad public access to knowledge, cultural heritage, and lifelong learning.

Its mission is to inspire libraries and museums to advance innovation, lifelong learning, and cultural and civic engagement. It provides leadership through research, policy development, and grant making.

Strategic Goals

- IMLS places the learner at the center and supports engaging experiences in libraries and museums that prepare people to be full participants in their local communities and our global society.
- IMLS promotes museums and libraries as strong community anchors that enhance civic engagement, cultural opportunities, and economic vitality.
- IMLS supports exemplary stewardship of museum and library collections and promotes the use of technology to facilitate discovery of knowledge and cultural heritage.
- IMLS advises the president and Congress on plans, policies, and activities to sustain and increase public access to information and ideas.
- IMLS achieves excellence in public management and performs as a model organization through strategic alignment of resources and prioritization of programmatic activities, maximizing value for the public.

There are 123,000 libraries and 35,000 museums in the United States. IMLS supports the full range of libraries, including public, academic, research, special, and tribal, and the full range of museums including art, history, science and technology, children's museums, historical societies, tribal museums, planetariums, botanic gardens, and zoos. Nearly 170 million people in the United States over

On January 15, 2015, Susan H. Hildreth completed her four-year term as IMLS director. Under her leadership, IMLS provided nearly $1 billion in support to libraries and museums, with a strong emphasis on early learning, STEM-related projects, and connectivity in libraries.

the age of 14 (69 percent of the population) are library users, and every year 148 million over the age of 18 visit a museum.

Overview

U.S. museums and libraries are at the forefront of the movement to create a nation of learners. As stewards of cultural heritage with rich, authentic content, they provide learning experiences for everyone. With built infrastructure in nearly every community in the nation, robust online networks, and dedicated and knowledgeable staff, they connect people to one another and to the full spectrum of human experience.

The role of IMLS is to provide leadership and funding for the nation's museums and libraries—resources these institutions need to fulfill their mission of becoming centers of learning for life, crucial to achieving personal fulfillment, a productive workforce, and an engaged citizenry.

The Museum and Library Services Act, which includes the Library Services and Technology Act (LSTA) and the Museum Services Act (MSA), authorizes IMLS to support the following activities:

LSTA

- Enhance coordination among federal programs that relate to library and information services
- Promote continuous improvement in library services in all types of libraries in order to better serve the people of the United States
- Facilitate access to resources in all types of libraries for the purpose of cultivating an educated and informed citizenry
- Encourage resource sharing among all types of libraries for the purpose of achieving economical and efficient delivery of library services to the public
- Promote literacy, education, and lifelong learning and enhance and expand the services and resources provided by libraries, including those services and resources relating to workforce development, 21st century skills, and digital literacy skills
- Enhance the skills of the current library workforce and recruit future professionals to the field of library and information services
- Ensure the preservation of knowledge and library collections in all formats and enable libraries to serve their communities during disasters
- Enhance the role of libraries within the information infrastructure of the United States in order to support research, education, and innovation
- Promote library services that provide users with access to information through national, state, local, regional, and international collaborations and networks

MSA

- Encourage and support museums in carrying out their public service role of connecting the whole of society to the cultural, artistic, historical, natural, and scientific understandings that constitute the nation's heritage

- Encourage and support museums in carrying out their educational role as core providers of learning and in conjunction with schools, families, and communities
- Encourage leadership, innovation, and applications of the most current technologies and practices to enhance museum services through international, national, regional, state, and local networks and partnerships
- Assist, encourage, and support museums in carrying out their stewardship responsibilities to achieve the highest standards in conservation and care of the nation's cultural, historic, natural, and scientific heritage to benefit future generations
- Assist, encourage, and support museums in achieving the highest standards of management and service to the public, and ease the financial burden borne by museums as a result of their increasing use by the public
- Support resource sharing and partnerships among museums, libraries, schools, and other community organizations
- Encourage and support museums as a part of economic development and revitalization in communities
- Ensure museums of various types and sizes in diverse geographic regions are afforded attention and support
- Support efforts at the state level to leverage museum resources and maximize museum services

A general provision of the Museum and Library Services Act calls for IMLS to develop and implement policy to ensure the availability of museum, library, and information services throughout the United States. Specific duties include the following: advising the president, Congress, and other federal agencies and offices on museum, library, and information services in order to ensure the creation, preservation, organization, and dissemination of knowledge; engaging federal, state, and local governmental agencies and private entities in assessing the needs of museum, library, and information services, and coordinating the development of plans, policies, and activities to meet such needs effectively; carrying out programs of research and development, data collection, and financial assistance to extend and improve the nation's museum, library, and information services; ensuring that museum, library, and information services are fully integrated into the information and education infrastructures.

Funding

In fiscal year (FY) 2014, Congress appropriated $180,909,000 for the programs authorized by LSTA. The Office of Library Services within IMLS, under the policy direction of the IMLS director and deputy director, administers LSTA programs. The office comprises the Division of State Programs, which administers the Grants to States program, and the Division of Discretionary Programs, which administers the National Leadership Grants for Libraries program; the Laura Bush 21st Century Librarian Program; the Native American Library Services program; and the Native Hawaiian Library Services program. IMLS presents annual awards to libraries through the National Medal for Museum and Library Service program.

Additionally, IMLS supports two award programs administered by the President's Committee on the Arts and the Humanities: the National Arts and Humanities Youth Program Awards and the National Student Poets Program.

Library Statistics

The president's budget request for FY 2014 included funds for IMLS to continue administering the Public Libraries Survey (PLS) and the State Library Administrative Agencies Survey. In addition to producing yearly reports of the survey data, IMLS provided shorter research products to highlight report findings. These brief reports leverage the survey data to address a wide range of public policy priorities, including education, employment, community and economic development, and telecommunications policy.

In the Library Statistics section of the IMLS website (http://www.imls.gov/research), visitors can link to data search tools, the latest available data for each survey, other publications, data files, and survey definitions.

Public Libraries Survey

Descriptive statistics for more than 9,000 public libraries are collected and disseminated annually through a voluntary census, the Public Libraries Survey (PLS). The survey is conducted through the Public Library Statistics Cooperative (PLSC, formerly the Federal-State Cooperative System [FSCS]). In FY 2014 IMLS completed the 26th collection of this data. In May 2014 final imputed data files for the FY 2012 Public Libraries Survey (PLS) were made available in the Data Sets section of the IMLS website. The PLS is designed as a universe survey whose FY 2012 frame consisted of 9,140 public libraries as identified by state library agencies (9,082 public libraries in the 50 states and the District of Columbia and 58 public libraries in the territories of Guam, the Northern Mariana Islands, Puerto Rico, and the U.S. Virgin Islands). The Compare Public Libraries Tool and the Find Public Libraries Tool on the IMLS website were updated with FY 2012 data, and a resource called Public Library Data Reports was produced using the Data Ferret tool developed by U.S. Census Bureau.

The survey collects identifying information about public libraries and each of their service outlets, including street address, city, county, zip code, and telephone number. Additional information is gathered on staffing; type of legal basis; type of geographic boundary; type of administrative structure; type of interlibrary relationship; type and number of public service outlets; operating revenue and expenditures; capital revenue and expenditures; size of collection (including number of electronic books, audio and video resources, and databases); and such service measures as number of reference transactions, interlibrary loans, circulation, public service hours, library visits, circulation of children's materials, number of programs (including programs for children and for young adults), program attendance, number of Internet terminals used by the general public, and number of users of electronic resources. This survey also collects several data items about outlets, including geo-location information (such as latitude and longitude), number of books-by-mail-only outlets, number of bookmobiles by bookmobile outlet, and square footage of the outlet.

The 50 states and the District of Columbia have participated in data collection from the survey's inception in 1989. In 1993 Guam, the Commonwealth of the Northern Mariana Islands, Puerto Rico, and the U.S. Virgin Islands also took part. The first release of Public Libraries Survey data occurred with the launch of the updated Compare Public Libraries Tool on the Library Statistics section of the IMLS website. The data used in this Web tool are final, but do not include imputations for missing data (imputation is a statistical means of providing an estimate for each missing data item).

An important feature of the public library data tools is the availability of locale codes for all administrative entities and outlets. These locale codes allow users to quickly identify which library outlets and administrative entities are located in cities, suburbs, towns, or rural areas. The locale codes are based on an address's proximity to an urbanized area (a densely settled core with densely settled surrounding areas). The locale code system classifies territory into four major types: city, suburban, town, and rural. Each type has three subcategories. For city and suburb, these gradations are based on population size: large, midsize, and small. Towns and rural areas are further distinguished by their distance from an urbanized area. They can be characterized as fringe, distant, or remote. The coding methodology was developed by the U.S. Census Bureau as a way to identify the location of public schools in the National Center for Education Statistics' (NCES's) Common Core of Data. Each library outlet and administrative entity survey has one of the 12 locale codes assigned to it.

Locale codes provide a new way to analyze library services. By incorporating objective measures of rurality and urbanicity into the data files, researchers and practitioners can benchmark services in a fundamentally different way by basing comparisons on community attributes as well as the attributes of the libraries themselves. In other words, library services in rural remote areas can now be compared with library services in other rural remote areas of the state or country using a standardized urbanicity/rurality metric that is applied consistently to each library. Once communities of interest have been selected, comparisons can be made to any data that are available in the survey whether financial, operational, or service output related.

State Library Administrative Agencies Survey

The State Library Administrative Agencies Survey collects and disseminates information about the state library administrative agencies in the 50 states and the District of Columbia. A State Library Administrative Agency (SLAA) is the official unit of state government charged with statewide library development and the administration of federal funds under the IMLS Grants to States program. SLAAs' administrative and developmental responsibilities affect the operation of thousands of public, academic, school, and special libraries. SLAAs provide important reference and information services to state governments and sometimes also provide service to the general public. SLAAs often administer state library and special operations such as state archives and libraries for the blind and physically handicapped and the state Center for the Book.

The SLAA Survey began in 1994 and was administered by NCES until 2007. Beginning with FY 1999 data, the survey used a Web-based data collection system and included imputations for missing data. IMLS has shifted to a biannual data collection of the survey. In FY 2014 the FY 2012 data file and final report were released.

National Medal for Museum and Library Service

The National Medal for Museum and Library Service honors outstanding institutions that make significant and exceptional contributions to their communities. Selected institutions demonstrate extraordinary and innovative approaches to public service, exceeding the expected levels of community outreach and core programs generally associated with its services. The medal includes a prize of $5,000 to each recipient, an awards ceremony held in Washington, D.C., and a visit from StoryCorps to interview community members about how the library or museum affected their lives. The 2014 ceremony was held at the White House on May 8.

Winners of the medal in 2014 were Brooklyn (New York) Botanic Garden; Chicago Public Library; the Children's Museum of Indianapolis; Las Vegas-Clark County Library District; Mid-Continent Public Library, Independence, Missouri; Mystic (Connecticut) Aquarium; North Carolina Museum of Natural Sciences, Raleigh; Octavia Fellin Public Library, Gallup, New Mexico; Sam Noble Oklahoma Museum of Natural History, Norman; and Yiddish Book Center, Amherst, Massachusetts.

State-Administered Programs

In FY 2014 approximately 85 percent ($154,848,000) of the annual federal appropriation under LSTA was distributed through the Grants to States program to SLAAs according to a formula set by the law. The formula consists of a base amount for each SLAA—the 50 states, Puerto Rico, and the District of Columbia receive $680,000 each; other U.S. territories receive $60,000 each—plus a supplemental amount based on population (Table 1).

SLAAs may use the appropriation for statewide initiatives and services. They may also distribute the funds through competitive subawards to, or cooperative agreements with, public, academic, research, school, or special libraries. For-profit and federal libraries are not eligible applicants. Grants to States funds have been used to meet the special needs of children, parents, teenagers, the unemployed, senior citizens, and the business community, as well as adult learners. Many libraries have partnered with community organizations to provide a variety of services and programs, including access to electronic databases, computer instruction, homework centers, summer reading programs, digitization of special collections, access to e-books and adaptive technology, bookmobile service, and development of outreach programs to the underserved. States are required by law to match the IMLS grant with non-federal funds at a 1-to-2 (non-federal to federal) ratio. No more than 4 percent of a state's program funds may be used for administrative costs.

**Table 1 / Library Services and Technology Act, State Allotments, FY 2014
(P.L. 113-76)**
Total Distributed to States: $154,848,000[1]

State	Federal Funds from IMLS (66%)[2]	State Matching Funds (34%)	Total Federal and State Funds
Alabama	$2,499,013	$1,287,370	$3,786,383
Alaska	955,925	492,446	1,448,371
Arizona	3,152,086	1,623,802	4,775,888
Arkansas	1,792,501	923,410	2,715,911
California	15,030,377	7,742,921	22,773,298
Colorado	2,636,913	1,358,410	3,995,323
Connecticut	2,034,387	1,048,018	3,082,405
Delaware	1,025,955	528,522	1,554,477
Florida	7,967,170	4,104,300	12,071,470
Georgia	4,422,103	2,278,053	6,700,156
Hawaii	1,205,222	620,872	1,826,094
Idaho	1,281,957	660,402	1,942,359
Illinois	5,536,935	2,852,360	8,389,295
Indiana	3,146,080	1,620,708	4,766,788
Iowa	1,839,676	947,712	2,787,388
Kansas	1,768,651	911,123	2,679,774
Kentucky	2,332,425	1,201,552	3,533,977
Louisiana	2,415,973	1,244,592	3,660,565
Maine	1,181,411	608,606	1,790,017
Maryland	2,899,835	1,493,854	4,393,689
Massachusetts	3,114,756	1,604,571	4,719,327
Michigan	4,328,074	2,229,614	6,557,688
Minnesota	2,709,174	1,395,635	4,104,809
Mississippi	1,806,004	930,366	2,736,370
Missouri	2,951,676	1,520,560	4,472,236
Montana	1,059,170	545,633	1,604,803
Nebraska	1,299,115	669,241	1,968,356
Nevada	1,720,752	886,448	2,607,200
New Hampshire	1,178,215	606,959	1,785,174
New Jersey	4,023,991	2,072,965	6,096,956
New Mexico	1,466,728	755,587	2,222,315
New York	7,632,818	3,932,058	11,564,876
North Carolina	4,173,865	2,150,173	6,324,038
North Dakota	943,921	486,262	1,430,183
Ohio	5,034,831	2,593,701	7,628,532
Oklahoma	2,119,065	1,091,640	3,210,705
Oregon	2,150,954	1,108,067	3,259,021
Pennsylvania	5,494,791	2,830,650	8,325,441
Rhode Island	1,076,202	554,407	1,630,609
South Carolina	2,461,931	1,268,267	3,730,198
South Dakota	994,366	512,249	1,506,615
Tennessee	3,115,490	1,604,949	4,720,439
Texas	10,510,319	5,414,407	15,924,726
Utah	1,757,101	905,173	2,662,274
Vermont	916,150	471,956	1,388,106
Virginia	3,693,415	1,902,668	5,596,083
Washington	3,281,761	1,690,604	4,972,365

State	Federal Funds from IMLS (66%)[2]	State Matching Funds (34%)	Total Federal and State Funds
West Virginia	1,379,918	710,867	2,090,785
Wisconsin	2,840,170	1,463,118	4,303,288
Wyoming	897,440	462,318	1,359,758
District of Columbia	918,531	473,183	1,391,714
Puerto Rico	2,038,457	1,050,114	3,088,571
American Samoa	80,642	0	80,642
Northern Marianas	79,303	0	79,303
Guam	120,499	0	120,499
Virgin Islands[3]	99,510	0	99,510
Pacific Territories[4]	254,300	131,003	385,303
Total[5]	$154,848,000	$79,574,448	$234,422,448

1 Maintenance of effort (MOE) reductions that resulted from MOE shortfalls reported on the FY 2011 Financial Status Report (reported and reviewed in FY 2013) have been applied to the FY 2014 allotment distribution. Those funds deducted from the states that did not meet their MOE requirement have been distributed proportionately across the states that did meet their FY 2011 MOE requirements.

2 IMLS federal funds are calculated using the current minimum base set into law (20 USC 9131[b]) and population figures from the U.S. Census Bureau.

Population data are pulled from the Bureau of the Census. Data used in the state allotment table are the most current published population estimates available on the first day of the fiscal year. Therefore, the population data used in the FY 2014 table reflect what was available on the Census Bureau website (www.census.gov/popest/states/index.html) on October 1, 2013.

Population data for American Samoa, the Commonwealth of the Northern Mariana Islands, Guam, the U.S. Virgin Islands, the Republic of the Marshall Islands, the Federated States of Micronesia, and the Republic of Palau are from the Census International Programs International Database (http://www.census.gov/population/international/data/idb/informationGateway.php). This table reflects what was available on October 1, 2013.

3 The matching requirement for Guam, American Samoa, the Commonwealth of the Northern Mariana Islands, and the U.S. Virgin Islands is waived pursuant to 48 U.S.C. § 1469a(d).

4 Aggregate allotments (including administrative costs) for the Republic of Palau, the Republic of the Marshall Islands, and the Federated States of Micronesia are awarded on a competitive basis to eligible applicants after taking into consideration recommendations from Mid-continent Research for Education and Learning (McREL).

5 Because of rounding to whole dollar amounts in the state allotments, some totals may be slightly adjusted to reflect actual total amounts.

A Special Rule, 20 USCA 9131(b)(3)(C), authorizes a small competitive grants program for four U.S. territories (Guam, American Samoa, the Commonwealth of Northern Mariana Islands, and the U.S. Virgin Islands) and three Freely Associated States (the Federated States of Micronesia, the Republic of the Marshall Islands, and the Republic of Palau). The funds for this grant program are taken from the total allotment for the Freely Associated States. In FY 2014 a total of $254,300 was available for the seven entities. This amount included a set-aside of 5 percent for the contractor for the Regional Educational Laboratory–Pacific, Mid-continent Research for Education and Learning (McREL) to facilitate the grants review process, in accordance with IMLS legislation. The total amount awarded in FY 2014, therefore, was $241,500.

The IMLS-funded programs and services delivered by each SLAA support the purposes and priorities set forth in LSTA. The SLAAs determine goals and objectives for the Grants to States funds through a planning process that includes statewide needs assessments. These goals and objectives are included in each state's statutorily required five-year plan on file with IMLS.

On a rotating basis, IMLS Grants to States program staff members conduct site visits to SLAAs to provide technical support and to monitor the states' success in administering the program. In 2014 program officers visited nine SLAAs in Arkansas, Colorado, Hawaii, Kentucky, Mississippi, Missouri, New Jersey, North Carolina, and Washington. Each site visit includes a critical review of the administration of the LSTA program at the SLAA as well as trips into the field to visit libraries that are recipients of subawards or beneficiaries of statewide IMLS-funded projects. For more information about state priorities and projects, see http://www.imls.gov/programs.

Discretionary Grants Programs

In FY 2014 IMLS's four library discretionary programs awarded the following total amounts: National Leadership Grants, $12,000,000; Laura Bush 21st Century Librarian Program, $10,117,529; Native American Library Services, $3,362,987; and Native Hawaiian Library Services, $551,569.

National Leadership Grants for Libraries

The National Leadership Grants for Libraries (NLG-Libraries) program provides funding for research and innovative model programs to enhance the quality of library services nationwide. National Leadership Grants are competitive and intended to produce results useful for the broader library community.

For FY 2014 there were three categories of National Leadership Grants for Libraries:

Advancing Digital Resources (maximum award: $500,000)

This category supports the creation, use, preservation, and presentation of significant digital resources, as well as the development of tools to manage digital assets, incorporating new technologies or new technology practice. This includes projects that develop and disseminate new tools to facilitate management, preservation, sharing, and use of digital resources; increase community access to institutional resources through innovative use of existing technology-based tools; develop or advance participation in library communities using social technologies in new ways; or develop new approaches or tools for digital curation.

Demonstration (maximum award: $500,000)

Demonstration projects use available knowledge to address key needs and challenges facing libraries and archives, and transform that knowledge into formal practice. This category includes projects that demonstrate and/or test new practices in library and/or archives operations; demonstrate how libraries and/or archives serve their communities by fostering public value and implementing systemic changes in the field; establish and/or test standards and tools for innovative learning; or demonstrate and/or test an expansion of preservation or conservation practices.

Research (maximum award: $500,000)

These grants support research projects that have the potential to improve library and archives practice, resource use, programs, and services. Both basic and applied research projects are encouraged. This category includes projects that evaluate the impact of library or archival services; investigate how learning takes place in libraries and archives, and how use of library and/or archival resources enhances learning; investigate how to improve the quality, effectiveness, or efficiency of library or archives management programs or services; investigate ways to enhance the archiving, preservation, management, discovery, and use of digital assets and resources; or investigate or conduct research to add new knowledge or make improvements in the conservation and preservation of collections.

The program received 167 complete and eligible proposals in FY 2014. Collectively, these proposals requested nearly $16 million. In September 2014 the program announced 54 awards to libraries and archives, totaling $12 million (for details, see http://www.imls.gov/recipients/grantsearch.aspx).

In addition to these awards to libraries and archives, remaining program funds were used to sponsor special initiatives, out-of-cycle special opportunities, and other projects, including 17 Sparks! Ignition Grants and multiple other small awards in support of such efforts as the National Medal awards.

Laura Bush 21st Century Librarian Program (maximum award: $500,000)

The Laura Bush 21st Century Librarian Program provides competitive grants to support projects to recruit and educate the next generation of librarians and library leaders; build institutional capacity in graduate schools of library and information science and develop faculty who will help in this endeavor; and support programs of continuing education and training in library and information science for librarians and library staff. In FY 2014 the program included the following categories:

Doctoral Programs

- To develop faculty to educate the next generation of library and archives professionals. In particular, to increase the number of students enrolled in doctoral programs that will prepare faculty to teach master's students who will work in school, public, academic, research, and special libraries and archives
- To develop the next generation of library and archives leaders to assume positions as library managers and administrators

Master's Programs

- To educate the next generation of librarians and archivists in nationally accredited graduate library programs to meet the evolving needs of the profession and society

Early Career Development Program

- To support the early career development of new faculty members in library and information science by supporting innovative research by untenured, tenure-track faculty

Research

- To investigate issues and trends affecting library and archival practices. (For all research projects, except Early Career Development Projects, all eligible library entities may apply, either individually or collaboratively.)

Programs to Build Institutional Capacity

- To develop or enhance curricula within graduate schools of library and information science to better meet the needs of cultural heritage and information professionals
- To broaden the library and information science curriculum by incorporating perspectives from other disciplines and fields of scholarship
- To develop projects or programs of study to increase the abilities of future library and archives professionals in developing the 21st century skills of their users, including information and digital literacy skills

Continuing Education

- To improve the knowledge, skills, and abilities of library and archives staff through programs of continuing education, both formal and informal, including such post-master's degree programs as certificates of advanced study, residencies, enhanced work experiences, and other training programs for professional staff

IMLS received a total of 98 applications in the 21st Century Librarian Program in FY 2014. A total of $10,117,529 was awarded in 38 grants (for details, see http://www.imls.gov/recipients/grantsearch.aspx). Matching funds equaled $4,291,455.

Native American/Native Hawaiian Library Services Grants

The Native American and Native Hawaiian Library Services program provides opportunities for improved library services to an important part of the nation's community of library users. The program offers three types of support:

- Basic library services grants in the amount of $6,000, which support core library operations on a noncompetitive basis for all eligible Indian tribes and Alaska Native villages and corporations that apply for such support
- Basic library services grants with a supplemental education/assessment option of $1,000 to provide funding for library staff to attend continuing education courses and/or training workshops onsite or offsite, for library staff to attend or give presentations at conferences related to library services, or to hire a consultant for an onsite professional library assessment
- Enhancement grants, which support new levels of library service for activities specifically identified under LSTA

Collectively, these programs received 244 applications in FY 2014. IMLS funded 233 of these proposals, totaling $3,362,987. This included basic grants and basic grants with the education/assessment option to 219 applicants, and 14 enhancement grants (for details, see http://www.imls.gov/recipients/grantsearch. aspx).

The Native Hawaiian Library Services program provides opportunities for improved library services through grants to nonprofit organizations that primarily serve and represent Native Hawaiians, as the term "Native Hawaiian" is defined in section 7207 of the Native Hawaiian Education Act (20 U.S.C. 7517). In FY 2014, IMLS awarded three grants in this program, totaling $551,569 (for details, see http://www.imls.gov/recipients/grantsearch.aspx).

Partnerships

Heritage Health Index II

A cooperative agreement with Washington, D.C.-based Heritage Preservation will update *A Public Trust at Risk: The Heritage Health Index Report on the State of America's Collections,* published in December 2005. This groundbreaking report, based on an extensive national survey, produced the first comprehensive data on the condition and preservation needs of U.S. collections held in archives, historical societies, libraries, museums, and scientific research organizations. Heritage Health Index II (HHI II) will examine the extent and effectiveness of preservation activities and initiatives since that time and will recommend actions to improve the care of collections and ensure that they will be available for public access in the future.

Early Learning

Libraries and museums have a long history of serving young children. These community anchor institutions form a well-established informal learning network and are a foundational part of the early learning landscape. In FY 2014 IMLS supported major early learning activities in numerous ways. The following are highlights:

- IMLS awarded $1.5 million in discretionary grants for early learning programming in libraries and museums, building upon $4.3 million in 2013 and $2.5 million awarded in 2012.
- It convened a meeting with Joan Lombardi, former U.S. Department of Education deputy assistant secretary; David Willis, Department of Health and Human Services division director of home visiting and early childhood systems; and library and museum experts to generate new networks and information sharing.
- It announced a partnership with BUILD to work intensively with five states to develop case studies and tools that will help strengthen early learning partnerships at the state and local levels.
- IMLS launched "Museums for All" to help address the economic divide in museum visitors and to give the neediest children a strong start. In partnership with the Association of Children's Museums, IMLS is working on a pilot program to enable low-income families to visit participating museums for a minimal fee.

- IMLS was recognized by the Campaign for Grade Level Reading as one of its 2014 "Pacesetter Partners." Ralph Smith, executive director of the Annie E. Casey Foundation, said, "No community that cares about all children reading by the end of third grade can afford not to have libraries and museums in the game, because of the resources, the expertise, the passion and creativity they bring to the cause of early literacy for all."

National Arts and Humanities Youth Program Awards

The National Arts and Humanities Youth Program (NAHYP) Awards are an initiative of the President's Committee on the Arts and Humanities, implemented in partnership with the National Endowment for the Arts, the National Endowment for the Humanities, and IMLS. The awards are the nation's highest honor for out-of-school, afterschool, and summer arts and humanities programs that celebrate the creativity of youth, particularly those from underserved communities. Libraries and museums are encouraged to apply.

Each year, the NAHYP awards recognize and support excellence in programs that open new pathways to learning, self-discovery, and achievement, in addition to presenting high-quality arts and humanities learning opportunities. The awards are presented at a White House ceremony. Award recipients receive $10,000 each, a plaque, and an opportunity to attend the Annual Awardees Conference in Washington, D.C., where they receive capacity-building and communications support designed to strengthen their organizations. The most recent award announcement was in November 2014. For more information, visit http://www.nahyp.org.

STEM Education, Makerspaces, and Learning Labs

Combining strengths in traditional and digital learning, libraries and museums are well positioned to build the skills needed in the 21st century. IMLS invested $23 million in 140 STEM (Science, Technology, Engineering, Math)-related projects in FY 2013–2014. Activities focusing on STEM learning for at-risk youth remain a priority for FY 2015 discretionary funding.

In May 2014 IMLS announced "Supporting Making in Museums and Libraries," an initiative with the Pittsburgh Children's Museum, the San Francisco Exploratorium, the North Carolina State University Libraries, and the Chicago Public Library to create a national Maker@Your Library and Museum program. With $425,192 in IMLS support, the project will draw on the expertise of 50 museum professionals and librarians to create tools to help libraries and museums launch effective makerspaces and programs. The result will be a freely accessible toolkit that will provide ideas, resources, and a framework that museums and libraries throughout the United States can use to create effective, collaborative makerspaces and programs.

IMLS continued to partner with the Joan Ganz Cooney Center at Sesame Street to support the 2014–2015 National STEM Video Challenge, which launched in October 2014. IMLS hopes to increase interest in STEM learning among youth by tapping into students' natural passion for playing and making video games while also developing systems thinking, problem solving, iterative design, and digital media literacy.

IMLS and the Mozilla Foundation teamed up in the summer of 2014 to help libraries and museums collaborate with other community organizations to host maker parties—volunteer-led events that teach Web literacy through play and hands-on making. The goal of this partnership was to teach the culture, mechanics, and citizenship of the Web, which are key skills for the future. Mozilla trained 100 lead librarians and museum professionals from across the country via online training to certify them as digital literacy skills trainers. Approximately 754 events were hosted by 107 libraries and branches during the three months of Maker Party 2014.

In partnership with the John D. and Catherine T. MacArthur Foundation, along with the Urban Libraries Council and the Association for Science and Technology Centers, IMLS has supported a national grant competition to create learning labs in libraries and museums. Inspired by the innovative YOUmedia teen space at the Chicago Public Library and innovations in science and technology centers, these labs help young people become creators of content rather than just consumers of it. The first and second cohorts of grantees, a total of 15 libraries and 9 museums, are partnering with a wide range of such institutions as libraries, museums, parks and recreation departments, media outlets, universities, and nonprofit community organizations.

In FY 2014 IMLS entered into a cooperative agreement with the Berkeley, California-based National Writing Project (NWP) to develop a Learning Labs Community of Practice. NWP is a professional development network that reaches more than 100,000 teachers of writing at all grade levels, and teachers in nearly all subjects, across the country. With $296,964 in support from IMLS, NWP will help build a community of educators committed to adapting, extending, and contributing to the curricula, program models, digital tools, and other prototypes that have been incubated in YOUmedia/Learning Labs. Activities will include the creation of an online micro-site to support professional development for mentors and other staff working in YOUmedia/Learning Labs. The project will also provide open access to resources and support that will help libraries and museums interested in the YOUmedia model to develop their own learning lab. Inspired by digital teen spaces in libraries and innovations in science and technology centers, these labs will help young people move beyond consuming content to making and creating it.

National Book Festival

IMLS partnered with the Library of Congress and the Chief Officers of State Library Agencies (COSLA) to sponsor the Pavilion of the States at the 2014 National Book Festival on August 31. The festival featured more than 100 authors, poets, and illustrators and its Convention Center venue in Washington, D.C., was filled to capacity.

National Digital Stewardship Residency

In collaboration with the Library of Congress, IMLS developed the National Digital Stewardship Residency (NDSR), an effort to place recent library and information school graduates in host institutions in the Washington, D.C., area for a year, giving the residents practical experience in digital curation projects and the host institutions support in achieving specific projects. All ten members of the first

NDSR cohort received jobs in the field by the end of the residency. IMLS and the Library of Congress renewed the project in 2014 for a second and third set of cohorts, and also funded similar NDSR programs in Boston and New York. All these efforts will increase the capacity of the library and archives professions to manage, preserve, and provide access to the nation's cultural heritage in digital formats.

National Student Poets Program

The President's Committee on the Arts and the Humanities and IMLS are partnering with the Alliance for Young Artists and Writers on the National Student Poets Program (NSPP). Five outstanding high school poets from across the country whose work exhibits exceptional creativity, dedication to craft, and promise are selected annually for a year of service as "national poetry ambassadors."

These National Student Poets are chosen from among the national medalists in the Scholastic Art and Writing Awards by a jury of accomplished authors and leaders in education and the arts. They receive college scholarships and opportunities to present their work at writing and poetry events throughout their term, as well as a stipend to complete a service/learning project. The third group of National Student Poets was appointed officially during a September 2014 ceremony at the White House, at which each poet had an opportunity to perform a selection of his or her poetry. The poets are encouraged to team with libraries or museums in their region for events throughout their year of service. Another round of Scholastic Art and Writing Awards launched in fall 2014. For more information, see http://www.artandwriting.org/the-awards/national-student-poets-program.

Federal Interagency Collaboration

People depend on libraries to deliver a wide range of information services, including government services, that are increasingly available only online. In the past three years, federal agencies increasingly sought partnerships with IMLS as they recognized the power that libraries have to reach the public. The following are examples of collaborative projects that have resulted:

- The U.S. Citizenship and Immigration Services (USCIS) signed a memorandum of understanding with IMLS pledging to support local libraries' services to new immigrants. Recent research shows that more than 55 percent of people who immigrated to the United States within the last 15 years use the public library at least once a week. More mock naturalization interviews take place at public libraries than at any other community institution. In FY 2014 IMLS worked with USCIS to conduct a webinar series to help librarians meet the needs of new immigrants.
- IMLS is working with the Consumer Financial Protection Bureau (CFPB) to help libraries access and use financial education tools. In FY 2014 IMLS partnered with CFPB to identify pilot sites for the development and testing of new tools for librarians. In April 2014 IMLS formalized a financial literacy partnership with CFPB, the Federal Deposit Insurance Corporation, the Federal Reserve Bank of Chicago, and the U.S. Department of Agri-

culture's Cooperative Extension Service. The partnership will help make financial information and educational resources available to the public. A series of monthly financial literacy webinars targeted to librarians began in July 2014. IMLS is also participating as an observer in the federal Financial Literacy and Education Commission (FLEC) and is facilitating connections between FLEC members and a variety of library networks.

- In July 2014 Congress passed the Workforce Opportunity and Investment Act. For the first time, the act recognized the role of libraries as partners helping to meet the training and workforce development needs in their communities. The language of the act builds upon the IMLS partnership with the U.S. Department of Labor's Employment and Training Administration to encourage partnerships between the federally sponsored American Job Center Network and public libraries to support workforce development and small business. In FY 2014 IMLS broadened its partnership for adult training and is now working with the Office of Career, Technical, and Adult Education (OCTAE) at the U.S. Department of Education to encourage effective collaborations between libraries and federally funded adult education programs.

- Over the past year, analysts in IMLS's Office of Planning, Research and Evaluation have provided technical support to help the staff of the Federal Communications Commission's (FCC's) Office of Strategic Planning and Policy Analysis to better understand the public library data collected by IMLS and how it might inform FCC's E-rate modernization planning. IMLS staff assisted with data analysis and provided its own analysis for Universal Service Administration Company (USAC) administrative data during the Notice of Proposed Rulemaking comment period. This new analysis of USAC data revealed significantly larger E-rate take-up rates than had been reported in previous studies or by FCC itself. A link to this analysis can be found at http://blog.imls.gov/?p=4778.

- Recognizing that 32 million Americans used a library computer for health information in just one year, the U.S. Health and Human Services' Centers for Medicare and Medicaid partnered with IMLS to help libraries access the online resources and community connections they need to meet patrons' health information needs. More than 1,000 library professionals participated in a series of related webinars in FY 2013 and FY 2014.

- IMLS works with a number of federal agencies through the Partners in Tourism initiative to advance the nation's National Tourism Strategy and spotlight the role of cultural heritage organizations in supporting economic development through tourism. In April 2014 IMLS highlighted the role of museums in local and national tourism efforts by participating in a panel with the National Endowment for the Humanities, the National Endowment for the Arts, and the American Express Foundation as part of the Cultural Heritage Exchange Conference.

- IMLS is an active participant in the Multi-Agency Informal Science Education Forum, which brings together representatives from a wide variety of federal agencies to share information and resources relating to STEM-focused programming. The quarterly meetings offer opportunities to exchange ideas, forge new partnerships, and reduce potential duplication of services.

* IMLS continues to administer a sub-initiative of First Lady Michelle Obama's Let's Move! program called Let's Move! Museums and Gardens. The initiative provides opportunities for millions of museum and garden visitors to learn about healthy food choices and promote physical activity through interactive exhibits and programs.

International Collaboration

Digging into Data

IMLS is a member of an international coalition of funding agencies that support the Digging into Data program, an effort to encourage partnerships in the use of data and the development of tools in the digital humanities field. The National Endowment for the Humanities, the National Science Foundation, and agencies from Canada, the United Kingdom, and the Netherlands are also partners.

Film Forward

Film Forward is an international touring program designed to enhance greater cultural understanding and dialogue in both the United States and abroad by engaging underserved audiences through the exhibition of films, workshops, and conversations with filmmakers. It is an initiative of the President's Committee on the Arts and Humanities and the Sundance Institute, in partnership with IMLS, the National Endowment for the Arts, and the National Endowment for the Humanities.

Evaluation of IMLS Programs

IMLS's evaluation strategy during FY 2014 continued to address the diverse needs of the Grants to States formula grant program and its discretionary grant programs. The work balanced capacity-building efforts to improve program and performance data with summative evaluations of completed grant projects. The following section highlights achievements during the year.

Measuring Success

The Measuring Success initiative is a long-term strategic planning effort begun in FY 2011 to improve performance reporting for the Grants to States program. The aim of the initiative is to increase the comparability of program data within and across the participating states. Standardization of program data will also increase the utility of the data for monitoring project accomplishments over time and comparing library service initiatives with other educational and social programming at the local level.

In FY 2014 IMLS worked collaboratively with 16 state partners to redesign the new State Program Reporting tool. These 16 pilot states not only are providing assistance in the redesign, review, and testing of the new reporting tool; they also have agreed to assist in training other states when the tool is deployed across the entire Grants to States program in FY 2015. Continued build-out of the new reporting tool in FY 2014 was enabled through a contract with the private firm Information International Associates.

IMLS Conferences and Activities

IMLS Focus

In FY 2014 IMLS hosted a series of three strategic meetings, each focused on a different priority. The sessions were designed to help inform future strategies, particularly for the agency's National Leadership Grant program. The first, at the New York Public Library on April 29, examined national digital initiatives. The second, at the San Francisco Public Library on May 15, addressed learning spaces in libraries, and the third, at the Chicago Public Library on June 5, focused on STEM subjects. More information, including convening videos and notes, is available at http://www.imls.gov/news/imls_focus.aspx.

WebWise

IMLS's 15th annual WebWise conference was held in February 2014 in Baltimore, addressing the theme "Anchoring Communities" and featuring presentations, workshops, and—as in previous years—an "unconference," where the content of sessions is created and managed by the participants during the course of the event, rather than in advance by one or more organizers (see http://blog.imls.gov/?p=4556#sthash.7maI025g.dpuf). WebWise explored digital technologies in libraries and museums, and two plenaries addressed the idea that technology offers institutions an opportunity rather than just a challenge.

Library Statistics State Data Coordinators Conference

The sixth IMLS-sponsored Library Statistics State Data Coordinators Conference was held in St. Louis in December 2013. There were 53 participants representing the 50 states, the District of Columbia, Puerto Rico, and Guam. The conference included training on data collection and input, a review of existing data elements included in the Public Libraries Survey, workshops on data presentation and analysis, and discussion and a comprehensive review of survey data elements for the FY 2014 survey and beyond.

Continuing Education

To develop a consensus around continuing education and professional development (CE/PD) priorities, IMLS continued to support the work of the Coalition to Advance Learning in Archives, Libraries and Museums, a collaboration of associations from all three professions. The purpose of the coalition is to work in deliberate coordination across organizational boundaries to devise and strengthen sustainable CE/PD programs that will transform the library, archives, and museum workforce in ways that lead to measurable impact on communities. Its goals are to encourage partnerships, share resources, avoid duplication of effort, and provide better services to the patrons of libraries, archives, and museums. To further those goals, IMLS has funded projects that explore collaborative leadership programs and that identify professional CE/PD needs that cross professional boundaries.

IMLS Website and Publications

The IMLS website (http://www.imls.gov) provides information on the various grant programs, the National Medal for Museum and Library Service, and funded projects, along with application forms and staff contacts. It also highlights model projects developed by libraries and museums and provides information about IMLS-sponsored conferences, publications, and studies. A grant search tool, detailing awarded IMLS grants, is at http://www.imls.gov/recipients/grantsearch. aspx.

In January 2014 IMLS released an FY 2013 Annual Report, which highlighted how the agency furthered education, cultural preservation, early learning, and workforce development through its grant making and other activities. The report is available online at http://www.imls.gov/assets/1/AssetManager/2013AnnualReport. pdf.

Through an electronic newsletter, *Primary Source,* and the IMLS blog "Up-Next," IMLS provides information on grant deadlines, success stories, and opportunities. Information on subscribing to the IMLS newsletter is also located on the website, along with guidelines for each of the grant programs and other publications.

IMLS is on twitter @US_IMLS and Facebook (http://www.facebook.com/USIMLS).

Part 3
Library/Information Science Education, Placement, and Salaries

Library Employment Sources on the Internet

Catherine Barr
Contributing Editor

Library school graduates of 2013 faced opportunities and challenges that required "luck, patience, and positive attitude," according to *Library Journal*'s article "Placements and Salaries 2014: Renaissance Librarians" [see the following article for the full report—*Ed.*]. But the overall starting salary was up 2.6 percent, the length of the job search briefer, and more permanent professional positions were available.

Librarians and information professionals have many options to consider when seeking employment both within and outside the library field. The following is not a comprehensive list of the hundreds of relevant job-related sites on the Internet. These are, however, some of the best starting places for a general job search in this ever-widening field. Many offer additional information that will be helpful to those considering a career in librarianship or a change in position, including advice on conducting a successful search, writing résumés, preparing for interviews, and negotiating salaries.

Before spending a lot of time on any website, users should check that the site has been updated recently and that out-of-date job listings no longer appear.

The Directory of Organizations in Part 6 of this volume may also prove useful, and many large libraries and library associations maintain Facebook pages that may give details of vacancies.

Background Information

The Bureau of Labor Statistics of the Department of Labor provides an overview of the work librarians do, average salaries in various sectors (schools, academia, government, and "other information services") at this page: http://www.bls.gov/oes/current/oes254021.htm. Maps show where the most jobs are located and where the salaries are highest. A useful companion page (http://www.bls.gov/ooh/Education-Training-and-Library/Librarians.htm#tab-1) looks at work environments, necessary qualifications, and similar occupations (with information on archivists, curators, museum technicians, and conservators; library technicians and assistants; and teachers).

The American Library Association (ALA) has a user-friendly introduction to librarianship at all levels—from pages and library assistants to managers and directors—at LibraryCareers.org (http://www.ala.org/educationcareers/careers/librarycareerssite/home). There are also links to discussions of career paths, education choices, and core competencies. This site will be particularly useful for young people considering a possible career in librarianship. A companion page is "Resources for Library Support Staff" (http://www.ala.org/offices/hrdr/library supportstaff/library_support_staff_resource_center).

San José State University's School of Library and Information Science has created a "Career Development" page (http://slisweb.sjsu.edu/resources/career_ development/index.htm) that aims to "help our students, alumni, and prospective students navigate a myriad of career opportunities, learn about emerging trends in the field, and develop an effective job search strategy." "Emerging Career Trends for Information Professionals: A Snapshot of Job Titles in Summer 2014" provides an interesting analysis of job listings and their requirements. A lively career blog at http://slisapps.sjsu.edu/blogs/career and links to career webinars are also useful.

The focus on alternatives to traditional librarianship is echoed in the many print and online publications about the profession, among them:

- The *Atlas of New Librarianship* by R. David Lankes (MIT, 2011)
- *Career Q&A: A Librarian's Real-Life, Practical Guide to Managing a Successful Career* by Susanne Markgren and Tiffany Eatman Allen (Information Today, 2013)
- "Getting the Library Job You Want" by Joseph Thompson, *Reference and User Services Quarterly* (Winter 2014)
- *The Librarian's Skillbook: 51 Essential Career Skills for Information Professionals* by Deborah Hunt and David Grossman (Information Edge, 2013)
- *LIS Career Sourcebook: Managing and Maximizing Every Stop of Your Career* by G. Kim Dority (Libraries Unlimited, 2012)
- *Making the Most of Your Library Career* ed. by Lois Stickell and Bridgette Sanders (ALA Editions, 2014)
- *The New Information Professional: Your Guide to Careers in the Digital Age* by Judy Lawson and Joanna Kroll (Neal-Schuman, 2010)
- *What Do Employers Want? A Guide for Library Science Students* by Priscilla K. Shontz and Richard A. Murray (Libraries Unlimited, 2012)

There are also many resources that address the challenges facing jobseekers and suggest strategies for success. A number of chats and webinars can be found on the ALA JobLIST site at http://joblist.ala.org/modules/jobseeker/multimedia. cfm. The April 2010 issue of *College and Research Library News* includes an article—"Making the Best of the Worst of Times: Global Turmoil and Landing Your First Library Job"—that looks at job listings and how to prepare for an interview. And http://opencoverletters.com provides actual examples of cover letters with details of names and institutions redacted.

Those who have succeeded in getting an interview will find these resources helpful:

- Congratulations! You've landed an interview: What do hiring committees really want?" by Megan Hodge and Nicole Spoor. *New Library World* Vol. 113 Iss: 3/4, pp.139–161 (2012). This article gives the results of a survey of members of library hiring committees, offering insight for jobseekers in the public and academic library fields.

• The Library Interview Question "Database," a spreadsheet on Google Drive available at http://tinyurl.com/InterviewQuestionsRepository, gives fascinating insight into the kinds of questions job applicants may encounter. Participants describe the level of interview, the kind of position involved, the questions they were asked and the questions they themselves asked in return.

• Finally, should you be agonizing over what to wear to an interview, visit http://librarianhirefashion.tumblr.com for photographs of suitable and unsuitable attire, with comments by librarians who hire.

General Sites/Portals

How to Apply for a Library Job

http://liswiki.org/wiki/HOWTO:Apply_for_a_library_job

A general guide with advice on phone, video, and in-person interviews.

ALA JobLIST

http://joblist.ala.org

Sponsored by the American Library Association and the Association of College and Research Libraries, this site is free for jobseekers, who can post their résumés and browse recent job postings or search jobs by library type, date, state, institution name, salary range, and other parameters offered in the advanced search function. Employers can choose from a menu of print and electronic posting combinations.

ALA JobLIST: Career Development Resources

http://joblist.ala.org/modules/jobseeker/controller.cfm

This ALA site lists job placement opportunities at forthcoming conferences, along with details of workshops and tips on various aspects of the job search. At the top of the page, you can do a quick search for job openings by state. Also available on this page are links to career assessment resources, advice on creating effective resumes and cover letters, general career information, and tips on job hunting, interviews, negotiating salaries, and so forth. A multimedia section includes webinars and podcasts on various aspects of job searches.

Canadian Library Association: Library Careers

http://www.cla.ca/AM/Template.cfm?Section=Library_Careers

The Canadian Library Association lists Canadian job openings here (select Job Search) and provides information on career development, plus guidance on recognition of foreign credentials.

San José State University Job Listing Sites and Resources

http://slisweb.sjsu.edu/career-development/job-search/job-listing-sites-and-resources

This page provides an extensive list of library employment sites as well as tips on conducting an effective job search, with webcasts and advice on creating an e-portfolio. A related page, Professional Associations (http://slisweb.sjsu.edu/resources/orgs.htm), is a comprehensive listing of organizations in the United States and abroad that will be helpful to jobseekers with specific interests.

INALJ

http://inalj.com

This community of information professionals working to help find and share jobs and job hunting advice is also present on Facebook, Twitter, and LinkedIn. Along with regularly updated, well-organized job listings (domestic and international), this site offers interesting articles and interviews, inspiring success stories, plus an extensive list of keywords for job searches that reveals the breadth of opportunities in the field. Check individual states for openings; the "last updated" date on splash pages may not apply.

Library Job Postings on the Internet

http://www.libraryjobpostings.org

Compiled by Sarah L. Johnson of Booth Library, Eastern Illinois University, author of "Career Development and Planning," in Ruddock, Bethan, ed., *The New Professional's Toolkit* (Facet, 2012), and coauthor of *The Information Professional's Guide to Career Development Online* (Information Today, Inc., 2002). Library Job Postings provides links to library employment sites in the United States and abroad, with easy access by location and by category of job; it will be useful for people seeking a job in a particular geographic area.

Metropolitan New York Library Council

http://metro.org/career-resources

A job board for library and related organizations in the New York City area, plus a calendar of events.

The Riley Guide

http://www.rileyguide.com

In addition to job listings (try http://www.rileyguide.com/info.html#lib to access positions suitable for librarians), the Riley Guide allows users to explore all aspects of job hunting, from proper preparation to résumés and cover letters, researching and targeting employers, and networking, interviewing, and negotiating salaries and job conditions.

Sites by Sector

Public Libraries

Public library openings can be found at all the general sites/portals listed above.

Careers in Public Librarianship

http://www.ala.org/pla/tools/careers

The Public Library Association offers information on public librarianship, with a webcast on finding and keeping public library jobs.

Competencies for Librarians Serving Children in Public Libraries

http://www.ala.org/ala/mgrps/divs/alsc/edcareeers/alsccorecomps

A detailed listing of skills and knowledge required to be a children's librarian in a public library.

School Libraries

School library openings can be found at many of the sites listed above and general education sites, and comprehensive employment sites such as Monster.com often include school library openings.

AASL: Recruitment to School Librarianship

http://www.ala.org/ala/mgrps/divs/aasl/aasleducation/recruitmentlib/aaslrecruitment.cfm

The American Association of School Librarians hosts this site, which describes the role of school librarians, salary and job outlooks, and mentoring programs; provides testimonials from working library media specialists; and offers state-by-state information on licensure, scholarships, library education, job hunting, mentoring, and recruitment efforts.

Special and Academic Libraries

AALL Career Center

http://www.aallnet.org/main-menu/Careers/career-center

Maintained by the American Association of Law Libraries, this site has an online job board and useful tips for job seekers (in academic libraries, court libraries, and law firms).

Careers in Law Librarianship

http://www.lawlibrarycareers.org

This excellent site answers the question "Is a career as a law librarian right for you?" and provides broad information on the profession, educational requirements, and available financial assistance.

Association of College and Research Libraries

http://www.ala.org/acrl

Under the heading Professional Tools, there are useful descriptions of various positions and information on recruitment and retention. Job listings are found at ALA JobLIST (see above).

ASIS&T: Careers

http://www.asist.org/careers.html

The Careers page maintained by the Information Association for the Information Age offers access to a Jobline, profiles of selected members, and continuing education information.

Association of Research Libraries: Leadership & Recruitment

http://www.arl.org/leadership-recruitment

In addition to user-friendly listings of openings at ARL member institutions and at other organizations, there is information on ARL's diversity programs plus a database of research library residency and internship programs.

Chronicle of Higher Education: Vitae

https://chroniclevitae.com

Listings can be browsed, with geographical options, using keywords. Articles and advice on job searching are also available.

EDUCAUSE Job Posting Service

http://www.educause.edu/Jobs

EDUCAUSE member organizations post positions "in the broad field of information technology in higher education."

HigherEdJobs.com

http://www.higheredjobs.com

The category "Libraries" is found under Administrative Positions.

Medical Library Association: Career Development

https://www.mlanet.org/professional-development/career_development

The Medical Library Association offers much more than job listings here, with brochures on medical librarianship, a video, career tips, and a mentor program.

Music Library Association Job Openings

http://www.musiclibraryassoc.org/?page=JobsAndCareers

Along with job postings and a résumé review service, this site features useful career resources.

SLA: Career Center

http://www.sla.org/career-center

The Career Center is the place to apply for jobs, post résumés, and find information on career enhancement.

Government
Library of Congress

http://www.loc.gov/hr/employment

An extensive survey of what it's like to work at the library, the kinds of employees the library is seeking, the organizational structure, benefits, current job openings, internships, fellowships, and volunteering.

National Archives and Records Administration

http://www.archives.gov/careers

In addition to information on employment opportunities, internships, and volunteering, NARA provides profiles of employees and interns, describing the kinds of work they do.

Serials

NASIG Jobs
http://nasigjobs.wordpress.com

Managed by the North American Serials Interest Group. Accepts serials-related job postings.

Library Periodicals
American Libraries

See ALA JobLIST above.

Library Journal

http://www.libraryjournal.com

Job listings are found under the Job Zone tab. The number of job openings under various headings is shown on the lower right. The Careers tab leads to archived articles relating to employment.

School Library Journal

http://www.schoollibraryjournal.com

Click on the Job Zone tab for access to a general list of job openings (jointly maintained with *Library Journal*). The number of job openings under the heading School Library/Media Center is shown on the lower right. The section on Careers (http://www.slj.com/category/careers) includes interesting features such as the results of *SLJ*'s 2013 Job Satisfaction Survey and "NYPL Panelists Explore Alternatives to Traditional Librarianship," in which children's librarians discuss their nontraditional careers.

Employment Agencies/Commercial Services

A number of employment agencies and commercial services in the United States and abroad specialize in library-related jobs. Among those that keep up-to-date listings on their websites are:

Advanced Information Management

http://www.aimusa.com

Specializes in librarians and support staff in a variety of types of libraries across the country.

LAC Group

http://careers.lac-group.com

An easy-to-use list of openings that can be sorted by function, location, and keyword. The LibGig site (http://www.libgig.com) was created by the LAC Group and offers news, career profiles, and résumé consultation.

Listservs and Networking Sites

Many listservs allow members to post job openings on a casual basis.

ALA Think Tank

https://www.facebook.com/groups/ALAthinkTANK

A lively Facebook group with nearly 12,000 members who post and comment on all aspects of librarianship.

LIBJOBS

http://www.ifla.org/en/mailing-lists

LIBJOBS is a mailing list for librarians and information professionals seeking employment. It is managed by the International Federation of Library Associations and Institutions (IFLA). Subscribers to this list receive posted job opportunities by e-mail.

LIS New Prof Network

https://twitter.com/lisnpn

A Twitter forum with news, blogs, and postings of general and specific interest (job openings, grants, and so forth).

PUBLIB

http://www.webjunction.org/documents/webjunction/PubLib_Overview.html

Public library job openings often appear on this list.

Blogs

hls: How Would You Hack Library School?

http://hacklibschool.wordpress.com

A blog that looks at various aspects of librarianship and its evolution.

Library Career People

http://librarycareerpeople.com

This attractive and user-friendly blog is maintained by librarians Tiffany Allen, Susanne Markgren, and Carrie Netzer Wajda and is intended to "create an enlightening discussion forum, and career development archive, of professional guidance and advice for librarians, library staff, and those thinking of entering the profession."

Placements and Salaries 2014: Renaissance Librarians

Stephanie L. Maatta

Luck, patience, and positive attitude were the keywords for members of the 2013 library and information science (LIS) graduating class. Graduates reported both positive experiences and challenges in their search for employment inside and outside the LIS field.

The overall average starting salary improved 2.6 percent, moving above $45,000 for the first time to $45,650. Other pointers toward an improving job market were revealed in a decline in the rate of unemployment, dropping to 4.3 percent of those reporting employment status, and an increase in the rate of permanent professional positions—69.6 percent of the job placements in 2013, up from 61.2 percent in 2012. The length of the job search appeared slightly shortened, with an average search of 4.2 months, ranging from 3.6 months in the Southwest to 4.7 months in the Southeast. Most reporting graduates cited job searches of three months, although some continued to seek a professional position as long as 20 months after graduation. Responses were received from 2,023 graduates, representing 44.3 percent of the graduates of the 40 LIS programs providing data.

While placements in school libraries continued to compose a smaller portion of the total placements, compared with previous years, jobs in that sector improved in number of placements and starting salaries, notably in the Southeast. Positions in digital content management, user interface design, and user experience continue to offer opportunity and growth.

Regionally, graduates accepting jobs in the West continued to enjoy the highest entry salaries, starting at approximately $55,631 (up by 2.2 percent); however, those landing in jobs in the Midwest saw the best salary increases, growing by 5.5 percent from $42,227 in 2012 to $44,555 in 2013. Other positive indicators included salary improvements among children's librarians ($41,938, up approximately 14.6 percent) and archivists ($41,656, up approximately 12 percent). Salary improvements were driven by the continued upward growth of wages in positions outside library and information science, especially those in private industry, which increased from $47,489 in 2012 to $56,327 in 2013.

Some of the gains were counterbalanced by flat starting salaries among academic librarians, which held steady at $42,458 nationwide (down a slim $141 from 2012) but were noticeably down 13.7 percent in the Southwest ($41,720 in 2012 compared with $35,988 in 2013). Graduates identifying as members of a minority group struggled to maintain the salary highs enjoyed by the previous year's class, losing momentum and rolling back 16 percent from an average starting salary of $52,931 in 2012 to $44,473 in 2013. Men who entered jobs in the Southeast experienced a similar reversal of fortunes, with salaries decreasing from $49,229 in 2012 to $43,409 in 2013 (a loss of 11.8 percent).

Stephanie L. Maatta is an assistant professor at Wayne State University, School of Library and Information Science, Detroit.

Adapted from *Library Journal,* October 15, 2014.

The dynamic nature of the LIS professions was clearly evident in the survey responses. While job titles did not vary from 2012 reports, a merging of responsibilities and an increasing number of jobs outside LIS suggested new and exciting ways of using skills learned during MLIS programs. Roles such as social media management, digital asset/digital content management, and project management appeared for a second year across the array of identified positions and in all types of library and information agencies. Individuals were as likely to be engaged in data analytics in academic institutions as private industry; digital content management was common in archives and public libraries.

User interface designers and user experience specialists found themselves working for academic institutions, private industry, and LIS vendors. While the average starting salaries decreased, dropping from $72,860 in 2012 to $70,026 in 2013, this group of graduates negotiated the highest level of wages of the graduating class: 53.4 percent higher than the average starting salary of all LIS grads. Among other roles, these graduates described their positions as bearing responsibility for front-end design of systems and for testing and research related to the user interface and interactions.

Digital content management jobs are still a small component of the overall job market—3.4 percent of all reported placements. However, jobs in this specialty were found through the United States and internationally with the highest concentration (21.3 percent) in the West. Salary levels were approximately 5.3 percent lower, averaging $46,917 in 2013 compared with $49,571 the previous year; however, they were still slightly higher than the overall average of $45,650 for starting salaries in 2013. Digital content management positions appeared in a variety of settings, most frequently in academic units within and outside the academic library, private industry, and archives (48.9 percent of the jobs fell into one of these three areas). Metadata, analytics, and standards research were among the featured skills used to describe the job; Web design and maintenance were often a component of the position.

Rearranging Roles

The traditional library and information science roles were not immune to the dynamics of a changing marketplace. New public and academic librarians spoke about their jobs in terms of "roving" positions; they changed their role based upon the needs of their organization, perhaps working circulation one day and providing literacy instruction the next. They emphasized they were not "just a reference librarian or just a cataloger" and were expected to be able to transition among roles as needed. The graduates were quick to suggest broader descriptions of their roles. For example, they felt "user services specialist" encompassed their responsibilities more accurately than being pigeonholed as adult services librarians or reference librarians, especially those who carried responsibilities in multiple departments. Similarly, interlibrary loan staff preferred the description "resource sharing" or "e-resource librarian" to incorporate all the materials and resources under their oversight.

(text continues on page 286)

Table 1 / Status of 2013 Graduates*

Region	Number of Schools Reporting	Number of Graduates Responding	Permanent Professional	Temporary Professional	Non-professional	Total	Graduates Outside of Profession	Unemployed or Status Unreported
Northeast	10	522	251	43	87	381	61	80
Southeast	13	376	233	6	18	257	23	28
Midwest	9	542	364	34	41	439	58	41
Southwest	4	211	141	4	17	162	20	25
West	4	372	154	18	23	195	34	53
Total	40	2,023	1,151	108	189	1,448	199	298

* Table based on survey responses from schools and individual graduates. Figures will not necessarily be fully consistent with some of the other data reported. Tables do not always add up, individually or collectively, since both schools and individuals omitted data in some cases.

Table 2 / Placements and Full-Time Salaries of 2013 Graduates/Summary by Region*

Region	Number of Placements	Number Responding			Low Salary		High Salary		Average Salary			Median Salary		
		Women	Men	Total	Women	Men	Women	Men	Women	Men	All	Women	Men	All
Northeast	272	186	30	218	$22,880	$24,000	$95,000	$105,000	$45,111	$49,313	$45,742	$43,000	$44,000	$43,000
Southeast	214	150	33	185	17,306	27,500	85,000	107,500	39,989	43,695	40,719	40,000	43,409	40,000
Midwest	235	150	29	182	21,000	27,000	80,000	105,000	43,125	51,886	44,555	41,495	45,000	42,000
Southwest	145	81	13	94	16,800	27,000	77,500	75,000	40,975	50,567	42,213	41,000	50,000	42,000
West	177	93	36	132	17,500	21,000	110,240	115,000	51,896	66,569	55,631	50,000	58,250	52,000
Canada/Intl.	36	17	8	25	25,439	19,000	85,437	85,000	53,536	44,425	50,499	51,500	44,200	45,300
Combined	1,339	692	158	860	$17,306	$19,000	$110,240	$115,000	$44,188	$52,110	$45,650	$42,000	$45,800	$42,550

* This table represents only salaries reported as full-time. Some data were reported as aggregate without breakdown by gender or region. Comparison with other tables will show different numbers of placements.

Table 3 / 2013 Total Graduates and Placements by School*

Schools	Graduates			Employed			Response Rate	
	Women	Men	Total	Women	Men	Total	No. Rec'd.	Rate
Alabama	89	34	123	19	3	24	31	25.2%
Albany	52	17	69	24	4	26	33	47.8
Buffalo	68	24	92	18	8	26	29	31.5
Catholic*	51	15	66	—	—	22	24	36.4
Clarion	173	24	197	29	9	39	45	22.8
Dominican	110	36	146	34	6	42	48	32.9
Drexel	178	44	222	53	13	68	83	37.4
Florida State	112	55	167	16	3	19	23	13.8
Hawaii	27	6	33	13	1	15	17	51.5
Illinois*	215	62	277	73	22	117	133	48.0
Indiana	150	57	207	37	8	45	52	25.1
Iowa	—	—	—	11	3	15	18	—
Kentucky	89	18	107	19	3	24	26	24.3
Long Island	101	20	121	2	—	2	2	1.7
Louisiana State	52	11	63	17	1	18	20	31.7
Michigan*	120	64	184	97	51	148	152	82.6
Missouri–Columbia	66	20	86	19	3	22	23	26.7
N.C. Central	160	49	209	—	—	—	—	—
N.C. Chapel Hill*	—	—	—	—	—	80	—	—
N.C. Greensboro	41	9	50	15	1	6	17	34.0
North Texas	—	—	—	62	12	74	91	—
Oklahoma	45	10	55	14	1	15	17	30.9
Pittsburgh	105	23	128	1	—	1	1	0.8
Pratt	110	26	136	18	5	23	27	19.9
Rutgers	121	29	150	47	11	59	68	45.3
San Jose*	—	—	553	—	—	216	241	43.5
Simmons	221	54	275	149	20	172	197	71.6
South Carolina	104	19	123	12	2	14	14	11.4
South Florida	87	11	98	26	2	28	31	31.6
Southern Mississippi	44	9	53	15	5	20	21	39.6
St. Catherine University	39	9	48	11	3	15	18	37.5
Syracuse	59	17	76	27	5	32	37	48.7
Tennessee	54	9	63	19	5	24	25	39.7
Texas (Austin)*	67	24	91	41	12	57	66	72.5
Texas Woman's	152	9	161	33	2	35	37	23.0
UCLA	60	12	72	18	3	22	29	40.3
Valdosta	55	17	72	11	2	14	15	20.8
Washington*	—	—	—	—	—	47	85	—
Wayne State	138	48	186	27	5	33	40	21.5
Wisconsin–Madison	72	15	87	47	7	56	58	66.7
Total	3,387	906	4,846	1,074	241	1,715		

Tables do not always add up, individually or collectively, since both schools and individuals omitted data.
* Some schools conducted their own survey and provided reports. This table represents placements of any kind. Comparison with other tables will show different numbers of placements.

(continued from page 283)

In an era of redefining and evolving job titles and responsibilities, there is a noticeable change in the types of positions being identified by new graduates. While on the surface it appears that many traditional jobs are disappearing, in reality many roles are being subsumed into other positions. Collection development, for example, made up less than 1 percent of the reported job titles, but primary responsibilities in collection management and maintenance appeared in 22.2 percent of the jobs described. Similarly, cataloging comprised 3 percent of the job assignments, but was included in 9.8 percent of the identified job responsibilities. Both collection development roles and cataloging appear across all types of libraries and archives and are described as components of digital collections and e-resource management in addition to standard library functions. Cataloging, in particular, was frequently linked with metadata and digital and archival processing when grads described their daily job functions. Both collection development ($47,375 in 2013) and cataloging ($39,148) experienced better-than-average salary growth compared with prior surveys—up 11.4 percent and 6.2 percent, respectively.

Teaching Is Trending

Another evolving area of responsibility for LIS grads is instruction and training. While a traditional role for many library and information specialists, especially in academic and school libraries, instruction has become a component of library services in a variety of employment contexts. New public librarians as well as academic librarians described efforts in digital literacy education, digital content development for e-learning, and tutoring. Individuals employed with LIS vendors, private industry, and nonprofit agencies also engaged in training and instruction. Approximately 22.4 percent of the reported jobs included instruction, education, or training as a component of their day-to-day activities; 4.2 percent of the reporting graduates indicated that instruction was their primary area of responsibility. Two of the new job titles appearing in the 2013 list are "learning services specialist" and "connected learning coordinator." Among other functions, instruction included authoring resources, creating learning objects, preparing standards and guidelines, and fostering instructional design.

Public Library Positions Rise

Public libraries continue to see growth and opportunity. In 2013 nearly 24 percent of the reported placements were in public libraries, up from 18.7 percent in 2012. Of equal note, the average starting salaries for public libraries increased by just over 4 percent, improving to $39,559 in 2013 (up $1,570 from 2012). This follows the pattern set between 2011 and 2012, when salaries for similar placements increased 1.7 percent. By far the most popular choice of jobs in public libraries falls within children's and youth services, making up 37.4 percent of the overall placements, with an average starting salary of $42,069. It was not unusual for many of the new public librarians to wear several hats, working across units rather than being tied to a single department. Technology, customer service, social media creation and management, and community outreach were all identified as likely tasks throughout a workday.

Beyond Academic Buildings

Approximately 9.8 percent of the 2013 grads who sought employment in academic institutions accepted positions in departments outside the library. These included working with information technology, learning management systems, and assessment. In addition to other academic units, 23.6 percent of the year's new professionals were hired as academic librarians in a variety of capacities; this was up from 21.2 percent in 2012. Regardless of whether in the academic library or in another unit, graduates placed a strong emphasis on working with and developing emerging technologies and e-resources. Digital project management and scholarly communication projects cropped up repeatedly in discussions of job roles and areas of responsibility.

While the reported numbers remained small, new archivists found improved rates of placement, with 5.4 percent of the jobs reported overall—up from 4.9 percent in 2012 and 2.9 percent in 2011. Approximately 40.5 percent of the newly filled archival positions were in the Northeast, down from 2012 when the figure was 44.7 percent. However, the Southeast realized the best growth in percentage of placements, rising to 13.9 percent from 12.7 percent the previous year. Along with the growth in reported placements came a bump in salary, climbing an average of $3,268 (approximately 8.4 percent) to $42,143 (up from $38,875 in 2012). The new archivists shared a growing focus on digital collections, database management, and metadata processes. A new role identified by a handful of the new grads was digital forensics.

Placements at special libraries (4.0 percent), government libraries (1.9 percent), and LIS vendors (1.4 percent) held steady in 2013. However, reports of placements in special libraries have fallen off in recent years, dropping from 6 percent in 2011 to 3.6 percent in 2012. This may signal, as some suggest, that hospital and corporate libraries, among others, are becoming obsolete, or it may indicate changing roles and titles within these situations. A very small number of new graduates were placed in other types of governmental agencies at the state and federal levels, including military, health, and law enforcement. Grads enumerated metadata, training, information technology, and project management as standard tasks in these types of positions.

Impact of Region and Demographics

There is no denying that location is everything in achieving higher-than-average starting salaries. For the 2013 graduating class, finding jobs in the West, especially in California and Washington, proved to be lucrative. Once again average salaries in the West ($55,631) outpaced the other regions by an average of 28.7 percent, though they did not have the same meteoric rise as previous years (2.2 percent compared with 9.3 percent in 2012 and 7 percent in 2011). With the exception of academic libraries, which experienced a 4 percent decline in average starting

(text continues on page 290)

Table 4 / Placements by Average Full-Time Salary of Reporting 2013 Graduates*

School	Average Salary			Median Salary		Low Salary		High Salary		Placements		Total Placements
	Women	Men	All	Women	Men	Women	Men	Women	Men	Women	Men	
Michigan	$58,471	$77,788	$65,047	$60,750	$76,250	$29,000	$19,000	$100,000	$115,000	62	32	148
Pratt	52,084	59,500	53,320	44,000	59,500	31,200	50,000	110,000	69,000	10	2	23
UCLA	54,068	54,667	52,960	52,300	55,000	20,000	49,000	110,240	60,000	17	3	22
Syracuse	49,480	51,875	49,879	45,000	48,750	32,000	45,000	82,000	65,000	20	4	32
San Jose	48,812	51,605	49,503	48,000	47,500	10,000	21,000	85,437	115,000	67	22	152
Hawaii	45,538	72,500	48,909	40,000	72,500	31,200	72,500	87,408	72,500	7	1	15
Catholic University	46,006	51,007	47,673	47,000	51,000	17,000	38,000	72,800	63,000	12	6	22
Rutgers	48,074	43,500	47,353	44,500	40,000	25,000	30,000	85,000	63,000	27	6	59
Illinois	43,337	51,557	46,009	41,800	49,500	28,800	29,120	85,000	105,000	44	18	75
Drexel	46,721	39,284	45,723	45,000	35,700	25,000	30,000	95,000	55,000	36	5	68
Florida State	45,885	44,000	45,616	43,500	44,000	21,120	36,000	65,000	52,000	12	2	19
Iowa	45,643	38,500	44,056	48,000	38,500	40,000	32,000	50,000	45,000	7	2	15
Simmons	42,828	51,846	44,012	42,000	45,000	18,000	26,000	68,000	98,000	97	13	172
Texas Woman's	43,553	45,750	43,762	40,000	45,750	25,500	45,000	69,000	46,500	19	2	35
St. Catherine University	44,071	36,000	43,278	37,000	36,000	25,000	36,000	65,000	36,000	7	1	15
Albany	44,500	36,333	42,867	40,000	35,000	35,000	30,000	70,000	44,000	12	3	26
Wayne State	44,207	37,750	42,626	43,840	35,500	28,454	30,000	77,000	50,000	14	4	33
Long Island	42,000	—	42,000	42,000	—	42,000	—	42,000	—	1	—	1

Valdosta	39,375	44,413	40,634	43,500	44,413	26,000	42,700	46,250	46,125	6	2	14
Wisconsin–Madison	39,978	44,010	40,632	41,000	43,030	17,500	27,000	56,500	59,000	31	6	56
Indiana	38,188	49,549	40,598	38,500	48,000	27,000	35,000	50,000	67,000	26	7	45
Dominican	41,744	36,067	39,868	41,000	37,700	22,000	27,000	56,000	43,500	22	3	42
North Texas	38,653	45,051	39,727	39,000	42,800	16,800	10,560	63,300	85,000	41	7	74
South Carolina	38,750	41,750	39,500	36,250	41,750	31,000	27,500	50,000	56,000	6	2	14
Clarion University	39,528	37,624	39,071	38,000	36,667	25,827	24,000	80,000	55,000	19	6	39
Tennessee	38,176	41,500	38,876	39,000	40,000	24,000	38,000	65,000	48,000	15	4	24
South Florida	39,201	33,000	38,836	40,000	33,000	10,000	33,000	56,000	33,000	16	1	28
Louisiana State	38,781	—	38,781	37,000	—	24,500	—	61,000	—	15	—	18
Oklahoma	38,084	—	38,084	38,639	—	28,808	—	45,000	—	10	—	15
Southern Mississippi	35,983	37,500	36,363	38,750	37,500	20,800	30,000	45,500	45,000	12	4	20
NC Greensboro	35,822	40,000	36,170	35,000	40,000	24,000	40,000	52,500	40,000	11	1	16
Buffalo	32,442	42,026	35,637	36,000	45,000	13,000	35,000	47,000	48,000	10	5	26
Kentucky	35,049	37,093	35,521	36,500	33,280	21,000	28,000	50,000	50,000	10	3	24
Alabama	33,499	36,644	34,627	33,475	39,933	13,000	28,000	44,105	42,000	19	3	24
Missouri–Columbia	32,511	33,000	32,552	30,000	33,000	21,000	33,000	48,000	33,000	11	1	22
Pittsburgh	25,000	—	25,000	25,000	—	25,000	—	25,000	—	1	—	1

* This table represents only placements and salaries reported as full-time. Some individuals or schools omitted some information, rendering information unusable. Comparisons with other tables will show different numbers for placements and salaries.

Table 5 / Average Salary for Starting Library Positions, 2009–2013

Year	Library Schools	Average Starting Salary	Increase in Average Salary	Percentage Change
2009	42	$42,215	$636	1.5
2010	38	42,556	341	0.8
2011	41	44,565	2,009	4.5
2012	41	44,503	-62	-0.1
2013	40	45,650	1,147	2.6

(continued from page 287)

salaries, there was a general trend toward higher salaries in all types of libraries and agencies in the West. Salaries for placements outside the LIS profession had the highest starting average ($71,416 compared with $45,650 overall) and phenomenal growth between 2012 and 2013, rising 40.7 percent from $50,747. Much of this can be attributed to the type of fields where grads were hired, including defense, aerospace, manufacturing, technology, and finance, and to the types of jobs they do, such as software engineering, data analytics, user experience, and user interface design.

Signs of economic recovery and progress were evident among graduates finding positions in the Midwest. While starting salaries ($44,555) continued to be slightly lower than the national average ($45,650), the gap narrowed considerably from nearly 5 percent ($42,427 compared with $44,503) in 2012 to 2.5 percent in 2013. Salary levels achieved by those in school libraries ($46,100, up 7.4 percent compared with 2012) and in other agencies ($53,029 with an increase of $6,719 from 2012) contributed to the healthy growth. Even public libraries in the Midwest experienced a modest rise in salary, moving from an average of $36,762 in 2012 to $38,194, a hike of 3.9 percent.

Grads landing in the Southeast experienced setbacks, with average starting salaries dropping by nearly 5 percent to $40,719. These grads saw falling salaries in school libraries ($42,125, down 5.3 percent); special libraries ($42,798, down 11 percent), which also saw lower placement rates; and archives ($40,625 compared with $50,750 a year earlier). As in other regions, the bright spots were in jobs outside libraries, which saw average starting salaries climbing to $52,724 (an increase of 11.5 percent over 2012 levels of $47,307). While Southeast public library salaries were flat in 2013 ($36,525 compared with $36,759 in 2012), men found salaries 22.3 percent higher than the previous year ($37,732 compared with $30,850).

Starting salaries for jobs in the Southwest were higher than the previous year at $42,213, but the increase (1.2 percent) did not quite recover the losses of 2012, which saw a decrease of 1.9 percent. Once again, academic librarians reported some of the most significant salary losses in the Southwest, dropping nearly 14 percent from $41,720 in 2012 to $35,988 in 2013. However, there were surprises in the overall salary growth for public librarians, which increased 8.7 percent ($38,552 compared with 2012 levels of $35,457), and among women (up 15 percent to $38,430) and grads reporting minority status (up 16.3 percent to $47,001).

Table 6 / Salaries of Reporting Professionals by Area of Job Assignment*

Assignment	No. Rec'd.	Percent of Total	Low Salary	High Salary	Average Salary	Median Salary
Access Services	42	3.0	$20,000	$80,000	$39,718	$40,000
Acquisitions	4	0.3	31,000	51,000	37,733	31,200
Administration	70	5.0	21,000	65,000	42,140	42,800
Adult Services	23	1.6	17,306	48,000	38,159	40,000
Archives	79	5.6	20,000	80,000	41,656	42,000
Automation/Systems	2	0.1	45,000	50,000	47,500	47,500
Cataloging & Classification	42	3.0	16,800	115,000	39,148	35,000
Children's Services	87	6.2	19,000	85,437	41,938	41,500
Circulation	51	3.6	19,000	67,000	33,601	31,000
Collection Development	8	0.6	26,000	63,000	47,375	48,500
Data Analytics	6	0.4	38,000	95,000	56,677	52,000
Database Management	18	1.3	21,000	68,000	46,214	43,000
Data Curation	4	0.3	48,000	67,000	53,250	49,000
Digital Content Management	47	3.4	25,000	82,000	46,917	45,000
Emerging Technologies	2	0.1	45,000	72,000	58,500	58,500
Government Documents	3	0.2	35,000	45,000	40,667	42,000
Indexing/Abstracting	1	0.1	52,000	52,000	52,000	52,000
Info Architecture	7	0.5	53,040	75,000	64,760	65,500
Info Technology	35	2.5	24,960	95,000	52,496	49,000
Instruction	59	4.2	27,000	98,000	48,324	46,000
Interlibrary Loans/Document Delivery	16	1.1	29,000	60,000	38,136	35,660
Knowledge Management	9	0.6	40,000	80,000	59,729	65,000
Metadata	16	1.1	31,200	60,000	45,038	43,000
Other	184	13.1	19,000	110,000	52,033	44,500
Public Services	60	0.7	24,000	77,300	41,075	40,000
Records Management	10	4.3	26,000	69,000	40,614	35,000
Reference/Info Services	208	14.9	20,000	110,240	43,688	42,000
Rights & Permissions	4	0.3	35,000	58,000	44,000	39,000
School Library Media Specialist	107	7.6	18,000	95,000	46,742	44,200
Social Media Management	5	0.4	40,000	40,000	40,000	40,000
Solo Librarian	30	2.1	24,000	63,000	40,135	40,000
Technical Services	37	2.6	22,000	65,000	42,719	45,000
Usability/User Experience/User Interface Design	57	4.1	37,000	115,000	70,026	72,500
YA/Teen Services	47	3.4	25,827	65,000	39,996	39,923
Total	1,400		$16,800	$115,000	$45,701	$42,800

* This table represents placements of any type reported by job assignment but only salaries reported as full-time. Some individuals omitted placement information, rendering some information unusable. Comparison with other tables will show different numbers of placements and average and median salaries.

Reported earnings in the Northeast remained relatively flat with a 1.5 percent uptick, moving from $45,077 in 2012 to $45,742 in 2013, a slim $665 increase. Archivists in the Northeast achieved the best overall salary growth. Their average starting salaries grew by 16.1 percent from $36,827 to $42,743. Salaries for other agencies grew at a much slower pace, rising 5.6 percent compared with an 18.6

(text continues on page 295)

Table 7 / Comparison of Salaries by Type of Organization*

	Total Placements	Placements		Low Salary		High Salary		Average Salary			Median Salary		
		Women	Men	Women	Men	Women	Men	Women	Men	All	Women	Men	All
Public Libraries													
Northeast	81	69	6	$24,000	$24,000	$58,400	$48,000	$40,602	$36,077	$39,923	$42,000	$36,064	$42,000
Southeast	78	64	13	17,306	30,000	59,400	50,000	36,223	37,732	36,525	36,531	35,000	36,100
Midwest	85	76	3	23,000	40,000	50,000	53,846	37,724	44,768	38,194	38,750	40,459	39,845
Southwest	51	48	2	20,000	48,000	55,000	65,000	38,430	56,500	38,552	38,000	56,500	38,500
West	40	30	5	25,827	39,000	77,300	56,000	51,681	51,200	51,576	51,972	54,000	52,945
Canada/International	9	3	3	45,000	25,000	62,400	52,000	50,800	35,000	42,900	45,000	28,000	45,000
All Public	349	183	33	17,306	24,000	77,300	65,000	39,363	40,645	39,559	40,000	40,000	40,000
School Libraries													
Northeast	54	52	2	25,000	42,719	95,000	98,000	49,107	70,360	50,095	47,000	70,360	47,000
Southeast	35	31	2	27,000	38,000	63,000	50,000	41,788	46,500	42,125	40,000	46,500	40,000
Midwest	17	15	1	30,200	42,000	77,000	42,000	46,473	42,000	46,100	48,000	42,000	45,500
Southwest	23	21	1	18,000	45,000	60,000	45,000	47,560	45,000	47,409	48,176	45,000	48,000
West	12	10	1	22,000	21,000	65,000	21,000	51,333	21,000	48,300	59,000	21,000	56,500
Canada/International	10	9	1	35,000	85,000	85,437	85,000	55,193	85,000	58,174	58,000	85,000	60,560
All School	163	115	8	18,000	21,000	95,000	98,000	47,403	53,340	47,789	45,000	43,860	45,000
College/University Libraries													
Northeast	81	38	8	24,000	33,000	80,000	65,000	42,087	49,213	43,326	41,000	46,500	41,500
Southeast	76	41	12	20,000	28,000	52,500	51,000	39,459	44,875	40,858	40,000	45,000	42,500
Midwest	75	41	7	24,000	27,000	67,000	44,000	40,652	37,929	40,464	40,000	38,000	40,000
Southwest	36	16	4	23,000	27,000	55,700	56,000	35,561	37,700	35,988	37,225	33,900	36,500
West	53	29	8	20,000	30,000	110,240	72,000	48,692	45,938	47,594	48,000	41,000	44,500
Canada/International	8	2	2	25,439	42,800	75,000	58,000	50,220	50,400	50,310	50,220	50,400	50,400
All Academic	345	172	46	20,000	27,000	110,240	72,000	41,845	44,746	42,458	41,000	43,750	42,000

Special Libraries													
Northeast	23	14	1	22,880	33,000	65,000	50,000	45,427	50,000	45,732	42,000	50,000	42,000
Southeast	9	6	2	30,000	50,000	62,000	52,000	43,398	41,000	42,798	41,193	41,000	41,193
Midwest	8	4	3	25,000	30,000	71,200	50,000	40,225	42,667	41,271	32,350	45,000	37,700
Southwest	6	4	1	49,000	40,000	65,000	40,000	54,250	40,000	51,400	51,500	40,000	51,000
West	10	6	3	38,000	17,500	68,000	49,000	53,600	28,833	45,344	53,300	20,000	49,000
All Special	59	34	11	30,000	17,500	71,200	67,000	44,288	45,973	44,700	42,000	49,000	42,100
Government Libraries													
Northeast	3	2	—	35,000	—	57,000	—	46,000	—	46,000	46,000	—	46,000
Southeast	12	8	1	24,000	53,040	62,500	53,040	41,438	53,040	42,727	38,000	53,040	38,000
Midwest	3	2	—	21,000	—	41,000	—	31,000	—	31,000	31,000	—	31,000
West	4	3	—	31,200	—	52,300	—	43,533	—	43,533	47,100	—	47,100
Canada/International	3	2	—	42,000	—	65,000	—	53,500	—	53,500	53,500	—	53,500
All Government	28	18	3	21,000	40,000	65,000	53,040	43,672	44,680	43,816	41,500	41,000	41,000
Archives													
Northeast	32	26	6	24,960	41,000	65,000	53,500	42,049	47,250	42,743	43,000	47,250	43,000
Southeast	11	7	4	30,000	27,500	48,000	52,000	40,917	39,750	40,625	42,500	39,750	42,500
Midwest	13	11	—	31,200	—	45,000	—	39,640	—	39,640	42,000	—	42,000
Southwest	9	9	1	25,000	52,000	45,000	52,000	36,800	52,000	36,800	38,000	52,000	38,000
West	10	9	1	40,000	42,000	60,000	42,000	48,833	42,000	47,857	49,000	42,000	48,000
Canada/International	1	—	1		45,600	—	45,600		45,600	45,600		45,600	45,600
All Archives	79	36	7	24,960	27,500	65,000	53,500	41,626	44,800	42,143	42,500	45,600	43,000

Table 7 / Comparison of Salaries by Type of Organization (cont.)

	Total Placements	Placements		Low Salary		High Salary		Average Salary			Median Salary		
		Women	Men	Women	Men	Women	Men	Women	Men	All	Women	Men	All
Vendors													
Northeast	12	10	2	$30,000	$31,200	$60,000	$43,000	$42,900	$37,100	$41,933	$40,000	$37,100	$40,000
Midwest	5	4	—	30,000	—	65,000	—	44,250	—	44,250	41,000	—	41,000
Southwest	1	1	—	16,800	—	16,800	—	16,800	—	16,800	16,800	—	16,800
West	1	1	—	40,000	—	40,000	—	40,000	—	40,000	40,000	—	40,000
All Vendors	20	16	3	16,800	40,000	65,000	70,000	40,875	51,000	42,474	40,000	43,000	40,000
Other Organizations													
Northeast	79	37	10	24,000	30,000	82,000	105,000	48,598	59,000	50,799	47,000	64,000	—
Southeast	39	17	4	30,000	39,933	85,000	107,500	50,559	64,608	52,724	43,000	55,500	—
Midwest	98	43	14	21,000	27,000	80,000	105,000	50,907	61,014	53,029	48,000	63,750	—
Southwest	42	9	3	33,000	64,000	77,500	75,000	51,167	68,667	55,542	43,000	67,000	—
West	59	23	18	36,000	46,000	100,000	115,000	61,411	85,667	71,416	61,000	85,750	—
Canada/International	5	—	1	—	19,000	—	19,000	—	19,000	19,000	—	19,000	—
All Other	348	135	51	17,000	19,000	110,000	115,000	51,827	68,973	56,327	48,000	68,000	50,000
Library Coops													
Northeast	1	1	—	30,000	—	30,000	—	30,000	—	30,000	30,000	—	30,000
Midwest	1	1	—	55,000	—	55,000	—	55,000	—	55,000	55,000	—	55,000
Southwest	1	1	—	—	—	—	—	—	—	45,000	—	—	45,000
All Library Coops	4	2	1	30,000	45,000	55,000	45,000	42,500	45,000	43,333	42,500	45,000	45,000

* This table represents only full-time salaries and all placements reported by type. Some individuals omitted placement information, rendering some information unusable.

(continued from page 291)
percent average growth overall (from $48,124 to $50,799). One positive outlook for the Northeast was the above average starting salary for men taking on jobs in academic libraries. Not only did they experience a 7 percent year-over-year increase ($49,213 compared with $46,000), but they also achieved salaries 7.8 percent higher than the overall rate of $45,650.

Salary growth for the 2013 graduating class made a positive move of 2.6 percent from $44,503 in 2012 to $45,650, finally breaking through the $45,000 barrier. Salaries for women ($44,188) mirrored the same growth rate of 2.6 percent as the overall starting averages, while men's salaries ($52,110) grew at a slightly higher rate of 3.5 percent. In a bit of a surprise, women accepting jobs in the West experienced flat salary growth between 2012 ($51,871) and 2013 ($51,896), while men in the same region had a growth spurt of 10.6 percent (from $60,211 to $66,569). The biggest salary increases for women came in the Midwest, with an average increase of 4.6 percent and an average starting salary of $43,125 (compared with $41,228 in 2012). By comparison, women and men in the Southeast suffered setbacks, with women ($38,989) losing 3.6 percent in salary compared with an eye-popping 11.2 percent decrease for men ($43,695).

The highest average salaries achieved by women were in other agencies, starting at $51,827, with the best wages obtained in private industry (averaging $48,699). Women also achieved better-than-average salaries in school libraries ($47,403), approximately 3.8 percent higher than the overall ($45,650), and 7.3 percent higher than the overall average for women ($44,188). Men also followed suit in other organizations, with an average starting salary of $68,973, coming in at 32.4 percent higher than average salaries reported by all men ($52,110).

In the 2013 survey, minority status more closely matched the other salary and placement trends than it has for some time. In previous reports, graduates self-identifying as members of minority groups earned higher average salaries (as much as 15.9 percent higher in 2012) than all of their counterparts. In 2013 this trend reversed when minority grads reported salaries 2.6 percent less than the overall average ($44,473 compared with $45,650). One of the most notable changes occurred in the Southeast. In 2012 reported salaries among minority graduates increased slightly more than 26 percent to $57,042; in 2013 all those gains were given up in a swift decline of 28 percent to $44,579. Salaries for minority graduates in the Midwest followed the same pattern as other graduates in the region, gaining 4.7 percent in average starting wages between 2012 ($49,926) and 2013 ($52,250).

For graduates claiming minority status, type of organization offered the greatest impact on salary. While overall salaries by type of agency were up, minority graduates experienced drops in most types. Public libraries, for example, exhibited a 4 percent increase in salaries ($39,559 compared with $38,029) for all reporting graduates; minority graduates in the same agencies saw a 6.2 percent decrease year to year ($38,047 in 2013 compared with $40,561 in 2012). Academic library salaries remained flat in 2013, but dropped from $48,174 in 2012 to $43,872 for minority placements (an 8.9 percent loss).

Women self-identifying as minority graduates, while continuing to earn more than all women (by 7.2 percent), lost some of the momentum of previous years with a cut of $3,942 (7.6 percent) in starting salary to $47,612. Men, on the other hand, saw a positive change in circumstances, with those self-identified as members of a minority group earning 7 percent more than the previous year's reports ($61,513 compared with $57,504). This also reversed the losses between 2011 and 2012 when minority men dropped $3,978 from their salaries.

The greatest improvements in salaries for minority grads occurred in school library positions ($53,857 compared with $46,867), which grew by nearly 15 percent, and for placements in special libraries ($46,167 compared with $42,823), up by 7.8 percent. Interestingly, the number of minority placements in both types of agencies was down slightly from 2012 placements.

Other Measures

Salary gains and losses only tell a portion of the placement story for the class. Of the 2,023 graduates responding to this survey, approximately 81.4 percent said they were employed. This was down slightly from the 2012 class when 85.6 percent reported employment of any sort. However, 66.9 percent of those employed were in a permanent, professional position, up from the previous year's report of 61.2 percent. Southeast grads enjoyed the best rate of permanence, reporting 83.2 percent of the jobs as permanent professional placement, also a significant improvement over 2012 when 66.7 percent reported permanent status.

Reports of jobs defined as temporary or contract positions, which often do not include the same benefits as permanent full-time employment (health care, paid days off, and so forth) declined from 10.5 percent in 2012 to 6.6 percent. This may be a signal of economic improvement, with employers regaining the ability to hire permanent staff. Several of the temporary positions fell outside LIS and into private industry, where grads described themselves as consultants and analysts, suggesting that job functions may change as organizations' needs do.

Graduates accepting positions outside LIS increased from 9.5 percent of 2012 placements to 12.1 percent in 2013. As in previous years, there was a wide range of employers outside the LIS profession, including government agencies, private industry, and nonprofit organizations. One graduate suggested that "Employers are beginning to recognize the importance of library science degrees." Jobs requiring research skills, such as those in legal and government research, grant writing expertise, and fund raising and donor development, were options explored by members of the 2013 graduating class. They also used skills in project management and social media to find positions in leading teams and developing the online presence of start-up companies and charitable organizations.

Approximately 32 percent of those who reported employment remained with an employer throughout their studies and after graduation. This continues a downward trend seen in previous years, dropping from a high of 47 percent in 2010 to 35 percent in 2012. As some grads were quick to point out, they already had a professional position within the organization, but needed degree credentials to be eligible for further promotion or endorsement. Public librarians (31.1 percent) were more likely to remain with a current employer, and approximately half of this group also reaped the benefits of earning an advanced degree. For some, this meant a promotion and/or a raise; for others, it offered greater mobility within the library system.

Academic librarians finally saw the fruits of their efforts, with 28.2 percent of those who held a position throughout their graduate studies achieving a raise, tenure status, or a promotion with the granting of the degree (up from the previous year when 17 percent received raises or promotions). For some academic librarians, however, earning an LIS degree was bittersweet. Several individuals shared disappointment in not finding an academic library position quickly because of the necessity of completing a second graduate degree before applying for professional positions.

While only 12.5 percent of school librarians reported remaining with the same school district before and after the completion of the degree, approximately 42 percent were able to take advantage of increased salaries and promotions. Some teachers remained in the classroom upon earning an LIS degree, but also took on the role of technologist or media supervisor. Others made the shift from the classroom to the school media center, but in some cases this meant they were assigned to multiple schools.

Advice for Future Colleagues

Once again, members of the graduating class shared their experiences and advice in their own words. As in previous years, a sense of real accomplishment was balanced by disappointment and frustration.

Among graduates who spoke about finding employment prior to graduation, approximately 37 percent had a job waiting for them when they received their degree. Some began their search well in advance of completing their studies, anticipating a competitive job market. Others waited until the semester before graduating because the positions they sought required the degree in hand. In a few cases, they experienced a delay from the time of offer prior to graduation to the start date after graduation, indicating the importance of the completed degree.

The résumé and CV were all-important for the 2013 graduating class. They recommended attending résumé-building workshops, having others proofread everything, and tailoring the résumé and cover letter for each application submitted—in some cases hundreds were sent out.

As in previous years, networking held high priority. Several grads indicated that "You have to know someone." Internships, paraprofessional jobs, and practicums were cited again as necessities to develop not only the skills needed but the contacts and relationships that may help in winning a job. Among the 2013 graduates, social networking became increasingly important. They engaged in social media to interact with potential employers and were recruited through these sources. Others maintained blogs and websites that were read by recruiters.

For many LIS grads, the search was a full-time job in itself. Besides polishing résumés and portfolios, this meant practicing interviewing skills and using informational interviews to learn about the current professional environment. The best suggestion shared by the graduating class of 2013 was this: "You are on the job hunt from the moment you enter into your MLIS program. Use your time wisely, make contacts, follow up, look for ways to differentiate yourself, and always be your best advocate—don't sell yourself short." They also said to "think more about the service you want to provide, and less about the place you will work."

The graduating class of 2013 offered similar reactions to the job search to those heard from previous classes. Those who landed a job just prior to or shortly after graduation felt "fortunate"; others found it necessary to compromise in the type of job they sought. Graduates cited another year of "not enough experience for an entry-level position" and "a competitive pool of applicants." Some advised those following in their footsteps to consider "second choice" options and "to be flexible" in approaching the range of jobs. One graduate suggested the second choice option might turn out to be the most fun.

Survey Methods

Responses were received through the institutional survey or via individuals representing 40 of the 49 LIS schools surveyed in the United States, as well as from 2,023 of the reported LIS graduates. Response rates varied among the programs, ranging from less than 1 percent of reported graduates to 83 percent. Approximately 44.3 percent of graduates from the participating LIS programs responded to the survey.

Several schools chose to conduct their own surveys and provide data for the *Library Journal* survey. These included Catholic University of America, University of Illinois, University of Michigan, University of North Carolina–Chapel Hill, San José State University, University of Texas at Austin, and University of Washington.

Schools were offered the choice of responding by paper or electronic survey, with most choosing the electronic format. Some graduates and schools reported incomplete information, rendering some data unusable. For schools that did not complete the institutional survey, data were taken from graduate surveys and thus are not full representation of all graduating classes.

Some schools that were unable to participate in the past were able to do so this year, including Clarion University of Pennsylvania, University of Hawaii, University of North Carolina–Greensboro, and Valdosta University.

The following schools declined to participate, did not respond to calls for participation, or had no graduate participation: University of Arizona, University of Denver, Emporia State University, Kent State University, University of Maryland, North Carolina Central, Queens College, University of Rhode Island, St. John's University, and University of Wisconsin at Milwaukee. North Carolina Central University provided graduation statistics, but graduates did not participate in the survey. The Canadian programs—including Alberta, British Columbia, Dalhousie, McGill, Montreal, Toronto, and Western Ontario—conduct their own annual salary and placements surveys and do not participate in the *Library Journal* survey. The University of Puerto Rico also does not participate.

Accredited Master's Programs in Library and Information Studies

This list of graduate programs accredited by the American Library Association is issued by the ALA Office for Accreditation. Regular updates and additional details appear on the Office for Accreditation's website at http://www.ala.org/CFApps/lisdir/index.cfm. A total of 145 U.S. and Canadian institutions offering both accredited and nonaccredited programs in librarianship are included in the 68th edition (2015–2016) of *American Library Directory* (Information Today, Inc.)

Northeast: D.C., Md., Mass., N.J., N.Y., Pa., R.I.

Catholic University of America, School of Arts and Sciences, Dept. of Lib. and Info. Science, 620 Michigan Ave. N.E., Washington, DC 20064. Bill Kules, chair. Tel. 202-319-5085, fax 319-5574, e-mail cua-slis@cua.edu, World Wide Web http://slis.cua.edu. Admissions contact: Louise Gray. Tel. 202-319-5085, fax 319-5574, e-mail grayl@cua.edu.

Clarion University of Pennsylvania, College of Business Admin. and Info. Sciences, Dept. of Lib. Science, 210 Carlson Lib. Bldg., Clarion, PA 16214. Linda L. Lillard, chair. Tel. 866-272-5612, fax 814-393-2150, World Wide Web http://www.clarion.edu/libsci. Admissions contact: Lois Dulavitch. Tel. 866-272-5612, e-mail ldulavitch@clarion.edu.

Drexel University, College of Computing and Informatics, 3141 Chestnut St., Philadelphia, PA 19104-2875. David E. Fenske, dean. Tel. 215-895-2474, fax 215-895-2494, e-mail istinfo@drexel.edu, World Wide Web http://www.cci.drexel.edu. Admissions contact: Matthew Lechtenburg. Tel. 215-895-1951, e-mail ml333@ischool.drexel.edu.

Long Island University, Palmer School of Lib. and Info. Science, C. W. Post Campus, 720 Northern Blvd., Brookville, NY 11548-1300. Valeda Dent, interim dir. Tel. 516-299-4109, fax 516-299-4168, e-mail palmer@cwpost.liu.edu, World Wide Web http://www.liu.edu/palmer. Admissions contact: Christine Prete. Tel. 516-299-2857, e-mail christine.prete@liu.edu.

Pratt Institute, School of Info. and Lib. Science, 144 W. 14 St., New York, NY 10011. Tula Giannini, dean. Tel. 212-647-7682, fax 202-367-2492, e-mail infosils@pratt.edu, World Wide Web http://www.pratt.edu/academics/information_and_library_sciences. Admissions contact: Quinn Lai. Tel. 212-647-7682, e-mail infosils@pratt.edu.

Queens College, City Univ. of New York, Grad. School of Lib. and Info. Studies, Rm. 254, Rosenthal Lib., 65-30 Kissena Blvd., Flushing, NY 11367-1597. Colleen Cool, chair. Tel. 718-997-3790, fax 718-997-3797, e-mail gc_gslis@qc.cuny.edu, World Wide Web http://www.qc.cuny.edu/academics/degrees/dss/gslis/Pages/default.aspx. Admissions contact: Roberta Brody. Tel. 718-997-3790, e-mail roberta_brody@qc.edu.

Rutgers University, School of Communication and Info., Dept. of Lib. and Info. Science, New Brunswick, NJ 08901-1071. Marie L. Radford, chair. Tel. 848-932-8797, fax 732-932-6916, e-mail mlis@comminfo.rutgers.edu, World Wide Web http://comminfo.rutgers.edu. Admissions contact: Kay Cassell. Tel. 732-932-7500 ext. 8264.

Saint John's University, College of Liberal Arts and Sciences, Div. of Lib. and Info. Science, 8000 Utopia Pkwy., Queens, NY 11439. Jeffery E. Olson, dir. Tel. 718-990-6200, fax 718-990-2071, e-mail dlis@stjohns.edu, World Wide Web http://www.stjohns.edu/dlis. Admissions contact: Deborah Martinez. Tel. 718-990-6200, e-mail dlis@stjohns.edu.

Simmons College, Grad. School of Lib. and Info. Science, 300 The Fenway, Boston, MA 02115. Eileen Abels, dean. Tel. 617-

521-2800, fax 617-521-3192, e-mail gslis@
simmons.edu, World Wide Web http://www.
simmons.edu/gslis. Admissions contact:
Sarah Petrakos. Tel. 617-521-2868, e-mail
gslisadm@simmons.edu.

Syracuse University, School of Info. Studies,
343 Hinds Hall, Syracuse, NY 13244. Elizabeth D. Liddy, dean. Tel. 315-443-2911,
fax 315-443-6886, e-mail ischool@syr.edu,
World Wide Web http://www.ischool.syr.
edu. Admissions contact: Jill Hurst-Wahl.
Tel. 315-443-2911, e-mail mslis@syr.edu.

University at Albany, State Univ. of New York,
College of Computing and Info., Dept. of
Info. Studies, Draper 113, 135 Western
Ave., Albany, NY 12222. Philip B. Eppard,
chair. Tel. 518-442-5110, fax 518-442-5367,
e-mail infostudies@albany.edu, World Wide
Web http://www.albany.edu/information
studies/index.php. Admissions contact:
Daphne Jorgensen. Tel. 518-442-5110, e-
mail djorgensen@albany.edu.

University at Buffalo, State Univ. of New
York, Graduate School of Educ., Lib. and
Info. Studies, 534 Baldy Hall, Buffalo, NY
14260-1020. Heidi Julien, chair. Tel. 716-
645-2412, fax 716-645-3775, e-mail ub-
lis@buffalo.edu, World Wide Web http://
gse.buffalo.edu/lis. Admissions contact:
Radhika Suresh. Tel. 716-645-2110, e-mail
gse-info@buffalo.edu.

University of Maryland, College of Info. Studies, 4105 Hornbake Bldg., College Park,
MD 20742. John Carlo Bertot, MLIS Program Dir. Tel. 301-405-2033, fax 301-314-
9145, e-mail ischooladmission@umd.edu,
World Wide Web http://ischool.umd.edu.
Admissions contact: Joanne Briscoe. Tel.
301-405-2038, e-mail ischooladmission@
umd.edu.

University of Pittsburgh, School of Info. Sciences, 135 N. Bellefield Ave., Pittsburgh, PA
15260. Sheila Corrall, chair. Tel. 412-624-
9420, fax 412-648-7001, e-mail lisinq@
mail.sis.pitt.edu, World Wide Web http://
www.ischool.pitt.edu. Admissions contact:
Debbie Day. Tel. 412-624-9420, e-mail
dday@sis.pitt.edu.

University of Rhode Island, Grad. School of
Lib. and Info. Studies, Rodman Hall, 94 W.
Alumni Ave., Kingston, RI 02881. Valerie
Karno, interim dir. Tel. 401-874-2878, fax
401-874-4964, e-mail gslis@etal.uri.edu,
World Wide Web http://www.uri.edu/artsci/
lsc.

Southeast: Ala., Fla., Ga., Ky., La., Miss., N.C., S.C., Tenn., P.R.

East Carolina University, College of Educ.,
Lib. Science Degree Program, Mailstop 172,
ECU, Greenville, NC 27858. John B. Harer,
program coord. Tel. 252-328-4389, fax 252-
328-4368, e-mail harerj@ecu.edu, World
Wide Web http://www.ecu.edu/cs-educ/idp/
lsed/index.cfm. Admissions contact: Camil-
la King. Tel. 252-328-6012, e-mail grad
school@ecu.edu.

Florida State University, College of Communication and Info., School of Lib. and
Info. Studies, 142 Collegiate Loop, P.O.
Box 3062100, Tallahassee, FL 32306-2100.
Kathleen Burnett, dir. Tel. 850-644-5775,
fax 850-644-9763, World Wide Web http://
slis.fsu.edu. Admissions e-mail slisgrad
admissions@admin.fsu.edu, tel. 850-644-
8121.

Louisiana State University, School of Lib.
and Info. Science, 267 Coates Hall, Baton
Rouge, LA 70803. Ed Holton, interim dir.
Tel. 225-578-3158, fax 225-578-4581, e-
mail slis@lsu.edu, World Wide Web http://
slis.lsu.edu. Admissions contact: LaToya
Coleman Joseph. E-mail lcjoseph@lsu.edu.

North Carolina Central University, School of
Lib. and Info. Sciences, P.O. Box 19586,
Durham, NC 27707. Irene Owens, dean.
Tel. 919-530-6485, fax 919-530-6402, e-
mail slisadmissions@nccu.edu, World Wide
Web http://www.nccuslis.org. Admissions
contact: Sofia Harrison.

University of Alabama, College of Communication and Info. Sciences, School of Lib.
and Info. Studies, Box 870252, Tuscaloosa,
AL 35487-0252. Ann E. Prentice, interim
dir. Tel. 205-348-4610, fax 205-348-3746,
e-mail info@slis.ua.edu, World Wide Web
http://www.slis.ua.edu. Admissions contact: Beth Riggs. Tel. 205-348-1527, e-mail
briggs@slis.ua.edu.

University of Kentucky, School of Lib. and
Info. Science, 320 Little Lib., Lexington,
KY 40506-0224. Jeffrey T. Huber, dir. Tel.

859-257-8876, fax 859-257-4205, e-mail ukslis@uky.edu, World Wide Web http://www.uky.edu/cis/slis. Admissions contact: Will Buntin. Tel. 859-257-3317, e-mail wjbunt0@uky.edu.

University of North Carolina at Chapel Hill, School of Info. and Lib. Science, CB 3360, 100 Manning Hall, Chapel Hill, NC 27599-3360. Gary Marchionini, dean. Tel. 919-962-8366, fax 919-962-8071, e-mail info@ils.unc.edu, World Wide Web http://www.sils.unc.edu. Admissions contact: Lara Bailey.

University of North Carolina at Greensboro, School of Educ., Dept. of Lib. and Info. Studies, 446 School of Educ. Bldg., Greensboro, NC 27402-6170. O. Lee Shiflett, interim chair. Tel. 336-334-3477, fax 336-334-4120, World Wide Web http://lis.uncg.edu. Admissions contact: Touger Vang. E-mail t_vang@uncg.edu.

University of Puerto Rico, Info. Sciences and Technologies, P.O. Box 21906, San Juan, PR 00931-1906. Mariano A. Maura, acting dir. Tel. 787-763-6199, fax 787-764-2311, e-mail egcti@uprrp.edu, World Wide Web http://egcti.upr.edu. Admissions contact: Migdalia Dávila-Perez. Tel. 787-764-0000 ext. 3530, e-mail migdalia.davila@upr.edu.

University of South Carolina, College of Mass Communications and Info. Studies, School of Lib. and Info. Science, 1501 Greene St., Columbia, SC 29208. Samantha K. Hastings, dir. Tel. 803-777-3858, fax 803-777-7938, e-mail hastings@sc.edu, World Wide Web http://www.libsci.sc.edu. Admissions contact: Tilda Reeder. Tel. 800-304-3153, e-mail tildareeder@sc.edu.

University of South Florida, College of Arts and Sciences, School of Lib. and Info. Science, 4202 E. Fowler Ave., CIS 1040, Tampa, FL 33620. James Andrews, dir. Tel. 813-974-3520, fax 813-974-6840, e-mail lisinfo@usf.edu, World Wide Web http://si.usf.edu. Admissions contact: Daniel Kahl. Tel. 813-974-8022, e-mail djkahl@usf.edu.

University of Southern Mississippi, College of Educ. and Psychology, School of Lib. and Info. Science, 118 College Drive, No. 5146, Hattiesburg, MS 39406-0001. Dorothy Elizabeth Haynes, dir. Tel. 601-266-4228, fax 601-266-5774, e-mail slis@usm.edu, World Wide Web http://www.usm.edu/slis. Admissions tel. 601-266-5137, e-mail graduatestudies@usm.edu.

University of Tennessee, College of Communication and Info., School of Info. Sciences, 451 Communication Bldg., Knoxville, TN 37996. Edwin M. Cortez, dir. Tel. 865-974-2148, fax 865-974-4967, World Wide Web http://www.sis.utk.edu. Admissions contact: Tanya Arnold. Tel. 865-974-2858, e-mail tnarnold@utk.edu.

Valdosta State Univ., Dept. of Info. Studies, 1500 N. Patterson St., Valdosta, GA 31698-0133. Linda R. Most, interim dept. head. Tel. 229-333-5966, fax 229-259-5055, e-mail mlis@valdosta.edu, World Wide Web http://www.valdosta.edu/mlis. Admissions contact: Sheila Peacock.

Midwest: Ill., Ind., Iowa, Kan., Mich., Minn., Mo., Ohio, Wis.

Dominican Univ., Grad. School of Lib. and Info. Science, 7900 W. Division St., River Forest, IL 60305. Kate Marek, dean. Tel. 708-524-6845, fax 708-524-6657, e-mail gslis@dom.edu, World Wide Web http://www.dom.edu/gslis. Admissions contact: Meagan Sather Tel. 708-524-6983, e-mail msather@dom.edu.

Emporia State University, School of Lib. and Info. Management, Campus Box 4025, 1 Kellogg Circle, Emporia, KS 66801-5415. Gwen Alexander, dean. Tel. 620-341-5203, fax 620-341-5233, e-mail sliminfo@emporia.edu, World Wide Web http://slim.emporia.edu. Admissions contact: Kathie Buckman. Tel. 620-341-5065, e-mail sliminfo@emporia.edu.

Indiana University, School of Informatics and Computing, Lib. and Info. Science, 1320 E. 10 St., LI 011, Bloomington, IN 47405-3907. Robert Schnabel, dean. Tel. 812-855-2018, fax 812-855-6166, e-mail ilsmain@indiana.edu, World Wide Web http://soic.iu.edu. Admissions contact: Rhonda Spencer.

Kent State University, School of Lib. and Info. Science, P.O. Box 5190, Kent, OH 44242-0001. Jeffrey Fruit, interim dir. Tel. 330-672-2782, fax 330-672-7965, e-mail slis inform@kent.edu, World Wide Web http://

www.kent.edu/slis. Admissions contact: Cheryl Tennant.

Saint Catherine University, School of Business and Leadership, Educ. and LIS, MLIS Program/Information Management Department, 2004 Randolph Ave. No. 4125, St. Paul, MN 55105. Deborah S. Grealy, assoc. dean/dir. Tel. 651-690-6802, fax 651-690-8724, e-mail imdept@stkate.edu, World Wide Web https:// www2.stkate.edu/mlis. Admissions contact: Kristina Sande. Tel. 651-690-6507, e-mail kmsande@stkate.edu.

University of Illinois at Urbana-Champaign, Grad. School of Lib. and Info. Science, 501 E. Daniel St., Champaign, IL 61820-6211. Allen Renear, interim dean. Tel. 217-333-3280, fax 217-244-3302, e-mail gslis@illinois.edu, World Wide Web http://www.lis.illinois.edu. Admissions contact: Penny Ames. Tel. 217-333-7197, e-mail pames@illinois.edu.

University of Iowa, Graduate College, School of Lib. and Info. Science, 3087 Main Lib., Iowa City, IA 52242-1420. David Eichmann, dir. Tel. 319-335-5707, fax 319-335-5374, e-mail slis@uiowa.edu, World Wide Web http://slis.grad.uiowa.edu. Admissions contact: Carol Ives. Tel. 319-335-5709, e-mail carol-ives@uiowa.edu.

University of Michigan, School of Info., 4322 North Quad, 105 S. State St., Ann Arbor, MI 48109-1285. Jeffrey Makie-Mason, dean. Tel. 734-763-2285, fax 734-764-2475, e-mail umsi.admissions@umich.edu, World Wide Web http://www.si.umich.edu. Admissions contact: Laura Elgas.

University of Missouri, College of Educ., School of Info. Science and Learning Technologies, 303 Townsend Hall, Columbia, MO 65211. Joi Moore, dir. Tel. 877-747-5868, fax 573-884-0122, e-mail sislt@missouri.edu, World Wide Web http://lis.missouri.edu. Admissions tel. 573-882-4546.

University of Wisconsin–Madison, College of Letters and Sciences, School of Lib. and Info. Studies, 600 N. Park St., Madison, WI 53706. Kristin Eschenfelder, dir. Tel. 608-263-2900, fax 608-263-4849, e-mail uw-slis@slis.wisc.edu, World Wide Web

http://www.slis.wisc.edu. Admissions contact: Tanya Cobb. Tel. 608-263-2909, e-mail student-services@slis.wisc.edu.

University of Wisconsin–Milwaukee, School of Info. Studies, P.O. Box 413, Milwaukee, WI 53211. Char Zahrt, assistant dean. Tel. 414-229-4707, fax 414-229-6699, e-mail soisinfo@uwm.edu, World Wide Web http://www4.uwm.edu/sois.

Wayne State University, School of Lib. and Info. Science, 106 Kresge Lib., Detroit, MI 48202. Stephen T. Bajjaly, assoc. dean. Tel. 313-577-1825, fax 313-577-7563, e-mail asklis@wayne.edu, World Wide Web http://www.slis.wayne.edu. Admissions contact: Matthew Fredericks. Tel. 313-577-2446, e-mail mfredericks@wayne.edu.

Southwest: Ariz., Okla., Texas

Texas Woman's University, School of Lib. and Info. Studies, P.O. Box 425438, Denton, TX 76204-5438. Ling Hwey Jeng, dir. Tel. 940-898-2602, fax 940-898-2611, e-mail slis@twu.edu, World Wide Web http://www.twu.edu/slis. Admissions contact: Brenda Mallory. E-mail bmallory@mail.twu.edu.

University of Arizona, College of Social and Behavioral Sciences, School of Info. Resources and Lib. Science, 1515 E. 1 St., Tucson, AZ 85719. P. Bryan Heidorn, dir. Tel. 520-621-3565, fax 520-621-3279, e-mail sirls@email.arizona.cdu, World Wide Web http://www.sirls.arizona.edu. Admissions contact: Geraldine Fragoso. Tel. 520-621-5230, e-mail gfragoso@u.arizona.edu.

University of North Texas, College of Info., Dept. of Lib. and Info. Sciences, 1155 Union Circle, No. 311068, Denton, TX 76203-5017. Suliman Hawamdeh, chair. Tel. 940-565-2445, fax 940-369-7600, e-mail lis-chair@unt.edu, World Wide Web http://lis.unt.edu. Admissions contact: Toby Faber. Tel. 940-565-2445, e-mail ci-advising@unt.edu.

University of Oklahoma, School of Lib. and Info. Studies, College of Arts and Sciences, 401 W. Brooks, Norman, OK 73019-6032. Cecelia Brown, dir. Tel. 405-325-3921, fax 405-325-7648, e-mail slisinfo@ou.edu,

World Wide Web http://www.ou.edu/cas/ slis. Admissions contact: Sarah Connelly.
University of Texas at Austin, School of Info., Suite 5.202, 1616 Guadalupe St., Austin, TX 78701-1213. Andrew Dillon, dean. Tel. 512-471-3821, fax 512-471-3971, e-mail info@ ischool.utexas.edu, World Wide Web http:// www.ischool.utexas.edu. Admissions contact: Carla Criner. Tel. 512-471-5654, e-mail criner@ischool.utexas.edu.

West: Calif., Colo., Hawaii, Wash.

San José State University, School of Lib. and Info. Science, 1 Washington Sq., San José, CA 95192-0029. Sandy Hirsh, dir. Tel. 408-924-2490, fax 408-924-2476, e-mail sjsu ischool@gmail.com, World Wide Web http://ischool.sjsu.edu. Admissions contact: Linda Main. Tel. 408-924-2494, e-mail lindxain@sjsu.edu.
University of California, Los Angeles, Graduate School of Educ. and Info. Studies, Dept. of Info. Studies, Box 951520, Los Angeles, CA 90095-1520. Jonathan Furner, chair. Tel. 310-825-8799, fax 310-206-3076, e-mail info@gseis.ucla.edu, World Wide Web http://is.gseis.ucla.edu. Admissions contact: Susan Abler. Tel. 310-825-5269, e-mail abler@gseis.ucla.edu.
University of Denver, Morgridge College of Educ., Lib. and Info. Science Program, 1999 E. Evans Ave., Denver, CO 80208-1700. Mary Stansbury, chair. Tel. 303-871-3587, fax 303-871-4456, e-mail mary.stansbury@ du.edu, World Wide Web http://www. du.edu/education. Admissions contact: Kristina Coccia. E-mail kristina.coccia@du.edu.
University of Hawaii, College of Natural Sciences, Lib. and Info. Science Program, 2550 McCarthy Mall, Honolulu, HI 96822. Andrew Wertheimer, chair. Tel. 808-956-7321, fax 808-956-5835, e-mail slis@hawaii.edu, World Wide Web http://www.hawaii.edu/lis.
University of Washington, The Information School, 370 Mary Gates Hall, Seattle, WA 98195-2840. Harry Bruce, dean. Tel. 206-685-9937, fax 206-616-3152, e-mail ischool@uw.edu, World Wide Web http://

ischool.uw.edu. Admissions contact: Tel. 206-543-1794, e-mail mlis@uw.edu.

Canada

Dalhousie University, School of Info. Management, Kenneth C. Rowe Management Bldg., Halifax, NS B3H 3J5. Louise Spiteri, dir. Tel. 902-494-3656, fax 902-494-2451, e-mail sim@dal.ca, World Wide Web http:// www.sim.management.dal.ca. Admissions contact: JoAnn Watson. Tel. 902-494-2471, e-mail joann.watson@dal.ca.
McGill University, School of Info. Studies, 3661 Peel St., Montreal, QC H3A 1X1. France Bouthillier, dir. Tel. 514-398-4204, fax 514-398-7193, e-mail sis@mcgill.ca, World Wide Web http://www.mcgill.ca/sis. Admissions contact: Kathryn Hubbard. Tel. 514-398-4204 ext. 0742, e-mail sis@mcgill. ca.
University of Alberta, School of Lib. and Info. Studies, 3-20 Rutherford S., Edmonton, AB T6G 2J4. Anna Altmann, interim dir. Tel. 780-492-4578, fax 780-492-2430, e-mail slis@ualberta.ca, World Wide Web http:// www.slis.ualberta.ca. Admissions contact: Lauren Romaniuk. Tel. 780-492-4140, e-mail slisadmissions@ualberta.ca.
University of British Columbia, School of Lib., Archival, and Info. Studies, Irving K. Barber Learning Centre, Suite 470, 1961 East Mall, Vancouver, BC V6T 1Z1. Caroline Haythornthwaite, dir. Tel. 604-822-2404, fax 604-822-6006, e-mail ischool.info@ubc.ca, World Wide Web http://www.slais.ubc.ca. Admissions contact: Dan Slessor. Tel. 604-822-2461, e-mail slais.ssc@ubc.ca.
Université de Montréal, École de Bibliothéconomie et des Sciences de l'Information, C.P. 6128, Succursale Centre-Ville, Montreal, QC H3C 3J7. Clément Arsenault, dir. Tel. 514-343-6044, fax 514-343-5753, e-mail ebsiinfo@ebsi.umontreal.ca, World Wide Web http://www.ebsi.umontreal.ca. Admissions contact: Alain Tremblay. Tel. 514-343-6044, e-mail alain.tremblay.1@umontreal. ca.
University of Ottawa, School of Info. Studies, Desmarais Bldg., Ottawa, ON K1N 6N5.

Tel. 613-562-5130, fax 613-562-5854, e-mail esis@uOttawa.ca, World Wide Web http://www.sis.uottawa.ca. Daniel Paré, interim dir. Admissions contact: Marisa Simard Swangha. Tel. 613-562-5800 ext. 3392, e-mail gradsi@uottawa.ca.

University of Toronto, Faculty of Info., 140 George St., Toronto, ON M5S 3G6. Seamus Ross, dean. Tel. 416-978-3202, fax 416-978-5762, e-mail inquire.ischool@utoronto.ca, World Wide Web http://www.ischool.utoronto.ca. Admissions contact: Adriana Rossini. Tel. 416-978-8589, e-mail adriana.rossini@utoronto.ca.

University of Western Ontario, Grad. Programs in Lib. and Info. Science, Faculty of Info. and Media Studies, Room 240, North Campus Bldg., London, ON N6A 5B7. Nick Dyer-Whitheford, acting dean; Pam McKenzie, assoc. dean. Tel. 519-661-4017, fax 519-661-3506, e-mail mlisinfo@uwo.ca, World Wide Web http://www.fims.uwo.ca. Admissions contact: Shelley Long.

Library Scholarship Sources

For a more complete list of scholarships, fellowships, and assistantships offered for library study, see *Financial Assistance for Library and Information Studies,* published annually by the American Library Association (ALA). The document is also available on the ALA website at http://www.ala.org/educationcareers/ sites/ala.org.educationcareers/files/content/scholarships/right_nav_pods/2014-2015%20FALIS%20Directory.pdf.

American Association of Law Libraries. (1) A varying number of scholarships of varying amounts for graduates of an accredited law school who are degree candidates in an ALA-accredited library school; (2) a varying number of scholarships of varying amounts for library school graduates working on a law degree and non-law graduates enrolled in an ALA-accredited library school; (3) the George A. Strait Minority Stipend for varying numbers of minority librarians working toward a library or law degree; and (4) a varying number of $200 scholarships for law librarians taking courses relating to law librarianship. For information, write to: AALL Scholarship Committee, 105 W. Adams, Suite 3300, Chicago, IL 60603.

American Library Association. (1) The David H. Clift Scholarship of $3,000 for a student who has been admitted to an ALA-accredited library school; (2) the Tom and Roberta Drewes Scholarship of $3,000 for library support staff; (3) the Mary V. Gaver Scholarship of $3,000 for an individual specializing in youth services; (4) the Miriam L. Hornback Scholarship of $3,000 for an ALA or library support staff member; (5) the Christopher J. Hoy/ERT Scholarship of $5,000 for a student who has been admitted to an ALA-accredited library school; (6) the Tony B. Leisner Scholarship of $3,000 for a library support staff member; (7) the Peter Lyman Memorial/Sage Scholarship in New Media of $2,500 for a student admitted to an ALA-accredited library school who will specialize in new media; (8) the Cicely Phippen Marks Scholarship of $1,500 for a student admitted to an ALA-accredited program who will specialize in federal librarianship; and (9) Spectrum Initiative Scholarships of $6,500 for a varying number of minority students admitted to a master's de-gree program at an ALA-accredited library school. For information, write to: ALA Scholarship Clearinghouse, 50 E. Huron St., Chicago, IL 60611, or see http://www.ala. org/scholarships.

ALA/Association for Library Service to Children. (1) The Bound to Stay Bound Books Scholarship of $7,500 each for four U.S. or Canadian citizens who have been admitted to an ALA-accredited master's or doctoral program, and who will work with children in a library for one year after graduation; and (2) the Frederic G. Melcher Scholarship of $6,000 each for two U.S. or Canadian citizens admitted to an ALA-accredited library school who will work with children in school or public libraries for one year after graduation. For information, write to: ALA Scholarship Clearinghouse, 50 E. Huron St., Chicago, IL 60611, or see http://www.ala. org/scholarships.

ALA/Association of College and Research Libraries Thomson Reuters. The WESS-SEES De Gruyter European Librarianship Study Grant of €2,500 for up to 30 consecutive days of study in Europe. Application is electronic only. For information, e-mail Chase Ollis at collis@ala.org.

ALA/Association of Specialized and Cooperative Library Agencies. Century Scholarship of up to $2,500 for a varying number of disabled U.S. or Canadian citizens admitted to an ALA-accredited library school. For information, write to: ALA Scholarship Clearinghouse, 50 E. Huron St., Chicago, IL 60611, or see http://www.ala.org/scholarships.

ALA/International Relations Committee. The Bogle Pratt International Library Travel Fund grant of $1,000 for a varying number of ALA members to attend a first international conference. For information, write to:

Michael Dowling, ALA/IRC, 50 E. Huron St., Chicago, IL 60611.

ALA/Library and Information Technology Association. (1) The LITA/Christian Larew Memorial Scholarship of $3,000 for a U.S. or Canadian citizen admitted to an ALA-accredited library school; (2) the LITA/OCLC Minority Scholarship in Library and Information Technology of $3,000 and (3) the LITA/LSSI Minority Scholarship of $2,500, each for a minority student admitted to an ALA-accredited program. For information, write to: ALA Scholarship Clearinghouse, 50 E. Huron St., Chicago, IL 60611, or see http://www.ala.org/scholarships.

ALA/Public Library Association. The Demco New Leaders Travel Grant Study Award of up to $1,500 for a varying number of PLA members with MLS degrees and five years or less experience. For information, write to: PLA Awards Program, ALA/PLA, 50 E. Huron St., Chicago, IL 60611.

American-Scandinavian Foundation. Fellowships and grants for 25 to 30 students, in amounts from $5,000 to $23,000, for advanced study in Denmark, Finland, Iceland, Norway, or Sweden. For information, write to: Fellowships and Grants, American-Scandinavian Foundation, 58 Park Ave., New York, NY 10026, or see http://www.amscan.org/fellowships_grants.html.

Association for Library and Information Science Education (ALISE). A varying number of research grants of up to $2,500 each for members of ALISE. For information, write to: ALISE, 2150 N.W. 107th St., Suite 205, Seattle, WA 98133.

Association of Bookmobile and Outreach Services (ABOS). (1) The Bernard Vavrek Scholarship of $1,000 for a student with a grade-point average of 3.0 or better admitted to an ALA-accredited program and interested in becoming an outreach/bookmobile librarian; (2) the John Philip Award of $300 to recognize outstanding contributions and leadership by an individual in bookmobile and outreach services; (3) the Carol Hole Conference Attendance Travel Grant of $500 for a public librarian working in outreach or bookmobile services. For information, write to President, ABOS, c/o AMIGOS Library Services, 3610 Barrett Office Drive, Suite 216, Ballwin, MO 63021.

Association of Jewish Libraries. The AJL Scholarship Fund offers up to two scholarships of $1,000 for MLS students who plan to work as Judaica librarians. For information, write to: Tina Weiss, AJL Scholarship Committee, Hebrew Union College, 1 W. 4th St., New York, NY 10012.

Association of Seventh-Day Adventist Librarians. The D. Glenn Hilts Scholarship of $1,200 for a member of the Seventh-Day Adventist Church in a graduate library program. For information, write to: Lori Curtis, Association of Seventh-Day Adventist Librarians, Loma Linda University, 11072 Anderson St., Loma Linda, CA 92350.

Beta Phi Mu. (1) The Sarah Rebecca Reed Scholarship of $2,000 for a person accepted in an ALA-accredited library program; (2) the Frank B. Sessa Scholarship of $1,500 for a Beta Phi Mu member for continuing education; (3) the Harold Lancour Scholarship of $1,750 for study in a foreign country relating to the applicant's work or schooling; (4) the Blanche E. Woolls Scholarship for School Library Media Service of $2,250 for a person accepted in an ALA-accredited library program; and (5) the Eugene Garfield Doctoral Dissertation Scholarship of $3,000 for a person who has approval of a dissertation topic. For information, write to Isabel Gray, Program Director, Beta Phi Mu, c/o Drexel University College of Computing and Informatics (CCI), 3141 Chestnut St., Philadelphia, PA 19104.

Canadian Association of Law Libraries. The Diana M. Priestly Scholarship of $2,500 for a student enrolled in an approved Canadian law school or accredited Canadian library school. For information, write to: Ann Marie Melvie, Librarian, Saskatchewan Court of Appeal, 2425 Victoria Ave., Regina, SK S4P 4W6.

Canadian Federation of University Women. (1) The Alice E. Wilson Award of $6,000 for five mature students returning to graduate studies in any field, with special consideration given to those returning to study after at least three years; (2) the Margaret McWilliams Pre-Doctoral Fellowship of $13,000 for a female student who has completed at least one full year as a full-time student in doctoral-level studies; (3) the Marion Elder Grant Fellowship of $11,000 for a full-time student at any level of a doctoral program; (4) the CFUW Memorial Fellowship of $10,000 for a student who is currently enrolled in a master's program in science, mathematics, or engineering in Canada or abroad; (5) the Beverly Jackson Fellowship of $2,000 for a student over the age of 35 at the time of application who is enrolled in graduate studies at an Ontario university; (6) the 1989 Ecole Polytechnique Commemorative Award of $7,000 for graduate studies in any field; (7) the Bourse Georgette LeMoyne award of $7,000 for graduate study in any field at a Canadian university (the candidate must be studying in French); (8) the Margaret Dale Philp Biennial Award of $3,000 for studies in the humanities or social sciences; and (9) the Canadian Home Economics Association Fellowship of $6,000 for a student enrolled in a postgraduate program in Canada. For information, write to: Fellowships Program Manager, Canadian Federation of University Women, 251 Bank St., Suite 305, Ottawa, ON K2P 1X3, Canada, or visit http://www.cfuw.org/en-ca/fellowships/fellowshipsandawards.aspx.

Canadian Library Association. (1) The CLA Dafoe Scholarship of $5,000 and (2) the H. W. Wilson Scholarship of $2,000, each given to a Canadian citizen or landed immigrant to attend an accredited Canadian library school; and (3) the Library Research and Development Grant of $1,000 for a member of the Canadian Library Association, in support of theoretical and applied research in library and information science. For information, write to: CLA Membership Services Department, Scholarship Committee, 1150 Morrison Drive, Suite 400, Ottawa, ON K2H 8S9, Canada.

Chinese American Librarians Association. (1) The Sheila Suen Lai Scholarship and the CALA Scholarship of Library and Information Science, each $500, to a Chinese descendant who has been accepted in an ALA-accredited program. For information, write to: MengXiong Liu, Clark Library, San José State University, 1 Washington Sq., San José, CA 95192-0028.

Church and Synagogue Library Association. The Muriel Fuller Memorial Scholarship of $200 (including texts) for a correspondence course offered by the association. For infor-

mation, write to: CSLA, 10157 S.W. Barbur Blvd., No. 102C, Portland, OR 97219-5957.

Council on Library and Information Resources. The Rovelstad Scholarship in International Librarianship, to enable a student enrolled in an accredited LIS program to attend the IFLA Annual Conference. For more information, write to: Rovelstad Scholarship, Council on Library and Information Resources, 1707 L St. N.W., Suite 650, Washington, DC 20036.

Massachusetts Black Librarians' Network. Two scholarships of at least $500 and $1,000 for minority students entering an ALA-accredited master's program in library science with no more than 12 semester hours completed toward a degree. For information, write to: Pearl Mosley, Chair, Massachusetts Black Librarians' Network, 17 Beech Glen St., Roxbury, MA 02119.

Medical Library Association. (1) The Cunningham Memorial International Fellowship of $3,500 for each of two health sciences librarians from countries other than the United States and Canada; (2) a scholarship of $5,000 for a person entering an ALA-accredited library program, with no more than one-half of the program yet to be completed; (3) a scholarship of $5,000 for a minority student studying health sciences librarianship; (4) a varying number of Research, Development, and Demonstration Project Grants of $100 to $1,000 for U.S. or Canadian citizens, preferably MLA members; (5) the Thomson Reuters/MLA Doctoral Fellowship of $2,000 for doctoral work in medical librarianship or information science; (6) the Rittenhouse Award of $500 for a student enrolled in an ALA-accredited library program or a recent graduate working as a trainee in a library internship program; and (7) the Librarians without Borders Ursula Poland International Scholarship of $5,000 for a librarian working in a U.S. or Canadian health sciences library. For information, write to: MLA Grants and Scholarships, Medical Library Association, 65 E. Wacker Place, Suite 1900, Chicago, IL 60601-7298.

Mountain Plains Library Association. A varying number of grants of up to $600 for applicants who are members of the association and have been for the preceding two years.

For information, write to: Judy Zelenski, Interim Executive Secretary, MPLA, 14293 W. Center Drive, Lakewood, SD 80228.

Society of American Archivists. (1) The F. Gerald Ham Scholarship of $7,500 for up to two graduate students in archival education at a U.S. university that meets the society's criteria for graduate education; (2) the Mosaic Scholarship of $5,000 for up to two U.S. or Canadian minority students enrolled in a graduate program in archival administration; (3) the Josephine Foreman Scholarship of $10,000 for a U.S. citizen or permanent resident who is a minority graduate student enrolled in a program in archival administration; (4) the Oliver Wendell Holmes Travel Award to enable foreign students involved in archival training in the United States or Canada to attend the SAA Annual Meeting; (5) the Donald Peterson Student Travel Award of up to $1,000 to enable graduate students or recent graduates to attend the meeting; and (6) the Harold T. Pinkett Minority Student Awards to enable minority students or graduate students to attend the meeting. For details, write to: Teresa Brinati, Society of American Archivists, 17 N. State St., Suite 1425, Chicago, IL 60607, or see http://www2.archivists.org/governance/handbook/section12.

Special Libraries Association. (1) Three $6,000 scholarships for students interested in special-library work; (2) the Plenum Scholarship of $1,000 and (3) the ISI Scholarship of $1,000, each also for students interested in special-library work; (4) the Affirmative Action Scholarship of $6,000 for a minority student interested in special-library work; and (5) the Pharmaceutical Division Stipend Award of $1,200 for a student with an undergraduate degree in chemistry, life sciences, or pharmacy entering or enrolled in an ALA-accredited program. For information on the first four scholarships, write to: Scholarship Committee, Special Libraries Association, 331 S. Patrick St., Alexandria, VA 22314-3501. For information on the Pharmaceutical Division Stipend, write to: Susan E. Katz, Awards Chair, Knoll Pharmaceuticals Science Information Center, 30 N. Jefferson St., Whippany, NJ 07981.

Library Scholarship and Award Recipients, 2014

Compiled by the staff of the *Library and Book Trade Almanac*

Scholarships and awards are listed by organization.

American Association of Law Libraries (AALL)

AALL and Thomson Reuters/George A. Strait Minority Scholarship. *Winners:* Kelly Lynn Anders, Anne Mira Guha, Lidia Koelbel, Esther Ojuri, Mahum Saulat Shere,

AALL Distinguished Lectureship. *Winner:* Richard Danner, professor of law and senior associate dean for information services, Duke University. *Topic:* "What We Know and How We Think About It."

AALL Grants. To enable law librarians to participate in professional educational opportunities at the AALL Annual Meeting or to engage in original research on topics important to law librarianship. *Winners:* Cynthia Bassett, Scott Burgh, Lindsey Carpino, Ericka Cohn, Sabrina Davis, DawnMarin Dell, Matthew Fluntz, Paul Gatz, Philip Johnson, Zanada Joyner, Rebecca Mattson, Lisa Mecklenberg Jackson, Lucie Olejnikova, Anupama Pal, Patrick Parsons, Akram Sadeghi Pari, Scott Uhl, Corrine Vogel, Janeen Williams, Andrew Winston.

AALL Marcia J. Koslov Scholarship. To an AALL member to finance conference or seminar attendance. *Winner:* Not awarded in 2014.

AALL Public Access to Government Information Award. *Winner:* Mississippi College of Law Library for its Library History Project.

AALL Spectrum Article of the Year Award. *Sponsor:* Wolters Kluwer. *Winners:* Ingrid Mattson and Linda-Jean Schneider for "Negotiating and Complying with Electronic Database License Agreements" (February 2013).

AALL/Wolters Kluwer Law and Business Research Grant. *Winners:* Phillip Gragg for "Upward Mobility and Career Prospects for the Dual Degree Librarian: A Quantitative Analysis of Our Profession and Projection of Career Opportunities Over the Next Two

Decades"; Shawn Nevers for "Research Practices of Attorneys."

Joseph L. Andrews Legal Literature Award. *Winners:* Ellyssa Kroski, New York Law Institute, for *Law Librarianship in the Digital Age* (Scarecrow); Barbara Berdahl, Glen Anderson, and Katherine Hedin for the website Walter F. Mondale: Spokesman for Reform and Justice in the U.S. Senate (http://mondale.law.umn.edu).

Emerging Leader Award. To recognize newer members who have made significant contributions to AALL and/or to the profession and have demonstrated the potential for leadership and continuing service. *Winner:* Janine Liebert, Los Angeles Law Library.

Marian Gould Gallagher Distinguished Service Award. To recognize extended and sustained service to law librarianship. *Winners:* Robert C. Berring, Jr., Walter Perry Johnson, Janis L. Johnston, Carol Avery Nicholson.

Innovations in Technology Award. To recognize an AALL member, special interest section, chapter, or library for innovative use of technology in the development and creation of an application or resource for law librarians or legal professionals. *Winner:* Mississippi College of Law Library for its Legislative History Project.

Law Library Advocate Award. To a law library supporter in recognition of his or her substantial contribution toward the advancement and improvement of a state, court, or county law library's service or visibility. *Winner:* Nancy Rice, chief justice, Colorado Supreme Court.

Law Library Journal Article of the Year. *Winner:* D. R. Jones for "Locked Collections: Copyright and the Future of Research Support."

Law Library Publications Award. *Winners:* (nonprint division) Margaret C. Clark for "International Responses to Syrian Conflict, Military Intervention, and Chemical Weapons"; (print division) Sacramento County

(California) Public Law Library for "Sacramento County Public Law Library: Step-by-Step Guides."

LexisNexis/John R. Johnson Memorial Scholarships. *Winners:* (library degree for law school graduates) Jessica Barile, Robert Beharriell, Anne Mira Guha, Lidia Koelbel, Jeremy James McCabe, Teresa Jean Myers, Cecily Harms Nicewicz, Lacy Rakestraw, Paul Riermaier, Mahum Saulat Shere, Shannon Stoneking, Corrine Vogel; (library degree for those without a law degree) Esther Ojuri; (dual library degree and law degree) Andrew William Lang.

LexisNexis Research Fund Grants. *Winners:* Melanie Knapp and Rob Wiley for "Comparison of Research Speed and Accuracy Using WestlawNext and Lexis Advance"; Andrea Alexander and Michelle Hook Dewey for "Building Bridges: Case Studies in Best Practices for Law Library and Career."

Minority Leadership Development Award. *Winner:* Stephanie Hayes, Florida State University College of Law Research Center.

Robert L. Oakley Advocacy Award. To recognize an AALL member who has been an outstanding advocate and has contributed significantly to the AALL policy agenda at the federal, state, local, or international level. *Winner:* Sarah G. Holterhoff, government information/reference librarian and associate professor of law librarianship, Valparaiso University Law School Library.

American Library Association (ALA)

ABC-CLIO/Greenwood Award for Best Book in Library Literature ($5,000). See "Literary Prizes, 2014" in Part 5.

ALA Excellence in Library Programming Award ($5,000). For a cultural/thematic library program or program series that engages the community in planning, sponsorship, and/or active participation, addresses an identified community need, and has a measurable impact. *Donor:* ALA Cultural Communities Fund. *Winners:* Kansas City Public Library and its community partners for their "Greetings from Kansas City" programs and exhibitions.

ALA Honorary Membership. To recognize outstanding contributions of lasting importance to libraries and librarianship. *Honoree:* Patricia Glass Schuman.

ALA/Information Today, Inc. Library of the Future Award ($1,500). For a library, consortium, group of librarians, or support organization for innovative planning for, applications of, or development of patron training programs about information technology in a library setting. *Donors:* Information Today, Inc., and IIDA. *Winners:* Queens Library, Jamaica, New York, for its "Enriching the Lives of a Challenged Community by Lending Tablets" in the wake of 2012's Hurricane Sandy.

Hugh C. Atkinson Memorial Award. For outstanding achievement (including risk taking) by academic librarians that has contributed significantly to improvements in library automation, management, and/or development or research. *Offered by:* ACRL, ALCTS, LITA, and LLAMA. *Winner:* Anne Kenney, Carl A. Kroch University Librarian, Cornell University.

Carroll Preston Baber Research Grant (up to $3,000). For innovative research that could lead to an improvement in library services to any specified group(s) of people. *Donor:* Eric R. Baber. *Winner:* David Loertcher for "The Impact of Co-Teaching on Learning When Classroom Teachers Team with Teacher Librarians: The Testing of an Unobtrusive Measurement Tool."

Beta Phi Mu Award ($1,000). For distinguished service in library education. *Donor:* Beta Phi Mu International Library and Information Science Honorary Society. *Winner:* Beth M. Paskoff, director, Louisiana State University School of Library and Information Science.

Bogle-Pratt International Library Travel Fund Award ($1,000). To ALA members to attend their first international conference. *Donors:* Bogle Memorial Fund and Pratt Institute School of Information and Library Science. *Winner:* Sai Deng, metadata librarian, University of Central Florida.

W. Y. Boyd Literary Award. See "Literary Prizes, 2014" in Part 5.

David H. Clift Scholarship ($3,000). To worthy U.S. or Canadian citizens enrolled in an

ALA-accredited program toward an MLS degree. *Winner:* Hannivett Nabahe.

Melvil Dewey Medal. To an individual or group for recent creative professional achievement in library management, training, cataloging and classification, and the tools and techniques of librarianship. *Donor:* OCLC. *Winner:* Robert A. Wolven, associate university librarian for bibliographic services and collection development, Columbia University Libraries

Tom and Roberta Drewes Scholarship ($3,000). To a library support staff member pursuing a master's degree in an ALA-accredited program. *Donor:* Quality Books. *Winner:* Lauren Stamm.

EBSCO/ALA Conference Sponsorship Award ($1,000). To enable librarians to attend the ALA Annual Conference. *Donor:* EBSCO. *Winners:* Elena Safia Azadbakht, Karen Grigg, Casey Hoeve, Julia Hutchins, Kimberly Miller, Stacy Schwartz, Erica W. Tyler.

Equality Award ($1,000). To an individual or group for an outstanding contribution that promotes equality in the library profession. *Donor:* Rowman & Littlefield. *Winner:* Ann K. Symons.

Elizabeth Futas Catalyst for Change Award ($1,000). A biennial award to recognize a librarian who invests time and talent to make positive change in the profession of librarianship. *Donor:* Elizabeth Futas Memorial Fund. *Winner:* Karen G. Schneider.

Loleta D. Fyan Public Library Research Grant (up to $5,000). For projects in public library development. *Donor:* Fyan Estate. *Winner:* Haslet (Texas) Public Library for its early science, technology, engineering and mathematics (STEM) education program for preteens, "Haslet Robotics Club."

Gale Cengage Learning Financial Development Award ($2,500). To a library organization for a financial development project to secure new funding resources for a public or academic library. *Donor:* Gale Cengage Learning. *Winner:* Cedar Park (Texas) Public Library for Fable Fest, an annual fundraising festival.

Mary V. Gaver Scholarship ($3,000). To a student pursuing an MLS degree and specializing in youth services. *Winner:* Alice Krebill.

Ken Haycock Award for Promoting Librarianship ($1,000). For significant contribution to public recognition and appreciation of librarianship through professional performance, teaching, or writing. *Winner:* Not awarded in 2014.

Miriam L. Hornback Scholarship ($3,000). To an ALA or library support staff person pursuing a master's degree in library science. *Winner:* Elizabeth Lieutenant.

Paul Howard Award for Courage ($1,000). To a librarian, library board, library group, or an individual for exhibiting unusual courage for the benefit of library programs or services. *Donor:* Paul Howard Memorial Fund. *Winner:* Not awarded in 2014.

John Ames Humphry/OCLC/Forest Press Award ($1,000). To one or more individuals for significant contributions to international librarianship. *Donor:* OCLC/Forest Press. *Winner:* Shali Zhang.

Tony B. Leisner Scholarship ($3,000). To a library support staff member pursuing a master's degree. *Donor:* Tony B. Leisner. *Winner:* Elizabeth Dobbins.

Joseph W. Lippincott Award ($1,000). For distinguished service to the library profession. *Donor:* Joseph W. Lippincott III. *Winner:* Maurice "Mitch" Freedman.

Peter Lyman Memorial/Sage Scholarship in New Media. To support a student seeking an MLS degree in an ALA-accredited program and pursing a specialty in new media. *Donor:* Sage Publications. *Winner:* Samuel Dodson.

James Madison Award. To recognize efforts to promote government openness. *Winners:* President Barack Obama's Review Group on Intelligence and Communications Technologies.

Marshall Cavendish Scholarship ($3,000). To a worthy U.S. or Canadian citizen to begin an MLS degree in an ALA-accredited program. *Winner:* Award discontinued.

Schneider Family Book Awards. See "Literary Prizes, 2014" in Part 5.

Scholastic Library Publishing Award ($1,000). To a librarian whose "unusual contributions to the stimulation and guidance of reading by children and young people exemplifies achievement in the profession." *Sponsor:* Scholastic Library Publishing. *Winner:* Sylvia M. Vardell, professor, School of Library and Information Studies, Texas Woman's University.

Scholastic Library Publishing National Library Week Grant ($3,000). For the best public awareness campaign in support of National Library Week. *Donor:* Scholastic Library Publishing. *Winner:* Arlington (Virginia) Public Library.

Lemony Snicket Prize for Noble Librarians Faced with Adversity ($3,000 plus a $1,000 travel stipend to enable attendance at the ALA Annual Conference). To honor a librarian who has faced adversity with integrity and dignity intact. *Sponsor:* Lemony Snicket (author Daniel Handler). *Winner:* Laurence Copel, youth outreach librarian and founder of the Lower Ninth Ward Street Library, New Orleans.

Spectrum Doctoral Fellowships. To provide full tuition support and stipends to minority U.S. and Canadian LIS doctoral students. *Donor:* Institute of Museum and Library Services. *Winners:* Not awarded in 2014.

Spectrum Initiative Scholarships ($5,000). To minority students admitted to ALA-accredited library schools. *Donors:* ALA and Institute of Museum and Library Services. *Winners:* Kelly Lynn Anders, Alonso Avila, Frances Ba, Dhyana Berry, Viviana Casillas-Serrano, Karen Chen, Mayra Corn, Meagan Daniels, Francisco de Vera, Rachel Deras, Olivia Dorsey, Jennifer Fuchikami, Juandamarie Gikandi, Lucero Gonzalez, Heather Green, Tiffany Henry, Jessica Humphries, Karen Hwang, Yvonne Ivey, Tova Johnson, Shih Fa Kao, Bradley Jermaine Kuykendall, Claudio Leon, Monica Lozano, John Edward Martin, LaTasha Martin, Maria de Lurdy Martinez-Serrano, Jhani Miller, Jerrod D. Moore, Amanda Moreno, Rebecca Nieto, Aaron Novinger, Cynthia Palacios, Hannah Rainey, Xochitl Rocha, Brittany Rodgers, Chi Chan Saeteurn, Maria Lourdes San Ramon, Alejandra Santana, Jennifer Scotten, Saguna Shankar, Jan Kiyoko Shiosaki, Camille Thomas, Jason Toms, Robbee Tonubbee, Patricia Valdovinos, Katherine Van Arsdale, Mai Xiong, April Ybarra, Darren Young.

Sullivan Award for Public Library Administrators Supporting Services to Children. To a library supervisor/administrator who has shown exceptional understanding and support of public library services to children. *Donor:* Peggy Sullivan. *Winner:* Luis Herrera, city librarian, San Francisco Public Library.

H. W. Wilson Library Staff Development Grant ($3,500). To a library organization for a program to further its staff development goals and objectives. *Donor:* H. W. Wilson Company. *Winner:* Martin County (Florida) Library System.

Women's National Book Association/Ann Heidbreder Eastman Grant ($500). To support library association professional development in a state in which WNBA has a chapter. *Winner:* Award suspended.

World Book/ALA Information Literacy Goal Awards ($5,000). To promote exemplary information literacy programs in public and school libraries. *Donor:* World Book. *Winners:* Award suspended.

American Association of School Librarians (AASL)

AASL/ABC-CLIO Leadership Grant (up to $1,750). To AASL affiliates for planning and implementing leadership programs at state, regional, or local levels. *Donor:* ABC-CLIO. *Winner:* Iowa Association of School Librarians.

AASL/Baker & Taylor Distinguished Service Award ($3,000). For outstanding contributions to librarianship and school library development. *Donor:* Baker & Taylor. *Winner:* Debra Kachel, Mansfield University.

AASL Collaborative School Library Award ($2,500). For expanding the role of the library in elementary and/or secondary school education. *Donor:* Upstart. *Winners:* Brenda Boyer, Alison Kocis-Westgate, and Josh Chambers, Kutztown (Pennsylvania) Area High School.

AASL Crystal Apple Award. To an individual, individuals, or group for a significant impact on school libraries and students. *Winner:* Marlene Woo-Lun.

AASL Distinguished School Administrators Award ($2,000). For expanding the role of the library in elementary and/or secondary school education. *Donor:* ProQuest. *Winner:* Arturo Cavazos, superintendent, Harlingen (Texas) Consolidated Independent School District.

AASL/Frances Henne Award ($1,250). To a school library media specialist with five or fewer years in the profession to attend an AASL regional conference or ALA Annual Conference for the first time. *Donor:* ABC-CLIO. *Winner:* Carolyn Stenzel, Chatham Hall School, Chatham, Virginia.

AASL Innovative Reading Grant ($2,500). To support the planning and implementation of an innovative program for children that motivates and encourages reading, especially with struggling readers. *Sponsor:* Capstone. *Winner:* Christina Genay, Quarles Elementary School, Winchester, Virginia, for her "School Bike Book Mobile Program."

AASL Research Grants (up to $2,500). *Sponsor:* Capstone. *Winners:* Award suspended.

Information Technology Pathfinder Award. To library media specialists for innovative approaches to microcomputer applications in the school library media center ($1,000 to the specialist, $500 to the library). *Donor:* Follett Software Company. *Winners:* (elementary) Susan Nottoli, Adolph Link School, Elk Grove Village, Illinois; (secondary) Louise Lankau, Summer Creek High School, Houston.

Intellectual Freedom Award ($2,000 plus $1,000 to the media center of the recipient's choice). To a school library media specialist and AASL member who has upheld the principles of intellectual freedom. *Donor:* ProQuest. *Winner:* Cathy Collins, Sharon (Massachusetts) High School.

National School Library Media Program of the Year Award ($10,000). For excellence and innovation in outstanding library media programs. *Donor:* Follett Library Resources. *Winners:* Eaglecrest High School, Centennial, Colorado; Kristin McKeown, school librarian.

Association for Library Collections and Technical Services (ALCTS)

ALCTS/LBI George Cunha and Susan Swartzburg Preservation Award ($1,250). To recognize cooperative preservation projects and/or individuals or groups that foster collaboration for preservation goals. *Sponsor:* Library Binding Institute. *Winner:* Thomas F. R. Clareson, senior consultant for digital and preservation services, LYRASIS.

ALCTS Presidential Citations for Outstanding Service. *Winners:* Alice Pearman, Jacob Ineichen, Holly Robertson and Annie Peterson, and OCLC Research.

Hugh C. Atkinson Memorial Award. *See under* American Library Association.

Ross Atkinson Lifetime Achievement Award ($3,000). To recognize the contribution of an ALCTS member and library leader who has demonstrated exceptional service to ALCTS and its areas of interest. *Donor:* EBSCO. *Winner:* Olivia M. A. Madison, Iowa State University.

Paul Banks and Carolyn Harris Preservation Award ($1,500). To recognize the contribution of a professional preservation specialist who has been active in the field of preservation and/or conservation for library and/or archival materials. *Donor:* Preservation Technologies. *Winner:* James M. Reilly, director, Image Permanence Institute, Rochester Institute of Technology.

Blackwell's Scholarship Award. See Outstanding Publication Award.

Ingram Coutts Award for Innovation in Electronic Resources Management ($2,000). To recognize significant and innovative contributions to electronic collections management and development practice. *Donor:* Coutts Information Services. *Winner:* Marie Kennedy.

First Step Award (Wiley Professional Development Grant) ($1,500). To enable librarians new to the serials field to attend the ALA Annual Conference. *Donor:* John Wiley & Sons. *Winner:* Chris Bulock, Southern Illinois University–Edwardsville.

Harrassowitz Award for Leadership in Library Acquisitions ($1,500). For significant contributions by an outstanding leader in the field of library acquisitions. *Donor:* Harrassowitz. *Winner:* Jenica P. Rogers, State University of New York, Potsdam.

Margaret Mann Citation (includes $2,000 scholarship award to the U.S. or Canadian library school of the winner's choice). To a cataloger or classifier for achievement in the areas of cataloging or classification. *Donor:* Online Computer Library Center (OCLC). *Winner:* Sara Shatford Layne.

Outstanding Collaboration Citation. For outstanding collaborative problem-solving efforts in the areas of acquisition, access, management, preservation, or archiving of library materials. *Winner:* The Alberta Library (TAL) for its selection of the OCLC group catalog as its provincial discovery tool for TAL Online.

Outstanding Publication Award (formerly the Blackwell's Scholarship Award) ($250). To honor the year's outstanding monograph, article, or original paper in the field of acquisitions, collection development, and related areas of resource development in libraries. *Winner:* Magda El-Sherbini for *RDA: Strategies for Implementation* (ALA Editions, 2013).

Esther J. Piercy Award ($1,500). To a librarian with no more than ten years' experience for contributions and leadership in the field of library collections and technical services. *Donor:* YBP Library Services. *Winner:* Patrick Carr.

Edward Swanson Memorial Best of *LRTS* Award. To the author(s) of the year's best paper published in the division's official journal. *Winners:* Wen-Ying Lu and Mary Beth Chambers for "PDA Consortium Style: The CU MyiLibrary Cataloging Experience."

Ulrich's Serials Librarianship Award ($1,500). For distinguished contributions to serials librarianship. *Sponsor:* ProQuest. *Winner:* Les Hawkins.

Association for Library Service to Children (ALSC)

ALSC/Baker & Taylor Summer Reading Program Grant ($3,000). For implementation of an outstanding public library summer reading program for children. *Donor:* Baker & Taylor. *Winner:* Ames (Iowa) Public Library.

ALSC/Booklist/YALSA Odyssey Award. To the producer of the best audiobook for children and/or young adults available in English in the United States. See Odyssey Award in "Literary Prizes, 2014" in Part 5.

ALSC/Candlewick Press "Light the Way: Library Outreach to the Underserved" Grant ($3,000). To a library conducting exemplary outreach to underserved populations. *Donor:* Candlewick Press. *Winner:* LGBT Center of Raleigh (North Carolina) Library.

May Hill Arbuthnot Honor Lectureship. To an author, critic, librarian, historian, or teacher of children's literature who prepares a paper considered to be a significant contribution to the field of children's literature. *Winner:* author Andrea Davis Pinkney.

Mildred L. Batchelder Award. See "Literary Prizes, 2014" in Part 5.

Louise Seaman Bechtel Fellowship ($4,000). For librarians with 12 or more years of professional-level work in children's library collections, to read and study at Baldwin Library, University of Florida, Gainesville. *Donor:* Bechtel Fund. *Winner:* Natalie Ziarnik, children's librarian, Ela Area Public Library District, Lake Zurich, Illinois.

Pura Belpré Award. See "Literary Prizes, 2014" in Part 5.

Bookapalooza Program Awards. To provide three libraries with a collection of materials that will help transform their collection. *Winners:* Talahi Community School, St. Cloud, Minnesota; North Shelby Library, Birmingham, Alabama; Northwood Elementary School, Crestview, Florida.

Bound to Stay Bound Books Scholarships ($7,000). For men and women who intend to pursue an MLS or other advanced degree and who plan to work in the area of library service to children. *Donor:* Bound to Stay Bound Books. *Winners:* Sylvia Aguiñaga, Omar Ramirez, Callen Nicole Taylor, Elissa Sperling.

Randolph Caldecott Medal. See "Literary Prizes, 2014" in Part 5.

Andrew Carnegie Medal for Excellence in Children's Video. To the U.S. producer of the most distinguished video for children in the previous year. *Sponsor:* Carnegie Corporation of New York. *Winners:* Paul R. Gagne and Melissa Reilly Ellard for "Bink & Gollie: Two for One" (Weston Woods).

Carnegie-Whitney Awards (up to $5,000). For the preparation of print or electronic reading lists, indexes, or other guides to library resources that promote reading or the use of library resources at any type of library. *Donors:* James Lyman Whitney and Andrew Carnegie Funds. *Winners:* Lauren Causey for "Annotated Bibliography of Diverse Nonfiction Children's and Young Adult Literature in the Social Sciences and Humanities"; Ruby Cheesman for "LDS Fiction Database: A Selected List"; Pingsheng Chen for "Welcome to America: A Resource Guide for Language, Culture, and Citizenship for ESL Students and Educators";

Keren Dali for "Biblio or Therapy? An Annotated Bibliography on Bibliotherapy for Librarians"; John DeLooper and Clifford Brooks for "Opera and Children's Literature: A Comprehensive Bibliography"; Jennifer France for "The Essential Wooden Boat Building Reading List"; Rachel Isaac-Menard for "The Use of Architecture for Political Means in the U.S.—A Multi-Disciplinary Research Guide and Webliography for Scholars"; Melissa Fisher Isaacs for "Religion in Kansas Project"; Amy Levine for "Booktalk Podcasts for Young Adults"; Claudette Newhall for "Cotton Mather: An Annotated Bibliography"; Danielle Renee Reed for "Flavor Science—Online Bibliography"; Beth Walker for "Annotated Manga/Graphic Novel Bibliography."

Century Scholarship ($2,500). For a library school student or students with disabilities admitted to an ALA-accredited library school. *Winner:* Michael L. Peterson.

Distinguished Service Award ($1,000). To recognize significant contributions to, and an impact on, library services to children and/or ALSC. *Winner:* Susan Roman.

Theodor Seuss Geisel Award. See "Literary Prizes, 2014" in Part 5.

Maureen Hayes Author/Illustrator Visit Award (up to $4,000). For an honorarium and travel expenses to make possible a library talk to children by a nationally known author/illustrator. *Sponsor:* Simon & Schuster Children's Publishing. *Winner:* Keene (New Hampshire) Public Library.

Frederic G. Melcher Scholarships ($6,000). To two students entering the field of library service to children for graduate work in an ALA-accredited program. *Winners:* Danielle Christine Crickman, Sheila Laurence Olson.

Estela and Raúl Mora Award ($1,000 and plaque). For exemplary programs celebrating Día de los Niños/Día de los Libros. *Winner:* Sioux Center (Iowa) Public Library.

John Newbery Medal. See "Literary Prizes, 2014" in Part 5.

Penguin Young Readers Group Awards ($600). To children's librarians in school or public libraries with ten or fewer years of experience to attend the ALA Annual Conference. *Donor:* Penguin Young Readers Group.

Winners: JoAnna Schofield, Rikki Unterbrink, Amanda Yother, Emily Dumas.

Robert F. Sibert Medal. See "Literary Prizes, 2014" in Part 5.

Laura Ingalls Wilder Medal. See "Literary Prizes, 2014" in Part 5.

Association of College and Research Libraries (ACRL)

ACRL Academic or Research Librarian of the Year Award ($5,000). For outstanding contribution to academic and research librarianship and library development. *Donor:* YBP Library Services. *Winner:* Tim Bucknall, University of North Carolina, Greensboro.

ACRL/CLS ProQuest Innovation in College Librarianship Award ($3,000). To academic librarians who show a capacity for innovation in the areas of programs, services, and operations; or creating innovations for library colleagues that facilitate their ability to better serve the library's community. *Winners:* Tish Hayes, Terra B. Jacobson, and Troy A. Swanson, Moraine Valley Community College Library.

ACRL/DLS Routledge Distance Learning Librarian Conference Sponsorship Award ($1,200). To an ACRL member working in distance-learning librarianship in higher education. *Sponsor:* Routledge/Taylor & Francis. *Winner:* Frederick Stielow, American Public University System (APUS).

ACRL/CJCLS Library Resources Leadership Award. *Winner:* David M. Rodriguez, Maricopa Community College District and Glendale (Arizona) Community College.

ACRL/EBSS Distinguished Education and Behavioral Sciences Librarian Award ($2,500). To an academic librarian who has made an outstanding contribution as an education and/or behavioral sciences librarian through accomplishments and service to the profession. *Donor:* John Wiley & Sons. *Winner:* Stephanie Davis-Kahl, Illinois Wesleyan University.

ACRL/STS Innovation in Science and Technology Librarianship Award ($3,000). To recognize creative, innovative approaches to solving problems or improving products and services in science and technology librarianship. *Sponsor:* IEEE. *Winner:* Not awarded in 2014.

ACRL/STS Oberly Award for Bibliography in the Agricultural or Natural Sciences. Awarded biennially for the best English-language bibliography in the field of agriculture or a related science in the preceding two-year period. *Donor:* Eunice Rockwood Oberly. *Winner:* Not awarded in 2014.

ACRL/WGSS Award for Career Achievement in Women and Gender Studies Librarianship. *Winner:* Laura Micham, David M. Rubenstein Rare Book and Manuscripts Library, Duke University.

ACRL/WGSS Award for Significant Achievement in Women and Gender Studies Librarianship. *Winner:* Not awarded in 2014.

Hugh C. Atkinson Memorial Award. *See under* American Library Association.

Coutts Nijhoff International West European Specialist Study Grant. See WESS-SEES De Gruyter European Librarianship Study Grant.

Miriam Dudley Instruction Librarian Award. For a contribution to the advancement of bibliographic instruction in a college or research institution. *Winner:* Esther Stampfer Grassian, University of California, Los Angeles.

Excellence in Academic Libraries Awards ($3,000). To recognize outstanding college and university libraries. *Donor:* YBP Library Services. *Winners:* (university) Cal Poly State University; (college) Lafayette College; (community college) Illinois Central College.

Instruction Section Innovation Award ($3,000). To librarians or project teams in recognition of a project that demonstrates creative, innovative, or unique approaches to information literacy instruction or programming. *Donor:* ProQuest. *Winners:* Meredith Farkas, Amy Hofer, Lisa Molinelli, and Kimberly Willson-St. Clair, Portland State University Libraries.

Marta Lange/Sage-CQ Press Award. To recognize an academic or law librarian for contributions to bibliography and information service in law or political science. *Donor:* Sage-CQ Press. *Winner:* Brian E. Coutts, Department of Library Public Services, Western Kentucky University.

Katharine Kyes Leab and Daniel J. Leab American Book Prices Current Exhibition Catalog Awards (citations). For the best catalogs

published by American or Canadian institutions in conjunction with exhibitions of books and/or manuscripts. *Sponsor:* Leab Endowment. *Winners:* (electronic exhibitions) John Carter Brown Library, Brown University, for *Sugar and Visual Imagination in the Atlantic World, circa 1600–1850*; (expensive) Bruce Peel Special Collections Library, University of Alberta, for *All Under Heaven: The Chinese World in Maps, Pictures, and Texts from the Collection of Floyd Sully*; (moderately expensive) Cushing Memorial Library and Archives, Texas A&M University, for *Deeper than Swords: Celebrating the Work of George R. R. Martin*; (inexpensive) Lewis Walpole Library, Yale University, for *Dancing on a Sunny Plain: The Life of Annie Burr Auchincloss Lewis*; (brochures) Rare Books and Manuscripts Library, University of Illinois at Urbana-Champaign, for *Marcel Proust: Writing Without End.*

Ilene F. Rockman Instruction Publication of the Year Award ($3,000). To recognize an outstanding publication relating to instruction in a library environment. *Sponsor:* Emerald Group. *Winner:* Wendy Holliday, Northern Arizona University, and Jim Rogers, Utah State University, for their article "Talking About Information Literacy: The Mediating Role of Discourse in a College Writing Classroom."

WESS-SEES De Gruyter European Librarianship Study Grant (formerly the Coutts Nijhoff International West European Specialist Study Grant) (€2,500). Supports research pertaining to European studies, librarianship, or the book trade. *Sponsor:* Walter de Gruyter Foundation for Scholarship and Research. *Winner:* Marta Mestrovic Deyrup, Seton Hall University.

Association of Library Trustees, Advocates, Friends, and Foundations (ALTAFF). See United for Libraries.

Association of Specialized and Cooperative Library Agencies (ASCLA)

ASCLA Cathleen Bourdon Service Award. To recognize an ASCLA personal member for outstanding service and leadership to the division. *Winner:* Not awarded in 2014.

ASCLA Exceptional Service Award. To recognize exceptional service to patients, the homebound, inmates, and to medical, nursing, and other professional staff in hospitals. *Winner:* (2013) Betsy Diamant-Cohen; (2014) Mary Beth Riedner.

ASCLA Leadership and Professional Achievement Award. To recognize leadership and achievement in the areas of consulting, multitype library cooperation, statewide service and programs, and state library development. *Winner:* Not awarded in 2014.

Francis Joseph Campbell Award. For a contribution of recognized importance to library service for the blind and physically handicapped. *Winner:* Chris Mundy, quality assurance specialist at Multistate Center East, a division of Clovernook Center for the Blind and Visually Impaired.

KLAS/National Organization on Disability Award for Library Service to People with Disabilities ($1,000). To a library organization to recognize an innovative project to benefit people with disabilities. *Donor:* Keystone Systems. *Winner:* Greenville County (South Carolina) Library System.

Black Caucus of the American Library Association (BCALA)

BCALA Trailblazer's Award. Presented once every five years in recognition of outstanding and unique contributions to librarianship. *Winner:* To be awarded next in 2015.

DEMCO/BCALA Excellence in Librarianship Award. To a librarian who has made significant contributions to promoting the status of African Americans in the library profession. *Winner:* Emily R. Guss, City Colleges of Chicago.

Ethnic and Multicultural Information and Exchange Round Table (EMIERT)

David Cohen Multicultural Award ($300). To recognize articles of significant research and publication that increase understanding and promote multiculturalism in North American libraries. *Donor:* Routledge. *Winner:* To be awarded next in 2016.

EMIERT Distinguished Librarian Award. Given biennially to recognize significant accomplishments in library services that are national or international in scope and that include improving, spreading, and promoting multicultural librarianship. *Winner:* To be awarded next in 2015.

Gale Multicultural Award ($1,000). For outstanding achievement and leadership in serving the multicultural/multiethnic community. *Donor:* Gale Research. *Winner:* Award suspended.

Exhibits Round Table (ERT)

Christopher J. Hoy/ERT Scholarship ($5,000). To an individual or individuals who will work toward an MLS degree in an ALA-accredited program. *Donor:* Family of Christopher Hoy. *Winner:* Angela Price.

Federal and Armed Forces Librarians Round Table (FAFLRT)

FAFLRT Achievement Award. For achievement in the promotion of library and information service and the information profession in the federal government community. *Winner:* Judith Proctor Cannan, Library of Congress.

FAFLRT Adelaide del Frate Conference Sponsorship Award ($1,000). To encourage library school students to become familiar with federal librarianship and ultimately seek work in federal libraries; for attendance at the ALA Annual Conference and activities of FAFLRT. *Winner:* Not awarded in 2014.

Distinguished Service Award (citation). To honor a FAFLRT member for outstanding and sustained contributions to the association and to federal librarianship. *Winner:* Eileen L. Welch, U.S. Department of Agriculture.

Cicely Phippen Marks Scholarship ($1,500). To a library school student with an interest in working in a federal library. *Winner:* Sue E. Graves, San José State University.

Rising Star Award. To a FAFLRT member new to the profession in a federal or armed forces library or government information management setting. *Winner:* Katie Rapp, National Institute of Standards and Technology.

Gay, Lesbian, Bisexual, and Transgender Round Table (GLBTRT)

Stonewall Book Awards. See "Literary Prizes, 2014" in Part 5.

Government Documents Round Table (GODORT)

James Bennett Childs Award. To a librarian or other individual for distinguished lifetime contributions to documents librarianship. *Winner:* Susan E. Tulis, Southern Illinois University, Carbondale.

Bernadine Abbott Hoduski Founders Award. To recognize documents librarians who may not be known at the national level but who have made significant contributions to the field of local, state, federal, or international documents. *Winner:* Marie Concannon, Missouri Regional Coordinator, Federal Depository Library Program.

Margaret T. Lane/Virginia F. Saunders Memorial Research Award. *Winners:* Walter Clark Wilson and William Curtis Ellis for their article "Surrogates Beyond Borders: Black Members of the United States Congress and the Representation of African Interests on the Congressional Foreign-Policy Agenda" in *Polity* 46.2 (2014): 255–273.

NewsBank/Readex Catharine J. Reynolds Award. To documents librarians for travel and/or study in the field of documents librarianship or an area of study benefiting their performance. *Donor:* NewsBank and Readex Corporation. *Winner:* Marianne Ryan, to support her continued study of the relationship between government information and baseball.

ProQuest/GODORT/ALA Documents to the People Award. To an individual, library, organization, or noncommercial group that most effectively encourages or enhances the use of government documents in library services. *Winner:* Andrea M. Morrison.

W. David Rozkuszka Scholarship ($3,000). To provide financial assistance to individuals currently working with government documents in a library while completing a master's program in library science. *Winner:* Stephanie L. Martin.

Intellectual Freedom Round Table (IFRT)

John Phillip Immroth Memorial Award for Intellectual Freedom ($500). For notable contribution to intellectual freedom fueled by personal courage. *Winner:* Not awarded in 2014.

Eli M. Oboler Memorial Award. See "Literary Prizes, 2014" in Part 5.

Library and Information Technology Association (LITA)

Hugh C. Atkinson Memorial Award. *See under* American Library Association.

Ex Libris Student Writing Award ($1,000 and publication in *Information Technology and Libraries*). For the best unpublished manuscript on a topic in the area of libraries and information technology written by a student or students enrolled in an ALA-accredited library and information studies graduate program. *Donor:* Ex Libris. *Winner:* Brighid Mooney Gonzales for "Linking Libraries to the Web: Linked Data and the Future of the Bibliographic Record."

LITA/Christian Larew Memorial Scholarship ($3,000). To encourage the entry of qualified persons into the library and information technology field. *Sponsor:* Informata.com. *Winner:* Adriana Rissetto Puckett.

LITA/Library Hi Tech Award. To an individual or institution for outstanding communication in library and information technology. *Donor:* Emerald Group. *Winners:* Victoria Reich and David S. H. Rosenthal for their collaboration to ensure the preservation of digital content through their creation and development of the LOCKSS Program.

LITA/LSSI Minority Scholarship in Library and Information Technology ($2,500). To encourage a qualified member of a principal minority group to work toward an MLS degree in an ALA-accredited program with emphasis on library automation. *Donor:* Library Systems and Services. *Winner:* Jason N. Toms.

LITA/OCLC Frederick G. Kilgour Award for Research in Library and Information Technology ($2,000 and expense-paid attendance at the ALA Annual Conference). To bring attention to research relevant to the development of information technologies. *Donor:* OCLC. *Winner:* Michael Buckland, University of California, Berkeley.

LITA/OCLC Minority Scholarship in Library and Information Technology ($3,000). To encourage a qualified member of a principal minority group to work toward an MLS degree in an ALA-accredited program with emphasis on library automation. *Donor:* OCLC. *Winner:* Olivia Dorsey.

LITA/OITP Award for Cutting-Edge Technology in Library Services. To honor libraries that are serving their communities with novel and innovative methods. *Winners:* Somerset County Library System, Bridgewater, New Jersey; Edmonton Public Library, Edmonton, Alberta, Canada; North Carolina State University, Raleigh; Penn State University Libraries.

Library History Round Table (LHRT)

Phyllis Dain Library History Dissertation Award. Given biennially to the author of a dissertation treating the history of books, libraries, librarianship, or information science. *Winner:* To be awarded next in 2015.

Donald G. Davis Article Award (certificate). Awarded biennially for the best article written in English in the field of U.S. and Canadian library history. *Winner:* Debra Gold Hansen for "Depoliticizing the California State Library: The Political and Professional Transformation of James Gillis, 1899–1917" in *Information & Culture: A Journal of History* 48:1 (2013).

Eliza Atkins Gleason Book Award. Presented every third year to the author of a book in English in the field of library history. *Winner:* To be awarded next in 2016.

Justin Winsor Library History Essay Award ($500). To the author of an outstanding essay embodying original historical research on a significant subject of library history. *Winner:* Kate Stewart, American Folklife Center, Library of Congress, for "The Man in the Rice Paddies Had Something to READ: Military Libraries and Intellectual Freedom in the Vietnam War."

Library Leadership and Management Association (LLAMA)

Hugh C. Atkinson Memorial Award. *See under* American Library Association.

John Cotton Dana Library Public Relations Awards. To libraries or library organizations of all types for public relations programs or special projects ended during the preceding year. *Donors:* H. W. Wilson Foundation and EBSCO. *Winners:* Birmingham (Alabama) Public Library for "Letter from Birmingham Jail: A Worldwide Celebration"; Champaign (Illinois) Public Library for "Show Some Library Love"; Kitsap Regional Library, Kitsap County, Washington, for its "Traveling Book Campaign"; James B. Hunt, Jr. Library, North Carolina State University, for "The Library of the Future"; Sacramento (California) Public Library for "The Poe Project"; Texas A & M University for "Deeper Than Swords: A Two-day Celebration of George R. R. Martin"; University of Texas, San Antonio, for "Ask Us Anything"; Wells County (Indiana) Public Library for "Your Go-To Spot."

Library Research Round Table (LRRT)

Jesse H. Shera Award for Distinguished Published Research. For a research article on library and information studies published in English during the calendar year. *Winner:* Paul Conway for "Preserving Imperfection: Assessing The Incidence of Digital Imaging Error in HaithTrust."

Jesse H. Shera Award for Support of Dissertation Research. To recognize and support dissertation research employing exemplary research design and methods. *Winner:* Not awarded in 2014.

Map and Geospatial Information Round Table (MAGIRT)

MAGIRT Honors Award. To recognize outstanding achievement and major contributions to map and geospatial librarianship. *Winner:* Gregory Allord, U.S. Geological Survey cartographer.

New Members Round Table (NMRT)

NMRT Annual Conference Professional Development Attendance Award (formerly the Marshall Cavendish Award) (tickets to the ALA Annual Conference event of the winners' choice). *Winners:* Tina Chan, Angela Fortin.

NMRT Professional Development Grant (formerly the 3M/NMRT Professional Development Grant). To new NMRT members to encourage professional development and participation in national ALA and NMRT activities. *Winner:* Samantha Helmick.

Shirley Olofson Memorial Award ($1,000). To an individual to help defray costs of attending the ALA Annual Conference. *Winner:* Katy DiVittorio.

Student Chapter of the Year Award. To an ALA student chapter for outstanding contributions to the association. *Winner:* Student Chapter at San José State University.

Office for Diversity

Achievement in Library Diversity Research Honor. To an ALA member who has made significant contributions to diversity research in the profession. *Winner:* Gerald Holmes, reference librarian and diversity coordinator, University of North Carolina at Greensboro.

Diversity Research Grants ($2,500). To the authors of research proposals that address critical gaps in the knowledge of diversity issues within library and information science. *Winners:* Shannon M. Oltmann for "In-Depth Investigation of LGBT Collections in School Media Centers"; Amy VanScoy and Kawanna Bright for "Including the Voice of Librarians of Color in Reference and Information Service Research"; Michelle Abate and Sarah Lightner for "Development of Texts that Mediate and Facilitate Diversity in Adolescent Classrooms."

Office for Information Technology Policy

L. Ray Patterson Copyright Award. To recognize an individual who supports the constitutional purpose of U.S. copyright law, fair use, and the public domain. *Sponsor:* Freedom to Read Foundation. *Winner:* Georgia Harper, scholarly communications advisor, University of Texas at Austin Libraries.

Office for Intellectual Freedom

Freedom to Read Foundation Gordon M. Conable Conference Scholarship. To enable a library school student or new professional to attend the ALA Annual Conference. *Winner:* John "Mack" Freeman.

Freedom to Read Foundation Roll of Honor (citation): To recognize individuals who have contributed substantially to the foundation. *Winner:* Herbert Krug.

Office for Literacy and Outreach Services (OLOS)

Jean E. Coleman Library Outreach Lecture. *Sponsor:* OLOS Advisory Committee. *Lecturer:* Virginia Bradley Moore. *Topic:* "Equality . . . Equity . . . Diversity: Libraries, Dr. Martin Luther King, Jr., and the Mission."

Public Library Association (PLA)

Baker & Taylor Entertainment Audio Music/Video Product Grant ($2,500 worth of audio music or video products). To help a public library to build or expand a collection of either or both formats. *Donor:* Baker & Taylor. *Winner:* Broadview (Illinois) Public Library District.

Gordon M. Conable Award ($1,500). To a public library staff member, library trustee, or public library for demonstrating a commitment to intellectual freedom and the Library Bill of Rights. *Sponsor:* LSSI. *Winner:* Smithville (Texas) Public Library.

Demco New Leaders Travel Grants (up to $1,500). To PLA members who have not attended a major PLA continuing education event in the past five years. *Winners:* Andrea Hirsh, Juneau (Alaska) Public Libraries; Zac Paul Matthews, Everett (Washington) Public Library; Emery M. Ortiz, Onslow County (North Carolina) Public Library; Michelle A. Moore, Missaukee County (Michigan) Library.

EBSCO Excellence in Small and/or Rural Public Service Award ($1,000). Honors a library serving a population of 10,000 or fewer that demonstrates excellence of service to its community as exemplified by an overall service program or a special program of significant accomplishment. *Donor:* EBSCO. *Winner:* Bertha Voyer Memorial Library, Honey Grove, Texas.

Allie Beth Martin Award ($3,000). To honor a public librarian who has demonstrated extraordinary range and depth of knowledge about books or other library materials and has distinguished ability to share that knowledge. *Donor:* Baker & Taylor. *Winner:* Rollie James Welch, Cleveland (Ohio) Public Library.

Polaris Innovation in Technology John Iliff Award. To a library worker, librarian, or library for the use of technology and innovative thinking as a tool to improve services to public library users. *Sponsor:* Polaris. *Winner:* Edmonton Public Library, Alberta, Canada.

Charlie Robinson Award. To honor a public library director who, over a period of seven years, has been a risk taker, an innovator, and/or a change agent in a public library. *Donor:* Baker & Taylor. *Winner:* Not awarded in 2014.

Romance Writers of America Library Grant ($4,500). To a library to build or expand a fiction collection and/or host romance fiction programming. *Donor:* Romance Writers of America. *Winner:* Red Wing (Minnesota) Public Library.

Upstart Innovation Award ($2,000). To recognize a public library's innovative achievement in planning and implementing a creative community service program. *Donor:* Upstart/Demco. *Winner:* Terrebonne Parish (Louisiana) Library for a multimedia program that facilitated teen participation in an investigation of the environmental, economic, and community issues affecting the parish, the state, and the region.

Public Programs Office

Sara Jaffarian School Library Program Award for Exemplary Humanities Programming ($4,000). To honor a K–8 school library that has conducted an outstanding humanities program or series. *Donors:* Sara Jaffarian and ALA Cultural Communities Fund. *Winner:* Perry Meridian Middle School, Indianapolis, Indiana.

Reference and User Services Association (RUSA)

ABC-CLIO Online History Award ($3,000). A biennial award to recognize a noteworthy online historical collection, an online tool tailored for the purpose of finding historical materials, or an online teaching aid stimulating creative historical scholarship. *Donor:* ABC-CLIO. *Winner:* To be awarded next in 2015.

ALA/RUSA Zora Neale Hurston Award. To recognize the efforts of RUSA members in promoting African American literature. *Sponsored by:* Harper Perennial Publishing. *Winner:* Grace Jackson-Brown, assistant professor of library science, University of Missouri.

Virginia Boucher-OCLC Distinguished ILL Librarian Award ($2,000). To a librarian for outstanding professional achievement, leadership, and contributions to interlibrary loan and document delivery. *Winner:* David Larsen, University of Chicago.

BRASS Academic Business Librarianship Travel Award ($1,250). To recognize a librarian new to the field of academic business librarianship and support his or her attendance at the ALA Annual Conference. *Sponsor:* Business Expert Press. *Winner:* Desirae Zingarelli-Sweet.

BRASS Award for Outstanding Service to Minority Business Communities ($2,000). To a librarian or library to recognize creation of an innovative service to a minority business community or achievement of recognition from that community for providing outstanding service. *Winner:* Award discontinued.

BRASS Emerald Research Grant Awards ($2,500). To an ALA member seeking support to conduct research in business librarianship. *Donor:* Emerald Group. *Winners:* Ilana Barnes and Tao Zhang.

BRASS Gale Cengage Learning Student Travel Award ($1,250). To enable a student enrolled in an ALA-accredited master's program to attend the ALA Annual Conference. *Donor:* Gale Cengage Learning. *Winner:* Katharine Macy.

Sophie Brody Medal. See "Literary Prizes, 2014" in Part 5.

BRASS Gale Cengage Learning Award for Excellence in Business Librarianship ($3,000). For distinguished activities in the field of business librarianship *Donor:* Gale Cengage Learning. *Winner:* Celia Ross.

BRASS Morningstar Public Librarian Support Award ($1,250). To support attendance at the ALA Annual Conference of a public librarian who has performed outstanding business reference service. *Donor:* Morningstar. *Winner:* Salvatore DiVincenzo.

Gale Cengage Learning Award for Excellence in Reference and Adult Library Services ($3,000). To recognize a library or library system for developing an imaginative and unique library resource to meet patrons' reference needs. *Donor:* Gale Cengage Learning. *Winner:* Northville (Michigan) District Library for its "Northville Historic Records" project.

Genealogical Publishing Company/History Section Award ($1,500). To encourage and commend professional achievement in historical reference and research librarianship. *Donor:* Genealogical Publishing Company. *Winner:* William Forsyth, Proquest.

MARS Achievement Recognition Certificate ("My Favorite Martian Award"). To recognize excellence in service to the RUSA section MARS—Emerging Technologies in Reference. *Winner:* Anne Houston, University of Virginia.

Isadore Gilbert Mudge Award ($5,000). For distinguished contributions to reference librarianship. *Donor:* Gale Cengage Learning. *Winner:* William Miller, Florida Atlantic University.

NoveList's Margaret E. Monroe Library Adult Services Award (citation). To a librarian for his or her impact on library service to adults. *Winner:* Diana Tixier Herald, Delta County (Colorado) Libraries.

Reference Service Press Award ($2,500). To the author or authors of the most outstanding article published in *RUSQ* during the preceding two volume years. *Donor:* Reference Service Press. *Winners:* Laura Saunders and Mary Wilkins Jordan for "Significantly Different? Reference Services Competencies in Public and Academic Libraries" (*RUSQ* 52: 3 Spring 2013).

John Sessions Memorial Award (plaque). To a library or library system in recognition of work with the labor community. *Donor:* Department for Professional Employees, AFL/CIO. *Winner:* Local History and Genealogy Department of Toledo-Lucas County (Ohio) Public Library.

Louis Shores Award. To an individual, team, or organization to recognize excellence in reviewing of books and other materials for libraries. *Winner:* Francine Graf, managing editor, *Choice*.

STARS—Atlas Systems Mentoring Award ($1,250). To a library practitioner new to the field of interlibrary loan, resource sharing, or electronic reserves, to attend the ALA Annual Conference. *Donor:* Atlas Systems. *Winner:* Jacob Kubrin.

Social Responsibilities Round Table (SRRT)

Jackie Eubanks Memorial Award ($500). To honor outstanding achievement in promoting the acquisition and use of alternative media in libraries. *Donor:* SRRT Alternatives in Publication Task Force. *Winner:* Not awarded in 2014.

Coretta Scott King Awards. See "Literary Prizes, 2014" in Part 5.

United for Libraries (formerly ALTAFF, Association of Library Trustees, Advocates, Friends, and Foundations)

Neal-Schuman Citizens-Save-Libraries Grants. To support library advocacy at the local level for libraries in financial difficulty. *Sponsor:* Neal-Schuman Foundation. *Winners:* (Cycle 1) Clarkston (Michigan) Independence District Library; Eisner Memorial Library, Red Bank, New Jersey; Friends of the Dallas (Texas) Public Library; Friends of the Long Beach (California) Public Library; Gladstone (Oregon) Public Library; Gilmanton (New Hampshire) Year-Round Library; Josephine Community Libraries (Grants Pass, Oregon); Pomona (California) Public Library; Salem-South Lyon (Michigan) District Library; Winona (Minnesota) Public Library; (Cycle 2) Berks County (Pennsylvania) Public Libraries; North Hampton (New Hampshire) Public Library; Santa Maria (California) Public Library; Shepherdstown (West Virginia) Public Library; Public Library of New London (Connecticut); Calaveras County (California) Library; Highland (Utah) City Library; Wicomico Public Library, Salisbury, Maryland; Stockton-San Joaquin County (California) Public Library System; Oakland (California) Public Library.

Trustee Citation. To recognize public library trustees for individual service to library development on the local, state, regional, or national level. *Winner:* Argiro Morgan, St. Tammany Parish (Louisiana) Library.

United for Libraries/Baker & Taylor Awards. To recognize library friends groups for outstanding efforts to support their libraries. *Donor:* Baker & Taylor. *Winners:* Friends of the Weber County Library, Ogden, Utah; Friends of the Peoria (Arizona) Public Library; Danville (Illinois) Library Foundation.

United for Libraries/Gale Outstanding Trustee Conference Grant Award ($850). *Donor:* Gale Cengage Learning. *Winner:* Donna Gerardi Riordan, Orcas Island (Washington) Public Library.

United for Libraries Major Benefactors Citation. To individuals, families, or corporate bodies that have made major benefactions to public libraries. *Winners:* Gordon and LaVerne Taylor, Kendrick B. Melrose.

United for Libraries Public Service Award. To a legislator who has been especially supportive of libraries. *Winners:* U.S. Sen. Patrick Leahy (D-Vt.), U.S. Rep. Jim Sensenbrenner (R-Wis.)

Young Adult Library Services Association (YALSA)

Baker & Taylor/YALSA Scholarship Grants ($1,000). To young adult librarians in public or school libraries to attend the ALA Annual Conference for the first time. *Donor:* Baker & Taylor. *Winners:* Jeanette Johnson, Lyndsey Runyan.

Dorothy Broderick Student Scholarship ($1,000). To enable a graduate student to attend the ALA Annual Conference for the first time. *Sponsor:* YALSA Leadership Endowment. *Winner:* Julia Hutchins.

BWI/YALSA Collection Development Grants ($1,000). To YALSA members who represent a public library and work directly with young adults, for collection development materials for young adults. *Donor:* Book Wholesalers, Inc. *Winners:* Jennifer McDonald, Carrie Wilson.

Margaret A. Edwards Award. See "Literary Prizes, 2014" in Part 5.

Great Books Giveaway (books, videos, CDs, and audiocassettes valued at a total of $25,000). *Winners:* (first place) Yakima Nation Library, Toppenish, Washington; (second place) Hilltop Pregnant Minors High School, San Francisco; (third place) Covington (Texas) Independent School District.

Frances Henne/YALSA/VOYA Research Grant ($1,000). To provide seed money to an individual, institution, or group for a project to encourage research on library service to young adults. *Donor:* Greenwood Publishing Group. *Winner:* Crystle Martin.

William C. Morris YA Debut Award. See "Literary Prizes, 2014" in Part 5.

Michael L. Printz Award. See "Literary Prizes, 2014" in Part 5.

YALSA/ABC-CLIO/Greenwood Publishing Group Service to Young Adults Achievement Award ($2,000). To a YALSA member who has demonstrated unique and sustained devotion to young adult services. *Donor:* Greenwood Publishing Group. *Winner:* Pam Spencer Holley.

YALSA/MAE Award ($500 for the recipient plus $500 for his or her library). For an exemplary young adult reading or literature program. *Sponsor:* Margaret A. Edwards Trust. *Winner:* Dawn Abron.

YALSA/Sagebrush Award. See YALSA/MAE Award.

American Society for Information Science and Technology (ASIS&T)

ASIS&T Award of Merit. For an outstanding contribution to the field of information science. *Winner:* Marjorie M. K. Hlava.

ASIS&T Best Information Science Books. *Winners:* Karine Nahon and Jeff Hemsley, for *Going Viral* (Polity); Robert J. Glushko, ed., for *The Discipline of Organizing* (MIT Press).

ASIS&T New Leaders Award. To recruit, engage, and retain new ASIS&T members and to identify potential for new leadership in the society. *Winners:* Devon Greyson, Maric Kramer, Jeremy L. McLaughlin, Agnes Mainka, Stephann Makri, Karen Miller, Anne Pepitone, Emily Vardell.

ASIS&T ProQuest Doctoral Dissertation Award ($1,000 plus expense-paid attendance at ASIS&T Annual Meeting). *Winner:* Amelia Acker for "Born Networked Records: A History of the Short Message Service Format."

ASIS&T Research in Information Science Award. For a systematic program of research in a single area at a level beyond the single study, recognizing contributions in the field of information science. *Winner:* Diane Kelly for "Research in Human-Centered Information Retrieval."

James M. Cretsos Leadership Award. *Winner:* Not awarded in 2014.

Watson Davis Award. For outstanding continuous contributions and dedicated service to the society. *Winner:* Vicki Gregory, Suffolk University.

Pratt Severn Best Student Research Paper Award. To encourage student research and writing in the field of information science. *Winner:* Curt Arledge for "Filled-in vs. Outline Icons: The Impact of Icon."

Thomson Reuters Doctoral Dissertation Proposal Scholarship ($2,000). *Winner:* Tiffany Chao for "Methods Metadata: Curating Scientific Research Data for Reuse."

Thomson Reuters Outstanding Teacher Award ($1,500). To recognize the unique teaching contribution of an individual as a teacher of information science. *Winner:* Michelle Kazmer, Florida State University.

John Wiley Best *JASIST* Paper Award. *Winners:* Max Hinne, Eduard Hoenkamp, Saskia Koldijk, Wessel Kraaij, Maya Sappelli, Maarten van der Heijden, and Suzan Verberne for "Reliability and Validity of Query Intent Assessments" (64:11).

Art Libraries Society of North America (ARLIS/NA)

ARLIS/NA Distinguished Service Award. To honor an individual whose exemplary service in art librarianship, visual resources curatorship, or a related field, has made an outstanding national or international contribution to art information. *Winner:* Joan Benedetti.

ARLIS/NA Wolfgang M. Freitag Internship Award ($3,000). To provide financial support for students preparing for a career in art librarianship or visual resource librarianship. *Winner:* Margit Wilson.

Melva J. Dwyer Award. To the creators of exceptional reference or research tools relating to Canadian art and architecture. *Winners:* Charlotte Townsend-Gault, Jennifer Dramer, and Ki-Ke-In, editors, for *Native Art of the Northwest Coast: A History of Changing Ideas* (University of British Columbia Press).

Gerd Muehsam Award. To one or more graduate students in library science programs to recognize excellence in a graduate paper or project. *Winner:* Jasmine Burns, for "Digital Facsimiles and the Modern Viewer: Medieval Manuscripts and Archival Practice in the Age of New Media."

H. W. Wilson Foundation Research Awards ($1,500). *Winners:* Bronwyn Dorhofer for her proposed website on the American photographer Nancy Ford Cones, "A Twilight Mood: The Pictorialist Photography of Nancy Ford Cones (1899–1932)"; Jaye Fishel for her project to create an online catalogue raisonné for Nexus Press, a publisher from 1989 to 2003 of artists' books and editions.

George Wittenborn Memorial Book Awards. See "Literary Prizes, 2014" in Part 5.

Asian/Pacific Americans Libraries Association (APALA)

APALA Scholarship ($1,000). For a student of Asian or Pacific background who is enrolled in, or has been accepted into, a master's or doctoral degree program in library and/or information science at an ALA-accredited school. *Winner:* Hannah Rainey.

APALA Travel Grant ($500). To a U.S. or Canadian citizen or permanent resident enrolled in a master's or doctoral degree program in library and/or information science at an ALA-accredited school, or a professional possessing a master's degree or doctoral degree in library and/or information science, to enable attendance at the ALA Annual Conference. *Winner:* Gerie Ventura.

Emerging Leaders Sponsorship. To fund participation in the 2014 class of the American Library Association's Emerging Leaders program (ELP). *Winner:* Arianna Sani Hussain.

Sheila Suen Lai Research Grant. To encourage APALA members to engage in research activities relative to library and information science in general and Asian Pacific American librarianship in particular. *Winner:* Not awarded in 2014.

Association for Library and Information Science Education (ALISE)

ALISE Award for Teaching Excellence. *Winner:* Renate Chancellor, Catholic University of America. *See also: Library Journal/ ALISE Excellence in Teaching Award*, below.

ALISE/Eugene Garfield Doctoral Dissertation Award. *Winner:* Youngseek Kim, University of Kentucky.

ALISE/Norman Horrocks Leadership Award. To recognize a new ALISE member who has demonstrated outstanding leadership qualities in professional ALISE activities. *Winner:* Shari A. Lee, St. John's University.

ALISE/LMC Paper Award. *Sponsor:* Libraries Unlimited/Linworth. *Winner:* Sharon McQueen, Old Dominion University.

ALISE/Pratt-Severn Faculty Innovation Award. To recognize innovation by full-time faculty members in incorporating evolving information technologies in the curricula of accredited master's degree programs in library and information studies. *Winner:* Not awarded in 2014.

ALISE Professional Contribution to Library and Information Science Education Award. *Winner:* Ling Hwey Jeng, Texas Woman's University.

ALISE/ProQuest Methodology Paper Competition. *Winner:* Angela Pollak, Western University.

ALISE Research Grant Awards (one or more grants totaling $5,000). *Winner:* Laurie Bonnici, University of Alabama.

ALISE Service Award. *Winner:* Sharon McQueen, Old Dominion University.

ALISE/Jean Tague Sutcliffe Doctoral Student Research Poster Competition. *Winners:* Jihee Beak, University of Wisconsin–Milwaukee; Patricia Condon, Simmons College; John D'Ignazio, Syracuse University; Jinxuan Ma, Florida State University; Mary-Jo Romaniuk, Queensland University of Technology.

ALISE/University of Washington Information School Youth Services Graduate Student Travel Award. To support the costs associated with travel to and participation in the ALISE Annual Conference. *Winner:* Natalie Greene Taylor, University of Maryland.

ALISE/Bohdan S. Wynar Research Paper Competition. *Winners:* Yi Shen, Johns Hopkins University; Virgil E. Varvel, Jr., University of Illinois at Urbana-Champaign.

Doctoral Students to ALISE Grant. To support the attendance of one or more promising LIS doctoral students at the ALISE Annual Conference. *Sponsor:* Libraries Unlimited/ Linworth. *Winners:* Adriana McCleer, University of Wisconsin–Milwaukee; Chaoqun Ni, Indiana University.

Library Journal/ALISE Excellence in Teaching Award (formerly the ALISE Award for Teaching Excellence in the Field of Library and Information Science Education). *Winner:* Paul T. Jaeger, associate professor, College of Information Studies, University of Maryland–College Park.

OCLC/ALISE Library and Information Science Research Grant Competition. To promote independent research that helps librarians integrate new technologies into areas of traditional competence and contributes to a better understanding of the library environment. *Winners:* June Abbas, University of Oklahoma; Denise Agosto, Drexel University; Leanne Bowler, University of Pittsburgh; Daqing He, University of Pittsburgh; Lynne McKechnie, Western University; Jung Sun Oh, University of Pittsburgh.

Association of Jewish Libraries (AJL)

AJL Scholarships ($1,000). For students enrolled in accredited library schools who plan to work as Judaica librarians. *Winners:* Marci Bayer, Ilya Slavutskiy.

Fanny Goldstein Merit Award. To honor loyal and ongoing contributions to the association and to the profession of Jewish librarianship. *Winner:* Joy Kingsolver.

Life Membership Award. To recognize outstanding leadership and professional contributions to the association and to the profession of Jewish librarianship. *Winner:* Heidi Lerner.

Association of Research Libraries

ARL Diversity Scholarships (stipend of up to $10,000). To a varying number of MLS students from under-represented groups who are interested in careers in research libraries. *Sponsors:* ARL member libraries and the Institute of Museum and Library Services. *Winners (2013–2015):* Joanna Chen, James Cheng, Andrea Devlin, Rhonda Evans, Pia Hunter, Rhonda Jones, Melissa Kahili, Rebecca Nieto, Paula Pascual, Conrad Pegues, Sarah Pham, Saira Raza, Joel Sanders, Nelson Santana, Madeline Sheldon.

Association of Seventh-Day Adventist Librarians

D. Glenn Hilts Scholarship ($1,500) for a member or members of the Seventh-Day Adventist Church who are enrolled in a graduate library program. *Winners:* Rebecca Brothers, Gina Lacson.

Beta Phi Mu

Beta Phi Mu Award. *See under* American Library Association.

Eugene Garfield Doctoral Dissertation Fellowships ($3,000). *Winners:* Amelia Acker, Kaitlin Costello, Lorraine Dong, Rhiannon Gainor, Katherine Howard, Aisha Johnson, Kyle Jones.

Harold Lancour Scholarship for Foreign Study ($1,750). For graduate study in a country related to the applicant's work or schooling. *Winner:* Katie McNirney.

Sarah Rebecca Reed Scholarship ($2,250). For study at an ALA-accredited library school. *Winners:* Gennie Gebhart, Pedro Gonzalez-Fernandez.

Frank B. Sessa Scholarship for Continuing Professional Education ($1,500). For continuing education for a Beta Phi Mu member. *Winner:* Hayley Johnson.

Blanche E. Woolls Scholarship ($2,250). For a beginning student in school library media services. *Winner:* Hailey Watkins.

Bibliographical Society of America (BSA)

BSA Fellowships ($1,500–$6,000). For scholars involved in bibliographical inquiry and research in the history of the book trades and in publishing history. *Winners:* (short-term fellowship) Tamara Atkin, "Play and Book: Drama, Reading, and the Invention of the Literary in Tudor England"; (BSA-ASECS Fellowship) Andrew Bricker, "The Eighteenth-Century Illicit Book Trade"; (short-term fellowship) Sonja Drimmer, "The Professionalization of Manuscript Illuminators in Late Medieval London"; (Pantzer Fellowship) John Garcia, "John Dunton's A Summer's Ramble: The Unpublished Narrative of a Bookseller's Travels in the Atlantic World, 1685–1705"; (Folter Fellowship) Daniel Hobbins, "Authorial Colophons in Late Medieval Manuscripts"; (Tanenbaum Fellowship) Robert Imes, "Chorography and Cartography: Domestic Travels, Domestic Maps"; (McCorison Fellowship) Heike Jablonski, "John Foxe in America: Publishing, Distributing, and Reading the Book of Martyrs in the United States"; (BSA-Mercantile Library Fellowship) Gary Kurutz, "Klondike and Alaska Gold Rushes: Descriptive Bibliography"; (Reese Fellowship) Amanda Laugesen, "Books for the World: The Franklin Book Program, American Publishers, and the Global Cultural Cold War"; (Senior Pantzer Fellowship) Michelle Levy,

"Women's Print History Project, 1750–1830"; (short-term fellowship) Jack Lynch, "The Shakespeare Phantom: The Lives of William Henry Ireland"; (short-term fellowship) Philip Palmer, "Copious Book, Book in Pieces: Material Readings of Thomas Coryate and the Early English Travelogue."

William L. Mitchell Prize for Research on Early British Serials ($1,000). Awarded triennially for the best single work published in the previous three years. *Winner:* Not awarded in 2014.

New Scholars Program. To promote the work of scholars who are new to the field of bibliography. *Winners:* Claire M. Bourne, John J. Garcia, L. Elizabeth Upper.

St. Louis Mercantile Library Prize in American Bibliography ($2,000). Awarded triennially for outstanding scholarship in the bibliography of American history and literature. *Sponsor:* St. Louis Mercantile Library, University of Missouri, St. Louis. *Winner:* Joseph J. Felcone for *Printing in New Jersey 1754–1800: A Descriptive Bibliography* (American Antiquarian Society, 2012).

Justin G. Schiller Prize for Bibliographical Work on Pre-20th Century Children's Books ($2,000). A triennial award to encourage scholarship in the bibliography of historical children's books. *Winner:* To be awarded next in 2016.

Canadian Library Association (CLA)

CLA Award for the Advancement of Intellectual Freedom in Canada. *Winner:* Dale Askey, now an associate librarian at McMaster University, for his commitment to intellectual freedom in the face of a defamation suit brought against him by an academic publisher whose products he had criticized in a blog post.

CLA/ACB Dafoe Scholarship (C$5,000). *Winner:* Alexander Herd.

CLA Best Poster Presentation Award. To recognize outstanding poster presentations on the basis of quality, knowledge of the presenter, relevance of content, and overall appearance of the poster. *Sponsor:* Dysart & Jones Associates. *Winners:* Marni Harrington and Annick Lapalme for "Profes-

sional Development beyond LIS Education: Building Bridges for Success."

CLA Robert H. Blackburn Distinguished Paper Award. To acknowledge notable published research. *Winner:* Cara Bradley, teaching and learning librarian, University of Regina, for "Information Literacy Articles in Science Pedagogy Journals," published in *Evidence Based Library and Information Practice* 8:4.

CLA Emerging Leader Award. To recognize a CLA member with less than five years' experience in the library field who demonstrates leadership or active participation in association work. *Sponsor:* Counting Opinions. *Winner:* Kayleigh Felice of the Bibliothèque Municipale de Gatineau.

CLA/Ken Haycock Award for Promoting Librarianship (C$1,000). For significant contributions to the public recognition and appreciation of librarianship. *Winner:* Not awarded in 2014.

CLA Library Research and Development Grant (C$1,000). *Winner:* Margaret Ann Wilkinson. *Topic:* "Developing a Guide for Education Institutions When Making Decisions about Relationships with Copyright Collectives."

CLA/Alan MacDonald Mentorship Award. To recognize the importance of mentorship to the library community. *Sponsor:* Canadian Electronic Library. *Winner:* Terri Tomchyshyn.

CLA/OCLC Award for Innovative Technology. *Donor:* OCLC Canada. *Winner:* The Alberta Library (TAL) for TAL Online's "Where Are You From?" (WAYF) application, interface, and administrative panel.

CLA Outstanding Service to Librarianship Award. *Donor:* ProQuest. *Winner:* Linda Cook, Edmonton Public Library.

CLA Student Article Award. *Winner:* Denise Scott for "The Language of Library Services for 'At-Risk' Youth."

CLA/H. W. Wilson Scholarship ($2,000). *Winner:* Zoe Dickinson.

W. Kaye Lamb Award for Service to Seniors. Awarded biennially to recognize a library that has developed an ongoing service, program, or procedure of benefit to seniors and/or a design and organization of buildings or facilities that improve access and encourage use by seniors. *Sponsors:* Ex Libris Association and CLA. *Winner:* Not awarded in 2014.

Angela Thacker Memorial Award. To honor teacher-librarians who have made contributions to the profession through publications, productions, or professional development activities. *Winner:* Carol Koechlin, school librarianship instructor, York University and the University of Toronto.

Catholic Library Association

Regina Medal. For continued, distinguished contribution to the field of children's literature. *Winner:* author Patricia Reilly Giff.

Chinese American Librarians Association (CALA)

CALA Conference Travel Grant. *Winners:* Ka-Chuen Gee, Mingyan Li, Kristy Lee, Jia Mi.

CALA Distinguished Service Award. To a librarian who has been a mentor, role model, and leader in the fields of library and information science. *Winner:* Yongyi Song, John F. Kennedy Memorial Library, California State University, Los Angeles.

CALA President's Recognition Award. *Winners:* Weiling Liu, Vincci Kwong.

CALA Scholarship of Library and Information Science ($1,000). *Winner:* Liya Deng.

Sheila Suen Lai Scholarship ($500). *Winner:* Yuehua Zhao.

Sally C. Tseng Professional Development Grant ($1,000). *Winner:* Not awarded in 2014.

Church and Synagogue Library Association (CSLA)

CSLA Award for Outstanding Congregational Librarian. For distinguished service to the congregation and/or community through devotion to the congregational library. *Winner:* Ruth White, chair, Library Advisory Committee, St. Stephen's Church, Sewickley, Pennsylvania.

CSLA Award for Outstanding Congregational Library. For responding in creative and innovative ways to the library's mission of

reaching and serving the congregation and/or the wider community. *Winner:* Not awarded in 2014.

CSLA Award for Outstanding Contribution to Congregational Libraries. For providing inspiration, guidance, leadership, or resources to enrich the field of church or synagogue librarianship. *Winner:* Not awarded in 2014.

Helen Keating Ott Award for Outstanding Contribution to Children's Literature. *Winner:* Not awarded in 2014.

Rodda Book Award. See "Literary Prizes, 2014" in Part 5.

Coalition for Networked Information (CNI)

Paul Evan Peters Award. Awarded biennially to recognize notable and lasting international achievements relating to high-performance networks and the creation and use of information resources and services that advance scholarship and intellectual productivity. *Sponsors:* Association of Research Libraries, CNI, EDUCAUSE. *Winner:* To be awarded next in 2015.

Paul Evan Peters Fellowship ($5,000 a year for two years). Awarded biennially to a student or students pursuing a graduate degree in librarianship or the information sciences. *Sponsors:* Association of Research Libraries, CNI, EDUCAUSE. *Winners:* Olivia Dorsey, Jordan Eschler.

Council on Library and Information Resources (CLIR)

CLIR Postdoctoral Fellowships in Scholarly Information Resources. *Current fellows:* Laura Aydelotte, Michael Bales, Meaghan Brown, Scout Calvert, Morgan Daniels, Rachel Deblinger, Anne Donlon, Annie Johnson, Emily McGinn, Monica Mercado, Paige Morgan, Alice Motes, Rikk Mulligan, Tim Norris, Charlotte Nunes, Jessica Otis, Philip Palmer, Alicia Peaker, Sarah Pickle, Andrew Rechnitz, Christopher Sawula, Meridith Beck Sayre, Emily Sherwood, Stephanie Simms, Plato Smith, Todd Suomela, Yun Tai, Ana Van Gulick; *Continuing current fellows:* Sayan Bhattacharyya, Alexandra Bolintineanu, Jonathan Cachat, Amy Chen, Margarita Corral, Matthew Davis, Jodi Flores, Nikolaus Fogle, John Kratz, Katie Rawson, Kendall Roark, Tamsyn Rose-Steel, Justin Schell, Matthew Sisk, Colleen Strawhacker, Ece Turnator, Bridget Whearty, Donna Wrublewski.

Mellon Fellowship Program for Dissertation Research in the Humanities in Original Sources (stipends of up to $20,000 to support dissertation research). Oscar Aguirre-Mandujano, Elisabeth Burton, Samuel Fury Childs Daly, Alexander Eastman, Edward Falk, Devin McGeehan Muchmore, Stuart McManus, Emma Otheguy, Bernadette Perez, Michael Polczynski, Paolo Savoia, Amanda Scott, Kathleen Tahk, Lucy Traverse, Benjamin Weber, Elizabeth Woodward, Ahyoung Yoo.

Rick Peterson Fellowship. To an early-career information technology professional or librarian who has reached beyond traditional boundaries to resolve a significant challenge facing digital libraries. *Cosponsors:* CLIR and the National Institute for Technology in Liberal Education (NITLE). *Winner:* Award suspended.

Rovelstad Scholarship in International Librarianship. To enable a student enrolled in an accredited LIS program to attend the IFLA World Library and Information Congress. *Winner:* Janetta Pegues, University of Wisconsin–Madison.

A. R. Zipf Fellowship in Information Management ($10,000). To a student enrolled in graduate school who shows exceptional promise for leadership and technical achievement. *Winner:* Award discontinued.

EDUCAUSE

EDUCAUSE Leadership Award. To acknowledge leadership in higher education information technology. *Winner:* Gordon Wishon, chief information officer, Arizona State University.

EDUCAUSE Rising Star Award. To recognize early-career information technology professionals who demonstrate exceptional achievement in the area of information technology in higher education. *Winner:* Katie

Vale, director of digital learning, Harvard School of Public Health.

Friends of the National Library of Medicine

Michael E. DeBakey Library Services Outreach Award. To recognize outstanding service and contributions to rural and underserved communities by a practicing health sciences librarian. *Winner:* Patricia Bradley, native and distance services librarian, University of New Mexico Health Sciences Library and Informatics Center (HSLIC).

Bill and Melinda Gates Foundation

Access to Learning Award ($1 million). To public libraries or similar organizations outside the United States for innovative programs that provide free public access to information technology. *Administered by:* Gates Foundation Global Libraries initiative. *Winner:* e-Library Nenasala Program of Sri Lanka, a government-run initiative to increase digital literacy and access to technology among the nation's poorest residents living in remote rural areas.

Institute of Museum and Library Services

National Medal for Museum and Library Service. For extraordinary civic, educational, economic, environmental, and social contributions ($5,000). *Winners:* (libraries) Chicago Public Library; Las Vegas-Clark County Library District; Mid-Continent Public Library, Independence, Missouri; Octavia Fellin Public Library, Gallup, New Mexico; Yiddish Book Center, Amherst, Massachusetts.

International Association of School Librarians (IASL)

Ken Haycock and Jean Lowrie Leadership Development Grants ($1,000). To enable applicants to attend their first IASL Annual Conference. *Winners:* Not awarded in 2014. IASL School Library Technology Innovation Award. *Winner:* Not awarded in 2014.

International Board on Books for Young People (IBBY)

IBBY-Asahi Reading Promotion Award ($10,000). Awarded biennially to projects that are making a lasting contribution to reading promotion for young people. *Offered by:* International Board on Books for Young People. *Sponsor:* Asahi Shimbun. *Winners:* The Children's Book Bank, Toronto, Canada, which supports childhood literacy by providing free books and literacy support to children in low-income neighborhoods in the Toronto area; PRAESA (the Project for the Study of Alternative Education in South Africa), in recognition of its more than 20 years' work in the field of children's multilingual literacy development.

International Federation of Library Associations and Institutions (IFLA)

Honorary Fellowship. For distinguished service to IFLA. *Winner:* Alex Byrne, IFLA president 2005–2007.

IFLA Medal. To a person or organization for a distinguished contribution either to IFLA or to international librarianship. *Winners:* Jesús Lau, Peter Johan Lor, Pascal Sanz.

Jay Jordan IFLA/OCLC Early Career Development Fellowships. To library and information science professionals from countries with developing economies who are in the early stages of their careers. *Winners:* Stanislava Gardasevic, Serbia; Nomsa Mathabela, Swaziland; Masimba Muziringa, Zimbabwe; Martin Julius Perez, Philippines; Sadaf Rafiq, Pakistan.

Dr. Shawky Salem Conference Grant (up to $1,900). To enable an expert in library and information science who is a national of an Arab country to attend the IFLA Conference for the first time. *Winner:* Bassim Faris, United Nations Relief and Work Agency (UNRWA), Amman, Jordan.

Frederick Thorpe Organizational Award (up to £15,000). To a library organization for development of service delivery to the visually impaired. *Sponsor:* Ulverscroft Foundation. *Winner:* Not awarded in 2014.

Ulverscroft Foundation/IFLA Libraries Serving Persons with Print Disabilities Section Best Practice Awards. To assist the development of library services for print-disabled people and foster cooperation between library services serving these persons. *Winner:* Not awarded in 2014.

Library Journal

DEMCO/LJ Paralibrarian of the Year Award. *Winner:* Clancy Poolz, Whitman County Rural Library District, Colfax, Washington.

Gale/LJ Library of the Year. *Sponsor:* Gale Cengage Learning. *Winner:* Edmonton (Alberta) Public Library.

Library Journal/ALISE Excellence in Teaching Award (formerly the ALISE Award for Teaching Excellence in the Field of Library and Information Science Education). *See under:* Association for Library and Information Science Education (ALISE).

LJ Best Small Library in America ($20,000). To honor a public library that profoundly demonstrates outstanding service to populations of 25,000 or less. *Co-sponsors: Library Journal* and the Bill and Melinda Gates Foundation. *Winner:* Pine River Public Library, Bayfield, Colorado.

LJ Librarian of the Year. *Winner:* Corinne Hill, Chattanooga Public Library.

Library of Congress

Library of Congress Literacy Awards. *Sponsor:* David M. Rubenstein. *Winners:* (David M. Rubenstein Prize, $150,000, for a groundbreaking or sustained record of advancement of literacy by any individual or entity) Room to Read, which operates in Africa and Southeast Asia and focuses on developing reading skills and the habit of reading among primary school children; (American Prize, $50,000, for a project developed and implemented successfully during the past decade for combating illiteracy and/or aliteracy) SMART (Start Making a Reader To-day), founded in 1992 to address the growing number of elementary school children who were reading significantly below grade level and now operating at more than 250 sites, serving approximately 9,000 children each year; (International Prize, $50,000, for the work of an individual, nation, or nongovernmental organization working in a specific country or region) The Mother Child Education Foundation (AÇEV), founded in 1993, the largest literacy organization in Turkey, operating a variety of projects designed to address family, adult, and early childhood literacy.

Library of Congress John W. Kluge Fellowship in Digital Studies Description. To promote examination of the impact of the digital revolution on society, culture, and international relations using the library's collections and resources. *Fellows:* Wendy Fok, Katrin Weller.

Library of Congress Prize for American Fiction. See "Literary Prizes, 2014" in Part 5.

Medical Library Association (MLA)

Virginia L. and William K. Beatty MLA Volunteer Service Award. To recognize a medical librarian who has demonstrated outstanding, sustained service to the Medical Library Association and the health sciences library profession. *Winner:* Janna Lawrence.

Estelle Brodman Award for the Academic Medical Librarian of the Year. To honor significant achievement, potential for leadership, and continuing excellence at midcareer in the area of academic health sciences librarianship. *Winner:* Julia Esparza.

Lois Ann Colaianni Award for Excellence and Achievement in Hospital Librarianship. To a member of MLA who has made significant contributions to the profession in the area of overall distinction or leadership in hospital librarianship. *Winner:* Heather N. Holmes.

Cunningham Memorial International Fellowships. For health sciences librarians from countries outside the United States and Canada, to provide for attendance at the MLA Annual Meeting and observation and super-vised work in one or more medical libraries. *Winner:* Not awarded in 2014.

Louise Darling Medal. For distinguished achievement in collection development in the health sciences. *Winner:* Library Network Office, Department of Veterans Affairs.

Janet Doe Lectureship. *Winner:* Margaret Moylan Bandy. *Topic:* "Pivoting: Leveraging Opportunities in a Turbulent Health Care Environment."

EBSCO/MLA Annual Meeting Grants (up to $1,000). To enable four health sciences librarians to attend the MLA Annual Meeting. *Winners:* Jennifer Deal, Vanessa Kitchin, Carolann Lee Curry, Heather Martin, and Amy Studer.

Ida and George Eliot Prize. To recognize a work published in the preceding calendar year that has been judged most effective in furthering medical librarianship. *Winners:* Joanne Gard Marshall, Julia Sollenberger, Sharon Easterby-Gannett, Lynn Kasner Morgan, Mary Lou Klem, Susan K. Cavanaugh, Kathleen Burr Oliver, Cheryl A. Thompson, Neil Romanosky, and Sue Hunter for "The Value of Library and Information Services in Patient Care: Results of a Multisite Study."

Carla J. Funk Governmental Relations Award ($500). To recognize a medical librarian who has demonstrated outstanding leadership in the area of governmental relations at the federal, state, or local level, and who has furthered the goal of providing quality information for improved health. *Sponsor:* Kent A. Smith. *Winner:* Donna Timm.

Murray Gottlieb Prize. For the best unpublished essay on the history of medicine and allied sciences written by a health sciences librarian. *Sponsor:* MLA History of the Health Sciences Section. *Winner:* Not awarded in 2014.

T. Mark Hodges International Service Award. To honor outstanding achievement in promoting, enabling, or delivering improved health information internationally. *Winner:* Paulraj Kirubanithi.

David A. Kronick Traveling Fellowship ($2,000). *Sponsor:* Bowden-Massey Foundation. *Winner:* Julie H. Schiavo.

Joseph Leiter NLM/MLA Lectureship. *Winner:* Terry J. Sejnowski. *Topic:* "The BRAIN Initiative: Connecting the Dots."

Donald A. B. Lindberg Research Fellowship ($10,000). To fund research aimed at expanding the research knowledge base, linking the information services provided by librarians to improved health care and advances in biomedical research. *Winner:* Deborah H. Charbonneau. *Topic:* "NIH Public Access and Data Sharing Policies: A Mixed-Methods Study."

Lucretia W. McClure Excellence in Education Award. To an outstanding educator in the field of health sciences librarianship and informatics. *Winner:* Michele R. Tennant.

John P. McGovern Award Lectureship. *Winner:* Aaron E. Carroll, M.D. *Topic:* "The Affordable Care Act: Health Care Reform Is Far From Over."

Majors/MLA Chapter Project of the Year Award. *Sponsor:* J. A. Majors Co. *Winner:* Medical Library Group of Southern California and Arizona.

Medical Informatics Section Career Development Grant ($1,500). To support a career development activity that will contribute to advancement in the field of medical informatics. *Winner:* Marci Brandenburg.

MLA Continuing Education Awards ($100–$500). *Winners:* Xan Goodman, Lynda J. Hartel.

MLA Scholarship (up to $5,000). For graduate study at an ALA-accredited library school. *Winner:* Allyson Mackay.

MLA Scholarship for Minority Students (up to $5,000). For graduate study at an ALA-accredited library school. *Winner:* Christina Meejung Czuhajewski.

Marcia C. Noyes Award. For an outstanding contribution to medical librarianship. *Winner:* Joanne Gard Marshall.

President's Award. To an MLA member for a notable or important contribution made during the past association year. *Winners:* J. Michael Homan and Heather Todd in recognition of their achievement in planning and coordinating the international meeting "One Health: Information in an Interdependent World."

Rittenhouse Award. For the best unpublished paper on medical librarianship submitted by a student enrolled in, or having been enrolled in, a course for credit in an ALA-accredited library school or a trainee in an internship program in medical librarianship. *Donor:* Rittenhouse Book Distributors. *Winner:* Laura L. Pavlech for "Evidence–Based Veterinary Medicine: Current Opinions and Barriers to Practice."

Thomson Reuters/Frank Bradway Rogers Information Advancement Award. To recognize outstanding contributions for the application of technology to the delivery of health science information, to the science of information, or to the facilitation of the delivery of health science information. *Sponsor:* Thomson Reuters. *Winner:* National Library of Medicine for MedlinePlus Connect.

Music Library Association

Carol June Bradley Award. To support studies that involve the history of music libraries or special collections. *Winners:* Not awarded in 2014.

Vincent H. Duckles Award. For the best book-length bibliography or other research tool in music. *Winners:* David Lasocki and Richard Griscom for *The Recorder: A Research and Information Guide,* 3rd edition (Routledge Music Bibliographies).

Dena Epstein Award for Archival and Library Research in American Music. To support research in archives or libraries internationally on any aspect of American music. *Winner:* Alice Miller Cotter (Princeton University) for research on John Adams' operas in Adams' private archive at his home in Berkeley, California, and other California collections.

Kevin Freeman Travel Grants. To colleagues who are new to the profession to enable them to attend the MLA Annual Meeting. *Winners:* Angela Pratesi, Jennifer Vaughn, Elin Williams.

Walter Gerboth Award. To members of the association who are in the first five years of their professional library careers, to assist research-in-progress in music or music librarianship. *Winner:* Not awarded in 2014.

Richard S. Hill Award. For the best article on music librarianship or article of a music-bibliographic nature. *Winner:* Christopher Reynolds for "Documenting the Zenith of Women Song Composers: A Database of

Songs Published in the United States and the British Commonwealth, ca. 1890–1930 in *Notes* 69:4 (2013).

MLA Citation. Awarded in recognition of contributions to the profession over a career. *Winner:* James P. Cassaro.

Eva Judd O'Meara Award. For the best review published in *Notes*. *Winner:* Erik Entwistle for his review of F. James Rybka's *Boshuslav Martinu: The Compulsion to Compose* in *Notes* 69:1 (2012).

A. Ralph Papakhian Special Achievement Award. To recognize extraordinary service to the profession of music librarianship over a relatively short period of time. *Winners:* Brenda Nelson-Strauss, Tracey Rudnick.

National Library Service for the Blind and Physically Handicapped, Library of Congress

Library of the Year Awards ($1,000). *Winners:* (network library of the year) New Hampshire State Library Talking Book Services; (subregional library of the year) Palm Beach County (Florida) Talking Books Library.

REFORMA (National Association to Promote Library and Information Services to Latinos and the Spanish-Speaking)

Elizabeth A. Martinez Lifetime Achievement Award. To recognize those who have achieved excellence in librarianship over an extended period of service and who have made significant and lasting contributions to REFORMA and the Latino community. *Winner:* Sandra Rios Balderrama.

REFORMA scholarships (up to $1,500). To students who qualify for graduate study in library science and who are citizens or permanent residents of the United States. *Winners:* Claudio Leon (Rose Treviño Memorial Scholarship), Maria de Lurdy Martinez Serrano (REFORMA scholarship).

Arnulfo D. Trejo Librarian of the Year Award. To recognize a librarian who has promoted and advocated services to the Spanish-speaking and Latino communities and made outstanding contributions to REFORMA. *Winner:* Salvador Avila, manager, Enterprise Branch, Las Vegas-Clark County Library District.

Society of American Archivists (SAA)

C. F. W. Coker Award for Description. To recognize creators of tools that enable archivists to produce more effective finding aids. *Winner:* Remixing Archival Metadata Project, University of Miami.

Distinguished Service Award. To recognize an archival institution, education program, nonprofit organization, or governmental organization that has given outstanding service to its public and has made an exemplary contribution to the archives profession. *Winner:* Not awarded in 2014.

Diversity Award. To an individual, group, or institution for outstanding contributions to advancing diversity within the archives profession, SAA, or the archival record. *Winners:* Recovering the U.S. Hispanic Literary Heritage Program, University of Houston; Jennifer O'Neal, University of Oregon Libraries.

Emerging Leader Award. To recognize early-career archivists who have completed archival work of broad merit, demonstrated significant promise of leadership, performed commendable service to the archives profession, or have accomplished a combination of these requirements. *Winner:* Beth Shields, Kentucky Department for Libraries and Archives.

Fellows' Ernst Posner Award. For an outstanding essay dealing with a facet of archival administration, history, theory, or methodology, published in *American Archivist*. *Winner:* Not awarded in 2014.

Josephine Forman Scholarship ($10,000). *Sponsor:* General Commission on Archives and History of the United Methodist Church. *Winner:* Joanna Chen (University of California, Los Angeles).

Elsie Ham and F. Gerald Ham Scholarship ($7,500). To recognize an individual's past performance in a graduate archival studies program and his or her potential in the field. *Winner:* William J. Levay, Pratt Institute.

Philip M. Hamer and Elizabeth Hamer Kegan Award. For individuals and/or institutions that have increased public awareness of a specific body of documents. *Winner:* Emma Goldman Papers Project.

Oliver Wendell Holmes Travel Award. To enable overseas archivists already in the United States or Canada for training to attend the SAA Annual Meeting. *Winner:* Not awarded in 2014.

J. Franklin Jameson Archival Advocacy Award. For individuals and/or organizations that promote greater public awareness of archival activities and programs. *Winner:* LGBT Center of Central Pennsylvania History Project.

Sister M. Claude Lane, O.P., Memorial Award. For a significant contribution to the field of religious archives. *Winner:* Judi Fergus, Arthur Moore Methodist Museum, Library and Archives, St. Simons Island, Georgia.

Waldo Gifford Leland Award. To encourage and reward writing of superior excellence and usefulness in the field of archival history, theory, or practice. *Winner:* Ellen Gruber Garvey for *Writing with Scissors: American Scrapbooks from the Civil War to the Harlem Renaissance* (Oxford University Press).

Theodore Calvin Pease Award. For the best student paper ($100 and publication in *American Archivist*). *Winner:* Joshua D. Hager, University of North Carolina at Chapel Hill, for "To Like or Not to Like: Understanding and Maximizing the Utility of Archival Outreach on Facebook."

Donald Peterson Student Travel Award (up to $1,000). To enable a student or recent graduate to attend the SAA Annual Meeting. *Winner:* Michelle Chiles, Simmons College.

Harold T. Pinkett Minority Student Award. To encourage minority students to consider careers in the archival profession, and to promote minority participation in SAA. *Winners:* Raquel Flores-Clemons, University of Illinois at Urbana-Champaign; Allan Jason Sarmiento, California State University, Sacramento.

Preservation Publication Award. To recognize an outstanding work published in North America that advances the theory or the practice of preservation in archival institu-

tions. *Winners:* Nancy Y. McGovern and Katherine Skinner, editors, for *Archivists' Guide to Archiving Video* (Witness).

SAA Fellows. To a limited number of members for their outstanding contribution to the archival profession. *Honored:* Mark Duffy, Michelle Light, Stephen E. Novak, Merrilee Proffitt, Frederick J. Stielow.

SAA Mosaic Scholarship ($5,000). To minority students pursuing graduate education in archival science. *Winners:* Rebecca Nieto, McGill University; Maria E. Sanchez-Tucker, University of Wisconsin–Milwaukee.

SAA Spotlight Award. To recognize the contributions of individuals who work for the good of the profession and of archival collections, and whose work would not typically receive public recognition. *Winner:* Kate Theimer, Spontaneous Scholarship Program.

Special Libraries Association (SLA)

SLA Copyright Clearance Center Rising Stars Award. To SLA members in the first five years of membership who demonstrate exceptional promise of leadership. *Winners:* Angela June Aranas Kent, Tanya Whippie, Sam Wiggins.

SLA John Cotton Dana Award. For exceptional support and encouragement of special librarianship. *Winner:* Cindy Hill.

SLA Dow Jones Innovate Award. To an SLA member who has consistently shown innovation, leadership, and creativity in the information profession and the association. *Winner:* Tracy Z. Maleeff.

SLA Fellows. *Honored:* Mary Ellen Bates, Tony Landolt, Catherine Lavallée-Welch, Daniel Lee, Leslie Reynolds.

SLA Hall of Fame Award. For outstanding performance and distinguished service to SLA. *Winners:* Anne Caputo, Jane Dysart, Ann Shea.

SLA Presidential Citations. To SLA members for notable or important contributions during the previous year that enhanced the association or furthered its goals and objectives. *Winners:* Not awarded in 2014.

Rose L. Vormelker Award. To SLA members for exceptional service through the education and mentoring of students and working professionals. *Winner:* Libby Trudell.

Theatre Library Association

Brooks McNamara Performing Arts Librarian Scholarship. *Winner:* Selena Chau, San José State University.

Louis Rachow Distinguished Service in Performing Arts Librarianship Award. For extraordinary contributions to performing arts librarianship. *Winner:* Jacqueline Z. Davis, Barbara G. and Lawrence A. Fleischman Executive Director, New York Public Library for the Performing Arts.

George Freedley Memorial Award. See "Literary Prizes, 2014" in Part 5.

Richard Wall Award. See "Literary Prizes, 2014" in Part 5.

Other Awards of Distinction

American Psychological Association Excellence in Librarianship Award ($2,500). For significant contributions to psychology and behavioral sciences librarianship. *Winner:* Frederick Lerner, retired information scientist at the National Center for PTSD, White River Junction, Vermont.

Robert B. Downs Intellectual Freedom Award. To recognize individuals or groups who have furthered the cause of intellectual freedom, particularly as it affects libraries and information centers and the dissemination of ideas. *Offered by:* Graduate School of Library and Information Science, University of Illinois at Urbana-Champaign. *Sponsor:* Libraries Unlimited/ABC-CLIO. *Winners:* the staff and board of trustees of the Orland Park (Illinois) Public Library for their policy of not filtering adult Internet access despite strong opposition.

I Love My Librarian Awards ($5,000, a plaque, and a $500 travel stipend to attend the awards ceremony). To recognize librarians for service to their communities, schools, and campuses. Winners are nominated by library patrons. *Sponsors:* Carnegie Corporation of New York and the *New York Times.* *Winners:* Michael Beller, F. W. Olin Library, Mills College, Oakland, California; Cherry Hamrick, Delta Township (Michigan) District Library; Jessica Elaine Holmes, Westridge Elementary School Library Media Center, Frankfort, Kentucky; Lynn Hancock Hurt, Brown Library at Virginia Western Community College, Roanoke; David Lopez, Santa Ana (California) Public Library; Christine Payne, Appoquinimink High School, Middletown, Delaware; Kevin M. Ray, Cleveland Public Library; Ciro Scardina, P.S. 18 School Library, Staten Island; Sarah A. Sugden, Waterville (Maine) Public Library; Frances Yates, Indiana University East Richmond.

RWA Librarian of the Year. To a librarian who demonstrates outstanding support of romance authors and the romance genre. *Offered by:* Romance Writers of America. *Winner:* Sean Gilmartin, Anythink Library, Thornton, Colorado.

USBBY Bridge to Understanding Award ($1,000). To acknowledge the work of adults who use books to promote international understanding among children. *Offered by:* United States Board on Books for Young People. *Winner:* Día Family Book Club, an extension of the El Día de los Niños/El Día de los Libros project of the Association for Library Service to Children (ALSC), American Library Association.

Women's National Book Association Award. Awarded biennially to a living American woman who derives part or all of her income from books and allied arts and who has done meritorious work in the world of books. *Offered by:* Women's National Book Association (WNBA). *Winner:* To be announced.

Part 4
Research and Statistics

Library Research and Statistics

Research and Statistics on Libraries and Librarianship in 2014

Kathy Rosa

Director, Office for Research and Statistics, American Library Association

Public, academic, and school libraries serve the information needs of the population. For most of them, adequate funding continues to be a challenge, but libraries strive to offer the innovative services and high-quality resources their patrons seek.

Public libraries are community anchors, providing print and digital books, databases, meeting spaces, and instruction on how to use new technologies. Public programs, from storytimes to author talks, have always been popular with patrons. The variety of programs today, including makerspaces and drop-in craft activities, reflects a changing world. The number of programs in public libraries has increased by 37.6 percent during the past eight years.[1] Children's programs are the most popular, with 65.6 million attendees during 2012.

Academic libraries serve the students, faculty, and staff of colleges and universities. Their collections include print and digital resources that support the college curriculum. Reference services and research support are evolving with the changes in technology. The librarian assists with reference work in person or by phone, e-mail, and online chat. Needs of students and faculty are also changing, and academic libraries are challenged to meet these requirements with little or no increase in budgets. One trend is to repurpose space, creating small group study spaces, quiet places, and learning labs for students. Faculty members are affected by the rapid changes in scholarly communications. Peer-reviewed print journals are often extremely expensive, and the growth in digital scholarly communication is rapid. Academic librarians must provide the scholarly resources that faculty need to further their research, and must do so while staying within a budget.

School libraries are integral to student learning. Research shows that students from schools with professionally staffed, fully equipped libraries score higher on achievement tests. The school librarian manages a diverse collection of resources that support the curriculum and the individual interests of students and teachers. In the best circumstance, the school has a professionally trained librarian prepared to guide students as they navigate and evaluate the vast and varied expanse of available information. But as vital as school libraries and librarians are, the number of professional staff is falling because of limits in funding.

This article discusses research and statistics about public, academic, and school libraries and librarianship. Each section covers the most recently available statistics about libraries and the notable research. Information sources include the American Library Association (ALA), the Institute of Museum and Library Services (IMLS), the Bureau of Labor Statistics, the Association of College and Research Libraries, the Association of Research Libraries, *Library Journal,* and the National Center for Education Statistics.

A listing of awards and grants conferred by professional associations is included. The winner's name, the award name, and the title of the qualifying work are listed for awards conferred by ALA and its divisions. The Association for Information Science and Technology (ASIS&T), the Association for Library and Information Science Education (ALISE), and the Medical Library Association are also included.

Public Libraries

Public libraries continue to recover from the recession of 2008. Revenue for the nation's nearly 17,000 public library outlets totaled $11.49 billion, a one-year decrease of 1.1 percent and a ten-year increase of 7.2 percent.[2] A *Library Journal*[3] survey found that 73 percent of libraries showed an increase in operating and salary budgets from 2013 to 2014, up from 68 percent the previous year, and from 60 percent the year before.

Revenue for public libraries comes largely from local, state, and federal governments. During the past ten years revenue from local government has increased by 7.2 percent, from 79.1 percent to 84.4 percent of the total. State government revenue to public libraries decreased by 37.2 percent during the same decade. Federal revenue to libraries saw a one-year increase of 3.6 percent. Donations and other non-government sources composed 8.2 percent of total revenue to public libraries; this category represents the largest increase in library revenue—13.3 percent.

Grants to States Program

IMLS provides funding to public libraries through the Grants to States program. Grant funds totaling $150 million are distributed to the State Library Administrative Agencies (SLAAs) every year based on population. SLAAs are the agencies charged by law with the extension and development of library services. They are located in each of the 50 states and the District of Columbia; the territories of Guam, American Samoa, Commonwealth of Puerto Rico, Commonwealth of the Northern Mariana Islands, and the U.S. Virgin Islands; and the "freely associated states" (Federated States of Micronesia, Republic of Palau, and Republic of the Marshall Islands).[4]

Chief Officers Survey

ALA conducted a survey of the chief officers of state library agencies during 2014.[5] The chief officers responded to the online survey between October 28 and December 3. The resulting report highlights changes in support for public library funding on a state level, reductions and closures, state collaborations, and broadband planning. ALA received responses from 47 of 50 states and from the District of Columbia; the non-respondents were West Virginia, Washington, Pennsylvania, and New York.

For states that provide direct state aid for public libraries, 45 percent reported no change from fiscal year (FY) 2014; 21 percent reported increased funding; and 17 percent reported decreased funding, with Missouri and Alabama reporting cuts of 9 percent to 10 percent or more.

Just under half (49 percent) of the responding states told ALA that their budgets were unchanged between FY 2014 and FY 2015 (five of those states operate on two-year budget calendars). For states with annual budgets, 38 percent reported flat funding. Twelve states reported budget increases for the state library, and another 12 states reported decreases.

Public Library Referenda

IMLS reports that nearly 300 million people, or more than 95 percent of the total U.S. population, live within the legal service area of a library. The people who reside in these areas pay taxes that help fund a library; in return they get free library cards and access to resources and services. Referenda to provide tax revenue for public libraries appear on local election ballots, and the outcome of local referenda is crucial given that nearly 85 percent of library funding comes from local sources.

During 2014 the ALA Office for Research and Statistics tracked 153 library referenda across 22 states.[6] Of the 126 measures, Ohio and Michigan led the way in sheer numbers. Ohio was a big winner, with 31 of 34 measures passed. Michigan voters approved 54 of 68 measures. The vote on library referenda determines whether libraries can support their operating budgets, make improvements, and stay current with technology resources. Passage of bonding referenda also is a main source of funds to build new libraries.

Notable Research on Public Libraries

The Digital Inclusion Survey[7] is a national survey that explores the digital inclusion roles of public libraries in four key areas: public access technology infrastructure resources and capacity (public access workstations, broadband connectivity, and so forth); digital content, services, and accessibility; digital literacy (including languages in which instruction is offered); and domain-specific services and programs (civic engagement, education, health and wellness, workforce/employment).

The study is conducted by ALA's Office for Research and Statistics and Office for Information Technology Policy, and by the Information Policy and Access Center at the University of Maryland. The International City/County Management Association and Community Attributes, Inc., served as partners. The study is funded by IMLS. Results included the following:

- Public libraries report an average download speed of 57 megabits per second (Mbps). City libraries report an average subscribed download speed of more than 100 Mbps, as compared with an average subscribed download speed of just over 21 Mbps for rural public libraries.

- Two-thirds of libraries overall report a desire to increase broadband connectivity. However, 58.8 percent of libraries said budgetary constraints affected their ability to increase bandwidth, while slightly less than one-third report that an outside entity makes the decisions regarding bandwidth.
- Nearly all (98.0 percent) public library outlets offer some form of technology training to patrons. City libraries were more likely to offer formal technology training than other libraries. For example, 77.6 percent of city libraries offer formal computer skills training compared with 57.9 percent of suburban libraries, 47.7 percent of town libraries, and 32.5 percent of rural libraries.
- Nearly all public libraries (99.5 percent) report offering education and learning programs. Almost all (98.4 percent) offer summer reading programs.
- A vast majority (95.0 percent) of libraries assist patrons with important employment resources.
- Nearly 80 percent of libraries offer programs that help patrons with job applications, such as interview skills and résumé development.
- A majority of libraries (72.2 percent) help patrons to access and use employment databases, as well as to access and use online business information resources (58.9 percent).
- Three-fourths of libraries overall offer community, civic engagement, or e-government programs. While 85 percent of city outlets offer these programs, only 70 percent of both town and rural libraries do so. Nearly all libraries offer patrons assistance in completing online government forms.
- An overall majority (57.9 percent) of libraries conduct health and wellness programs. Nearly half (46.3 percent) of rural libraries offer these programs, and nearly three-fourths of suburban libraries.
- More than half (55.9 percent) of libraries offer programs that promote the development of healthy lifestyles.

Academic Libraries

College students recognize the importance of academic libraries. When asked about their library experience, 33 percent of first-year students and 47 percent of seniors agreed that the library at their institution contributed "very much" to their knowledge, skills, and personal development.[8] The majority of students report that they use the library in person and online. Students reported visiting the library in person daily (22.7 percent), weekly (34.7 percent), monthly (15.4 percent), rarely (19.6 percent), and never (7.6 percent); they report using online information resources or services through the library daily (13.2 percent), weekly (35.1 percent), monthly (22.9 percent), rarely (22.9 percent), and never (7.6 percent).[9]

Academic librarians are nimbly managing financial resources and space allocation to meet the learning needs of students and support the research needs of faculty. Doctoral/research institutions spent an average of $6,305,337 for collections, with 74.3 percent toward ongoing purchases. Baccalaureate schools spent an average of $462,929, with 70.6 percent toward ongoing purchases. Institutions offering associate degrees spent 54.8 percent of their $144,062 materials budget on ongoing purchases.[10]

A total of 232 new academic library buildings were completed in the United States and Puerto Rico between 2000 and 2014.[11] Four new academic libraries were completed in 2014, and many existing library spaces were being repurposed. In a survey, 63 percent of respondents reported redesigning space to maximize areas for quiet study space, group study, writing/tutoring centers, technology learning areas, and to increase seating.[12]

Staffing

Doctoral/research institutions employed an average of 49.58 professional staff; comprehensive institutions employed an average of 10.8; baccalaureate schools employed an average of 6, and associate degree institutions employed an average of 5.24, according to a recent survey.[13]

Academic libraries provided 26.3 percent of all jobs for new library school graduates in 2013, down from 33.3 percent in 2012. The most recent survey of first-year students found that 0.7 percent planned to become a librarian.[14]

Salaries

Academic library expenditures for salaries and wages accounted for 55.4 percent of total expenditures on average. Salaries and wages constituted 74.1 percent of total library expenditures for associate degree institutions, 51.4 percent for baccalaureate, 52.3 percent for comprehensive schools, and 43.8 percent for doctoral/research institutions.[15]

The average salary for academic librarians was $53,000.[16] New academic librarians earned an average of $42,000, down from $42,599 in 2012.

Two-thirds of academic librarians received a salary increase of 3.4 percent in 2013. Although most of the raises were cost-of-living or merit pay increases, 9 percent of academic librarians received increases as the result of a job change.

Trends

The evolving role of the library, competition for space and funding, and the changing nature of scholarly publishing are just a few of the challenges facing academic librarians. One role of the Research Planning and Review Committee of the Association of College and Research Libraries (ACRL), a division of ALA, is to consider these challenges and identify trends. In 2014 the committee identified deeper collaboration as the underlying theme of the 2014 top trends.[17] The trends, listed below, provide numerous opportunities for research collaboration in the academic and research library community.

Data

- New initiatives and collaborative opportunities
- Cooperative roles for researchers, repositories, and journal publishers
- Partnerships related to discovery and re-use of data
- Device neutral digital services

Evolving Openness in Higher Education

- Open access
- Open education

Student Success

- Funding, student success initiatives, and accreditation
- Libraries, student success, and demonstrating value

Competency-Based Learning

Altmetrics

Digital Humanities

- Student success initiatives, competency-based learning, altmetrics, and digital humanities

Notable Research on Academic Libraries

The Association of Research Libraries (ARL) surveys member institutions about current research library policies and practices. The results, published as SPEC Kits, are intended to help academic librarians manage change and improve performance. New SPEC Kits[18] in 2014 included the following:

SPEC Kit 345: Shared Print Programs (December 2014)—This SPEC Kit explores the extent of ARL member libraries' participation in shared print programs, the type and scope of programs in which they choose to participate, the rationale for participation, the value and benefits the programs provide to ARL and other libraries, and the roles different libraries are playing in them.

SPEC Kit 344: Talent Management (November 2014)—An investigation of the following areas relating to talent management: talent strategy, recruitment and hiring, retention, employee engagement, job classification management, compensation management, performance assessment, competencies, professional development planning, and leadership and succession planning.

SPEC Kit 343: Library Support for Faculty/Researcher Publishing (October 2014)—This SPEC Kit explores ARL member libraries' activities relating to support of faculty and researcher publishing of scholarly works. It investigates the level and variety of services ARL libraries are providing to support, facilitate, and participate in the publishing activities of the faculty and researchers they serve, whether through the reframing of existing traditional library services or the development of new services.

SPEC Kit 342: Next-Gen Learning Spaces (September 2014)—This SPEC Kit includes examples of learning spaces, instruction spaces, floor plans and maps, marketing for spaces, programs, and instruction, space use policies and procedures, job descriptions and organization charts, and planning and assessment documents.

SPEC Kit 341: Digital Collections Assessment and Outreach (August 2014)—An investigation of what methods ARL member libraries use to maintain the relevancy of their locally curated digital library collections, and to continue to sustain, grow, capture return on investment, and enhance existing resources through outreach and assessment. The survey also explores current practices for integrating digital resources into the research, teaching, and learning environment.

SPEC Kit 340: Open Source Software (July 2014)—This SPEC Kit investigates ARL member libraries' adoption and/or development of open source software for functions such as integrated library systems (ILS), discovery layer, electronic resource management, interlibrary loan, digital asset management, institutional repository, course reserve, streaming media, study room scheduler, digital preservation, publishing, floor maps, data warehouse, and other library-related purposes.

School Libraries

Many states continue to struggle to keep school libraries open and staffed with credentialed librarians. In California during 2012–2013 there were 802 teacher librarians for 6,156,604 students, a drop from the previous year when there were 834 teacher librarians for a student enrollment of 6,149,704. That makes California's 2012–2013 ratio of librarians to students 1:7,677.[19] During the last three years Chicago Public Schools have decreased the number of school librarians from 454 to 254.[20] In Colorado the total number of students rose by 5.2 percent from 2007 to 2011 (from 801,867 to 843,316) while the number of school librarians fell by 9 percent.[21]

From 2005 to 2011, the number of school librarians declined more than other school staff.[22] The total number of school librarians increased by less than 1 percent from school year 2005–2006 to 2006–2007, then steadily dropped each academic year thereafter. The decreases were 0.11 percent in 2007–2008, 1.07 percent in 2008–2009, 2.34 percent in 2009–2010, and 4.27 percent in 2010–2011.

Table 1 / Total Staff and Percentage Changes by Job Function

School Year	Total Staff	% Change	Number of Teachers	% Change	Number of Guidance Staff	% Change	Number of Librarians	% Change
2005–2006	6,122,358		3,136,921		103,268		54,068	
2006–2007	6,163,962	0.68	3,180,396	1.39	103,823	0.54	54,445	0.70
2007–2008	6,215,635	0.84	3,178,142	-0.07	105,519	1.63	54,385	-0.11
2008–2009	6,328,318	1.81	3,221,917	1.38	107,802	2.16	53,802	-1.07
2009–2010	6,355,351	0.43	3,209,637	-0.38	107,564	-0.22	52,541	-2.34
2010–2011	6,195,207	-2.52	3,099,095	-3.44	105,079	-2.31	50,300	-4.27

Credentials of School Librarians

School librarian credentials vary among states. Most states require a school librarian to have a teaching certificate and then coursework or a master's degree in library and information science. A comparison of school library staffing from 2007–2008[23] to 2011–2012[24] reveals that the numbers of school library staff who held classroom teaching certificates or a master's degree in a library-related major were down by 8.9 percent and 4.4 percent, respectively. The percentage of school library staff who held a state library media certificate was up by 17 percent.

Table 2 / Comparing School and Staffing Survey Data for
2007–2008 and 2011–2012

Total Paid Professional Library Staff in the SASS Sample	Percent Who Were State-Certified Classroom Teachers	Percent Who Had a Master's Degree in a Library-Related Major	Percent Who Are State-Certified Library Media Specialists
81,790	71.9	56.2	65.9
88,520	63.0	51.8	82.9
6,730	-8.9	-4.4	17.0

Source: National Center for Education Statistics
Note: Percentages will not add to 100 due to the possibility that staff may hold more than one of the listed credentials.

Notable Research on School Libraries

The peer-reviewed journal *School Library Research* is the successor to *School Library Media Research* and *School Library Media Quarterly Online*. Three new research articles are available in volume 18.[25] The three examine the motivation to seek out information, science-focused collaboration between pre-service school librarians and pre-service elementary teachers, and school library advocacy efforts. The articles can be found on the American Association of School Librarians (AASL) website at www.ala.org/aasl/slr. They are "The Information-Seeking Behavior of Intrinsically Motivated Elementary School Children of a Collectivist Culture" by Sherry Crow; "Preparing Pre-Service School Librarians for Science-Focused Collaboration with Pre-Service Elementary Teachers: The Design and Impact of a Cross-Class Assignment" by Casey Rawson, Janice Anderson, and Sandra Hughes-Hassell; and "Union-Active School Librarians and School Library Advocacy: A Modified Case Study of the British Columbia Teacher-Librarians' Association and the British Columbia Teachers' Federation" by Ann Dutton Ewbank.

Awards and Grants That Honor and Support Excellent Research

The professional library associations offer many awards and grants to recognize and encourage research. The 2014 awards and grants here are listed under the name of the sponsoring association and, in the case of ALA, by the awarding division, in alphabetical order. More-detailed information about the prizes and prizewinners can be found at the association websites.

American Library Association

Carroll Preston Baber Research Grant
Winner: David Loertscher for "The Impact of Co-Teaching on Learning When Classroom Teachers Team with Teacher Librarians: The Testing of an Unobtrusive Measurement Tool."

Jesse H. Shera Award for Excellence in Published Research
Winner: Paul Conway for "Preserving Imperfection: Assessing the Incidence of Digital Imaging Error in HathiTrust" in *Preservation, Digital Technology, and Culture* 42(1), 17–30.

Association for Information Science and Technology

ASIS&T Best Information Science Book Award
Winners: Karine Nahon and Jeff Hemsley, for *Going Viral* (Polity); Robert J. Glushko, ed., for *The Discipline of Organizing* (MIT Press).

John Wiley Best JASIST *Paper*
Winners: Suzane Verberne, Maarten van der Heijden, Max Hinne, Maya Sappelli, Saskia Koldijk, Eduard Hoenkamp, and Wessel Kraaij for "Reliability and Validity of Query Intent Assessments" (Vol. 64, issue 11)

Pratt Severn Best Student Research Paper Award
Winner: Curt Arledge for "Filled-in vs. Outline Icons: The Impact of Icon."

ProQuest Doctoral Dissertation
Winner: Amelia Acker for "Born Networked Records: A History of the Short Message Service Format." University of California, Los Angeles, 2014.

Research in Information Science
Winner: Diane Kelly for "Research in Human-Centered Information Retrieval."

Thomson Reuters Doctoral Dissertation Proposal Scholarship
Winner: Tiffany Chao for "Methods Metadata: Curating Scientific Research Data for Reuse."

Watson Davis Award
Winner: Vicki Gregory, Suffolk University.

Association for Library and Information Science Education (ALISE)

ALISE/Eugene Garfield Doctoral Dissertation Competition
Winner: Youngseek Kim for "Institutional and Informational Influences on Scientists' Data Sharing Behaviors."

ALISE Research Grant Competition
Winner: Laurie Bonnici (University of Alabama) for "Non-Verbal Communication in Information Behavior: Ischemic Stroke and Partial Facial Paralysis."

ALISE/Bohdan S. Wynar Research Paper Competition
Winners: Yi Shen, Johns Hopkins University, and Virgil E. Varvel, University of Illinois at Urbana-Champaign, for "Data Management: Consulting at the Johns Hopkins University."

Library and Information Technology Association/OCLC

Frederick G. Kilgour Award for Research in Library and Information Technology
Winner: Michael Buckland, University of California, Berkeley.

Association of College and Research Libraries (ACRL)

Academic/Research Librarian of the Year Award
Winner: Tim Bucknall.

Ilene F. Rockman Instruction Publication of the Year Award
Winners: Wendy Holliday and Jim Rogers for their article "Talking About Information Literacy: The Mediating Role of Discourse in a College Writing Classroom."

WESS-SEES De Gruyter European Librarianship Study Grant
Winner: Marta Mestrovic Deyrup for her project "C'era una Volta: A Guide to Print Materials Published by and About the Italian Minority Communities of Dalmatia and Istria in the 20th and 21st Centuries."

Medical Library Association

Janet Doe Lectureship
Winner: Margaret Moylan Bandy for "Pivoting: Leveraging Opportunities in a Turbulent Health Care Environment."

Donald A. B. Lindberg Research Fellowship
Winner: Deborah H. Charbonneau for "NIH Public Access and Data Sharing Policies: A Mixed-Methods Study."

Notes

1. Institute of Museum and Library Services. IMLS 2012 Public Library Survey Results Announced. Retrieved February 20, 2015, from http://www.imls.gov/imls_2012_public_library_survey_results_announced.aspx.

2. Ibid.

3. Peet, L. (2015). "Paying for People: Budgets and Funding." *Library Journal.* Retrieved from http://lj.libraryjournal.com/2015/02/budgets-funding/paying-for-people-budgets-funding/#_.

4. Grants to State Library Administrative Agencies. Institute of Museum and Library Services. Retrieved from http://www.imls.gov/programs.

5. Rose, N. (2015). Survey of Chief Officers of State Library Agencies (COSLA). Available from the American Library Association. Office for Research and Statistics.

6. Rosa, K. "An Overview of How States Performed in the November Ballots." *American Libraries.* Retrieved from http://www.americanlibrariesmagazine.org/article/referenda-roundup-2014.

7. Digital Inclusion Survey Results and Reports. (2014). Retrieved from http://digitalinclusion.umd.edu/content/reports.

8. National Survey of Student Engagement, 2014 Topical Module: Experiences with Information Literacy. Available at http://nsse.iub.edu/2014_institutional_report/pdf/Modules/NSSE1420Module20Summary-Experiences20with20Information20Literacy.pdf.

9. University of Houston Student Survey. (2014). Retrieved from http://www.uhd.edu/library/about/Student_Survey_2013.pdf.

10. 2013 Academic Library Trends and Statistics, ACRL, 2014.

11. Stewart, Christopher. *Building with Purpose: A Quantitative Overview and Analysis of New U.S. Academic Library Construction, 2000–2014.* ACRL, 2015.

12. 2013 Academic Library Trends and Statistics. ACRL, 2014.

13. Stephanie L. Maatta, "Placements & Salaries 2014: Public, Academic and Special Libraries," *Library Journal,* October 15, 2014. Available at http://lj.libraryjournal.com/2014/10/placements-and-salaries/2014-survey/public-academic-and-special-libraries.

14. John H. Pryor, et al. The American Freshman: National Norms Fall 2014. (2015) Los Angeles, California: Higher Education Research Institute, UCLA. Available at: http://heri.ucla.edu/monographs/TheAmericanFreshman2014.pdf.

15. 2013 Academic Library Trends and Statistics, ACRL, 2014.

16. "Payday: LJ Salary Survey 2014, Data Tables." *Library Journal,* July 3, 2014. Available at http://lj.libraryjournal.com/2014/07/careers/payday-lj-salary-survey-2014-data-tables/#table4.

17. "Top Trends in Academic Libraries." *College & Research Library News.* (June 2014). Retrieved from http://crln.acrl.org/content/75/6/294.full.

18. SPEC Kits can be found on the Association of Research Libraries Website at http://publications.arl.org/SPEC_Kits.

19. "Statistics About California School Libraries." Retrieved from http://www.cde.ca.gov/ci/cr/lb/schoollibrstats08.asp.

20. "Librarians Are a Luxury Chicago Public Schools Can't Afford." (2014). Retrieved from http://www.npr.org/blogs/ed/2014/09/01/344905087/librarians-are-a-luxury-chicago-public-schools-cant-afford.

21. Fast Facts. Colorado Library Research Services. (2012). Retrieved from http://www.lrs.org/documents/fastfacts/308_School_Librarian_Numbers_2004_2011.pdf.

22. Schools and Staffing Survey results are found in the following documents
NCES 2013-312 *Characteristics of Public and Private Elementary and Secondary Schools in the United States: Results from the 2011–12 Schools and Staffing Survey.* First Look.
NCES 2013-314 *Characteristics of Public and Private Elementary and Secondary School Teachers in the United States: Results from the 2011–12 Schools and Staffing Survey.* First Look.
NCES 2012-327 *Public Elementary and Secondary School Student Enrollment and Staff Counts from the Common Core of Data: School Year 2010–11.*
NCES 2011-347 *Public Elementary and Secondary School Student Enrollment and Staff Counts from the Common Core of Data: School Year 2009–10.*
NCES 2010-347 *Public Elementary and Secondary School Student Enrollment and Staff from the Common Core of Data: School Year 2008–09.*
NCES 2010-309 *Public Elementary and Secondary School Student Enrollment and Staff from the Common Core of Data: School Year 2007–08.*
NCES 2009-305 *Public Elementary and Secondary School Student Enrollment and Staff from the Common Core of Data: School Year 2006–07.*
NCES 2007-352 *Public Elementary and Secondary School Student Enrollment, High School Completions, and Staff from the Common Core of Data: School Year 2005–06.*

23. *Characteristics of Public and Bureau of Indian Education Elementary and Secondary School Library Media Centers in the United States: Results from the 2007–08 Schools and Staffing Survey.* First Look. Retrieved from http://nces.ed.gov/pubs2009/2009322.pdf#page=16&zoom=150,13,0.

24. *Characteristics of Public Elementary and Secondary School Library Media Centers in the United States: Results from the 2011–12 Schools and Staffing Survey.* First Look. Retrieved from http://nces.ed.gov/pubs2013/2013315.pdf.

25. *School Library Research (SLR)* Vol. 18. (2015) Retrieved from http://www.ala.org/aasl/slr/vol18.

Public Library Data at Home and Abroad:
An Exploration of Data from Four Countries

Robert E. Molyneux

Stephen Abram

Garry Cannon

This study reports the results of an examination of public library data from four countries (Australia, three provinces in Canada, New Zealand, and the United States).

We focus on two categories of these data collection efforts. One is the core of data elements common to most of them. As will be seen, many of the reported data from these different series seem to be comparable. This category of data suggests that librarians in these four countries have common functions and concerns and seek to learn more about their libraries by similar kinds of measures.

The second category of these efforts is the set of data that are not in all of these collection efforts. We briefly survey these kinds of variables, but they are worthy of a closer look.

Of these four countries, the United States has the largest population served and the most public libraries. It also has the most mature data collection effort. It is national, has been published for a number of years, and is well documented. The other three countries, though, have serious data collection efforts and in many cases have surveyed new measures of public library activity that it might benefit the United States—as well as the other data collection efforts—to examine. Data in this category are diverse and largely unique. They report on different aspects of digital data that suggest promising directions for research and also other possibilities that might allow better understanding of libraries.

Overview

Why do libraries collect data? There are a number of reasons, of course. Today's decision-makers often require data to be used in allocating budgets for civic projects, and librarians in those situations will be involved in working with data in budget presentations. In many cases, the data about libraries are collected at a regional government level or, in the case of colleges and universities, both governments and associations may compile library data. With these latter kinds of collection efforts, the aim may be broader than budgets for a few libraries, extending to questions about all libraries in an area. When governments participate, the collection of data may well involve information policy—an important factor for any government whose citizens are competing in a world market.

However, library data were published before the notion arose of using data to support decisions or in information policy planning. That fact means they fulfill other purposes. In his 1835 *Statistical Essay on the Libraries of Vienna and the World,*[1] Adriano Balbi was motivated by pride in Vienna and believed that its libraries were among the best in the world. He collected such data as he could find and ranked the libraries by size of volumes reportedly held in an attempt to make his case. His motivation, in part, was bragging rights, but in the end his discussion of problems with the library data he dealt with still offers useful observations 180 years later.

The Gerould Statistics[2] is a compilation of a series of U.S. academic library data started by James Thayer Gerould with the 1907–1908 compilation of five variables from 14 university libraries. The series expanded over the years and was published annually through the 1962–1963 academic year when the series was continued by the Association of Research Libraries (ARL). The data were published with the institutions reporting listed in alphabetical order, but from the earliest years a number of the originals show handwritten rankings by number of volumes reportedly held. Today ARL continues publishing ranks of libraries by different variables, but in order by the magnitude of that variable. These ranks reappear in other publications, widening their influence. In fact, a faculty member or university administrator may not know much about the details of running the library, but he or she may well be aware if the library has dropped from 20th to 30th in that list. Library directors can then point out when budgets are discussed that the library is falling behind its peer institutions. Something similar occurs with public libraries as these kinds of ratings are also used in their budget discussions. Ranking of libraries by quantitative measures is an old exercise.

There are also other uses of library data compilations. Ontario and New Zealand (see "Sources of Data" below) in their published data list the integrated library system used by their public libraries, and one can look for nearby libraries that have a given system to see how it works, either for advice or as part of research on changing a library's system. These data compilations, then, can be a directory to locate similar libraries in a given matter of interest.

Examining these data discloses a rich vein of information about these libraries. We only scratch the surface in this report.

Common Data Elements

Table 1 shows a sample of apparently common data from libraries in Australia, three provinces in Canada (British Columbia, Ontario, and Manitoba), New Zealand, and the United States. There are others, but this sample will provide an introduction. We use data collected and published nominally for 2012. The matter of dates is discussed with information on the sources used here.

This table presents reported public library data for 2012 in order by the four countries and the regions where reported. Given that we have states, territories, and provinces, we will use the generic "regions" when referring to more than one.

The first two rows have national summary data from Australia and the United States in boldface. Both nations also publish data from their various regions and those regional data are included in the body of the table. In those two cases, then, we have both regional and national summary data.

Let us look briefly in those first two rows at the U.S. summary figure for population served. We see that U.S. public libraries serve 303 million people. The total population served for all these libraries is given at the bottom of the

(text continues on page 355)

Table 1 / Sample of Common Public Library Data Elements

Country	State/Province/Territory	Population Served	Cardholders/ Members	Total Circulation	In-Person Visits	Reference Transactions	Total Staff	Internet Terminals Used by Public	Total Operating Expenditures $
AUS	**Australia**	**22,680,500**	**9,999,492***	**180,794,120**	**110,255,850***	**12,389,703**	**7,567**	**9,974**	**1,010,000,000***
US	**United States**	**303,113,633**	**170,770,302**	**2,422,538,191**	**1,498,894,429**	**284,543,995**	**136,982**	**271,687**	**10,743,358,638**
AUS	Australia Capital Territory	374,700	229,271	3,090,717	1,963,294	29,198	99	76	13,470,000
AUS	New South Wales	7,290,300	3,188,109	47,720,855	35,002,039	5,343,777	2,357	3,027	332,140,000
AUS	Northern Territory	234,800	79,249	1,014,087	1,020,086	104,321	99	89	10,560,000
AUS	Queensland	4,560,100	2,000,854	39,629,608	20,439,282	2,001,073	1,503	2,226	201,060,000
AUS	South Australia	1,654,800	899,555	16,850,921	11,058,032	588,761	737	945	114,350,000
AUS	Tasmania	512,000	138,292	4,755,821	3,075,654	64,316	N/A	518	22,760,000
AUS	Victoria	5,623,500	2,538,072	51,336,800	27,627,855	2,618,740	1,687	2,218	208,860,000
AUS	Western Australia	2,430,300	995,794	16,395,311	10,069,578	1,639,517	1,086	875	107,200,000
CAN	British Columbia	4,525,221	2,096,657	57,015,567	30,957,826	3,721,323	2,252	3,303	221,612,493
CAN	Manitoba	1,066,810	511,436	8,249,250	4,244,084	—	454	836	—
CAN	Ontario	13,151,825	4,913,281	133,957,766	72,529,650	7,475,450	6,593	—	641,086,137
NZ	**New Zealand**	**4,414,090**	**2,063,093**	**53,256,697**	**37,349,155**	**2,491,568**	**2,081**	**—**	**266,047,750**
US	Alabama	4,779,736	2,519,236	20,997,336	17,010,830	4,375,988	1,795	5,276	94,867,541
US	Alaska	648,733	443,576	4,604,130	3,358,432	446,946	306	779	32,872,289
US	Arizona	6,482,505	3,422,112	50,655,828	28,121,005	4,365,109	2,189	5,296	175,445,306
US	Arkansas	2,643,928	1,635,503	14,258,573	10,816,729	2,043,178	950	2,246	67,948,315
US	California	37,678,127	21,966,469	231,683,802	163,570,057	23,340,954	11,176	20,340	1,181,515,874
US	Colorado	5,059,050	3,417,947	66,065,031	32,774,319	4,329,429	3,007	5,874	243,979,258
US	Connecticut	3,574,097	1,779,083	34,086,955	24,404,598	3,890,359	2,347	4,353	197,902,778
US	Delaware	897,934	417,768	6,283,400	4,561,619	463,903	322	576	24,741,891
US	District of Columbia	632,323	321,544	3,363,313	2,546,796	919,789	418	900	36,972,424

US	Florida	13,031,381	10,208,157	126,432,886	82,460,245	30,948,863	6,179	15,735	501,081,343
US	Georgia	13,459,546	4,564,784	43,529,545	33,351,403	9,661,011	2,767	7,516	180,438,626
US	Hawaii	1,374,810	981,737	6,924,263	5,347,164	689,909	555	453	31,089,929
US	Idaho	1,385,848	784,014	15,114,743	9,441,138	1,255,529	747	1,651	43,465,328
US	Illinois	11,702,600	4,978,251	120,491,025	77,447,598	13,875,236	8,733	13,858	701,939,170
US	Indiana	6,100,143	3,791,353	77,578,562	38,663,561	5,208,670	4,451	8,383	297,084,666
US	Iowa	2,992,002	2,047,632	29,126,922	19,518,720	1,880,628	1,685	4,486	110,895,138
US	Kansas	2,467,707	1,701,112	26,374,729	14,731,174	2,034,423	1,719	3,649	106,486,991
US	Kentucky	4,369,356	2,472,391	29,708,255	19,870,274	3,795,367	2,190	4,497	132,267,144
US	Louisiana	4,601,893	2,610,550	20,664,469	16,829,969	3,971,830	2,565	5,054	182,878,982
US	Maine	1,202,073	763,560	9,638,661	7,129,155	667,827	668	1,893	41,643,480
US	Maryland	5,699,478	3,290,865	57,212,709	29,209,021	8,320,716	3,305	4,531	251,357,006
US	Massachusetts	6,584,353	3,426,313	64,827,848	42,650,826	5,466,267	3,614	6,070	272,862,580
US	Michigan	9,832,470	5,232,500	86,964,120	55,525,753	9,565,212	4,827	12,081	374,672,622
US	Minnesota	5,332,246	4,260,035	56,232,412	26,211,333	3,430,178	2,167	5,675	196,545,167
US	Mississippi	2,984,890	1,449,099	8,309,506	9,669,062	1,508,207	1,196	2,696	47,220,751
US	Missouri	5,466,502	3,365,430	54,476,559	30,385,105	4,052,115	3,112	4,932	203,510,000
US	Montana	988,533	464,262	7,535,351	4,678,960	447,928	378	1,248	22,656,477
US	Nebraska	1,453,012	1,038,112	13,638,104	8,763,610	886,035	813	2,801	50,145,582
US	Nevada	2,721,794	1,325,468	20,096,391	11,127,581	1,788,041	669	1,654	78,686,875
US	New Hampshire	1,002,752	811,850	11,406,956	7,580,567	819,161	798	1,425	55,144,343
US	New Jersey	8,708,750	4,746,885	61,606,942	48,061,530	8,262,130	4,801	7,867	450,848,028
US	New Mexico	1,654,445	1,042,244	9,466,902	7,506,392	1,047,435	659	1,920	45,187,346
US	New York	-9,378,102	9,940,655	158,242,286	115,247,666	30,076,039	11,944	17,856	1,122,679,060
US	North Carolina	9,669,244	5,573,568	55,515,553	40,644,178	10,805,807	2,848	7,246	192,200,178
US	North Dakota	623,296	282,487	4,193,957	2,385,110	379,259	230	663	15,017,643
US	Ohio	11,541,952	9,089,977	189,563,218	87,376,219	20,378,409	8,932	11,980	659,213,729
US	Oklahoma	3,076,121	1,964,200	21,985,301	14,378,840	2,943,356	1,391	2,994	109,083,048
US	Oregon	3,695,088	2,029,303	63,699,158	23,255,307	2,705,466	1,804	3,035	183,409,995

Table 1 / Sample of Common Public Library Data Elements *(cont.)*

Country	State/Province/Territory	Population Served	Cardholders/ Members	Total Circulation	In-Person Visits	Reference Transactions	Total Staff	Internet Terminals Used by Public	Total Operating Expenditures $
US	Pennsylvania	12,411,451	5,337,951	69,133,176	46,879,095	7,775,636	4,476	7,885	305,934,152
US	Rhode Island	1,051,302	482,127	7,491,949	6,092,066	742,644	576	1,426	44,383,579
US	South Carolina	4,652,360	2,595,764	25,854,042	18,301,086	3,480,229	1,872	3,823	114,701,234
US	South Dakota	752,824	414,648	6,684,939	3,998,307	474,152	361	973	22,488,642
US	Tennessee	6,231,419	3,353,178	26,245,287	20,895,473	3,512,573	1,772	4,896	104,308,919
US	Texas	23,449,049	12,627,631	129,657,778	75,186,773	15,003,671	6,686	19,150	435,706,700
US	Utah	2,814,871	1,780,901	38,084,065	19,142,011	3,414,192	1,233	1,974	91,089,116
US	Vermont	611,040	333,570	4,698,790	3,926,690	528,906	337	1,082	22,364,660
US	Virginia	7,865,333	4,685,425	76,132,262	39,646,073	7,355,277	3,686	5,699	258,782,230
US	Washington	6,697,131	4,155,782	81,146,191	43,095,638	5,339,960	3,598	6,906	348,649,926
US	West Virginia	1,808,350	905,125	6,504,905	5,830,894	668,865	638	1,405	33,987,699
US	Wisconsin	5,703,525	3,538,530	63,366,031	35,648,456	4,668,129	3,022	6,164	214,547,500
US	Wyoming	568,158	399,638	4,983,075	3,640,021	533,052	468	815	30,457,378
	Total	348,952,079	190,423,965	2,855,811,591	1,754,230,964	310,622,039	155,930	285,800	**

Totals exclude double counting from Australia and the United States. Dollar amounts are in local currencies.

*In these cases, the totals reported by National and State Libraries Australasia do not agree with the sum of the states' and territories' reported data.

**Given the different values of the four currencies, a total would have no meaning.

(continued from page 351)

table and it is 349 million. U.S. libraries, then, serve more than the other libraries combined. There are 51 U.S. reporting regions—50 states plus the District of Columbia. There are 12 reporting regions for the non-U.S. libraries. We can expect that there will be a U.S. bias reflected in the data tables.

Among the 12 reporting regions is New Zealand, the libraries of which serve a bit more than 4 million. New Zealand's figures are also in bold.

The totals at the bottom exclude Australian and U.S. totals, hence avoiding double counting. In addition to the 349 million people served by these libraries, almost 2.9 billion items were circulated from them in one year.

Before looking at these data analytically, there are a few points to note. One is a characteristic of all data: missing items. Manitoba's raw reports have very sparse data for financial figures and certainly not enough for the totals to indicate anything reasonable about the province's libraries. The figures are available for a few libraries, but not for all.

The second point to note regards the central question of comparability. Are the reported data for items from these four countries libraries measuring the same thing? Is "population served"—the term in the United States—the same as Ontario's "Population (Resident)?" Ontario has other kinds of population figures because a number of its municipalities contract with others for library service. Whether "Population (Contracting)" figures should be included as a part of the served population to be comparable with the U.S. figures is impossible to say given the lack of documentation. The numbers of the contracting population are small and for now they are not included.

New Zealand reports "Stats NZ 2012 Estimated Population Projections." Apparently, there is an agency there that provides the population projection figures.

In the United States, the 51 regions rely on a number of means of estimating this number and, worse, there are two kinds of "Population Served"—"Population Served" and "Unduplicated Population Served."

What, the patient reader asks, is an "unduplicated" person? As it happens, the 50 states and the District of Columbia have different ways of determining what a served population is. In addition, who is "served" by a library varies. In some states, all people are eligible for library service, but in others this is not the case. You might move in to a new house and visit "your" library the first time and find you are not in the area that "your" library serves. Worse, you may live in an area that no library "serves." Moreover, there are states where one might be in an area served by more than one library. How can libraries in states with these various methods of defining the served population be compared when the most common means of comparison of public libraries is to use the population served? That is, for example, the total number of circulations divided by the number of people in the served population? Tables 2 and 3 look at circulations per capita in more detail; but with states defining "population served" differently, per capitas will not be comparable.

For our purposes, it will be sufficient to note that a number of people gave this matter thought and came up with the notion of the "Unduplicated Population," which is created by a mathematical operation on the raw figures. We use this number here for the U.S. population served for each state as has long been the custom with these data.

What we have done, then, is defer to the compilers closest to the libraries and their data. We found three cases of apparent mathematical errors in the Australian data and wrote to the agency that published them, but they did not respond. We use the reported number even though we are skeptical and, in these cases, the number we believe to be correct would show their libraries in a better light, at least in terms of the order in which their libraries would fall in these tables.

There are more data points from what appear to be common data elements, but these will suffice as a sample. The existence of these common elements suggests that public libraries in these countries not only have common tasks, but that the librarians in charge are interested in measuring a central set of aspects of these libraries and the people who use them.

Comparability

To examine comparability we adopt a means of ranking public libraries by regions from the survey of U.S. public libraries currently compiled and published by the Institute of Museum and Library Services (IMLS.) This method has been used for years and consists of ranks of states by a set of variables converted to per capita measures. These tables are among the most popular output of this data collection effort.

There is no magic test to tell us when these data are measuring the same thing exactly the same way. What we rely on is our experience with libraries and data to make observations. Library data are usually unaudited and are created by a variety of methods and by people with varying skills and time to devote to reporting data. The data used here are compiled and vetted by government agencies that likely employ analysts to examine the raw data and question odd reported values.

Table 2 / U.S. State Ranks by Circulations per Capita, FY 2012*

Rank	State	Circulations per Capita	Population Served	Total Annual Circulations
1	Oregon	17.24	3,695,088	63,699,158
2	Ohio	16.42	11,541,952	189,563,218
3	Utah	13.53	2,814,871	38,084,065
4	Colorado	13.06	5,059,050	66,065,031
5	Indiana	12.72	6,100,143	77,578,562
6	Washington	12.12	6,697,131	81,146,191
7	New Hampshire	11.38	1,002,752	11,406,956
8	Wisconsin	11.11	5,703,525	63,366,031
9	Idaho	10.91	1,385,848	15,114,743
10	Kansas	10.69	2,467,707	26,374,729
11	Minnesota	10.55	5,332,246	56,232,412
12	Illinois	10.30	11,702,600	120,491,025
13	Maryland	10.04	5,699,478	57,212,709
14	Missouri	9.97	5,466,502	54,476,559
15	Massachusetts	9.85	6,584,353	64,827,848

16	Iowa	9.73	2,992,002	29,126,922
17	Virginia	9.68	7,865,333	76,132,262
18	Connecticut	9.54	3,574,097	34,086,955
19	Nebraska	9.39	1,453,012	13,638,104
20	South Dakota	8.88	752,824	6,684,939
21	Michigan	8.84	9,832,470	86,964,120
22	Wyoming	8.77	568,158	4,983,075
23	New York	8.17	19,378,102	158,242,286
24	Maine	8.02	1,202,073	9,638,661
25	Arizona	7.81	6,482,505	50,655,828
26	Vermont	7.69	611,040	4,698,790
27	Montana	7.62	988,533	7,535,351
28	Nevada	7.38	2,721,794	20,096,391
29	Oklahoma	7.15	3,076,121	21,985,301
30	Rhode Island	7.13	1,051,302	7,491,949
31	Alaska	7.10	648,733	4,604,130
32	New Jersey	7.07	8,708,750	61,606,942
33	Delaware	7.00	897,934	6,283,400
34	Kentucky	6.80	4,369,356	29,708,255
35	North Dakota	6.73	623,296	4,193,957
36	Florida	6.64	19,031,381	126,432,886
37	California	6.15	37,678,127	231,683,802
38	North Carolina	5.74	9,669,244	55,515,553
39	New Mexico	5.72	1,654,445	9,466,902
40	Pennsylvania	5.57	12,411,451	69,133,176
41	South Carolina	5.56	4,652,360	25,854,042
42	Texas	5.53	23,449,049	129,657,778
43	Arkansas	5.39	2,643,928	14,258,573
44	District of Columbia	5.32	632,323	3,363,313
45	Hawaii	5.04	1,374,810	6,924,263
46	Louisiana	4.49	4,601,893	20,664,469
47	Alabama	4.39	4,779,736	20,997,336
48	Tennessee	4.21	6,231,419	26,245,287
49	Georgia	4.16	10,459,546	43,529,545
50	West Virginia	3.60	1,808,350	6,504,905
51	Mississippi	2.78	2,984,890	8,309,506
	United States	8.00	303,113,633	2,422,538,191
	Median==>	7.70		

*Includes the District of Columbia

Table 2 shows an example of how this calculation is presented for the libraries in the 50 states and the District of Columbia. The states are in order by the descending circulations per capita. The columns Population Served and Total Annual Circulations are the variables used to calculate the circulations per capita and are included for reference.

There are two aspects of this table that bear further scrutiny. The first is the use of per capitas as discussed above, that is, number of circulations per member of the population served by a library rather than the raw number of circulations. Looking at Table 1, we can see that libraries in Oregon with 3.7 million population served have a smaller number of circulations than Ohio with its 11.5 million population served, but Oregon's libraries have a higher circulation for each in the population served.

In academic data, the general practice is to put the institutions in order by the raw numbers, while in public library data institutions are often placed in order by the variable analyzed divided by the number in the population served. The IMLS set has tables ranking states by more than 20 such per capita measures, and in assembling data for this study, it was found that similar per capitas are calculated commonly in the data series examined here. Given the widely varying sizes of the collections of libraries from the regions, using per capitas allows us to get a picture not of the raw size of the libraries but how they are used by the population served.

The second aspect of this table to note is the range of these numbers. Looking at the per capita figures first, Table 2 shows that Oregon has a statewide average of more than 17 annual circulations for each person in the population served while Mississippi has less than 3. From these data, one can be confident that Oregon residents are heavier users of their libraries than are Mississippi residents, but that both have libraries. The Southeastern states show lower circulations per capita than those in the upper Midwest and West. These numbers and ranks, generally, persist over time and are functions of such factors as history, demographics, and culture. However, we see through these data that public libraries are used differently depending on such factors. The range of numbers occurs with the raw numbers too. The largest state in terms of population is California with almost 38 million, and the smallest is Wyoming with fewer than 600,000. This type of distribution of numbers is called "skewed,"[3] which is another characteristic of library data. Variation in these numbers generated by libraries, then, is expected. The skewness of public library data makes comparisons difficult. How can one compare very large libraries with very small libraries? Per capitas such as circulations per capita—that is, per individual in the population—are often used in informal and in published comparisons.

Now, we move on to Table 3 and analysis of these data. What might they tell us about public libraries in these three other countries and what might we glean about public libraries in general?

Table 3 is an expansion of Table 2 with matching data from the libraries outside the United States. We see all regions in our dataset in order by circulations per capita, so we have added them to the data presented in Table 2. In addition to those regions, we include national summary data from Australia and the United States in order. A quick glance at the table shows the circulation per capita data from the various regions reporting fall within the range we saw in Table 2, but with the new data we see that British Columbia is 6th in the table and the U.S. state it is contiguous to is 7th. The first ranked U.S. state, Oregon, is contiguous to Washington and one might speculate that there are commonalities between the libraries and residents of these two states and British Columbia.

Mississippi still has the lowest circulations per capita and Australia's Northern Territory, at 4.3, has the lowest figure for the additions.

Given New Zealand's relative size, its summary data are included here with those of the various other regions. Australia's summary data are almost tied with

Table 3 / Ranks by Circulations per Capita for Australia, Canada, New Zealand, and the United States

Rank	Country	State/Province/ Territory	Circulations per Capita	Population Served	Total Annual Circulations
1	US	Oregon	17.24	3,695,088	63,699,158
2	US	Ohio	16.42	11,541,952	189,563,218
3	US	Utah	13.53	2,814,871	38,084,065
4	US	Colorado	13.06	5,059,050	66,065,031
5	US	Indiana	12.72	6,100,143	77,578,562
6	CAN	British Columbia	12.60	4,525,221	57,015,567
7	US	Washington	12.12	6,697,131	81,146,191
8	**NZ**	**New Zealand**	**12.07**	**4,414,090**	**53,256,697**
9	US	New Hampshire	11.38	1,002,752	11,406,956
10	US	Wisconsin	11.11	5,703,525	63,366,031
11	US	Idaho	10.91	1,385,848	15,114,743
12	US	Kansas	10.69	2,467,707	26,374,729
13	US	Minnesota	10.55	5,332,246	56,232,412
14	US	Illinois	10.30	11,702,600	120,491,025
15	AUS	South Australia	10.20	1,654,800	16,850,921
16	CAN	Ontario	10.19	13,151,825	133,957,766
17	US	Maryland	10.04	5,699,478	57,212,709
18	US	Missouri	9.97	5,466,502	54,476,559
19	US	Massachusetts	9.85	6,584,353	64,827,848
20	US	Iowa	9.73	2,992,002	29,126,922
21	US	Virginia	9.68	7,865,333	76,132,262
22	US	Connecticut	9.54	3,574,097	34,086,955
23	US	Nebraska	9.39	1,453,012	13,638,104
24	AUS	Tasmania	9.30	512,000	4,755,821
25	AUS	Victoria	9.10	5,623,500	51,336,800
26	US	South Dakota	8.88	752,824	6,684,939
27	US	Michigan	8.84	9,832,470	86,964,120
28	US	Wyoming	8.77	568,158	4,983,075
29	AUS	Queensland	8.70	4,560,100	39,629,608
30	AUS	Australia Capital Territory	8.20	374,700	3,090,717
31	US	New York	8.17	19,378,102	158,242,286
32	US	Maine	8.02	1,202,073	9,638,661
33	**AUS**	**Australia**	**8.00**	**22,680,500**	**180,794,120**
34	**US**	**United States**	**7.99**	**303,113,633**	**2,422,538,191**
35	US	Arizona	7.01	6,182,505	50,655,828
36	CAN	Manitoba	7.73	1,066,810	8,249,250
37	US	Vermont	7.69	611,040	4,698,790
38	US	Montana	7.62	988,533	7,535,351
39	US	Nevada	7.38	2,721,794	20,096,391
40	US	Oklahoma	7.15	3,076,121	21,985,301
41	US	Rhode Island	7.13	1,051,302	7,491,949
42	US	Alaska	7.10	648,733	4,604,130
43	US	New Jersey	7.07	8,708,750	61,606,942
44	US	Delaware	7.00	897,934	6,283,400
45	US	Kentucky	6.80	4,369,356	29,708,255
46	US	North Dakota	6.73	623,296	4,193,957

Table 3 / Ranks by Circulations per Capita for Australia, Canada,
New Zealand, and the United States (cont.)

Rank	Country	State/Province/ Territory	Circulations per Capita	Population Served	Total Annual Circulations
47	AUS	Western Australia	6.70	2,430,300	16,395,311
48	US	Florida	6.64	19,031,381	126,432,886
49	AUS	New South Wales	6.50	7,290,300	47,720,855
50	US	California	6.15	37,678,127	231,683,802
51	US	North Carolina	5.74	9,669,244	55,515,553
52	US	New Mexico	5.72	1,654,445	9,466,902
53	US	Pennsylvania	5.57	12,411,451	69,133,176
54	US	South Carolina	5.56	4,652,360	25,854,042
55	US	Texas	5.53	23,449,049	129,657,778
56	US	Arkansas	5.39	2,643,928	14,258,573
57	US	District of Columbia	5.32	632,323	3,363,313
58	US	Hawaii	5.04	1,374,810	6,924,263
59	US	Louisiana	4.49	4,601,893	20,664,469
60	US	Alabama	4.39	4,779,736	20,997,336
61	AUS	Northern Territory	4.30	234,800	1,014,087
62	US	Tennessee	4.21	6,231,419	26,245,287
63	US	Georgia	4.16	10,459,546	43,529,545
64	US	West Virginia	3.60	1,808,350	6,504,905
65	US	Mississippi	2.78	2,984,890	8,309,506
		Totals ==>		348,952,079	2,855,811,591
		Median ==>	8.00		

the summary U.S. data at 8 circulations per capita. The median, or central figure, for all values for circulations per capita for all regions is also 8.

The largest Canadian province in terms of population, Ontario, is tied with South Australia with 10.2 circulations per capita while the largest Australian state, New South Wales, reports 6.5 circulations per capita for 2012.

It appears from Table 3 that we can combine data from these various sources and that these data show similarities in libraries in these various regions. In the data world, there are always limits though. Table 4 has another table of ranks by percentage of population served who are "registered borrowers," to use the U.S. terminology. In Australia there are "registered library users." All of these datasets recognize that there is a group that are in the population served and a second group within that population of individuals who have library cards or are active users. In Manitoba and New Zealand, they are reported as "members." Ontario and British Columbia have "active cardholders."

People who do not have library cards benefit from having libraries nearby even if they never "use" them. This case is clear to anyone who understands what libraries do. Sadly, although costs are usually relatively easy to measure, benefits are rather harder. We do not know how to measure the benefits to those who do not join and get library cards. What we can do is measure actual users.

Table 4 presents the regions in order by the results of a calculation: what percentage of the "Population Served" is a "member" or "cardholder?" The U.S. state

Table 4 / Percentage of Population Served Who Are Cardholders/Members

	Country	State/Province/ Territory	% of Population Card-holders/ Members	Cardholders/ Members	Population Served	Circulations per Cardholder/ Member	Circulations per Capita
1	US	New Hampshire	81.0	811,850	1,002,752	14.05	11.38
2	US	Minnesota	79.9	4,260,035	5,332,246	13.20	10.55
3	US	Ohio	78.8	9,089,977	11,541,952	20.85	16.42
4	US	Nebraska	71.4	1,038,112	1,453,012	13.14	9.39
5	US	Hawaii	71.4	981,737	1,374,810	7.05	5.04
6	US	Wyoming	70.3	399,638	568,158	12.47	8.77
7	US	Kansas	68.9	1,701,112	2,467,707	15.50	10.69
8	US	Iowa	68.4	2,047,632	2,992,002	14.22	9.73
9	US	Alaska	68.4	443,576	648,733	10.38	7.10
10	US	Colorado	67.6	3,417,947	5,059,050	19.33	13.06
11	US	Oklahoma	63.9	1,964,200	3,076,121	11.19	7.15
12	US	Maine	63.5	763,560	1,202,073	12.62	8.02
13	US	Utah	63.3	1,780,901	2,814,871	21.38	13.53
14	US	New Mexico	63.0	1,042,244	1,654,445	9.08	5.72
15	US	Indiana	62.2	3,791,353	6,100,143	20.46	12.72
16	US	Washington	62.1	4,155,782	6,697,131	19.53	12.12
17	US	Wisconsin	62.0	3,538,530	5,703,525	17.91	11.11
18	US	Arkansas	61.9	1,635,503	2,643,928	8.72	5.39
19	US	Missouri	61.6	3,365,430	5,466,502	16.19	9.97
20	AUS	Australia Capital Territory	61.0	229,271	374,700	13.48	8.20
21	US	Virginia	59.6	4,685,425	7,865,333	16.25	9.68
22	US	California	58.3	21,966,469	37,678,127	10.55	6.15
23	US	Maryland	57.7	3,290,865	5,699,478	17.39	10.04
24	US	North Carolina	57.6	5,573,568	9,669,244	9.96	5.74
25	US	Louisiana	56.7	2,610,550	4,601,893	7.92	4.49
26	US	Kentucky	56.6	2,472,391	4,369,356	12.02	6.80
27	US	Idaho	56.6	784,014	1,385,848	19.28	10.91
28	**US**	**United States**	**56.3**	**170,770,302**	**303,113,633**	**14.19**	**7.99**
29	US	South Carolina	55.8	2,595,764	4,652,360	9.96	5.56
30	US	South Dakota	55.1	414,648	752,824	16.12	8.88
31	US	Oregon	54.9	2,029,303	3,695,088	31.39	17.24
32	US	Vermont	54.6	333,570	611,040	14.09	7.69
33	US	New Jersey	54.5	4,746,885	8,708,750	12.98	7.07
34	US	Texas	53.9	12,627,631	23,449,049	10.27	5.53
35	US	Tennessee	53.8	3,353,178	6,231,419	7.83	4.21
36	US	Florida	53.6	10,208,157	19,031,381	12.39	6.64
37	US	Michigan	53.2	5,232,500	9,832,470	16.62	8.84
38	US	Arizona	52.8	3,422,112	6,482,505	14.80	7.81
39	US	Alabama	52.7	2,519,236	4,779,736	8.33	4.39
40	US	Massachusetts	52.0	3,426,313	6,584,353	18.92	9.85
41	US	New York	51.3	9,940,655	19,378,102	15.92	8.17
42	US	District of Columbia	50.9	321,544	632,323	10.46	5.32
43	US	West Virginia	50.1	905,125	1,808,350	7.19	3.60

Table 4 / Percentage of Population Served Who Are Cardholders/Members *(cont.)*

	Country	State/Province/ Territory	% of Population Card- holders/ Members	Cardholders/ Members	Population Served	Circulations per Cardholder/ Member	Circulations per Capita
44	AUS	South Australia	50.0	899,555	1,654,800	18.73	10.20
45	US	Connecticut	49.8	1,779,083	3,574,097	19.16	9.54
46	US	Nevada	48.7	1,325,468	2,721,794	15.16	7.38
47	US	Mississippi	48.5	1,449,099	2,984,890	5.73	2.78
48	CAN	Manitoba	47.9	511,436	1,066,810	16.13	7.73
49	US	Montana	47.0	464,262	988,533	16.23	7.62
50	**NZ**	**New Zealand**	**46.7**	**2,063,093**	**4,414,090**	**25.81**	**12.07**
51	US	Delaware	46.5	417,768	897,934	15.04	7.00
52	CAN	British Columbia	46.3	2,096,657	4,525,221	27.19	12.60
53	**AUS**	**Australia**	**46.3**	**9,999,492**	**22,680,500**	**18.08**	**8.00**
54	US	Rhode Island	45.9	482,127	1,051,302	15.54	7.13
55	US	North Dakota	45.3	282,487	623,296	14.85	6.73
56	AUS	Victoria	45.0	2,538,072	5,623,500	20.23	9.10
57	AUS	Queensland	44.0	2,000,854	4,560,100	19.81	8.70
58	AUS	New South Wales	44.0	3,188,109	7,290,300	14.97	6.50
59	US	Georgia	43.6	4,564,784	10,459,546	9.54	4.16
60	US	Pennsylvania	43.0	5,337,951	12,411,451	12.95	5.57
61	US	Illinois	42.5	4,978,251	11,702,600	24.20	10.30
62	AUS	Western Australia	41.0	995,794	2,430,300	16.46	6.70
63	CAN	Ontario	37.4	4,913,281	13,151,825	27.26	10.19
64	AUS	Northern Territory	34.0	79,249	234,800	12.80	4.30
65	AUS	Tasmania	27.0	138,292	512,000	34.39	9.30
		Median ==>	54.5			15.00	8.00

of New Hampshire is the leader at 81 percent. The Australian Capital Territory (ACT) is the first non-U.S. region at 61 percent and so on. The smallest percentage is Tasmania at 27 percent. Tasmania's place is curious because in Table 3 we saw that Tasmania was well above the mean circulations per capita and 24th in that list. The 27 percent figure seems improbable.

Let us probe a bit further and look at the column headed "Circulations per Cardholder/Member" and compare this column to the "Circulations per Capita" column. As we can expect, focusing on "active" users, circulations per this smaller number are greater. And this number gives us another view of the world these libraries inhabit: use by active cardholders.

What is the difference between the two figures, that is, circulations per capita and circulations per cardholder? It varies a good bit. The greatest difference is with Tasmania. In fact, if this table were in order by "Circulations per Cardholder/ Member," the order for the first five would be Tasmania, Oregon, Ontario, British Columbia, and New Zealand. Tasmania, then, goes from worst in percentage of cardholders to first in terms of circulations per cardholder. This reminds us why we "weigh" evidence. But it seems unlikely that all of these regions are measuring this variable in the same way, does it not?

What might affect the measurement of cardholders?

- Although it is a common practice to require membership or a card to use services of a library such as its computers, that is not a universal practice. It varies even within the libraries in Ontario, for example.
- Even though in the library community we realize that the registered members use a library more, it appears that the many ways in which we measure this number are not compatible.

In Ontario, an "Active Cardholder" has used the library in the last two years. British Columbia reports the number of cardholders at "year-end." In the 51 reporting agencies in the United States, practices vary widely. Note that the Australian regions show generally lower numbers of members/cardholders than their U.S. counterparts although the available documentation does not help to indicate detail about how these libraries define the variable. Given what we see in this table and the suggestions from available documentation, one can speculate that the non-U.S. libraries are stricter in their measurement of this variable than are the U.S. libraries. If a library does not weed out members who are not actively using a library, the reported number of members will rise. Even people who died or those who have moved out of a library's service area will be counted.

We are looking at one year's data, and it often happens that data practices may vary from library to library or region to region but be consistent over time. Analyzing this variable over time might well be a useful way of looking at this matter in spite of these apparent differences in measurement. The regions may define it differently, but over time we can observe trends. The library world rarely uses or publishes data more than one year at a time, but two of us (Abram and Molyneux) have used just such a method to follow changes in "Active Cardholders" at Ontario's public libraries.

Expenditures

The data examined in the tables given here relate to people and their behavior, which should be relatively similar in the regions we have used. However, financial figures are much harder to compare. All four countries have a national currency called a "dollar," but their values fluctuate. The Association of Research Libraries has U.S. and Canadian members, and publishes a number each year that allows a consistent comparison of the two currencies. In the case of four currencies, one could calculate a similar number, but given the gyrations in currencies recently it is not clear that such an effort would provide a useful means of comparison now. More difficult would be the purchasing parity of the various currencies for library materials. To take a simple example: do books in Australia cost the same as books in the United States? It appears not, but this is a difficult question. Canada has restrictions on library purchasing that channel purchases to Canadian publishers when available in Canada. How such laws affect prices is not clear.

Given the differences in currency, per capita measures will not tell us much at this stage, although it is commonly calculated in the sources of these data. If we cannot yet make this kind of comparison, can we still use these data to examine library finances? One useful statistic is percentage of the Total Operating Expenditures spent on collections.

Table 5 has these two expenditure figures, Total Operating Expenditures and Expenditures for Collections, and is in order by the descending percentage of Total Expenditures for Collections.

Table 5 / Expenditures for Collections as a Percent of Total Operating Expenditures

Rank	Country	State/Province/Territory	% of Total Expenditures for Collections	$ Expenditures for Collections	$ Total Operating Expenditures
1	AUS	Australian Capital Territory	19.6	2,640,000	13,470,000
2	AUS	Victoria	16.6	34,580,000	208,860,000
3	US	Missouri	16.4	33,332,181	203,510,000
4	US	Utah	16.3	14,849,855	91,089,116
5	US	North Dakota	15.8	2,380,227	15,017,643
6	US	New Mexico	15.5	6,993,682	45,187,346
7	US	Oklahoma	15.1	16,513,144	109,083,048
8	AUS	Queensland	15.0	30,140,000	201,060,000
9	US	West Virginia	14.6	4,952,216	33,987,699
10	US	Ohio	14.4	94,752,145	659,213,729
11	**NZ**	**New Zealand**	**14.4**	**38,185,893**	**266,047,750**
12	US	Arkansas	14.3	9,746,939	67,948,315
13	US	Nebraska	14.3	7,168,441	50,145,582
14	US	Indiana	14.2	42,094,856	297,084,666
15	US	Kentucky	14.0	18,491,303	132,267,144
16	US	Arizona	13.9	24,322,319	175,445,306
17	US	South Dakota	13.8	3,104,246	22,488,642
18	US	Colorado	13.3	32,444,201	243,979,258
19	US	South Carolina	13.3	15,240,433	114,701,234
20	US	Washington	13.2	45,965,708	348,649,926
21	US	Texas	13.0	56,762,448	435,706,700
22	US	Iowa	12.9	14,254,704	110,895,138
23	US	Maryland	12.8	32,248,375	251,357,006
24	US	Montana	12.6	2,856,044	22,656,477
25	US	Nevada	12.5	9,848,675	78,686,875
26	US	Kansas	12.4	13,156,464	106,486,991
27	**AUS**	**Australia**	**12.3**	**123,850,000**	**1,010,000,000***
28	US	Massachusetts	12.2	33,268,335	272,862,580
29	CAN	British Columbia	12.1	26,824,930	221,612,493
30	US	Tennessee	12.0	12,490,684	104,308,919
31	US	Florida	11.9	59,597,419	501,081,343
32	US	Louisiana	11.5	21,000,474	182,878,982
33	AUS	Northern Territory	11.5	1,210,000	10,560,000
34	US	Illinois	11.4	80,328,599	701,939,170
35	US	Wisconsin	11.4	24,542,407	214,547,500
36	**US**	**United States**	**11.4**	**1,222,040,297**	**10,743,358,638**
37	US	Alabama	11.2	10,663,055	94,867,541
38	US	Pennsylvania	11.1	34,055,985	305,934,152
39	US	Idaho	11.1	4,804,876	43,465,328
40	US	Michigan	11.1	41,409,821	374,672,622
41	US	Minnesota	11.0	21,673,033	196,545,167
42	US	New Hampshire	10.9	6,032,165	55,144,343

43	US	Vermont	10.9	2,430,934	22,364,660
44	CAN	Ontario	10.6	68,191,904	641,086,137
45	US	Delaware	10.6	2,617,233	24,741,891
46	US	North Carolina	10.4	20,081,347	192,200,178
47	AUS	Western Australia	10.4	11,120,000	107,200,000
48	AUS	Tasmania	10.3	2,350,000	22,760,000
49	US	Virginia	10.3	26,701,253	258,782,230
50	US	Oregon	10.1	18,469,190	183,409,995
51	US	Maine	9.9	4,130,307	41,643,480
52	US	Connecticut	9.8	19,445,793	197,902,778
53	AUS	New South Wales	9.8	32,460,000	332,140,000
54	US	New Jersey	9.5	42,824,290	450,848,028
55	US	Alaska	9.4	3,084,447	32,872,289
56	US	Georgia	9.3	16,846,171	180,438,626
57	US	Hawaii	9.3	2,882,625	31,089,929
58	US	Wyoming	9.0	2,737,181	30,457,378
59	US	Mississippi	8.8	4,141,924	47,220,751
60	US	New York	8.7	97,853,147	1,122,679,060
61	US	Rhode Island	8.5	3,788,063	44,383,579
62	US	California	8.5	100,418,596	1,181,515,874
63	AUS	South Australia	8.2	9,350,000	114,350,000
64	US	District of Columbia	6.1	2,242,337	36,972,424
65	CAN	Manitoba	n.a.	n.a.	n.a.
		Median==>	11.5		

Dollar amounts are in local currencies.

*The total reported by the National and State Libraries Australasia does not agree with the sum of the states' and territories' reported data.

The range in this table is from a low of 6 percent for the District of Columbia to a high of almost 20 percent for the libraries of the Australian Capital Territory. The median is 11.5 percent. From a traditional view of what a modern public library does, that number seems low. That is, if libraries exist to house collections, the library should be buying materials; however, the modern library has much more going on than collections. Many of those "collections" are digital and it is possible that digital purchases are not included in these figure. Staff expenditures for these libraries would be useful to have, but that number is generally not available. It seems a reasonable speculation that, over time, the percentage of expenditures on traditional collections has declined while similar figures on expenditures for computers and digital resources have increased. Do libraries spend more on staff to support these efforts? We cannot tell broadly. That seems an important question because the rapidly changing library world places a great deal of stress on library employees.

Potentially Useful Variables in a Few Data Compilations

One striking aspect of these data collection efforts is their attempts to create measures of the impact of the digitization of information on libraries; but there are other interesting facets. What data librarians collect or do not collect is not only a function of common problems and functions but also a function of history, law, and custom. It is interesting to see what is being collected by only one or two of these efforts. A sample follows.

Australia gathers "Percentage of collection purchased in previous 5 years." This number ranges from 39 percent for South Australia to 75 percent for Queensland. According to Table 5, Queensland's libraries spent 15 percent of their total operating expenditures on collections while South Australia's expenditure was 8.2 percent. With this number, the reader has a quick indication of which libraries have the newer materials.

British Columbia has a strong series. The reports have a great deal of detail not found in other data series and breakdowns of many variables into small constituent elements. This resource could inform discussions on possible new variables to add to any data collection effort. One that is particularly interesting is "website and catalogue page views." The provincial total was 128 million and the Vancouver Public Library had 54 million of them. This seems an obvious number to collect, particularly when it should be a relatively easy thing to count, and a library's website is a major part of a library's presence these days. Of the data series surveyed, British Columbia and Manitoba are the only ones that report this number for their libraries.

Manitoba is relatively small in population and, as a result, has a smaller data effort than British Columbia, but it reports detailed data on electronic resources (use of EBSCO Hosts, circulation of e-books and audiobooks), and also documents facilities including floor space for each building.

New Zealand's spreadsheet is well organized, with a number of per capita measures. An interesting unique number is the percentage of "issues" ("circulations" in the United States) that are "patron self-issues" as opposed to "staff issues." Twenty-seven of the reporting library agencies have self-issue facilities. The median figure is 47 percent and the high is 73 percent at Horowhenua District; Auckland Council with three times the total circulations is at 64 percent. What an interesting number. There are a few library agencies reporting numbers so low that one might suspect that they have just added the capability for patrons to check materials out, a supposition that a glance back to previous years appears to confirm. For libraries that have had this capability for some time, why is the percentage not higher? (And what must the savings be in staff time that they can devote to other activities?)

Ontario, the Canadian province with the largest population, has one of the most substantial data collection and publication efforts of those outside the United States. The data include quite detailed financial breakdowns. There are also breakouts of collections (titles held, volumes held, databases, CD ROMs) by language: English, French, and other.

As mentioned earlier, the U.S. public library data collection is mature and continually improving. Data have been collected since 1987 and there is a long record of excellent documentation of these data as well as reports assessing aspects of these libraries.

Conclusion

In surveying the data series used here, it became clear that our colleagues in these countries are facing many of the same problems as U.S. public libraries and, as we show, measure a core of similar activities. In addition, they also developed other measures that we will briefly introduce here. We suggest that an examination of this category of measures may improve the U.S. data collection efforts. We also suggest that a cooperative exchange of information between those involved in these data collection efforts and others, may be a useful group to build a bottom-up understanding of measuring libraries.

It is another characteristic of annual library data series that it takes about three years for a new variable to yield useful numbers. It takes that long to work out the bugs in new definitions and to create a means to measure new things. Using the experience of colleagues in other countries who have already collected a variable that may be useful to measure should reduce the time to yield useful information. Given how fast the library world is changing these days, speeding up the process from planning to data would help us implement new capabilities. Measures of digital library content, collections, and use particularly would benefit from a careful look at the ways in which these regions have attempted to catch this lightning in a data bottle.

When one stands in a public library or examines pictures of public libraries in various countries, they look similar; however, when one examines their underlying data, one often sees differences in staffing patterns and the allocation of resources. This provokes a question: what methods of provisioning library services work best? For instance, how could we organize funding, staffing, and so forth to best supply public library service? This question is complex enough given that many factors that affect libraries such as history, custom, culture, economics, and demographics. But the more we know, the better.

Sources of Data

These sources are readily available, are available for 2012 to the best we can determine, and the libraries measured have many commonalities with U.S. public libraries.

Australia's public library data come from the *Australian Public Libraries Statistical Report, 2011–2012*. Compiled by Regional Access and Public Libraries, State Library of Queensland, July 2013 (http://www.nsla.org.au/publication/annual-australian-public-library-statistics), accessed February 7, 2015. This publication was issued under the copyright of the National and State Libraries Australasia (http://www.nsla.org.au).

The report has a summary of the data collection efforts of the various Australian states and territories and what has been done here is to collect data from these different efforts and publish them in one source. We use the regional totals. The data are in pdf and are available from 1996–1997 to 2012–2013.

Canada's data used in this study come from three of its provinces. Canadian public library data are not collected nationally. Only three provinces had published data for 2012:

British Columbia's data are compiled by the Ministry of Education, Libraries and Literacy Branch. A compiled version of the annual data from 2002–2013 are available in xls and csv formats (http://catalogue.data.gov.bc.ca/dataset/bc-public-libraries-statistics-2002-present). The Survey Questions and Instructions are also available at http://www.bced.gov.bc.ca/pls/reports.htm. These publications provide good documentation for the data themselves, including definitions and how calculations are done. The 2012 spreadsheet was used for this study.

Manitoba's public library data are compiled by the province's Tourism, Culture, Heritage, Sport and Consumer Protection agency, Public Library Services Branch, and are available for 2008 to 2014. The 2012 data were used in this study (https://mb.countingopinions.com/index.php?page_id=4).

Ontario's public library data are compiled by the Ministry of Tourism, Culture and Sport. Data in pdf format for 1999–2013 are available at http://www.mtc.gov.on.ca/en/libraries/statistics.shtml. This page also has what appears to be the only publicly available documentation of this effort. Each year is divided into more than 60 different files by the size of the library and the activity being measured. This organization makes it easier for working librarians to focus on the specific data of libraries of like size, but those wishing to analyze all Ontario's public libraries or the libraries over time will find this source cumbersome. However, each year's Summary and Comparison tables will give the reader an overview of the state of the province's libraries. The data used in this study came from the 2012 Summary and Comparison. For deeper analysis, the best source is the tables published in csv format: https://www.ontario.ca/data/ontario-public-library-statistics. As of February 27, 2015, these data are available for 1999–2010.

New Zealand's public library data are published in xls format by Public Libraries of New Zealand (http://www.publiclibrariesofnewzealand.org.nz). Statistics are available for 2004/2005–2013/2014. The data used here are from the 2011/2012 spreadsheet.

The U.S. public library data come from the Institute of Museum and Library Services' (http://www.imls.gov) *Public Library Survey for Fiscal Year 2012*. The institute publishes three series of annual data on public libraries, and we use data from the *Public Library State Summary/State Characteristics Data File* (http://www.imls.gov/research/pls_data_files.aspx). This file has summary data from all public libraries for each state and some territories of the United States. We have not used data from Guam or Puerto Rico for this study.

IMLS continues a data collection effort that began in 1988 and a timeline of this remarkable series is available at http://drdata.lrs.org/FSCS_History.pdf.

Notes

1. Balbi, Adriano. *A Statistical Essay on the Libraries of Vienna and the World*. Vienna, Che Frédéric Volke, 1835. Translated by Larry Barr and Janet L. Barr, McFarland, 1986.
2. Molyneux, Robert. *The Gerould Statistics, 1907/08–1961/62*. 2nd ed., slightly revised, 2010. http://www.libqual.org/documents/admin/2012/2010_Molyneux_Gerould.pdf.

3. "How the Largest Public Libraries Affect Libraries in General." *Library and Book Trade Almanac,* v. 59, 369–380 (2014).

About the Authors

Robert E. Molyneux has worked on compiling, documenting, and analyzing library data for more than 30 years and has taught a variety of library school classes dealing with the integration of computers and networking technology in libraries.

Stephen Abram is a library sector leader having worked on research, LIS education, association leadership, advocacy, and market and product development for 37 years. He writes about the future, library sector trends and user dynamics and is author of the Stephen's Lighthouse blog.

Garry Cannon has worked with academic, government, legal, and public libraries and for technology vendors serving the library industry for more than 25 years. Throughout the Asia Pacific region, he has met and worked with a wide variety of library professionals seeking to improve their service offerings. For this reason he created Cannon Global to provide consulting and product-related services to the market. His interests lie at the intersection of service provision, funding, and the inevitable justification of the supporting evidence.

Number of Libraries in the United States and Canada

Statistics are from *American Library Directory (ALD) 2014–2015* (Information Today, Inc., 2014). Data are exclusive of elementary and secondary school libraries.

Libraries in the United States

Public Libraries	16,826*
Public libraries, excluding branches	9,634†
Main public libraries that have branches	1,408
Public library branches	7,192
Academic Libraries	3,695*
Community college	1,139
Departmental	200
Law	0
Medical	6
Religious	8
University and college	2,556
Departmental	1,258
Law	190
Medical	238
Religious	248
Armed Forces Libraries	260*
Air Force	74
Medical	5
Army	122
Medical	25
Marine Corps	12
Navy	52
Law	1
Medical	10
Government Libraries	955*
Law	372
Medical	140
Special Libraries (excluding public, academic, armed forces, and government)	5,936*
Law	773
Medical	1,217
Religious	454
Total Special Libraries (including public, academic, armed forces, and government)	7,179
Total law	1,336
Total medical	1,641
Total religious	925
Total Libraries Counted(*)	27,672

Libraries in Regions Administered by the United States

Public Libraries	28*
Public libraries, excluding branches	10†
Main public libraries that have branches	3
Public library branches	18
Academic Libraries	37*
Community college	3
Departmental	3
Medical	0
University and college	34
Departmental	21
Law	3
Medical	2
Religious	1
Armed Forces Libraries	2*
Air Force	1
Army	1
Navy	0
Government Libraries	3*
Law	1
Medical	1
Special Libraries (excluding public, academic, armed forces, and government)	6*
Law	3
Medical	1
Religious	1
Total Special Libraries (including public, academic, armed forces, and government)	14
Total law	7
Total medical	4
Total religious	2
Total Libraries Counted(*)	76

Libraries in Canada

Public Libraries	2,023*
Public libraries, excluding branches	792†
Main public libraries that have branches	139
Public library branches	1,231
Academic Libraries	332*
Community college	78
Departmental	12
Medical	0
Religious	1
University and college	254
Departmental	179

Law	16
Medical	19
Religious	34
Government Libraries	223*
Law	36
Medical	6
Special Libraries (excluding public, academic, armed forces, and government)	698*
Law	92
Medical	155
Religious	22
Total Special Libraries (including public, academic, armed forces, and government)	810
Total law	144
Total medical	180
Total religious	76
Total Libraries Counted(*)	3,276

Summary

Total U.S. Libraries	27,672
Total Libraries Administered by the United States	76
Total Canadian Libraries	3,276
Grand Total of Libraries Listed	31,024

Note: Numbers followed by an asterisk are added to find "Total libraries counted" for each of the three geographic areas (United States, U.S.-administered regions, and Canada). The sum of the three totals is the "Grand total of libraries listed" in *ALD*. For details on the count of libraries, see the preface to the 67th edition of *ALD—Ed.*

†Federal, state, and other statistical sources use this figure (libraries *excluding* branches) as the total for public libraries.

Library Acquisition Expenditures, 2013–2014: U.S. Public, Academic, Special, and Government Libraries

The information in these tables is taken from the 2014–2015 edition of *American Library Directory* (*ALD*) (Information Today, Inc.). The tables report acquisition expenditures by public, academic, special, and government libraries.

The total number of libraries in the United States and in regions administered by the United States listed in this 67th edition of *ALD* is 27,412, including 16,826 public libraries, 3,695 academic libraries, 5,936 special libraries, and 955 government libraries.

Understanding the Tables

Number of libraries includes only those U.S. libraries in *ALD* that reported annual acquisition expenditures (1,904 public libraries, 778 academic libraries, 122 special libraries, and 44 government libraries). Libraries that reported annual income but not expenditures are not included in the count. Academic libraries include university, college, and junior college libraries. Special academic libraries, such as law and medical libraries, that reported acquisition expenditures separately from the institution's main library are counted as independent libraries.

The amount in the *total acquisition expenditures* column for a given state is generally greater than the sum of the categories of expenditures. This is because the total acquisition expenditures amount also includes the expenditures of libraries that did not itemize by category.

Figures in *categories of expenditure* columns represent only those libraries that itemized expenditures. Libraries that reported a total acquisition expenditure amount but did not itemize are only represented in the total acquisition expenditures column.

Table 1 / Public Library Acquisition Expenditures

State	Number of Libraries	Total Acquisition Expenditures	Books	Other Print Materials	Periodicals/ Serials	Manuscripts & Archives	AV Equipment	AV Materials	Microforms	Electronic Reference	Preservation
Alabama	26	18,176,749	1,309,303	9,400	42,905	2,000	297	208,049	2,013	4,661	400
Alaska	17	2,441,646	915,682	17,832	87,382	0	0	271,419	500	228,709	6,871
Arizona	23	18,407,227	3,190,779	210,477	194,111	575	14,000	1,267,578	30,481	713,973	0
Arkansas	16	4,599,452	2,321,017	20,564	71,282	0	23,105	726,833	302	557,570	5,000
California	74	82,109,305	32,842,893	1,602,416	2,990,287	9,000	43,417	8,482,217	124,693	8,312,883	88,887
Colorado	36	17,309,821	6,371,063	15,300	490,542	0	17,200	3,345,865	1,000	1,479,280	200
Connecticut	66	21,389,044	4,516,953	6,139	1,197,584	1,605	11,646	1,059,152	16,284	1,163,042	43,517
Delaware	7	706,467	166,110	0	6,408	0	0	29,234	0	3,635	0
District of Columbia	0	0	0	0	0	0	0	0	0	0	0
Florida	35	30,707,957	12,436,706	206,519	899,634	0	146,545	5,583,078	19,353	3,148,600	4,140
Georgia	17	8,185,756	1,434,006	42,253	79,989	0	3,081	364,519	2,350	287,028	945
Hawaii	1	3,881,055	1,975,964	38,182	142,634	0	518,497	0	38,549	1,167,229	0
Idaho	10	412,420	111,305	500	0	0	0	14,224	0	14,064	0
Illinois	99	32,307,592	10,140,869	81,992	709,705	3,000	75,113	3,548,534	53,467	4,030,402	26,369
Indiana	67	26,565,339	11,504,235	12,000	1,079,055	0	90,515	4,452,860	152,653	2,800,749	75,647
Iowa	66	7,270,782	2,252,913	70,195	197,709	0	8,913	682,074	3,555	346,349	0
Kansas	40	10,378,589	2,565,490	125,222	859,061	15	23,600	944,643	3,554	702,220	400
Kentucky	23	9,508,241	3,358,964	93,950	189,882	0	81,271	1,191,912	13,065	849,439	22,000
Louisiana	9	8,281,914	2,710,127	5,000	302,186	0	90,792	809,789	54,882	1,709,535	0
Maine	50	1,616,696	861,558	1,350	120,124	2,000	5,350	143,572	800	242,758	1,000
Maryland	3	10,640,301	1,823,665	0	85,337	0	0	974,786	0	175,455	0
Massachusetts	89	20,394,939	3,897,955	96,894	477,790	0	6,014	1,147,739	34,959	525,307	3,700
Michigan	86	32,714,353	7,406,428	177,030	535,717	0	140,831	2,098,330	12,506	1,551,281	2,102
Minnesota	37	75,012,857	2,437,432	3,903	86,761	0	0	515,059	180	186,690	516
Mississippi	10	1,441,628	637,845	0	104,151	0	0	106,142	26,000	137,488	3,247

State										
Missouri	34	26,596,139	5,534,147	100,000	500,681	0	25,796	2,735,157	44,736	1,884,800	150
Montana	19	1,108,939	511,256	73,040	90,507	200	10,316	120,192	2,873	108,874	2,500
Nebraska	31	2,238,098	1,315,101	273,449	43,817	0	47	69,138	40	333,836	2,346
Nevada	5	932,628	128,500	1,193	10,558	0	0	34,634	0	20,000	0
New Hampshire	65	2,518,465	1,073,593	131	131,304	0	7,428	271,633	14,680	111,168	7,050
New Jersey	74	28,300,589	13,525,698	118,407	1,310,812	500	21,500	3,748,101	105,249	2,518,251	4,350
New Mexico	14	3,920,100	1,918,388	215,399	58,510	0	6,000	376,046	10,213	489,465	0
New York	142	53,566,925	17,478,897	90,057	1,368,760	5,000	316,188	3,831,538	75,713	2,581,714	22,403
North Carolina	26	11,171,889	6,802,064	1,334,289	235,167	0	31,840	803,089	10,072	465,423	0
North Dakota	16	1,726,646	738,528	4,085	86,654	0	35,000	135,890	3,500	124,820	1,000
Ohio	73	118,079,854	22,681,907	314,297	3,405,820	6,921	32,856	11,638,094	322,656	9,396,862	220,893
Oklahoma	12	13,220,818	5,227,732	11,544	878,083	0	0	1,981,725	3,520	2,000,701	0
Oregon	40	8,874,976	3,341,582	15,027	365,027	0	5,000	1,144,893	23,699	304,220	1,872,003
Pennsylvania	77	20,909,430	4,818,815	895,879	914,497	156,260	9,748	2,476,744	177,510	1,269,309	251,375
Rhode Island	8	9,874,188	693,792	71,214	59,754	0	0	120,060	70	831,299	1,300
South Carolina	17	11,569,722	5,372,657	46,957	137,700	5,000	7,500	2,085,944	0	950,989	10,832
South Dakota	18	2,062,692	989,007	16,756	97,149	0	395	389,781	50	128,587	0
Tennessee	24	5,900,200	1,497,450	0	140,459	0	16,600	361,304	1,200	538,149	1,724
Texas	97	55,003,147	9,858,605	332,282	832,783	0	272,843	1,807,600	56,872	2,013,134	38,150
Utah	11	3,833,367	2,023,678	1,203	65,063	245,000	0	851,771	30,367	419,209	70,000
Vermont	47	1,335,599	586,871	311	26,455	0	0	118,578	276	21,973	500
Virginia	32	12,990,765	4,779,087	148,148	447,456	44,810	0	1,267,559	42,325	1,282,173	1,339,701
Washington	23	19,373,260	2,681,967	557,156	111,313	0	54,230	633,853	622	595,063	400
West Virginia	16	4,110,271	1,517,955	4,086	98,200	9,000	24,000	252,048	13,810	872,489	2,900
Wisconsin	64	7,374,900	3,039,355	75,495	245,382	0	17,277	970,216	11,892	289,224	2,700
Wyoming	12	1,337,130	345,751	500	38,177	0	6,000	68,701	55	18,388	0
Puerto Rico	0	0	0	0	0	0	0	0	0	0	0
Total	1,904	872,407,867	235,671,645	7,538,023	22,650,324	490,886	2,200,751	76,261,897	1,543,146	59,908,467	4,137,218
Estimated % of Acquisition Expenditures			27.01	0.86	2.60	0.06	0.25	8.74	0.18	6.87	0.47

Table 2 / Academic Library Acquisition Expenditures

State	Number of Libraries	Total Acquisition Expenditures	Books	Other Print Materials	Periodicals/ Serials	Manuscripts & Archives	AV Equipment	AV Materials	Microforms	Electronic Reference	Preservation
Alabama	13	13,836,921	1,439,651	8,031	3,286,184	0	10,000	120,913	97,741	1,777,198	71,387
Alaska	5	6,777,613	560,433	20,000	2,446,408	0	300	77,387	16,807	938,392	18,827
Arizona	8	2,626,277	366,162	2,500	196,349	4,997	5,203	108,081	28,227	1,595,988	7,748
Arkansas	7	10,140,356	1,472,505	495,153	6,031,667	34,264	1,000	28,972	122,257	1,028,746	9,187
California	59	88,367,648	5,810,742	252,861	10,861,881	4,199	46,109	341,313	177,688	12,631,439	310,189
Colorado	14	21,653,097	1,381,144	23,852	2,283,843	0	0	126,343	19,428	3,181,416	68,037
Connecticut	12	8,944,758	1,339,163	250	4,130,416	262	80,000	94,091	7,918	1,476,402	52,788
Delaware	4	10,533,103	78,468	0	595,297	0	0	0	0	300,019	3,000
District of Columbia	4	16,518,550	1,435,677	110,000	5,900,251	0	0	3,267	34,380	1,825,723	47,000
Florida	30	34,029,013	5,571,612	857,238	14,561,358	0	26,000	491,690	177,194	11,626,515	185,371
Georgia	21	16,113,238	1,179,552	2,000	1,961,400	0	3,673	114,371	76,214	2,203,571	50,868
Hawaii	1	91,232	0	0	0	0	0	0	0	0	0
Idaho	4	9,324,254	368,331	54,040	1,886,540	0	0	11,776	0	597,018	24,910
Illinois	29	69,739,584	8,920,938	1,010	16,406,885	0	31,200	272,798	57,368	2,999,526	134,500
Indiana	21	35,129,168	3,446,701	39,211	16,506,532	0	18	182,827	19,169	2,281,189	72,760
Iowa	16	25,015,234	2,305,010	476,638	4,371,752	0	26,550	94,438	42,545	2,178,958	78,787
Kansas	17	9,025,301	1,098,477	24,000	6,451,414	3,000	5,918	63,740	41,492	839,672	52,825
Kentucky	12	20,377,048	913,393	12,495	3,594,421	132	2,864	146,934	80,345	1,931,670	22,922
Louisiana	9	4,540,533	336,824	2,935	2,539,820	500	0	5,935	36,508	1,248,435	41,421
Maine	3	10,140,624	1,285,489	177,656	7,393,257	0	0	44,800	53,849	475,000	32,730
Maryland	12	12,139,895	1,673,705	6,209	8,219,911	14,926	0	79,259	18,894	1,517,232	67,292
Massachusetts	26	187,079,207	2,300,049	35,056	8,670,652	36,000	47,000	269,534	42,629	8,153,066	185,275
Michigan	28	24,722,316	2,691,535	138,714	9,663,557	31,203	40,000	179,793	1,448,981	6,912,166	62,306
Minnesota	18	13,556,397	2,061,596	10,000	5,071,016	300	54,455	259,592	67,722	1,325,749	117,409
Mississippi	6	3,501,369	341,867	0	1,364,201	0	1,000	35,353	116,000	1,324,052	44,200

State											
Missouri	17	12,252,795	528,627	10,411	1,722,978	8,767	4,000	97,174	132,857	626,949	36,117
Montana	4	374,177	164,234	0	154,583	0	10,000	9,000	3,000	20,000	0
Nebraska	8	13,397,120	508,056	86,211	2,216,984	15,000	0	78,638	71,643	1,531,321	14,126
Nevada	2	415,295	136,754	0	11,877	0	0	15,908	217	49,926	613
New Hampshire	5	8,922,284	1,195,724	0	4,180,222	0	0	700	21,116	1,351,794	76,271
New Jersey	12	9,565,113	1,501,495	69,154	2,744,732	1,000	0	77,330	25,708	2,257,575	7,603
New Mexico	5	3,541,864	137,311	0	2,685,913	11,802	0	19,878	16,450	112,334	28,574
New York	52	77,704,052	7,872,974	266,606	22,164,198	27,796	192,385	503,921	174,955	17,444,305	432,311
North Carolina	29	85,902,758	4,119,229	42,297	12,263,168	1,000	1,112,895	449,184	399,005	3,455,773	126,723
North Dakota	3	3,125,817	399,806	10,000	2,049,935	0	1,080	36,752	684	577,816	16,594
Ohio	34	43,711,249	5,123,866	104,195	8,455,607	1,007	14,206	242,280	172,410	6,847,196	204,383
Oklahoma	10	6,528,601	755,444	1,866	2,443,689	2,000	0	130,646	16,270	2,232,888	10,213
Oregon	16	28,132,438	1,468,321	0	5,039,305	0	38,779	109,872	0	1,173,967	55,554
Pennsylvania	32	24,422,394	3,965,821	54,744	9,358,134	45,300	51,743	346,173	179,742	4,105,850	212,489
Rhode Island	4	2,121,036	508,550	2,100	948,070	17,500	0	57,971	8,000	561,553	17,292
South Carolina	17	11,733,145	2,147,577	53,414	2,881,967	20,000	10,000	110,263	79,726	2,365,429	99,896
South Dakota	4	3,144,200	271,897	0	784,243	0	5,958	14,415	12,872	553,540	18,333
Tennessee	14	18,769,623	865,397	0	1,515,072	0	0	26,860	68,400	2,802,270	8,063
Texas	38	50,448,232	5,355,525	59,602	13,939,322	6,250	164,102	220,130	256,372	6,548,898	166,465
Utah	5	6,986,569	1,188,698	0	3,094,967	0	5,000	66,500	3,500	877,180	5,383
Vermont	5	1,581,941	269,284	0	860,042	1,451	5,000	37,146	1,956	373,382	4,180
Virginia	27	42,038,331	7,413,491	615,565	17,630,287	47,962	28,414	241,817	126,792	8,659,775	172,579
Washington	14	15,594,587	2,099,936	0	7,904,319	14,564	46,000	248,005	7,900	1,705,600	24,598
West Virginia	14	3,531,955	278,118	2,052	454,633	6,750	23,300	40,426	52,944	948,339	10,778
Wisconsin	18	23,469,164	797,744	1,964	1,570,392	1,879	21,000	151,396	57,608	1,843,687	17,429
Wyoming	3	7,480,309	3,458,937	0	2,201,321	0	0	13,200	0	863,481	0
Puerto Rico	7	6,319,100	793,468	1,000	4,661,824	5,000	29,490	44,940	0	766,183	9,800
Total	778	1,165,136,885	101,705,308	4,131,030	278,332,796	364,811	2,144,642	6,543,732	4,673,483	141,026,153	3,538,106
Estimated % of Acquisition Expenditures			8.73	0.35	23.89	0.03	0.18	0.56	0.40	12.10	0.30

Table 3 / Special Library Acquisition Expenditures

State	Number of Libraries	Total Acquisition Expenditures	Category of Expenditures (in U.S. dollars)								
			Books	Other Print Materials	Periodicals/ Serials	Manuscripts & Archives	AV Equipment	AV Materials	Microforms	Electronic Reference	Preservation
Alabama	0	0	0	0	0	0	0	0	0	0	0
Alaska	0	0	0	0	0	0	0	0	0	0	0
Arizona	5	20,824	3,500	0	324	0	0	0	0	0	1,000
Arkansas	0	0	0	0	0	0	0	0	0	0	0
California	14	411,491	52,083	2,000	171,417	0	1,000	1,100	0	65,891	3,000
Colorado	1	10,000	7,000	0	1,000	0	0	2,000	0	0	0
Connecticut	1	1,000	0	0	0	0	0	0	0	0	0
Delaware	0	0	0	0	0	0	0	0	0	0	0
District of Columbia	2	285,000	43,000	0	95,000	0	0	0	2,000	145,000	0
Florida	2	13,600	4,650	0	7,500	0	0	0	0	0	600
Georgia	0	0	0	0	0	0	0	0	0	0	0
Hawaii	0	0	0	0	0	0	0	0	0	0	0
Idaho	0	0	0	0	0	0	0	0	0	0	0
Illinois	9	2,995,200	91,600	30,500	149,700	200	1,500	2,000	1,500	102,500	4,700
Indiana	1	3,075	275	0	120	500	0	0	680	0	1,500
Iowa	3	213,058	35,362	0	12,408	0	0	0	155,288	0	0
Kansas	2	12,581	4,400	4,000	4,081	0	0	0	0	0	100
Kentucky	0	0	0	0	0	0	0	0	0	0	0
Louisiana	1	18,000	5,000	0	13,000	0	0	0	0	0	0
Maine	1	200	0	0	0	0	0	0	0	0	0
Maryland	3	166,950	23,150	0	130,450	50	0	0	0	12,000	100
Massachusetts	2	79,391	0	0	0	0	0	0	0	0	0
Michigan	1	12,000	3,000	500	3,600	0	0	400	0	0	0
Minnesota	2	54,850	21,350	5,000	11,500	0	0	1,000	0	16,000	0
Mississippi	0	0	0	0	0	0	0	0	0	0	0

State											
Missouri	1	67,500	24,000	0	29,500	0	0	0	0	14,000	0
Montana	1	17,348	15,848	0	0	0	0	0	0	1,500	0
Nebraska	2	2,600	950	0	1,500	0	0	0	0	0	0
Nevada	1	1,000	0	0	0	0	0	0	0	0	0
New Hampshire	2	92,000	16,000	10,000	5,000	20,000	0	0	0	32,000	9,000
New Jersey	4	21,200	9,000	0	5,000	0	0	6,000	6,000	0	1,200
New Mexico	2	12,500	0	0	0	0	0	0	0	0	0
New York	22	959,933	388,223	50	88,450	20,000	3,800	18,782	1,000	46,306	158,320
North Carolina	0	0	0	0	0	0	0	0	0	0	0
North Dakota	2	11,598	2,660	0	5,475	2,000	0	0	0	0	1,463
Ohio	9	709,823	90,980	550	73,858	1,892	150	1,798	0	33,019	12,047
Oklahoma	3	101,050	15,000	1,250	36,800	12,000	20,000	1,000	3,000	12,000	0
Oregon	1	600	200	0	0	0	0	0	0	400	0
Pennsylvania	3	173,557	30,108	47,812	29,259	18,351	0	9,671	10,000	3,322	25,034
Rhode Island	1	75,313	44,726	0	5,000	15,387	0	0	0	0	10,200
South Carolina	1	29,600	14,000	0	5,000	0	0	6,000	3,000	0	0
South Dakota	0	0	0	0	0	0	0	0	0	0	0
Tennessee	2	26,000	12,500	0	6,000	0	500	3,000	0	4,000	0
Texas	6	1,865,360	38,556	43,992	2,393	500	670	765	0	814,000	2,056
Utah	1	75,000	5,000	5,000	10,000	0	5,000	0	0	50,000	0
Vermont	0	0	0	0	0	0	0	0	0	0	0
Virginia	5	377,723	101,968	12,600	51,230	39,903	48,265	5,224	4,200	27,975	86,358
Washington	1	1,500	0	0	0	0	0	0	0	0	0
West Virginia	0	0	0	0	0	0	0	0	0	0	0
Wisconsin	2	85,500	5,300	0	20,000	0	0	0	0	60,000	0
Wyoming	0	0	0	0	0	0	0	0	0	0	0
Puerto Rico	0	0	0	0	0	0	0	0	0	0	0
Total	122	9,003,925	1,109,389	163,254	974,565	130,783	80,885	58,740	180,668	1,439,913	316,678
Estimated % of Acquisition Expenditures			12.32	1.81	10.82	1.45	0.90	0.65	2.01	15.99	3.52

Table 4 / Government Library Acquisition Expenditures

State	Number of Libraries	Total Acquisition Expenditures	Books	Other Print Materials	Periodicals/ Serials	Manuscripts & Archives	AV Equipment	AV Materials	Microforms	Electronic Reference	Preservation
								Category of Expenditures (in U.S. dollars)			
Alabama	2	626,295	243,777	0	575	0	0	0	0	381,472	471
Alaska	0	0	0	0	0	0	0	0	0	0	0
Arizona	0	0	0	0	0	0	0	0	0	0	0
Arkansas	0	0	0	0	0	0	0	0	0	0	0
California	10	2,242,897	595,673	10,000	526,222	0	0	3,740	6,207	8,000	324,620	1,950
Colorado	0	0	0	0	0	0	0	0	0	0	0
Connecticut	0	0	0	0	0	0	0	0	0	0	0
Delaware	1	50,000	7,000	1,000	9,000	0	0	0	0	33,000	0
District of Columbia	0	0	0	0	0	0	0	0	0	0	0
Florida	1	19,545	3,750	0	14,170	0	0	1,625	0	0	0
Georgia	0	0	0	0	0	0	0	0	0	0	0
Hawaii	0	0	0	0	0	0	0	0	0	0	0
Idaho	0	0	0	0	0	0	0	0	0	0	0
Illinois	0	0	0	0	0	0	0	0	0	0	0
Indiana	0	0	0	0	0	0	0	0	0	0	0
Iowa	0	0	0	0	0	0	0	0	0	0	0
Kansas	2	789,260	296,852	0	400,491	0	0	0	0	85,690	6,227
Kentucky	0	0	0	0	0	0	0	0	0	0	0
Louisiana	2	1,050,279	91,080	0	42,318	0	0	1,000	0	41,663	0
Maine	1	257,079	0	0	0	0	0	0	0	0	0
Maryland	3	589,000	358,000	11,800	196,000	0	0	7,700	0	0	3,500
Massachusetts	3	348,868	195,036	0	0	0	0	0	0	68,332	7,500
Michigan	1	35,000	0	0	0	0	0	0	0	0	0
Minnesota	2	134,500	18,000	0	61,500	0	0	0	0	55,000	0
Mississippi	0	0	0	0	0	0	0	0	0	0	0

Missouri	0	0	0	0	0	0	0	0	0	0
Montana	1	425,961	328,391	0	0	0	0	0	97,570	0
Nebraska	0	0	0	0	0	0	0	0	0	0
Nevada	1	768,769	562,656	0	10,803	0	0	3,151	186,357	5,802
New Hampshire	1	70,000	0	0	0	0	0	0	0	0
New Jersey	0	0	0	0	0	0	0	0	0	0
New Mexico	0	0	0	0	0	0	0	0	0	0
New York	3	1,367,180	0	0	0	0	0	0	0	5,300
North Carolina	0	0	0	0	0	0	0	0	0	0
North Dakota	1	40,000	5,000	0	30,000	0	0	0	5,000	0
Ohio	0	0	0	0	0	0	0	0	0	0
Oklahoma	0	0	0	0	0	0	0	0	0	0
Oregon	0	0	0	0	0	0	0	0	0	0
Pennsylvania	4	575,000	71,500	0	500	0	0	0	10,000	0
Rhode Island	1	43,425	9,961	0	31,764	0	814	0	886	0
South Carolina	0	0	0	0	0	0	0	0	0	0
South Dakota	0	0	0	0	0	0	0	0	0	0
Tennessee	0	0	0	0	0	0	0	0	0	0
Texas	0	0	0	0	0	0	0	0	0	0
Utah	0	0	0	0	0	0	0	0	0	0
Vermont	0	0	0	0	0	0	0	0	0	0
Virginia	1	63,090	13,355	0	42,453	0	6,271	0	1,011	0
Washington	0	0	0	0	0	0	0	0	0	0
West Virginia	1	650,000	50,000	0	400,000	0	0	0	200,000	0
Wisconsin	2	91,000	45,000	0	0	0	0	0	36,000	0
Wyoming	0	0	0	0	0	0	0	0	0	0
Puerto Rico	0	0	0	0	0	0	0	0	0	0
Total	44	10,237,148	2,895,031	22,800	1,765,796	3,740	23,617	11,151	1,526,601	30,750
Estimated % of Acquisition Expenditures			28.28	0.22	17.25	0.04	0.23	0.11	14.91	0.30

Highlights of IMLS and NCES Surveys

The Institute of Museum and Library Services (IMLS) and the National Center for Education Statistics (NCES) collect and disseminate statistical information about libraries in the United States and its outlying areas. Two major surveys are conducted by NCES, the Academic Libraries Survey and the School Library Media Centers Survey; two others, the Public Libraries Survey and the State Library Agencies Survey, were formerly conducted by NCES, but are now handled by IMLS.

This article presents highlights from three of the most recently conducted surveys. For more information, see "National Center for Education Statistics" in Part 1 and "Institute of Museum and Library Services, Office of Library Services" in Part 2 of this volume.

Public Libraries

The following are highlights from the IMLS report *Public Libraries in the United States Survey, Fiscal Year 2012*, released in December 2014.

Library Use

- In FY 2012 there were 1.5 billion in-person visits to public libraries across the United States, the equivalent of more than 4.1 million visits each day. Although this reflects a ten-year increase of 20.7 percent, there has been a decrease in physical visitation since a peak in FY 2009.
- Visitation per capita was 4.9, a one-year decrease of 2.7 percent and ten-year increase of 10.2 percent.
- U.S. public libraries had 170.6 million registered borrowers, a six-year increase of 5.4 percent.
- Librarians and staff fielded 284.3 million reference transactions in FY 2012, a one-year decrease of 3.0 percent.
- More than 2.2 billion materials were circulated in public libraries, similar to FY 2011, and a ten-year increase of 28.0 percent.

Staffing

- Public libraries employed 136,851 full-time equivalent (FTE) staff, with 46,808 librarian FTEs. This was at the same level as FY 2011, following losses after the recession.
- Use of library services, such as circulation and visitation, showed an increase immediately following the recession, followed by a decrease back down to pre-recession levels.

Public Access Computer Use

- There were 271,146 public access computers in public libraries, representing a one-year increase of 3.7 percent, and there were 340.5 million use sessions of public access computers. Although this has declined in recent years, the survey result was similar to FY 2011 levels. The report discusses this finding in light of the increase of personal digital devices such as smartphones.

Circulation

- In FY 2012 there were 2.2 billion materials circulated in public libraries, a ten-year increase of 28.0 percent. Public libraries circulated 852.0 million children's materials, accounting for 35.2 percent of total circulation and representing a ten-year increase of 25.07 percent.
- Circulation per capita was 8.0, a one-year decrease of 1.72 percent but a ten-year increase of 16.79 percent.

Program Attendance

- A total of 92.6 million people attended public library programs in FY 2012. This was a one-year increase of 4.1 percent and an eight-year increase of 37.6 percent. Total attendance per 1,000 people was 306.0; in other words, for every 1,000 people in a library service area, there were 306.0 attendees at a public library program. Average attendance was 23.1 people per program.
- There were 64.5 million attendees at programs for children, a one-year increase of 3.5 percent and a ten-year increase of 24.2 percent.
- Children's programs at public libraries are among the most popular. Out of all program attendees, 69.6 percent attended a program for children. Attendance at children's programs per 1,000 children in the legal service area was 711.75.
- Programs for young adults were attended by 5.7 million, a one-year increase of 6.8 percent. Attendance at young adult programs per 1,000 young adults was 352.8.

Operating Expenditures

- Total operating expenditures for public libraries totaled $10.7 billion in FY 2012, a one-year decrease of 1.8 percent and a ten-year increase of 7.1 percent, after adjusting for inflation. The majority of expenditures—67.6 percent—went to staffing expenses, which includes salaries and benefits.
- The $7.3 billion spent on staffing reflects a 12.0 percent increase over ten years, most of which is the result of the rising cost of benefits, which has increased by 51.0 percent over a decade.
- Public libraries spent $1.2 billion on collections materials in FY 2012, a ten-year decrease of 15.6 percent. Expenditures for collections accounted for 11.4 percent of total operating expenditures, a ten-year decrease of 21.3 percent. Expenditures on electronic materials have been increasing steadily, almost doubling (rising 92.2 percent) since data on this element were first collected in FY 2003. Expenditures on electronic materials account for 16.7 percent of all collections expenditures.

Collections

- The average collection size across all public libraries was 110,708.0 items (median = 42,833.5), including printed materials, e-books, and audio and video materials. There was much variability across libraries, with collection sizes ranging from 314 to 23,246,282 items. Across all public libraries, there were 783.9 million volumes of print materials. Digital holdings at public libraries continued a long increase.

- A total of 5,733 public libraries reported having e-books as part of their collections, ranging from one to 273,885 e-books. The average number of e-books was 15,206.6, and the median was 6,280.

Revenue

- Revenue for public libraries was $11.5 billion. This was similar to FY 2011 levels, after adjusting for inflation. Revenue declined after a peak in FY 2009, but was up 7.2 percent over ten years.

- In the aggregate, most (84.4 percent) of public library revenue came from local government sources. Funding from local governments increased by 6.7 percent over the past ten years, from 79.1 percent in FY 2002. Revenue from state government sources was $788.0 million, comprising 6.9 percent of total revenue. This is a one-year decrease of 10.1 percent, and a ten-year decrease of 37.2 percent (after adjusting for inflation). Federal revenue to libraries was $60.1 million, a one-year increase of 3.6 percent. Total revenue per capita was $37.98 in FY 2012.

State Library Administrative Agencies

The following are highlights from the IMLS report *State Library Administrative Agencies Survey, Fiscal Year 2012,* released in May 2014.

Revenue and Expenditures

- State Library Administrative Agency (SLAA) revenues totaled nearly $1 billion in fiscal year (FY) 2012, which represented a 27 percent decrease from FY 2003 and a 12 percent decrease from FY 2010.

- Revenues from the federal government for all SLAAs totaled $181.6 million in FY 2012. State revenues totaled $766.2 million, which included $265.8 million received from the states to support SLAA operation, $455.6 million in state aid to libraries, and $40.9 million received from the states for any other purposes (such as interagency transfers).

- Total expenditures for FY 2012 across all SLAAs were $995.5 million, which represented a 26 percent decrease from FY 2003 and an 11 percent decrease from FY 2010. When looking across the types of expenditures, $640.6 million went toward financial assistance to libraries, $335.4 million went toward operating expenditures, $14.8 million was allocated to other services, and $2.5 million was spent on capital outlay.

- More than $89 million of LSTA (Library Services and Technology Act) funds was used to support access to technology and information resources for libraries in 2012, and $36 million went toward programs and services for lifelong learning.

Workforce and Staff Development

- In FY 2012 SLAAs employed 2,814 full-time equivalent (FTE) staff, which was a decrease of 5 percent from 2010.
- In FY 2012 a total of 360 staff (13 percent of all budgeted FTEs) was reported within the service of administration, more than 600 budgeted FTEs (22 percent) were reported within library development, and 1,354 budgeted FTEs (48 percent) were reported within library services.

Services

- A total of 40 SLAAs funded or facilitated digitization programs and services in 2012, and 15 SLAAs provided preservation and conservation services to public libraries and library cooperatives.
- During FY 2012 the number of library service transactions that served the general public and state government employees reported by SLAAs included library visits (29,051), circulation transactions (45,971), reference transactions (15,992), and interlibrary loan services provided to another library (6,222) and received from another library (2,368).
- Fifty SLAAs funded summer reading programs and continuing education programs for public libraries in FY 2012.

Identification and Governance

- Of the 50 states and the District of Columbia, three SLAAs (Michigan, New York, and Tennessee) were located within the legislative branch in state government, and 48 were located within the executive branch.
- Thirty-seven of the 51 SLAAs reported having allied operations in addition to their SLAA functions, ten reported state archives and state records management services, and eight reported some other type of allied operation.

School Libraries

The following are highlights from the NCES publication *Characteristics of Public Elementary and Secondary School Library Media Centers in the United States: Results from the 2011–2012 Schools and Staffing Survey* (NCES 2013-315).

- During the 2011–2012 school year, 79,000 of the 85,500 traditional public schools in the United States reported having a library media center, while 2,200 of the 4,500 public charter schools reported having one.
- About two-thirds (67 percent) of library media centers in traditional public schools had full-time, paid, state-certified library media center specialists,

while one-third (33 percent) of those in public charter schools had this type of staff. In traditional public schools, 20 percent of library media centers did not have any paid, state-certified library media center specialists (full or part time), and 56 percent of those in public charter schools did not have this type of staff.

- The percentage of paid, professional library media center staff with a master's degree in a library-related major field was 52 percent for all public schools, 52 percent in traditional public schools, and 27 percent in public charter schools.

- During the 2010–2011 school year, public school library media centers spent an average of $9,340 for all information resources. This included an average of $6,010 for the purchase of books and $490 for the purchase of audio/video materials.

- The number of holdings in public library media centers per 100 students was 2,188 for book titles and 81 for audio/video materials at the end of the 2010–2011 school year.

- Public school library media centers provided technological services, including automated catalog(s) for student and/or staff use (88 percent), laptops for staff use outside the library media center (54 percent), laptops for student use outside the library media center (40 percent), and technology to assist students and/or staff with disabilities (31 percent).

- The percentage of library media centers with computer workstations for student and/or staff use was 97 percent in traditional public schools and 88 percent in public charter schools. Of the library media center computer workstations, 95 percent had Internet access. Among all public school library media centers, 86 percent provided student access to online, licensed databases.

- For classes and other activities, 61 percent of public school library media centers had both flexible scheduling (available as needed) and regular scheduling (previously specified times), while 19 percent had only flexible scheduling, and 19 percent had only regular scheduling. The percentage of public school library media centers that were available for independent student use was 89 percent during regular school hours, 57 percent before school, and 54 percent after school.

- About one-fourth (24 percent) of public school library media centers were open to community members who do not attend the school and do not have children who attend the school. Of these, 61 percent had workstations that community members could use to access the Internet.

- Public school library media centers supported programs that encourage students to read (65 percent) and family literacy activities (36 percent). Per 100 students in the school, there was an average of 100 student visits to the library media center and 110 books or other materials checked out during a full week of school.

Library Buildings 2014: Commons Sense

Bette-Lee Fox

Managing Editor, *Library Journal*

The library construction projects completed between July 1, 2013, and June 30, 2014, seem to have found common purpose around a common theme: community. Many of the 16 academic projects and 84 public library capital efforts find themselves at the center of their neighborhoods. Whether large or small, on an expansive budget or a shoestring, these facilities strengthen ties among their constituencies and between learning and entertainment.

The new Frederick E. Berry Library and Learning Commons at Salem (Massachusetts) State University reinforces its sense of openness and transparency through a pleated glass wall on the north façade that draws students inside. The Pierce College Library Learning Crossroads Building, Woodland Hills, California, integrates learning and social interaction, combining a food court, the library, a tutoring center, a computer commons, and a Student Success Center. Oxnard (California) College Library Learning Resource Center is based around hub-and-spoke architecture and a network of pathways that act as a pivot for campus connectivity.

Augustana College's Center for Student Life in Rock Island, Illinois, brings under one roof the Thomas Tredway Library, a student center, and the college dining center. American Jewish University in Bel Air, California, converted an underused driveway and parking garage to expand the Bel and Jack Ostrow Library, a joint resource open both to the community and to scholarly research.

The mother of all communal projects is Virginia's new Tidewater Community College/City of Virginia Beach Joint-Use Library. With a village-inspired motif, the 125,000-square-foot facility features meeting rooms, a multipurpose room, a cafe, an open commons area, a computer lab, study spaces, a children's section, and a teen zone.

Parks and Yards

The North Beach Branch of the San Francisco Public Library is the first phase of the Joe DiMaggio Playground and North Beach Public Library Master Plan, a civic pavilion in the park that responds to the "rhythm of the buildings on the street." The Pico Branch of California's Santa Monica Public Library is located in the 9.5-acre Virginia Avenue Park. The campus-like setting includes the branch library and its freestanding Annex, an 818-square-foot community room, a community center, a teen center, a recreational facility, and a general-purpose meeting space. The Prairie West Branch of Siouxland Libraries in Sioux Falls, South Dakota, was built on the edge of a park, echoed by its blue-and green interior.

Hennepin County Library–Walker sits at one of the busiest intersections in Minneapolis, next to a city park and near a transit center and biking trails. The Arlington Hills Community Center in nearby St. Paul is a combined library and recreation center. A noteworthy joint program is its Createch Studio, a teen-orient-

Adapted from *Library Journal*, November 15, 2014

ed tech lab. The complex encompasses a full-court gym and a fitness room, along with athletic fields and a plaza for public performances.

The Fort Myers (Florida) Regional Library campus comprises the Fort Myers Regional Library, the Talking Books Library/meeting rooms/conference center, and an expansive outdoor plaza designed for concerts, bazaars, farmers markets, youth activities, outdoor movie nights, art festivals, food festivals, craft fairs, and parking.

The Back of the Yards Branch of the Chicago Public Library, built in conjunction with the Back of the Yards College Preparatory High School, serves all levels of the community through STEM-based programs for youngsters and teens and, for adults, book discussions, financial planning seminars, and CyberNavigator technology assistance. A disused 7,778-square-foot elementary school was transformed into the Rio Linda Branch of California's Sacramento Public Library, doubling the branch's space and providing a children's area, a teen room, an adult browsing area, and 22 public access computers.

The diversity of the neighborhood of the East Boston Branch of the Boston Public Library is celebrated by stone pavers on the exterior that show the name of and distance to the capital cities of the top 21 countries of origin of the residents of East Boston.

The Embudo Valley Library and Community Center in New Mexico is a non-profit public library located in an unincorporated village. The nearly $708,000 project was supported entirely through donations and grants. The Hollidaysburg (Pennsylvania) Area Public Library encompasses an outdoor patio and amphitheater, as well as a 12-foot gazebo. A kitchen is adjacent to the 100-seat community room, and the Armed Forces Room houses a coffee bar and a plaque recognizing local veterans.

Maker Spaces and More

In Arizona, the Mesa Public Library Red Mountain Branch Library's THINKspot is a collaborative makerspace featuring an AV and photography studio and the latest technology (3-D printer, SMART boards, conferencing systems, and more), with mobile furnishings to encourage collaboration. The Brand Library and Art Center, a branch of the Glendale (California) Library Arts and Culture Department, is housed in a repurposed 1904 mansion. The materials collection and the site's accompanying recital hall, art gallery, and performance plaza make the library both a research center and a lively arts venue.

The Fort York Branch of Toronto Public Library offers the system's first branch digital innovation hub. The Savage Branch/STEM Education Center of Howard County Library System in Laurel, Maryland, includes a HiTech classroom in which students create robotic projects and apps. The remodeled Library 21c, the main and system headquarters of Pikes Peak Library District, Colorado Springs, presents a business and entrepreneurial center, conference space, print/copy services, and an AV production studio, plus cafe/catering services, a 400-seat performance/meeting venue, two Maker spaces, two gaming labs, and an exhibit gallery.

The Ames Free Library in Easton, Massachusetts, turned the 1854 Queset House into a 21st-century learning commons. Its first "author-in-residence," Kate Klise, wrote, "The[se] clever folks . . . bought this ridiculously pretty house. . . and turned it into a, well, community clubhouse of sorts . . . a place for people of all ages to meet that's not school or home or work. Or Starbucks."

The Barrington (Illinois) Area Library redefines its connection to the community through smart rooms, media labs, makerspaces, a business center, an Internet cafe, and a reading commons. The Niles (Illinois) Public Library, created on the lower level a teen space called the Underground, providing an informal lounge area for this important constituency. The Ridgefield (Connecticut) Library turned a 1903 historic building into a teen center, a technology center, and study and meeting rooms that function as part of a cultural campus with a recently renovated movie theater.

The Bibliothèque de Brossard Georgette-Lepage in Brossard, Quebec, tore down a wall between two basement storage rooms to create a large room the youth contingent calls SODA, with zones for working, reading, socializing, and relaxing.

The Kenton County (Kentucky) Public Library's Covington Branch is the new civic hub in the city's downtown. An atrium visually connects interior to exterior and all three floors of the building to one another. A large clerestory window brings needed light to the main level reading and study area.

Carnegie Revival

The Washington Heights Branch of the New York Public Library revived its 1914 Renaissance Revival Carnegie building, using 3,600 square feet of the second floor for a children's reading room. The 1918 Carnegie-built Athol (Massachusetts) Library is in one of the most economically depressed towns in the state, yet residents supported the economic, social, and environmental benefits of a Platinum-level Leadership in Energy and Environmental Design (LEED)-certified restoration.

The West Tisbury (Massachusetts) Free Public Library created an inviting front porch and gardens that provide outdoor seating. The high-ceilinged lower level of the East Hampton (New York) Library features the state-of-the-art Baldwin Family Lecture Room, with space for programs, meetings, film screenings, readings, lectures, and book events.

The Arlington Branch of the Cranston (Rhode Island) Public Library was renovated within the Cranston Senior Center. A lobby space serves seniors and is also a study spot for neighborhood teens. The remodeled Madison (Wisconsin) Public Library includes an art gallery, public meeting rooms, and an outdoor terrace that overlooks the green roof. The third-floor commons can be rented for private events.

Three recovery projects also stood out: at Cedar Rapids (Iowa) Public Library, destroyed in a 2008 flood; Pratt City Library in Birmingham, Alabama, victim of 2005's Hurricane Katrina; and the Coney Island branch of Brooklyn Public Library, damaged by 2012's Superstorm Sandy.

Inventive, creative, environmentally respectful, forward-thinking—each of the year's projects shares an underlying principle: to serve best the communities that support them. They have done so with uncommonly awe-inspiring results.

Table 1 / New Academic Buildings, Additions, and Renovations, 2014

Institution	Type	Status	Project Cost	Gross Area (Sq. Ft.)	Sq. Ft. Cost	Constr. Cost	Furniture/ Equip. Cost	Book Capacity	Architect
Frederick E. Berry Library & Learning Commons, Salem State University, MA	N		$74,000,000	128,000	$421.88	$54,000,000	$300,000	253,000	Shepley Bulfinch
Jerry Falwell Library, Liberty University, Lynchburg, VA	N		n.a.	190,000	273.68	52,000,000	n.a.	500,000	VMDO Architects
Pierce College Library Learning Crossroads Building, Los Angeles Community College District, Woodland Hills, CA	N		50,000,000	119,000	327.73	39,000,000	n.a.	110,000	Paul Murdoch Architects
**Tidewater Community College/City of Virginia Beach Joint-Use Library	N		41,756,598	125,000	202.33	25,291,717	9,400,000	20,184 l.f.	Carrier Johnson + CULTURE; RRMM Architects; Anderson Brulé Architects
Oxnard College Library Learning Resource Center, Oxnard College, Ventura County Community College District, CA	N		17,500,000	37,250	340.94	12,700,000	n.a.	100,000	Paul Murdoch Architects
McMillen Library, Indiana Tech, Fort Wayne	N		2,227,000	9,135	232.62	2,125,000	101,000	n.a.	Schenkel Shultz Architecture
Truax Campus Library, Madison College, WI	A		22,148,385	16,500	n.a.	n.a.	n.a.	n.a.	Plunkett Raysich Architects
John Hay Library, Brown University, Providence	R		14,974,937	100,131	106.82	10,695,501	113,225	3,000,000	Selldorf Architects
John T. Richardson Library, DePaul University, Chicago	R		4,500,000	29,500	108.47	3,200,000	500,000	100,000	Vasilko Architects
Georgia State University Library, Atlanta	R		1,200,000	3,300	181.82	600,000	600,000	n.a.	Collins Cooper Carusi

Library	Type								Architect
John W. Hicks Undergraduate Library, Purdue University, West Lafayette, IN	R		930,440	10,000	49.04	490,440	440,000	432	GMB Architecture; McGee Designhouse
Dr. Peter W. Addiego Health Sciences Library, Nassau University Medical Center, East Meadow, NY	R		n.a.	4,600	181.52	835,000	n.a.	n.a.	Ehasz Giacalone Associates; Stalco Construction
Perry-Castaneda Library, University of Texas at Austin	R		725,000	5,000	120.00	600,000	125,000	n.a.	Edwards + Mulhausen Interior Design
MacOdrum Library, Carleton University, Ottawa, Ont.	A&R	Total	27,200,000	113,800	202.99	23,100,000	690,000	n.a.	Diamond Schmitt Architects
		New	n.a.	67,800	299.41	20,300,000	690,000	n.a.	
		Renovated	n.a.	46,000	60.87	2,800,000	n.a.	n.a.	
Thomas Tredway Library, Augustana College, Rock Island, IL	A&R	Total	21,000,000	69,000	272.46	18,800,000	1,015,198	120,000	BLDD Architects
		New	n.a.	n.a.	n.a.	n.a.	n.a.	n.a.	
		Renovated	n.a.	n.a.	n.a.	n.a.	n.a.	n.a.	
Bel and Jack Ostrow Library, American Jewish University, Bel Air, CA	A&R	Total	n.a.	n.a.	n.a.	n.a.	n.a.	n.a.	Paul Murdoch Architects
		New	n.a.	n.a.	n.a.	n.a.	n.a.	n.a.	
		Renovated	n.a.	25,000	200.00	5,000,000	n.a.	n.a.	

** Joint-use project with public library; see more info on public library tables

TYPE: N = New Buildings; A = Additions; R = Renovations; A&R = Additions & Renovations n.a. = not available; l.f. = linear feet

Table 2 / New Public Library Buildings, 2014

	Pop. ('000)	Code	Project Cost	Const. Cost	Gross Area (Sq. Ft.)	Sq. Ft. Cost	Equip. Cost	Other Costs	Federal Funds	State Funds	Local Funds	Gift Funds	Architect
California													
Pico Rivera	64	B	$13,024,269	$8,840,891	16,199	$545.77	$1,000,000	$3,183,378	0	0	$13,024,269	0	Carde Ten Architects
San Francisco	17	B	14,331,220	10,061,435	8,500	1,183.70	500,000	3,765,426	0	0	13,831,220	$500,000	Leddy Maytum Stacy Architects
Santa Monica	22	B	9,700,000	7,162,000	8,690	824.16	680,000	1,858,000	0	0	9,700,000	0	Koning Eizenberg Architecture
Colorado													
Carbondale	8	B	6,185,905	3,702,973	13,000	284.84	544,703	1,262,913	0	0	5,909,770	276,135	Humphries Poli; Willis Pember
Glenwood Springs	12	B	6,545,646	4,551,042	15,686	290.13	369,223	625,381	0	0	6,413,741	131,905	Humphries Poli Architects
Florida													
Fort Myers	202	B	20,142,557	16,361,733	43,135	379.32	1,172,718	2,608,106	0	0	18,735,972	1,456,000	BSSW Architects, Inc.
Georgia													
Cumming	54	B	6,429,042	4,559,433	24,580	185.49	800,000	1,069,609	0	$2,000,000	5,860,578	0	Craig, Gaulden, Davis
Illinois													
Chicago	44	B	1,174,416	943,804	8,300	113.71	154,881	75,731	0	0	1,174,416	0	STL Architects, Inc.
Iowa													
Cedar Rapids	258	MS	44,513,000	23,454,679	94,000	249.52	7,967,717	5,580,934	$25,520,330	10,000,000	4,800,000	4,195,670	OPN Architects, Inc.
Massachusetts													
East Boston	40	B	17,360,988	10,045,600	14,878	675.20	1,085,000	4,630,388	0	7,255,988	10,105,000	0	William Rawn Associates
Granby	6	M	4,802,173	3,733,500	12,600	296.31	100,790	752,883	0	2,603,663	1,711,576	701,934	Johnson Roberts Associates
Westwood	14	M	12,398,165	9,148,365	32,026	285.65	818,000	2,431,800	0	3,883,915	9,300,000	690,000	Finegold Alexander & Associates
Minnesota													
Minneapolis	49	B	11,214,969	8,660,829	30,000	288.69	682,686	1,871,454	0	0	11,214,969	0	VJAA
Saint Paul	30	n.a.	15,493,208	10,262,950	41,155	249.37	619,972	3,439,728	0	0	15,493,208	0	HGA Architects & Engineers

Symbol Code: B=Branch Library; BS=Branch and System Headquarters; M=Main Library; MS=Main and System Headquarters; n.a.=not available.

Location		Code											Architect
New Hampshire													
Bethlehem	3	M	1,700,000	1,200,000	5,000	240.00	200,000	300,000	50,000	0	90,000	1,560,000	E.H. Danson Associates
New Mexico													
Dixon	1	M	707,968	553,620	3,000	184.54	50,000	54,348	47,208	0	0	660,760	Autotroph Design
New York													
Staten Island	n.a.	B	11,837,318	7,254,616	10,000	725.46	574,850	3,303,852	0	740,042	11,097,277	0	A*PT Architecture
Ohio													
Columbus	12	B	6,973,835	4,046,432	14,985	270.03	293,291	2,133,843	0	0	6,973,835	0	NBBJ Architects
Garfield Heights	29	B	11,512,740	9,387,788	30,000	313.93	928,232	935,020	0	0	11,512,740	0	Bostwick Design Partnership
North Royalton	31	B	10,651,209	8,182,936	30,000	272.76	1,042,766	900,507	0	0	10,651,209	0	Richard Fleischmann + Partners
Parma	58	B	13,563,654	10,307,945	42,918	240.17	1,272,709	1,101,700	0	0	13,563,654	0	Design Group
Pennsylvania													
Annville	22	M	960,000	740,000	7,000	105.71	26,000	0	0	0		960,000	None
Hollidaysburg	24	M	3,000,500	2,192,000	11,364	192.93	100,000	575,000	0	1,550,000		1,450,000	Kasun Architects, Inc.
South Carolina													
Hanahan	16	B	2,075,095	1,549,095	6,700	231.21	156,000	130,000	0	38,000	2,037,095	0	SGA Architecture
South Dakota													
Sioux Falls	31	M	3,504,490	2,806,000	15,720	178.50	365,390	333,100	0	0	3,504,490	0	Architecture Incorporated
Virginia													
Virginia Beach*	40	n.a.	41,756,598	25,291,717	125,000	202.33	9,400,000	3,799,922	0	36,491,639	5,264,959	0	Carrier Johnson; RRMM; Anderson
Washington													
Federal Way	92	B	7,786,000	5,428,000	15,000	361.87	1,207,000	1,151,000	0	0	7,786,000	0	SRG Partnership
Wisconsin													
Cedarburg	11	M	6,329,226	5,325,691	22,537	236.31	442,998	560,537	0	0	6,200,000	730,000	Engberg Anderson
Canada													
Toronto, Ont.	27	B	9,192,000	6,502,000	16,000	406.38	1,447,745	1,242,255	0	0	9,192,000	0	KPMB Architects

*Joint-use public and academic project, also listed under Academic New Buildings

Symbol Code: B=Branch Library; BS=Branch and System Headquarters; M=Main Library; MS=Main and System Headquarters; n.a.=not available.

Table 3 / Public Library Buildings, Additions and Renovations, 2014

	Pop. ('000)	Code	Project Cost	Const. Cost	Gross Area (Sq. Ft.)	Sq. Ft. Cost	Equip. Cost	Other Costs	Federal Funds	State Funds	Local Funds	Gift Funds	Architect
Alabama													
Birmingham	19	B	$1,771,599	$1,498,420	8,000	$187.30	$268,179	$5,000	$100,000	$150,000	$1,403,420	$118,180	Herrington Architects; Chasm Architecture
Arizona													
Goodyear	80	B	2,325,471	552,636	10,363	53.30	308,985	113,850	0	0	2,325,471	0	Dick & Fritsche
Mesa	409	B	350,133	219,374	2,239	97.98	55,759	75,000	0	0	350,133	0	Emc2 Group Architect
California													
Glendale	192	B	6,766,371	5,306,889	26,000	204.11	431,224	1,028,258	0	0	8,185,228	0	Gruen Associates; Offenhauser/Mekeel
Lennox	23	B	8,336,000	5,388,500	10,826	497.74	691,000	2,256,500	0	0	0	8,336,000	Cwa Aia, Inc.
Rio Linda	15	B	1,326,000	830,000	7,778	106.71	326,000	170,000	1,318,000	0	8,000	0	Architectural Nexus
San Carlos	34	B	1,460,000	1,255,000	21,836	57.47	85,000	120,000	0	0	928,000	532,000	Anderson Brulé Architects
Colorado													
Colorado Springs	178	MS	10,650,000	4,050,000	112,883	35.88	2,200,000	650,000	0	129,000	9,086,000	1,785,000	Humphries Poli Architects
Connecticut													
Ridgefield	24	M	20,756,170	17,781,545	43,671	407.17	1,070,449	1,904,176	0	500,000	7,498,331	12,758,120	Newman Architects Pc
District of Columbia													
Washington	25	B	10,199,995	9,000,000	17,000	529.41	449,995	750,000	0	0	10,199,995	0	Bell Architects
Florida													
Jupiter	57	B	1,681,604	1,142,103	24,950	45.80	336,437	203,064	0	0	1,681,604	0	Colomé & Associates, Inc.
Tampa	343	B	2,527,000	1,967,000	13,640	144.21	400,000	160,000	0	0	2,855,000	116,819	Long & Associates
Valrico	272	B	2,410,000	1,850,000	12,520	147.76	400,000	160,000	0	0	2,855,000	0	Long & Associates

Symbol Code: B=Branch Library; BS=Branch and System Headquarters; M=Main Library; MS=Main and System Headquarters; n.a.=not available.

Illinois

Barrington	44	MS	8,786,000	6,636,000	60,000	110.60	1,500,000	650,000	0	0	8,800,000	0	Engberg Anderson
Lincolnshire	41	M	1,230,000	800,000	33,000	24.24	320,000	110,000	0	0	1,230,000	0	Product Architecture + Design
Niles	30	M	5,252,000	380,000	62,000	61.29	752,000	700,000	0	59,000	5,193,400	0	Product Architecture + Design

Indiana

Kewanna	10	M	1,193,000	1,100,000	8,588	128.08	5,000	88,000	500,000	0	650,000	50,000	Mohler Architects, Pc

Iowa

Nevada	7	M	2,253,959	1,738,500	17,000	102.26	306,523	208,936	0	0	1,120,000	1,133,959	Feh Associates, Inc.

Kentucky

Covington	50	B	12,445,000	10,139,000	64,700	156.70	1,211,000	1,095,000	0	0	12,195,980	249,020	Designgroup

Maryland

Laurel	25	B	6,075,000	4,110,000	24,000	171.25	1,215,000	750,000	0	0	6,075,000	0	Grimm + Parker
Mt. Airy	24	B	503,031	394,336	16,431	24.00	95,025	13,670	0	157,000	346,031	0	Rubeling & Associates

Massachusetts

Athol	12	M	8,500,000	6,726,000	20,068	335.16	359,000	1,390,000	0	0	3,730,000	197,000	Tappé Associates, Inc.
Foxborough	17	M	10,806,053	7,974,589	32,638	244.33	750,450	2,081,014	0	0	7,500,000	540,000	Lib Architects
Holyoke	40	M	14,500,000	11,900,000	40,515	293.72	700,000	1,900,000	2,400,000	4,367,594	5,600,000	2,200,000	Finegold Alexander + Associates
North Easton	23	M	448,745	285,334	9,000	31.70	59,051	104,360	0	40,000	150,000	260,000	James Thomas Architect
West Tisbury	3	M	6,668,649	5,226,650	13,551	385.70	249,410	1,192,589	0	2,982,544	1,500,000	2,186,105	Oudens Ello Architecture

Nebraska

Yutan	2	M	73,137	65,469	1,708	38.33	1,281	6,387	0	0	73,137	0	Steve Eveans Architect Pc

New Jersey

Maywood	10	M	577,964	270,123	5,070	53.28	270,904	36,937	0	0	577,964	0	Arcari + Iovino
Norwood	6	M	652,985	506,235	5,150	98.30	75,000	71,750	0	0	652,985	0	Arcari + Iovino

New Mexico

Hobbs	43	M	3,372,180	2,811,635	41,171	68.29	404,955	155,590	0	0	3,372,180	0	Teske Architects

Symbol Code: B=Branch Library; BS=Branch and System Headquarters; M=Main Library; MS=Main and System Headquarters; n.a.=not available.

Table 3 / Public Library Buildings, Additions and Renovations, 2014 *(cont.)*

	Pop. ('000)	Code	Project Cost	Const. Cost	Gross Area (Sq. Ft.)	Sq. Ft. Cost	Equip. Cost	Other Costs	Federal Funds	State Funds	Local Funds	Gift Funds	Architect
New York													
Brooklyn*	34	B	$2,700,000	$1,800,000	6,000	$300.00	$900,000	0	$1,076,827	$358,323	$1,214,850	$50,000	Beatty Harvey Coco Architects
Brooklyn	15	B	1,500,005	1,020,005	11,655	87.52	480,000	0	508,463	10,694	730,843	250,000	Beatty Harvey Coco Architects
Commack	118	B	4,469,271	3,468,368	13,074	265.29	394,534	$606,369	0	247,402	4,215,682	6,187	Bbs Architects
East Hampton	16	M	7,000,000	5,500,000	10,000	550.00	550,000	950,000	0	417,000	0	6,583,000	Robert A.M. Stern Architects; Skolnick Design
New York	n.a.	B	9,673,408	7,526,311	18,986	396.41	574,758	1,572,339	0	1,710,244	6,434,754	1,528,410	Dattner Architects; Andrew Berman Architect
Plainview	28	n.a.	338,650	182,800	4,290	42.60	132,350	23,500	0	122,383	216,267	0	John A. Grillo Architects
Staten Island	n.a.	B	15,351,338	9,262,054	12,000	771.83	641,223	3,803,707	0	95,082	14,764,677	491,581	Andrew Berman Architect
Ohio													
Avon	21	B	231,803	104,470	10,400	10.05	92,983	33,350	0	0	231,803	0	Arkinetics
Cincinnati	12	B	1,242,727	1,080,454	1,144	944.45	113,773	48,500	0	0	1,242,727	0	K4 Architecture
Euclid	48	M	1,133,409	942,068	28,193	33.42	53,073	138,268	0	0	1,116,909	16,500	Holzheimer, Bolek + Meehan (HBM)
Lodi	5	B	2,390,365	1,706,533	7,000	243.80	65,221	618,611	0	0	2,390,365	0	Prime Engineering/HBM Architects
Parma	58	B	14,465,548	12,617,320	28,826	437.70	787,181	1,061,047	0	0	14,465,548	0	Holzheimer, Bolek + Meehan (HBM)
Oregon													
Newberg	23	M	385,000	195,000	3,600	54.17	125,000	65,000	0	0	0	385,000	DJ Architecture

Symbol Code: B=Branch Library; BS=Branch and System Headquarters; M=Main Library; MS=Main and System Headquarters; n.a.=not available.

*FEMA still owes the library more than $1 million for a portion of this work as the damage was caused by Superstorm Sandy in 2012

Symbol Code: B=Branch Library; BS=Branch and System Headquarters; M=Main Library; MS=Main and System Headquarters; n.a.=not available.

Six-Year Cost Summary

	Fiscal 2009	Fiscal 2010	Fiscal 2011	Fiscal 2012	Fiscal 2013	Fiscal 2014
Number of new buildings	80	70	62	34	27	29
Number of ARRs	90	55	89	73	47	55
Sq. ft. new buildings	1,772,434	1,608,324	1,555,598	898,865	470,167	717,973
Sq. ft. ARRs	1,942,810	1,271,709	1,672,664	1,375,307	715,380	1,164,355
New Buildings						
Construction cost	$486,722,590	$453,517,944	$454,425,651	$263,313,088	$139,136,298	$212,257,074
Equipment cost	54,212,351	49,087,060	47,836,977	30,533,085	16,184,831	34,002,671
Site cost	37,658,061	28,981,431	35,104,201	14,215,747	28,272,719	18,929,131
Other cost	75,202,090	110,238,949	113,525,121	53,113,752	29,983,512	49,676,815
Total—Project cost	656,020,880	669,591,384	650,871,920	361,175,672	212,079,360	314,866,191
ARRs—Project cost	482,214,848	234,485,743	447,583,852	241,643,154	145,668,398	260,983,928
New & ARR project cost	$1,138,235,728	$904,077,127	$1,098,455,772	$602,818,826	$357,747,758	$575,850,119

Symbol Code: ARR—Additions, Renovations, and Remodels

Funding Sources

	Fiscal 2009	Fiscal 2010	Fiscal 2011	Fiscal 2012	Fiscal 2013	Fiscal 2014
Federal, new buildings	$17,049,910	$8,038,118	$5,854,589	$38,465,599	$1,000,000	$25,617,538
Federal, ARRs	7,873,278	10,657,831	9,270,750	18,882,075	1,684,211	6,239,463
Federal, Total	$24,923,188	$18,695,949	$15,125,339	$57,347,674	$2,684,211	$31,857,001
State, new buildings	$63,038,118	$67,097,479	$43,548,440	$19,558,708	$9,570,111	64,563,247
State, ARRs	40,827,176	27,486,827	33,147,756	9,286,208	2,017,590	19,563,872
State, Total	$103,865,294	$94,584,306	$76,696,196	$28,844,916	$11,587,701	$84,127,119
Local, new buildings	$518,738,443	$558,427,058	$567,608,480	$284,164,989	$192,466,192	215,147,978
Local, ARRs	392,376,170	251,796,891	348,642,090	184,662,609	133,692,708	188,446,449
Local, Total	$911,114,613	$810,223,949	$916,250,570	$468,827,598	326,158,900	$403,594,427
Gift, new buildings	$58,532,660	$45,898,678	$37,374,332	$19,573,952	$12,366,431	13,312,404
Gift, ARRs	42,456,942	15,599,975	58,733,738	29,367,511	8,996,727	50,361,901
Gift, Total	$100,989,602	$61,498,653	$96,108,070	$48,941,463	$21,363,158	$63,674,305
Total—Funds Used	$1,140,892,697	$985,002,857	$1,104,180,175	$603,961,651	$361,793,970	$583,252,852

Symbol Code: ARR—Additions, Renovations, and Remodels

Public Library State Rankings, 2012

State	Library Visits per Capita	Registered Users per Capita	Circulation Transactions per Capita	Interlibrary Loans Received per 1,000 Population	Average Public-use Computers per Outlet
Alabama	46	35	47	27	19
Alaska	25	9	31	35	45
Arizona	35	37	25	31	4
Arkansas	38	18	43	43	40
California	34	21	37	20	16
Colorado	10	10	4	18	5
Connecticut	3	42	18	14	17
Delaware	27	46	33	6	18
District of Columbia	40	40	44	50	1
Florida	36	34	36	48	2
Georgia	51	49	49	22	12
Hawaii	42	5	45	51	43
Idaho	4	26	9	25	36
Illinois	6	51	12	8	21
Indiana	13	15	5	28	11
Iowa	8	8	16	19	47
Kansas	18	7	10	11	41
Kentucky	32	25	34	42	7
Louisiana	45	24	46	39	29
Maine	16	11	23	7	48
Maryland	26	22	13	32	3
Massachusetts	9	38	15	4	33
Michigan	21	36	21	12	15
Minnesota	29	2	11	15	27
Mississippi	48	44	51	47	37
Missouri	22	19	14	23	32
Montana	30	45	27	16	38
Nebraska	17	4	19	37	42
Nevada	39	43	28	30	14
New Hampshire	1	1	7	17	51
New Jersey	23	31	32	13	20
New Mexico	33	14	39	45	23
New York	19	39	24	9	25
North Carolina	37	23	38	49	13
North Dakota	43	48	35	21	44
Ohio	2	3	2	5	24
Oklahoma	31	12	29	44	30
Oregon	14	30	1	2	31
Pennsylvania	44	50	40	10	35
Rhode Island	20	47	30	3	8
South Carolina	41	27	41	36	10
South Dakota	24	28	20	33	49
Tennessee	47	33	48	41	22
Texas	50	32	42	34	6

State	Library Visits per Capita	Registered Users per Capita	Circulation Transactions per Capita	Interlibrary Loans Received per 1,000 Population	Average Public-use Computers per Outlet
Utah	5	13	3	46	28
Vermont	7	29	26	24	50
Virginia	28	20	17	40	26
Washington	11	16	6	38	9
West Virginia	49	41	50	26	46
Wisconsin	15	17	8	1	34
Wyoming	12	6	22	29	39

State	Public-use Internet Computers per 5,000 Population	Print Materials per Capita	Current Print Serial Subscriptions per 1,000 Population	Audio Physical Units per 1,000 Population	Video Physical Units per 1,000 Population
Alabama	20	39	50	43	45
Alaska	17	16	7	22	3
Arizona	39	51	44	41	39
Arkansas	34	31	38	47	31
California	50	45	42	42	43
Colorado	18	35	29	21	14
Connecticut	13	6	19	7	6
Delaware	47	43	17	34	30
District of Columbia	8	38	39	35	25
Florida	35	48	41	40	32
Georgia	45	50	51	51	50
Hawaii	51	30	48	18	46
Idaho	15	22	28	26	24
Illinois	16	14	10	2	13
Indiana	9	10	14	5	4
Iowa	4	9	2	10	11
Kansas	5	12	13	20	7
Kentucky	27	40	6	39	36
Louisiana	21	28	11	45	27
Maine	3	2	8	16	10
Maryland	40	34	30	13	33
Massachusetts	30	3	18	11	12
Michigan	14	18	20	17	17
Minnesota	23	23	25	25	34
Mississippi	32	42	43	50	47
Missouri	33	21	16	23	29
Montana	12	25	31	37	35
Nebraska	1	8	5	24	20
Nevada	49	49	46	29	26
New Hampshire	7	1	1	3	2
New Jersey	31	20	24	8	21
New Mexico	19	27	34	32	38
New York	29	17	12	15	16

State	Public-use Internet Computers per 5,000 Population	Print Materials per Capita	Current Print Serial Subscriptions per 1,000 Population	Audio Physical Units per 1,000 Population	Video Physical Units per 1,000 Population
North Carolina	43	47	45	49	51
North Dakota	24	15	23	30	28
Ohio	25	13	3	1	1
Oklahoma	28	32	40	31	44
Oregon	37	26	27	14	15
Pennsylvania	48	37	33	27	42
Rhode Island	10	7	26	33	23
South Carolina	36	41	36	44	41
South Dakota	11	11	22	28	22
Tennessee	41	44	49	46	48
Texas	38	46	47	48	49
Utah	46	29	32	9	18
Vermont	2	4	4	12	8
Virginia	44	33	37	36	40
Washington	26	36	21	19	19
West Virginia	42	24	35	38	37
Wisconsin	22	19	15	6	5
Wyoming	6	5	9	4	9

State	Total Paid FTE Staff per 25,000 Population	Paid FTE Librarians per 25,000 Population	ALA-MLS Librarians per 25,000 Population	Other Paid FTE Staff per 25,000 Population
Alabama	38	31	44	39
Alaska	28	28	28	24
Arizona	44	47	35	31
Arkansas	41	45	48	30
California	46	48	31	43
Colorado	10	27	13	8
Connecticut	7	5	2	13
Delaware	42	34	38	41
District of Columbia	8	21	3	5
Florida	45	43	29	40
Georgia	50	51	46	44
Hawaii	33	37	14	28
Idaho	21	32	40	12
Illinois	4	8	6	4
Indiana	5	13	10	3
Iowa	14	3	25	33
Kansas	6	7	20	7
Kentucky	24	10	33	32
Louisiana	17	18	26	18
Maine	11	6	11	25
Maryland	12	17	18	14
Massachusetts	19	9	5	26
Michigan	25	26	12	23

State	Total Paid FTE Staff per 25,000 Population	Paid FTE Librarians per 25,000 Population	ALA-MLS Librarians per 25,000 Population	Other Paid FTE Staff per 25,000 Population
Minnesota	32	35	22	29
Mississippi	35	14	50	49
Missouri	13	33	49	6
Montana	37	24	41	46
Nebraska	16	12	32	21
Nevada	51	49	45	50
New Hampshire	2	1	1	16
New Jersey	18	30	9	11
New Mexico	36	29	39	37
New York	9	19	7	10
North Carolina	47	50	36	42
North Dakota	39	22	42	48
Ohio	3	15	8	1
Oklahoma	30	20	30	35
Oregon	26	36	19	15
Pennsylvania	40	42	27	34
Rhode Island	20	16	4	20
South Carolina	34	38	21	27
South Dakota	27	11	43	36
Tennessee	49	46	51	45
Texas	48	44	37	47
Utah	31	39	34	22
Vermont	15	2	24	38
Virginia	29	40	17	17
Washington	22	41	15	9
West Virginia	43	25	47	51
Wisconsin	23	23	16	19
Wyoming	1	4	23	2

State	Total Operating Revenue per Capita	State Operating Revenue per Capita	Local Operating Revenue per Capita	Other Operating Revenue per Capita
Alabama	46	27	45	26
Alaska	11	26	10	24
Arizona	36	42	34	49
Arkansas	37	14	39	39
California	33	41	27	30
Colorado	9	47	8	17
Connecticut	8	35	9	4
Delaware	38	8	42	40
District of Columbia	4	49	?	51
Florida	41	22	37	43
Georgia	49	12	48	47
Hawaii	44	2	51	32
Idaho	29	28	26	19
Illinois	2	11	1	12
Indiana	12	9	12	20

State	Total Operating Revenue per Capita	State Operating Revenue per Capita	Local Operating Revenue per Capita	Other Operating Revenue per Capita
Iowa	24	33	20	11
Kansas	15	20	14	7
Kentucky	20	21	17	27
Louisiana	14	24	13	41
Maine	25	37	33	3
Maryland	16	3	24	9
Massachusetts	21	25	19	14
Michigan	19	32	16	21
Minnesota	23	18	21	13
Mississippi	51	10	50	29
Missouri	18	31	15	18
Montana	43	39	41	33
Nebraska	26	38	22	23
Nevada	30	5	36	35
New Hampshire	6	45	5	10
New Jersey	7	34	4	22
New Mexico	35	16	35	45
New York	3	13	6	2
North Carolina	45	19	44	46
North Dakota	39	15	40	28
Ohio	1	1	32	1
Oklahoma	27	30	23	37
Oregon	13	36	11	15
Pennsylvania	40	7	46	8
Rhode Island	17	4	29	5
South Carolina	42	23	38	48
South Dakota	34	50	30	42
Tennessee	50	43	47	44
Texas	48	48	43	50
Utah	32	40	25	36
Vermont	28	51	31	6
Virginia	31	17	28	38
Washington	5	44	3	34
West Virginia	47	6	49	31
Wisconsin	22	29	18	25
Wyoming	10	46	7	16

State	Total Operating Expenditures per Capita	Total Collection Expenditures per Capita	Total Staff Expenditures per Capita	Salaries and Wages Expenditures per Capita
Alabama	45	46	46	45
Alaska	10	20	10	17
Arizona	37	30	39	44
Arkansas	39	31	43	42
California	31	44	29	34
Colorado	13	5	14	11
Connecticut	5	9	3	2

State	Total Operating Expenditures per Capita	Total Collection Expenditures per Capita	Total Staff Expenditures per Capita	Salaries and Wages Expenditures per Capita
Delaware	35	40	34	35
District of Columbia	2	35	1	1
Florida	38	39	41	43
Georgia	49	50	49	49
Hawaii	44	47	42	32
Idaho	30	36	32	30
Illinois	1	3	6	3
Indiana	12	2	15	14
Iowa	23	19	19	20
Kansas	15	11	17	16
Kentucky	32	23	35	36
Louisiana	18	21	24	26
Maine	25	34	21	18
Maryland	14	8	12	13
Massachusetts	17	13	16	10
Michigan	19	24	22	24
Minnesota	24	27	23	23
Mississippi	51	51	51	51
Missouri	22	6	25	22
Montana	43	41	40	41
Nebraska	27	16	26	25
Nevada	34	32	33	33
New Hampshire	6	7	4	5
New Jersey	9	17	7	4
New Mexico	36	25	36	8
New York	3	14	2	38
North Carolina	46	48	45	46
North Dakota	42	29	44	40
Ohio	4	1	8	7
Oklahoma	26	10	28	28
Oregon	11	15	11	15
Pennsylvania	41	42	38	39
Rhode Island	16	33	13	12
South Carolina	40	38	37	37
South Dakota	33	26	31	29
Tennessee	50	49	50	50
Texas	48	45	47	47
Utah	29	12	30	31
Vermont	21	28	20	19
Virginia	28	37	27	27
Washington	8	4	9	9
West Virginia	47	43	48	48
Wisconsin	20	22	18	21
Wyoming	7	18	5	6

Notes

FTE = full-time equivalent.

Per capita and per population are based on the total unduplicated population of legal service areas.

The District of Columbia, although not a state, is included in the state rankings. Special care should be used in comparing its data to state data.

Caution should be used in making comparisons with the state of Hawaii, as Hawaii reports only one public library for the entire state.

An ALA-MLS is a master's degree from a program of library and information studies accredited by the American Library Association

Total operating expenditures includes total staff expenditures, collection expenditures, and other operating expenditures. State rankings of other operating expenditures are not included in this report.

Total staff expenditures include expenditures for salaries and wages and benefits. State rankings of employee benefits expenditures are not included in this report.

Source: Compiled by Carol Collier from *Public Libraries in the United States Survey: Fiscal Year 2012,* Institute of Museum and Library Services, 2014.

Book Trade Research and Statistics

Hachette-Amazon Row Leads 2014 Publishing News

Jim Milliot
Editorial Director, *Publishers Weekly*

The longest-running story in book publishing in 2014 was the dispute over e-book sale terms between Amazon and the Hachette Book Group.

The disagreement stemmed from negotiations between Amazon and Hachette over the discount the online retailer would receive on the price of e-books. While negotiations over discounts between publishers and accounts are a routine part of the business and often lead to wrangling between the parties, the negotiations between Amazon and Hachette became a national issue when Amazon stopped taking pre-orders on new Hachette books and also made it difficult to order many Hachette print books.

The issue became public in May and lasted until fall. Until the deal was reached, Hachette and Amazon criticized each other in the press, columnists and media commentators weighed in (often on the side of Hachette), the issue of a possible investigation into Amazon antitrust practices was raised, and authors took sides. While some authors supported Amazon, a larger group formed an organization called Authors United whose primary goal was to limit the "collateral damage" suffered by authors whose sales were being hurt during the dispute. The Hachette-Amazon battle was viewed by many as a defining moment in the book industry, arguing that Amazon's decision to use its power in the marketplace against Hachette was the beginning of an era when the retailer would be able to determine many industry practices.

When the two sides finally reached an agreement, the settlement was a bit anticlimactic as several weeks earlier Amazon had reached a deal with Simon & Schuster with much less rancor. Under its sales agreement with Amazon, S&S signed a multiyear deal that covered terms on both its print and digital books. As part of its agreement on e-books, S&S moved back to a version of "agency pricing" under which S&S sets the price for e-books. Under the wholesale model, which is used to sell print books, Amazon and other vendors receive a discount of about 50 percent off the cover price of a book and can sell it at whatever price they choose.

Publishers have been concerned that Amazon's strategy to offer deep discounts on e-books would destroy the market for print books, while also driving many of Amazon's online competitors out of business, leaving it the only major bookseller of print and e-books. It was this fear that led to the Hachette-Amazon battle. With the S&S deal as a model, Amazon and Hachette reached essentially the same agreement in November.

Both Hachette and Amazon said they were happy with the deal; both Hachette and S&S noted that the agreement "maintains the author's share of income generated by e-book sales."

It was the fear of Amazon's dominance that led five publishers to collude with Apple to fix e-book prices several years ago. Although the publishers that were charged by the Justice Department with collusion settled, Apple itself chose to go to trial; it lost in spring 2013. It then appealed that decision, and in December oral arguments in the case were heard.

At stake for Apple is up to $400 million. In an agreement approved by Judge Denise Cote in November 2014, Apple agreed to pay $400 million to consumers if it loses the appeal, $50 million if the decision is remanded to a lower court for further proceedings, and nothing if it wins. There is also the possibility that Apple will appeal the new decision, a process that could go to the Supreme Court.

The federal lawsuit was only one of the e-book price-fixing cases Apple was contending with in 2014. The company was also fighting a suit brought by most state attorneys general and a consumer class action suit. In the spring, however, Apple agreed to settle with both the states and the class action.

Acquisitions Rise

With the exception of the Penguin-Random House merger in 2013, acquisitions within book publishing had been relatively scarce since the Great Recession of 2008–2009. That changed in 2014. The number of deals rose, including an acquisition involving one of the country's largest trade houses, HarperCollins, which bought one of the largest independent publishers, Harlequin. Harper paid C$455 million for Toronto-based Harlequin, which had sales in 2013 of about C$400 million. Harper said it acquired the company to speed both its international expansion and to accelerate growth of digital content (about a quarter of Harlequin's revenue comes from e-books). Harlequin generates about 40 percent of its revenues from titles published in languages other than English and has offices in more than 30 countries.

Following the completion of the purchase on August 1, Harper moved quickly to take advantage of Harlequin's global presence by rebranding Harlequin's German office as HarperGermany; it will use that company to begin publishing German-language titles. Harper intends to rebrand Harlequin offices in other countries in much the same way and to publish commercial fiction in local languages.

The second-biggest deal of the year was one that didn't get completed. In late June the Hachette Book Group agreed to acquire the Perseus Book Group and then sell Perseus's distribution arm to Ingram. The deal was originally set to be completed at the end of July, but—just days before the expected close—notices were sent to Perseus employees explaining that the parties were not able to finish the transaction by the end of the month. The deal was still expected to be completed by the end of August, but only a few weeks later the purchase was called off. The only statement came from Perseus, which noted that the three parties "could not reach an agreement on everything necessary to close the transaction."

One of the reasons behind Hachette's bid for Perseus was to add more nonfiction titles to its list, and in November it reached an agreement to acquire Black Dog & Leventhal, publisher of 250 illustrated titles and other nonfiction works. That purchase closed in early 2015. (For more deals, see the "Mergers and Acquisitions" section below.)

The future of Barnes & Noble was another major story in 2014. In the middle of the year, the board of directors of the country's largest bricks-and-mortar bookstore chain approved a plan for the company to move forward with examining the possibility of separating its retail trade stores from Nook Media, the division that houses its Nook digital assets as well as its college stores. The Nook digital business continued to shrink in 2014 as sales of both its hardware and digital content units fell.

To prepare for the eventual separation, which the company hopes will occur by the middle of the second quarter of 2015, B&N bought back the investments made in Nook Media in 2012 by Microsoft and Pearson. Through the buy-back, B&N hopes to simplify the process of splitting up the company. Although B&N executives have said they will separate the retail stores from Nook Media, at the time this article was prepared B&N had not announced a firm plan, and there was speculation that it would try to keep the trade stores and the college stores together while splitting off just the digital business.

One reason B&N executives feel confident about operating its retail business as a stand-alone unit is the improved outlook for print book sales. The threat that sales of e-books would overwhelm print book sales and lead to massive closings of physical bookstores largely passed in 2014 as unit sales of print books rose for the first time since e-books exploded in the market in 2010. According to Nielsen BookScan, unit sales of print books rose 2.4 percent in 2014 over 2013, to 635 million units. (BookScan captures about 80 percent of all print book sales.) The increase was driven by a 3.4 percent increase in sales through the retail and club channel, which includes traditional bookstores plus Amazon; it offset a decline in sales through the mass merchandiser channel, which fell 1.8 percent. Sales of children's books, both print and digital, did exceptionally well in 2014; unit sales of children's fiction print books rose 12.0 percent, while print units of children's nonfiction books increased 15.6 percent. Print units of adult nonfiction also rose during the year, climbing 1.4 percent, while sales of adult fiction fell 7.9 percent.

The children's segment benefitted from a number of blockbuster titles in the year, included the three titles in the Divergent trilogy, books tied to the movie *Frozen,* a series of Minecraft books, and a number of John Green titles led by *The Fault in Our Stars.* In the adult segment, *Killing Patton* by Bill O'Reilly and Martin Dugard was the top nonfiction seller in 2014, selling more than 1.2 million copies in print, while *Gone Girl* was the leader in fiction, selling more than 962,000 copies in print. The top five e-book sellers on Amazon during the year were *The Fault in Our Stars, Gone Girl, Divergent, The Goldfinch,* and *Insurgent.*

Shakeouts

The disruption in the book market in recent years caused by the growth of digital publishing and bookselling led to a number of companies exploring ways to take advantage of the changes. Although a few startups closed prior to 2014, the majority of these companies remained in business hoping that sustained profitability was just around the corner. That changed in 2014 as much more of a shakeout took place, with several companies closing down and others being sold.

Among those that closed was Bilbary, the online retail site founded in December 2011 by former Waterstones chief executive Tim Coates. Originally started with the intention of selling e-books to consumers and libraries, the company first encountered trouble when publishers became reluctant to add their e-books to Bilbary's library-lending program. Still, Bilbary had amassed about 380,000 e-books from more than 7,000 publishers on its site by early 2014. As it sought to focus more on consumer sales, however, the company was unable to raise enough new funds and closed in April. Togather.com was another company that made a slight change to its original business plan, but failed to gain traction in 2014. Started in 2012 by author Andrew Kessler, Togather's original goal was to create a platform that allowed authors or their fans to propose an author event and get commitments from fans planning to attend, well before the event was scheduled to be held. Kessler later modified his approach to focus on large institutions and signed a deal with B&N College in late 2013, through which B&N would use Togather to research and promote book events aimed at students using its campus stores. Togather suspended operations in the spring, however, citing disagreements with investors.

Paperight, founded by Arthur Attwell and based in Cape Town, South Africa, offered a platform that allowed copy shops to become print-on-demand (POD)-driven bookstores in what Attwell called "distributed print-on-demand." Late in 2014 Attwell announced that Paperight would close down at the end of the year.

Readmill, conceived as a social reading app in December 2011 by Henrik Berggren, shut down in summer 2014 with much of its staff joining Dropbox. In a farewell note on the Readmill site, Berggren acknowledged that the company had "failed to create a sustainable platform for reading." Based in Berlin, it had tried various ways to add publisher content and build consumer traffic, including reaching a deal with Penguin U.K. that allowed customers to buy directly from the publisher and read the titles via their Readmill apps. In the end, Readmill could not attract enough customers willing to buy content through the app.

Another company that closed in 2014 was Graphicly. Originally launched as a platform to distribute digital comics and other visual works, Graphicly repositioned itself several times over the years. In its last iteration Graphicly focused on its digital publishing platform, which allowed publishers or self-publishers to upload, convert, and distribute digital content across a wide range of mobile devices and e-book marketplaces. Following its closing in May, a number of key Graphicly staff members joined Blurb as part of that company's efforts to enhance its self-publishing offerings.

Restructuring

Startups were not the only companies that underwent changes in 2014. A little more than two months after the deal to sell the Perseus Books Group to Hachette and Ingram fell apart, Perseus CEO David Steinberger implemented a restructuring aimed at streamlining the publisher's operations. As a result, Steinberger created two new group roles, appointing Susan Weinberg senior vice president, group publisher, and naming Mark Suchomel to the new post of president, client services. Three executives left as part of the reorganization, including Running Press publisher Chris Navratil. Steinberger also reached outside the company to hire a new senior vice president for operations, Raymond Floyd, whose background includes 13 years with General Electric. He will report to Perseus COO Charles Gallagher.

Other promotions included that of Matty Goldberg to the new role of president of publishing, client and sales development, while Sabrina McCarthy was appointed senior vice president of group sales, taking Goldberg's old post. McCarthy, who had headed up Perseus Distribution Client Services, was succeeded in that role by Heidi Sachner. Jeff Tegge, who was Suchomel's second in command at Legato, will now head that unit. The only other jobs eliminated in the reorganization were those of Patrick Kirk, who was a project manager, and Scott Edinburgh, who was in business development.

In a major reorganization of the editorial operations of Penguin Random House last fall, PRH CEO Markus Dohle created the Penguin Publishing Group, which put all Penguin adult imprints under Madeline McIntosh, who was named president of the new unit. Previously, Penguin's adult imprints operated under the Penguin Adult and Berkley/NAL groups. The selection of McIntosh, who had been PRH's COO and president of U.S. operations, resulted in the departure of publishing veteran Susan Petersen Kennedy, who left the company at the end of 2014.

The move of McIntosh from COO to publisher also led to the promotion of Nihar Malaviya and Jaci Updike to new roles with added responsibilities. Malaviya is now executive vice president and COO, PRH U.S., and Updike is president of sales, PRH U.S. Updike's appointment—from senior vice president, director, adult sales—put her in charge of all of PRH's sales operations, with Felicia Frazier, senior vice president, director, PRH Young Readers Sales, and Cyrus Kheradi, senior vice president, director, PRH International Sales and Marketing, and director, East Asia Business Development, reporting to Updike.

In a reorganization at Simon & Schuster that saw the merger of the house's digital department with its corporate marketing department, Liz Perl was promoted to executive vice president, chief marketing officer, and Ellie Hirschhorn, who was executive vice president, chief digital officer, left the company.

Hachette eliminated 28 positions in June, about 3 percent of its workforce. As part of the restructuring, Hachette closed its Business Plus imprint and folded the titles into the Grand Central Publishing list. Rick Wolff, founder of Business Plus, was let go; he resurfaced at Houghton Mifflin Harcourt, where he was hired to start a new business line.

McGraw-Hill Education restructured its domestic education operations under Peter Cohen, who had been president of its K–12 group. Cohen was named to the newly created position of group president of U.S. Education. In his new role, Cohen is responsible for McGraw-Hill Education's U.S. K–12, Higher Education, and Assessment groups. In related changes, Christine Willig, formerly the K–12 group's senior vice president of products, was promoted to be the new president of the K–12 group. Ellen Haley continues in her role as president of the company's assessment group. Brian Kibby, president of the Higher Education group, left the company.

The American Booksellers Association (ABA) and the American Booksellers Foundation for Free Expression (ABFFE) integrated ABFFE's operations with ABA's. Beginning January 1, 2015, ABFFE became a distinct group within ABA, and ABFFE president Chris Finan became its director.

Judith Regan, who formed her own multimedia unit at Phaidon, Regan Arts, late in 2013 announced her first staff appointments. Michael Szczerban, was named senior editor, moving from Simon & Schuster. Szczerban will acquire both fiction and nonfiction titles. Ron Hogan, former contributing editor at Shelf Awareness and senior editor at Galley Cat, joined Regan Arts as editor, acquiring fiction and nonfiction. Fritz Brantley, an editor and marketer at Routledge, was named associate editor.

The bankruptcy court overseeing Cengage Learning's Chapter 11 proceedings approved the company's plan of reorganization in the spring. Cengage filed for Chapter 11 in July 2013 and under the reorganization plan, the company cut its debt by more than $4 billion and received $1.7 billion in new financing.

Mergers and Acquisitions

The maturation of the digital book market led two companies to make multiple deals in 2014. Open Road acquired two of its e-book publishing competitors in the first half of the year, buying E-Reads and Premiere Digital in deals that added about 1,500 titles to its marketing and distribution network. In a similar move, Vook bought two digital-content companies to add to its distribution and marketing platform. In September it bought Byliner and two months later acquired Coliloquy. Byliner, founded by John Tayman in 2011, was an effort to publish and sell long-form journalism online. In June 2014 reports surfaced that the venture was struggling "to reach the level of growth we'd been hoping for . . . ," according to an e-mail sent to Byliner authors. Those financial problems eventually led Byliner to be sold to Vook, which bought between 60 and 70 Byliner titles.

Coliloquy was founded in 2011 in Palo Alto, California, by Lisa Rutherford and Wayne Lue, to create enhanced e-books and apps that allow readers to make choices while reading that affect the outcome of the book. The company published more than 30 titles and expanded into middle-grade storytelling. Following the purchase, Vook says it will continue to use the Coliloquy brand.

At the very beginning of 2014 online retailer startup Zola Books acquired the assets of Bookish. Bookish was founded by Penguin Group USA, Hachette Book Group, and Simon & Schuster with the goal of creating a book discovery website that would also sell books from all publishers.

A newcomer to book publishing, Start Publishing, a division of Start Media, made two purchases in the year and signed a distribution deal. The company's focus is on building its presence in the e-book market, and that was the driver behind its agreement with Mason Crest to distribute Mason's e-books to the trade market, as well its purchase of e-book publisher Whiskey Creek Press. Its second purchase of the year, Cleis Press and its Viva Editions and Tempted Romance units, was its largest to date and involved the purchase of print assets as well as Cleis's e-book offerings. Rowman & Littlefield started the year making a niche purchase, acquiring the book program from Alban Institute, and in May bought Globe Pequot Press, one of the country's largest regional publishers. In a deal that merged the country's two largest publishers of local history titles, Arcadia Publishing bought the History Press. Courier Corp., whose main business is printing, sold its Creative Homeowner unit to Fox Chapel for $1 million. Skyhorse Publishing paid $1.6 million for the assets of Good Books, which had filed for bankruptcy. In a significant purchase by a Chinese publisher of an American publisher, Phoenix Media bought the children's division of Publications International.

Audiobook publisher Recorded Books was involved in two deals in the year. In January the company was acquired by the investment group Wasserstein & Co. and in May Recorded Books, with Wasserstein's backing, bought HighBridge Audio.

People

At the beginning of 2014 Barnes & Noble, Inc., which has been without a CEO since William Lynch resigned in July 2013, promoted Michael Huseby to the post. Huseby joined B&N in March 2012 as CFO and was named president of B&N and CEO of Nook Media following Lynch's resignation. With his promotion, Huseby oversees all of B&N's operations. Mitch Klipper, CEO of the Retail Group, and Max Roberts, CEO of Barnes & Noble College, report to Huseby, as does the Nook Media unit. Also early in 2014 Baker & Taylor appointed George Coe CEO and president, succeeding Arnie Wight who retired January 15. Coe had run B&T's library division. Dan Reynolds, CEO and president of Workman imprints Storey and Timber, was named CEO of Workman Publishing Company. McGraw Hill Professional's Keith Fox joined Phaidon Press as CEO. Michael Serbinis, founder and CEO of Kobo, gave up his CEO role and was succeeded by Takahito "Taka" Aiki.

In December 2014 Amazon announced that Daphne Durham, publisher of adult trade and children's at Amazon Publishing, would leave the company on January 16, 2015. She was succeeded by Mikyla Bruder, head of global marketing for Amazon Publishing, who assumed publisher responsibilities for Montlake Romance, Thomas & Mercer, Skyscape, Lake Union, 47North and Jet City Comics. Bruder is based in Seattle. Durham took over at Amazon Publishing from Larry Kirshbaum in 2013.

Jan Johnson left her post as publisher of the Red Wheel/Weiser group of imprints, becoming publisher emerita. Johnson had led the group since November 2000. Debra Polansky was named publishing director, books, at the Reader's Digest Association. Amy Einhorn, who left her eponymous imprint at Penguin Random House, joined Macmillan's Flatiron Books imprint as senior vice president and publisher. Alessandra Bastagli joined Nation Books as its new editorial director. Rick Horgan, formerly vice president, executive editor at Crown, joined Scribner with the same title. Michael Sand, executive editor at Little, Brown, was appointed vice president, publisher, adult trade at Abrams.

Evan Schnittman, brought on by Hachette Book Group in May 2012 to help make the company's sales and marketing efforts more compatible with the growth in digital sales, left the publisher December 12. With this departure, HBG eliminated the position of chief marketing and sales officer, which it had created for Schnittman. To lead its sales operation, HBG promoted Chris Murphy to senior vice president, group sales director. Also at HBG Stacy Creamer was named vice president and executive editor of Hachette Books, the newly announced imprint at Hachette, built off of the Hyperion backlist.

Megan Lynch was named editorial director at Ecco, succeeding Lee Boudreaux who decamped the HarperCollins imprint to oversee her own unit at Hachette. Lynch was a senior editor at Riverhead. Margot Schupf was named publisher of Time Home Entertainment, the book and bookazine publishing division of Time Inc., succeeding Jim Childs, who left the company to become publisher at Rowman & Littlefield. Schupf joined the division as vice president, associate publisher in June.

Stuart Applebaum, the dean of corporate communications directors in the publishing industry, was named emeritus executive vice president, corporate communications at Penguin Random House, and Claire von Schilling was promoted to senior vice president, director, corporate communications and will run the day-to-day operations of the department. Also at PRH the publisher created a consumer marketing development and operations group led by Amanda Close.

Jennifer Crewe was named president and director at Columbia University Press after serving as interim director for nine months, and after a career of three decades with the press. Lia Ronnen was appointed publisher of Workman imprint Artisan. Ronnen replaced Ann Bramson, who will now acquire books across Workman imprints in the newly created role of executive director, special projects. Mara Anastas was named publisher of S&S's Aladdin Books and Simon Pulse imprints, succeeding Bethany Buck, who left the company in April 2014. St. Martin's marketing executive Matthew Baldacci moved to Scholastic as vice president of marketing for the Scholastic Trade Publishing division.

Stephanie Kip Rostan was named partner at the Levine Greenberg Agency and the name of the firm was changed to the Levine Greenberg Rostan Literary Agency. Verso Advertising appointed Martha Otis president effective October 1, succeeding Denise Berthiaume, who stepped down from running the day-to-day operations of the firm to become chairman.

Midwest Tape appointed Tammy Faxel publisher of its audiobook and video division, Dreamscape Media. Faxel has served as director of business development since July 2014. Prior to that, she was leader of business development at Brilliance Publishing. Following the decision by Irv Myers to step down as president and CEO of New Leaf Distributing at the end of 2014, New Leaf owner Santosh Krinsky took over Myers's responsibilities.

Mary Rasenberger, a lawyer and six-year Copyright Office and Library of Congress veteran, took over as executive director of the Authors Guild on November 3. She succeeded Paul Aiken, who will continue to consult for the guild. In 2013 Aiken announced that he had ALS, also known as Lou Gehrig's Disease. Amy Stolls was appointed director of literature for the National Endowment for the Arts. Electric Literature editor Benjamin Samuel was named the new program manager for the National Book Foundation.

Among well-known industry figures who died in 2014 were Coffee House Press founding publisher Allan Kornblum, who died at his home in St. Paul, Minnesota, on November 23 of complications from chronic lymphocytic leukemia, a disease that he had been battling since a 2006 diagnosis. He was 65. Marcus Boggs, former editorial director and publisher at Rowman & Littlefield, died November 1 at the age of 66. Frederick Gale Ruffner, Jr., founder of Gale Research Co., passed away August 12 at the age of 88 following a long illness. Oscar Dystel, a pioneer of mass market paperbacks and one-time CEO of Bantam Books, died at the age of 101.

Bestsellers

Since the merger of Random House and Penguin in 2013, the only question in terms of the bestsellers lists has been which company would come in second, and the Hachette Book Group took the honors in 2014. Hachette titles occupied 17 percent of *Publishers Weekly*'s hardcover bestseller slots in 2014 compared with 40 percent for PRH. Hachette had a greater presence on the bestsellers list than HarperCollins and Simon & Schuster despite those companies having more books hit the list. Hachette managed to top its competitors by having a number of long-running bestselling books. *The Goldfinch* was on the hardcover fiction list for 42 weeks and *Grain Brain* stayed on the hardcover nonfiction list for 39 weeks. *David and Goliath* and *I Am Malala* remained on the nonfiction list for 31 and 24 weeks, respectively.

Penguin Random House placed a total of 235 books on the hardcover bestsellers lists in 2014, easily topping the 74 for HarperCollins. PRH's longest-running fiction hardcover bestseller was *Sycamore Row*, which stayed on the list for 18 weeks; in nonfiction *Everything I Need to Know I Learned from a Golden Book* remained on the list for 29 weeks.

In paperback, PRH had a 38 percent share of all bestseller slots, placing 167 titles on *Publishers Weekly*'s trade paperback and mass market lists. Hachette took second place with 55 bestsellers and a 16 percent share of paperback slots. PRH divisions did particularly well in mass market paperback with five of the six longest-running sellers published by a PRH imprint—*Inferno, Sycamore Row, Gone Girl, A Dance with Dragons,* and *The Racketeer.* The three longest-running trade paperbacks were also from PRH—*The Power of Habit* (43 weeks), *Gone Girl* (36), and *The Boys in the Boat* (31).

Prices of U.S. and Foreign Published Materials

Narda Tafuri
Editor, ALA ALCTS Library Materials Price Index Editorial Board

The Library Materials Price Index (LMPI) Editorial Board of the American Library Association's Association for Library Collections and Technical Services' Publications Committee continues to monitor prices for a range of library materials from sources within North America and from other key publishing centers around the world.

The U.S. Consumer Price Index (CPI) increased by 0.8 percent in 2014. This is the lowest increase of the CPI since 2008. CPI data are obtained from the Bureau of Labor Statistics Web site at http://www.bls.gov.

The U.S. Periodical Price Index (USPPI) (Table 1) reestablished by Stephen Bosch in 2014, continues in this year's article using data provided by EBSCO Information Services. Readers are reminded that the new USPPI is based on a mix of both print and online pricing that is a more accurate representation of an average library's journal collection. The base year for this table is set to 2010. Percent changes in average prices from previous years are noted in the chart below under the category "Periodicals."

The 2012 and 2013 figures for Tables 3 (hardcover books), 6 (mass market paperback books), 7 (U.S. paperback books), 7A (audiobooks), and 7B (U.S. e-books), have been restated for this year's article due to late updates to the data.

| | | Percent Change | | |
Index	2010	2011	2012	2013	2014
CPI	1.5	3.0	1.7	1.5	0.8
Periodicals	n.a.	4.6	5.9	6.1	6.1
Legal serials services	3.5	11.0	6.1	10.5	11.3
*Hardcover books	5.54	0.87	5.18	-2.57	3.07
+Academic books	12.4	4.6	8.0	6.3	n.a.
+Academic e-books	13.7	-0.3	23.0	6.5	n.a.
+Textbooks	0.7	3.5	10.6	-1.2	n.a.
College books	-2.3	4.6	2.15	4.21	-0.60
*Mass market paperbacks	1.94	2.34	1.00	-0.28	0.85
*Trade paperbacks	7.30	-9.99	31.96	-12.31	0.71
*Audiobooks	-1.19	-4.39	-10.96	-4.76	-0.59
*U.S. e-books	-6.07	-41.17	-6.37	22.03	-17.30
++Serials	n.a.	n.a.	5.8	6.5	5.8
++Online serials	n.a.	n.a.	6.3	7.0	6.3
British academic books	0.16	2.77	10.81	1.67	1.0

n.a. = not available
* = figures revised based on BISAC categories
+Beginning with 2009, new data source
++Data set changes each year

U.S. Published Materials

Tables 1 through 7B indicate average prices and price indexes for library materials published primarily in the United States. These indexes are U.S. Periodicals (Table 1), Legal Serials Services (Table 2), U.S. Hardcover Books (Table 3), North American Academic Books (Table 4), North American Academic E-Books (Table 4A), North American Academic Textbooks (Table 4B), U.S. College Books (Table 5), U.S. Mass Market Paperback Books (Table 6), U.S. Paperbacks (Excluding Mass Market) (Table 7), U.S. Audiobooks (Table 7A), and U.S. E-Books (Table 7B).

Periodical and Serials Prices

The U.S. Periodical Price Index (USPPI) (Table 1) was reestablished by Stephen Bosch in 2014 and is updated for 2015 using data supplied by EBSCO Information Services. This report includes 2010–2015 data indexed to the base year of 2010. The title list used in the new Table 1 differs from previous versions, so a new base year is appropriate. Table 1 is based on a selected set of titles that, as much as possible will remain as the base for future comparisons. The data in Table 1 are created from a print preferred data pull, but about half the data in the index ends up being online pricing so that the data provide a strong mix of both print and online pricing. The subscription prices used are publishers' list prices, excluding publisher discount or vendor service charges. The pricing data for 2010–2014 was based on a single report that pulled pricing information for a static set of titles for the five-year period. The pricing data for 2015 is based on that set of titles, but is not an exact match due to changes that occur with serial titles. Some titles fell off the list while others on the list had pricing available that did not have pricing available in 2014.

The USPPI in 2015 treats a little more than 5,900 titles in comparison with the original title list, which covered only about 3,700 titles. The previous versions of the USPPI treated Russian translations as a separate category. Russian translations are no longer a focus of this index. These were once seen as a major cost factor, but this is no longer the case and therefore their inclusion in or exclusion from the index no longer makes sense. There are Russian translation titles in the index, but they are not reported separately.

The main barrier to reestablishing this index was the difficulty of maintaining the title list and obtaining standard retail pricing for titles on the list. Changes in serial titles due to ceased publication, movement to open access, mergers, combining titles in packages, moving to direct orders, and publication delays are a few of the situations that can affect compilers' ability to obtain current pricing information. The new index retained that part of the title list from the previous index that remained viable and added new titles to that list based on data from EBSCO on the most frequently ordered serials in their system. From that list of serials, titles were selected for the new index to ensure that the distribution by subject was similar to the distribution in the original index. There are more titles in the selected title set than the number of titles that produced prices over the past six years. This should allow the current index to be sustainable into the future as titles fall off the list and

(text continues on page 420)

Table 1 / U.S. Periodicals: Average Prices and Price Indexes 2010–2015

Index Base 2010 = 100

Subject	LC Class	Titles	2010 Average Price	2011 Average Price	2012 Average Price	2013 Average Price	2014 Average Price	2015 Average Price	Price Increase 2014–2015	Price Index (Base = 2010)
Agriculture	S	246	$579.48	$610.84	$641.43	$687.22	$726.67	$780.01	7.3%	134.6
Anthropology	GN	50	373.64	391.31	411.00	430.83	453.36	428.52	-5.5	114.7
Arts and architecture	N	115	112.39	116.80	120.62	125.24	130.70	180.35	38.0	160.5
Astronomy	QB	28	1,793.08	1,662.27	1,753.73	2,049.88	2,186.19	2,083.50	-4.7	116.2
Biology	QH	330	2,053.06	2,160.88	2,288.26	2,405.68	2,535.65	2,727.29	7.6	132.8
Botany	QK	55	1,361.09	1,419.23	1,491.68	1,583.36	1,667.34	1,646.31	-1.3	121.0
Business and economics	HA-HJ	492	351.29	370.36	389.34	410.55	434.12	480.98	10.8	136.9
Chemistry	QD	124	3,396.26	3,605.69	3,808.31	4,024.45	4,244.38	4,335.51	2.1	127.7
Education	L	229	354.92	371.24	389.92	409.63	433.05	499.55	15.4	140.8
Engineering	T	542	1,244.39	1,323.70	1,405.36	1,486.54	1,584.81	1,692.44	6.8	136.0
Food science	TX	51	356.17	373.62	394.64	416.09	439.51	617.45	40.5	173.4
General science	Q	97	998.51	1,051.67	1,109.61	1,153.60	1,218.88	1,401.48	15.0	140.4
General works	A	131	85.84	87.93	90.73	95.41	99.14	106.87	7.8	124.5
Geography	G-GF	84	670.60	644.52	684.72	783.49	836.61	872.34	4.3	130.1

Subject	LC class	Titles							% change	Index
Geology	QE	74	1,368.79	1,424.96	1,514.90	1,603.07	1,699.34	1,648.20	-3.0	120.4
Heath sciences	R	803	1,009.55	1,068.74	1,147.17	1,224.65	1,309.43	1,402.65	7.1	138.9
History	C,D,E,F	312	202.39	210.80	221.80	231.75	245.88	277.95	13.0	137.3
Language and literature	P	277	168.12	176.34	185.63	194.56	205.49	232.29	13.0	138.2
Law	K	251	214.01	220.92	231.72	239.11	251.93	297.45	18.1	139.0
Library science	Z	107	290.02	303.75	321.24	336.34	355.38	376.47	5.9	129.8
Math and computer science	QA	329	1,242.13	1,300.45	1,367.86	1,406.66	1,480.16	1,623.12	9.7	130.7
Military and naval science	U,V	28	239.90	272.80	285.07	301.03	288.80	276.33	-4.3	115.2
Music	M	49	82.18	86.03	89.24	92.24	95.74	151.67	58.4	184.5
Philosophy and religion	B-BD, BH-BX	212	232.37	240.32	253.08	266.63	281.45	316.77	12.6	136.3
Physics	QC	148	2,845.54	2,794.21	2,944.32	3,282.05	3,499.54	3,538.93	1.1	124.4
Political science	J	103	312.76	324.99	340.45	362.82	382.91	562.63	46.9	179.9
Psychology	BF	111	648.21	683.75	726.61	767.19	828.57	970.19	17.1	149.7
Recreation	GV	86	69.79	72.50	81.14	84.44	90.20	122.06	35.3	174.9
Social sciences	H	41	351.40	369.57	388.63	410.60	435.17	645.60	48.4	183.7
Sociology	HM-HX	240	482.59	508.78	538.51	567.96	608.13	717.56	18.0	148.7
Technology	TA-TT	136	535.73	564.70	592.24	624.46	679.00	723.65	6.6	135.1
Zoology	QL	117	1,454.26	1,527.59	1,613.42	1,675.90	1,762.83	1,816.13	3.0	124.9
Total		5,998	$843.46	$882.38	$934.48	$991.39	$1,051.73	$1,114.32	6.0%	132.1

Compiled by Stephen Bosch, University of Arizona, based on subscription information supplied by EBSCO Information Services.

(continued from page 417)

pricing becomes available for titles that may have been delayed, or are no longer in memberships, etc.

The first five years of data showed fairly consistent price changes across subject areas due to the fact that the pricing data took a historical look at the prices of the exact same set of journals. The data for 2015 is based on the same title lists, but is not the exact same list of titles as the data for 2010–2014 due to the factors mentioned above that can impact pricing availability. Across subject areas, the changes in price were more volatile this year, but the overall 6 percent increase mirrors increases seen in other pricing studies. Also at the subject level the sample sizes are smaller so a few changes can cause a large swing in the overall price for that area.

Direct comparisons between Table 1 and Table 8 should still be avoided, especially at the subject level. Both tables show the overall rate of increase in serial prices to be close to 6 percent; however, beyond that point there is little that can reasonably be compared. Table 8 has higher overall average prices in most areas, and this is due to the survey's largest set of data coming from the ISI Citation Indexes, which include higher impact—and consequently more expensive—journals. Table 1 is a broader mix of journals that attempts to reflect the collections in an average library; therefore the mix contains more trade and popular titles than would be found in the ISI indexes. These journals tend to be cheaper, with lower average prices. Differences in data sets will yield different results.

The most important trend seen in this data (Table 1) is that increases in prices have remained fairly constant since the economic recovery began in 2010. Price increases have hovered around 6 percent annually during that time. Science does not dominate the list of subjects with the largest price increases. The subject areas that displayed the largest increases were quite varied: recreation, arts and architecture, food science, political science, social sciences, and music. Average prices for journals in the science and technology areas are still far higher than in other areas, and that trend continues, with the average cost of chemistry journals being $4,335 and of physics journals being $3,538.

In this price index, as in similar price indexes, the data are less accurate at describing price changes the smaller the sample becomes. For that reason, drawing conclusions about price changes in subject areas with a limited number of titles will be less accurate than for large areas or the broader price survey. Price changes are far more volatile where smaller data sets are used. For example, military and naval science (about 28 titles) showed average price of $285 (2012), $301 (2013), $288 (2014), and $276 (2015). If a specific inflation figure only for military and naval science is needed, it would be better to look at an average over the period or the overall number for the price study (6.0 percent) than to use the actual numbers year-by-year. The variation in pricing is too volatile in smaller sample sizes to be comparable on a year-to-year basis. In a small sample size the change in just one or two titles could easily have a large impact on the overall price for an area.

More extensive reports from the periodical price index have been published annually in the April 15 issue of *Library Journal* through 1992, in the May issue of *American Libraries* 1993 to 2002, and in the October 2003 issue of *Library Resources and Technical Services*.

The Legal Serials Services Index (Table 2) has been compiled by Ajaye Bloomstone using data collected from a number of different legal serials vendors. The base year for this index is 2009. This index presents price data covering the years 2009 through 2015.

Vendors were asked again to provide cost data on particular titles with the assumption that the title/set has been held by a large academic research law library, and the cost recorded in the index is that for the upkeep of the title in question, *not* the cost incurred in purchasing a new set. A nuance of legal publishing is that for some of the larger legal publishers, hard prices for a calendar year are not set at the beginning of the year but halfway through, so in some cases only price estimates are available for this article. Legal serials services can be updated as new editions, regular/irregular updates ("releases") throughout the year, or added/revised volumes, and the price for a title may increase or decrease from one year to the next, depending on plans for keeping a title current. It should be noted that although legal serials in print format continue to be produced, titles seem to be migrating, albeit slowly, to an electronic-only format. Some prices were provided for several titles with the caveat "no longer available for new sales." This statement would lead one to believe that the publication is being phased out. Either the title might no longer be available as a print product, or it may cease publication entirely, in any format.

Table 2 / Legal Serials Services:
Average Prices and Price Indexes, 2009–2015

Index Base: 2009 = 100

Year	Number of Titles	Average Price	Percent Change	Index
2009	217	$1,658.20	n.a.	100.0
2010	217	1,716.30	3.5%	103.5
2011	217	1,905.20	11.0	114.9
2012	217	2,020.83	6.1	124.1
2013	217	2,233.00	10.5	134.7
2014	217	2,486.04	11.3	149.9
2015	217	2,831.00	13.9	170.7

Book Prices

Tables 3 (hardcover books), 6 (mass market paperbacks), 7 (other—trade—paperbacks), 7A (audiobooks), and 7B (e-books), prepared by Catherine Barr, are derived from data provided by book wholesaler Baker & Taylor. Figures for 2012 and 2013 are revised to reflect late updates to the Baker & Taylor database; the 2014 figures given here may be similarly revised in next year's tables and should be considered preliminary. These five tables use the Book Industry Study Group's BISAC categories; for more information on the BISAC categories, visit http://www.bisg.org. The BISAC juvenile category (fiction and nonfiction) has been divided into children's and young adult.

(text continues on page 427)

Table 3 / Hardcover Books: Average Prices and Price Indexes, 2011–2014

Index Base: 2005 = 100

BISAC Category	2005 Average Prices	2011 Final Volumes	2011 Final Average Prices	2011 Final Index	2012 Final Volumes	2012 Final Average Prices	2012 Final Index	2013 Final Volumes	2013 Final Average Prices	2013 Final Index	2014 Preliminary Volumes	2014 Preliminary Average Prices	2014 Preliminary Index
Antiques and collectibles	$71.07	150	$53.07	74.7	124	$69.56	97.9	137	$70.41	99.1	140	$62.74	88.3
Architecture	66.99	743	77.19	115.2	762	80.66	120.4	879	88.92	132.7	789	89.04	132.9
Art	62.33	1,686	71.06	114.0	1,821	73.02	117.2	2,042	71.34	114.5	1,852	76.70	123.1
Bibles	48.05	221	46.28	96.3	199	37.46	78.0	197	37.43	77.9	129	34.17	71.1
Biography and autobiography	46.20	1,711	49.00	106.1	1,713	49.42	107.0	1,939	44.12	95.5	1,745	46.87	101.5
Body, mind and spirit	26.76	155	30.18	112.8	132	37.32	139.5	237	31.99	119.5	164	44.14	164.9
Business and economics	120.56	4,105	136.53	113.2	4,126	139.77	115.9	4,386	150.18	124.6	4,258	140.17	116.3
Children	23.14	11,704	26.80	115.8	11,920	22.97	99.3	12,179	23.78	102.8	12,619	23.74	102.6
Comics and graphic novels	32.75	801	34.64	105.8	735	37.86	115.6	639	37.53	114.6	646	39.40	120.3
Computers	113.07	884	138.05	122.1	981	167.06	147.7	880	139.41	123.3	904	158.35	140.0
Cooking	28.68	972	30.82	107.5	1,135	29.05	101.3	1,215	29.54	103.0	1,202	28.82	100.5
Crafts and hobbies	28.82	218	30.44	105.6	210	31.13	108.0	195	29.10	101.0	201	28.47	98.8
Design	59.41	441	68.63	115.5	504	64.87	109.2	399	62.97	106.0	394	67.74	114.0
Drama	60.81	138	40.77	67.0	72	76.98	126.6	76	74.53	122.6	79	77.29	127.1
Education	95.10	1,569	130.14	136.8	1,616	132.56	139.4	1,747	118.72	124.8	1,884	117.81	123.9
Family and relationships	25.37	229	33.72	132.9	213	43.07	169.8	265	36.53	144.0	214	43.78	172.6
Fiction	28.37	4,491	29.51	104.0	4,421	30.23	106.6	5,155	30.29	106.8	4,590	29.94	105.5
Foreign language study	116.89	158	136.08	116.4	221	115.16	98.5	270	115.33	98.7	213	100.52	86.0
Games	32.07	112	34.75	108.4	122	36.01	112.3	111	40.05	124.9	92	39.20	122.2
Gardening	38.20	118	40.00	104.7	134	39.94	104.6	115	37.42	98.0	97	31.32	82.0
Health and fitness	54.05	321	60.01	111.0	321	73.38	135.8	378	64.67	119.6	348	57.89	107.1
History	88.17	4,543	82.80	93.9	4,950	86.46	98.1	5,030	86.61	98.2	5,327	93.00	105.5
House and home	31.51	90	38.30	121.5	88	44.73	142.0	108	35.83	113.7	92	34.92	110.8
Humor	19.00	199	19.33	101.7	245	19.77	104.1	246	19.94	104.9	279	24.11	126.9

Language arts and disciplines	120.71	1,587	115.71	95.9	1,147	131.89	109.3	1,253	141.23	117.0	1,244	142.87	118.4
Law	155.28	1,756	179.16	115.4	1,900	178.81	115.2	1,966	178.70	115.1	1,966	176.08	113.4
Literary collections	74.92	357	88.34	117.9	258	96.92	129.4	282	90.16	120.3	256	88.97	118.8
Literary criticism	123.84	1,964	120.90	97.6	2,027	123.34	99.6	1,990	121.24	97.9	2,124	121.12	97.8
Mathematics	144.88	1,030	135.56	93.6	963	151.30	104.4	910	133.13	91.9	917	126.95	87.6
Medical	156.54	2,976	165.38	105.6	3,546	180.38	115.2	3,443	185.17	118.3	3,439	197.82	126.4
Music	77.63	488	91.25	117.5	524	90.51	116.6	534	89.37	115.1	507	89.14	114.8
Nature	67.75	400	73.56	108.6	371	89.94	132.8	470	84.27	124.4	421	88.10	130.0
Performing arts	71.74	534	82.49	115.0	574	90.23	125.8	583	94.64	131.9	673	92.46	128.9
Pets	25.45	122	21.16	83.1	93	23.98	94.2	107	25.64	100.7	105	24.76	97.3
Philosophy	127.22	1,004	96.68	76.0	1,169	105.35	82.8	1,291	105.67	83.1	1,320	104.61	82.2
Photography	56.77	822	60.45	106.5	865	85.88	151.3	801	93.22	164.2	827	66.36	116.9
Poetry	36.58	318	35.16	96.1	287	41.58	113.7	420	33.92	92.7	358	33.61	91.9
Political science	103.39	2,578	110.27	106.7	2,654	112.81	109.1	2,608	113.25	109.5	2,972	111.81	108.1
Psychology	93.85	1,082	119.76	127.6	1,100	140.31	149.5	1,171	131.91	140.6	1,204	145.32	154.8
Reference	202.23	599	351.48	173.8	499	396.56	196.1	409	356.07	176.1	394	319.21	157.8
Religion	62.29	2,370	73.53	118.0	2,730	81.93	131.5	2,804	77.10	123.8	2,490	80.31	128.9
Science	203.44	3,459	194.96	95.8	3,331	195.83	96.3	3,325	194.94	95.8	3,480	193.93	95.3
Self-help	22.43	219	23.92	106.6	265	24.74	110.3	377	28.15	125.5	284	25.45	113.5
Social science	96.17	3,069	105.66	109.9	3,139	115.79	120.4	3,335	115.72	120.3	3,334	134.68	140.0
Sports and recreation	38.77	645	44.69	115.3	658	51.66	133.2	690	47.29	122.0	605	61.24	158.0
Study aids	105.28	20	96.26	91.4	14	110.60	105.1	14	116.17	110.3	19	92.75	88.1
Technology and engineering	187.80	2,633	167.64	89.3	2,653	175.47	93.4	2,540	172.73	92.0	2,609	183.88	97.9
Transportation	68.68	326	61.92	90.2	225	66.85	97.3	316	71.76	104.5	240	85.35	124.3
Travel	37.11	340	42.35	114.1	205	49.73	134.0	205	41.30	111.3	177	38.82	104.6
True crime	29.28	73	31.48	107.5	70	32.37	110.6	87	28.20	96.3	78	28.71	98.1
Young adult	50.17	2,602	37.47	74.7	2,256	36.87	73.5	1,965	30.98	61.8	2,159	33.63	67.0
Totals	$80.36	69,132	$90.32	112.4	70,288	$95.00	118.2	72,721	$92.56	115.2	72,460	$95.40	118.7

Compiled by Catherine Barr from data supplied by Baker & Taylor.

423

Table 4 / North American Academic Books: Average Prices and Price Indexes 2011–2013

Index Base: 1989 = 100

Subject Area	LC Class	1989 No. of Titles	1989 Average Price	2011 No. of Titles	2011 Average Price	2012 No. of Titles	2012 Average Price	2013 No. of Titles	2013 Average Price	2013 % Change 2012–2013	2013 Index
Agriculture	S	897	$45.13	1,321	$100.51	1,402	$106.66	1,361	$99.44	-6.8%	220.3
Anthropology	GN	406	32.81	558	101.56	563	105.27	581	101.62	-3.5	309.7
Botany	QK	251	69.02	283	139.62	356	161.26	307	156.65	-2.9	227.0
Business and economics	H	5,979	41.67	11,237	103.11	11,058	115.17	11,242	117.50	2.0	282.0
Chemistry	QD	577	110.61	686	214.45	787	259.27	754	238.81	-7.9	215.9
Education	L	1,685	29.61	4,728	88.90	4,768	95.15	4,573	96.65	1.6	326.4
Engineering and technology	T	4,569	64.94	8,089	135.40	8,769	147.53	8,470	157.88	7.0	243.1
Fine and applied arts	M-N	3,040	40.72	7,866	63.68	7,098	65.76	7,174	69.08	5.1	169.6
General works	A	333	134.65	115	76.52	162	97.19	148	110.81	14.0	82.3
Geography	G	396	47.34	1,219	108.35	1,241	131.13	1,171	120.75	-7.9	255.1
Geology	QE	303	63.49	298	115.36	321	138.07	320	217.42	57.5	342.5
History	C-D-E-F	5,549	31.34	10,729	74.99	9,857	73.31	10,301	83.35	13.7	265.9
Home economics	TX	535	27.10	878	48.94	1,043	51.81	1,059	67.40	30.1	248.7
Industrial arts	TT	175	23.89	322	44.03	430	45.58	363	43.71	-4.1	183.0
Law	K	1252	51.10	6,277	126.55	6,139	136.38	5,758	161.29	18.3	315.6
Library and information science	Z	857	44.51	867	88.75	812	106.91	878	108.53	1.5	243.8
Literature and language	P	10,812	24.99	21,247	60.21	21,813	61.12	23,203	69.50	13.7	278.1
Mathematics and computer science	QA	2,707	44.68	4,295	106.72	4,820	122.99	4,495	133.96	8.9	299.8
Medicine	R	5,028	58.38	9,613	114.54	9,249	130.09	8,711	128.67	-1.1	220.4
Military and naval science	U-V	715	33.57	812	71.69	891	83.37	928	81.76	-1.9	243.6
Philosophy and religion	B	3,518	29.06	8,706	88.74	8,314	84.73	8,392	97.28	14.8	334.7
Physical education and recreation	GV	814	20.38	1,914	67.58	2,102	64.92	2,170	85.89	32.3	421.4
Physics and astronomy	QB	1,219	64.59	1,669	134.88	1,811	145.95	1,761	149.09	2.2	230.8
Political science	J	1,650	36.76	3,863	105.19	3,905	110.71	3,721	106.53	-3.8	289.8
Psychology	BF	890	31.97	1,889	85.09	1,990	99.96	1,983	115.22	15.3	360.4
Science (general)	Q	433	56.10	611	115.87	717	139.25	593	128.18	-8.0	228.5
Sociology	HM	2,742	29.36	7,273	89.96	7,044	98.63	7,260	114.34	15.9	389.5
Zoology	QH,L,P,R	1,967	71.28	3,117	147.90	3,375	157.49	3,147	161.11	2.3	226.0
Average for all subjects		59,299	$41.69	120,482	$93.26	120,837	$100.69	120,822	$107.02	6.3%	256.7

Compiled by Stephen Bosch, University of Arizona, from electronic data provided by Ingrams Content Group (Coutts Information Services) and YBP Library Services. The data represent all titles (includes hardcover, trade, and paperback books, as well as annuals) treated for all approval plan customers serviced by the vendors. This table covers titles published or distributed in the United States and Canada during the calendar years listed.

This index does include paperback editions and electronic books. The inclusion of these items does impact pricing in the index.

Table 4A / North American Academic E-Books: Average Prices and Price Indexes 2011–2013

Index Base: 2007 = 100

Subject Area	LC Class	2007 No. of Titles	2007 Average Price	2011 No. of Titles	2011 Average Price	2012 No. of Titles	2012 Average Price	2013 No. of Titles	2013 Average Price	2013 % Change 2012–2013	2013 Index
Agriculture	S	894	$128.59	793	$125.68	748	$150.01	730	$137.60	-8.3%	107.0
Anthropology	GN	382	105.28	357	109.99	367	130.70	317	125.90	-3.7	119.6
Botany	QK	287	168.18	169	169.98	224	176.14	197	170.44	-3.2	101.3
Business and economics	H	9807	97.25	8,796	106.45	7,369	136.31	6,684	138.84	1.9	142.8
Chemistry	QD	934	213.76	675	258.38	595	280.25	526	268.27	-4.3	125.5
Education	L	2565	107.62	2,707	108.27	2,848	126.02	2,422	125.68	-0.3	116.8
Engineering and technology	T	7176	133.60	5,662	144.34	5,365	193.12	5,069	204.78	6.0	153.3
Fine and applied arts	M-N	1141	84.30	1,802	84.88	1,898	114.59	1,749	116.21	1.4	137.8
General works	A	60	107.85	43	115.99	83	121.94	67	109.96	-9.8	102.0
Geography	G	888	132.67	833	119.81	752	147.60	623	164.58	11.5	124.1
Geology	QE	201	136.49	196	129.39	209	181.01	189	314.30	73.6	230.3
History	C-D-E-F	4452	93.55	6,288	91.40	5,352	111.36	4,800	116.44	4.6	124.5
Home economics	TX	255	104.31	245	72.80	384	125.74	449	112.76	-10.3	108.1
Industrial arts	TT	20	52.73	157	150.98	72	70.54	86	72.30	2.5	137.1
Law	K	1743	99.61	2,591	153.51	3,034	174.94	2,461	200.43	14.6	201.2
Library and information science	Z	308	74.70	525	91.94	413	123.84	439	119.44	-3.6	159.9
Literature and language	P	5517	90.59	8,582	100.63	9,027	111.29	8,953	123.27	10.8	136.1
Mathematics and computer science	QA	4285	102.93	3,357	121.44	2,759	149.91	2,376	181.42	21.0	176.3
Medicine	R	7420	123.59	7,184	127.12	5,957	170.07	5,466	170.38	0.2	137.9
Military and naval science	U-V	684	82.89	645	71.69	503	110.54	499	106.19	-3.9	128.1
Philosophy and religion	B	3612	93.77	5,648	115.85	4,609	137.82	4,146	146.45	6.3	156.2
Physical education and recreation	GV	610	96.00	1,114	79.19	1,059	101.69	922	102.68	1.0	107.0
Physics and astronomy	QB	1965	142.11	1,350	136.13	1,372	179.48	1,158	187.49	4.5	131.9
Political science	J	2447	102.72	2,695	114.27	2,823	130.94	2,177	135.39	3.4	131.8
Psychology	BF	1113	83.51	1,290	92.65	1,214	132.04	1,033	163.63	23.9	195.9
Science (general)	Q	468	117.19	528	119.86	427	144.13	346	148.23	2.8	126.5
Sociology	HM	4139	98.02	4,883	100.82	4,400	131.34	3,966	151.15	15.1	154.2
Zoology	QH,L,P,R	3394	154.01	2,442	170.60	2,190	180.24	1,967	206.60	14.6	134.2
Average for all subjects		66,767	$110.82	71,557	$115.86	66,053	$142.52	59,817	$151.77	6.5%	137.0

Compiled by Stephen Bosch, University of Arizona, from electronic data provided by Ingrams Content Group (formerly Coutts Information Services), and YBP Library Services. The data represents all e-book titles treated for all approval plan customers serviced by the vendors. This table covers titles published or distributed in the United States and Canada during the calendar years listed. It is important to note that e-books that were released in a given year may have been published in print much earlier.

Table 4B / North American Academic Text Books: Average Prices and Price Indexes 2011–2013

Index Base: 2007 = 100

Subject Area	LC Class	2007 No. of Titles	2007 Average Price	2011 No. of Titles	2011 Average Price	2012 No. of Titles	2012 Average Price	2013 No. of Titles	2013 Average Price	2013 % Change 2012–2013	2013 Index
Agriculture	S	68	$134.75	120	$118.80	100	$140.37	62	$131.30	-6.5%	97.4
Anthropology	GN	40	89.15	59	88.71	75	108.16	35	114.63	6.0	128.6
Botany	QK	4	98.00	17	114.79	14	185.04	9	207.69	12.2	211.9
Business and economics	H	666	110.18	1,556	113.53	1,378	140.60	849	139.79	-0.6	126.9
Chemistry	QD	80	138.70	169	154.21	155	186.00	99	154.16	-17.1	111.2
Education	L	235	79.58	667	82.90	589	103.20	322	99.91	-3.2	125.5
Engineering and technology	T	668	106.13	1,736	120.21	1,128	133.28	835	136.07	2.1	128.2
Fine and applied arts	M-N	82	73.69	173	86.78	179	111.44	104	107.49	-3.5	145.9
General works	A	1	48.00	4	80.88	8	116.81	3	120.33	3.0	250.7
Geography	G	59	100.42	190	110.18	150	127.39	91	134.77	5.8	134.2
Geology	QE	26	118.28	56	117.57	46	137.67	30	138.20	0.4	116.8
History	C-D-E-F	72	78.41	205	78.84	207	97.25	106	90.00	-7.5	114.8
Home economics	TX	54	68.23	46	87.78	71	106.75	50	105.95	-0.7	155.3
Industrial arts	TT	13	73.90	23	821.82	27	88.60	14	87.95	-0.7	119.0
Law	K	163	87.67	513	105.89	543	116.61	316	113.67	-2.5	129.7
Library and information science	Z	24	65.54	49	76.14	42	75.03	24	75.73	0.9	115.5
Literature and language	P	269	71.35	864	78.90	787	93.32	382	91.06	-2.4	127.6
Mathematics and computer science	QA	732	91.42	1,544	112.26	1,072	124.39	783	108.08	-13.1	118.2
Medicine	R	1210	126.37	3,357	130.46	2,046	138.27	1,596	135.40	-2.1	107.1
Military and naval science	U-V	10	104.58	24	98.38	29	129.40	12	75.62	-41.6	72.3
Philosophy and religion	B	85	55.51	216	65.42	232	73.94	122	73.20	-1.0	131.9
Physical education and recreation	GV	47	72.14	118	87.56	110	108.93	62	121.16	11.2	167.9
Physics and astronomy	QB	237	107.05	537	116.51	323	130.77	258	119.37	-8.7	111.5
Political science	J	104	74.21	277	84.69	265	105.94	148	102.16	-3.6	137.7
Psychology	BF	120	100.17	327	95.86	287	128.83	174	132.07	2.5	131.8
Science (general)	Q	24	111.30	64	87.63	65	102.40	35	99.37	-3.0	89.3
Sociology	HM	330	84.88	844	88.31	815	103.14	489	104.24	1.1	122.8
Zoology	QH,L,P,R	250	116.73	511	120.33	431	136.35	256	137.69	1.0	118.0
Average for all subjects		5,673	$102.52	14,266	$111.69	11,174	$123.56	7,266	$122.07	-1.2%	119.1

Compiled by Stephen Bosch, University of Arizona, from electronic data provided by YBP Library Services and Ingrams Content Group. The data represent all textbook titles treated for all approval plan customers serviced by the vendors. This table covers titles published or distributed in the United States and Canada during the calendar years listed.

This index does include paperback editions. The inclusion of these items does impact pricing in the index.

(continued from page 421)
Average book prices generally declined in 2013, with only e-books showing gains. List prices for hardcovers overall (Table 3) fell 2.57 percent. Mass market paperback prices (Table 6) dipped 0.28 percent and trade paperbacks (Table 7) declined 12.31 percent. Audiobook prices (Table 7A) have been falling since 2009, losing a further 4.76 percent in 2013. After declining for several years, e-book prices registered an increase of 22.03 percent.

The North American Academic Books Price Indexes (Tables 4, 4A, and 4B) are prepared by Stephen Bosch. The current version of North American Academic Books: Average Prices and Price Indexes, 2011–2013 (Table 4) should not be compared with the versions published in 2009 or previous years. The North American Academic Books Price Index (NAABPI) now contains many more titles in the source data, which has affected the index considerably. This is due to the fact that Coutts treats far more titles in its approval programs than the former Blackwell Book Services. For indexes published prior to 2009 Blackwell was a supplier of data for the index. Blackwell was purchased in 2011 by YBP and the vendor data used to create the index changed at that time. After 2009 the data comes from Ingram and YBP; prior to 2009 the data came from Blackwell and YBP. The year-to-year comparisons from 2007 on (indexes published since 2009) are now based on this new data model, and the changes in price and number of titles are not as dramatic as when looking at comparable data in the indexes that were published prior to 2009.

The overall average price for books in the NAABPI for 2013 increased 6.3 percent, a slight dip from the 8.0 percent seen the previous year. The average price increased to $107.02 from $100.69. The number of titles was relatively unchanged, so increasing prices will pressure library budgets. The increase this year was primarily due to rising costs for books that cost more than $120. Many of these books are e-books. As they are more expensive than print books, and this year the overall e-book index showed a price increase of 6.5 percent, higher e-books prices were a driver in the overall price increase of academic books for 2013. E-books make up about 20 percent of the base table.

Since 2008 two additional indexes have been available, one for e-books only (Table 4A) and another for textbooks (Table 4B). Both of these indexes are of high interest to users. Based on that input, the indexes continue to be published with the base index year set to 2007. In the academic market, it has always been assumed that e-books are more expensive than their print counterparts. Users might be surprised to find that the cheaper versions of e-books, available to consumers through such channels as Amazon and the Apple Store, are not available to libraries at similar prices, if they are available at all. The new index clearly points out the difference in price: the average price of an e-book in 2013 was $151.77 while the average price for all books was $107.02. The average price of a print book drops to $81.00 if the e-books are removed from the overall index. The high price for e-books is not that surprising as most pricing models for academic e-books generally charge a large percentage of the list print price for access to the e-books. Multi-user licenses are an even larger percentage. In most situations, even single-user academic e-book titles are more expensive than their print counterparts. Responding to customer demands, vendors offer e-books on multiple platforms with multiple pricing models; consequently there can be multiple prices for the same title. Only the first instance of a unique ISBN is included in the data, so if the same book was treated by a vendor from one e-book aggregator and then treated again from another aggregator, only the first instance of the e-book is in the index. Also, if different pricing models are available the single user price is supplied. Where multiple prices are available for different use models, the lowest price is provided. Because electronic access is where the market is going, it is appropriate to have e-books as a separate index. It is also important to note that the e-book market is rapidly changing. The availability of additional pricing models could be a factor in the upward shift in e-book prices.

The cost of textbooks has been a hot topic on many college campuses. The index for textbooks documents price changes in this area. The data show that textbooks tend to be much more expensive than other types of books, with an average price of $122.07 in 2013. There was a slight decrease in the average price, down 1.2 percent after a 10.6 percent increase in 2012. This is still not good news for students, who are essentially hostages of the textbook market. Textbooks are still expensive and the prices are not dropping significantly despite pressure on the textbook market from alternative sources such as rental services for either print or electronic versions. "E" versions are included in the textbook index, so a migration to "e" format does not seem to be lowering costs. This is not much consolation for cash-strapped students.

The average price of North American academic books in 2013 (Table 4) increased by 6.3 percent as compared with the 2012 average price. This is mainly due to a large increase in the number of titles treated in the higher part of the price bands ($120 and up) as well as a large increase in the top price band. Nearly all price bands showed only modest growth, or no growth, in the number of titles between 2010 and 2013 except for the price band above $120, which showed very large increases. This led to a large increase in the average price for all books. The increase in the upper price bands was primarily due to increases in e-books; their prices average well above the $120 threshold. Take e-books out of the sample and the upper price bands shrink considerably. See Figure 1.

Figure 1 / Comparison of Titles in Sample Grouped by Price

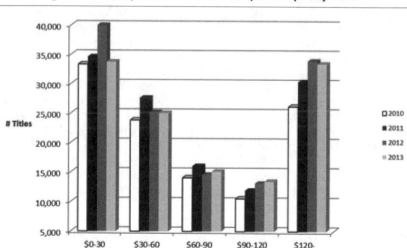

(text continues on page 444)

Table 5 / U.S. College Books: Average Prices and Price Indexes 1989, 2012–2014

Index Base for all years: 1989 = 100

Subject	1989 No. of Titles	1989 Avg. Price per Title	2012 No. of Titles	2012 Avg. Price per Title	2012 Indexed to 1989	2012 Indexed to 2011	2013 No. of Titles	2013 Avg. Price per Title	2013 Indexed to 1989	2013 Indexed to 2012	2014 No. of Titles	2014 Avg. Price per Title	2014 Indexed to 1989	2014 Indexed to 2013	Percent Change 2013–2014
GENERAL*	19	$40.19	n.a.	n.a.	n.a.	n.a.	n.a.	n.a.	n.a.	n.a.	n.a.	n.a.	n.a.	n.a.	n.a.
HUMANITIES	21	$32.33	99	$69.36	214.5	113.9	92	$69.95	216.4	100.9	110	$74.73	231.1	1.5	6.8%
Art and architecture	276	55.56	176	68.40	123.1	105.9	189	64.93	116.9	94.9	186	62.00	111.6	1.5	-4.5
Fine arts**	n.a.	n.a.	117	67.49	n.a.	103.1	90	65.66	n.a.	97.3	87	60.99	n.a.	1.4	-7.1
Architecture**	n.a.	n.a.	58	75.15	n.a.	111.0	51	72.09	n.a.	95.9	63	88.46	n.a.	1.7	22.7
Photography	24	44.11	31	63.50	144.0	122.4	45	56.60	128.3	89.1	37	60.00	136.0	1.9	6.0
Communication	42	32.70	85	68.36	209.1	93.0	95	71.68	219.2	104.9	114	65.00	198.8	1.3	-9.3
Language and literature	110	35.17	122	73.30	208.4	104.6	118	70.83	201.4	96.6	115	89.67	255.0	1.8	26.6
Africa and Middle East**	n.a.	n.a.	21	66.77	n.a.	104.4	22	52.80	n.a.	79.1	18	59.32	n.a.	2.1	12.3
Asia and Oceania**	n.a.	n.a.	20	61.66	n.a.	78.2	16	65.30	n.a.	105.9	21	59.37	n.a.	1.4	-9.1
Classical	75	43.07	27	94.71	219.9	102.6	32	87.87	204.0	92.8	39	85.24	197.9	1.1	-3.0
English and American	547	30.27	412	70.77	233.8	102.7	399	72.45	239.3	102.4	365	80.44	265.7	1.5	11.0
Germanic	38	32.18	29	71.17	221.2	104.7	29	73.44	228.2	103.2	30	66.44	206.5	1.2	-9.5
Romance	97	30.30	67	69.54	229.5	101.2	63	77.37	255.3	111.3	66	76.29	251.8	1.3	-1.4
Slavic	41	27.92	13	50.78	181.9	91.6	16	56.07	200.8	110.4	10	85.40	305.9	2.7	52.3
Other	63	25.09	n.a.	n.a.	n.a.	n.a.	n.a.	n.a.	n.a.	n.a.	n.a.	n.a.	n.a.	n.a.	n.a.
Performing Arts	20	29.41	27	62.56	212.7	135.9	17	59.85	203.5	95.7	37	70.72	240.5	2.0	18.2
Film	82	33.00	148	66.69	202.1	102.7	152	77.23	234.0	115.8	146	74.68	226.3	1.3	-3.3
Music	156	35.34	137	66.48	188.1	102.1	165	70.44	199.3	106.0	141	68.10	192.7	1.4	-3.3
Theater and dance	58	34.18	37	68.87	201.5	98.0	53	67.24	196.7	97.6	49	70.75	207.0	1.6	5.2
Philosophy	185	37.25	236	71.79	192.7	102.2	243	75.30	202.1	104.9	241	76.70	205.9	1.4	1.9
Religion	174	33.49	259	83.71	250.0	137.3	233	66.32	198.0	79.2	271	68.68	205.1	1.6	3.6
TOTAL HUMANITIES	2,009	$36.09	2,121	$68.96	191.1	103.1	2,120	$70.53	195.4	102.3	2,146	$73.21	202.9	1.5	3.8

Table 5 / U.S. College Books: Average Prices and Price Indexes 1989, 2012–2014 (cont.)

Index Base for all years: 1989 = 100

Subject	1989		2012				2013				2014				
	No. of Titles	Avg. Price per Title	No. of Titles	Avg. Price per Title	Indexed to 1989	Indexed to 2011	No. of Titles	Avg. Price per Title	Indexed to 1989	Indexed to 2012	No. of Titles	Avg. Price per Title	Indexed to 1989	Indexed to 2013	Percent Change 2013–2014
SCIENCE AND TECHNOLOGY	99	$46.90	104	$57.10	121.7	98.5	95	$68.77	146.6	120.4	102	$59.53	126.9	1.3	-13.4
History of science and technology	74	40.56	77	59.84	147.5	118.0	68	47.47	117.0	79.3	85	54.60	134.6	2.4	15.0
Astronautics and astronomy	22	50.56	50	52.82	104.5	94.4	46	65.56	129.7	124.1	57	57.52	113.8	1.3	-12.3
Biology	97	51.01	136	81.29	159.4	110.7	148	72.46	142.1	89.1	154	72.99	142.7	1.4	0.5
Botany	29	63.91	75	90.52	141.6	127.6	70	82.34	128.8	91.0	62	91.94	143.9	1.4	11.7
Zoology	53	49.21	95	68.49	139.2	112.3	114	73.03	148.4	106.6	139	58.54	119.0	1.1	-19.8
Chemistry	21	70.76	46	90.74	128.2	94.5	26	107.12	151.4	118.1	36	86.65	122.5	0.8	-19.1
Earth science	34	79.44	100	82.49	103.8	128.9	105	81.36	102.4	98.6	115	84.08	105.8	1.3	3.3
Engineering	87	66.74	60	98.52	147.6	96.5	69	98.47	147.5	99.9	58	91.42	137.0	0.9	-7.2
Health sciences	94	34.91	155	60.78	174.1	104.8	146	59.12	169.3	97.3	162	66.98	191.9	1.9	13.3
Information and computer science	70	40.35	73	69.63	172.6	99.4	82	59.15	146.6	84.9	62	72.94	180.8	2.1	23.3
Mathematics	60	48.53	92	64.44	132.8	92.2	91	65.88	135.8	102.2	85	62.64	129.1	1.4	-4.9
Physics	22	43.94	53	52.85	120.3	80.6	49	66.47	151.3	125.8	51	58.96	134.2	1.3	-11.3
Sports and physical education	18	27.46	47	80.83	294.4	126.5	46	59.12	215.3	73.1	54	69.08	251.6	2.0	16.8
TOTAL SCIENCE	780	$49.54	1,163	$71.29	143.9	105.4	1,155	$70.27	141.8	98.6	1,222	$69.20	139.7	1.4	-1.5
SOCIAL AND BEHAVIORAL SCIENCES	92	$37.09	158	$70.11	189.0	102.1	172	$69.48	187.3	99.1	126	$81.26	219.1	1.7	17.0
Anthropology	96	39.94	126	68.60	171.8	100.2	127	82.06	205.5	119.6	123	84.95	212.7	1.3	3.5
Business management and labor	145	35.72	169	56.52	158.2	104.0	161	62.04	173.7	109.8	160	65.21	182.6	1.7	5.1
Economics	332	40.75	264	63.84	156.7	108.2	225	60.24	147.8	94.4	247	60.59	148.7	1.7	0.6
Education	71	34.50	162	70.85	205.4	101.9	155	65.31	189.3	92.2	138	73.24	212.3	1.7	12.1

History, geography, and area studies	59	42.10	125	66.85	158.8	93.2	142	76.21	181.0	114.0	117	68.10	161.8	1.2	-10.6
Africa	44	34.85	44	67.96	195.0	104.1	36	71.76	205.9	105.6	34	71.62	205.5	1.4	-0.2
Ancient history**	n.a.	n.a.	66	80.73	n.a.	108.5	50	88.88	n.a.	110.1	41	102.96	n.a.	1.3	15.8
Asia and Oceania	76	34.75	84	66.78	192.2	108.0	62	69.43	199.8	104.0	92	71.77	206.5	1.5	3.4
Central and Eastern Europe**	n.a.	n.a.	74	54.03	n.a.	84.1	60	63.73	n.a.	118.0	59	72.77	n.a.	1.8	14.2
Latin America and Caribbean	42	37.23	66	63.00	169.2	104.5	65	60.74	163.1	96.4	67	65.86	176.9	1.8	8.4
Middle East and North Africa	30	36.32	38	72.37	199.3	119.3	42	60.23	165.8	83.2	35	74.43	204.9	2.1	23.6
North America	349	30.56	416	49.91	n.a.	105.2	384	63.47	207.7	127.2	441	49.60	162.3	1.2	-21.9
United Kingdom**	n.a.	n.a.	88	78.10	n.a.	97.2	89	78.40	n.a.	100.4	86	72.12	n.a.	1.2	-8.0
Western Europe	287	42.08	134	68.45	162.7	98.3	123	74.59	177.3	109.0	122	75.99	180.6	1.4	1.9
Political science	28	33.56	2	105.00	312.9	79.3	3	39.98	119.1	38.1	4	112.49	335.2	7.0	181.4
Comparative politics	236	37.82	195	70.51	186.4	96.9	213	70.22	185.7	99.6	202	69.93	184.9	1.4	-0.4
International relations	207	35.74	170	67.30	188.3	92.9	183	70.52	197.3	104.8	177	73.64	206.0	1.5	4.4
Political theory	59	37.76	86	58.54	155.0	99.1	89	59.86	158.5	102.3	85	62.83	166.4	1.8	5.0
U.S. politics	212	29.37	246	56.52	192.4	101.2	211	54.32	185.0	96.1	241	63.49	216.2	2.2	16.9
Psychology	179	36.36	114	73.84	203.1	115.2	137	81.60	224.4	110.5	96	75.08	206.5	1.1	-8.0
Sociology	178	36.36	230	69.04	189.9	107.1	216	71.22	195.9	103.2	193	78.79	216.7	1.6	10.6
BEHAVIORAL SCIENCES	2,722	$36.43	3,057	$64.19	176.2	102.3	2,945	$68.03	186.7	106.0	2,886	$68.19	187.2	1.5	0.2
TOTAL GENERAL, HUMANITIES, SCIENCE AND SOCIAL SCIENCE	5,511	$38.16	6,341	$67.09	175.8	103.1	6,220	$69.30	181.6	103.3	6,254	$70.11	183.7	1.5	1.2
REFERENCE	636	$61.02	37	$93.04	152.5	101.8	28	$117.48	192.5	126.3	40	$98.18	160.9	0.7	-16.4
Humanities**	n.a.	n.a.	138	110.23	n.a.	87.2	116	103.51	n.a.	93.9	136	114.67	n.a.	1.1	10.8
Science and technology**	n.a.	n.a.	43	151.19	n.a.	110.8	70	193.49	n.a.	128.0	43	134.78	n.a.	0.4	-30.3
Social and behavioral sciences**	n.a.	n.a.	210	136.53	n.a.	94.7	185	153.64	n.a.	112.5	178	134.98	n.a.	0.6	-12.1
TOTAL REFERENCE	636	$61.02	428	$125.76	206.1	93.5	399	$143.52	235.2	114.1	397	$124.29	203.7	0.6	-13.4
GRAND TOTAL	6,147	$40.52	6,769	$70.80	174.7	102.1	6,619	$73.78	182.1	104.2	6,651	$73.34	181.0	1.3	-0.6%

Compiled by Frederick Lynden, Brown University.

* General category no longer appears after 1999.

** Began appearing as separate sections after 1989.

n.a. = not available

Table 6 / U.S. Mass Market Paperback Books: Average Prices and Price Indexes, 2011–2014

Index Base: 2005 = 100

BISAC Category	2005 Average Prices	2011 Final Volumes	2011 Final Average Prices	2011 Final Index	2012 Final Volumes	2012 Final Average Prices	2012 Final Index	2013 Volumes	2013 Average Prices	2013 Index	2014 Volumes	2014 Average Prices	2014 Index
Antiques and collectibles	$7.69	5	$8.79	114.3	5	$8.99	116.9	5	$8.99	116.9	4	$8.99	116.9
Architecture	n.a.	n.a.	n.a.	n.a.	n.a.	n.a.	n.a.	n.a.	n.a.	n.a.	n.a.	n.a.	n.a.
Art	n.a.	n.a.	n.a.	n.a.	n.a.	n.a.	n.a.	n.a.	n.a.	n.a.	n.a.	n.a.	n.a.
Bibles	n.a.	n.a.	n.a.	n.a.	n.a.	n.a.	n.a.	n.a.	n.a.	n.a.	n.a.	n.a.	n.a.
Biography and autobiography	7.83	8	8.62	110.1	4	6.73	86.0	3	9.66	123.4	6	8.98	114.7
Body, mind and spirit	7.11	17	7.93	111.5	14	8.13	114.3	14	8.13	114.3	2	9.99	140.5
Business and economics	12.47	2	7.99	64.1	1	7.99	64.1	n.a.	n.a.	n.a.	n.a.	n.a.	n.a.
Children	5.29	253	6.56	124	240	6.49	122.7	217	6.70	126.7	197	6.36	120.2
Comics and graphic novels	8.47	n.a.	n.a.	n.a.	n.a.	n.a.	n.a.	n.a.	n.a.	n.a.	n.a.	n.a.	n.a.
Computers	n.a.	n.a.	n.a.	n.a.	n.a.	n.a.	n.a.	n.a.	n.a.	n.a.	n.a.	n.a.	n.a.
Cooking	7.50	1	7.99	106.5	n.a.	n.a.	n.a.	n.a.	n.a.	n.a.	n.a.	n.a.	n.a.
Crafts and hobbies	n.a.	n.a.	n.a.	n.a.	n.a.	n.a.	n.a.	n.a.	n.a.	n.a.	n.a.	n.a.	n.a.
Design	n.a.	n.a.	n.a.	n.a.	n.a.	n.a.	n.a.	n.a.	n.a.	n.a.	n.a.	n.a.	n.a.
Drama	6.32	1	8.95	141.6	2	4.95	78.3	n.a.	n.a.	n.a.	n.a.	n.a.	n.a.
Education	n.a.	n.a.	n.a.	n.a.	n.a.	n.a.	n.a.	n.a.	n.a.	n.a.	n.a.	n.a.	n.a.
Family and relationships	6.98	1	8.99	128.8	n.a.	n.a.	n.a.	n.a.	n.a.	n.a.	n.a.	n.a.	n.a.
Fiction	6.34	3,997	6.97	109.9	3,894	7.05	111.2	3,524	7.00	110.4	3,534	7.09	111.8
Foreign language study	n.a.	n.a.	n.a.	n.a.	n.a.	n.a.	n.a.	n.a.	n.a.	n.a.	1	6.99	n.a.
Games	7.14	n.a.	n.a.	n.a.	n.a.	n.a.	n.a.	1	9.99	139.9	4	9.87	138.2
Gardening	n.a.	n.a.	n.a.	n.a.	n.a.	n.a.	n.a.	n.a.	n.a.	n.a.	n.a.	n.a.	n.a.
Health and fitness	7.43	11	8.17	110	16	8.24	110.9	8	8.24	110.9	3	9.33	125.6
History	7.90	7	8.56	108.4	3	8.66	109.6	3	9.99	126.5	2	9.99	126.5
House and home	5.99	n.a.	n.a.	n.a.	n.a.	n.a.	n.a.	n.a.	n.a.	n.a.	n.a.	n.a.	n.a.
Humor	6.99	1	3.5	50.1	n.a.	n.a.	n.a.	2	8.00	114.4	n.a.	n.a.	n.a.

Language arts and disciplines	6.99	n.a.	n.a.	n.a.	n.a.	n.a.	n.a.	n.a.	n.a.	n.a.	1	7.99	114.3
Law	n.a.	n.a.	n.a.	n.a.	n.a.	n.a.	n.a.	n.a.	n.a.	n.a.	n.a.	n.a.	n.a.
Literary collections	n.a.	1	7.95	n.a.	2	5.95	n.a.	n.a.	n.a.	n.a.	1	4.95	n.a.
Literary criticism	7.95	1	9.99	125.7	n.a.	n.a.	n.a.	n.a.	n.a.	n.a.	n.a.	n.a.	n.a.
Mathematics	n.a.	n.a.	n.a.	n.a.	n.a.	n.a.	n.a.	n.a.	n.a.	n.a.	n.a.	n.a.	n.a.
Medical	7.83	1	n.a.	n.a.	1	8.99	114.8	n.a.	n.a.	n.a.	1	7.99	102
Music	7.95	1	7.95	n.a.	n.a.	n.a.	n.a.	n.a.	n.a.	n.a.	n.a.	n.a.	n.a.
Nature	n.a.	n.a.	n.a.	n.a.	1	7.99	n.a.	n.a.	n.a.	n.a.	1	n.a.	n.a.
Performing arts	8.25	2	8.99	109.2	1	9.99	121.4	1	10.99	133.5	1	10.99	133.5
Pets	n.a.	1	7.99	n.a.	1	n.a.	n.a.	1	7.99	n.a.	n.a.	n.a.	n.a.
Philosophy	7.45	n.a.	n.a.	n.a.	n.a.	n.a.	n.a.	n.a.	n.a.	n.a.	n.a.	n.a.	n.a.
Photography	n.a.	n.a.	n.a.	n.a.	n.a.	n.a.	n.a.	n.a.	n.a.	n.a.	n.a.	n.a.	n.a.
Poetry	5.75	1	7.95	138.3	2	7.45	129.6	3	6.62	115.1	n.a.	n.a.	n.a.
Political science	7.97	1	5.95	n.a.	n.a.	n.a.	n.a.	n.a.	n.a.	n.a.	1	9.99	n.a.
Psychology	7.97	1	7.99	100.3	n.a.	n.a.	n.a.	n.a.	n.a.	n.a.	n.a.	n.a.	n.a.
Reference	6.85	2	7.99	116.6	3	8.31	121.3	3	6.49	94.7	5	12.89	188.2
Religion	9.96	3	7.99	80.2	2	7.49	75.2	n.a.	n.a.	n.a.	n.a.	n.a.	n.a.
Science	n.a.	n.a.	n.a.	n.a.	n.a.	n.a.	n.a.	n.a.	n.a.	n.a.	n.a.	n.a.	n.a.
Self-help	12.45	1	7.99	64.2	1	7.99	64.2	n.a.	n.a.	n.a.	n.a.	n.a.	n.a.
Social science	7.08	n.a.	n.a.	n.a.	1	9.99	141.1	n.a.	n.a.	n.a.	n.a.	n.a.	n.a.
Sports and recreation	7.62	1	7.99	104.9	1	7.99	104.9	n.a.	n.a.	n.a.	n.a.	n.a.	n.a.
Study aids	n.a.	n.a.	n.a.	n.a.	n.a.	n.a.	n.a.	n.a.	n.a.	n.a.	n.a.	n.a.	n.a.
Technology and engineering	n.a.	n.a.	n.a.	n.a.	n.a.	n.a.	n.a.	n.a.	n.a.	n.a.	n.a.	n.a.	n.a.
Transportation	12.95	n.a.	n.a.	n.a.	n.a.	n.a.	n.a.	n.a.	n.a.	n.a.	n.a.	n.a.	n.a.
Travel	n.a.	n.a.	n.a.	n.a.	n.a.	n.a.	n.a.	n.a.	n.a.	n.a.	n.a.	n.a.	n.a.
True crime	7.19	44	7.83	108.9	38	8.31	115.6	26	8.49	118.1	22	9.06	126.0
Young adult	6.46	47	8.48	131.3	44	8.94	138.4	44	9.22	142.7	21	8.80	136.2
Totals	$6.34	4,411	$6.99	110.3	4,276	$7.06	111.4	3,855	$7.04	111.0	3,806	$7.10	112.0

Compiled by Catherine Barr from data supplied by Baker & Taylor.

n.a. = not available

Table 7 / U.S. Paperback Books (Excluding Mass Market): Average Prices and Price Indexes, 2011–2014

Index Base: 2005 = 100

BISAC Category	2005 Average Prices	2011 Final Volumes	2011 Final Average Prices	2011 Final Index	2012 Final Volumes	2012 Final Average Prices	2012 Final Index	2013 Final Volumes	2013 Final Average Prices	2013 Final Index	2014 Preliminary Volumes	2014 Preliminary Average Prices	2014 Preliminary Index
Antiques and collectibles	$24.80	158	$25.85	104.2	160	$31.34	126.4	134	$34.08	137.4	141	$38.56	155.5
Architecture	38.90	739	42.71	109.8	639	42.72	109.8	780	43.74	112.4	669	45.68	117.4
Art	31.28	1,706	37.64	120.3	1,718	37.93	121.3	1,697	41.70	133.3	1,630	38.07	121.7
Bibles	36.87	755	41.08	111.4	641	44.66	121.1	808	41.74	113.2	768	44.77	121.4
Biography and autobiography	19.19	4,946	18.93	98.6	2,648	20.10	104.7	3,092	19.80	103.2	2,861	20.34	106.0
Body, mind and spirit	17.48	1,717	17.88	102.3	1,061	18.35	105.0	1,013	18.31	104.7	855	17.97	102.8
Business and economics	71.12	5,789	68.02	95.6	9,050	86.29	121.3	7,243	88.39	124.3	6,351	86.70	121.9
Children	11.11	9,474	11.05	99.5	10,137	13.83	124.5	10,360	12.31	110.8	11,315	12.78	115.0
Comics and graphic novels	12.75	3,415	16.24	127.4	2,206	16.39	128.5	1,834	16.73	131.2	2,102	17.60	138.0
Computers	57.01	3,495	71.41	125.3	4,289	93.80	164.5	3,636	85.88	150.6	3,382	80.90	141.9
Cooking	18.30	1,242	19.80	108.2	1,297	20.48	111.9	1,190	20.06	109.6	1,244	19.58	107.0
Crafts and hobbies	18.49	1,091	19.41	105.0	1,079	19.52	105.6	1,201	18.40	99.5	1,160	18.61	100.6
Design	32.87	414	42.72	130.0	386	41.48	126.2	327	38.64	117.6	306	42.20	128.4
Drama	16.40	559	18.80	114.6	504	19.60	119.5	611	20.09	122.5	566	20.19	123.1
Education	35.10	3,565	41.21	117.4	4,189	45.94	130.9	4,195	48.89	139.3	4,168	53.50	152.4
Family and relationships	17.10	1,288	17.87	104.5	763	19.18	112.2	767	19.42	113.6	749	20.94	122.5
Fiction	15.74	18,402	18.22	115.8	11,063	17.07	108.4	13,231	17.00	108.0	12,633	17.17	109.1
Foreign language study	41.90	1,247	36.30	86.6	1,224	42.66	101.8	1,006	52.51	125.3	1,322	38.68	92.3
Games	16.53	705	16.61	100.5	665	15.75	95.3	619	15.64	94.6	536	17.70	107.1
Gardening	20.59	249	23.33	113.3	236	23.60	114.6	194	22.83	110.9	155	22.22	107.9
Health and fitness	22.81	1,477	26.98	118.3	1,181	27.90	122.3	1,095	26.30	115.3	1,094	26.36	115.6
History	33.53	7,456	36.45	108.7	6,978	42.43	126.5	6,513	37.88	113.0	7,188	36.81	109.8
House and home	19.33	153	20.43	105.7	148	23.49	121.5	145	20.08	103.9	946	95.86	495.9
Humor	12.96	581	14.97	115.5	395	14.18	109.4	353	14.39	111.0	336	14.97	115.5

Language arts and disciplines	49.14	1,835	72.19	146.9	2,282	77.38	157.5	1,875	73.94	150.5	2,045	76.82	156.3
Law	60.92	3,220	70.43	115.6	3,492	76.71	125.9	3,154	76.13	125.0	3,498	77.66	127.5
Literary collections	28.07	541	29.36	104.6	492	35.11	125.1	474	34.38	122.5	651	21.07	75.1
Literary criticism	31.99	1,750	38.50	120.4	1,597	44.22	138.2	1,587	40.32	126.0	2,015	39.66	124.0
Mathematics	75.77	1,611	81.10	107.0	2,618	97.95	129.3	1,479	86.74	114.5	1,465	82.70	109.1
Medical	64.27	6,107	83.04	129.2	8,268	93.79	145.9	5,120	96.56	150.2	4,684	96.89	150.8
Music	22.66	2,837	24.53	108.3	2,683	25.89	114.3	2,653	24.31	107.3	1,914	28.63	126.3
Nature	26.90	586	35.86	133.3	651	37.45	139.2	564	31.58	117.4	579	30.28	112.6
Performing arts	27.85	938	32.40	116.3	922	38.65	138.8	867	35.48	127.4	879	35.02	125.7
Pets	18.86	235	18.70	99.2	217	18.19	96.4	154	18.87	100.1	141	18.31	97.1
Philosophy	31.40	1,587	42.41	135.1	1,481	49.07	156.3	1,522	44.41	141.4	1,612	44.05	140.3
Photography	27.74	541	32.14	115.9	514	33.57	121.0	445	34.43	124.1	420	35.40	127.6
Poetry	16.09	3,811	16.26	101.1	1,959	16.55	102.9	2,399	16.62	103.3	2,252	17.54	109.0
Political science	45.65	3,472	41.07	90.0	3,522	48.73	106.7	3,555	47.80	104.7	3,529	46.79	102.5
Psychology	45.74	1,685	53.84	117.7	2,039	70.42	154.0	1,944	67.22	147.0	2,204	57.10	124.8
Reference	52.54	1,217	89.01	169.4	1,022	107.43	204.5	823	100.88	192.0	871	96.20	183.1
Religion	20.54	8,639	20.58	100.2	7,158	22.98	111.9	7,968	22.24	108.3	7,386	23.52	114.5
Science	71.05	4,685	99.37	139.9	7,680	93.93	132.2	4,523	90.07	126.8	4,442	87.50	123.2
Self-help	16.36	2,043	17.31	105.8	1,440	17.32	105.9	1,291	17.72	108.3	1,135	18.55	113.4
Social science	36.83	4,013	43.93	119.3	5,442	54.44	147.8	4,502	50.07	135.9	4,447	51.03	138.6
Sports and recreation	21.82	1,310	24.79	113.6	1,118	23.47	107.6	1,111	23.88	109.4	1,174	24.07	110.3
Study aids	30.90	985	33.84	109.5	590	41.74	135.1	535	47.44	153.5	1,681	44.39	143.7
Technology and engineering	85.80	2,426	105.98	123.5	4,519	101.91	118.8	2,805	101.16	117.9	3,835	105.34	122.8
Transportation	40.19	458	36.76	91.5	405	34.48	85.8	427	39.45	98.2	447	36.22	90.1
Travel	19.18	2,513	19.82	103.3	2,160	20.28	105.7	1,736	20.64	107.6	1,709	20.57	107.2
True crime	17.71	227	19.00	107.3	169	18.79	106.1	169	19.84	112.0	169	19.07	107.7
Young adult	14.06	2,555	18.59	132.2	3,315	17.19	122.3	2,169	16.83	119.7	2,911	18.57	132.1
Totals	$33.90	132,450	$37.86	111.7	130,412	$49.96	147.4	117,895	$43.81	129.2	120,572	$44.12	130.1

Compiled by Catherine Barr from data supplied by Baker & Taylor.

Table 7A / U.S. Audiobooks: Average Prices and Price Indexes, 2011–2014

Index Base: 2005 = 100

BISAC Category	2005 Average Prices	2011 Final Volumes	2011 Final Average Prices	2011 Final Index	2012 Volumes	2012 Average Prices	2012 Index	2013 Volumes	2013 Average Prices	2013 Index	2014 Volumes	2014 Average Prices	2014 Index
Antiques and collectibles	n.a.	n.a.	n.a.	n.a.	n.a.	n.a.	n.a.	n.a.	n.a.	n.a.	n.a.	n.a.	n.a.
Architecture	$68.95	3	$39.97	58.0	2	$32.45	47.1	7	$42.82	62.1	n.a.	n.a.	n.a.
Art	57.51	9	40.36	70.2	12	37.40	65.0	3	29.95	52.1	9	$39.32	68.4
Bibles	47.08	10	44.49	94.5	23	49.94	106.1	20	81.48	173.1	11	70.88	150.6
Biography and autobiography	37.68	749	51.25	136.0	1,018	47.08	124.9	1,199	41.12	109.1	968	41.19	109.3
Body, mind and spirit	26.74	103	37.62	140.7	126	35.99	134.6	244	26.93	100.7	177	27.98	104.6
Business and economics	42.11	401	45.20	107.3	475	38.25	90.8	452	34.51	82.0	610	29.83	70.8
Children	26.57	978	34.74	130.7	1,283	32.05	120.6	1,713	40.92	154.0	976	34.39	129.4
Comics and graphic novels	n.a.	29	19.99	n.a.	4	37.48	n.a.	2	14.99	n.a.	n.a.	n.a.	n.a.
Computers	41.39	12	53.99	130.4	4	42.73	103.2	2	52.47	126.8	18	41.26	99.7
Cooking	14.45	14	42.77	296.0	14	44.91	310.8	20	47.19	326.6	14	49.06	339.5
Crafts and hobbies	n.a.	n.a.	n.a.	n.a.	1	24.95	n.a.	3	24.95	n.a.	5	24.78	n.a.
Design	n.a.	n.a.	n.a.	n.a.	3	57.30	n.a.	1	29.95	n.a.	n.a.	n.a.	n.a.
Drama	23.45	104	28.03	119.5	111	24.09	102.7	100	32.53	138.7	59	25.86	110.3
Education	27.46	34	44.04	160.4	37	34.92	127.2	33	39.25	142.9	32	36.84	134.2
Family and relationships	24.58	110	41.20	167.6	143	43.07	175.2	119	35.16	143.0	122	32.38	131.7
Fiction	41.47	7,174	48.19	116.2	11,408	41.85	100.9	11,434	38.34	92.5	11,227	38.57	93.0
Foreign language study	70.04	223	50.61	72.3	178	65.81	94.0	114	69.35	99.0	218	74.12	105.8
Games	32.68	5	46.98	143.8	5	44.98	137.6	n.a.	n.a.	n.a.	5	47.18	144.4
Gardening	n.a.	n.a.	n.a.	n.a.	5	31.99	n.a.	n.a.	n.a.	n.a.	n.a.	n.a.	n.a.
Health and fitness	26.61	110	47.00	176.6	99	43.08	161.9	131	42.91	161.3	111	41.16	154.7
History	41.61	446	59.36	142.7	610	50.35	121.0	480	47.52	114.2	476	51.88	124.7
House and home	25.00	1	34.95	139.8	3	55.32	221.3	4	29.98	119.9	1	9.99	40.0
Humor	29.60	103	40.46	136.7	77	33.05	111.7	70	37.80	127.7	98	32.93	111.3

Subject													
Language arts and disciplines	60.84	38	44.87	73.8	26	55.28	90.9	14	40.79	67.0	11	38.17	62.7
Law	55.32	7	70.42	127.3	18	51.04	92.3	16	64.24	116.1	12	61.41	111.0
Literary collections	24.71	33	51.64	209.0	35	39.87	161.3	18	37.09	150.1	42	53.88	218.0
Literary criticism	26.41	188	30.59	115.8	95	33.38	126.4	11	48.62	184.1	7	13.56	51.3
Mathematics	n.a.	1	24.95	n.a.	3	51.32	n.a.	5	38.97	n.a.	5	20.59	n.a.
Medical	153.72	24	45.74	29.8	24	49.26	32.0	24	40.98	26.7	12	37.74	24.6
Music	29.83	57	48.44	162.4	51	45.86	153.7	34	41.10	137.8	20	60.37	202.4
Nature	28.92	44	46.71	161.5	13	51.60	178.4	25	42.26	146.1	23	46.63	161.2
Performing arts	25.78	9	65.08	252.4	16	34.42	133.5	45	39.34	152.6	59	39.75	154.2
Pets	33.05	25	43.14	130.5	20	42.93	129.9	30	39.28	118.9	13	37.05	112.1
Philosophy	35.30	73	46.86	132.7	42	39.76	112.6	38	29.62	83.9	25	32.02	90.7
Photography	n.a.	n.a.	n.a.	n.a.	n.a.	n.a.	n.a.	n.a.	n.a.	n.a.	n.a.	n.a.	n.a.
Poetry	22.87	16	23.03	100.7	16	27.28	119.3	19	26.39	115.4	38	39.07	170.8
Political science	42.66	220	48.22	113.0	236	46.61	109.3	166	45.06	105.6	130	44.80	105.0
Psychology	35.70	91	48.58	136.1	85	39.45	110.5	73	43.95	123.1	96	32.57	91.2
Reference	21.20	19	42.62	201.0	11	35.44	167.2	5	49.77	234.8	8	25.99	122.6
Religion	26.52	465	31.81	119.9	577	33.05	124.6	675	29.06	109.6	692	28.46	107.3
Science	39.86	90	54.30	136.2	117	42.30	106.1	95	41.15	103.2	98	41.78	104.8
Self-help	23.58	197	41.65	176.6	386	36.91	156.5	212	31.10	131.9	228	30.45	129.1
Social science	35.73	102	48.64	136.1	116	43.50	121.7	111	38.11	106.7	101	35.70	99.9
Sports and recreation	28.46	38	45.51	159.9	37	44.06	154.8	48	39.93	140.3	52	38.52	135.3
Study aids	41.85	2	27.66	66.1	5	147.63	352.8	1	24.99	59.7	5	131.00	313.0
Technology and engineering	61.47	26	46.41	75.5	11	40.07	65.2	8	36.61	59.6	9	52.09	84.7
Transportation	28.00	1	24.95	89.1	7	46.27	165.2	10	48.68	173.9	5	52.39	187.1
Travel	41.91	20	61.17	146.0	49	35.88	85.6	37	35.89	85.6	9	47.76	114.0
True crime	35.97	36	50.04	139.1	80	45.29	125.9	136	39.89	110.9	93	33.87	94.2
Young adult	35.68	960	41.71	116.9	1,461	34.55	96.8	1,271	42.20	118.3	1,251	42.93	120.3
Totals	$40.49	13,400	$45.89	113.3	19,178	$40.86	100.9	19,278	$38.92	96.1	18,181	$38.69	95.6

Table 7B / U.S. E-Books: Average Prices and Price Indexes, 2011–2014

Index Base: 2008 = 100

BISAC Category	2008 Average Prices	2011 Final Volumes	2011 Final Average Prices	2011 Final Index	2012 Final Volumes	2012 Final Average Prices	2012 Final Index	2013 Final Volumes	2013 Final Average Prices	2013 Final Index	2014 Preliminary Volumes	2014 Preliminary Average Prices	2014 Preliminary Index
Antiques and collectibles	$55.97	229	$21.46	38.3	168	$22.62	40.4	177	$20.96	37.4	121	$16.48	29.4
Architecture	70.50	312	60.38	85.6	830	47.86	67.9	823	63.80	90.5	903	165.17	234.3
Art	45.41	729	16.89	37.2	1,339	21.41	47.1	1,812	18.09	39.8	1,847	15.54	34.2
Bibles	25.79	113	11.34	44.0	165	13.37	51.8	495	8.76	34.0	211	10.65	41.3
Biography and autobiography	14.58	3,824	10.23	70.2	8,544	18.07	123.9	8,156	15.10	103.6	9,050	18.47	126.7
Body, mind and spirit	12.41	1,378	11.54	93.0	2,744	12.90	103.9	1,984	11.94	96.2	1,737	10.11	81.5
Business and economics	57.52	7,198	40.64	70.7	12,688	41.17	71.6	11,760	56.43	98.1	9,025	51.18	89.0
Children	12.01	14,867	16.42	136.7	23,942	10.63	88.5	20,257	11.53	96.0	20,124	14.36	119.6
Comics and graphic novels	25.04	269	6.02	24.0	628	6.68	26.7	551	7.31	29.2	1,726	6.18	24.7
Computers	66.87	4,383	61.72	92.3	4,881	70.64	105.6	4,170	54.38	81.3	3,133	52.95	79.2
Cooking	20.20	1,561	12.42	61.5	2,680	11.55	57.2	3,437	12.45	61.6	2,599	11.88	58.8
Crafts and hobbies	14.35	785	15.26	106.3	1,270	10.45	72.8	1,388	10.22	71.2	878	12.16	84.7
Design	36.04	104	33.69	107.4	221	25.27	70.1	193	26.00	72.1	120	27.47	76.2
Drama	29.49	2,758	3.19	10.8	2,256	7.19	24.4	1,629	7.91	26.8	1,746	9.40	31.9
Education	51.98	1,787	50.25	96.7	3,878	47.65	91.7	5,038	51.32	98.7	3,821	42.31	81.4
Family and relationships	19.88	1,210	10.13	51.0	2,208	13.81	69.5	1,927	28.32	142.5	1,930	15.22	76.6
Fiction	8.71	56,776	4.83	55.5	108,916	9.68	111.1	94,876	6.55	75.2	106,409	6.60	75.8
Foreign language study	43.01	304	19.69	45.8	903	23.06	53.6	1,589	16.08	37.4	1,576	16.24	37.8
Games	17.73	324	10.79	60.9	492	8.42	47.5	506	9.43	53.2	665	8.48	47.8
Gardening	20.40	169	13.34	65.4	408	14.41	70.6	360	13.77	67.5	301	11.93	58.5
Health and fitness	18.54	1,988	13.20	71.2	3,179	13.49	72.8	3,562	17.61	95.0	2,960	11.40	61.5
History	57.53	4,163	33.22	57.7	9,697	32.46	56.4	9,775	39.71	69.0	10,665	31.86	55.4
House and home	22.89	187	14.90	65.1	309	12.89	56.3	425	10.39	45.4	287	9.45	41.3
Humor	11.27	619	7.53	66.8	1,297	12.39	109.9	1,085	8.81	78.2	1,032	9.46	83.9

Language arts and disciplines	93.27	1,075	59.54	63.8	2,009	45.28	48.5	2,413	52.09	55.8	1,843	69.69	74.7
Law	81.23	872	76.17	93.8	2,132	72.99	89.9	1,745	94.15	115.9	1,268	89.95	110.7
Literary collections	24.50	1,757	4.41	18.0	1,823	9.95	40.6	1,468	13.90	56.7	1,451	11.32	46.2
Literary criticism	86.62	936	50.59	58.4	2,444	36.90	42.6	2,336	61.37	70.8	1,585	76.03	87.8
Mathematics	106.16	1,332	95.28	89.8	1,973	74.53	70.2	1,434	84.14	79.3	1,072	88.28	83.2
Medical	135.21	4,299	100.28	74.2	5,638	95.97	71.0	4,242	98.63	72.9	2,902	96.70	71.5
Music	33.83	4,390	14.12	41.7	18,723	4.85	14.3	1,942	30.36	89.7	1,196	30.53	90.2
Nature	59.76	527	32.10	53.7	934	38.90	65.1	1,017	33.08	55.4	729	32.09	53.7
Performing arts	38.06	863	26.70	70.2	1,231	28.74	75.5	1,599	39.69	104.3	1,239	31.94	83.9
Pets	15.91	581	11.17	70.2	716	14.76	92.8	750	8.41	52.9	376	9.96	62.6
Philosophy	79.19	948	44.17	55.8	2,304	37.51	47.4	2,676	56.26	71.0	1,956	53.72	67.8
Photography	30.30	387	18.19	60.0	471	18.89	62.3	535	22.02	72.7	513	19.22	63.4
Poetry	13.66	1,807	5.73	41.9	2,398	7.18	52.6	3,047	6.93	50.7	3,555	6.48	47.4
Political science	59.03	2,208	43.34	73.4	4,959	41.13	69.7	5,129	50.02	84.7	3,520	56.61	95.9
Psychology	65.30	2,139	49.01	75.1	3,023	44.76	68.5	4,119	139.89	214.2	2,988	92.36	141.4
Reference	48.33	788	19.77	40.9	1,392	24.74	51.2	1,543	82.84	171.4	3,959	25.10	51.9
Religion	27.29	5,669	17.29	63.4	9,644	17.76	65.1	9,800	20.59	75.4	10,444	16.56	60.7
Science	210.57	3,634	131.61	62.5	5,935	102.09	48.5	4,491	105.83	50.3	3,805	114.67	54.5
Self-help	14.15	2,497	8.10	57.2	4,978	13.50	95.4	4,299	29.36	207.5	4,704	9.09	64.2
Social science	69.42	2,240	53.61	77.2	4,446	54.35	78.3	6,941	79.66	114.8	4,154	71.53	103.0
Sports and recreation	22.44	1,223	17.09	76.2	2,607	17.82	79.4	2,727	19.47	86.8	1,790	17.50	78.0
Study aids	21.95	859	9.20	41.9	13,402	22.96	104.6	6,142	18.79	85.6	4,708	18.52	84.4
Technology and engineering	153.73	2,831	123.20	80.1	4,044	118.05	76.8	3,886	114.23	74.3	3,262	144.23	93.8
Transportation	35.47	193	19.12	53.9	323	24.34	68.6	327	26.12	73.6	307	21.65	61.0
Travel	15.61	2,745	9.10	58.3	3,686	9.74	62.4	2,546	10.96	70.2	2,026	10.64	68.2
True crime	11.60	321	8.81	75.9	621	15.87	136.8	616	12.03	103.7	511	12.65	109.1
Young adult	8.83	2,821	21.47	243.1	5,980	17.11	193.8	6,502	13.60	154.0	6,612	14.06	159.2
Totals	$57.38	155,979	$24.48	42.7	301,479	$22.92	39.9	260,247	$27.97	48.7	255,341	$23.13	40.3

Compiled by Catherine Barr from data supplied by Baker & Taylor.

Table 8 / Average Price of Serials, Based on Titles in Select Serial Indexes, 2011–2015

Subject	LC Class	Avg. No. of Titles	2011 Avg. Price	2012 Avg. Price	2011–12 % of Price Increase	2013 Avg. Price	2012–13 % of Price Increase	2014 Avg. Price	2013–14 % of Price Increase	2015 Avg. Price	2014–15 % of Price Increase
Agriculture	S	289	$989	$1,039	5.1%	$1,117	7.4%	$1,181	5.8%	$1,253	6.1%
Anthropology	GN	92	367	386	5.1	413	7.0	443	7.2	465	5.1
Arts and architecture	N	198	249	263	5.6	281	6.9	302	7.5	319	5.9
Astronomy	QB	50	1,885	2,002	6.2	2,195	9.6	2,299	4.7	2,488	8.2
Biology	QH	812	2,054	2,170	5.6	2,293	5.6	2,409	5.1	2,559	6.2
Botany	QK	94	1,556	1,641	5.5	1,744	6.2	1,845	5.8	1,931	4.7
Business and economics	HA-HJ	835	763	811	6.3	865	6.7	920	6.4	980	6.5
Chemistry	QD	308	3,595	3,783	5.2	3,970	5.0	4,143	4.4	4,310	4.0
Education	L	415	492	518	5.2	561	8.4	597	6.3	637	6.7
Engineering	T	680	1,913	2,030	6.1	2,166	6.7	2,305	6.4	2,443	6.0
Food science	TX	64	855	908	6.2	976	7.5	1,041	6.7	1,112	6.9
General science	Q	167	935	1,010	8.0	1,061	5.0	1,118	5.4	1,229	10.0
General works	A	216	124	128	3.5	135	5.0	141	5.0	149	5.3
Geography	G-GF	182	876	935	6.8	1,030	10.1	1,099	6.8	1,175	6.9
Geology	QE	121	1,545	1,637	6.0	1,780	8.7	1,883	5.8	2,003	6.4
Health sciences	R	1,980	1,111	1,182	6.4	1,278	8.1	1,366	6.9	1,460	6.9
History	C,D,E,F	697	266	283	6.3	301	6.4	320	6.4	341	6.4

Subject	Code									
Language and literature	P	752	242	256	5.6	272	6.4	276	1.3	291	5.6
Law	K	280	255	273	7.0	285	4.7	302	5.8	327	8.3
Library science	Z	130	327	340	4.1	358	5.2	377	5.4	399	5.8
Math and computer science	QA	337	1,480	1,557	5.2	1,587	1.9	1,676	5.6	1,744	4.0
Military and naval science	U,V	60	260	274	5.5	286	4.0	276	-3.3	321	16.1
Music	M	105	200	210	4.7	228	8.7	240	5.3	252	5.0
Philosophy and religion	B-BD BH-BX	497	247	261	5.8	278	6.6	296	6.6	316	6.5
Physics	QC	336	3,195	3,375	5.6	3,615	7.1	3,795	5.0	3,916	3.2
Political science	J	208	468	496	5.9	527	6.4	561	6.3	598	6.6
Psychology	BF	284	677	712	5.1	761	6.9	822	8.1	881	7.1
Recreation	GV	71	286	313	9.5	338	7.9	367	8.4	392	7.0
Social sciences	H	108	509	533	4.8	569	6.8	604	6.1	642	6.2
Sociology	HM-HX	570	601	635	5.7	681	7.2	727	6.8	781	7.4
Technology	TA-TT	129	1,192	1,256	5.4	1,334	6.1	1,428	7.1	1,508	5.6
Zoology	QL	180	1,310	1,384	5.6	1,451	4.8	1,536	5.9	1,618	5.4
Totals		11,247	$1,033	$1,094	5.8%	$1,165	6.5%	$1,233	5.8%	$1,306	5.9%

Data on serial pricing supplied by EBSCO are based on titles indexed in ISI Arts and Humanities Citation Index, ISI Science Citation Index, ISI Social Sciences Citation Index, EBSCO Academic Search Premier, and EBSCO Masterfile Premier

Table 8A / Average Price of Online Serials, Based on Titles in Select Serial Indexes, 2011–2015

Subject	LC Class	Average No. of Titles 2011–15	2011 Avg. Price	2012 Avg. Price	2011–12 % of Price Increase	2013 Avg. Price	2012–13 % of Price Increase	2014 Avg. Price	2013–14 % of Price Increase	2015 Avg. Price	2014–15 % of Price Increase
Agriculture	S	58	$711	$736	3.6%	$774	5.1%	$810	4.7%	$850	4.9%
Anthropology	GN	26	538	561	4.3	614	9.4	659	7.4	703	6.6
Arts and architecture	N	54	440	465	5.5	497	6.8	543	9.3	584	7.5
Astronomy	QB	9	523	555	6.1	579	4.3	617	6.5	672	8.9
Biology	QH	195	1,439	1,526	6.0	1,604	5.1	1,705	6.3	1,815	6.4
Botany	QK	22	911	958	5.2	1,026	7.2	1,070	4.3	1,120	4.6
Business and economics	HA-HJ	249	1,283	1,365	6.4	1,463	7.1	1,551	6.0	1,652	6.5
Chemistry	QD	83	3,437	3,655	6.4	3,890	6.4	4,131	6.2	4,326	4.7
Education	L	213	662	693	4.7	756	9.0	804	6.4	865	7.6
Engineering	T	135	1,427	1,509	5.8	1,665	10.4	1,771	6.3	1,878	6.0
Food science	TX	18	1,386	1,475	6.4	1,577	6.9	1,682	6.7	1,802	7.1
General science	Q	48	847	947	11.9	1,034	9.2	1,109	7.3	1,221	10.1
General works	A	17	519	541	4.4	575	6.1	607	5.6	641	5.6
Geography	G-GF	75	968	1,052	8.7	1,136	8.0	1,210	6.5	1,296	7.1
Geology	QE	24	721	793	10.1	870	9.7	934	7.4	1,019	9.0
Health sciences	R	533	848	911	7.5	967	6.2	1,043	7.8	1,098	5.3
History	C,D,E,F	235	406	427	5.1	455	6.7	485	6.6	519	6.9
Language and literature	P	221	385	405	5.2	428	5.8	410	-4.1	433	5.6

Law	K	44	431	465	7.9	491	5.6	520	5.9	588	13.0
Library science	Z	48	328	339	3.5	358	5.6	379	5.9	395	4.2
Math and computer science	QA	64	1,290	1,358	5.3	1,421	4.6	1,524	7.3	1,602	5.1
Military and naval science	U,V	20	442	461	4.3	476	3.2	432	-9.1	540	24.9
Music	M	37	335	350	4.3	382	9.2	402	5.1	429	6.8
Philosophy and religion	B-BD BH-BX	152	256	270	5.4	286	6.0	307	7.3	331	7.9
Physics	QC	91	3,311	3,530	6.6	3,822	8.3	4,032	5.5	4,226	4.8
Political science	J	102	574	608	6.0	650	6.8	692	6.6	739	6.7
Psychology	BF	116	745	799	7.3	863	8.0	934	8.3	992	6.2
Recreation	QV	28	517	574	11.0	612	6.7	667	9.0	707	6.0
Social sciences	H	38	629	659	4.8	699	6.1	742	6.1	780	5.1
Sociology	HM-I-X	256	746	787	5.6	846	7.5	907	7.1	981	8.3
Technology	TA-TT	39	1,510	1,585	5.0	1,681	6.0	1,776	5.6	1,894	6.7
Zoology	QL	32	603	634	5.1	670	5.6	746	11.4	795	6.6
Totals		3,282	$929	$988	6.3%	$1,057	7.0%	$1,124	6.3%	$1,194	6.2%

Compiled by Stephen Bosch, University of Arizona, from data on serial pricing for titles available in online format supplied by EBSCO and is based on titles indexed in ISI Arts and Humanities Citation Index, ISI Science Citation Index, ISI Social Sciences Citation Index, EBSCO Academic Search Premier, and EBSCO Masterfile Premier.

(continued from page 428)

One thing that really stands out when looking at the data by price band is that the highest end of the price bands ($120 and up) has seen huge growth in the past four years, close to doubling in overall costs from $5.8 million (2010) to $9.6 million (2013). The impact on pricing from the titles in the $120-and-up price band is confirmed if you look at the actual dollar values in groups (sum of all prices for titles in the group). It is clear that the increase in the top end of the index was the main component in the overall increase in the index for 2013. Although the $0–$30 price area has the largest number of titles, dollar-wise it remains the smallest portion as far as total cost (sum of all prices) goes in the index. The increase in the prices in the upper end of the index was what added to the overall level of increase. Since 2007 the cost (titles X prices) for books pricing above $120 has increased by 259 percent, while the overall costs for all books increased 120 percent. The increases in the costs of books in the upper price band represents 91 percent of the entire increase over the period covered. Again, e-books are a significant driver in that increase as within the price bands the average price remains fairly constant except for the area with prices above $120, which showed a 62 percent increase over the past four years. See Figures 2 and 3.

Figure 2 / Comparison of Total Costs in Sample Grouped by Price

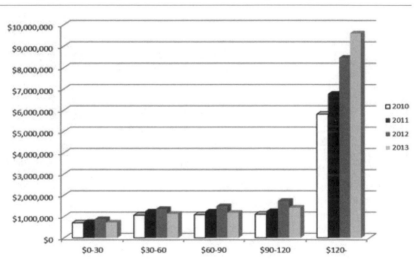

Figure 3 / Comparison of Total Costs for E-Books in Sample Grouped by Price

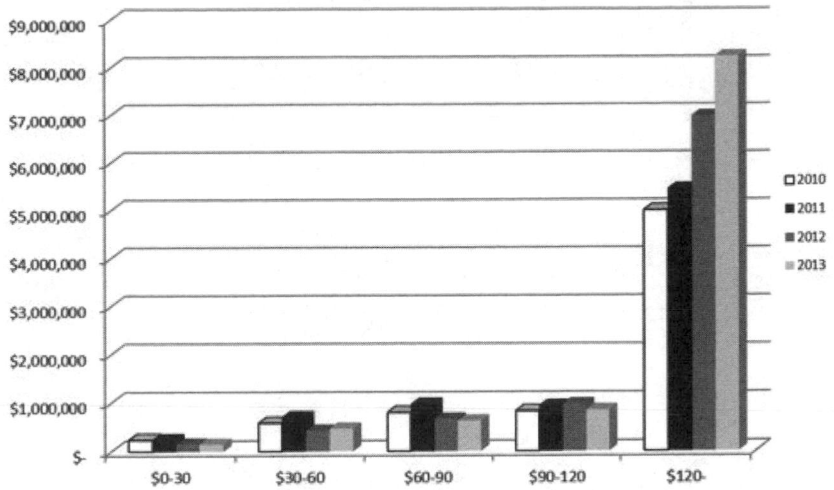

The data used for this index are derived from all titles treated by the Ingram Content Group (formerly Coutts Information Services) and YBP Library Services in their approval plans during the calendar years listed. The index includes e-books as well as paperback editions as supplied by these vendors, and this inclusion of paperbacks and e-books as distributed as part of the approval plans has clearly influenced the prices reflected in the index figures. The index is inclusive of the broadest categories of materials because that is the marketplace in which academic libraries operate, and the index attempts to chart price changes that impact that market.

E-books are also now being treated in a separate index (Table 4A), so the differences in the indexes will be interesting to observe. Currently the vast majority of titles are not published in both print and "e" version, so the number of titles in the e-book index should remain smaller than the broader index. It is safe to say that in the future the number of titles in the broader index could decline and at the same time the number of e-books should rise, especially as we see more publishers move to electronic versions of their books. Many e-book pricing models add extra charges of as much as 50 percent to 100 percent to the retail price. This pricing model is reflected in the higher prices for e-books. The overall price for e-books did show a decline from 2007 to 2009, but in 2011 to 2013 the prices shot up again. The year 2012 saw the largest price increase (23 percent) since the inception of the index and the overall trend does seem to be going up. The index does clearly show that for the library market, e-books are much more expensive than print. Many publishers and e-book aggregators are still adding "e" versions of print books from backlists, and these are showing up in the index; this is also the basis for the wide swings in numbers of titles in the index from year to year.

(text continues on page 448)

Table 9 / British Academic Books: Average Prices and Price Indexes 2009–2014

Index Base: 2009 = 100

Subject	LC Class	2009		2011		2012		2013		2014			
		No. of Titles	Average Price (£)	No. of Titles	Average Price (£)	No. of Titles	Average Price (£)	No. of Titles	Average Price (£)	No. of Titles	Average Price (£)	% Change 2013–2014	Index
Agriculture	S	140	53.96	177	58.83	183	69.29	163	68.55	134	73.28	6.9%	134.1
Anthropology	GN	109	53.60	111	59.74	145	45.73	124	55.11	109	57.63	4.6	114.0
Botany	QK	22	145.94	39	85.29	45	97.50	33	81.54	35	74.78	-8.3	64.0
Business and economics	H-HJ	1,634	59.08	1,690	61.77	2,022	71.12	1,877	71.29	1,911	71.19	-0.1	119.7
Chemistry	QD	88	101.14	87	116.07	144	155.82	96	149.82	91	125.67	-16.1	128.6
Education	L	386	49.70	456	52.98	547	64.36	440	64.49	517	64.50	0.0	128.2
Engineering and technology	T-TS	796	60.97	715	68.90	741	76.09	758	78.35	788	76.69	-4.1	122.1
Fine and applied arts	M, N	762	38.43	949	41.29	1,092	42.40	1,005	43.35	1,009	44.54	2.8	116.1
General works	A	15	76.73	24	69.50	26	78.67	17	91.58	32	72.25	-21.1	102.5
Geography	G-GF, GR-GT	233	54.43	294	56.70	276	63.59	268	64.44	245	67.55	4.8	125.3
Geology	QE	41	53.80	35	57.97	51	79.33	34	77.70	33	59.80	-23.0	119.8
History	C,D,E,F	1,572	43.41	1,586	43.28	1,880	44.74	1,690	44.63	1,725	48.11	7.8	110.7
Home economics	TX	59	39.02	34	48.40	47	61.06	58	67.22	38	63.79	-5.1	168.1
Industrial arts	TT	21	24.32	42	36.62	42	25.47	37	35.50	27	45.43	28.0	182.6

Law	K	1,117	76.13	1,159	78.79	1,312	87.74	1,264	88.46	1,253	88.30	-0.2	116.0
Library and information science	Z	98	60.32	104	61.51	105	65.96	100	59.99	106	69.71	16.2	118.0
Literature and language	F	2,928	34.77	3,526	32.71	3,966	37.34	3,448	37.25	3,553	38.95	4.6	112.9
Mathematics and computer science	QA	216	49.30	245	55.79	266	54.93	212	61.40	180	54.91	-10.6	113.1
Medicine	R	1,110	48.50	1,177	55.02	1,280	55.88	1,126	60.74	1,113	63.10	3.9	127.6
Military and naval sciences	U, V	112	48.42	133	46.35	163	57.71	173	48.95	201	50.67	3.5	110.6
Philosophy and religion	B-BD, BH-BX	1,091	45.65	1,151	48.65	1,293	54.67	1,074	53.96	1,187	52.78	1.7	119.3
Physics and astronomy	QB, QC	196	54.73	215	64.76	240	68.87	221	72.08	161	72.29	0.3	129.6
Political Science	J	621	59.74	671	62.95	797	69.98	732	66.67	794	65.82	-1.3	113.1
Psychology	BF	195	44.46	264	46.77	297	50.93	266	54.88	295	63.42	15.6	139.3
Science (general)	Q	45	41.65	60	51.05	72	72.50	47	54.85	54	57.89	5.5	146.4
Sociology	HM-HX	958	59.36	1,069	54.31	1,195	57.01	1,111	63.65	1,221	64.89	1.9	109.9
Sports & Recreation	GV	181	30.90	145	46.83	202	56.70	165	54.18	170	61.49	13.5	176.5
Zoology	QH, QL-QR	336	62.59	370	77.75	434	84.57	396	81.41	285	79.00	-3.0	125.4
Total, All Books		15,082	50.42	16,528	51.94	18,863	57.51	16,935	58.47	17,267	59.05	1.0%	116.4

Compiled by George Aulisio, University of Scranton, based on information provided by YBP U.K./Baker & Taylor

(continued from page 445)

The price index for textbooks (Table 4B) shows a 1.2 percent decrease for overall prices between 2012 and 2013. Despite the decrease, overall textbook prices are higher than regular books. These are indicators that the angst experienced by students as they purchase their texts is well justified as prices appear to be much higher than for regular academic books.

Price changes vary, as always, among subject areas. This year there were many double-digit increases in subject areas, and a few areas showed price decreases. This is a normal occurrence. What is not normal is the fact that a third of the subject areas showed double-digit price increases. This is probably caused by increases in e-book publishing in these subject areas, especially in large expensive online reference works and encyclopedias. STM and social science publishers have tended to be early adopters of e-books and have been publishing e-books for a while. The large price increases in science and the social sciences reflect the availability and higher pricing of e-books in these areas.

It is good to remember that price indexes become less accurate at describing price changes the smaller the sample becomes. Geology and physical education are small samples and show very large price changes, but to conclude that all books in those areas increased or decreased at like amounts is not correct. These areas have a small sample size (fewer than 1,000 titles) and the inclusion/exclusion of just a few large expensive items can have a major impact on prices for the category. The increases in geology, for example, were due to a few very expensive titles that showed up in the data. Because the sample is very small, these titles caused the overall price to jump dramatically.

The U.S. College Books Price Index (Table 5), prepared by Frederick C. Lynden, contains price and index number data for the years 2012 through 2014 (index base year of 1989), and also the percentage change in price between 2013 and 2014.

Data for the index were compiled from 6,974 reviews of books published in *Choice* during 2014. Expensive titles ($500 or more) were omitted from the analysis, thus the total number of titles reported is smaller than the actual number of books reviewed in 2014. This index includes some paperback prices; as a result, the average book price is less than if only hardcover books were included.

The average price for humanities titles in 2014 increased by 3.80 percent from the previous year, whereas the average price for science and technology titles decreased again slightly at a rate of 1.52 percent. Finally, the average price for social and behavioral sciences increased only slightly at a rate of 0.23 percent. Combined, the overall subject area increase was 1.17 percent. For all titles, which include reference, there was a small dip of 0.60 percent, caused primarily by the large decrease in reference title average prices. More and more reference titles are being published online these days.

For 2014, the overall price average for books in the four major sections of *Choice*—humanities, science and technology, social and behavioral sciences, and reference—was $73.34, a 0.60 percent decrease compared with the average 2013 book price of $73.78. Reference books calculated separately had an average price decrease of 13.4 percent over the previous year, with a 2014 average price of $124.29 (after items $500 or higher were removed) compared with last year's average price of $143.52. Excluding reference books, however, the 2014 average price was $70.11, a 1.17 percent increase over the average 2013 price of $69.30.

Questions regarding this index should be addressed to the author: Frederick Lynden, Retired Director, Scholarly Communication and Library Research, Brown University Library, Providence, RI 02912 (e-mail flynden@stanfordalumni.org).

Foreign Prices

During 2014 the dollar made significant gains against the Canadian dollar, euro, British pound sterling, and Japanese yen. The fall in oil prices may have been a factor in the dollar's renewed strength.

Dates	12/31/10*	12/31/11*	12/31/12*	12/31/13*	12/31/14*
Canada	1.0200	1.0180	0.9950	1.0640	1.1580
Euro	0.7700	0.7650	0.7590	0.7260	0.8220
U.K.	0.6400	0.6370	0.6180	0.6050	0.6420
Japan	83.8300	78.0000	86.1600	105.0100	119.4500

* Data from Bureau of Fiscal Services. U.S. Treasury Department (http://www.fiscal.treasury.gov/ fsreports/rpt/treasRptRateExch/treasRptRateExch_home.htm).

Serials Prices

Average Price of Serials (Table 8) and Average Price of Online Serials (Table 8A), compiled by Stephen Bosch, provide the average prices and percent increases for serials based on titles in select serials indexes. The serials included here are published in the United States as well as overseas and are indexed in the ISI Arts and Humanities Citation Index, ISI Science Citation Index, ISI Social Sciences Citation Index, EBSCO Academic Search Premier, and EBSCO Masterfile Premier.

Tables 8 and 8A cover prices for periodicals and serials for a five-year period, 2011 through 2015. The 2015 pricing is the actual renewal pricing for 2015 for serials that were indexed in the selected products. These tables are derived from pricing data supplied by EBSCO Information Services and reflect broad pricing changes aggregated from titles that are indexed in the five major products mentioned above. The U.S. Periodicals: Average Prices and Price Indexes (USPPI) (Table 1) is based on price changes seen in a static set of approximately 5,900 serial titles. The Average Price of Serials (Table 8) is based on a much broader set of titles, approximately 11,000; however, the titles are not static, so this pricing study does not rise to the level of a price index. This study is still useful in showing price changes for periodicals. The indexes selected for this price survey were deemed to be fairly representative of serials that are frequently purchased in academic and public libraries. There are some foreign titles in the indexes, so the scope is broader and this may give a better picture of the overall price pressures experienced in libraries. Table 8 contains both print and online serials pricing. Table 8A is a subset of the titles treated in Table 8 and contains only online serials pricing.

The most important trend seen in the data in Table 8 is that increases in prices have remained fairly constant since the economic recovery began. Price increases have hovered around 6 percent annually since 2011. For titles with online availability (Table 8A), the rates of increase are even higher, averaging 6.5 percent over the past five years. There is a difference between the average prices for print serials and online serials, so, at least for this set of data, online formats do cost less than their print counterparts. This may have more to do with pricing policy at large publishers as opposed to online versions actually being cheaper than print versions. Several large publishers have made online pricing available only through custom quotes, so there is no standard retail price and the pricing data is not available for this survey. As these titles tend to be more expensive than titles from other publishers, this affects the overall prices, making them lower.

Another interesting trend is that the science areas do not dominate the list of subjects with the largest price increases. The subject areas that displayed large increases were quite varied. Military and naval science, general science, law, astronomy, sociology, psychology, and recreation saw higher increases than most areas. Most of these areas showed the highest increases in the online table (Table 8A) as well. Average prices of journals in the science and technology areas are by far higher than in other areas and that trend continues, with the average cost of chemistry and physics journals being $4,310 and $3,916, respectively. Although these STM titles are not inflating at high rates, the impact of a 4 percent increase in a $4,000 title is much higher than a 9 percent increase on a $300 title. Online journals (Table 8A) showed similar average prices for chemistry ($4,326) and physics ($4,226).

In this price study, as in similar price surveys, the data become less accurate at describing price changes as the sample becomes smaller. For that reason, drawing conclusions about price changes in subject areas with a limited number of titles will be less accurate than for large areas or the broader price survey. Price changes are far more volatile where smaller data sets are used. For example, military and naval science (about 60 titles) showed price changes of 5.5 percent, 4.0 percent, -3.3 percent, and 16.1 percent between 2012 and 2015. Librarians are encouraged to look at an average price change over the period (military and naval science averaged 5.6 percent) or the overall number for the price study (5.9 percent) to calculate inflation. Year-to-year price changes are too unstable to be used for this purpose.

Book Prices

British Academic Books (Table 9), compiled by George Aulisio, indicates the average prices and price indexes from 2011 through 2014. The percent of change in titles and average price is calculated for 2013 to 2014 and the index price shows the percent of change between 2014 and the base year of 2009. This index is compiled using data from YBP and utilizes prices from cloth editions except when not available. YBP U.K. also profiles select titles from continental Europe and Africa. The index does not separate out more expensive reference titles. Small numbers of titles that include higher-priced reference sets may not be reliable indicators of price changes. This table does not include e-book prices.

Data on "Total, All Books" production illustrates the sum total of the LC Classes profiled in this table, not the sum total of all books profiled by YBP. In 2014 British academic books saw a 1.96 percent increase from 16,935 titles to

17,267 titles. According to YBP's industry insights, they anticipate another modest 1 percent to 2 percent increase in U.K. academic titles in 2015.

The average price in British pounds has increased moderately each year since 2009. In 2014 there was a 1.96 percent increase in book production and a moderate price increase of 1.0 percent, bringing the average price across all books profiled to £59.05. The 2014 overall average price increase of 1.0 percent is above the United Kingdom's Consumer Price Index, which, according to the Office of National Statistics, was at a very modest 0.5 percent inflation in December 2014 (http://www.ons.gov.uk).

Table 9 shows how average prices have increased or decreased in comparison with the 2009 base year. For 2014 the overall index price for all LC subjects profiled in this table is at 116.4 percent. Though British academic books were slightly above the Consumer Price Index on average, price increases were rather reasonable. All LC classes are currently above their 2009 base prices, except for botany, which is now at 64.0 percent of the 2009 base price. The highest increases in comparison with the 2009 base prices are industrial arts (182.6 percent), sports and recreation (176.5 percent), home economics (168.1 percent), and science (general) (146.4 percent). The large individual price increase from 2013 to 2014 in industrial arts (27.97 percent) is likely due to the small sample size, which in 2014 was 27 titles. Additional double-digit percent increases in average price in library and information science (16.21 percent), psychology (15.56 percent), and sports and recreation (13.49 percent), as well as large price decreases in geology (-23.0 percent), general works (-21.1 percent), and chemistry (-16.1 percent) are also likely due to small sample sizes with the possibility of a few titles being released at prices that were much higher or much lower than the average listed price.

Based on historical data, industry insights, and general economic data, YBP forecasts for 2015 a 3 percent to 4 percent increase in the price of United Kingdom print books. In addition, YBP notes that e-book pricing is linked to print book pricing and therefore speculates that e-books will see a similar price increase in 2015 (http://www.ybp.com/book_price_update.html).

Using the Price Indexes

Librarians are encouraged to monitor trends in the publishing industry and changes in economic conditions when preparing budget forecasts and projections. The ALA ALCTS Library Materials Price Index Editorial Board endeavors to make information on publishing trends readily available by sponsoring the annual compilation and publication of price data contained in Tables 1 to 9. The indexes cover newly published library materials and document prices and rates of percent changes at the national and international level. They are useful benchmarks against which local costs can be compared, but because they reflect retail prices in the aggregate, they are not a substitute for cost data that reflect the collecting patterns of individual libraries, and they are not a substitute for specific cost studies.

Differences between local prices and those found in national indexes arise partially because these indexes exclude discounts, service charges, shipping and handling fees, and other costs that a library might incur. Discrepancies may also relate to a library's subject coverage; mix of titles purchased, including both current and backfiles; and the proportion of the library's budget expended on domestic or foreign materials. These variables can affect the average price paid by an individual library, although the individual library's rate of increase may not differ greatly from the national indexes.

LMPI is interested in pursuing studies that would correlate a particular library's costs with the national prices. The group welcomes interested parties to its meetings at ALA Annual and Midwinter conferences.

The Library Materials Price Index Editorial Board consists of compilers George Aulisio, Catherine Barr, Ajaye Bloomstone, Stephen Bosch, Kittie Henderson, Frederick C. Lynden, and editor Narda Tafuri.

Book Title Output and Average Prices: 2010–2014

Catherine Barr
Contributing Editor

Constance Harbison
Baker & Taylor

Overall American book title output has generally showed growing strength since the economic downturn, but this recovery has been uneven. After reaching a high of 210,772 in 2012 (up from 2009's 178,841), the revised figures for 2013 show a dip to 198,488. Preliminary figures for 2014, however, indicate a rebound. (Preliminary figures are likely to be revised upward as late-arriving materials are added to the database.) The number of titles published dropped by 5.5 percent in 2008 and 0.66 percent in 2009, but rose by 4.2 percent in 2010, 2.25 percent in 2011, and 10.62 percent in 2012 before declining 5.83 percent in 2013.

The figures for this edition of the *Library and Book Trade Almanac* were provided by book wholesaler Baker & Taylor and are based on the Book Industry Study Group's BISAC categories. The BISAC juvenile category (fiction and nonfiction) has been divided into children's and young adult. Figures for 2012 and 2013 have been restated, reflecting late updates to the Baker & Taylor database. Figures for 2014 are preliminary.

For more information on the BISAC categories, visit http://www.bisg.org.

Output by Format and by Category

Revised results for 2013 were mixed. Output of hardcover titles continued a slow rise with an increase of 3.46 percent, hardcovers less than $81 were up 4.90 percent after a drop of 1.78 percent, mass market paperbacks fell 9.82 percent on the heels of a decline of 3.06 percent in 2012, and trade paperbacks were down 9.60 percent. The rapid increase in audiobook output stalled in 2013 (after soaring more than 43 percent in 2012), and e-books, which had scored an impressive gain of 93.28 percent in 2012, found their momentum slowing, with a decline of 13.70 percent in 2013.

Output of fiction, a key category, grew 13.07 percent in 2013 after a drop of 8.64 percent in 2012; preliminary results for 2014 suggested another dip. Output of hardcover fiction priced at less than $81 rebounded a little more than 17 percent in 2013, but prospects for 2014 did not seem so rosy. In the paperback sector, mass market fiction dropped 9.50 percent in 2013, while trade fiction rose 19.60 percent; prospects for 2014 appeared healthy. Audiobook fiction held steady in 2013, up a modest 0.23 percent. E-book fiction output, after climbing steadily for several years, has begun to fluctuate; the 2013 total is down 12.89 percent, but preliminary results for 2014 suggest a return to the level of 2012.

The important juveniles category is broken down into children's (PreK–6) and young adult (YA; grades 7–12) titles. Overall children's books output has been rising slowly but steadily, with a revised increase of 1.84 percent in 2013 and a prediction of a much larger jump in 2014. Hardcover books priced at less than

$81 rose 1.94 percent in 2013, while mass market lost 9.58 percent and trade paperbacks rose 2.20 percent in the same period. Children's audiobooks and e-books showed inconsistent growth, with audiobooks up 33.52 percent in 2013; e-books fell 15.39 percent in 2013, following a jump of 61.04 percent in 2012.

Output of YA titles rose a revised 8.81 percent in 2012, but registered a decline of 25.60 percent in 2013; preliminary data for 2014, however, showed a rebound of 16.29 percent. Hardcover titles priced at less than $81 continue to lose ground, falling 9.88 percent in 2013; mass market paperbacks held steady; and trade paperbacks fell 34.57 percent. YA audiobook production sagged 13 percent in 2012) but e-books posted an 8.73 percent hike.

A review of overall output in nonfiction categories (Table 1) shows the usual variations. Of the 51 categories, 32 lost ground in 2013. Categories with significant output that registered interesting results in 2013 were biography and autobiography (up 15.33 percent), business and economics (down 12.7 percent), computers (down 14.71 percent), medical (down 27.72 percent), science (down 29.0 percent), and travel (down 17.87 percent). Preliminary figures for 2014 indicated that many of these trends would be reversed.

Average Book Prices

Book prices declined in 2013 with only e-books showing gains. List prices for hardcovers overall (Table 2) fell 2.57 percent; hardcovers under $81 (Table 3) fell 2 cents (0.06 percent) but showed some recovery in preliminary data for 2014. Mass market paperback (Table 4) prices dipped 0.35 percent and trade paperbacks (Table 5) declined 12.31 percent. Audiobook prices (Table 6) have been falling since 2009, losing a further 4.76 percent in 2013. After declining for several years, e-book prices registered an increase of 22.03 percent.

Average book prices for fiction were generally down in 2013. Hardcover fiction titles priced at less than $81 edged up 38 cents (1.32 percent). Mass market fiction prices dipped 0.64 percent although there were signs of recovery in 2014; trade paperback fiction was down 0.42 percent. Audiobook fiction prices were down 8.39 percent, and e-book pricing plunged 32.33 percent, wiping out much of the gains made in 2012.

Average prices for hardcovers under $81 in the important children's category have been fairly stable over the last few years, climbing 1.55 percent in 2013. Children's mass market paperback prices also have moved in a tight range, posting a gain of 3.26 percent in 2013; the more important sector of trade paperbacks saw prices drop 10.97 percent. Children's audiobook prices rose an unexpected 27.69 percent and e-book prices were up 8.53 percent with promise of a further hike in 2014.

Prices for young adult materials fell 8.90 percent in the hardcovers under $81 sector in 2013 but looked set to recover in 2014. Mass market prices were up 3.04 percent, while trade paperbacks were down 2.08 percent, again with higher prices on the horizon in 2014. YA audiobook prices recovered 22.14 percent, reversing a sharp decline in 2012; e-book prices have been retreating since 2011 (down a further 20.51 percent in 2013) but looked stronger in preliminary data for 2014.

Prices fell in 32 of the categories in the hardcover sector in 2012 (Table 2) and early figures for 2013 showed declines in 29 categories.

Table 1 / American Book Production, 2010–2014

BISAC Category	2010	2011	2012	2013	2014
Antiques and collectibles	366	294	289	278	285
Architecture	1,495	1,468	1,402	1,661	1,462
Art	3,213	3,325	3,554	3,751	3,489
Bibles	614	976	840	1,005	897
Biography and autobiography	4,105	4,496	4,365	5,034	4,611
Body, mind, and spirit	1,189	1,324	1,207	1,264	1,021
Business and economics	10,024	9,813	13,811	12,057	10,947
Children	20,562	21,300	22,461	22,874	24,185
Comics and graphic novels	2,542	4,212	2,941	2,473	2,748
Computers	4,312	4,391	5,379	4,588	4,406
Cooking	2,131	2,142	2,435	2,409	2,448
Crafts and hobbies	1,271	1,301	1,291	1,398	1,372
Design	878	856	894	727	702
Drama	875	606	578	687	648
Education	4,955	4,923	5,996	6,108	6,232
Family and relationships	1,064	981	977	1,032	965
Fiction	17,971	21,211	19,379	21,911	20,759
Foreign language study	1,464	1,463	1,483	1,360	1,561
Games	955	792	787	733	632
Gardening	359	368	370	309	252
Health and fitness	1,601	1,654	1,544	1,512	1,492
History	11,975	11,634	12,007	11,616	12,563
House and home	290	230	236	254	1,038
Humor	651	626	640	601	615
Language arts and disciplines	3,985	3,530	3,549	3,239	3,513
Law	4,925	4,979	5,476	5,268	5,566
Literary collections	998	870	752	756	908
Literary criticism	3,580	3,673	3,628	3,582	4,145
Mathematics	2,549	2,781	4,100	2,604	2,584
Medical	8,574	9,021	12,572	9,087	8,766
Music	3,541	3,313	3,222	3,194	2,432
Nature	944	948	1,045	1,040	1,013
Performing arts	1,569	1,449	1,502	1,459	1,557
Pets	388	330	310	262	246
Philosophy	2,447	2,465	2,836	2,854	2,966
Photography	1,345	1,359	1,379	1,249	1,249
Poetry	2,015	2,321	2,248	2,822	2,610
Political science	6,703	5,925	6,239	6,187	6,543
Psychology	2,882	2,817	3,327	3,314	3,486
Reference	1,601	1,687	1,537	1,241	1,272
Religion	9,550	9,117	9,927	10,821	9,940
Science	7,782	8,266	12,575	8,928	8,902
Self-help	1,379	1,336	1,707	1,678	1,422
Social science	7,353	7,056	8,708	7,932	7,853
Sports and recreation	1,968	1,836	1,777	1,803	1,781
Study aids	1,519	999	626	549	1,700
Technology and engineering	4,907	5,060	7,971	5,827	7,046
Transportation	800	769	631	744	687
Travel	2,953	2,778	2,367	1,944	1,887
True crime	316	299	277	282	269
Young adult	4,909	5,163	5,618	4,180	5,095
Totals	186,344	190,533	210,772	198,488	200,768

Table 2 / Hardcover Average Per-Volume Prices, 2011–2014

BISAC Category	2011			2012			2013			2014		
	Vols.	$ Total	Prices	Vols.	$ Total	Prices	Vols.	$ Total	Prices	Vols.	$ Total	Prices
Antiques and collectibles	150	$7,960.50	$53.07	124	$8,625.88	$69.56	137	$9,645.86	$70.41	140	$8,782.95	$62.74
Architecture	743	57,353.10	77.19	762	61,463.81	80.66	879	78,162.37	88.92	789	70,254.92	89.04
Art	1,686	119,808.64	71.06	1,821	132,964.53	73.02	2,042	145,666.13	71.34	1,852	142,045.75	76.70
Bibles	221	10,228.39	46.28	199	7,454.48	37.46	197	7,373.67	37.43	129	4,407.64	34.17
Biography and autobiography	1,711	83,835.30	49.00	1,713	84,650.53	49.42	1,939	85,549.24	44.12	1,745	81,785.35	46.87
Body, mind, and spirit	155	4,678.47	30.18	132	4,926.32	37.32	237	7,582.01	31.99	164	7,238.56	44.14
Business and economics	4,105	560,439.24	136.53	4,126	576,674.56	139.77	4,386	658,692.42	150.18	4,258	596,832.97	140.17
Children	11,704	313,717.81	26.80	11,920	273,799.03	22.97	12,179	289,575.11	23.78	12,619	299,533.10	23.74
Comics and graphic novels	801	27,745.57	34.64	735	27,823.54	37.86	639	23,984.39	37.53	646	25,450.18	39.40
Computers	884	122,038.70	138.05	981	163,883.97	167.06	880	122,678.32	139.41	904	143,145.84	158.35
Cooking	972	29,952.24	30.82	1,135	32,966.80	29.05	1,215	35,887.62	29.54	1,202	34,637.84	28.82
Crafts and hobbies	218	6,636.46	30.44	210	6,536.84	31.13	195	5,674.81	29.10	201	5,722.50	28.47
Design	441	30,266.36	68.63	504	32,696.54	64.87	399	25,125.39	62.97	394	26,688.97	67.74
Drama	138	5,625.83	40.77	72	5,542.87	76.98	76	5,664.42	74.53	79	6,106.12	77.29
Education	1,569	204,182.22	130.14	1,616	214,220.22	132.56	1,747	207,398.98	118.72	1,884	221,948.34	117.81
Family and relationships	229	7,722.37	33.72	213	9,173.95	43.07	265	9,679.73	36.53	214	9,369.47	43.78
Fiction	4,491	132,527.00	29.51	4,421	133,663.96	30.23	5,155	156,133.62	30.29	4,590	137,422.62	29.94
Foreign language study	158	21,500.20	136.08	221	25,450.95	115.16	270	31,138.49	115.33	213	21,411.00	100.52
Games	112	3,891.77	34.75	122	4,392.79	36.01	111	4,445.18	40.05	92	3,606.40	39.20
Gardening	118	4,720.14	40.00	134	5,352.22	39.94	115	4,302.83	37.42	97	3,037.98	31.32
Health and fitness	321	19,262.41	60.01	321	23,555.04	73.38	378	24,446.29	64.67	348	20,145.53	57.89
History	4,543	376,140.58	82.80	4,950	427,995.44	86.46	5,030	435,654.69	86.61	5,327	495,402.68	93.00
House and home	90	3,447.30	38.30	88	3,935.94	44.73	108	3,869.64	35.83	92	3,212.99	34.92

Humor	199	3,847.01	19.33	245	4,842.66	19.77	246	4,904.26	19.94	279	6,728.03	24.11
Language arts and disciplines	1,587	183,632.32	115.71	1,147	151,273.33	131.89	1,253	176,961.29	141.23	1,244	177,732.83	142.87
Law	1,756	314,608.71	179.16	1,900	339,733.91	178.81	1,966	351,320.68	178.70	1,966	346,169.00	176.08
Literary collections	357	31,536.51	88.34	258	25,004.52	96.92	282	25,425.94	90.16	256	22,776.27	88.97
Literary criticism	1,964	237,447.45	120.90	2,027	250,008.05	123.34	1,990	241,276.93	121.24	2,124	257,249.87	121.12
Mathematics	1,030	139,631.75	135.56	963	145,702.22	151.30	910	121,150.65	133.13	917	116,412.45	126.95
Medical	2,976	492,181.51	165.38	3,546	639,621.95	180.38	3,443	637,534.42	185.17	3,439	680,299.70	197.82
Music	488	44,531.57	91.25	524	47,428.36	90.51	534	47,725.59	89.37	507	45,192.28	89.14
Nature	400	29,422.57	73.56	371	33,365.99	89.94	470	39,604.58	84.27	421	37,089.29	88.10
Performing arts	534	44,052.03	82.49	574	51,791.11	90.23	583	55,173.00	94.64	673	62,226.83	92.46
Pets	122	2,580.92	21.16	93	2,230.43	23.98	107	2,743.61	25.64	105	2,599.71	24.76
Philosophy	1,004	97,070.12	96.68	1,169	123,149.48	105.35	1,291	136,417.24	105.67	1,320	138,078.97	104.61
Photography	822	49,691.09	60.45	865	74,284.98	85.88	801	74,673.01	93.22	827	54,875.62	66.36
Poetry	318	11,181.99	35.16	287	11,933.43	41.58	420	14,247.45	33.92	358	12,033.89	33.61
Political science	2,578	284,265.43	110.27	2,654	299,398.54	112.81	2,608	295,365.76	113.25	2,972	332,312.40	111.81
Psychology	1,082	129,576.30	119.76	1,100	154,343.99	140.31	1,171	154,471.48	131.91	1,204	174,962.69	145.32
Reference	599	210,538.27	351.48	499	197,881.61	396.56	409	145,633.70	356.07	394	125,767.10	319.21
Religion	2,370	174,269.39	73.53	2,730	223,678.07	81.93	2,804	216,178.58	77.10	2,490	199,973.24	80.31
Science	3,459	674,361.10	194.96	3,331	652,311.72	195.83	3,325	648,160.05	194.94	3,480	674,882.22	193.93
Self-help	219	5,239.28	23.92	265	6,556.76	24.74	377	10,612.57	28.15	284	7,227.49	25.45
Social science	3,069	324,271.08	105.66	3,139	363,460.96	115.79	3,335	385,918.04	115.72	3,334	449,033.31	134.68
Sports and recreation	645	28,825.82	44.69	658	33,995.43	51.66	690	32,626.76	47.29	605	37,050.66	61.24
Study aids	20	1,925.29	96.26	14	1,548.35	110.60	14	1,626.34	116.17	19	1,762.30	92.75
Technology and engineering	2,633	441,397.42	167.64	2,653	465,522.95	175.47	2,540	438,736.77	172.73	2,609	479,745.15	183.88
Transportation	326	20,185.88	61.92	225	15,040.36	66.85	316	22,676.69	71.76	240	20,483.44	85.35
Travel	340	14,400.62	42.35	205	10,193.81	49.73	205	8,466.10	41.30	177	6,871.49	38.82
True crime	73	2,298.15	31.48	70	2,265.72	32.37	87	2,453.13	28.20	78	2,239.15	28.71
Young adult	2,602	97,498.64	37.47	2,256	83,170.95	36.87	1,965	60,866.15	30.98	2,159	72,601.94	33.63
Totals	69,132	$6,244,148.82	$90.32	70,288	$6,677,489.86	$95.00	72,721	$6,731,281.98	$92.56	72,460	$6,912,567.02	$95.40

Table 3 / Hardcover Average Per-Volume Prices, Less Than $81, 2011–2014

BISAC Category	2011 Vols.	2011 $ Total	2011 Prices	2012 Vols.	2012 $ Total	2012 Prices	2013 Vols.	2013 $ Total	2013 Prices	2014 $ Total	2014 Vols.	2014 Prices
Antiques and collectibles	124	$4,832.07	$38.97	95	$3,639.00	$38.31	111	$4,385.44	$39.51	$4,474.52	111	$40.31
Architecture	531	26,758.87	50.39	516	26,135.33	50.65	553	29,614.62	53.55	25,443.43	484	52.57
Art	1,339	62,333.12	46.55	1,413	66,651.03	47.17	1,539	73,169.81	47.54	65,302.97	1,364	47.88
Bibles	207	7,484.93	36.16	191	6,581.52	34.46	194	7,043.73	36.31	4,307.65	128	33.65
Biography and autobiography	1,529	47,544.96	31.10	1,536	47,993.56	31.25	1,800	56,905.75	31.61	49,483.71	1,598	30.97
Body, mind, and spirit	146	3,789.58	25.96	124	3,175.32	25.61	227	6,249.01	27.53	3,456.21	153	22.59
Business and economics	1,618	66,319.32	40.99	1,587	68,982.27	43.47	1,637	71,973.43	43.97	71,623.30	1,578	45.39
Children	11,226	217,931.06	19.41	11,652	223,824.32	19.21	11,878	231,707.87	19.51	246,378.78	12,310	20.01
Comics and graphic novels	766	23,644.60	30.87	698	22,543.70	32.30	598	19,354.66	32.37	18,555.39	597	31.08
Computers	228	13,644.29	59.84	180	11,008.45	61.16	203	12,376.54	60.97	13,483.61	216	62.42
Cooking	949	25,459.16	26.83	1,116	30,160.17	27.03	1,189	31,554.44	26.54	32,301.12	1,189	27.17
Crafts and hobbies	211	5,976.56	28.32	209	5,536.84	26.49	188	4,874.41	25.93	5,130.23	196	26.17
Design	352	17,121.41	48.64	411	19,224.47	46.77	325	15,414.14	47.43	15,230.67	312	48.82
Drama	112	2,624.48	23.43	41	1,710.41	41.72	43	2,040.50	47.45	1,790.62	40	44.77
Education	497	26,169.88	52.66	477	26,369.70	55.28	555	28,609.06	51.55	32,794.35	662	49.54
Family and relationships	208	4,844.78	23.29	183	4,152.36	22.69	241	6,018.43	24.97	4,154.14	173	24.01
Fiction	4,462	125,949.05	28.23	4,372	125,821.29	28.78	5,117	149,228.84	29.16	131,604.77	4,557	28.88
Foreign language study	47	2,280.52	48.52	101	5,930.85	58.72	123	6,929.41	56.34	5,608.38	97	57.82
Games	106	3,103.78	29.28	119	3,752.79	31.54	103	3,312.25	32.16	2,796.42	86	32.52
Gardening	114	4,245.14	37.24	127	4,232.27	33.32	109	3,299.33	30.27	2,762.98	95	29.08
Health and fitness	262	7,824.20	29.86	230	7,166.08	31.16	272	7,484.95	27.52	7,875.47	274	28.74
History	2,749	119,506.01	43.47	2,865	125,275.28	43.73	2,869	124,866.01	43.52	126,141.55	2,864	44.04
House and home	86	2,809.40	32.67	83	3,384.21	40.77	107	3,774.64	35.28	2,947.99	90	32.76

Humor	198	3,722.01	18.80	243	4,652.71	19.15	246	4,904.26	19.94	277	6,478.04	23.39
Language arts and disciplines	600	35,250.83	58.75	300	17,141.02	57.14	303	17,567.25	57.98	250	15,084.76	60.34
Law	263	14,269.14	54.26	319	18,678.81	58.55	337	19,522.76	57.93	293	17,037.83	58.15
Literary collections	210	9,172.96	43.68	141	5,669.72	40.21	144	5,810.13	40.35	159	6,113.87	38.45
Literary criticism	779	44,425.92	57.03	787	46,707.71	59.35	770	44,932.52	58.35	774	46,650.80	60.27
Mathematics	188	11,725.87	62.37	186	11,201.81	60.22	189	11,211.19	59.32	225	14,062.73	62.50
Medical	397	22,552.35	56.81	392	21,524.94	54.91	343	18,455.52	53.81	284	16,110.89	56.73
Music	309	13,585.82	43.97	313	14,173.73	45.28	298	13,525.14	45.39	302	13,777.13	45.62
Nature	270	9,520.87	35.26	230	8,416.78	36.59	283	9,708.98	34.31	244	8,834.92	36.21
Performing arts	274	13,364.73	48.78	319	15,524.46	48.67	284	14,339.70	50.49	308	15,651.33	50.82
Pets	122	2,580.92	21.16	93	2,230.43	23.98	107	2,743.61	25.64	104	2,499.71	24.04
Philosophy	481	25,282.98	52.56	476	26,754.50	56.21	513	28,262.86	55.09	491	27,568.11	56.15
Photography	719	34,351.66	47.78	756	36,270.44	47.98	696	33,340.41	47.90	721	34,470.94	47.81
Poetry	301	8,760.54	29.10	259	7,488.59	28.91	406	11,495.00	28.31	336	9,186.49	27.34
Political science	910	43,026.72	47.28	913	42,160.00	46.18	888	43,344.45	48.81	952	48,512.33	50.96
Psychology	446	22,949.08	51.46	366	18,870.64	51.56	334	16,287.17	48.76	344	16,905.22	49.14
Reference	202	6,492.48	32.14	181	6,063.91	33.50	168	5,194.40	30.92	150	4,666.00	31.11
Religion	1,593	54,819.43	34.41	1,713	56,736.05	33.12	1,848	62,519.67	33.83	1,549	56,580.27	36.53
Science	579	27,707.21	47.85	496	22,933.51	46.24	553	25,342.81	45.83	538	26,061.93	48.44
Self-help	217	5,024.33	23.15	262	6,259.77	23.89	368	9,402.57	25.55	280	6,672.49	23.83
Social science	1,320	69,515.12	52.66	1,100	60,821.33	55.29	1,197	65,490.50	54.71	1,048	58,497.51	55.82
Sports and recreation	572	17,643.62	30.85	572	17,875.67	31.25	606	19,233.32	31.74	503	15,956.77	31.72
Study aids	15	649.59	43.31	9	478.70	53.19	9	406.64	45.18	14	648.60	46.33
Technology and engineering	280	15,773.29	56.33	202	11,123.96	55.07	236	13,604.34	57.65	227	12,997.85	57.26
Transportation	270	9,767.73	36.18	180	6,882.24	38.23	244	9,828.02	40.28	164	6,880.30	41.95
Travel	325	9,925.47	30.54	181	5,460.97	30.17	186	5,834.20	31.37	164	5,121.05	31.23
True crime	71	2,068.15	29.13	68	1,949.77	28.67	87	2,453.13	28.20	78	2,239.15	28.71
Young adult	2,472	70,155.32	28.38	2,115	57,481.72	27.18	1,906	47,192.20	24.76	2,062	53,892.85	26.14
Totals	42,252	$1,426,281.31	$33.76	41,498	$1,394,785.11	$33.61	43,530	$1,462,140.02	$33.59	42,015	$1,422,808.13	$33.86

Table 4 / Mass Market Paperbacks Average Per-Volume Prices, 2011–2014

BISAC Category	2011 Vols.	2011 $ Total	2011 Prices	2012 Vols.	2012 $ Total	2012 Prices	2013 Vols.	2013 $ Total	2013 Prices	2014 Vols.	2014 $ Total	2014 Prices
Antiques and collectibles	5	$43.95	$8.79	5	$44.95	$8.99	5	$44.95	$8.99	4	$35.96	$8.99
Architecture	n.a.	n.a.	n.a.	n.a.	n.a.	n.a.	n.a.	n.a.	n.a.	n.a.	n.a.	n.a.
Art	n.a.	n.a.	n.a.	n.a.	n.a.	n.a.	n.a.	n.a.	n.a.	n.a.	n.a.	n.a.
Bibles	n.a.	n.a.	n.a.	n.a.	n.a.	n.a.	n.a.	n.a.	n.a.	n.a.	n.a.	n.a.
Biography and autobiography	8	68.92	8.62	4	26.92	6.73	3	28.98	9.66	6	53.90	8.98
Body, mind and spirit	17	134.83	7.93	14	113.86	8.13	14	113.86	8.13	2	19.98	9.99
Business and economics	2	15.98	7.99	1	7.99	7.99	n.a.	n.a.	n.a.	n.a.	n.a.	n.a.
Children	253	1,658.44	6.56	240	1,557.60	6.49	217	1,454.30	6.70	197	1,253.01	6.36
Comics and graphic novels	n.a.	n.a.	n.a.	n.a.	n.a.	n.a.	n.a.	n.a.	n.a.	n.a.	n.a.	n.a.
Computers	n.a.	n.a.	n.a.	n.a.	n.a.	n.a.	n.a.	n.a.	n.a.	n.a.	n.a.	n.a.
Cooking	1	7.99	7.99	n.a.	n.a.	n.a.	n.a.	n.a.	n.a.	n.a.	n.a.	n.a.
Crafts and hobbies	n.a.	n.a.	n.a.	n.a.	n.a.	n.a.	n.a.	n.a.	n.a.	n.a.	n.a.	n.a.
Design	n.a.	n.a.	n.a.	n.a.	n.a.	n.a.	n.a.	n.a.	n.a.	n.a.	n.a.	n.a.
Drama	1	8.95	8.95	2	9.90	4.95	n.a.	n.a.	n.a.	n.a.	n.a.	n.a.
Education	n.a.	n.a.	n.a.	n.a.	n.a.	n.a.	n.a.	n.a.	n.a.	n.a.	n.a.	n.a.
Family and relationships	1	8.99	8.99	n.a.	n.a.	n.a.	n.a.	n.a.	n.a.	n.a.	n.a.	n.a.
Fiction	3,997	27,865.23	6.97	3,894	27,441.26	7.05	3,524	24,674.87	7.00	3,534	25,065.23	7.09
Foreign language study	n.a.	n.a.	n.a.	n.a.	n.a.	n.a.	n.a.	n.a.	n.a.	1	6.99	6.99
Games	n.a.	n.a.	n.a.	n.a.	n.a.	n.a.	1	9.99	9.99	4	39.47	9.87
Gardening	n.a.	n.a.	n.a.	n.a.	n.a.	n.a.	n.a.	n.a.	n.a.	n.a.	n.a.	n.a.
Health and fitness	11	89.89	8.17	16	131.85	8.24	8	65.92	8.24	3	27.98	9.33
History	7	59.89	8.56	3	25.97	8.66	3	29.98	9.99	2	19.98	9.99
House and home	n.a.	n.a.	n.a.	n.a.	n.a.	n.a.	n.a.	n.a.	n.a.	n.a.	n.a.	n.a.

Humor	1	3.50	3.50	n.a.	n.a.	n.a.	2	15.99	8.00	n.a.	n.a.	n.a.
Language arts and disciplines	n.a.	n.a.	n.a.	n.a.	n.a.	n.a.	n.a.	n.a.	n.a.	1	7.99	7.99
Law	1	7.95	7.95	2	11.90	5.95	n.a.	n.a.	n.a.	1	4.95	4.95
Literary collections	1	9.99	9.99	n.a.	n.a.	n.a.	n.a.	n.a.	n.a.	n.a.	n.a.	n.a.
Literary criticism	n.a.	n.a.	n.a.	1	8.99	8.99	n.a.	n.a.	n.a.	n.a.	n.a.	n.a.
Mathematics	n.a.	n.a.	n.a.	n.a.	n.a.	n.a.	n.a.	n.a.	n.a.	n.a.	n.a.	n.a.
Medical	1	7.95	7.95	1	8.99	8.99	n.a.	n.a.	n.a.	1	7.99	7.99
Music	n.a.	n.a.	n.a.	1	7.99	7.99	n.a.	n.a.	n.a.	n.a.	n.a.	n.a.
Nature	n.a.	n.a.	n.a.	1	9.99	9.99	n.a.	n.a.	n.a.	n.a.	n.a.	n.a.
Performing arts	2	17.98	8.99	1	9.99	9.99	1	10.99	10.99	1	10.99	10.99
Pets	1	7.99	7.99	n.a.	n.a.	n.a.	1	7.99	7.99	n.a.	n.a.	n.a.
Philosophy	n.a.	n.a.	n.a.	n.a.	n.a.	n.a.	n.a.	n.a.	n.a.	n.a.	n.a.	n.a.
Photography	n.a.	n.a.	n.a.	n.a.	n.a.	n.a.	n.a.	n.a.	n.a.	n.a.	n.a.	n.a.
Poetry	1	7.95	7.95	2	14.90	7.45	3	19.85	6.62	1	9.99	9.99
Political science	1	5.95	5.95	n.a.	n.a.	n.a.	n.a.	n.a.	n.a.	n.a.	n.a.	n.a.
Psychology	1	7.99	7.99	n.a.	n.a.	n.a.	n.a.	n.a.	n.a.	n.a.	n.a.	n.a.
Reference	2	15.98	7.99	3	24.93	8.31	3	19.48	6.49	5	64.46	12.89
Religion	3	23.97	7.99	2	14.98	7.49	n.a.	n.a.	n.a.	n.a.	n.a.	n.a.
Science	n.a.	n.a.	n.a.	n.a.	n.a.	n.a.	n.a.	n.a.	n.a.	n.a.	n.a.	n.a.
Self-help	1	7.99	7.99	1	7.99	7.99	n.a.	n.a.	n.a.	n.a.	n.a.	n.a.
Social science	n.a.	n.a.	n.a.	1	9.99	9.99	n.a.	n.a.	n.a.	n.a.	n.a.	n.a.
Sports and recreation	1	7.99	7.99	1	7.99	7.99	n.a.	n.a.	n.a.	n.a.	n.a.	n.a.
Study aids	n.a.	n.a.	n.a.	n.a.	n.a.	n.a.	n.a.	n.a.	n.a.	n.a.	n.a.	n.a.
Technology and engineering	n.a.	n.a.	n.a.	n.a.	n.a.	n.a.	n.a.	n.a.	n.a.	n.a.	n.a.	n.a.
Transportation	n.a.	n.a.	n.a.	n.a.	n.a.	n.a.	n.a.	n.a.	n.a.	n.a.	n.a.	n.a.
Travel	n.a.	n.a.	n.a.	n.a.	n.a.	n.a.	n.a.	n.a.	n.a.	n.a.	n.a.	n.a.
True crime	44	344.56	7.83	38	315.62	8.31	26	220.74	8.49	22	199.30	9.06
Young adult	47	398.53	8.48	44	393.54	8.94	44	405.49	9.22	21	184.80	8.80
Totals	4,411	$30,839.33	$6.99	4,276	$30,189.11	$7.06	3,855	$27,123.38	$7.04	3,806	$27,012.97	$7.10

n.a. = not available

Table 5 / Trade Paperbacks Average Per-Volume Prices, 2011–2014

BISAC Category	2011			2012			2013			2014		
	Vols.	$ Total	Prices	Vols.	$ Total	Prices	Vols.	$ Total	Prices	Vols.	$ Total	Prices
Antiques and collectibles	158	$4,084.94	$25.85	160	$5,013.82	$31.34	134	$4,566.36	$34.08	141	$5,437.11	$38.56
Architecture	739	31,559.04	42.71	639	27,300.28	42.72	780	34,116.40	43.74	669	30,562.60	45.68
Art	1,706	64,211.49	37.64	1,718	65,165.45	37.93	1,697	70,760.81	41.70	1,630	62,057.82	38.07
Bibles	755	31,013.64	41.08	641	28,627.08	44.66	808	33,723.64	41.74	768	34,382.32	44.77
Biography and autobiography	4,946	93,609.40	18.93	2,648	53,221.08	20.10	3,092	61,211.50	19.80	2,861	58,199.89	20.34
Body, mind, and spirit	1,717	30,695.43	17.88	1,061	19,473.64	18.35	1,013	18,548.80	18.31	855	15,365.34	17.97
Business and economics	5,789	393,764.09	68.02	9,050	780,896.45	86.29	7,243	640,206.62	88.39	6,351	550,600.13	86.70
Children	9,474	104,689.10	11.05	10,137	140,160.48	13.83	10,360	127,532.60	12.31	11,315	144,572.90	12.78
Comics and graphic novels	3,415	55,465.86	16.24	2,206	36,152.82	16.39	1,834	30,688.26	16.73	2,102	36,987.72	17.60
Computers	3,495	249,579.85	71.41	4,289	402,287.48	93.80	3,636	312,263.01	85.88	3,382	273,600.63	80.90
Cooking	1,242	24,597.47	19.80	1,297	26,565.72	20.48	1,190	23,876.96	20.06	1,244	24,352.04	19.58
Crafts and hobbies	1,091	21,175.04	19.41	1,079	21,060.03	19.52	1,201	22,092.46	18.40	1,160	21,590.51	18.61
Design	414	17,684.75	42.72	386	16,011.01	41.48	327	12,635.01	38.64	306	12,914.63	42.20
Drama	559	10,506.88	18.80	504	9,877.77	19.60	611	12,276.55	20.09	566	11,426.25	20.19
Education	3,565	146,902.07	41.21	4,189	192,424.29	45.94	4,195	205,089.19	48.89	4,168	222,980.40	53.50
Family and relationships	1,288	23,020.33	17.87	763	14,635.11	19.18	767	14,891.95	19.42	749	15,685.17	20.94
Fiction	18,402	335,323.99	18.22	11,063	188,817.39	17.07	13,231	224,869.74	17.00	12,633	216,967.21	17.17
Foreign language study	1,247	45,261.94	36.30	1,224	52,211.37	42.66	1,006	52,823.03	52.51	1,322	51,130.84	38.68
Games	705	11,712.67	16.61	665	10,473.76	15.75	619	9,683.93	15.64	536	9,487.28	17.70
Gardening	249	5,810.32	23.33	236	5,568.52	23.60	194	4,429.50	22.83	155	3,444.57	22.22
Health and fitness	1,477	39,849.21	26.98	1,181	32,951.74	27.90	1,095	28,800.53	26.30	1,094	28,834.76	26.36
History	7,456	271,738.66	36.45	6,978	296,049.18	42.43	6,513	246,690.58	37.88	7,188	264,597.87	36.81
House and home	153	3,125.76	20.43	148	3,476.67	23.49	145	2,911.52	20.08	946	90,683.41	95.86

Humor	581	8,694.93	14.97	395	5,600.19	14.18	353	5,080.69	14.39	336	5,029.46	14.97
Language arts and disciplines	1,835	132,469.86	72.19	2,282	176,575.76	77.38	1,875	138,631.62	73.94	2,045	157,100.53	76.82
Law	3,220	226,786.54	70.43	3,492	267,877.35	76.71	3,154	240,111.09	76.13	3,498	271,662.82	77.66
Literary collections	541	15,881.19	29.36	492	17,272.72	35.11	474	16,297.53	34.38	651	13,719.38	21.07
Literary criticism	1,750	67,367.67	38.50	1,597	70,624.89	44.22	1,587	63,991.81	40.32	2,015	79,907.78	39.66
Mathematics	1,611	130,653.27	81.10	2,618	256,435.84	97.95	1,479	128,287.47	86.74	1,465	121,151.77	82.70
Medical	6,107	507,144.40	83.04	8,268	775,462.20	93.79	5,120	494,390.86	96.56	4,684	453,809.74	96.89
Music	2,837	69,596.60	24.53	2,683	69,462.84	25.89	2,653	64,490.23	24.31	1,914	54,806.15	28.63
Nature	586	21,015.68	35.86	651	24,378.54	37.45	564	17,812.75	31.58	579	17,532.13	30.28
Performing arts	938	30,390.41	32.40	922	35,636.18	38.65	867	30,763.02	35.48	879	30,783.88	35.02
Pets	235	4,395.04	18.70	217	3,947.06	18.19	154	2,905.68	18.87	141	2,582.13	18.31
Philosophy	1,587	67,304.33	42.41	1,481	72,676.07	49.07	1,522	67,585.08	44.41	1,612	71,007.59	44.05
Photography	541	17,387.11	32.14	514	17,254.98	33.57	445	15,322.60	34.43	420	14,866.52	35.40
Poetry	3,811	61,979.20	16.26	1,959	32,424.44	16.55	2,399	39,871.76	16.62	2,252	39,490.38	17.54
Political science	3,472	142,581.41	41.07	3,522	171,638.93	48.73	3,555	169,930.99	47.80	3,529	165,134.84	46.79
Psychology	1,685	90,713.21	53.84	2,039	143,593.12	70.42	1,944	130,675.88	67.22	2,204	125,855.42	57.10
Reference	1,217	108,322.32	89.01	1,022	109,796.48	107.43	823	83,020.83	100.88	871	83,788.46	96.20
Religion	8,639	177,831.51	20.58	7,158	164,496.45	22.98	7,968	177,182.12	22.24	7,386	173,681.86	23.52
Science	4,685	465,535.92	99.37	7,680	721,360.56	93.93	4,523	407,368.35	90.07	4,442	388,669.37	87.50
Self-help	2,043	35,371.73	17.31	1,440	24,946.68	17.32	1,291	22,879.76	17.72	1,135	21,053.49	18.55
Social science	4,013	176,295.60	43.93	5,442	296,247.46	54.44	4,502	225,414.83	50.07	4,447	226,940.90	51.03
Sports and recreation	1,310	32,479.61	24.79	1,118	26,237.08	23.47	1,111	26,533.25	23.88	1,174	28,258.19	24.07
Study aids	985	33,330.29	33.84	590	24,629.18	41.74	535	25,382.01	47.44	1,681	74,621.03	44.39
Technology and engineering	2,426	257,108.54	105.98	4,519	460,536.17	101.91	2,805	283,766.44	101.16	3,835	403,962.43	105.34
Transportation	458	16,835.71	36.76	405	13,963.19	34.48	427	16,844.59	39.45	447	16,191.31	36.22
Travel	2,513	49,806.57	19.82	2,160	43,811.42	20.28	1,736	35,825.83	20.64	1,709	35,159.38	20.57
True crime	227	4,313.89	19.00	169	3,175.80	18.79	169	3,352.46	19.84	169	3,223.14	19.07
Young adult	2,555	47,506.66	18.59	3,315	56,976.06	17.19	2,169	36,503.03	16.83	2,911	54,043.75	18.57
Totals	132,450	$5,014,481.13	$37.86	130,412	$6,515,458.76	$49.96	117,895	$5,164,911.51	$43.81	120,572	$5,319,895.23	$44.12

Table 6 / Audiobook Average Per-Volume Prices, 2011–2014

BISAC Category	2011 Vols.	2011 $ Total	2011 Prices	2012 Vols.	2012 $ Total	2012 Prices	2013 Vols.	2013 $ Total	2013 Prices	2014 Vols.	2014 $ Total	2014 Prices
Antiques and collectibles	n.a.	n.a.	n.a.	n.a.	n.a.	n.a.	n.a.	n.a.	n.a.	n.a.	n.a.	n.a.
Architecture	3	$119.90	$39.97	2	$64.90	$32.45	7	$299.77	$42.82	n.a.	n.a.	n.a.
Art	9	363.27	40.36	12	448.82	37.40	3	89.85	29.95	9	$353.91	$39.32
Bibles	10	444.86	44.49	23	1,148.54	49.94	20	1,629.54	81.48	11	779.70	70.88
Biography and autobiography	749	38,389.55	51.25	1,018	47,926.38	47.08	1,199	49,301.08	41.12	968	39,869.60	41.19
Body, mind, and spirit	103	3,874.54	37.62	126	4,535.13	35.99	244	6,571.37	26.93	177	4,952.28	27.98
Business and economics	401	18,126.12	45.20	475	18,167.31	38.25	452	15,599.57	34.51	610	18,197.46	29.83
Children	978	33,971.16	34.74	1,283	41,118.66	32.05	1,713	70,102.79	40.92	976	33,563.51	34.39
Comics and graphic novels	29	579.71	19.99	4	149.92	37.48	2	29.98	14.99	n.a.	n.a.	n.a.
Computers	12	647.86	53.99	4	170.92	42.73	2	104.94	52.47	18	742.73	41.26
Cooking	14	598.74	42.77	14	628.78	44.91	20	943.75	47.19	14	686.78	49.06
Crafts and hobbies	n.a.	n.a.	n.a.	1	24.95	24.95	3	74.85	24.95	5	123.88	24.78
Design	n.a.	n.a.	n.a.	3	171.90	57.30	1	29.95	29.95	n.a.	n.a.	n.a.
Drama	104	2,915.63	28.03	111	2,673.74	24.09	100	3,253.44	32.53	59	1,525.64	25.86
Education	34	1,497.28	44.04	37	1,292.12	34.92	33	1,295.19	39.25	32	1,178.72	36.84
Family and relationships	110	4,531.51	41.20	143	6,158.90	43.07	119	4,183.77	35.16	122	3,950.17	32.38
Fiction	7,174	345,701.76	48.19	11,408	477,403.65	41.85	11,434	438,350.32	38.34	11,227	432,988.02	38.57
Foreign language study	223	11,285.56	50.61	178	11,713.66	65.81	114	7,905.87	69.35	218	16,157.83	74.12
Games	5	234.91	46.98	5	224.88	44.98	n.a.	n.a.	n.a.	5	235.90	47.18
Gardening	n.a.	n.a.	n.a.	5	159.93	31.99	n.a.	n.a.	n.a.	n.a.	n.a.	n.a.
Health and fitness	110	5,170.40	47.00	99	4,265.01	43.08	131	5,621.79	42.91	111	4,568.96	41.16
History	446	26,475.56	59.36	610	30,713.03	50.35	480	22,808.11	47.52	476	24,694.41	51.88
House and home	1	34.95	34.95	3	165.97	55.32	4	119.92	29.98	1	9.99	9.99

Category												
Humor	103	4,167.81	40.46	77	2,544.95	33.05	70	2,646.17	37.80	98	3,227.52	32.93
Language arts and disciplines	38	1,705.23	44.87	26	1,437.29	55.28	14	571.08	40.79	11	419.85	38.17
Law	7	492.96	70.42	8	918.69	51.04	16	1,027.88	64.24	12	736.88	61.41
Literary collections	33	1,704.26	51.64	35	1,395.31	39.87	18	667.57	37.09	42	2,263.06	53.88
Literary criticism	188	5,750.62	30.59	95	3,170.80	33.38	11	534.78	48.62	7	94.94	13.56
Mathematics	1	24.95	24.95	3	153.97	51.32	5	194.87	38.97	5	102.96	20.59
Medical	24	1,097.85	45.74	24	1,182.32	49.26	24	983.42	40.98	12	452.88	37.74
Music	57	2,761.16	48.44	51	2,338.88	45.86	34	1,397.49	41.10	20	1,207.41	60.37
Nature	44	2,055.28	46.71	3	670.79	51.60	25	1,056.48	42.26	23	1,072.54	46.63
Performing arts	9	585.74	65.08	6	550.68	34.42	45	1,770.38	39.34	59	2,345.53	39.75
Pets	25	1,078.57	43.14	20	858.69	42.93	30	1,178.29	39.28	13	481.64	37.05
Philosophy	73	3,420.46	46.86	42	1,669.98	39.76	38	1,125.56	29.62	25	800.54	32.02
Photography	n.a.	n.a.	n.a.	n.a.	n.a.	n.a.	n.a.	n.a.	n.a.	n.a.	n.a.	n.a.
Poetry	16	368.54	23.03	16	436.52	27.28	19	501.50	26.39	38	1,484.47	39.07
Political science	220	10,608.99	48.22	236	10,999.82	46.61	166	7,480.77	45.06	130	5,823.64	44.80
Psychology	91	4,420.40	48.58	85	3,353.42	39.45	73	3,208.55	43.95	96	3,126.47	32.57
Reference	19	809.77	42.62	11	389.81	35.44	5	248.87	49.77	8	207.91	25.99
Religion	465	14,790.98	31.81	577	19,067.79	33.05	675	19,613.56	29.06	692	19,693.63	28.46
Science	90	4,887.33	54.30	117	4,949.55	42.30	95	3,909.06	41.15	98	4,094.52	41.78
Self-help	197	8,205.68	41.65	386	14,247.32	36.91	212	6,593.63	31.10	228	6,942.12	30.45
Social science	102	4,961.38	48.64	116	5,045.79	43.50	111	4,229.66	38.11	101	3,605.30	35.70
Sports and recreation	38	1,729.47	45.51	37	1,630.38	44.06	48	1,916.81	39.93	52	2,003.15	38.52
Study aids	2	55.32	27.66	5	738.13	147.63	1	24.99	24.99	5	654.98	131.00
Technology and engineering	26	1,206.57	46.41	11	440.78	40.07	8	292.84	36.61	9	468.83	52.09
Transportation	1	24.95	24.95	7	323.86	46.27	10	486.78	48.68	5	261.95	52.39
Travel	20	1,223.46	61.17	49	1,758.00	35.88	37	1,327.79	35.89	9	429.84	47.76
True crime	36	1,801.29	50.04	30	3,623.44	45.29	136	5,424.56	39.89	93	3,149.66	33.87
Young adult	960	40,041.92	41.71	1,451	50,472.17	34.55	1,271	53,638.33	42.20	1,251	53,703.96	42.93
Totals	13,400	$614,944.21	$45.89	19,178	$783,696.23	$40.86	19,278	$750,367.52	$38.92	18,181	$703,435.67	$38.69

n.a. = not available

Table 7 / E-Book Average Per-Volume Prices, 2011–2014

BISAC Category	2011 Vols.	2011 $ Total	2011 Prices	2012 Vols.	2012 $ Total	2012 Prices	2013 Vols.	2013 $ Total	2013 Prices	2014 Vols.	2014 $ Total	2014 Prices
Antiques and collectibles	229	$4,913.87	$21.46	168	$3,800.79	$22.62	177	$3,709.06	$20.96	121	$1,994.43	$16.48
Architecture	312	18,837.60	60.38	830	39,720.21	47.86	823	52,510.47	63.80	903	149,150.46	165.17
Art	729	12,309.78	16.89	1,339	28,673.78	21.41	1,812	32,775.88	18.09	1,847	28,701.95	15.54
Bibles	113	1,281.94	11.34	165	2,206.87	13.37	495	4,333.81	8.76	211	2,246.77	10.65
Biography and autobiography	3,824	39,105.73	10.23	8,544	154,373.76	18.07	8,156	123,126.02	15.10	9,050	167,188.61	18.47
Body, mind, and spirit	1,378	15,899.16	11.54	2,744	35,389.78	12.90	1,984	23,684.99	11.94	1,737	17,552.54	10.11
Business and economics	7,198	292,515.94	40.64	12,688	522,358.69	41.17	11,760	663,595.41	56.43	9,025	461,918.33	51.18
Children	14,867	244,048.77	16.42	23,942	254,440.89	10.63	20,257	233,647.32	11.53	20,124	289,043.25	14.36
Comics and graphic novels	269	1,619.40	6.02	628	4,192.87	6.68	551	4,026.22	7.31	1,726	10,658.38	6.18
Computers	4,383	270,498.10	61.72	4,881	344,797.66	70.64	4,170	226,748.54	54.38	3,133	165,893.03	52.95
Cooking	1,561	19,388.60	12.42	2,680	30,965.36	11.55	3,437	42,783.24	12.45	2,599	30,875.19	11.88
Crafts and hobbies	785	11,979.56	15.26	1,270	13,268.39	10.45	1,388	14,188.74	10.22	878	10,676.06	12.16
Design	104	4,023.47	38.69	221	5,584.31	25.27	193	5,018.09	26.00	120	3,296.81	27.47
Drama	2,758	8,809.25	3.19	2,256	16,231.91	7.19	1,629	12,878.07	7.91	1,746	16,419.05	9.40
Education	1,787	89,804.00	50.25	3,878	184,802.91	47.65	5,038	258,550.05	51.32	3,821	161,667.57	42.31
Family and relationships	1,210	12,252.48	10.13	2,208	30,502.48	13.81	1,927	54,580.56	28.32	1,930	29,365.15	15.22
Fiction	56,776	274,064.81	4.83	108,916	1,054,636.72	9.68	94,876	621,737.05	6.55	106,409	701,874.08	6.60
Foreign language study	304	5,986.97	19.69	903	20,823.78	23.06	1,589	25,544.34	16.08	1,576	25,595.77	16.24
Games	324	3,495.71	10.79	492	4,142.80	8.42	506	4,769.22	9.43	665	5,641.10	8.48
Gardening	169	2,254.01	13.34	408	5,880.82	14.41	360	4,956.98	13.77	301	3,591.25	11.93
Health and fitness	1,988	26,236.83	13.20	3,179	42,891.46	13.49	3,562	62,711.65	17.61	2,960	33,730.41	11.40
History	4,163	138,309.34	33.22	9,697	314,778.53	32.46	9,775	388,187.94	39.71	10,665	339,808.37	31.86
House and home	187	2,787.16	14.90	309	3,982.29	12.89	425	4,415.55	10.39	287	2,712.22	9.45

Humor	619	4,660.76	7.53	1,297	16,071.41	12.39	1,085	9,553.43	8.81	1,032	9,761.10	9.46
Language arts and disciplines	1,075	64,004.71	59.54	2,009	90,968.66	45.28	2,413	125,698.00	52.09	1,843	128,445.54	69.69
Law	872	66,422.78	76.17	2,132	155,611.00	72.99	1,745	164,290.91	94.15	1,268	114,059.54	89.95
Literary collections	1,757	7,757.14	4.41	1,823	18,146.74	9.95	1,468	20,401.17	13.90	1,451	16,427.73	11.32
Literary criticism	936	47,348.25	50.59	2,444	90,185.27	36.90	2,336	143,363.07	61.37	1,585	120,503.20	76.03
Mathematics	1,332	126,913.95	95.28	1,973	147,047.70	74.53	1,434	120,663.77	84.14	1,072	94,641.38	88.28
Medical	4,299	431,112.16	100.28	5,638	541,053.54	95.97	4,242	418,405.81	98.63	2,902	280,614.74	96.70
Music	4,390	62,006.71	14.12	18,723	90,863.68	4.85	1,942	58,965.00	30.36	1,196	36,512.72	30.53
Nature	527	16,917.81	32.10	934	36,334.47	38.90	1,017	33,638.81	33.08	729	23,395.74	32.09
Performing arts	863	23,042.10	26.70	1,231	35,374.70	28.74	1,599	63,467.86	39.69	1,239	39,569.07	31.94
Pets	581	6,492.44	11.17	716	10,566.72	14.76	750	6,307.08	8.41	376	3,745.39	9.96
Philosophy	948	41,871.46	44.17	2,304	86,422.67	37.51	2,676	150,551.22	56.26	1,956	105,085.10	53.72
Photography	387	7,038.13	18.19	471	8,895.05	18.89	535	11,782.68	22.02	513	9,862.29	19.22
Poetry	1,807	10,345.56	5.73	2,398	17,226.54	7.18	3,047	21,126.49	6.93	3,555	23,045.02	6.48
Political science	2,208	95,687.88	43.34	4,959	203,959.25	41.13	5,129	256,538.87	50.02	3,520	199,265.46	56.61
Psychology	2,139	104,824.79	49.01	3,023	135,309.18	44.76	4,119	576,196.82	139.89	2,988	275,975.31	92.36
Reference	788	15,578.45	19.77	1,392	34,439.38	24.74	1,543	127,825.45	82.84	3,959	99,356.95	25.10
Religion	5,669	98,002.50	17.29	9,644	171,278.22	17.76	9,800	201,788.49	20.59	10,444	172,965.23	16.56
Science	3,634	478,281.26	131.61	5,935	605,906.19	102.09	4,491	475,304.15	105.83	3,805	436,326.25	114.67
Self-help	2,497	20,217.11	8.10	4,978	67,191.81	13.50	4,299	126,240.06	29.36	4,704	42,763.30	9.09
Social science	2,240	120,078.07	53.61	4,446	241,646.49	54.35	6,941	552,934.85	79.66	4,154	297,118.15	71.53
Sports and recreation	1,223	20,906.04	17.09	2,607	46,467.69	17.82	2,727	53,090.88	19.47	1,790	31,331.22	17.50
Study aids	859	7,903.67	9.20	13,402	307,735.80	22.96	6,142	115,383.65	18.79	4,708	87,180.54	18.52
Technology and engineering	2,831	348,789.41	123.20	4,044	477,385.35	118.05	3,886	443,909.28	114.23	3,262	470,486.56	144.23
Transportation	193	3,689.30	19.12	323	7,862.59	24.34	327	8,542.62	26.12	307	6,647.12	21.65
Travel	2,745	24,973.53	9.10	3,686	35,907.30	9.74	2,546	27,895.98	10.96	2,026	21,559.44	10.64
True crime	321	2,826.65	8.81	621	9,853.58	15.87	616	7,412.95	12.03	511	6,461.99	12.65
Young adult	2,821	60,577.82	21.47	5,980	102,305.51	17.11	6,502	88,454.31	13.60	6,612	92,944.84	14.06
Totals	155,979	$3,818,692.92	$24.48	301,479	$6,910,463.55	$22.92	260,247	$7,278,212.86	$27.97	255,341	$5,905,651.70	$23.13

U.S. Book Exports and Imports: 2010–2013: Shift to Digital Evident, But Print Very Much Alive

Albert N. Greco

Gabelli School of Business, Fordham University
E-mail agreco@fordham.edu

Balance of Trade

The goal of the U.S. Government since 1790 has been to have a positive balance of trade; that is, the total dollar volume of exported goods or products should exceed the dollar volume of imported goods and services. If this occurs, a trade surplus is generated. Unfortunately, the United States generally imports more than it exports, resulting in a trade deficit. For example, between 2010 and 2013, U.S. firms had exports totaling $8.44 trillion while imports reached $10.50 trillion, resulting in a deficit of $2.06 trillion. For detailed historical information about U.S. exports and imports, see http://www.census.gov/foreign-trade/statistics/historical.

The U.S. Department of Commerce, International Trade Commission (ITC) is the source of all book export and import unit and revenue data in this article. ITC uses tariff and trade data to compile its statistics. When new datasets become available, ITC updates previously released statistical tables. Therefore there were changes in export and import revenues and units for certain book categories for 2010–2012 in the ITC datasets as of October 1, 2014. All of the ITC updates were incorporated into the tables and narratives here.

Because of significant declines in export and import totals for dictionaries and thesauruses, encyclopedias, and art books, these categories are not included in this analysis. Export and import tallies for 2010–2013 are included for five book categories: textbooks; religious books (Bibles, testaments, prayer books, and so forth); technical, scientific, and professional books; hardcover books; and mass market (rack-sized) paperback books. Note that data for individual categories may not add up to totals due to statistical rounding.

Fortunately, the U.S. book publishing industry is a positive-balance-of-trade industry in terms of total revenues. Between 2010 and 2013, ITC reported that the "big five" book categories posted $6.29 billion in exports and $4.35 billion in imports. This created a positive balance of trade of $1.94 billion. However, a review of book export and import units revealed an anomaly. While book export units for 2010–2013 were at the 982.65 million level, the import unit totals were 1,228.36 million, giving a deficit of 245.71 million. Many of the imported books were printed and published abroad; but a significant number were printed (not printed and published) abroad for U.S. publishers because the unit manufacturing costs for certain classifications of books were lower than the cost to print these books in the United States. This was true, for example, of religious books and

The author and the editors of the *Library and Book Trade Almanac* are grateful for the considerable assistance of Jim Rice of the International Trade Commission (ITC) for his help in obtaining detailed statistical databases for 2010–2013.

textbooks imported from China. Table 1 lists U.S. book trade revenues and units from 2010 through 2013.

Table 1 / U.S. Trade in Books: Exports, Imports, and Balance of Trade, 2010–2013

	Revenues ($'000)			Units ('000)		
	Exports	Imports	Balance of Trade	Exports	Imports	Balance of Trade
2010	1,534,313	1,211,697	322,616	223,573	338,820	-115,247
2011	1,546,397	1,078,401	467,996	232,065	309,074	-77,009
2012	1,610,629	1,069,963	540,666	270,439	290,141	-19,702
2013	1,597,529	991,837	605,631	256,572	290,329	-33,757
Total	6,288,868	4,351,898	1,936,970	982,649	1,228,364	-245,715

Book Exports

U.S. book publishers are generally successful in exporting their fiction and nonfiction titles. However, exports depend on attracting the interest of foreign distributors or retailers, and on their ability to purchase these books. Total export revenues increased 4.97 percent between 2010 and 2012, but the results for 2012–2013 showed a 0.8 percent decline. Two of the five categories (mass market paperbacks and religious books; see Table 2) saw declines in revenues between 2012–2013. In terms of export units, the declines were more widespread. While gains were evident between 2010 and 2012 (up 20.96 percent), between 2012 and 2013 four of the five categories saw declines (technical, scientific, and professional books; textbooks; religious books; and mass market paperbacks), resulting in a 5.1 percent drop in units. Table 3 lists the details.

U.S. textbooks have long been adopted by colleges and universities in other countries, especially textbooks in the fields of mathematics, the sciences, and business administration. An analysis of the United States' top ten export markets revealed that five posted declines between 2012 and 2013, triggering deficits in both revenues and units. Table 4 has the figures.

Table 2 / U.S. Exports of Books: 2010–2013 Revenues
($'000)

Category	2010	2011	2012	2013	Percent Change 2012–2013
Textbooks	452,217	464,478	456,010	478,493	4.9
Religious Books (Bibles, Testaments, Prayer Books, and Other Religious Books)	91,556	103,939	97,024	89,375	-7.9
Hardcover Books	222,132	251,711	277,400	285,245	2.8
Technical, Scientific, Professional Books	454,001	339,506	311,183	275,743	7.9
Mass Market Paperback Books	314,407	386,763	469,012	468,673	-0.1
Total	1,534,313	1,546,397	1,610,629	1,597,529	-0.8

Table 3 / U.S. Exports of Books: 2010–2013
('000 Units)

Category	2010	2011	2012	2013	Percent Change 2012–2013
Textbooks	45,291	46,356	41,866	40,350	-3.6
Religious Books (Bibles, Testaments, Prayer Books, and Other Religious Books)	34,623	36,174	32,149	30,548	-5.0
Hardcover Books	25,512	27,225	31,148	31,274	0.4
Technical, Scientific, Professional Books	30,481	21,383	20,888	18,729	-10.3
Mass Market Paperback Books	87,666	100,927	144,388	135,671	-6.0
Total	223,573	232,065	270,439	256,572	-5.1

Table 4 / U.S. Exports of Textbooks: Top Ten Markets 2012–2013

	Revenues ($'000)			Units ('000)		
	2012	2013	Percent Change 2012–2013	2012	2013	Percent Change 2012–2013
United Kingdom	126,671	163,472	29.1	9,436	10,842	14.9
Canada	87,406	83,153	-4.9	6,872	6,372	-7.3
Australia	22,810	24,568	7.7	1,792	2,183	21.8
Singapore	25,634	20,710	-19.2	2,849	1,937	-32.0
United Arab Emirates	15,569	19,277	23.8	991	869	-12.3
South Korea	25,736	18,382	-28.6	2,567	1,427	-44.4
Saudi Arabia	5,896	16,359	177.5	372	1,211	225.5
China	10,149	12,599	24.1	351	604	72.3
Mexico	13,398	12,219	-8.8	1,952	2,309	18.3
Japan	15,197	9,486	-37.6	1,096	768	-29.9

Table 5 / U.S. Exports of Bibles, Testaments, Prayer Books, and Other Religious Books: Top Ten Markets 2012–2013

	Revenues ($'000)			Units ('000)		
	2012	2013	Percent Change 2012–2013	2012	2013	Percent Change 2012–2013
Canada	18,378	16,705	-9.1	3,507	3,428	-2.3
United Kingdom	7,638	7,610	-0.4	4,004	3,709	-7.4
Nigeria	8,370	7,145	-14.6	2,413	2,276	-5.7
Mexico	6,657	6,863	3.1	3,131	1,828	-41.6
Colombia	3,926	3,153	-19.7	1,024	786	-23.3
Australia	3,778	3,049	-19.3	1,262	900	-28.7
Chile	2,224	2,552	14.8	900	1,113	23.7
Argentina	3,423	2,540	-25.8	1,601	661	-58.7
Peru	1,951	2,512	28.8	881	956	8.4
Brazil	2,349	2,484	5.7	918	1,083	17.9

Table 6 / U.S. Exports of Hardcover Books: Top Ten Markets 2012–2013

	Revenues ($'000)			Units ('000)		
	2012	2013	Percent Change 2012–2013	2012	2013	Percent Change 2012–2013
Canada	187,942	195,068	3.8	21,674	22,495	3.8
United Kingdom	36,479	42,832	17.4	3,547	3,649	2.9
Australia	8,004	6,269	-21.7	802	684	-14.8
Japan	7,034	3,686	-47.6	669	291	-56.5
India	1,975	3,403	72.3	304	531	74.7
United Arab Emirates	1,542	2,591	68.0	152	236	56.0
Netherlands	1,894	2,526	33.3	118	215	82.0
Mexico	588	2,449	316.7	67	219	224.8
Singapore	2,259	2,409	6.7	241	253	4.8
China	2,904	2,285	-21.3	446	263	-41.2

Table 7 / U.S. Exports of Technical, Scientific, and Professional Books: Top Ten Markets 2012–2013

	Revenues ($'000)			Units ('000)		
	2012	2013	Percent Change 2012–2013	2012	2013	Percent Change 2012–2013
Canada	107,332	91,291	-14.9	8,387	7,122	-15.2
United Kingdom	30,738	29,147	-5.2	1,972	2,184	10.8
Japan	33,008	28,659	-13.2	1,104	951	-13.9
Mexico	27,650	20,553	-25.7	2,897	2,824	-2.5
India	12,025	11,690	-2.8	395	377	-4.7
Australia	14,429	11,679	-19.1	426	342	-19.8
Hong Kong	8,846	7,343	-17.0	172	129	-25.0
Singapore	4,941	7,226	46.3	325	400	23.1
Germany	7,600	7,074	-6.9	278	211	-24.4
China	7,124	6,591	-7.5	291	276	-5.0

Table 8 / U.S. Book Exports of Mass Market Paperbacks (Rack-Sized): Top Ten Markets 2012–2013

	Revenues ($'000)			Units ('000)		
	2012	2013	Percent Change 2012–2013	2012	2013	Percent Change 2012–2013
United Kingdom	158,160	179,378	13.4	46,430	46,470	0.1
Canada	165,859	152,004	-8.4	57,589	52,779	-8.4
Singapore	18,931	23,801	25.7	4,760	5,831	22.5
Australia	15,698	16,053	2.3	5,457	5,084	-6.8
Japan	13,185	11,296	-14.3	3,872	2,917	-24.7
Philippines	15,605	10,642	-31.8	4,240	2,923	-31.1
Brazil	13,880	10,637	-23.4	3,589	2,563	-28.6
South Africa	8,770	6,375	-27.3	2,137	1,287	-39.8
Sweden	3,692	6,351	72.0	863	1,466	70.0
China	10,392	6,026	-42.0	2,441	1,481	-39.3

This pattern of fewer export sales was also evident in the analysis of religious books (Table 5); hardcover books (Table 6); technical, scientific, and professional books (Table 7); and mass market paperbacks (Table 8). Why did these declines take place? They were due to two global trends. First, as more individuals abroad adopt e-readers or tablets, the export of physical books is bound to decline. Second—and perhaps the more important reason—the international economic environment was cloudy in 2013, and the outlook for 2014 was unsettling. The International Monetary Fund (IMF) was reported in October as having "sounded the alarm on the health of the Eurozone economy, warning there is a 4 in 10 chance that the single currency area will slide into its 3rd recession since the financial crisis [of 2007–2008]" (Giles and Wagstyl). Talley remarked that "the world's export engines are sputtering." Greco, Milliot, and Wharton address these global economic patterns.

Book Imports

It has been well documented in various newspapers and industry studies and in *Publishers Weekly* that e-books accounted for about a third of all books sold in the United States in 2013 (Greco). This transformation in format had a positive impact on some publishers' margins. On the other hand, bricks-and-mortar bookstores, both major chains such as Barnes and Noble and the independents, have seen a loss of physical book sales. The net result of book content delivered on electronic devices has been a decline, and a steep one, in physical books imported into the United States.

Total revenues generated by imports fell consistently in all five book categories between 2010 and 2013, with a 7.3 percent decline in the total tallies just between 2012 and 2013. Table 9 outlines these trends. Unit totals for those years were down in three of the five categories. Religious books plunged 77.3 percent between 2012 and 2013; see Table 10).

Table 9 / U.S. Imports of Books: 2010–2013
($'000)

Category	2010	2011	2012	2013	Percent Change 2012–2013
Textbooks	259,525	219,583	196,678	172,587	-12.2
Religious Books (Bibles, Testaments, Prayer Books, and Other Religious Books)	132,097	135,623	138,197	125,868	-8.9
Hardcover Books	532,845	466,345	469,955	446,932	-4.9
Technical, Scientific, Professional	198,021	185,265	175,121	162,378	-7.3
Mass Market Paperback Books	89,209	71,585	90,012	84,072	-6.6
Total	1,211,697	1,078,401	1,069,963	991,837	-7.3

Table 10 / U.S. Imports of Books: 2010–2013
('000 Units)

Category	2010	2011	2012	2013	Percent Change 2012–2013
Textbooks	45,302	33,190	31,450	27,976	-11.1
Religious Books (Bibles, Testaments, Prayer Books, and Other Religious Books)	363	857	864	196	-77.3
Hardcover Books	199,362	174,249	164,153	164,680	0.3
Technical, Scientific, Professional	48,058	62,055	41,165	46,025	11.8
Mass Market Paperback Books	45,735	38,723	52,509	51,452	-2.0
Total	338,820	309,074	290,141	290,329	0.1

All of the major U.S. textbook publishers started to de-emphasize printed textbooks in 2007 with the launch of CourseSmart, a major provider of electronic textbooks and digital course materials. This transformation from print to digital textbooks (and digital learning systems and solutions) accelerated in 2012 and 2013 because nearly all higher education students by then had computers (desktops, laptops, tablets). Revenues and units for print textbooks declined precipitously between 2012 and 2013, and the prognosis is dismal. Pearson PLC's Prentice Hall textbook unit has about 60 percent of textbooks available in digital formats, and it hopes to reach the 80 percent mark in 2016. Cengage Learning, McGraw-Hill, John Wiley, Macmillan, and others are positioning their product lines away from print, although their digital footprint is smaller than Pearson's. Table 11 illustrates changes in textbook imports.

Similar trends were evident for religious books (Table 12); hardbound books (Table 13); technical, scientific, and professional books (Table 14); and mass market paperbacks (Table 15).

Table 11 / U.S. Imports of Textbooks: Top Ten Markets 2012–2013

	Revenues ($'000)			Units ('000)		
	2012	2013	Percent Change 2012–2013	2012	2013	Percent Change 2012–2013
Canada	45,287	41,096	-9.3	7,752	7,735	-0.2
China	45,751	39,982	-12.6	12,122	10,914	-10.0
United Kingdom	48,089	37,912	-21.2	3,051	2,474	-18.9
Singapore	10,138	9,552	-5.8	2,288	2,272	-0.7
Australia	3,015	6,545	117.1	56	81	45.1
India	3,278	5,035	53.6	241	261	8.5
Hong Kong	10,110	3,632	-64.1	842	619	-26.5
Mexico	3,420	3,385		720	475	-34.0
United Arab Emirates	4,016	2,803	-30.2	300	200	-33.3
France	1,597	2,717	70.1	202	291	43.8

Table 12 / U.S. Imports of Bibles, Testaments, Prayer Books, and
Other Religious Books: Top Ten Markets 2012–2013

	Revenues ($'000)			Units ('000)		
	2012	2013	Percent Change 2012–2013	2012	2013	Percent Change 2012–2013
China	63,820	61,700	-3.3	298	80	-73.2
South Korea	21,062	18,966	-10.0	—	—	—
Israel	8,017	7,025	-12.4	—	—	—
Colombia	12,280	4,521	-63.2	0	0	n.a.
Germany	2,154	4,441	106.2	0	0	n.a.
Japan	1,402	4,052	189.1	0	2	n.a.
Italy	4,423	3,141	-29.0	0	1	n.a.
United Kingdom	4,057	3,111	-23.3	3	25	614.8
Mexico	2,588	2,620	1.3	42	23	-45.3
Canada	1,456	2,001	37.5	10	0	n.a.

Note: "n.a." indicates that the annual percentage change cannot be calculated. Dashes indicate that no ITC unit data was available for that country.

Table 13 / U.S. Imports of Hardbound Books: Top Ten Markets 2012–2013

	Revenues ($'000)			Units ('000)		
	2012	2013	Percent Change 2012–2013	2012	2013	Percent Change 2012–2013
China	303,047	280,475	-7.4	133,390	132,160	-0.9
United Kingdom	45,777	45,240	-1.2	3,209	3,683	14.8
Italy	23,842	23,887	0.2	1,722	1,734	0.7
Singapore	19,824	14,719	-25.8	8,937	7,417	-17.0
Canada	14,433	14,582	1.0	3,390	3,475	2.5
Hong Kong	13,031	14,567	11.8	3,992	5,202	30.3
Germany	9,516	11,269	18.4	1,444	1,537	6.5
India	4,277	6,226	45.6	1,004	711	-29.2
Spain	5,418	4,866	-10.2	1,134	685	-39.6
Malaysia	3,047	4,199	37.8	892	1,956	119.2

Table 14 / U.S. Imports of Technical, Scientific, and Professional Books:
Top Ten Markets 2012–2013

	Revenues ($'000)			Units ('000)		
	2012	2013	Percent Change 2012–2013	2012	2013	Percent Change 2012–2013
China	49,489	39,764	-19.7	16,246	15,768	-2.9
Canada	23,713	24,829	4.7	3,598	3,599	0.1
United Kingdom	21,749	21,434	-1.5	2,070	2,332	12.6
Japan	18,028	19,717	9.4	2,330	3,409	46.3
Germany	11,474	14,070	22.6	886	722	-18.5
Mexico	6,189	6,307	1.9	7,580	12,499	64.9
India	7,708	5,505	-28.6	2,033	2,729	34.2
Italy	5,700	4,053	-28.9	644	431	-33.1

Table 15 / U.S. Imports of Mass Market Paperbacks (Rack-Sized): Top Ten Markets 2012–2013

	Revenues ($'000)			Units ('000)		
	2012	2013	Percent Change 2012–2013	2012	2013	Percent Change 2012–2013
China	53,708	54,198	0.9	36,238	38,957	7.5
Canada	11,723	10,218	-12.8	5,365	4,582	-14.8
United Kingdom	6,716	3,639	-45.8	1,517	653	-56.9
Singapore	3,006	2,271	-24.4	2,258	1,671	-26.0
Italy	1,429	2,020	41.4	244	244	0.0
Korea	1,185	2,003	69.0	799	1,013	26.9
Malaysia	3,276	1,984	-39.4	2,349	1,765	-24.9
Spain	1,575	1,609	2.1	1,004	955	-4.8
Hong Kong	2,568	1,402	-45.4	1,088	598	-45.0
Germany	1,455	1,278	-12.2	362	281	-22.6

Conclusions

Despite dire predictions from some that print is dead, that bookstores will disappear, and that all content (books, magazines, newspapers, and professional information) will migrate to the cloud, all available data clearly indicate that print is quite alive. Content formats and delivery systems have undergone substantive changes in the last decade, but years after the launch of the Kindle, the Nook, the iPad, and other e-reading devices, we are still buying and reading printed books. The export and import trends outlined in this article reveal that in 2013 more than $1.5 billion worth of printed books (256.6 million books) were exported, and nearly $1 billion worth (more than 290.3 million books) were imported into the United States.

References

Chris Giles and Stefan Wagstyl. "IMF Warns of Third Eurozone Recession Since the Financial Crisis," *Financial Times,* October 8, 2014, p. 1. Also see Nahid Kalbasi Anaraki. "Effects of Euro Devaluation on Eurozone Exports," *International Journal of Economics and Finance* 6, 2(February 2014): 19–24.

Albert N. Greco. *The Economics of the Publishing and Information Industries: The Search for Yield in a Disintermediated World* (Routledge, 2015): 1–39. Also see Alexandr Vashchilko. "Vertically Related Markets, Tariffs, and Technology Adoption," *Journal of Economics* 110, 3 (November 2013): 273–286; Abdul Abiad, Prachi Mishra, and Petia Topalova. "Does Trade Evolve in the Aftermath of Financial Crises?" *IMF Economic Review* 62, 2(June 2014): 213–247; Mary Amiti, Oleg Itskhoki, and Josef Konings. "Importers, Exporters, and Exchange Rate Disconnect," *American Economic Review* 104, 7(July 2014): 1942–1978.

Albert N. Greco, Jim Milliot, and Robert M. Wharton. *The Book Publishing Industry,* 3rd ed. (Routledge, 2014), pp. 78–84.

Ian Talley. "Devaluation Gains Currency," *Wall Street Journal,* October 6, 2014, p. A2.

Number of Book Outlets
in the United States and Canada

The *American Book Trade Directory* (Information Today, Inc.) has been published since 1915. Revised annually, it features lists of booksellers, wholesalers, periodicals, reference tools, and other information about the U.S. and Canadian book markets. The data shown in Table 1, the most current available, are from the 2015–2016 edition of the directory.

The 15,387 stores of various types shown are located throughout the United States, Canada, and regions administered by the United States. "General" bookstores stock trade books and children's books in a general variety of subjects. "College" stores carry college-level textbooks. "Educational" outlets handle school textbooks up to and including the high school level. "Mail order" outlets sell general trade books by mail and are not book clubs; all others operating by mail are classified according to the kinds of books carried. "Antiquarian" dealers sell old and rare books. Stores handling secondhand books are classified as "used." "Paperback" stores have more than 80 percent of their stock in paperbound books. Stores with paperback departments are listed under the appropriate major classification ("general," "department store," "stationer," and so forth). Bookstores with at least 50 percent of their stock on a particular subject are classified by subject.

Table 1 / Bookstores in the United States and Canada, 2014

Category	United States	Canada
Antiquarian General	552	48
Antiquarian Mail Order	208	5
Antiquarian Specialized	104	3
Art Supply Store	53	1
College General	2,833	136
College Specialized	104	6
Comics	187	26
Computer Software	2	0
Cooking	248	12
Department Store	1,515	14
Educational*	170	27
Federal Sites†	232	1
Foreign Language*	15	2
General	2,515	479
Gift Shop	106	6
Juvenile*	69	15
Mail Order General	52	6
Mail Order Specialized	256	10
Metaphysics, New Age, and Occult	121	18
Museum Store and Art Gallery	453	28
Nature and Natural History	36	4
Newsdealer	20	2
Office Supply	9	1
Other‡	2,204	371
Paperback§	43	2

Religious*	1,351	125
Self Help/Development	15	5
Stationer	3	3
Toy Store	37	35
Used*	415	68
Totals	13,928	1,459

* Includes Mail Order Shops for this topic, which are not counted elsewhere in this survey.

† National Historic Sites, National Monuments, and National Parks.

‡ Stores specializing in subjects or services other than those covered in this survey.

§ Includes Mail Order. Excludes used paperback bookstores, stationers, drugstores, or wholesalers handling paperbacks.

Review Media Statistics

Compiled by the staff of the *Library and Book Trade Almanac*

Number of Books and Other Media Reviewed by Major Reviewing Publications 2013–2014

	Adult		Juvenile		Young Adult		Total	
	2013	2014	2013	2014	2013	2014	2013	2014
Booklist[1]	4,197	n.a.	3,035	n.a.	—	—	8,182	n.a.
Bookmarks	662	692	—	—	24	30	686	722
BookPage[2]	625	605	80	98	37	48	742	751
Bulletin of the Center for Children's Books[3]	—	—	892	1,024	—	—	892	1,024
Chicago Tribune Sunday Book Section[4]	1,580	1,610	340	345	—	—	1,920	1,955
Choice[5]	7,080	6,664	—	—	—	—	7,080	6,664
Horn Book Guide	—	—	3,148	3,289	987	936	4,135	4,225
Horn Book Magazine[6]	5	—	356	399	171	176	532	575
Kirkus Reviews[4]	3,816	3,890	3,164	3,305	—	—	6,980	7,195
Library Journal[7]	6,081	5,524	—	—	—	—	6,081	5,524
Library Media Connection (LMC)[8]	—	—	1,704	1,704	—	—	1,704	1,704
New York Journal of Books[9]	1,387	n.a.	45	n.a.	200	n.a.	1,632	n.a.
New York Review of Books[10]	n.a.	n.a.	—	—	—	—	n.a.	n.a.
New York Times Sunday Book Review	864	n.a.	n.a.	n.a.	—	—	864	n.a.
Publishers Weekly[11]	6,729	6,469	1,915	1,842	—	—	8,644	8,571
School Library Journal[4]	230	124	5,403	5,763	—	—	6,448	6,630
Washington Post Book World	900	900	60	36	—	—	960	936

n.a. = not available

1 All figures are for a 12-month period from September 1 to August 31. YA books are included in the juvenile total. Included in the overall total are adult books recommended for YA readers and other media such as audio, video, and databases.

2 In 2014 *BookPage* also published 36 audio reviews. Of the total, 309 reviews were online-only; of these, 198 were of adult works, 82 juvenile, and 29 young adult. The grand total of reviews for the year was 1,096.

3 All figures are for a 12-month period beginning September and ending July/August. YA books are included in the juvenile total. The *Bulletin* also published eight professional titles.

4 YA books are included in the juvenile total. In 2014 the *Chicago Tribune* also reviewed 155 digital reading apps and other works; *Kirkus* also reviewed 130 iPad apps; and *School Library Journal* also reviewed 749 other works.

5 All materials reviewed in *Choice* are scholarly publications intended for undergraduate libraries. The total for 2014 includes 310 Internet resources.

6 *Horn Book Magazine* also reviewed 11 audiobooks.

7 *Library Journal* also published approximately 600 "Xpress reviews" online only, and approximately 1,400 works were included in "Prepub Alert."

8 *LMC* publishes 284 reviews of book and nonbook materials for children and young adults in grades K–12 in 6 issues each school year. In Vol. 32 (August/September 2013 to May/June 2014) the total included approximately 50 reviews of professional books/websites.

9 *New York Journal of Books,* which began publication in 2010, is online only.

10 *New York Review of Books* in 2010 published 280 articles dealing directly with books or other media. These articles treated a cumulative 435 individual items, of which 10 were films, 2 operas, 2 television series, 3 plays, and 24 art exhibitions. The remainder (394) were adult books. Figures for subsequent years were unavailable.

11 Of the total of 8,571 reviews, 1,567 were online only. A total of 260 audiobooks are included in *Publishers Weekly's* total count.

Part 5
Reference Information

Bibliographies

The Librarian's Bookshelf

Karen Muller

Librarian, American Library Association

Valerie Hawkins

Library Reference Assistant, American Library Association

Most of the books on this selective bibliography have been published since 2011; a few earlier titles are retained because of their continuing importance. Many are also available as e-books.

General

ALA Glossary of Library and Information Science. 4th ed. By Michael Levine-Clark and Toni M. Carter. ALA Editions, 2013.

American Library Directory, 2015-2016. Information Today, Inc., 2015. 2v. Print and online.

Annual Review of Information Science and Technology (ARIST). Ed. by Blaise Cronin. Information Today, Inc., 2010-.

Encyclopedia of Library and Information Science. 3rd ed. Ed. by Miriam A. Drake. CRC, 2009. Print and online.

Introduction to the Library and Information Professions. 2nd ed. By Roger C. Greer, Robert J. Grover, and Susan G. Fowler. Libraries Unlimited, 2013.

Library and Book Trade Almanac, 2015. Ed. by Dave Bogart. Information Today, Inc., 2015.

Library and Information Science: A Guide to Key Literature and Sources. By Michael F. Bemis. ALA Editions, 2014.

Library and Information Science Source. EBSCO Publishing. Online database.

Library World Records. 2nd ed. By Godfrey Oswald. McFarland, 2009.

The Whole Library Handbook 5: Current Data, Professional Advice, and Curiosa. Ed. by George Eberhart. American Library Association, 2013.

Academic Libraries

Embedded Librarianship: What Every Academic Librarian Should Know. Ed. by Alice L. Daugherty and Michael F. Russo. Libraries Unlimited, 2013.

Library Assessment in Higher Education. by Joseph R. Matthews. Libraries Unlimited, 2015.

Managing the Small College Library. By Rachel Applegate. Libraries Unlimited, 2010.

Twenty-First Century Access Services: On the Front Line of Academic Librarianship. Ed. by Michael J. Krasulski, Jr. and Trevor A. Dawes. Association of College and Research Libraries, 2013.

Administration

Balancing the Books: Accounting for Librarians. By Rachel A. Kirk. Libraries Unlimited, 2013.

The Complete Library Trustee Handbook. By Sally Gardner Reed and Jillian Kolonick. Neal-Schuman, 2010.

Exploring Digital Libraries: Foundations, Practice, Prospects. By Karen Calhoun. Neal-Schuman, 2014.

Getting Started with Evaluation. By Peter Hernon, Robert E. Dugan, and Joseph R. Matthews. ALA Editions, 2014

How to Thrive as a Solo Librarian. Ed. by Carol Smallwood, Melissa J. Clapp. Scarecrow, 2012.

Implementing for Results: Your Strategic Plan in Action. By Sandra Nelson. American Library Association, 2009.

Joint Libraries: Models That Work. By Claire B. Gunnels, Susan E. Green, and Patricia M. Butler. American Library Association, 2012.

Library and Information Center Management. 8th ed. By Barbara B. Moran, Robert D. Stueart, and Claudia J. Morner. Libraries Unlimited, 2013.

Management Basics for Information Professionals. 3rd ed. By Camila A. Alire and G. Edward Evans. Neal-Schuman, 2013.

Managing in the Middle: the Librarian's Handbook. Ed. by Robert Farrell and Kenneth Schlesinger. ALA Editions, 2013.

Moving Materials: Physical Delivery in Libraries. Ed. by Valerie Horton and Bruce Smith. American Library Association, 2010.

New Planning for Results: A Streamlined Approach. By Sandra Nelson. Public Library Association, 2001.

Strategic Planning for Results. By Sandra Nelson. American Library Association, 2008.

Useful, Usable, Desirable: Applying User Experience Design to Your Library. By Aaron Schmidt and Amanda Etches. American Library Association, 2014.

What Every Library Director Should Know. By Susan Carol Curzon. Rowman & Littlefield, 2014.

Advocacy and Funding

Activism and the School Librarian: Tools for Advocacy and Survival. Ed. by Deborah D. Levitov. Libraries Unlimited, 2012.

ALA Book of Library Grant Money. 9th ed. Ed. by Nancy Kalikow Maxwell. American Library Association, 2014.

Beyond Book Sales: The Complete Guide to Raising Real Money for Your Library. Ed. by

Susan Dowd for Library Strategies, a consulting group of the Friends of the Saint Paul Public Library. Neal-Schuman, 2014.

A Book Sale How-to Guide: More Money, Less Stress. By Pat Ditzler and JoAnn Dumas. American Library Association, 2012.

Grassroots Library Advocacy. By Lauren Comito, Aliqae Geraci, and Christian Zabriskie. American Library Association, 2012.

Librarian's Handbook for Seeking, Writing, and Managing Grants. By Sylvia D. Hall-Ellis, Stacey L. Bowers, Christopher Hudson, Claire Williamson, and Joanne Patrick. Libraries Unlimited, 2011.

The Lone Arranger: Succeeding in a Small Repository. By Christina Zamon. Society of American Archivists, 2012.

Say It With Data: A Concise Guide to Making Your Case and Getting Results. Priscille Dando. ALA Editions, 2014.

School Libraries Matter. Ed. by Mirah J. Dow. Libraries Unlimited, 2013.

Archives and Special Collections

Archives: Principles and Practices. By Laura A. Millar. Neal-Schuman, 2010.

Digitization and Digital Archiving: A Practical Guide for Librarians. By Elizabeth R. Leggett. Rowman & Littlefield, 2014.

Health Sciences Librarianship. Ed. by M. Sandra Wood. Rowman & Littlefield, 2014.

Rare Books and Special Collections. By Sidney E. Berger. Neal-Schuman, 2014.

Special Libraries: A Survival Guide. By James M. Matarazzo and Toby Pearlstein with the assistance of Sylvia James. Libraries Unlimited, 2013.

Starting, Strengthening, and Managing Institutional Repositories: A How-to-Do-It Manual. By Jonathan A. Nabe. Neal-Schuman, 2010.

Buildings and Space Planning

The Academic Library Building in the Digital Age: A Study of Construction, Planning, and Design of New Library Space. By Christopher Stewart. Association of College and Research Libraries, 2010.

Building Blocks for Planning Functional Library Space. 3rd ed. By the Library Leadership and Management Association. Scarecrow, 2011.

Building Science 101: A Primer for Librarians. By Lynn M. Piotrowicz and Scott Osgood. American Library Association, 2010.

Countdown to a New Library: Managing the Building Project. 2nd ed. By Jeannette Woodward. American Library Association, 2010.

Planning Academic and Research Library Buildings. 3rd ed. By Philip D. Leighton and David C. Weber. American Library Association, 1999.

The Power of Play: Designing Early Learning Spaces. By Dorothy Stoltz, Marisa Conner, and James Bradberry. ALA Editions, 2015.

Teen Spaces: The Step-by-Step Library Makeover. 2nd ed. By Kimberly Bolan. American Library Association, 2009.

Cataloging and Bibliographic Control

Cataloging Correctly for Kids: An Introduction to the Tools. 5th ed. By Sheila S. Intner and Joanna F. Fountain. American Library Association, 2011.

Information Resource Description: Creating and Managing Metadata. By Philip Hider. ALA Editions, 2013.

Introduction to Cataloging and Classification. 11th ed. By Daniel N. Joudrey, Arlene G. Taylor, and David P. Miller. Libraries Unlimited, 2015.

Introduction to Indexing and Abstracting. 4th ed. By Donald Cleveland and Ana Cleveland. Libraries Unlimited, 2013.

Maxwell's Handbook for RDA: Resource Description and Access: Explaining and Illustrating RDA: Resource Description and Access Using MARC21. By Robert L. Maxwell. ALA Editions, 2013.

RDA: Resource Description and Access Print. Joint Steering Committee for Development of RDA (JSC). American Library Association, 2011-. Looseleaf.

RDA and Serials Cataloging. By Ed Jones. ALA Editions, 2013.

RDA Made Simple: A Practical Guide to the New Cataloging Rules. By Amy Hart. Libraries Unlimited, 2014.

RDA Toolkit. Joint Steering Committee for Development of RDA (JSC). American Library Association, 2011-. Online resource.

Children's and Young Adult Services and Materials

The Collection Program in Schools: Concepts and Practices. 5th ed. By Kay Bishop. Libraries Unlimited, 2013.

The Coretta Scott King Awards, 1970-2014. ALA Editions, 2015.

Diversity Programming for Digital Youth. By Jamie Campbell Naidoo. Libraries Unlimited, 2014.

Evaluating Teen Services and Programs. By Sarah Flowers. Neal-Schuman, 2012.

The Handbook for Storytellers. By Judy Freeman and Caroline Feller Bauer. ALA Editions, 2015.

Integrating Young Adult Literature Through the Common Core Standards. Rachel L. Wadham and Jonathan W. Ostenson. Libraries Unlimited, 2013.

Managing Children's Services in Libraries. 4th ed. By Adele M. Fasick and Leslie Edmonds Holt. Libraries Unlimited, 2013.

The Newbery and Caldecott Awards 2015: A Guide to the Medal and Honor Books. Association for Library Service to Children/ American Library Association, 2015.

Pura Belpré Awards: Celebrating Latino Authors and Illustrators. By Rose Zertuche Trevino. ALA Editions, 2006.

Young Adults Deserve the Best: YALSA's Competencies in Action. By Sarah Flowers. American Library Association, 2010.

Collection Development*Choice's Outstanding Academic Titles, 2007-2011.* Ed. by Rebecca Ann Bartlett. Association of College and Research Libraries, 2012.

Developing and Managing Electronic Collections: The Essentials. By Peggy Johnson. ALA Editions, 2013.

Floating Collections: A Collection Development Model for Long-Term Success. By

Wendy K. Bartlett. Libraries Unlimited, 2014.

Fundamentals of Collection Development and Management. 3rd ed. By Peggy Johnson. American Library Association, 2014.

Getting Started with Demand-Driven Acquisitions for E-Books. By Theresa S. Arndt. ALATechsource, 2015.

Rethinking Collection Development and Management. By Becky Albitz, Christine Avery, and Diane Zabel. Libraries Unlimited, 2014.

Copyright and Other Legal Issues

Complete Copyright for K–12 Librarians and Educators. By Carrie Russell. American Library Association, 2012

The Copyright Book: A Practical Guide. 6th ed. By William S. Strong. MIT Press, 2014.

Copyright Law for Librarians and Educators: Creative Strategies and Practical Solutions. 3rd ed. By Kenneth D. Crews. American Library Association, 2012.

Intellectual Property for Nonprofit Organizations and Associations. By Jefferson C. Glassie, Eileen Morgan Johnson, and Dana O. Lynch. ASAE Association Management Press, 2012.

The Librarian's Legal Companion for Licensing Information Resources and Services. By Tomas A. Lipinski. Neal-Schuman, 2013.

Owning and Using Scholarship: An IP Handbook for Teachers and Researchers. By Kevin L. Smith. ACRL, 2014.

Privacy and Confidentiality Issues: A Guide for Libraries and Their Lawyers. By Theresa Chmara. American Library Association, 2009.

History

The Book: A Global History. Ed. by Michael F. Suarez and H. R. Woudhuysen. Oxford University Press, 2013.

The Great Depression: Its Impact on Forty-six Large American Public Libraries: An Inquiry Based on a Content Analysis of Published Writings of Their Directors. By Robert Scott Kramp. Library Juice Press, 2010.

Historical Dictionary of Librarianship. By Mary Ellen Quinn. Rowman & Littlefield, 2014.

Libraries and the Reading Public in Twentieth-Century America. By Christine Pawley and Louise S. Robbins. University of Wisconsin Press, 2013.

The Library Beyond the Book. By Jeffrey T. Schnapp and Matthew Battles. Harvard University Press, 2014.

Main Street Public Library. By Wayne Weigand. University of Iowa Press, 2011.

When Books Went to War: The Stories that Helped Us Win World War II. Molly Guptill Manning. Houghton Mifflin Harcourt, 2014.

Human Resources and Leadership

Being Indispensable: A School Librarian's Guide to Becoming an Invaluable Leader. Ruth Toor and Hilda K. Weisburg. American Library Association, 2011.

Coaching in the Library: A Management Strategy for Achieving Excellence. 2nd ed. By Ruth F. Metz. American Library Association, 2011.

Communicating Professionally: A How-to-Do-It Manual for Librarians. By Catherine Sheldrick Ross and Kirsti Nilsen. Neal-Schuman, 2013.

Fundamentals of Library Supervision. By Joan Giesecke and Beth McNeil. American Library Association, 2010.

Handbook of Academic Writing for Librarians. Rev. ed. By Christopher Vance Hollister. ACRL, 2014.

Hiring, Training, and Supervising Library Shelvers. By Patricia Tunstall. American Library Association, 2010.

Interpersonal Skills, Theory, and Practice: The Librarian's Guide to Becoming a Leader. By Brooke E. Sheldon. Libraries Unlimited, 2010.

Staff Development: A Practical Guide. 4th ed. Ed. by Andrea Wigbels Stewart, Carlette Washington-Hoagland, and Carol T. Zsulya. ALA Editions, 2013.

Success with Library Volunteers. By Leslie Edmonds Holt and Glen E. Holt. Libraries Unlimited, 2014.

Succession Planning in the Library: Developing Leaders, Managing Change. By Paula M. Singer with Gail Griffith. American Library Association, 2010.

Information Literacy

Concise Guide to Information Literacy. By Scott Lanning. Libraries Unlimited, 2012

Designing Online Learning: A Primer for Librarians. Ed. by Susan Alman, Christinger Tomer, and Margaret L. Lincoln. Libraries Unlimited, 2012.

Fundamentals of Library Instruction. By Monty L. McAdoo. American Library Association, 2012.

How to Teach: A Practical Guide for Librarians. By Beverley E. Crane. Rowman & Littlefield, 2014.

Metaliteracy: Reinventing Information Literacy to Empower Learners. By Thomas P. Mackey and Trudi E. Jacobson. Neal Schuman, 2014.

The One-Shot Library Instruction Survival Guide. By Heidi E. Buchanan and Beth A. McDonough. ALA Editions, 2014.

Reference and Instructional Services for Information Literacy Skills in School Libraries. 3rd ed. By Scott Lanning. Libraries Unlimited, 2014.

Web of Deceit: Misinformation and Manipulation in the Age of Social Media. Ed. by Anne P. Mintz. CyberAge Books, 2012.

Intellectual Freedom

Banned Books Resource Guide. American Library Association/Office of Intellectual Freedom, 2014.

Books Under Fire: A Hit List of Banned and Challenged Children's Books. By Pat Scales. ALA Editions, 2015.

Intellectual Freedom for Teens: A Practical Guide for Young Adult and School Librarians. By Kristin Fletcher-Speak and Kelly Tyler. ALA Editions, 2014.

Intellectual Freedom Manual. 8th ed. American Library Association/Office of Intellectual Freedom, 2010.

Library Ethics. By Jean L. Preer. Libraries Unlimited, 2008.

The Library Juice Press Handbook of Intellectual Freedom: Concepts, Cases and Theories. By Mark Alfino and Laura Koltutsky. Library Juice Press, 2014.

Sex in the Library: A Guide to Sexual Content in Teen Literature. By Mary Jo Heller and Aarene Storms. VOYA Press, 2013.

VOYA's Guide to Intellectual Freedom for Teens. By Margaret Auguste. VOYA Press, 2012.

Librarians and LIS Principles

Foundations of Library and Information Science. 3rd ed. By Richard E. Rubin. Neal-Schuman, 2010.

Information Services Today: An Introduction. By Sandra Hirsh. Rowman & Littlefield, 2015.

Introduction to Information Science and Technology. By Charles H. Davis and Debora Shaw. Information Today, Inc., 2011.

Knowledge Management: An Introduction. By Kevin C. Desouza and Scott Paquette. Neal-Schuman, 2011.

Neal-Schuman Library Technology Companion: A Basic Guide for Library Staff. 4th ed. By John J. Burke. Neal-Schuman, 2013.

Outreach, Programming, and Services

Assistive Technologies in the Library. By Barbara T. Mates; with contributions by William R. Reed IV. American Library Association, 2011.

Blueprint for a Job Center at Your Library. By Bernice Kao and Megan Pittsley-Fox. Libraries Unlimited, 2014.

Crash Course in Gaming. By Suellen S. Adams. Libraries Unlimited, 2014.

Dragons in the Stacks: A Teen Librarian's Guide to Tabletop Role-Playing. By Steven A. Torres-Roman and Cason E. Snow. Libraries Unlimited, 2015.

Easy Information Sources for ESL, Adult Learners, and New Readers. By Rosemarie Riechel. Neal-Schuman, 2008.

El Día de los niños/El día de los libros: Building a Culture of Literacy in Your Community through Día. By Jeanette Larson. American Library Association, 2011.

Hola, Amigos! A Plan for Latino Outreach. By Susana G. Baumann. Libraries Unlimited, 2010.

Libraries and the Affordable Care Act: Helping the Community Understand Health-Care Options. By Francisca Goldsmith. ALA Editions, 2015.

Library Services for Adults in the 21st Century. By Elsie A. Rogers Halliday Okobi. Libraries Unlimited, 2014.

Library Services for Multicultural Patrons: Strategies to Encourage Library Use. Ed. by Carol Smallwood and Kim Becnel. Scarecrow, 2013.

Lifelong Learning in Public Libraries: Principles, Programs, and People. By Donna L. Gilton. Scarecrow, 2012.

Literacy: A Way Out for At-Risk Youth. By Jennifer Sweeney. Libraries Unlimited, 2012.

Makerspaces: Top Trailblazing Projects. By Caitlin A. Bagley. ALA, 2014.

The Prison Library Primer: A Program for the Twenty-First Century. By Brenda Vogel. Scarecrow Press, 2009.

School Library Makerspaces: Grades 6-12. By Leslie Preddy. Libraries Unlimited, 2012.

Serving Grandfamilies in Libraries: A Handbook and Programming Guide. By Sarah Gough, Pat Feehan, and Denise R. Lyons. Scarecrow, 2014.

Small Business and the Public Library: Strategies for a Successful Partnership. By Luise Weiss, Sophia Serlis-McPhillips, and Elizabeth Malafi. American Library Association, 2011.

Streamlined Library Programming: How to Improve Services and Cut Costs. By Daisy Porter-Reynolds. Libraries Unlimited, 2014.

Successful Community Outreach: A How-to-Do-It Manual for Librarians. By Barbara Blake, Robert S. Martin, and Yunfei Du. Neal-Schuman, 2011.

Technology and Literacy: 21st Century Library Programming for Children and Teens. By Jennifer Nelson and Keith Braafladt. American Library Association, 2012.

Technology Training in Libraries. By Sarah Houghton-Jan. Neal-Schuman, 2010.

Preservation, Disaster Response, and Security

Disaster Response and Planning for Libraries. 3rd ed. By Miriam B. Kahn. American Library Association, 2012.

Guide to Security Considerations and Practices for Rare Book, Manuscript, and Special Collection Libraries. Ed. by Everett C. Wilkie, Jr. Association of College and Research Libraries, 2011.

The Library Security and Safety Guide to Prevention, Planning, and Response. By Miriam B. Kahn. American Library Association, 2008.

Personal Archiving: Preserving Our Digital Heritage. Ed. by Donald T. Hawkins. Information Today, Inc., 2013.

Practical Digital Preservation: A How-to Guide for Organizations of Any Size. By Adrian Brown. Neal-Schuman, 2013.

The Preservation Management Handbook: A 21st-Century Guide for Libraries, Archives, and Museums. Ed. by D. R. Harvey and Martha R. Mahard. Rowman & Littlefield, 2014.

Public Libraries

IFLA Public Library Service Guidelines. Ed. by Christie Koontz and Barbara Gubbin. De Gruyter Saur, 2010.

Opportunity for All: How Library Policies and Practices Impact Public Internet Access: The U.S. IMPACT Study: A Research Initiative Examining the Impact of Free Access to Computers and the Internet in Public Libraries. By Samantha Becker et al. IMLS, 2011. Free.

Public Libraries and Resilient Cities. Ed. by Michael Dudley. American Library Association, 2013.

Public Libraries in the 21st Century. By Ann E. Prentice. Libraries Unlimited, 2011.

The Public Library Policy Writer: A Guidebook with Model Policies on CD-ROM. By Jeanette C. Larson and Herman L. Totten. Neal-Schuman, 2008.

Small Public Library Management. By Jane Pearlmutter and Paul Nelson. American Library Association, 2012.

Public Relations/Marketing

Building a Buzz: Libraries and Word-of-Mouth Marketing. By Peggy Barber and Linda Wallace. American Library Association, 2010.

Crash Course in Dealing with Difficult Library Customers. By Shelley Mosley, Dennis C. Tucker, and Sandra Van Winkle. Libraries Unlimited, 2014.

DIY Programming and Book Displays: How to Stretch Your Programming Without Stretching Your Budget and Staff. By Amanda Moss Struckmeyer and Svetha Hetzler. Libraries Unlimited, 2010.

Face2Face Using Facebook, Twitter, and Other Social Media Tools to Create Great Customer Connections. By David Lee King. Information Today, Inc., 2012.

Listening to the Customer. By Peter Hernon and Joseph R. Matthews. Libraries Unlimited, 2011.

Marketing and Social Media: A Guide for Libraries, Archives, and Museums. By Christie Koontz, and Lorri M. Mon. Rowman & Littlefield, 2014.

Marketing Your Library: Tips and Tools That Work. Ed. by Carol Smallwood, Vera Gubnitskaia, and Kerol Harrod. McFarland, 2012.

The Mobile Marketing Handbook: A Step-by-Step Guide to Creating Dynamic Mobile Marketing Campaigns. 2nd ed. By Kim Dushinski. Information Today, Inc., 2012.

Start a Revolution: Stop Acting Like a Library. By Benn Bizzle and Maria Flora. ALA Editions, 2015.

Readers Advisory

Children's Literature in Action: A Librarian's Guide. 2nd ed. By Sylvia M. Vardell. Libraries Unlimited, 2014.

Diversity in Youth Literature: Opening Doors Through Reading. By Jamie Campbell Naidoo and Sarah Park Dahlen. American Library Association, 2013.

The Mother of All Booklists: The 500 Most Recommended Nonfiction Reads for Ages 3 to 103. By William Patrick Martin. Rowman & Littlefield, 2014.

Outstanding Books for the College Bound: Titles and Programs for a New Generation. Ed. by Angela Carstensen. American Library Association, 2011.

The Reader's Advisory Handbook. Ed. by Jessica E. Moyer and Kaite Mediatore Stover. American Library Association, 2010.

Readers' Advisory Service for Children and 'Tweens. By Penny Peck. Libraries Unlimited, 2010.

Serving Boys Through Readers' Advisory. By Michael Sullivan. American Library Association, 2010.

The Slow Book Revolution: Creating a New Culture of Reading on College Campuses and Beyond. Ed. by Meagan Lacy. Libraries Unlimited, 2014.

Women's Fiction: A Guide to Popular Reading Interests. Rebecca Vnuk and Nanette Donohue. Libraries Unlimited, 2013.

Reference Services

Conducting the Reference Interview: A How-to-Do-It Manual for Librarians. 2nd ed. By Catherine Sheldrick Ross, Kristi Nilsen, and Marie L. Radford. Neal-Schuman, 2009.

Essential Reference Services For Today's School Media Specialists. 2nd ed. By Scott Lanning and John Bryner. Libraries Unlimited, 2010.

Fundamentals of Managing Reference Collections. By Carol A. Singer. ALA Editions, 2012.

Fundamentals of Reference. By Carolyn Mulac. American Library Association, 2012.

Guide to Reference. http://www.guidetoreference.org. American Library Association. Online database.

Implementing an Inclusive Staffing Model for Today's Reference Services: A Practical Guide for Librarians. By Julia K. Nims, Paula Storm, and Robert Stevens. Rowman & Littlefield, 2014.

Implementing Virtual Reference Services: A LITA Guide. Ed. by Beth C. Thomsett-Scott. ALA TechSource, 2013.

Interlibrary Loan Practices Handbook. 3rd ed. Ed. by Cheri L. Weible and Karen L. Janke. American Library Association, 2011.

Legal Reference for Librarians: How and Where to Find the Answers. By Paul D. Healey. ALA Editions, 2014.

The Librarian as Information Consultant: Transforming Reference for the Information Age. By Sarah Anne Murphy. American Library Association, 2011.

Reference and Information Services: An Introduction. 4th ed. Ed. by Richard E. Bopp and Linda C. Smith. Libraries Unlimited, 2011.

Reference Sources and Services for Youth. By Meghan Harper. Neal-Shuman, 2011.

Strauss's Handbook of Business Information: A Guide for Librarians, Students, and Researchers. 3rd ed. By Rita W. Moss and David G. Ernsthausen. Libraries Unlimited, 2012.

Training Paraprofessionals for Reference Service. By Pamela J. Morgan. Neal-Schuman, 2008.

Research and Statistics

Academic Library Trends and Statistics. Association of College and Research Libraries/American Library Association Annual. Print and online.

The ALA-APA Salary Survey 2012: Librarian—Public and Academic. ALA-Allied Professional Association. American Library Association, 2012. Print and online.

ARL Annual Salary Survey. Association of Research Libraries. Annual. Print and online.

ARL Statistics. Association of Research Libraries. Annual. Print and online.

Assessing Information Needs: Managing Transformative Library Services. By Robert J. Grover, Roger C. Greer, and John Agada. Libraries Unlimited, 2010.

Knowledge into Action: Research and Evaluation in Library and Information Science. By Danny P. Wallace and Connie Van Fleet. Libraries Unlimited, 2012.

PLAmetrics: a PLDS Online Database. Public Library Association/American Library Association. Online database.

Public Libraries in the United States Survey. Institute of Museum and Library Services. Annual. Online only. Free.

Research Methods in Information. 2nd ed. By Alison Jane Pickard and Susan Childs. Neal-Schuman, 2013.

School Libraries

Empowering Learners: Guidelines for School Library Programs. American Association of School Librarians, 2009.

Enhancing Teaching and Learning: A Leadership Guide for School Librarians. By Jean Donham. Neal-Schuman, 2013.

Guide for Developing and Evaluating School Library Programs. 7th ed. By Nebraska Educational Media Association. Libraries Unlimited, 2010.

Independent School Libraries: Perspectives on Excellence. Ed. by Dorcas Hand. Libraries Unlimited, 2010.

The School Library Manager. 5th ed. By Blanche Woolls, Ann C. Weeks, and Sharon Coatney. Libraries Unlimited, 2014.

The School Library Media Specialist's Policy and Procedure Writer. By Elizabeth Downs. Neal-Schuman, 2010.

Standards for the 21st-Century Learner. American Association of School Librarians, 2007.

Standards for the 21st-Century Learner in Action. American Association of School Librarians, 2009.

21st Century Learning in School Libraries: Putting the AASL Standards to Work. Ed. by Kristin Fontichiaro. Libraries Unlimited, 2009.

Technical Services

Electronics Resources Management in the Academic Library: A Professional Guide. By Karin Wikoff. Libraries Unlimited, 2012.

Integrated Library Systems: Planning, Selecting, and Implementing. By Desiree Webber and Andrew Peters. Libraries Unlimited, 2010.

Introduction to Technical Services. 8th ed. By C. Edward Evans, Sheila S. Intner, and Jean Weihs. Libraries Unlimited, 2011.

Library Automation: Core Concepts and Practical Systems Analysis. 3rd ed. By Dania Bilal. Libraries Unlimited, 2014.

Trends

Academic Libraries and Research Data Services Current Practices and Plans for the

Future; an ACRL White Paper. By Carol Tenopir, Ben Birch, and Suzie Allard. Association of College and Research Libraries, a division of the American Library Association, 2012.

Are Libraries Obsolete? An Argument for Relevance in the Digital Age. By Mark Y. Herring. McFarland, 2014.

Ecology, Economy, Equity: The Path to a Carbon-Neutral Library. Mandy Henk. ALA Editions, 2014.

Global Mobile: Applications and Innovations for the Worldwide Mobile Ecosystem. Ed. by Peter A. Bruck and Madanmohan Rao. Information Today, Inc., 2013.

Greening Libraries. Ed. by Monika Antonelli and Mark McCullough. Library Juice, 2012.

Growing Young Minds: How Museums and Libraries Create Lifelong Learners. Institute of Museum and Library Services, 2013. http://purl.fdlp.gov/GPO/gpo38726.

Library 2020: Today's Leading Visionaries Describe Tomorrow's Library. By Joseph Janes. Scarecrow, 2013.

Open Conversations: Public Learning in Libraries and Museums. By David Carr. Libraries Unlimited, 2011.

Reflecting on the Future of Academic and Public Libraries. Ed. by Peter Hernon and Joseph R Matthews. ALA Editions, 2013.

Reinventing the Library for Online Education. Frederick J. Stielow. ALA, 2014.

UContent: The Information Professional's Guide to User-Generated Content. By Nicholas G. Tomaiuolo. Information Today, Inc., 2012.

Without a Net: Librarians Bridging the Digital Divide. By Jessamyn C. West. Libraries Unlimited, 2011.

Periodicals

This listing of key library periodical publications includes ISSNs for print and online formats; in general, newsletters are not included. Titles have been verified against the EBSCO database as active periodicals.

Against the Grain (1043-2094)

American Archivist (print, 0360-9081; online, 2165-6274)

American Libraries (0002-9769)

American Libraries Direct (online, 1559-369X)

Ariadne (1361-3200)

Archival Science (print, 1389-0166; online, 1573-7519)

Art Documentation (print, 0730-7187; online, 2161-9417)

Behavioral and Social Sciences Librarian (print , 0163-9269; online, 1544-4546)

Booklist (0006-7385); *Booklist Online* (2163-5544)

Bottom Line: Managing Library Finances (print + online, 0888-045X; online, 2054-1724)

Cataloging and Classification Quarterly (print, 0163-9374; online, 1544-4554)

Catholic Library World (0008-820X)

Children and Libraries: The Journal of the Association for Library Service to Children (print + online, 1542-9806)

CHOICE: Current Reviews for Academic Libraries (print, 0009-4978; online, 1523-8253)

Code4Lib Journal (1940-5758)

Collection Building (print + online, 0160-4953; online 2054-5592)

Collection Management (print, 0146-2679; online, 1545-2549)

College & Research Libraries (online, 2150-6701)

Computers in Libraries (1041-7915)

D-Lib Magazine (1082-9873)

DttP: A Quarterly Journal of Government Information Practice & Perspective (0091-2085)

Electronic Library (print + online, 0264-0473; online, 1758-616X)

Electronic Journal of Knowledge Management (1479-4411)

First Monday (1396-0466)

Government Information Quarterly (0740-624X)

Horn Book Magazine (0018-5078)

IFLA Journal (print, 0340-0352; online, 1745-2651)

In the Library with the Lead Pipe (1944-6195)

Indexer (print, 0019-4131; online 1756-0632)

Information & Culture (print + online, 2164-8034; online, 2166-3033)

Information Outlook (print + online, 1091-0808; online, 1938-3819)

Information Research—An International Electronic Journal (1368-1613)

Information Standards Quarterly (print + online, 1041-0031; online, 2161-6205)

Information Technology and Libraries (online, 2163-5226)

Interlending & Document Supply (print + online, 0264-1615; online 1758-5848)

International Journal of Geographical Information Science (print 1365-8816; online 1362-3087)

Internet @ Schools (print 1546-4636; online 2156-843X)

Internet Reference Services Quarterly (print, 1087-5301; online, 1540-4749)

Issues in Science and Technology Librarianship (online, 1092-1206)

Journal of Academic Librarianship (0099-1333)

Journal of Documentation (print + online, 0022-0418; online, 1758-7379)

Journal of Education for Library and Information Science (0748-5786)

Journal of Electronic Resources Librarianship (print, 1941-126X; online, 1941-1278)

Journal of Information Ethics (print, 1061-9321; online, 1941-2894)

Journal of Information Science (print, 0165-5515; online, 1741-6485)

Journal of Interlibrary Loan, Document Delivery and Information Supply (print + online, 1072-303X

Journal of Librarianship & Information Science (print, 0961-0006; online, 1741-6477)

Journal of Library Administration (print, 0193-0826; online, 1540-3564)

Journal of Library Metadata (print, 1938-6389; online, 1937-5034)

Journal of Research on Libraries and Young Adults (2157-3980)

Journal of the American Society for Information Science and Technology (print, 2330-1635; online, (2330-1643)

Journal of Archival Organization (print, 1533-2748; online, 1533-2756)

Journal of the Medical Library Association (print, 1536-5050; online, 1558-9439)

Journal of Web Librarianship (print, 1932-2909; online, 1932-2917)

Knowledge Quest (1094-9046)

Law Library Journal (0023-9283)

Legal Reference Services Quarterly (print, 0270-319X; online, 1540-949X)

Library & Archival Security (print, 0196-0075; online, 1540-9511)

Library & Information Science Research (LIBRES) (0740-8188)

Library Collections Acquisitions & Technical Services (print, 1464-9055; online, 1873-1821)

Library Hi-Tech Journal (0737-8831)

Library Journal (0363-0277)

Library Leadership & Management (online, 1945-886X)

Library Management (print + online, 0143-5124; online, 1758-7921)

The Library Quarterly (print, 0024-2519; online, 1549-652X)

Library Resources & Technical Services, eLRTS (online, 2159-9610)

Library Technology Reports (print, 0024-2586; online, 1945-4538)

Library Trends (print, 0024-2594; online, 1559-0682)

Library Worklife: HR E-News for Today's Leaders (1550-3534)

Librarysparks (1544-9092)

New Review of Children's Literature and Librarianship (print, 1361-4541; online, 1740-7885)

News from the Library of Congress (1046-1663)

Newsletter on Intellectual Freedom (online, 1945-4546)

Notes (Music Library Association) (print, 0027-4380; online, 1534-150X)

Online Searcher (2324-9684)

portal: Libraries and the Academy (print, 1531-2542; online, 1530-7131)

Preservation Digital Technology & Culture (print, 2195-2957; online, 2195-2965)

Public Libraries (0163-5506; some content online at http://publiclibrariesonline.org)

Public Library Quarterly (print, 0161-6846; online, 1541-1540)

Publishing Research Quarterly (print, 1053-8801; online, 1936-4792)

RBM: A Journal of Rare Books, Manuscripts, and Cultural Heritage (print 1529-6407; online 2150-668X)

Reference & User Services Quarterly (online, 1094-9054)

Reference Librarian (print, 0276-3877; online, 1541-1117)

Reference Services Review (print + online, 0090-7324; online, 2054-1716)

Research Libraries Issues (1947-4911)
School Library Journal (0362-8930)
School Library Research (2165-1019)
The Scout Report (Online, 1092-3861)
Serials Librarian (print, 0361-526X; online, 1541-1095)
Serials Review (print, 0098-7913; online, 1879-095X)
State of America's Libraries Report (annual, online only)
Technical Services Quarterly (print, 0731-7131; online, 1555-3337)
Technicalities (0272-0884)
Theological Librarianship (1937-8904)
Voice of Youth Advocates (*VOYA*) (0160-4201)
Young Adult Library Services (1541-4302)

Blogs

(All sites checked March 3, 2015)

025.431: The Dewey Blog. Jonathan Furner, editor (http://ddc.typepad.com)
AASL Blog (http://www.aasl.ala.org/aaslblog)
ACRL Insider (http://acrl.ala.org/acrlinsider)
ACRLog (http://acrlog.org)
American Libraries: The Scoop (http://americanlibrariesmagazine.org/blogs)
ALSC Blog (http://www.alsc.ala.org/blog)
Annoyed Librarian (http://lj.libraryjournal.com/blogs/annoyedlibrarian)
AOTUS: Collector in Chief. By David Ferriero (http://blogs.archives.gov/aotus)
Archivesblogs: A syndicated collection of blogs by and for archivists (http://archivesblogs.com/category/eng)
ASCLA Blog (http://ascla.ala.org/blog)
Attempting Elegance. By Jennica Rogers (http://www.attemptingelegance.com)
Awful Library Books. By Holly Hibner and Mary Kelly (http://awfullibrarybooks.net)
Bibliographic Wilderness (http://bibwild. wordpress.com)
Blogging Censorship (http://ncac.org/blog)
Blue Skunk. By Doug Johnson (http://dougjohnson.squarespace.com)
The Booklist Reader (http://www.booklistreader.com)
Celeripedean. By Jennifer Eustis (http://celeripedean.wordpress.com)
Copyfight: the Politics of IP. By Donna Wentworth, Ernest Miller, Elizabeth Rader, Jason Schultz, Wendy Seltzer, Aaron Schwartz, and Adam Wexelblat (http://copyfight.corante.com)
Copyrightlaws.com. By Lesley Ellen Harris (http://www.copyrightlaws.com)
Deeplinks. From Electronic Frontier Foundation (https://www.eff.org/deeplinks)
Designing Better Libraries: Exploring the Application of Design, Innovation, and New Media to Create Better Libraries and User Experiences (http://dbl.lishost.org/blog)
The Digital Shift (http://www.thedigitalshift.com)
Digitization 101. By Jill Hurst-Wahl (http://hurstassociates.blogspot.com)
District Dispatch. By the ALA Washington Office (http://www.districtdispatch.org)
Early Word. By Nora Rawlinson (http://www.earlyword.com)
A Fuse #8 Production. By Elizabeth Bird (http://blog.schoollibraryjournal.com/afuse-8production)
Go to Hellman. By Eric Hellman (http://go-to-hellman.blogspot.com)
Hack Library School (http://hacklibraryschool.com)
Hangingtogether.org (http://hangingtogether.org)
Hey Jude. By Judy O'Connell (http://heyjude.wordpress.com)
The Hub: Your Connection to Teen Reads. By the Young Adult Library Services Association (http://www.yalsa.ala.org/thehub)
INFOdocket. By Gary Price and Shirl Kennedy (http://infodocket.com)
Information Wants to Be Free. By Meredith Farkas (http://meredith.wolfwater.com/wordpress).
John Battelle's Searchblog. (http://battellemedia.com)
The Krafty Librarian (http://kraftylibrarian.com)
Leads from LLAMA (http://www.llama.ala.org/llamaleads)
Librarian.net. By Jessamyn West (http://www.librarian.net)
LibrarianInBlack. By Sarah Houghton-Jan (http://librarianinblack.net/librarianinblack)
Library as Incubator Project. By Laura Damon-Moore, Erinn Batykefer, and Christina Endres (http://www.libraryasincubatorproject.org)

Library History Buff Blog. By Larry T. Nix (http://libraryhistorybuff.blogspot.com)

Library Juice. By Rory Litwin (http://libraryjuicepress.com/blog)

Library of Congress Blog (http://blogs.loc.gov/loc)

A Library Writer's Blog. By Corey Seeman (http://librarywriting.blogspot.com)

Librarycity (http://librarycity.org)

Law Librarians of Congress (http://blogs.loc.gov/law)

LIS News. By Blake Carver (http://lisnews.org)

LITA Blog (http://litablog.org)

The 'M' Word—Marketing in Libraries. By Kathy Dempsey (http://themwordblog.blogspot.com)

NeverEndingSearch. By Joyce Valenza (http://blogs.slj.com/neverendingsearch)

NMRT Notes (http://www.nmrt.ala.org/notes)

No Shelf Required. By Sue Polanka (http://www.libraries.wright.edu/noshelfrequired)

Office for Intellectual Freedom Blog (http://www.oif.ala.org/oif)

Pattern Recognition. By Jason Griffey (http://www.jasongriffey.net/wp)

Peer to Peer Review. By Barbara Fister (http://lj.libraryjournal.com/author/bfister)

Planet Cataloging (http://planetcataloging.org)

Preservation & Conservation Administration News (http://prescan.wordpress.com)

RA for All (http://raforall.blogspot.com)

RDA Toolkit Blog (http://www.rdatoolkit.org/blog)

Reader's Advisor Online (http://www.readersadvisoronline.com/blog)

RIPS Law Librarian (http://ripslawlibrarian.wordpress.com)

RUSA Blog (http://rusa.ala.org/blog)

SarahGlassmeyer(dot)com (http://sarahglassmeyer.com)

The Signal: Digital Preservation (http://blogs.loc.gov/digitalpreservation)

Swiss Army Librarian. By Brian Herzog (http://www.swissarmylibrarian.net)

Tame the Web: Libraries and Technology. By Michael Stephens (http://tametheweb.com)

Teen Librarian Toolbox. By Karen Jensen, Stephanie Wilkes, Christie Ross Gibrich, and Heather Booth (http://www.teenlibrariantoolbox.com)

Techsoup for libraries (http://www.techsoupforlibraries.org/blog)

TechSource Blog. By Jason Griffey, Tom Peters, Kate Sheehan, Michael Stephens, Cindi Trainor, Michelle Boule, and Richard Wallis (http://www.alatechsource.org/blog)

TeleRead: News and views on e-books, libraries, publishing and related topics (http://www.teleread.com)

The Unquiet Librarian (http://theunquietlibrarian.wordpress.com)

Walt at Random. By Walt Crawford (http://walt.lishost.org)

YALSA Blog (http://yalsa.ala.org/blog)

Ready Reference

How to Obtain an ISBN

Beat Barblan
United States ISBN/SAN Agency

The International Standard Book Numbering (ISBN) system was introduced into the United Kingdom by J. Whitaker & Sons Ltd. in 1967 and into the United States in 1968 by R. R. Bowker. The Technical Committee on Documentation of the International Organization for Standardization (ISO TC 46) is responsible for the international standard.

The purpose of this standard is to "establish the specifications for the International Standard Book Number (ISBN) as a unique international identification system for each product form or edition of a monographic publication published or produced by a specific publisher." The standard specifies the construction of an ISBN, the rules for assignment and use of an ISBN, and all metadata associated with the allocation of an ISBN.

Types of monographic publications to which an ISBN may be assigned include printed books and pamphlets (in various product formats); electronic publications (either on the Internet or on physical carriers such as CD-ROMs or diskettes); educational/instructional films, videos, and transparencies; educational/instructional software; audiobooks on cassette or CD or DVD; braille publications; and microform publications.

Serial publications, printed music, and musical sound recordings are excluded from the ISBN standard as they are covered by other identification systems.

The ISBN is used by publishers, distributors, wholesalers, bookstores, and libraries, among others, in 217 countries and territories as an ordering and inventory system. It expedites the collection of data on new and forthcoming editions of monographic publications for print and electronic directories used by the book trade. Its use also facilitates rights management and the monitoring of sales data for the publishing industry.

The "new" ISBN consists of 13 digits. As of January 1, 2007, a revision to the ISBN standard was implemented in an effort to substantially increase the numbering capacity. The 10-digit ISBN identifier (ISBN-10) is now replaced by the ISBN 13-digit identifier (ISBN-13). All facets of book publishing are now expected to use the ISBN-13, and the ISBN agencies throughout the world are now issuing only ISBN-13s to publishers. Publishers with existing ISBN-10s need to convert their ISBNs to ISBN-13s by the addition of the EAN prefix 978 and recalculation of the new check digit:

ISBN-10: 0-8352-8235-X
ISBN-13: 978-0-8352-8235-2

When the inventory of the ISBN-10s has been exhausted, the ISBN agencies will start assigning ISBN-13s with the "979" prefix instead of the "978." There is no 10-digit equivalent for 979 ISBNs.

Construction of an ISBN

An ISBN currently consists of 13 digits separated into the following parts:

1 A prefix of "978" for an ISBN-10 converted to an ISBN-13
2 Group or country identifier, which identifies a national or geographic grouping of publishers
3 Publisher identifier, which identifies a particular publisher within a group
4 Title identifier, which identifies a particular title or edition of a title
5 Check digit, the single digit at the end of the ISBN that validates the ISBN-13

For more information regarding ISBN-13 conversion services provided by the U.S. ISBN Agency at R. R. Bowker, LLC, visit the ISBN Agency Web site at http://www.isbn.org, or contact the U.S. ISBN Agency at isbn-san@bowker.com.

Publishers requiring their ISBNs to be converted from the ISBN-10 to ISBN-13 format can use the U.S. ISBN Agency's free ISBN-13 online converter at http://isbn.org/converterpub.asp. Publishers can also view their ISBNs online by accessing their personal account at http://www.myidentifiers.com.

Displaying the ISBN on a Product or Publication

When an ISBN is written or printed, it should be preceded by the letters ISBN, and each part should be separated by a space or hyphen. In the United States, the hyphen is used for separation, as in the following example: ISBN 978-0-8352-8235-2. In this example, 978 is the prefix that precedes the ISBN-13, 0 is the group identifier, 8352 is the publisher identifier, 8235 is the title identifier, and 2 is the check digit. The group of English-speaking countries, which includes the United States, Australia, Canada, New Zealand, and the United Kingdom, uses the group identifiers 0 and 1.

The ISBN Organization

The administration of the ISBN system is carried out at three levels—through the International ISBN Agency in the United Kingdom, through the national agencies, and through the publishing houses themselves. The International ISBN Agency, which is responsible for assigning country prefixes and for coordinating the worldwide implementation of the system, has an advisory panel that represents the International Organization for Standardization (ISO), publishers, and libraries. The International ISBN Agency publishes the *Publishers International ISBN Directory,* which is a listing of all national agencies' publishers with their assigned ISBN publisher prefixes. R. R. Bowker, as the publisher of *Books In Print* with its extensive and varied database of publishers' addresses, was the obvious place to initiate the ISBN system and to provide the service to the U.S. publishing industry. To date, the U.S. ISBN Agency has entered more than 180,000 publishers into the system.

ISBN Assignment Procedure

Assignment of ISBNs is a shared endeavor between the U.S. ISBN Agency and the publisher. Publishers can apply online through the ISBN Agency's website www.myidentifiers.com. Once the order is processed, an e-mail confirmation will be sent with instructions for managing the account. The publisher then has the responsibility to assign an ISBN to each title, keep an accurate record of each number assigned, and register each title in the *Books In Print* database at www.myidentifiers.com. It is the responsibility of the ISBN Agency to validate assigned ISBNs and keep a record of all ISBN publisher prefixes in circulation.

ISBN implementation is very much market-driven. Major distributors, wholesalers, retailers, and so forth recognize the necessity of the ISBN system and request that publishers register with the ISBN Agency. Also, the ISBN is a mandatory bibliographic element in the International Standard Bibliographical Description (ISBD). The Library of Congress Cataloging in Publication (CIP) Division directs publishers to the agency to obtain their ISBN prefixes.

Location and Display of the ISBN

On books, pamphlets, and other printed material, the ISBN shall be printed on the verso of the title leaf or, if this is not possible, at the foot of the title leaf itself. It should also appear on the outside back cover or on the back of the jacket if the book has one (the lower right-hand corner is recommended). The ISBN shall also appear on any accompanying promotional materials following the provisions for location according to the format of the material.

On other monographic publications, the ISBN shall appear on the title or credit frames and any labels permanently affixed to the publication. If the publication is issued in a container that is an integral part of the publication, the ISBN shall be displayed on the label. If it is not possible to place the ISBN on the item or its label, then the number should be displayed on the bottom or the back of the container, box, sleeve, or frame. It should also appear on any accompanying material, including each component of a multi-type publication.

Printing of ISBN in Machine-Readable Coding

All books should carry ISBNs in the EAN-13 bar code machine-readable format. All ISBN EAN-13 bar codes start with the EAN prefix 978 for books. As of January 1, 2007, all EAN bar codes should have the ISBN-13 appearing immediately above the bar code in eye-readable format, preceded by the acronym "ISBN." The recommended location of the EAN-13 bar code for books is in the lower right-hand corner of the back cover (see Figure 1).

Figure 1 / Printing the ISBN in Bookland/EAN Symbology

Five-Digit Add-On Code

In the United States, a five-digit add-on code is used for additional information. In the publishing industry, this code is used for price information. The lead digit of the five-digit add-on has been designated a currency identifier, when the add-on is used for price. Number 5 is the code for the U.S. dollar, 6 denotes the Canadian dollar, 1 the British pound, 3 the Australian dollar, and 4 the New Zealand dollar. Publishers that do not want to indicate price in the add-on should print the code 90000 (see Figure 2).

Figure 2 / Printing the ISBN Bookland/EAN Number in Bar Code with the Five-Digit Add-On Code

978 = ISBN Bookland/EAN prefix   90000 means no information
5 = Code for U.S. $ in the add-on code
2499 = $24.99

Reporting the Title and the ISBN

After the publisher reports a title to the ISBN Agency, the number is validated and the title is listed in the many R. R. Bowker hard-copy and electronic publications, including *Books in Print; Forthcoming Books; Paperbound Books in Print; Books in Print Supplement; Books Out of Print; Books in Print Online; Books in Print Plus-CD ROM; Children's Books in Print; Subject Guide to Children's Books in Print; Books Out Loud: Bowker's Guide to AudioBooks; Bowker's Complete Video Directory; Software Encyclopedia; Software for Schools;* and other specialized publications.

For an ISBN application and information, visit the ISBN Agency website at www.myidentifiers.com, call the toll-free number 877-310-7333, fax 908-795-3515, or write to the United States ISBN Agency, 630 Central Ave., New Providence, NJ 07974.

The ISSN, and How to Obtain One

U.S. ISSN Center
Library of Congress

In the early 1970s the rapid increase in the production and dissemination of information and an intensified desire to exchange information about serials in computerized form among different systems and organizations made it increasingly clear that a means to identify serial publications at an international level was needed. The International Standard Serial Number (ISSN) was developed and became the internationally accepted code for identifying serial publications.

The ISSN is an international standard, ISO 3297: 2007, as well as a U.S. standard, ANSI/NISO Z39.9. The 2007 edition of ISO 3297 expands the scope of the ISSN to cover continuing resources (serials, as well as updating databases, looseleafs, and some websites).

The number itself has no significance other than as a brief, unique, and unambiguous identifier. The ISSN consists of eight digits in Arabic numerals 0 to 9, except for the last ("check") digit, which can be an X. The numbers appear as two groups of four digits separated by a hyphen and preceded by the letters ISSN—for example, ISSN 1234-5679.

The ISSN is not self-assigned by publishers. Administration of the ISSN is coordinated through the ISSN Network, an intergovernmental organization within the UNESCO/UNISIST program. The ISSN Network consists of national ISSN centers, coordinated by the ISSN International Centre, located in Paris. National ISSN Centers are responsible for registering serials published in their respective countries. Responsibility for the assignment of ISSN to titles from multinational publishers is allocated among the ISSN Centers in which the publisher has offices. A list of these publishers and the corresponding ISSN centers is located on the ISSN International Centre's website, http://www.issn.org.

The ISSN International Centre handles ISSN assignments for international organizations and for countries that do not have a national center. It also maintains and distributes the ISSN Register and makes it available in a variety of products, most commonly via the ISSN Portal, an online subscription database. The ISSN Register is also available via Z39.50 access, and as a data file. Selected ISSN data can also be obtained in customized files or database extracts that can be used, for example, to check the accuracy or completeness of a requestor's list of titles and ISSN. Another available ISSN service is OAI-PMH, a customizable "harvesting" protocol through which external applications can automatically and regularly gather new and updated metadata on a defined schedule. The ISSN Register contains bibliographic records corresponding to each ISSN assignment as reported by national ISSN centers. The database contains records for more than 1.7 million ISSNs.

The ISSN is used all over the world by serials publishers to identify their serials and to distinguish their titles from others that are the same or similar. It is used by subscription services and libraries to manage files for orders, claims, and back issues. It is used in automated check-in systems by libraries that wish to process receipts more quickly. Copyright centers use the ISSN as a means to collect and disseminate royalties. It is also used as an identification code by postal services and legal deposit services. The ISSN is included as a verification element in interlibrary lending activities and for union catalogs as a collocating device. In recent years, the ISSN has been incorporated into bar codes for optical recognition of serial publications and into the standards for the identification of issues and articles in serial publications. Other growing uses for the ISSN are in online systems where it can serve to connect catalog records or citations in abstracting and indexing databases with full-text journal content via OpenURL resolvers or reference linking services, and as an identifier and link in archives of electronic and print serials.

Because serials are generally known and cited by title, assignment of the ISSN is inseparably linked to the key title, a standardized form of the title derived from information in the serial issue. Only one ISSN can be assigned to a title in a particular medium. For titles issued in multiple media—e.g., print, online, CD-ROM—a separate ISSN is assigned to each medium version. If a major title change occurs or the medium changes, a new ISSN must be assigned. Centers responsible for assigning ISSNs also construct the key title and create an associated bibliographic record.

A significant new feature of the 2007 ISSN standard is the Linking ISSN (ISSN-L), a mechanism that enables collocation or linking among different media versions of a continuing resource. The Linking ISSN allows a unique designation (one of the existing ISSNs) to be applied to all media versions of a continuing resource while retaining the separate ISSN that pertains to each version. When an ISSN is functioning as a Linking ISSN, the eight digits of the base ISSN are prefixed with the designation "ISSN-L." The Linking ISSN facilitates search, retrieval, and delivery across all medium versions of a serial or other continuing resource for improved ISSN functionality in OpenURL linking, search engines, library catalogs, and knowledge bases. The 2007 standard also supports interoperability by specifying the use of ISSN and ISSN-L with other systems such as DOI, OpenURL, URN, and EAN bar codes. ISSN-L was implemented in the ISSN Register in 2008. To help ISSN users implement the ISSN-L in their databases, two free tables are available from the ISSN International Centre's home page: one lists each ISSN and its corresponding ISSN-L; the other lists each ISSN-L and its corresponding ISSNs.

In the United States, the U.S. ISSN Center at the Library of Congress is responsible for assigning and maintaining the ISSNs for all U.S. serial titles. Publishers wishing to have an ISSN assigned should download an application from the Center's website, and mail, e-mail, or fax the form to the U.S. ISSN Center. Assignment of the ISSN is free, and there is no charge for use of the ISSN.

To obtain an ISSN for a U.S. publication, or for more information about ISSN in the United States, libraries, publishers, and other ISSN users should visit the U.S. ISSN Center's website, http://www.loc.gov/issn, or contact the U.S. ISSN Center, U.S. Programs, Law, and Literature, Library of Congress, 101 Independence Ave. S.E., Washington, DC 20540-4284 (telephone 202-707-6452, fax 202-707-6333, e-mail issn@loc.gov).

For information about ISSN products and services, and for application procedures that non-U.S. parties should use to apply for an ISSN, visit the ISSN International Centre's website, http://www.issn.org, or contact the International Centre at 45 rue de Turbigo, 75003 Paris, France (telephone 33-1-44-88-22-20, fax 33-1-40-26-32-43, e-mail issnic@issn.org).

How to Obtain an SAN

Beat Barblan
United States ISBN/SAN Agency

SAN stands for Standard Address Number. The SAN system, an American National Standards Institute (ANSI) standard, assigns a unique identification number that is used to positively identify specific addresses of organizations in order to facilitate buying and selling transactions within the industry. It is recognized as the identification code for electronic communication within the industry.

For purposes of this standard, the book industry includes book publishers, book wholesalers, book distributors, book retailers, college bookstores, libraries, library binders, and serial vendors. Schools, school systems, technical institutes, and colleges and universities are not members of this industry, but are served by it and therefore included in the SAN system.

The purpose of the SAN is to ease communications among these organizations, of which there are several hundreds of thousands that engage in a large volume of separate transactions with one another. These transactions include purchases of books by book dealers, wholesalers, schools, colleges, and libraries from publishers and wholesalers; payments for all such purchases; and other communications between participants. The objective of this standard is to establish an identification code system by assigning each address within the industry a unique code to be used for positive identification for all book and serial buying and selling transactions.

Many organizations have similar names and multiple addresses, making identification of the correct contact point difficult and subject to error. In many cases, the physical movement of materials takes place between addresses that differ from the addresses to be used for the financial transactions. In such instances, there is ample opportunity for confusion and errors. Without identification by SAN, a complex record-keeping system would have to be instituted to avoid introducing errors. In addition, problems with the current numbering system—such as errors in billing, shipping, payments, and returns—are significantly reduced by using the SAN system. The SAN also eliminates one step in the order fulfillment process: the "look-up procedure" used to assign account numbers. Previously a store or library dealing with 50 different publishers was assigned a different account number by each of the suppliers. The SAN solved this problem. If a publisher prints its SAN on its stationery and ordering documents, vendors to whom it sends transactions do not have to look up the account number, but can proceed immediately to process orders by SAN.

Libraries are involved in many of the same transactions as book dealers, such as ordering and paying for books and charging and paying for various services to other libraries. Keeping records of transactions—whether these involve buying, selling, lending, or donations—entails operations suited to SAN use. SAN stationery speeds up order fulfillment and eliminate errors in shipping, billing, and crediting; this, in turn, means savings in both time and money.

History

Development of the Standard Address Number began in 1968 when Russell Reynolds, general manager of the National Association of College Stores (NACS), approached R. R. Bowker and suggested that a "Standard Account Number" system be implemented in the book industry. The first draft of a standard was prepared by an American National Standards Institute (ANSI) Committee Z39 subcommittee, which was co-chaired by Reynolds and Emery Koltay of Bowker. After Z39 members proposed changes, the current version of the standard was approved by NACS on December 17, 1979.

Format

The SAN consists of six digits plus a seventh *Modulus 11* check digit; a hyphen follows the third digit (XXX-XXXX) to facilitate transcription. The hyphen is to be used in print form, but need not be entered or retained in computer systems. Printed on documents, the Standard Address Number should be preceded by the identifier "SAN" to avoid confusion with other numerical codes (SAN XXXXXXX).

Check Digit Calculation

The check digit is based on *Modulus 11*, and can be derived as follows:

1. Write the digits of the basic number.   2 3 4 5 6 7
2. Write the constant weighting factors associated with each position by the basic number.   7 6 5 4 3 2
3. Multiply each digit by its associated weighting factor.   14 18 20 20 18 14
4. Add the products of the multiplications. $14 + 18 + 20 + 20 + 18 + 14 = 104$
5. Divide the sum by Modulus 11 to find the remainder. $104 \div 11 = 9$ plus a remainder of 5
6. Subtract the remainder from the Modulus 11 to generate the required check digit. If there is no remainder, generate a check digit of zero. If the check digit is 10, generate a check digit of X to represent 10, since the use of 10 would require an extra digit. $11 - 5 = 6$
7. Append the check digit to create the standard seven-digit Standard Address Number.   SAN 234-5676

SAN Assignment

R. R. Bowker accepted responsibility for being the central administrative agency for SAN, and in that capacity assigns SANs to identify uniquely the addresses of organizations. No SANs can be reassigned; in the event that an organization should cease to exist, for example, its SAN would cease to be in circulation entirely. If an organization using an SAN should move or change its name with no change in ownership, its SAN would remain the same, and only the name or address would be updated to reflect the change.

The SAN should be used in all transactions; it is recommended that the SAN be imprinted on stationery, letterheads, order and invoice forms, checks, and all other documents used in executing various book transactions. The SAN should always be printed on a separate line above the name and address of the organization, preferably in the upper left-hand corner of the stationery to avoid confusion with other numerical codes pertaining to the organization, such as telephone number, zip code, and the like.

SAN Functions

The SAN is strictly a Standard Address Number, becoming functional only in applications determined by the user; these may include activities such as purchasing, billing, shipping, receiving, paying, crediting, and refunding. It is the method used by Pubnet and PubEasy systems and is required in all electronic data interchange communications using the Book Industry Systems Advisory Committee (BISAC) EDI formats. Every department that has an independent function within an organization could have a SAN for its own identification.

For additional information or to make suggestions, write to ISBN/SAN Agency, R. R. Bowker, LLC, 630 Central Ave., New Providence, NJ 07974, call 877-310-7333, or fax 908-795-3515. The e-mail address is san@bowker.com. A SAN can be ordered online through the website www.myidentifiers.com, or an application can be requested by e-mail through san@bowker.com.

Distinguished Books

Notable Books of 2014

The Notable Books Council of the Reference and User Services Association, a division of the American Library Association, selected these titles for their significant contribution to the expansion of knowledge or for the pleasure they can provide to adult readers.

Fiction

Denfield, Rene. *The Enchanted* (Harper).

Doerr, Anthony. *All the Light We Cannot See* (Scribner).

Flanagan, Richard. *Narrow Road to the Deep North* (Knopf).

Harkaway, Nick. *Tigerman* (Knopf).

Lee, Chang-Rae. *On Such a Full Sea* (Riverhead).

McEwan, Ian. *The Children Act* (Nan A. Talese).

Mitchell, David. *The Bone Clocks* (Random).

Ness, Patrick. *The Crane Wife* (Penguin).

Powers, Richard. *Orfeo* (Norton).

Rash, Ron. *Something Rich and Strange: Selected Stories* (Ecco).

Toews, Miriam. *All My Puny Sorrows* (McSweeneys).

Nonfiction

Birmingham, Kevin. *The Most Dangerous Book: The Battle for James Joyce's 'Ulysses'* (Penguin).

Blum, Howard. *Dark Invasion: 1915 Germany's Secret War and the Hunt for the First Terrorist Cell in America* (Harper).

Bragg, Rick. *Jerry Lee Lewis: His Own Story* (Harper).

Eig, Jonathan. *The Birth of the Pill: How Four Crusaders Reinvented Sex and Launched a Revolution* (Norton).

Greenwald, Glenn. *No Place to Hide: Edward Snowden, the NSA, and the U.S. Surveillance State* (Holt).

Jager, Eric. *Blood Royal: A True Tale of Crime and Detection in Medieval Paris* (Little, Brown).

Kolbert, Elizabeth. *The Sixth Extinction: An Unnatural History* (Holt).

Lepore, Jill. *The Secret History of Wonder Woman* (Knopf).

Macy, Beth. *Factory Man* (Little, Brown).

Sides, Hampton. *In the Kingdom of Ice: The Grand and Terrible Polar Voyage of the USS Jeanette* (Doubleday).

Stark, Lizzie. *Pandora's DNA: Tracing the Breast Cancer Genes Through History, Science, and One Family Tree* (Chicago Review).

Stevenson, Bryan. *Just Mercy: A Story of Justice and Redemption* (Spiegel & Grau).

Poetry

Fairchild, B. H. *The Blue Buick: New and Selected Poems* (Norton).

Hirsch, Edward. *Gabriel: A Poem* (Knopf).

Best Fiction for Young Adults

Each year a committee of the Young Adult Library Services Association (YALSA), a division of the American Library Association, compiles a list of the best fiction appropriate for young adults ages 12 to 18. Selected on the basis of each book's proven or potential appeal and value to young adults, the titles span a variety of subjects as well as a broad range of reading levels.

Alexander, Kwame. *The Crossover* (Houghton).

Anderson, Laurie Halse. *The Impossible Knife of Memory* (Viking).

Bassoff, Leah, and Laura DeLuca. *Lost Girl Found* (Groundwood).

Brown, Rachel Manija, and Sherwood Smith. *Stranger* (Viking).

Carleson, J. C. *The Tyrant's Daughter* (Knopf).

Combs, Sarah. *Breakfast Served Anytime* (Candlewick).

Fine, Sarah. *Of Metal and Wishes* (Simon & Schuster).

Foley, Jessie Ann. *The Carnival at Bray* (Elephant Rock).

Fombelle, Timothée de. *Vango: Between Sky and Earth* (Candlewick).

Giles, Gail. *Girls Like Us* (Candlewick).

Green, Sally. *Half Bad* (Viking).

Griffin, Adele. *The Unfinished Life of Addison Stone* (Soho Teen).

Hattemer, Kate. *The Vigilante Poets of Selwyn Academy* (Knopf).

Herbach, Geoff. *Fat Boy vs. the Cheerleaders* (Sourcebooks).

Hosie, Donna. *The Devil's Intern* (Holiday).

Howe, Katherine. *Conversion* (Putnam).

Hubbard, Jenny. *And We Stay* (Delacorte).

Johnston, E. K. *The Story of Owen: Dragon Slayer of Trondheim* (Carolrhoda).

Kiely, Brendan. *The Gospel of Winter* (Simon & Schuster).

Kiernan, Celine. *Into the Grey* (Candlewick).

King, A. S. *Glory O'Brien's History of the Future* (Little, Brown).

Knudsen, Michelle. *Evil Librarian* (Candlewick).

Kuehn, Stephanie. *Complicit.* (St. Martin's/Griffin).

Kulper, Kendall. *Salt and Storm* (Little, Brown).

LaCour, Nina. *Everything Leads to You* (Dutton).

LaFevers, Robin. *Mortal Heart* (Harcourt).

Lockhart, E. *We Were Liars* (Delacorte).

Lu, Marie. *The Young Elites* (Putnam).

Maas, Sarah J. *Heir of Fire* (Bloomsbury).

Maciel, Amanda. *Tease* (HarperCollins).

Magoon, Kekla. *How It Went Down* (Holt).

Maguire, Gregory. *Egg & Spoon* (Candlewick).

Miller, Lauren. *Free to Fall* (HarperTeen).

Moracho, Cristina. *Althea & Oliver* (Viking).

Nelson, Jandy. *I'll Give You the Sun* (Dial).

Parsons, Mark Huntley. *Road Rash* (Knopf).

Pearson, Mary E. *The Kiss of Deception* (Holt).

Pratt, Non. *Trouble* (Simon & Schuster).

Quintero, Isabel. *Gabi, a Girl in Pieces* (Cinco Puntos).

Reynolds, Jason. *When I Was the Greatest* (Atheneum).

Ritter, William. *Jackaby* (Algonquin).

Rutkoski, Marie. *The Winner's Curse* (Farrar, Straus and Giroux).

Schrefer, Eliot. *Threatened* (Scholastic).

Sedgwick, Marcus. *She Is Not Invisible* (Roaring Brook).

Smith, Andrew. *Grasshopper Jungle* (Dutton).

Smith, Andrew. *100 Sideways Miles* (Simon & Schuster).

Spears, Kat. *Sway* (St. Martin's/Griffin).

Templeman, McCormick. *The Glass Casket* (Delacorte).

Tripp, Ben. *The Accidental Highwayman* (Tor).

Venkatraman, Padma. *A Time to Dance* (Penguin).

Vlahos, Len. *The Scar Boys* (Egmont).

Waller, Sharon Biggs. *A Mad, Wicked Folly* (Viking).

Walton, Leslye. *The Strange and Beautiful Sorrows of Ava Lavender* (Candlewick).

Westerfeld, Scott. *Afterworlds* (Simon & Schuster).

Whaley, John Corey. *Noggin* (Atheneum).

Wiles, Deborah. *Revolution* (Scholastic).

White, Kiersten, and Jim Di Bartolo, illustrator. *In the Shadows* (Scholastic).

Wood, Fiona. *Wildlife* (Little, Brown).

Quick Picks for Reluctant Young Adult Readers

The Young Adult Library Services Association, a division of the American Library Association, annually chooses a list of outstanding titles that will stimulate the interest of reluctant teen readers. This list is intended to attract teens who, for whatever reason, choose not to read.

The list includes fiction and nonfiction titles published from late 2013 through 2014.

Fiction

Alender, Katie. *Famous Last Words* (Scholastic).

Alender, Katie. *Marie Antoinette, Serial Killer* (Scholastic).

Alexander, Kwame. *The Crossover* (Houghton Mifflin Harcourt).

Armentrout, Jennifer L. *Don't Look Back* (Disney-Hyperion).

Belton, Claire. *I am Pusheen the Cat* (Simon & Schuster).

Bernard, Romily. *Find Me* (HarperCollins).

Blount, Patty. *Some Boys* (Sourcebooks).

Brown, Jennifer. *Torn Away* (Little, Brown).

Carroll, Emily. *Through the Woods* (Simon & Schuster).

Coates, Jan L. *Rocket Man* (Red Deer).

Cooner, Donna. *Can't Look Away* (Scholastic).

Demetrios, Heather. *Something Real* (Macmillan).

Deuker, Carl. *Swagger* (Houghton Mifflin Harcourt).

Doctorow, Cory, and Jen Wang. *In Real Life* (Roaring Brook).

Ewing, Lynne. *The Lure* (HarperCollins).

Fantaskey, Beth. *Buzz Kill* (Houghton Mifflin Harcourt).

Farizan, Sara. *Tell Me Again How A Crush Should Feel* (Workman).

Feutl, Rita. *Bike Thief* (Orca).

Giles, Lamar. *Fake ID* (HarperCollins).

Green, S. E. *Killer Instinct* (Simon & Schuster).

Higgins, M. G. *I'm Just Me* (Saddleback Educational).

Kang, Lydia. *Control* (Penguin).

Kuderick, Madeleine. *Kiss of Broken Glass* (HarperCollins).

Magoon, Kekla. *How it Went Down* (Macmillan).

Maihack, Mike. *Cleopatra in Space No. 1: Target Practice* (Scholastic).

Mathieu, Jennifer. *The Truth About Alice* (Roaring Brook).

Moore, Peter. *V Is For Villain* (Disney-Hyperion).

Northrop, Michael. *Surrounded by Sharks* (Scholastic).

Polak, Monique. *Straight Punch* (Orca).

Quintero, Isabel. *Gabi, A Girl in Pieces* (Cinco Puntos).

Sakugawa, Yumi. *I Think I Am in Friend-Love With You* (F+W Media).

Scott, Jerry, and Jim Borgman. *Zits: Shredded* (HarperCollins).

Sheff, Nic. *Schizo* (Penguin).

Sitomer, Alan Lawrence. *Caged Warrior* (Disney-Hyperion).

Smith, Jennifer E. *The Geography of You and Me* (Little, Brown).

Strohmeyer, Sarah. *The Secrets of Lily Graves* (HarperCollins).

Walters, Eric. *The Rule of Three: Fight for Power* (Farrar, Straus and Giroux).

Watkins, Steve. *Juvie* (Candlewick).

West, Kasie. *On the Fence* (HarperCollins).

Wilson, G. Willow, and Adrian Alphona, illustrator. *Ms. Marvel: No Normal* (Marvel).

Yang, Gene Luen, and Sonny Liew, illustrator. *The Shadow Hero* (Roaring Brook).

Zarr, Sara, and Tara Altebrando. *Roomies* (Little, Brown).

Nonfiction

Boyer, Crispin. *This Or That? The Wacky Book of Choices to Reveal the Hidden You* (National Geographic Children's Books).

Brown, Box. *Andre The Giant: Life and Legend* (Roaring Brook).

Burcaw, Shane. *Laughing at My Nightmare* (Roaring Brook).

Butcher, Christina. *Braids, Buns, and Twists! Step-by-Step Tutorials for 82 Fabulous Hairstyles* (Chronicle).

Capps, Tyler. *Cooking Comically: Recipes So Easy You'll Actually Make Them* (Penguin).

Carmindy. *Bloom: A Girl's Guide to Growing Up Gorgeous* (Penguin).

Coefield, Sasha. *DIY Braids: From Crowns to Fishtails, Easy, Step-by-Step Hair-Braiding.* (F+W Media/Adams Media).

Crockett, Alexandra. *Metal Cats* (power-House).

Dakota, Heather, and Ali Castro, illustrator. *Zombie Apocalypse Survival Guide* (Scholastic).

Enz, Tammy, and Agnieszka Biskup. *Batman Science: The Real-World Science Behind Batman's Gear* (Capstone).

Ganter, Chris. *Graffiti School: A Student Guide with Teacher's Manual* (Thames & Hudson).

Gownley, Jimmy. *The Dumbest Idea Ever!* (Scholastic).

Kidd, Chip. *Go: A Kidd's Guide to Graphic Design.* (Workman).

Knapp, Andrew. *Find Momo: A Photography Book.* (Quirk).

Latta, Sara, and G. E. Gallas, illustrator. *Scared Stiff: Everything You Need to Know About 50 Famous Phobias* (Zest).

Lee, Hannah. *Cool Nail Art: 30 Step-by-Step Designs to Rock Your Fingers and Toes.* (F+W Media).

Maletsky, Sophie. *Sticky Fingers: DIY Duct Tape Projects. Easy to Pick Up, Hard to Put Down.* (Zest).

McNeil, Legs, and Gillian McCain. *Dear Nobody: The True Diary of Mary Rose* (Sourcebooks).

McNeill, Suzanne. *Friendship Bracelets All Grown Up: Hemp, Floss, and Other Boho Chic Designs to Make* (Fox Chapel).

Prince, Liz. *Tomboy: A Graphic Memoir* (Zest).

Rivera, Mariano, and Wayne Coffey. *The Closer: Young Readers Edition.* (Little, Brown).

Shoket, Ann. *Seventeen Ultimate Guide to College: Everything You Need to Know to Walk Onto Campus and Own It!* (Perseus).

Stanton, Brandon. *Humans of New York* (St. Martin's).

Thomson, Ruth. *Photos Framed: A Fresh Look at the World's Most Memorable Photographs* (Candlewick).

Voltz, Stephen and Fritz Grobe. *How to Build a Hovercraft: Air Cannons, Magnet Motors, and 25 Other Amazing DIY Science Projects* (Chronicle).

What's Your Style? Series

Kenney, Karen Latchana. *Boho Fashion* (Lerner).

St. John, Amanda. *Edgy Fashion* (Lerner).

Kenney, Karen Latchana. *Hipster Fashion* (Lerner).

Kenney, Karen Latchana. *Preppy Fashion* (Lerner).

Watson, Stephanie. *Streetwear Fashion.* (Lerner).

Amazing Audiobooks for Young Adults

Each year a committee of the Young Adult Library Services Association, a division of the American Library Association, compiles a list of the best audiobooks for young adults ages 12 to 18. The titles are selected for their teen appeal and recording quality, and because they enhance the audience's appreciation of any written work on which the recordings may be based. While the list as a whole addresses the interests and needs of young adults, individual titles need not appeal to this entire age range but rather to parts of it.

Nonfiction

The Port Chicago 50: Disaster, Mutiny, and the Fight for Civil Rights by Steve Sheinkin, read by Dominic Hoffman. Listening Library, 3 hours and 50 minutes, 3 discs.

Thomas Jefferson: President and Philosopher by Jon Meacham, read by Edward Herrmann. Books on Tape, 4 hours and 56 minutes, 4 discs.

Fiction

ACID by Emma Pass, read by Fiona Hardingham with Nicholas Guy Smith and Suzan Crowley. Listening Library, 10 hours and 48 minutes, 9 discs.

Curtsies and Conspiracies by Gail Carriger, read by Moira Quick. Hachette Audio, 9 hours and 30 minutes, 8 discs.

Define Normal by Julie Anne Peters, read by Christine Lakin. Hachette, 5 hours and 30 minutes, digital download.

Divided We Fall by Trent Reedy, read by Andrew Eiden. Scholastic Audio, 10 hours and 43 minutes, digital download.

Dreams of Gods and Monsters by Laini Taylor, read by Khristine Hvam. Hachette Audio, 18 hours, 14 discs.

Fat Boy vs. the Cheerleaders by Geoff Herbach, read by Nick Podehl. Brilliance Audio, 5 hours and 49 minutes, 1 MP3 disc.

Five, Six, Seven, Nate! by Tim Federle, read by the author. Simon & Schuster, 7 hours, 6 discs.

Glory O'Brien's History of the Future by A. S. King, read by Christine Lakin. Hachette Audio, 7 hours and 5 minutes, digital download.

Half Bad by Sally Green, read by Carl Prekopp. Recorded Books, 8 hours and 30 minutes, 7 discs.

Hollow City by Ransom Riggs, read by Kirby Heyborne. Blackstone Audio, 11 hours and 30 minutes, 10 discs.

The Impossible Knife of Memory by Laurie Halse Anderson, read by Julia Whelan and Luke Daniels. Brilliance Audio, 9 hours, 8 discs.

Jackaby by William Ritter, read by Nicola Barber. HighBridge Audio, 7 hours and 30 minutes, 6 discs.

The Killing Woods by Lucy Christopher, read by Fiona Hardingham and Shaun Grindell. Blackstone Audio, 9 hours and 30 minutes, 8 discs.

Love Letters to the Dead by Ava Dellaira, read by Julia Whelan. Brilliance Audio, 8 hours and 30 minutes, 1 MP3 disc.

Noggin by John Corey Whaley, read by Kirby Heyborne. Simon & Schuster, 8 hours and 30 minutes, 7 discs.

Raging Star by Moira Young, read by Heather Lind. Simon & Schuster, 11 hours, 10 discs.

Rebel Belle by Rachel Hawkins, read by Amy Rubinate. Dreamscape, 9 hours and 24 minutes, 8 discs.

Revolution by Deborah Wiles, read by Stacey Aswad and Francois Battiste with J. D. Jackson and Robin Miles. Listening Library, 12 hours and 10 minutes, 10 discs.

The Scandalous Sisterhood of Prickwillow Place by Julie Berry, read by Jayne Entwistle. Listening Library, 9 hours and 24 minutes, 8 discs.

The Shadows by Megan Chance, read by Karen Peakes. Brilliance Audio, 9 hours and 28 minutes, 1 MP3 disc.

Skink—No Surrender by Carl Hiaasen, read by Kirby Heyborne. Listening Library, 7 hours and 50 minutes, 7 discs.

Sway by Kat Spears, read by Nick Podehl. Brilliance Audio, 6 hours and 56 minutes, 1 MP3 disc.

We Were Liars by E. Lockhart, read by Ariadne Meyers. Listening Library, 6 hours and 30 minutes, 5 discs.

When I Was the Greatest by Jason Reynolds, read by J. B. Adkins. Listening Library, 6 hours and 3 minutes, 5 discs.

The Whispering Skull by Jonathan Stroud, read by Katie Lyons. Listening Library, 11 hours and 37 minutes, 9 discs.

White Space by Ilsa J. Bick, read by Kathleen McInerney. Brilliance Audio, 15 hours and 47 minutes, 2 MP3 discs.

William Shakespeare's Star Wars Collection by Ian Doescher, read by Danny Davis, Jonathan Davis, Ian Doescher, Jeff Gurner, January LaVoy, and Marc Thompson. Random House Audio, 10 hours and 30 minutes, 15 discs.

The Reading List

Established in 2007 by the Reference and User Services Association (RUSA), a division of the American Library Association, this list highlights outstanding genre fiction that merits special attention by general adult readers and the librarians who work with them.

RUSA's Reading List Council, which consists of 12 librarians who are experts in readers' advisory and collection development, selects books in eight categories: Adrenaline (suspense, thrillers, and action adventure), Fantasy, Historical Fiction, Horror, Mystery, Romance, Science Fiction, and Women's Fiction.

Adrenaline

Broken Monsters by Lauren Beukes (Mulholland).

Fantasy

The Goblin Emperor by Katherine Addison (Tor).

Historical Fiction

Bitter Greens by Kate Forsyth (Thomas Dunne).

Horror

The Lesser Dead by Christopher Buehlman (Penguin).

Mystery

Murder at the Brightwell by Ashley Weaver (Minotaur).

Romance

A Bollywood Affair by Sonali Dev (Kensington).

Science Fiction

The Martian by Andy Weir (Crown).

Women's Fiction

My Real Children by Jo Walton (Tor).

The Listen List

Established in 2010 by the Reference and User Services Association (RUSA), the Listen List highlights outstanding audiobooks that merit special attention by general adult listeners and the librarians who work with them.

They are chosen by RUSA's Listen List Council, which annually selects a list of 12 titles that may include fiction, nonfiction, poetry, and plays. To be eligible, titles must be available for purchase and circulation by libraries. An annotated version of the list on the RUSA website includes more information on each choice.

The Bees by Laline Paull, narrated by Orlagh Cassidy. Blackstone Audio/HarperAudio.

Furious Cool: Richard Pryor and the World That Made Him by David Henry and Joe Henry, narrated by Dion Graham. Tantor Media.

The Home Place by Carrie La Seur, narrated by Andrus Nichols. Blackstone Audio/HarperAudio.

The Invention of Wings by Sue Monk Kidd, narrated by Jenna Lamia and Adepero Oduye. Penguin Audio/Recorded Books.

Lord of Scoundrels by Loretta Chase, narrated by Kate Reading. Blackstone Audio.

The Martian by Andy Weir, narrated by R. C. Bray. Podium Publishing.

Moonraker by Ian Fleming, narrated by Bill Nighy. Blackstone Audio.

The Moonstone by Wilkie Collins, narrated by Ronald Pickup, Joe Marsh, Fenella Woolgar, Sam Dale, Jonathan Oliver, Jamie Parker, Sean Barrett, David Timson, John Foley, and Benjamin Soames. Naxos AudioBooks.

Queen of the Tearling by Erika Johansen, narrated by Katherine Kellgren. Blackstone Audio.

The Silkworm by Robert Galbraith, narrated by Robert Glenister. Blackstone Audio/Hachette Audio.

Station Eleven by Emily St. John Mandel, narrated by Kirsten Potter. Books on Tape/Random House Audio.

The Things They Carried by Tim O'Brien, narrated by Bryan Cranston. Brilliance Audio.

Alex Awards

The Alex Awards are given to ten books written for adults that have special appeal to young adults ages 12 through 18. The winning titles are selected by a committee of the Young Adult Library Services Association (YALSA), a division of the American Library Association, from among the previous year's publishing. The award is sponsored by the Margaret A. Edwards Trust.

Doerr, Anthony. *All the Light We Cannot See* (Scribner).

Darnielle, John. *Wolf in White Van* (Farrar, Straus and Giroux).

Ebrahim, Zak, and Jeff Giles. *The Terrorist's Son: A Story of Choice* (Simon & Schuster).

Koryta, Michael. *Those Who Wish Me Dead* (Little, Brown).

Levine, James A. *Bingo's Run* (Spiegel & Grau).

Minato, Kanae, and Stephen Snyder, translator. *Confessions* (Mulholland).

Ng, Celeste. *Everything I Never Told You* (Penguin).

Racculia, Kate. *Bellweather Rhapsody* (Houghton Mifflin Harcourt).

Scalzi, John. *Lock In* (Tor).

Weir, Andy. *The Martian* (Crown).

Outstanding International Books, 2014

The United States Board on Books for Young People (USBBY), the U.S. national section of the International Board on Books for Young People (IBBY), compiles an annual list of outstanding books originating outside the United States that represent the best in children's literature from around the world.

Grades Pre-K–2

Arnaldo, Monica. *Arto's Big Move,* illustrated by the author (Owlkids).

Camcam, Princesse. *Fox's Garden,* illustrated by the author (Enchanted Lion).

Davies, Nicola. *The Promise,* illustrated by Laura Carlin (Candlewick).

Dubuc, Marianne. *The Lion and the Bird,* illustrated by the author (Enchanted Lion).

Haughton, Chris. *Shh! We Have a Plan,* illustrated by the author (Candlewick).

Kalluck, Celina. *Sweetest Kulu,* illustrated by Alexandria Neonakis (Inhabit).

Lagercranta, Rose. *My Heart Is Laughing,* illustrated by Eva Eriksson (Gecko).

Luxbacher, Irene. *Mr. Frank,* illustrated by the author (Groundwood).

Uegaki, Chieri. *Hana Hashimoto, Sixth Violin,* illustrated by Qin Leng (Kids Can).

Vallat, Christelle. *Celia,* illustrated by Stéphanie Augusseau (Peter Pauper).

Van Hout, Mies. *Surprise,* illustrated by the author (Lemniscaat).

Grades 3–5

Adderson, Caroline. *Norman, Speak!* illustrated by Qin Leng (Groundwood).

Cole, Tom Clohosy. *Wall,* illustrated by the author (Candlewick/Templar).

Grill, William. *Shackleton's Journey,* illustrated by the author (Nobrow/Flying Eye).

Hold, Stian. *Anna's Heaven,* illustrated by the author (Eerdmans).

Jordan-Fenton, Christy, and Margaret Pokiak Fenton. *Not My Girl,* illustrated by Gabrielle Grimard (Annick).

Kuhlmann, Torben. *Lindbergh: The Tale of a Flying Mouse,* illustrated by the author (NorthSouth).

Landmann, Bimba. *In Search of the Little Prince: The Story of Antoine de Saint-Exupéry,* illustrated by the author (Eerdmans).

Millard, Glenda. *Once a Shepherd,* illustrated by Phil Lesnie (Candlewick).

Schmidt, Annie M. G. *A Pond Full of Ink,* illustrated by Sieb Posthuma (Eerdmans).

Smith, David J. *If . . . A Mind-Bending New Way of Looking at Big Ideas and Numbers,* illustrated by Steve Adams (Kids Can).

Tan, Shaun. *Rules of Summer,* illustrated by the author (Scholastic).

Van Leeuwen, Joke. *The Day My Father Became a Bush,* illustrated by the author (Gecko).

Walser, David, reteller. *The Glass Mountain: Tales from Poland,* illustrated by Jan Pienkowski (Candlewick).

Walters, Eric. *Hope Springs,* illustrated by Eugenie Fernandes (Tundra).

Grades 6–8

Abirached, Zeina. *I Remember Beirut,* illustrated by the author (Lerner).

Bassoff, Leah, and Laura DeLuca. *Lost Girl Found* (Groundwood).

Boyne, John. *Stay Where You Are and Then Leave,* illustrated by Oliver Jeffers (Holt).

Das, Amrita. *Hope Is a Girl Selling Fruit,* illustrated by the author (Tara).

Dillon, Patrick. *The Story of Buildings: From the Pyramids to the Sydney Opera House and Beyond,* illustrated by Stephen Biesty (Candlewick).

French, Simon. *My Cousin's Keeper* (Candlewick).

Mateo, José Manuel. *Migrant: The Journey of a Mexican Worker,* illustrated by Javier Martinez Pedro (Abrams).

McKay, Sharon E. *The End of the Line* (Annick).

Prins, Marcel; and Peter Henk Steenhuis. *Hidden Like Anne Frank: Fourteen True Stories of Survival.* (Scholastic).

Ramstein, Anne-Margot, and Matthias Arégui. *Before After,* illustrated by the authors (Candlewick).

Shyam, Bhajju, with Gita Wolf and Sirish Rao. *The London Jungle Book,* illustrated by the author (Tara).

Grades 9–12

Bass, Karen. *Graffiti Knight* (Pajama).

Charleyboy, Lisa, and Mary Beth Leatherdale, eds. *Dreaming in Indian: Contemporary Native American Voices* (Annick).

Maier, Corinne. *Marx: An Illustrated Biography,* illustrated by Anne Simon (Nobrow).

Sarn, Amelie. *I Love I Hate I Miss My Sister* (Random).

Shraya, Vivek. *God Loves Hair,* illustrated by Juliana Neufeld (Arsenal Pulp).

Zail, Suzy. *Playing for the Commandant* (Candlewick).

Notable Children's Videos

These DVD titles are selected by a committee of the Association for Library Service to Children, a division of the American Library Association. Recommendations are based on originality, creativity, and suitability for children.

Brave Girl: Clara and the Shirtwaist Makers' Strike of 1909. Dreamscape Media, 9 minutes. Ages 5–9.

The Duckling Gets a Cookie!? Weston Woods, 7 minutes. Ages 3–8.

Each Kindness. Weston Woods, 8 minutes. Ages 5–8.

Exclamation Mark. Weston Woods, 6 minutes. Ages 4–8.

Extra Yarn. Weston Woods, 7 minutes. Ages 4–8.

Getting Through It: Kids Talk about Divorce. Human Relations Media, 19 minutes. Ages 10–14.

Honey Badgers: Masters of Mayhem. PBS, 53 minutes. Ages 5 and up.

Locomotive. Dreamscape Media, 24 minutes. Ages 6–10.

Me and My Moulton. National Film Board of Canada, 14 minutes. Ages 6 and up.

Me . . . Jane. Weston Woods, 8 minutes. Ages 4–8.

A Nation's Hope: The Story of Boxing Legend Joe Lewis. Dreamscape Media, 10 minutes. Ages 6–10.

No Fish Where to Go. National Film Board of Canada, 12 minutes. Ages 8 and up.

One Cool Friend. Weston Woods, 12 minutes. Ages 4–8.

This Is Not My Hat. Weston Woods, 5 minutes. Ages 4–8.

You Are In Charge of Your Body: A Sexual Abuse Prevention Curriculum. Human Relations Media, 34 minutes. Ages 10–14.

Notable Recordings for Children

This list of notable CD recordings for children was selected by the Association for Library Service to Children, a division of the American Library Association. Recommended titles are chosen by children's librarians and educators on the basis of their originality, creativity, and suitability.

Angus and Sadie. Listening Library. Ages 5–9. The story of two border collie pups growing up on a farm in Maine is read by Wendy Carter.

Betty Bunny Didn't Do It. Live Oak Media, book and CD. Ages 3–6. Katherine Kellgren tells of how Betty Bunny learns the importance of being honest.

The Boundless. Brilliance Audio. Ages 9–14. Nick Podehl narrates this steam punk adventure involving the longest train in the world.

Brown Girl Dreaming. Listening Library. Ages 9 and up. Award-winning author Jacqueline Woodson reads from her verse memoir about growing up in South Carolina and New York.

Deep in the Swamp. Live Oak Media, book and CD. Ages 3–8. In story and song, Tom Chapin explores the creatures and plant life of a swamp.

The Duckling Gets a Cookie!? Weston Woods, book and CD. Ages 3–8. Mo Willems and his daughter dramatize a humorous exchange between Pigeon and Duckling.

Egg & Spoon. Candlewick on Brilliance Audio. Ages 12 and up. Colorful characters including Baba Yaga star in this historical fantasy set in Tsarist Russia, voiced by Michael Page.

Exclamation Mark. Weston Woods, book and CD. Ages 5–9. The tale of a lonely exclamation mark who learns to appreciate his own strengths.

The Family Romanov: Murder, Rebellion and the Fall of Imperial Russia. Listening Library. Ages 12 and up. The story of the reign and downfall of the Romanov family.

Five, Six, Seven, Nate! Simon & Schuster Audio. Ages 10 and up. Author Tim Federle takes listeners backstage as Nate Foster prepares for his Broadway debut.

H.O.R.S.E.: A Game of Imagination and Basketball. Live Oak Media, book and CD. Ages 6 and up. Christopher Myers and Dion

Graham narrate a game of one-upmanship on the basketball court.

Ice Whale. Recorded Books. Ages 10 and up. The sights and sounds of the Arctic world fill this story of a Yup'ik family and a bowhead whale whose lives are intertwined for many generations.

If I Ever Get Out of Here. Listening Library. Ages 12 and up. Author Eric Gansworth infuses humor into the painful seventh-grade year of a bright, Beatles-loving Tuscarora boy.

In a Heartbeat. Laura Doherty. Ages 2–6. Children will sing along with Doherty's mix of upbeat and calming songs in a variety of musical styles.

Josephine: The Dazzling Life of Josephine Baker. Recorded Books, book and CD. Ages 8 and up. Lizan Mitchell portrays the ups and downs of entertainer Josephine Baker's life with passion and depth.

The Key That Swallowed Joey Pigza. Listening Library. Ages 10–14. Author Jack Gantos brings Joey Pigza's saga full circle as Joey attempts to put things right for both himself and his baby brother.

The Madman of Piney Woods. Listening Library. Ages 10–14. J. D. Jackson and Kirby Heyborne tell the story of two boys, one the descendant of slaves and the other of Irish immigrants, in this companion story to *Elijah of Buxton.*

The Misadventures of the Family Fletcher. Listening Library. Ages 8–12. The Fletcher family's "misadventures" are brought to life through the humorous narration of Dan Woren.

One Cool Friend. Weston Woods, book and CD. Ages 4–8. Jazzy music and a trio of narrators dramatize the escapades of Proper Elliot, his eccentric father, and their newly acquired penguin.

Ophelia and the Marvelous Boy. Listening Library. Ages 8–12. Jayne Entwistle's narration highlights both the drama and the pathos in this adaptation of the Hans Christian Andersen tale *The Snow Queen.*

Percy Jackson's Greek Gods. Listening Library. Ages 10 and up. Jesse Bernstein brings out the humor and irreverence in this retelling of the stories of the Greek gods.

Rain Reign. Brilliance Audio. Ages 9–12. Laura Hamilton narrates the story of an 11-year-old girl with autism.

Revolution. Listening Library. Ages 10 and up. A full-cast audio collage of documentary materials provides the background for two young people's experiences during the "Freedom Summer" of 1964.

The Scandalous Sisterhood of Prickwillow Place. Listening Library. Ages 11 and up. Jayne Entwistle creates distinct personalities for each character in this farcical Victorian murder mystery.

A Snicker of Magic. Scholastic Audiobooks. Ages 8–12. Natural-born poet Felicity Pickle (voiced by Cassandra Morris) rallies the townsfolk to bring the magic back to Midnight Gulch.

Through the Woods: An Appalachian Adventure. Okee Dokee Music, CD and DVD. All ages. The Okee Dokee Brothers and a host of folk musicians take listeners on an adventure in a toe-tapping album of mountain music.

Under the Freedom Tree. Recorded Books, book and CD. Ages 6 and up. With a reading featuring all the gravitas that the subject deserves, Myra Lucretia Taylor tells the story of an important episode in the Civil War.

Winterfrost. Candlewick on Brilliance Audio. Ages 7–12. Amy McFadden narrates the Christmastime story set in Denmark of how Bettina must retrieve her baby sister from a spiteful nisse.

Notable Children's Books

A list of notable children's books is selected each year by the Notable Children's Books Committee of the Association for Library Service to Children, a division of the American Library Association. Recommended titles are selected by children's librarians and educators based on originality, creativity, and suitability for children. [See "Literary Prizes, 2014" later in Part 5 for Caldecott, Newbery, and other award winners—*Ed.*]

Books for Younger Readers

The Adventures of Beekle: The Unimaginary Friend by Dan Santat, illustrated by the author (Little, Brown).

The Baby Tree by Sophie Blackall, illustrated by the author (Penguin/Nancy Paulsen).

Beautiful Moon: A Child's Prayer by Tonya Bolden, illustrated by Eric Velasquez (Abrams).

Blizzard by John Rocco, illustrated by the author (Disney-Hyperion).

A Boy and a Jaguar by Alan Rabinowitz, illustrated by CáTia Chien (Houghton Mifflin Harcourt).

The Chicken Squad: The First Misadventure by Doreen Cronin, illustrated by Kevin Cornell (Simon & Schuster).

A Dance Like Starlight: One Ballerina's Dream by Kristy Dempsey, illustrated by Floyd Cooper (Penguin).

Dory Fantasmagory by Abby Hanlon, illustrated by the author (Penguin/Dial).

Draw! by Raúl Colón, illustrated by the author (Simon & Schuster).

Early Bird by Toni Yuly, illustrated by the author (Feiwel and Friends).

The Farmer and the Clown by Marla Frazee, illustrated by the author (Simon & Schuster).

The Farmer's Away! Baa! Neigh! by Anne Vittur Kennedy, illustrated by the author (Candlewick).

Feathers: Not Just for Flying by Melissa Stewart, illustrated by Sarah S. Brannen (Charlesbridge).

Firebird by Misty Copeland, illustrated by Christopher Myers (Penguin).

Firefly July: A Year of Very Short Poems selected by Paul B. Janeczko, illustrated by Melissa Sweet (Candlewick).

Flashlight by Lizi Boyd, illustrated by the author (Chronicle).

Fox's Garden by Princesse Camcam, illustrated by the author (Enchanted Lion).

Froodle by Antoinette Portis, illustrated by the author (Roaring Brook).

Gaston by Kelly DiPucchio, illustrated by Christian Robinson (Simon & Schuster).

Green Is a Chile Pepper by Roseanne Greenfield Thong, iIllustrated by John Parra (Chronicle).

Handle with Care: An Unusual Butterfly Journey by Loree Griffin Burns, photographed by Ellen Harasimowicz (Millbrook/Lerner).

Have You Seen My Dragon? by Steve Light, illustrated by the author (Candlewick).

Hi, Koo! A Year of Seasons by Jon J. Muth, illustrated by the author (Scholastic).

The Iridescence of Birds: A Book about Henri Matisse by Patricia MacLachlan, illustrated by Hadley Hooper (Roaring Brook).

Little Melba and Her Big Trombone by Katheryn Russell-Brown, illustrated by Frank Morrison (Lee & Low).

Little Roja Riding Hood by Susan Middleton Elya, illustrated by Susan Guevara (Penguin).

Mama Built a Little Nest by Jennifer Ward, illustrated by Steve Jenkins (Simon & Schuster).

The Most Magnificent Thing by Ashley Spires, illustrated by the author (Kids Can).

Mr. Putter and Tabby Turn the Page by Cynthia Rylant, illustrated by Arthur Howard (Houghton Mifflin Harcourt).

My Teacher is a Monster! (No, I am Not) by Peter Brown, illustrated by the author (Little, Brown).

Nana in the City by Lauren Castillo, illustrated by the author (Clarion).

Naptime by Iris De Moüy, illustrated by the author, translated by Shelley Tanaka (Groundwood).

The Noisy Paint Box: The Colors and Sounds of Kandinsky's Abstract Art by Barb Rosenstock, illustrated by Mary Grandpré (Knopf).

The Pigeon Needs a Bath! by Mo Willems, illustrated by the author (Disney-Hyperion).

Queen Victoria's Bathing Machine by Gloria Whelan, illustrated by Nancy Carpenter (Simon & Schuster).

Sam and Dave Dig a Hole by Mac Barnett, illustrated by Jon Klassen (Candlewick).

Shh! We Have a Plan by Chris Haughton, illustrated by the author (Candlewick).

Star Stuff: Carl Sagan and the Mysteries of the Cosmos by Stephanie Roth Sisson, illustrated by the author (Roaring Brook).

Tap Tap Boom Boom by Elizabeth Bluemle, illustrated by G. Brian Karas (Candlewick).

Telephone by Mac Barnett, illustrated by Jen Corace (Chronicle).

Tiny Creatures: The World of Microbes by Nicola Davies, illustrated by Emily Sutton (Candlewick).

Viva Frida by Yuyi Morales, illustrated by the author (Roaring Brook).

Waiting Is Not Easy! by Mo Willems, illustrated by the author (Disney-Hyperion).

Water Rolls, Water Rises: El Agua Rueda, el Agua Sube by Pat Mora, illustrated by Meilo So, translated by Adriana Domínguez and Pat Mora (Lee & Low).

Weeds Find a Way by Cindy Jenson-Elliott, illustrated by Carolyn Fisher (Simon & Schuster).

Winter Bees and Other Poems of the Cold by Joyce Sidman, illustrated by Rick Allen (Houghton Mifflin Harcourt).

Work, An Occupational ABC by Kellen Hatanaka, illustrated by the author (House of Anansi).

You Are (Not) Small by Anna Kang, illustrated by Christopher Weyant (Two Lions).

Middle Readers

Absolutely Almost by Lisa Graff (Penguin/Philomel).

Arcady's Goal by Eugene Yelchin, illustrated by the author (Holt).

Angel Island: Gateway to Gold Mountain by Russell Freedman, Chinese poems translated by Evans Chan (Clarion).

Before After by Anne-Margot Ramstein and Matthias Arégui, illustrated by the authors (Candlewick).

Brown Girl Dreaming by Jacqueline Woodson (Penguin).

The Boundless by Kenneth Oppel (Simon & Schuster).

The Case of the Vanishing Little Brown Bats: A Scientific Mystery by Sandra Markle (Millbrook).

Chasing Cheetahs: The Race to Save Africa's Fastest Cats by Sy Montgomery, photographs by Nic Bishop (Houghton Mifflin Harcourt).

Dare the Wind: The Record-Breaking Voyage of Eleanor Prentiss and the Flying Cloud by Tracey Fern, illustrated by Emily Arnold McCully (Farrar, Straus and Giroux).

El Deafo by Cece Bell, color by David Lasky (Abrams/Amulet).

Eye to Eye: How Animals See the World by Steve Jenkins, illustrated by the author (Houghton Mifflin Harcourt).

The Fourteenth Goldfish by Jennifer L. Holm (Random).

Freedom Summer: The 1964 Struggle for Civil Rights in Mississippi by Susan Goldman Rubin (Holiday).

The Great Greene Heist by Varian Johnson (Scholastic).

Half a Chance by Cynthia Lord (Scholastic).

Harlem Hellfighters by J. Patrick Lewis, illustrated by Gary Kelley (Creative Editions).

Hello, I'm Johnny Cash by G. Neri, illustrated by A. G. Ford (Candlewick).

Hidden: A Child's Story of the Holocaust by Loïc Dauvillier, illustrated by Marc Lizano, color by Greg Salsedo, translated by Alexis Siegel (First Second).

Hope Is a Ferris Wheel by Robin Herrera (Abrams/Amulet).

I Lived on Butterfly Hill by Marjorie Agosín, illustrated by Lee White (Simon & Schuster).

Josephine: The Dazzling Life of Josephine Baker by Patricia Hruby Powell, illustrated by Christian Robinson (Chronicle).

Kinda Like Brothers by Coe Booth (Scholastic).

Lowriders in Space by Cathy Camper, illustrated by Raúl the Third (Chronicle).

The Luck Uglies by Paul Durham, illustrated by Pétur Antonsson (HarperCollins).

Mikis and the Donkey by Bibi Dumon Tak, illustrated by Philip Hopman, translated by Laura Watkinson (Eerdmans).

The Misadventures of the Family Fletcher by Dana Alison Levy (Random).

A Moose Boosh: A Few Choice Words about Food by Eric-Shabazz Larkin (Readers to Eaters).

Mysterious Patterns: Finding Fractals in Nature by Sarah C. Campbell, photographs by the author and Richard P. Campbell (Boyds Mills).

Neighborhood Sharks: Hunting with the Great Whites of California's Farallon Islands by Katherine Roy, illustrated by the author (Roaring Brook).

Nest by Esther Ehrlich (Random).

Once Upon an Alphabet by Oliver Jeffers, illustrated by the author (Penguin).

Rain Reign by Ann M. Martin (Feiwel and Friends).

The Red Pencil by Andrea Davis Pinkney, illustrated by Shane W. Evans (Little, Brown).

Separate Is Never Equal: Sylvia Mendez and Her Family's Fight for Desegregation by Duncan Tonatiuh, illustrated by the author (Abrams).

Sisters by Raina Telgemeier, illustrated by the author (Scholastic/Graphix).

A Snicker of Magic by Natalie Lloyd (Scholastic).

Three Bird Summer by Sara St. Antoine (Candlewick).

The Turtle of Oman by Naomi Shihab Nye (HarperCollins).

Under the Egg by Laura Marx Fitzgerald (Penguin/Dial).

West of the Moon by Margi Preus (Abrams).

The Whispering Town by Jennifer Elvgren, illustrated by Fabio Santomauro (Kar-Ben).

The Witch's Boy by Kelly Barnhill (Algonquin/Workman).

Older Readers

Because They Marched: The People's Campaign for Voting Rights That Changed America by Russell Freedman (Holiday House).

Caminar by Skila Brown (Candlewick).

The Crossover by Kwame Alexander (Houghton Mifflin Harcourt).

The Family Romanov: Murder, Rebellion and the Fall of Imperial Russia by Candace Fleming (Schwartz & Wade).

How I Discovered Poetry by Marilyn Nelson, illustrated by Hadley Hooper (Penguin/Dial).

The Night Gardener by Jonathan Auxier (Abrams).

Nine Open Arms by Benny Lindelauf, illustrated by Dasha Tolstikova, translated by John Nieuwenhuizen (Enchanted Lion).

The Port Chicago 50: Disaster, Mutiny, and the Fight for Civil Rights by Steve Sheinkin (Roaring Brook).

Portraits of Hispanic American Heroes by Juan Felipe Herrera, illustrated by Raúl Colón (Penguin/Dial).

Revolution: The Sixties Trilogy, Book Two by Deborah Wiles (Scholastic).

This One Summer by Mariko Tamaki, illustrated by Jillian Tamaki (First Second).

A Time to Dance by Padma Venkatraman (Penguin).

All Ages

The Right Word: Roget and His Thesaurus by Jen Bryant, illustrated by Melissa Sweet (Eerdmans).

The Scraps Book: Notes from a Colorful Life by Lois Ehlert, illustrated by the author (Simon & Schuster).

Take Away the A: An Alphabeast of a Book! by Michaël Escoffier, illustrated by Kris DiGiacomo (Enchanted Lion).

Bestsellers of 2014

Children's, YA Titles Lead List of Top Selling Books

Clare Swanson

News Editor, *Publishers Weekly*

Led by John Green's *The Fault in Our Stars,* the top of the 2014 print bestseller list was dominated by children's and young adult titles that sold more than 1 million copies. Green's novel, adapted into a film that premiered in June 2014, sold more than 1.8 million paperbacks last year, according to Nielsen BookScan, which tracks approximately 80 percent of print book sales.

The ninth book in Jeff Kinney's Diary of a Wimpy Kid series, *The Long Haul,* landed at No. 2, selling more than 1.5 million copies in 2014 (and in a relatively short period of time—the book went on sale November 4). Roughly 20 percent of *The Long Haul*'s total sales occurred in the first week, when the book moved nearly 320,000 units, the highest first-week sales of the year. The three books in Veronica Roth's wildly popular young adult Divergent trilogy, *Divergent* (1.4 million copies sold), *Insurgent* (1.3 million), and *Allegiant* (1.2 million), hit No. 3, No. 4, and No. 6, respectively.

In fact, according to Nielsen, the only adult title to sell more than 1 million print copies last year was *Killing Patton,* the fourth book in Bill O'Reilly and Martin Dugard's Killing series. The book, released September 23, sold 1.19 million copies, landing at No. 5. The book also topped the adult nonfiction list, followed by Sarah Young's *Jesus Calling,* which moved more than 700,000 copies in the year.

In addition to *The Fault in Our Stars,* other books with big-screen adaptations thrived in 2014. Gillian Flynn's 2012 phenomenon *Gone Girl,* adapted into a film released in October, took the No. 1 spot on the adult fiction list (the movie-tie in claimed the No. 4 spot), and the No. 7 spot on the overall bestseller list. The first film based on Roth's series, *Divergent,* hit theaters in mid-March (the big-screen version of *Insurgent* was released soon afterward, and the final book, *Allegiant,* was to be split into two subsequent films).

Frozen, a Golden Book by Victoria Saxon based on the Disney sensation of the same name (the highest-grossing animated film of all time), sold more than 780,000 copies, hitting No. 10 on the overall list and in eighth place on the juvenile list, where it was joined by four other Frozen series books. The August film adaptation of Gayle Forman's young adult novel *If I Stay* sent that book up the bestseller list throughout the year—it netted nearly 750,000 copies in 2014 (the hardcover, released in April 2009, sold roughly 40,000 copies in its first year on sale, according to Nielsen).

Laura Hillenbrand's *Unbroken* hit No. 3 on the adult nonfiction list, selling more than 660,000 copies. The book, first published in 2012, was adapted into a film by Angelina Jolie and premiered on Christmas Day.

Adapted from *Publishers Weekly,* January 2, 2015.

Digital Hits

Turning to digital, Green's *The Fault in Our Stars* also topped Amazon's Kindle bestseller list, followed by *Gone Girl* at No. 2. Donna Tartt's *The Goldfinch,* winner of the 2014 Pulitzer Prize for fiction, hit No. 4 on Amazon's list (the book came in at No. 5 on the adult fiction print list).

Once again, the 2014 charts revealed that—with the exception of *Unbroken* at No. 10—fiction still outperforms nonfiction digitally. *Killing Patton,* the topselling adult nonfiction title in print and the only adult print title to sell more than 1 million copies last year, didn't land in the top 50 on Amazon's Kindle list for 2014 (at the end of the year it sat at No. 56).

Top Ten Print Bestsellers, 2014

1. *The Fault in Our Stars* (trade paper). John Green. Penguin/Speak. 1,813,574.
2. *The Long Haul.* Jeff Kinney. Abrams/Amulet. 1,560,410.
3. *Divergent.* Veronica Roth. HarperCollins/Tegen. 1,426,292.
4. *Insurgent.* Veronica Roth. HarperCollins/Tegen. 1,310,210.
5. *Killing Patton.* Bill O'Reilly and Martin Dugard. Holt. 1,190,152.
6. *Allegiant.* Veronica Roth. HarperCollins/Tegen. 1,146,369.
7. *Gone Girl.* Gillian Flynn. Broadway. 962,797.
8. *The Fault in Our Stars* (movie tie-in). John Green. Penguin/Speak. 923,182.
9. *The Fault in Our Stars* (hardcover). John Green. Dutton. 769,065.
10. *Frozen.* Victoria Saxon. Random/Disney. 784,691.

Top 10 Amazon Kindle Bestsellers, 2014

1. *The Fault in Our Stars.* John Green. Penguin/Speak.
2. *Gone Girl.* Gillian Flynn. Crown.
3. *Divergent.* Veronica Roth. HarperCollins/Tegen.
4. *The Goldfinch.* Donna Tartt. Little, Brown.
5. *Insurgent.* Veronica Roth. HarperCollins/Tegen.
6. *Allegiant.* Veronica Roth. HarperCollins/Tegen.
7. *The Husband's Secret.* Liane Moriarty. Putnam.
8. *If I Stay.* Gayle Forman. Penguin/Speak.
9. *Orphan Train.* Christina Baker Kline. Morrow.
10. *Unbroken.* Laura Hillenbrand. Random.

Source: Amazon. Sales are through December 30, 2014.

Nielsen BookScan Adult Fiction Top 20

1. *Gone Girl* (trade paper). Gillian Flynn. Broadway. 962,797.
2. *Gray Mountain.* John Grisham. Doubleday. 619,578.

3. *Orphan Train.* Christina Baker Kline. Morrow. 493,654.
4. *Gone Girl* (movie tie-in) Gillian Flynn. Broadway. 458,245.
5. *The Goldfinch.* Donna Tartt. Little, Brown. 428,643.
6. *Gone Girl* (mass market). Gillian Flynn. Broadway. 415,253.
7. *To Kill a Mockingbird.* Harper Lee. Grand Central. 382,587.
8. *Sycamore Row.* John Grisham. Dell. 359,902.
9. *Revival.* Stephen King. Scribner. 344,871.
10. *Fifty Shades of Grey.* EL James. Vintage. 324,172.
11. *Inferno.* Dan Brown. Anchor. 322,319.
12. *The Invention of Wings.* Sue Monk Kidd. Viking. 312,882.
13. *Mr. Mercedes.* Stephen King. Scribner. 308,334.
14. *Shadow Spell.* Nora Roberts. Berkley. 298,605.
15. *Edge of Eternity.* Ken Follett. Dutton. 290,607.
16. *The Great Gatsby.* F. Scott Fitzgerald. Scribner. 287,777.
17. *The Best of Me* (movie tie-in). Nicholas Sparks. Grand Central. 286,960.
18. *Never Go Back.* Lee Child. Dell. 281,674.
19. *Hope to Die.* James Patterson. Little, Brown. 277,071.
20. *All the Light We Cannot See.* Anthony Doerr. Scribner. 247,789.

Nielsen BookScan Adult Nonfiction Top 20

1. *Killing Patton.* Bill O'Reilly and Martin Dugard. Holt. 1,190,152.
2. *Jesus Calling.* Sarah Young. Thomas Nelson. 706,837.
3. *Unbroken* (trade paper). Laura Hillenbrand. Random. 665,585.
4. *Strengths Finder 2.0.* Tom Rath. Gallup. 517,071.
5. *Make It Ahead.* Ina Garten. Clarkson Potter. 512,872.
6. *41: A Portrait of My Father.* George W. Bush. Crown. 488,891.
7. *Heaven Is for Real* (trade paper). Todd Burpo. Thomas Nelson. 468,581.
8. *Heaven Is for Real* (movie tie-in). Todd Burpo. Thomas Nelson. 462,719.
9. *The Boys in the Boat.* Daniel James Brown. Penguin. 417,251.
10. *Guinness World Records 2015.* Guinness World Records. Guinness. 383,760
11. *The Five Love Languages.* Gary Chapman. Northfield. 347,790.
12. *One Nation.* Ben Carson. Penguin/Sentinel. 343,743.
13. *Wild: From Lost to Found on the Pacific Coast Trail.* Cheryl Strayed. Vintage. 337,945.
14. *Killing Jesus.* Bill O'Reilly and Martin Dugard. Holt. 315,489.
15. *Yes Please.* Amy Poehler. Morrow/Dey Street. 300,230.
16. *Unbroken* (movie tie-in). Laura Hillenbrand. Random. 293,910.
17. *What If.* Randall Munroe. Houghton Mifflin Harcourt. 281,714.
18. *The Official SAT Study Guide.* College Board. College Board. 277,253.
19. *Unbroken* (hardcover). Laura Hillenbrand. Random. 266,479.

20. *Hard Choices.* Hillary Rodham Clinton. Simon & Schuster. 260,814.

Nielsen BookScan Juvenile Top 20

1. *The Fault in Our Stars* (trade paper). John Green. Penguin/Speak. 1,813,574.
2. *The Long Haul.* Jeff Kinney. Abrams/Amulet. 1,560,410.
3. *Divergent.* Veronica Roth. HarperCollins/Tegen. 1,426,292.
4. *Insurgent.* Veronica Roth HarperCollins/Tegen. 1,310,210.
5. *Allegiant.* Veronica Roth HarperCollins/Tegen. 1,146,369.
6. *The Fault in Our Stars* (movie tie-in). John Green. Penguin/Speak. 923,182.
7. *The Fault in Our Stars* (hardcover). John Green. Dutton. 796,065.
8. *Frozen.* Victoria Saxon. Random/Disney. 784,691.
9. *If I Stay.* Gayle Forman. Penguin/Speak. 747,935.
10. *Looking for Alaska.* John Green. Penguin/Speak. 738,518.
11. *The Maze Runner.* James Dashner. Delacorte. 696,021.
12. *Frozen: Journey to the Ice Palace.* Frank Berrios. Random/Disney. 682,146.
13. *Minecraft: Redstone Handbook.* Scholastic. Scholastic. 678,978.
14. *Minecraft: Essential Handbook.* Scholastic. Scholastic. 671,500.
15. *Four.* Veronica Roth. HarperCollins/Tegen. 651,383.
16. *Frozen: Big Snowman.* Tish Rabe. Random/Disney. 603,803.
17. *Hard Luck.* Jeff Kinney. Abrams/Amulet. 598,654.
18. *Paper Towns.* John Green. Penguin/Speak. 577,449.
19. *Frozen: A Tale of Two Sisters.* Melissa Lagonegro. Random/Disney. 557,547.
20. *Frozen: Troll Magic.* Courtney Carbone. Random/Disney. 499,643.

Note: The Blood of Olympus, book five in Rick Riordan's Heroes of Olympus series, failed to make the juvenile top 20 because it is sold under two separate ISBNs, even though it is the same book. A special edition for Barnes & Noble sold 209,356 copies while the regular hardcover sold 445,128 copies. The combined sales of 654,484 copies sold would place the book in the 16th spot on the juvenile list.

Literary Prizes, 2014

Compiled by the staff of the *Library and Book Trade Almanac*

ABC-CLIO/Greenwood Award for Best Book in Library Literature ($5,000). To recognize works that improve library management principles and practice, understanding and application of new techniques, or further the education of librarians or other information specialists. *Sponsor:* ABC-CLIO. *Administered by:* American Library Association. *Winner:* Robert Maxwell for *Maxwell's Handbook for RDA: Explaining and Illustrating RDA—Resource Description and Access Using MARC21* (ALA Editions).

Academy of American Poets Fellowship ($25,000). For outstanding poetic achievement. *Offered by:* Academy of American Poets. *Winner:* Tracy K. Smith.

Jane Addams Children's Book Awards. For children's books that effectively promote the cause of peace, social justice, world community, and equality. *Offered by:* Women's International League for Peace and Freedom and the Jane Addams Peace Association. *Winners:* (younger children), Michelle Markel and Melissa Sweet, illustrator, for *Brave Girl: Clara and the Shirtwaist Makers' Strike of 1909* (Balzer & Bray); (older children) Jewell Parker Rhodes for *Sugar* (Little, Brown).

Aesop Prize. For outstanding work in children's folklore, both fiction and nonfiction. *Offered by:* American Folklore Society. *Winners:* Shiho S. Nunes and Lak-Khee Tay-Audouard, illustrator, for *Chinese Fables: "The Dragon Slayer" and Other Timeless Tales of Wisdom* (Tuttle).

Agatha Awards. For mystery writing in the method exemplified by author Agatha Christie. *Offered by:* Malice Domestic Ltd. *Winners:* (contemporary novel) Hank Phillippi Ryan for *The Wrong Girl* (Forge); (first novel) Leslie Budewitz for *Death Al Dente* (Berkley Prime Crime); (historical) Charles Todd for *A Question of Honor* (William Morrow); (children's/YA) Chris Grabenstein for *Escape from Mr. Lemoncello's Library* (Random); (nonfiction) Daniel Stashower for *The Hour of Peril: The Secret Plot to Murder Lincoln Before the Civil War* (Minotaur); (short story) Art Taylor for "The Care and Feeding of House Plants" in *Ellery Queen Mystery Magazine* (Dell).

Ambassador Book Awards. To honor an exceptional contribution to the interpretation of life and culture in the United States. *Offered by:* English-Speaking Union of the United States. *Winners:* Award suspended since 2011.

American Academy of Arts and Letters Award of Merit ($25,000). Given annually, in rotation, for the short story, sculpture, novel, poetry, drama, and painting. *Offered by:* American Academy of Arts and Letters. *Winner:* Donna Dennis (sculpture).

American Academy of Arts and Letters Awards in Literature ($7,500). To honor writers of fiction and nonfiction, poets, dramatists, and translators of exceptional accomplishment. *Offered by:* American Academy of Arts and Letters. *Winners:* Kati Agocs, Don Bartlett, Emily Fragos, George Green, Rajiv Joseph, James Longenbach, Eric Puchner, Jean Valentine, Brenda Wineapple.

American Academy of Arts and Letters Gold Medals for distinguished achievement in belles lettres and criticism, biography, fiction, history, poetry, and drama. *Offered by:* American Academy of Arts and Letters. *Winner:* Natalie Zemon Davis (history).

American Academy of Arts and Letters Rome Fellowships. For a one-year residency at the American Academy in Rome for young writers of promise. *Offered by:* American Academy of Arts and Letters. *Winners:* Krys Lee, Liz Moore.

American Book Awards. For literary achievement by people of various ethnic backgrounds. *Offered by:* Before Columbus Foundation. *Winners:* Andrew Bacevich for *Breach of Trust: How Americans Failed Their Soldiers and Their Country* (Metropolitan); Joshua Bloom and Waldo E. Martin for *Black Against Empire: The History and Politics of the Black Panther Party* (University of California Press); Juan Delgado (poetry) and Thomas McGovern (photography) for *Vital Signs* (Heyday); Alex Espinoza for

The Five Acts of Diego León (Random); Jonathan Scott Holloway for *Jim Crow Wisdom: Memory and Identity in Black America Since 1940* (University of North Carolina Press); Joan Naviyuk Kane for *Hyperboreal* (University of Pittsburgh Press); Jamaica Kincaid for *See Now Then* (Farrar, Straus & Giroux); Tanya Olson for *Boyishly* (Yes-Yes); Sterling D. Plumpp for *Home/Bass* (Third World); Emily Raboteau for *Searching For Zion: The Quest for Home in the African Diaspora* (Atlantic Monthly); Jerome Rothenberg with Heriberto Yepez for *Eye of Witness: A Jerome Rothenberg Reader* (Commonwealth); Nick Turse for *Kill Anything That Moves: The Real American War in Vietnam* (Metropolitan); Margaret Wrinkle for *Wash* (Atlantic Monthly); Koon Woon for *Water Chasing Water* (Kaya); (anti-censorship award) Armond White; (lifetime achievement) Michael Parenti.

American Indian Youth Literature Awards. Offered biennially to recognize excellence in books by and about American Indians. *Offered by:* American Indian Library Association. *Winners:* (picture book) Tomson Highway and John Rombough, illustrator, for *Caribou Song* (Fifth House); (middle school) Tim Tingle for *How I Became a Ghost: A Choctaw Trail of Tears Story* (Roadrunner); (young adult) Joseph Bruchac for *Killer of Enemies* (Tu).

American Poetry Review/Honickman First Book Prize in Poetry ($3,000 and publication of the book). To encourage excellence in poetry and to provide a wide readership for a deserving first book of poems. *Winner:* Katherine Bode-Lang for *The Reformation* (American Poetry Review).

Américas Book Award for Children's and Young Adult Literature. To recognize U.S. works of fiction, poetry, folklore, or selected nonfiction that authentically and engagingly portray Latin America, the Caribbean, or Latinos in the United States. *Sponsored by:* Consortium of Latin American Studies Programs (CLASP). *Winners:* Susan Roth and Cindy Trumbore for *Parrots Over Puerto Rico* (Lee & Low).

Rudolfo and Patricia Anaya Lecture on the Literature of the Southwest. To honor a Chicano or Chicana fiction writer. *Offered by:* National Hispanic Cultural Center, University of New Mexico. *Winner:* Ana Castillo.

Hans Christian Andersen Awards. Awarded biennially to an author and an illustrator whose body of work has made an important and lasting contribution to children's literature. *Offered by:* International Board on Books for Young People (IBBY). *Sponsor:* Nami Island, Inc. *Winners:* (writer) Nahoko Uehashi, Japan; (illustrator) Roger Mello, Brazil.

Hans Christian Andersen Literature Award (500,000 Danish kroner, about $73,000). To a writer whose work can be compared with that of Andersen. *Offered by:* Hans Christian Andersen Literary Committee. *Winner:* Salman Rushdie.

Anthony Awards. For superior mystery writing. *Offered by:* Boucheron World Mystery Convention. *Winners:* (novel) William Kent Krueger for *Ordinary Grace* (Atria); (first novel) Matt Coyle for *Yesterday's Echo* (Oceanview); (paperback original) Catriona McPherson for *As She Left It* (Midnight Ink); (children's/YA) Joelle Charbonneau for *The Testing* (Houghton Mifflin); (short story) John Connolly for "The Caxton Private Lending Library and Book Depository" in *Bibliomysteries* (Mysterious Bookshop); (critical or nonfiction Work) Daniel Stashower for *The Hour of Peril: The Secret Plot To Murder Lincoln Before the Civil War* (Minotaur).

Asia Society Bernard Schwartz Book Award ($20,000). *Winner:* Gary Bass for *The Blood Telegram: Nixon, Kissinger, and a Forgotten Genocide* (Knopf).

Asian Literary Prize (formerly the Man Asian Literary Prize). For a novel by an Asian writer, either written in English or translated into English, and published in the previous calendar year. *Winner:* Award suspended in 2013.

Asian/Pacific American Awards for Literature. For books that promote Asian/Pacific American culture and heritage. *Sponsor:* Asian/Pacific American Librarians Association (APALA). *Winners:* (picture book) Ji-li Jiang for *Red Kite, Blue Kite* (Disney/Hyperion); (children's) Cynthia Kadohata for *The Thing About Luck* (Atheneum); (young adult) Leza Lowitz and Shogo Oketani for *Jet Black and the Ninja Wind* (Tuttle); (adult fiction) Ruth Ozeki for *A Tale for the Time Being* (Viking); (adult nonfiction) Cindy I-Fen Cheng for *Citizens of Asian America: Democracy and Race during the Cold War* (New York University Press).

Audio Publishers Association awards (Audies). To recognize excellence in audiobooks. *Winners:* (audiobook of the year, humor, and narration by the author or authors) *Still Foolin' 'Em: Where I've Been, Where I'm Going, and Where the Hell Are My Keys?* by Billy Crystal, read by the author (Macmillan); (distinguished achievement in production) *The Storm King—Stories, Narratives, Poems: Spoken Words Set to a World of Music* by Pete Seeger, read by the author, presented by Jeff Haynes (Hachette); (solo narration, female) *The Twelve Clues of Christmas: A Royal Spyness Mystery* by Rhys Bowen, read by Katherine Kellgren (Audible); (solo narration, male, and literary fiction) *The Goldfinch* by Donna Tartt, read by David Pittu (Hachette); (nonfiction) *David and Goliath: Underdogs, Misfits, and the Art of Battling Giants* by Malcolm Gladwell, read by the author (Hachette); (biography/memoir) *The Elephant Whisperer: My Life With the Herd in the African Wild* by Lawrence Anthony with Graham Spence, read by Simon Vance (Tantor Media); (history) *Devil in the Grove: Thurgood Marshall, the Groveland Boys, and the Dawn of a New America* by Gilbert King, read by Peter Francis James (Harper); (inspirational/faith-based fiction) *A Story of God and All of Us* (based on the television miniseries "The Bible") by Roma Downey and Mark Burnett, read by Keith David and the authors (Hachette); (inspirational/faith-based nonfiction) *Keeping Hope Alive: One Woman, 90,000 Lives Changed* by Hawa Abdi, Sarah J. Robbins, read by Robin Miles (Hachette); (business/educational) *Leadership Secrets of the Salvation Army* by Robert Watson and Ben Brown, read by Bob Souer (eChristian); (personal development) *You Are a Badass: How to Stop Doubting Your Greatness and Start Living an Awesome Life* by Jen Sincero, read by the author (Tantor Media); (fiction) *Doctor Sleep* by Stephen King, read by Will Patton (Simon & Schuster); (classic) *The Complete Sherlock Holmes: The Heirloom Collection* by Arthur Conan Doyle, read by Simon Vance (Brilliance); (short stories/collections) *Sherlock Holmes in America* by Jon L. Lellenberg, Martin H. Greenberg, and Daniel Stashower, editors, read by Graeme Malcolm (Audible); (romance) *The Longest Ride* by Nicholas Sparks, read by January LaVoy and Ron McLarty (Hachette); (erotica) *Carrie's Story: An Erotic S/M Novel* by Molly Weatherfield, read by Shana Savage (Audible); (science fiction) *Captain Vorpatril's Alliance: Vorkosigan Saga, Book 15* by Lois McMaster Bujold, read by Grover Gardner (Blackstone); (paranormal) *Reviver* by Seth Patrick, read by Ari Fliakos (Macmillian); (fantasy) *Wisp of a Thing: A Novel of the Tufa, Book 2* by Alex Bledsoe, read by Stefan Rudnicki (Blackstone); (mystery) *Unleashed: Andy Carpenter, Book 11* by David Rosenfelt, read by Grover Gardner (Listen & Live); (thriller/suspense) *The Hit* by David Baldacci, read by Ron McLarty and Orlagh Cassidy (Hachette); (children's, ages 0–8) *Hooray for Anna Hibiscus* by Atinuke, read by Mutiyat Ade-Salu (Recorded Books); (children's, ages 8–12) *Matilda* by Roald Dahl, read by Kate Winslet (Penguin); (teens) *Viva Jacquelina! Bloody Jack, Book 10* by L. A. Meyer, read by Katherine Kellgren (Listen & Live); (audio drama) *Oliver Twist* (Focus on the Family series) by Charles Dickens, adapted by Paul McCusker, read by Joe Holgate, Henry Goodman, Bill Sykes, Geoffrey Palmer, Roy Hudd, Finty Williams, and a full cast (Tyndale); (multi-voiced performance) *World War Z: An Oral History of the Zombie War* by Max Brooks, read by Martin Scorsese, Alfred Molina, and a full cast (Random); (original work) *Thirteen* by Scott Harrison, Dan Abnett, Cavan Scott, Kim Newman, Kaaron Warren, George Mann, and Simon Clark, read by Kirby Heyborne, Stefan Rudnicki, Theodore Bikel, Paul Boehmer, Scott Brick, Gabrielle de Cuir, Samantha Eggar, Harlan Ellison, Susan Hanfield, Roxanne Hernandez, Janis Ian, Rex Linn, Richard McGonagle, Jim Meskimen, Emily Rankin, John Rubinstein, Christian Rummel, Vikas Adams, Nathan Dana Aldritch, Alison Bews, Emily Bews, Kelly Catey, Sunil Malhotra, Kathe Mazur, Taylor Meskimen, Arthur Morey, Karyn O'Bryant, Lisa Renee Pitts, and Judy Young (Spokenworld Audio/

Ladbroke Audio); (lifetime achievement) George Guidall.

Bad Sex in Fiction Award (United Kingdom). To "draw attention to the crude, badly written, often perfunctory use of redundant passages of sexual description in the modern novel, and to discourage it." *Sponsor: Literary Review. Winner:* Ben Okri for *The Age of Magic* (Head of Zeus).

Baileys Women's Prize for Fiction (United Kingdom) (formerly the Orange Prize for Fiction) (£30,000). For the best novel written by a woman and published in the United Kingdom. *Winner:* Eimear McBride for *A Girl is a Half-formed Thing* (Coffee House).

Bakeless Literary Prizes. For promising new writers. *Offered by:* Bread Loaf Writers' Conference of Middlebury College. *Winners:* Award discontinued in 2013.

Bancroft Prizes ($10,000). For books of exceptional merit and distinction in American history, American diplomacy, and the international relations of the United States. *Offered by:* Columbia University. *Winners:* Ira Katznelson for *Fear Itself: The New Deal and the Origins of Our Time* (Liveright); Ari Kelman for *A Misplaced Massacre: Struggling Over the Memory of Sand Creek* (Harvard University Press).

Barnes & Noble Discover Great New Writers Awards. To honor a first novel and a first work of nonfiction by American authors. *Offered by:* Barnes & Noble. *Winners:* (fiction) Anthony Marra for *A Constellation of Vital Phenomena* (Hogarth); (nonfiction) Justin St. Germain for *Son of a Gun: A Memoir* (Random)

Mildred L. Batchelder Award. To the American publisher of a children's book originally published in a language other than English and subsequently published in English in the United States. *Offered by:* American Library Association, Association for Library Service to Children. *Winner:* Enchanted Lion for *Mister Orange* by Truus Matti, translated by Laura Watkinson.

BBC National Short Story Award (United Kingdom) (£15,000). *Winner:* Lionel Shriver for "Kilifi Creek."

Beacon of Freedom Award. For the best title introducing American history, from colonial times through the Civil War, to young readers. *Offered by:* Williamsburg (Virginia) Regional Library and the Colonial Williamsburg Foundation. *Winner:* Laurie Calkhoven for *Will at the Battle of Gettysburg* (Boys of Wartime series) (Dutton).

Pura Belpré Awards. To a Latino/Latina writer and illustrator whose work portrays, affirms, and celebrates the Latino cultural experience in an outstanding work of literature for children and youth. *Offered by:* American Library Association, Association for Library Service to Children. *Winners:* (writer) Meg Medina for *Yaqui Delgado Wants to Kick Your Ass* (Candlewick); (illustrator) Yuyi Morales, author and illustrator of *Niño Wrestles the World* (Roaring Brook).

Helen B. Bernstein Book Award for Excellence in Journalism ($15,000). To a journalist who has written at book length about an issue of contemporary concern. *Offered by:* New York Public Library. *Winner:* Dan Fagin for *Toms River: A Story of Science and Salvation* (Bantam).

Black Caucus of the American Library Association (BCALA) Literary Awards. *Winners:* (fiction) James McBride for *The Good Lord Bird* (Riverhead); (nonfiction) Craig Steven Wilder for *Ebony and Ivy: Race, Slavery, and the Troubled History of America's Universities* (Bloomsbury); (first novelist award, to acknowledge outstanding achievement in writing and storytelling by a first-time fiction writer) Edward Kelsey Moore for *The Supremes at Earl's All-You-Can-Eat* (Knopf); (poetry) Nikki Giovanni for *Chasing Utopia: A Hybrid* (William Morrow); (outstanding contribution to publishing citation) Ahmir "Questlove" Thompson for *Soul Train: The Music, Dance, and Style of a Generation* (Harper Design).

Irma Simonton Black and James H. Black Award for Excellence in Children's Literature. To a book for young children in which the text and illustrations work together to create an outstanding whole. *Offered by:* Bank Street College of Education. *Winner:* Mo Willems for *That Is Not a Good Idea!* (Balzer + Bray).

James Tait Black Memorial Prize (United Kingdom) (£10,000). To recognize literary excellence in fiction and biography. *Offered by:* University of Edinburgh. *Winners:* (fiction) Jim Crace for *Harvest* (Picador);

(biography) Hermione Lee for *Penelope Fitzgerald: A life* (Chatto & Windus).

James Tait Black Prize for Drama (United Kingdom) (£10,000). *Offered by:* University of Edinburgh in partnership with the National Theatre of Scotland and in association with the Traverse Theatre. *Winner:* Rory Mullarkey for *Cannibals.*

Blue Peter Book of the Year (United Kingdom). To recognize excellence in children's books. Winners are chosen by a jury of viewers, ages 8–12, of the BBC television children's program "Blue Peter." *Winners:* (best story) Katherine Rundell for *Rooftoppers* (Faber); (best book with facts) Tony Robinson and Del Thorpe, illustrator, for *Weird World of Wonders: World War II* (Macmillan).

Rebekah Johnson Bobbitt National Prize for Poetry ($10,000). *Offered biennially by:* Library of Congress. *Winner:* Patricia Smith for *Shoulda Been Jimi Savannah.*

Bookseller/Diagram Prize for Oddest Title of the Year. *Sponsor: The Bookseller* magazine. *Winner:* co-authors Mats & Enzo for *How to Poo on a Date* (Prion).

BookSense Book of the Year Awards. See Indies Choice Book Awards.

Boston Globe/Horn Book Awards. For excellence in children's literature. *Winners:* (fiction) Andrew Smith for *Grasshopper Jungle* (Dutton); (nonfiction) Steve Sheinkin for *The Port Chicago 50: Disaster, Mutiny, and the Fight for Civil Rights (Roaring Brook); (picture book)* Peter Brown for *Mr. Tiger Goes Wild* (Little, Brown).

W. Y. Boyd Literary Award ($5,000). For a military novel that honors the service of American veterans during a time of war. *Offered by:* American Library Association. *Donor:* W. Y. Boyd II. *Winner:* Ralph Peters for *Hell or Richmond* (Forge).

Branford Boase Award (United Kingdom). To the author and editor of an outstanding novel for young readers by a first-time writer. *Winners:* C. J. (Chelsey) Flood and editor Venetia Gosling for *Infinite Sky* (Simon & Schuster).

Michael Braude Award for Light Verse ($5,000). *Offered triennially by:* American Academy of Arts and Letters. *Winner:* To be awarded next in 2015.

Bridport International Creative Writing Prizes (United Kingdom). For poetry and short stories. *Offered by:* Bridport Arts Centre. *Winners:* (poetry, £5,000) Natalya Anderson for "Clear Recent History"; (short story, £5,000) Tracy Slaughter for "Scenes of a Long Term Nature"; (flash fiction, 250-word maximum, £1,000) Kit de Waal for "Romans Chapter 1 Verse 29."

British Council Award for ELT writing (£2,000). To celebrate the best writing for English language teaching. *Winners:* Gavin Dudeney, Nicky Hockly, and Mark Pegrum for *Digital Literacies* (Pearson).

British Fantasy Awards. *Offered by:* British Fantasy Society. *Winners:* (novel) Sofia Samatar for *A Stranger in Olondria* (Small Beer); (horror novel) Lauren Beukes for *The Shining Girls* (HarperCollins); (novella) Sarah Pinborough for *Beauty* (Gollancz); (short story) Carole Johnstone for "Signs of the Times" in *Black Static* No. 33 (TTA); (anthology) Jonathan Oliver, editor, for *End of the Road* (Solaris); (collection) Stephen Volk for *Monsters in the Heart* (Gray Friar); (comic/graphic novel) Becky Cloonan for "Demeter"; (artist) Joey Hi-Fi; (nonfiction) Justin Landon and Jared Shurin, editors, for *Speculative Fiction 2012* (Jurassic London); (magazine/periodical) Neil Clarke, Sean Wallace, and Kate Baker, editors, for *Clarkesworld* (Wyrm); (film/television episode) David Benioff and D. B. Weiss for "Game of Thrones: The Rains of Castamere" (HBO); (newcomer) Ann Leckie for *Ancillary Justice* (Orbit); (British Fantasy Society Special Award, The Karl Edward Wagner Award) Farah Mendlesohn.

Sophie Brody Medal. For the U.S. author of the most distinguished contribution to Jewish literature for adults, published in the preceding year. *Donors:* Arthur Brody and the Brodart Foundation. *Offered by:* American Library Association, Reference and User Services Association. *Winner:* Yossi Klein Halevi for *Like Dreamers: The Story of the Israeli Paratroopers Who Reunited Jerusalem and Divided a Nation* (HarperCollins).

Witter Bynner Poetry Fellowships ($10,000). To encourage poets and poetry. *Sponsor* Witter Bynner Foundation for Poetry. *Winners:* Fanonne Jeffers, James Adam York.

Caine Prize for African Writing (£10,000). For a short story by an African writer, published in English. *Winner:* Okwiri Oduor for "My

Father's Head" in *Feast, Famine and Potluck* (Short Story Day Africa).

Randolph Caldecott Medal. For the artist of the most distinguished picture book. *Offered by:* American Library Association, Association for Library Service to Children. *Winner:* Brian Floca, writer and illustrator, for *Locomotive* (Atheneum).

California Book Awards. To California residents to honor books of fiction, nonfiction, and poetry published in the previous year. *Offered by:* Commonwealth Club of California. *Winners:* (fiction) Karen Joy Fowler for *We Are All Completely Beside Ourselves* (Putnam/Marian Wood); (first fiction) Anthony Marra for *A Constellation of Vital Phenomena* (Hogarth); (nonfiction) Eric Schlosser for *Command and Control: Nuclear Weapons, the Damascus Accident, and the Illusion of Safety* (Penguin); (poetry) Brenda Hillman for *Seasonal Works With Letters On Fire* (Wesleyan University Press); (juvenile) *Marissa Moss for Barbed Wire Baseball* (Abrams); (young adult) Tom McNeal for *Far Far Away* (Knopf); (contribution to publishing) Heyday Books for *Deborah Valoma: Scrape the Willow Until It Sings—The Words and Work of Basket Maker Julia Parker,* photographs by Lee Fatherree; (Californiana) Ronald M. George, retired California Supreme Court chief justice, for *Chief: The Quest for Justice in California* (University of California, Berkeley: Public Policy Press).

John W. Campbell Award. For the best new science fiction or fantasy writer whose first work of science fiction or fantasy was published in a professional publication in the previous two years. *Offered by:* Dell Magazines. *Winner:* Sofia Samatar for *A Stranger in Olondria* (Small Beer).

John W. Campbell Memorial Award. For science fiction writing. *Offered by:* Center for the Study of Science Fiction. *Winners:* Marcel Theroux for *Strange Bodies* (Farrar, Straus & Giroux).

Canadian Library Association Book of the Year for Children. *Sponsor:* Library Services Centre. *Winner:* Allan Stratton for *Curse of the Dream Witch* (Scholastic Canada).

Canadian Library Association Amelia Frances Howard-Gibbon Illustrator's Award. *Sponsor:* Library Services Centre. *Winner:* Jon Klassen for *The Dark,* written by Lemony Snicket (HarperCollins).

Canadian Library Association Young Adult Book Award. *Winner:* Karen Bass for *Graffiti Knight* (Pajama).

Andrew Carnegie Medal for Excellence in Fiction and Nonfiction. For adult books published during the previous year in the United States. *Sponsors:* Carnegie Corporation of New York, ALA/RUSA, and *Booklist. Winners:* (fiction) Donna Tartt for *The Goldfinch* (Little, Brown); (nonfiction) Doris Kearns Goodwin for *The Bully Pulpit: Theodore Roosevelt, William Howard Taft, and the Golden Age of Journalism* (Simon & Schuster).

Carnegie Medal (United Kingdom). See CILIP Carnegie Medal.

Center for Fiction Flaherty-Dunnan First Novel Prize. See Flaherty-Dunnan First Novel Prize.

Chicago Folklore Prize. For the year's best folklore book. *Offered by:* American Folklore Society. *Winner:* David A. McDonald for *My Voice Is My Weapon: Music, Nationalism, and the Poetics of Palestinian Resistance* (Duke University Press).

Chicago Tribune Nelson Algren Short Story Award ($5,000). For unpublished short fiction. *Offered by: Chicago Tribune. Winner:* Ben Hoffman for "This Will All Be Over Soon."

Chicago Tribune Heartland Prize for Fiction ($7,500). *Offered by: Chicago Tribune. Winner:* Daniel Woodrell for *The Maid's Version* (Little, Brown).

Chicago Tribune Heartland Prize for Nonfiction ($7,500). *Offered by: Chicago Tribune. Winner:* Jesmyn Ward for *Men We Reaped* (Bloomsbury).

Chicago Tribune Literary Prize. For a lifetime of literary achievement by an author whose body of work has had great impact on American society. *Offered by: Chicago Tribune. Winner:* musician and author Patti Smith.

Chicago Tribune Young Adult Literary Prize. To recognize a distinguished literary career. *Winner:* James Patterson.

Children's Africana Book Awards. To recognize and encourage excellence in children's books about Africa. *Offered by:* Africa Access, African Studies Association. *Winners:* (young children) Archbishop Desmond

Tutu, Douglas Abrams, and A. G. Ford, illustrator, for *Desmond and the Very Mean Word, A Story of Forgiveness* (Candlewick); Mubina Hassanali Kirmani and Tony Siema, illustrator, for *Bundle of Secrets: Savita Returns Home* (CreateSpace); (older readers) Monica Edinger and Robert Byrd, illustrator, for *Africa Is My Home: A Child of the Amistad* (Candlewick); Anna Cottrell, Agbotadua Togbi Kumassah, and Kwabena Poku, illustrator, for *Once Upon a Time in Ghana: Traditional Stories Retold in English* (Afram).

Children's Book Council of Australia Book of the Year Awards. *Winners:* (older readers) Fiona Wood for *Wildlife* (Pan Macmillan Australia); (younger readers) Catherine Jinks for *City of Orphans: A Very Unusual Pursuit* (Allen & Unwin); (early childhood) Jan Ormerod and Andrew Joyner, illustrator, for *The Swap* (Little Hare); (picture book) Shaun Tan for *Rules of Summer* (Hachette Australia).

Children's Poet Laureate ($25,000). For lifetime achievement in poetry for children. Honoree holds the title for two years. *Offered by:* The Poetry Foundation. *Winner:* Kenn Nesbitt.

Cholmondeley Awards for Poets (United Kingdom) (£1,500). For a poet's body of work and contribution to poetry. *Winners:* W. N. Herbert, Jeremy Hooker, John James, Glynn Maxwell, and Denise Riley.

CILIP Carnegie Medal (United Kingdom). For the outstanding children's book of the year. *Offered by:* CILIP: The Chartered Institute of Library and Information Professionals (formerly the Library Association). *Winner:* Kevin Brooks for *The Bunker Diary* (Penguin).

CILIP Kate Greenaway Medal and Colin Mears Award (United Kingdom) (£5,000 plus £500 worth of books donated to a library of the winner's choice). For children's book illustration. *Offered by:* CILIP: The Chartered Institute of Library and Information Professionals. *Winner:* Jon Klassen for *This Is Not My Hat* (Walker).

Arthur C. Clarke Award. For the best science fiction novel published in the United Kingdom. *Offered by:* British Science Fiction Association. *Winner:* Ann Leckie for *Ancillary Justice* (Orbit).

David Cohen Prize for Literature (United Kingdom) (£40,000). Awarded biennially to a living British writer, novelist, poet, essayist, or dramatist in recognition of an entire body of work written in the English language. *Offered by:* David Cohen Family Charitable Trust. *Winner:* To be awarded next in 2015.

Matt Cohen Award: In Celebration of a Writing Life (C$20,000). To a Canadian author whose life has been dedicated to writing as a primary pursuit, for a body of work. *Offered by:* Writers' Trust of Canada. *Sponsors:* Marla and David Lehberg. *Winner:* Susan Musgrave.

Commonwealth Book Prize (United Kingdom) (£10,000). To reward and encourage new Commonwealth fiction and ensure that works of merit reach a wider audience outside their country of origin. *Offered by:* Commonwealth Institute. *Winner:* The prize, formerly known as the Commonwealth Writers' Prize, was discontinued after the 2013 competition.

Commonwealth Short Story Prize (United Kingdom) (£5,000). To reward and encourage new short fiction by Commonwealth writers. *Offered by:* Commonwealth Institute. (Overall winner and regional winner, Africa) Jennifer Nansubuga Makumbi (Uganda) for "Let's Tell This Story Properly"; (regional winner, Asia) Sara Adam Ang (Singapore) for "A Day in the Death"; (regional winner, Canada and Europe) Lucy Caldwell (United Kingdom) for "Killing Time"; (regional winner, Caribbean) Maggie Harris (Guyana) for "Sending for Chantal"; (regional winner, Pacific) Lucy Treloar (Australia) for "The Dog and the Sea."

Costa Book Awards (United Kingdom) (£5,000 plus an additional £25,000 for Book of the Year). For literature of merit that is readable on a wide scale. *Offered by:* Booksellers Association of Great Britain and Costa Coffee. *Winners:* (biography and Book of the Year) Helen Macdonald for *H is For Hawk* (Cape); (novel) Ali Smith for *How to Be Both* (Hamish Hamilton); (first novel) Emma Healey for *Elizabeth Is Missing* (Harper); (poetry) Jonathan Edwards for *My Family and Other Superheroes* (Seren); (children's) Kate Saunders for *Five Children on the Western Front* (Faber).

Costa Short Story Award (United Kingdom) *Winners:* (first place, £3,500) Zoe Gilbert for "Fishskin, Hareskin"; (second place, £1,500) Paula Cunningham for "The Matchboy"; (third place, £500) Joanne Meek for "Jellyfish."

Crab Orchard Review Literary Prizes ($2,000 and publication in *Crab Orchard Review.* *Winners:* (Jack Dyer Fiction Prize) Troy Ehlers for "Five Deaths of Ellie Marsh"; (John Guyon Literary Nonfiction Prize) Allison Backous Troy for "Inertia"; (Richard Peterson Poetry Prize) Nandi Comer for "Detroit, Llorona, My Heart, My City," "Loosing Between Manholes and Myths," and "The Warning."

Crime Writers' Association (CWA) Dagger Awards (United Kingdom). *Winners:* (diamond dagger, for significant contribution to crime writing) Simon Brett; (gold dagger, for best novel) Wiley Cash for *This Dark Road to Mercy* (Doubleday); (Ian Fleming steel dagger, for best thriller) Robert Harris for *An Officer and a Spy* (Random); (John Creasey dagger, for best new crime writer) Ray Celestin for *The Axeman's Jazz* (Mantle); (international dagger, for a work translated into English) Arturo Pérez-Reverte and T. Frank Wynne, translator, for *The Siege* (Weidenfeld); (nonfiction dagger) Adrian Levy and Cathy Scott-Clark for *The Siege* (Viking); (CWA Dagger in the Library, for a body of work) Sharon (SJ) Bolton; (debut dagger, for a previously unpublished crime writer) Jody Sabral for *The Movement*; (short story) John Harvey for "Fedora" in *Deadly Pleasures* (Severn House); (CWA Endeavour historical dagger, for the best historical crime novel) Antonia Hodgson for *The Devil in the Marshalsea* (Hodder & Stoughton).

Roald Dahl Funny Prize (United Kingdom) (£2,500). *Offered by:* Booktrust. *Winners:* Award suspended until 2016.

Benjamin H. Danks Award ($20,000). To a promising young writer, playwright, or composer, in alternate years. *Offered by:* American Academy of Arts and Letters. *Winner:* fiction writer Yiyun Li.

Dartmouth Medal. For creating current reference works of outstanding quality and significance. *Donor:* Dartmouth College. *Offered by:* American Library Association,

Reference and User Services Division. *Winner:* Bloomsbury Publishing for the six-volume *Mammals of Africa.*

Derringer Awards. To recognize excellence in short crime and mystery fiction. *Sponsor:* Short Mystery Fiction Society. *Winners:* (flash story, up to 1,000 words) Stephen D. Rogers for "Luck is What You Make" in *Crime Factory,* May 2013); (short story, 1,001–4,000 words) Robert Lopresti for "The Present" in *Strand Magazine,* February–May 2013); (long story, 4001–8,000 words) Ray Daniel for "Give Me a Dollar" in *Best New England Crime Stories 2014: Stone Cold* (Level Best); (novelette, 8,001–20,000 words) Melodie Campbell for "The Goddaughter's Revenge" (Orca); Edward D. Hoch Memorial Golden Derringer for Lifetime Achievement) Ed Gorman.

Diagram Prize for Oddest Title of the Year. See Bookseller/Diagram Prize for Oddest Title of the Year.

Philip K. Dick Award. For a distinguished science fiction paperback published in the United States. *Sponsor:* Philadelphia Science Fiction Society and the Philip K. Dick Trust. *Winner:* Ben H. Winters for *Countdown City* (Quirk).

Digital Book Awards. To recognize high-quality digital content available to readers as e-books and enhanced digital books. *Sponsor:* Digital Book World. *Winners:* (e-book, flowable: adult fiction) John Ashbery for *Chinese Whispers* (Open Road); (e-book, flowable: adult nonfiction) Sheila Heti, Heidi Julavits, and Leanne Shapton for *Women in Clothes* (Penguin); (e-book, flowable: children's) Laurie S. Sutton for *You Choose: Scooby-Doo! The Terror of the Bigfoot Beast* (Capstone); (e-book, fixed format/enhanced: adult fiction) Neil Gaiman for *The Truth Is a Cave in the Black Mountains* (Morrow); (e-book, fixed format/enhanced: adult nonfiction) Shauna Miller for *Penny Chic: How to Be Stylish on a Real Girl's Budget* (Little, Brown); (e-book, fixed format/enhanced: children's) Kyo Maclear, Danielle Mulhall, and Laura Brady for *Virginia Wolf* (Kids Can).

DSC Prize for South Asian Literature ($50,000). To recognize outstanding literature from or about the South Asian region and raise awareness of South Asian culture around the world. *Sponsor:* DSC Limited. *Winner:* Jhumpa Lahiri for *The Lowland* (Knopf).

Dundee International Book Prize (Scotland) (£10,000 and publication by Cargo). For an unpublished novel on any theme, in any genre. *Winner:* Amy Mason for *The Other Ida.*

Dundee Picture Book Award (Scotland) (£1,000). To recognize excellence in storytelling for children. The winner is chosen by the schoolchildren of Dundee. *Winner:* Rachel Bright for *Love Monster and the Last Chocolate* (HarperCollins).

Educational Writers' Award (United Kingdom) (£2,000). For noteworthy educational nonfiction for children. *Offered by:* Authors' Licensing and Collecting Society and Society of Authors. *Winners:* Jon Richards and Ed Simkins for *The World in Infographics: Animal Kingdom* (Wayland).

Margaret A. Edwards Award ($2,000). To an author whose book or books have provided young adults with a window through which they can view their world and which will help them to grow and to understand themselves and their role in society. *Donor: School Library Journal. Winner:* Markus Zusak for *The Book Thief* (Random), *Fighting Ruben Wolfe* (Scholastic), *Getting the Girl* (Scholastic), and *I Am the Messenger* (Random).

T. S. Eliot Prize for Poetry (United Kingdom) (£20,000). *Offered by:* Poetry Book Society. *Winner:* David Harsent for *Fire Songs* (Faber).

Encore Award (United Kingdom) (£10,000). Awarded biennially for the best second novel of the previous two years. *Offered by* Society of Authors. *Sponsor:* Lucy Astor. *Winner:* Evie Wyld for *All the Birds, Singing* (Pantheon).

European Union Prize for Literature (€5,000). To recognize outstanding European writing. *Sponsors:* European Commission, European Booksellers Federation, European Writers' Council, Federation of European Publishers. *Winners:* (Albania) Ben Blushi for *Othello, the Moor of Vlora*; (Bulgaria) Milen Ruskov for *Summit*; (Czech Republic) Jan Nemec for *A History of Light*; (Greece) Makis Tsitas for *God Is My Witness*; (Iceland) Oddny Eir for *Land of Love, Plan of Ruins*; (Latvia)

Janis Jonevs for *Jelgava '94*; (Liechtenstein) Armin Ohri for *The Dark Muse*; (Malta) Pierre J. Mejlak for *What the Night Lets You Say*; (Montenegro) Ognjen Spahic for *Head Full of Joy*; (Netherlands) Marente de Moor for *The Dutch Maiden*; (Serbia) Ugljesa Sajtinac for *Quite Modest Gifts*; (Turkey) Birgul Oguz for *Aha*; (United Kingdom) Evie Wyld for *All the Birds, Singing.*

Fairfax Prize ($10,000). For a body of work that has "made significant contributions to American and international culture." *Sponsors:* Fairfax County (Virginia) Public Library Foundation and George Mason University. *Winner:* Richard Russo.

FIELD Poetry Prize ($1,000). For a booklength poetry collection. *Offered by: FIELD: Contemporary Poetry and Poetics. Winner:* Carol Potter for *Some Slow Bees* (Oberlin College Press).

FIL Literary Award in Romance Languages (formerly the Juan Rulfo International Latin American and Caribbean Prize (Mexico) ($150,000). For lifetime achievement in any literary genre. *Offered by:* Juan Rulfo International Latin American and Caribbean Prize Committee. *Winner:* Italian novelist, playwright, writer, and translator Claudio Magris.

Financial Times/Goldman Sachs Business Book of the Year Award (£30,000). To recognize books that provide compelling and enjoyable insight into modern business issues. *Winners:* Thomas Piketty and Arthur Goldhammer, translator, for *Capital in the Twenty-First Century* (Belknap).

Flaherty-Dunnan First Novel Prize ($10,000). *Offered by:* Center for Fiction, Mercantile Library of New York. *Winner:* Tiphanie Yanique for *Land of Love and Drowning* (Riverhead).

Sid Fleischman Award for Humor. See Golden Kite Awards.

ForeWord Reviews Book of the Year Awards ($1,500). For independently published books. *Offered by: ForeWord Reviews* magazine. *Winners:* (editor's choice prize, fiction) Kelly Luce for *Three Scenarios in Which Hana Sasaki Grows a Tail* (A Strange Object); (editor's choice prize, nonfiction) Kristen Gresh and Michket Krifa for *She Who Tells a Story* (MFA).

E. M. Forster Award ($20,000). To a young writer from England, Ireland, Scotland, or Wales, for a stay in the United States. *Offered by:* American Academy of Arts and Letters. *Winner:* Sarah Hall.

Forward Prizes (United Kingdom). For poetry. *Offered by: The Forward. Winners:* (best collection, £10,000), Kei Miller for *The Cartographer Tries to Map a Way to Zion* (Carcanet); (best first collection, £5,000) Liz Berry for *Black Country* (Random); (best single poem, £1,000) Stephen Santus for "In a Restaurant."

H. E. Francis Short Story Competition ($1,000). For an unpublished short story no more than 5,000 words in length. *Sponsors:* Ruth Hindman Foundation and English Department, University of Alabama, Huntsville. *Winner:* Sandra Hunter for "Against the Stranger."

Josette Frank Award. For a work of fiction in which children or young people deal in a positive and realistic way with difficulties in their world and grow emotionally and morally. *Offered by:* Bank Street College of Education and the Florence M. Miller Memorial Fund. *Winner:* Elizabeth Wein for *Rose Under Fire* (Disney/Hyperion).

George Freedley Memorial Award. For the best English-language work about live theater published in the United States. *Offered by:* Theatre Library Association. *Winner:* Alisa Solomon for *Wonder of Wonders: A Cultural History of 'Fiddler on the Roof'* (Metropolitan).

French-American Foundation Translation Prizes ($10,000). For a translation or translations from French into English of works of fiction and nonfiction. *Offered by:* French-American Foundation. *Donor:* Florence Gould Foundation. *Winners:* (fiction) Adriana Hunter for her translation of *Eléctrico W* by Hervé Le Tellier (Other); (nonfiction) Alison Dundy and Nicholas Elliott for their translation of *The Falling Sky* by Davi Kopenawa and Bruce Albert (Harvard University Press).

Frost Medal. To recognize achievement in poetry over a lifetime. *Offered by:* Poetry Society of America. *Winner:* Gerald Stern.

Lewis Galantière Award. Awarded biennially for a literary translation into English from any language other than German. *Offered*

by: American Translators Association. *Winner:* Juliet Winters Carpenter for her translation from Japanese of Minae Mizumura's *A True Novel* (Other).

Galaxy National Book Awards. See Specsavers National Book Awards.

Theodor Seuss Geisel Award. For the best book for beginning readers. *Offered by:* American Library Association, Association for Library Service to Children. *Winner:* Greg Pizzoli for *The Watermelon Seed,* illustrated by the author (Disney/Hyperion).

David Gemmell Legend Awards for Fantasy. For novels published for the first time in English during the year of nomination. *Winners:* (Legend Award for best fantasy novel) Mark Lawrence for *Emperor of Thorns* (Broken Empire No.3) (Ace); (Morningstar Award for best debut novel) Brian McClellan for *Promise of Blood* (Power Mage trilogy) (Orbit); (Ravenheart Award for best cover art) Jason Chan for *Emperor of Thorns* (Ace).

Giller Prize (Canada). See Scotiabank Giller Prize.

Gival Press Novel Award ($3,000 and publication by Gival Press). *Winner:* Elizabeth Harris for *Mayhem: Three Lives of a Woman.*

Giverny Award. For an outstanding children's science picture book. *Offered by:* 15 Degree Laboratory. *Winner:* Lori Nichols, author and illustrator, for *Maple* (Nancy Paulsen).

Alexander Gode Medal. To an individual or institution for outstanding service to the translation and interpreting professions. *Offered by:* American Translators Association. *Winner:* Not awarded in 2014.

Goldberg Prize for Jewish Fiction by Emerging Writers ($2,500). To highlight new works by contemporary writers exploring Jewish themes. *Offered by:* Foundation for Jewish Culture. *Donor:* Samuel Goldberg and Sons Foundation. *Winner:* Award suspended in 2014.

Golden Duck Awards for Excellence in Children's Science Fiction Literature. *Sponsored by:* Super-Con-Duck-Tivity. *Winners:* (picture book) Jeffrey Brown for *Vader's Little Princess* (Chronicle); (Eleanor Cameron Award for middle grades books) Ray O'Ryan for *Hello Nebulon* and *Journey to Juno* (Little Simon); (Hal Clement Award for young adult books) Dan Krokos for *The Planet Thieves* (Starscape).

Golden Kite Awards. For children's books. *Offered by:* Society of Children's Book Writers and Illustrators. *Winners:* (picture book text) Pat Zietlow Miller for *Sophie's Squash* (Random); (picture book illustration) Peter Brown for *Mr. Tiger Goes Wild* (Little, Brown); (fiction) Tim Federle for *Better Nate than Ever* (Simon & Schuster); (nonfiction) David Meissner for *Call of the Klondike* (Boyds Mills); (Sid Fleischman Award for Humor) Bill Konigsberg for *Openly Straight* (Arthur A. Levine).

Governor General's Literary Awards (Canada) (C$25,000, plus C$3,000 to the publisher). For works, in English and in French, of fiction, nonfiction, poetry, drama, and children's literature, and for translation. *Offered by:* Canada Council for the Arts. *Winners:* (fiction, English) Thomas King for *The Back of the Turtle* (HarperCollins); (fiction, French) Andrée A. Michaud for *Bondrée* (Editions Québec Amérique); (nonfiction, English) Michael Harris for *The End of Absence: Reclaiming What We've Lost in a World of Constant Connection* (HarperCollins); (nonfiction, French) Gabriel Nadeau-Dubois for *Tenir Tête* (Lux Editeur); (poetry, English) Arleen Paré for *Lake of Two Mountains* (Brick); (poetry, French) José Acquelin for *Anarchie de la Lumière* (Editions du Passage); (drama, English) Jordan Tannahill for *Age of Minority: Three Solo Plays* (Playwrights Canada); (drama, French) Carole Fréchette for *Small Talk* (Leméac Editeur); (children's literature, text, English) Raziel Reid for *When Everything Feels like the Movies* (Arsenal Pulp); (children's literature, text, French) Linda Amyot for *Le Jardin d'Amsterdam* (Leméac Editeur); (children's literature, illustration, English) Jillian Tamaki for *This One Summer*, written by Mariko Tamaki (Groundwood); (children's literature, illustration, French) Marianne Dubuc for *Le Lion et l'Oiseau*, written by Marianne Dubuc (Editions de la Pastèque); (translation, French to English) Peter Feldstein for *Paul-Emile Borduas: A Critical Biography* by François-Marc Gagnon (McGill-Queen's University Press); (translation, English to French) Daniel Poliquin for *L'Indien Malcommode: Un Portrait Inat-*

tendu des Autochtones d'Amérique du Nord by Thomas King (Editions du Boréal).

Dolly Gray Children's Literature Awards. Presented biennially for fiction or biographical children's books with positive portrayals of individuals with developmental disabilities. *Offered by:* Council for Exceptional Children, Division on Autism and Developmental Disabilities. *Winners:* To be offered next in 2015.

Kate Greenaway Medal and Colin Mears Award. See CILIP Kate Greenaway Medal.

Eric Gregory Awards (United Kingdom) (£4,000). For a published or unpublished collection by poets under the age of 30. *Winners:* Sophie Collins, Emily Hasler (Lorrie Scott), Martha Sprackland, Chloe Stopa-Hunt, David Tait.

Griffin Poetry Prizes (Canada) (C$65,000). To a living Canadian poet or translator and a living poet or translator from any country, which may include Canada. *Offered by:* Griffin Trust. *Winners:* (international) Brenda Hillman for *Seasonal Works with Letters on Fire* (Wesleyan University Press); (Canadian) Anne Carson for *Red Doc>* (Cape).

Gryphon Award ($1,000). To recognize a noteworthy work of fiction or nonfiction for younger children. *Offered by:* The Center for Children's Books. *Winners:* Jon Scieszka and Mac Barnett, and Matthew Myers, illustrator, for *Battle Bunny* (Simon & Schuster).

Guardian Children's Fiction Prize (United Kingdom) (£1,500). For an outstanding children's or young adult novel. *Offered by:* The *Guardian*. *Winner:* Piers Torday for *The Dark Wild* (Viking).

Guardian First Book Award (United Kingdom) (£10,000). To recognize a first book. *Offered by:* The *Guardian*. *Winner:* Colin Barrett for the short story collection *Young Skins* (Cape).

Dashiell Hammett Prize. For a work of literary excellence in the field of crime writing by a U.S. or Canadian writer. *Offered by:* North American Branch, International Association of Crime Writers. *Winner:* Richard Lange for *Angel Baby* (Mulholland).

Hatchet Job of the Year (United Kingdom). To reward book critics who have the courage to overturn received opinion, and who do so with style. *Sponsor:* The Fish Society. *Winner:* A. A. Gill for his *Sunday Times* review of *Morrissey: Autobiography* by singer-songwriter Steven Patrick Morrissey (Penguin Classics).

R. R. Hawkins Award. For the outstanding professional/scholarly work of the year. *Offered by:* Association of American Publishers. *Winner:* Thomas Piketty and Arthur Goldhammer, translator, for *Capital in the Twenty-First Century* (Belknap Press of Harvard University Press).

Anthony Hecht Poetry Prize ($3,000 and publication by Waywiser Press). For an unpublished first or second book-length poetry collection. *Winner:* Geoffrey Brock for *Voices Bright Flags.*

Drue Heinz Literature Prize ($15,000 and publication by University of Pittsburgh Press). For short fiction. *Winner:* Kent Nelson for *The Spirit Bird.*

O. Henry Awards. See PEN/O. Henry Prize.

William Dean Howells Medal. In recognition of the most distinguished novel published in the preceding five years. *Offered by:* American Academy of Arts and Letters. *Winner:* To be awarded next in 2015.

Hugo Awards. For outstanding science fiction writing. *Offered by:* World Science Fiction Convention. *Winners:* (novel) Ann Leckie for *Ancillary Justice* (Orbit); (novella) Charles Stross for *Equoid* (Tor.com); (novelette) Mary Robinette Kowal for "The Lady Astronaut of Mars" (maryrobinettekowal.com/Tor.com); (short story) John Chu for "The Water That Falls on You from Nowhere" (Tor.com); (related work) Kameron Hurley for "We Have Always Fought: Challenging the Women, Cattle and Slaves Narrative" (in the online fanzine "A Dribble of Ink"); (graphic story) Randall Munroe for "Time" (XKCD); (dramatic presentation, long form) Alfonso Cuarón and Jonás Cuarón for *Gravity* (Warner Bros.); (dramatic presentation, short form) David Benioff and D. B. Weiss for *Game of Thrones: The Rains of Castamere* (HBO).

Hurston/Wright Legacy Awards. To writers of African American descent for a book of fiction, a book of nonfiction, and a book of poetry. *Offered by:* Hurston/Wright Foundation. *Winners:* (fiction) NoViolet Bulawayo for *We Need New Names* (Reagan Arthur); (nonfiction) Craig Steven Wilder for *Ebony and Ivy: Race, Slavery, and the Troubled History of America's Universities* (Bloomsbury); (poetry) Amaud Jamaul Johnson for *Darktown Follies* (Tupelo).

IMPAC Dublin Literary Award (Ireland) (€100,000). For a book of high literary merit, written in English or translated into English; if translated, the author receives €75,000 and the translator €25,000. *Offered by:* IMPAC Corp. and the City of Dublin. *Winner:* Juan Gabriel Vásquez and Anne McLean, translator from Spanish, for *The Sound of Things Falling* (Riverhead).

Independent Foreign Fiction Prize (United Kingdom) (£5,000 each for author and translator). For a work of fiction by a living author that has been translated into English from any other language and published in the United Kingdom. *Sponsor:* Arts Council England. *Winners:* Hassan Blasim, for his short story collection *The Iraqi Christ,* and Jonathan Wright, translator from Arabic (Comma).

Indies Choice Book Awards (formerly BookSense Book of the Year Awards). Chosen by owners and staff of American Booksellers Association member bookstores. *Winners:* (adult fiction) Kate Atkinson for *Life After Life* (Reagan Arthur); (adult nonfiction) Daniel James Brown for *The Boys in the Boat: Nine Americans and Their Epic Quest for Gold at the 1936 Berlin Olympics* (Viking); (adult debut) Anthony Marra for *A Constellation of Vital Phenomena* (Hogarth); (young adult) Rainbow Rowell for *Eleanor and Park* (St. Martin's Griffin).

International Prize for Arabic Fiction ($50,000 and publication in English). To reward excellence in contemporary Arabic creative writing. *Sponsors:* Booker Prize Foundation, Emirates Foundation for Philanthropy. *Winner:* Ahmed Saadawi for *Frankenstein in Baghdad* (Penguin).

IRA Children's and Young Adult Book Awards. For first or second books in any language published for children or young adults. *Offered by:* International Reading Association. *Winners:* (primary fiction) Stacy McAnulty for *Dear Santasaurus* (Boyds Mills); (primary nonfiction) Kathryn Selbert for *War Dogs: Churchill and Rufus* (Charlesbridge); (intermediate fiction) Liesl Shurtliff for *Rump: The True Story of Rumpelstiltskin* (Knopf); (intermediate nonfiction) Brian

McLachlan for *Draw Out the Story: Ten Secrets to Creating Your Own Comics* (Owlkids); (young adult fiction) Rainbow Rowell for *Eleanor and Park* (St. Martin's Griffin).

Rona Jaffe Foundation Writers' Awards ($30,000). To identify and support women writers of exceptional talent in the early stages of their careers. *Offered by:* Rona Jaffe Foundation. *Winners:* Olivia Clare, Karen Hays, Danielle Jones-Pruett, T. L. Khleif, Mara Naselli, Solmaz Sharif.

Jerusalem Prize (Israel). Awarded biennially to a writer whose works best express the theme of freedom of the individual in society. *Offered by:* Jerusalem International Book Fair. *Winner:* To be awarded next in 2015.

Jewish Book Council Awards. *Winners:* (Jewish Book of the Year) Ileene Smith, editorial director, and series editors Steven J. Zipperstein and Anita Shapira of Yale University Press for Yale's Jewish Lives Series; (American Jewish studies) Adam D. Mendelsohn for *The Rag Race: How Jews Sewed Their Way to Success in America and the British Empire* (NYU Press); (biography, autobiography, memoir) George Prochnik for *The Impossible Exile: Stefan Zweig at the End of the World* (Other); (children's and young adult) Devra Lehmann for *Spinoza: The Outcast Thinker* (Namelos); (contemporary Jewish life and practice) Shlomo M. Brody for *A Guide to the Complex: Contemporary Halakhic Debates* (Maggid); (education and Jewish identity) Elie Holzer with Orit Kent for *A Philosophy of Havruta: Understanding and Teaching the Art of Text Study in Pairs* (Academic Studies); (fiction) David Bezmozgis for *The Betrayers* (Little, Brown); (history) Yohanan Petrovsky-Shtern for *The Golden Age Shtetl: A New History of Jewish Life in East Europe* (Princeton University Press); (Holocaust) James A. Grymes for *Violins of Hope: Violins of the Holocaust—Instruments of Hope and Liberation in Mankind's Darkest Hour* (Harper Perennial); (illustrated children's book) Allison Ofanansky and Elsa Oriol, illustrator, for *The Patchwork Torah* (Kar-Ben); (modern Jewish thought and experience) Jay Goldmintz and Jonathan Sacks for *The Koren Ani Tefillah Siddur* (Koren); (outstanding debut fiction) Stuart Rojstaczer for *The Mathematician's Shiva* (Penguin); (scholarship)

Louis H. Feldman, James L. Kugel, and Lawrence H. Schiffman, editors, for *Outside the Bible: Ancient Jewish Writings Related to Scripture* (Jewish Publication Society); (Sephardic culture) Julia Phillips Cohen and Sarah Abrevaya Stein, editors, for *Sephardi Lives: A Documentary History, 1700–1950* (Stanford University Press); (women's studies) Kathryn Hellerstein for *A Question of Tradition: Women Poets in Yiddish, 1586–1987* (Stanford University Press); (writing based on archival material) Julia Phillips Cohen for *Becoming Ottomans: Sephardi Jews and Imperial Citizenship in the Modern Era* (Oxford University Press).

Samuel Johnson Prize for Nonfiction (United Kingdom) (£25,000). For an outstanding work of nonfiction. *Sponsor:* British Broadcasting Corporation. *Donor:* Anonymous. *Winner:* Helen Macdonald for *H is For Hawk* (Cape).

Sue Kaufman Prize for First Fiction ($5,000). For a first novel or collection of short stories. *Offered by:* American Academy of Arts and Letters. *Winner:* Manuel Gonzales for *The Miniature Wife and Other Stories* (Riverhead)

Ezra Jack Keats Awards. For children's picture books. *Offered by:* New York Public Library and the Ezra Jack Keats Foundation. *Winners:* (new writer award) Ame Dyckman for *Tea Party Rules,* illustrated by K. G. Campbell (Viking); (new illustrator award) Christian Robinson for *Rain!,* written by Linda Ashman (Houghton Mifflin Harcourt).

Kerlan Award. To recognize singular attainments in the creation of children's literature and in appreciation for generous donation of unique resources to the Kerlan Collection for the study of children's literature. *Offered by:* Kerlan Children's Literature Research Collections, University of Minnesota. *Winners:* Linda Sue Park, Russell Freedman.

Coretta Scott King Book Awards ($1,000). To an African American author and illustrator of outstanding books for children and young adults. *Offered by:* American Library Association, Ethnic and Multicultural Exchange Round Table (EMIERT). *Winners:* (author) Rita Williams-Garcia for *P.S. Be Eleven* (Amistad); (illustrator) Bryan Collier for *Knock Knock: My Dad's Dream for Me,* written by Daniel Beaty (Little, Brown).

Coretta Scott King/John Steptoe Award for New Talent. To offer visibility to a writer or illustrator at the beginning of a career. *Sponsor:* Coretta Scott King Book Award Committee. *Winner:* Theodore Taylor III, illustrator of *When the Beat was Born: DJ Kool Herc and the Creation of Hip Hop,* written by Laban Carrick Hill (Roaring Brook).

Coretta Scott King/Virginia Hamilton Award for Lifetime Achievement. Given in even-numbered years to an African American author, illustrator, or author/illustrator for a body of books for children or young adults. In odd-numbered years, the award honors substantial contributions through active engagement with youth, using award-winning African American literature for children or young adults. *Winners:* authors Patricia and Frederick McKissack.

Kirkus Prize ($50,000). For outstanding fiction, nonfiction, and young readers literature. *Offered by Kirkus: Reviews. Winners:* (fiction) Lily King for *Euphoria* (Atlantic Monthly); (nonfiction) Roz Chast for *Can't We Talk About Something More Pleasant?* (Bloomsbury); (young readers) Kate Samworth for *Aviary Wonders Inc.: Spring Catalog and Instruction Manual* (Clarion).

Lambda Literary Awards. To honor outstanding lesbian, gay, bisexual, and transgender (LGBT) literature. *Offered by:* Lambda Literary Foundation. *Winners:* (transgender fiction) Trish Salah for *Wanting in Arabic* (TSAR); (gay general fiction) Luis Negron and translator Suzanne Jill Levine for *Mundo Cruel: Stories* (Seven Stories); (lesbian general fiction) Chinelo Okparanta for *Happiness, Like Water* (Houghton Mifflin Harcourt); (LGBT debut fiction) Nik Nicholson for *Descendants of Hagar* (AuthorHouse); (transgender nonfiction) Mattilda Bernstein Sycamore for *The End of San Francisco* (City Lights); (bisexual nonfiction) Maria San Filippo for *The B Word: Bisexuality in Contemporary Film and Television* (Indiana University Press); (LGBT nonfiction) Hilton Als for *White Girls* (McSweeney's); (gay poetry) Rigoberto González for *Unpeopled Eden* (Four Way); (lesbian poetry) Ana Bozicevic for *Rise in the Fall* (Birds); (gay mystery) Janice Law for *The Prisoner of the Riviera: A Francis Bacon Mystery* (MysteriousPress.com); (lesbian mystery) Katherine

V. Forrest for *High Desert* (Spinsters Ink); (gay memoir/biography) Jerry Rosco, editor, for *A Heaven of Words: Last Journals, by Glenway Wescott* (University of Wisconsin Press); (lesbian memoir/biography) Barrie Jean Borich for *Body Geographic* (University of Nebraska Press); (gay romance) TJ Klune for *Into This River I Drown* (Dreamspinner); (lesbian romance) Andrea Bramhall for *Clean Slate* (Bold Strokes); (gay erotica) Alex Jeffers for *The Padisah's Son and the Fox* (Lethe); (lesbian erotica) Sacchi Green, editor, for *Wild Girls Wild Nights: True Lesbian Sex Stories* (Cleis); (LGBT anthology) Karen Martin and Makhosazana Xaba for *Queer Africa: New and Collected Fiction* (MaThoko's); (LGBT children's/young adult) Sara Farizan for *If You Could Be Mine* (Algonquin), and David Levithan for *Two Boys Kissing* (Knopf); (LGBT drama) Michel Marc Bouchard for *Tom at the Farm* (Talonbooks); (LGBT graphic novel) Nicole J. Georges for *Calling Dr. Laura: A Graphic Memoir* (Houghton Mifflin Harcourt); (LGBT science fiction/fantasy/horror) Melissa Scott and Amy Griswold for *Death by Silver* (Lethe); (LGBT studies) Christina B. Hanhardt for *Safe Space: Gay Neighborhood History and the Politics of Violence* (Duke University Press).

Harold Morton Landon Translation Award ($1,000). For a book of verse translated into English. *Offered by:* Academy of American Poets. *Winner:* W. S. Merwin for *Selected Translations* (Copper Canyon).

David J. Langum, Sr. Prize in American Historical Fiction ($1,000). To honor a book of historical fiction published in the previous year. *Winner:* Gary Schanbacher for *Crossing Purgatory* (Pegasus).

David J. Langum, Sr. Prize in American Legal History or Biography ($1,000). For a university press book that is accessible to the educated general public, rooted in sound scholarship, with themes that touch upon matters of general concern. *Winner:* Whitney Strub for *Obscenity Rules: Roth v. United States and the Long Struggle over Sexual Expression* (University Press of Kansas).

Lannan Foundation Literary Awards and Fellowships. To recognize young and mid-career writers of distinctive literary merit who demonstrate potential for continued outstanding work. *Offered by:* Lannan Foundation. *Winners:* (awards) (lifetime achievement) Steve Erickson, Joseph Stroud; (poetry) Claudia Rankine; (fellowships) (fiction) Mitchell S. Jackson; (poetry) Jill McDonough, Adrian Matejka, Jamaal May.

Latner Writers' Trust Poetry Prize (C$25,000). To a writer with an exceptional body of work in the field of poetry. *Winner:* Ken Babstock.

James Laughlin Award ($5,000). To commend and support a second book of poetry. *Offered by:* Academy of American Poets. *Winner:* Brian Blanchfield for *A Several World* (Nightboat).

Claudia Lewis Award. For the year's best poetry book or books for young readers. *Offered by:* Bank Street College of Education and the Florence M. Miller Memorial Fund. *Winner:* Joyce Sidman and Pamela Zagarenski, illustrator, for *What the Heart Knows: Chants, Charms, and Blessings* (Houghton Mifflin Harcourt)

Library of Congress Prize for American Fiction. To honor an American literary writer whose body of work is distinguished for its mastery of the art and for its originality of thought and imagination. *Offered by:* Library of Congress. *Winner:* E. L. Doctorow.

Ruth Lilly and Dorothy Sargent Rosenberg Poetry Fellowships ($25,800). To emerging poets to support their continued study and writing of poetry. *Offered by:* the Poetry Foundation. *Winners:* Hannah Gamble, Solmaz Sharif, Danez Smith, Ocean Vuong, and Wendy Xu.

Ruth Lilly Poetry Prize ($100,000). To a U.S. poet in recognition of lifetime achievement. *Offered by:* the Poetry Foundation. *Winner:* Nathaniel Mackey.

Astrid Lindgren Memorial Award (Sweden) (5 million kroner, approximately $582,000). In memory of children's author Astrid Lindgren, to honor outstanding children's literature and efforts to promote it. *Offered by:* Government of Sweden and the Swedish Arts Council. *Winner:* Swedish author Barbro Lindgren.

Locus Awards. For science fiction writing. *Offered by:* Locus Publications. *Winners:* (science fiction novel) James S. A. Corey for *Abaddon's Gate* (Orbit); (fantasy novel) Neil Gaiman for *The Ocean at the End of the Lane* (Morrow); (young adult book) Catherynne M. Valente for *The Girl Who Soared Over Fairyland and Cut the Moon in Two* (Feiwel & Friends); (first novel) Ann Leckie for *Ancillary Justice* (Orbit); (novella) Catherynne M. Valente for *Six-Gun Snow White* (Subterranean); (novelette) Neil Gaiman for "The Sleeper and the Spindle" (Rags and Bones); (short story) Caitlín R. Kiernan for "The Road of Needles" in *Once Upon a Time: New Fairy Tales* (Prime); (anthology) George R. R. Martin and Gardner Dozois, editors, for *Old Mars* (Bantam); (collection) Connie Willis for *The Best of Connie Willis* (Del Rey); (nonfiction) Jeff VanderMeer for *Wonderbook: The Illustrated Guide to Creating Imaginative Fiction* (Abrams Image); (art book) Cathy Fenner and Arnie Fenner, editors, for *Spectrum 20: The Best in Contemporary Fantastic Art* (Underwood).

London Book Festival Awards. To honor books worthy of further attention from the international publishing community. *Winners:* (general fiction and grand prize) Aaron T. Brownell for *Progression: A Sara Grey Tale* (iUniverse); (general nonfiction) Jason Lassen for *Hollywood Clown* (self-published); (children's) Delfeayo Marsalis and Reginald W. Butler, illustrator, for *No Cell Phone Day* (Kidstown); (young adult) F. T. Camargo for *Shanti and the Magic Mandala* (Lodestone); (business) Blanca De La Rosa for *Empower Yourself for an Amazing Career* (Balboa); (biography/autobiography/memoir) John Espinosa Nelson for *Where Excuses Go to Die* (Highrise); (how to) Dianna M. Young with Robert H. Mottram for *Think Like Your Dog and Enjoy the Rewards* (Island); (wild card) Edward Zellem for *Mataluna: 151 Afghan Pashto Proverbs* (Cultures Direct); (poetry) Dr. Neal Hall, M.D. for *Winter's a-Comin' Still* (surgeonpoet.com); (spiritual) Steven Manchester for *Twelve Months* (Story Plant); (romance) Evelyn Price for *A Man Above Reproach* (Montlake); (photography/art) Kathy L'amour, et al., for *Louis L'amour's 'Law of the Desert Born'* (Bantam); (science fiction) Milo Behr for *Beowulf: A Bloody Calculus* (self-published); (cookbooks) Mansour Gorji for *Zing! By Gorji* (Zing By Gorji Cookbook); (history) John N. Powers for *Bean Camp to Briar Patch: Life in the POW Camps of Korea and Vietnam* (Cronin).

Elizabeth Longford Prize for Historical Biography (United Kingdom) (£5,000). *Sponsors:* Flora Fraser and Peter Soros. *Winner:* Charles Moore for *Margaret Thatcher: The Authorized Biography, Volume One: Not For Turning* (Allen Lane).

Los Angeles Times Book Prizes. To honor literary excellence. *Offered by: Los Angeles Times. Winners:* (biography) Marie Arana for *Bolivar: American Liberator* (Simon & Schuster); Sheri Fink for *Five Days at Memorial: Life and Death in a Storm-Ravaged Hospital* (Crown); (fiction) Ruth Ozeki for *A Tale for the Time Being* (Viking); (Art Seidenbaum Award for First Fiction) NoViolet Bulawayo for *We Need New Names* (Reagan Arthur); (graphic novel/comics) Ulli Lust for *Today is the Last Day of the Rest of Your Life* (Fantagraphics); (history) Christopher Clark for *The Sleepwalkers: How Europe Went to War in 1914* (HarperCollins); (mystery/thriller) J. K. Rowling (writing As Robert Galbraith) for *The Cuckoo's Calling* (Mulholland); (poetry) Ron Padgett for *Collected Poems* (Coffee House); (science and technology) Alan Weisman for *Countdown: Our Last, Best Hope for a Future on Earth?* (Little, Brown); (young adult literature) Gene Luen Yang for *Boxers and Saints* (First Second); (Robert Kirsch Award for lifetime achievement) Susan Straight; (innovator's award) John Green.

Amy Lowell Poetry Traveling Scholarship. For one or two U.S. poets to spend one year outside North America in a country the recipients feel will most advance their work. *Offered by:* Amy Lowell Poetry Traveling Scholarship. *Winner:* Sam Taylor.

J. Anthony Lukas Awards. For nonfiction writing that demonstrates literary grace, serious research, and concern for an important aspect of American social or political life. *Offered by:* Columbia University Graduate School of Journalism and the Nieman Foundation for Journalism at Harvard. *Winners:* (Lukas Book Prize, $10,000) Sheri Fink for *Five Days at Memorial: Life and Death in a Storm-Ravaged Hospital* (Crown); (Mark Lynton History Prize, $10,000) Jill Lepore for *Book of Ages: The Life and Opinions of Jane Franklin* (Knopf); (Work-in-Progress Award, $30,000) Adrienne Berard for *When Yellow Was Black: The Untold Story of the First Fight for Desegregation in Southern Schools* (Beacon).

Macavity Awards. For excellence in mystery writing. *Offered by:* Mystery Readers International. *Winners:* (mystery novel) William Kent Krueger for *Ordinary Grace* (Atria); (first mystery) Terry Shames for *A Killing at Cotton Hill* (Seventh Street); (short story) Art Taylor for "The Care and Feeding of Houseplants" in *Ellery Queen Mystery Magazine,* March-April 2013; (nonfiction) Daniel Stashower for *The Hour of Peril: The Secret Plot to Murder Lincoln Before the Civil War* (Minotaur); (Sue Feder Historical Mystery Award) David Morrell for *Murder as a Fine Art* (Little, Brown).

McKitterick Prize (United Kingdom) (£4,000). To an author over the age of 40 for a first novel, published or unpublished. *Winner:* Gabriel Weston for *Dirty Work* (Little, Brown).

Man Booker International Prize (United Kingdom) (£60,000). Awarded biennially to a living author for a significant contribution to world literature. *Offered by:* Man Group. *Winner:* To be awarded next in 2015.

Man Booker Prize for Fiction (United Kingdom) (£50,000). For the best novel written in English by a Commonwealth author. *Offered by:* Booktrust and the Man Group. *Winner:* Richard Flanagan for *The Narrow Road to the Deep North* (Chatto & Windus).

Lenore Marshall Poetry Prize ($25,000). For an outstanding book of poems published in the United States. *Offered by:* Academy of American Poets. *Winner:* Rigoberto González for *Unpeopled Eden* (Four Way).

Mason Award ($10,000). To honor an author whose body of work has made extraordinary contributions to bringing literature to a wide reading public. *Sponsors:* George Mason University and Fall for the Book. *Winner:* Jodi Picoult.

Somerset Maugham Awards (United Kingdom) (£2,500). For works in any genre except drama by a writer under the age of 35, to enable young writers to enrich their work by gaining experience of foreign countries. *Winners:* (£4,000) Nadifa Mohamed for *The Orchard of Lost Souls* (Simon & Schuster), Daisy Hildyard for *Hunters in the Snow* (Cape); (£2,000) Amy Sackville for *Orkney* (Granta).

Addison M. Metcalf Award in Literature ($2,000). Awarded biennially in alternation with the Addison M. Metcalf Award in Art, to a young writer of great promise. *Offered by:* American Academy of Arts and Letters. *Winner:* To be awarded next in 2015.

Vicky Metcalf Award for Literature for Young People (Canada) (C$20,000). To a Canadian writer of children's literature for a body of work. *Offered by:* Metcalf Foundation. *Winner:* Cary Fagan.

Midwest Booksellers Choice Awards. *Offered by:* Midwest Booksellers Association. *Winners:* (fiction) Nickolas Butler for *Shotgun Lovesongs* (St. Martin's); (nonfiction) Robin Wall Kimmerer for *Braiding Sweetgrass* (Milkweed); (poetry) Joyce Sidman for *What the Heart Knows* (Houghton Mifflin Harcourt); (children's—middle grade and young adult) Kate DiCamillo and K. G. Campbell, illustrator, for *Flora and Ulysses: The Illuminated Adventures* (Candlewick); (picture book) Richard T. Morris and Tom Lichtenheld, illustrator, for *This is a Moose* (Little, Brown).

William C. Morris YA Debut Award. To honor a debut book published by a first-time author writing for teens and celebrating impressive new voices in young adult literature. *Offered by:* American Library Association, Young Adult Library Services Association. *Donor:* William C. Morris Endowment. *Winner:* Stephanie Kuehn for *Charm and Strange* (St. Martin's Griffin).

Gustavus Myers Awards. For outstanding books that extend understanding of the root causes of bigotry. *Offered by:* Gustavus Myers Center for the Study of Bigotry and Human Rights in North America. *Winners:* Awarded suspended in 2009 when the center closed for lack of funds.

Mythopoeic Fantasy Awards. To recognize fantasy or mythic literature for children and adults that best exemplifies the spirit of the Inklings, a group of fantasy writers that includes J. R. R. Tolkien, C. S. Lewis, and Charles Williams. *Offered by:* Mythopoeic Society. *Winners:* (adult literature) Helene Wecker for *The Golem and the Jinni* (HarperCollins); (children's literature) Holly Black for *Doll Bones* (Margaret K. McElderry); (Mythopoeic Scholarship Award in Inklings Studies) Jason Fisher, editor, for *Tolkien and the Study of His Sources: Critical Essays* (McFarland); (Mythopoeic Scholarship Award in Myth and Fantasy Studies) G. Ronald Murphy for *Tree of Salvation: Yggdrasil and the Cross in the North* (Oxford University Press).

National Book Awards. To celebrate the best in American literature. *Offered by:* National Book Foundation. *Winners:* (fiction) Phil Klay for *Redeployment* (Penguin); (nonfiction) Evan Osnos for *Age of Ambition: Chasing Fortune, Truth, and Faith in the New China* (Farrar, Straus & Giroux); (poetry) Louise Glück for *Faithful and Virtuous Night* Farrar, Straus & Giroux); (young people's literature) Jacqueline Woodson for *Brown Girl Dreaming* (Penguin).

National Book Awards (United Kingdom). See Specsavers National Book Awards.

National Book Critics Circle Awards. For literary excellence. *Offered by:* National Book Critics Circle. *Winners:* (fiction) Chimamanda Ngozi Adichie for *Americanah* (Knopf); (nonfiction) Sheri Fink for *Five Days at Memorial: Life and Death in a Storm-Ravaged Hospital* (Crown); (biography) Leo Damrosch for *Jonathan Swift: His Life and His World* (Yale University Press); (autobiography) Amy Wilentz for *Farewell, Fred Voodoo: A Letter From Haiti* (Simon & Schuster); (poetry) Frank Bidart for *Metaphysical Dog* (Farrar, Straus & Giroux); (criticism) Franco Moretti for *Distant Reading* (Verso); (Nona Balakian Citation for Excellence in Reviewing) Katherine A. Powers; (Ivan Sandrof Lifetime Achievement Award) author, translator, and essayist Rolando Hinojosa-Smith.

National Book Foundation Literarian Award for Outstanding Service to the American Literary Community. *Offered by:* National Book Foundation. *Winner:* Kyle Zimmer, president and co-founder, First Book.

National Book Foundation Medal for Distinguished Contribution to American Letters ($10,000). To a person who has enriched the nation's literary heritage over a life of service or corpus of work. *Offered by:* National Book Foundation. *Winner:* Ursula K. Le Guin.

National Translation Awards ($5,000). To honor translators whose work has made a valuable contribution to literary translation into English. *Offered by:* American Literary Translators Association. *Winners:* Eugene Ostashevsky and Matvei Yankelevich, translators from Russian, for *Alexander Vvedensky: An Invitation for Me to Think* (NYRB Poets); (Lucien Stryk Asian Translation Prize) Jonathan Chaves for *Every Rock a Universe: The Yellow Mountains and Chinese Travel Writing* (Floating World Editions).

Nebula Awards. For science fiction writing. *Offered by:* Science Fiction and Fantasy Writers of America (SFWA). *Winners:* (novel) Ann Leckie for *Ancillary Justice* (Orbit); (novella) Vylar Kaftan for *The Weight of the Sunrise* in *Asimov's,* February 2013; (novelette) Aliette de Bodard for "The Waiting Stars" in *The Other Half of the Sky* (Candlemark & Gleam); (short story) Rachel Swirsky for "If You Were a Dinosaur, My Love" in *Apex,* March 2013); (Ray Bradbury Award for Outstanding Dramatic Presentation) Alfonso Cuarón and Jonás Cuarón for *Gravity* (Warner Bros.); (Andre Norton Award for Young Adult Science Fiction and Fantasy) Nalo Hopkinson for *Sister Mine* (Grand Central); (Damon Knight Grand Master Award) Samuel R. Delany.

John Newbery Medal. For the most distinguished contribution to literature for children. *Offered by:* American Library Association, Association for Library Service to Children. *Winner:* Kate DiCamillo and K. G. Campbell, illustrator, for *Flora and Ulysses: The Illuminated Adventures* (Candlewick).

Nimrod Literary Awards ($2,000 plus publication). *Offered by:* Nimrod International Journal of Prose and Poetry. *Winners:* (Pablo Neruda Prize in Poetry) Mary-Alice Daniel for "Disease Map" and other poems; (Katherine Anne Porter Prize in Fiction) Shobha Rao for "Kavitha and Mustafa."

Nobel Prize in Literature (Sweden). For the total literary output of a distinguished career. *Offered by:* Swedish Academy. *Winner:* Patrick Modiano.

Eli M. Oboler Memorial Award. Given biennially to an author of a published work in English or in English translation dealing with issues, events, questions, or controversies in the area of intellectual freedom. *Offered by:* Intellectual Freedom Round Table, American Library Association. *Winner:* June Pinnell-Stephens for *Protecting Intellectual Freedom in Your Public Library: Scenarios from the Front Lines* (ALA Editions).

Flannery O'Connor Awards for Short Fiction. For collections of short fiction. *Offered by:* University of Georgia Press. *Winners:* Karin Lin-Greenberg for *Faulty Predictions*, Monica McFawn for *Bright Shards of Someplace Else* (both UGA Press).

Frank O'Connor Short Story Award (£25,000). An international award for a collection of short stories. *Offered by:* Munster Literature Centre, Cork, Ireland. *Sponsor:* Cork City Council. *Winner:* Colin Barrett for *Young Skins* (Cape).

Oddest Book Title of the Year Award. See Bookseller/Diagram Prize for Oddest Title of the Year.

Scott O'Dell Award for Historical Fiction ($5,000). *Offered by: Bulletin of the Center for Children's Books,* University of Chicago. *Winner:* Kirkpatrick Hill for *Bo at Ballard Creek* (Holt).

Odyssey Award. To the producer of the best audiobook for children and/or young adults available in English in the United States. *Sponsors:* American Library Association, ALSC/Booklist/YALSA. *Winner:* Listening Library for *Scowler* by Daniel Kraus, narrated by Kirby Heyborne.

Seán Ó Faoláin Short Story Competition (€1,500 and publication in the literary journal *Southword. Offered by:* Munster Literature Centre, Cork, Ireland. *Winner:* Susan Maier-Moul for "'Pleasure."

Dayne Ogilvie Prize (Canada) (C$4,000). To an emerging Canadian writer from the LGBT community who demonstrates promise through a body of quality work. *Offered by:* Writers' Trust of Canada. *Sponsor:* Robin Pacific. *Winner:* Tamai Kobayashi.

Orange Award for New Writers (United Kingdom) (£10,000). For a first novel or short story collection written by a woman and published in the United Kingdom. *Offered by:* Orange plc and Arts Council London. *Winner:* Award discontinued in 2011.

Orbis Pictus Award for Outstanding Nonfiction for Children. *Offered by:* National Council of Teachers of English. *Winners:* Jen Bryant and Melissa Sweet, illustrator, for *A Splash of Red: The Life and Art of Horace Pippin* (Knopf).

Orion Book Awards ($3,000). To recognize books that deepen connection to the natural world, present new ideas about mankind's relationship with nature, and achieve excellence in writing. *Sponsors: Orion Magazine* and the Geraldine R. Dodge Foundation. *Winners:* (fiction) Margaret Atwood for *MaddAddam* (Nan A. Talese); (nonfiction) Kathleen Jamie for *Sightlines: A Conversation with the Natural World* (Experiment).

Oxford-Weidenfeld Translation Prize. *Winner:* Susan Wicks for her translation of Valérie Rouzeau's *Talking Vrouz* (Arc).

PEN Award for Poetry in Translation ($3,000). For a book-length translation of poetry from any language into English, published in the United States. *Offered by:* PEN American Center. *Winners:* Karen Emmerich and Edmund Keeley for their translation from Greek of *Diaries of Exile* by Yannis Ritsos (Archipelago).

PEN/Saul Bellow Award for Achievement in American Fiction ($25,000). Awarded biennially to a distinguished living American author of fiction. *Offered by:* PEN American Center. *Winner:* Louise Erdrich.

PEN/Bellwether Prize for Socially Engaged Fiction ($25,000). Awarded biennially to the author of a previously unpublished novel that addresses issues of social justice and the impact of culture and politics on human relationships. *Founder:* Barbara Kingsolver. *Winner:* Ron Childress for "And West Is West," to be published by Algonquin.

PEN Beyond Margins Awards. See PEN Open Book Awards.

PEN/Robert W. Bingham Prize ($25,000). To a writer whose first novel or short story collection represents distinguished literary achievement and suggests great promise. *Offered by:* PEN American Center. *Winner:* Shawn Vestal for *Godforsaken Idaho* (Little A/New Harvest).

PEN/Diamonstein-Spielvogel Award for the Art of the Essay ($10,000). For a book of essays by a single author that best exemplifies the dignity and esteem of the essay form. *Winner:* James Wolcott for *Critical Mass* (Doubleday).

PEN/ESPN Award for Literary Sports Writing ($5,000). To a living writer or writers for exceptional contributions to the field of literary sports writing. *Winner:* Mark Fainaru-Wada and Steve Fainaru for *League of Denial* (Crown Archetype).

PEN/ESPN Lifetime Achievement Award for Literary Sports Writing ($5,000). For a writer whose body of work represents an exceptional contribution to the field. *Winner:* Dave Anderson.

PEN/Faulkner Award for Fiction ($15,000). To honor the year's best work of fiction published by an American. *Winner:* Karen Joy Fowler for *We Are All Completely Beside Ourselves* (Putnam/Marian Wood).

PEN/John Kenneth Galbraith Award ($10,000). Given biennially for a distinguished book of general nonfiction. *Offered by:* PEN American Center. *Winner:* To be awarded next in 2015.

PEN/Heim Translation Fund Grants ($3,300). To support the translation of book-length works of fiction, creative nonfiction, poetry, or drama that have not previously appeared in English or have appeared only in an egregiously flawed translation. *Winners:* Kurt Beals, Eric M. B. Becker, David Burnett, Janet Hong, Paul Hoover, Andrea G. Labinger, Sergey Levchin, Zachary Ludington, J. Bret Maney, Philip Metres and Dimitri Psurtsev, Sayuri Okamoto, Benjamin Paloff, Miranda Richmond Mouillot, Thom Satterlee, Sholeh Wolpé.

PEN/Ernest Hemingway Foundation Award. For a distinguished work of first fiction by an American. *Offered by:* PEN New England. *Winner:* NoViolet Bulawayo for *We Need New Names* (Reagan Arthur).

PEN/O. Henry Prize. For short stories of exceptional merit, in English, published in U.S. and Canadian magazines. *Winners:* Mark Haddon for "The Gun" in *Granta*; Stephen Dixon for "Talk" in the *American Reader*; Tessa Hadley for "Valentine" in the *New Yorker*; Olivia Clare for "Pétur" in *Ecotone*; David Bradley for "You Remember the Pin Mill" in *Narrative*; Kirstin Valdez Quade for "Nemecia" in *NarrativeMagazine.com*; Dylan Landis for "Trust" in *Tin House*; Allison Alsup for "Old Houses" in *New Orleans Review*; Halina Duraj for "Fatherland" in *Harvard Review*; Chanelle Benz for "West of the Known" in the *American Reader*; William Trevor for "The Women" in the *New Yorker* Colleen Morrissey for "Good Faith" in the *Cincinnati Review*;

Robert Anthony Siegel for "The Right Imaginary Person" in *Tin House*; Louise Erdrich for "Nero" in the *New Yorker*; Rebecca Hirsch Garcia for "A Golden Light" in the *Threepenny Review*; Chinelo Okparanta for "Fairness" in *Subtropics*; Kristen Iskandrian for "The Inheritors" in *Tin House*; Michael Parker for "Deep Eddy" in *Southwest Review*; Maura Stanton for "Oh Shenandoah" in *New England Review*; Laura van den Berg for "Opa-locka" in the *Southern Review*.

PEN/Steven Kroll Award ($5,000). To an author of exceptional writing in an illustrated children's book. *Winner:* Bil Lepp for *The King of Little Things,* illustrated by David T. Wenzel (Peachtree).

PEN/Nora Magid Award ($2,500). Awarded biennially to honor a magazine editor who has contributed significantly to the excellence of the publication he or she edits. *Winners:* To be awarded next in 2015.

PEN/Malamud Award. To recognize a body of work that demonstrates excellence in the art of short fiction. *Winner:* To be announced.

PEN/Ralph Manheim Medal for Translation. Given triennially to a translator whose career has demonstrated a commitment to excellence. *Winner:* To be awarded next in 2015.

PEN/Phyllis Naylor Working Writer Fellowship ($5,000). To a published author of children's or young adults' fiction to aid in completing a book-length work in progress. *Offered by:* PEN American Center. *Winner:* Linda Oatman High for "The Taste of Elephant Tears."

PEN New England Awards. For works of fiction, nonfiction, and poetry by New England writers or with New England topics or settings. *Winners:* (fiction) Jennifer Haigh for *News From Heaven* (Harper); (nonfiction) Doug Bauer for *What Happens Next* (University of Iowa Press), (poetry) Karen Skofield for *Frost in Low Areas* (Zone 3).

PEN New England Susan P. Bloom Children's Book Discovery Award. For noteworthy unpublished children's or young adult literature. *Winners:* Rebecca Roan for the picture book "Dragons Get Colds Too"; Pamela Sonn for the nonfiction picture book "Jedediah Buxton, The Human Calculator"; Mackenzie Van Engelenhoven for the YA novel "The Shadow Boys Are Breaking."

PEN New England Henry David Thoreau Prize for Literary Excellence in Nature Writing. *Winner:* T. C. Boyle.

PEN Open Book Award (formerly PEN Beyond Margins Award) ($1,000). For book-length writings by authors of color, published in the United States during the current calendar year. *Offered by:* PEN American Center. *Winners:* Ruth Ellen Kocher for *domina Un/blued* (Tupelo); Nina McConigley for *Cowboys and East Indians* (FiveChapters).

PEN/Joyce Osterweil Award for Poetry ($5,000). A biennial award given in odd-numbered years to recognize a new and emerging American poet. *Offered by:* PEN American Center. *Winner:* To be awarded next in 2015.

PEN/Laura Pels Foundation Awards for Drama. To recognize a master American dramatist, an American playwright in mid-career, and an emerging American playwright. *Offered by:* PEN American Center. *Winners:* (master dramatist, $7,500) David Rabe; (mid-career, $7,500) Donald Margulies; (emerging playwright, $2,500) Laura Marks.

PEN Prison Writing Awards. To provide support and encouragement to prison inmates whose writing shows merit or promise. *Offered by:* PEN American Center. *Winners:* (poetry) E. R. Hayson for "An Ordinary Prison"; (fiction) Thomas Whitaker for "Manufacturing Anomie"; (essay) Thomas Whitaker for "A Nothing Would Do as Well"; (memoir) Steve Bartholomew for "Son of the District"; (drama) Mylrell Minner for "Desert World."

PEN Translation Prize ($3,000). To promote the publication and reception of translated world literature in English. *Winners:* Joanne Turnbull and Nikolai Formozov for their translation from Russian of *Autobiography of a Corpse* by Sigizmund Krzhizhanovsky (New York Review of Books).

PEN/Voelcker Award for Poetry. Given in even-numbered years to an American poet at the height of his or her powers. *Offered by:* PEN American Center. *Winner:* Frank Bidart.

PEN/Jacqueline Bograd Weld Award for Biography ($5,000). To the author of a distinguished biography published in the United States during the previous calendar year. *Offered by:* PEN American Center. *Win-

ner: Linda Leavell for *Holding On Upside Down: The Life and Work of Marianne Moore* (Farrar, Straus & Giroux).

PEN/E. O. Wilson Literary Science Writing Award ($10,000). For a book of literary nonfiction on the subject of the physical and biological sciences. *Winner:* Carl Hart for *High Price* (Harper).

Maxwell E. Perkins Award. To honor an editor, publisher, or agent who has discovered, nurtured, and championed writers of fiction in the United States. *Offered by:* Center for Fiction, Mercantile Library of New York. *Winner:* Nicole Aragi, agent, Aragi Inc.

Phoenix Awards. To the authors of English-language children's books that failed to win a major award at the time of publication 20 years earlier. *Winners:* Gary Soto for *Jesse* (Houghton Mifflin Harcourt); (picture book award) Raymond Briggs for *The Bear* (Julia MacRae).

Edgar Allan Poe Awards. For outstanding mystery, suspense, and crime writing. *Offered by:* Mystery Writers of America. *Winners:* (novel) William Kent Krueger for *Ordinary Grace* (Simon & Schuster); (first novel) Jason Matthews for *Red Sparrow* (Simon & Schuster); (paperback original) Alex Marwood for *The Wicked Girls* (Penguin); (fact crime) Daniel Stashower for *The Hour of Peril: The Secret Plot to Murder Lincoln Before the Civil War* (Minotaur); (critical/biographical) Erik Dussere for *America is Elsewhere: The Noir Tradition in the Age of Consumer Culture* (Oxford University Press); (short story) John Connolly for "The Caxton Private Lending Library and Book Depository" (Mysterious Bookshop); (juvenile) Amy Timberlake for *One Came Home* (Random); (young adult) Annabel Pitcher for *Ketchup Clouds* (Hachette); (television episode) Allan Cubitt for "The Fall," Episode 1 (Netflix); (Robert L. Fish Memorial Award) Jeff Soloway for "The Wentworth Letter" in *Criminal Element's Malfeasance Occasional* (St. Martin's); (grand master) Robert Crais, Carolyn Hart; (Simon & Schuster Mary Higgins Clark Award) Jenny Milchman for *Cover of Snow* (Random).

Poets Out Loud Prize ($1,000 and publication by Fordham University Press). For a book-length poetry collection. *Sponsor:* Fordham University. *Winners:* Daneen Wardrop for

"Cyclorama"; Terrence Chiusano for "On Generation and Corruption: Poems."

Katherine Anne Porter Award ($20,000). Awarded biennially to a prose writer of demonstrated achievement. *Offered by:* American Academy of Arts and Letters. *Winner:* Sherman Alexie.

Michael L. Printz Award. For excellence in literature for young adults. *Offered by:* American Library Association, Young Adult Library Services Association. *Winner:* Marcus Sedgwick for *Midwinterblood* (Roaring Brook).

V. S. Pritchett Memorial Prize (United Kingdom) (£1,000). For a previously unpublished short story. *Offered by:* Royal Society of Literature. *Winner:* Alice Jolly for "Ray the Rottweiler."

Pritzker Military Library Literature Award ($100,000). To recognize a living author for a body of work that has profoundly enriched the public understanding of American military history. *Sponsor:* Tawani Foundation. *Winner:* Antony Beevor.

Prix Aurora Awards (Canada). For science fiction. *Winners:* (novel) Julie E. Czerneda for *A Turn of Light* (DAW); (young adult novel) Kelley Armstrong for *The Rising* (Doubleday Canada); (short fiction) Ryan McFadden for "Ghost in the Machine" in *The Puzzle Box* (Edge Science Fiction and Fantasy); (poem/song) Eileen Kernaghan for "Night Journey: West Coast" in *Tesseracts Seventeen* (Edge Science Fiction and Fantasy); (graphic novel) Peter Chiykowski for the webcomic *Rock, Paper, Cynic*; (related work) *On Spec* (Copper Pig Writers' Society).

Prix Goncourt (France). For "the best imaginary prose work of the year." *Offered by:* Société des Gens des Lettres. *Winner:* Lydie Salvayre's for *Pas Pleurer* (*Don't Cry*) (French and European Publications).

Pulitzer Prizes in Letters ($10,000). To honor distinguished work dealing preferably with American themes. *Offered by:* Columbia University Graduate School of Journalism. *Winners:* (fiction) Donna Tartt for *The Goldfinch* (Little, Brown); (drama) Annie Baker for *The Flick*; (history) Alan Taylor for *The Internal Enemy: Slavery and War in Virginia, 1772–1832* (Norton); (biography/autobiography) Megan Marshall for *Marga-*

ret Fuller: A New American Life (Houghton Mifflin Harcourt); (poetry) Vijay Seshadri for *3 Sections* (Graywolf); (general nonfiction) Dan Fagin for *Toms River: A Story of Science and Salvation* (Bantam).

Raiziss/De Palchi Translation Award ($5,000 prize and a $25,000 fellowship, awarded in alternate years). For a translation into English of a significant work of modern Italian poetry by a living translator. *Offered by:* Academy of American Poets. *Winner:* Luigi Bonaffini for his translation of *The Bedroom* by Attilio Bertolucci (Chelsea Editions)

RBC Bronwen Wallace Award for Emerging Writers (C$5,000) (Canada). For a writer under the age of 35 who has not yet been published in book form. *Sponsor:* RBC Foundation. *Winner:* Erin Frances Fisher for the short story "Girl."

Arthur Rense Poetry Prize ($20,000). Awarded triennially to an exceptional poet. *Offered by:* American Academy of Arts and Letters. *Winner:* Ellen Bryant Voigt.

John Llewellyn Rhys Prize (United Kingdom) (£5,000). For a work of literature by a British or Commonwealth author 35 or younger and published in the United Kingdom. *Offered by:* Booktrust. *Winner:* Award suspended in 2011.

Harold U. Ribalow Prize. For Jewish fiction published in English. *Sponsor:* Hadassah magazine. *Winner:* Helene Wecker for *The Golem and the Jinni* (HarperCollins).

Rita Awards. *Offered by:* Romance Writers of America. *Winners:* (first book) Laura Drake for *The Sweet Spot* (Grand Central); (contemporary romance) Molly O'Keefe for *Crazy Thing Called Love* (Random); (short contemporary) Leah Ashton for *Why Resist a Rebel?* (Harlequin); (erotic) J. Kenner for *Claim Me* (Random); (historical) Sarah MacLean for *No Good Duke Goes Unpunished* (Avon); (inspirational) Carla Laureano for *Five Days in Skye* (David C. Cook); (paranormal) Susanna Kearsley for *The Firebird* (Sourcebooks); (novella) Jane Porter for *Take Me, Cowboy* (Tule); (suspense) Carolyn Crane for *Off the Edge* (self published).

Rita Golden Heart Awards. For worthy unpublished romance manuscripts. *Offered by:* Romance Writers of America. *Winners:* (contemporary) Suzanne Kaufman Kalb for "Too Good to Be True"; (short contemporary) Sarah Cannon for "Yesterday's Promise"; (historical) Lenora Bell for "Charlene and the Duchess Factory"; (inspirational) Kristi Ann Hunter for "My Lord Valet"; (paranormal) Marni Folsom for "Beyond the Fire"; (suspense) Denny S. Bryce for "Chasing Damn"; (young adult) McCall Hoyle for "The Thing with Feathers."

Rodda Book Award. To recognize a book that exhibits excellence in writing and has contributed significantly to congregational libraries through promotion of spiritual growth. The award is given to books for adults, young adults, and children on a rotational basis. *Offered by:* Church and Synagogue Library Association. *Winner:* (children's book), Sally Lloyd-Jones and Jago, illustrator, for *Thoughts to Make Your Heart Sing* (Zonderkidz).

Rogers Writers' Trust Fiction Prize (Canada) (C$25,000). To a Canadian author of a novel or short story collection. *Offered by:* Rogers Communications. *Winner:* Miriam Toews for *All My Puny Sorrows* (Knopf Canada).

Sami Rohr Prize for Jewish Literature ($100,000). For emerging writers of Jewish literature. *Offered by:* Family of Sami Rohr. *Winner:* Matti Friedman for *The Aleppo Codex: A True Story of Obsession, Faith, and the Pursuit of an Ancient Bible* (Algonquin).

Rosenthal Foundation Award ($10,000). To a young novelist of considerable literary talent. *Offered by:* American Academy of Arts and Letters. *Winner:* Laura Van Den Berg for *The Isle of Youth* (FSG Originals).

Royal Society of Literature Benson Medal (United Kingdom). To recognize meritorious works in poetry, fiction, history and belles lettres, honoring an entire career. The recipient may be someone who is not a writer but has done conspicuous service to literature. *Winners:* Deirdre La Faye, Jane Austen scholar and author of the biography *Jane Austen: A Family Record*; Russian scholar and writer Valentina Polukhina.

Royal Society of Literature Jerwood Awards for Nonfiction (United Kingdom). For authors engaged on their first major commissioned works of nonfiction. *Offered by:* Royal Society of Literature. *Winners:* (£10,000) Laurence Scott for "The Four-Dimensional Human"; (£5,000) Minocher Dinshaw for

"A Life of Sir Steven Runciman"; writer and editor Aida Edemariam for an as yet untitled biography of the author's grandmother.

Royal Society of Literature Ondaatje Prize (United Kingdom) (£10,000). For a distinguished work of fiction, nonfiction, or poetry evoking the spirit of a place. *Offered by:* Royal Society of Literature. *Winner:* Alan Johnson for *This Boy: A Memoir of a Childhood* (Bantam).

Juan Rulfo International Latin American and Caribbean Prize. See FIL Literary Award in Romance Languages.

Saltire Society Scotland Literary Awards. To recognize noteworthy work by writers of Scottish descent or living in Scotland, or by anyone who deals with the work or life of a Scot or with a Scottish problem, event, or situation. *Offered by:* Saltire Society. *Sponsors:* Creative Scotland, the National Library of Scotland, the Scottish Poetry Library, the Scottish Historical Review Trust, Tamdhu Speyside Single Malt Scotch Whisky. *Winners (book of the year £5,000, individual categories £2,000):* (Scottish research book and book of the year) Bob Harris and Charles McKean for *The Scottish Town in the Age of Enlightenment 1740–1820* (Edinburgh University Press); (literary book of the year) Ali Smith for *How to be Both* (Hamish Hamilton); (poetry book of the year) Alexander Hutchison for *Bones and Breath* (Salt); (first book) Niall Campbell for *Moontide* (Bloodaxe); (history book) Steve Bruce for *Scottish Gods: Religion in the Modern Scotland 1900–2012* (Edinburgh University Press); (Scottish publisher of the year, £4,000) Sandstone Press.

Carl Sandburg Literary Awards. To honor a significant body of work that has enhanced public awareness of the written word. *Sponsor:* Chicago Public Library Foundation. *Winners:* (fiction) novelist and screenwriter Larry McMurtry; (nonfiction) biographer Doris Kearns Goodwin; (21st Century Award, for significant recent achievement by a Chicago-area writer) Veronica Roth, author of the "Divergent" trilogy.

Schneider Family Book Awards ($5,000). To honor authors and illustrators for books that embody artistic expressions of the disability experience of children and adolescents. *Offered by:* American Library Association.

Donor: Katherine Schneider. *Winners:* (ages 0–8) Jen Bryant and Melissa Sweet, illustrator, for *A Splash of Red: The Life and Art of Horace Pippin* (Knopf); (ages 9–13) Merrie Haskell for *Handbook for Dragon Slayers* (HarperCollins); (ages 14–18) Elizabeth Wein for *Rose Under Fire* (Hyperion).

Scotiabank Giller Prize (Canada) (C$100,000 first place, C$10,000 to each of the finalists). For the best Canadian novel or short story collection written in English. *Offered by:* Giller Prize Foundation and Scotiabank. *Winners:* Sean Michaels for *Us Conductors* (Random Canada); (finalists) David Bezmozgis for *The Betrayers* (HarperCollins); Frances Itani for *Tell* (HarperCollins); Heather O'Neill for *The Girl Who Was Saturday Night* (HarperCollins); Miriam Toews for *All My Puny Sorrows* (Knopf Canada); Padma Viswanathan for *The Ever After of Ashwin Rao* (Random Canada).

Scottish Mortgage Investment Trust Book Awards. *Sponsor:* Scottish Arts Council. *Donor:* Scottish Mortgage Investment Trust. *Winners:* Awards discontinued in 2013.

Shamus Awards. To honor mysteries featuring independent private investigators. *Offered by:* Private Eye Writers of America. *Winners:* (hardcover novel) Brad Parks for *The Good Cop* (Minotaur); (first novel) Lachlan Smith for *Bear Is Broken* (Mysterious); (original paperback) P. J. Parrish for *Heart of Ice* (Pocket); (short story) Max Allan Collins and Mickey Spillane for "So Long, Chief" in *Strand Magazine*; (indie novel) M. Ruth Myers for *Don't Dare a Dame* (Tuesday House); (Shamus Award for Lifetime Achievement) Sue Grafton; (Hammer Award for Best Series Character) Sue Grafton for Kinsey Millhone; (St. Martin's/PWA Award, for an unpublished novel) Grant Bywaters for *The Red Storm.*

Roger Shattuck Prize for Criticism ($5,000). To support and encourage emerging critics. *Offered by:* Center for Fiction, Mercantile Library of New York. *Winner:* Not awarded in 2014.

Shelley Memorial Award ($6,000 to $9,000). To a poet or poets living in the United States, chosen on the basis of genius and need. *Offered by:* Poetry Society of America. *Winner:* Bernadette Mayer.

Robert F. Sibert Medal. For the most distinguished informational book for children. *Offered by:* American Library Association, Association for Library Service to Children. *Winner:* Susan L. Roth and Cindy Trumbore for *Parrots over Puerto Rico* (Lee & Low).

Society of Authors Traveling Scholarships (United Kingdom) (£2,500). *Winners:* Eimear McBride, Daljit Nagra, Michela Wrong.

Specsavers National Book Awards (United Kingdom) (formerly the Galaxy National Book Awards, earlier the British Book Awards). *Winners:* (book of the year and writer of the year) Jessie Burton for *The Miniaturist* (Pan Macmillan); (crime/thriller) Terry Hayes for *I Am Pilgrim* (Transworld); (autobiography/biography) Alan Johnson for *Please, Mister Postman* (Transworld); (food and drink) Yotam Ottolenghi for *Plenty More* (Ebury); (children's book and audiobook) David Walliams for *Awful Auntie* (HarperCollins); (international author of the year) Karen Joy Fowler for *We Are All Completely Beside Ourselves* (Putnam/Marian Wood); (popular fiction) Nathan Filer for *The Shock of the Fall* (HarperCollins); (nonfiction) Nina Stibbe for *Love, Nina* (Penguin); (UK author of the year) David Nicholls for *Us* (Hodder & Stoughton).

Spur Awards. *Offered by:* Western Writers of America. *Winners:* (contemporary novel) James Lee Burke for *Light of the World* (Simon & Schuster); (historical novel) Henry Chappell for *Silent We Stood* (Texas Tech University Press); (traditional novel) Gary Schanbacher for *Crossing Purgatory* (Pegasus); (first novel) Anne Hillerman for *Spider Woman's Daughter* (HarperCollins); (historical nonfiction) Mark Lee Gardner for *Shot all to Hell: Jesse James, the Northfield Raid, and the Wild West's Greatest Escape* (Morrow); (contemporary nonfiction) William Philpott for *Vacationland: Tourism and Environment in the Colorado High Country* (University of Washington Press); (nonfiction biography) Earle Labor for *Jack London: An American Life* (Farrar, Straus & Giroux); (juvenile fiction) Ellen Gray Massey for *Papa's Gold* (Pen-L); (juvenile nonfiction) Jean A. Lukesh for *Eagle of Delight: Portrait of the Plains Indian Girl in the White House* (Field Mouse Produc-

tions); (storyteller) Ginger Wadsworth and Daniel San Souci for *Yosemite's Songster: One Coyote's Story* (Yosemite Conservancy); (short fiction) Brett Cogburn for "Cabin Fever" (High Hill); (short nonfiction) Mark Lee Gardner for "The Other James Brother" (Wild West); (poem) Amy Glynn Greacen for "Chamise" (Orion); (song) Waddie Mitchell and Juni Fisher for "Still There" (Red Geetar Music); (documentary script) M. Smoker for "Indian Relay" (Dye Works Film).

Wallace Stevens Award ($100,000). To recognize outstanding and proven mastery in the art of poetry. *Offered by:* Academy of American Poets. *Winner:* Robert Hass.

Bram Stoker Awards. For superior horror writing. *Offered by:* Horror Writers Association. *Winners:* (novel) Stephen King for *Doctor Sleep* (Scribner); (first novel) Rena Mason for *The Evolutionist* (Nightscape); (young adult novel) Joe McKinney for *Dog Days* (JournalStone); (graphic novel) Caitlín R. Kiernan for *Alabaster: Wolves* (Dark Horse); (long fiction) Gary Braunbeck "The Great Pity" in *Chiral Mad 2* (Written Backwards); (short fiction) David Gerrold for "Night Train to Paris" in the *Magazine of Fantasy and Science Fiction,* January/February 2013; (screenplay) Glen Mazzara for "The Walking Dead: Welcome to the Tombs" (AMC TV); (lifetime achievement) Stephen Jones, R. L. Stine.

Stonewall Book Awards. *Offered by:* Gay, Lesbian, Bisexual, and Transgender Round Table, American Library Association. *Winners:* (Barbara Gittings Literature Award) Hilary Sloin for *Art on Fire* (Bywater); (Israel Fishman Nonfiction Award) David McConnell for *American Honor Killings: Desire and Rage Among Men* (Akashic); Lori Duron for *Raising My Rainbow: Adventures in Raising a Fabulous, Gender Creative Son* (Broadway); (Mike Morgan and Larry Romans Children's and Young Adult Literature Award) Kirstin Cronn-Mills for *Beautiful Music for Ugly Children* (Flux); E. E. Charlton-Trujillo for *Fat Angie* (Candlewick).

Story Prize ($20,000). For a collection of short fiction. *Offered by: Story* magazine. *Winner:* George Saunders for *Tenth of December* (Random).

Flora Stieglitz Straus Award. For nonfiction books that serve as an inspiration to young readers. *Offered by:* Bank Street College of Education and the Florence M. Miller Memorial Fund. *Winner:* Michelle Markel and Melissa Sweet, illustrator, for *Brave Girl: Clara and the Shirtwaist Makers' Strike of 1909* (Balzer + Bray).

Theodore Sturgeon Memorial Award. For the year's best short science fiction. *Offered by:* Center for the Study of Science Fiction. *Winner:* Sarah Pinsker for "In Joy, Knowing the Abyss Behind" in the online magazine *Strange Horizons,* July 2013.

Sunburst Awards for Canadian Literature of the Fantastic (C$1,000). *Winners:* (adult) Ruth Ozeki for *A Tale for the Time Being* (Penguin Canada); (young adult) Charles de Lint for *The Cats of Tanglewood Forest* (Little, Brown).

Sunday Times EFG Short Story Award (United Kingdom) (£30,000). To an author from any country for an English-language story of 6,000 words or less *Winner:* Adam Johnson for "Nirvana."

Tanizaki Junichiro Prize (Japan) (1 million yen, approximately $8,450). For a full-length work of fiction or drama by a professional writer. *Offered by:* Chuokoron-Shinsha, Inc. *Winner:* Hikaru Okuizumi for *Tokyo Jijoden* (Tokyo Autobiography).

Charles Taylor Prize for Literary Nonfiction (Canada) (C$25,000). To honor a book of creative nonfiction widely available in Canada and written by a Canadian citizen or landed immigrant. *Offered by:* Charles Taylor Foundation. *Winner:* Thomas King for *The Inconvenient Indian: A Curious Account of Native People in North America* (Doubleday Canada).

Sydney Taylor Children's Book Awards. For a distinguished contribution to Jewish children's literature. *Offered by:* Association of Jewish Libraries. *Winners:* (younger readers) Laurel Snyder and Catia Chien, illustrator, for *The Longest Night: A Passover Story* (Schwartz & Wade); (older readers) Patricia Polacco for *The Blessing Cup* (Simon & Schuster); (teen readers) Neal Bascomb for *The Nazi Hunters: How a Team of Spies and Survivors Captured the World's Most Notorious Nazi* (Scholastic).

Sydney Taylor Manuscript Competition ($1,000). For the best fiction manuscript appropriate for readers ages 8–13, both Jewish and non-Jewish, revealing positive aspects of Jewish life, and written by an unpublished author. *Winner:* Susan Krawitz for *Viva, Rose.*

Theatre Library Association Award. See Richard Wall Memorial Award.

Dylan Thomas Prize (United Kingdom) (£30,000). For a published or produced literary work in the English language, written by an author under 30. *Offered by:* University of Wales. *Winner:* Joshua Ferris for *To Rise Again at a Decent Hour* (Viking).

Thriller Awards. *Offered by:* International Thriller Writers. *Winners:* (hardcover novel) Andrew Pyper for *The Demonologist* (Simon & Schuster); (paperback original) Jennifer McMahon for *The One I Left Behind* (Morrow); (first novel) Jason Matthews for *Red Sparrow* (Scribner); (e-book original) Rebecca Cantrell for *The World Beneath* (self published); (young adult) Cristin Terrill for *All Our Yesterdays* (Hyperion); (short story) Twist Phelan for "Footprints in Water" in *Ellery Queen Mystery Magazine*; (ThrillerMaster award for career achievement and outstanding contributions to the genre) Scott Turow.

Thurber Prize for American Humor ($5,000). For a humorous book of fiction or nonfiction. *Offered by:* Thurber House. *Winner:* John Kenney for *Truth in Advertising* (Touchstone).

Tom-Gallon Trust Award (United Kingdom) (£1,000). For a short story. *Offered by:* Society of Authors. *Sponsor:* Authors' Licensing and Collecting Society. *Winner:* Benjamin Myers for "The Folk Song Singer."

Betty Trask Prize and Awards (United Kingdom). To Commonwealth writers under the age of 35 for "romantic or traditional" first novels. *Offered by:* Society of Authors. *Winners:* (Betty Trask Prize, £10,000) Nathan Filer for *The Shock of the Fall* (HarperCollins); (Betty Trask Awards, £3,750) NoViolet Bulawayo for *We Need New Names* (Reagan Arthur), Sam Byers for *Idiopathy* (Fourth Estate), Mave Fellowes for *Chaplin and Company* (Cape), Matt Greene for *Ostrich* (Weidenfeld).

Kate Tufts Discovery Award ($10,000). For a first or very early book of poetry by an emerging poet. *Offered by:* Claremont Graduate School. *Winner:* Yona Harvey for *Hemming the Water* (Four Way).

Kingsley Tufts Poetry Award ($100,000). For a book of poetry by a mid-career poet. *Offered by:* Claremont Graduate School. *Winner:* Afaa Michael Weaver for *The Government of Nature* (University of Pittsburgh Press).

21st Century Award. To honor recent achievement in writing by an author with ties to Chicago. See Carl Sandburg Literary Awards.

UKLA Children's Book Awards (United Kingdom). *Sponsor:* United Kingdom Literacy Association. *Winners:* (ages 3–6) Jon Klassen for *This is not my Hat* (Walker); (ages 7–11) Andri Snaer Magnason, Julian Meldon D'Arcy, translator, and Áslaug Jónsdóttir, illustrator, for *The Story of the Blue Planet* (Pushkin); (ages 12–16) Michael Williams for *Now is the Time for Running* (Tamarind).

Ungar German Translation Award ($1,000). Awarded biennially for a distinguished literary translation from German into English that has been published in the United States. *Offered by:* American Translators Association. *Winner:* To be awarded next in 2015.

John Updike Award ($20,000). Given biennially to a writer in mid-career who has demonstrated consistent excellence. *Offered by:* American Academy of Arts and Letters. *Winner:* To be awarded next in 2015.

VCU/Cabell First Novelist Award ($5,000). For a first novel published in the previous year. *Offered by:* Virginia Commonwealth University. *Winner:* Helene Wecker for *The Golem and the Jinni* (HarperCollins).

Harold D. Vursell Memorial Award ($10,000). To a writer whose work merits recognition for the quality of its prose style. *Offered by:* American Academy of Arts and Letters. *Winner:* Daniel Mendelsohn.

Amelia Elizabeth Walden Award ($5,000). To honor a book relevant to adolescents that has enjoyed a wide teenage audience. *Sponsor:* Assembly on Literature for Adolescents, National Council of Teachers of English. *Winner:* Rainbow Rowell for *Eleanor and Park* (St. Martin's Griffin).

Richard Wall Memorial Award (formerly the Theatre Library Association Award). To honor an English-language book of exceptional scholarship in the field of recorded performance, including motion pictures, television, and radio. *Offered by:* Theatre Library Association. *Winner:* Glenn Frankel for *The Searchers: The Making of an American Legend* (Bloomsbury USA).

George Washington Book Prize ($50,000). To recognize an important new book about America's founding era. *Offered by:* Washington College and the Gilder Lehrman Institute of American History. *Winner:* Andrew Jackson O'Shaughnessy for *The Men Who Lost America: British Leadership, the American Revolution, and the Fate of the Empire* (Yale University Press).

Carole Weinstein Poetry Prize ($10,000). To poets with strong connections to the Commonwealth of Virginia who have made a "significant recent contribution to the art of poetry." *Winner:* Rita Dove.

Hilary Weston Writers' Trust Prize for Nonfiction (C$60,000) (Canada). *Winner:* Naomi Klein for *This Changes Everything: Capitalism vs. the Climate* (Knopf Canada).

Hilary Weston Writers' Trust Prize for Student Nonfiction (C$2,500 plus C$1,000 for the winner's school, and publication on Macleans.ca and Writerstrust.com) (Canada). For students in grades 9–12. *Winner:* Ashley Ash for "No One's Girl."

Whitbread Book Awards. See Costa Book Awards.

E. B. White Award ($10,000). For achievement in children's literature. *Offered by:* American Academy of Arts and Letters. *Winner:* Not awarded in 2014.

E. B. White Read-Aloud Awards. For children's books with particular appeal as read-aloud books. *Offered by:* American Booksellers Association/Association of Booksellers for Children. *Winners:* (picture book) Drew Daywalt and Oliver Jeffers, illustrator, for *The Day the Crayons Quit* (Philomel); (middle readers) Kate DiCamillo and K. G. Campbell, illustrator, for *Flora and Ulysses: The Illuminated Adventures* (Candlewick).

Whiting Writers' Awards ($50,000). For emerging writers of exceptional talent and promise. *Offered by:* Mrs. Giles Whiting Foundation. *Winners:* To be awarded next in 2015.

Walt Whitman Award ($5,000). To a U.S. poet who has not published a book of poems in a standard edition. *Offered by:* Academy of American Poets. *Winner:* Hannah Sanghee Park for "The Same—Different."

Richard Wilbur Award ($1,000 and publication by University of Evansville Press). For a book-length poetry collection. *Winner:* Maryann Corbett for "Mid Evil."

Laura Ingalls Wilder Award. Awarded biennially to an author or illustrator whose books have made a substantial and lasting contribution to children's literature. *Offered by:* American Library Association, Association for Library Service to Children. *Winner:* To be awarded next in 2015.

Thornton Wilder Prize for Translation ($20,000). To a practitioner, scholar, or patron who has made a significant contribution to the art of literary translation. *Offered by:* American Academy of Arts and Letters. *Winner:* David Hinton.

Robert H. Winner Memorial Award ($2,500). To a mid-career poet over 40 who has published no more than one book of poetry. *Offered by:* Poetry Society of America. *Winner:* Dore Kiesselbach.

George Wittenborn Memorial Book Awards. To North American art publications that represent the highest standards of content, documentation, layout, and format. *Offered by:* Art Libraries Society of North America (ARLIS/NA). *Winners:* Sara Sapire and Michelle Komie (Yale University Press), Brenda Danilowitz (the Josef and Anni Albers Foundation), and Phillip Tiongson and Abby Palmer (Potion Design) for the "Interaction of Color by Josef Albers" app for iPad.

Thomas Wolfe Prize and Lecture. To honor writers with distinguished bodies of work. *Offered by:* Thomas Wolfe Society and University of North Carolina at Chapel Hill. *Winner:* Sandra Cisneros.

Thomas Wolfe Fiction Prize ($1,000). For a short story that honors Thomas Wolfe. *Offered by:* North Carolina Writers Network. *Winners:* Susan Levi Wallach for "A Still Life"; Jude Whelchel for "Mother in a Boneyard World."

Helen and Kurt Wolff Translator's Prize ($10,000). For an outstanding translation from German into English, published in the United States. *Offered by:* Goethe Institut Inter Nationes, New York. *Winner:* Shelley Frisch for her translation of Reiner Stach's *Kafka—Die Jahre der Erkenntnis (Kafka—The Years of Insight)* (Princeton University Press).

World Fantasy Convention Awards. For outstanding fantasy writing. *Offered by:* World Fantasy Convention. *Winners:* (novel) Sofia Samatar for *A Stranger in Olondria* (Small Beer); (novella) Andy Duncan and Ellen Klages for *Wakulla Springs* (Tor.com); (short story) Caitlín R. Kiernan for "The Prayer of Ninety Cats" in *Subterranean* magazine); (anthology) George R. R. Martin and Gardner Dozois, editors, for *Dangerous Women* (Tor); (collection) Caitlín R. Kiernan for *The Ape's Wife and Other Stories* (Subterranean Press).

Writers' Trust Distinguished Contribution Award (Canada). To an individual or an organization in recognition of their long-standing involvement with the Writers' Trust of Canada. *Winner:* Not awarded in 2014.

Writers' Trust Engel/Findley Award (C$25,000). To a Canadian writer predominantly of fiction, for a body of work. *Winner:* Joan Thomas.

Writers' Trust Poetry Prize. See Latner Writers' Trust Poetry Prize.

Writers' Trust Shaughnessy Cohen Prize for Political Writing (Canada) (C$25,000). For a nonfiction book that captures a subject of political interest. *Sponsor:* CTV. *Winner:* Paul Wells for *The Longer I'm Prime Minister: Stephen Harper and Canada, 2006–* (Vintage Canada).

Writers' Trust/McClelland & Stewart Journey Prize (Canada) (C$10,000). To a new, developing Canadian author for a short story or an excerpt from a novel in progress. *Offered by:* McClelland & Stewart. *Winner:* Tyler Keevil for "Sealskin" in *New Orphic Review* (Vol. 16. No. 2).

Writers' Trust Hilary Weston Prize for Nonfiction (Canada). See Hilary Weston Writers' Trust of Canada Prize for Nonfiction.

YALSA Award for Excellence in Nonfiction. For a work of nonfiction published for young adults (ages 12–18). *Offered by:* American Library Association, Young Adult Library Services Association. *Winner:* Neal Bascomb for *The Nazi Hunters: How a*

Team of Spies and Survivors Captured the World's Most Notorious Nazi (Scholastic).

Young Lions Fiction Award ($10,000). For a novel or collection of short stories by an American under the age of 35. *Offered by:* Young Lions of the New York Public Library. *Winner:* Paul Yoon for *Snow Hunters* (Simon & Schuster).

Morton Dauwen Zabel Award ($10,000). Awarded biennially, in rotation, to a progressive and experimental poet, writer of fiction, or critic. *Offered by:* American Academy of Arts and Letters. *Winner:* poet Claudia Rankine.

Zoetrope Short Fiction Prizes. *Offered by: Zoetrope: All-Story. Winners:* (first, $1,000) Dara Kell for "Small Holding"; (second, $500) Lauren Schenkman for "Numb"; (third, $250) Josh Sheridan for "The Narrators."

Charlotte Zolotow Award. For outstanding writing in a picture book published in the United States in the previous year. *Offered by:* Cooperative Children's Book Center, University of Wisconsin–Madison. *Winners:* Lemony Snicket for *The Dark,* illustrated by Jon Klassen (Little, Brown).

Part 6
Directory of Organizations

Directory of Library and Related Organizations

Networks, Consortia, and Other Cooperative Library Organizations

This list is taken from the current edition of *American Library Directory* (Information Today, Inc.), which includes additional information on member libraries and primary functions of each organization.

United States

Alabama

Alabama Health Libraries Assn., Inc. (AL-HeLa), Lister Hill Lib., Univ. of Alabama, Birmingham 35294-0013. SAN 372-8218. Tel. 205-975-8313, fax 205-934-2230. *Pres.* Lee Vacovich.

Library Management Network, Inc. (LMN), 2132 6th Ave S.E., Suite 106, Decatur 35601. SAN 322-3906. Tel. 256-308-2529, fax 256-308-2533. *Systems Coord.* Charlotte Moncrief.

Marine Environmental Sciences Consortium, Dauphin Island Sea Laboratory, Dauphin Island 36528. SAN 322-0001. Tel. 251-861-2141, fax 251-861-4646, e-mail disl@disl.org. *Coord.* John Dindo.

Network of Alabama Academic Libraries, c/o Alabama Commission on Higher Education, Montgomery 36104. SAN 322-4570. Tel. 334-242-2211, fax 334-242-0270. *Dir.* Ron P. Leonard.

Alaska

Alaska Library Network (ALN), 344 W. Third Ave., No. 125, Anchorage 99501-0585. SAN 371-0688. Tel. 907-269-6567, e-mail aln@alaska.gov. *Dir.* Nina Malyshev.

Arkansas

Mid-America Law Library Consortium (MALLCO), UALR Bowen School of Law Lib., 1203 McMath Ave., Little Rock 72202. Tel. 501-324-9980. Exec. *Dir.* Susan Goldner.

Northeast Arkansas Hospital Library Consortium, 223 E. Jackson, Jonesboro 72401. SAN 329-529X. Tel. 870-972-1290, fax 870-931-0839. *Dir.* Karen Crosser.

California

49-99 Cooperative Library System, c/o Southern California Lib. Cooperative, Monrovia 91016. SAN 301-6218. Tel. 626-359-6111, fax 626-359-0001. *Dir.* Diane R. Satchwell.

Bay Area Library and Information Network (BayNet), 1462 Cedar St., Berkeley 94702. SAN 371-0610. Tel. 415-355-2826, e-mail infobay@baynetlibs.org. *Pres.* Debbie Abilock.

Califa, 32 W. 25 Ave., Suite 201, San Mateo 94403. Tel. 650-572-2746, fax 650-349-5089, e-mail califa@califa.org. *Exec. Dir.* Linda Crowe.

Claremont University Consortium (CUC), 150 E. 8 St., Claremont 91711. Tel. 909-621-

8026; 909-621-8150, fax 909-621-8681. *CEO* Stig Lanesskog.

Consumer Health Information Program and Services (CHIPS), 12350 Imperial Hwy., Norwalk 90650. SAN 372-8110. Tel. 562-868-4003, fax 562-868-4065, e-mail reference services@gw.colapl.org. *Libn.* James Balducki.

Consortium for Open Learning, 333 Sunrise Ave., No. 229, Roseville 95661-3480. SAN 329-4412. Tel. 916-788-0660, fax 916-788-0696. *Operations Mgr.* Sandra Scott-Smith.

Gold Coast Library Network, 3437 Empresa Drive, Suite C, San Luis Obispo 93401-7355. Tel. 805-543-6082, fax 805-543-9487. *Admin. Dir.* Maureen Theobald.

National Network of Libraries of Medicine–Pacific Southwest Region (NN/LM-PSR), Louise M. Darling Biomedical Lib., Los Angeles 90095-1798. SAN 372-8234. Tel. 310-825-1200, fax 310-825-5389, e-mail psr-nnlm@library.ucla.edu. *Dir.* Judy Consales.

Nevada Medical Library Group (NMLG), Barton Memorial Hospital Lib., South Lake Tahoe 96150. SAN 370-0445. Tel. 530-543-5844, fax 530-541-4697. *Senior Exec. Coord.* Laurie Anton.

Northern and Central California Psychology Libraries (NCCPL), 2040 Gough St., San Francisco 94109. SAN 371-9006. Tel. 415-771-8055. *Pres.* Marianne Morgan.

Northern California Assn. of Law Libraries (NOCALL), 268 Bush St., No. 4006, San Francisco 94104. SAN 323-5777. E-mail admin@nocall.org. *Pres.* Coral Henning.

Peninsula Libraries Automated Network (PLAN), 2471 Flores St., San Mateo 94403-4000. SAN 371-5035. Tel. 650-349-5538, fax 650-349-5089. *Dir., Information Technology.* Monica Schultz.

San Bernardino, Inyo, Riverside Counties United Library Services (SIRCULS), 555 W. 6th St., San Bernadino 92410. Tel. 909-381-8257, fax 909-888-3171, e-mail ils@inlandlib.org. *Exec. Dir.* Vera Skop.

San Francisco Biomedical Library Network (SFBLN), San Francisco General Hospital UCSF/Barnett-Briggs Medical Lib., San Francisco 94110. SAN 371-2125. Tel. 415-206-6639, e-mail fishbon@ucsfmedctr.org.

Santa Clarita Interlibrary Network (SCIL-NET), Powell Lib., Santa Clarita 91321.

SAN 371-8964. Tel. 661-362-2271, fax 661-362-2719. *Libn.* John Stone.

Serra Cooperative Library System, c/o San Diego Public Lib., San Diego 92101. SAN 301-3510. Tel. 619-232-1225. *Exec. Dir.* Rosario Garza.

Southern California Library Cooperative (SCLC), 248 E. Foothill Blvd., Suite 101, Monrovia 91016-5522. SAN 371-3865. Tel. 626-359-6111, fax 626-359-0001, e-mail sclchq@socallibraries.org. *Dir.* Diane R. Satchwell.

Colorado

Automation System Colorado Consortium (ASCC), c/o Delta Public Lib., Delta 81416. Tel. 970-872-4317. *Technology Consultant* Connie Wolfrom.

Colorado Alliance of Research Libraries, 3801 E. Florida Ave., Suite 515, Denver 80210. SAN 322-3760. Tel. 303-759-3399, fax 303-759-3363. *Exec. Dir.* Alan Charnes.

Colorado Assn. of Law Libraries, P.O. Box 13363, Denver 80201. SAN 322-4325. Tel. 303-492-7535, fax 303-492-2707. *Pres.* Tracy Leming.

Colorado Council of Medical Librarians (CCML), P.O. Box 101058, Denver 80210-1058. SAN 370-0755. Tel. 303-724-2124, fax 303-724-2154. *Pres.* Melissa Kovac.

Colorado Library Consortium (CLiC), 7400 E. Arapahoe Rd., Suite 75, Centennial 80112. SAN 371-3970. Tel. 303-422-1150, fax 303-431-9752. *Exec. Dir.* Jim Duncan.

Connecticut

Bibliomation, 32 Crest Rd., Middlebury 06762. Tel. 203-577-4070, fax 203-577-4077. *CEO* Mike Simonds.

Connecticut Library Consortium, 234 Court St., Middletown 06457-3304. SAN 322-0389. Tel. 860-344-8777, fax 860-344-9199, e-mail clc@ctlibrarians.org. *Exec. Dir.* Jennifer Keohane.

Council of State Library Agencies in the Northeast (COSLINE), Connecticut State Lib., Hartford 06106. SAN 322-0451. Tel. 860-757-6510, fax 860-757-6503.

CTW Library Consortium, Olin Memorial Lib., Middletown 06459-6065. SAN 329-4587.

Tel. 860-685-3887, fax 860-685-2661. *Man. Dir.* Patricia Tully.

Hartford Consortium for Higher Education: 31 Pratt St., 4th fl., Hartford 06103. SAN 322-0443. Tel. 860-702-3801, fax 860-241-1130. *Exec. Dir.* Martin Estey.

Libraries Online, Inc. (LION), 100 Riverview Center, Suite 252, Middletown 06457. SAN 322-3922. Tel. 860-347-1704, fax 860-346-3707. *Exec. Dir.* Alan Hagyard.

Library Connection, Inc., 599 Matianuck Ave., Windsor 06095-3567. Tel. 860-298-5322, fax 860-298-5328. *Exec. Dir.* George Christian.

Delaware

Central Delaware Library Consortium, Dover Public Lib., Dover 19901. SAN 329-3696. Tel. 302-736-7030, fax 302-736-5087. *Dir.* Margery Kirby Cyr.

District of Columbia

Council for Christian Colleges and Universities, 321 8th St. N.E., Washington 20002. SAN 322-0524. Tel. 202-546-8713, fax 202-546-8913, e-mail council@cccu.org. *Pres.* Paul R. Corts.

District of Columbia Area Health Science Libraries (DCAHSL), P.O. Box 96920, Washington 20090. SAN 323-9918. Tel. 202-863-2518, fax 202-484-1595, e-mail mtalia ferro@aamc.org; *Pres.* Linda Todd.

FEDLINK/Federal Library and Information Network, c/o Federal Lib. and Info. Center Committee, Washington 20540-4935. SAN 322-0761. Tel. 202-707-4800, fax 202-707-4818, e-mail flicc@loc.gov. *Mgr.* S. Lynn McDonald.

Interlibrary Users Assn. (IUA), c/o Urban Institute Lib., Washington 20037. SAN 322-1628. Tel. 202-261-5534, fax 202-223-3043. *Pres.* Nancy L. Minter.

Washington Theological Consortium, 487 Michigan Ave. N.E., Washington 20017-1585. SAN 322-0842. Tel. 202-832-2675, fax 202-526-0818, e-mail wtc@washtheo con.org. *Exec. Dir.* Larry Golemon.

Florida

Florida Library Information Network, R. A. Gray Bldg., Tallahassee 32399-0250. SAN 322-0869. Tel. 850-245-6600, fax 850-245-6744, e-mail library@dos.myflorida.com. *Bureau Chief* Cathy Moloney.

Northeast Florida Library Information Network (NEFLIN), 2233 Park Ave., Suite 402, Orange Park 32073. Tel. 904-278-5620, fax 904-278-5625, e-mail office@neflin.org. *Exec. Dir.* Brad Ward.

Panhandle Library Access Network (PLAN), Five Miracle Strip Loop, Suite 8, Panama City Beach 32407-3850. SAN 370-047X. Tel. 850-233-9051, fax 850-235-2286. *Exec. Dir.* William P. Conniff.

SEFLIN/Southeast Florida Library Information Network, Inc, Wimberly Lib., Office 452, Boca Raton 33431. SAN 370-0666. Tel. 561-208-0984, fax 561-208-0995. *Exec. Dir.* Jeannette Smithee.

Southwest Florida Library Network (SWFLN), 13120 Westlinks Terrace, Unit 3, Fort Myers 33913. Tel. 239-225-4225, fax 239-225-4229, e-mail swfln@fgcu.edu. *Exec. Dir.* Luly Castro.

Tampa Bay Library Consortium, Inc., 1202 Tech Blvd., Suite 202, Tampa 33619. SAN 322-371X. Tel. 813-740-3963; 813-622-8252, fax 813-628-4425. *Exec. Dir.* Charlie Parker.

Tampa Bay Medical Library Network: Medical Lib., Department 7660, Saint Petersburg 33701. SAN 322-0885. Tel. 727-767-8557. *Chair* Joshua Brown.

Georgia

Atlanta Health Science Libraries Consortium, Fran Golding Medical Lib. at Scottish Rite, Atlanta 30342-1600. Tel. 404-785-2157, fax 404-785-2155. *Pres.* Kate Daniels.

Atlanta Regional Council for Higher Education (ARCHE), 50 Hurt Plaza, Suite 735, Atlanta 30303-2923. SAN 322-0990. Tel. 404-651-2668, fax 404-880-9816, e-mail arche@ atlantahighered.org. *Pres.* Michael Gerber.

Georgia Interactive Network for Medical Information (GAIN), c/o Mercer Univ. School of Medicine, Macon 31207. SAN 370-0577. Tel. 478-301-2515, fax 478-301-2051, e-mail gain.info@gain.mercer.edu. *Program Coord.* David Greenebaum.

Georgia Online Database (GOLD), c/o Georgia Public Lib. Service, Atlanta 30345-4304. SAN 322-094X. Tel. 404-235-7200, fax 404-235-7201. *Project Mgr.* Elaine Hardy.

LYRASIS, 1438 W. Peachtree St. N.W., Suite 200, Atlanta 30309-2955. SAN 322-0974. Tel. 404-892-0943, fax 404-892-7879. *Exec. Dir.* Kate Nevins.

Metro Atlanta Library Assn. (MALA), P.O. Box 14948, Atlanta 30324. SAN 378-2549. Tel. 678-915-7207, fax 678-915-7471, e-mail mala-a@comcast.net. *Pres.* Steven Vincent.

Hawaii

Hawaii Library Consortium (HLC), http://web.hawaii.edu/hlc. Tel. 808-875-2408. *Pres.* Christian DeLay.

Hawaii-Pacific Chapter, Medical Library Assn. (HPC-MLA), Health Sciences Lib., Honolulu 96813. SAN 371-3946. Tel. 808-692-0810, fax 808-692-1244. *Chair* A. Lee Adams.

Idaho

Canyon Owyhee Library Group (COLG), 203 E. Owyhee Ave., Homedale 83628. Tel. 208-337-4613, fax 208-337-4933. *Pres.* Peggy Rabe.

Cooperative Information Network (CIN), 8385 N. Government Way, Hayden 83835-9280. SAN 323-7656. Tel. 208-772-5612, fax 208-772-2498.

LYNX Consortium, c/o Boise Public Lib., Boise 83702-7195. SAN 375-0086. Tel. 208-384-4238, fax 208-384-4025.

Western Council of State Libraries, Inc., Idaho Commission for Libraries, Boise 83702-6055. Tel. 208-334-2150, fax 208-334-4016. *Pres.* Ann Joslin.

Illinois

Areawide Hospital Library Consortium of Southwestern Illinois (AHLC), c/o St. Elizabeth Hospital Health Sciences Lib., Belleville 62222. SAN 322-1016. Tel. 618-234-2120 ext. 2011, fax 618-222-4614.

Assn. of Chicago Theological Schools (ACTS), Univ. of St. Mary of the Lake, Mundelein

60060-1174. SAN 370-0658. Tel. 847-566-6401. *Chair* Thomas Baima.

Center for Research Libraries, 6050 S. Kenwood, Chicago 60637-2804. SAN 322-1032. Tel. 773-955-4545, fax 773-955-4339. *Pres.* Bernard F. Reilly.

Chicago and South Consortium, Jackson Park Hospital and Medical Center, Chicago 60649-3993. SAN 322-1067. Tel. 773-947-7653. *Coord.* Andrew Paradise.

Chicago Area Museum Libraries (CAML), c/o Lib., Field Museum, Chicago 60605-2496. SAN 371-392X. Tel. 312-665-7970, fax 312-665-7893. *Museum Libn.* Christine Giannoni.

Committee on Institutional Cooperation, 1819 S. Neil St., Suite D, Champaign 61820-7271. Tel. 217-333-8475, fax 217-244-7127, e-mail cic@staff.cic.net. *Dir.* Barbara Mcfadden Allen.

Consortium of Academic and Research Libraries in Illinois (CARLI), 100 Trade Center Drive, Suite 303, Champaign 61820. SAN 322-3736. Tel. 217-244-7593, fax 217-244-7596, e-mail support@carli.illinois.edu. *Exec. Dir.* Susan Singleton.

Council of Directors of State University Libraries in Illinois (CODSULI), Southern Illinois Univ. School of Medicine Lib., Springfield 62702-4910. SAN 322-1083. Tel. 217-545-0994, fax 217-545-0988.

East Central Illinois Consortium, Booth Lib., Eastern Illinois Univ., Charleston 61920. SAN 322-1040. Tel. 217-581-7549, fax 217-581-7534. *Mgr.* Stacey Knight-Davis.

Fox Valley Health Science Library Consortium, c/o Delnor-Community Hospital, Geneva 60134. SAN 329-3831. Tel. 630-208-4299.

Heart of Illinois Library Consortium, 511 N.E. Greenleaf, Peoria 61603. SAN 322-1113. *Chair* Leslie Menz.

Illinois Library and Information Network (IL-LINET), c/o Illinois State Lib., Springfield 62701-1796. SAN 322-1148. Tel. 217-782-2994, fax 217-785-4326. *Dir.* Anne Craig.

LIBRAS, Inc., North Park Univ., Chicago 60625-4895. SAN 322-1172. Tel. 773-244-5584, fax 773-244-4891. *Pres.* David Malone.

Metropolitan Consortium of Chicago, Chicago School of Professional Psychology, Chicago 60610. SAN 322-1180. Tel. 312-329-6633, fax 312-644-6075. *Coord.* Margaret White.

National Network of Libraries of Medicine–
Greater Midwest Region (NN/LM-GMR),
c/o Lib. of Health Sciences, Univ. of Illinois at Chicago, Chicago 60612-4330. SAN
322-1202. Tel. 312-996-2464, fax 312-996-
2226. *Dir.* Kathryn Carpenter.

Network of Illinois Learning Resources in
Community Colleges (NILRC), P.O. Box
120, Blanchardville 53516-0120. Tel. 608-
523-4094, fax 608-523-4072. *Business Mgr.*
Lisa Sikora.

System Wide Automated Network (SWAN),
c/o Metropolitan Lib. System, Burr Ridge
60527-5783. Tel. 630-734-5000, fax 630-
734-5050. *Dir.* Aaron Skog.

Indiana

Central Indiana Health Science Libraries Consortium, Indiana Univ. School of Medicine
Lib., Indianapolis 46202. SAN 322-1245.
Tel. 317-274-8358, fax 317-274-4056. *Officer* Elaine Skopelja.

Consortium of College and University Media
Centers (CCUMC), Indiana Univ., Bloomington 47405-1223. SAN 322-1091. Tel. 812-
855-6049, fax 812-855-2103, e-mail ccumc
@ccumc.org. *Exec. Dir.* Aileen Scales.

Evansville Area Library Consortium, 3700
Washington Ave., Evansville 47750. SAN
322-1261. Tel. 812-485-4151, fax 812-485-
7564. *Coord.* Jane Saltzman.

Evergreen Indiana Consortium, Indiana State
Lib., Indianapolis 46202. Tel. 317-234-
6624, fax 317-232-0002. *Coord.* Anna Go-
ben.

Iowa

Consortium of User Libraries (CUL), Lib. for
the Blind and Physically Handicapped, Des
Moines 50309-2364. Tel. 515-281-1333, fax
515-281-1378; 515-281-1263.

Dubuque (Iowa) Area Library Information
Consortium, c/o Burton Payne Lib., N.E.
Iowa Community College, Peosta 52068.
Tel. 563-556-5110 ext. 269, fax 563-557-
0340. *Coord.* Deb Seiffert.

Iowa Private Academic Library Consortium
(IPAL), http://www.ipalgroup.org. SAN
329-5311. Tel. 712-749-2127, 712-749-
2203, fax 712-749-2059, e-mail library@
bvu.edu. *Chair* Paul Waelchli.

Polk County Biomedical Consortium, c/o
Broadlawns Medical Center Lib., Des
Moines 50314. SAN 322-1431. Tel. 515-
282-2394, fax 515-282-5634. *Treas.* Elaine
Hughes.

Quad City Area Biomedical Consortium, Great
River Medical Center Lib., West Burlington
52655. SAN 322-435X. Tel. 319-768-4075,
fax 319-768-4080. *Coord.* Sarah Goff.

Sioux City Library Cooperative (SCLC), c/o
Sioux City Public Lib., Sioux City 51101-
1203. SAN 329-4722. Tel. 712-255-2933
ext. 255, fax 712-279-6432. *Chair* Betsy
Thompson.

State of Iowa Libraries Online (SILO), State
Lib. of Iowa, Des Moines 50319. SAN
322-1415. Tel. 515-281-4105, fax 515-281-
6191. *State Libn.* Mary Wegner.

Kansas

Associated Colleges of Central Kansas
(ACCK), 210 S. Main St., McPherson
67460. SAN 322-1474. Tel. 620-241-5150,
fax 620-241-5153.

Dodge City Library Consortium, c/o Coman-
che Intermediate Center, Dodge City 67801.
SAN 322-4368. Tel. 620-227-1609, fax 620-
227-4862.

State Library of Kansas/Statewide Resource
Sharing Div., 300 S.W. 10 Ave., Room 343
N., Topeka 66612-1593. SAN 329-5621.
Tel. 785-296-3875, fax 785-368-7291. *Dir.*
Jeff Hixon.

Kentucky

Assn. of Independent Kentucky Colleges and
Universities (AIKCU), 484 Chenault Rd.,
Frankfort 40601. SAN 322-1490. Tel. 502-
695-5007, fax 502-695-5057. *Pres.* Gary S.
Cox.

Eastern Kentucky Health Science Information
Network (EKHSIN), c/o Camden-Carroll
Lib., Morehead 40351. SAN 370-0631. Tel.
606-783-6860, fax 606-784-2178. *Lib. Dir.*
Tammy Jenkins.

Kentuckiana Metroversity, Inc., 109 E. Broadway, Louisville 40202. SAN 322-1504. Tel.
502-897-3374, fax 502-895-1647.

Kentucky Medical Library Assn., VA Medical Center, Lib. Serices 142D, Louisville
40206-1499. SAN 370-0623. Tel. 502-287-

6240, fax 502-287-6134. *Head Libn.* Gene M. Haynes.

Theological Education Assn. of Mid America (TEAM-A), Southern Baptist Theological Seminary, Louisville 40280. SAN 377-5038. Tel. 502-897-4807, fax 502-897-4600. *Dir., Info. Resources* Ken Boyd.

Louisiana

Central Louisiana Medical Center Library Consortium (CLMLC), 2495 Shreveport Hwy., 142D, Alexandria 71306. Tel. 318-619-9102, fax 318-619-9144, e-mail clmlc 8784@yahoo.com. *Coord.* Miriam J. Brown.

Health Sciences Library Assn. of Louisiana (HSLAL), NSU Shreveport Nursing Lib., Shreveport 71101. SAN 375-0035. *Pres.* Paula Craig.

Loan SHARK, State Lib. of Louisiana, Baton Rouge 70802. SAN 371-6880. Tel. 225-342-4920, 342-4918, fax 225-219-4725. *Head, Access Services* Kytara A. Gaudin.

LOUIS/Louisiana Library Network, Info. Technology Services, Baton Rouge 70803. *Exec. Dir.* Sara Zimmerman.

New Orleans Educational Telecommunications Consortium, 6400 Press Dr., New Orleans 70126. SAN 329-5214. Tel. 504-524-0350, e-mail noetc@noetc.org.

Southeastern Chapter of the American Assn. of Law Libraries (SEAALL), c/o Supreme Court of Louisiana, New Orleans 70130-2104. Tel. 504-310-2405, fax 504-310-2419. *Pres.* Francis Norton.

Maine

Health Science Library Information Consortium (HSLIC), 211 Marginal Way, No 245, Portland 04101. SAN 322-1601. Tel. 207-795-2561, fax 207-795-2569. *Chair* Kathy Brunjes.

Maryland

Maryland Interlibrary Loan Organization (MILO), c/o Enoch Pratt Free Lib., Baltimore 21201-4484. SAN 343-8600. Tel. 410-396-5498, fax 410-396-5837, e-mail milo@prattlibrary.org. *Mgr.* Emma E. Beaven.

National Network of Libraries of Medicine (NN/LM), National Lib. of Medicine, Bethesda 20894. SAN 373-0905. Tel. 301-496-4777, fax 301-480-1467. *Dir.* Angela Ruffin.

National Network of Libraries of Medicine–Southeastern Atlantic Region (NN/LM-SEA), Univ. of Maryland Health Sciences and Human Services Lib., Baltimore 21201-1512. SAN 322-1644. Tel. 410-706-2855, fax 410-706-0099, e-mail hshsl-nlmsea@hshsl.umaryland.edu. *Dir.* Mary J. Tooey.

U.S. National Library of Medicine (NLM), 8600 Rockville Pike, Bethesda 20894. SAN 322-1652. Tel. 301-594-5983, fax 301-402-1384, e-mail custserv@nlm.nih.gov. *Coord.* Martha Fishel.

Washington Research Library Consortium (WRLC), 901 Commerce Drive, Upper Marlboro 20774. SAN 373-0883. Tel. 301-390-2000, fax 301-390-2020. *Exec. Dir.* Mark Jacobs.

Massachusetts

Boston Biomedical Library Consortium (BBLC), c/o Dana Farber Cancer Trust, Boston 02115. SAN 322-1725. *Pres.* Christine Fleuried.

Boston Library Consortium, Inc., 10 Milk St., Suite 354, Boston 02108. SAN 322-1733. Tel. 617-262-0380, fax 617-262-0163, e-mail admin@blc.org. *Exec. Dir.* Susan Stearns.

Cape Libraries Automated Materials Sharing Network (CLAMS), 270 Communication Way, Unit 4E, Hyannis 02601. SAN 370-579X. Tel. 508-790-4399, fax 508-771-4533. *Exec. Dir.* Gayle Simundza.

Central and Western Massachusetts Automated Resource Sharing (C/W MARS), 67 Millbrook St., Suite 201, Worcester 01606. SAN 322-3973. Tel. 508-755-3323 ext. 30, fax 508-755-3721. *Exec. Dir.* Joan Kuklinski.

Cooperating Libraries of Greater Springfield (CLGS), Springfield Technical Community College, Springfield 01102. SAN 322-1768. Tel. 413-755-4565, fax 413-755-6315, e-mail lcoakley@stcc.edu. *Coord.* Lynn Coakley.

Fenway Libraries Online, Inc. (FLO), c/o Wentworth Institute of Technology, Boston 02115. SAN 373-9112. Tel. 617-442-2384, fax 617-442-1519. *Exec. Dir.* Walter Stine.

Massachusetts Health Sciences Libraries Network (MAHSLIN), Lamar Soutter Lib.,

Univ. of Massachusetts Medical School, Worcester 01655. SAN 372-8293. http://nahsl.libguides.com/mahslin/home. *Pres.* Donna Beales.

Merrimack Valley Library Consortium, 1600 Osgood St., North Andover 01845. SAN 322-4384. Tel. 978-557-1050, fax 978-557-8101, e-mail netmail@mvlc.org. *Exec. Dir.* Lawrence Rungren.

Minuteman Library Network, 10 Strathmore Rd., Natick 01760-2419. SAN 322-4252. Tel. 508-655-8008, fax 508-655-1507. *Exec. Dir.* Susan McAlister.

National Network of Libraries of Medicine–New England Region (NN/LM-NER), Univ. of Massachusetts Medical School, Shrewsbury 01545-2732. SAN 372-5448. Tel. 508-856-5979, fax 508-856-5977. *Dir.* Elaine Martin.

North of Boston Library Exchange, Inc. (NOBLE), 26 Cherry Hill Drive, Danvers 01923. SAN 322-4023. Tel. 978-777-8844, fax 978-750-8472. *Exec. Dir.* Ronald A. Gagnon.

Northeast Consortium of Colleges and Universities in Massachusetts (NECCUM), Merrimack College, North Andover 01845. SAN 371-0602. Tel. 978-556-3400, fax 978-556-3738. *Pres.* Richard Santagati.

Northeastern Consortium for Health Information (NECHI), Lowell General Hospital Health Science Lib., Lowell 01854. SAN 322-1857. Tel. 978-937-6247, fax 978-937-6855. *Libn.* Donna Beales.

SAILS, Inc., 10 Riverside Dr., Suite 102, Lakeville 02347. SAN 378-0058. Tel. 508-946-8600, fax 508-946-8605, e-mail support@sailsinc.org. *Pres.* Francis Ward.

Western Massachusetts Health Information Consortium, Baystate Medical Center Health Sciences Lib., Springfield 01199. SAN 329-4579. Tel. 413-794-1865, fax 413-794-1974. *Pres.* Susan La Forter.

Michigan

Detroit Area Consortium of Catholic Colleges, c/o Sacred Heart Seminary, Detroit 48206. SAN 329-482X. Tel. 313-883-8500, fax 313-883-8594. *Dir.* Chris Spilker.

Detroit Area Library Network (DALNET), 6th Floor SEL, 5048 Gullen Mall, Detroit 48202. Tel. 313-577-6789, fax 313-577-1231, info@dalnet.org. *Exec. Dir.* Steven K. Bowers.

Lakeland Library Cooperative, 4138 Three Mile Rd. N.W., Grand Rapids 49534-1134. SAN 308-132X. Tel. 616-559-5253, fax 616-559-4329. *Dir.* Sandra Wilson.

The Library Network (TLN), 41365 Vincenti Ct., Novi 48375. SAN 370-596X. Tel. 248-536-3100, fax 248-536-3099. *Dir.* James Pletz.

Michigan Health Sciences Libraries Assn. (MHSLA), 1407 Rensen St., Suite 4, Lansing 48910. SAN 323-987X. Tel. 517-394-2774, fax 517-394-2675. *Pres.* Sheila Bryant.

Mideastern Michigan Library Cooperative, 503 S. Saginaw St., Suite 839, Flint 48502. SAN 346-5187. Tel. 810-232-7119, fax 810-232-6639. *Dir.* Denise Hooks.

Mid-Michigan Library League, 210 1/2 N Mitchell, Cadillac 49601-1835. SAN 307-9325. Tel. 231-775-3037, fax 231-775-1749. *Dir.* James Lawrence.

PALnet, 1040 W Bristol Rd., Flint 48507. Tel. 810-766-4070. *Dir.* Vince Molosky.

Southeastern Michigan League of Libraries (SEMLOL), Lawrence Technological Univ., Southfield 48075. SAN 322-4481. Tel. 248-204-3000, fax 248-204-3005. *Treas.* Gary Cocozzoli.

Southwest Michigan Library Cooperative, Willard Public Library, Battle Creek, 49017. SAN 308-2156. Tel. 269-968-8166, e-mail rhulsey@willard.lib.mi.us. *Dir.* John Mohney.

Suburban Library Cooperative (SLC), 44750 Delco Blvd., Sterling Heights 48313. SAN 373-9082. Tel. 586-685-5750, fax 586-685-3010. *Dir.* Tammy Turgeon.

Upper Peninsula of Michigan Health Science Library Consortium, c/o Marquette Health System Hospital, Marquette 49855. SAN 329-4803. Tel. 906-225-3429, fax 906-225-3524. *Lib. Mgr.* Janis Lubenow.

Upper Peninsula Region of Library Cooperation, Inc., 1615 Presque Isle Ave., Marquette 49855. SAN 329-5540. Tel. 906-228-7697, fax 906-228-5627. *Treas.* Suzanne Dees.

Valley Library Consortium, 3210 Davenport Ave., Saginaw 48602-3495. Tel. 989-497-0925, fax 989-497-0918. *Exec. Dir.* Randall Martin.

Minnesota

Capital Area Library Consortium (CALCO), c/o Minnesota Dept. of Transportation, Lib. MS155, Saint Paul 55155. SAN 374-6127. Tel. 651-296-5272, fax 651-297-2354. *Libn.* Shirley Sherkow.

Central Minnesota Libraries Exchange (CMLE), Miller Center, Room 130-D, Saint Cloud 56301-4498. SAN 322-3779. Tel. 320-308-2950, fax 320-654-5131, e-mail cmle@stcloudstate.edu. *Dir.* Patricia A. Post.

Cooperating Libraries in Consortium (CLIC), 1619 Dayton Ave., Suite 204, Saint Paul 55104. SAN 322-1970. Tel. 651-644-3878, fax 651-644-6258. *Exec. Dir.* Ruth Dukelow.

Metronet, 1619 Dayton Ave., Suite 314, Saint Paul 55104. SAN 322-1989. Tel. 651-646-0475, fax 651-649-3169, e-mail information @metrolibraries.net. *Exec. Dir.* Ann Walker Smalley.

Metropolitan Library Service Agency (MELSA), 1619 Dayton Ave., No. 314, Saint Paul 55104-6206. SAN 371-5124. Tel. 651-645-5731, fax 651-649-3169, e-mail melsa@ melsa.org. *Exec. Dir.* Chris D. Olson.

MINITEX Library Information Network, 15 Andersen Lib., Univ. of Minnesota–Twin Cities, Minneapolis 55455-0439. SAN 322-1997. Tel. 612-624-4002, fax 612-624-4508. *Dir.* Valerie Horton.

Minnesota Library Information Network (MnLINK), Univ. of Minnesota–Twin Cities, Minneapolis 55455-0439. Tel. 612-624-8096, fax 612-624-4508. *Info. Specialist* Nick Banitt.

Minnesota Theological Library Assn. (MTLA), Luther Seminary Lib., Saint Paul 55108. SAN 322-1962. Tel. 651-641-3447. *Chair* David Stewart.

Northern Lights Library Network, 103 Graystone Plaza, Detroit Lakes 56501-3041. SAN 322-2004. Tel. 218-847-2825, fax 218-847-1461, e-mail nloffice@nlln.org. *Exec. Dir.* Kathy B. Enger.

Southeastern Libraries Cooperating (SELCO), 2600 19th St. N.W., Rochester 55901-0767. SAN 308-7417. Tel. 507-288-5513, fax 507-288-8697. *Exec. Dir.* Ann Hutton.

Southwest Area Multicounty Multitype Interlibrary Exchange (SAMMIE), 109 S. 5

St., Suite 30, Marshall 56258-1240. SAN 322-2039. Tel. 507-532-9013, fax 507-532-2039, e-mail info@sammie.org. *Exec. Dir.* Shelly Grace.

Twin Cities Biomedical Consortium (TCBC), c/o Fairview Univ. Medical Center, Minneapolis 55455. SAN 322-2055. Tel. 612-273-6595, fax 612-273-2675. *Mgr.* Colleen Olsen.

Mississippi

Central Mississippi Library Council (CMLC), c/o Millsaps College Lib., Jackson 39210. SAN 372-8250. Tel. 601-974-1070, fax 601-974-1082. *Admin./Treas.* Tom Henderson.

Mississippi Electronic Libraries Online (MELO), Mississippi State Board for Community and Junior Colleges, Jackson 39211. Tel. 601-432-6518, fax 601-432-6363, e-mail melo@colin.edu. *Dir.* Audra Kimball.

Missouri

Greater Western Library Alliance (GWLA), 5109 Cherry St., Kansas City 64110. Tel. 816-926-8765, fax 816-926-8790. *Exec. Dir.* Joni Blake.

Health Sciences Library Network of Kansas City (HSLNKC), Univ. of Missouri–Kansas City Health Sciences Lib., Kansas City 64108-2792. SAN 322-2098. Tel. 816-235-1880, fax 816-235-6570. *Dir.* Peggy Mullaly-Quijas.

Kansas City Library Service Program (KCLSP), 14 W. 10 St., Kansas City 64105.Tel. 816-701-3520, fax 816-701-3401, e-mail kclcsupport@kclibrary.org. *Dir. of Business and Library Systems* Steven Knapp.

Mid-America Library Alliance/Kansas City Metropolitan Library and Information Network, 15624 E. 24 Hwy., Independence 64050. SAN 322-2101. Tel. 816-521-7257, fax 816-461-0966. *Exec. Dir.* Susan Burton.

Saint Louis Regional Library Network, 341 Sappington Rd., Saint Louis 63122. SAN 322-2209. Tel. 314-395-1305.

Nebraska

ICON Library Consortium, McGoogan Lib. of Medicine, Univ. of Nebraska, Omaha 68198-6705. Tel. 402-559-7099, fax 402-559-5498.

Nevada

Desert States Law Library Consortium, Wiener-Rogers Law Lib., William S. Boyd School of Law, Las Vegas 89154-1080. Tel. 702-895-2400, fax 702-895-2416. *Collection Development Libn.* Matthew Wright.

Information Nevada, Interlibrary Loan Dept., Nevada State Lib. and Archives, Carson City 89701-4285. SAN 322-2276. Tel. 775-684-3328, fax 775-684-3330. *Asst. Admin., Lib. and Development Services* Karen Starr.

New Hampshire

GMILCS, Inc., 1701B Hooksett Rd., Hooksett 03106. Tel. 603-485-4286, fax 603-485-4246, e-mail helpdesk@gmilcs.org. *Systems Libn.* Kevin French.

Health Sciences Libraries of New Hampshire and Vermont, Breene Memorial Lib., New Hampshire Hospital, Concord 03246. SAN 371-6864. Tel. 603-527-2837, fax 603-527-7197. *Admin. Coord.* Anne Conner.

Librarians of the Upper Valley Coop. (LUV Coop), c/o Hanover Town Lib., Etna 03750. SAN 371-6856. Tel. 603-643-3116. *Coord.* Barbara Prince.

Merri-Hill-Rock Library Cooperative, c/o Kimball Lib., Atkinson 03811-2299. SAN 329-5338. Tel. 603-362-5234, fax 603-362-4791. *Dir.* Jon Godfrey.

New Hampshire College and University Council, 3 Barrell Court, Suite 100, Concord 03301-8543. SAN 322-2322. Tel. 603-225-4199, fax 603-225-8108. *Pres.* Thomas R. Horgan.

Nubanusit Library Cooperative, c/o Peterborough Town Lib., Peterborough 03458. SAN 322-4600. Tel. 603-924-8040, fax 603-924-8041.

New Jersey

Basic Health Sciences Library Network (BHSL), Overlook Hospital Health Science Lib., Summit 07902. SAN 371-4888. Tel. 908-522-2886, fax 908-522-2274. *Coord.* Pat Regenberg.

Bergen Passaic Health Sciences Library Consortium, c/o Health Sciences Lib., Englewood Hospital and Medical Center, Englewood 07631. SAN 371-0904. Tel. 201-894-3069, fax 201-894-9049. *Coord.* Lia Sabbagh.

Burlington Libraries Information Consortium (BLINC), 5 Pioneer Blvd., Westampton 08060. Tel. 609-267-9660, fax 609-267-4091, e-mail hq@bcls.lib.nj.us. *Dir.* Ranjna Das.

Libraries of Middlesex Automation Consortium (LMxAC), 1030 Saint Georges Ave., Suite 203, Avenel 07001. SAN 329-448X. Tel. 732-750-2525, fax 732-750-9392. *Exec. Dir.* Eileen Palmer.

LibraryLinkNJ, New Jersey Library Cooperative, 44 Stelton Rd., Suite 330, Piscataway 08854. SAN 371-5116. Tel. 732-752-7720, fax 732-752-7785. *Exec. Dir.* Cheryl O'Connor.

Monmouth-Ocean Biomedical Information Consortium (MOBIC), Community Medical Center, Toms River 08755. SAN 329-5389. Tel. 732-557-8117, fax 732-557-8354. *Libn.* Reina Reisler.

Morris Automated Information Network (MAIN), c/o Morris County Lib., 30 East Hanover Ave., Whippany 07981. SAN 322-4058. Tel. 973-631-5353, fax 973-631-5366. *Dir.* Jeremy Jenynak.

Morris-Union Federation, 214 Main St., Chatham 07928. SAN 310-2629. Tel. 973-635-0603, fax 973-635-7827.

New Jersey Health Sciences Library Network (NJHSN), Overlook Hospital Lib., Summit 07902. SAN 371-4829. Tel. 908-522-2886, fax 908-522-2274. *Lib. Mgr.* Patricia Regenberg.

New Jersey Library Network, Lib. Development Bureau, Trenton 08608. SAN 372-8161. Tel. 609-278-2640 ext. 152, fax 609-278-2650. *Assoc. State Libn. for Lib. Development* Kathleen Moeller-Peiffer.

Virtual Academic Library Environment (VALE), William Paterson Univ. Lib., Wayne 07470-2103. Tel. 973-720-3179, fax 973-720-3171. *Coord.* Judy Avrin.

New Mexico

Estacado Library Information Network (ELIN), 509 N. Shipp, Hobby 88240. Tel. 505-397-9328, fax 505-397-1508.

New Mexico Consortium of Academic Libraries, Dean's Office, Albuquerque 87131-0001. SAN 371-6872. *Pres.* Ruben Aragon.

New Mexico Consortium of Biomedical and Hospital Libraries, c/o St. Vincent Hospital, Santa Fe 87505. SAN 322-449X. Tel. 505-820-5218, fax 505-989-6478. *Chair* Albert Robinson.

New York

Academic Libraries of Brooklyn, Long Island Univ. Lib. LLC 517, Brooklyn 11201. SAN 322-2411. Tel. 718-488-1081, fax 718-780-4057.

Associated Colleges of the Saint Lawrence Valley, SUNY Potsdam, Potsdam 13676-2299. SAN 322-242X. Tel. 315-267-3331, fax 315-267-2389. *Exec. Dir.* Anneke J. Larrance.

Brooklyn-Queens-Staten Island-Manhattan-Bronx Health Sciences Librarians (BQSIMB), 150 55th St., Brooklyn 11220. Tel. 718-630-7200, fax 718-630-8918. *Pres.* Irina Meyman.

Capital District Library Council (CDLC), 28 Essex St., Albany 12206. SAN 322-2446. Tel. 518-438-2500, fax 518-438-2872. *Exec. Dir.* Kathleen Gundrum.

Central New York Library Resources Council (CLRC), 6493 Ridings Rd., Syracuse 13206-1195. SAN 322-2454. Tel. 315-446-5446, fax 315-446-5590. *Exec. Dir.* Debby Emerson.

ConnectNY, Rochester Institute of Technology, Rochester 14623. Tel. 585-475-2050. *Exec. Dir.* Bart Harloe.

Library Assn. of Rockland County (LARC), P.O. Box 917, New City 10956-0917. Tel. 845-359-3877. *Pres.* Sara Nugent.

Library Consortium of Health Institutions in Buffalo (LCHIB), Abbott Hall, SUNY at Buffalo, Buffalo 14214. SAN 329-367X. Tel. 716-829-3900 ext. 143, fax 716-829-2211, e-mail hubnet@buffalo.edu; ulb-lchib@buffalo.edu. *Exec. Dir.* Martin E. Mutka.

Long Island Library Resources Council (LILRC), 627 N. Sunrise Service Rd., Bellport 11713. SAN 322-2489. Tel. 631-675-1570. *Dir.* Herbert Biblo.

Medical and Scientific Libraries of Long Island (MEDLI), c/o Palmer School of Lib. and Info. Science, Brookville 11548. SAN 322-4309. Tel. 516-299-2866, fax 516-299-4168. *Chair* Mary Westermann-Cicio.

Metropolitan New York Library Council (METRO), 57 E. 11 St., 4th flr., New York 10003-4605. SAN 322-2500. Tel. 212-228-2320, fax 212-228-2598. *Exec. Dir.* Jason Kucsma.

New England Law Library Consortium (NELLCO), 80 New Scotland Ave., Albany 12208. SAN 322-4244. Tel. 518-694-3025, fax 518-694-3027. *Exec. Dir.* Tracy L. Thompson.

New York State Higher Education Initiative (NYSHEI), 22 Corporate Woods Blvd., Albany 12211-2350. Fax 518-432-4346, e-mail nyshei@nyshei.org. *Exec. Dir.* Jason Kramer.

Northeast Foreign Law Libraries Cooperative Group, Columbia Univ. Lib., New York 10027. SAN 375-0000. Tel. 212-854-1411, fax 212-854-3295. *Coord.* Silke Sahl.

Northern New York Library Network, 6721 U.S. Hwy. 11, Potsdam 13676. SAN 322-2527. Tel. 315-265-1119, fax 315-265-1881, e-mail info@nnyln.org. *Exec. Dir.* John J. Hammond.

Rochester Regional Library Council, 390 Packetts Landing, Fairport 14450. SAN 322-2535. Tel. 585-223-7570, fax 585-223-7712, e-mail rrlc@rrlc.org. *Exec. Dir.* Kathleen M. Miller.

South Central Regional Library Council, Clinton Hall, Ithaca 14850. SAN 322-2543. Tel. 607-273-9106, fax 607-272-0740, e-mail scrlc@scrlc.org. *Exec. Dir.* Mary-Carol Lindbloom.

Southeastern New York Library Resources Council (SENYLRC), 21 S. Elting Corners Rd., Highland 12528-2805. SAN 322-2551. Tel. 845-883-9065, fax 845-883-9483. *Exec. Dir.* John L. Shaloiko.

SUNYConnect, Office of Lib. and Info. Services, Albany 12246. Tel. 518-443-5577, fax 518-443-5358. *Asst. Provost for Lib. and Info. Services* Carey Hatch.

United Nations System Electronic Information Acquisitions Consortium (UNSEIAC), c/o United Nations Lib., New York 10017. SAN 377-855X. Tel. 212-963-2026, fax 212-963-2608, e-mail unseiac@un.org. *Coord.* Kikuko Maeyama.

Western New York Library Resources Council, 4455 Genesee St., Buffalo 14225. SAN 322-2578. Tel. 716-633-0705, fax 716-633-1736. *Exec. Dir.* Sheryl Knab.

North Carolina

AHEC Digital Library, http://library.ncahec. net. *Dir.* Diana McDuffee.

Association of Southeastern Research Libraries (ASERL), 226A Bostock Lib., Durham 27708. SAN 322-1555. Tel. 919-681-2531, fax 919-681-0805. *Pres.* Lynn Sutton.

Cape Fear Health Sciences Information Consortium, 1601 Owen Drive, Fayetteville 28301. SAN 322-3930. Tel. 910-671-5046, fax 910-671-5337. *Dir.* Katherine Mcginniss.

North Carolina Community College System, 200 W. Jones St., Raleigh 27603-1379. SAN 322-2594. Tel. 919-807-7100, fax 919-807-7175; 919-807-7164. *Assoc. V.P. for Learning Technology Systems* Bill Randall.

Triangle Research Libraries Network, Wilson Lib., Chapel Hill 27514-8890. SAN 329-5362. Tel. 919-962-8022, fax 919-962-4452. *Interim Dir.* Lisa Croucher.

Western North Carolina Library Network (WNCLN), c/o Ramsey Lib., 1 University Heights, Asheville 28804. Tel. 828-668-2368. *Network Libn.* Ben Shirley.

North Dakota

Central Dakota Library Network, Morton Mandan Public Lib., Mandan 58554-3149. SAN 373-1391. Tel. 701-667-5365, e-mail mortonmandanlibrary@cdln.info. *Dir.* Kelly Steckler.

Mid-America Law Library Consortium (MALLCO), Univ. of North Dakota School of Law, Grand Forks 58202. SAN 371-6813. Tel. 701-777-2204, fax 701-777-4956. *Interim Dir.* Rhonda Schwartz.

Tri-College University Libraries Consortium, NDSU Downtown Campus, Fargo 58102. SAN 322-2047. Tel. 701-231-8170, fax 701-231-7205. *In Charge* Sonia Hohnadel.

Ohio

Assn. of Christian Librarians (ACL), P.O. Box 4, Cedarville 45314. Tel. 937-766-2255, fax 937-766-5499, e-mail info@acl.org. *Pres.* Frank Quinn.

Central Ohio Hospital Library Consortium, 127 S. Davis Ave., Columbus 43222. SAN 371-084X. Tel. 614-234-5214, fax 614-234-1257, e-mail library@mchs.com. *Dir.* Stevo Roksandic.

Christian Library Consortium (CLC), c/o ACL, Cedarville 45314. Tel. 937-766-2255, fax 937-766-5499, e-mail info@acl.org. *Coord.* Beth Purtee.

Columbus Area Library and Information Council of Ohio (CALICO), c/o Westerville Public Lib., Westerville 43081. SAN 371-683X. Tel. 614-882-7277, fax 614-882-5369.

Consortium of Popular Culture Collections in the Midwest (CPCCM), c/o Popular Culture Lib., Bowling Green 43403-0600. SAN 370-5811. Tel. 419-372-2450, fax 419-372-7996. *Head Libn.* Nancy Down.

Five Colleges of Ohio, 102 Allen House, Gambier 43022. Tel. 740-427-5377, fax 740-427-5390, e-mail ohiofive@gmail.com. *Exec. Dir.* Susan Palmer.

Northeast Ohio Regional Library System (NEO-RLS), 1580 Georgetown Rd., Hudson 44236. SAN 322-2713. Tel. 330-655-0531, fax 330-655-0568. *Exec. Dir.* Catherine Hakala-Ausperk.

Northwest Regional Library System (NORWELD), 181½ S. Main St., Bowling Green 43402. SAN 322-273X. Tel. 419-352-2903, fax 419-353-8310. *Exec. Dir.* Arline V. Radden.

OCLC Online Computer Library Center, Inc., 6565 Kilgour Place, Dublin 43017-3395. SAN 322-2748. Tel. 614-764-6000, fax 614-718-1017, e-mail oclc@oclc.org. *Pres./CEO* Skip Pritchard.

Ohio Health Sciences Library Assn. (OHSLA), Medical Lib., South Pointe Hospital, Warrensville Heights 44122. Tel. 216-491-7454, fax 216-491-7650. *Pres.* Stevo Roksandic.

Ohio Library and Information Network (OhioLINK), 35 E. Chestnut St., 8th fl., Columbus 43215-2541. SAN 374-8014. Tel. 614-485-6722, fax 614-228-1807, e-mail info@ohiolink.edu. *Exec. Dir.* Gwen Evans.

Ohio Network of American History Research Centers, Ohio Historical Society Archives-Lib., Columbus 43211-2497. SAN 323-9624. Tel. 614-297-2510, fax 614-297-2546, e-mail reference@ohiohistory.org.

Ohio Public Library Information Network (OPLIN), 2323 W. 5 Ave., Suite 130, Columbus 43204. Tel. 614-728-5252, fax 614-728-5256, e-mail support@oplin.org. *Exec. Dir.* Stephen Hedges.

OHIONET, 1500 W. Lane Ave., Columbus 43221-3975. SAN 322-2764. Tel. 614-486-2966, fax 614-486-1527. *Exec. Officer* Michael P. Butler.

SEO (Serving Every Ohioan) Library Center, 40780 Marietta Rd., Caldwell 43724. SAN 356-4606. *Dir.* Dianna Clark.

Southeast Regional Library System (SERLS), 252 W. 13 St., Wellston 45692. SAN 322-2756. Tel. 740-384-2103, fax 740-384-2106, e-mail dirserls@oplin.org. *Dir.* Jay Burton.

SWON Libraries Consortium, 10250 Alliance Rd., Suite 225, Blue Ash 45242. SAN 322-2675. Tel. 513-751-4422, fax 513-751-0463, e-mail info@swonlibraries.org. *Exec. Dir.* Melanie A. Blau-McDonald.

Southwestern Ohio Council for Higher Education (SOCHE), Miami Valley Research Park, Dayton 45420-4015. SAN 322-2659. Tel. 937-258-8890, fax 937-258-8899, e-mail soche@soche.org.

State Assisted Academic Library Council of Kentucky (SAALCK), c/o SWON Libs., Cincinnati 45241. SAN 371-2222. Tel. 513-751-4422, fax 513-751-0463, e-mail saalck @saalck.org. *Exec. Dir.* Anne Abate.

Theological Consortium of Greater Columbus (TCGC), Trinity Lutheran Seminary, Columbus 43209-2334. Tel. 614-384-4646, fax 614-238-0263. *Lib. Systems Mgr.* Ray Olson.

Oklahoma

Greater Oklahoma Area Health Sciences Library Consortium (GOAL), Resource Center, Mercy Memorial Health Center, Ardmore 73401. SAN 329-3858. Tel. 580-220-6625, fax 580-220-6599. *Pres.* Catherine Ice.

Oklahoma Health Sciences Library Assn. (OHSLA), HSC Bird Health Science Lib., Univ. of Oklahoma, Oklahoma City 73190. SAN 375-0051. Tel. 405-271-2285 ext. 48755, fax 405-271-3297.

Oregon

Chemeketa Cooperative Regional Library Service, c/o Chemeketa Community College, Salem 97305-1453. SAN 322-2837. Tel. 503-399-5105, fax 503-399-7316, e-mail contact@cclrs.org. *Dir.* John Goodyear.

Gorge LINK Library Consortium, c/o Hood River County Lib., Hood River 97031. Tel. 541-386-2535, fax 541-386-3835, e-mail gorgelinklibrary@gorge.net. *System Admin.* Jayne Guidinger.

Library Information Network of Clackamas County (LINCC), 16239 S.E. McLoughlin Blvd., Suite 208, Oak Grove 97267-4654. SAN 322-2845. Tel. 503-723-4888, fax 503-794-8238. *Lib. System Analyst* George Yobst.

Orbis Cascade Alliance, 2288 Oakmont Way, Eugene 97401. SAN 377-8096. Tel. 541-246-2470. *Chair.* Jay Starratt.

Oregon Health Sciences Libraries Assn. (OHSLA), Oregon Health and Science Univ. Lib., Portland 97239-3098. SAN 371-2176. Tel. 503-494-3462, fax 503-494-3322, e-mail library@ohsu.edu.

Portland Area Library System (PORTALS), Port Community College, SYLIB202, Portland 97219. Tel. 503-977-4571, fax 503-977-4977. *Coord.* Roberta Richards.

Southern Oregon Library Federation, c/o Klamath County Lib., Klamath Falls 97601. SAN 322-2861. Tel. 541-882-8894, fax 541-882-6166. *Dir.* Andy Swanson.

Washington County Cooperative Library Services, 111 N.E. Lincoln St., MS No. 58, Hillsboro 97124-3036. SAN 322-287X. Tel. 503-846-3222, fax 503-846-3220. *Mgr.* Eva Calcagno.

Pennsylvania

Associated College Libraries of Central Pennsylvania, c/o 648 State St., Lancaster 17603. E-mail webmaster@aclcp.org. *Chair* Maureen O'Brien Dermott.

Berks County Library Assn. (BCLA), Reading Public Lib., Reading 19602. SAN 371-0866. Tel. 610-478-9035; 610-655-6350. *Pres.* Jennifer Balas.

Central Pennsylvania Consortium (CPC), Dickinson College, Carlisle 17013. SAN 322-2896. Tel. 717-245-1984, fax 717-245-1807, e-mail cpc@dickinson.edu. *Pres.* Katherine Haley Will.

Central Pennsylvania Health Sciences Library Assn. (CPHSLA), Office for Research Protections, Pennsylvania State Univ., University Park 16802. SAN 375-5290. Fax 814-865-1775. *Pres.* Tracie Kahler.

Cooperating Hospital Libraries of the Lehigh Valley Area, Estes Lib., Saint Luke's Hospital, Bethlehem 18015. SAN 371-0858. Tel. 610-954-3407, fax 610-954-4651. *Chair* Sharon Hrabina.

Delaware Valley Information Consortium (DEVIC), St. Mary Medical Center Medical Lib., Langhorne 19047. Tel. 215-710-2012, fax 215-710-4638.

Eastern Mennonite Associated Libraries and Archives (EMALA), 2215 Millstream Rd., Lancaster 17602. SAN 372-8226. Tel. 717-393-9745, fax 717-393-8751. *Chair* Edsel Burdge.

Greater Philadelphia Law Library Assn. (GPLLA), Wolf, Block, Schorr and Solis-Cohen LLP Lib., 25th flr., Philadelphia 19103. SAN 373-1375. *Pres.* Nicole Snyder.

HSLC/Access PA (Health Science Libraries Consortium), 3600 Market St., Suite 550, Philadelphia 19104-2646. SAN 323-9780. Tel. 215-222-1532, fax 215-222-0416, e-mail support@hslc.org. *Exec. Dir.* Maryam Phillips.

Interlibrary Delivery Service of Pennsylvania (IDS), c/o Bucks County IU, No. 22, Doylestown 18901. SAN 322-2942. Tel. 215-348-2940 ext. 1620, fax 215-348-8315, e-mail ids@bucksiu.org. *Admin. Dir.* Pamela Newman Dinan.

Keystone Library Network, Dixon Univ. Center, Harrisburg 17110-1201. Tel. 717-720-4088, fax 717-720-4453. *Coord.* Mary Lou Sowden.

Laurel Highlands Health Science Library Consortium, 361 Sunrise Rd., Dayton 16222. SAN 322-2950. Tel. 814-341-0242, fax 814-266-8230. *Dir.* Rhonda Yeager.

Lehigh Valley Assn. of Independent Colleges, 130 W. Greenwich St., Bethlehem 18018. SAN 322-2969. Tel. 610-625-7888, fax 610-625-7891. *Exec. Dir.* Diane Dimitroff.

Montgomery County Library and Information Network Consortium (MCLINC), 301 Lafayette St., 2nd flr., Conshohocken 19428. Tel. 610-238-0580, fax 610-238-0581, e-mail webmaster@mclinc.org. *Pres.* Anne Frank.

National Network of Libraries of Medicine– Middle Atlantic Region (NN/LM-MAR), Univ. of Pittsburgh, Pittsburgh 15261. E-mail nnlmmar@pitt.edu. *Exec. Dir.* Renae Barger.

Northeastern Pennsylvania Library Network, c/o Marywood Univ. Lib., Scranton 18509-1598. SAN 322-2993. Tel. 570-348-6260, fax 570-961-4769. *Exec. Dir.* Catherine H. Schappert.

Northwest Interlibrary Cooperative of Pennsylvania (NICOP), Mercyhurst College Lib., Erie 16546. SAN 370-5862. Tel. 814-824-2190, fax 814-824-2219. *Archivist* Earleen Glaser.

Pennsylvania Library Assn., 220 Cumberland Pkwy, Suite 10, Mechanicsburg 17055. Tel. 717-766-7663, fax 717-766-5440. *Exec. Dir.* Glenn R. Miller.

Philadelphia Area Consortium of Special Collections Libraries (PACSCL), P.O. Box 22642, Philadelphia 19110-2642. Tel. 215-985-1445, fax 215-985-1446, email lblanchard@pacscl.org. *Exec. Dir.* Laura Blanchard.

Southeastern Pennsylvania Theological Library Assn. (SEPTLA), c/o Biblical Seminary, Hatfield 19440. SAN 371-0793. Tel. 215-368-5000 ext. 234. *Chair* Daniel La-Valla.

State System of Higher Education Library Cooperative (SSHELCO), c/o Bailey Lib., Slippery Rock 16057. Tel. 724-738-2630, fax 724-738-2661. *Dir.* Philip Tramdack.

Susquehanna Library Cooperative (SLC), Stevenson Lib., Lock Haven Univ., Lock Haven 17745. SAN 322-3051. Tel. 570-484-2310, fax 570-484-2506. *Interim Dir. of Lib. and Info. Services* Joby Topper.

Tri-State College Library Cooperative (TCLC), c/o Rosemont College Lib., Rosemont 19010-1699. SAN 322-3078. Tel. 610-525-0796, fax 610-525-1939, e-mail office@tclclibs.org. *Coord.* Ellen Gasiewski.

Rhode Island

Library of Rhode Island Network (LORI), c/o Office of Lib. and Info. Services, Providence 02908-5870. SAN 371-6821. Tel. 401-574-9300, fax 401-574-9320. *Lib. Services Dir.* Howard Boksenbaum.

Ocean State Libraries (OSL), 300 Centerville Rd., Suite 103S, Warwick 02886-0226. SAN 329-4560. Tel. 401-738-2200, fax 401-736-8949, e-mail support@oslri.net. *Exec. Dir.* Joan Gillespie.

South Carolina

Charleston Academic Libraries Consortium (CALC), P.O. Box 118067, Charleston 29423-8067. SAN 371-0769. Tel. 843-574-6088, fax 843-574-6484. *Chair* Drucie Gullion.

Partnership Among South Carolina Academic Libraries (PASCAL), 1333 Main St., Suite 305, Columbia 29201. Tel. 803-734-0900, fax 803-734-0901. *Exec. Dir.* Rick Moul.

South Carolina AHEC, c/o Medical Univ. of South Carolina, Charleston 29425. SAN 329-3998. Tel. 843-792-4431, fax 843-792-4430. *Exec. Dir.* David Garr.

South Carolina Library Network, 1430 and 1500 Senate St., Columbia 29201. SAN 322-4198. Tel. 803-734-8666, fax 803-734-8676. *Dir., Lib. Development* Denise Lyons.

South Dakota

South Dakota Library Network (SDLN), 1200 University, Unit 9672, Spearfish 57799-9672. SAN 371-2117. Tel. 605-642-6835, fax 605-642-6472. *Dir.* Warren Wilson.

Tennessee

Consortium of Southern Biomedical Libraries (CONBLS), Meharry Medical College, Nashville 37208. SAN 370-7717. Tel. 615-327-6728, fax 615-327-6448. *Chair* Barbara Shearer.

Knoxville Area Health Sciences Library Consortium (KAHSLC), Univ. of Tennessee Preston Medical Lib., Knoxville 37920. SAN 371-0556. Tel. 865-305-9525, fax 865-305-9527. *Pres.* Cynthia Vaughn.

Tennessee Health Science Library Assn. (THeSLA), Holston Valley Medical Center Health Sciences Lib., Kingsport 37660. SAN 371-0726. Tel. 423-224-6870, fax 423-224-6014. *Coord., Lib. Services* Sharon M. Brown.

Tri-Cities Area Health Sciences Libraries Consortium (TCAHSLC), James H. Quillen College of Medicine, East Tennessee State Univ., Johnson City 37614. SAN 329-4099. Tel. 423-439-6252, fax 423-439-7025. *Dir.* Biddanda Ponnappa.

Texas

Abilene Library Consortium, 3305 N. 3 St., Suite 301, Abilene 79603. SAN 322-4694. Tel. 325-672-7081, fax 325-672-7082. *Coord.* Edward J. Smith.

Amigos Library Services, Inc., 14400 Midway Rd., Dallas 75244-3509. SAN 322-3191. Tel. 972-851-8000, fax 972-991-6061, e-mail amigos@amigos.org. *Pres./CEO* Bonnie Juergens.

Council of Research and Academic Libraries (CORAL), P.O. Box 290236, San Antonio 78280-1636. SAN 322-3213. Tel. 210-458-4885. *Coord.* Rosemary Vasquez.

Del Norte Biosciences Library Consortium, El Paso Community College, El Paso 79998. SAN 322-3302. Tel. 915-831-4149, fax 915-831-4639. *Coord.* Kristin Sanchez.

Harrington Library Consortium, 413 E. 4 Ave., Amarillo 79101. SAN 329-546X. Tel. 806-378-6037, fax 806-378-6038. *Dir.* Donna Littlejohn.

Health Libraries Information Network (Health LINE), Univ. of Texas Southwestern Medical Center Lib., Dallas 75390-9049. SAN 322-3299. Tel. 214-648-2626, fax 214-648-2826.

Houston Area Library Automated Network (HALAN), Houston Public Lib., Houston 77002. Tel. 832-393-1411, fax 832-393-1427, e-mail website@hpl.lib.tx.us. *Chief* Judith Hiott.

Houston Area Research Library Consortium (HARLiC), c/o Univ. of Houston Libs., Houston 77204-2000. SAN 322-3329. Tel. 713-743-9807, fax 713-743-9811. *Pres.* Dana Rooks.

National Network of Libraries of Medicine–South Central Region (NN/LM-SCR), c/o HAM-TMC Library, Houston 77030-2809. SAN 322-3353. Tel. 713-799-7880, fax 713-790-7030, e-mail nnlm-scr@exch.library.tmc.edu. *Dir.* L. Maximillian Buja.

South Central Academic Medical Libraries Consortium (SCAMeL), c/o Lewis Lib.-UNTHSC, Fort Worth 76107. SAN 372-8269. Tel. 817-735-2380, fax 817-735-5158. *Dir.* Daniel Burgard.

Texas Council of Academic Libraries (TCAL), VC/UHV Lib., Victoria 77901. SAN 322-337X. Tel. 361-570-4150, fax 361-570-4155. *Chair* Joe Dahlstrom.

Texas Navigator Group, P.O. Box 12927, Austin 78711. SAN 322-3396. Tel. 512-463-5406, fax 512-936-2306. *Coord.* Sue Bennett.

Texas State Library and Archives Commission (TexSHARE), P.O. Box 12927, Austin 78711. Tel. 512-463-5465, fax 512-936-2306, e-mail texshare@tsl.state.tx.us. *Consortia Services* Beverley Shirley.

Utah

National Network of Libraries of Medicine–MidContinental Region (NN/LM-MCR), Spencer S. Eccles Health Sciences Lib., Univ. of Utah, Salt Lake City 84112-5890. SAN 322-225X. Tel. 801-587-3412, fax 801-581-3632. *Dir.* Wayne J. Peay.

Utah Academic Library Consortium (UALC), Univ. of Utah, Salt Lake City 84112-0860. SAN 322-3418. Tel. 801-581-7701, 801-581-3852, fax 801-585-7185, e-mail UALC mail@library.utah.edu. *Fiscal Agent* Carol Jost.

Utah Health Sciences Library Consortium, c/o Spencer S. Eccles Health Sciences Lib., Univ. of Utah, Salt Lake City 84112-5890. SAN 376-2246. Tel. 801-585-5743, fax 801-581-3632. *Chair* Emily Eresuma.

Vermont

North Atlantic Health Sciences Libraries, Inc. (NAHSL), Dana Medical Lib., Univ. of Vermont Medical School, Burlington 05405. SAN 371-0599. Tel. 508-656-3483, fax 508-656-0762. *Chair* Cindy Stewart.

Vermont Resource Sharing Network, c/o Vermont Dept. of Libs., Montpelier 05609-0601. SAN 322-3426. Tel. 802-828-3261, fax 802-828-1481. *Ref. Libn.* Gerrie Denison.

Virgin Islands

Virgin Islands Library and Information Network (VILINET), c/o Div. of Libs., Archives, and Museums, Saint Thomas 00802. SAN 322-3639. Tel. 340-773-5715, fax 340-773-3257, e-mail info@vilinet.net. *Territorial Dir. of Libs., Archives, and Museums* Ingrid Bough.

Virginia

American Indian Higher Education Consortium (AIHEC), 121 Oronoco St., Alexandria 22314. SAN 329-4056. Tel. 703-838-0400, fax 703-838-0388, e-mail info@aihec.org.

Lynchburg Area Library Cooperative, c/o Sweet Briar College Lib., Sweet Briar 24595. SAN 322-3450. Tel. 434-381-6315, fax 434-381-6173.

Lynchburg Information Online Network (LION), 2315 Memorial Ave., Lynchburg 24503. SAN 374-6097. Tel. 434-381-6311, fax 434-381-6173. *Dir.* John G. Jaffee.

NASA Libraries Information System–NASA Galaxie, NASA Langley Research Center, MS 185-Technical Lib., Hampton 23681-2199. SAN 322-0788. Tel. 757-864-2356, fax 757-864-2375. *Branch Head* Manjula Ambur.

Richmond Academic Library Consortium (RALC), James Branch Cabell Lib., Virginia Commonwealth Univ., Richmond 23284. SAN 322-3469. Tel. 804-828-1110, fax 804-828-1105. *Univ. Libn.* John E. Ulmschneider.

Southside Virginia Library Network (SVLN), Longwood Univ., Farmville 23909-1897. SAN 372-8242. Tel. 434-395-2431; 434-395-2433, fax 434-395-2453. *Dir.* Suzy Szasz.

United States Army Training and Doctrine Command (TRADOC)/Lib. Program Office, U.S. Army Hq TRADOC, Fort Monroe 23651. SAN 322-418X. Tel. 757-788-2155, fax 757-788-5544. *Dir.* Amy Loughran.

Virginia Independent College and University Library Assn., c/o Mary Helen Cochran Lib., Sweet Briar 24595. SAN 374-6089. Tel. 434-381-6139, fax 434-381-6173. *Dir.* John Jaffee.

Virginia Tidewater Consortium for Higher Education (VTC), 4900 Powhatan Ave., Norfolk 23529. SAN 329-5486. Tel. 757-683-3183, fax 757-683-4515, e-mail lgdotolo@aol.com. *Pres.* Lawrence G. Dotolo.

Virtual Library of Virginia (VIVA), George Mason Univ., Fairfax 22030. Tel. 703-993-4652, fax 703-993-4662. *Dir.* Katherine Perry.

Washington

Cooperating Libraries in Olympia (CLIO), Evergreen State College Library, L2300, Olympia 98505. SAN 329-4528. Tel. 360-867-6260, fax 360-867-6790. *Dean, Lib. Services* Lee Lyttle.

Inland NorthWest Health Sciences Libraries (INWHSL), P.O. Box 10283, Spokane 99209-0283. SAN 370-5099. Tel. 509-368-6973, fax 509-358-7928. *Treas.* Robert Pringle.

National Network of Libraries of Medicine–Pacific Northwest Region (NN/LM-PNR), T-344 Health Sciences Bldg., Univ. of Washington, Seattle 98195. SAN 322-3485. Tel. 206-543-8262, fax 206-543-2469, e-mail nnlm@u.washington.edu. *Assoc. Dir.* Catherine Burroughs.

Palouse Area Library Information Services (PALIS), c/o Neill Public Lib., Pullman 99163. SAN 375-0132. Tel. 509-334-3595, fax 509-334-6051. *Dir.* Andriette Pieron.

Washington Idaho Network (WIN), Foley Center Lib., Gonzaga Univ., Spokane 99258. Tel. 509-323-6545, fax 509-324-5904, e-mail winsupport@gonzaga.edu. *Pres.* Eileen Bell-Garrison.

Wisconsin

Fox River Valley Area Library Consortium (FRVALC), c/o Polk Lib., Univ. of Wisconsin–Oshkosh, Oshkosh 54901. SAN 322-3531. Tel. 920-424-3348, 920-424-4333, fax 920-424-2175.

Fox Valley Library Council, c/o OWLS, Appleton 54911. SAN 323-9640. Tel. 920-832-6190, fax 920-832-6422. *Pres.* Joy Schwarz.

North East Wisconsin Intertype Libraries, Inc. (NEWIL), 515 Pine St., Green Bay 54301. SAN 322-3574. Tel. 920-448-4413, fax 920-448-4420. *Coord.* Jamie Matczak.

Northwestern Wisconsin Health Science Library Consortium, c/o Gundersen Lutheran Medical Center, Lacrosse 54601. Tel. 608-775-5410, fax 608-775-6343. *Treas.* Eileen Severson.

South Central Wisconsin Health Science Library Consortium, c/o Fort Healthcare Medical Lib., Fort Atkinson 53538. SAN 322-4686. Tel. 920-568-5194, fax 920-568-5195. *Coord.* Carrie Garity.

Southeastern Wisconsin Health Science Library Consortium, Veterans Admin. Center Medical Lib., Milwaukee 53295. SAN 322-3582. Tel. 414-384-2000 ext. 42342, fax 414-382-5334. *Coord.* Janice Curnes.

Southeastern Wisconsin Information Technology Exchange, Inc. (SWITCH), 3401 South 39th St., P.O. Box 343922, Room FO 237A Milwaukee 53234-3922. Tel. 414-382-6710. *Coord.* Jennifer Schmidt.

University of Wisconsin System School Library Education Consortium (UWSSLEC), Graduate and Continuing Educ., Univ. of Wisconsin–Whitewater, Whitewater 53190. Tel. 262-472-1463, fax 262-472-5210, e-mail lenchoc@uww.edu. *Co-Dir.* E. Anne Zarinnia.

Wisconsin Library Services (WILS), 1360 Regent St., No. 121, Madison 53715-1255. Tel. 608-216-8399, e-mail information@wils.org. *Dir.* Stef Morrill.

Wisconsin Public Library Consortium (WPLC), c/o WILS, 1360 Regent St., No. 121, Madison 53715-1255. Tel. 608-216-8399, e-mail information@wils.org.

Wisconsin Valley Library Service (WVLS), 300 N. 1 St., Wausau 54403. SAN 371-3911. Tel. 715-261-7250, fax 715-261-7259. *Dir.* Marla Rae Sepnafski.

WISPALS Library Consortium, c/o Gateway Technical College, Kenosha 53144-1690. Tel. 262-564-2602, fax 262-564-2787. *Coord.* Kelly Kroes.

Wyoming

WYLD Network, c/o Wyoming State Lib., Cheyenne 82002-0060. SAN 371-0661. Tel. 307-777-6339, fax 307-777-6289, e-mail wyldstaff@will.state.wy.us. *State Libn.* Lesley Boughton.

Canada

Alberta

The Alberta Library (TAL), 6-14, 7 Sir Winston Churchill Sq., Edmonton T5J 2V5. Tel. 780-414-0805, fax 780-414-0806, e-mail admin@thealbertalibrary.ab.ca. *CEO* Maureen Woods.

Council of Prairie and Pacific University Libraries (COPPUL), LCR Admin. Suite, 6th fl. TFDL, Calgary T2N 1N4. Tel. 403-220-8133, fax 403-282-1218. *Exec. Dir.* Andrew Waller.

NEOS Library Consortium, Cameron Lib., 5th flr., Edmonton T6G 2J8. Tel. 780-492-0075, fax 780-492-8302. *Mgr.* Anne Carr-Wiggin.

British Columbia

British Columbia Academic Health Council (BCAHC), 402-1770 W. 7 Ave., Vancouver V6J 4Y6. Tel. 604-739-3910 ext. 228, fax 604-739-3931, e-mail info@bcahc.ca. *CEO* Laureen Styles.

British Columbia College and Institute Library Services, Langara College Lib., Vancouver V5Y 2Z6. SAN 329-6970. Tel. 604-323-5639, fax 604-323-5544, e-mail cils@langara.bc.ca. *Dir.* Mary Anne Epp.

British Columbia Electronic Library Network (BCELN), WAC Bennett Lib., 7th flr., Simon Fraser Univ., Burnaby V5A 1S6. Tel. 778-782-7003, fax 778-782-3023, e-mail office@eln.bc.ca. *Exec. Dir.* Anita Cocchia.

Council of Prairie and Pacific University Libraries (COPPUL), c/o Bennett Lib., Burnaby V5A 1S6. Tel. 778-782-9404, fax 778-782-3023. *Exec. Dir.* Gwen Bird.

Electronic Health Library of British Columbia (e-HLbc), c/o Bennett Lib., Burnaby V5A 1S6. Tel. 778-782-5440, fax 778-782-3023, e-mail info@ehlbc.ca. *Coord.* JoAnne Newyear-Ramirez.

Public Library InterLINK, 5489 Byrne Rd., No 158, Burnaby V5J 3J1. SAN 318-8272. Tel. 604-517-8441, fax 604-517-8410, e-mail info@interlinklibraries.ca. *Operations Mgr.* Rita Avigdor.

Manitoba

Manitoba Library Consortium, Inc. (MLCI), c/o Lib. Admin., Univ. of Winnipeg, Winnipeg R3B 2E9. SAN 372-820X. Tel. 204-786-9801, fax 204-783-8910. *Chair* Patricia Burt.

Nova Scotia

Maritimes Health Libraries Assn. (MHLA-ABSM), W. K. Kellogg Health Sciences Lib., Halifax B3H 1X5. SAN 370-0836. Tel. 902-494-2483, fax 902-494-3750. *Libn.* Shelley McKibbon.

NOVANET, 84 Chain Lake Drive, Suite 402, Halifax B3S 1A2. SAN 372-4050. Tel. 902-453-2461, fax 902-453-2369, e-mail office@novanet.ns.ca. *Mgr.* Bill Slauenwhite.

Ontario

Canadian Assn. of Research Libraries (Association des Bibliothèques de Recherche du Canada), 203-309 Cooper St., Ottawa K2P 0G5. SAN 323-9721. Tel. 613-482-9344, fax 613-562-5297, e-mail info@carl-abrc.ca. *Exec. Dir.* Brent Roe.

Canadian Health Libraries Assn. (CHLA-ABSC), 39 River St., Toronto M5A 3P1. SAN 370-0720. Tel. 416-646-1600, fax 416-646-9460, e-mail info@chla-absc.ca. *Pres.* Miriam Ticoll.

Canadian Research Knowledge Network (CRKN), Preston Sq., Tower 2, Ottawa K1S 1N4. Tel. 613-907-7040, fax 866-903-9094. *Exec. Dir.* Deb deBruijn.

Consortium of Ontario Libraries (COOL), 111 Peter St., Suite 902, Toronto M5V 2H1. Tel. 416-961-1669, fax 416-961-5122. *Dir.* Barbara Franchetto.

Hamilton and District Health Library Network, c/o St Josephs Healthcare Hamilton, Sherman Lib., Room T2305, Hamilton L8N 4A6. SAN 370-5846. Tel. 905-522-1155 ext. 3410, fax 905-540-6504. *Coord.* Jean Maragno.

Health Science Information Consortium of Toronto, c/o Gerstein Science Info. Center, Univ. of Toronto, Toronto M5S 1A5. SAN 370-5080. Tel. 416-978-6359, fax 416-971-2637. *Exec. Dir.* Miriam Ticoll.

Ontario Council of University Libraries (OCUL), 130 Saint George St., Toronto M5S 1A5. Tel. 416-946-0578, fax 416-978-6755. *Exec. Dir.* Kathy Scardellato.

Ontario Library Consortium (OLC), c/o Georgina Public Lib., Keswick L4P 3P7. *Pres.* Mary Baxter.

Parry Sound and Area Access Network, c/o Parry Sound Public Lib., Parry Sound P2A 1E3. Tel. 705-746-9601, fax 705-746-9601, e-mail pspl@vianet.ca. *Chair* Laurine Tremaine.

Perth County Information Network (PCIN), c/o Stratford Public Lib., Stratford N5A 1A2. Tel. 519-271-0220, fax 519-271-3843, e-mail webmaster@pcin.on.ca. *CEO* Sam Coglin.

Shared Library Services (SLS), Woodstock General Hospital, Woodstock N4V 0A4. SAN 323-9500. Tel. 519-421-4233, ext. 2735, fax 519-421-4236. *Libn.* Linda Wilcox.

Southwestern Ontario Health Libraries and Information Network (SOHLIN), London Health Sciences Centre, London N6A 5W9. Tel. 519-685-8500, ext. 56038. *Pres.* Sandra McKeown.

Toronto Health Libraries Assn. (THLA), 3409 Yonge St., Toronto M4N 2L0. SAN 323-9853. Tel. 416-485-0377, fax 416-485-6877, e-mail medinfoserv@rogers.com. *Pres.* Graziela Alexandria.

Quebec

Assn. des Bibliothèques de la Santé Affiliées a l'Université de Montréal (ABSAUM), c/o Health Lib., Univ. of Montreal, Montreal H3C 3J7. SAN 370-5838. Tel. 514-343-6826, fax 514-343-2350. *Dir.* Monique St-Jean.

Canadian Heritage Information Network (CHIN), 15 Eddy St., 4th flr., Gatineau K1A 0M5. SAN 329-3076. Tel. 819-994-1200, fax 819-994-9555, e-mail service@chin.gc.ca. *Acting Exec. Dir.* Claudette Levesque.

Réseau BIBLIO de l'Ouatouais, 2295 Saint-Louis St., Gatineau, Quebec J8T 5L8. SAN 319-6526. Tel. 819-561-6008. *Exec. Gen.* Sylvie Thibault.

National Library and Information-Industry Associations, United States and Canada

AIIM—The Association for Information and Image Management

President and CEO, John F. Mancini
1100 Wayne Ave., Suite 1100, Silver Spring, MD 20910
800-477-2446, 301-587-8202, e-mail aiim@aiim.org
World Wide Web http://www.aiim.org
European Office: 8 Canalside, Lowesmoor Wharf, Worcester WR1 2RR, England
Tel. 44-1905-727600, fax 44-1905-727609, e-mail info@aiim.org.uk

Object

AIIM is an international authority on enterprise content management, the tools and technologies that capture, manage, store, preserve, and deliver content in support of business processes. Founded in 1943.

Officers

Chair Paul Engel, VeBridge; *V. Chair* Anthony Peleska, Minnesota Housing Finance Agency; *Treas.* Daniel Antion, American Nuclear Insurers; *Past Chair* Timothy Elmore, Federal Credit Union.

Publication

Connect (weekly, memb., online).

American Association of Law Libraries

Executive Director, Kate Hagan
105 W. Adams St., Suite 3300, Chicago, IL 60603
312-939-4764, fax 312-431-1097, e-mail khagan@aall.org
World Wide Web http://www.aallnet.org

Object

The American Association of Law Libraries (AALL) is established for educational and scientific purposes. It shall be conducted as a nonprofit corporation to promote and enhance the value of law libraries to the public, the legal community, and the world; to foster the profession of law librarianship; to provide leadership in the field of legal information; and to foster a spirit of cooperation among the members of the profession. Established 1906.

Membership

Memb. 5,000+. Persons officially connected with a law library or with a law section of a state or general library, separately maintained. Associate membership available for others. Dues (Indiv.) $222; (Associate) $222; (Retired) $56; (Student) $56. Year. July–June.

Officers (2014–2015)

Pres. Holly M. Riccio. E-mail hriccio@omm. com; *V.P.* Keith Ann Stiverson. E-mail kstivers@kentlaw.iit.edu; *Secy.* Katherine K. Coolidge. E-mail kcoolidge@bulkley.com; *Treas.* Gail Warren. E-mail gail.warren.56@comcast.net; *Past Pres.* Steven P. Anderson. E-mail steve.anderson@courts.state.md.us.

Executive Board Members

John W. Adkins. E-mail jadkins@sdlawlibrary.org; Femi Cadmus. E-mail femi.cadmus@cornell.edu; Amy J. Eaton. E-mail aeaton@perkinscoie.com; Kenneth J. Hirsh. E-mail hirshkh@ucmail.uc.edu; Donna Nixon. E-mail dnixon@email.unc.edu; Suzanne Thorpe. E-mail s-thor@umn.edu.

American Indian Library Association

President, Zora Sampson
World Wide Web http://www.ailanet.org

Object

To improve library and information services for American Indians. Founded in 1979; affiliated with American Library Association in 1985.

Membership

Any person, library, or other organization interested in working to improve library and information services for American Indians may become a member. Dues (Inst.) $40; (Indiv.) $20; (Student) $10.

Officers (July 2014–June 2015)

Pres. Zora Sampson (Choctaw). E-mail sampsonz@uwplatt.edu; *V.P./Pres.-Elect* Paulita Aguilar. E-mail paulita@unm.edu; *Secy.* Angela Thornton (Cherokee Nation). E-mail athornton@hdpl.org; *Treas.* Carlene Engstrom (Salish/Kootenai). E-mail carleneengstrom@yahoo.com; *Past Pres.* Heather Devine (Eastern Shawnee); *Exec. Dir.* Jody Gray (Cheyenne River Lakota); *Membs. at Large* (2014–2016) Antonio Arce; (2013–2015) Omar Poler (Mole Lake Sokaogon Chippewa Community); Valarie Kingsland (Inupiaq).

Publication

AILA Newsletter (irregular). *Ed.* Danielle Geller (Navajo).

American Library Association

Executive Director, Keith Michael Fiels
50 E. Huron St., Chicago, IL 60611
800-545-2433, 312-280-1392, fax 312-440-9374
World Wide Web http://www.ala.org

Object

The mission of the American Library Association (ALA) is to provide leadership for the development, promotion, and improvement of library and information services and the profession of librarianship in order to enhance learning and ensure access to information for all. Founded 1876.

Memb. (Indiv.) 52,841; (Inst.) 2,415; (Corporate) 183; (Total) 55,439 (as of November 2014). Any person, library, or other organization interested in library service and librarians. Dues (Indiv.) 1st year, $67; 2nd year, $102; 3rd year and later, $135; (Trustee and Assoc. Memb.) $61; (Lib. Support Staff) $48; (Student) $35; (Foreign Indiv.) $81; (Non-salaried/Unemployed/Retired) $48; (Inst.) $175 and up, depending on operating expenses of institution.

Officers (2014–2015)

Pres. Courtney L. Young, Penn State Univ. E-mail cly11@psu.edu; *Pres.-Elect* Sari Feldman, Cuyahoga County Public Library. E-mail sfeldman@cuyahogalibrary.org; *Past Pres.* Barbara K. Stripling, iSchool, Syracuse Univ. E-mail bstripli@syr.edu; *Treas.* Mario M. Gonzalez, Passaic (New Jersey) Public Lib. E-mail mgonzalez@passaicpubliclibrary.org.

Executive Board

Robert E. Banks (2015), Peter Hepburn (2017), Alexia Hudson-Ward (2015), Sara Kelly Johns (2016), John A. Moorman (2015), James G. Neal (2016), Gina Persichini (2017), Gail A. Schlachter (2017).

Endowment Trustees

Rodney M. Hersberger, Kate Nevins, Robert Randolph Newlen, Siobhan A. Reardon, Teri R. Switzer; *Exec. Board Liaison* Mario M. Gonzalez; *Staff Liaisons* Keith D. Brown, Gregory L. Calloway.

Divisions

See the separate entries that follow: American Assn. of School Libns.; Assn. for Lib. Collections and Technical Services; Assn. for Lib. Service to Children; Assn. of College and Research Libs.; Assn. of Specialized and Cooperative Lib. Agencies; Lib. Leadership and Management Assn.; Lib. and Info. Technology Assn.; Public Lib. Assn.; Reference and User Services Assn.; United for Libraries; Young Adult Lib. Services Assn.

Publications

ALA Handbook of Organization (online).
American Libraries (6 a year with occasional digital supplements; memb.; organizations $70; foreign $80; single copy $11.50).
Booklist (22 a year with 4 *Book Links* print issues and access to *Booklist Online*; U.S. and Canada $147.50; foreign $170; single copy $9).

Round Table Chairs

(ALA staff liaison in parentheses)
Ethnic and Multicultural Information Exchange. Katherine Trouern-Trend (John Amundsen).

Exhibits. Kelly Coyle-Crivelli (Paul Graller).

Federal and Armed Forces Libraries. Amanda J. Wilson (Rosalind Reynolds).

Games and Gaming. Diane Robson (Jenny Levine).

Gay, Lesbian, Bisexual, and Transgender. Ann K. Symons (John Amundsen).

Government Documents. Helen Sheehy (Rosalind Reynolds).

Intellectual Freedom. Dave Trudeau (Shumeca Pickett).

International Relations. Robin Kear (Delin Guerra).

Learning. Jennifer L. Fenton (Kimberly Redd).

Library History. Dominique Renee Daniel (Norman Rose).

Library Instruction. Jennifer Corbin (Beatrice Calvin).

Library Research. Jennifer W. Arns (Norman Rose).

Library Support Staff Interests. Valentin Colon (Beatrice Calvin).

Map and Geospatial Information. Paige Andrew (Danielle M. Alderson).

New Members. Megan Hodge (Kimberly Redd).

Retired Members. Mary Elizabeth Wendt (Danielle M. Alderson).

Social Responsibilities. Nicole Winslow (John Amundsen).

Staff Organizations. Leon S. Bey (Kimberly Redd).

Sustainability. Ashley Jones (John Amundsen).

Video. Laura Jenemann (Danielle M. Alderson).

Committee Chairs

(ALA staff liaison in parentheses)

Accreditation (Standing). Mary Stansbury (Laura Dare).

American Libraries Advisory (Standing). Sandra Hirsh (Laurie Borman).

Appointments (Standing). Sari Feldman (Kerri Price).

Awards (Standing). Eric D. Suess (Cheryl Malden).

Budget Analysis and Review (Standing). Patricia A. Wand (Keith D. Brown).

Chapter Relations (Standing). Ann H. Hamilton (Michael Dowling).

Committee on Committees (Elected Council Committee). Sari Feldman (Lois Ann Gregory-Wood).

Conference Committee (Standing). Walter L. Betts (Paul Graller).

Conference Program Coordinating Team. Walter L. Betts (Paul Graller).

Constitution and Bylaws (Standing). James R. Rettig (JoAnne M. Kempf).

Council Orientation (Standing). Joseph M. Eagan (Lois Ann Gregory-Wood).

Diversity (Standing). Alanna Aiko Moore (Michelle Harrell Washington).

Education (Standing). Susan Roman (Lorelle R. Swader).

Election (Standing). Sarah Ann Long (Lois Ann Gregory-Wood).

Human Resource Development and Recruitment (Standing). Neely Tang (Lorelle R. Swader).

Information Technology Policy Advisory (Standing). Daniel R. Lee (Alan Inouye).

Intellectual Freedom (Standing). J. Douglas Archer (Nanette Perez).

International Relations (Standing). Loida A. Garcia-Febo (Michael P. Dowling).

Legislation (Standing). Vivian R. Wynn (Adam M. Eisgrau).

Library Advocacy (Standing). Gina J. Millsap (Marci Merola).

Literacy (Standing). Cynthia Czesak (Michelle Harrell Washington).

Literacy and Outreach Services Advisory (Standing). John C. Sandstrom (Michelle Harrell Washington).

Membership (Standing). Laurel M. Bliss (Cathleen Bourdon).

Membership Meetings. Mike L. Marlin (Lois Ann Gregory-Wood).

Nominating. Larry P. Neal (JoAnne M. Kempf).

Organization (Standing). Mary E. Rzepczynski (Kerri Price).

Policy Monitoring (Standing). Henry R. Stewart, Jr. (Lois Ann Gregory-Wood).

Professional Ethics (Standing). Martin L. Garnar (Deborah Caldwell-Stone).

Public and Cultural Programs Advisory (Standing). Timothy P. Grimes (Deborah A. Robertson).

Public Awareness (Standing). Nancy R. Dowd (Cathleen Bourdon).

Publishing (Standing). Anders C. Dahlgren (Donald E. Chatham).

Research and Statistics (Standing). Linda Hofschire (Kathy Rosa).

Resolutions. Larry Romans (Lois Ann Gregory-Wood).

Rural, Native, and Tribal Libraries of All Kinds. Miriam C. Nauenburg (Michelle Harrell Washington).

Scholarships and Study Grants. Min Chou (Lorelle R. Swader).

Status of Women in Librarianship (Standing). Sandy Wee (Lorelle R. Swader).

Training, Orientation, and Leadership Development. Gary W. White (Lorelle R. Swader).

Website Advisory. John Morris Jackson II (Sherri L. Vanyek).

American Library Association
American Association of School Librarians

Executive Director, Sylvia Knight Norton
50 E. Huron St., Chicago, IL 60611
312-280-4382, 800-545-2433 ext. 4382, fax 312-280-5276, e-mail aasl@ala.org
World Wide Web http://www.aasl.org

Object

The American Association of School Librarians empowers leaders to transform teaching and learning. AASL works to ensure that all members of the field collaborate to provide leadership in the total education program; participate as active partners in the teaching/learning process; connect learners with ideas and information; and prepare students for lifelong learning, informed decision making, a love of reading, and the use of information technologies.

Established in 1951 as a separate division of the American Library Association.

Membership

Memb. 7,000+. Open to all libraries, school librarians, interested individuals, and business firms, with requisite membership in ALA.

Officers (2014–2015)

Pres. Terri Grief; *Pres.-Elect* Leslie Preddy; *Treas.* Robbie Nickel; *Past Pres.* Gail K. Dickinson.

Board of Directors

Kathy Carroll, Audrey P. Church, Gail Dickinson, Valerie Edwards, Catherine G. Evans, Jessica Gillis, Carlyn J. Gray, Terri Grief, Lisa Hathcock, Jody K. Howard, Eileen Kern, Michelle Luhtala, Robbie Nickel, Susan M. Nickel, Sylvia Knight Norton (ex officio), Devona J. Pendergrass, Leslie Preddy, Ken Stewart, Sarah Thornbery, Steven Yates.

Publications

AASL Hotlinks (mo.; electronic, memb.).

Knowledge Quest (5 a year; $50, $60 outside U.S.). *Ed.* Meg Featheringham. E-mail mfeatheringham@ala.org.

School Library Research (electronic, free, at http://www.ala.org/aasl/slr). *Eds.* Ruth Small. E-mail drruth@syr.edu; Mega Subramaniam. E-mail manis2@gmail.com.

Section Leadership

AASL/ESLS Executive Committee. Judy T. Bivens, Audrey P. Church, Karen Gavigan, Sue Kimmel, Rebecca Morris.

AASL/ISS Executive Committee. Cheri Estes Dobbs, Catherine G. Evans, Sarah Jane Levin, Yapha Mason.

AASL/SPVS Executive Committee. Mary Keeling, Kathryn Roots Lewis, Margaret Montgomery, Devona J. Pendergrass, Amy Short.

Committee Chairs

AASL/ACRL Interdivisional Committee on Information Literacy. Jennifer Fabbi.

AASL/ALSC/YALSA Joint Committee on School/Public Library Cooperation. Jenna Nemec-Loise (ALSC).

Advocacy. Hilda Weisburg.

Affiliate Assembly. Carrie Turner.

Alliance for Association Excellence. Robbie Nickel.

American University Press Book Selection. Annemarie Roscello.

Annual Conference. Elizabeth Friese.

Awards. Bonnie J. Grimble.

Banned Websites Awareness Day. Michelle Luhtala.

Best Apps for Teaching and Learning. Melissa Jacobs-Israel.

Best Websites for Teaching and Learning. Heather Moorefield-Lang.

Beyond Words Grant Jury. Elaine E. Steinberg.

Blog Group. Susi Parks Grissom, Frances Reeve.

Bylaws and Organization. Rebecca J. Pasco.

CAEP Coordinating Committee. Sherry Crow.

Fall Forum (National Institute) 2014. Steven Yates.

Leadership Development Committee. Gail Dickinson.

Legislation. Carl Jay Bansbach.

National Conference. Debra Kay Logan, Katherine E. Lowe.

Research/Statistics. Sue Kimmel.

School Library Month Committee. Susan Hess.

Standards and Guidelines Implementation. Nina Kemps.

Editorial Board Chairs

Essential Links Editorial Board. Mary Jo Richmond.

Knowledge Quest Editorial Board. Rebecca Jane Morris.

School Library Research Editorial Board. Ruth Small, Mega Subramaniam.

Task Force Chairs

Committee Review. Frances R. Roscello.

Community of Scholars. Jeffrey DiScala.

External Relations. To be announced.

Presidential Initiative. To be announced.

65th Celebration. Carl A. Harvey.

STEM. Susan Kowalski.

Underserved Student Populations. Juanita Jameson.

Awards Committee Chairs

ABC-CLIO Leadership Grant. Floyd Clark Pentlin.

Collaborative School Library Award. Beth Kabes.

Distinguished School Administrator Award. Krista K. Britton.

Distinguished Service Award. Rocco A. Staino.

Frances Henne Award. Pamela Jo Renfrow.

Information Technology Pathfinder Award. Carolyn J. Starkey.

Innovative Reading Grant. Sharon K. Carvell.

Intellectual Freedom Award. Michelle F. Bayuk.

National School Library Program of the Year Award. Nancy Everhart.

Roald Dahl's Miss Honey Social Justice Award. Terrence E. Young.

Advisory Group Staff Liaisons

Professional Development. Jennifer Habley.

Publications. Stephanie Book.

American Library Association
Association for Library Collections and Technical Services

Executive Director, Charles Wilt
50 E. Huron St., Chicago, IL 60611
800-545-2433 ext. 5030, fax 312-280-5033, e-mail cwilt@ala.org
World Wide Web http://www.ala.org/alcts

Object

The Association for Library Collections and Technical Services (ALCTS) envisions an environment in which traditional library roles are evolving. New technologies are making information more fluid and raising expectations. The public needs quality information anytime, anyplace. ALCTS provides frameworks to meet these information needs.

ALCTS provides leadership to the library and information communities in developing principles, standards, and best practices for creating, collecting, organizing, delivering, and preserving information resources in all forms. It provides this leadership through its members by fostering educational, research, and professional service opportunities. ALCTS is committed to quality information, universal access, collaboration, and lifelong learning.

Standards—Develop, evaluate, revise, and promote standards for creating, collecting, organizing, delivering, and preserving information resources in all forms.

Best practices—Research, develop, evaluate, and implement best practices for creating, collecting, organizing, delivering, and preserving information resources in all forms.

Education—Assess the need for, sponsor, develop, administer, and promote educational programs and resources for lifelong learning.

Professional development—Provide opportunities for professional development through research, scholarship, publication, and professional service.

Interaction and information exchange—Create opportunities to interact and exchange information with others in the library and information communities.

Association operations—Ensure efficient use of association resources and effective delivery of member services.

Established in 1957; renamed in 1988.

Membership

Memb. 3,800. Any member of the American Library Association may elect membership in this division according to the provisions of the bylaws.

Officers (2014–2015)

Pres. Mary Page, Univ. of Central Florida., P.O. Box 162666. Orlando, FL 32816. Tel. 407-823-2564, fax 407-823-2529, e-mail mary.page@ucf.edu; *Pres.-Elect* Norm Medeiros, Haverford College, 370 Lancaster Ave., Haverford, PA 19041. Tel. 610-896-1173, e-mail nmedeiro@haverford.edu; *Past Pres.* Genevieve Owens, Williamsburg Regional Libs., 7700 Croaker Rd., Williamsburg, VA 23188. Tel. 757-259-7777, fax 757-259-4079, e-mail gowens@wrl.org; *Councilor* Andy Hart, Univ. of North Carolina, CB#3910 Davis Lib., Chapel Hill, NC 27514. Tel. 912-962-8047, e-mail ashart@email.unc.edu.

Address correspondence to the executive director.

Board of Directors

Jennifer Bowen, Keri Cascio, Melinda Reagor Flannery, Elaine Franco, Regina Gong, Andy Hart, Michael Levine-Clark, Lucas Mak, Kara McClurken, Norm Medeiros, Meg Mering, Rebecca Mugridge, Genevieve Owens, Mary Page, Vicki Sipe, Lisa Spagnolo, Karla Strieb, Charles Wilt, Jennifer Young.

Publications

ALCTS News (q.; free; posted at http://www.ala.org/alcts). *Ed.* Rebecca Mugridge, Univ.

Libs., Univ. at Albany, SUNY, UAB 121, Albany, NY 12222. Tel. 518-437-5062, e-mail rmugridge@albany.edu.

Library Resources and Technical Services (LRTS) (q.; nonmemb. $100; international $100). Electronic only. *Ed.* Mary Beth Weber, Technical and Automated Services Dept., Rutgers Univ. Libs., 47 Davidson Rd., Piscataway, NJ 08854. Tel. 732-445-0500, fax 732-445-5888, e-mail mbfecko@rci.rutgers.edu.

Section Chairs

Acquisitions. Lisa Spagnolo.
Cataloging and Metadata Management. Melinda Reagor Flannery.
Collection Management. Michael Levine-Clark.
Continuing Resources. Jennifer Young.
Preservation and Reformatting. Kara McClurken.

Committee Chairs

Affiliate Relations. Elaine Franco.
ALCTS Outstanding Publications Award Jury. Rene Erlandson.
Hugh C. Atkinson Memorial Award (ALCTS/ACRL/LLAMA/LITA). Nancy Gibbs.
Ross Atkinson Lifetime Achievement Award Jury. Emily McElroy.
Budget and Finance. Vicki Sipe.
Continuing Education. Maria Pinkas.
Fund Raising. Lenore England.
International Relations. Qiang Jin.
Leadership Development. Donia Conn.
LRTS Editorial Board. Mary Beth Weber.

Membership. Susan Wynne.
Nominating. Carolynne Myall.
Organization and Bylaws. Lucas Mak.
Outstanding Collaboration Citation Jury. Ginger Williams.
Esther J. Piercy Award Jury. Harriet Lightman.
Planning. Meg Mering.
Program. Susan Davis, Reeta Sinha.
Publications. Mary Miller.
Edward Swanson Memorial Best of *LRTS* Award Jury. Arthur Miller.

Interest Group Chairs

Authority Control (ALCTS/LITA). Nathan Putnam.
Creative Ideas in Technical Services. Erin Leach.
Electronic Resources. Jeanne Castro.
Functional Requirements for Bibliographic Records (FRBR). Scott Piepenburg.
Linked Library Data (ALCTS/LITA). Violeta Ilik, Sarah Quimby.
MARC Formats (ALCTS/LITA). Carolyn Hansen, Victoria Mueller.
New Members. Elyssa Gould, Deana Groves.
Newspapers. Brian Geiger.
Public Libraries Technical Services. Carolyn Saccucci.
Role of the Professional in Academic Research Technical Service Departments. Christine Dulaney, Harriet Wintermute.
Scholarly Communications. Doug Way.
Technical Services Directors of Large Research Libraries. Jennifer Marill.
Technical Services Managers in Academic Libraries. Amy Lana.
Technical Services Workflow Efficiency. Margaret Glerum, Michael Winecoff.

American Library Association
Association for Library Service to Children

Executive Director, Aimee Strittmatter
50 E. Huron St., Chicago, IL 60611
312-280-2163, 800-545-2433 ext. 2163, fax 312-280-5271, e-mail alsc@ala.org
World Wide Web http://www.ala.org/alsc

Object

The core purpose of the Association for Library Service to Children (ALSC) is to create a better future for children through libraries. Its primary goal is to lead the way in forging excellent library services for all children. ALSC offers creative programming, information about best practices, continuing education, an awards and media evaluation program, and professional connections. Founded in 1901.

Membership

Memb. 4,000. Open to anyone interested in library services to children. For information on dues, see ALA entry.

Address correspondence to the executive director.

Officers

Pres. Ellen Riordan; *V.P./Pres.-Elect* Andrew Medlar; *Past Pres.* Starr LaTronica; *Fiscal Officer* Diane Foote; *Div. Councilor* Lisa Von Drasek.

Directors

Rita Auerbach, Gretchen Caserotti, Doris Gebel, Jamie Campbell Naidoo, Julie Roach, Michael Santangelo, Megan Schliesman, Kay Weisman.

Publications

ALSC Matters! (q., electronic; memb. Not available by subscription.)

Children and Libraries: The Journal of the Association for Library Service to Children (q.; print and online; memb; nonmemb. $50; foreign $60).

Everyday Advocacy Matters (q., electronic; memb. Not available by subscription.)

Committee Chairs

AASL/ALSC/YALSA Interdivisional Committee on School/Public Library Cooperation. Jenna Nemec-Loise.

Advocacy and Legislation. Robyn M. Lupa.

ALSC/Booklist/YALSA Odyssey Award Selection 2015. Dawn Rutherford.

ALSC/Booklist/YALSA Odyssey Award Selection 2016. Jennifer Duffy.

Arbuthnot Honor Lecture 2015. Sue McCleaf Nespeca.

Arbuthnot Honor Lecture 2016. Julie Corsaro.

Arbuthnot Honor Lecture 2017. Ellen Ruffin.

Mildred L. Batchelder Award 2015. Diane Janoff.

Mildred L. Batchelder Award 2016. Elizabeth Stalford.

Pura Belpré Award 2015. Tim Wadham.

Pura Belpré Award 2016. Ana-Elba Pavon.

Budget. Paula Holmes.

Randolph Caldecott Award 2015. Junko Yokota.

Randolph Caldecott Award 2016. Rachel Payne.

Andrew Carnegie Medal/Notable Children's Videos 2015. Caitlin Dixon Jacobson.

Andrew Carnegie Medal/Notable Children's Videos 2016. Lizabeth Deskins.

Children and Libraries Advisory Committee. Judi Moreillon.

Children and Technology. Amy Graves.

Distinguished Service Award 2015. Julie Cummins.

Distinguished Service Award 2016. Julie A. Corsaro.

Early Childhood Programs and Services. Matthew McLain.

Education. Nina Lindsay.

Every Child Ready to Read Oversight. Dorothy M. Stoltz.

Theodor Seuss Geisel Award 2015. Kevin Delecki.

Theodor Seuss Geisel Award 2016. Robin Lynn Smith.

Grant Administration Committee. Susan A. M. Poulter.

Great Websites. Lara Crews, Lisa Taylor.

Intellectual Freedom. Heather Acerro.

Interdivisional Committee on School/Public Library Partnerships. Jenna Nemec-Loise.

Liaison with National Organizations. Lori Coffey Hancock, Beth Munk.

Library Service to Special Population Children and Their Caregivers. Africa S. Hands.

Local Arrangements (San Francisco). Christy Estrovitz.

Managing Children's Services. Thomas J. Barthelmess.

Membership. Amanda Jean Roberson.

John Newbery Award 2015. Randall Enos.

John Newbery Award 2016. Ernie Cox.

Nominating 2015. Mary Fellows.

Nominating 2016. Jan S. Watkins.

Notable Children's Books. Maralita L. Freeny.

Notable Children's Recordings. Barbara Scotto.

Odyssey Award 2015. Dawn M. Rutherford.

Odyssey Award 2016. Cindy Lombardo.

Oral History. Deborah Sharon Cooper.

Organization and Bylaws. Samuel Eddington, Vicky Smith.

Program Coordinating. Patricia Ann Carleton.

Public Awareness. Amy E. Koester.

Quicklists Consulting. Krista K. Britton, Mary R. Voors.

Charlemae Rollins President's Program. Christine D. Caputo, Carol K. Phillips.

Scholarships. Miriam Budin.

School Age Programs and Service. Amber Lea Creger.

Robert F. Sibert Award 2015. Deborah Taylor.

Robert F. Sibert Award 2016. Elizabeth Overmeyer.

Special Collections and Bechtel Fellowship. Mary Beth Dunhouse.

Laura Ingalls Wilder Award 2015. Karen Nelson Hoyle.

Laura Ingalls Wilder Award 2016. Chrystal Carr-Jeter.

American Library Association
Association of College and Research Libraries

Executive Director, Mary Ellen K. Davis
50 E. Huron St., Chicago, IL 60611-2795
312-280-2523, 800-545-2433 ext. 2523, fax 312-280-2520, e-mail acrl@ala.org
World Wide Web http://www.ala.org/acrl

Object

The Association of College and Research Libraries (ACRL) leads academic and research librarians and libraries in advancing learning and transforming scholarship. Founded 1940.

Membership

Memb. 11,172. For information on dues, see ALA entry.

Officers

Pres. Karen A. Williams, Univ. of Arizona, Tucson, AZ 85718-9531. Tel. 520-621-6432, fax 520-621-9733, e-mail karenwilliams@email.arizona.edu; *Pres.-Elect* Ann Campion Riley, Univ. of Missouri, Columbia, MO 65201. Tel. 573-882-1685, fax 573 882-8044, email rileyac@missouri.edu; *Past Pres.* Trevor A. Dawes, Washington Univ. in St. Louis, St. Louis, MO 63130-4862. Tel. 314-935-5410, fax 314-935-4045, e-mail tadawes@wustl.edu;

Budget and Finance Chair Cynthia K. Steinhoff, Anne Arundel Community College, 101 College Pkwy., Arnold, MD 21012-1895. Tel. 410-777-2483, fax 410-777-4483, e-mail ck steinhoff@aacc.edu; *ACRL Councilor* Douglas K. Lehman, Wittenberg Univ., P.O. Box 7207, Springfield, OH 45501-7207. Tel. 937-327-7016, fax 937-327-6139, e-mail dlehman@wittenberg.edu.

Board of Directors

Officers; John P. Culshaw, Julie Ann Garrison, Julia M. Gelfand, Irene M. H. Herold, Marilyn Nabua Ochoa, Loretta R. Parham, Kim Leeder Reed, Susan Barnes Whyte.

Publications

Choice (12 a year; $429; Canada and Mexico $465; other international $549). *Ed.* Mark Cummings.

Choice Reviews-on-Cards (available only to subscribers of *Choice* and/or *Choice Reviews Online*) $529; Canada and Mexico $565; other international $659).

Choice Reviews Online 2.0 (academic libraries FTE 10,000+, $625; academic libraries FTE 2,500–9,999, $589; academic libraries FTE fewer than 2,500, $555; school libraries K–12, $375; foreign academic libraries [includes Mexico and Canada] $619; public libraries, $530; government libraries, $600; other libraries, $600; publishers/dealers, $600).

College & Research Libraries (C&RL) (6 a year; open access online-only). *Ed.* Scott Walter.

College & Research Libraries News (C&RL News) (11 a year; memb.; nonmemb. $54; Canada and other PUAS countries $59; other international $64). *Ed.* David Free.

Publications in Librarianship (formerly ACRL Monograph Series) (occasional). *Ed.* To be announced.

RBM: A Journal of Rare Books, Manuscripts, and Cultural Heritage (s. ann.; $48; Canada and other PUAS countries $54; other international $64). *Ed.* Jennifer K. Sheehan.

Committee and Task Force Chairs

AASL/ACRL Information Literacy (interdivisional). Jennifer Leigh Fabbi, Mary O. Keeling.

Academic/Research Librarian of the Year Award. Tyrone Heath Cannon.

ACRL Academic Library Trends and Statistics Survey. Robert E. Dugan.

ACRL 2015 Colleagues Committee. Julia M. Gelfand, Karin A. Trainer.

ACRL 2015 Contributed Papers. Beth McNeil, Janice D. Welburn.

ACRL 2015 Coordinating Committee (Portland). Lori Goetsch.

ACRL 2015 Innovations. Heidi Steiner Burkhardt, Beth Filar-Williams.

ACRL 2015 Invited Papers. Adele L. Barsh, Lisa Janicke Hinchliffe.

ACRL 2015 Keynote Speakers. Elizabeth A. Dupuis, Maggie Farrell.

ACRL 2015 Local Arrangements. Rachel Bridgewater, Dena Holiman Hutto.

ACRL 2015 Panel Sessions. Elizabeth Blakesley, Scott Walter.

ACRL 2015 Poster Sessions. Kim Leeder Reed, Tanner Wray III.

ACRL 2015 Preconference. Penny M. Beile, Jennifer Leigh Fabbi.

ACRL 2015 Roundtable Discussions. John P. Culshaw, Rita Cecilia Knight.

ACRL 2015 Scholarships. Latrice Booker, Adriana Gonzalez.

ACRL 2015 TechConnect Presentations. Heidi Gauder, John Leonard.

ACRL 2015 Virtual Conference. Ameet Doshi, Melanie Hawks.

ACRL 2015 Workshop Programs. Elizabeth L. Bagley, Madeleine Charney.

ACRL/LLAMA Interdivisional Committee on Building Resources. Frank R. Allen, Felice E. Maciejewski.

Appointments. John M. Budd.

Hugh C. Atkinson Memorial Award. Nancy Jean Gibbs.

Budget and Finance. Cynthia K. Steinhoff.

Choice Editorial Board. Peggy Seiden.

College & Research Libraries Editorial Board. Scott Walter.

College & Research Libraries News Editorial Board. Cassandra Kvenild.

Diversity. Martha Alvarado Parker.

Excellence in Academic Libraries Award. Steven J. Bell.

Government Relations. Jonathan Miller.

Immersion Program. Elin Anne O'Hara-Gonya.

Information Literacy Standards. Jeanne R. Davidson.

Dr. E. J. Josey Spectrum Scholar Mentor Program. Harriett E. Green.

Leadership Recruitment and Nomination. Gillian S. Gremmels.

Liaison Assembly. Elizabeth G. McClenney.

Liaison Coordinating. Lori J. Phillips.

Liaison Grants. Andrea M. Falcone.

Liaisons Training and Development. Elizabeth G. McClenney.

Membership. Kathy M. Irwin.

New Publications Advisory. Barbara Irene Dewey.

President's Program Planning Committee, 2015. Deborah B. Dancik.

Professional Development. Paul A. Sharpe.

Publications Coordinating. Priscilla J. Finley.

Publications in Librarianship Editorial Board. To be announced.

RBM Editorial Board. Jennifer Karr Sheehan.

Research Planning and Review. Jeanne R. Davidson.

Resources for College Libraries Editorial Board. E. Chisato Uyeki.

Section Membership. Katie E. Gibson, Dalena Estelle Hunter.

Standards. Susanna D. Boylston.

Student Learning and Information Literacy. Carrie Donovan.

Value of Academic Libraries. Lynn Silipigni Connaway.

Discussion Group Chairs

Assessment. Charla M. Gilbert, Nancy B. Turner.

Balancing Baby and Book. Laura Bonella.

Continuing Education/Professional Development. Rich Paustenbaugh.

Copyright. Tomas A. Lipinski.

First Year Experience. Danielle L. Rowland.

Heads of Public Services. Patricia Flanagan.

Information Commons. Carolyn L. Cunningham, Michael Whitchurch.

International Perspectives on Academic and Research Libraries. Evviva Weinraub Lajoie.

Leadership. Rudy Leon.

Library and Information Science Collections. Cynthia H. Krolikowski, Daniel G. Tracy.

Library Support for Massive Open Online Courses (MOOCs). Kyle Kenneth Courtney, Michele Ostrow.

Media Resources. Monique L. Threatt.

MLA International Bibliography. Sarah G. Wenzel.

New Members. Tyler Dzuba, Elizabeth Psyck.

Personnel Administrators and Staff Development Officers. Leo G. Agnew, Tiffany Allen.

Philosophical, Religious, and Theological Studies. Wayne Bivens-Tatum.

Popular Cultures. Jenny E. Robb.

Scholarly Communications. Devin Savage.

Student Retention. Jaime Corris Hammond, Nicole Pagowsky.

Undergraduate Libraries. Doug Worsham.

Interest Group Conveners

Academic Library Services to International Students. Arianne Hartsell-Gundy, Qing Meade.

Digital Badges. Cinthya Ippoliti, Emily L. Rimland.

Digital Curation. Megan Toups.

Digital Humanities. Zach Coble.

Health Sciences. Julie Planchon Wolf.

Image Resources. Kasia Leousis.

Librarianship in For-Profit Educational Institutions. Julie Evener.

Library and Information Science (LIS) Education. Michael A. Crumpton.

Library Marketing and Outreach Interest Group. Virginia A. Alexander, Adam Haigh.

Numeric and Geospatial Data Services in Academic Libraries. Jeremy Darrington.

Residency. Tarida Anantachai.

Technical Services. Gwen Gregory.

Universal Accessibility. John Siegel.

Virtual Worlds. JJ Jacobson.

Section Chairs

African American Studies Librarians. Malaika Grant.
Anthropology and Sociology. Erin F. Gratz.
Arts. Ngoc-Yen Tran.
Asian, African, and Middle Eastern. Jingfeng Xia.
College Libraries. Erin T. Smith.
Community and Junior College Libraries. Theresa C. Stanley.

Distance Learning. Alice Daugherty.
Education and Behavioral Sciences. Dana Scott Peterman.
Instruction. Mark Szarko.
Law and Political Science. Jeremy Darrington.
Literatures in English. Laura Lynne Taddeo.
Rare Books and Manuscripts. R. Arvid Nelsen.
Science and Technology. Marianne Stowell Bracke.
Slavic and East European. Kirill Tolpygo.
University Libraries. Marilyn Myers.
Western European Studies. Sarah Sussman.
Women and Gender Studies. Diane M. Fulkerson.

American Library Association
Association of Specialized and Cooperative Library Agencies

Executive Director, Susan Hornung
50 E. Huron St., Chicago, IL 60611-2795
312-280-4395, 800-545-2433 ext. 4395, fax 312-280-5273, e-mail shornung@ala.org
World Wide Web http://www.ala.org/ascla

Object

The Association for Specialized and Cooperative Library Agencies (ASCLA) enhances the effectiveness of library service by advocating for and providing high-quality networking, enrichment, and educational opportunities for its diverse members, who represent state library agencies, libraries serving special populations, library cooperatives, and library consultants. ASCLA's members are

• Librarians, library agencies, and staff serving populations with special needs, such as those with sensory, physical, health, or behavioral conditions or those who are incarcerated or detained
• Librarians and staff of state library agencies, and state library consultants—organizations created or authorized by state governments to promote library services
• Library networks and cooperatives, organizations of one or more types of libraries—academic, public, special, or school—that collaborate to maximize the funds available for provision of library services to all citizens; they may serve a

community, a metropolitan area, a region, or a statewide or multistate area
• Consultants, independent or contract librarians, as well as those who work outside traditional library settings

Member activity is centered around interest groups.

Membership

Memb. 800+. For information on dues, see ALA entry.

Officers and Directors (2014–2015)

Pres. Kathleen Moeller-Peiffer; *Pres.-Elect* Rhonda K. Puntney Gould; *Past Pres.* Sara G. Laughlin; *Div. Councilor* Lizbeth Bishoff; *Secy.* Tracy Byerly; *Dirs.-at-Large* Jana R. Fine, Raye L. Oldham; *Dir., Cooperatives and Networks* Gregory Pronevitz; *Dirs., Special Populations* Christopher John Corrigan, Lily J. Sacharow; *Dir., Lib. Consultants/Independent*

Libns. Allan Martin Kleiman; *Dir., State Lib. Agencies* Shannon O'Grady.

Interest Group Leaders

Alzheimer's and Related Dementias. Mary Beth Riedner.

Bridging Deaf Cultures @ your library. Alec McFarlane.

Collaborative Digitization. Sandra McIntyre.

Consortial eBooks. Dee Brennan, Veronda Pitchford.

Consortium Management Discussion. Sheryl Knab.

Future of Libraries. Peggy Cadigan.

Interlibrary Cooperation. To be announced.

Library Consultants. Carson Block.

Library Services for Youth in Custody. Camden Eadoin Tadhg.

Library Services to People with Visual or Physical Disabilities that Prevent Them from Reading Standard Print. Carli Spina.

Library Services to the Incarcerated and Detained. Elizabeth Marshak.

LSTA Coordinators. Katie McDonough.

Physical Delivery. James E. Pletz.

State Library Agencies—Library Development. Carol Desch.

Tribal Librarians. Lillian Chavez.

Universal Access. Marti Goddard.

Youth Services Consultants. Sharon Rawlins.

For more information on ASCLA interest groups, see http://www.ala.org/ascla/ascla ourassoc/asclainterest/list.

Publication

Interface (q.; online). *Ed.* Anne Abate. E-mail anne@librarydiscountnetwork.com.

Committees

Accessibility Assembly; Awards; Board of Directors; Conference Programming; Executive; Finance and Planning; Guidelines for Library and Information Services for the American Deaf Community; Interest Group Coordinating; Membership; Nominating; Online Learning; President's Program Planning; Publications; Web Presence.

For more information on ASCLA committees, see http://www.ala.org/ascla/asclaour assoc/asclarosters/rosters.

American Library Association
Library and Information Technology Association

Executive Director, Mary C. Taylor
50 E. Huron St., Chicago, IL 60611
312-280-4267, 800-545-2433, e-mail mtaylor@ala.org
World Wide Web http://www.lita.org

Object

As a center of expertise about information technology, the Library and Information Technology Association (LITA) leads in exploring and enabling new technologies to empower libraries. LITA members use the promise of technology to deliver dynamic library collections and services.

LITA educates, serves, and reaches out to its members, other ALA members and divisions, and the entire library and information community through its publications, programs, and other activities designed to promote, develop, and aid in the implementation of library and information technology.

Membership

Memb. 2,900. For information on dues, see ALA entry.

Officers (2014–2015)

Pres. Rachel Vacek; *V.P.* Thomas P. Dowling; *Past Pres.* Cindi Trainor.

Directors

Aimee Fifarek, Cody Hanson, S. G. Ranti Junus, Bohyun Kim, Jennifer Reiswig, Jennifer Emanuel Taylor, Andromeda Yelton, *Div. Councilor* Aaron Dobbs.

Publication

Information Technology and Libraries (*ITAL*) (open source at http://ejournals.bc.edu/ojs/index.php/ital/issue/current). *Ed.* Robert Gerrity. For information or to send manuscripts, contact the editor.

American Library Association
Library Leadership and Management Association

Executive Director, Kerry Ward
50 E. Huron St., Chicago, IL 60611
312-280-5032, 800-545-2433 ext. 5032, fax 312-280-5033
e-mail kward@ala.org
World Wide Web http://www.ala.org/llama

Object

The Library Leadership and Management Association (LLAMA) Strategic Plan sets out the following:

Mission: The Library Leadership and Management Association advances outstanding leadership and management practices in library and information services by encouraging and nurturing individual excellence in current and aspiring library leaders.

Vision: As the foremost organization developing present and future leaders in library and information services, LLAMA provides a welcoming community where aspiring and experienced library leaders and library supporters from all types of libraries can seek and share knowledge and skills in leadership, administration, and management in a manner that creates meaningful transformation in libraries around the world.

Core Values: LLAMA believes advancing leadership and management excellence is achieved by fostering the following values—exemplary and innovative service to and for our members, and leadership development and continuous learning opportunities for our members.

Established in 1957.

Membership

Memb. 3,900+. For information on dues, see ALA entry.

Officers (2014–2015)

Pres. Diane Bruxvoort. E-mail dbruxvoort@abdn.ac.uk; *Pres.-Elect* Jeff Steely; *Treas.* James Rettig; *Past Pres.* Catherine Friedman.

Address correspondence to the executive director.

Publication

Library Leadership and Management (*LL&M*) (open access at http://journals.tdl.org/llm/index.php/llm). *Ed.* Bradford Lee Eden. E-mail brad.eden@valpo.edu.

Section Chairs

Buildings and Equipment. Melissa B. Bennett.
Fund Raising and Financial Development. James Michael Thompson.
Human Resources Marcy L. Simons.

Library Organization and Management. Leo S. Lo.
Measurement, Assessment, and Evaluation. Lisa R. Horowitz.

New Professionals. Tyler Dzuba.
Public Relations and Marketing. Kimberly Terry.
Systems and Services. Paul A. Sharpe.

American Library Association
Public Library Association

Executive Director, Barbara A. Macikas
50 E. Huron St., Chicago, IL 60611
312-280-5752, 800-545-2433 ext. 5752, fax 312-280-5029, e-mail pla@ala.org
World Wide Web http://www.pla.org

The Public Library Association (PLA) has specific responsibility for

1. Conducting and sponsoring research about how the public library can respond to changing social needs and technical developments
2. Developing and disseminating materials useful to public libraries in interpreting public library services and needs
3. Conducting continuing education for public librarians by programming at national and regional conferences, by publications such as the newsletter, and by other delivery means
4. Establishing, evaluating, and promoting goals, guidelines, and standards for public libraries
5. Maintaining liaison with relevant national agencies and organizations engaged in public administration and human services, such as the National Association of Counties, the Municipal League, and the Commission on Postsecondary Education
6. Maintaining liaison with other divisions and units of ALA and other library organizations, such as the Association for Library and Information Science Education and the Urban Libraries Council
7. Defining the role of the public library in service to a wide range of user and potential user groups
8. Promoting and interpreting the public library to a changing society through legislative programs and other appropriate means

9. Identifying legislation to improve and to equalize support of public libraries

PLA enhances the development and effectiveness of public librarians and public library services. This mission positions PLA to

- Focus its efforts on serving the needs of its members
- Address issues that affect public libraries
- Commit to quality public library services that benefit the general public

The goals of PLA are

- Advocacy and Awareness: PLA is an essential partner in public library advocacy.
- Leadership and Transformation: PLA is the leading source for learning opportunities to advance transformation of public libraries.
- Literate Nation: PLA will be a leader and valued partner of public libraries' initiatives to create a literate nation.
- Organizational Excellence: PLA is positioned to sustain and grow its resources to advance the work of the association.

Membership

Memb. 8,000+. Open to all ALA members interested in the improvement and expansion of public library services to all ages in various types of communities.

Officers (2014–2015)

Pres. Larry Neal, Clinton-Macomb (Michigan) Public Lib. E-mail lneal@cmpl.org; *Pres.-Elect* Vailey Oehlke, Multonomah County (Oregon) Lib. E-mail vaileyo@multcolib.org; *Past Pres.* Carolyn Anthony, Skokie (Illinois) Public Lib. E-mail canthony@skokielibrary.info.

Publication

Public Libraries (bi-mo.; memb.; nonmemb. $65; foreign $75; single copy $10). *Ed.* Kathleen Hughes, PLA, 50 E. Huron St., Chicago, IL 60611. E-mail khughes@ala.org.

Committee Chairs

Baker & Taylor Entertainment Audio Music/Video Product Award. Nick Taylor.

Budget and Finance. Clara Nalli Bohrer.

Gordon M. Conable Award Jury. Susan Wray.

Continuing Education Advisory Group. James D. Cooper.

DEMCO New Leaders Travel Grant Jury. Marla J. Ehlers.

EBSCO Excellence in Small and/or Rural Public Library Service Award. Luren E. Dickinson.

Intellectual Freedom. Robert Hubsher.

Leadership Development. Karen Danczak-Lyons.

Legislation and Advocacy. Jan W. Sanders.

Allie Beth Martin Award Jury. Kristen Rae Allen-Vogel.

Membership Advisory Group. Richard Kong.

Nominating 2015. Eva D. Poole.

Performance Measurement Task Force. Denise Marie Davis.

Charlie Robinson Award Jury. Skip Auld.

PLA 2016 Local Arrangements. Diane Lapierre.

PLA 2016 National Conference. Marcellus Turner.

PLA 2016 National Conference Program Subcommittee. Pamela Sandlian Smith.

PLA/ALSC Every Child Ready to Read Oversight Committee. Dorothy M. Stoltz.

PLA Annual Conference Program Subcommittee. Trisha A. Burns.

PLDS Statistical Report Advisory. Kristin Whitehair.

Polaris Innovation in Technology John Iliff Award. Tricia Bengel.

Public Libraries Advisory. Monique Le Conge Ziesenhenne.

Romance Writers of America Library Grant Jury. Kara A. Kohn.

Technology. Brian Auger.

Upstart Library Innovation Award Jury. Monica Harris.

American Library Association
Reference and User Services Association

Executive Director, Susan Hornung
50 E. Huron St., Chicago, IL 60611
800-545-2433 ext. 4395, 312-280-4395, fax 312-280-5273, e-mail shornung@ala.org
World Wide Web http://www.ala.org/rusa

Object

The Reference and User Services Association (RUSA) is responsible for stimulating and supporting excellence in the delivery of general library services and materials, and the provision of reference and information services, collection development, readers' advisory, and resource sharing for all ages, in every type of library.

The specific responsibilities of RUSA are:

1. Conduct of activities and projects within the association's areas of responsibility

2. Encouragement of the development of librarians engaged in these activities, and stimulation of participation by members of appropriate type-of-library divisions

3. Synthesis of the activities of all units within the American Library Association that have a bearing on the type of activities represented by the association

4. Representation and interpretation of the association's activities in contacts outside the profession

5. Planning and development of programs of study and research in these areas for the total profession

6. Continuous study and review of the association's activities

Membership

Memb. 3,800+

Officers (2014–2015)

Pres. Joseph Thompson; *Pres.-Elect* Liane Taylor; *Secy.* Erin Rushton; *Past Pres.* M. Kathleen Kern; *Div. Councilor* Jennifer C. Boettcher.

Publications

Reference & User Services Quarterly (online only at http://rusa.metapress.com) (memb.). *Ed.* Barry Trott, Williamsburg Regional Lib., 7770 Croaker Rd., Williamsburg, VA 23188-7064. E-mail btrott@wrl.org.

RUSA Update, (q., online newsletter, at http://www.rusa.ala.org/rusaupdate).

Sections

Business Reference and Services (BRASS); Collection Development and Evaluation (CODES); History (HS); MARS: Emerging Technologies in Reference (MARS); Reference Services (RSS); Sharing and Transforming Access to Resources (STARS).

Committees

Access to Information; AFL-CIO/ALA Library Service to Labor Groups; Andrew Carnegie Medals for Excellence in Fiction and Nonfiction; Awards Coordinating; Board of Directors; Budget and Finance; Conference Program Coordinating; Executive; Free School (subcommittee); Gale Cengage Award for Excellence in Reference and Adult Services; Isadore Gilbert Mudge Award; Just Ask Council (ad hoc); Learning Opportunities Task Force (ad hoc); John Sessions Memorial Award; Margaret E. Monroe Library Adult Services Award; Membership; Nominating; Organization and Planning; President's Program Planning; Professional Development; Publications and Communications; *Reference & User Services Quarterly* Editorial Advisory; Reference Service Press Awards; Resource Development Committee (ad hoc); Review Professional Competencies for Reference and User Services Librarians; Review Task Force (ad hoc);

Standards and Guidelines; Strategic Plan Co-ordinating Task Force (ad hoc); Task Force on Legislative Issues (ad-hoc); Trends Task Force.

For section committees, and committee chairpersons, see http://www.ala.org/rusa/contact/rosters#rss.

American Library Association
United for Libraries: Association of Library Trustees, Advocates, Friends, and Foundations

Executive Director, Sally Gardner Reed
109 S. 13 St., Suite 117B, Philadelphia, PA 19107
312-280-2161, fax 215-545-3821, e-mail sreed@ala.org
World Wide Web http://www.ala.org/united

Object

United for Libraries was founded in 1890 as the American Library Trustee Association (ALTA). It was the only division of the American Library Association (ALA) dedicated to promoting and ensuring outstanding library service through educational programs that develop excellence in trusteeship and promote citizen involvement in the support of libraries. ALTA became an ALA division in 1961. In 2008 the members of ALTA voted to expand the division to more aggressively address the needs of friends of libraries and library foundations, and through a merger with Friends of Libraries USA (FOLUSA) became the Association of Library Trustees, Advocates, Friends and Foundations (ALTAFF). In 2012 members voted to add "United for Libraries" to its title.

Memb. 5,200. Open to all interested persons and organizations. For dues and membership year, see ALA entry.

Officers (2013–2014)

Pres. Rod Wagner; *Pres-Elect* Christine Lind Hage; *Councilor* Susan Schmidt; *Past Pres.* Gail Guidry Griffin.

Publications

Citizens-Save-Libraries: A Power Guide for Successful Advocacy.
The Complete Trustee Handbook.
Even More Great Ideas for Libraries and Friends.
101+ Great Ideas for Libraries and Friends.
The Voice for America's Libraries (q.; memb.).

Committee Chairs

Annual Conference Program. Robin Hoklotubbe.
Library Issues. Jeff Smith.
Newsletter and Website Advisory. Cindy Friedemann.
Nominating. Susan Schmidt.
PLA Conference Program. Deloris Lynch.
United for Libraries Leaders Orientation. Peggy Danhof.

American Library Association
Young Adult Library Services Association

Executive Director, Beth Yoke
50 E. Huron St., Chicago, IL 60611
312-280-4390, 800-545-2433 ext. 4390, fax 312-280-5276, e-mail yalsa@ala.org
World Wide Web http://www.ala.org/yalsa
YALSA blog http://yalsa.ala.org/blog, The Hub (http://yalsa.ala.org/thehub),
Wiki (http://wikis.ala.org/yalsa), Twitter (http://twitter.com/yalsa)
Facebook (http://www.facebook.com/YALSA)

Object

In every library in the nation, high-quality library service to young adults is provided by a staff that understands and respects the unique informational, educational, and recreational needs of teenagers. Equal access to information, services, and materials is recognized as a right, not a privilege. Young adults are actively involved in the library decision making process. The library staff collaborates and cooperates with other youth-serving agencies to provide a holistic, community-wide network of activities and services that support healthy youth development. To ensure that this vision becomes a reality, the Young Adult Library Services Association (YALSA)

1. Advocates extensive and developmentally appropriate library and information services for young adults ages 12 to 18
2. Promotes reading and supports the literacy movement
3. Advocates the use of information and digital technologies to provide effective library service
4. Supports equality of access to the full range of library materials and services, including existing and emerging information and digital technologies, for young adults
5. Provides education and professional development to enable its members to serve as effective advocates for young people
6. Fosters collaboration and partnerships among its individual members with the library community and other groups involved in providing library and information services to young adults
7. Influences public policy by demonstrating the importance of providing library and information services that meet the unique needs and interests of young adults
8. Encourages research and is in the vanguard of new thinking concerning the provision of library and information services for youth

Membership

Memb. 5,100. Open to anyone interested in library services for and with young adults. For information on dues, see ALA entry.

Officers

Pres. Christopher Shoemaker. E-mail cinf-0master@gmail.com; *Pres.-Elect* Candice Mack. E-mail cmack@lapl.org; *Div. Councilor* Vicki Emery. E-mail vemery@fcps.edu; *Fiscal Officer* Linda W. Braun. E-mail lbraun2000@gmail.com; *Secy.* Carrie Kausch. E-mail ckaush@gmail.com; *Past Pres.* Shannon Peterson. E-mail shannon.peterson@gmail.com.

Directors

Maureen Hartman, Joy Kim, Gretchen Kolderup, Jennifer Korn, Carla Land, Nicola McDonald, Rachel McDonald, Krista McKenzie, Jack Martin, Sarah Sogigian, Sarah Townsend.

Publications

Journal of Research on Libraries and Young Adults (q.) (online, open source, peer-reviewed). *Ed.* Denise Agosto.

Young Adult Library Services (q.) (memb.; nonmemb. $70; foreign $80). *Ed.* Linda W. Braun.

YALSA E-News (weekly, memb.). *Ed.* Anna Lam.

American Merchant Marine Library Association (AMMLA)

Executive Director, Roger T. Korner
104 Broadway, Jersey City, NJ 07306
201-369-1100, fax 201-369-1105, e-mail ussammla@ix.netcom.com
World Wide Web http://unitedseamensservice.org

Object

Known as "the public library of the high seas," AMMLA provides ship and shore library service for American-flag merchant vessels and for the Military Sealift Command, the U.S. Coast Guard, and other waterborne operations of the U.S. government. Established in 1921.

In 2012 it distributed more than 23,000 books and magazines to American Merchant Marine, the U.S. Navy and Coast Guard, and seafarers of allied nations. A total of 240 libraries were mailed to U.S. merchant vessels transporting supplies to U.S. forces.

Executive Committee

Pres. Edward R. Morgan; *Chair* F. Anthony Naccarato; *Secy.* Donald E. Kadlac; *Treas.* William D. Potts; *Gen. Counsel* John L. DeGurse, Jr.; *V.P.s* Thomas J. Bethel, Capt. Timothy A. Brown, James Capo, David Cockroft, Capt. Remo Di Fiore, Yoji Fujisawa, John Halas, Richard P. Hughes, Michael B. Jewell, Rene Lioeanjie, George E. Murphy, Conrado F. Oca, Michael Sacco, Richard L. Trumka.

American Theological Library Association

Executive Director, Brenda Bailey-Hainer
300 S. Wacker Drive, Suite 2100, Chicago, IL 60606-6701
888-665-2852, 312-454-5100, fax 312-454-5505, e-mail atla@atla.com
World Wide Web http://www.atla.com

Mission

The mission of the American Theological Library Association (ATLA) is to foster the study of theology and religion by enhancing the development of theological and religious libraries and librarianship.

Membership

(Inst.) 249; (International Inst.) 19; (Indiv.) 401; (Student) 99; (Lifetime) 92; (Affiliates) 69.

Officers

Pres. Beth Bidlack, Burke Lib. at Union Theological Seminary, New York. E-mail beth.bidlack@columbia.edu; *V.P.* Kelly Campbell, John Bulow Campbell Lib., Columbia Theological Seminary, Decatur, Ga.; *Secy.* Stephen Z. Perisho, Seattle Pacific Univ. Lib., Seattle; *Past Pres.* Andrew Keck, Luther Seminary, 2481 Como Ave., St. Paul, MN 55108.

Directors

H. D. "Sandy" Ayer, Jennifer Bartholomew, Carrie M. Hackney, Andrew Keck, Amy E. Limpitlaw, Timothy D. Lincoln, Melody Layton McMahon, Matthew Ostercamp, Eileen K. Saner.

Publications

ATLA Indexes in MARC Format (q.).

ATLA Religion Database, 1949– (q., on EB-SCO, Ovid).

ATLASerials, 1949– (q., full-text, on EBSCO, Ovid).

ATLA Catholic Periodical and Literature Index (q., on EBSCO).

Old Testament Abstracts (ann., on EBSCO).

New Testament Abstracts (ann., on EBSCO).

Proceedings (ann.; memb.; nonmemb. $60). *Ed.* Tawny Burgess.

Research in Ministry: An Index to Doctor of Ministry Project Reports (ann.) online. *Ed.* Justin Travis.

Archivists and Librarians in the History of the Health Sciences

President, Stephen E. Novak
E-mail sen13@columbia.edu
World Wide Web http://www.alhhs.org

Object

The association was established exclusively for educational purposes, to serve the professional interests of librarians, archivists, and other specialists actively engaged in the librarianship of the history of the health sciences by promoting the exchange of information and by improving the standards of service.

Membership

Memb. Approximately 150.

Officers

Pres. Stephen E. Novak. E-mail sen13@columbia.edu; *Secy.* Phoebe Evans Letocha. E-mail pletocha@jhmi.edu; *Treas.* Barbara J. Niss. E-mail barbara.niss@mssm.edu; *Past Pres.* Christopher Lyons. E-mail christopher.lyons@mcgill.ca; *Membs.-at-Large* Elisabeth Brander, Deborah Coltham, Bob Vietrogoski, Renee Ziemer.

Publication

Watermark (q.; memb.). *Ed.* Martha Stone, Massachusetts General Hospital. E-mail mstone@partners.org

ARMA International

President, Fred Pulzello
ARMA International, 11880 College Blvd., Suite 450, Overland Park, KS 66210
800-422-2762, 913-341-3808, fax 913-341-3742
World Wide Web http://www.arma.org

Object

To advance the practice of records and information management as a discipline and a profession; to organize and promote programs of research, education, training, and networking within that profession; to support the enhancement of professionalism of the membership; and to promote cooperative endeavors with related professional groups.

Membership

Approximately 26,000 in more than 30 countries. Annual dues $175; Chapter dues vary.

Officers

Pres. Fred Pulzello; *Past-Pres.* Julie J. Colgan; *Pres.-Elect* Peter Kurilecz; *Treas.* Brenda Prowse.

Directors

Patricia Burns, Robert E. Calabrese, Tod Chernikoff, Melissa G. Dederer, Tera Ladner, Peggy Neal, Alison North, Denise Pickett, Marc Simpson, Richard Vestuto.

Publication

Information Management (IM) (bi-mo.).

Art Libraries Society of North America

President, Carole Ann Fabian
Executive Director, Robert J. Kopchinski
414-908-4954 ext. 136, e-mail r.kopchinski@arlisna.org
World Wide Web https://www.arlisna.org

Object

The object of the Art Libraries Society of North America (ARLIS/NA) is to foster excellence in art librarianship and visual resources curatorship for the advancement of the visual arts. Established 1972.

Membership

Memb. 1,000+. Dues (Inst./Business Affiliate) $145; (Introductory) $90 (one-year limit); (Indiv.) $120; (Student) $50 (three-year limit); (Retired/Unemployed) $60. Year. Jan. 1–Dec. 31. Membership is open to all those interested in visual librarianship, whether they be professional librarians, students, library assistants, art book publishers, art book dealers, art historians, archivists, architects, slide and photograph curators, or retired associates in these fields.

Officers

Pres. Carole Ann Fabian, Avery Architectural and Fine Arts Lib., Columbia Univ., 1172 Amsterdam Ave., MC0301, New York, NY 10027. Tel. 212-854-3068, e-mail caf2141@columbia. edu; *V.P./Pres.-Elect* Kristen Regina, Hillwood Estate, Museum and Gardens, Washington, D.C. Tel. 202-243-3934, e-mail kregina@

hillwoodmuseum.org; *Secy.* Eric Wolf, the Menil Collection, 1511 Branard St., Houston, TX 77006. Tel. 713-525-9426, e-mail ewolf@menil.org; *Treas.* Mark Pompelia, Rhode Island School of Design, Providence. Tel. 401-709-5935, e-mail mpompeli@risd.edu; *Past Pres.* Gregory P. J. Most, National Gallery of Art, Washington, DC 20565. Tel. 202-842-6100, e-mail g-most@nga.gov.

Address correspondence to Robert J. Kopchinski, Technical Enterprises, Inc., 7044 S. 13 St., Oak Creek, WI 53154.

Publications

ARLIS/NA Update (bi-mo.; memb.).
Art Documentation (2 a year; memb., subscription).
Handbook and List of Members (ann.; memb.).
Occasional papers (price varies).
Miscellaneous others (request current list from headquarters).

Asian/Pacific American Librarians Association

Executive Director, Buenaventura "Ven" Basco
P.O. Box 677593, Orlando, FL 32867-7593
E-mail buenaventura.basco@ucf.edu
World Wide Web http://www.apalaweb.org

Object

To provide a forum for discussing problems and concerns of Asian/Pacific American librarians; to provide a forum for the exchange of ideas by Asian/Pacific American librarians and other librarians; to support and encourage library services to Asian/Pacific American communities; to recruit and support Asian/Pacific American librarians in the library/information science professions; to seek funding for scholarships in library/information science programs for Asian/Pacific Americans; and to provide a vehicle whereby Asian/Pacific American librarians can cooperate with other associations and organizations having similar or allied interests. Founded in 1980; incorporated 1981; affiliated with American Library Association 1982.

Membership

Approximately 300. Open to all librarians and information specialists of Asian/Pacific descent working in U.S. libraries and information centers and other related organizations, and to others who support the goals and purposes of the association. Asian/Pacific Americans are defined as people residing in North America who self-identify as Asian/Pacific American.

Officers (July 2014–June 2015)

Pres. Eileen K. Bosch, Bowling Green State Univ. E-mail ebosch@bgsu.edu; *V.P./Pres.-Elect* Janet H. Clarke, Stony Brook Univ. Libs. E-mail janet.clarke@stonybrook.edu; *Secy.* Sarah Jeong, Wake Forest Univ. E-mail jeongsh@wfu.edu; *Treas.* Dora Ho, Los Angeles Public Lib. E-mail dorah2005@gmail.com; *Past Pres.* Eugenia Beh, Massachusetts Institute of Technology. E-mail eugenia_beh@yahoo.com; *Board Membs.-at-Large* Anna Coats, Melissa Cardenas-Dow, Paolo Gujilde, Annie Pho.

Publication

APALA Newsletter (q.).

Committee Chairs

Constitution and Bylaws. Paul Lai.
Family Literacy Focus. Lessa Pelayo-Lozada.
Finance and Fund Raising. Sandy Wee.
Literature Awards. Ven Basco, Dora Ho.
Membership. Maria Pontillas.
Newsletter and Publications. Melissa Cardenas-Dow, Gary A. Colmenar.
Nominating. Eugenia Beh.

Program Planning, 2015. Janet Clarke, Peter Spyers-Duran.
Publicity. Holly Okuhara, Ngoc-Yen Tran.

Scholarships and Awards. Tassanee Chitcharoen, Valeria Molteni.
Web. Alvin Dantes.

Association for Information Science and Technology

Executive Director, Richard B. Hill
8555 16th St., Suite 850, Silver Spring, MD 20910
301-495-0900, fax 301-495-0810, e-mail asis@asis.org
World Wide Web http://www.asist.org

Object

The Association for Information Science and Technology (ASIS&T, formerly the American Society for Information Science and Technology) provides a forum for the discussion, publication, and critical analysis of work dealing with the design, management, and use of information, information systems, and information technology.

Membership

Regular Memb. (Indiv.) 1,100; (Student) 500; (Early/Transitional Professional) 140; (Developing Nation) 30; (Inst.) 120. Dues (Indiv.) $140; Early/Transitional Professional $65; Developing Nation (varies by category); (Student) $40; (Inst.) $650 and $800.

Officers

Pres. Sandra G. Hirsh, San José State Univ.; *Pres.-Elect* Nadia Caidi, Univ. of Toronto; *Treas.* Vicki Gregory, Univ. of South Florida; *Past Pres.* Harry Bruce, University of Washington.

Address correspondence to the executive director.

Directors

June Abbas, Jamshid Beheshti, Lynn Silipigni Connaway, Sanda Erdelez, Lauren D. Harrison, Fidelia Ibekwe-SanJuan.

Publications

Periodicals

Journal of the Association for Information Science and Technology. Available with ASIS&T membership or from Wiley Blackwell.
Bulletin of the Association for Information Science and Technology (online only).
Proceedings of the ASIS&T Annual Meeting. Available from ASIS&T.

Books and Monographs

ASIST Thesaurus of Information Science, Technology, and Librarianship, 3rd ed.
Computerization Movements and Technology Diffusion: From Mainframes to Ubiquitous Computing.
Covert and Overt.
Digital Inclusion.
Editorial Peer Review: Its Strengths and Weaknesses.
Electronic Publishing: Applications and Implications.
Evaluating Networked Information Services: Techniques, Policy and Issues.
From Print to Electronic: The Transformation of Scientific Communication.
Historical Information Science.
Historical Studies in Information Science.
The History and Heritage of Scientific and Technological Information Systems.
Information and Emotion: The Emergent Affective Paradigm in Information Behavior Research and Theory.
Information Management for the Intelligent Organization, 3rd ed.
Information Need: A Theory Connecting Information Search to Knowledge Formation.

Information Representation and Retrieval in the Digital Age, 2nd ed.
Intelligent Technologies in Library and Information Service Applications.
International Perspectives on the History of Information Science and Technology.
Introduction to Information Science and Technology.
Introductory Concepts in Information Science, 2nd ed.
Knowledge Management: The Bibliography.
Knowledge Management for the Information Professional.
Knowledge Management in Practice: Connections and Context.
Knowledge Management Lessons Learned: What Works and What Doesn't.

The New Digital Scholar.
The Next Digital Scholar.
Powering Search: The Role of Thesauri in New Information Environments.
Scholarly Metrics Under the Microscope.
Statistical Methods for the Information Professional.
Theories of Information Behavior.
The Web of Knowledge: A Festschrift in Honor of Eugene Garfield.

The above books and monographs are available from Information Today, Inc., 143 Old Marlton Pike, Medford, NJ 08055. Many are available as e-books.

Association for Library and Information Science Education

Executive Director, Andrew Estep
ALISE Headquarters, 2150 N. 107 St., Suite 205, Seattle WA 98133
Tel. 206-209-5267, fax 206-367-8777, e-mail office@alise.org
World Wide Web http://www.alise.org

The Association for Library and Information Science Education (ALISE) is an independent nonprofit professional association whose mission is to promote excellence in research, teaching, and service for library and information science education through leadership, collaboration, advocacy, and dissemination of research. Its enduring purpose is to promote research that informs the scholarship of teaching and learning for library and information science, enabling members to integrate research into teaching and learning. The association provides a forum in which to share ideas, discuss issues, address challenges, and shape the future of education for library and information science. Founded in 1915 as the Association of American Library Schools, it has had its present name since 1983.

Membership

700+ in four categories: Personal, Institutional, International Affiliate Institutional, and Associate Institutional. Personal membership is open to anyone with an interest in the association's objectives.

Officers (2015–2016)

Pres. Samantha K. Hastings, Univ. of South Carolina. E-mail hastings@sc.edu; *V.P./Pres.-Elect* Louise Spiteri, Dalhousie Univ. E-mail louise.spiteri@dal.ca; *Secy.-Treas.* Denice Adkins, Univ. of Missouri. E-mail adkinsde@missouri.edu; *Dirs.* Laurie Bonnici, Univ. of Alabama; Carol L. Tilley, Univ. of Illinois at Urbana-Champaign; *Past Pres.* Clara Chu, Univ. of North Carolina–Greensboro. E-mail cmchu@uncg.edu.

Publication

Journal of Education for Library and Information Science (JELIS) (q.). *Ed.* Peta Wellstead, Open Polytechnic of New Zealand/ Kuratini Tuwhera. E-mail jeliseditor@alise. org.

Association for Rural and Small Libraries

201 E. Main St., Suite 1405, Lexington, KY 40507
Tel. 859-514-9178, e-mail szach@amrms.com
World Wide Web http://www.arsl.info

Object

The Association for Rural and Small Libraries (ARSL) was established in 1978, in the Department of Library Science at Clarion University of Pennsylvania, as the Center for Study of Rural Librarianship.

ARSL is a network of people throughout the United States dedicated to the positive growth and development of libraries. ARSL believes in the value of rural and small libraries, and strives to create resources and services that address national, state, and local priorities for libraries situated in rural communities.

Its objectives are

- To organize a network of members concerned about the growth and development of useful library services in rural and small libraries
- To provide opportunities for the continuing education of members
- To provide mechanisms for members to exchange ideas and to meet on a regular basis
- To cultivate the practice of librarianship and to foster a spirit of cooperation among members of the profession, enabling them to act together for mutual goals
- To serve as a source of current information about trends, issues, and strategies
- To partner with other library and nonlibrary groups and organizations serving rural and small library communities
- To collect and disseminate information and resources that are critical to this network
- To advocate for rural and small libraries at the local, state, and national levels

Officers

Pres. Donna Brice, Eastern Lancaster County Lib., 11 Chestnut, New Holland, PA 17557. Tel. 717-354-0525, e-mail dbrice@elanco library.org; *V.P./Pres.-Elect* Lisa Lewis, Tel. 520-226-6063, e-mail minefee2001@yahoo. com; *Past Pres.* Tena Hanson, Estherville Public Lib., 613 Central Ave., Estherville, IA 51334. Tel. 712-362-7731, e-mail thanson librarian@gmail.com.

Association of Academic Health Sciences Libraries

Executive Director, Louise S. Miller
2150 N. 107 St., Suite 205, Seattle, WA 98133
206-367-8704, fax 206-367-8777, e-mail aahsl@sbims.com
World Wide Web http://www.aahsl.org

Object

The Association of Academic Health Sciences Libraries (AAHSL) comprises the libraries serving the accredited U.S. and Canadian medical schools belonging to or affiliated with the Association of American Medical Colleges. Its goals are to promote excellence in academic health science libraries and to ensure that the next generation of health practitioners is trained in information-seeking skills that enhance the quality of health care delivery, education, and research. Founded in 1977.

Membership

Memb. 150+. Full membership is available to nonprofit educational institutions operating a school of health sciences that has full or provisional accreditation by the Association of American Medical Colleges. Full members are represented by the chief administrative officer of the member institution's health sciences library. Associate membership (and nonvoting representation) is available to organizations having an interest in the purposes and activities of the association. For dues information, contact the association.

Officers

Pres. (2014–2015) Paul Schoening, Bernard Becker Medical Lib., Washington Univ. School of Medicine. Tel. 314-362-3119, e-mail pas@wusm.wustl.edu; *Pres.-Elect (2014–2015)* Ruth Riley, School of Medicine Lib., Univ. of South Carolina. Tel. 803-216-3220, e-mail ruth.riley@uscmed.sc.edu; *Past Pres.* A. James Bothmer, Health Sciences Lib./Learning Resources Center, Creighton Univ. Tel. 402-280-5120, e-mail jbothmer@creighton.edu; *Secy./Treas. (2013–2016)* Kathryn Carpenter, Lib. of the Health Sciences, Univ. of Illinois at Chicago. Tel. 312-996-8966, e-mail khc@uic.edu.

Directors

Barbara Epstein (2012–2015), Health Sciences Lib. System, Univ. of Pittsburgh. Tel. 412-648-8866, e-mail bepstein@pitt.edu; Neville Prendergast (2013–2016), Rudolph Matas Lib. of the Health Sciences, Tulane Univ. Medical Center. Tel. 614-292-4852, e-mail nprender@tulane.edu; Pamela Bradigan (2014–2017), Health Sciences Lib., Ohio State Univ. Tel. 212-263-6990, e-mail pamela.bradigan@osumc.edu.

Association of Christian Librarians

Executive Director, Janelle Mazelin
P.O. Box 4, Cedarville, Ohio 45314
Tel. 937-766-2255, fax 937-766-5499, e-mail info@acl.org

Object

The mission of the Association of Christian Librarians (ACL) is to strengthen libraries through professional development of evangelical librarians, scholarship, and spiritual encouragement for service in higher education. ACL is a growing community that integrates faith, ministry, and academic librarianship through development of members, services, and scholarship.

Founded 1957.

Membership

500+ at about 150 institutions. Membership is open to those who profess the Christian faith as outlined by the association's statement of faith, and are employed at an institution of higher education. Associate memberships are available for non-librarians who both agree with ACL's statement of faith and are interested in libraries or librarianship.

Officers

Pres. (2012–2016) Frank Quinn, Point Loma Nazarene Univ.; *V.P. (2011–2015)* Rodney Birch, George Fox Univ.; *Secy. (2014–2017)* Denise Nelson, Point Loma Nazarene Univ., *Treas. (2008–-2016)* Sheila O. Carlblom; *Dirs.-at-Large* Jennifer Ewing, Nate Farley, Alison Jones, Linda Poston, Paul Roberts, Bob Triplett.

Association of Independent Information Professionals

8550 United Plaza Blvd., Suite 1001, Baton Rouge, LA 70809
225-408-4400, fax 225-408-4422, e-mail office@aiip.org
World Wide Web http://www.aiip.org

Object

Members of the Association of Independent Information Professionals (AIIP) are owners of firms providing such information-related services as online and manual research, document delivery, database design, library support, consulting, writing, and publishing.

The objectives of the association are

- To advance the knowledge and understanding of the information profession
- To promote and maintain high professional and ethical standards among its members
- To encourage independent information professionals to assemble to discuss common issues
- To promote the interchange of information among independent information professionals and various organizations
- To keep the public informed of the profession and of the responsibilities of the information professional

Membership

Memb. 50+.

Officers

Pres. Connie Clem, Clem Information Strategies. E-mail president@aiip.org; *Pres.-Elect* June Boyle, CeRCo Research and Consulting;

Secy. Joann M. Wleklinski, Wleklinski Information Services; *Treas.* Marilyn Harmacek, MHC Info Solutions; *Past Pres.* Jocelyn Sheppard, Red House Consulting.

Publications

AIIP Connections (q.).
Membership Directory (ann.).
Professional papers series.

Association of Jewish Libraries

P.O. Box 1118, Teaneck, NJ 07666
201-371-3255
World Wide Web http://www.jewishlibraries.org

Object

The Association of Jewish Libraries (AJL) is an international professional organization that fosters access to information and research in all forms of media relating to all things Jewish. The association promotes Jewish literacy and scholarship and provides a community for peer support and professional development.

AJL membership is open to individuals and libraries, library workers, and library supporters. There are two divisions within AJL: RAS (Research Libraries, Archives, and Special Collections) and SSC (Schools, Synagogues, and Centers). The diverse membership includes libraries in synagogues, JCCs, day schools, yeshivot, universities, Holocaust museums, and the Library of Congress. Membership is drawn from North America and places beyond, including China, the Czech Republic, the Netherlands, Israel, Italy, South Africa, Switzerland, and the United Kingdom.

Goals

The association's goals are to

- Maintain high professional standards for Judaica librarians and recruit qualified individuals into the profession
- Facilitate communication and exchange of information on a global scale
- Encourage quality publication in the field in all formats and media, print, digital, and so forth, and to stimulate publication of high-quality children's literature
- Facilitate and encourage establishment of Judaica library collections

- Enhance information access for all through application of advanced technologies
- Publicize the organization and its activities in all relevant venues: stimulate awareness of Judaica library services among the public at large; promote recognition of Judaica librarianship within the wider library profession; and encourage recognition of Judaica library services by other organizations and related professions
- Ensure continuity of the association through sound management, financial security, effective governance and a dedicated and active membership

AJL conducts an annual convention in the United States or Canada in late June.

Membership

Memb. 600. Year: Oct.–Sept. For dues information, contact Sheryl Stahl at sstahl@huc.edu.

Officers (2014–2016)

Pres. Yaffa Weisman; *V.P./Pres.-Elect* Amalia Warshenbrot; *V.P. Membership* Sheryl Stahl; *Secy.* Marga Hirsch; *Treas.* Deborah Stern; *Past Pres.* Heidi Estrin; *V.P. Development* James P. Rosenbloom; *RAS Pres.* Sharon Benamou; *SSC Pres.* Aimee Lurie.

Address correspondence to info@jewishlibraries.org.

Publications

AJL Conference Proceedings.

AJL News (q., digital).
AJL Reviews (q., digital).
Judaica Librarianship (annual, digital).

Association of Research Libraries

Executive Director, Elliott Shore
21 Dupont Circle N.W., Suite 800, Washington, D.C. 20036
202-296-2296, fax 202-872-0884, e-mail arlhq@arl.org
World Wide Web http://www.arl.org

Object

The Association of Research Libraries (ARL) is a nonprofit organization of 125 research libraries in the United States and Canada. ARL's mission is to influence the changing environment of scholarly communication and the public policies that affect research libraries and the diverse communities they serve. ARL pursues this mission by advancing the goals of its member research libraries, providing leadership in public and information policy to the scholarly and higher education communities, fostering the exchange of ideas and expertise, facilitating the emergence of new roles for research libraries, and shaping a future environment that leverages its interests with those of allied organizations.

Membership

Memb. 125. Membership is institutional. Dues: $26,744 for 2015.

Officers

Pres. Deborah Jakubs, Duke Univ.; *V.P./Pres.-Elect* Larry Alford, Univ. of Toronto; *Past Pres.* Carol Pitts Diedrichs, Ohio State Univ.

Board of Directors

Larry Alford, Univ. of Toronto; David H. Carlson (ex officio), Texas A&M Univ.; Mary Case, Univ. of Illinois at Chicago; Carol Pitts Diedrichs, Ohio State Univ.; Susan Gibbons, Yale Univ.; Thomas Hickerson, Univ. of Calgary; Jeffrey L. Horrell (ex officio), Dartmouth College; Deborah Jakubs, Duke Univ.; Richard E. Luce, Univ. of Oklahoma; Bonnie MacEwan, Auburn Univ.; Mary Ann Mavrinac, Univ. of Rochester; Brian E. C. Schottlaender (ex officio), Univ. of California, San Diego; Elliott Shore (ex officio), ARL; Ann Thornton, New York Public Lib.; John Wilkin, Univ. of Illinois at Urbana-Champaign.

Publications

Research Library Issues: A Report from ARL, CNI, and SPARC (4 per year).
ARL Academic Health Sciences Library Statistics (ann.).
ARL Academic Law Library Statistics (ann.).
ARL Annual Salary Survey (ann.).
ARL Statistics (ann.).
SPEC Kit series (4 a year).

Committee and Working Group Chairs

Accessibility and Universal Design Working Group. Ed Van Gemert, Univ. of Wisconsin–Madison.
Advancing Scholarly Communication. Brian E. C. Schottlaender, Univ. of California, San Diego.
ARL Licensing Working Group. Jay Starratt, Washington State Univ.
Diversity and Leadership. Joyce Backus, National Lib. of Medicine.
E-Research Working Group. Harriette Hemmasi, Brown Univ.
Fair Use and Related Exemptions Working Group. Betsy Wilson, Univ. of Washington.

Influencing Public Policies. David Carlson, Texas A&M Univ.

Membership. Sarah Thomas, Harvard Univ.

Regional Federal Depository Libraries Working Group. Judith C. Russell, Univ. of Florida.

Statistics and Assessment. Robert E. Fox, Jr., Univ. of Louisville.

Strategic Thinking and Design Transition Team. Brian E. C. Schottlaender, Univ. of California, San Diego.

Transforming Research Libraries. Jeffrey Horrell, Dartmouth College.

Transforming Special Collections in the Digital Age Working Group, Thomas Hickerson, Univ. of Calgary.

ARL Membership

Non-university Libraries

Boston Public Lib.; Center for Research Libs.; Lib. of Congress; National Agricultural Lib.; National Archives and Records Administration; National Lib. of Medicine; National Research Council Canada, Knowledge Management; New York Public Lib.; New York State Lib.; Smithsonian Institution Libs.

University Libraries

Alabama; Albany (SUNY); Alberta; Arizona; Arizona State; Auburn; Boston College; Boston Univ.; Brigham Young; British Columbia; Brown; Buffalo (SUNY); Calgary; California, Berkeley; California, Davis; California, Irvine; California, Los Angeles; California, Riverside; California, San Diego; California, Santa Barbara; Case Western Reserve; Chicago; Cincinnati; Colorado; Colorado State; Columbia; Connecticut; Cornell; Dartmouth; Delaware; Duke; Emory; Florida; Florida State; George Washington; Georgetown; Georgia; Georgia Inst. of Technology; Guelph; Harvard; Hawaii; Houston; Howard; Illinois, Chicago; Illinois, Urbana-Champaign; Indiana; Iowa; Iowa State; Johns Hopkins; Kansas; Kent State; Kentucky; Laval; Louisiana State; Louisville; McGill; McMaster; Manitoba; Maryland; Massachusetts; Massachusetts Inst. of Technology; Miami (Florida); Michigan; Michigan State; Minnesota; Missouri; Montreal; Nebraska, Lincoln; New Mexico; New York; North Carolina; North Carolina State; Northwestern; Notre Dame; Ohio; Ohio State; Oklahoma; Oklahoma State; Oregon; Ottawa; Pennsylvania; Pennsylvania State; Pittsburgh; Princeton; Purdue; Queen's (Kingston, Ontario); Rice; Rochester; Rutgers; Saskatchewan; South Carolina; Southern California; Southern Illinois; Stony Brook (SUNY); Syracuse; Temple; Tennessee; Texas; Texas A&M; Texas Tech; Toronto; Tulane; Utah; Vanderbilt; Virginia; Virginia Tech; Washington; Washington (Saint Louis); Washington State; Waterloo; Wayne State; Western Ontario; Wisconsin; Yale; York.

Association of Vision Science Librarians

Co-Chairs, D. J. Matthews, Kristin Motte
World Wide Web http://www.avsl.org

Object

To foster collective and individual acquisition and dissemination of vision science information, to improve services for all persons seeking such information, and to develop standards for libraries to which members are attached. Founded in 1968.

Officers

Co-Chairs D. J. Matthews, Marshall B. Ketchum Univ. E-mail djmatthews@ketchum.edu; Kristin Motte, New England College of Optometry. E-mail mottek@neco.edu; *Treas.* Elaine Wells, Harold Kohn Vision Science Lib., SUNY College of Optometry; *Member-ship Chair* Christine Weber, Illinois College of Optometry.

Publications

Guidelines for Vision Science Librarians.
Opening Day Book, Journal and AV Collection List–Visual Science.
Standards for Vision Science Libraries.
Union List of Vision-Related Serials (irreg.).

Meetings

Annual meeting held in the fall, mid-year mini-meeting with the Medical Library Association.

Beta Phi Mu
(International Library and Information Studies Honor Society)

Executive Director, Alison M. Lewis
Drexel University, College of Computing and Informatics
Philadelphia, PA 19104
215-895-5959, fax 215-895-2494, e-mail alewis@drexel.edu or betaphimu@drexel.edu
World Wide Web http://www.beta-phi-mu.org

Object

To recognize distinguished achievement in and scholarly contributions to librarianship, information studies, or library education, and to sponsor and support appropriate professional and scholarly projects relating to these fields. Founded at the University of Illinois in 1948.

Membership

Memb. 36,000. Eligibility for membership in Beta Phi Mu is by invitation of the faculty from institutions where the American Library Association, or other recognized accrediting agency approved by the Beta Phi Mu Executive Board, has accredited or recognized a professional degree program. Candidates must be graduates of a library and information science program and fulfill the following requirements: complete the course requirements leading to a master's degree with a scholastic average of 3.75 where A equals 4 points, or complete a planned program of advanced study beyond the master's degree which require full-time study for one or more academic years with a scholastic average of 3.75 where A equals 4.0. Each chapter or approved institution is allowed to invite no more than 25 percent of the annual graduating class, and the faculty of participating library schools must attest to their initiates' professional promise.

Officers

Pres. Eileen Abels, Graduate School of Lib. and Info. Science, Simmons College, Boston; V.P. Charles McElroy, Florida State Univ. Lib.

Directors

Susan W. Alman, Lynn Silipigni Connaway, Marie Radford, Vinette Thomas, Elaine Yontz.

Publications

Beta Phi Mu Scholar Series. Available from Rowman & Littlefield, Publishers, 4501 Forbes Blvd., Suite 200, Lanham, MD 20706. Ed. Lorraine J. Haricombe; Assoc. Ed. Keith Russell.

Newsletter. The Pipeline (biennial; electronic only). Ed. Isabel Gray.

Chapters

Alpha. Univ. of Illinois at Urbana-Champaign, Grad. School of Lib. and Info. Science; Gamma. Florida State Univ., College of Communication and Info.; Epsilon. Univ. of North Carolina at Chapel Hill, School of Info. and Lib. Science; Theta. Pratt Inst., Grad. School of Lib. and Info. Science; Iota. Catholic Univ. of America, School of Lib. and Info. Science; Univ. of Maryland, College of Info. Studies; Lambda. Univ. of Oklahoma, School of Lib. and Info. Studies; Xi. Univ. of Hawaii at Manoa, School of Lib. and Info. Studies; Omicron. Rutgers Univ., Grad. School of Communication, Info., and Lib. Studies; Pi. Univ. of Pittsburgh, School of Info. Sciences; Rho. Kent State Univ., School of Lib. and Info. Science; Sigma. Drexel Univ., College of Computing and Informatics; Phi. Univ. of Denver, Grad. School of Lib. and Info. Science; Psi. Univ. of Missouri at Columbia, School of Lib. and Info. Science; Omega. San Jose State Univ., School of Lib. and Info. Science; Beta Beta. Simmons College, Grad. School of Lib. and Info. Science; Beta Delta. State Univ. of New York at Buffalo, Dept. of Lib. and Info. Studies; Beta Epsilon. Emporia State Univ., School of Lib. and Info. Management; Beta Zeta. Louisiana State Univ., School of Lib. and Info. Science; Beta Eta. Univ. of Texas at Austin, Grad. School of Lib. and Info. Science; Beta Iota. Univ. of Rhode Island, Grad. School of Lib. and Info. Studies; Beta Kappa. Univ. of Alabama, School of Lib. and Info. Studies; Beta Lambda. Texas Woman's Univ., School of Lib. and Info. Sciences; Beta Mu. Long Island Univ., Palmer School of Lib. and Info. Science; Beta Xi. North Carolina Central Univ., School of Lib. and Info. Sciences; Beta Omicron. Univ. of Tennessee at Knoxville, School of Info. Sciences; Beta Pi. Univ. of Arizona, School of Info. Resources and Lib. Science; Beta Rho. Univ. of Wisconsin at Milwaukee, School of Info.; Beta Sigma. Clarion Univ. of Pennsylvania, Dept. of Lib. Science; Beta Phi. Univ. of South Florida, School of Lib. and Info. Science; Beta Psi. Univ. of Southern Mississippi, School of Lib. and Info. Science; Beta Omega. Univ. of South Carolina, College of Lib. and Info. Science; Beta Beta Epsilon. Univ. of Wisconsin at Madison, School of Lib. and Info. Studies; Beta Beta Theta. Univ. of Iowa, School of Lib. and Info. Science; Beta Beta Kappa. Univ. of Puerto Rico, Grad. School of Info. Sciences and Technologies; Pi Lambda Sigma. Syracuse Univ., School of Info. Studies; Beta Beta Mu. Valdosta State Univ., School of Lib. and Info. Science; Beta Beta Nu. Univ. of North Texas, College of Info.; Beta Beta Xi. St. Catherine Univ., Master of Lib. and Info. Science program.

Bibliographical Society of America

Executive Secretary, Michèle E. Randall
P.O. Box 1537, Lenox Hill Sta., New York, NY 10021
212-452-2710 (tel./fax), e-mail bsa@bibsocamer.org
World Wide Web http://www.bibsocamer.org

Object

To promote bibliographical research and to issue bibliographical publications. Organized in 1904.

Membership

Memb. Dues (Indiv.) $65; (Sustaining) $250; (Contributing) $100; (Student) $20; (Inst.) $100; (Lifetime) $1,250. Year. Jan.–Dec.

Officers

Pres. Martin Antonetti, Smith College. E-mail mantonet@smith.edu; *V.P.* John Crichton, Brick Row Book Shop, San Francisco. E-mail jcrichton@brickrow.com; *Secy.* Barbara Heritage, Rare Book School. E-mail beh7v@virginia.edu; *Treas.* G. Scott Clemons, Brown Brothers Harriman. E-mail scott.clemons@bbh.com.

Council

(2015) Christina Geiger, Michael Suarez, David J. Supino, Michael Thompson; (2016) John A. Buchtel, Gerald Cloud, David Alan Richards, Marcia Reed; (2017) William T. LaMoy, Nina Musinsky, George Ong, Heather Wolfe.

Publication

Papers of the Bibliographical Society of America (q.; memb.).

Bibliographical Society of Canada
(La Société Bibliographique du Canada)

President, Linda Quirk
World Wide Web http://www.bsc-sbc.ca/index.html
360 Bloor St. W., P.O. Box 19035, Toronto, ON M5S 3C9

Object

The Bibliographical Society of Canada is a bilingual (English/French) organization that has as its goal the scholarly study of the history, description, and transmission of texts in all media and formats, with a primary emphasis on Canada, and the fulfillment of this goal through the following objectives:

- To promote the study and practice of bibliography: enumerative, historical, descriptive, analytical, and textual
- To further the study, research, and publication of book history and print culture

- To publish bibliographies and studies of book history and print culture
- To encourage the publication of bibliographies, critical editions, and studies of book history and print culture
- To promote the appropriate preservation and conservation of manuscript, archival, and published materials in various formats
- To encourage the utilization and analysis of relevant manuscript and archival sources as a foundation of bibliographical scholarship and book history

- To promote the interdisciplinary nature of bibliography, and to foster relationships with other relevant organizations nationally and internationally
- To conduct the society without purpose of financial gain for its members, and to ensure that any profits or other accretions to the society shall be used in promoting its goal and objectives

Membership

The society welcomes as members all those who share its aims and wish to support and participate in bibliographical research and publication.

Officers

Pres. Linda Quirk. E-mail president@bsc-sbc.ca; *1st V.P.* Nancy Earle; *2nd V.P.* Ruth Panofsky; *Secy.* Greta Golick. E-mail secretary@bsc-sbc.ca; *Assoc. Secy.* Roger Meloche; *Treas.* Tom Vincent; *Past Pres.* Janet Friskney.

Publications

Papers of the Bibliographical Society of Canada/Cahiers de la Société Bibliographique du Canada (s. ann).
The Bulletin/Le Bulletin (s. ann).

For a full list of the society's publications, see http://www.library.utoronto.ca/bsc/publicationseng.html.

Black Caucus of the American Library Association

President, Kelvin A. Watson
P.O. Box 1738, Hampton, VA 23669
World Wide Web http://www.bcala.org

Mission

The Black Caucus of the American Library Association (BCALA) serves as an advocate for the development, promotion, and improvement of library services and resources for the nation's African American community and provides leadership for the recruitment and professional development of African American librarians. Founded in 1970.

Membership

Membership is open to any person, institution, or business interested in promoting the development of library and information services for African Americans and other people of African descent and willing to maintain good financial standing with the organization. The membership is currently composed of librarians and other information professionals, library support staff, libraries, publishers, authors, vendors, and other library-related organizations in the United States and abroad. Dues (Lifetime)

$500; (Corporate) $200; (Institutional) $60; (Regular) $45; (Library Support Staff) $20; (Student) $10; (Retired) $0.

Officers

Pres. Kelvin A. Watson. E-mail kantoniow@yahoo.com; *V.P./Pres.-Elect* Denyvetta Davis; *Secy.* kYmberly Keeton; *Past Pres.* Jerome Offord, Jr.

Executive Board

Richard Ashby, Bettye Black, Wanda K. Brown, Elizabeth Jean Brumfield, Rudolf Clay, Eboni Curry, Tiffany A. Duck, Michele Fenton, Emily Guss, Andrew P. Jackson, Karen Lemons, Carol Nurse, Kirby McCurtis, Monya Tomlinson.

Publication

BCALA Newsletter (bi-mo; memb.).

Canadian Association for Information Science
(L'Association Canadienne des Sciences de l'Information)

President, Diane Rasmussen Pennington
World Wide Web http://www.cais-acsi.ca

Object

To promote the advancement of information science in Canada and encourage and facilitate the exchange of information relating to the use, access, retrieval, organization, management, and dissemination of information.

Officers

Pres. Diane Rasmussen Pennington, Ashford Univ. E-mail diane.m.rasmussen@gmail.com; *Secy.* Deborah Hicks, Univ. of Alberta. E-mail deborah.hicks@ualberta.ca; *Treas.* Anatoliy Gruzd, Dalhousie Univ. E-mail gruzd@dal.ca.

Membership

Institutions and individuals interested in information science and involved in the gathering, organization, and dissemination of information (such as information scientists, archivists, librarians, computer scientists, documentalists, economists, educators, journalists, and psychologists) and who support CAIS's objectives can become association members.

Publication

Canadian Journal of Information and Library Science. *Ed.* Clément Arsenault, Univ. de Montréal. E-mail clement.arsenault@umontreal.ca.

Canadian Association of Research Libraries
(Association des Bibliothèques de Recherche du Canada)

Executive Director, Susan Haigh
309 Cooper St., Suite 203, Ottawa, ON K2P 0G5
613-482-9344 ext. 101, e-mail info@carl-abrc.ca
World Wide Web http://www.carl-abrc.ca

Membership

The Canadian Association of Research Libraries (CARL), established in 1976, is the leadership organization for the Canadian research library community. The association's members are the 29 major academic research libraries across Canada together with Library and Archives Canada and the Canada Institute for Scientific and Technical Information (CISTI). Membership is institutional, open primarily to libraries of Canadian universities that have doctoral graduates in both the arts and the sciences. CARL is an associate member of the Association of Universities and Colleges of Canada (AUCC) and is incorporated as a not-for-profit organization under the Canada Corporations Act.

Mission

The association provides leadership on behalf of Canada's research libraries and enhances their capacity to advance research and higher education. It promotes effective and sustainable scholarly communication, and public policy that enables broad access to scholarly information.

Officers (2013–2015)

Pres. Gerald Beasley, Univ. of Alberta; *V.P./ Pres.-Elect* Martha Whitehead, Queen's Univ.; *Secy.* Lynda Gadoury, Université du Québec à Montréal; *Treas.* Donna Bourne-Tyson, Dalhousie Univ.; *Past Pres.* Thomas Hickerson, Univ. of Calgary. E-mail tom.hickerson@ ucalgary.ca; *Dirs.* Jonathan Bengtson, Univ. of Victoria; Vivian Lewis, McMaster Univ.; *Exec. Dir.* Susan Haigh. E-mail susan.haigh@carl-abrc.ca.

Member Institutions

Univ. of Alberta, Univ. of British Columbia, Brock Univ., Univ. of Calgary, Carleton Univ., CISTI (Canada Institute for Scientific and Technical Information), Concordia Univ., Dalhousie Univ., Univ. of Guelph, Université Laval, Lib. and Archives Canada, McGill Univ., McMaster Univ., Univ. of Manitoba, Memorial Univ. of Newfoundland, Université de Montréal, Univ. of New Brunswick, Univ. of Ottawa, Université du Québec à Montréal, Queen's Univ., Univ. of Regina, Ryerson Univ., Univ. of Saskatchewan, Université de Sherbrooke, Simon Fraser Univ., Univ. of Toronto, Univ. of Victoria, Univ. of Waterloo, Univ. of Western Ontario, Univ. of Windsor, York Univ.

Canadian Library Association
(Association Canadienne des Bibliothèques)

Executive Director, Valoree McKay
1150 Morrison Drive, Suite 400, Ottawa, ON K1Y 0K4
613-232-9625 ext. 306, fax 613-563-9895, e-mail vmckay@cla.ca
World Wide Web http://www.cla.ca

Object

The Canadian Library Association (CLA) is the national voice for Canada's library communities. CLA champions library values and the value of libraries, influences public policy affecting libraries, inspires and supports learning, and collaborates to strengthen the library community. The association represents Canadian librarianship to the federal government and media, carries on international liaison with other library associations and cultural agencies, offers professional development programs, and supports such core library values as intellectual freedom and access to information, particularly for disadvantaged populations. Founded in 1946, CLA is a not-for-profit voluntary organization governed by an elected executive council.

Membership

Memb. (as of December 2014) (Indiv.) 957; (Inst.) 249; (Corporate) 50; (Associate) 27.

Open to individuals, institutions, library boards, and groups interested in librarianship and in library and information services.

Officers

Pres. Sandra Singh, Vancouver Public Lib., 350 W. Georgia St., Vancouver, BC V6B 6B1. Tel. 604-331-4007, e-mail sandra.singh@vpl.ca; *V.P./Pres.-Elect* Rosemary Bonanno, Vancouver Island Regional Lib. E-mail rbonanno@ virl.bc.ca; *Treas.* Michael Ridley, Univ. of Guelph. E-mail mridley@uoguelph.ca; *Past Pres.* Marie DeYoung, Saint Mary's Univ. E-mail marie.deyoung@smu.ca.

Publications

Feliciter: Linking Canada's Information Professionals (6 a year; electronic).
CLA Digest (bi-w.; electronic newsletter).

Catholic Library Association

President, Sara B. Baron
8550 United Plaza Blvd., Suite 1001, Baton Rouge, LA 70809
Tel. 225-408-4417, e-mail cla@cathla.org
World Wide Web http://www.cathla.org

Object

The promotion and encouragement of Catholic literature and library work through cooperation, publications, education, and information. Founded in 1921.

Membership

Memb. 1,000. Dues $55–$500. Year. July–June.

Officers

Pres. Sara B. Baron, Regent Univ. Lib., Virginia Beach. E-mail sbaron@regent.edu; *V.P./Pres.-Elect* Mary Kelleher, Univ. of St. Thomas, Houston. E-mail kellehm@stthom.edu; *Past Pres.* Malachy R. McCarthy, Claretian Missionaries Archives, Chicago. E-mail mmccarthy@cathla.org.

Address correspondence to the executive director.

Executive Board

Officers; Susan B. Finney; Cait C. Kokolus; Pat Lawton; Ann O'Hara.

Publication

Catholic Library World (q.; memb.; nonmemb. $125). *General Ed.* Sigrid Kelsey.

Chief Officers of State Library Agencies

Executive Director, Timothy Cherubini
201 E. Main St., Suite 1405, Lexington, KY 40507
859-514-9826, fax 859-514-9166, e-mail tcherubini@cosla.org
World Wide Web http://www.cosla.org

Object

Chief Officers of State Library Agencies (COSLA) is an independent organization of the chief officers of state and territorial agencies designated as the state library administrative agency and responsible for statewide library development. Its purpose is to identify and address issues of common concern and national interest; to further state library agency relationships with federal government and national organizations; and to initiate cooperative action for the improvement of library services to the people of the United States.

COSLA's membership consists solely of these top library officers, variously designated as state librarian, director, commissioner, or executive secretary. The organization provides a continuing mechanism for dealing with the problems and challenges faced by these officers. Its work is carried on through its members, a board of directors, and committees.

Board of Directors (2014–2016)

Pres. Kendall Wiggin, State Libn., Connecticut State Lib., 231 Capitol Ave., Hartford, CT 06106. Tel. 860-757-6510, e-mail kendall.wiggin@ct.gov; *V.P./Pres.-Elect* Sandra Treadway, Libn. of Virginia, Lib. of Virginia, 800 E. Broad St., Richmond, VA 23219. Tel. 804-692-

3535, e-mail sandra.treadway@lva.virginia.gov; *Treas.* Stacey Aldrich, Deputy Secy. for Libs., Office of Commonwealth Libs., Pennsylvania Dept. of Educ., 607 South Drive, Forum Bldg., Room 200, Harrisburg, PA 17120-0600. Tel. 717-787-2646, e-mail saldrich@pa.gov; *Secy.* Kurt Kiefer, State Libn., Div. for Libraries, Technology, and Community Learning, Wisconsin Dept. of Public Instruction, P.O. Box 7841, Madison, WI 53707. Tel. 608-266-2205, e-mail kurt.kiefer@dpi.wi.gov;

Past Pres. Ann Joslin, State Libn., Idaho Commission for Libs., 325 W. State St., Boise, ID 83702. Tel. 208-334-2150, e-mail ann.joslin@libraries.idaho.gov; *Dirs.* Cal Shepard, State Libn., North Carolina State Lib., 4640 Mail Service Center, Raleigh, NC 27699-4640. Tel. 919-807-7410, e-mail cal.shepard@ncdcr.gov; Charles Sherrill, State Libn. and Archivist, Tennessee State Lib. and Archives, 403 Seventh Ave. North, Nashville, TN 37243. Tel. 615-741-7996, e-mail chuck.sherrill@tn.gov.

Chinese American Librarians Association

Executive Director, Li Fu
E-mail ailifaha@gmail.com
World Wide Web http://cala-web.org

Object

To enhance communications among Chinese American librarians as well as between Chinese American librarians and other librarians; to serve as a forum for discussion of mutual problems and professional concerns among Chinese American librarians; to promote Sino-American librarianship and library services; and to provide a vehicle whereby Chinese American librarians can cooperate with other associations and organizations having similar or allied interests.

Membership

Memb. About 600. Membership is open to anyone interested in the association's goals and activities. Dues (Regular) $30; (International/Student/Non-salaried) $15; (Inst.) $100; (Affiliated) $100; (Life) $300.

Officers

Pres. Carol Kachuen Gee. E-mail kachuen.gee@lehman.cuny.edu; *V.P./Pres.-Elect* Lian Ruan. E-mail lruan@illinois.edu; *Incoming V.P./Pres.-Elect*; *Treas.* Hong Miao. E-mail miao hong818@gmail.com; *Past Pres.* Lisa Zhao. E-mail zhzhls200@gmail.com.

Publications

CALA Newsletter (2 a year; memb.; online). *Eds.* Priscilla Yu. E-mail pcyu@illinois.edu; Sai Deng. E-mail saideng@gmail.com.
Journal of Library and Information Science (*JLIS*) (2 a year). *Editorial Board Chair* (2012–2015) Chengzhi Wang, Columbia Univ. Libs. E-mail cw2165@columbia.edu.
Membership Directory (memb.).
Occasional Paper Series (OPS) (online). *Ed.* (2012–2015) Yunshan Ye. E-mail yye@jhu.edu.

Church and Synagogue Library Association

10157 S.W. Barbur Blvd., No.102C, Portland, OR 97219
503-244-6919, 800-542-2752, fax 503-977-3734, e-mail csla@worldaccessnet.com
World Wide Web http://www.cslainfo.org

Object

The Church and Synagogue Library Association (CSLA) provides educational guidance in the establishment and maintenance of congregational libraries.

Its purpose is to act as a unifying core for congregational libraries; to provide the opportunity for a mutual sharing of practices and problems; to inspire and encourage a sense of purpose and mission among congregational librarians; to study and guide the development of congregational librarianship toward recognition as a formal branch of the library profession. Founded in 1967.

Membership

Memb. 1,000. Dues (Inst.) $200; (Affiliated) $100; (Church or Synagogue) $70 ($75 foreign); (Indiv.) $50 ($55 foreign).

Officers

Pres. Cheryl Cutchin; *1st V.P./Pres.-Elect* to be announced; *2nd V.P.* Maria Isabel Garcia; *Treas.* Alice Campbell; *Past Pres.* Evelyn Pockrass; *Ed., Congregational Libraries Today* Sue Poss; *Admin.* Judith Janzen.

Executive Board

Officers; committee chairs.

Publications

Bibliographies (4; price varies).
Congregational Libraries Today (q.; memb.; nonmemb. $50; Canada $60).
CSLA Guides (price varies).

Coalition for Networked Information

Executive Director, Clifford A. Lynch
21 Dupont Circle, Suite 800, Washington, DC 20036
202-296-5098, fax 202-872-0884, e-mail http://www.cni.org/contact
World Wide Web http://www.cni.org
Twitter http://twitter.com/cni_org
YouTube https://www.youtube.com/cnivideo
Vimeo http://vimeo.com/cni

Mission

The Coalition for Networked Information (CNI) promotes the transformative promise of networked information technology for the advancement of scholarly communication and the enrichment of intellectual productivity.

Membership

Memb. 232. Membership is institutional. Dues $7,500. Year. July–June.

Steering Committee

John P. Barden, Univ. of Rochester; Daniel Cohen, Digital Public Lib. of America; Joseph D. Combs, Vanderbilt Univ.; Rebecca A. Graham, Univ. of Guelph; Geneva L. Henry, George Washington Univ.; Thomas C. Leonard, Univ. of California, Berkeley; Clifford A. Lynch (ex officio), Coalition for Networked Information; Diana G. Oblinger (ex officio) EDUCAUSE; Elliott Shore (ex officio), Assn. of Research Libs.; John Unsworth, Brandeis Univ.; Donald J. Waters, Andrew W. Mellon Foundation.

Publication

CNI-Announce (subscribe by e-mail to cni-announce-subscribe@cni.org).
Periodic reports (http://www.cni.org/resources/publications/other-publications-by-cni-staff).

Council on Library and Information Resources

1707 L St. N.W., Suite 650, Washington, DC 20036
202-939-4750, fax 202-600-9628
World Wide Web http://www.clir.org

Object

In 1997 the Council on Library Resources (CLR) and the Commission on Preservation and Access (CPA) merged and became the Council on Library and Information Resources (CLIR). CLIR is an independent, nonprofit organization that forges strategies to enhance research, teaching, and learning environments in collaboration with libraries, cultural institutions, and communities of higher learning.

CLIR promotes forward-looking collaborative solutions that transcend disciplinary, institutional, professional, and geographic boundaries in support of the public good. CLIR identifies and defines the key emerging issues relating to the welfare of libraries and the constituencies they serve, convenes the leaders who can influence change, and promotes collaboration among the institutions and organizations that can achieve change. The council's interests embrace the entire range of information resources and services from traditional library and archival materials to emerging digital formats. It assumes a particular interest in helping institutions cope with the accelerating pace of change associated with the transition into the digital environment.

While maintaining appropriate collaboration and liaison with other institutions and organizations, CLIR operates independently of any particular institutional or vested interests. Through the composition of its board, it brings the broadest possible perspective to bear upon defining and establishing the priority of the issues with which it is concerned.

Board

CLIR's Board of Directors currently has 23 members.

Officers

Chair David Gift, Internet2; *Pres.* Charles Henry. E-mail chenry@clir.org; *V. Chair* Leslie Weir, Univ. of Ottawa; *Treas.* Kathleen Fitzpatrick, Modern Language Assn.

Address correspondence to headquarters.

Publications

Annual Report.
CLIR Issues (bi-mo.).
Technical reports.

Federal Library and Information Network

Interim Executive Director, Kathryn Mendenhall
Library of Congress, Washington, DC 20540-4935
202-707-4800, World Wide Web http://www.loc.gov/flicc

Object

The Federal Library and Information Network (FEDLINK) is an organization of federal agencies working together to achieve optimum use of the resources and facilities of federal libraries and information centers by promoting common services, coordinating and sharing available resources, and providing continuing professional education for federal library and information staff. FEDLINK serves as a forum for discussion of the policies, programs, procedures, and technologies that affect federal libraries and the information services they provide to their agencies, to Congress, the federal courts, and the public.

Membership

The FEDLINK voting membership is composed of representatives of the following U.S. federal departments and agencies: Each of the national libraries (the Library of Congress, National Agricultural Library, National Library of Education, National Library of Medicine, and the National Transportation Library); each cabinet-level executive department, as defined

in 5 U.S.C. § 101; additional departments and agencies (the Defense Technical Information Center; departments of the Air Force, Army, and Navy; Executive Office of the President, Government Accountability Office, General Services Administration, Government Printing Office, Institute of Museum and Library Services, National Aeronautics and Space Administration, National Archives and Records Administration, National Technical Information Service [Department of Commerce], Office of Management and Budget, Office of Personnel Management, Office of Scientific and Technical Information [Department of Energy], Office of the Director of National Intelligence, and the Smithsonian Institution); the U.S. Supreme Court and the Administrative Office of the U.S. Courts; the District of Columbia; and other federal independent agencies and government corporations.

Officers

Co-Chairs Kathryn Mendenhall and Mark Sweeney, Library of Congress.

Address correspondence to the interim executive director.

Medical Library Association

Executive Director, Carla Funk
65 E. Wacker Place, Suite 1900, Chicago, IL 60601-7298
312-419-9094, fax 312-419-8950, e-mail info@mlahq.org
World Wide Web http://www.mlanet.org

Object

The Medical Library Association (MLA) is a nonprofit professional education organization with nearly 4,000 health sciences information professional members and partners worldwide. MLA provides lifelong educational opportunities, supports a knowledge base of health information research, and works with a global network of partners to promote the importance of high-quality information for improved health to the health care community and the public.

Membership

Memb. (Inst.) 400+; (Indiv.) 3,200+, in more than 50 countries. Institutional members are medical and allied scientific libraries. Individual members are people who are (or were at the time membership was established) engaged in professional library or bibliographic work in medical and allied scientific libraries or people who are interested in medical or allied scientific libraries. Members can be affiliated with one or more of MLA's more than 20 special-interest sections and its regional chapters.

Officers

Pres. Linda Walton. E-mail linda-walton@uiowa.edu; *Pres.-Elect* Michelle Kraft. E-mail kraftm@ccf.org; *Secy.* Sandra Franklin; *Treas.* Chris Shaffer; *Past Pres.* Dixie Jones.

Directors

Kris Alpi (2016), Melissa De Santis (2017), Angela Dixon (2016), Julia Esparza (2015), Sandra Franklin (2016), Heidi Heilemann (2017), Teresa L. Knott (2017), Jodi L. Philbrick (2016), Chris Shaffer (2015).

Publications

Journal of the Medical Library Association (q.; $190).
MLA News (10 a year; $120).

Music Library Association

8551 Research Way, Suite 180, Middleton, WI 53562
608-836-5825, fax 608-831-8200, e-mail mla@areditions.com
World Wide Web http://www.musiclibraryassoc.org

Object

The Music Library Association provides a professional forum for librarians, archivists, and others who support and preserve the world's musical heritage. To achieve this mission, it

- Provides leadership for the collection and preservation of music and information about music in libraries and archives
- Develops and delivers programs that promote continuing education and professional development in music librarianship
- Ensures and enhances intellectual access to music for all by contributing to the development and revision of national and international codes, formats, and other standards for the bibliographic control of music
- Ensures and enhances access to music for all by facilitating best practices for housing, preserving, and providing access to music
- Promotes legislation that strengthens music library services and universal access to music
- Fosters information literacy and lifelong learning by promoting music reference services, library instruction programs, and publications
- Collaborates with other groups in the music and technology industries, government, and librarianship, to promote its mission and values

Membership

Memb. 1,200+. Dues (Inst.) $135; (Indiv.) $100; (Retired or Assoc.) $70; (Paraprofessional) $55; (Student) $45. (Foreign, add $10.) Year. July–June.

Officers

Pres. Michael Colby. E-mail mdcolby@ucdavis. edu; *V.P./Pres.-Elect* Michael Rogan. E-mail michael.rogan@tufts.edu; *Recording Secy.* Lisa Shiota. E-mail lshi@loc.gov; *Admin. Officer* Paul Cary. E-mail pcary@bw.edu; *Past Pres.* Jerry L. McBride. E-mail jerry.mcbride@ stanford.edu.

Members-at-Large

(2013–2015) Stephanie Bonjack, Michael J. Duffy IV, Rick McRae; (2014–2016) Damian Iseminger, Tracey Rudnick, John Shepard.

Publications

MLA Index and Bibliography Series (irreg.; price varies).
MLA Newsletter (q.; memb.).
MLA Technical Reports (irreg.; price varies).
Music Cataloging Bulletin (mo.; online subscription only, $35).
Notes (q.; indiv. $85; inst. $100).

National Association of Government Archives and Records Administrators

1450 Western Ave., Suite 101, Albany, NY 12203
518-694-8472, World Wide Web http://www.nagara.org

Object

Founded in 1984, the National Association of Government Archives and Records Administrators (NAGARA) is a nationwide association of local, state, and federal archivists and records administrators, and others interested in improved care and management of government records. NAGARA promotes public awareness of government records and archives management programs, encourages interchange of information among government archives and records management agencies, develops and implements professional standards of government records and archival administration, and encourages study and research into records management problems and issues.

Membership

Most NAGARA members are federal, state, and local archival and records management agencies.

Officers

Pres. Tanya Marshall, Vermont State Archives and Records Admin., 1078 U.S. Route 2, Middlesex, Montpelier 05633-7701. Tel. 802-828-0405, fax 802-828-3710, e-mail tanya.marshall@sec.state.vt.us; *Pres.-Elect* Pari Swift, Ohio Attorney General`s Office, 30 E. Broad St., Co-lumbus 43215-3428. Tel. 614-466-1356, e-mail pari.swift@ohioattorneygeneral.gov; *V.P.* Cathi Carmack, Tennessee State Lib. and Archives, 403 7th Ave. North, Nashville 37243. Tel. 615-253-3468, fax 615-532-5315 e-mail Cathi. Carmack@tn.gov; *Secy.* Jannette Goodall, City of Austin, 301 W. 2 St., P.O. Box 1088, Austin 78767. Tel. 512-974-9045, e-mail jannette. goodall@austintexas.gov; *Treas.* Galen Wilson, National Archives and Records Admin., 3150 Springboro Rd., Dayton, OH 45439-1883. Tel. 937-425-0613, e-mail galen.wilson@nara.gov; *Past Pres.* Daphne DeLeon, Nevada State Lib. and Archives, 100 N. Stewart St., Carson City, NV 89701-4285. Tel. 775-684-3315, fax 775-684-3311, e-mail ddeleon@nevadaculture.org.

Directors

Debbie Bahn, Patricia Franks, Anne Mills, Arian Ravanbakhsh, Shawn Rounds, Michael Sherman, Amelia Winstead.

Publications

Clearinghouse (q.; memb.).

Crossroads (q.; memb.).

Government Records Issues (series).

Preservation Needs in State Archives.

Program Reporting Guidelines for Government Records Programs.

National Federation of Advanced Information Services

Executive Director, Marcie Granahan
801 Compass Way, Suite 201, Annapolis, MD 21401
443-221-2980, fax 443-221-2981, e-mail nfais@nfais.org
World Wide Web http://www.nfais.org

Object

The National Federation of Advanced Information Services (NFAIS) is an international nonprofit membership organization composed of leading information providers. Its membership includes government agencies, nonprofit scholarly societies, private sector businesses, and libraries. NFAIS is committed to promoting the value of credible, high-quality content. It serves all groups that create, aggregate, organize, or facilitate access to such information. In order to improve members' capabilities and to contribute to their ongoing success, NFAIS provides opportunities for education, advocacy, and a forum in which to address common interests. Founded in 1958.

Membership

Memb. 60. Full members are organizations whose main focus is any of the following activities: information creation, organization, aggregation, dissemination, access, or retrieval. Organizations are eligible for associate member status if they do not meet the qualifications for full membership.

Officers (2014–2015)

Pres. Chris McCue, CAS; *Pres.-Elect* Mary Sauer-Games, OCLC; *Secy.* Lynn Willis, American Psychological Assn.; *Treas.* Christopher Burghardt, Thomson Reuters; *Past Pres.* Suzanne BeDell, Elsevier.

Directors

Brenda Bailey-Hainer, American Theological Lib. Assn.; Nancy Blair-DeLeon; Chris Cole, National Agricultural Lib.; Don Hagen, National Technical Info. Service; Cynthia Murphy, Thomson Reuters IP Solutions; Deborah Ozga, National Lib. of Medicine; Judith Russell, Univ. of Florida; Judy Salk, Elsevier; Peter Simon, NewsBank.

Staff

Exec. Dir. Marcie Granahan. E-mail mgranahan @nfais.org; *Dir., Professional Development* Jill O'Neill. E-mail jilloneill@nfais.org.

Publications

For a detailed list of NFAIS publications, go to http://www.nfais.org/publications.

National Information Standards Organization (NISO)

Executive Director, Todd Carpenter
3600 Clipper Mill Rd., Suite 302, Baltimore, MD 21211
301-654-2512, fax 410-685-5278, e-mail nisohq@niso.org
World Wide Web http://www.niso.org

Object

The National Information Standards Organization (NISO) fosters the development and maintenance of standards that facilitate the creation, persistent management, and effective interchange of information so that it can be trusted for use in research and learning. To fulfill this mission, NISO engages libraries, publishers, information aggregators, and other organizations that support learning, research, and scholarship through the creation, organization, management, and curation of knowledge. NISO works with intersecting communities of interest and across the entire lifecycle of an information standard. NISO standards apply both traditional and new technologies to the full range of information-related needs, including discovery, retrieval, repurposing, storage, metadata, business information, and preservation.

NISO also develops and publishes recommended practices, technical reports, white papers, and information publications. NISO holds regular educational programs on standards, technologies, and related topics where standards-based solutions can help solve problems. These programs include webinars, online virtual conferences, in-person forums, and teleconferences.

Experts from the information industry, libraries, systems vendors, and publishing participate in the development of NISO standards and recommended practices. The standards are approved by the consensus body of NISO's voting membership, representing libraries, publishers, vendors, government, associations, and private businesses and organizations. NISO is supported by its membership and grants.

NISO is a not-for-profit association accredited by the American National Standards Institute (ANSI) and serves as the U.S. Technical Advisory Group Administrator to ISO/TC 46 Information and Documentation as well as the secretariat for ISO/TC 46/SC 9, Identification and Description.

Membership

Voting Members: 80+. Open to any organization, association, government agency, or company willing to participate in and having substantial concern for the development of NISO standards. Library Standards Alliance Members: 60+. Open to any academic, public, special, or government-supported library interested in supporting the mission of NISO.

Officers

Chair Gerry Grenier, IEEE; *V. Chair/Chair-Elect* Mike Teets, OCLC; *Treas.* Janice Fleming, American Psychological Assn.; *Past Chair* Heather Reid, Copyright Clearance Center.

Directors

Marian Hollingsworth, Thomson Reuters; Evan Owens, Cenveo Publisher Services; Oliver Pesch, EBSCO; Barbara Preece, Loyola/Notre Dame Lib.; Chris Shillum, Elsevier; B. Tommie Usdin, Mulberry Technologies; Tyler Walters, Virginia Tech Univ. Libs.; Keith Webster, Carnegie Mellon Univ.; Jabin White, ITHAKA.

Publications

Information Standards Quarterly (print: $130/year domestic, $165/year international, back issues $36; electronic version available in open access from the NISO website).

NISO Newsline (free e-newsletter released on the first Wednesday of each month; distributed by e-mail and posted on the NISO website).

Working Group Connection (free quarterly e-newsletter supplement to *Newsline* that provides updates on the activities of NISO's working groups; distributed by e-mail and posted on the NISO website).

For other NISO publications, see the article "National Information Standards Organization (NISO) Standards" later in Part 6 of this volume.

NISO's published standards, recommended practices, and technical reports are available free of charge as downloadable PDF files from the NISO website (http://www.niso.org). Hardcopy documents are available for sale from the website.

Patent and Trademark Resource Center Association

World Wide Web http://www.ptrca.org

Object

The Patent and Trademark Resource Center Association (PTRCA) provides a support structure for the more than 80 patent and trademark resource centers (PTRCs) affiliated with the U.S. Patent and Trademark Office (USPTO). The association's mission is to discover the interests, needs, opinions, and goals of the PTRCs and to advise USPTO in these matters for the benefit of PTRCs and their users, and to assist USPTO in planning and implementing appropriate services. Founded in 1983 as the Patent Depository Library Advisory Council; name changed to Patent and Trademark Depository Library Association in 1988; became an American Library Association affiliate in 1996. In 2011 the association was renamed the Patent and Trademark Resource Center Association.

Membership

Open to any person employed in a patent and trademark resource center library whose responsibilities include the patent and trademark collection. Affiliate membership is also available. Dues $65 in 2015.

Officers (2014–2015)

Pres. Spruce Fraser. E-mail sfraser@slpl.org; *V.P./Pres.-Elect* Karen Kitchens. E-mail karen. kitchens@wyo.gov; *Secy.* Suzanne Reinman. E-mail suzanne.reinman@okstate.edu; *Treas.* Jim Miller. E-mail jmiller2@umd.edu; *Past Pres.* Ran Raider. E-mail ran.raider@wright. edu.

Divisional Representatives

(Academic) Connie Wu (2013–2015). E-mail conniewu@rutgers.edu; Lisha Li (2014–2016). E-mail lisha.li@library.gatech.edu; (Public) Mary Kordyban (2013–2015). E-mail mkordyban@detroitpubliclibrary.org; Irene Yelovich (2014–2016). E-mail yelovichi@carnegielibrary.org.

Publication

PTRCA Journal. Electronic at http://ptrca.org/newsletters. *Ed.* Suzanne Reinman. E-mail suzanne.reinman@okstate.edu.

Polish American Librarians Association

President, Ronald V. Stoch
P.O. Box 7232, Prospect Heights, IL 60070-7232
World Wide Web http://www.palalib.org

Object

The mission of the Polish American Librarians Association (PALA) is to positively affect services provided to library patrons of Polish descent and individuals interested in Polish culture.

The organization's vision is

* To enhance professional knowledge by developing forums for discussion and networks of communication among library staff working with Polish collections and patrons of Polish origin
* To promote understanding and respect among all cultures by expanding the means to access reliable, current information about Polish and Polish American culture
* To promote Polish American librarianship
* To provide opportunities for cooperation with other library associations

Founded in 2009.

Membership

Membership is open to librarians, students of library schools, library support staff, and others who support the vision of PALA. Dues (Regular) $25; (Support Staff, Student, Retired, Unemployed) $15.

Officers

Pres. Ronald V. Stoch, 1827 N. 74 Ct., Elmwood Park, IL 60707. Tel. 708-453-9274, e-mail yukon981973@att.net; *V.P./Pres.-Elect* Joanna Klos, Wood Dale Public Lib. Dist., 520 N. Wood Dale Rd., Wood Dale, IL 60191. Tel. 630-766-6762, fax 630-766-5715, e-mail jklos@wooddalelibrary.org; *Secy.* Pamela Cipkowski, Creek Public Lib. Dist., 1405 S. Park Ave., Streamwood, IL 60107. Tel. 630-483-4946, e-mail secretary@palalib.org; *Treas.* Malgorzata Bylinska, Arlington Heights Memorial Lib., 500 N. Dunton Ave., Arlington Heights, IL 60004. Tel. 847-870-4401; *Past Pres.* Elizabeth Marszalik, Oak Park Public Lib., 834 Lake St., Oak Park, IL 60301. Tel. 708-697-6917, e-mail emarszalik@oppl.org; *Dirs.-at-Large* Diane Bartkowiak, Wanda Jacak, Grazyna Krzycka-Langguth, Felice E. Maciejewski, Renata Schneider; *Exec. Dir.* Leonard Kniffel, 2743 N. Greenview Ave., Chicago, IL 60614. Tel. 773-935-3635, e-mail lkniffe@sbcglobal.net.

REFORMA (National Association to Promote Library and Information Services to Latinos and the Spanish-Speaking)

President, Silvia Cisneros
P.O. Box 832, Anaheim, CA 92815
Tel. 209-379-5637, e-mail info@reforma.org
World Wide Web http://www.reforma.org

Object

Promoting library services to the Spanish-speaking for nearly 40 years, REFORMA, an affiliate of the American Library Association, works in a number of areas to advance the development of library collections that include Spanish-language and Latino-oriented materials; the recruitment of more bilingual and bicultural professionals and support staff; the development of library services and programs that meet the needs of the Latino community; the establishment of a national network among individuals who share its goals; the education of the U.S. Latino population in regard to the availability and types of library services; and lobbying efforts to preserve existing library resource centers serving the interest of Latinos.

Membership

Memb. 800+. Membership is open to any person who is supportive of the goals and objectives of REFORMA.

Officers

Pres. Silvia Cisneros, Santa Ana Public Lib., 26 Civic Center Plaza, Santa Ana, CA 92701. Tel. 714-647-5244, e-mail president@reforma. org; *V.P./Pres.-Elect* Beatriz Guevara, Charlotte Mecklenburg Lib./Independence Regional Lib., 6000 Conference Drive, Charlotte, NC 28212. Tel. 704-416-4833, e-mail vice-president@ reforma.org; *Secy./Recorder* Louis Munoz, Brooklyn Public Lib. Tel. 718-230-2417, e-mail secretary@reforma.org; *Treas.* Sarah Dahlen, California State Univ., Monterey Bay. Tel. 831-582-4432, e-mail treasurer@reforma. org; *Memb.-at-Large* Cristina Ramirez, Richmond (Virginia) Public Lib. Tel. 804-646-

8488, e-mail cristina.ramirez@richmondgov. com; *Past Pres.* Isabel Espinal, W. E. B. Du Bois Lib., Univ. of Massachusetts. Tel. 413-545-6817, e-mail past-president@reforma.org.

Committees

Pura Belpré Award. Ana E. Pavon.
Children's and Young Adult Services. Lucía González, Celia Perez.
Education. Lori S. Mestre.
Finance. Isabel Espinal.
Information Technology. Juan Carlos Rodríguez.
International Relations. Ady Huertas.
Legislative. Angélica Fortín, Millie González.
Librarian of the Year Award. Roxana Benavides.
Membership. Juan Carlos Rodriguez, Jose Miguel Ruiz.
Nominations. Maria Kramer.
Organizational Development. Martha A. Parker.
Program. Beatriz Guevara.
National Conferences. Jacqueline Ayala, Loanis Menéndez-Cuesta
Public Relations. David Lopez.
Recruitment and Mentoring. Minerva Alaniz.
Scholarship. Mary A. Donley.
Translations. Nicanor Diaz.

Publication

REFORMA (online newsletter).

Meetings

General membership and board meetings take place at the American Library Association Midwinter Meeting and Annual Conference.

Society for Scholarly Publishing

Executive Director, Ann Mehan Crosse
10200 W. 44 Ave., Suite 304, Wheat Ridge, CO 80033
303-422-3914, fax 720-881-6101, e-mail info@sspnet.org or amcrosse@kellencompany.com
World Wide Web http://www.sspnet.org

Object

To draw together individuals involved in the process of scholarly publishing. This process requires successful interaction of the many functions performed within the scholarly community. The Society for Scholarly Publishing (SSP) provides the leadership for such interaction by creating opportunities for the exchange of information and opinions among scholars, editors, publishers, librarians, printers, booksellers, and all others engaged in scholarly publishing.

Membership

Memb. 1,180+. Open to all with an interest in the scholarly publishing process and dissemination of information. Dues (New Member) $160; (Indiv. Renewal) $175; (Libn.) $85; (Early Career) $80; (Student) $40; (Supporting Organization) $1,750; (Sustaining Organization) $4,100. Year. Jan.–Dec.

Executive Committee

Pres. Howard Ratner, *CHOR, Inc.* E-mail hratner @chorusaccess.org; *Pres.-Elect* Ann Michael, DeltaThink. E-mail ann.michael@deltathink. com; *Past Pres.* Kent Anderson, AAAS/Science. Email kanderso@aaas.org; *Secy./Treas.* Byron Laws, vPrompt eServices. Email byron @vprompt.com.

Directors

Jocelyn Dawson, Emilie Delquie, Marian Hollingsworth, Michelle Norell, Jennifer Pesanelli, Jean Shipman, David Smith, Heather Staines, Greg Suprock.

Meetings

An annual meeting is held in late May/early June. SSP also conducts a Librarian Focus Group (February), the Spring Seminar Series (May/early June), and the Fall Seminar Series (September).

Society of American Archivists

Executive Director, Nancy P. Beaumont
17 N. State St., Suite 1425, Chicago, IL 60602
866-722-7858, 312-606-0722, fax 312-606-0728, e-mail nbeaumont@archivists.org
World Wide Web http://www.archivists.org

Object

Founded in 1936, the Society of American Archivists (SAA) is North America's oldest and largest national archival professional association. Representing more than 6,000 individual and institutional members, SAA promotes the value and diversity of archives and archivists and is the preeminent source of professional resources and the principal communication hub for American archivists.

Membership

Memb. 6,200+. Dues (Indiv.) $50 to $250, graduated according to salary; (Assoc. domestic) $100; (Student or Bridge) $50; (Inst.) $300; (Sustaining Inst.) $550.

Officers (2014–2015)

Pres. Kathleen Roe, Troy Archival Consulting. Tel. 518-961-1550, e-mail kathleen.d.roe@gmail.com; *V.P.* Dennis Meissner, Minnesota Historical Society; *Treas.* Mark Duffy, Archives of the Episcopal Church.

Staff

Exec. Dir. Nancy Beaumont. E-mail nbeaumont@archivists.org; *Admin., Web and Information Systems* Matt Black. E-mail mblack@archivists.org; *Dir., Publishing* Teresa Brinati. E-mail tbrinati@archivists.org; *Educ. Program Coord.* Mia Capodilupo. E-mail mcapodilupo@archivists.org; *Dir., Educ.* Solveig De Sutter. E-mail sdesutter@archivists.org; *Dir., Finance and Admin.* Peter Carlson. E-mail pcarlson@archivists.org; *Mgr., Service Center* Carlos Salgado. E-mail csalgado@archivists.org; *Program Coord.* René Craig. E-mail rcraig@archivists.org; *Editorial and Production Coord.* Anne Hartman. E-mail ahartman@archivists.org; *Educ. Program Coord.* Ania Jaroszek. E-mail ajaroszek@archivists.org; *Service Center Reps.* Lee Gonzalez. E-mail lgonzalez@archivists.org; Jeanette Spears. E-mail jspears@archivists.org.

Publications

American Archivist (2 a year) individual print or online edition, $169; print and online, $199; institutional, $209 print or online, $259 print and online). *Ed.* Gregory Hunter; *Reviews Ed.* Amy Cooper Cary.

Archival Outlook (bi-mo.; memb.). *Eds.* Teresa Brinati, Anne Hartman.

Software and Information Industry Association

1090 Vermont Ave. N.W., Washington, DC 20005-4095
202-289-7442, fax 202-289-7097
World Wide Web http://www.siia.net

The Software and Information Industry Association (SIIA) was formed January 1, 1999, through the merger of the Software Publishers Association (SPA) and the Information Industry Association (IIA).

Membership

Memb. 800+ companies. Open to companies that develop software and digital information content. For details on membership and dues, see the SIIA website, http://www.siia.net.

Staff

Pres. Kenneth Wasch. E-mail kwasch@siia.net; *CFO* Tom Meldrum; *Gen. Counsel and Senior V.P.* Keith Kupferschmid; *Senior V.P.* Tom Davin; *V.P.s* Jennifer Baranowski, Karen Billings, Eileen Bramlet, Rhianna Collier, Eric Fredell, Luis Hernandez, Mark MacCarthy, Michael Marchesano; *Senior Dirs.* Matthew Kinsman, David LeDuc, Mark Schneiderman, Katrina Styles-Hunt.

Board of Directors

Ann Amstutz-Hayes, Scholastic; Richard Atkinson, Adobe Systems; Simon Beale; Mark Bohannon, Red Hat; Cynthia Braddon (chair), McGraw Hill Financial; Antoinette Bush, Dow Jones; Denise Elliott, Kiplinger Washington Editors; Kate Friedrich, Thomson Reuters; Randall Hopkins, NASDAQ OMX; Stephen Laster, McGraw Hill Education; Bernard McKay, Intuit; Jason Mahler, Oracle; Douglas Manoni, SourceMedia; Steve Manzo, Reed Elsevier; Peter Marney, Wiley; Chuck Melley, Pearson; Timothy Sheehy, IBM; Johanna Shelton, Google; Neal Vitale, 1105 Media; Ken Wasch, SIIA.

SPARC

Executive Director, Heather Joseph
21 Dupont Circle, Suite 800, Washington, DC 20036
202-296-2296, fax 202-872-0884, e-mail sparc@arl.org
World Wide Web http://www.sparc.arl.org

SPARC, the Scholarly Publishing and Academic Resources Coalition, is a global organization that promotes expanded sharing of scholarship in the networked digital environment. It is committed to faster and wider sharing of outputs of the research process to increase the impact of research, fuel the advancement of knowledge, and increase the return on research investments.

Developed by the Association of Research Libraries, SPARC has become a catalyst for change. Its pragmatic focus is to stimulate the emergence of new scholarly communication models that expand the dissemination of scholarly research and reduce financial pressures on libraries. Action by SPARC in collaboration with stakeholders—including authors, publishers, and libraries—builds on the unprecedented opportunities created by the networked digital environment to advance the conduct of scholarship.

SPARC's role in stimulating change focuses on

- Educating stakeholders about the problems facing scholarly communication and the opportunities for them to play a role in achieving positive change

- Advocating policy changes that advance scholarly communication and explicitly recognize that dissemination of scholarship is an essential, inseparable component of the research process
- Incubating demonstrations of new publishing and sustainability models that benefit scholarship and academe

SPARC is a visible advocate for changes in scholarly communication that benefit more than the academic community alone. Founded in 1997, it has expanded to represent more than 800 academic and research libraries in North America, the United Kingdom, Europe, and Japan.

Membership

SPARC membership is open to international academic and research institutions, organizations, and consortia that share an interest in creating a more open and diverse marketplace for scholarly communication. Dues are scaled by membership type and budget. For more information, visit SPARC's website at http://www.sparc.arl.org/membership, SPARC Europe at http://www.sparceurope.org, or SPARC Japan at http://www.nii.ac.jp/sparc.

Publications

HowOpenIsIt? Open Access Spectrum (2014 revision) by Greg Tananbaum.
North American Campus-Based Open Access Funds: A Five-Year Progress Report (2014) by Greg Tananbaum.
Article-Level Metrics: A SPARC Primer (2013) by Greg Tananbaum.
The Collective Provision of Open Access Resources (2013) by Raym Crow in collaboration with Knowledge Exchange.
Implementing an Open Data Policy (2013) by Greg Tananbaum.
You've Signed the Boycott, Now What? A SPARC Guide for Campus Action (2012) (http://www.arl.org/sparc/bm~doc/sparc_boycott_next_steps.pdf).
Open-Access Journal Publishing Resource Index (2011) by Raym Crow.
Library Publishing Services: Strategies for Success (2011) by Raym Crow, October

Ivins, Allyson Mower, Daureen Nesdill, Mark Newton, Julie Speer, and Charles Watkinson.
Library Publishing Services: Strategies for Success Report, Version 1.0 (2011) by Raym Crow, October Ivins, Allyson Mower, Daureen Nesdill, Mark Newton, Julie Speer, and Charles Watkinson.
Campus-Based Open-Access Publishing Funds: A Practical Guide to Design and Implementation (2010) by Greg Tananbaum.
Campus-Based Publishing Partnerships: A Guide to Critical Issues (2009) by Raym Crow.
Income Models for Open Access: An Overview of Current Practice (2009) by Raym Crow.
The Right to Research: The Student Guide to Opening Access to Scholarship (2008), part of a campaign to engage students on the issue of research access.
Greater Reach for Research: Expanding Readership Through Digital Repositories (2008), the initiative to educate faculty on the benefits of open repositories and emerging research access policies.
Author Rights (2006), an educational initiative and introduction to the SPARC Author Addendum, a legal form that enables authors of journal articles to modify publishers' copyright transfer agreements and allow authors to keep key rights to their articles.
"Open Access News Blog," daily updates on the worldwide movement for open access to science and scholarship, written by Peter Suber and cosponsored by SPARC.
SPARC Open Access Newsletter, a monthly roundup of developments relating to open access publishing, written by Peter Suber.
SPARC e-news, SPARC's monthly newsletter featuring SPARC activities, an industry roundup, upcoming workshops and events, and articles relating to developments in scholarly communication.
Publishing Cooperatives: An Alternative for Society Publishers (2006) by Raym Crow.
Sponsorships for Nonprofit Scholarly and Scientific Journals: A Guide to Defining and Negotiating Successful Sponsorships (2005) by Raym Crow.

A more-complete list of SPARC publications, including brochures, articles, and guides, is available at http://www.sparc.arl.org/resources.

Special Libraries Association (SLA)

Interim Executive Director, Cindy Shamel
Interim Strategic Director Ulla de Stricker
331 S. Patrick St., Alexandria, VA 22314
703-647-4900, fax 703-647-4901, e-mail resources@sla.org
World Wide Web http://www.sla.org

Mission

The Special Libraries Association promotes and strengthens its members through learning, advocacy, and networking initiatives.

Strategic Vision

SLA is a global association of information and knowledge professionals who are employed in every sector of the economy. Its members thrive where data, information, and knowledge intersect, and its strategic partners support SLA because they believe in the association's mission and the future of its members. SLA's goal is to support information professionals as they contribute, in their varied and evolving roles, to the opportunities and achievements of organizations, communities, and society.

Membership

Memb. 9,000+ in 75 countries. Dues (Organizational) $750; (Indiv.) $114–$200; (Student/Retired/Salary less than $18,000 income per year) $40.

Officers

Pres. Jill Strand. E-mail jillstrand@gmail.com; *Pres.-Elect* Tom Rink. E-mail rink@nsuok.edu; *Treas.* John DiGilio. E-mail jdigilio@reedsmith.com; *Chapter Cabinet Chair* James King. E-mail james.king@nih.gov; *Chapter Cabinet Chair-Elect* Kim Silk. E-mail kimberly.silk@rotman.utoronto.ca; *Div. Cabinet Chair* Juliane Schneider. E-mail juliane_schneider@hms.harvard.edu; *Div. Cabinet Chair-Elect* Ruth Kneale. E-mail rkneale@nso.edu; *Past Pres.* Kate Arnold. E-mail katearnold64@yahoo.co.uk.

Directors

Officers; Kevin Adams, Catherine Lavalee-Welch; Moy McIntosh, Bethan Ruddock.

Publication

Information Outlook (memb., nonmemb. $125/yr.)

Theatre Library Association

c/o New York Public Library for the Performing Arts
40 Lincoln Center Plaza, New York, NY 10023
E-mail theatrelibraryassociation@gmail.com
World Wide Web http://www.tla-online.org

Object

To further the interests of collecting, preserving, and using theater, cinema, and performing arts materials in libraries, museums, and private collections. Founded in 1937.

Membership

Memb. 300. Dues (Indiv.) $25–$50, (Inst.) $75–$95. Year. Jan.–Dec.

Officers

Pres. Nancy Friedland, Columbia Univ.; *V.P.* Angela Weaver, Univ. of Washington; *Exec. Secy.* Laurie Murphy, New York Univ.; *Treas.* Colleen Reilly, Slippery Rock Univ.

Executive Board

Noreen Barnes, Diana Bertolini, Jody Blake, John Calhoun, Leahkim Gannett, Tanisha Jones, Beth Kattelman, Diana King, Doug Reside, Kenneth Schlesinger, Morgen Stevens-Garmon, Joseph Tally, Annemarie van Roessel; *Honorary* Louis A. Rachow; *Legal Counsel* Georgia Harper.

Publications

Broadside (3 a year; memb.). *Ed.* Angela Weaver.
Performing Arts Resources (occasional; memb.).
Membership Directory (annual; memb.). *Ed.* Laurie Murphy.

Committee Chairs

Book Awards. Linda Miles, Tiffany Nixon.
Conference Planning. Angela Weaver.
Membership. Beth Kattelman.
Nominating. Kenneth Schlesinger.
Professional Awards. Francesca Marini.
Publications. Leakhim Gannett.
Strategic Planning. Angela Weaver.
Website Editorial. David Nochimson, Angela Weaver.

Urban Libraries Council

CEO and President, Susan B. Benton
125 S. Wacker Drive, Suite 1050, Chicago, IL 60606
312-676-0999, fax 312-676-0950, e-mail info@urbanlibraries.org
World Wide Web http://www.urbanlibraries.org

Object

Since 1971 the Urban Libraries Council (ULC) has worked to strengthen public libraries as an essential part of urban life. A member organization of North America's leading public library systems, ULC serves as a forum for research widely recognized and used by public and private sector leaders. Its members are thought leaders dedicated to leadership, innovation, and the continuous transformation of libraries to meet community needs.

ULC's work focuses on helping public libraries to identify and utilize skills and strategies that match the challenges of the 21st century.

Membership

Membership is open to public libraries and to corporate partners specializing in library-related materials and services. The organization also offers associate memberships.

Officers (2014–2015)

Chair Karen "Kari" Glover; *V. Chair/Chair-Elect* Matthew K. Poland; *Secy./Treas.* Jan Harder; *Past Chair* Melanie Huggins; *Member-at-Large* Michael Sherrod.

Officers serve one-year terms, members of the executive board two-year terms. New officers are elected and take office at the summer annual meeting of the council.

Executive Board

Ruth Anna, Jill Bourne, Rhea Brown Lawson, Irvin Mayfield, William H. Meadows, Vailey Oehlke, Mary Blankenship Pointer, Gloria Rubio-Cortés, Gary A. Wasdin, Ed Williams, Rashad Young.

State, Provincial, and Regional Library Associations

The associations in this section are organized under three headings: United States, Canada, and Regional. Both the United States and Canada are represented under Regional associations.

United States

Alabama

Memb. 1,200. Publication. *The Alabama Librarian* (q.).

Pres. Wendy Stephens, 204 California St., Huntsville 35801. Tel. 256-520-1878, e-mail wendysteadmanstephens@gmail.com; *Pres.-Elect* Paula Laurita, Athens-Limestone Public Lib., 405 E. South St., Athens 35611. Tel. 256-232-1233, e-mail drago.biblioteche@gmail.com; *Secy.* James Gilbreath, Brown Mackie College Lib., 105 Vulcan Rd., Suite 400, Birmingham 35209. Tel. 205-909-1554, e-mail jgilbreath@brownmackie.edu; *Treas.* John Gantt, Auburn Univ. at Montgomery, P.O. Box 244023, Montgomery 36124-4023. Tel. 334-244-3781, e-mail jgantt2@aum.edu; *Past Pres.* Jeff Simpson, Lib./Wallace Hall, 501 University Ave., Troy 36082. Tel. 334-670-3257, e-mail jsimpson25000@outlook.com; *Assn. Admin.* Angela Moore.

Address correspondence to the association, 6030 Monticello Drive, Montgomery 36117. Tel. 334-414-0113, e-mail allibraryassoc@gmail.com.

World Wide Web http://allanet.org.

Alaska

Memb. 450+. Publication. *Newspoke* (q.) (online at http://akla.org/newspoke).

Pres. Karen Jensen. E-mail kljensen@alaska.edu; *Pres.-Elect* Patty Brown. E-mail director@haineslibrary.org; *Secy.* Maeghan Kearney. E-mail maeghan.kearney@alaska.gov; *Interim Treas.* Robert Barr. E-mail robert_barr@juneau.lib.ak.us; *Conference Coords.* MJ Grande. E-mail mjgrande@juneau.lib.ak.us; Linda Wynne. E-mail lindaleewynne@gmail.com; *Past Pres.* Stacey Glaser. E-mail sglaser@alaska.edu; *Exec. Officer* Patty Linville. E-mail eo@akla.org.

Address correspondence to the secretary, Alaska Lib. Assn., P.O. Box 81084, Fairbanks 99708. E-mail akla@akla.org.

World Wide Web http://www.akla.org.

Arizona

Memb. 1,000. Term of Office. Nov.–Nov. Publication. *AzLA Newsletter* (mo.).

Pres. Dan Stanton, Arizona State Univ. Libs. Tel. 480-965-1798, e-mail danton@asu.edu or president@azla.org; *Pres.-Elect* Amber Mathewson, Pima County Public Lib. Tel. 520-594-5650, e-mail amber.mathewson@pima.gov; *Secy.* Joyce Martin, Labriola National American Indian Data Center, ASU Libs. Tel. 480-965-0298, e-mail joyce.martin@asu.edu; *Treas.* Denise Keller, Pinal County Lib. Dist., Florence 85132. Tel. 520-866-6457, e-mail denise.keller@pinalcountyaz.gov; *Past Pres.* Ann Boles, Wickenburg Public Lib. Tel. 928-533-2276, e-mail ann.boles@gmail.com; *Exec. Secy.* Debbie J. Hanson, Arizona Lib. Assn., 950 E. Baseline Rd., No. 104-1025, Tempe 85283. Tel. 480-609-3999, fax 480-609-3939, e-mail admin@azla.org.

Address correspondence to the executive secretary.

World Wide Web http://www.azla.org.

Arkansas

Memb. 600. Publication. *Arkansas Libraries* (bi-mo.).

Pres. Devona Pendergrass, Mountain Home H.S. Tel. 870-425-2541, e-mail dpendergrass@mtnhome.k12.ar.us; *V.P./Pres.-Elect* Jud Copeland, Univ. of Central Arkansas, Conway. Tel. 501-499-5414, e-mail jcopeland@uca.edu; *Secy./Treas.* Jamie Melson, Central Arkansas Lib. System, Little Rock. Tel. 501-918-3074, e-mail jamiem@cals.lib.ar.us; *Past Pres.* Trish Miller, Remington College, Little Rock. Tel. 501-312-0007, e-mail trish.miller@remington college.edu; *Exec. Admin.* Lynda Hampel, Arkansas Lib. Assn., P.O. Box 958, Benton 72018-0958. Tel. 501-860-7585, fax 501-778-4014, e-mail arlib2@sbcglobal.net.

Address correspondence to the executive administrator.

World Wide Web http://www.arlib.org.

California

Memb. 2,500. Publication. *CLA Insider* (online).

Pres. Robert Karatsu, Rancho Cucamonga Public Lib. E-mail robert.karatsu@cityofrc.us; *V.P./Pres.-Elect* Misty Jones, San Diego Public Lib. System. E-mai lmnjones@sandiego.gov; *Secy.* Hillary Theyer, Torrance Public Lib. E-mail librarylady16@yahoo.com; *Treas.* Beth Wrenn-Estes, San José State Univ. E-mail bwestes@mac.com; *Past Pres.* Deborah Doyle, CALTAC. E-mail zorrah@gmail.com; *Interim Exec. Dir.* Natalie Cole. Tel. 650-376-0886, e-mail execdir@cla-net.org or ncole@cla-net.org

Address correspondence to the executive director, California Lib. Assn., 2471 Flores St., San Mateo 94403. Tel. 650-376-0886, fax 650-539-2341.

World Wide Web http://www.cla-net.org.

Colorado

Pres. Kari May, Elbert County Lib. Dist. E-mail director@elbertcountylibrary.org; *V.P./Pres.-Elect* Joanna Primus, Community College of Aurora. E-mail joanna.primus@ccaurora.edu; *Secy.* Dinah Kress, Prairie Hills Elementary School. E-mail dinah.kress@asd20.org; *Treas.* Mike Varnet, Pikes Peak Lib. Dist. E-mail mvarnet@ppld.org; *Past Pres.* Stephen Sweeney. E-mail stephen.sweeney@archden.org; *Business Mgr.* Jesse Haynes; *Business Admin.* Amanda Rewerts.

Address correspondence to the president, Colorado Assn. of Libs., 12011 Tejon St., Suite 700, Westminster 80234. Tel. 303-463-6400, fax 303-458-0002.

World Wide Web http://www.cal-webs.org.

Connecticut

Memb. 1,000+. Term of Office. July–June. Publication. *CLA Today* (online). E-mail editor@ctlibrarians.org.

Pres. Dawn La Valle, Connecticut State Lib., 231 Capitol Ave., Hartford 06106. Tel. 860-757-6665, e-mail dawn.lavalle@ct.gov; *V.P./Pres.-Elect* Beth A Crowley, Scranton Memorial Lib., 801 Boston Post Rd., Madison 06443. Tel. 203 245-7365, e-mail crowleyb@madisonct.org; *Recording Secy.* Michele Martin, Greenwich Lib., 101 W. Putnam Ave., Greenwich 06830. Tel. 203-625-6533, e-mail mmartin@greenwichlibrary.org; *Treas.* Nicole Greco, Milford Public Lib., 57 New Haven Ave., Milford 06460. Tel. 203-783-3307, e-mail ngreco@ci.milford.ct.us; *Past Pres.* Richard Conroy, Essex Lib. Assn., 33 West Ave., Essex 06426. Tel. 860-767-1560, e-mail rconroy @essexlib.org.

Address correspondence to Connecticut Lib. Assn., 234 Court St., Middletown 06457. Tel. 860-346-2444, fax 860-344-9199, e-mail cla@ctlibrarians.org.

World Wide Web http://www.ctlibrary association.org.

Delaware

Memb. 200+. Publication. *DLA Bulletin* (online only).

Pres. Beth Borene, Bear Public Lib., 101 Governors Place, Bear 19701. Tel. 302-838-3300, e-mail eborene@nccde.org; *V.P.* Laurel Ferris, John Eugene Derrickson Memorial Lib., Delaware Technical Community College, 333 N. Shipley St., Wilmington 19801. Tel. 302-573-5431, e-mail lferris@dtcc.edu; *Secy.* Janice Haney, Appoquinimink H.S., 1080 Bunker Hill Rd., Middletown 19709. E-mail janice.haney@appo.k12.de.us; *Treas.* Ed Goyda, Lewes Public Lib., 111 Adams Ave., Lewes 19958. E-mail ed.goyda@lib.de.us; *Past Pres.* Christine Payne, Appoquinimink H.S., 1080 Bunker Hill Rd., Middletown 19709. Tel. 302-449-3840, e-mail christine.payne@appo.k12.de.us; *Exec. Dir.* Cathay Keough, Delaware Div. of Libs., 121 Martin Luther King, Jr. Blvd. N., Dover 19901. Tel. 302-983-1430, e-mail cathay.keough@lib.de.us.

World Wide Web http://www2.lib.udel.edu/dla.

District of Columbia

Memb. 300+. Term of Office. July–June. Publication. *Capital Librarian* (s. ann.).

Pres. Christina Bailey. E-mail dclapresident @gmail.com; *V.P./Pres.-Elect* Julius C. Jefferson, Jr. E-mail dclavicepresident@gmail.com; *Secy.* Victor Benitez. E-mail dclasecretary@gmail.com; *Treas.* TaChalla Ferris. E-mail dclatreasurer@gmail.com; *Past Pres.* Amanda J. Wilson.

Address correspondence to the association, Box 14177, Benjamin Franklin Sta., Washington 20044.

World Wide Web http://www.dcla.org.

Florida

Memb. (Indiv.) 1,000+. Publication. *Florida Libraries* (s. ann.).

Pres. (2013–2016) Linda McCarthy, Florida Virtual Campus. Tel. 850-922-6044, e-mail lmccarthy@flvc.org; *V.P./Pres.-Elect (2014–2017)* Gene Coppola, Palm Harbor Lib. Tel. 727-784-3332 ext. 3001, e-mail gene@phlib. org; *Secy. (2013–2015)* Anne Haywood, Bruton Memorial Lib. Tel. 813-757-9215, e-mail ahaywood@plantcitygov.com; *Treas. (2014–2016)* Sarah Hammill, Florida International Univ. Tel. 305-348-3009, e-mail hammills@fiu.edu; *Past Pres.* Gladys Roberts, Polk County Lib. Cooperative. Tel. 863-519-7958, e-mail gladys.roberts@mypclc.info; *Exec. Dir.* Martina Brawer, Florida Lib. Assn., 541 E. Tennessee St., Suite 103, Tallahassee 32308. Tel. 850-270-9205, fax 850-270-9405, e-mail martina. brawer@comcast.net.

Address correspondence to the executive director.

World Wide Web http://www.flalib.org.

Georgia

Memb. 800+. Publication. *Georgia Library Quarterly. Ed.* Virginia Feher, Univ. of North Georgia. Tel. 706-310-6305, e-mail virginia. feher@ung.edu.

Pres. Lace Keaton, Newton County Lib. System; *1st V.P./Pres.-Elect* Cathy Jeffrey, Clayton State Univ. Tel. 678-466-4336, e-mail cathy jeffrey@clayton.edu; *2nd V.P./Membership Chair* Karen Manning, Georgia Tech Lib. and Info. Center. Tel. 404-385-8353, e-mail km17@mail.gatech.edu; *Secy.* Ariel Turner, Horace W. Sturgis Lib., Kennesaw State Univ. Tel. 470-578-6273, e-mail aturne93@kennesaw.

edu; *Treas.* Ashley Dupuy, Kennesaw State Univ.; *Past Pres.* Susan Morris, Univ. of Georgia. Tel. 706-542-0642, e-mail smorris@uga. edu.

Address correspondence to the president, Georgia Lib. Assn., P.O. Box 793, Rex 30273-0793.

World Wide Web http://gla.georgialibraries. org.

Hawaii

Memb. 250. Publication. HLA Blog, "Hawaii Library Association" (http://hawaiilibraryassociation.blogspot.com).

Pres. Tim Arnold, Meader Lib., Hawaii Pacific Univ. Tel. 808-544-9330, e-mail tarnold@hpu.edu; *V.P./Pres.-Elect* Kimball Boone, Brigham Young Univ.–Hawaii; *Secy.* Susan Hammer, Mid-Pacific Institute; *Treas.* Jude Y. Yang, University of Hawaii at Manoa; *Past Pres.* Christina Abelardo, Sgt. Yano Lib., Schofield Barracks. E-mail christinathelibrarian@gmail.com.

Address correspondence to the association at P.O. Box 4441, Honolulu 96812-4441 or by e-mail at hawaii.library.association@gmail. com.

World Wide Web http://hla.chaminade.edu.

Idaho

Memb. 420. Term of Office. Oct.–Oct.

Pres. Becky Proctor, West Junior H.S., 8371 W. Salt Creek Court, Boise 83709. Tel. 208-854-6456, e-mail becky.proctor@boiseschools. org; *V.P./ Pres.-Elect* Kristi Haman, Ada Community Lib., Boise 83709. Tel. 208-362-0181 ext.124, e-mail khaman@adalib.org; *Secy.* Kathleen McVey, Meridian Lib. Dist.,1326 W. Cherry Lane, Meridian 83642. Tel. 208-888-4451, e-mail kathleen@mld.org; *Treas.* Danielle Persinger, College of Western Idaho, P.O. Box 3010, Nampa 83653. Tel. 208-562-2154, e-mail daniellepersinger@cwidaho.cc; *Past Pres.* Rami Attebury, Univ. of Idaho Lib., P.O. Box 442350, Moscow 88344-2350. Tel. 208-885-2503, e-mail rattebur@uidaho.edu.

Address correspondence to the association, P.O. Box 8533, Moscow 83844.

World Wide Web http://www.idaholibraries. org.

Illinois

Memb. 3,500. Publication. *ILA Reporter* (bi-mo.).

Pres. Jeannie Dilger, La Grange Public Lib., 10 W. Cossitt Ave., La Grange 60525. Tel. 708-215-3273, fax 708-352-1620, e-mail dilgerj@ lagrangelibrary.org; *V.P./Pres.-Elect* Betsy Adamowski, Wheaton Public Lib., 225 N. Cross St. Wheaton 60187-5376. Tel. 630-668-1374, fax 630-668-1465, e-mail betsy@wheatonlibrary.org; *Treas.* Leora Siegel, Lenhardt Lib., Chicago Botanic Garden, 1000 Lake Cook Rd., Glencoe 60022. Tel. 847-835-8202, fax 847-835-6885, e-mail lsiegel@chicagobotanic. org; *Past Pres.* Su Erickson, Robert Morris Univ., 905 Meridan Lake Drive, Aurora 60504. Tel. 630-375-8209, fax 630-375-8193, e-mail serickson@robertmorris.edu; *Exec. Dir.* Robert P. Doyle, Illinois Lib. Assn., 33 W. Grand Ave., Suite 401, Chicago 60654-6799. Tel. 312-644-1896, fax 312-644-1899, e-mail doyle@ila.org.

Address correspondence to the executive director.

World Wide Web http://www.ila.org.

Indiana

Indiana Lib. Federation. Memb. 2,000+. Publications. *Indiana Libraries* (s. ann.). *Ed.* Kristi Palmer, IUPUI Univ. Lib., 755 W. Michigan, Indianapolis 46202. Tel. 317-274-8230, e-mail klpalmer@iupui.edu; *Focus on Indiana Libraries* (11 a year, memb.). *Ed.* Diane J. Bever, Kokomo Lib., Indiana Univ., 2300 S. Washington St., P.O. Box 9003, Kokomo 46904-9003. Tel. 765-455-9345, fax 765-455-9276, e-mail dbever@iuk.edu.

Pres. Beverly Gard, Hancock County Public Lib., Greenfield. Tel. 317-462-5141, e-mail bevjgard@gmail.com; *Pres.-Elect* Robyn Young, Avon Community School Corp., 7575 E. CR 150 S., Avon 46123. Tel. 317-544-5031, e-mail rryoung@avon-schools.org; *Secy.* Kathy Burnette, Discovery Middle School, Granger. Tel. 574-674-6010, e-mail teach46530@gmail. com; *Treas.* Amy Harshbarger, Logan Lib., Rose-Hulman Institute of Technology, Terre Haute. E-mail harshbarg@rose-hulman.edu; *Past Pres.* Marcia Learned Au, Evansville Vanderburgh Public Lib., Evansville. E-mail mau@evpl.org; *Exec. Dir.* Susan Akers. Tel. 317-257-2040 ext. 101, e-mail sakers@ilfonline.org.

Address correspondence to Indiana Lib. Federation, 941 E. 86 St., Suite 260, Indianapolis 46240. Tel. 317-257-2040, fax 317-257-1389.

World Wide Web http://www.ilfonline.org.

Iowa

Memb. 1,500. Publication. *Catalyst* (bi-mo.).

Pres. Sarah Willeford; *V.P./Pres.-Elect* Duncan Stewart; *Secy.* Marilyn Murphy; *Treas.* Nancy Trask; *Past Pres.* Mary Heinzman.

Address correspondence to the association, 6919 Vista Drive, West Des Moines 50266. Tel. 515-282-8192.

World Wide Web http://www.iowalibraryassociation.org.

Kansas

Kansas Lib. Assn. Memb. 1,500. Term of Office. July–June. Publication. *KLA Connects* (q.).

Pres. Terri Summey, Emporia State Univ. Libs. and Archives, Campus Box 4051, Emporia 66801. Tel. 620-341-5058, e-mail tsummey @emporia.edu; *V.P.* Kelly Fann, Lawrence Public Lib., 707 Vermont St., Lawrence 66044. Tel. 785-843-3833, e-mail kfann@lawrence. lib.ks.us; *2nd V.P.* Kim Gile, Johnson County Lib., 9875 W. 87 St., Overland Park 66212. Tel. 913-826-4600 ext. 64479, e-mail gilek@ jocolibrary.org; *Secy.* Julie Hildebrand, Independence Public Lib., 220 E. Maple St., Independence 67301. Tel. 620-331-3030, e-mail julie.hildebrand@iplks.org; *Treas.* Gary Landeck, Atchison Public Lib., 401 Kansas Ave., Atchison 66002. Tel. 913-367-1902 ext. 208, e-mail glandeck@atchisonlibrary.org; *Past Pres.* Cathy Reeves, Dodge City Public Lib., 1001 N. 2 Ave., Dodge City 67801. Tel. 620-225-0248, e-mail cathyr@dcpl.info; *Exec. Secy.* Cary Pressley.

Address correspondence to the president, Kansas Lib. Assn., 1020 S.W. Washburn, Topeka 66604. Tel. 785-580-4518, fax 785-580-4595, e-mail kansaslibraryassociation@yahoo. com.

World Wide Web http://www.kslibassoc.org.

Kentucky

Memb. 1,600. Publication. *Kentucky Libraries* (q.).

Pres. Laura Whayne, Kentucky Transportation Center, 176 Raymond Bldg., Lexington 40506. Tel. 859-257-2155, e-mail laura. whayne@uky.edu; *Pres.-Elect* Julie Howe, Somerset Community College, Laurel North Campus, Bldg. 2, Room 125, 100 University Drive, Somerset 40741. Tel. 606-878-4724, e-mail julie.howe@kctcs.edu; *Secy.* Dave Schroeder, Kenton County Public Lib., Admin. Center, 2171 Chamber Center Drive, Ft. Mitchell 41017. Tel. 859-578-3600, e-mail dave. schroeder@kentonlibrary.org; *Past Pres.* Brenda Metzger, McCracken County H.S., 6530 New Hwy. 60 W., Paducah 42001. Tel. 270-538-4356, e-mail brenda.metzger@mccracken. kyschools.us; *Exec. Dir.* Tom Underwood, 1501 Twilight Trail, Frankfort 40601. Tel. 502-223-5322, fax 502-223-4937, e-mail info@ kylibasn.org.

Address correspondence to the executive director.

World Wide Web http://www.klaonline.org

Louisiana

Memb. 1,000+. Term of Office. July–June. Publication. *Louisiana Libraries* (q.). *Ed.* Celise Reech-Harper. Tel. 337-463-6217 ext. 22, e-mail celise@beau.org.

Pres. Robert Bremer. Tel. 985-448-4657, e-mail robert.bremer@nicholls.edu; *1st V.P./ Pres.-Elect* Paula Clemmons. Tel. 337-433-5246, e-mail pclemmons@episcopaldayschool. org; *2nd V.P.* Kathlyn Bowersox. Tel. 225-771-2666, e-mail kathlyn_bowersox@subr. edu; *Secy.* Holly Priestley. Tel. 318-327-1490, e-mail hpriestley@oplib.org; *Past Pres.* Vivian McCain. Tel. 318-251-5030, e-mail vmccain@ mylpl.org.

Address correspondence to Louisiana Lib. Assn., 8550 United Plaza Blvd., Suite 1001, Baton Rouge 70809. Tel. 225-922-4642, 877-550-7890, fax 225-408-4422, e-mail office@ llaonline.org.

World Wide Web http://www.llaonline.org.

Maine

Maine Lib. Assn. Memb. 950. Publication. *MLA-to-Z* (q., online).

Pres. Nissa Flanagan, Merrill Memorial Lib., 215 Main St., Yarmouth 04096. Tel. 207-846-4763, e-mail nflanagan@maine.rr.com;

V.P./Pres.-Elect Bryce Cundick, Mantor Lib., Univ. of Maine at Farmington, 116 South St., Farmington 04938-1998. Tel. 207-240-7565, e-mail bryce.cundick@maine.edu; *Secy.* Lisa Shaw. E-mail librarydirector@cariboumaine. org; *Treas.* Michael Dignan, Paris Public Lib., 37 Market Sq., Paris 04291-1509. Tel. 207-743-6994, e-mail mdignan@paris.lib. me.us; *Past Pres.* Andi Jackson-Darling, Falmouth Memorial Lib., 5 Lunt Rd., Falmouth 04105. Tel. 207-781-2351, e-mail ajdarling@ falmouth.lib.me.us; *Business Mgr.* Edna Comstock. E-mail mla1@gwi.net.

Address correspondence to the association, P.O. Box 634, Augusta 04332-0634. Tel. 207-441-1410.

World Wide Web http://mainelibraries.org.

Maryland

Maryland Lib. Assn. Memb. 1,000+. Term of Office. July–July. Publication. *The Crab* (q., online). *Ed.* Annette Haldeman. E-mail annette. haldeman@mlis.state.md.us.

Pres. John Venditta; *1st V.P./Pres.-Elect* Mary Hastler; *Secy.* Katy Sullivan; *Treas.* Daria Parry; *Past Pres.* Carrie Willson-Plymire; *Exec. Dir.* Margaret Carty. E-mail mcarty@carr.org.

Address correspondence to the association, 1401 Hollins St., Baltimore 21223. Tel. 410-947-5090, fax 410-947-5089, e-mail mla@ mdlib.org.

World Wide Web http://www.mdlib.org.

Massachusetts

Massachusetts Lib. Assn. Memb. (Indiv.) 1,000; (Inst.) 100. Publication. *Bay State Libraries* (q.).

Pres. Maureen Ambrosino, Westborough Public Lib., 55 W. Main St., Westborough 01581. Tel. 508-871-5280, e-mail mambrosino@town.westborough.ma.us; *V.P.* Eric Poulin, Nahman-Watson Lib., Greenfield Community College, 1 College Drive, Greenfield 01301. Tel. 413-775-1834, e-mail pouline@ gcc.mass.edu; *Secy.* Debby Conrad, SAILS Lib. Network, 10 Riverside Drive, Suite 102, Lakeville 02347. Tel. 508-946-8600, e-mail dconrad@sailsinc.org; *Treas.* Ryan Livergood, Robbins Lib., 700 Massachusetts Ave., Arlington 02476. Tel. 781-316-3200, e-mail rlivergood@minlib.net; *Past Pres.* Elizabeth

Marcus, Brockton Public Lib., 304 Main St., Brockton 02301. Tel. 508-580-7890 ext. 101, e-mail emarcus@cobma.us; *Exec. Mgr.* Sarah Hagan, Massachusetts Lib. Assn., P.O. Box 240813, Boston 01730. Tel. 781-698-7764, e-mail manager@masslib.org.

Address correspondence to the executive manager.

World Wide Web http://www.masslib.org.

Michigan

Memb. 1,200+. Publication. *MLA Weekly* (e-newsletter).

Pres. Asante Cain, Grand Rapids Public Lib.; *Pres.-Elect* Leslie Warren, Olson Lib., Northern Michigan Univ.; *Treas.* Richard Schneider, Muskegon Dist. Lib.; *Past Pres.* Cathy Wolford, DALNET.

Address correspondence to Gail Madziar, Exec. Dir., Michigan Lib. Assn., 3410 Belle Chase Way, Suite 100, Lansing 48911. Tel. 517-394-2774 ext. 224, e-mail madziarg@mlcnet.org.

World Wide Web http://www.mla.lib.mi.us.

Minnesota

Memb. 1,100. Term of Office. (*Pres., Pres.-Elect*) Jan.–Dec.

Pres. Maggie Snow, Anoka County Lib. E-mail maggie.snow@co.anoka.mn.us; *Pres.-Elect* Margaret Stone, Washington County Lib. E-mail margaret.stone@co.washington.mn.us; *Secy.* Laura Morlcok, St. Catherine Univ. MLIS Program. E-mail llmorlock@stkate.edu; *Treas.* Jennifer Hootman, MINITEX. E-mail hootm001@umn.edu; *Past Pres.* Michele Mc-Graw, Hennepin County Lib. E-mail mmcgraw@hclib.org.

Address correspondence to the association, 400 S. 4 St., Suite 401-223, Minneapolis 55415. Tel. 877-867-0982, 612-294-6549, e-mail mla@management-hq.com.

World Wide Web http://www.mnlibrary association.org.

Mississippi

Memb. 625. Term of Office. Jan.–Dec. Publication. *Mississippi Libraries* (q.).

Pres. Patsy C. Brewer, Waynesboro-Wayne County Lib. Tel. 601-735-2268, e-mail wlib@wwcls.lib.ms.us; *V.P.* Molly McManus, U.S. Army Engineer Research and Development Center, Vicksburg. Tel. 601-634-4122, e-mail molly.s.mcmanus@usace.army.mil; *Secy.* Selina Swink, Lake Public Lib. Tel. 601-775-3560, e-mail sswink@cmrls.lib.ms.us; *Treas.* Blair Booker, Holmes Community College. Tel. 601-605-3303, e-mail bbooker@holmescc.edu; *Past Pres.* Amanda Clay Powers, MSU-Mitchell Memorial Lib. Tel. 662-325-7677, e-mail apowers@library.msstate.edu; *MLA Admin.* Barbara J. Price, P.O. Box 13687, Jackson 39236-3687. Tel. 601-981-4586, e-mail info@misslib.org.

Address correspondence to the administrator.

World Wide Web http://www.misslib.org.

Missouri

Memb. 800+. Term of Office. Jan.–Dec. Publication. *MO INFO* (bi-mo.).

Pres. Christina Prucha, Logan Univ. E-mail christina.prucha@logan.edu; *Pres.-Elect* Sharla Lair, MOBIUS Consortium, Columbia; *Past Pres.* Gerald S. Brooks, St. Louis Public Lib. E-mail gbrooks@slpl.org.

Address correspondence to the president.

World Wide Web http://www.molib.org.

Montana

Memb. 600. Term of Office. July–June. Publication. *Focus* (bi-mo.).

Pres. Sheila Bonnand, Renne Lib., MSU, P.O. Box 173320, Bozeman 59717. Tel. 406-994-4130, e-mail sbonnand@montana.edu; *V.P./Pres.-Elect* Dawn Kingstad, Glendive Public Lib., P.O. Box 576, Glendive 59330. Tel. 406-989-1561, e-mail booksrus@midrivers.com; *Secy./Treas.* Lisa Mecklenberg Jackson, State Law Lib. of Montana, 215 N. Sanders, P.O. Box 203004, Helena 59620. Tel. 406-444-3660, e-mail lisameckjack@gmail.com; *Past Pres.* Beth Boyson, Bozeman Public Lib., 626 Main St., Bozeman 59715. Tel. 406-582-2402, fax 406-582-2424, e-mail bboyson@bozeman.net; *Admin. Dir.* Debbi Kramer, P.O. Box 1352, Three Forks 59752. Tel. 406-579-3121, fax 406-285-3091, e-mail debkmla@hotmail.com.

Address correspondence to the administrative director.

World Wide Web http://www.mtlib.org.

Nebraska

Term of Office. Jan.–Dec.

Pres. Gayle Roberts, Blair Public Lib. E-mail groberts@ci.blair.ne.us; *V.P./Pres.-Elect* Julee Hector, Lincoln City Libs. E-mail j.hector@lincolnlibraries.org; *Secy.* Terry Wingate, Omaha Public Libs. E-mail twingate @omahalibrary.org; *Treas.* Megan Klein-Hewitt, Omaha Public Libs. E-mail nlatreasurer @gmail.com; *Past Pres.* Robin Clark, Sump Memorial Lib. E-mail robin.r.clark@gmail. com; *Exec. Dir.* Michael Straatmann.

Address correspondence to the executive director, P.O. Box 21756, Lincoln 68542-1756. Tel. 402-216-0727, e-mail nlaexecutivedirector @gmail.com.

World Wide Web http://nebraskalibraries. site-ym.com.

Nevada

Memb. 450. Term of Office. Jan.–Dec. Publication. *Nevada Libraries* (q.).

Pres. Carol Lloyd, Churchill County Lib. E-mail celloyd@clan.lib.nv.us; *Pres.-Elect* Scott Clonan, Las Vegas-Clark County Lib. Dist. E-mail clonans@lvccld.org; *Treas.* Tammy Westergard, Carson City Lib. E-mail twestergard @carson.org; *Past Pres.* Ann-Marie White, Las Vegas-Clark County Lib. System. E-mail whitea@lvccld.org; *Exec. Secy.* Kristy Isla. E-mail ardainia@yahoo.com.

Address correspondence to the executive secretary.

World Wide Web http://www.nevada libraries.org.

New Hampshire

Memb. 700. Publication. *NHLA News* (q.).

Pres. Amy Lapointe, Amherst Town Lib., 14 Main St., Amherst 03031. Tel. 603-673-2288, e-mail alapointe@amherstlibrary.org; *V.P./Pres.-Elect* Jenn Hosking, Nashua Public Lib., 2 Court St., Nashua 03060. Tel. 603-589-4621, e-mail jenn.hosking@nashualibrary. org; *Secy.* Mary White, Howe Lib., 13 South St., Hanover 03755. Tel. 603-640-3267, e-mail mary.h.white@thehowe.org; *Treas.* Cara Barlow, Derry Public Lib., 64 E. Broadway, Derry 03038. Tel. 603-432-6128, e-mail carab@ derrypl.org; *Past Pres.* Linda Taggart, Nashua

Public Lib., 2 Court St., Nashua 03060. Tel. 603-589-4600, e-mail linda.taggart@nashua library.org.

Address correspondence to the association, c/o New Hampshire State Lib., Attn: Michael York, State Libn., 20 Park St., Concord 03301-6314.

World Wide Web http://nhlibrarians.org.

New Jersey

Memb. 1,800. Term of Office. July–June. Publication. *New Jersey Libraries NEWSletter* (q.).

Pres. Terrie McColl, New Milford Public Lib., 200 Dahlia Ave., New Milford 07646. Tel. 201-262-1221, e-mail mccoll@bccls.org; *V.P.* James Keehbler, Piscataway Public Lib., 500 Hoes Lane, Piscataway 08854. Tel. 732-463-1633, fax 908-463-1007, e-mail jkeehbler@ piscatawaylibrary.org; *2nd V.P.* Keith McCoy, Somerset County Lib. System, Bridgewater Lib., 1 Vogt Drive, Bridgewater 08807. Tel. 908-526-4016 ext.128, e-mail kmccoy@sclibnj. org; *Secy.* Leslie Kahn, Newark Public Lib., 5 Washington St., Newark 07102. Tel. 973-733-7820, fax 973-733-5648, e-mail lkahn@npl. org; *Treas.* Chris Carbone, South Brunswick Public Lib., 110 Kingston Lane, Monmouth Junction 08852. Tel. 732-329-4000 ext. 7287, fax 732-329-0573, e-mail ccarbone@sbpl.info; *Past Pres.* Eileen Palmer, Libs. of Middlesex Automation Consortium, 1030 St. Georges Ave., Suite 203, Avenel 00701. Tel. 732-750-2525, e-mail empalmer@lmxac.org; *Exec. Dir.* Patricia Tumulty, NJLA, P.O. Box 1534, Trenton 08607. Tel. 609-394-8032, fax 609-394-8164, e-mail ptumulty@njla.org.

Address correspondence to the executive director.

World Wide Web http://www.njla.org.

New Mexico

Memb. 550. Term of Office. Apr.–Apr. Publication. *NMLA Bulletin* (online, 6 a year).

Pres. Janice Kowemy. E-mail lagunapueblo-nsn.gov; *V.P./Pres.-Elect* Sharon Jenkins. E-mail djenkins@nmsu.edu; *Secy.* Melanie Chavez. E-mail melchavez10@gmail.com; *Treas.* Paulita Aguilar. E-mail paulita@unm. edu; *Past Pres.* Mary Ellen Pellington. E-mail mepellington@ci.gallup.nm.us.

Address correspondence to the association, Box 26074, Albuquerque 87125. Tel. 505-400-7309, e-mail contact@nmla.org.
World Wide Web http://nmla.org.

New York

Memb. 4,000. Term of Office. Nov.–Nov. Publication. *NYLA e-Bulletin* (q.). *Pres.* Geoffrey S. Kirkpatrick. Tel. 518-439-9314, e-mail geoff@bethpl.org; *Pres.-Elect* Debby Emerson. Tel. 315-446-5446, e-mail demerson@clrc.org; *Treas.* Timothy G. Burke. Tel. 518-437-9882, e-mail tim.burke@uhls.lib.ny.us; *Past Pres.* Sara Kelly Johns. Tel. 518-891-2339, e-mail skjohns@gmail.com.

Address correspondence to Jeremy Johannesen, executive director, New York Lib. Assn., 6021 State Farm Rd., Guilderland 12084. Tel. 800-252-6952 ext. 101 or 518-432-6952, fax 518-427-1697, e-mail director@nyla.org.
World Wide Web http://www.nyla.org.

North Carolina

Memb. 1,100. Term of Office. Oct.–Oct. Publications. *North Carolina Library Association E-news* (online, bi-mo.). *Ed.* Marilyn Schuster, Local Documents/Special Collections, Univ. of North Carolina–Charlotte. E-mail mbschust@email.uncc.edu; *North Carolina Libraries* (online, 2 a year). *Ed.* Ralph Scott, Joyner Lib., East Carolina Univ., Greenville 27858. Tel. 252-328-0265, e-mail scottr@ecu.edu.

Pres. Dale Cousins, Wake County Public Libs., 404 Perry St., Raleigh 27605. Tel. 919-856-6726, e-mail dale.cousins@wakegov.com; *V.P./Pres.-Elect* Rodney Lippard, Rowan-Cabarrus Community College, P.O. Box 1595, Salisbury 28145. Tel. 704-216-3686, e-mail rodney.lippard@rccc.edu; *Secy.* To be announced; *Treas.* M. J. Wilkerson, Alamance County Public Libs., 342 S. Spring St., Burlington 27215. Tel. 336-513-4753, e-mail mgoodrum@alamancelibraries.org; *Past Pres.* Wanda Brown, Z. Smith Reynolds Lib., Wake Forest Univ., Box 7777 Reynolda Sta., Winston-Salem 27109. Tel. 336-758-5094, e-mail brownw@wfu.edu; *Admin. Asst.* Kim Parrott, North Carolina Lib. Assn., 1841 Capital Blvd., Raleigh 27604. Tel. 919-839-6252, fax 919-839-6253, e-mail nclaonline@gmail.com.

Address correspondence to the administrative assistant.
World Wide Web http://www.nclaonline.org.

North Dakota

Memb. (Indiv.) 300+. Term of Office. Sept.–Sept. Publication. *The Good Stuff* (q.). *Ed.* Marlene Anderson, Bismarck State College Lib., Box 5587, Bismarck 58506-5587. Tel. 701-224-5578, fax 701-224-5551, e-mail marlene.anderson@bismarckstate.edu.

Pres. Greta Guck, Leach Public Lib., 417 Second Ave. N, Wahpeton 58075-4416. Tel. 701-642-5732, e-mail greta.leachplib@midconetwork.com; *Pres.-Elect* Stephen Banister, Minot State Univ. Tel. 701-858-3855, fax 701-858-3581, e-mail stephen.banister@minotstateu.edu; *Secy.* Mary Lorenz, Grand Forks Public Lib. Tel. 701-772-8116, fax 701-772-1379, e-mail mary.lorenz@gflibrary.com; *Treas.* Michael Safratowich, UND Lib. of the Health Sciences. Tel. 701-777-2602, fax 701-777-4790, e-mail michael.safratowich@med.und.edu; *Past Pres.* Victor Lieberman, Chester Fritz Lib., Univ. of North Dakota. Tel. 701-777-4639, fax 701-777-3319, e-mail victor.lieberman@library.und.edu.

Address correspondence to the president.
World Wide Web http://www.ndla.info.

Ohio

Memb. 2,700+. Term of Office. Jan.–Dec. Publication. *Access* (memb., weekly, online). *Pres.* Jeff Winkle, Findlay Hancock County Public Lib. Tel. 419-422-1712, e-mail winkleje@findlaylibrary.org; *V.P./Pres.-Elect* Alan Radnor, Bexley Public Lib. Tel. 614-464-6326; *Secy./Treas.* Deborah Dubois, Mansfield-Richland County Public Lib. Tel. 419-522-3001, e-mail ddubois@mrcpl.org; *Past Pres.* Meg Delaney, Toledo-Lucas County Public Lib. Tel. 419-259-5333, e-mail meg.delaney@toledolibrary.org; *Exec. Dir.* Douglas S. Evans. E-mail devans@olc.org.

Address correspondence to the executive director, OLC, 1105 Schrock Rd., Suite 440, Columbus 43229-1174. Tel. 614-410-8092, fax 614-410-8098, e-mail olc@olc.org.
World Wide Web http://www.olc.org.

Oklahoma

Memb. (Indiv.) 1,000; (Inst.) 60. Term of Office. July–June. Publication. *Oklahoma Librarian* (bi-mo.).
Pres. Shari Clifton; *V.P./Pres.-Elect* Calypso Gilstrap; *Secy.* Chris Kennedy; *Treas.* Tim Miller; *Past Pres.* Lynda Reynolds; *Exec. Dir.* Kay Boies, 300 Hardy Drive, P.O. Box 6550, Edmond 73083. Tel. 405-525-5100, fax 405-525-5103, e-mail exec_director@oklibs.org.
Address correspondence to the executive director.
World Wide Web http://www.oklibs.org.

Oregon

Memb. (Indiv.) 1,000+. Publications. *OLA Hotline* (bi-w.), *OLA Quarterly.*
Pres. Candice Watkins, Clatsop Community College Lib. E-mail cwatkins@clatsopcc.edu; *V.P./Pres.-Elect* Jane Corry, Multnomah County Lib. E-mail janec@multcolib.org; *Secy.* Stephanie Debner, Mt. Hood Community College Lib. E-mail stephanie.debner@mhcc.edu; *Treas.* Valery King, Oregon State Univ. Lib. E-mail valery.king@oregonstate.edu; *Past Pres.* Penny Hummel, Canby Public Lib. E-mail phummel.ola@gmail.com; *Assn. Mgr.* Shirley Roberts. E-mail sroberts.ola@gmail.com.
Address correspondence to Oregon Lib. Assn., P.O. Box 3067, La Grande 97850. Tel. 541-962-5824, e-mail olaweb@olaweb.org.
World Wide Web http://www.olaweb.org.

Pennsylvania

Memb. 1,900+. Term of Office. Jan.–Dec. Publication. *PaLA Bulletin* (10 a year).
Pres. Janis Stubbs, Delaware County Lib. System. Tel. 610-891-8622, e-mail jstubbs@delcolibraries.org; *1st V.P.* David Schappert, Marywood Univ. Tel. 570-961-4764, e-mail dschappert@gmail.com; *2nd V.P./Conference Chair* Chris Snyder, Bucks County Free Lib. Tel. 215-348-9083, e-mail snyderc@buckslib.org; *3rd V.P.* Carolyn Blatchley, Cumberland County Lib. Tel. 717-240-5379, e-mail cblatchley@ccpa.net; *Treas.* Marguerite Dube, Chester County Lib. Tel. 610-280-2645, e-mail mdube@ccls.org; *Past Pres.* Paula Gilbert, Martin Lib. Tel. 717-846-5300, e-mail pgilbert@yorklibraries.org; *Exec. Dir.* Glenn R. Miller, Pennsylvania Lib. Assn., 220 Cumberland Pkwy., Suite 10, Mechanicsburg 17055. Tel. 717-766-7663, fax 717-766-5440, e-mail glenn@palibraries.org.
Address correspondence to the executive director.
World Wide Web http://www.palibraries.org.

Rhode Island

Memb. (Indiv.) 350+; (Inst.) 50+. Term of Office. June–June. Publication. *RILA Bulletin.*
Eds. Brandi Kenyon, Andria Tieman. E-mail rilabulletin@gmail.com.
Pres. Jenifer Bond, Douglas and Judith Krupp Lib., Bryant Univ., Smithfield 02917. Tel. 401-232-6299, e-mail jbond2@bryant.edu; *V.P./Pres.-Elect* Aaron Coutu, Cumberland Lib. Tel. 401-333-2552 ext. 5, e-mail acoutu@cumberlandlibrary.org; *Secy.* Emily Grace LeMay. E-mail secretary@rilibraryassoc.org; *Treas.* Patricia Lombardi. Tel. 401-232-6296, e-mail treasurer@rilibraryassoc.org; *Past Pres.* Eileen Dyer, Cranston Public Lib., 140 Sockanossett Cross Rd., Cranston 02920. Tel. 401-943-9080 ext. 119, e-mail eadyer@gmail.com.
Address correspondence to Rhode Island Library Assn., P.O. Box 6765, Providence 02940.
World Wide Web http://www.rilibraries.org.

South Carolina

Memb. 350+. Term of Office. Jan.–Dec. Publication. *News and Views.*
Pres. Crystal Johnson, Richland Lib., 2916 Broad River Rd., Columbia 29210. Tel. 803-772-6675, e-mail cjohnson@richlandlibrary.com; *1st V.P./Conference Chair* John Kennerly, Erskine College, P.O. Box 188, 1 Depot St., Due West 29639. Tel. 864-379-8788, e-mail kennerly@erskine.edu; *2nd V.P.* Amber Conger, Richland Lib., 1431 Assembly St., Columbia 29212. Tel. 803-929-3401, e-mail aconger@richlandlibrary.com; *Secy.* Virginia Alexander, USC Upstate, 800 University Way, Spartanburg 29303. Tel. 864-503-5735, e-mail alexanva@uscupstate.edu; *Treas.* Sarah Hood, J. Drake Edens Lib., Columbia College, 1301 Columbia College Drive, Columbia 29203. Tel. 803-786-3570, e-mail shood@columbiasc.edu; *Past Pres.* Edward Rock, Clemson Univ. Libs., Box 343001, Clemson 29643. Tel. 864-656-1879, e-mail erock@clemson.edu; *Exec.*

Secy. Donald Wood, SCLA, P.O. Box 1763, Columbia 29202. Tel. 803-252-1087, fax 803-252-0589. E-mail scla@capconsc.com. Address correspondence to the executive secretary. World Wide Web http://www.scla.org.

South Dakota

Memb. (Indiv.) 450+; (Inst.) 60+. Publication. *Book Marks* (q.). *Ed.* Melissa Weber, Canistota School Lib., Canistota 57012. E-mail bookmarkssd@gmail.com. *Pres.* Amber Wilde, Grace Balloch Memorial Lib., Spearfish. E-mail amber.wilde@cityofspearfish.com; *V.P./Pres.-Elect* Kathy Jacobs-Wibbels, Yankton Community Lib. E-mail kwibbles@cityofyankton.org; *Recording Secy.* Nita Gill, Brookings Public Lib. E-mail ngill@cityofbrookings.org; *Past Pres.* Scott Ahola, Black Hills State Univ., Spearfish. E-mail scott.ahola@bhsu.edu; *Exec. Secy./Treas.* Laura G. Olson, Canton Public Lib. E-mail sdlaest@gmail.com. Address correspondence to the executive secretary, SDLA, 28363 472nd Ave., Worthing 57077-5722. Tel. 605-372-0235, e-mail sdlaest@gmail.com. World Wide Web http://www.sdlibraryassociation.org.

Tennessee

Memb. 600+. Term of Office. July–June. Publications. *Tennessee Libraries* (q.). *Ed.* Amy York. E-mail ayork@mtsu.edu; *TLA Newsletter* (q.). *Ed.* Anthony Prince. E-mail aprince1@tnstate.edu. Both online at http://www.tnla.org. *Pres.* Susan Jennings. E-mail suzyjenn620@gmail.com; *V.P./Pres.-Elect* Pam Dennis. E-mail pdennis@memphis.edu; *Recording Secy.* Heather Lanier. E-mail lanierh@brentwood-tn.org; *Past Pres.* Ruth Kinnersley. E-mail rkinnersley@trevecca.edu; *Exec. Dir.* Annelle R. Huggins, Tennessee Lib. Assn., Box 241074, Memphis 38124. Tel. 901-485-6952, e-mail arhuggins1@comcast.net. Address correspondence to the executive director. World Wide Web http://tnla.org.

Texas

Memb. 6,500+. Term of Office. Apr.–Apr. Publications. *Texas Library Journal* (q.), *TLACast* (9 a year). *Pres.* Sharon Amastae; *Pres.-Elect* Susan Mann; *Treas.* Gretchen Pruett; *Past Pres.* Yvonne Chandler; *Exec. Dir.* Patricia H. Smith, TXLA, 3355 Bee Cave Rd., Suite 401, Austin 78746-6763. Tel. 512-328-1518, fax 512-328-8852, e-mail pats@txla.org or tla@txla.org. Address correspondence to the executive director. World Wide Web http://www.txla.org.

Utah

Memb. 650. Publication. *Utah Libraries News* (q.) (online at http://www.ula.org/newsletter). *Pres.* Pamela Martin, Merrill Cazier Lib., Utah State Univ., 3000 Old Main Hill, Logan 84322. Tel. 435-797-2685, fax 435-797-2677, e-mail pamela.martin@usu.edu; *V.P./Pres.-Elect* Dustin Fife, San Juan County Lib., 25 W. 300 South, Blanding 84511. Tel. 435-678-2335, e-mail d.t.fife@sanjuancounty.org; *Recording Secy.* Andrea Payant, USU Merrill-Cazier Lib. E-mail andrea.payant@usu.edu; *Treas.* Javaid Lal. E-mail jlal@ula.org; *Past Pres.* Patricia Hull, Magna Branch, Salt Lake County Lib. System, 8339 W. 3500 South, Magna 84044. Tel. 801-944-7626, e-mail phull@slcolibrary.org; *Exec. Dir.* Barbara Hopkins, Canyons School Dist. Tel. 801-810-7149, e-mail barbaraw.hopkins@gmail.com. Address correspondence to the executive director, Utah Lib. Assn., P.O. Box 708155, Sandy 84070-8155. World Wide Web http://www.ula.org.

Vermont

Memb. 400. Publication. *VLA News* (q.). *Pres.* Toni Josey. E-mail vermontlibrariespresident@gmail.com; *V.P./Pres.-Elect* Virgil Fuller, Chelsea Public Lib., 296 Vermont Route 1110, Chelsea 05038. Tel. 802-685-2188, e-mail vermontlibrariesvicepresident@gmail.com; *Secy.* Sarah Costa, Aldrich Public Lib., 6 Washington St., Barre 05641. Tel. 802-839-5045, e-mail sbjackman@gmail.com; *Treas.* James Allen, Bailey/Howe Lib., Univ. of Vermont, 538 Main St., Burlington 05405. Tel. 802-656-3254, e-mail jpallen@uvm.edu; *Past*

Pres. Amber Billey, Bailey/Howe Lib., Univ. of Vermont, 538 Main St., Burlington 05405-0036. Tel. 802-656-8568, e-mail amber.billey @uvm.edu.

Address correspondence to VLA, Box 803, Burlington 05402.

World Wide Web http://www.vermont libraries.org.

Virginia

Memb. 950+. Term of Office. Oct.–Oct. Publication. *Virginia Libraries* (q.).

Pres. Suzy Szasz Palmer, Greenwood Lib., Longwood Univ., 201 High St., Farmville 23909. Tel. 434-395-2083, e-mail palmerss@ longwood.edu; *Pres.-Elect* Martha Hutzel, England Run Branch, Central Rappahannock Regional Lib., 806 Lyons Blvd., Fredericksburg 22406. Tel. 540-899-1703, e-mail mhutzel @crrl.org; *2nd V.P.* Shari Henry, Westover Branch, Arlington Public Lib., 1644 N. McKinley Rd., Arlington 22205. Tel. 703-228-5261, e-mail shenry@arlingtonva.us; *Secy.* Cindy S. Church, Lib. of Virginia, 800 E. Broad St., Richmond 23219-8000. Tel. 804-692-3773, e-mail cindy.church@lva.virginia.gov; *Treas.* Nathan Flinchum, Roanoke Public Libs., 706 S. Jefferson St. S.W., Roanoke 24016. Tel. 540-853-2073, e-mail nathan.flinchum@roanokeva.gov; *Past Pres.* Kevin Smith, Yorktown Public Lib., 100 Long Green Blvd., Yorktown 23693. Tel. 757-890-5134, e-mail smithk@yorkcounty. gov; *Exec. Dir.* Lisa Varga, P.O. Box 56312, Virginia Beach 23456. Tel. 757-689-0594, fax 757-447-3478, e-mail vla.lisav@cox.net.

Address correspondence to the executive director.

World Wide Web http://www.vla.org.

Washington

Memb. (Indiv.) 742, (Inst.) 47. Publications. *Alki: The Washington Library Association Journal* (3 a year). *Ed.* Joyce Hansen, Seattle Public Lib., 1000 Fourth Ave., Seattle 98104. Tel. 206-713-9497, e-mail alkieditor@alki.org; *Connect* (e-newsletter, mo.).

Pres. Nancy Ledeboer, Spokane County Lib. Dist. Tel. 509-893-8200, e-mail nledeboer@ scld.org; *V.P./Pres.-Elect* Darcy Brixey, Bellevue Regional Lib. Tel. 425-450-1765. E-mail dbrixey@kcls.org; *Secy./Treas.* Phil Heikkinen,

Orcas Island Public Lib. Tel. 360-376-2308, e-mail pheikkinen@orcaslibrary.org; *Past Pres.* Jennifer Wiseman, King County Lib. System. Tel. 425-369-3221, e-mail jlwiseman@kcls. org; *Exec. Dir.* Dana Murphy-Love, WLA, 23607 Hwy. 99, Suite 2-C, Edmonds 98026. Tel. 425-967-0739, e-mail dana@wla.org.

Address correspondence to the executive director.

World Wide Web http://www.wla.org.

West Virginia

Memb. 650+. Publication. *West Virginia Libraries* (6 a year). *Ed.* Pamela K. Coyle, Martinsburg-Berkeley County Public Lib., 101 W. King St., Martinsburg 25401. Tel. 304-267-8933, fax 304-267-9720, e-mail pam.coyle@ martin.lib.wv.us.

Pres. Amy Lilly, Raleigh County Public Lib., 221 N. Kanawha St., Beckley 25801. Tel. 304-255-0511 ext. 100, e-mail amy.lilly@ raleigh.lib.wv.us; *1st V.P./Pres.-Elect* Emilee Seese, Ritchie County Public Lib., P.O. Box 122, Ellenboro 26346. Tel. 304-643-5122, fax 304-643-4019, e-mail seesee@mail.mln. lib.wv.us; *2nd V.P.* Ivonne Martinez, Mountaintop Public Lib., P.O. Box 217, 384 Quail Ridge Rd., Thomas 26292. Tel. 304-463-4582, fax 304-463-5789, e-mail ivonne.martinez@ mail.nln.lib.wv.us; *Secy.* Jessica Tapia, WVU Libs., P.O. Box 6069, 1549 University Ave., Morgantown 26506. Tel. 304-293-0312, e-mail jessica.tapia@mail.wvu.edu; *Treas.* Brian E. Raitz, Parkersburg and Wood County Public Lib., 3100 Emerson Ave., Parkersburg 26104-2414. Tel. 304-420-4587 ext. 11, fax 304-420-4589, e-mail raitzb@mail.mln.lib.wv.us; *Past Pres.* Beth Royall, Evansdale Lib., West Virginia Univ. Libs., P.O. Box 6105, Morgantown 26506-6105. Tel. 304-293-9755, fax 304-293-7330, e-mail beth.royall@mail.wvu.edu.

Address correspondence to the president.

World Wide Web http://www.wvla.org.

Wisconsin

Memb. 1,900. Term of Office. Jan.–Dec. Publication. *WLA Newsletter* (q.).

Pres. John Politz, McIntyre Lib., UW–Eau Claire. Tel. 715-836-4827, e-mail pollitjh@ uwec.edu; *Pres.-Elect* Pamela Westby, Middleton Public Lib., Middleton. Tel. 608-827-7425, e-mail pamela@midlibrary.org; *Treas.* Jen Gerber, Oscar Grady Public Lib., Saukville. Tel. 262-284-6022, e-mail jgerber@esls.lib. wi.us; *Past Pres.* Krista L. Ross, Southwest Wisconsin Lib. System, Fennimore. Tel. 608-822-3393, e-mail kross@swls.org; *Exec. Dir.* Plumer Lovelace. E-mail lovelace@wisconsin libraries.org.

Address correspondence to the association, 4610 S. Biltmore Lane, No. 100, Madison 53718-2153. Tel. 608-245-3640, fax 608-245-3646, e-mail wla@wisconsinlibraries.org.

World Wide Web http://wla.wisconsin libraries.org.

Wyoming

Memb. 450+. Term of Office. Oct.–Oct.

Pres. Rebecca Lehman, Campbell County Public Lib. Tel. 307-682-3223, e-mail president @wyla.org; *V.P.* Sid Stanfill. E-mail vice president @wyla.org; *Past Pres.* Richard Landreth, Westwood H.S./4J Elementary Libs. E-mail landreth@ccsd.k12.wy.us; *Exec. Secy.* Laura Grott, P.O. Box 1387, Cheyenne 82003-1387. Tel. 307-632-7622, fax 307-638-3469, e-mail executivesecretary@wyla.org.

Address correspondence to the executive secretary.

World Wide Web http://www.wyla.org.

Canada

Alberta

Memb. 500. Term of Office. May–Apr. Publication. *Letter of the LAA* (q.).

Pres. Karen Hildebrandt, Concordia Univ. College of Alberta. E-mail president@laa. ca; *1st V.P.* Jason Openo, Medicine Hat College. E-mail 1stvicepresident@laa.ca; *2nd V.P.* Norene James, Grant MacEwan Univ. E-mail 2ndvicepresident@laa.ca; *Treas.* Jackie Flowers, Calgary Public Lib. E-mail treasurer@ laa.ca; *Past Pres.* Lisa Hardy, Calgary Public Lib. E-mail pastpresident@laa.ca; *Exec. Dir.* Christine Sheppard, 80 Baker Crescent N.W., Calgary T2L 1R4. Tel. 403-284-5818, fax 403-282-6646, e-mail info@laa.ca.

Address correspondence to the executive director.

World Wide Web http://www.laa.ca.

British Columbia

Memb. 750+. Term of Office. April–April. Publication. *BCLA Browser* (q.; online at http://bclabrowser.ca). *Ed.* Leanna Jantzi. E-mail browser@bcla.bc.ca.

Pres. Heather Buzzell, Penticton Public Lib.; *Past Pres.* Gwen Bird, Council of Prairie and Pacific Univ. Libs.; *Exec. Dir.* Annette De-Faveri. E-mail execdir@bcla.bc.ca.

Address correspondence to the association, 900 Howe St., Suite 150, Vancouver V6Z 2M4. Tel. 604-683-5354, e-mail exdir@bcla.bc.ca.

World Wide Web http://www.bcla.bc.ca.

Manitoba

Memb. 500+. Term of Office. May–May. Publications. *Newsline* (mo.); *Manitoba Libraries* (mo., online, open access journal).

Pres. Camille Callison, Elizabeth Dafoe Lib., Univ. of Manitoba, Winnipeg. Tel. 204-480-1054, e-mail president@mla.mb.ca; *V.P.* Alix-Rae Stefanko. E-mail awards@mla. mb.ca; *Secy.* Evelyn Bruneau, Elizabeth Dafoe Lib., Univ. of Manitoba, Winnipeg. Tel. 204-474-6780, e-mail evelyn_bruneau@umanitoba. ca; *Treas.* Laura Hochheim, Neil John Maclean Health Sciences Lib., Univ. of Manitoba, Winnipeg. Tel. 204-480-1346, e-mail laura.hochheim @umanitoba.ca; *Past Pres.* Dawn Bassett, Canadian Grain Commission. E-mail dbassett69 @gmail.com.

Address correspondence to the association, 606-100 Arthur St., Winnipeg R3B 1H3. Tel. 204-943-4567, e-mail manitobalibrary@gmail. com.

World Wide Web http://www.mla.mb.ca.

Ontario

Memb. 5,000+. Publications. *Access* (q.); *Teaching Librarian* (3 a year).

Pres. Jane Hilton, Whitby Public Lib. E-mail janehilton.ca@gmail.com; *V.P./Pres.-Elect* Todd Kyle, Newmarket Public Lib. E-mail tkyle@newmarketpl.ca; *Treas.* Lesa Balch, Kitchener Public Lib. E-mail lesa.balch@kpl. org; *Past Pres.* Anita Brooks Kirkland. E-mail anitabk@bythebrooks.ca; *Exec. Dir.* Shelagh Paterson. E-mail spaterson@accessola.com.

Address correspondence to the association, 2 Toronto St., Toronto M5C 2B6. Tel. 416-363-

3388 or 866-873-9867, fax 416-941-9581 or 800-387-1181, e-mail info@accessola.com. World Wide Web http://www.accessola. com.

Quebec

Memb. (Indiv.) 100+. Term of Office. May–April. Publication. *ABQLA Bulletin* (3 a year). *Pres.* Shannon Babcock. E-mail shannon. babcock@mels.gouv.qc.ca; *V.P.* Sonia Smith. E-mail sonia.smith@mcgill.ca; *Treas.* Anne Wade. E-mail wada@education.concordia.ca; *Past Pres.* Robin Canuel. E-mail robin.canuel @mcgill.ca; *Exec. Secy.* Margaret Goldik, P.O. Box 26717, CPS Beaconsfield, Beaconsfield H9W 6G7. Tel./fax 514-697-0146, e-mail abq-la@abqla.qc.ca.

Address correspondence to the executive secretary.

World Wide Web http://www.abqla.qc.ca.

Saskatchewan

Memb. 200+. Publication. *Forum* (q.). *Pres.* Gwen Schmidt, Saskatoon Public Lib. 311 23rd St., Saskatoon S7K 0J6. Tel. 306-975-7606, e-mail gwen.m.schmidt@gmail.com; *V.P., Membership and Publications* Michael Shires, Dr. John Archer Lib., Univ. of Regina. Tel. 306-585-4493, e-mail michael.shires@ uregina.ca; *V.P., Advocacy and Development* Gillian Nowlan, Dr. John Archer Lib., Univ. of Regina. Tel. 306-337-2434, e-mail gillian. nowlan@uregina.ca; *Treas.* Deborah McConkey, Horizon College and Seminary Lib., 1303 Jackson Ave., Saskatoon S7H 2M9. Tel. 306-374-6655, e-mail library@horizon.edu; *Exec. Dir.* Judy Nicholson, SLA Office, No. 15, 2010 7th Ave., Regina S4R 1C2. Tel. 306-780-9413, fax 306-780-9447, e-mail slaexdir@sasktel. net.

Address correspondence to the executive director.

World Wide Web http://www.saskla.ca.

Regional

Atlantic Provinces: N.B., N.L., N.S., P.E.I.

Memb. (Indiv.) 320+; (Inst.) Publication. *APLA Bulletin* (4 a year).

Pres. Crystal Rose, Ferriss Hodgett Lib., Grenfell Campus, Memorial Univ. of Newfoundland, 20 University Drive, Corner Brook A2H 5G4. Tel. 709-637-6236 or 709-637-2183, e-mail crose@grenfell.mun.ca; *V.P./Pres.-Elect* Lynn Somers, Nova Scotia Provincial Library, Dept. of Communities, Culture, and Heritage, 1741 Brunswick St., Halifax NS B3J 3X8. Tel. 902 424-4852, fax 902-424-0633; *V.P., Membership* Suzanne van den Hoogen, Angus L. Macdonald Lib., St. Francis Xavier Univ., P.O. Box 5000, Antigonish, NS B2G 2W5. Tel. 902-867-4535, e-mail svandenh@stfx.ca; *V.P. Nova Scotia* Stan Orlov, Mount Saint Vincent Univ., 166 Bedford Hwy., Halifax, NS B3M 2J6. Tel. 902-457-6212, fax 902-457-6445, e-mail stan.orlov@msvu.ca; *V.P. New Brunswick* Leah Brisco, New Brunswick Public Lib. Service, 250 King St., P.O. Box 6000, Fredericton, NB E3B 5H1. Tel. 506-453-3442, e-mail leah. brisco@gnb.ca; *V.P. Newfoundland and Labrador* Krista Godfrey, Queen Elizabeth II Lib., Memorial Univ. of Newfoundland, St. John's, NL A1B 3Y1. Tel. 709-864-3753, e-mail kgodfrey@mun.ca; *V.P. Prince Edward Island* Patricia Doucette, Holland College, 140 Weymouth St., Charlottetown, PE C1A 4Z1. Tel. 902-566-9558, e-mail pmdoucette@holland-college.com; *Secy.* Anne Bowden, Dr. C. R. Barrett Lib., Marine Institute, Memorial Univ. of Newfoundland, P.O. Box 4920, St. John's, NL A1C 5R3. Tel. 709-778-0445, e-mail anne. bowden@mi.mun.ca; *Treas.* Gail Fraser, W. K. Kellogg Health Sciences Lib., Dalhousie Univ., P.O. Box 15000, Halifax, NS B3H 4R2. E-mail gail.fraser@dal.ca; *Past Pres.* Louise White, Marine Institute, Memorial Univ. of Newfoundland, P.O. Box 4920, St. John's, NL A1C 5R3. Tel. 709-757-0719, e-mail louise.white@ mi.mun.ca.

Address correspondence to Atlantic Provinces Lib. Assn., c/o SIM, Kenneth C. Rowe Mgt. Bldg., Dalhousie Univ., Suite 4010, 6100 University Ave., Halifax, NS B3H 4R2.

World Wide Web http://www.apla.ca.

Mountain Plains: Ariz., Colo., Kan., Mont., Neb., Nev., N.Dak., N.Mex., Okla., S.Dak., Utah, Wyo.

Memb. 700. Term of Office. Oct.–Oct. Publications. *MPLA Newsletter* (bi-mo., online only). *Ed.* Abby Moore, I. D. Weeks Lib., Univ. of

South Dakota, 414 E. Clark St., Vermillion 57069. Tel. 605-677-6094, e-mail editor@mpla.us.

Pres. Annie Epperson, Michener Lib., Univ. of Northern Colorado, Campus Box 48, Greeley 80639-0091. Tel. 970-351-1535, fax 970-351-2963, president@mpla.us; *V.P./Pres.-Elect* Eric Stroshane, North Dakota State Lib. E-mail vicepresident@mpla.us; *Recording Secy.* Valerie Nye, Inst. of American Indian Arts, Santa Fe. E-mail secretary@mpla.us; *Past Pres.* Wendy Wendt, Grand Forks Public Lib. Tel. 701-772-8116, fax 701-771-1379, e-mail past president@mpla.us; *Exec. Secy.* Judy Zelenski, 14293 W. Center Drive, Lakewood, CO 80228. Tel. 303-985-7795, e-mail execsecretary@mpla.us.

Address correspondence to the executive secretary.

World Wide Web http://www.mpla.us.

New England: Conn., Maine, Mass., N.H., R.I., Vt.

Memb. (Indiv.) 650+. Term of Office. Nov.–Oct. Publication. *NELA News* (online, mo.).

Pres. Stephen Spohn, Massachusetts Lib. System, Marlborough. E-mail president@nelib.org; *V.P./Pres.-Elect* Deb Hoadley, Massachusetts Lib. System, Marlborough. Tel. 508-357-2121, e-mail vice-president@nelib.org; *Secy.* Betsy Solon. E-mail secretary@nelib.org; *Treas.* Denise Van Zanten, Manchester City Lib., Manchester, N.H. E-mail treasurer@nelib.org; *Senior Dir.* Amy Howlett, Vermont Dept. of Libs., Chester. E-mail director-sr@nelib.org; *Junior Dir.* Meaghan Thompson, Turner Free Lib., Randolph, Mass. E-mail director-jr@nelib.org; *Admin.* Robert Scheier, New England Lib. Assn., 55 N. Main St., Unit 49, Belchertown, MA 01007. Tel. 413-813-5254, e-mail library-association-administrator@nelib.org.

World Wide Web http://www.nelib.org.

Pacific Northwest: Alaska, Idaho, Mont., Ore., Wash., Alberta, B.C.

Memb. 170+. Term of Office. Aug.–Aug. Publication. *PNLA Quarterly. Ed.* Mary Bolin, 322B Love Lib., Univ. of Nebraska, P.O. Box 881140, Lincoln, NE 68588-4100. Tel. 402-472-4281, e-mail mbolin2@unlnotes.unl.edu.

Pres. Honore Bray, Missoula Public Lib., Missoula, Mont. Tel. 406-721-2665, e-mail hbray@missoula.lib.mt.us; *1st V.P./Pres.-Elect* Gwendolyn Haley, Spokane County (Washington) Lib. Dist.; *2nd V.P.* Jay Peters, Coquitlam Public Lib., 575 Poirier St., Coquitlam, BC V3J 6A. Tel. 604-937-4148 ext. 4248, e-mail jpeters@library.coquitlam.bc.ca; *Secy.* Candice Stenstrom, Public Lib. InterLINK, 5489 Byrne Rd., Burnaby, BC V5J 3J1. Tel. 604-437-8441, fax 604-437-8410, e-mail candice.stenstrom@interlink; *Treas.* Katie Cargill, Eastern Washington Univ. Libs., 816 F St., Cheney, WA 99004. Tel. 509-999-6714, e-mail kcargill@ewu.edu; *Past Pres.* Kelsey Keyes, Albertsons Lib., Boise State Univ., Boise, ID. Tel. 208-426-1139, e-mail kelseykeyes@boisestate.edu.

Address correspondence to the president, Pacific Northwest Lib. Assn.

World Wide Web http://www.pnla.org.

Southeastern: Ala., Ark., Fla., Ga., Ky., La., Miss., N.C., S.C., Tenn., Va., W.Va.

Memb. 500. Publication. *The Southeastern Librarian (SELn)* (q.). *Ed.* Perry Bratcher, 503A Steely Lib., Northern Kentucky Univ., Highland Heights, KY 41099. Tel. 859-572-6309, fax 859-572-6181, e-mail bratcher@nku.edu.

Pres. Camille McCutcheon. E-mail cmccutcheon@uscupstate.edu; *V.P.* Linda Suttle Harris. *Secy.* Sue Alexander; *Treas.* Beverly James; *Past Pres.* Gordon N. Baker, Clayton State Univ. Lib. E-mail gordonbaker@clayton.edu.

Address correspondence to Southeastern Lib. Assn., Admin. Services, P.O. Box 950, Rex, GA 30273-0950. Tel. 770-961-3520, fax 770-961-3712.

World Wide Web http://selaonline.org.

State and Provincial Library Agencies

The state library administrative agency in each of the U.S. states will have the latest information on its state plan for the use of federal funds under the Library Services and Technology Act (LSTA). The directors and addresses of these state agencies are listed below.

Alabama

Nancy C. Pack, Dir., Alabama Public Lib. Service, 6030 Monticello Drive, Montgomery 36130-6000. Tel. 334-213-3901, fax 334-213-3993, e-mail npack@apls.state.al.us. World Wide Web http://statelibrary.alabama.gov.

Alaska

Linda S. Thibodeau, State Libn. and Dir., Alaska Dept. of Educ., Div. of Libs., Archives, and Museums, P.O. Box 110571, Juneau 99811. Tel. 907-465-2911, fax 907-465-2151, e-mail linda.thibodeau@alaska.gov. World Wide Web http://library.state.ak.us.

Arizona

Joan Clark, State Libn., Arizona State Lib., Archives, and Public Records, 1700 W. Washington, Phoenix 85007. Tel. 602-926-4035, fax 602-256-7983, e-mail jclark@azlibrary.gov. World Wide Web http://www.lib.az.us.

Arkansas

Carolyn Ashcraft, State Libn., Arkansas State Lib., 900 W. Capitol, Suite 100, Little Rock 72201-3108. Tel. 501-682-1526, fax 501-682-1899, e-mail carolyn@library.arkansas.gov. World Wide Web http://www.library.arkansas.gov.

California

Greg Lucas, State Libn., California State Lib., P.O. Box 942837, Sacramento 94237-0001. Tel. 916-323-9750, fax 916-323-9768, e-mail greg.lucas@library.ca.gov. World Wide Web http://www.library.ca.gov.

Colorado

Eugene Hainer, Dir. and State Libn., Colorado State Lib., Rm. 309, 201 E. Colfax Ave., Denver 80203-1799. Tel. 303-866-6733, fax 303-866-6940, e-mail hainer_g@cde.state.co.us. World Wide Web http://www.cde.state.co.us/cdelib.

Connecticut

Kendall F. Wiggin, State Libn., Connecticut State Lib., 231 Capitol Ave., Hartford 06106. Tel. 860-757-6510, fax 860-757-6503, e-mail kendall.wiggin@ct.gov. World Wide Web http://www.cslib.org.

Delaware

Annie Norman, State Libn. and Dir., Delaware Div. of Libs., 121 Martin Luther King Jr. Blvd. N., Dover 19901. Tel. 302-257-3001, fax 302-739-8436, e-mail annie.norman@state.de.us. World Wide Web http://www.state.lib.de.us.

District of Columbia

Richard Reyes-Gavilan, Exec. Dir., District of Columbia Public Lib., 901 G St. N.W., Suite 400, Washington 20001-4599. Tel. 202-727-1101, fax 202-727-1129, e-mail rrg@dc.gov. World Wide Web http://www.dclibrary.org.

Florida

Judith A. Ring, State Libn., Div. of Lib. and Info. Services, R. A. Gray Bldg., 500 S. Bronough St., Tallahassee 32399-0250. Tel. 850-245-6604, fax 850-488-2746, e-mail jring@dos.state.fl.us. World Wide Web http://dlis.dos.state.fl.us/library.

Georgia

Julie Walker, State Libn., Georgia Public Lib. Services, 1800 Century Place, Suite 150, Atlanta 30345-4304. Tel. 404-235-7140, fax 404-235-7201, e-mail jwalker@georgialibraries.org. World Wide Web http://www.georgialibraries.org.

Hawaii

Richard Burns, State Libn., Hawaii State Public Lib. System, 44 Merchant St., Honolulu 96813. Tel. 808-586-3704, fax 808-586-3715, e-mail stlib@librarieshawaii.org. World Wide Web http://www.librarieshawaii.org.

Idaho

Ann Joslin, State Libn., Idaho Commission for Libs., 325 W. State St., Boise 83702-6072. Tel. 208-334-2150, fax 208-334-4016, e-mail ann.joslin@libraries.idaho.gov. World Wide Web http://libraries.idaho.gov.

Illinois

Anne Craig, Dir., Illinois State Lib., 300 S. 2 St., Springfield 62701-1703. Tel. 217-782-2994, fax 217-785-4326, e-mail acraig@ilsos.net. World Wide Web http://www.cyberdriveillinois.com/departments/library/home.html.

Indiana

Jacob Speer, Dir. and State Libn., Indiana State Lib., 315 W. Ohio St., Indianapolis 46202. Tel. 317-232-3693, fax 317-232-3728, e-mail jspeer1@library.in.gov. World Wide Web http://www.in.gov/library.

Iowa

Barbara Corson, Interim State Libn., State Lib. of Iowa, 1112 E. Grand Ave., Des Moines 50319. Tel. 515-281-4105, fax 515-281-6191, e-mail barb.corson@lib.state.ia.us. World Wide Web http://www.statelibraryofiowa.org.

Kansas

Jo Budler, State Libn., State Lib. of Kansas, Rm. 312-N, 300 S.W. 10 Ave., Topeka 66612-1593. Tel. 785-296-5466, fax 785-296-6650, e-mail jo.budler@library.ks.gov. World Wide Web http://www.kslib.info.

Kentucky

Wayne Onkst, State Libn. and Commissioner, Kentucky Dept. for Libs. and Archives, P.O. Box 537, 300 Coffee Tree Rd., Frankfort 40602-0537. Tel. 502-564-8300 ext. 312, fax 502-564-5773, e-mail wayne.onkst@ky.gov. World Wide Web http://www.kdla.ky.gov.

Louisiana

Rebecca Hamilton, State Libn., State Lib. of Louisiana, P.O. Box 131, 701 N. 4 St., Baton Rouge 70821-0131. Tel. 225-342-4923, fax 225-219-4804, e-mail rhamilton@crt.state.la.us. World Wide Web http://www.state.lib.la.us.

Maine

James Ritter, State Libn., Maine State Lib., 64 State House Sta., Augusta 04333-0064. Tel. 207-287-5620, fax 207-287-5624, e-mail linda.lord@maine.gov. World Wide Web http://www.state.me.us/msl.

Maryland

Irene Padilla, Asst. State Superintendent for Libs., State Dept. of Educ., Div. of Lib. Development and Services, 200 W. Baltimore St., Baltimore 21201. Tel. 410-767-0435, fax 410-333-2507, e-mail ipadilla@msde.state.md.us. World Wide Web http://www.marylandpublicschools.org/MSDE/divisions/library.

Massachusetts

Dianne Carty, Dir., Massachusetts Board of Lib. Commissioners, 98 N. Washington St., Suite 401, Boston 02114-1933. Tel. 617-725-1860 ext. 222, fax 617-725-0140, e-mail dianne.carty@state.ma.us. World Wide Web http://mblc.state.ma.us.

Michigan

Randy Riley, State Libn., Lib. of Michigan, 702 W. Kalamazoo St., P.O. Box 30007, Lansing 48909-7507. Tel. 517-373-5860, fax 517-373-5700, e-mail rileyr@michigan.gov. World Wide Web http://www.michigan.gov/libraryofmichigan.

Minnesota

Jennifer R. Nelson, Dir. of State Lib Services, Minnesota State Lib. Agency, Div. of State Lib. Services, Dept. of Educ., 1500 Hwy. 36 W., Roseville 55113-4266. Tel. 651-582-8791, fax

651-582-8752, e-mail jennifer.r.nelson@state. mn.us. World Wide Web http://education.state. mn.us/MDE/stusuc/lib.statelibserv/index.html.

Mississippi

Susan Cassagne, Exec. Dir., Mississippi Lib. Commission, 3881 Eastwood Drive, Jackson 39211. Tel. 601-432-4039, fax 601-432-4480, e-mail susan@mlc.lib.ms.us. World Wide Web http://www.mlc.lib.ms.us.

Missouri

Barbara A. Reading, State Libn., Missouri State Lib., P.O. Box 387, 600 W. Main, Jefferson City 65102-0387. Tel. 573-526-4783, fax 573-751-3612, e-mail barbara.reading@ sos.mo.gov. World Wide Web http://www.sos. mo.gov/library.

Montana

Jennie Stapp, State Libn., Montana State Lib., 1515 E. 6 Ave., P.O. Box 201800, Helena 59620-1800. Tel. 406-444-3116, fax 406-444-0266, e-mail jstapp2@mt.gov. World Wide Web http://msl.mt.gov.

Nebraska

Rodney G. Wagner, Dir., Nebraska Lib. Commission, Suite 120, The Atrium, 1200 N St., Lincoln 68508-2023. Tel. 402-471-4001, fax 402-471-2083, e-mail rod.wagner@nebraska. gov. World Wide Web http://www.nlc.nebraska. gov.

Nevada

Daphne DeLeon, State Lib. and Archives Admin., Nevada State Lib. and Archives, 100 N. Stewart St., Carson City 89710-4285. Tel. 775-684-3315, fax 775-684-3311, e-mail ddeleon@ admin.nv.gov. World Wide Web http://nsla. nv.gov.

New Hampshire

Michael York, State Libn., New Hampshire State Lib., 20 Park St., Concord 03301-6314. Tel. 603-271-2397, fax 603-271-6826, e-mail michael.york@dcr.nh.gov. World Wide Web http://www.state.nh.us/nhsl.

New Jersey

Mary Chute, State Libn., New Jersey State Lib., P.O. Box 520, Trenton 08625-0520. Tel. 609-278-2640 ext. 101, fax 609-278-2652, e-mail mchute@njstatelib.org. World Wide Web http://www.njstatelib.org.

New Mexico

Michael Delello, Interim State Libn., New Mexico State Lib., 1209 Camino Carlos Rey, Santa Fe 87507. Tel. 505-827-6354, fax 505-476-9761, e-mail michael.delello@state.nm.us. World Wide Web http://www.nmstatelibrary. org.

New York

Bernard A. Margolis, State Libn. and Assistant Commissioner for Libs., New York State Lib., Room 10C34, 222 Madison Ave., Albany 12230. Tel. 518-486-4865, fax 518-486-6880, e-mail bmargolis@mail.nysed.gov. World Wide Web http://www.nysl.nysed.gov.

North Carolina

Caroline "Cal" Shepard, State Libn., State Lib. of North Carolina, Admin. Section, 4640 Mail Service Center, 109 E. Jones St., Raleigh 27699-4640. Tel. 919-807-7410, fax 919-733-8748, e-mail cal.shepard@ncdcr.gov. World Wide Web http://statelibrary.ncdcr.gov.

North Dakota

Mary J. Soucie, State Libn., North Dakota State Lib., 604 E. Boulevard Ave., Dept. 250, Bismarck 58505-0800. Tel. 701-328-2492, fax 701-328-2040, e-mail msoucie@nd.gov. World Wide Web http://ndsl.lib.state.nd.us.

Ohio

Beverly Cain, State Libn., State Lib. of Ohio, Suite 100, 274 E. 1 Ave., Columbus 43201. Tel. 614-644-6843, fax 614-466-3584, e-mail bcain@library.ohio.gov. World Wide Web http://www.library.ohio.gov.

Oklahoma

Susan C. McVey, Dir., Oklahoma Dept. of Libs., 200 N.E. 18 St., Oklahoma City 73105-

3298. Tel. 405-522-3173, fax 405-522-1077, e-mail smcvey@oltn.odl.state.ok.us. World Wide Web http://www.odl.state.ok.us.

Oregon

MaryKay Dahlgreen, State Libn., Oregon State Lib., 250 Winter St. N.E., Salem 97301. Tel. 503-378-4367, fax 503-585-8059, e-mail marykay.dahlgreen@state.or.us. World Wide Web http://oregon.gov/OSL.

Pennsylvania

Stacey Aldrich, Deputy Secy. of Educ. and Commissioner for Libs., Pennsylvania Office of Commonwealth Libs., 607 South Drive, Harrisburg 17120-0600. Tel. 717-783-2466, fax 717-772-3265, e-mail saldrich@pa.gov. World Wide Web http://www.portal.state.pa.us/portal/server.pt/community/bureau_of_state_library/8811.

Rhode Island

Karen Mellor, Acting Chief Lib. Officer, Rhode Island Office of Lib. and Info. Services, 1 Capitol Hill, second flr., Providence 02908-5803. Tel. 401-574-9304, fax 401-574-9320, e-mail karen.mellor@olis.ri.gov. World Wide Web http://www.olis.ri.gov.

South Carolina

Leesa Benggio, Acting Dir., South Carolina State Lib., 1430 Senate St., P.O. Box 11469, Columbia 29211. Tel. 803-734-8668, fax 803-734-8676, e-mail lbenggio@statelibrary.sc.gov. World Wide Web http://www.statelibrary.sc.gov.

South Dakota

Daria Bossman, State Libn., South Dakota State Lib., 800 Governors Drive, Pierre 57501-2294. Tel. 605-773-3167, fax 605-773-6962, e-mail daria.bossman@state.sd.us. World Wide Web http://library.sd.gov.

Tennessee

Chuck Sherrill, State Libn. and Archivist, Tennessee State Lib. and Archives, 403 Seventh Ave. N., Nashville 37243-0312. Tel. 615-741-7996, fax 615-532-9293, e-mail chuck.sherrill@tn.gov. World Wide Web http://www.tennessee.gov/tsla.

Texas

Mark Smith, Dir. and Libn., Texas State Lib. and Archives Commission, 1201 Brazos St., P.O. Box 12927, Austin 78711-2927. Tel. 512-463-6856, fax 512-463-5436, e-mail msmith@tsl.state.tx.us. World Wide Web http://www.tsl.state.tx.us.

Utah

Donna Jones Morris, Dir. and State Libn., Utah State Lib. Div., Suite A, 250 N. 1950 W., Salt Lake City 84116-7901. Tel. 801-715-6770, fax 801-715-6767, e-mail dmorris@utah.gov. World Wide Web http://library.utah.gov.

Vermont

Martha Reid, State Libn., Vermont Dept. of Libs., 109 State St., Montpelier 05609. Tel. 802-828-3265, fax 802-828-2199, e-mail martha.reid@mail.dol.state.vt.us. World Wide Web http://dol.state.vt.us.

Virginia

Sandra G. Treadway, Libn. of Virginia, Lib. of Virginia, 800 E. Broad St., Richmond 23219-8000. Tel. 804-692-3535, fax 804-692-3594, e-mail sandra.treadway@lva.virginia.gov. World Wide Web http://www.lva.virginia.gov.

Washington

Rand Simmons, State Libn., Washington State Lib., Office of the Secy. of State, 6880 Capitol Blvd., P.O. Box 42460, Olympia 98504. Tel. 360-570-5585, fax 360-586-7575, e-mail rand.simmons@sos.wa.gov. World Wide Web http://www.sos.wa.gov/library.

West Virginia

Karen Goff, Dir./State Libn., West Virginia Lib. Commission, Cultural Center, 1900 Kanawha Blvd. E., Charleston 25305. Tel. 304-558-2041, fax 304-558-2044, e-mail karen.e.goff@wv.gov. World Wide Web http://www.librarycommission.wv.gov.

Wisconsin

Kurt Kiefer, Asst. State Superintendent, Wisconsin Dept. of Public Instruction, Div. for Libs. and Technology, P.O. Box 7841, Madison 53707-7841. Tel. 608-266-2205, fax 608-266-9207, e-mail kurt.kiefer@dpi.wi.gov. World Wide Web http://dlt.dpi.wi.gov.

Wyoming

Lesley Boughton, State Libn., Wyoming State Lib., 2800 Central Ave., Cheyenne 82002. Tel. 307-777-5911, fax 307-777-6289, e-mail lbough@wyo.gov. World Wide Web http://www-wsl.state.wy.us.

American Samoa

Justin H. Maga, Acting Territorial Libn., Feleti Barstow Public Lib., P.O. Box 997687, Pago Pago, AS 96799. Tel. 684-633-5816, fax 684-633-5823, e-mail justinmaga@gmail.com. World Wide Web http://fbpl.org.

Federated States of Micronesia

Augustine Kohler, Acting Dir., National Archives, Culture, and Historic Preservation, P.O. Box PS 175, Palikir, Pohnpei, FM 96941. Tel. 691-320-2343, fax 691-320-5634, e-mail hpo@mail.fm. World Wide Web http://www.fsmgov.org.

Guam

Sandra Stanley, Admin. Officer, Guam Public Lib. System, 254 Martyr St., Hagatna 96910-5141. Tel. 671-475-4765, fax 671-477-9777, e-mail sandra.stanley@gpls.guam.gov. World Wide Web http://gpls.guam.gov.

Northern Mariana Islands

John Oliver Gonzales, Exec. Dir., CNMI Joeten-Kiyu Public Lib., P.O. Box 501092, Saipan, MP 96950-1092. Tel. 670-235-7324, fax 670-235-7550, e-mail joetenkiyupublic library@gmail.com. World Wide Web http://www.cnmilibrary.com.

Palau

Sinton Soalablai, Chief of School Mgt., Palau Ministry of Educ., P.O. Box 189, Koror, PW 96940. Tel. 680-488-2952, fax 680-488-8465, e-mail ssoalablai@palaumoe.net. World Wide Web http://palaugov.net.

Puerto Rico

Miguel A. Hernández, Dir., Lib. and Info. Services Program, Puerto Rico Dept. of Educ., P.O. Box 190759, San Juan 00919-0759. Tel. 787-773-3564, fax 787-753-6945, e-mail hernandez _mi@de.gobierno.pr. World Wide Web http://www.de.gobierno.pr/tags/bibliotecas.

Republic of the Marshall Islands

Amenta Matthew, Exec. Dir., Alele Museum, Lib., National Archives, P.O. Box 629, Majuro, MH 96960. Tel. 692-455-5707, fax 692-625-3226, e-mail alelemuseum@gmail.com. World Wide Web http://alelemuseum.tripod.com/index.html.

U.S. Virgin Islands

Ingrid Bough, Territorial Dir., Div. of Libs., Archives, and Museums, Dept. of Planning and Natural Resources, 1122 King St., Christiansted, St. Croix, VI 00820. Tel. 340-773-5715, fax 340-773-5327, e-mail ingrid.bough@dpnr.vi.gov. World Wide Web http://www.virgin islandspace.org/division%20of%20libraries/dlamhome.htm.

Canada

Alberta

Diana Davidson, Dir., Public Lib. Services Branch, Alberta Municipal Affairs, 803 Standard Life Centre, 10405 Jasper Ave., Edmonton T5J 4R7. Tel. 780-415-0284, fax 780-415-8594, e-mail diana.davidson@gov.ab.ca or libraries@gov.ab.ca. World Wide Web http://www.municipalaffairs.alberta.ca/alberta_libraries.cfm.

British Columbia

Beverley Shaw, Dir., Public Lib. Services Branch, Ministry of Educ., P.O. Box 9161, Stn. Prov. Govt., Victoria V8W 9H3. Tel. 250-415-1662, fax 250 953-4985, e-mail bev.shaw@gov.bc.ca. World Wide Web http://www.bced.gov.bc.ca/pls.

Manitoba

Dir., Public Lib. Services, Manitoba Dept. of Tourism, Culture, Heritage, Sport and Consumer Protection, 300-1011 Rosser Ave., Brandon R7A OL5. Tel. 204-726-6590, fax 204-726-6868, e-mail pls@gov.mb.ca. World Wide Web http://www.gov.mb.ca/chc/pls/index.html.

New Brunswick

Sylvie Nadeau, Exec. Dir., New Brunswick Public Lib. Service, Place 2000, 250 King St., P.O. Box 6000, Fredericton E3B 5H1. Tel. 506-453-2354, fax 506-444-4064, e-mail sylvie.nadeau@gnb.ca. World Wide Web http://www.gnb.ca/0003/index-e.asp.

Newfoundland and Labrador

Shawn Tetford, Exec. Dir., Provincial Info. and Lib. Resources Board, 48 St. George's Ave., Stephenville A2N 1K9. Tel. 709-643-0902, fax 709-643-0925, e-mail stetford@nlpl.ca. World Wide Web http://www.nlpl.ca.

Northwest Territories

Alison Hopkins, Territorial Libn., NWT Lib. Services, 75 Woodland Drive, Hay River X0E 1G1. Tel. 867-874-6531, fax 867-874-3321, e-mail alison_hopkins@gov.nt.ca. World Wide Web http://www.nwtpls.gov.nt.ca.

Nova Scotia

Jennifer Evans, Dir., Provincial Libn., Nova Scotia Provincial Lib., 3770 Kempt Rd., Halifax B3K 4X8. Tel. 902-424-2457, fax 902-424-0633, World Wide Web http://www.library.ns.ca.

Nunavut

Ron Knowling, Mgr., Nunavut Public Lib. Services, Box 270, Baker Lake X0C 0A0. Tel. 867-793-3353, fax 867-793-3360, e-mail rknowling@gov.nu.ca. World Wide Web http://www.publiclibraries.nu.ca.

Ontario

Rod Sawyer, Ontario Government Ministry of Tourism, Culture, and Sport, Hearst Block, 900 Bay St., Toronto M7A 2E1. Tel. 416-326-9326. World Wide Web http://www.mtc.gov.on.ca/en/libraries/contact.shtml.

Ontario Lib. Service–North, 334 Regent St., Sudbury P3C 4E2. Tel. 705-675-6467. World Wide Web http://www.olsn.ca. Joyce Cunningham, Chair.

Southern Ontario Lib. Service, No. 1504, 1 Yonge St., Toronto M5E 1E5. Tel. 416-961-1669, fax 416-961-5122. World Wide Web http://www.sols.org. Barbara Franchetto, CEO. E-mail bfranchetto@sols.org.

Prince Edward Island

Public Lib. Service of Prince Edward Island, P.O. Box 7500, Morell C0A 1S0. Tel. 902-961-7320, fax 902-961-7322, e-mail plshq@gov.pe.ca. World Wide Web http://www.library.pe.ca.

Quebec

Christiane Barbe, Chair and CEO, Bibliothèque et Archives Nationales du Québec (BAnQ), 2275 rue Holt, Montreal H2G 3H1. Tel. 800-363-9028 or 514-873-1100, fax 514-873-9312, info@banq.qc.ca. World Wide Web http://www.banq.qc.ca/portal/dt/accueil.jsp.

Saskatchewan

Brett Waytuck, Provincial Libn., Provincial Lib. and Literacy Office, Ministry of Educ., 409A Park St., Regina S4N 5B2. Tel. 306-787-2972, fax 306-787-2029, e-mail brett.waytuck@gov.sk.ca. World Wide Web http://www.education.gov.sk.ca/provincial-library/public-library-system.

Yukon Territory

Julie Ourom, Dir., Public Libs., Community Development Div., Dept. of Community Services, Government of Yukon, P.O. Box 2703, Whitehorse Y1A 2C6. Tel. 867-667-5447, fax 867-393-6333, e-mail julie.ourom@gov.yk.ca. World Wide Web http://www.ypl.gov.yk.ca.

State School Library Media Associations

Alabama

Children's and School Libns. Div., Alabama Lib. Assn. Memb. 600+. Publication. *The Alabama Librarian* (q.).

Chair Susan Cordell, Sta. 33, Univ. of West Alabama, Livingston 35470. Tel. 205-652-5421, fax 205-652-3706, e-mail scordell@uwa.edu; *V. Chair/Chair-Elect* Cendy Cooper, Tarrant Middle/H.S., 91 Black Creek Rd., Tarrant 35217. Tel. 205-849-0172, e-mail cooperc@tarrant.k12.al.us; *Past Chair* Carolyn Starkey, Buckhorn H.S., 25 Warren Rd., Albertville 35950. Tel. 256-302-1009, e-mail admin@jojo-starkey.com.

Address correspondence to the association administrator, Alabama Lib. Assn., 6030 Monticello Drive, Montgomery 36117. Tel. 334-414-0113, e-mail allibraryassoc@gmail.com.

World Wide Web http://allanet.org.

Alaska

Alaska Assn. of School Libns. Memb. 100+. Publication. *The Puffin* (3 a year), online at http://akasl.org/puffin-newsletter. *Ed.* Alta Collins, Northern Lights ABC School, Anchorage. E-mail collins_alta@asdk12.org.

Pres. Deborah Rinio, North Pole Middle School, Fairbanks. E-mail akasl.president@gmail.com; *Pres.-Elect* Dona Helmer, College Gate Elementary, Anchorage. E-mail helmer_dona@asdk12.org; *Secy.* Amelia Mitchell, Ryan Middle School, Northstar, Fairbanks; *Treas.* Laura Guest, Turnagain Elementary, Anchorage. E-mail guest_laura@asdk12.us; *Past Pres.* Wendy Stout, Larson Elementary, Wasilla. E-mail wendy.stout@matsuk12.us.

World Wide Web http://www.akasl.org.

Arizona

Teacher-Libn. Div., Arizona Lib. Assn. Memb. 1,000. Term of Office. Jan.–Dec. Publication. *AZLA Newsletter.*

Chair Shirley Berow, Desert Harbor Elementary, 15585 N. 91 Ave., Peoria 85382. Tel. 623-486-6216, e-mail sberow@cox.net.

Address correspondence to the chairperson.

World Wide Web http://www.azla.affiniscape.com.

Arkansas

Arkansas Assn. of School Libns., div. of Arkansas Lib. Assn.

Chair Wendy Rickman, Univ. of Central Arkansas, Conway 72035. Tel. 501-450-5431, e-mail arasl@uca.edu; *Past Chair* Erin Shaw, Greenbrier Middle School, 13 School Drive, Greenbrier 72058. Tel. 501-679-2113, e-mail shawe@greenbrierschools.org.

Address correspondence to the president.

World Wide Web http://www.arlib.org/organization/aasl/index.php.

California

California School Lib. Assn. Memb. 1,200+. Publications. *CSLA Journal* (2 a year). *Ed.* Jeanne Nelson. E-mail nelson.jeanne914@gmail.com; *CSLA Newsletter* (10 a year, memb., via e-mail).

(State Board) *Pres.* Liz Dodds, Bullard H.S., 5445 N. Palm Ave., Fresno 93704. Tel. 559-451-4405, e-mail liz.dodds@gmail.com; *Pres.-Elect* Beth Olshewsky, 1290 Ridder Park Drive, MC232, San José 95131-2304. Tel. 408-453-6670, fax 408-453-6815, e-mail beth_olshewsky@sccoe.org; *Secy.* Nina Jackson; *Treas.* Kathie Maier; *Past Pres.* Janice Gilmore-See; (Northern Region) *Pres.* Jessica Lee; *Pres.-Elect* Lisa Bishop; (Southern Region) *Pres.* Sondra Keckley; *Pres.-Elect* Sharlene Paxton.

Address correspondence to the association at 6444 E. Spring St., No. 237, Long Beach 90815-1553. Tel./fax 888-655-8480, e-mail info@csla.net.

World Wide Web http://www.csla.net.

Colorado

Colorado Assn. of School Libns. Memb. 250+.

Pres. Megan McQuinn, Farrell B. Howell ECE-8, Denver. E-mail megan_mcquinn@dpsk12.org.

World Wide Web http://www.cal-webs. org/?page=CASL.

Connecticut

Connecticut Assn. of School Libs. (formerly Connecticut Educ. Media Assn.). Memb. 500+. Term of Office. July–June.

Pres. Mary Ellen Minichiello. E-mail meminichiello@milforded.org; *V.P.* Shelley Stedman. E-mail slstedman@hotmail.com; *Recording Secy.* Christopher Barlow. E-mail christophbarlow@sbcglobal.net; *Treas.* Jody Pillar. E-mail pillarj@gilbertschool.org; *Past Pres.* Sara Kelley-Mudie. E-mail librarian. skm@gmail.com; *Admin. Secy.* Anne Weimann, 25 Elmwood Ave., Trumbull 06611. Tel. 203-372-2260, e-mail aweimann@snet.net.

Address correspondence to the administrative secretary.

World Wide Web http://www.ctcasl.com.

Delaware

Delaware School Lib. Assn., div. of Delaware Lib. Assn. Memb. 100+. Publications. *DSLA Newsletter* (online; irreg.); column in *DLA Bulletin* (3 a year).

Pres. Jen Delgado, Henry B. duPont Middle School, 735 Meeting House Rd., Hockessin 19707. Tel. 302-239-3420, e-mail jennifer. delgado@redclay.k12.de.us; *V.P./Pres.-Elect* Bonnie Gaus, May B. Leasure School, 1015 Church Rd., Newark 19702. Tel. 302-454-2103 ext. 408, fax 302-454-2109, e-mail gausb@ christina.k12.de.us; *Secy.* Tamara Carr. E-mail tcarr@caravel.org; *Past Pres.* Janice Haney, Appoquinimink H.S., 1080 Bunker Hill Rd., Middletown 19709. E-mail janice.haney@ appo.k12.de.us.

Address correspondence to the president.

World Wide Web http://www2.lib.udel.edu/ dla/divisions/dsla13.htm.

District of Columbia

District of Columbia Assn. of School Libns. Memb. 8. Publication. *Newsletter* (4 a year).

Pres. André Maria Taylor. E-mail diva librarian2@aol.com.

Address correspondence to André Maria Taylor, 330 10th St. N.E., Washington, DC 20002. Tel. 301-502-4203.

Florida

Florida Assn. for Media in Educ. Memb. 1,400+. Term of Office. Nov.–Oct. Publication. *Florida Media Quarterly. Ed.* Maggie Josephson.

Pres. Michelle Jarret. E-mail jarrettm@ osceola.k12.fl.us; *Pres.-Elect* Lucretia Miller. E-mail millerL7@duvalschools.org; *Secy.* Andrea Parisi; *Treas.* Lorri Cosgrove. E-mail cosgrol@stjohns.k12.fl.us; *Past Pres.* Henry Haake. E-mail henry.haake@polk-fl.net.

Address correspondence to FAME, P.O. Box 4778, Haines City 33845-4778. Tel. 813-380-5673, e-mail floridamediaed@gmail.com.

World Wide Web http://www.floridamedia. org.

Georgia

Georgia Assn. of School Libns.

Chair Lucy Green, Georgia Southern Univ. E-mail lgreen@georgiasouthern.edu; *Chair-Elect* Stephanie Jones, Georgia Southern Univ., P.O. Box 8131, Statesboro 30460-8131. Tel. 912-478-5250, e-mail sjones@georgiasouthern.edu.

Address correspondence to School Lib. Media Div., Georgia Lib. Assn., P.O. Box 793, Rex, GA 30273.

World Wide Web http://gla.georgialibraries. org/div_media.htm.

Georgia Lib. Media Assn. Memb. 700+.

Pres. Beth Miller; *Pres.-Elect* Debbie Sandford; *Secy.* Janelle McClure; *Treas.* Lora Taft; *Past Pres.* Andy Spinks; *Exec. Dir.* Lasa Joiner.

Address correspondence to GLMA Executive Office, 2711 Irvin Way, Suite 111, Decatur 30030. Tel. 404-299-7700, fax 404-299-7029, e-mail glma@jlh-consulting.com.

World Wide Web http://www.glma-inc.org.

Hawaii

Hawaii Assn. of School Libns. Memb. 145. Term of Office. June–May. Publication. *HASL Newsletter* (3 a year).

Pres. Sherry Rose; *V.P., Programming* Nalani Naluai; *V.P., Membership* Diane Mokuau; *Corresponding Secy.* Terry Heckman; *Recording Secy.* Deb Peterson; *Treas.* Danielle Fujii.

Address correspondence to the association, P.O. Box 235284, Honolulu 96823.

World Wide Web https://sites.google.com/site/haslsite.

Idaho

Educ. Media Div., Idaho Lib. Assn. Memb. 40+.

Chair Sara Murphy, Meridian Middle School, West Ada School Dist. E-mail murphy. sara@meridianschools.org; *Chair-Elect* Jessica Bowman, Sandpoint Middle School, Lake Pend Oreille School Dist. E-mail bowm9663@gmail.com; *Past Chair* Debbie Jenson, Fairmont Junior H.S., Boise School Dist. Tel. 208-854-4796, e-mail deborah.jenson@boiseschools.org.

Address correspondence to the chairperson. World Wide Web http://www.idaholibraries.org/about-us/officersdivisionscommittees/educational-media-division.

Illinois

Illinois School Lib. Media Assn. Memb. 1,000. Term of Office. July–June. Publications. *ISL-MA News* (4 a year); *Linking for Learning: The Illinois School Library Media Program Guidelines* (3rd ed., 2010); *Powerful Libraries Make Powerful Learners: The Illinois Study.*

Pres. Stephanie Stieglitz, Lane School, Hinsdale. E-mail sstieglitz@d181.org; *Pres.-Elect* Angie Green, Illini Bluffs SD No. 327, Glasford. E-mail angela.green0905@gmail.com; *Secy.* Christy Semande, Canton USD 66, Canton. E-mail csemande@yahoo.com; *Treas.* Lauren Ochs, Warrensburg-Latham H.S., Warrensburg. E-mail ochsl@wl.k12.il.us; *Past Pres.* Debra Turner, Metea Valley H.S., 1801 N. Eola Rd., Aurora, IL 60502. Tel. 630-375-8851. E-mail debbie_turner@ipsd.org; *Exec. Secy./Membership* Becky Robinson, ISLMA, P.O. Box 1326, Galesburg 61402-1326. Tel. 309-341-1099, e-mail ISLMAexsec@gmail.com.

World Wide Web http://www.islma.org.

Indiana

Assn. of Indiana School Library Educators (AISLE). Publications. *Focus on Indiana Libraries* (mo.); *Indiana Libraries* (q.).

Pres. Gigi Shook, Center Grove H.S., 2717 S. Morgantown Rd., Greenwood 46143. Tel. 317-881-0581, e-mail shookg@centergrove.k12.in.us; *V.P.* Michelle Houser, 1000 E. North Adams Drive, Decatur 46733. Tel. 260-724-7121 ext. 2143, e-mail houserm@nadams.k12.in.us; *Secy.* Liz Green, Mitchell Elementary, 2809 W. Purdue Ave., Muncie 47304. Tel. 765-747-5413, e-mail lgreen@muncie.k12.in.us; *Treas.* Debbie Acord, Wells County Public Lib., 200 W. Washington St., Bluffton 46714. Tel. 260-824-1612, e-mail debbie.acord@gmail.com; *Past Pres.* Susie Highley, Creston Middle School, 10925 E. Prospect, Indianapolis 46239. Tel. 812-532-6806, fax 812-532-6891, e-mail shighley@warren.k12.in.us.

Address correspondence to the association, c/o Indiana Lib. Federation, 941 E. 86 St., Suite 260, Indianapolis 46240. Tel. 317-257-2040, fax 317-257-1389, e-mail ilf@indy.net.

World Wide Web http://www.ilfonline.org/?AISLE.

Iowa

Iowa Assn. of School Libns., div. of the Iowa Lib. Assn. Memb. 180+. Term of Office. Jan.–Jan. Publication. *IASL Journal* (online, 4 a year).

Chair Dixie Forcht. E-mail dixieforcht@gmail.com; *V. Chair* Kathrine Rogers. E-mail kathrine.rogers@mcsdonline.org; *Secy./Treas.* Sue Inhelder. E-mail sinhelder@marshalltown.k12.ia.us; *Past Chair* Christine Sturgeon. E-mail csturgeon@mnwcougars.com.

Address correspondence to the chairperson. World Wide Web http://www.iasl-ia.org.

Kansas

Kansas Assn. of School Libns. Memb. 600. Publication. *KASL News* (online, q.).

Pres. Nancy McFarlin. E-mail kaslpresident@gmail.com; *Pres.-Elect* Marla Wigton. E-mail kaslpresidentelect@gmail.com; *Secy.* Sharon Parks. E-mail kaslsecretary@gmail.com; *Treas.* Brenda Lemon. E-mail kasltreasurer@gmail.com; *Past Pres.* Carmaine Ternes; E-mail kaslpastpresident@gmail.com; *Exec. Secy.* Barb Bahm. E-mail kaslexecsecretary@gmail.com.

Address correspondence to the executive secretary.

World Wide Web http://kasl.typepad.com/kasl.

Kentucky

Kentucky Assn. of School Libns. (KASL), section of Kentucky Lib. Assn. Memb. 600+. Publication. *KASL Newsletter* (q.).

Pres. Lisa Hughes, Lone Oak Intermediate School, 300 Cumberland Ave., Paducah 42001. Tel. 270-538-4160, e-mail lisa.hughes@mccracken.kyschools.us; *Pres.-Elect* James Allen. E-mail james.allen@oldham.kyschools.us; *Secy.* Renee Hale. E-mail renee.hale@warren.kyschools.us; *Treas.* Fred Tilsley. E-mail ftilsley@windstream.net; *Past Pres.* Janet Wells, Rockcastle County H.S. Tel. 606-256-4816, e-mail janet.wells@rockcastle.kyschools.us.

Address correspondence to the president.

World Wide Web http://www.kysma.org.

Louisiana

Louisiana Assn. of School Libns., section of Louisiana Lib. Assn. Memb. 230. Term of Office. July–June.

Pres. Kristy Sturm. Tel. 337-521-7411 ext. 18919, e-mail kasturm@lpssonline.com; *1st V.P./Pres.-Elect* Jade Calais. Tel. 337-521-7950, fax 337-521-7951, e-mail rjrcampbell@lpssonline.com; *2nd V.P.* Desiree Alexander. E-mail educatoralexander@gmail.com; *Secy.* Janet Gary. Tel. 337-364-3927, fax 337-365-9681, e-mail jgary@iberia.k12.la.us; *Past Pres.* Amanda Graves. Tel. 225-383-0397 ext.118, e-mail agraves@catholichigh.org.

Address correspondence to the association, c/o Louisiana Lib. Assn., 8550 United Plaza Blvd., Suite 1001, Baton Rouge 70809. Tel. 225-922-4642, fax 225-408-4422, e-mail office@llaonline.org.

World Wide Web http://llaonline.org/sig/lasl.php.

Maine

Maine Assn. of School Libs. Memb. 200+.

Pres. Joyce Lucas, Winslow H.S. E-mail jolukeme@gmail.com; *Pres.-Elect* Tina Taggart, Foxcroft Academy. E-mail tina.taggart@staff.foxcroftacademy.org; *Secy.* Janet Patterson. E-mail janet.patterson.mls@gmail.com; *Treas.* Dorothy Hall-Riddle. E-mail dorothy hallriddle@gmail.com; *Past Pres.* Eileen Broderick. E-mail ebroderick@rus10.org; *Business Mgr.* Edna Comstock, MASL, P.O. Box 634,

Augusta 04332-0634. Tel. 207-441-1410, e-mail masl@gwi.net.

Address correspondence to the president.

World Wide Web http://www.maslibraries.org.

Maryland

Maryland Assn. of School Libns. (formerly Maryland Educ. Media Organization).

Pres. Mary Jo Richmond, Frederick County Public Schools. E-mail president@maslmd.org; *Secy.* Linda S. Langr, High Point H.S., Prince George's County Public Schools. E-mail secretary@maslmd.org; *Treas.* Lynda Baker, Frederick County Public Schools. E-mail treasurer@maslmd.org; *Past Pres.* Michele Forney, Prince George's County Public Schools. E-mail michele.forney@gmail.com.

Address correspondence to the association, Box 21127, Baltimore 21228.

World Wide Web http://maslmd.org.

Massachusetts

Massachusetts School Lib. Assn. Memb. 800. Publication. *MSLA Forum* (3 a year).

Pres. Judi Paradis, Plympton Elementary, Waltham. Tel. 781-314-5767, e-mail jparadis@maschoolibraries.org; *Pres.-Elect* Anita Cellucci, Westborough H.S. Tel. 508-836-7720 ext. 5180; *Secy.* Carrie Tucker, E. Bridgewater H.S. Tel. 508-378-5841; *Treas.* Linda Friel. E-mail lafriel@maschoolibraries.org; *Past Pres.* Valerie Diggs, Chelmsford H.S. Tel. 978-251-5111; *Exec. Dir.* Kathy Lowe, Massachusetts School Lib. Assn., P.O. Box 658, Lunenburg 01462. Tel. 978-582-6967, e-mail klowe@maschoolibraries.org.

Address correspondence to the executive director.

World Wide Web http://www.maschoolibraries.org.

Michigan

Michigan Assn. for Media in Educ. Memb. 1,200. Publications. *Media Spectrum* (2 a year); *MAME Newsletter* (6 a year).

Pres. Kathy Lester, East Middle School, 1042 S. Mill St., Plymouth 48170. Tel. 734-416-4951, e-mail kathyl@mimame.org; *Pres.-Elect* Gwenn Marchesano, Pioneer Middle School, 46081 Ann Arbor Rd., Plymouth

48170. Tel. 734-416-7561, e-mail gmarchesano @mimame.org; *Secy.* Jeanna Walker, Portage Public Schools, 1000 Idaho St., Portage 49024. Tel. 269-323-5489, e-mail jwalker@portageps. org; *Past Pres.* Tom Stream, 15681 High Ridge Drive, Grand Haven 49417. Tel. 616-842-3335, e-mail tom.stream@mimame.org.

Address correspondence to MAME, 1407 Rensen, Suite 3, Lansing 48910. Tel. 517-394-2808, fax 517-394-2096, e-mail mame@mimame.org.

World Wide Web http://www.mimame.org.

Minnesota

Info. and Technology Educators of Minnesota (ITEM) (formerly Minnesota Educ. Media Organization). Memb. 400+. Term of Office. July–June.

Pres. Mary Mehsikomer, TIES, 1667 Snelling Ave. N., St. Paul 55108. Tel. 651-999-6510, e-mail mary.mehsikomer@ties.k12. mn.us; *Co-Pres.-Elect* Andi Bodeau, Bloomington Public Schools. E-mail bodeaua@gmail. com; Jen Legatt, Hopkins Public Schools. E-mail jen.m.legatt@gmail.com; *Secy.* Rosalyn Obando, Richfield Middle School, 7461 Oliver Ave. S., Richfield 55423. Tel. 612-798-6400, e-mail rjobando@gmail.com; *Treas.* Robin Weber, Isanti 55040. Tel. 763-464-1503, e-mail weber@usinternet.com; *Past Co-Pres.* Karen Qualey, Hubert Olson Middle School, 4551 W. 102 St., Bloomington 55437. E-mail karenjoy113@gmail.com; Donna Ohlgren, Oak View Elementary, 6710 E. Fish Lake Rd., Maple Grove 55369. E-mail ohlgrend@gmail. com; *Admin. Asst.* Deanna Sylte, P.O. Box 130555, Roseville 55113. Tel. 651-771-8672, e-mail admin@memoweb.org.

World Wide Web http://mnitem.org.

Mississippi

School Lib. Section, Mississippi Lib. Assn. Memb. 1,300.

Chair Holly Gray, Tupelo High Schools. Tel. 662-841-8979, e-mail ehgray@gmail.com. *Exec. Secy.* Barbara J. Price.

Address correspondence to School Section, Mississippi Lib. Assn., P.O. Box 13687, Jackson 39236-3687. Tel. 601-981-4586, e-mail info@misslib.org.

World Wide Web http://www.misslib.org.

Missouri

Missouri Assn. of School Libns. Memb. 1,000. Term of Office. July–June. Publication. *Connections* (q.).

Pres. Lysha Thompson, Miller County R-3 Schools. E-mail lthompson@tuscumbialions. k12.mo.us; *1st V.P./Pres.-Elect* Margaret Sullivan, Rockwood Summit H.S., Marquette H.S., Rockwood School Dist. E-mail sullivan margaret@rockwood.k12.mo.us; *2nd V.P.* Amy Taylor, Lee's Summit West H.S. E-mail amy. taylor@leesummit.k12.mo.us; *Secy.* Rene Burress, Univ. of Central Missouri. E-mail burress@ucmo.edu; *Treas.* Kris Baughman, Eastwood Hills Elementary, Raytown C-2 School Dist. E-mail kris.baughman@raytown schools.org; *Past Pres.* Ellen Wickham, Raytown South H.S. E-mail wickhame@raytown schools.org.

Address correspondence to the association, P.O. Box 684, Jefferson City 65102. Tel. 573-635-6044, e-mail info@maslonline.org.

World Wide Web http://www.maslonline. org.

Montana

School Lib. Div., Montana Lib. Assn. Memb. 200+. Publication. *FOCUS* (published by Montana Lib. Assn.) (q.).

Chair Dana Carmichael, Whitefish Middle School, 221 Peregrine Lane, Whitefish 59937. Tel. 406-862-8650, e-mail carmichaeld@wfps. k12.mt.us; *V. Chair* Niki Keuch, Chief Joseph Middle School, 4255 Kimberwicke, Bozeman 59718. Tel. 406-522-6307, e-mail nkeuch@ gmail.com; *Past Chair* Lisa Lykins, Glacier H.S., 851 N. Main St., Kalispell 59901. Tel. 406-261-2338, e-mail lykinsl@sd5.k12.mt.us; *Exec. Dir., Montana Lib. Assn.* Debbi Kramer, P.O. Box 1352, Three Forks 59752. Tel. 406-579-3121, e-mail debkmla@hotmail.com.

World Wide Web http://www.mtlib.org.

Nebraska

Nebraska School Libns. Assn. Memb. 300+. Term of Office. July–June. Publication. *NSLA News* (q.).

Pres. Beth Kabes. E-mail bkabes@esu7. org; *Pres.-Elect* Laura Pietsch. E-mail laura. pietsch@ops.org; *Secy.* Stephanie Dannehl. E-mail sdannehl@esu11.org; *Treas.* Angie

Richeson. E-mail aricheso@esu10.org; *Past Pres.* Sherry Crow. E-mail crowsr@unk.edu; *Exec. Secy.* Kim Gangwish. E-mail contact nsla@gmail.com.

Address correspondence to the executive secretary, Bellevue West H.S., 1501 Thurston Ave., Bellevue 68123.

World Wide Web http://www.neschoolli-brarians.org.

Nevada

Nevada School and Children Libns. Section, Nevada Lib. Assn. Memb. 120.

Chair Shar Murphy, Honors Academy of Literature. E-mail ms.shar@academyoflit.org; *Past Chair* Carla Land, Las Vegas-Clark County Lib. Dist. E-mail landc@lvccld.org; *Exec. Secy.* Kristy Isla. E-mail ardainia@yahoo.com.

Address correspondence to the executive secretary.

World Wide Web http://www.nevadalibraries.org/handbook/nscls.html.

New Hampshire

New Hampshire School Lib. Media Assn. Memb. 250+. Term of Office. July–June. Publication. *Online News* (winter, spring; online and print).

Pres. Carol Sweny, Henniker Community School. E-mail cdsweny@comcast.net; *V.P.* Donna Zecha, Hopkinton Middle/H.S. Lib., Contoocook. E-mail hophslibrary@hopkinton schools.org; *Recording Secy.* Caitlin Ahearn. E-mail cahearn@londonderry.org; *Treas.* Helen Burnham, Lincoln Street School, Exeter. E-mail hburnham@sau16.org; *Past Pres.* Pam Harland, Sanborn Regional H.S., Kingston. E-mail pharland@sau17.org.

Address correspondence to the president, NHSLMA, Box 418, Concord 03302-0418.

World Wide Web World Wide Web http://nhslma.org.

New Jersey

New Jersey Assn. of School Libns. (NJASL). Memb. 1,000+. Term of Office. Aug.–July.

Pres. Arlen Kimmelman, Clearview Regional H.S., Mullica Hill. E-mail president@njasl.org; *Pres.-Elect* Janet Clark, Cleveland Street School, Orange. E-mail presidentelect@njasl.org; *V.P.* Bruce DuBoff, Pennsauken Intermediate School and Howard M. Phifer Middle School, Pennsauken. E-mail vicepresident@njasl.org; *Recording Secy.* Michelle McGreivey. E-mail recordingsecretary@njasl.org; *Treas.* Jean Stock. E-mail treasurer@njasl.org; *Past Pres.* Pam Gunter. E-mail immediatepastpresident@njasl.org.

Address correspondence to Elizabeth McArthur, Mgr., NJASL, P.O. Box 460, Collingswood 08108. E-mail associationmanager@njasl.org.

World Wide Web http://www.njasl.org.

New York

Section of School Libns., New York Lib. Assn., 6021 State Farm Rd., Guilderland, NY 12084. Tel. 518-432-6952, fax 518-427-1697, e-mail info@nyla.org†. Memb. 800+. Term of Office. Nov.–Oct. Publications. *SLMSGram* (q.); participates in *NYLA Bulletin* (mo. except July and Aug.).

Pres. Jill Leinung. E-mail mfleinung@gmail.com; *Pres.-Elect* Susan Polos; *Past Pres.* Karen Sperrazza. E-mail krnsprzz@gmail.com.

World Wide Web http://nylassl.weebly.com.

North Carolina

North Carolina School Lib. Media Assn. Memb. 1,000+. Term of Office. Nov. Oct.

Pres. Joanna Gerakios, Pitt County Schools. Tel. 252-830-3516, fax 252-830-0206, e-mail gerakij@pitt.k12.nc.us; *Pres.-Elect* Walter Carmichael, Kimmel Farm Elementary, Winston Salem 27127. Tel. 336-703-6760, fax 336-784-4427, e-mail ncslmawalter@gmail.com; *Secy.* Jennifer Umbarger, Rogers-Herr Middle School, Durham Public Schools, Durham 27707. Tel. 919-560-3970 ext. 70235, e-mail jennifer.umbarger@dpsnc.net; *Treas.* Laura Bowers, Westwood Elementary, West Jefferson 28694. Tel. 336-877-2921, e-mail laura.bowers@ashe.k12.nc.us; *Past Pres.* Joann Absi, New Hanover County Schools, Wilmington 28412. Tel. 910-790-2360, fax 910-790-2356, e-mail joann.absi@nhcs.net.

Address correspondence to the president.

World Wide Web http://www.ncslma.org.

North Dakota

School Lib. and Youth Services Section, North Dakota Lib. Assn. Memb. 100. Publication. *The Good Stuff* (q.).

Chair Amber Emery, Fargo Public Lib. Tel. 701-241-1495,fax701-241-8581,e-mailaemery @cityoffargo.com.

World Wide Web http://ndlaonline.org.

Ohio

Ohio Educ. Lib. Media Assn. Memb. 1,000. Publications. *OELMA News* (3 a year); *Ohio Media Spectrum* (q.).

Pres. Angela Wojtecki, Nordonia Hills H.S., 8006 S. Bedford Drive, Macedonia 44056. Tel. 330-908-6030, e-mail oelma.awojtecki@ gmail.com; *V.P.* Liz Deskins, Hilliard Bradley H.S. 4629 Shaler Drive, Columbus 43228. Tel. 614-870-1641; *Secy.* Karen Gedeon, Cuyahoga Falls Middle School, 1057 Thornton Court, Macedonia 44056. Tel. 330-467-2017, e-mail kgedeon2@gmail.com; *Treas.* Lisa Barnes Prince, Stanton Middle School, 1175 Hudson Rd., Kent 44240. E-mail lbarnesprince@att. net; *Past Pres.* Susan Yutze. E-mail oelmasdy@ gmail.com; *Dir. of Services* Kate Brunswick, 17 S. High St., Suite 200, Columbus 43215. Tel. 614-221-1900, fax 614-221-1989, e-mail kate@assnoffices.com.

Address correspondence to the director of services.

World Wide Web http://www.oelma.org.

Oklahoma

Oklahoma School Libns. Div., Oklahoma Lib. Assn. Memb. 200+. Publication. *Oklahoma Librarian.*

Chair Kristi Merchant. E-mail oksl@oklibs. org; *Past Chair* Earon Cunningham.

Address correspondence to the chairperson, School Libs. Div., Oklahoma Lib. Assn., P.O. Box 6550, Edmond, OK 73083. Tel. 405-348-0506.

World Wide Web http://www.oklibs.org/ ?page=OKSL.

Oregon

Oregon Assn. of School Libs. Memb. 600. Publication. *Interchange* (3 a year).

Pres. Stephanie Thomas. E-mail president@ oasl.olaweb.org; *Pres.-Elect* Robin Rolfe. E-mail presidentelect@oasl.olaweb.org; *Secy.* Jenny Takeda. E-mail secretary@oasl.olaweb. org; *Treas.* Stuart Levy. E-mail treasurer@oasl. olaweb.org; *Past Pres.* Nancy Sullivan. E-mail pastpresident@oasl.olaweb.org.

Address correspondence to the association, P.O. Box 3067, La Grande 97850.

World Wide Web http://ola.memberclicks. net/oasl-home.

Pennsylvania

Pennsylvania School Libns. Assn. Memb. 800+.

Pres. Michael Nailor. E-mail mnailor@psla. org; *V.P./Pres.-Elect* Allison Burrell. E-mail aburrell@psla.org; *Secy.* Lindsey Long. E-mail pslaboard@psla.org; *Treas.* Natalie Hawley. E-mail pslaboard@psla.org; *Past Pres.* Eileen Kern. E-mail ekern@psla.org.

Address correspondence to the president.

World Wide Web http://www.psla.org.

Rhode Island

School Libns. of Rhode Island (formerly Rhode Island Educ. Media Assn.). Memb. 350+.

Pres. Jane Perry. *V.P.* Sarah Hunicke; *Secy.* Lisa Casey; *Treas.* Jen Simoneau; *Past Pres.* Darshell Silva.

World Wide Web http://www.slri.info.

South Carolina

South Carolina Assn. of School Libns. Memb. 900. Term of Office. July–June.

Pres. Diana Carr. E-mail dcarr@richland one.org; *V.P./Pres.-Elect* Jennifer Tazerouti; *Secy.* Andi Fansher. E-mail andifansher@ gmail.com; *Treas.* Gloria Coleman; *Past Pres.* Anne Lemieux. E-mail lemieux.anne@gmail. com; *Exec. Secy.* Diane Ervin. E-mail ervin scasl@gmail.com.

Address correspondence to the association, P.O. Box 2442, Columbia 29202. Tel./fax 803-492-3025.

World Wide Web http://www.scasl.net.

South Dakota

South Dakota School Lib. Media Section, South Dakota Lib. Assn., 28363 472nd Ave.,

Worthing 57077. Tel. 605-372-0235. Memb. 140+. Term of Office. Oct.–Sept.
Chair Sharlene Lien, Discovery Elementary, Sioux Falls. E-mail sharlene.lien@k12.sd.us.

Tennessee

Tennessee Assn. of School Libns. Memb. 450. Term of Office. Jan.–Dec. Publication. *TASL Talks.*
Pres. Lora Ann Black, Stewart County H.S. E-mail loraannblack.tasl@gmail.com; *V.P./ Pres.-Elect* Mindy Nichols, Crockett County H.S. E-mail mindy.nichols.tasl@gmail.com; *Secy.* Shannon Minner, Reeves Rogers Elementary. E-mail shannon.minner.tasl@gmail.com; *Treas.* Nancy Dickinson, Hillsboro Elementary. E-mail tasltennessee@gmail.com; *Past Pres.* Mona Batchelor, McKenzie H.S. E-mail mona.batchelor.tasl@gmail.com.
Address correspondence to the president.
World Wide Web http://www.tasltn.org.

Texas

Texas Assn. of School Libns., div. of Texas Lib. Assn. Memb. 4,000+. Term of Office. Apr.–Mar.
Chair Julie Briggs. E-mail julie.briggs@ risd.org; *Chair-Elect* Renee Dyer. E-mail rdyer @wisd.us; *Secy.* Jill Bellomy. E-mail jill bellomy@gmail.com; *Past Chair* Karen Kessel. E-mail karen_kessel@yahoo.com.
Address correspondence to Texas Lib. Assn., 3355 Bee Cave Rd., Suite 401, Austin 78746. Tel. 512-328-1518, fax 512-328-8852, e-mail tla@txla.org.
World Wide Web http://www.txla.org/ groups/tasl.

Utah

Utah Educ. Lib. Media Assn. Memb. 500+. Publication. *UELMA Newsletter* (q.).
Pres. Jessica Moody, Olympus Junior H.S., 2217 E. 4800 S., Holladay 84117-5309. Tel. 385-646-5224, e-mail jmoody@graniteschools. org; *Pres.-Elect* Michelle Miles, Riverton H.S., 12476 S. 2700 W., Riverton 84065. Tel. 801-256-5800, e-mail michelle.miles@jordan district.org; *Secy.* Nikki Ann Gregerson, Granite School Dist., 2500 S. State St., Salt Lake City. Tel. 801-824-8478, e-mail ngregerson

@graniteschools.org; *Past Pres.* Amanda Porter, Rocky Mountain Middle School, 800 W. School House Way, Heber City 84032. Tel. 435-654-9350 ext. 2610, e-mail amanda.porter @wasatch.edu; *Exec. Dir.* Brian Rollins. Tel. 801-232-6531, e-mail brollins04@comcast. net.
Address correspondence to the executive director.
World Wide Web http://www.uelma.org.

Vermont

Vermont School Lib. Assn. (formerly Vermont Educ. Media Assn.). Memb. 220+. Term of Office. May–May. Publication. *VSLA Newsletter Online* (q.).
Pres. Linda McSweeney, Stowe Middle/ H.S., 413 Barrows Rd., Stowe 05672. Tel. 802-253-7229, e-mail linda.mcsweeney@lssuvt. org; *Pres.-Elect* Kathy Lawrence. E-mail klawrence@ccsuvt.org; *Secy.* Kate Davie, Blue Mountain Union School, 2420 Rte. 302, Wells River 05081. Tel. 802-757-2711 ext.1142, e-mail kate.davie@bmuschool.org; *Treas.* Susan Monmaney, Montpelier H.S., 5 High School Drive, Montpelier 05602. Tel. 802-225-8020, e-mail susanm@mpsvt.org; *Past Pres.* Denise Wentz, Allen Brook School, 497 Talcott Rd., Williston 05495. Tel. 802-879-5848, e-mail dwentz@cssu.org.
Address correspondence to the president.
World Wide Web https://sites.google.com/ site/vermontschoollibraries/home.

Virginia

Virginia Assn. of School Libns. (VAASL) (formerly Virginia Educ. Media Assn. [VEMA]). Memb. 1,200. Term of Office. Nov.–Nov. Publication. *VAASL Voice* (q.).
Pres. Eileen Godwin. E-mail president@ vaasl.org; *Pres.-Elect* Carolyn Vibbert. E-mail presidentelect@vaasl.org; *Secy.* Schenell Agee. E-mail secretary@vaasl.org; *Treas.* Judy Deichman. E-mail treasurer@vaasl.org; *Past Pres.* Lori Donovan. E-mail pastpresident@ vaasl.org; *Exec. Dir.* Margaret Baker. Tel. 540-416-6109, e-mail executive@vaasl.org.
Address correspondence to the association, P.O. Box 2015, Staunton 24402-2015. Tel. 540-416-6109.
World Wide Web http://vaasl.org.

Washington

Washington Lib. Media Assn. Memb. 700+. Term of Office. Oct.–Oct. Publication. *Medium* (3 a year). *Ed.* Jodeana Kruse. E-mail medium @wlma.org.

Pres. Sharyn Merrigan. E-mail president@ wlma.org; *Pres.-Elect* Craig Seasholes. E-mail pres-elect@wlma.org; *V.P.* Carrie Willenbring. E-mail vicepresident@wlma.org; *Secy.* Kimberly Rose. E-mail secretary@wlma.org; *Treas.* Merrilyn Tucker. E-mail treasurer@wlma. org; *Past Pres.* Anne Bingham. E-mail past president@wlma.org.

Address correspondence to the association. E-mail wlma@wlma.org.

World Wide Web http://www.wlma.org.

West Virginia

School Lib. Div., West Virginia Lib. Assn. Memb. 50. Term of Office. Nov.–Nov. Publication. *WVLA School Library News* (5 a year).

Chair Lynda Suzie Martin, Brookhaven Elementary, 147 Estate Drive, Morgantown 26508. Tel. 304-282-0147, e-mail library nbct@gmail.com; *Past Chair* Cathy Davis, East Fairmont Junior H.S., 1 Orion Lane, Fairmont 26554. Tel. 304-367-2123, e-mail davisc57@ hotmail.com.

Address correspondence to the chairperson. World Wide Web http://www.wvla.org.

Wisconsin

Wisconsin Educ. Media and Technology Assn. Memb. 1,100+. Publication. *WEMTA Dispatch* (q.).

Pres. Donna Smith. E-mail president@ wemta.org; *Pres.-Elect* Kim Bannigan. E-mail pres-elect@wemta.org; *Secy.* Eileen Schroeder. E-mail secretary@wemta.org; *Treas.* Renee Disch. E-mail treasurer@wemta.org; *Past Pres.* Joel VerDuin. E-mail joelverduin@ yahoo.com.

Address correspondence to WEMTA, P.O. Box 44578, Madison 53744-4578. Tel. 608-848-1232, fax 608-848-9266, e-mail wemta@ wiscow.com.

World Wide Web http://www.wemta.org.

Wyoming

Teacher-Libn. Interest Group, Wyoming Lib. Assn. Memb. 100+.

Group Leader Laura Miller. E-mail lamiller @ccsd.k12.wy.us.

Address correspondence to the group leader. World Wide Web https://sites.google.com/ site/wlateacherlibrarians.

International Library Associations

International Association of Agricultural Information Specialists

Federico Sancho Guevara, President
IAALD, P.O. Box 63, Lexington, KY 40588-0063
Fax 859-257-8379, e-mail info@iaald.org
World Wide Web http://www.iaald.org

Object

The International Association of Agricultural Information Specialists (IAALD) facilitates professional development of and communication among members of the agricultural information community worldwide. Its goal is to enhance access to and use of agriculture-related information resources. To further this mission, IAALD will promote the agricultural information profession, support professional development activities, foster collaboration, and provide a platform for information exchange. Founded 1955.

Membership

Memb. 400+ in more than 75 countries. Dues (Inst.) US$130; (Indiv.) US$60.

Officers

Pres. Federico Sancho Guevara (Costa Rica); *V.P./Pres.-Elect* Peter Walton (Australia); *Secy.-Treas.* Toni Greider (USA); *Past Pres.* Edith Hesse (Austria).

Board Members

Krishan Bheenick (Mauritius), Jerry Miner (Canada), Jaron Porciello (USA), Margaret Sraku-Lartey (Ghana).

Publication

Agricultural Information Worldwide (q.) (memb.).

International Association of Law Libraries

Jeroen Vervliet, President
Peace Palace Library, The Hague, Netherlands
Tel. 31-70-302-4242, e-mail j.vervliet@ppl.nl
World Wide Web http://www.iall.org

Object

The International Association of Law Libraries (IALL) is a worldwide organization of librarians, libraries, and other persons or institutions concerned with the acquisition and use of legal information emanating from sources other than their jurisdictions and from multinational and international organizations.

IALL's purpose is to facilitate the work of librarians who acquire, process, organize, and provide access to foreign legal materials. IALL has no local chapters but maintains liaison with national law library associations in many countries and regions of the world.

Membership

More than 800 members in more than 50 countries on five continents.

Officers

Pres. Jeroen Vervliet, Peace Palace Lib., Carnegieplein 2, 2517 KJ The Hague, Netherlands. Tel. 31-70-302-4242, e-mail j.vervliet@ppl.nl; *1st V.P.* Ruth Bird, Bodleian Law Lib., Univ. of Oxford, St. Cross Bldg., Manor Rd., Oxford OX1 3UR, England. Tel. 44-1865-271451, fax 44-1865-271475, e-mail ruth.bird@bodleian. ox.ac.uk; *2nd V.P.* Bård Tuseth, Dept. of Public and International Law Lib., Domus Bibliotheca, Karl Johansgt. 47, 0162 Oslo, Norway. Tel. 47-2285-9494, fax 47-2285-9493, e-mail b.s.tuseth@ub.uio.no; *Secy.* Barbara Garavaglia, Univ. of Michigan Law Lib., Ann Arbor, MI 48109-1210. Tel. 734-764-9338, fax 734-764-5863, e-mail bvaccaro@umich.edu; *Treas.* Xinh Luu, Univ. of Virginia Law Lib., 580 Massie Rd., Charlottesville, VA 22903. E-mail xtl5d@virginia.edu; *Past Pres.* Petal Kinder, High Court of Australia, Parkes Place, Parkes, Canberra, ACT 2600. Tel. 61-2-6270-6922, fax 61-2-6273-2110, e-mail pkinder@hcourt.gov. au.

Board Members

Kristina Alayan, Duke Univ. School of Law; Daniel Boyer, Nahum Gelber Law Lib., McGill Univ.; Kurt Carroll, Lib. of Congress; Lily Echiverri, Univ. of the Philippines; Mark D. Engsberg (ex officio), MacMillan Law Lib., Emory Univ. School of Law, Atlanta; David Gee, Inst. of Advanced Legal Studies, Univ. of London; Marci Hoffman (ex officio), Univ. of California, Berkeley, School of Law Lib.; Kerem Kahvecioglu, Istanbul Bilgi Univ., Istanbul; Ivo Vogel, Sondersammelgebiet und Virtuellen Fachbibliothek Recht, Berlin.

Publication

International Journal of Legal Information (IJLI) (3 a year; memb.).

International Association of Music Libraries, Archives, and Documentation Centres

Pia Shekhter, Secretary-General
Gothenburg University Library, P.O. Box 210, SE 405 30 Gothenburg, Sweden
Tel. 46-31-786-4057, cell 46-703-226-092, fax 46-31-786-40-59, e-mail secretary@iaml.info.
World Wide Web http://www.iaml.info.

Object

The object of the International Association of Music Libraries, Archives, and Documentation Centres (IAML) is to promote the activities of music libraries, archives, and documentation centers and to strengthen the cooperation among them; to promote the availability of all publications and documents relating to music and further their bibliographical control; to encourage the development of standards in all areas that concern the association; and to support the protection and preservation of musical documents of the past and the present.

Membership

Memb. 1,700.

Board Members

Pres. Barbara Dobbs Mackenzie, *Répertoire International de Littérature Musicale (RILM)*, New York. E-mail president@iaml.info; *Secy.-Gen.* Pia Shekhter, Gothenburg Univ. Lib., Box 210, SE 405 30 Gothenburg. Tel. 46-31-786-40-57; *Treas.* Thomas Kalk, Stadtbüchereien Düsseldorf. E-mail treasurer@iaml.info; *V.P.s*

Stanisław Hrabia, Uniwersytet Jagiellonski, Kraków; Antony Gordon, British Lib., London; Johan Eeckeloo, Koninklijk Conservatorieum, Brussels; Joseph Hafner, McGill Univ., Montreal; *Past Pres.* Roger Flury, National Lib. of New Zealand (retired), P.O. Box 1467, Wellington.

Publication

Fontes Artis Musicae (4 a year; memb.). *Ed.* Maureen Buja, Hong Kong Gold Coast Block 22, Flat 1-A, 1 Castle Peak Rd., Tuen Mun, NT, Hong Kong. Tel. 852-2146-8047, e-mail fontes@iaml.info.

Professional Branches

Archives and Music Documentation Centres. *Chair* Marie Cornaz, Bibliothèque Royale de Belgique, Brussels. E-mail archives@iaml.info.
Broadcasting and Orchestra Libraries. *Chair* Nienke de Boer, Holland Symfonia, Haarlem. E-mail broadcasting@iaml.info.
Libraries in Music Teaching Institutions. *Chair* Johan Eeckeloo, Koninklijk Conservatorium, Brussels. E-mail teaching@iaml.info.

Public Libraries. *Chair* Carolyn Dow, Polley Music Lib., Lincoln City Libs., Lincoln, Nebraska. E-mail publiclibraries@iaml.info.
Research Libraries. *Chair* Thomas Leibnitz. Musiksammlung der Österreichischen Nationalbibliothek, Vienna. E-mail research libraries@iaml.info.

Subject Commissions

Audio-Visual Materials. *Chair* Andrew Justice. University of North Texas, Denton. E-mail av@iaml.info.
Bibliography. *Chair* Rupert Ridgewell, British Lib., London. E-mail bibliography@iaml.info.
Cataloguing. *Chair* Joseph Hafner. McGill Univ., Montreal. E-mail cataloguing@iaml.info.
Service and Training. *Chair* Jane Gottlieb. Juilliard School, New York. E-mail service@iaml.info.
Sub-commission on Unimarc. *Chair* Isabelle Gauchet Doris. Centre de Documentation de la Musique Contemporaine, Paris. E-mail unimarc@iaml.info.

International Association of School Librarianship

Kathleen Combs, Executive Director
65 E. Wacker Place, Suite 1900, Chicago, IL 60601
e-mail iasl@mlahq.org
World Wide Web http://iasl-online.mlanet.org

Mission and Objectives

The mission of the International Association of School Librarianship (IASL) is to provide an international forum for those interested in promoting effective school library programs as viable instruments in the education process. IASL also provides guidance and advice for the development of school library programs and the school library profession. IASL works in cooperation with other professional associations and agencies.

Membership is worldwide and includes school librarians, teachers, librarians, library advisers, consultants, education administrators, and others who are responsible for library and information services in schools. The membership also includes professors and instructors in universities and colleges where there are programs for school librarians, and students who are undertaking such programs.

The objectives of IASL are to advocate the development of school libraries throughout all countries; to encourage the integration of school library programs into the instruction and curriculum of the school; to promote the professional preparation and continuing education of school library personnel; to foster a sense of community among school librarians in all parts of the world; to foster and extend relationships between school librarians and other professionals in connection with children and youth; to foster research in the field of school librarianship and the integration of its findings with pertinent knowledge from related fields; to promote the publication and dissemination of information about successful advocacy and program initiatives in school librarianship; to share information about programs and materials for children and youth throughout the international community; and to initiate and coordinate activities, conferences, and other projects in the field of school librarianship and information services.

Founded 1971.

Membership

Approximately 600.

Officers and Executive Board

Pres. Diljit Singh, Malaysia; *V.P.s.* Mihaela Banek Zorica, Association Operations, Croatia; Kay Hones, Association Relations, USA; Elizabeth Greef, Advocacy and Promotion, Australia; *Treas.* Katy Manck, USA; *Dirs.* Geraldine Howell, Oceania; Busi Dlamini, Africa–Sub Sahara; Lourdes T. David, East Asia; Luisa Marquardt, Europe; Dianne Oberg, Canada; Madhu Bhargava, International Schools; Nancy Everhart, USA; Ayse Yuksel-Durukan, North Africa/Middle East; Hanna Chaterina George, Asia; Paulette Stewart, Latin America/Caribbean.

Publications

Proceedings of annual conferences (available on the EBSCO, Proquest, and Gale Cengage databases).
School Libraries Worldwide (http://www.iasl-online.org/publications/slw/index.html), the association's refereed research and professional journal (2 a year).
IASL Newsletter (http://www.iasl-online.org/publications/newsletter.html) (4 a year).

International Association of Scientific and Technological University Libraries (IATUL)

President, Reiner Kallenborn
World Wide Web http://www.iatul.org

Object

The main object of the International Association of Scientific and Technological University Libraries (IATUL) is to provide a forum where library directors and senior managers can meet to exchange views on matters of current significance and to provide an opportunity for them to develop a collaborative approach to solving problems. IATUL also welcomes into membership organizations that supply services to university libraries, if they wish to be identified with the association's activities.

Membership

250+ in 60 countries.

Officers

Pres. Reiner Kallenborn, Technische Universität München, Munich, Germany; *V.P.* Gwendolyn Ebbett, Univ. of Windsor, Ontario, Canada; *Secy.* Elisha R. T. Chiware, Cape Peninsula Univ. of Technology, South Africa; *Treas.* Irma Pasanen, Aalto Univ. Lib., Helsinki, Finland.

Publication

IATUL Conference Proceedings (on IATUL website, http://www.iatul.org) (ann.).

International Council on Archives

David A. Leitch, Secretary-General
60 rue des Francs-Bourgeois, 75003 Paris, France
Tel. 33-1-40-27-63-06, fax 33-1-42-72-20-65, e-mail ica@ica.org
World Wide Web http://www.ica.org

Object

The mission of the International Council on Archives (ICA) is to establish, maintain, and strengthen relations among archivists of all lands, and among all professional and other agencies or institutions concerned with the custody, organization, or administration of archives, public or private, wherever located. Established 1948.

Membership

Memb. Approximately 1,400 (representing nearly 200 countries and territories).

Officers

Pres. David Fricker, Australia; *V.P.s* Andreas Kellerhals, Switzerland; Henri Zuber, France.

Executive Board

Haman bin Mohammed al-Dhawyani, Oman; Atakitty Assefa Asgedom, Ethiopia; Esther Cruces Blanco, Spain; Paola Caroli, Italy; Eric Sze Choong, Singapore; Bryan Corbett, Canada; Margaret Crockett, United Kingdom; Jaime Antunes da Silva, Brazil; Deborah Jenkins, United Kingdom; Antoine Lumenganeso Kiobe, Congo; Alphonse Labitan, Benin; Hervé Lemoine, France; Emilie Gagnet Leumas, United States; William J. Maher, United States; Milovan Misic, Switzerland; Francis Mwangi, Kenya; Donghoon Park, South Korea; Günther Schefbeck, Austria; Amela Silipa, Western Samoa; Kenth Sjöblom, Finland; David Sutton, United Kingdom; Rita Tjien-Fooh, Suriname; Sarah Tyacke, United Kingdom; F. J. W. Van Kan, Netherlands; Karel Velle, Belgium; Amatuni Virabyan, Armenia; Geir Magnus Walderhaug, Norway; Saroja Wettasinghe, Sri Lanka.

Publications

Comma (memb.) (2 a year, memb.).
Flash (2 a year; memb.).
Guide to the Sources of the History of Nations (Latin American Series, 11 vols. pub.; Africa South of the Sahara Series, 20 vols. pub.; North Africa, Asia, and Oceania Series, 15 vols. pub.).
Guide to the Sources of Asian History (English-language series [India, Indonesia, Korea, Nepal, Pakistan, Singapore], 14 vols. pub.; national language series [Indonesia, Korea, Malaysia, Nepal, Thailand], 6 vols. pub.; other guides, 3 vols. pub.).

International Federation of Film Archives
(Fédération Internationale des Archives du Film)

Secretariat, 42 rue Blanche, B-1060 Brussels, Belgium
Tel. 32-2-538-30-65, fax 32-2-534-47-74, e-mail info@fiafnet.org
World Wide Web http://www.fiafnet.org

Object

Founded in 1938, the International Federation of Film Archives (FIAF) brings together not-for-profit institutions dedicated to rescuing films and any other moving-image elements considered both as cultural heritage and as historical documents.

FIAF is a collaborative association of the world's leading film archives whose purpose has always been to ensure the proper preservation and showing of motion pictures. More than 150 archives in more than 75 countries collect, restore, and exhibit films and cinema documentation spanning the entire history of film.

FIAF seeks to promote film culture and facilitate historical research, to help create new archives around the world, to foster training and expertise in film preservation, to encourage the collection and preservation of documents and other cinema-related materials, to develop cooperation between archives, and to ensure the international availability of films and cinema documents.

Officers

Pres. Eric Le Roy; *Secy.-Gen.* Michael Loebensten; *Treas.* Jon Wengström.

Address correspondence to Christophe Dupin, Senior Administrator, c/o FIAF Secretariat. E-mail c.dupin@fiafnet.org.

Publications

Journal of Film Preservation.
International Index to Film Periodicals.
FIAF International Filmarchive database (OVID).
FIAF International Index to Film Periodicals (ProQuest).

For additional FIAF publications, see http://www.fiafnet.org.

International Federation of Library Associations and Institutions

Jennefer Nicholson, Secretary-General
P.O. Box 95312, 2509 CH The Hague, Netherlands
Tel. 31-70-314-0884, fax 31-70-383-4827
E-mail ifla@ifla.org, World Wide Web http://www.ifla.org

Object

The object of the International Federation of Library Associations and Institutions (IFLA) is to promote international understanding, cooperation, discussion, research, and development in all fields of library activity, including bibliography, information services, and the education of library personnel, and to provide a body through which librarianship can be represented in matters of international interest. IFLA is the leading international body representing the interests of library and information services and their users. It is the global voice of the library and information profession. Founded 1927.

Officers and Governing Board

Pres. Sinikka Sipilä, Finnish Lib. Assn.; *Pres.-Elect* Donna Scheeder, Lib. of Congress; *Treas.* Frédéric Blin, Bibliothèque Nationale et Universitaire de Strasbourg.

Governing Board

Kent Skov Andreasen (Denmark), Ingrid Bon (Netherlands), Genevieve Clavel-Merrin (Switzerland), Loida Garcia-Febo (United States), Ngian Lek Choh (Singapore), Barbara Lison (Germany), Inga Lundén (Sweden), Ellen Ndeshi Namhila (Namibia), and Glòria Pérez-Salmerón (Spain), plus the chairs of the IFLA Professional Committee and divisions.

Publications

IFLA Annual Report.
IFLA Journal (4 a year).
IFLA Professional Reports.
IFLA Publications Series.
IFLA Series on Bibliographic Control.
International Preservation News.

American Membership

Associations

American Lib. Assn., Assn. for Lib. and Info. Science Educ., Assn. of Research Libs., Chief Officers of State Lib. Agencies, Medical Lib. Assn., Special Libs. Assn., Urban Libs. Council, Chinese American Libns. Assn., Polish American Lib. Assn.

Institutional Members

More than 100 libraries and related institutions are institutional members or consultative bodies and sponsors of IFLA in the United States (out of a total of more than 1,000 globally), and more than 100 are individual affiliates (out of a total of more than 300 affiliates globally).

International Organization for Standardization

Rob Steele, Secretary-General
ISO Central Secretariat, Chemin de Blandonnet 8, CP 401
1214 Vernier, Geneva, Switzerland
Tel. 41-22-749-01-11, fax 41-22-733-34-30, e-mail central@iso.org
World Wide Web http://www.iso.org

Object

The International Organization for Standardization (ISO) is a worldwide federation of national standards bodies, founded in 1947, at present comprising 163 members, one in each country. The object of ISO is to promote the development of standardization and related activities in the world with a view to facilitating international exchange of goods and services, and to developing cooperation in the spheres of intellectual, scientific, technological, and economic activity. The scope of ISO covers international standardization in all fields except electrical and electronic engineering standardization, which is the responsibility of the International Electrotechnical Commission (IEC). The results of ISO technical work are published as international standards.

Officers

Pres. Zhang Xiaogang, China; *V.P. (Policy)* John Walter, Canada; *V.P. (Technical Management)* Elisabeth Stampfl-Blaha, Austria; *V.P. (Finance)* Olivier Peyrat, France; *Treas.* Miguel Payró, Argentina/United Kingdom.

Technical Work

The technical work of ISO is carried out by more than 200 technical committees. These include:

ISO/TC 46—Information and documentation (Secretariat, Association Française de Normalization, 11 ave. Francis de Pressensé, 93571 La Plaine Saint-Denis, Cedex, France). Scope: Standardization of practices relating to libraries, documentation and information centers, indexing and abstracting services, archives, information science, and publishing.

ISO/TC 37—Terminology and language and content resources (Secretariat, INFOTERM, Aichholzgasse 6/12, 1120 Vienna, Austria, on behalf of Österreichisches Normungsinstitut). Scope: Standardization of principles, methods, and applications relating to terminology and other language and content resources in the contexts of multilingual communication and cultural diversity.

ISO/IEC JTC 1—Information technology (Secretariat, American National Standards Institute, 25 W. 43 St., 4th fl., New York, NY 10036). Scope: Standardization in the field of information technology.

Publications

ISO Annual Report.
ISOfocus (6 a year).
ISO International Standards.
ISO Online information service on World Wide Web (http://www.iso.org).

Foreign Library Associations

The following is a list of regional and national library associations around the world. A more complete list can be found in *International Literary Market Place* (Information Today, Inc.).

Regional

Africa

Standing Conference of Eastern, Central, and Southern African Lib. and Info. Assns. (SCECSAL), c/o Swaziland Lib. Assn., P.O. Box 2309, Mbabane H100, Swaziland. Tel. 268-404-2633, fax 268-404-3863, e-mail fmkhonta@uniswacc.uniswa.sz, World Wide Web http://www.swala.sz.

The Americas

Assn. of Caribbean Univ., Research, and Institutional Libs. (ACURIL), P.O. Box 21609, San Juan, Puerto Rico 00931-1906. Tel. 787-763-6199, e-mail executivesecretariat@acuril.org. *Pres.* Dorcas R. Bowler; *Exec. Secy.* Luisa Vigo-Cepeda.

Seminar on the Acquisition of Latin American Lib. Materials (SALALM), c/o *Exec. Secy.* Hortensia Calvo, SALALM Secretariat, Latin American Lib., 422 Howard Tilton Memorial Lib., Tulane Univ., 7001 Freret St., New Orleans, LA 70118-5549. Tel. 504-247-1366, fax 504-247-1367, e-mail salalm@tulane.edu, World Wide Web http://www.salalm.org. *Pres.* Luis Gonzales. E-mail luisgonz@indiana.edu.

Asia

Congress of Southeast Asian Libns. (CONSAL), c/o Jl Salemba Raya 28A, Jakarta 10430, Indonesia. Tel. 21-310-3554, World Wide Web http://www.consal.org. *Secy.-Gen.* Aristianto Hakim.

The Commonwealth

Commonwealth Lib. Assn. (COMLA), P.O. Box 144, Mona, Kingston 7, Jamaica. Tel. 876-978-2274, fax 876-927-1926, e-mail comla72@yahoo.com. *Interim Pres.* Elizabeth Watson.

National and State Libs. Australasia, c/o State Lib. of Victoria, 328 Swanston St., Melbourne, Vic. 3000, Australia. Tel. 3-8664-7512, fax 3-9639-4737, e-mail nsla@slv.vic.gov.au, World Wide Web http://www.nsla.org.au. *Chair* Alan Smith.

U.K. Library and Archives Group on Africa (SCOLMA, formerly the Standing Conference on Lib. Materials on Africa), c/o Marion Wallace, Social Science Collections and Research, British Lib., St. Pancras, 96 Euston Rd., London NW1 2DB, England. Tel. 20-7412-7829, World Wide Web http://scolma.org.

Europe

Ligue des Bibliothèques Européennes de Recherche (LIBER) (Assn. of European Research Libs.), Postbus 90407, 2509 LK The Hague, Netherlands. Tel. 070-314-07-67, fax 070-314-01-97, e-mail liber@kb.nl, World Wide Web http://www.libereurope.eu. *Pres.* Kristiina Hormia Poutancn. E-mail kristiina.hormia@helsinki.fi; *V.P.* Jeannette Frey. E-mail jeannette.frey@bcu.unil.ch; *Secy.-Gen.* Ann Matheson. E-mail a.matheson@tinyworld.co.uk.

National

Argentina

Asociación de Bibliotecarios Graduados de la República Argentina (ABGRA) (Assn. of Graduate Libns. of Argentina), Parana 918, 2do Piso, C1017AAT Buenos Aires. Tel. 11-4811-0043, fax 11-4816-3422, e-mail info@abgra.org.ar, World Wide Web http://www.abgra.org.ar. *Pres.* Antonio Bellofatto; *V.P.* Tatiana María Carsen; *Secy.-Gen.* Mirta Estela Villalba.

Australia

Australian Lib. and Info. Assn., Box 6335, Kingston, ACT 2604. Tel. 2-6215-8222, fax 2-6282-2249, e-mail enquiry@alia.org.au, World Wide Web http://www.alia.org.au. *Pres.* Damian Lodge; *CEO* Sue McKerracher. E-mail sue.mckerracher@alia.org.au.
Australian Society of Archivists, P.O. Box A623, Sydney South, NSW 1235. Tel. 618-8411-5550, e-mail office@archivists.org.au, World Wide Web http://www.archivists.org.au. *Pres.* Kylie Percival; *V.P.* Adelaide Parr.

Austria

Österreichische Gesellschaft für Dokumentation und Information (Austrian Society for Documentation and Info.), c/o OGDI, Wollzeile 1-3, P.O. Box 43, 1022 Vienna. E-mail office@oegdi.at, World Wide Web http://www.oegdi.at. *Secy.-Gen.* Hermann Huemer. E-mail hermann.huemer@oegdi.at.
Vereinigung Österreichischer Bibliothekarinnen und Bibliothekare (VOEB) (Assn. of Austrian Libns.), Vorarlberg State Lib., Fluherstr. 4, 6900 Bregenz. E-mail voeb@ub.tuwein.ac.at, World Wide Web http://www.univie.ac.at/voeb/php. *Pres.* Werner Schlacher, Universitätsbibliothek Graz, Universitätsplatz 3, 8010 Graz. E-mail werner.schlacher@uni-graz.at.

Bangladesh

Bangladesh Assn. of Libns., Info. Scientists and Documentalists (BALID), 67/B, Rd. 9/A, Dhanmondi, Dhaka 1209. *Chair* Mirza Mohd Rezaul Islam. E-mail balidbd@gmail.com.

Barbados

Lib. Assn. of Barbados, P.O. Box 827E, Bridgetown, Barbados. E-mail milton@uwichill.edu.bb. *Pres.* Junior Browne.

Belgium

Archief- en Bibliotheekwezen in België (Belgian Assn. of Archivists and Libns.), Keizerslaan 4, 1000 Brussels. Tel. 2-519-53-93, fax 2-519-56-10.

Association Belge de Documentation/Belgische Vereniging voor Documentatie (Belgian Assn. for Documentation), Chaussée de Wavre 1683, B-1160 Brussels. Tel. 2-675-58-62, fax 2-672-74-46, e-mail abdbvd@abd-bvd.be, World Wide Web http://www.abd-bvd.be. *Pres.* Guy Delsaut. E-mail guy.delsaut@skynet.be; *Secy.-Gen.* Marc Van Den Bergh. E-mail mvdbergh@serv.be.
Association Professionnelle des Bibliothécaires et Documentalistes (Assn. of Libns. and Documentation Specialists), Chaussée de Charleroi 85, 5000 Namur, Belgique. Tel. 71-52-31-93, fax 71-52-23-07, World Wide Web http://www.apbd.be. *Pres.* Françoise Dury.
Vlaamse Vereniging voor Bibliotheek-, Archief-, en Documentatiewezen (Flemish Assn. of Libns., Archivists, and Documentalists), Statiestraat 179, B-2600 Berchem, Antwerp. Tel. 3-281-44-57, e-mail vvbad@vvbad.be, World Wide Web http://www.vvbad.be. *Coord.* Bruno Vermeeren.

Belize

Belize National Lib. Service and Info. System (BNLSIS), P.O. Box 287, Belize City. Tel. 223-4248, fax 223-4246, e-mail nls@btl.net, World Wide Web http://www.nlsbze.bz. *Chief Libn.* Joy Ysaguirre.

Bolivia

Centro Nacional de Documentación Cientifica y Tecnológica (National Scientific and Technological Documentation Center), Av. Mariscal Santa Cruz 1175, Esquina c Ayacucho, La Paz. Tel. 02-359-583, fax 02-359-586, e-mail iiicndct@huayna.umsa.edu.bo, World Wide Web http://www.bolivian.com/industrial/cndct.

Bosnia and Herzegovina

Drustvo Bibliotekara Bosne i Hercegovine (Libns. Society of Bosnia and Herzegovina), Zmaja od Bosne 8B, 71000 Sarajevo. Tel. 33-275-5325, fax 33-212-435, e-mail nubbih@nub.ba, World Wide Web http://www.nub.ba. *Pres.* Nevenka Hajdarovic. E-mail nevenka@nub.ba.

Botswana

Botswana Lib. Assn., Box 1310, Gaborone. Tel. 371-750, fax 371-748, World Wide Web http://www.bla.org.bw. *Pres.* Kgomotso Radijeing. E-mail president@bla.org.bw.

Brazil

Associação dos Arquivistas Brasileiros (Assn. of Brazilian Archivists), Av. Presidente Vargas 1733, Sala 903, 20210-030 Rio de Janiero RJ. Tel. 21-2507-2239, fax 21-3852-2541, e-mail aab@aab.org.br, World Wide Web http://www.aab.org.br. *Pres.* Margareth da Silva.

Brunei Darussalam

Persatuan Perpustakaan Negara Brunei Darussalam (National Lib. Assn. of Brunei), c/o Class 64 Lib., SOASC, Jalan Tengah, Bandar Seri Begawan BS8411. Fax 2-222-330, e-mail pobox.bla@gmail.com, World Wide Web http://bruneilibraryassociation.word press.com. *Hon. Secy.* Hjh Rosnani. E-mail rosnaniy@hotmail.com.

Cameroon

Assn. des Bibliothécaires, Archivistes, Documentalistes et Muséographes du Cameroun (Assn. of Libns., Archivists, Documentalists, and Museum Curators of Cameroon), BP 14077, Yaoundé. World Wide Web http://www.abadcam.sitew.com. *Pres.* Jérôme Ndjock.

Chile

Colegio de Bibliotecarios de Chile (Chilean Lib. Assn.), Avda. Diagonal Paraguay 383, Torre 11, Oficina 122, 6510017 Santiago. Tel. 2-222-5652, e-mail cbc@bibliotecarios.cl, World Wide Web http://www.bibliotecarios. cl. *Pres.* Gabriela Pradenas Bobadilla; *Secy.-Gen.* Victor Candia Arancibia.

China

Lib. Society of China, 33 Zhongguancun S, Beijing 100081. Tel. 10-8854-5283, fax 10-6841-7815, e-mail ztxhmsc@nlc.gov. cn, World Wide Web http://www.nlc.gov.cn. *Dir.* Zhou Heping.

Colombia

Asociación Colombiana de Bibliotecólogos y Documentalistas (Colombian Assn. of Libns. and Documentalists), Calle 21, No. 6-58, Oficina 404, Bogotá D.C. Tel. 1-282-3620, fax 1-282-5487, e-mail secretaria@ ascolbi.org, World Wide Web http://www. ascolbi.org. *Pres.* Marisol Goyeneche Reina.

Congo (Republic of)

Assn. des Bibliothécaires, Archivistes, Documentalistes et Muséologues du Congo (ABADOM) (Assn. of Librarians, Archivists, Documentalists, and Museologists of Congo), BP 3148, Kinshasa-Gombe. *Pres.* Desire Didier Tengeneza. E-mail didier teng@yahoo.fr.

Côte d'Ivoire

Direction des Archives Nationales et de la Documentation, BP V 126, Abidjan. Tel. 20-21-75-78. *Dir.* Venance Bahi Gouro.

Croatia

Hrvatsko Knjiznicarsko Drustvo (Croatian Lib. Assn.), c/o National and Univ. Lib., Hrvatske bratske zajednice 4, 10 000 Zagreb. Tel./fax 1-615-93-20, e-mail hkd@nsk.hr, World Wide Web http://www.hkdrustvo.hr. *Pres.* Marijana Misetic. E-mail mmisetic@ffzg.hr.

Cuba

Asociación Cubana de Bibliotecarios (AS-CUBI) (Lib. Assn. of Cuba), P.O. Box 6670, Havana. Tel. 7-555-442, fax 7-816-224, e-mail ascubi@bnjm.cu, World Wide Web http://www.bnjm.cu/ascubi. *Chair* Margarita Bellas Vilariño. E-mail ascubi@bnjm.cu.

Cyprus

Kypriakos Synthesmos Vivliothicarion (Lib. Assn. of Cyprus), c/o Pedagogical Academy, P.O. Box 1039, Nicosia.

Czech Republic

Svaz Knihovniku a Informacnich Pracovniku Ceske Republiky (SKIP) (Assn. of Lib. and Info. Professionals of the Czech Republic),

National Lib., Klementinum 190, 110 00
Prague 1. Tel. 221-663-379, fax 221-663-
175, e-mail skip@nkp.cz, World Wide Web
http://skipcr.cz. *Pres.* Roman Giebisch. E-
mail roman.giebisch@nkp.cz.

Denmark

Arkivforeningen (Archives Society), c/o Rig-
sarkivet, Rigsdagsgarden 9, 1218 Copenhagen. Tel. 3392-3310, fax 3315-3239, World
Wide Web http://www.arkivarforeningen.
no. *Chair* Lars Schreiber Pedersen. E-mail
lape02@frederiksberg.dk.

Danmarks Biblioteksforening (Danish Lib.
Assn.), Vartov, Farvergade 27D, 1463 Copenhagen K. Tel. 3325-0935, fax 3325-
7900, e-mail db@db.dk, World Wide Web
http://www.db.dk. *Pres.* Steen Bording Andersen. E-mail sba@byr.aarhus.dk.

Danmarks Forskningsbiblioteksforening
(Danish Research Lib. Assn.), c/o Statsbib-
lioteket, Tangen 2, 8200 Arhus N. Tel. 89-
46-22-07, e-mail df@statsbiblioteket.dk,
World Wide Web http://www.dfdf.dk. *Pres.*
Michael Cotta-Schønberg. E-mail mcs@
kb.dk; *Secy.* Hanne Dahl.

Dansk Musikbiblioteks Forening (Assn.
of Danish Music Libs.), c/o Koge Lib.,
Kirkestr. 18, 4600 Koge. E-mail sekretariat
@dmbf.nu, World Wide Web http://www.
dmbf.nu. *Pres.* Emilie Wieth-Knudsen. E-
mail emwk@ltk.dk.

Kommunernes Skolebiblioteksforening (Assn.
of Danish School Libs.), Farvergade 27 D,
2 sal, 1463 Copenhagen K. Tel. 33-11-13-
91, e-mail ksbf@ksbf.dk, World Wide Web
http://www.ksbf.dk. *Dir.* Gitte Frausing. E-
mail gf@ksbf.dk.

Ecuador

Asociación Ecuatoriana de Bibliotecarios (Ec-
uadoran Lib. Assn.), c/o Casa de la Cultura
Ecuatoriana, Casillas 87, Quito. E-mail
asoecubiblio@gmail.com. *Pres.* Eduardo
Puente. E-mail epuente@flacso.edu.ec.

El Salvador

Asociación de Bibliotecarios de El Salvador
(ABES) (Assn. of Salvadorian Libns.), Jar-
dines de la Hacienda Block D pje, 19 No.
158, Ciudad Merliot, Antiguo Cuscatlan,

La Libertad. Tel. 503-2534-8924, fax 523-
2228-2956, e-mail abeselsalvador@gmail.
com. *Co-Chairs* Ernesto Jonathan Menjivar,
Ana Yensi Vides.

Finland

Suomen Kirjastoseura (Finnish Lib. Assn.),
Runeberginkatu 15 A 23, 00100 Helsinki.
Tel. 44-522-2941, e-mail info@fla.fi, World
Wide Web http://www.fla.fi. *Exec. Dir.*
Sinikka Sipilä.

France

Association des Archivistes Français (Assn.
of French Archivists), 8 rue Jean-Marie
Jego, 75013 Paris. Tel. 1-46-06-39-44,
fax 1-46-06-39-52, e-mail secretariat@
archivistes.org, World Wide Web http://
www.archivistes.org. *Pres.* Katell Auguié;
Secy. Marie-Edith Enderlé-Naud.

Association des Bibliothécaires Français
(Assn. of French Libns.), 31 rue de Chab-
rol, F-75010 Paris. Tel. 1-55-33-10-30, fax
1-55-30-10-31, e-mail info@abf.asso.fr,
World Wide Web http://www.abf.asso.fr.
Pres. Anne Verneuil; *Gen. Secy.* Sophie Rat.

Association. des Professionnels de l'Information et de la Documentation (Assn. of Info.
and Documentation Professionals), 25 rue
Claude Tillier, F-75012 Paris. Tel. 1-43-72-
25-25, fax 1-43-72-30-41, e-mail adbs@
adbs.fr, World Wide Web http://www.adbs.
fr. *Co-Pres.* Anne-Marie Libmann, Véro-
nique Mesguich; *CEO* Karine Cuney.

Germany

Arbeitsgemeinschaft der Spezialbibliotheken
(Assn. of Special Libs.), c/o Herder-Insti-
tute eV, Bibliothek, Gisonenweg 5-7, 35037
Marburg. Tel. 6421-184-151, fax 6421-
184-139, e-mail geschaeftsstelle@aspb.de,
World Wide Web http://aspb.de. *Chair* Henning Frankenberger. E-mail frankenberger@
mpisoc.mpg.de.

Berufsverband Information Bibliothek (Assn.
of Info. and Lib. Professionals), Gartenstr.
18, 72764 Reutlingen. Tel. 7121-3491-0,
fax 7121-3004-33, e-mail mail@bib-info.
de, World Wide Web http://www.bib-info.
de. *Deputy Chairs* Tom Becker. E-mail tom.
becker@fh-koeln.de; Petra Kille. E-mail

kille@ub.uni-kl.de; *Acting Managing Dir.* Bernd Raja. E-mail schleh@bib-info.de.

Deutsche Gesellschaft für Informationswissenschaft und Informationspraxis eV (German Society for Information Science and Practice eV), Windmühlstr. 3, 603294 Frankfurt-am-Main. Tel. 69-43-03-13, fax 69-490-90-96, e-mail mail@dgi-info.de, World Wide Web http://www.dgi-info.de. *Pres.* Reinhard Karger, German Research Center for Artificial Intelligence.

Deutscher Bibliotheksverband eV (German Lib. Assn.), Fritschestr. 27–28, 10585 Berlin. Tel. 30-644-98-99-10, fax 30-644-98-99-29, e-mail dbv@bibliotheksverband.de, World Wide Web http://www.bibliotheksverband. de. *Pres.* Gudrun Heute-Bluhm.

VdA—Verband Deutscher Archivarinnen und Archivare (Assn. of German Archivists), Woerthstr. 3, 36037 Fulda. Tel. 661-29-109-72, fax 661-29-109-74, e-mail info@vda.archiv. net, World Wide Web http://www.vda.archiv. net. *Chair* Irmgard Christa Becker.

Verein Deutscher Bibliothekare eV (Society of German Libns.), Universitaetsbibliothek München, Geschwister-Scholl-Platz 1, 80539 Munich. Tel. 89-2180-2420, e-mail geschaeftsstelle@vdb-online.org, World Wide Web http://www.vdb-online.org. *Chair* Klaus-Rainer Brintzinger, Munich Univ. Lib., Geschwister-Scholl-Platz 1, 80539 Munich. E-mail vorsitzender@vdb-online.org.

Ghana

Ghana Lib. Assn., Box GP 4105, Accra. Tel. 244-17-4930, e-mail ghanalibassoc@gmail. com, World Wide Web http://gla-net.org. *Pres.* Perpetua S. Dadzie; *V.P.* Samuel B. Aggrey.

Greece

Enosis Hellinon Bibliotekarion (Assn. of Greek Libns.), Skoufa 52, P.O. Box 10672, Athens. Tel./fax 210-330-2128, e-mail info@eebep.gr, World Wide Web http:// www.eebep.gr. *Pres.* George Glossa. E-mail glossiotis@gmail.com; *Gen. Secy.* Rena Choremi-Thomopoulou. E-mail rhoremi@ hotmail.com.

Guyana

Guyana Lib. Assn., c/o National Lib., P.O. Box 10240, Georgetown.

Hong Kong

Hong Kong Lib. Assn., GPO Box 10095, Hong Kong, China. E-mail hkla@hkla.org, World Wide Web http://www.hkla.org. *Pres.* Bryant McEntyre. E-mail mbmcentire@yahoo. com.

Hungary

Magyar Könyvtárosok Egyesülete (Assn. of Hungarian Libns.), H-1054, Hold u 6, Budapest. Tel./fax 1-311-8634, e-mail mke@ oszk.hu, World Wide Web http://www.mke. oszk.hu. *Pres.* Klara Bakos; *Secy. Gen.* Miklós Fehér.

Iceland

Upplysing—Felag bokasafns-og upplysingafraeoa (Information—The Icelandic Lib. and Info. Science Assn.), Lyngas 18, 210 Gardabaer. Tel. 354-864-6220, e-mail upplysing@upplysing.is, World Wide Web http://www.upplysing.is.

India

Indian Assn. of Special Libs. and Info. Centres, P-291, CIT Scheme 6M, Kankurgachi, Kolkata 700-054. Tel. 33-2362-9651, e-mail iaslic@vsnl.net, World Wide Web http://www.iaslic1955.org.in. *Pres.* Barun Mukherjee. *Gen. Secy.* Pijushkanti Panigrahi. E-mail panigrahipk@yahoo.com.

Indian Lib. Assn., A/40-41, Flat 201, Ansal Bldg., Mukerjee Nagar, New Delhi 110009. Tel./fax 11-2765-1743, e-mail dvs-srcc@ rediffmail.com, World Wide Web http:// www.ilaindia.net. *Pres.* Ashu Shokeen. E-mail shokeen_ashu@rediffmail.com; *Gen. Secy.* Pardeep Rai. E-mail raipardeep@ gmail.com.

Indonesia

Ikatan Pustakawan Indonesia (Indonesian Lib. Assn.), 11 Jalan Medan Merdeka Selatan, Jakarta 10110. Tel./fax 21-385-5729, e-mail pi2012_2015@yahoo.com, World Wide Web http://ipi.pnri.go.id.

Ireland

Cumann Leabharlann na hEireann (Lib. Assn. of Ireland), c/o 138–144 Pearce St., Dublin 2. E-mail president@libraryassociation.ie, World Wide Web http://www.libraryassociation. ie. *Pres.* Jane Cantwell. E-mail president@ libraryassociation.ie.

Israel

Israeli Center for Libs., 22 Baruch Hirsch St., P.O. Box 801, 51108 Bnei Brak. Tel. 03-6180151, fax 03-5798048, e-mail meida@ gmail.com or icl@icl.org.il; World Wide Web http://www.icl.org.il.

Italy

Associazione Italiana Biblioteche (Italian Lib. Assn.), Biblioteca Nazionale Centrale, Viale Castro Pretorio 105, 00185 Rome RM. Tel. 6-446-3532, fax 6-444-1139, e-mail aib@legalmail.it, World Wide Web http:// www.aib.it. *CEO* Enrica Manenti. E-mail manenti@aib.it.

Jamaica

Lib. and Info. Assn. of Jamaica, P.O. Box 125, Kingston 5. Tel./fax 876-927-1614, e-mail liajapresident@yahoo.com, World Wide Web http://www.liaja.org.jm. *Pres.* Viviene Kerr-Williams. E-mail vskwilliams@gmail. com.

Japan

Info. Science and Technology Assn., Sasaki Bldg., 2-5-7 Koisikawa, Bunkyo-ku, Tokyo 112-0002. Tel. 3-3813-3791, fax 3-3813-3793, e-mail infosta@infosta.or.jp, World Wide Web http://www.infosta.or.jp.

Nihon Toshokan Kyokai (Japan Lib. Assn.), 1-11-14 Shinkawa, Chuo-ku, Tokyo 104 0033. Tel. 3-3523-0811, fax 3-3523-0841, e-mail info@jla.or.jp, World Wide Web http://www.jla.or.jp. *Pres.* Shiomi Noboru.

Senmon Toshokan Kyogikai (Japan Special Libs. Assn.), c/o Japan Lib. Assn., Bldg. F6, 1-11-14 Shinkawa Chuo-ku, Tokyo 104-

0033. Tel. 3-3537-8335, fax 3-3537-8336, e-mail jsla@jsla.or.jp, World Wide Web http://www.jsla.or.jp.

Jordan

Jordan Lib. and Info. Assn., P.O. Box 6289, Amman 11118. Tel./fax 6-462-9412, e-mail jorla_1963@yahoo.com, World Wide Web http://www.jorla.org. *Pres.* Omar Mohammad Jaradat.

Kenya

Kenya Assn. of Lib. and Info. Professionals (formerly Kenya Lib. Assn.), Buruburu, P.O. Box 49468, 00100 Nairobi. Tel. 20-733-732-799, e-mail gitachur@yahoo.com, World Wide Web http://www.kenyalibrary association.or.ke. *Chair* Rosemary Gitachu.

Korea (Democratic People's Republic of)

Lib. Assn. of the Democratic People's Republic of Korea, c/o Grand People's Study House, P.O. Box 200, Pyongyang. E-mail korea@ korea-dpr.com.

Korea (Republic of)

Korean Lib. Assn., San 60-1, Banpo-dong, Seocho-gu, Seoul 137-702. Tel. 2-535-4868, fax 2-535-5616, e-mail license@kla. kr, World Wide Web http://www.kla.kr.

Laos

Association des Bibliothécaires Laotiens (Lao Lib. Assn.), c/o Direction de la Bibliothèque Nationale, Ministry of Educ., BP 704, Vientiane. Tel. 21-21-2452, fax 21-21-2408, e-mail bailane@laotel.com.

Latvia

Latvian Libns. Assn., Terbatas iela 75, Riga LV-1001. Tel./fax 6731-2791, e-mail lbb@ lbi.lnb.lv, World Wide Web http://www.lnb. lv.

Lebanon

Lebanese Lib. Assn., P.O. Box 13-5053, Beirut 1102 2801. Tel. 1-786-456, e-mail kjaroudy@lau.edu.lb, World Wide Web http://www.llaweb.org. *Pres.* Randa Chidiac. E-mail randachidiac@usek.edu.lb.

Lesotho

Lesotho Lib. Assn., Private Bag A26, Maseru 100. Tel. 213-420, fax 340-000, e-mail s.mohai@nul.ls. *Contact* Makemang Ntsasa.

Lithuania

Lietuvos Bibliotekininku Draugija (Lithuanian Libns. Assn.), S Dariaus ir S Gireno g 12, LT-59212 Birstonas. Tel./fax 8-319-65760, e-mail lbd.sekretore@gmail.com, World Wide Web http://www.lbd.lt. *Pres.* Irma Kleiziene. E-mail bmb@is.lt.

Luxembourg

Association Luxembourgeoise des Bibliothécaires, Archivistes, et Documentalistes (ALBAD) (Luxembourg Assn. of Libns., Archivists, and Documentalists), c/o National Lib. of Luxembourg, BP 295, L-2012 Luxembourg. Tel. 352-22-97-55-1, fax 352-47-56-72, World Wide Web http://www.albad.lu. *Pres.* Jean-Marie Reding; *Secy. Gen.* Bernard Linster. E-mail bernard.linster@hotmail.com.

Malawi

Malawi Lib. Assn., c/o Univ. Libn., P.O. Box 429, Zomba. Tel. 524-265, fax 525-255, World Wide Web http://www.mala.mw. *Pres.* Fiskani Ngwire; *Secy. Gen.* Robin Mwanga.

Malaysia

Persatuan Pustakawan Malaysia (Libns. Assn. of Malaysia), P.O. Box 12545, 50782 Kuala Lumpur. Tel./fax 3-2694-7390, e-mail ppm55@po.jaring.my, World Wide Web http://ppm55.org.

Mali

Association Malienne des Bibliothécaires, Archivistes et Documentalistes (Mali Assn. of Libns., Archivists, and Documentalists) (AMBAD), BP E4473, Bamako. Tel. 20-

29-94-23, fax 20-29-93-76, e-mail dnbd@afribone.net.ml.

Malta

Malta Lib. and Info. Assn. (MaLIA), c/o Univ. of Malta Lib., Msida MSD 2080. E-mail info@malia-malta.org, World Wide Web http://www.malia-malta.org. *Chair* Mark Camilleri.

Mauritania

Association Mauritanienne des Bibliothécaires, Archivistes, et Documentalistes (Mauritanian Assn. of Libns., Archivists, and Documentalists), c/o Bibliothèque Nationale, BP 20, Nouakchott. Tel. 525-18-62, fax 525-18-68, e-mail bibliothequenationale@yahoo.fr.

Mauritius

Mauritius Lib. Assn., Ministry of Educ. Public Lib., Moka Rd., Rose Hill. Tel. 403-0200, fax 454-9553. *Pres.* Abdool Fareed Soogali.

Mexico

Asociación Mexicana de Bibliotecarios (Mexican Assn. of Libns.), Angel Urraza 817-A, Colonia Del Valle, Benito Juárez, Mexico DF, CP 03100. Tel. 55-55-75-33-96, e-mail correo@ambac.org.mx, World Wide Web http://www.ambac.org.mx. *Pres.* María Asunción Mendoza Becerra; *V.P.* Armendáriz Saúl Sánchez.

Myanmar

Myanmar Lib. Assn., c/o National Lib. of Myanmar, 85 Thirimingalar Yeiktha Lane, Kabar Aye Pagoda Rd., Yankin Township, Yangon. Tel. 1-662-470, e-mail myanmarlibraryassociation.mla@gmail.com, World Wide Web https://www.facebook.com/pages/Myanmar-Library-Association/759155320812626.

Nepal

Nepal Lib. Assn., GPO 2773, Kathmandu. Tel. 977-1-441-1318, e-mail info@nla.org.np, World Wide Web http://www.nla.org.np. *Pres.* Prakash Kumar Thapa. E-mail kyammuntar@yahoo.com.

The Netherlands

KNVI—Koninklijke Nederlandse Vereniging van Informatieprofessionals (Royal Dutch Association of Information Professionals) (formerly Nederlandse Vereniging voor Beroepsbeoefenaren in de Bibliotheek-Informatie-en Kennissector or Netherlands Assn. of Libns., Documentalists, and Info. Specialists), Mariaplaats 3, 3511 LH Utrecht. Tel. 30-233-0050, e-mail info@knvi.net, World Wide Web http://http://knvi.net. *Chair* Michel Wesseling. E-mail m.g.wesseling@gmail.com.

New Zealand

New Zealand Lib. Assn. (LIANZA), P.O. Box 12212, Thorndon, Wellington 6144. Tel. 4-801-5542, fax 4-801-5543, e-mail officeadmin@lianza.org.nz, World Wide Web http://www.lianza.org.nz. *Pres.* Corin Haines. E-mail librarianboy@gmail.com; *Pres.-Elect* Kris Wehipeihana. E-mail kris.wehipeihana@toiwhakaari.ac.nz; *Exec. Dir.* Joanna Matthew. E-mail joanna@lianza.org.nz.

Nicaragua

Asociación Nicaraguense de Bibliotecarios y Profesionales Afines (ANIBIPA) (Nicaraguan Assn. of Libns.), Bello Horizonte, Tope Sur de la Rotonda 1/2 cuadra abajo, J-11-57, Managua. Tel. 277-4159, e-mail anibipa@hotmail.com. *Pres.* Yadira Roque. E-mail r-yadira@hotmail.com.

Nigeria

National Lib. of Nigeria, Sanusi Dantata House, Central Business District, PMB 1, Abuja GPO 900001. Tel. 805-536-5245, fax 9-234-6773, e-mail info@nla-ng.org, World Wide Web http://www.nla-ng.org. *Pres.* Alhaji Rilwanu Abdulsala.

Norway

Arkivarforeningen (Assn. of Archivists), Fredrik Glads gate 1, 0482 Oslo. Tel. 913-16-895, e-mail imb@steria.no, World Wide Web http://www.arkivforeningen.no. *Chair* Inge Manfred Bjorlin. E-mail inge.bjorlin@gmail.com.

Norsk Bibliotekforening (Norwegian Lib. Assn.), Postboks 6540, 0606 Etterstad, Oslo. Tel. 23-24-34-30, fax 22-67-23-68, e-mail nbf@norskbibliotekforening.no, World Wide Web http://www.norskbibliotekforening.no. *Gen. Secy.* Hege Newth Nouri. E-mail hege.newth.nouri@norskbibliotekforening.no.

Pakistan

Library Promotion Bureau, Karachi Univ. Campus, P.O. Box 8421, Karachi 75270. Tel./fax 21-3587-6301. *Pres.* Ghaniul Akram Sabzwari, 4213 Heritage Way Drive, Fort Worth, TX 76137. E-mail gsabzwari@hotmail.com, World Wide Web http://www.lpb-pak.com,.

Panama

Asociación Panameña de Bibliotecarios (Lib. Assn. of Panama), c/o Biblioteca Interamericana Simón Bolivar, Estafeta Universitaria, Panama City. E-mail biblis2@arcon.up.ac.pa, World Wide Web https://www.facebook.com/asociacionpanamenabibliotecarios/info.

Paraguay

Asociación de Bibliotecarios Graduados del Paraguay (Assn. of Paraguayan Graduate Libns.), Facultad Politecnica, Universidad Nacional de Asunción, 2160 San Lorenzo. Tel. 21-585-588, e-mail abigrap@pol.una.py, World Wide Web http://www.pol.una.py/abigrap. *Chair* Emilce Sena Correa. E-mail esena@pol.una.py.

Peru

Asociación de Archiveros del Perú (Peruvian Assn. of Archivists), Av. Manco Capac No. 1180, Dpto 201, La Victoria, Lima. Tel. 1-472-8729, fax 1-472-7408, e-mail contactos@adapperu.com. *Pres.* Juan Manuel Serrano Valencia.

Philippines

Assn. of Special Libs. of the Philippines, c/o Goethe-Institut Philippinen, G/4-5/F Adamson Centre, 121 Leviste St., Salcedo Village,

1227 Makati City. Tel. 2-840-5723, e-mail aslpboard@yahoo.com.ph, World Wide Web http://aslpwiki.wikispaces.com. *Pres.* Brinerdine G. Alejandrino. Philippine Libns. Assn., Room 301, National Lib. Bldg., T. M. Kalaw St., 1000 Ermita, Manila. Tel. 525-9401. World Wide Web http://plai.org.ph. *Pres.* Elizabeth R. Peralejo.

Poland

Stowarzyszenie Bibliotekarzy Polskich (Polish Libns. Assn.), al Niepodleglosci 213, 02-086 Warsaw. Tel. 22-825-83-74, fax 22-825-53-49, e-mail biuro@sbp.pl, World Wide Web http://www.sbp.pl. *Chair* Elizabeth Stefanczyk. E-mail e.stefanczyk@bn.org.pl; *Secy. Gen.* Marzena Przybysz.

Portugal

Associação Portuguesa de Bibliotecários, Arquivistas e Documentalistas (Portuguese Assn. of Libns., Archivists, and Documentalists), Rua Morais Soares, 43C, 1 Dto e Frte, 1900-341 Lisbon. Tel. 21-816-19-80, fax 21-815-45-08, e-mail apbad@apbad.pt, World Wide Web http://www.apbad.pt.

Puerto Rico

Sociedad de Bibliotecarios de Puerto Rico (Society of Libns. of Puerto Rico), Apdo 22898, San Juan 00931-2898. Tel./fax 787-764-0000, World Wide Web http://www.sociedadbibliotecarios.org. *Pres.* Juan Vargas. E-mail juan.vargas3@upr.edu.

Russia

Rossiiskaya Bibliotechnaya Assotsiatsiya (Russian Lib. Assn.), 18 Sadovaya St., St. Petersburg 191069. Tel./fax 812-110-5861, e-mail rba@nlr.ru, World Wide Web http://www.rba.ru. *Exec. Secy.* Elena Tikhonova.

Senegal

Association Sénégalaise des Bibliothécaires, Archivistes et Documentalistes (Senegalese Assn. of Libns., Archivists, and Documentalists), BP 2006, Dakar RP, Université Cheikh Anta Diop, Dakar. Tel. 77-651-00-

33, fax 33-824-23-79, e-mail asbad200@hotmail.com, World Wide Web http://www.asbad.org. *Pres.* Lawrence Gomis Baaya; *Secy. Gen.* Alassane Ndiath.

Serbia and Montenegro

Jugoslovenski Bibliografsko Informacijski Institut, Terazije 26, 11000 Belgrade. Tel. 11-2687-836, fax 11-2687-760.

Sierra Leone

Sierra Leone Assn. of Archivists, Libns., and Info. Scientists, c/o Sierra Leone Lib. Board, Rokel St., P.O. Box 326, Freetown. Tel. 022-220-758.

Singapore

Lib. Assn. of Singapore, National Lib. Board, 100 Victoria St., No. 14-01, Singapore 188064. Tel. 6332-3255, fax 6332-3248, e-mail lassec@las.org.sg, World Wide Web http://www.las.org.sg. *Pres.* Lee Cheng Ean. E-mail president@las.org.sg.

Slovenia

Zveza Bibliotekarskih Druötev Slovenije (Union of Assns. of Slovene Libns.), Turjaöka 1, 1000 Ljubljana. Tel. 1-2001-176, fax 1-4257-293, e-mail info@zbds-zveza.si, World Wide Web http://www.zbds-zveza.si. *Pres.* Sabina Fras Popovic. E-mail sabina.fras-popovic@mb.sik.si.

South Africa

Lib. and Info. Assn. of South Africa, P.O. Box 1598, Pretoria 0001. Tel. 12-328-2010, fax 12-323-4912, e-mail liasa@liasa.org.za, World Wide Web http://www.liasa.org.za. *Pres.* Ujala Satgoor. E-mail president@liasa.org.za.

Spain

Federación Española de Archiveros, Bibliotecarios, Museólogos y Documentalistas (ANABAD) (Spanish Federation of Assns. of Archivists, Libns., Archaeologists, Museum Curators, and Documentalists), de las Huertas, 37, 28014 Madrid. Tel. 91-575-

1727, fax 91-578-1615, e-mail anabad@
anabad.org, World Wide Web http://www.
anabad.org. *Pres.* Miguel Ángel Gacho San-
tamaría.

Sri Lanka

Sri Lanka Lib. Assn., Sri Lanka Professional Centre 275/75, Stanley Wijesundara
Mawatha, Colombo 7. Tel./fax 11-258-
9103, e-mail slla@slltnet.lk, World Wide
Web http://www.slla.org.lk. *Pres.* Shivanthi
Weerasinghe; *Gen. Secy.* Lilamani Amer-
asekera.

Swaziland

Swaziland Lib. Assn. (SWALA), P.O. Box
2309, Mbabane H100. Tel. 404-2633, fax
404-3863.

Sweden

Svensk Biblioteksförening Kansli (Swedish
Lib. Assn.), World Trade Center, D5, Box
70380, 107 24 Stockholm. Tel. 8-545-
132-30, fax 8-545-132-31, e-mail info@
biblioteksforeningen.org, World Wide Web
http://www.biblioteksforeningen.org. *Chair*
Calle Nathanson; *Secy. Gen.* Niclas Lindberg. E-mail nl@biblioteksforeningen.org.
Svensk Förening för Informationsspecialister
(Swedish Assn. for Info. Specialists), Box
2001, 135 02 Tyresö. E-mail kansliet@sfis.
nu, World Wide Web http://www.sfis.nu/om.
Chair Ann-Christin Karlén Gramming. E-
mail ann-christin.karlen@vinge.se.
Svenska Arkivsamfundet (Swedish Archival Society), Association Hall, Virkesvä-
gen 26, 120 30 Stockholm. E-mail info@
arkivsamfundet.se, World Wide Web http://
www.arkivsamfundet.se.

Switzerland

Bibliothek Information Schweiz/Bibliothèque
Information Suisse/Biblioteca Informazione
Swizzera/Library Information Switzerland
(BIS), Bleichemattstrasse 42, 5000 Aarau.
Tel. 41-62-823-19-38, fax 41-62-823-19-39,
e-mail info@bis.ch. *Managing Dir.* Hans
Ulrich Locher. E-mail halo.locher@bis.info.
Verein Schweizer Archivarinnen und Archivare
(Assn. of Swiss Archivists), Schweizeri-
sches Bundesarchiv, Büro Pontri GmbH,
Solohurnstr. 13, Postfach CH-3322, Urte-
nen Schönbühl. Tel. 41-31-312-26-66, fax
41-31-312-26-68, e-mail info@vsa-aas.ch,
World Wide Web http://www.vsa-aas.org.
Pres. Claudia Engler.

Taiwan

Lib. Assn. of the Republic of China (LAROC),
20 Zhongshan South Rd., Taipei 10001. Tel.
2-2361-9132, fax 2-2370-0899, e-mail lac@
msg.ncl.edu.tw, World Wide Web http://
www.lac.org.tw.

Tanzania

Tanzania Lib. Assn., P.O. Box 33433, Dar es
Salaam. Tel./fax 255-744-296-134, e-mail
tla_tanzania@yahoo.com, World Wide Web
http://www.tla.or.tz.

Thailand

Thai Lib. Assn., 1346 Akarnsongkhro 5 Rd.,
Klongchan, Bangkapi, Bangkok 10240.
Tel. 02-734-9022, fax 02-734-9021, e-mail
tla2497@yahoo.com, World Wide Web
http://tla.or.th.

Trinidad and Tobago

Lib. Assn. of Trinidad and Tobago, P.O. Box
1275, Port of Spain. Tel. 868-687-0194,
e-mail info@latt.org.tt, World Wide Web
http://www.latt.org.tt. *Pres.* Selwyn Rod-
ulfo.

Tunisia

Association Tunisienne des Documentalistes,
Bibliothécaires et Archivistes (Tunisian
Assn. of Documentalists, Libns., and Archi-
vists), BP 380, 1000 Tunis RP. Tel. 895-450.

Turkey

Türk Kütüphaneciler Dernegi (Turkish Libns.
Assn.), Necatibey Cad Elgun Sok 8/8,
06440 Kizilay, Ankara. Tel. 312-230-13-
25, fax 312-232-04-53, e-mail tkd.dernek@
gmail.com, World Wide Web http://www.
kutuphaneci.org.tr. *Pres.* Ali Fuat Kartal.

Uganda

Uganda Lib. and Info. Assn., P.O. Box 8147, Kampala. Tel. 772-488-937, e-mail info@ulia.or.ug. *Pres.* Constant Okello-Obura; *Gen. Secy.* Simon Engitu.

Ukraine

Ukrainian Lib. Assn., Vasylkovska 12, Office 5, Code 5, 01004, Kyiv. Tel. 380-44-239-74-87, fax 380-44-35-45-47, e-mail u_b_a@ukr.net, World Wide Web http://www.uba.org.ua.

United Kingdom

Archives and Records Assn., UK and Ireland (formerly the Society of Archivists), Prioryfield House, 20 Canon St., Taunton TA1 1SW, England. Tel. 1823-327-077, fax 1823-271-719, e-mail societyofarchivists@archives.org.uk, World Wide Web http://www.archives.org.uk. *Chief Exec.* John Chambers; *Chair* David Mander.

ASLIB, the Assn. for Info. Management, Howard House, Wagon Lane, Bingley BD16 1WA, England. Tel. 01274-777-700, fax 01274-785-201, e-mail support@aslib.com, World Wide Web http://www.aslib.com.

Bibliographical Society, Institute of English Studies, Senate House, Malet St., London WC1E 7HU, England. E-mail admin@bibsoc.org.uk, World Wide Web http://www.bibsoc.org.uk. *Pres.* Henry Woudhuysen. E-mail president@bibsoc.org.uk.

Chartered Institute of Lib. and Info. Professionals (CILIP) (formerly the Lib. Assn.), 7 Ridgmount St., London WC1E 7AE, England. Tel. 20-7255-0500, fax 20-7255-0501, e-mail info@cilip.org.uk, World Wide Web http://www.cilip.org.uk. *Pres.* Jan Parry. E-mail jan.parry@cilip.org.uk; *Chief Exec.* Annie Mauger. E-mail annie.mauger@cilip.org.uk.

School Lib. Assn., 1 Pine Court, Kembrey Park, Swindon SN2 8AD, England. Tel. 1793-530-166, fax 1793-481-182, e-mail info@sla.org.uk, World Wide Web http://www.sla.org.uk. *Pres.* Kevin Crossley-Holland; *Chair* Karen Horsfield; *Dir.* Tricia Adams.

Scottish Lib. and Info. Council, 151 W. George St., Glasgow G2 2JJ, Scotland. Tel. 141-228-4790, e-mail info@scottishlibraries.org, World Wide Web http://www.scottishlibraries.org. *CEO* Amina Shah. E-mail a.shah@scottishlibraries.org.

Society of College, National, and Univ. Libs (SCONUL) (formerly Standing Conference of National and Univ. Libs.), 94 Euston St., London NW1 2HA, England. Tel. 20-7387-0317, fax 20-7383-3197, e-mail info@sconul.ac.uk, World Wide Web http://www.sconul.ac.uk. *Chair* Liz Jolly; *Exec. Dir.* Ann Rossiter.

Uruguay

Agrupación Bibliotecológica del Uruguay (Uruguayan Lib. and Archive Science Assn.) and Asociación de Bibliotecólogos del Uruguay (Uruguayan Libns. Assn.), Eduardo V. Haedo 2255, CP 11200, Montevideo. Tel. 2409-9989, e-mail abu@adinet.com.uy. *Pres.* Alicia Ocaso.

Vietnam

Hôi Thu-Vien Viet Nam (Vietnam Lib. Assn.), National Lib. of Vietnam, 31 Trang Thi, Hoan Kiem, 10000 Hanoi. Tel. 4-3825-5397, fax 4-3825-3357, e-mail info@nlv.gov.vn, World Wide Web http://www.nlv.gov.vn.

Zambia

Zambia Lib. Assn., P.O. Box 38636, 10101 Lusaka. *Chair* Benson Njobvu. E-mail benson njobvu@hotmail.com.

Zimbabwe

Zimbabwe Lib. Assn., Harare City Lib., Civic Centre, Rotten Row, P.O. Box 1987, Harare. Tel. 263-773-060-307, e-mail info@zimla.co.za, World Wide Web http://zimbabwe reads.org/zimla. *Chair* T. G. Bohwa.

Directory of Book Trade and Related Organizations

Book Trade Associations, United States and Canada

For more extensive information on the associations listed in this section, see the annual edition of *Literary Market Place* (Information Today, Inc.).

AIGA—The Professional Assn. for Design (formerly American Institute of Graphic Arts), 164 Fifth Ave., New York, NY 10010. Tel. 212-807-1990, fax 212-807-1799, e-mail aiga@aiga.org, World Wide Web http://www.aiga.org. *Pres.* Sean Adams, Adams-Morioka, Inc. E-mail sean_a@adamsmorioka.com; *Secy.-Treas.* Darralyn Rieth. E-mail darralynrieth@gmail.com; *Exec. Dir.* Richard Grefé. E-mail grefe@aiga.org.

American Book Producers Assn. (ABPA), 151 W. 19 St., third fl., New York, NY10011. Tel. 212-675-1363, fax 212-675-1364, e-mail office@ABPAonline.org, World Wide Web http://www.abpaonline.org. *Pres.* Richard Rothschild; *V.P.* Nancy Hall; *Treas.* Valerie Tomaselli; *Admin.* Kirsten Hall.

American Booksellers Assn., 200 White Plains Rd., Tarrytown, NY 10591. Tel. 800-637-0037, 914-591-2665, fax 914-591-2720, World Wide Web http://www.bookweb.org. *Pres.* Steve Bercu, BookPeople, Austin. Tel. 512-472-5050, e-mail steve@bookpeople.com; *V.P./Secy.* Betsy Burton, The King's English Bookshop, Salt Lake City. Tel. 801-484-9100, e-mail btke@comcast.net; *CEO* Oren Teicher. E-mail oren@bookweb.org.

American Literary Translators Assn. (ALTA), Univ. of Texas at Dallas, 800 W. Campbell Rd., Mail Sta. JO51, Richardson, TX 75080. Tel. 972-883-2092, fax 972-883-6303, World Wide Web http://www.utdallas.edu/alta. *Managing Dir.* Erica Mena. E-mail erica@literarytranslators.org.

American Printing History Assn., Box 4519, Grand Central Sta., New York, NY 10163-4519. World Wide Web http://www.printinghistory.org. *Pres.* Robert McCamant; *Exec. Secy.* Lyndsi Barnes. E-mail secretary@printinghistory.org.

American Society for Indexing, 1628 E. Southern Ave., No. 9-223, Tempe, AZ 85282. Tel. 480-245-6750, e-mail info@asindexing.org, World Wide Web http://www.asindexing.org. *Pres.* Charlee Trantino. E-mail president@asindexing.org; *V.P./Pres.-Elect* Fred Leise. E-mail presidentelect@asindexing.org; *Exec. Dir.* Gwen Henson. E-mail gwen@asindexing.org.

American Society of Journalists and Authors, 1501 Broadway, Suite 403, New York, NY 10036. Tel. 212-997-0947, fax 212-937-2315, e-mail asjaoffice@asja.org, World Wide Web http://www.asja.org. *Pres.* Randy Dotinga. E-mail president@asja.org; *V.P.* Sherry Beck Paprocki. E-mail vicepresident@asja.org; *Exec. Dir.* Alexandra Cantor Owens.

American Society of Media Photographers, 150 N. 2 St., Philadelphia, PA 19106. Tel. 215-451-2767, fax 215-451-0880, e-mail mopsik@asmp.org, World Wide Web http://www.asmp.org. *Pres.* Gail Mooney. E-mail mooney@asmp.org; *V. Chair* Jenna Close; *Exec. Dir.* Eugene Mopsik.

American Society of Picture Professionals, 201 E. 25 St., No. 11C, New York, NY 10010. Tel. 516-500-3686, e-mail director@aspp.com, World Wide Web http://www.aspp.

com. *Pres.* Cecilia de Querol. E-mail president@aspp.com; *Exec. Dir.* Sam Merrell. E-mail director@aspp.com.

American Translators Assn., 225 Reinekers Lane, Suite 590, Alexandria, VA 22314. Tel. 703-683-6100, fax 703-683-6122, e-mail ata@atanet.org, World Wide Web http://www.atanet.org. *Pres.* Caitilin Walsh; *Pres.-Elect* David C. Rumsey; *Secy.* Boris Silversteyn; *Treas.* Ted R. Wozniak; *Exec. Dir.* Walter W. Bacak, Jr. E-mail walter@atanet.org.

Antiquarian Booksellers Assn. of America, 20 W. 44 St., No. 507, New York, NY 10036-6604. Tel. 212-944-8291, fax 212-944-8293, e-mail inquiries@abaa.org, World Wide Web http://www.abaa.org. *Pres.* Thomas Goldwasser; *V.P./Secy.* Mary Gilliam; *Treas.* Charles Kutcher; *Exec. Dir.* Susan Benne. E-mail sbenne@abaa.org.

Assn. Media and Publishing, 12100 Sunset Hills Road, Suite 130, Reston, VA 20190. Tel. 703-234-4063, fax 703-435-4390, e-mail info@associationmediaandpublishing.org, World Wide Web http://www.association mediaandpublishing.org. *Pres.* Kim Howard; *V.P.* Erin Pressley; *Exec. Dir.* Elissa Myers. Tel. 703-234-4107, e-mail elissa@association mediaandpublishing.org.

Assn. of American Publishers, 71 Fifth Ave., New York, NY 10003. Tel. 212-255-0200, fax 212-255-7007. Washington Office 455 Massachusetts Ave. N.W., Suite 700, Washington, DC 20001. Tel. 202-347-3375, fax 202-347-3690, World Wide Web http://www.publishers.org. *Pres./CEO* Tom Allen. E-mail tallen@publishers.org; *General Counsel and V.P., Government Affairs* Allan R. Adler. E-mail adler@publishers.org; *Exec. Dir., Higher Educ.* David Anderson. E-mail danderson@publishers.org; *Exec. Dir., Pre-K–12 Learning Group* Jay Diskey. E-mail jdiskey@publishers.org; *Senior Dir., Pre-K–12 Learning Group* Susan Fletcher. E-mail sfletcher@publishers.org; *V.P.* Tina Jordan. E-mail tjordan@publishers.org; *Dir., Membership Marketing* Gail Kump. E-mail gkump@publishers.org; *Exec. Dir., Digital, Environmental and Accessibility Affairs* Ed McCoyd. E-mail emccoyd@publishers.org; *Strategic Partnerships Exec.* Jo-Ann McDevitt. E-mail jmcdevitt@publishers.org; *Dir., Free Expression Advocacy* Judith Platt. E-mail jplatt@publishers.org; *Exec. Dir., International Copyright Enforcement and Trade Policy* M. Lui Simpson. E-mail lsimpson@publishers.org; *V.P. and Exec. Dir., Professional and Scholarly Publishing* John Tagler. E-mail jtagler@publishers.org.

Assn. of American University Presses, 28 W. 36 St., Suite 602, New York, NY 10018. Tel. 212-989-1010, fax 212-989-0275, e-mail info@aaupnet.org, World Wide Web http://aaupnet.org. *Pres.* Barbara Kline Pope, National Academies Press; *Pres.-Elect* Meredith Babb, Univ. Press of Florida; *Past Pres.* Philip Cercone, McGill-Queen's Univ. Press; *Exec. Dir.* Peter Berkery. Tel. 212-989-1010 ext. 29, e-mail pberkery@aaupnet.org.

Assn. of Canadian Publishers, 174 Spadina Ave., Suite 306, Toronto, ON M5T 2C2. Tel. 416-487-6116, fax 416-487-8815, World Wide Web http://www.publishers.ca. *Pres.* Erin Creasy, ECW Press, 2120 Queen St. E., Suite 200 Toronto, ON M4E 1E2. Tel. 416-694-3348, fax 416-698-9906, e-mail erin@ecwpress.com; *V.P./Treas.* Matt Williams, House of Anansi/Groundwood, 110 Spadina Ave., Suite 801, Toronto, ON M5V 2M5. Tel. 416-363-4343, fax 416-363-1017, e-mail matt@anansi.ca; *Exec. Dir.* Carolyn Wood. Tel. 416-487-6116 ext. 222, e-mail carolyn_wood@canbook.org.

Assn. of Educational Publishers (AEP). Merged in 2013 with the School Division of the Assn. of American Publishers (AAP).

Audio Publishers Assn., 100 N. 20 St., Suite 400, Philadelphia, PA 19103. Tel. 215-564-2729, e-mail info@audiopub.org; World Wide Web http://www.audiopub.org. *Pres.* Michele Cobb; *V.P.* Linda Lee; *V.P., Member Communications* Robin Whitten; *Secy.* Janet Benson; *Treas.* Sean McManus; *Exec. Dir.* Denise Daniels.

Authors Guild, 31 E. 32 St., seventh fl., New York, NY 10016. Tel. 212-563-5904, fax 212-564-5363, e-mail staff@authorsguild.org, World Wide Web http://www.authorsguild.org. *Pres.* Roxana Robinson; *V.P.s* Judy Blume, Richard Russo, James Shapiro; *Secy.* Pat Cummings; *Treas.* Peter Petre.

Book Industry Study Group, 145 W. 45 St., Suite 601, New York, NY 10017. Tel. 646-336-7141, fax 646-336-6214, e-mail info@

bisg.org, World Wide Web http://www.bisg. org. *Chair* Tara Catogge, Quarto Publishing; *V. Chair* Andrew Savikas, Safari Books Online; *Secy.* Fran Toolan, Firebrand Technologies; *Treas.* Maureen McMahon, Kaplan Publishing; *Exec. Dir.* Len Vlahos. E-mail len@bisg.org.

Book Manufacturers' Institute, 2 Armand Beach Drive, Suite 1B, Palm Coast, FL 32137. Tel. 386-986-4552, fax 386-986-4553, e-mail info@bmibook.com, World Wide Web http://www.bmibook.org. *Pres.* Jac B. Garner, Webcrafters; *Exec. V.P./Secy.* Daniel N. Bach; *V.P./Pres.-Elect* Kent H. Larson, Bridgeport National Bindery; *Treas.* Paul Genovese, Lake Book Manufacturing. Address correspondence to the executive vice president.

Bookbuilders of Boston, 115 Webster Woods Lane, North Andover, MA 01845. Tel. 781-378-1361, fax 419-821-2171, e-mail office @bbboston.org, World Wide Web http://www.bbboston.org. *Pres.* Jamie Carter. E-mail jcarter@copyright.com; *1st V.P.* Christopher Hartman. E-mail hartman.cg@gmail.com; *2nd V.P.* Tom Delano. E-mail tom.delano@gmail.com; *Treas.* James Taylor. E-mail jtaylor@vistahigherlearning.com; *Clerk* Laura Wind. E-mail lwind@bedford stmartins.com.

Bookbuilders West. See Publishing Professionals Network.

Canadian Booksellers Assn. Now part of Retail Council of Canada. Toronto office: 1255 Bay St., Suite 902, Toronto, ON M5R 2A9.

Canadian International Standard Numbers (ISN) Agency, c/o Published Heritage, Lib. and Archives Canada, 395 Wellington St., Ottawa, ON K1A 0N4. Tel. 866-578-7777 (toll-free) or 613-996-5115, World Wide Web http://www.collectionscanada.ca/isn/index-e.html.

Canadian Printing Industries Assn., P.O. Box 58033, Orleans Garden, 1619 Orleans Blvd., Ottawa, ON K1C 7E2. Tel. 613-236-7208, toll free (Canada and USA) 800-267-7280, fax 613-232-1334, World Wide Web http://www.cpia-aci.ca. *Chair* Sandy Stephens, Informco; *Exec. Dir.* Brian Ellis. E-mail brian ellis@cpia-aci.ca.

CBA: The Assn. for Christian Retail (formerly Christian Booksellers Association), 9240 Explorer Drive, Suite 200, Colorado Springs, CO 80920. Tel. 719-265-9895, fax 719-272-3510, e-mail info@cbaonline.org, World Wide Web http://www.cbaonline. org. *Chair* Sue Smith, Baker Book House; *V. Chair* Robin Hogan, Christian Cultural Center Bookstore.

Chicago Book Clinic. See Midwest Publishing Assn.

Children's Book Council, 54 W. 39 St., 14th fl., New York, NY 10018. Tel. 212-966-1990, fax 212-966-2073, e-mail cbc.info@cbc books.org, World Wide Web http://www.cbc books.org. *Chair* Betsy Groban, Houghton Mifflin Harcourt; *V. Chair* Jon Anderson, Simon & Schuster; *Exec. Dir.* Robin Adelson. E-mail robin.adelson@cbcbooks.org.

Christian Booksellers Association. See CBA: The Assn. for Christian Retail.

Copyright Society of the USA, 1 E. 53 St., eighth fl., New York, NY 10022. World Wide Web http://www.csusa.org. *Pres.* Eric J. Schwartz; *V.P.* Nancy E. Wolff; *Secy.* Judith Finell; *Treas.* Michael Donaldson; *Dir. Operations* Kaitland Kubat.

Council of Literary Magazines and Presses, 154 Christopher St., Suite 3C, New York, NY 10014. Tel. 212-741-9110, fax 212-741-9112, e-mail info@clmp.org, World Wide Web http://www.clmp.org. *Co-chairs* Nicole Dewey, Gerald Howard; *Exec. Dir.* Jeffrey Lependorf. E-mail jlependorf@clmp.org.

Educational Book and Media Assn. (formerly Educational Paperback Assn.), P.O. Box 3363, Warrenton, VA 20188. Tel. 540-318-7770, e-mail info@edupaperback.org, World Wide Web http://www.edupaperback. org. *Pres.* Jennifer Allen; *V.P.* Jill Faherty; *Treas.* Joyce Skokut; *Past Pres.* Dan Walsh.

Evangelical Christian Publishers Assn., 9633 S. 48 St., Suite 140, Phoenix, AZ 85044. Tel. 480-966-3998, fax 480-966-1944, e-mail info@ecpa.org, World Wide Web http://www.ecpa.org. *Pres. and CEO* Mark W. Kuyper.

Graphic Artists Guild, 32 Broadway, Suite 1114, New York, NY 10004. Tel. 212-791-3400, fax 212-792-0333, e-mail admin@ gag.org, World Wide Web http://www. graphicartistsguild.org. *Pres.* Haydn S. Adams. E-mail president@gag.org; *V.P.* Lara Kisielewska; *Exec. Dir.* Patricia McKiernan. E-mail admin@gag.org.

Great Lakes Independent Booksellers Assn., c/o Exec. Dir. Deb Leonard, 2113 Roosevelt, Ypsilanti, MI 48197. Tel. 888-736-3096, fax 734-879-11291, e-mail deb@gliba.org, World Wide Web http://www.gliba.org. *Pres.* Tom Lowry, Lowry's Books, 22 N. Main St., Three Rivers, MI 49093. Tel. 269-273-7323, e-mail hiphop@net-link.net.

Guild of Book Workers, 521 Fifth Ave., New York, NY 10175. Tel. 212-292-4444, e-mail secretary@guildofbookworkers.org, World Wide Web http://www.guildofbook workers.org. *Pres.* Mark Andersson. E-mail president@guildofbookworkers.org; *V.P.* Bexx Caswell. E-mail vicepresident@guildofbookworkers.org.

Horror Writers Assn., P.O. Box 56687, Sherman Oaks, CA 91413. E-mail hwa@horror.org, World Wide Web http://www.horror.org. *Pres.* Rocky Wood. E-mail president@horror.org; *V.P.* Lisa Morton. E-mail vp@horror.org; *Secy.* Joe McKinney. E-mail secretary@horror.org; *Treas.* Leslie Klinger. E-mail treasurer@horror.org.

IAPHC—The Graphic Professionals Resource Network (formerly the International Assn. of Printing House Craftsmen), P.O. Box 2549, Maple Grove, MN 55311-7549. Tel. 800-466-4274 (toll-free) or 763-560-1620, fax 763-560-1350, e-mail headquarters@iaphc.org, World Wide Web http://www.iaphc.org. *Pres./CEO* Kevin P. Keane. E-mail kkeane1069@aol.com.

Independent Book Publishers Assn. (formerly PMA), 1020 Manhattan Beach Blvd., Suite 204, Manhattan Beach, CA 90266. Tel. 310-546-1818, fax 310-546-3939, e-mail info@ibpa-online.org, World Wide Web http://www.ibpa-online.org. *Chair* Deltina Hay, Dalton Publishing, 9101 La Cresada Drive, No. 1934, Austin, TX 78749. Tel. 512-567-4955; *Exec. Dir.* Angela Bole. Tel. 310-546-1818, e-mail angela@ibpa-online.org; *COO/Secy.* Terry Nathan. E-mail terry@ibpa-online.org.

International Standard Book Numbering U.S. Agency, 630 Central Ave., New Providence, NJ 07974. Tel. 888-269-5372, fax 908-219-0188, e-mail isbn-san@bowker.com, World Wide Web http://www.isbn.org. *Dir., Identifier Services* Beat Barblan.

Jewish Book Council, 520 Eighth Ave., fourth fl., New York, NY 10018. Tel. 212-201-2920, fax 212-532-4952, e-mail jbc@jewishbooks.org, World Wide Web http://www.jewishbookcouncil.org. *Pres.* Lawrence J. Krule; *V.P.* Judith Lieberman; *Secy.* Mimi S. Frank.

Library Binding Institute/Hardcover Binders International, 4400 PGA Blvd., Suite 600, Palm Beach Gardens, FL 33410. Tel. 561-745-6821, fax 561-775-0089, e-mail info@lbibinders.org, World Wide Web http://www.lbibinders.org. *Pres.* Duncan Campbell, Campbell-Logan Bindery. E-mail duncan@campbell-logan.com; *Exec. Dir.* Debra Nolan. E-mail dnolan@lbibinders.org.

Midwest Independent Publishers Assn. (MIPA), P.O. Box 18536, St. Paul, MN 55118-0536. Tel. 651-917-0021 or 651-917-0021, World Wide Web http://www.mipa.org. *Pres.* Sherry Roberts, Roberts Group. Tel. 952-322-4005, e-mail sherry@editorialservice.com; *Secy.* Judith Palmateer, Amber Skye Publishing. Tel. 651-452-0463, e-mail jpalmateer0463@comcast.net; *Treas.* Dorie McClelland, Spring Book Design. Tel. 651-457-0258, e-mail dorie@springbookdesign.com.

Midwest Publishing Assn., 275 N. York St., Suite 401, Elmhurst, IL 60126. Tel. 630-833-4220, e-mail info@midwestpublish.org, World Wide Web http://www.midwestpublish.org. *Pres.* Del Bishop, The Bishop Group, 3 Burning Oak Trail, Barrington Hills, IL 60019. Tel. 847-462-1877, e-mail bishopgroup@comcast.nct.

Miniature Book Society. *Pres.* Stephen Byrne. E-mail sb@finalscore.demon.co.uk; *V.P.* Jim Brogan; *Secy.* Gail Faulkner; *Treas.* Karen Nyman. World Wide Web http://www.mbs.org.

Minnesota Book Publishers' Roundtable. E-mail information@publishersroundtable.org, World Wide Web http://www.publishersroundtable.org. *Pres.* Katie Nickerson, Univ. of Minnesota Press, 111 Third Ave. S., Suite 290, Minneapolis, MN 55401. E-mail nickerso@umn.edu; *V.P.* Kate Kjorlien, Hazelden Publishing, 15251 Pleasant Valley Rd., Center City, MN 55012. E-mail kkjorlien@hazelden.org.

Mountains and Plains Independent Booksellers Assn., 3278 Big Spruce Way, Park City, UT 84098. Tel. 435-649-6079, fax 435-649-6105, e-mail laura@mountainsplains.org,

World Wide Web http://www.mountains plains.org. *Pres.* Andrea Avantaggio, Maria's Bookshop, 960 Main Ave., Durango, CO 81301. Tel. 970-247-1438, fax 970-247-5916, e-mail andrea@mariasbookshop.com; *Exec. Dir.* Laura Ayrey.

MPA—The Assn. of Magazine Media (formerly Magazine Publishers of America), 757 Third Ave., 11th fl., New York, NY 10017. Tel. 212-872-3700, e-mail mpa@magazine. org, World Wide Web http://www.magazine. org. *Pres. and CEO* Mary Berner. Tel. 212-872-3710, e-mail president@magazine.org.

NAPL (formerly National Assn. for Printing Leadership), 1 Meadowlands Plaza, Suite 1511, East Rutherford, NJ 07073. Tel. 800-642-6275, 201-634-9600, fax 201-634-0324, e-mail info@napl.org, World Wide Web http://www.napl.org. *Pres./CEO* Joseph P. Truncale. E-mail jtruncale@napl. org.

National Assn. of College Stores, 500 E. Lorain St., Oberlin, OH 44074-1294. Tel. 800-622-7498, 440-775-7777, fax 440-775-4769, e-mail info@nacs.org, World Wide Web http://www.nacs.org. *Pres.* Todd Summer; *Pres.-Elect* Anthony Martin; *CEO* Brian Cartier. E-mail bcartier@nacs.org.

National Book Foundation, 90 Broad St., Suite 604, New York, NY 10004. Tel. 212-685-0261, fax 212-213-6570, e-mail national book@nationalbook.org, World Wide Web http://www.nationalbook.org. *Pres./CEO* David Steinberger, Perseus Books Group; *V.P.* Morgan Entrekin, Grove/Atlantic; *Exec. Dir.* Harold Augenbraum. E-mail haugenbraum @nationalbook.org.

National Coalition Against Censorship (NCAC), 19 Fulton St., Suite 407, New York, NY 10038. Tel. 212-807-6222, fax 212-807-6245, e-mail ncac@ncac.org, World Wide Web http://www.ncac.org. *Exec. Dir.* Joan E. Bertin; *Dirs.* Jon Anderson, Michael Bamberger, Joan E. Bertin, Judy Blume, Susan Clare, Martha Gershun, Robie Harris, Phil Harvey, Michael Jacobs, Eric M. Freedman, Chris Peterson, Larry Siems, Emily Whitfield.

New Atlantic Independent Booksellers Assn. (NAIBA), 2667 Hyacinth St., Westbury, NY 11590. Tel. 516-333-0681, fax 516-333-0689, e-mail info@naiba.com, World Wide Web http://www.newatlanticbooks.

com. *Pres.* Mark LaFramboise, Politics and Prose; *V.P.* Todd Dickinson, Aaron's Books; *Exec. Dir.* Eileen Dengler.

New England Independent Booksellers Assn. (NEIBA), 1955 Massachusetts Ave., Cambridge, MA 02140-1405, e-mail steve@ neba.org, World Wide Web http://www.new englandbooks.org. *Pres.* Suzanna Hermans, Oblong Books & Music, Rhinebeck, NY; *V.P.* Susan Mercier, Edgartown Books, Edgartown, MA; *Exec. Dir.* Steve Fischer.

New York Center for Independent Publishing (formerly the Small Press Center), c/o General Society of Mechanics and Tradesmen Lib., 20 W. 44 St., New York, NY 10036. Tel. 212-764-7021, e-mail info@nycip.org, World Wide Web http://nycip.wordpress. com.

Northern California Independent Booksellers Assn., The Presidio, 1007 General Kennedy Ave., P.O. Box 29169, San Francisco, CA 94129. Tel. 415-561-7686, fax 415-561-7685, e-mail office@nciba.com, World Wide Web http://www.nciba.com. *Pres.* Calvin Crosby; *V.P.* John Russel; *Exec. Dir.* Hut Landon.

PEN American Center, Div. of International PEN, 588 Broadway, Suite 303, New York, NY 10012. Tel. 212-334-1660, fax 212-334-2181, e-mail pen@pen.org, World Wide Web http://www.pen.org. *Pres.* Peter Godwin; *Exec. V.P.* John Troubh; *V.P.s* Jeri Laber, Joanne Leedom-Ackerman, Annette Tapert; *Secy.* Theresa Rebeck; *Treas.* John Oakes; *Exec. Dir.* Susanne Nossel. E-mail snossel@pen.org.

Periodical and Book Assn. of America, 481 Eighth Ave., Suite 526, New York, NY 10001. Tel. 212-563-6502, fax 212-563-4098, World Wide Web http://www.pbaa. net. *Pres.* Jay Annis. E-mail jannis@taunton. com; *Chair* William Michalopoulos. E-mail wmichalopoulos@hearst.com; *Exec. Dir.* Lisa W. Scott. E-mail lisawscott@hotmail. com; *Assoc. Dir.* Jose Cancio. E-mail jcancio @pbaa.net.

Publishers Marketing Assn. (PMA). See Independent Book Publishers Assn.

Publishing Professionals Network (formerly Bookbuilders West), 9328 Elk Grove Blvd., Suite 105, Elk Grove, CA 95624. Tel. 415-670-9564, e-mail operations@bookbuilders. org, World Wide Web http://pubpronetwork.

org. *Pres.* David Zielonka; *V.P.* Tona Pearce Myers.

Romance Writers of America, 14615 Benfer Rd., Houston, TX 77069. Tel. 832-717-5200, fax 832-717-5201, e-mail info@rwa.org, World Wide Web http://www.rwa.org. *Pres.* Cindy Kirk. E-mail cindykirk@aol.com; *Pres.-Elect* Diane Kelly. E-mail diane@dianekelly.com; *Exec. Dir.* Allison Kelley. E-mail allison.kelley@rwa.org.

Science Fiction and Fantasy Writers of America, P.O. Box 3238, Enfield, CT 06083-3238. World Wide Web http://www.sfwa.org. *Pres.* Steven Gould. E-mail president@sfwa.org; *V.P.* Cat Rambo. E-mail vp@sfwa.org; *Secy.* Susan Forest. E-mail secretary@sfwa.org; *CFO* Bud Sparhawk. E-mail treasurer@sfwa.org; *Operations Mgr.* Kate Baker. E-mail office@sfwa.org.

Society of Children's Book Writers and Illustrators (SCBWI), 8271 Beverly Blvd., Los Angeles, CA 90048. Tel. 323-782-1010, fax 323-782-1892, e-mail scbwi@scbwi.org, World Wide Web http://www.scbwi.org. *Pres.* Stephen Mooser. E-mail stephenmooser@scbwi.org; *Exec. Dir.* Lin Oliver.

Society of Illustrators (SI), 128 E. 63 St., New York, NY 10065. Tel. 212-838-2560, fax 212-838-2561, e-mail info@societyillustrators.org, World Wide Web http://www.societyillustrators.org. *Pres.* Tim O'Brien; *Exec. V.P.* Victor Juhasz; *V.P.* Kar-en Green; *Secy.* Leslie Cober-Gentry; *Exec. Dir.* Anelle Miller. E-mail anelle@societyillustrators.org.

Southern Independent Booksellers Alliance (SIBA), 3806 Yale Ave., Columbia, SC 29205. Tel. 803-994-9530, fax 309-410-0211, e-mail info@sibaweb.com, World Wide Web http://www.sibaweb.com. *Exec. Dir.* Wanda Jewell. E-mail wanda@sibaweb.com.

Western Writers of America, c/o Candy Moulton, 271 CR 219, Encampment, WY 82325 Tel. 307-329-8942, e-mail wwa.moulton@gmail.com, World Wide Web http://www.westernwriters.org. *Pres.* Sherry Monahan; *V.P.* Kirk Ellis; *Past Pres.* Dusty Richards; *Exec. Dir./Secy.-Treas.* Candy Moulton.

Women's National Book Assn., P.O. Box 237, FDR Sta., New York, NY 10150. Tel./fax 212-208-4629, e-mail info@wnba-books.org, World Wide Web http://www.wnba-books.org. *Pres.* Carin Siegfried, 7308 Quail Meadow Lane, Charlotte, NC 28210. Tel. 704-608-6559, e-mail carinsiegfried@earthlink.net; *V.P./Pres.-Elect* Jane Kinney-Denning, 1629 NYS Rt. 94, New Windsor, NY 12533. Tel. 845-496-1593, e-mail jdenning@pace.edu; *Secy.* Shannon Janeczek; *Treas.* Gloria Toler; *Past Pres.* Valerie Tomaselli.

International and Foreign Book Trade Associations

For Canadian book trade associations, see the preceding section, "Book Trade Associations, United States and Canada." For a more extensive list of book trade organizations outside the United States and Canada, with more detailed information, consult *International Literary Market Place* (Information Today, Inc.), which also provides extensive lists of major bookstores and publishers in each country.

International

African Publishers' Network, c/o Ghana Book Publishers Assn. (GBPA), P.O. Box LT 471, Lartebiokorshie, Accra, Ghana. Tel. 233-21-912765, e-mail ghanabookpubs@yahoo.com.

Afro-Asian Book Council, 4835/24 Ansari Rd., New Delhi 110002, India. Tel. 11-2325-8865, fax 11-2326-7437, e-mail afro@aabcouncil.org, World Wide Web http://www.aabcouncil.org. *Secy.-Gen.* Sukumar Das. E-mail sukumar4das21@gmail.com; *Dir.* Saumya Gupta. E-mail sgupta@aabcouncil.org.

Centro Régional para el Fomento del Libro en América Latina y el Caribe (CERLALC) (Regional Center for Book Promotion in Latin America and the Caribbean), Calle 70, No. 9-52, Bogotá, Colombia. Tel. 1-540-2071, fax 1-541-6398, e-mail libro@cerlalc.com, World Wide Web http://www.cerlalc.org. *Dir.* Fernando Zapata López.

Federation of European Publishers, rue Montoyer 31, Boîte 8, 1000 Brussels, Belgium. Tel. 2-770-11-10, fax 2-771-20-71, e-mail info@fep-fee.eu, World Wide Web http://www.fep-fee.eu. *Pres.* Pierre Dutilleul; *Dir.-Gen.* Anne Bergman-Tahon.

International Board on Books for Young People (IBBY), Nonnenweg 12, 4003 Basel, Switzerland. Tel. 61-272-29-17, fax 61-272-27-57, e-mail ibby@ibby.org, World Wide Web http://www.ibby.org. *Exec. Dir.* Elizabeth Page.

International League of Antiquarian Booksellers (ILAB), c/o Rue Toepffer 5, Case postale 499, 1211 Geneva 12, Switzerland. E-mail secretary@ilab.org, World Wide Web http://www.ilab.org. *Pres.* Norbert Donhofer; *Gen. Secy.* Ulrich Hobbeling.

International Publishers Assn. (Union Internationale des Editeurs), 23 ave. de France, CH-1202 Geneva, Switzerland. Tel. 22-704-1820, e-mail secretariat@internationalpublishers.org, World Wide Web http://www.internationalpublishers.org. *Pres.* Youngsuk Chi; *Secy.-Gen.* Jens Bammel.

STM: The International Assn. of Scientific, Technical, and Medical Publishers, 267 Banbury Rd., Oxford OX2 7HT, England. Tel. 44-1865-339-321, fax 44-1865-339-325, e-mail info@stm-assoc.org, World Wide Web http://www.stm-assoc.org. *CEO* Michael Mabe.

National

Argentina

Cámara Argentina del Libro (Argentine Book Assn.), Av. Belgrano 1580, 4 piso, C1093AAQ Buenos Aires. Tel. 11-4381-8383, fax 11-4381-9253, e-mail cal@editores.org.ar, World Wide Web http://www.editores.org.ar. *Pres.* Isaac Rubizal.

Fundación El Libro (Book Foundation), Yrigoyen 1628, 5 piso, C1089AAF Buenos Aires. Tel. 11-4370-0600, fax 11-4370-0607, e-mail fundacion@el-libro.com.ar, World Wide Web http://www.el-libro.org.ar. *Admin. Mgr.* Daniel Monzo; *Chair* Martin Gremmelspacher.

Australia

Australian and New Zealand Assn. of Antiquarian Booksellers (ANZAAB), Apartment 1, 122 Raglan St., Mosman, NSW 2088. E-mail admin@anzaab.com, World Wide Web http://www.anzaab.com. *Pres.* Jörn Harbeck; *Secy.* Rachel Robarts.

Australian Booksellers Assn., 828 High St., Unit 9, Kew East, Vic. 3102. Tel. 3-9859-7322, fax 3-9859-7344, e-mail mail@aba.org.au, World Wide Web http://www.aba.

org.au. *Pres.* Patricia Genat; *CEO* Joel Becker.

Australian Publishers Assn., 60/89 Jones St., Ultimo, NSW 2007. Tel. 2-9281-9788, e-mail apa@publishers.asn.au, World Wide Web http://www.publishers.asn.au. *Pres.* Louise Adler; *CEO* Maree McCaskill. E-mail maree.mccaskill@publishers.asn.au.

Austria

Hauptverband des Österreichischen Buchhandels (Austrian Publishers and Booksellers Assn.), Grünangergasse 4, A-1010 Vienna. Tel. 1-512-15-35-26, fax 1-512-84-82, e-mail sekretariat@hvb.at, World Wide Web http://www.buecher.at. *Mgr.* Inge Kralupper. E-mail kralupper@hvb.at.

Verband der Antiquare Österreichs (Austrian Antiquarian Booksellers Assn.), Grünangergasse 4, A-1010 Vienna. Tel. 1-512-1535-14, e-mail sekretariat@hvb.at, World Wide Web http://www.antiquare.at.

Belarus

National Book Chamber of Belarus, 31a V Khoruzhei Str., Rm. 707, 220002 Minsk. Tel. 17-289-33-96, fax 17-334-78-47, World Wide Web http://natbook.org.by. *Dir.* Elena V. Ivanova. E-mail elvit@natbook.org.by.

Belgium

Boek.be (formerly Vlaamse Boekverkopersbond, Flemish Booksellers Assn.), Te Buelaerlei 37, 2140 Borgerhout. Tel. 03-230-89-23, fax 3-281-22-40, World Wide Web http://www.boek.be. *CEO* Geert Joris; *Communication Mgr.* Patricia De Laet. E-mail patricia.delaet@boek.be.

Vlaamse Uitgevers Vereniging (Flemish Publishers Assn.). See Boek.be.

Bolivia

Cámara Boliviana del Libro (Bolivian Book Chamber), Calle Capitan Ravelo No. 2116, 682 La Paz. Tel. 2-211-3264, e-mail cabolib@entelnet.bo, World Wide Web http://www.cabolib.org.bo. *Gen. Mgr.* Ana Patricia Navarro.

Brazil

Cámara Brasileira do Livro (Brazilian Book Assn.), Rua Cristiano Viana 91, Jardim Paulista, 05411-000 Sao Paulo-SP. Tel./fax 11-3069-1300, e-mail cbl@cbl.org.br, World Wide Web http://www.cbl.org.br. *Pres.* Karine Goncalves Pansa.

Sindicato Nacional dos Editores de Livros (Brazilian Publishers Assn.), Rue da Ajuda 35-18 andar, 20040-000 Rio de Janeiro-RJ. Tel. 21-2533-0399, fax 21-2533-0422, e-mail snel@snel.org.br, World Wide Web http://www.snel.org.br. *Pres.* Sonia Machado Jardim.

Chile

Cámara Chilena del Libro AG (Chilean Assn. of Publishers, Distributors, and Booksellers), Av. Libertador Bernardo O'Higgins 1370, Oficina 501, Santiago. Tel. 2-672-0348, fax 2-687-4271, e-mail prolibro@tie.cl, World Wide Web http://www.camlibro.cl. *Pres.* Arturo Infante.

Colombia

Cámara Colombiana del Libro (Colombian Book Assn.), Calle 35, No. 5A 05, Bogotá. Tel. 57-1-323-01-11, fax 57-1-285-10-82, e-mail camlibro@camlibro.com.co, World Wide Web http://www.camlibro.com.co. *Exec. Chair* Enrique González Villa; *Secy.-Gen.* José Manuel Ramirez Sarmiento.

Czech Republic

Svaz ceských knihkupcu a nakladatelu (Czech Publishers and Booksellers Assn.), P.O. Box 177, 110 01 Prague. Tel. 224-219-944, fax 224-219-942, e-mail sckn@sckn.cz, World Wide Web http://www.sckn.cz. *Chair* Martin Vopěnka.

Denmark

Danske Boghandlerforening (Danish Booksellers Assn.), Slotsholmsgade 1 B, 1216 Copenhagen K. Tel. 3254-2255, fax 3254-0041, e-mail ddb@bogpost.dk, World Wide Web http://www.boghandlerforeningen.dk. *Chair* Mogens Eliasson.

Danske Forlæggerforening (Danish Publishers Assn.), Børsen DK-1217 Copenhagen K. Tel. 45-33-15-66-88, e-mail danishpublishers@danishpublishers.dk, World Wide Web http://www.danskeforlag.dk.

Ecuador

Cámara Ecuatoriana del Libro, Avda. Eloy Alfaro, N29-61 e Inglaterra, Edf. Eloy Alfaro, 9 no. piso, Quito. Tel. 2-5533-11, fax 2-222-150, e-mail celnp@uio.satnet.net, World Wide Web http://celibro.org.ec. *Pres.* Fabian Luzuriaga.

Egypt

General Egyptian Book Organization (GEBO), P.O. Box 235, Cairo 11511. Tel. 2-257-7531, fax 2-257-54213, e-mail info@gebo.gov.eg, World Wide Web http://www.gebo.gov.eg. *Chair* Nasser Al-Ansary.

Estonia

Estonian Publishers Assn., Roosikrantsi 6-207,10119 Tallinn. Tel. 372-644-9866, fax 372-617-7550, e-mail kirjastusteliit@eki.ee, World Wide Web http://www.estbook.com. *Managing Dir.* Kaidi Urmet.

Finland

Kirjakauppaliitto Ry (Booksellers Assn. of Finland), Urho Kekkosen Katu 8 C 34b, 00100 Helsinki. Tel. 9-6899 112, e-mail toimisto@kirjakauppaliitto.fi, World Wide Web http://www.kirjakauppaliitto.fi. *CEO* Katriina Jaakkola.

Suomen Kustannusyhdistys (Finnish Book Publishers Assn.), P.O. Box 177, Lönnrotinkatu 11 A, FIN-00121, Helsinki. Tel. 358-9-228-77-250, fax 358-9-612-1226, World Wide Web http://www.kustantajat.fi/en. *Chair* Pasi Vainio; *Dir.* Sakari Laiho.

France

Bureau International de l'Edition Française (BIEF) (International Bureau of French Publishing), 115 blvd. Saint-Germain, F-75006 Paris. Tel. 01-44-41-13-13, fax 01-46-34-63-83, e-mail info@bief.org, World Wide Web http://www.bief.org. *Pres.* Vera Michalski-Hoffmann; *CEO.* Jean-Guy Boin.
New York Branch French Publishers Agency, 853 Broadway, Suite 1509, New York, NY 10003-4703. Tel./fax 212-254-4540, World Wide Web http://frenchpubagency.com.

Cercle de la Librairie (Circle of Professionals of the Book Trade), 35 rue Grégoire-de-Tours, F-75006 Paris. Tel. 01-44-41-28-00, fax 01-44-41-28-65, e-mail commercial@electre.com, World Wide Web http://www.electre.com.

Syndicat de la Librairie Française, Hotel Massa, 38 rue du Faubourg Saint-Jacques, F-75014 Paris. Tel. 01-53-62-23-10, fax 01-53-62-10-45, e-mail contact@union-librarie.fr, World Wide Web http://www.syndicat-librairie.fr. *Mgr.* Guillaume Husson.

Syndicat National de la Librairie Ancienne et Moderne (SLAM) (National Assn. of Antiquarian and Modern Booksellers), 4 rue Gît-le-Coeur, F-75006 Paris. Tel. 01-43-29-46-38, fax 01-43-25-41-63, e-mail slam-livre@wanadoo.fr, World Wide Web http://www.slam-livre.fr. *Pres.* Frederic Castaing.

Syndicat National de l'Edition (SNE) (National Union of Publishers), 115 blvd. Saint-Germain, F-75006 Paris. Tel. 01-44-41-40-50, fax 01-44-41-40-77, World Wide Web http://www.sne.fr. *Pres.* Vincent Mountain.

Germany

Börsenverein des Deutschen Buchhandels e.V. (Stock Exchange of German Booksellers), Braubachstr. 16, 60311 Frankfurt-am-Main. Tel. 49-69-1306-0, fax 49-69-1306-201, e-mail info@boev.de, World Wide Web http://www.boersenverein.de. *CEO* Alexander Skipis.

Verband Deutscher Antiquare e.V. (German Antiquarian Booksellers Assn.), Geschäftsstelle, Seeblick 1, 56459 Elbingen. Tel. 6435-90-91-47, fax 6435-90-91-48, e-mail buch@antiquare.de, World Wide Web http://www.antiquare.de. *Chair* Christian Hesse.

Greece

Hellenic Federation of Publishers and Booksellers, 73 Themistocleous St., 106 83 Athens. Tel. 2103-300-924, fax 2133-301-617, e-mail secretary@poev.gr, World Wide Web http://www.poev.gr. *Pres.* Annie Ragia; *Secy.-Gen.* Nicholas Stathatos.

Hungary

Magyar Könyvkiadók és Könyvterjesztök Egyesülése (Assn. of Hungarian Publishers and Booksellers), Postfach 130, 1367 Budapest. Tel. 1-343-2540, fax 1-343-2541, e-mail mkke@mkke.hu, World Wide Web http://www.mkke.hu. *Managing Dir.* Péter László Zentai.

Iceland

Félag Islenskra Bókaútgefenda (Icelandic Publishers Assn.), Baronsstig 5, 101 Reykjavik. Tel. 511-8020, fax 511-5020, e-mail fibut@fibut.is, World Wide Web http://www.bokautgafa.is. *Chair* Egill Örn Jóhannsson.

India

Federation of Indian Publishers, Federation House, 18/1C Institutional Area, Aruna Asaf Ali Marg, New Delhi 110067. Tel. 11-2696-4847, fax 11-2686-4054, e-mail fip1@sify.com, World Wide Web http://www.fipindia.org. *Exec. Dir.* P. K. Arora.

Indonesia

Ikatan Penerbit Indonesia (Assn. of Indonesian Book Publishers), Jl. Kalipasir 32, Cikini Jakarta Pusat 10330. Tel. 21-3190-2532, fax 21-3192-6124, e-mail sekretariat@ikapi.org, World Wide Web http://www.ikapi.org.

Ireland

Publishing Ireland/Foilsiu Eireann (formerly CLÉ: The Irish Book Publishers' Assn.), 25 Denzille Lane, Dublin 2. Tel. 639-4868, e-mail info@publishingireland.com, World Wide Web http://www.publishingireland.com. *Pres.* Michael McLouglin. E-mail president@publishingireland.com.

Israel

Book Publishers' Assn. of Israel, 29 Carlebach St., 67132 Tel Aviv. Tel. 3-561-4121, fax 3-561-1996, e-mail info@tbpai.co.il, World Wide Web http://www.tbpai.co.il. *Chair* Rachel Edelman.

Italy

Associazione Italiana Editori (Italian Publishers Assn.), Corso di Porta Romana 108, 20122 Milan. Tel. 2-89-28-0800, fax 2-89-28-0860, e-mail aie@aie.it, World Wide Web http://www.aie.it. *Dir.* Alfieri Lorenzon.

Associazione Librai Antiquari d'Italia (Antiquarian Booksellers Assn. of Italy), Via dei Bononcini 24, 41121 Modena. Tel. 347 646-9147, fax 06 9293-3756, e-mail alai@alai.it, World Wide Web http://www.alai.it. *Pres.* Fabrizio Govi.

Japan

Antiquarian Booksellers Assn. of Japan, 27 Sakamachi, Shinjuku-ku, Tokyo 160-0002. Tel. 3-3357-1417, fax 3-3356-8730, e-mail abaj@abaj.gr.jp, World Wide Web http://www.abaj.gr.jp. *Pres.* Masaji Yagi.

Japan Assn. of International Publications (formerly Japan Book Importers Assn.), c/o UPS, 1-32-5 Higashi-shinagawa, Shinagawa-ku, Toyko 140-0002. Tel. 3-5479-7269, fax 3-5479-7307, e-mail office@jaip.jp, World Wide Web http://www.jaip.jp. *Exec. Dir.* Takashi Yamakawa.

Japan Book Publishers Assn., 6 Fukuro-machi, Shinjuku-ku, Tokyo 162-0828. Tel. 3-3268-1302, fax 3-3268-1196, e-mail research@jbpa.or.jp, World Wide Web http://www.jbpa.or.jp. *Pres.* Masahiro Oga.

Kenya

Kenya Publishers Assn., P.O. Box 42767, Nairobi 00100. Tel. 20-375-2344, e-mail info@kenyapublishers.org, World Wide Web http://www.kenyapublishers.org. *Chair* Lawrence Njagi.

Korea (Republic of)

Korean Publishers Assn., 105-2 Sagan-dong, Jongro-gu, Seoul 110-190. Tel. 735-2701-4, fax 2-738-5414, e-mail webmaster@kpa21.or.kr, World Wide Web http://eng.kpa21.or.kr. *Pres.* Sok-Ghee Baek.

Latvia

Latvian Publishers' Assn., Baznicas iela 37-3, LV-1010 Riga. Tel./fax 67-217-730, e-mail lga@gramatizdeveji.lv, World Wide Web http://www.gramatizdeveji.lv. *Pres.* Renāte Punka.

Lithuania

Lithuanian Publishers Assn., The Capitol, 5-317, LT-01108 Vilnius. Tel./fax 5-261-77-40, e-mail info@lla.lt, World Wide Web http://www.lla.lt. *Pres.* Remigijus Jokubauskas; *Exec. Dir.* Aida Dobkevičiūtė.

Malaysia

Malaysian Book Publishers' Assn., No. 7-6, Block E2, Jl PJU 1/42A, Dataran Prima, 47301 Petaling Jaya, Selangor. Tel. 3-7880-5840, fax 3-7880-5841, e-mail info@mabopa.com.my, World Wide Web http://www.mabopa.com.my. *Pres.* Husammuddin Haji Yaacub.

Mexico

Cámara Nacional de la Industria Editorial Mexicana (Mexican Publishers' Assn.), Holanda No. 13, Col. San Diego Churubusco, Deleg. Coyoacan, 04120 Mexico DF. Tel. 155-56-88-20-11, fax 155-56-04-31-47, e-mail contacto@caniem.com, World Wide Web http://www.caniem.com. *Pres.* José Ignacio Echeverría.

The Netherlands

KVB—Koninklijke Vereeniging van het Boekenvak (Royal Society for the Book Trade), P.O. Box 12040, AA Amsterdam-Zuidoost. Tel. 20-624-02-12, fax 20-620-88-71, e-mail info@kvb.nl, World Wide Web http://www.kvb.nl. *Dir.* Marty Langeler.

Nederlands Uitgeversverbond (Royal Dutch Publishers Assn.), Postbus 12040, 1100 A A Amsterdam. Tel. 20-430-9150, fax 20-430-9199, e-mail info@nuv.nl, World Wide Web http://www.nuv.nl. *Pres.* Loek Hermans.

Nederlandsche Vereeniging van Antiquaren (Netherlands Assn. of Antiquarian Booksellers), Singel 319, 1012 WJ Amsterdam. Tel. 70-364-98-40, fax 70-364-33-40, e-mail info@nvva.nl, World Wide Web http://www.nvva.nl. *Pres.* Frank Rutten.

Nederlandse Boekverkopersbond (Dutch Booksellers Assn.), Postbus 32, 3720 AA Bilthoven. Tel. 30-228-79 56, fax 30-228-45-66, e-mail info@boekbond.nl, World Wide Web http://www.boekbond.nl. *Pres.* Dick Anbeek.

New Zealand

Booksellers New Zealand, Featherstone St., P.O. Box 25033, Wellington 6011. Tel. 4-472-1908, fax 4-472-1912, e-mail info@booksellers.co.nz, World Wide Web http://www.booksellers.co.nz. *Chair* Mary Sangster; *CEO* Lincoln Gould.

Nigeria

Nigerian Publishers Assn., GPO Box 2541, Dugbe, Ibadan. Tel. 2-751-5352, e-mail info@nigerianpublishers.org, World Wide Web http://www.nigerianpublishers.org. *Pres.* N. O. Okereke.

Norway

Norske Bokhandlerforening (Norwegian Booksellers Assn.), Øvre Vollgate 15, 0158 Oslo. Tel. 22-40-45-40, fax 22-41-12-89, e-mail post@bokogsamfunn.no, World Wide Web http://www.bokogsamfunn.no. *Editor* Dag H. Nestegard.

Norske Forleggerforening (Norwegian Publishers Assn.), Øvre Vollgate 15, 0158 Oslo. Tel. 22-00-75-80, fax 22-33-38-30, e-mail dnf@forleggerforeningen.no, World Wide Web http://www.forleggerforeningen.no. *Chair* Tom Harald Jenssen; *CEO* Kristenn Einarsson.

Peru

Cámara Peruana del Libro (Peruvian Publishers Assn.), Av. Cuba 427, Jesús María, Apdo. 10253, Lima 11. Tel. 1-472-9516, fax 1-265-0735, e-mail cp-libro@cpl.org.pe, World Wide Web http://www.cpl.org.pe. *Pres.* Coronado Germán Vallenas.

Philippines

Philippine Educational Publishers Assn., c/o St. Mary's Publishing Corporation, 1308 P. Guevarra St., Sta. Cruz, Manila. Tel. 2-734-7790, fax 2-735-0955.

Poland

Polish Society of Book Editors, Holy Cross 30, lok 156, 00-116 Warsaw. Tel. 22-407-77-30, e-mail ptwk@ptwk.pl, World Wide Web http://www.wydawca.com.pl. *Dir.* Maria Kuisz.

Władze Stowarzyszenia Księgarzy Polskich (Assn. of Polish Booksellers), ul. Mazowiecka 6.8 def. 414, 00-048 Warsaw. Tel./fax 0-22-827-93-81, e-mail skp@ksiegarze.org. pl, World Wide Web http://www.ksiegarze. org.pl. *Chair* Waldemar Janaszkiewicz.

Portugal

Associação Portuguesa de Editores e Livreiros (Portuguese Assn. of Publishers and Booksellers), Av. dos Estados Unidas da America 97, 6 Esq., 1700-167 Lisbon. Tel. 21-843-51-80, e-mail geral@apel.pt, World Wide Web http://www.apel.pt. *Pres.* João Alvim.

Russia

Assn. of Book Publishers of Russia, ul. B. Nikitskaya 44, 121069 Moscow. Tel. 495-202-1174, fax 495-202-3989, e-mail askibook@ gmail.com, World Wide Web http://www. aski.ru. *Pres.* Konstantin V. Chechenev.

Rossiiskaya Knizhnaya Palata (Russian Book Chamber), Kremlin Embankment, 1.09, Bldg. 8, 19019 Moscow. Tel. 495-688-96-89, fax 495-688-99-91, e-mail info@book chamber.ru, World Wide Web http://www. bookchamber.ru. *Dir. Gen.* Elena Nogina.

Serbia and Montenegro

Assn. of Yugoslav Publishers and Booksellers, Kneza Milosa 25/I, 11000 Belgrade. Tel. 11-642-533, fax 11-646-339.

Singapore

Singapore Book Publishers Assn., 86 Marine Parade Central No. 03-213, Singapore 440086. Tel. 6344-7801, fax 6344-0897, e-mail info@singaporebookpublishers.sg, World Wide Web http://www.singapore bookpublishers.sg. *Pres.* Triena Noeline Ong.

Slovenia

Zdruzenie Zaloznikov in Knjigotrzcev Slovenije Gospodarska Zbornica Slovenije (Assn. of Publishers and Booksellers of Slovenia), Dimieva ulica 13, SI 1000 Ljubljana. Tel. 1-5898-000, fax 1-5898-100, e-mail info@ gzs.si, World Wide Web http://www.gzs.si/ slo.

South Africa

Publishers Assn. of South Africa (PASA), P.O. Box 18223, Wynberg 7824. Tel. 21-762-9083, fax 21-762-2763, e-mail pasa@publish sa.co.za, World Wide Web http://www. publishsa.co.za. *Chair* Mandla Balisa; *Exec. Dir.* Brian Wafawarowa.

South African Booksellers Assn. (formerly Associated Booksellers of Southern Africa), P.O. Box 870, Bellville 7535. Tel. 21-945-1572, fax 21-945-2169, e-mail saba@ sabooksellers.com, World Wide Web http:// sabooksellers.com. *Chair and Pres.* Sydwell Molosi.

Spain

Federación de Gremios de Editores de España (Federation of Spanish Publishers Assns.), Cea Bermúdez 44-2, 28003 Madrid. Tel. 91-534-51-95, fax 91-535-26-25, e-mail fgee@fge.es, World Wide Web http://www. federacioneditores.org. *Pres.* Xavier Mallafré; *Exec. Dir.* Antonio María Ávila.

Sri Lanka

Sri Lanka Book Publishers Assn., 53 Maligakanda Rd., Colombo 10. Tel./fax 0094-112-696-821, fax, e-mail bookpub@sltnet. lk, World Wide Web http://www.book publishers.lk. *Pres.* Vijitha Yapa.

Sudan

Sudanese Publishers' Assn., c/o Institute of African and Asian Studies, Khartoum Univ., P.O. Box 321, Khartoum 11115. Tel. 11-77-0022. *Dir.* Al-Amin Abu Manga Mohamed.

Sweden

Svenska Förläggareföreningen (Swedish Publishers Assn.), Queen St. 97, S-11360 Stockholm. Tel. 8-736-19-40, e-mail info@ forlaggare.se, World Wide Web http://www. forlaggare.se. *Pres. and Dir.* Kristina Ahlinder.

Switzerland

Swiss Booksellers and Publishers Association (SBVV), Alder Strasse 40, P.O. Box 8034, Zurich. Tel. 44-421-36-00, fax 44-421-36-18, e-mail info@sbvv.ch, World Wide Web https://www.sbvv.ch. *CEO* Dani Landolf.

Thailand

Publishers and Booksellers Assn. of Thailand, 83/159 Moo Chinnakhet 2, Ngam Wong Wan Rd., Tungsonghong Lak Si, Bangkok 10210. Tel. 2-954-9560-4, fax 2-954-9566, e-mail info@pubat.or.th, World Wide Web http://www.pubat.or.th. *Pres.* Charun Homtientong.

Uganda

Uganda Publishers Assn., P.O. Box 7732, Kampala. Tel. 414-286-093, fax 414-286-397. *Chair* David Kibuuka; *Gen. Secy.* Martin Okia.

United Kingdom

Antiquarian Booksellers Assn., Sackville House, 40 Piccadilly, London W1J 0DR, England. Tel. 20-7439-3118, fax 20-7439-3119, e-mail admin@aba.org.uk, World Wide Web http://www.aba.org.uk. *Admin.* Clare Pedder; *Secy.* Tony Russ.

Assn. of Learned and Professional Society Publishers, 1-3 Ship St., Shoreham-by-Sea, West Sussex BN43 5DH, England. Tel. 1275-858-837, World Wide Web http://www.alpsp.org. *Chief Exec.* Audrey McCulloch.

Booktrust, Book House, 45 East Hill, Wandsworth, London SW18 2QZ, England. Tel. 20-8516-2977, fax 20-8516-2978, e-mail query@booktrust.org.uk, World Wide Web http://www.booktrust.org.uk. *Pres.* Michael Morpurgo; *Chair* Karen Brown.

Publishers Assn., 29B Montague St., London WC1B 5BW, England. Tel. 20-7691-9191, fax 20-7691-9199, e-mail mail@publishers. org.uk, World Wide Web http://www. publishers.org.uk. *Pres.* Dominic Knight; *Chief Exec.* Richard Mollet.

Scottish Book Trust, Sandeman House, Trunk's Close, 55 High St., Edinburgh EH1 1SR, Scotland. Tel. 131-524-0160, e-mail info@ scottishbooktrust.com, World Wide Web http://www.scottishbooktrust.com. *CEO* Marc Lambert.

Welsh Books Council (Cyngor Llyfrau Cymru), Castell Brychan, Aberystwyth, Ceredigion SY23 2JB, Wales. Tel. 1970-624-151, fax 1970-625-385, e-mail info@wbc.org. uk, World Wide Web http://www.cllc.org. uk. *Chief Exec.* Elwyn Jones.

Uruguay

Cámara Uruguaya del Libro (Uruguayan Publishers Assn.), Colon 1476, Apdo. 102, 11000 Montevideo. Tel. 2-916-93-74, fax 2-916-76-28, e-mail gerencia@camara dellibro.com.uy, World Wide Web http:// www.camaradellibro.com.uy. *Pres.* Alicia Guglielmo.

Venezuela

Cámara Venezolana del Libro (Venezuelan Publishers Assn.), Av. Andrés Bello, Centro Andrés Bello, Torre Oeste 11, piso 11, of. 112-0, Caracas 1050. Tel. 212-793-1347, fax 212-793-1368, e-mail cavelibrocgeneral @gmail.com, World Wide Web http://www. cavelibro.org. *Pres.* Ivan Dieguez Vazquez; *Exec. Dir.* Dalila Da Silva.

Zambia

Booksellers Assn. of Zambia, P.O. Box 51109, 10101 Lusaka. E-mail bpaz@zamtel.zm.

Zimbabwe

Zimbabwe Book Publishers Assn., P.O. Box 3041, Harare. Tel. 4-773-236, fax 4-754-256.

National Information Standards Organization (NISO)

Content and Collection Management

ANSI/NISO Z39.2-1994 (R2009)	Information Interchange Format ISBN 978-1-937522-23-0
ANSI/NISO Z39.14-1997 (R2015)	Guidelines for Abstracts ISBN 978-1-937522-44-5
ANSI/NISO Z39.18-2005 (R2010)	Scientific and Technical Reports— Preparation, Presentation, and Preservation ISBN 978-1-937522-21-6
ANSI/NISO Z39.19-2005 (R2010)	Guidelines for the Construction, Format, and Management of Monolingual Controlled Vocabularies ISBN 978-1-937522-22-3
ANSI/NISO Z39.23-1997 (S2015)	Standard Technical Report Number Format and Creation ISBN 978-1-937522-45-2
ANSI/NISO Z39.29-2005 (R2010)	Bibliographic References ISBN 978-1-937522-26-1
ANSI/NISO Z39.32-1996 (R2012)	Information on Microfiche Headers ISBN 978-1-937522-29-2
ANSI/NISO Z39.41-1997 (S2015)	Placement Guidelines for Information on Spines ISBN 978-1-937522-46-9
ANSI/NISO Z39.43-1993 (R2011)	Standard Address Number (SAN) for the Publishing Industry ISBN 978-1-937522-28-5
ANSI/NISO Z39.48-1992 (R2009)	Permanence of Paper for Publications and Documents in Libraries and Archives ISBN 978-1-937522-30-8
ANSI/NISO Z39.71-2006 (R2011)	Holdings Statements for Bibliographic Items ISBN 978-1-937522-31-5
ANSI/NISO Z39.73-1994 (R2012)	Single-Tier Steel Bracket Library Shelving ISBN 978-1-937522-32-2
ANSI/NISO Z39.74-1996 (R2012)	Guides to Accompany Microform Sets ISBN 978-1-937522-40-7

ANSI/NISO Z39.78-2000 (R2010)	Library Binding ISBN 978-1-937522-33-9
ANSI/NISO Z39.84-2005 (R2010)	Syntax for the Digital Object Identifier ISBN 978-1-937522-34-6
ANSI/NISO Z39.85-2012	The Dublin Core Metadata Element Set ISBN 978-1-937522-14-8
ANSI/NISO Z39.86-2005 (R2012)	Specifications for the Digital Talking Book ISBN 978-1-937522-35-3
ANSI/NISO Z39.96-2012	JATS: Journal Article Tag Suite ISBN 978-1-937522-10-0
ANSI/NISO Z39.98-2012	Authoring and Interchange Framework for Adaptive XML Publishing Specification ISBN 978-1-937522-07-0
ANSI/NISO/ISO 12083-1995 (R2009)	Electronic Manuscript Preparation and Markup ISBN 978-1-880124-20-8

Standards for Discovery to Delivery

ANSI/NISO Z39.19-2005 (R2010)	Guidelines for the Construction, Format, and Management of Monolingual Controlled Vocabularies ISBN 978-1-937522-22-3
ANSI/NISO Z39.50-2003 (S2014)	Information Retrieval (Z39.50) Application Service Definition and Protocol Specification ISBN 978-1-937522-42-1
ANSI/NISO Z39.83-1-2012	NISO Circulation Interchange Part 1: Protocol (NCIP) version 2.02 ISBN 978-1-937522-03-2
ANSI/NISO Z39.83-2-2012	NISO Circulation Interchange Protocol (NCIP) Part 2: Implementation Profile 1, version 2.02 ISBN 978-1-937522-04-9
ANSI/NISO Z39.85-2012	The Dublin Core Metadata Element Set ISBN 978-1-937522-14-8
ANSI/NISO Z39.87-2006 (R2011)	Data Dictionary—Technical Metadata for Digital Still Images ISBN 978-1-937522-37-7
ANSI/NISO Z39.88-2004 (R2010)	The OpenURL Framework for Context- Sensitive Services ISBN 978-1-937522-38-4
ANSI/NISO Z39.89-2003 (S2014)	The U.S. National Z39.50 Profile for Library Applications ISBN 978-1-937522-43-8

ANSI/NISO Z39.99-2014   ResourceSync Framework Specification
ISBN 978-1-937522-19-3

Business Information

ANSI/NISO Z39.7-2013   Information Services and Use: Metrics and
Statistics for Libraries and Information
Providers—Data Dictionary
ISBN 978-1-937522-15-5

ANSI/NISO Z39.93-2014   The Standardized Usage Statistics
Harvesting Initiative (SUSHI) Protocol
ISBN 978-1-937522-47-6

Preservation and Storage

ANSI/NISO Z39.32-1996 (R2012)   Information on Microfiche Headers
ISBN 978-1-937522-29-2

ANSI/NISO Z39.48-1992 (R2009)   Permanence of Paper for Publications and
Documents in Libraries and Archives
ISBN 978-1-937522-30-8

ANSI/NISO Z39.73-1994 (R2012)   Single-Tier Steel Bracket Library Shelving
ISBN 978-1-937522-32-2

ANSI/NISO Z39.78-2000 (R2010)   Library Binding
ISBN 978-1-937522-33-9

In Development/NISO Initiatives

NISO develops new standards, reports, and best practices on a continuing basis to support its ongoing standards development program. NISO working groups are currently developing or exploring the following:

- Alternative Metrics Recommended Practices
- Bibliographic Vocabulary Use and Reuse; Vocabulary Documentation; and Vocabulary Preservation
- Journal Article Versions (JAV) Addendum (NISO RP-8-201x)
- Protocol for Exchanging Serial Content (NISO RP-23-201x)
- Standard Interchange Protocol (SIP) (NISO Z39.100-201x)
- Permanence of Paper for Publications and Documents in Libraries and Archives (revision to Z39.48)
- SUSHI Lite (NISO TR-06-201x)

NISO Recommended Practices

A Framework of Guidance for Building Good Digital Collections, 3rd ed., 2007
      ISBN 978-1-880124-74-1

NISO RP-2005-01	Ranking of Authentication and Access Methods Available to the Metasearch Environment ISBN 978-1-880124-89-5
NISO RP-2005-02	Search and Retrieval Results Set Metadata ISBN 978-1-880124-88-8
NISO RP-2005-03	Search and Retrieval Citation Level Data Elements ISBN 978-1-880124-87-1
NISO RP-2006-01	Best Practices for Designing Web Services in the Library Context ISBN 978-1-880124-86-4
NISO RP-2006-02	NISO Metasearch XML Gateway Implementers Guide ISBN 978-1-880124-85-7
NISO RP-6-2012	RFID in U.S. Libraries ISBN 978-1-937522-02-5
NISO RP-7-2012	SERU: A Shared Electronic Resource Understanding ISBN 978-1-937522-08-7
NISO RP-8-2008	Journal Article Versions (JAV) ISBN 978-1-880124-79-6
NISO RP-9-2014	KBART: Knowledge Bases and Related Tools ISBN 978-1-937522-41-4
NISO RP-10-2010	Cost of Resource Exchange (CORE) Protocol ISBN 978-1-880124-84-0
NISO RP-11-2011	ESPReSSO: Establishing Suggested Practices Regarding Single Sign-On ISBN 978-1-880124-98-7
NISO RP-12-2012	Physical Delivery of Library Resources ISBN 978-1-937522-01-8
NISO RP-14-2014	NISO SUSHI Protocol: COUNTER-SUSHI Implementation Profile ISBN 978-1-937522-45-2
NISO RP-15-2013	Recommended Practices for Online Supplemental Journal Article Materials ISBN 978-1-937522-12-4
NISO RP-16-2013	PIE-J: The Presentation and Identification of E-Journals ISBN 978-1-937522-05-6
NISO RP-17-2013	Institutional Identification: Identifying Organizations in the Information Supply Chain ISBN 978-1-937522-11-7
NISO RP-20-2014	Open Discovery Initiative: Promoting Transparency in Discovery ISBN 978-1-937522-42-1

NISO RP-21-2013   Improving OpenURLs Through Analytics (IOTA):
Recommendations for Link Resolver Providers
ISBN 978-1-937522-18-6

NISO RP-22-2015   Access License and Indicators
ISBN 978-1-937522-49-0

NISO RP-24-2015   Transfer Code of Practice, version 3.0
ISBN 978-1-937522-40-7

NISO Technical Reports

NISO TR01-1995   Environmental Guidelines for the Storage of Paper Records
by William K. Wilson
ISBN 978-1-800124-21-5

NISO TR02-1997   Guidelines for Indexes and Related Information Retrieval
Devices
by James D. Anderson
ISBN 978-1-880124-36-9

NISO TR03-1999   Guidelines for Alphabetical Arrangement of Letters and
Sorting of Numerals and Other Symbols
by Hans H. Wellisch
ISBN 978-1-880124-41-3

NISO TR04-2006   Networked Reference Services: Question/Answer
Transaction Protocol
ISBN 978-1-880124-71-0

NISO TR-05-2013   IOTA Working Group Summary of Activities and
Outcomes
ISBN 978-1-937522-17-9

Other NISO Publications

The Case for New Economic Models to Support Standardization
by Clifford Lynch
ISBN 978-1-880124-90-1

The Exchange of Serials Subscription Information
by Ed Jones
ISBN 978-1-880124-91-8

The Future of Library Resource Discovery
by Marshall Breeding
ISBN 978-1-937522-41-4

Information Standards Quarterly (ISQ) [NISO quarterly open access magazine]
ISSN 1041-0031

Internet, Interoperability and Standards—Filling the Gaps
by Janifer Gatenby
ISBN 978-1-880124-92-5

Issues in Crosswalking Content Metadata Standards
by Margaret St. Pierre and William P. LaPlant
ISBN 978-1-880124-93-2

Making Good on the Promise of ERM: A Standards and Best Practices Discussion Paper
by the ERM Data Standards and Best Practices Review Steering Committee
ISBN 978-1-9357522-00-1

Metadata Demystified: A Guide for Publishers
by Amy Brand, Frank Daly, and Barbara Meyers
ISBN 978-1-880124-59-8

The Myth of Free Standards: Giving Away the Farm
by Andrew N. Bank
ISBN 978-1-880124-94-9

NISO Newsline [free monthly e-newsletter]
ISSN 1559-2774

NISO Working Group Connection (free quarterly supplement to Newsline)
Patents and Open Standards
by Priscilla Caplan
ISBN 978-1-880124-95-6

The RFP Writer's Guide to Standards for Library Systems
by Cynthia Hodgson
ISBN 978-1-880124-57-4

Streamlining Book Metadata Workflow
by Judy Luther
ISBN 978-1-880124-82-6

Understanding Metadata
ISBN 978-1-880124-62-8

Up and Running: Implementing Z39.50: Proceedings of a Symposium Sponsored by the State Library of Iowa
edited by Sara L. Randall
ISBN 978-1-880124-33-8

Z39.50: A Primer on the Protocol
ISBN 978-1-880124-35-2

Z39.50 Implementation Experiences
ISBN 978-1-880124-51-2

NISO standards are available online at http://www.niso.org/standards. Recommended Practices, Technical Reports, White Papers, and other publications are available on the NISO website at http://www.niso.org/publications.

For more information, contact NISO, 3600 Clipper Mill Rd., Suite 302, Baltimore, MD 21211. Tel. 301-654-2512, fax 410-685-5278, e-mail nisohq@niso.org, World Wide Web http://www.niso.org.

Calendar, 2015–2024

The list below contains information on association meetings or promotional events that are, for the most part, national or international in scope. State and regional library association meetings are also included. To confirm the starting or ending date of a meeting, which may change after the *Library and Book Trade Almanac* has gone to press, contact the association directly. Addresses of library and book trade associations are listed in Part 6 of this volume. For information on additional book trade and promotional events, see *Literary Market Place* and *International Literary Market Place,* published by Information Today, Inc., and other library and book trade publications such as *Library Journal, School Library Journal,* and *Publishers Weekly.* The American Library Association (ALA) keeps an online calendar at http://www.ala.org/conferencesevents/planning-calendar. An Information Today events calendar can be found at http://www.infotoday.com/calendar.shtml.

2015

May

12–13	Streaming Media East	New York
12–15	Florida Library Assn.	Orlando
13–15	Utah Library Assn.	St. George
14–17	Warsaw Book Fair	Warsaw, Poland
14–18	Turin International Book Fair	Turin, Italy
19	Vermont Library Assn.	Burlington
27–28	Rhode Island Library Association	Newport
27–29	BookExpo America (BEA)	New York
29–June 14	Madrid Book Fair	Madrid, Spain

June

3–5	Canadian Assn. for Information Science (CAIS)	Ottawa
3–5	IFLA President's Meeting 2015	Istanbul, Turkey
3–5	Specialized Information Publishers Association	Washington, DC
3–6	Canadian Library Assn. National Conference and Trade Show	Ottawa

June 2015 *(cont.)*

4–5	Fifth Annual Conference on Information and Religion	Kent, OH
7–11	Assn. of Caribbean University, Research and Institutional Libraries (ACURIL)	Paramaribo, Suriname
8–11	Assn. of Christian Librarians	Jefferson City, TN
8–11	Congress of Southeast Asian Librarians (CONSAL)	Bangkok, Thailand
10–12	Assn. of Canadian Publishers Annual Meeting	Toronto
14–16	Special Libraries Assn.	Boston
17–21	Seoul International Book Fair	Seoul, South Korea
18–20	Assn. of American University Presses	Denver
22–24	Tennessee Library Assn.	Memphis
24–26	Assn. of European Research Libraries (LIBER)	London, UK
25–30	American Library Assn. Annual Conference	San Francisco
28–July 2	International Assn. of School Librarianship (IASL)	Maastricht, Netherlands

July

1–4	Tokyo International Book Fair	Tokyo, Japan
15–21	Hong Kong Book Fair	Hong Kong
18–21	American Assn. of Law Libraries (AALL)	Philadelphia
22–25	National Assn. of Government Archives and Records Administrators (NAGARA)	Austin
28–30	Science and Information Conference 2015	London, UK

August

5–7	Pacific Northwest Library Assn.	Vancouver, WA
15–21	81st IFLA General Conference and Assembly	Cape Town, South Africa
16–22	Society of American Archivists	Cleveland
26–30	Beijing International Book Fair	Beijing, China

September

2–7	Moscow International Book Fair	Moscow, Russia
16–19	Kentucky Library Assn./Kentucky Assn. of School Libraries	Louisville
17–18	Web Search University 2015	Arlington, VA
23–25	South Dakota Library Assn.	Rapid City
23–25	Wyoming Library Assn./Mountain Plains Library Assn.	Cheyenne
24–27	Göteborg Book Fair	Gothenburg, Sweden

| 28–Oct. 2 | Ohio Library Council | Cincinnati |
| 30–Oct. 2 | Kansas Library Assn./Missouri Library Assn. | Kansas City |

October

1–2	Idaho Library Assn.	Boise
4–6	Arkansas Library Assn.	Little Rock
4–7	Pennsylvania Library Assn.	State College
5–8	American Assn. of School Librarians	Columbus, OH
7–9	Georgia Council of Media Organizations	Athens
7–9	Ohio Library Council	Cincinnati
8–9	Minnesota Library Assn.	St. Paul
13–14	Nevada Library Assn.	Fallon
14–16	Assn. of Bookmobile and Outreach Services	St. Charles, IL
14–16	Iowa Library Assn.	Council Bluffs
14–16	Nebraska Library Assn.	Lincoln
14–18	Frankfurt Book Fair	Frankfurt, Germany
20–21	Internet Librarian International 2015	London, UK
20–23	Mississippi Library Assn.	Natchez
20–23	North Carolina Library Assn.	Greensboro
21–23	New Mexico Library Assn.	Albuquerque
21–24	New York Library Assn.	Lake Placid
21–24	South Carolina Library Assn.	Columbia
22–24	Colorado Assn. of Libraries	Loveland
22–24	Illinois Library Conference	Peoria
22–24	Virginia Library Assn.	Williamsburg
22–25	Helsinki Book Fair	Helsinki, Finland
25–27	New England Library Assn./New Hampshire Library Assn.	Manchester
26–28	Internet Librarian 2015	Monterey, CA
26–Nov. 2	Belgrade International Book Fair	Belgrade, Serbia
28–30	Michigan Library Assn.	Novi

November

2–5	KMWorld 2015	Washington, DC
3–6	Wisconsin Library Assn.	Madison
4–6	International Conference on Knowledge Management (ICKM)	Osaka, Japan
5–7	California Library Assn.	Pasadena
5–10	Association for Information Science and Technology (ASIS&T)	St. Louis
7–10	Istanbul International Book Fair	Istanbul, Turkey

November 2015 *(cont.)*

12–15	Buch Wien International Book Fair	Vienna, Austria
16–18	Indiana Library Federation	Indianapolis
17–18	Streaming Media West	Huntington Beach, CA
18–20	Arizona Library Assn.	Flagstaff
18–23	Salon du Livre de Montréal	Montreal, QC
25–27	International Symposium on Information Management	Guangzhou, China
25–29	Moscow International Book Fair	Moscow, Russia
26–27	Bibliographical Society of Australia and New Zealand	Melbourne
28–Dec. 6	Guadalajara International Book Fair	Guadalajara, Mexico

December

13–16	International Conference on Information Systems (ICIS)	Fort Worth, TX

2016

January

5–8	Hawaii International Conference on System Sciences	Poipu, Kauai
22–26	American Library Assn. Midwinter Meeting	Boston

April

5–9	Public Library Assn.	Denver
19–22	Texas Library Assn.	Houston

May

4–6	Maryland Library Assn.	Ocean City
12–16	BookExpo America (BEA)	Chicago

June

23–28	American Library Assn. Annual Conference	Orlando

October

12–14	Iowa Library Assn.	Dubuque
16–19	Pennsylvania Library Assn.	Pocono Manor

2017

January

20–24   American Library Assn. Midwinter Meeting   Atlanta

March

22–25   Assn. of College and Research Libraries   Baltimore

April

19–22   Texas Library Assn.   San Antonio

May

3–5   Maryland Library Assn.   Ocean City

June

22–27   American Library Assn. Annual Conference   Chicago

November

9–12   American Assn. of School Librarians   Phoenix

2018

January

19–23   American Library Assn. Midwinter Meeting   Los Angeles

March

20–24   Public Library Assn.   Philadelphia

April

10–13   Texas Library Assn.   Dallas

June

21–26   American Library Assn. Annual Conference   New Orleans

2019

January

25–29   American Library Assn. Midwinter Meeting   Seattle

April 2019

2–5   Texas Library Assn.   Austin

June

20–25   American Library Assn. Annual Conference   Washington, DC

2020
January

17–21   American Library Assn. Midwinter Meeting   Philadelphia

March

31–April 3 Texas Library Assn.   Houston

June

25–28   American Library Assn. Annual Conference   Chicago

2021
January

22–26   American Library Assn. Midwinter Meeting   Indianapolis

June

24–29   American Library Assn. Annual Conference   San Francisco

2022
January

21–25   American Library Assn. Midwinter Meeting   San Antonio

June

23–28   American Library Assn. Annual Conference   Philadelphia

2023
January

27–31   American Library Assn. Midwinter Meeting   New Orleans

June

22–27   American Library Assn. Annual Conference   Chicago

2024

February

9–13   American Library Assn. Midwinter Meeting   Denver

June

27–July 2   American Library Assn. Annual Conference   San Diego

Acronyms

A

AALL. American Association of Law Libraries

AASL. American Association of School Librarians

ABA. American Booksellers Association

ABFFE. American Booksellers Foundation for Free Expression

ABOS. Association of Bookmobile and Outreach Services

ACRL. Association of College and Research Libraries

AFSIC. National Agricultural Library, Alternative Farming Systems Information Center

AGRICOLA. Agricultural OnLine Access

AGRIS. Agricultural Science and Technology database

AiA. American Library Association, grants and contributions, Assessment in Action

AIIM. The Association for Information and Image Management

AIIP. Association of Independent Information Professionals

AILA. American Indian Library Association

AJL. Association of Jewish Libraries

ALA. American Library Association

ALC. Association of Christian Librarians

ALCTS. Association for Library Collections and Technical Services

ALIC. National Archives and Records Administration, Archives Library Information Center

ALISE. Association for Library and Information Science Education

ALS. National Center for Education Statistics, Academic Library Survey

ALSC. Association for Library Service to Children

ALTAFF. Association of Library Trustees, Advocates, Friends, and Foundations

AMMLA. American Merchant Marine Library Association

APALA. Asian/Pacific American Librarians Association

ARL. Association of Research Libraries

ARLIS/NA. Art Libraries Society of North America

ARSL. Association for Rural and Small Libraries

ASCLA. Association of Specialized and Cooperative Library Agencies

ASIS&T. Association for Information Science and Technology

ATLA. American Theological Library Association

AWIC. Animal Welfare Information Center

B

BCALA. Black Caucus of the American Library Association

BEA. BookExpo America

BHL. Biodiversity Heritage Library

BIBFRAME. bibliographic framework initiative

BSA. Bibliographical Society of America

C

CAIS. Canadian Association for Information Science

CALA. Chinese-American Librarians Association

CARL. Canadian Association of Research Libraries

CFBP. Customer Financial Protection Bureau

CFUW. Canadian Federation of University
Women
CGP. Catalog of Government Publications
CIA. Central Intelligence Agency
CLA. Canadian Library Association
CLA. Catholic Library Association
CLIR. Council on Library and Information
Resources
CNI. Coalition for Networked Information
COSLA. Chief Officers of State Library
Agencies
CRS. Congressional Research Service
CSLA. Church and Synagogue Library
Association
CUL. Columbia University Libraries

D

DBCR. Digitized Bound Congressional
Record
DLF. Digital Library Federation
DPL. Denver Public Library
DPLA. Digital Public Library of America
DRM. Digital rights management
DTIC. Defense Technical Information
Center

E

EAR. National Technical Information
Service, Export Administration
Regulations
EDB. National Technical Information
Service, Energy Science and
Technology Database
EMIERT. American Library Association,
Ethnic and Multicultural Information
and Exchange Round Table
ERA. National Archives and Records
Administration, Electronic Records
Archives
ERIC. Education Resources Information
Center
ERT. American Library Association,
Exhibits Round Table

F

FAFLRT. American Library Association,
Federal and Armed Forces Librarians
Round Table

FAIFE. International Federation of Library
Associations and Institutions,
Freedom of Access to Information
and Freedom of Expression
FDLP. Government Printing Office, Federal
Depository Library Program
FDsys. Federal Digital System
FEDLINK. Federal Library and Information
Network
FEDRIP. National Technical Information
Service, FEDRIP (Federal Research
in Progress Database)
FIAF. International Federation of Film
Archives
FNIC. National Agricultural Library, Food
and Nutrition Information Center
FRCs. National Archives and Records
Administration, Federal Records
Centers
FSRIO. National Agricultural Library, Food
Safety Research Information Office
FSRS. National Technical Information
Service, Federal Science Repository
Service
FTRF. Freedom to Read Foundation

G

GLBTRT. American Library Association,
Gay, Lesbian, Bisexual, and
Transgender Round Table
GODORT. American Library Association,
Government Documents Round Table
GPO. Government Printing Office

H

HBG. Hachette Book Group

I

IAALD. International Association of
Agricultural Information Specialists
IACs. Defense Technical Information
Center, Information Analysis Centers
IALL. International Association of Law
Libraries
IAML. International Association of
Music Libraries, Archives and
Documentation Centres

IASL. International Association of School Librarianship
IBBY. International Board on Books for Young People
ICA. International Council on Archives
ICBS. International Committee of the Blue Shield
ICTs. information and communications technologies
IFLA. International Federation of Library Associations and Institutions
IFRT. American Library Association, Intellectual Freedom Round Table
ILS. Government Printing Office, Integrated Library System
IMLS. Institute of Museum and Library Services
ISBN. International Standard Book Number
ISO. International Organization for Standardization
ISOO. National Archives and Records Administration, Information Security Oversight Office
ISSN. International Standard Serial Number
ITS. Information Technology Services Office

L

LAC. Library and Archives Canada
LCA. Library Copyright Alliance
LCDP. Association of Research Libraries, Leadership and Career Development Program
LCI. Leading Change Institute
LEED. Library buildings, LEED (Leadership in Energy and Environmental Design) certification
LHHS. Labor, Health, and Human Services Appropriations Bill
LHRT. American Library Association, Library History Round Table
LIS. Library/information science
LITA. Library and Information Technology Association
LJ. Library Journal
LLAMA. Library Leadership and Management Association
LRRT. American Library Association, Library Research Round Table
LSCM. Government Printing Office, Library Services and Content Management
LSTA. Library Services and Technology Act

M

MAGIRT. American Library Association, Map and Geospatial Information Round Table
MLA. Medical Library Association; Music Library Association
MSA. Museum Services Act

N

NAGARA. National Association of Government Archives and Records Administrators
NAL. National Agricultural Library
NARA. National Archives and Records Administration
NBRII. National Bibliographic Records Inventory Initiative
NCBI. National Center for Biotechnology Information
NCES. National Center for Education Statistics
NDC. National Archives and Records Administration, National Declassification Center
NDIIPP. National Digital Information Infrastructure and Preservation Program
NDNP. Newspapers, National Digital Newspaper Program
NDSA. National Digital Stewardship Alliance
NDSR. National Digital Stewardship Residency
NEH. National Endowment for the Humanities
NFAIS. National Federation of Advanced Information Services
NIH. National Institutes of Health
NISIC. National Agricultural Library, National Invasive Species Information Center
NISO. National Information Standards Organization
NLE. National Library of Education
NLM. National Library of Medicine
NLS. National Library Service for the Blind and Physically Handicapped
NMRT. American Library Association, New Members Round Table

NTIS. National Technical Information Service

NTRL. National Technical Information Service, National Technical Reports Library

O

OA. open access

OLOS. American Library Association, Office for Literacy and Outreach Services

P

PALA. Polish American Librarians Association

PCC. Program for Cooperative Cataloging

PLA. Public Library Association

PLS. public libraries, IMLS Public Libraries Survey

PRH. Penguin Random House

PTDLA. Patent and Trademark Depository Library Association

R

RDA. Library of Congress, Resource Description and Access

RIC. National Agricultural Library, Rural Information Center

RUSA. Reference and User Services Association

S

SAA. Society of American Archivists

SAN. Standard Address Number

SIBF. American Library Association, Sharjah International Book Fair

SIIA. Software and Information Industry Association

SLA. Special Libraries Association

SLAA. State Library Administrative Agency

SPARC. Scholarly Publishing and Academic Resources Coalition

SRRT. American Library Association, Social Responsibilities Round Table

SRS. National Technical Information Service, Selected Research Service

SSP. Society for Scholarly Publishing

STEM. Education, STEM (science, technology, engineering, and mathematics)

T

TLA. Theatre Library Association

TPS. Teaching with Primary Sources Program

TRAC. Trusted Repository Audit Checklist

U

ULC. Urban Libraries Council

UNT. University of North Texas

USBBY. United States Board on Books for Young People

USCIS. United States Citizenship and Immigration Service

V

VHP. History, Veterans History Project

W

WDL. World Digital Library

WIOA. Workforce Innovation and Opportunity Act

WIPO. World Intellectual Property Organization

WISE. Web-based Information Science Education Consortium

WNC. World News Connection

WQIC. National Agricultural Library, Water Quality Information Center

Y

YALSA. Young Adult Library Services Association

Index of Organizations

Please note that many cross-references refer to entries in the Subject Index.

Subject Index

Please note that many cross-references refer to entries in the Index of Organizations.

A